Anatomy of Wonder

Anatomy of Wonder

A Critical Guide to Science Fiction

Fifth Edition

Neil Barron

LIBRARIES
UNLIMITED
A Member of the Greenwood Publishing Group

Westport, Connecticut • London

British Library Cataloguing in Publication Data is available.

Copyright © 2004 by Neil Barron

ISBN: 1-59158-171-0

First published in 2004

Libraries Unlimited, 88 Post Road West, Westport, CT 06881
A Member of the Greenwood Publishing Group, Inc.
www.lu.com

Printed in the United States of America

The paper used in this book complies with the
Permanent Paper Standard issued by the National
Information Standards Organization (Z39.48-1984).

10   9   8   7   6   5   4   3   2   1

TO ANNE

The End of Science Fiction

By Lisel Mueller

This is not fantasy, this is our life.
We are the characters
who have invaded the moon,
who cannot stop their computers.
We are the gods who can unmake
the world in seven days.

Both hands are stopped at noon.
We are beginning to live forever,
in lightweight, aluminum bodies
with numbers stamped on our backs.
We dial our words like Muzak.
We hear each other through water.

The genre is dead. Invent something new.
Invent a man and a woman
naked in a garden,
invent a child that will save the world,
a man who carries his father
out of a burning city.
Invent a spool of thread
that leads a hero to safety,
invent an island on which he abandons
the woman who saved his life
with no loss of sleep over his betrayal.

Invent us as we were
before our bodies glittered
and we stopped bleeding:
invent a shepherd who kills a giant,
a girl who grows into a tree,
a woman who refuses to turn
her back on the past and is changed to salt,
a boy who steals his brother's birthright
and becomes the head of a nation.

Invent real tears, hard love,
slow-spoken, ancient words,
difficult as a child's
first steps across a room.

Reprinted by permission of Louisiana State University Press from *Alive Together: New and Selected Poems* by Lisel Mueller. Copyright © 1966 by Lisel Mueller.

Contents

III. The Secondary Literature—Annotated Bibliography

How to Use This Guide

Anatomy of Wonder is divided into three parts. Part I provides a succinct but detailed critical history of science fiction, i.e., the "primary" literature. Early examples of proto-science fiction are discussed in Chapter 1, before the genre received its current name. Later chapters show the complex evolution of the field to the early 21st century. Hundreds of books and many magazines and films are briefly mentioned in Chapters 1 to 5, showing the growing popularity of science fiction (SF) as a literary and extra-literary genre.

Part II is a natural extension of Part I, in which more than 1,400 novels, individually authored story collections, and multiply authored anthologies are critically examined in more detail. These books were judged the best, better, or historically important of the many thousands published since the 16th century. (See Chapter 6 for statistics on SF publishing.) While some plot summary is provided to suggest what each book is "about," the emphasis throughout is on the distinctive qualities and merits (or weaknesses) of the book. Cross-references to similar books are usually provided.

Part III provides a comprehensive survey of the "secondary" literature, i.e., books and other resources that investigate printed fiction and related areas, such as films and illustration. SF fans have vigorously discussed their hobby since the 1920s, and academic scholars—some of them former fans—began to add their voices beginning in the 1940s. Today several hundred books—popular and academic—discussing fantastic literature, film, and illustration are published annually in English alone. Almost 700 of the best of them are discussed in Part III, along with chapters on teaching SF and a directory of libraries containing significant collections of science fiction.

Here is a sample fiction annotation, with each of the most common elements explained:

①   **②**   **③**

Herbert, Frank, U.S., 1920–1986

④ ⑤   **⑥**   **⑦ ⑧**   **⑨**

*II-524.   Dune. Chilton, 1965. Series: Dune

⑩

The first of a seven-volume best-selling series is the story of a selectively bred messiah who acquires paranormal powers by use of the spice that is the main product of the desert planet Arrakis, and uses these powers to prepare for the ecological renewal of the world. Politics and metaphysics are tightly bound into a remarkably detailed and coherent pattern; an imaginative tour de force. The series as a whole is overinflated, the later revisitations of the theme being prompted more by market success than by the discovery of new things to do with it. The series demonstrates how a good SF writer's ability to build a coherent and convincing hypothetical world can serve the purpose of making philosophical and sociological questions concrete; the series thus becomes a massive thought experiment in social philosophy, and is more considerable as such **⑪** than Asimov's Foundation series or Bradley's Darkover series. *House Atreides* (1999) by Frank Herbert's son Brian and Kevin J. Anderson is the first in a surprisingly well-done series of prequels to the original books. It has now reached five volumes, with at least one more planned. Three films have also been made based on the series. **⑫**(BS/ML)

⑬Awards: Hugo, Nebula

⑭Themes: Ecology, Future history, Life on other worlds, Politics

1. **Author**, with less-used portion of name shown in parentheses. All books are entered under the most common name used by the author, even if a pseudonym. Annotations of novels and collections are sequenced by author surname. Anthologies, following current library practice, are grouped at the end and are sequenced by title, with editors shown in the author index.

2. **Nationality**, shown by name of country.

3. **Birth and death years**.

4. **Best book**, designated by an asterisk. See complete best book list in Chapter 16.

5. **Entry number**. Entry numbers with the Roman numeral prefix II are found in Part II, Primary Literature. Entry numbers starting 6– to 15– can be found in Part III, Secondary Literature

6. **Title**, including any subtitle.

7. **Publisher** of the first edition of the book. Many books have been reprint-

ed repeatedly. In some cases, specific editions are recommended because the text is more reliable or there is an introduction by the author or a critic.

8. **Year** of first book publication; earlier magazine publication is often noted.

9. **Series name.** Chapter 16 lists all books in annotated series of three or more titles.

10. **Annotation** providing a critical evaluation and a succinct plot summary or description of the book's contents.

11. **Cross-references** to books with similar or contrasting plots or themes are usually provided.

12. **Contributor initials.** In this example, Brian Stableford wrote the original annotation, and Michael Levy revised it. The YA annotations retained from the fourth edition were written by Francis Molson and Susan Miles (only Molson's initials are used), sometimes revised by Michael Levy or Paul Carter. See list of contributors.

13. **Awards received.** See Chapter 16 for an explanation of the principal awards.

14. **Themes.** One or more themes are shown for most novels and themed anthologies and for many works of nonfiction, notably more than 60 books annotated in Chapter 9.

Preface

Most science fiction, like fiction generally, is undistinguished. (See the publication figures in Chapter 6 to understand why this must be so.) *Anatomy of Wonder* has always sought to identify the best, better, or historically important works of fiction and the related nonfiction that analyzes, explains, and helps put the fiction in perspective. The guide serves multiple audiences:

- The casually curious reader who is skeptical and wonders how much, if any, of this "Buck Rogers stuff" is really worth reading (as a percentage of the large total, not much is).

- The devoted fan, who often thinks *he* (mostly he—see Chapter 6 for some demographics) knows the field thoroughly. He may be surprised at the very wide variety of distinguished work, old and new.

- SF buffs who wish to match their interests and favorite books against those of the guide's very knowledgeable contributors, who strove for infallibility without pretending to it.

- Librarians, most of whom are not SF readers but who need an easy-to-use source to answer questions, advise readers, and placate the intimidating know-it-all fan.

- Collection development librarians who are unwilling to settle for a (usually) randomly selected SF collection and want to acquire at least some of the best books listed in Chapter 16 to add balance and historical depth.

- Teachers, from el-hi to college, who are either teaching a science fiction course or want to use a work of science fiction in a course in anthropology, politics, history, or women's studies, among many other fields.

- Futurists who are looking over the near horizon, exploring possible future scenarios and seeking new ideas or works that question traditional assumptions.

- Scholars relatively new to the study of SF who need an overview of previous research.
- Anyone seeking the sense of discovery provided by the best SF, in the meaning suggested by the Hungarian American biochemist Albert Szent-Györgyi, winner of the 1937 Nobel Prize for physiology or medicine, who said: "Discovery consists of seeing what everyone else has seen and thinking what no one else has thought."

Here are some of the key improvements in this new edition:

- The historical/critical narrative essays now follow one another in Part I, providing a succinct, balanced survey of SF from its earliest progenitors to summer 2004. Chapters 1, 2, and 5 were completely rewritten, with all the other chapters thoroughly revised.
- The approximately 1,400 entries in Part II, the annotated fiction bibliography, document and amplify the essays. All authors of novels and collections are now in a single A–Z alphabet under their most commonly used name; cross-references from pseudonyms are included. Little or no use of the author index is necessary.
- All anthologies follow and are now sequenced by title, following current library practice, with editors included in the author index.
- Young adult (YA) SF is now integrated with the essays and the fiction bibliography and is clearly labeled. The target teenage audience for YA books often ignores the well-meaning efforts of publishers and librarians and reads as much or more nominally adult SF. Adult readers should ignore the YA tag, for the best YA books are fully equal to their "adult" counterparts. A complete list of the 159 annotated YA books, 37 of them new to this edition, appears in Chapter 16.
- SF literature and film do not exist in a vacuum. To provide a historical context, a selective chronology of the more important books and films and sci-tech discoveries and developments is available in the Book Companion section of the Libraries Unlimited Web site (http://lu.com).
- The theme index is much more detailed. Contributors were asked to assign at least one, and sometimes several, theme headings to each novel, some anthologies, and some works of nonfiction.
- When the fourth edition of *Anatomy of Wonder* was compiled in the early 1990s, the World Wide Web was far more rudimentary than today. Web site addresses and often e-mail addresses now appear throughout the guide, and Chapter 8 annotates some of the best sites and cross-references online sources that are discussed in other chapters. Online sources help keep this guide current.
- The earliest period of SF has been partially mapped by various scholars, among whom one of the most distinguished is Brian Stableford, who wrote a new Chapter 1, revised Chapter 2, and explored the earlier years in his *Scientific Romance in Britain 1880–1950* [9-184].

- The best books listing was enlarged by adding to contributor and outsider reader choices the selections in several best books guides.
- Two sections of the fourth edition have been dropped. SF poetry is a relatively minor and very specialized field that, in my judgment, has never produced major works. The audience for comics overlaps but is largely distinct from that for SF (the annual comic-con in San Diego attracts many times the number attending even the largest world SF conventions).

Librarians have often been disappointed with "new" or "revised" editions, only to find the changes cosmetic and the additional cost incommensurate with the claimed improvements. Let me reassure them: every edition of *Anatomy of Wonder* has been extensively revised and updated, with useful new features added whenever possible. This fifth edition is no exception. Here is a summary of the key changes since the fourth edition (1995). A great many of the entries retained from that edition have been revised. Many annotations discuss more than one book (as in series), but the entry is counted only once here.

Chapter	Entries	New Entries	Retained Entries	Comments
Front matter				Detailed chronology added
1	151	92	59	Completely rewritten and expanded
2	161	46	115	Revised, with many new entries
3	248	1	247	221 adult, 25 YA retained
4	370	4	366	Chapter 4 covered 1963 to 1994 in 4th ed.
5	485	245	240	YA fiction, formerly Chapter 5, is now integrated with adult fiction
6				More-detailed discussion of SF reader demographics, themes
7	36	14	22	Multiple-author reference works moved to Chapter 10
8				Online sources (new). Web sites also appear in multiple chapters
9	255	103	152	Rapid growth in critical studies
10	173	82	92	Multiple-author guides moved here
11	83	36	47	Updated tables and introduction
12	96	51	45	Comics dropped
13	35	10	25	Discussion of fandom added
14	27	11	16	Extensively updated
15	69	2	67	OPAC Web site addresses added
16				List of YA books added
Theme index				More fiction indexed more thoroughly

Looking Back—A Personal Reminiscence

A careful reader of the fourth edition of this guide may recall that I said it was to be the last edition I planned to edit, having plowed the ground repeatedly. It would have been had not four grant applications for a projected book (having nothing to do with fantastic literature) been turned down. Maybe, I then thought, I can get it *right* the fifth time. I hope I did. So far as I know, no SF reference book has gone through five editions.

This guide had its origin in three bibliographic essays in *Choice*, an excellent book review journal targeted mostly to academic libraries. When no one picked up on my idea for such a guide, I enlisted the help of a handful of academics, none of whom I'd then met personally. The first edition, in 1976, was less than half the length of this fifth edition, with the chapters on secondary aids reflecting the then rudimentary stage of scholarship and the limited recognition of the field as worthy of study. In spite of its inadequacies, it was selected as an outstanding reference book by a division of the American Library Association and sold about 9,300 copies in cloth and paper, far more than any later edition. Later editions were also well reviewed and nominated for awards.

The second (1981) and third (1987) editions added coverage of SF not translated into English in an attempt to offset the insularity of monolingual readers. Unfortunately, the economics of publishing and the rapid growth in the primary and secondary literature made retention of this coverage impossible in later editions.

In "The Erosion of Wonder," an autobiographical piece published in *Fantasy Commentator* 51, Fall 1998, I traced the reasons for my declining interest in SF. It is appropriate to end this reminiscence with my concluding words from that essay:

> But if I no longer find much SF plausible, for reasons I have only sketched, the memories linger. Like you, I have explored the dead sea bottoms of Barsoom, joined Carson Napier in the misty mythical forests of Venus, admired Martin Padway's efforts to prevent darkness from falling, worshipped "she who must be obeyed," sensed a Mr. Hyde on the fringes of my own consciousness, and witnessed the Time Traveller 30 million years hence, shivering on a dying earth. Names jostle one another: Robida, Verne, Wells, Doyle, Čapek, Campbell, Merritt, Stapledon, Weinbaum, William, Zamiatin, joined by Aldiss, Ballard, Blish, Bishop, Bradbury, Brunner, Compton, Dick, Disch, Ellison, Heinlein, Lem, Malzberg, Silverberg, Sladek, Sturgeon, Tiptree and Waldrop. Other figures huddle indistinctly on the fringes of memory.
>
> Is there any example of SF that, even roughly, parallels my erratic journey through SF? The closest analogue I could think of is the life of David Selig, the protagonist of *Dying Inside*, whose tragic sensibility opposes the facile optimism of too much SF. His final words can serve as mine:
>
> *The world is white outside and gray within. I accept that. I think life will be more peaceful. Silence will become my mother tongue. There will be discoveries and revelations, but no upheavals. Perhaps some color will come back into the world for me, later on. Perhaps.*

Contributors

Each edition of this guide has drawn on the knowledge and enthusiasm of its many contributors, as well as on many of the books by the scholars and fans annotated in Part III. (The preface to the fourth edition acknowledges the help of all contributors up to 1995.) We certainly couldn't have done it without them or one another.

Neil Barron was an active fan in the late 1940s and early 1950s. He edited the four previous editions of this guide, has written more than 700 published book reviews, and in 1982 received the Pilgrim award for his overall contributions to SF and fantasy scholarship. His companion guide, *Fantasy and Horror* (1999), won the best nonfiction award from the International Horror Guild. Comments welcome at writeneil@charter.net.

Walter Albert is retired from the University of Pittsburgh, where he taught French and Italian literature. His interest in the visual arts dates back to an early obsession with horror and fantasy films.

Robert E. Briney is a mathematician and computer scientist with a lifelong interest in fantasy, SF, mystery fiction, and fantastic art. He contributed to Chapter 12.

Paul A. Carter was professor of history at the University of Arizona until his retirement. His *The Creation of Tomorrow* [9-46] is a highly regarded history of American SF in the magazines.

William G. Contento worked as a System Support Engineer for Cray Inc. (a supercomputer firm) from 1980 to 2003 and as an author/editor/publisher for Locus Press since 1985.

Hal W. Hall won the Pilgrim award in 2000 for his many bibliographic works, print and online; see Chapters 7 and 8. He is a librarian at Texas A&M University.

Paul Kincaid, a critic and reviewer for many years, is a former administrator of the British SF Association and current administrator of the Arthur C. Clarke award. His collection of critical essays, *What It Is We Do When We Read Science Fiction?* (Wildside Press/Borgo Press), is scheduled for late 2004 publication. He assisted Michael Levy. His wife is Maureen Kincaid Speller.

Michael Klossner is a librarian at the Arkansas State Library, Little Rock, and has an extensive knowledge of fantastic cinema.

Dennis M. Kratz, a specialist in medieval culture, is a professor of Arts and Humanities at the University of Texas, Dallas, where he teaches graduate and undergraduate courses in SF and fantasy and is also a specialist in translation.

Rob(ert) Latham, of the University of Iowa's English Department, contributed to Chapters 4 and 11. He is also one of the editors of *Science Fiction Studies*.

Michael M. Levy is a professor of English and chair of the department at the University of Wisconsin–Stout. He is also past president of the SF Research Association and current president of the International Association of the Fantastic in the Arts.

Richard L. McKinney, American-born, has lived in Sweden since 1968. A student counselor and librarian at Lund University until his retirement in 2002, he has read, studied, and lectured on and written about SF most of his adult life.

Susan G. Miles, a former reference librarian at Central Michigan University, is now special projects librarian at Northwestern Michigan College. She and Francis Molson wrote the chapter on young adult SF for the 1995 edition of this guide.

Joseph Milicia teaches courses in SF film and television at the University of Wisconsin–Sheboygan. He is a regular contributor to *The New York Review of Science Fiction*.

Francis J. Molson is a retired professor of English from Central Michigan University and the author of *Children's Fantasy* (1989). His pioneering survey of YA science fiction was part of the first (1976) edition of this guide.

Michael A. Morrison is a professor of physics and general education and an adjunct professor of English at the University of Oklahoma. He is the author of *Understanding Quantum Physics*. He wrote many of the original annotations for Chapter 10.

Joe Sanders retired from the English Department at Lakeland Community College in Mentor, Ohio. He edited *Science Fiction Fandom* [13-33, 9-168].

Maureen Kincaid Speller, wife of Paul Kincaid, is a long-time critic and reviewer who assisted Michael Levy. She formerly administered the British SF Association and edited its newsletter for some years.

Brian Stableford is not only the author of considerable fantastic fiction but is one of SF's most knowledgeable critics and historians. In 1987, he received the Distinguished Scholarship Award of the International Association for the Fantastic in the Arts. In 1999, he received the SF Research Association's Pilgrim award.

Gary K. Wolfe has been a dean and professor at Roosevelt University, Chicago, for many years and is the author of *The Known and the Unknown* [9-202] and co-author of a study of Harlan Ellison [10-63]. He was awarded the Pilgrim by the SFRA in 1987 and the Distinguished Scholarship Award of the IAFA in 1988.

Outside readers for this edition were:

John Clute, co-editor of *The Encyclopedia of Science Fiction* [7-21], principal editor of *The Encyclopedia of Fantasy* [7-33], and a distinguished British critic.

Don D'Ammassa, a reviewer of fantastic fiction for many years for *Science Fiction Chronicle* (now *Chronicle*).

James Gunn, now retired from the University of Kansas's English Department. He is one of the SF field's outstanding scholars and teachers and an author of SF.

David Hartwell, an editor with Tor Books. He has edited many prize-winning anthologies and is one of the editors of *The New York Review of Science Fiction* [13-18].

Special thanks to *Barbara Ittner* and *Catherine Barr,* my editors, who put up with endless questions and my frustrations over computer matters. They will sympathize with the comments of James Thurber, from the foreword to his 1950 fantasy, *The 13 Clocks:*

> I must apologize to my publishers . . . who were forced to keep up with the constant small changes I insisted on making all the time, even in galley proofs. In the end they took the book away from me, on the ground that it was finished and that I was just having fun tinkering with clocks and running up and down secret stairs. They had me there.

The Primary
Literature—
A Critical History

CHAPTER 1

The Emergence of Science Fiction, 1516–1914

Brian Stableford

The Origins of Science Fiction

The idea of "science fiction" is recent; the term was first coined in 1851 but was not used again until 1929, when it began to gradually displace rival terms such as "scientific romance" and "scientifiction." Its use thereafter was so promiscuous that there was never any possibility of obtaining a clear definition of the term's scope, and none of the many working definitions that have been produced for particular critical and historical purposes has ever recruited sufficient adherents to be standardized. For a valuable discussion of the many definitions of science fiction and related terms including speculative fiction, see Wolfe's glossary [7-29].

Any attempt to construct a retrospective history of the "science fiction" that was published before the label came into being is, in consequence, doomed to be controversial. There is no agreement as to how far that history can be projected back in time or what relative importance ought to be attached to works that can be connected to modern science fiction by some thematic element or detectable chain of literary influence.

Science fiction (abbreviated SF in this guide, rather than sf or sci-fi or other variations) did not simply spring into being; various pre-existing genres of fiction generated—over a long period of time—works that took aboard aspects of

3

the scientific imagination (itself a problematic concept given that the word *science* changed its meaning considerably between its Latin origins and its acquisition of something like its modern meaning in the 18th century). The two genres most hospitable to such intrusions were "utopias" in the broadest sense—accounts of hypothetical societies, which were used either to satirize existing society or to illustrate political schemes for its betterment—and "fantastic voyages," which were often developed as vehicles for wondrous invention for its own sake, although they were also routinely employed as framing devices for utopias.

Early accounts of hypothetical societies formulated as experiments in political philosophy, of which the most famous is Plato's *Republic* (4th century B.C.), are inevitably concerned with knowledge as a good and the organization of society's traffic in that good, but have little or no consciousness of the relevance of technology as a key determinant of social norms, let alone as an agent of social change. While clearly ancestral to modern SF, the vast majority of works in what eventually came to be identified as the "Utopian tradition"—after Thomas More's satirical account of *Utopia* (1516)—cannot qualify as SF. It was not until some such works acquired an awareness of the roles played by science and technology in social change *and began to use that awareness as a subject matter*, in order to explore its implications, that they became sensibly describable as "science fiction."

The most obvious foundation stone of this kind is the unfortunately incomplete *New Atlantis* (written ca. 1617; published 1627) by Francis Bacon—a crucial contributor to the development of the modern philosophy of science and one of the first to attempt a description of its fundamental method—although the importance of technological progress to social reform was also recognized by Johann Valentin Andreae's *Christianopolis* (1619) and Tommaso Campanella's *Civitas Solis* [*The City of the Sun*] (written 1602; published 1623). These key precedents were, however, largely ignored by most utopian writers during the next two centuries, who relegated scientific and technological advancement to a minor role while matters of social, religious, and political reform remained center-stage, even in such imaginatively adventurous texts as Gabriel de Foigny's *La terre australe connu* [*The Southern Land Discovered*; trans. as *The Southern Land, Known*] (written 1676; published 1693).

One notable early exception to this generalization was Margaret Cavendish's surreal account of *The Blazing World* (1666), but that seemed too bizarre to exert any influence. Other 17th-century writers who took account of scientific progress tended to be less enthusiastic about it; Baconian optimism prompted a backlash of hostility from those who perceived a threat to religious values in the materialistic encouragements of technology. The first work of proto-SF to be sufficiently influential to create a mini-genre was (perhaps unfortunately) of this anti-scientific kind; the third imaginary voyage undertaken by Jonathan Swift's Lemuel Gulliver in *Gulliver's Travels* (1726) was merciless in its assault on the pretensions of science and the ambitions of scientists. Among the "Gulliveriana" whose prolific production was encouraged by Swift's example, however, were several works that took great delight in the exercise of an imagination partly guided by scientific possibility. The most interesting include Ludvig Holberg's *Journey to the World Underground* (1741) and Giovanni Casanova's *Icosameron* (1788).

A new exemplar of great importance was provided in pre-Revolutionary France when Louis-Sébastien Mercier placed his own hypothetical ideal society in the future rather than on some remote island, representing it as a lineal descendant of an actual city—Paris—in *L'an deux mille quatre cent quarante* [*The Year 2440*; trans. as *Memoirs of the Year Two Thousand Five Hundred*] (1771). Such a move made it necessary to establish processes of social change—including the contribution made thereto by technological development—as a central issue in prospective political reorganization. Mercier's decision to do so had been greatly encouraged by the recent emergence in France of the Marquis de Condorcet's philosophy of progress, which proposed that scientific and technological progress is an intrinsically virtuous influence in human affairs. Opposition to this notion was already in place, and the intellectual war that was joined in regard to this principle became such an important generator of texts that warrant description as "science fiction" that the whole history of the genre can be seen as an ongoing argument about the extent to which the extension of knowledge and the elaboration of technology can improve or detract from the quality of human life.

All of the pre-Mercierian utopias cited above had used imaginary voyages as frameworks, but the imaginary voyage story had always been more than a vehicle for accounts of hypothetical societies. Its inventors had discovered at a very early stage the opportunities offered by travelers' tales for telling lies of a wondrous kind, and the genre had always exploited the fashion in which the credulity of an audience, who have been assured that they are listening to a true account of an actual experience, can be gradually stretched until it extends far beyond the breaking point dictated by rational skepticism. Modern SF inherited this tendency, too; its arguments about the rewards and penalties of scientific and technological advancements have always taken place in a context defined by the sheer delight of extravagant invention—an exuberant celebration of the power a writer has to make *anything at all* happen in the world within his text merely by saying so.

Marvel-packed travelers' tales such as the *Odyssey* are obviously ancestral to a great deal of modern SF—there are more science-fictional transfigurations of the *Odyssey* than of any other literary text—but their relationship to the genre is a peculiar one. On the one hand, it is frankly antithetical, in that the marvelous apparatus of the *Odyssey* is frankly supernatural, thus locating it within a worldview that science—and hence SF—claims to have rejected and replaced. On the other hand, the "sense of wonder" to which such works appeal is as fundamental to the aesthetics of SF as it is to the aesthetics of many other kinds of fantasy.

The tension created by this odd combination of blatant antithesis and intimate kinship is responsible for many of the disputes as to which kinds of texts can qualify as SF and which cannot, and deeply confuses characterizations of SF in terms of its literary and social significance. This confusion is reflected in many individual texts and entire subgenres that are frankly chimerical, in the sense that they not only combine rationally incompatible worldviews but actually draw narrative energy from their confrontation. One can see the beginnings of this productive confusion in such vigorous travelers' tales as Robert Paltock's *Life and Adventures of Peter Wilkins* (1751).

Voyages into the Unknown

For the early teller of travelers' tales, the ultimate improbability was a voyage to the Moon, which retained that status for centuries after such tales began to be written down. For this reason, the Roman satirist Lucian formulated his scathing parody of travelers' tales as an account of a voyage to the Moon, and gave it the heavily ironic title *True History* (2nd century A.D.). Many subsequent writers did likewise, but the increase of knowledge eventually wrought a dramatic change in human understanding of what kind of entity the Moon is, and gradually but drastically amended calculations as to the likelihood of a journey to that destination. The transformation of the lunar voyage from manifest absurdity to imaginable project—and eventually to plannable enterprise—was one of the key threads in the emergence of SF as a genre.

Another significant pioneer of the scientific method, John Kepler, was the first person to use a lunar voyage—conscientiously cast as a visionary fantasy—as a serious exploration of the nature of the Moon and its place in the solar system, in *Somnium* [*Dream*] (written 1609; published 1634). Like Bacon's *New Atlantis*, the exemplar was not widely copied; most subsequent accounts of lunar voyages remained calculatedly farcical. However, Francis Godwin's unrepentantly absurd *The Man in the Moone* (1638) appeared in the same year as John Wilkins's earnest essay celebrating the *Discovery of a World in the Moon* (1638). A supplement was added to the latter work in 1640 proposing that men would one day journey to the moon, and the influence of both works was cleverly combined in Cyrano de Bergerac's flamboyant *L'autre monde* [*The Other World*], fragments of which were published in 1657 and 1662.

Such speculations were problematic in Roman Catholic France, where the Copernican theory of the heliocentric solar system was still considered heretical, and it was not until Bernard de Fontenelle published his enormously popular *Entretiens sur la pluralité des mondes* [*Conversations on the Plurality of Worlds*] (1686) that the idea became a safer topic for discussion; Cyrano's exemplar also languished unheeded for many years. Inevitably, however, lunar voyages began to take aboard more and more baggage from scientific speculations about the actual condition of the lunar surface and the difficulties inherent in crossing sublunar space. The lunar voyage in Ralph Morris's *Life and Astonishing Adventures of John Daniel* (1751) is brief, but it marks the beginning of this kind of transition in English fiction.

Even the more earnest uses of the imaginary voyage framework extended beyond the depiction of hypothetical societies. Such adventures could easily extend to accounts of the cosmic context of human existence, especially if the voyages in question were visionary. Like travelers' tales, dream stories came with a built-in assumption of fanciful falsehood, but with a compensating mythology of oracular revelation. Such bold accounts of earnest visions as the one contained in Dante's *Divina Commedia* [*Divine Comedy*] (written ca. 1307–1321) were inevitably founded in contemporary cosmological theory, and thus functioned as exemplars in need of replacement as those theories were modified; for this reason the *Divine Comedy* is as prolific a source of transfigurations as the *Odyssey*, including numerous key works of SF as well as other kinds of fantasy.

Because cosmic voyages usually include lunar voyages, the two evolutionary threads are sometimes treated as one, although their implications are significantly different. Works such as Athanasius Kircher's *Itinerarium Exstaticum* [*Ecstatic Journey*] (1656) continued to illustrate cosmologies rendered redundant by the progress of astronomical science, but some images presented as authentic religious revelations, most notably Emmanuel Swedenborg's *Arcana Coelestia* (experienced 1743–1745; published 1749–1756), took aboard a good deal of insight from physics, geology, and mathematics, as did such religious allegories as *Voyages de Mylord Céton dans les sept planètes* [*Lord Seaton's Voyages to the Seven Planets*] (1765) by Marie-Anne de Roumier-Robert.

Mercier's *L'an deux mille quatre cent quarante* was cast as a visionary fantasy, thus claiming quasi-oracular authority, and Mercier also wrote a whole series of *Songes et visions philosophiques* [*Philosophical Dreams and Visions*] (1768), including *Nouvelles de la lune* [*News from the Moon*], whose description of a universe that the disincarnate souls of the dead are free to roam, while the enlightened make progress toward further phases of evolution, was a similarly significant exemplar. Whenever 17th- and 18th-century imaginary voyages found it convenient to cross interplanetary space, however, their facilitating devices inevitably became phantasmagorical, thus limiting their potential as fictions based in rational speculation. Dreaming was also the only plausible means of gaining narrative access to the future throughout the 17th and 18th centuries; the only apparent alternative—sleeping for a long time—was unattractive because there was no easy way to transmit information gained in that way back to the present.

In the meantime, however, the gradual removal of *terra incognita* from maps of the earth's surface helped to force utopian and satirical images into more distant imaginative territories, both in space and in time. Madame Robert was not the only writer to anticipate modern techniques of fabulation by borrowing magical means of travel from folklore for apologetic use as a facilitating device to open up the whole array of worlds within the solar system. The remoter regions of the southern hemisphere remained useful to such writers as Restif de la Bretonne in *La découverte australe par un homme volant* [*The Exploration of the Southern Continent by a Flying Man*] (1781), but Restif soon elected to go much further afield in *Les Posthumes* [*Posthumous Correspondence*] (written 1789; published 1800).

A significant variation on the cosmic voyage theme was introduced in Voltaire's *conte philosophique Micromégas* [*Micromegas*] (1752), which brought visitors to Earth from Sirius and Saturn. This key example of early SF was not immediately influential, but the group of tales to which it belonged—some of which use flagrantly fantastic apparatus, although the most famous, *Candide*, is naturalistic—marked a significant historical watershed by their flat rejection of the whole theistic way of thinking and all the philosophical follies based thereon. Their insistence on attempting to see "the world as it is"—"Le Monde comme il va, vision de Babouc" (1746; trans. as "The World as It Is") was the first of the *contes philosophiques*—while retaining the ambition to extend that sight beyond the limits of everyday human experience was fundamental to the imaginative projects whose instruments would include intellectually serious SF.

Many French works, along with several translations from English, were reprinted in a 36-volume series of *Voyages imaginaires* [*Imaginary Voyages*], published by Charles Garnier in 1787–1789. This attempt to define and exemplify a genre might have been even more influential had it not been interrupted by the Revolution; even so, it provided a vital landmark for later explorers of the imaginary voyage tradition whose interests were more scientifically inclined. Chief among these were Camille Flammarion, who included many of its constituent works in the pioneering history of cosmological speculative fiction he constructed in *Les mondes imaginaires et les mondes réels* [*Imaginary Worlds and Real Worlds*] (1864), and Jules Verne, who described his own works, collectively, as *Voyages extraordinaires* [*Extraordinary Voyages*].

Many post-enlightenment imaginary voyages, moved by an escapist impulse, remained entirely untouched by the desire to see "the world as it is," but even those whose primary motivation was whimsical often took aboard proto–science-fictional elements. In the early years of the 19th century, such hybrids began to emerge with considerable regularity, notable early examples including William Bilderdijk's *Kort verhaal van eene aanmerklijke luchtreis en nieuwe planeetokdekking* [*A Short Account of a Remarkable Aerial Voyage and the Discovery of a New Planet*] (1813) and Adam Seaborn's *Symzonia* (1820).

Problems of Progress

The optimistic "euchronian" mode of utopian speculation introduced by Mercier's *L'an deux mille quatre cent quarante* was soon exploited for the production of more cynical accounts of futurity. The optimism of the Marquis de Condorcet's philosophy of progress was soon blighted by the aftermath of the French Revolution (whose victims included Condorcet). Constantin-François Volney set out an antithetical philosophy in *Les Ruines, ou Méditations sur les révolutions des empires* (1791), which suggested that history was cyclic and progress a mere phase leading to decadence and decline.

This alternative view of future development soon found literary expression in Cousin de Grainville's *Le dernier homme* [*The Last Man*] (1805). But the pessimism that infected French culture even more deeply—when the aftermath of Napoleon Bonaparte's defeat instituted a whole series of swiftly aborted schemes for reform—was further reflected in Louis Geoffroy's groundbreaking exercise in alternative history *Napoleon apocryphe* [*The Apocryphal Napoleon*] (1836), Emile Souvestre's pioneering dystopian fantasy *Le Monde tel qu'il sera* [*The World as It Will Be*] (1846) (English trans. by I. F. Clarke, Wesleyan Univ. Press, 2004), Charles Defontenay's account of life on *Star ou Psi de Cassiopée, histoire merveilleuse de l'un des mondes de l'espace* [*Star, or Psi Cassiopeae; The Marvellous*

History of One of the Worlds in Space] (1854), and Edmond About's account of the revival from suspended animation of one of Napoleon's officers in *L'homme à l'oreille cassée* [*The Man with the Broken Ear*] (1861).

The lessons of French history were not wasted on the English-speaking world, and philosophical disputes about the reliability of progress soon crept into lunar voyages including Joseph Atterley's *A Voyage to the Moon* (1827) and Chrysostom Trueman's *The History of a Voyage to the Moon* (1864), Herrmann Lang's pioneering future war story *The Air Battle* (1859) and such ambivalent utopias as Lord Lytton's *The Coming Race* (1871) and Samuel Butler's *Erewhon* (1872). As the 19th century progressed, the Industrial Revolution brought technological progress to the urgent attention of the middle-class writers and readers of Europe and America, thus creating scope for the development of a genre of fiction that examined a broad spectrum of possibilities arising from mechanical and social progress. The dearth of ready-made narrative formats and strategies for the production of such works is clearly demonstrated by the first great experimentalist in that as-yet-unnameable genre, Edgar Allan Poe.

Poe's earliest poem to see eventual publication was "Sonnet—to Science," written in the early 1820s, and his unfortunately terminated career culminated with *Eureka* (1848), an extraordinary poetic essay on the nature of the universe newly revealed by astronomical telescopes. The imaginative thread connecting these two works was only occasionally visible in Poe's output, and the results of his experiments went unappreciated by contemporary critics, but his innovative flair can now be more accurately judged. Although the prefatory essay that Poe attached to reprints of his lunar voyage story "The Unparalleled Adventures of One Hans Pfaall" (1835; revised 1840) was profoundly ironic, it proved prophetic in highlighting the fundamental problem implicit in extending travelers' tales beyond the earth's surface. In spite of its disingenuousness, Poe's call for more "verisimilitude" in interplanetary fiction became the first tentative manifesto for modern SF.

As well as introducing marginal science-fictional devices into the sea stories "MS. Found in a Bottle" (1833) and *The Narrative of Arthur Gordon Pym* (1838), Poe experimented with various obsolete narrative devices as carriers of futuristic speculation. "The Conversation of Eiros and Charmion" (1839) is a dialogue of the dead whose protagonists recall the near-future destruction of Earth by a comet. "The Colloquy of Monos and Una" (1841) also features conversational spirits. "Mesmeric Revelation" (1844) attempts to add a new authority to visionary fantasy, and mesmerism also features in "A Tale of the Ragged Mountains" (1844) and "The Facts in the Case of M. Valdemar" (1845).

Nathaniel Hawthorne, Poe's contemporary, described imaginary scientific experiments in several of his moral tales, but his deep suspicion of the scientific worldview set him firmly in the antagonistic tradition; "The Birthmark" (1843) and "Rappaccini's Daughter" (1844) are early exemplars of a skeptical attitude deploring the excesses and perversions of what would nowadays be called "scientism." Most other 19th-century American writers following in Poe's footsteps were inclined to a similar caution. Problems of perception, ironically enhanced by technology and visionary ambition, are skeptically treated in such stories as

Lucretia P. Hale's "The Spider's Eye" (1856), Fitz-James O'Brien's "The Diamond Lens" (1858), and J. P. Whelpley's "The Atoms of Chladni" (1860). Meanwhile, scientific curiosity leads to perverse ends in such ambivalent tales as Mary Putnam Jacobi's "A Martyr to Science" (1869), Alvey A. Adee's "The Life-Magnet" (1870), Charles de Kay's "Manmat'ha" (1876), and W. H. Rhodes's "Phases in the Life of John Pollexfen" (1876).

It was not until the advent of such prolific but quickly forgotten journalist-writers as Edward Page Mitchell and Robert Duncan Milne in the late 1870s that Poe's experimental ambition was carried robustly forward in his own country. Edward Everett Hale, author of the spaceflight satire "The Brick Moon" (1869) and the essay in alternative history "Hands Off!" (1881), was unable to take science-fictional devices seriously, and Frank R. Stockton showed similar limitations in such early flights of fancy as "The Water-Devil" (1874) and "A Tale of Negative Gravity" (1884). Mitchell tended to a similar lightheartedness, but Milne demonstrated that there was room in such fiction for a certain seriousness of purpose as well as very abundant scope for melodrama.

A few British writers contemporary with Poe grappled in similar fashion with the problem of finding appropriate narrative frameworks for scientific speculation. Sir Humphry Davy's *Consolations in Travel* (1830) includes a visionary fantasy whose cosmological and moral implications are extrapolated in a series of dialogues. Robert Hunt, a significant pioneer of the popularization of science, followed his discourse on *The Poetry of Science* (1848) with the metaphysical fantasy *Panthea* (1849), which also employs visionary fantasy as a means of extrapolating scientific speculations. Hunt's *The Poetry of Science* inspired William Wilson to coin the term "science-fiction" in *A Little Earnest Book Upon a Great Old Subject* (1851), but the only example Wilson could come up with was R. H. Horne's *The Poor Artist* (1850), a mannered fable in which an artist discovers the wonders of nature as perceived by the eyesights of different creatures.

Modern historians often attribute the origins of British scientific romance to the works of Mary Shelley, although the Gothic trappings of *Frankenstein* (1818) place it within the tradition of anti-science fiction and *The Last Man* (1826) is a magnification of her mourning. The case is bolstered by the fact that both works eventually became formative templates heading powerful traditions of imaginative fiction; the *Frankenstein* formula of an artifact run amok, thus bringing about the downfall of its creator, became established in the latter decades of the 19th century as the principal formula of anti-science fiction, while *The Last Man* is ancestral to a rich tradition of elegiac British disaster stories carried forward by Richard Jefferies's *After London* (1885).

One early work derivative of *Frankenstein* that offered some tentative championship of progress was *The Mummy! A Tale of the Twenty-Second Century* (1827) by Jane Webb. But such explorations of future possibility remained few and highly tentative for half a century thereafter, until Edward Maitland's *By and By* (1873) and Andrew Blair's *Annals of the Twenty-Ninth Century* (1874) finally reintroduced futuristic fiction into Victorian three-decker fiction. It never thrived there, but as in America—albeit on a more limited scale and in a more conservative vein—it gradually obtained a more secure foothold in popular magazines. That infiltration received a spectacular boost when the May 1871 issue of *Blackwood's* published an account by George Chesney of "The Battle of Dorking," which describes a catastrophic British military defeat in the face of a German invasion. The story was inspired by the ignominious failure of the French to hold back Bismarck's invading forces during the previous year; by the fact that Napoleon III's capitulation at Sedan in September had been followed by the establishment of the Paris Commune, which collapsed under siege in January; and by the fact that the Prussian king, Wilhelm I, had been proclaimed German Emperor ten days before.

Quickly reprinted as a bestselling pamphlet, *The Battle of Dorking* called forth scores of replies in kind. Almost all the replies followed its example in featuring contemporary technology, but the excitement stimulated by the affair provided a significant precedent and the new subgenre continued to generate a trickle of texts throughout the 1880s. In the meantime, new influences from France began to boost interest in modestly futuristic fiction in another sector of the literary marketplace.

The Advent of Vernian Romance

With the aid of Charles Baudelaire, their French translator, Poe's works became highly influential in France, and it was in that nation that the cause of finding more appropriate narrative frameworks for science fiction was taken up most urgently and most adventurously. H. le Hon's "L'an 7860 de l'ère chrétienne" ["7860 A.D."] (1860) was a particularly bold futuristic extrapolation, while the essayist X. B. Saintine included several cosmological and biological fantasias in his collections, including "Courses astronomiques" ["Astronomical Excursions"] and "Une autre visite! Une autre planète!" ["Another Visit! Another Planet!"] in *La seconde vie* [*The Second Life*] (1864). Adrien Robert's "La guerre de 1894" ["The War of 1894"] in *Contes fantasques et fantastiques* [*Odd and Fantastic Tales*] (1865) offered a further anticipation of the future war genre. Jules Verne toyed briefly with Poesque short fiction before deciding that the imaginary voyage offered far more scope for technological speculation. Although he was eventually to pay tribute to Poe's influence by writing a sequel to *The Narrative of Arthur Gordon Pym, Le sphinx des glaces* [*The Sphinx of the Ice-Fields*] (1897)—which contrived a bathetic naturalistic reduction of all its ominous wonders—Verne set Poe's methods firmly aside in becoming the great pioneer of carefully constrained extrapolations of contemporary technology, employing various hypothetical locomotive technologies in imaginary projects in exploration and tourism. Verne made the most convincing 19th-century attempt to import a measure of verisimilitude into an extraterrestrial voyage in *De la terre à la lune* [*From the Earth to the Moon*] (1865), paying the price of his good conscience by refusing to land his moonshot—because he had no plausible way to return it to Earth—so that his voyagers merely made a trip *Autour de la lune* [*Around the Moon*] (1870).

Verne's earliest *voyages extraordinaires* included his most boldly imaginative works, including *Voyage au centre de la terre* [*Journey to the Centre of the Earth*] (1863) and *Vingt mille lieues sous les mers* [*Twenty Thousand Leagues Under the Sea*] (1870). But his publisher, P.-J. Hetzel, apparently refused to publish an adventurous vision of the future that Verne penned in the early 1860s; if the text published as *Paris au XXe siècle* [*Paris in the 20th Century*] (1994) is genuine, it offers a glimpse of the writer that Verne might have become had he not been persuaded that the secret of success was moderation. *Voyage au centre de la terre* was read in manuscript by George Sand, who was immediately inspired to write *Laura: Voyage dans le cristal* [*Laura: Journey Within the Crystal*] (1864), and it was also read by the Comte de Villiers de l'Isle Adam, who similarly adapted Vernian romance to his own Romantic purposes; but Verne's literary influence was limited in later years by Hetzel's insistence on serializing his novels in an educational magazine for young readers. Although Verne's own works were read by adults as well as children, the works of other "Vernian" writers—who sprang up in considerable profusion in France, Britain, and Germany—were routinely marketed as "boys' books."

The imaginative discipline imposed on Verne by Hetzel became so stern that a few of the more adventurous works credited to Verne in his later years owed their imaginative reach to contributions made by his enthusiastic disciple Paschal Grousset—who signed himself André Laurie—or by his son Michel Verne. Verne was, however, solely responsible for the extraterrestrial fantasy *Hector Servadac* [also trans. as *Off on a Comet*] (1877) and the flying-machine story *Robur le conquérant* [*Robur the Conqueror*, trans. as *The Clipper of the Clouds*] (1886). The most important of the works Verne rewrote from Grousset's original scripts was *Les Cinq cents millions de la begum* [*The Begum's Five Hundred Millions*; trans. as *The Begum's Fortune*] (1879), which contrasts utopian and dystopian images of technological development, while the most impressive of the "collaborations" to which Michel signed his father's name was the fantasy of cyclic history "L'Eternel Adam" ["The Eternal Adam"] (1910).

Poe's inspiration is also manifest—along with that of Humphry Davy—in the works of Camille Flammarion, another pioneer of the popularization of science. Although Flammarion was more imaginatively ambitious than Verne, he struggled in vain to find narrative formats appropriate to his ambition. Three fictionalized essays collected in *Récits de l'infini* [*Stories of Infinity*] (1872) included *Lumen* (separately published 1887), in which a human questioner interrogates a disembodied soul, modeled on those featured in Mercier's "Nouvelles de la lune," whose ability to travel faster than light has allowed him to view his former incarnations on many alien worlds, each of which has life forms adapted to its particular physical circumstances. Flammarion subsequently incorporated synoptic accounts of *Lumen*'s cosmic scheme into other patchwork essays, including *Uranie* [*Urania*] (1889). His account of *La fin du monde* [*The End of the World*; trans. as *Omega*] (1893) is also fragmentary; the rhapsodic prose poem with which it concludes is clearly derivative of *Eureka*.

The most prolific of Verne's French disciples were Pierre d'Ivoi and Gustave le Rouge, but there were many others, including Jules Lermina, Louis Boussenard, René Thévenin, George Le Faure, and "Captain Danrit." The weekly *Journal des Voyages* (launched in 1875 as *Sur Terre et Mer*, retitled 1877), a magazine of Vernian romance that played host to many of these writers, published more than a thousand issues in its first series, which ended in 1896, and more than a thousand more in four more series whose final one concluded in 1949. The illustrator Albert Robida, who was to become the great caricaturist of *La guerre au vingtième siècle* [*War in the 20th Century*] (1883) began his career with the parodic series *Voyages très extraordinaires de Saturnin Farandoul dans les 5 ou 6 parties du monde et dans tous les pays connus et même inconnus de M. Jules Verne* [*Saturnin Farandoul's Very Extraordinary Voyages in the Five or Six Continents and in all the Nations Known—and Even Unknown—to M. Jules Verne*] (1879).

Verne's influence was, however, by no means confined to France. *Journey to the Centre of the Earth* was one of the earliest novels picked up for serialization by the British boys' papers (Poe's *Narrative of Arthur Gordon Pym* was another) and extraordinary voyages became a regular feature therein. The most adventurous writers of that kind of fiction included Francis Henry Atkins, who wrote as "Frank Aubrey" and "Fenton Ash," and George C. Wallis; "Herbert Strang" and Gordon Stables were more restrained. The leading German Vernians included Robert Kraft, F. W. Mader, Carl Grunert, and Oskar Hoffmann; the 165 issues of the magazine *Der Luftpirat und sein lenkbares Luftschiff* [*The Air Pirate and His Dirigible Airship*] (1908–1911) featured fiction that soon left Earth's atmosphere to range throughout the solar system.

Vernian fiction in America quickly became distinctive because of its adaptation to a new cultural context. Locomotion remained a key issue, but it was focused on the actual adventure in large-scale logistics that was then being conducted as colonists took formal possession of the western reaches of the continent, in which railroads played a central role. Stories about young inventors producing machines that might help to tame the "wild" West quickly came to constitute one of several commercial genres fabricated by the publishers of "dime novels." Edward S. Ellis's pioneering account of *The Steam Man of the Prairies* (1868) was a hybrid SF western, which anticipated the manner in which American SF would adopt and fervently commit itself to the myth of the "frontier" and the necessity of its "conquest." Most of the items in the various series featuring young inventors such as Frank Reade and Tom Edison, Jr., were similar in nature. Although English Vernian fiction was always enthusiastic about linking technological inventiveness with colonial adventurism, the British Empire was already in decline and the imperial ambitions of other European nations were similarly frustrated; only the internally expansive U.S. was able to mythologize space as a "final frontier" waiting to be pioneered and conquered.

The myth of the West as a place where the future was to be found and made was sufficiently powerful to enable American Vernian fiction to outstrip the ambitions of European Vernians. Writers including Frank R. Stockton, in *The Great War Syndicate* (1889) and *The Great Stone of Sardis* (1898), John Jacob Astor in *A Journey in Other Worlds* (1894), and Garrett P. Serviss in *The Moon Metal* (1900) and *A Columbus of Space* (1909) began to pave the way for the development of a new kind of popular fiction that celebrated technology as a means of illimitable economic and physical expansion. By the time these foundation stones had been laid, however, American popular fiction was moving into a new medium, and hence into a new era, that was soon to submerge this kind of interplanetary romance within another kind whose ambitions were conspicuously less hard-headed.

The Advent of Scientific Romance

The establishment of Vernian fiction in Britain to complement the kind of alarmist fiction popularized by George Chesney helped add further impetus to a new vogue for utopian fiction sparked by Lytton's *Coming Race* and Butler's *Erewhon*. The politics of progress continued to be debated in a variety of contexts. W. H. Hudson's *A Crystal Age* (1887) was far ahead of its time in its extrapolation of themes that could not yet be labeled "ecological," while Walter Besant's *The Revolt of Man* (1882) was one of several novels inspired by the suffragette movement. Besant followed it up with the more profoundly meditative *The Inner House* (1888), which exposed the prospect of biotechnological longevity to a suspicious gaze. Similar issues were foreshadowed in works of interplanetary fiction, including Percy Greg's *Across the Zodiac* (1880) and Hugh MacColl's *Mr Stranger's Sealed Packet* (1889).

Alongside such works, the spectrum of *contes philosophiques* was further broadened by such idiosyncratic additions as Edwin Abbott's *Flatland* (1884) and Robert Louis Stevenson's *Strange Case of Dr Jekyll and Mr Hyde* (1886), both of which inspired interesting variants. Such trends spread to the colonies, where native traditions of fantastic fiction were founded in Canada, Australia, and New Zealand, whose more interesting products included James de Mille's *Strange Manuscript Found in a Copper Cylinder* (1888) and the utopian extravaganza begun in Godfrey Sweven's *Riallaro* (1901).

The advent in Britain in the late 1880s and early 1890s of a large number of new "middlebrow" newspapers and magazines generated fierce circulation wars, one of whose corollaries was an experimental frame of mind on the part of several significant proprietors. One of the gimmicks they tried was the revivification of future-war fiction, initially in the same modest vein as *The Battle of Dorking*. But this time, the competition called forth much bigger and more violent imagery, in which technologies of warfare not yet developed—the airship, the submarine, and more powerful explosives—were employed in wars that engulfed the entire world. Such works quickly co-opted the legacy of the more imaginative utopias as well as that of Chesneyan military alarmism. The relatively pedestrian account of "The Great War of 1892"—which was compiled by military experts including Rear-Admiral Colomb, and which was serialized in 1891–1892—was rapidly upstaged by George Griffith's *The Angel of the Revolution* (1893), in which heroic "Terrorists" trash the world before bringing a quasi-socialistic utopia out of its ruins.

Griffith's fervent anti-imperialistic sentiments immediately called forth a right-wing backlash in E. Douglas Fawcett's account of the exploits of *Hartmann the Anarchist,* introducing a second front to the war of melodramatic exploitation. Other journalists instructed by their employers to write future-war serials included Louis Tracy, author of *The Final War* (1896), and William le Queux, whose works in that vein culminated in the groundbreaking newspaper serial reprinted as *The Invasion of 1910* (1906). Griffith's casual deployment of as-yet-nonexistent arms and armor was rapidly standardized, as was his insistence that the next great war would be a worldwide affair involving a crucial settlement of nationalistic and imperialist accounts.

Because Britain was in the throes of political disputes in which disillusioned anti-imperialists were scornfully stigmatized as "little Englanders," writers there found it easier to contemplate a world stage than American writers, who were still preoccupied with affairs internal to their nation. But British writers could not be optimistic about their nation's role upon the world stage, and they lacked any sense of a "frontier" that they could extrapolate, unlike the Americans. This globalized but essentially conservative worldview kept the British speculative imagination tightly focused on the spherical surface of the earth, and securely bound thereto. Although a handful of writers—including Robert William Cole in *The Struggle for Empire* (1900)—followed Andrew Blair's example in imagining the extension of the British Empire into and beyond the solar system, the majority regarded interplanetary adventures as mere excursions, like the ones featured in Robert Cromie's *A Plunge into Space* (1890), Ellsworth Douglass's *Pharaoh's Broker* (1899), George Griffith's *A Honeymoon in Space* (1900), and Edwin Lester Arnold's *Lt Gullivar Jones* (1905).

The escalation of conflict in the renewed future-war genre proceeded so rapidly that when Griffith began work on his last future-war story in 1906, *The Lord of Labour* (published posthumously in 1911), his weapons of choice were nuclear missiles and disintegrator rays. The hastily popularized discovery of X-rays by Wilhelm Röntgen in 1895, followed in 1896 by Antoine Becquerel's discovery of atomic radiation, had administered a powerful stimulus to the science-fictional imagination, which the future-war story was perfectly equipped to exploit. Biological warfare was added to the mix by T. Mullett Ellis's *Zalma* (1895) and further extrapolated by M. P. Shiel in *The Yellow Danger* (1898).

Although the expansion of the future-war genre into a broader speculative genre, which journalists and reviewers labeled "scientific romance," was tentatively begun by others, one writer in particular soon came to be regarded as exemplary: H. G. Wells. Precedents had been set for Wellsian speculative fiction by such *contes philosophiques* as Grant Allen's "Pausodyne" (1881) and "A Child of the Phalanstery" (1884), as well as Besant's *The Inner House.* But Wells imported such a powerful narrative energy and such imaginative bravado into his works that he effortlessly surpassed the accomplishments of all his competitors. The flood of new periodicals provided the perfect arena for Wells to conduct his experiments in speculation, which began as brief provocative essays such as "The Man of the Year Million" (1893).

Wells had already written a much longer essay of that kind, "The Chronic Argonauts" (1888), for a periodical of his own, but the only way he could adapt it for the commercial magazines was to turn it into something more reminiscent of a novel; he required two further attempts before finalizing the text as *The Time Machine* (1895). Recognizing that futuristic visions—whether or not they were mesmerically induced—no longer commanded the least shred of plausibility, Wells took advantage of articles by C. H. Hinton that were collected in *Scientific Romances* (1886), which had popularized the idea of time as a "fourth dimension," to provide an apologetic jargon for a new facilitating device that would open the entirety of future time to exploration. Such an imaginative device had little or nothing in common with Jules Verne's earnest extrapolations of locomotive technology—as Verne was quick to complain—but Wells understood far better than the Frenchman how necessary some such literary device had become as a means of liberating the future as an imaginative space for serious speculative endeavor.

Wells's time machine was the most spectacular example of a series of such facilitating devices, whose accumulation opened up the farther reaches of time and space to a kind of rational enquiry that had previously been severely handicapped by its imprisonment in obsolete narrative frameworks. The anti-gravity technology of Cavorite, employed by Wells in *The First Men in the Moon* (1901), followed examples provided by Chrysostom Trueman, Percy Greg, and Robert Cromie in providing spaceships with a means of propulsion that could take them anywhere they needed to go with a minimum of fuss. In between these two key works, Wells published *The Island of Dr Moreau* (1896), *The Invisible Man* (1897), "A Story of the Days to Come" (1897), *The War of the Worlds* (1898), and *When the Sleeper Wakes* (1899), as well as numerous shorter moral fables in melodramatic guise, including "The Star" (1897) and "The Crystal Egg" (1897).

After 1901, however, and despite their manifest design for repeated deployment, Wells never used the time machine or Cavorite again; nor did he invent any other new facilitating device of a similar kind. He resisted application of the term "scientific romance" to his work, and in the lists of his previous publications that were included in his novels he refused to make any distinction between speculative fictions seemingly based on scientific premises and works such as the angelic fantasy *The Wonderful Visit* (1895) and the mermaid story *The Sea Lady* (1902), grouping them all together as "Fantastic and Imaginative Romances." The reasons for Wells's refusal to discriminate between these various categories of fantasy are complex, involving matters of reputation as well as matters of definition, but it serves to emphasize that all his works in this realm are, in essence, Voltairean *contes philosophiques* whose primary function—in their author's eyes—was to reconstruct moral expectations in the context of a modern worldview. The modernity of that worldview was largely constituted, for Wells, by the advent of the Darwinian theory of evolution, but the purpose of his advocacy was always political. Looking backward from the year 2000 and beyond, we can now see seven of the long works that Wells published between 1895 and 1901 as foundation stones of modern SF. But he was not attempting to found a new genre, and when he finally assented to their description as "scientific romances" (allowing the phrase to be used as the title of a 1933 omnibus), he was scathingly dismissive of them precisely because he felt that in being relegated to genre status they had lost almost all their intended and potential impact as literary propaganda.

Although he wrote several more utopias and future war novels after 1901, and began *The Food of the Gods* (1904) as a scientific romance before abruptly changing direction halfway to convert it into a political tract, Wells deliberately avoided the narrative strategy that had been the innovative essence of his most successful early works. On the other hand, he remained perfectly willing to develop moral fables in more traditional forms, employing the lost race story in "The Country of the Blind" (1904), miraculous fantasy in *In the Days of the Comet* (1906), Biblical allegory in *The Undying Fire* (1919), and visionary fantasy in *The Dream* (1923). His defection from the genre he founded was to prove as influential, in its way, as the foundation stones he had provided, lending ironic support to the common opinion that this genre was, after all, intrinsically frivolous and innately inferior to serious naturalistic fiction.

The Wellsian Legacy in Europe

The first philosophical novel subjecting the possibilities of futuristic fiction to scrupulous analysis, Anatole France's *Sur la pierre blanche* [*On the White Stone*] (1903), hailed H. G. Wells as the only writer prepared to venture into the future as an open-minded explorer rather than as a vulgar prophet intent on painting his own hopes or anxieties on its blank canvas. This judgment was probably colored by France's contemplation of Gabriel Tarde's *Fragment d'histoire future* [*Fragment of a Future History*; trans. as *Underground Man*] (1896). As soon as the 20th century had begun, Wells, moved by the earnest passion of his socialist convictions, gave up wide-ranging exploration of an infinite range of future possibility in favor of a much less interesting quest to discover and comment upon the particular form that the future actually would take—a quest whose plausibility he argued (mistakenly) in a lecture reprinted as *The Discovery of the Future* (1902) and had already begun to carry forward in his pioneering work of "futurology"—*Anticipations* (1901). Although his first formal utopian fantasy, *A Modern Utopia* (1905), remained conscientiously aware that its propositions were contingent on political decisions, such later texts as *Men Like Gods* (1923) and *The Shape of Things to Come* (1933) offered themselves as prophecies of a more definite kind.

The sole exception to the 20th-century degeneration of Wells's proto-science-fictional ambitions was his work in the future-war subgenre, to which he was a latecomer. The distinctiveness of his contribution is rooted in the fact that he was virtually alone among its writers in deploring the destruction that a new war might bring. His anticipation of tank warfare in "The Land Ironclads" (1903) was followed up by an account of *The War in the Air* (1908) as witnessed by its potential victims. These two stories now seem far more prophetic than the jingoistic flood of novels that took it for granted that "the war to end war" would be won by the British—and thus provided the slogan under which the actual Great War could recruit its cannon fodder. But in this respect too, Wells relented; his atomic war story *The World Set Free* (1914) was the first of several works in which he welcomed the prospect of a destruction of civilization, on the grounds that nothing less would clear the way for socialist reconstruction.

However disappointing the eventual development of Wells's career may seem to modern connoisseurs of science fiction, his early work offered a striking revelation to writers enthusiastic to work on wider and more spectacular stages than naturalistic fiction, whether their interests were melodramatic, extrapolative, or fabulatory. There was, inevitably, a certain parting of the ways between writers whose primary interest was in futuristic and otherworldly costume drama and writers who were seriously concerned to explore future possibilities associated with the advancement of science and technology; but Wells gave abundant imaginative ammunition to both—with the result that the overlap between the two remained considerable, and the artful combination of the two kinds of ambition was able to exploit a powerful synergy.

In spite of his own withdrawal from the field of battle, there was no shortage of 20th-century writers ambitious to write the Wellsian fiction that he had abandoned, bravely risking the critical disgust that he had meekly accepted and echoed. Many of the writers recruited to the future-war subgenre diversified their output into other fields of speculative fiction, taking inspiration from various examples set by Wells. George Griffith led the way, followed by W. Laird Clowes in the satirical *The Great Peril* (1893), Fred T. Jane in the breezily apocalyptic *The Violet Flame* (1899), and M. P. Shiel in the more flamboyantly profound apocalyptic fantasy *The Purple Cloud* (1900). The proto-Wellsian Grant Allen continued work in that vein in his quasi-anthropological study titled *The British Barbarians* (1895), while popular writers such as Arthur Conan Doyle, Joseph Conrad, and Rudyard Kipling began to dabble productively in speculative fiction, and G. K. Chesterton and E. M. Forster began to construct ideological replies to Wells in his own currency. It was not long before neo-Wellsians including Francis Hernaman-Johnson and J. D. Beresford made their appearance, beginning to carry the cause of scientific romance forward, while further breadth was added by writers adventurous to diversify its scope, including William Hope Hodgson. This activity was, however, curbed as the popular periodicals moved beyond their experimental phase, having discovered that other genres—especially detective fiction—were more popular with larger audiences.

In France, the continuing influence of Poe, Verne, and Flammarion was quickly combined with Wellsian elements by such writers as J. H. Rosny aîné, the pioneer of the novel of prehistory. Rosny had already adapted that subgenre to more adventurous speculation in the alien visitation story "Les Xipéhuz" ["The Xipehuz"] (1887) and had dabbled in Flammarionesque visionary fantasy in "La légende sceptique" ["The Skeptical Legend"] (1889), but the influences of Flammarion and Wells were fruitfully combined in "La mort de la terre" ["The Death of the Earth"] (1910). Albert Robida, who had built a career as a writer and illustrator by cleverly satirizing Jules Verne and future-war fiction, also became more adventurous toward the end of his career, in such novels as the time-reversal fantasy *L'horloge des siècles* [*The Clock of the Centuries*] (1902), while new writers such as Maurice Renard imported Wellsian elements into their Vernian fantasies from the very beginning. Flammarionesque notions of serial extraterrestrial reincarnation remained important in French speculative fiction, providing a logic for the striking visionary fantasy *Force ennemie* [*Hostile Force*] (1903) by John-Antoine Nau, which won the first Prix Goncourt.

In Germany, a speculative tradition to rival those of Verne in France and Wells in Britain might have taken root if a prospectus laid out by Kurd Lasswitz had attracted more attention, but it was not until Verne and Wells had been imported that Lasswitz published the monumental *Auf zwei Planeten* [*On Two Planets*] (1897) and the highly imaginative Paul Scheerbart began to write the *Astrale Noveletten* [*Astral Novellas*] that were collected in 1912. In Russia, too, a tradition founded in the works of the neo-alchemical fantasist Vladimir Odoevsky began to bear robust speculative fruit in stories such as Valery Brussof's "Respublika yuzhnavo kresta" ["The Republic of the Southern Cross"] (1905), Alexander Kuprin's "Tost" ["A Toast"] (1906), and Alexander Bogdanov's *Krasnaia zvezda* [*Red Star*] (1908). It is conceivable that the German and Russian traditions, like the French, might have continued to thrive even as the British tradition ran into difficulties, but all of them were doomed to fall into a dark abyss in 1914, when the future war so long anticipated in European fiction finally arrived.

The impact of that historical break on the futuristic imagination cannot be underestimated; the brutal interruption of the pattern of social and technological development cut the ground away from all extrapolative lines of thought. Save for anticipations of the way in which the war itself would develop—which were almost entirely taken over by the necessity of maintaining and rebuilding morale—futuristic speculation was put into suspended animation until the normal course of political affairs could be resumed.

Nor was this effect confined to futuristic speculation; escapist fantastic voyages were also devastated as they came to be seen as a kind of intellectual treason. That is, the desire to escape to more hospitable fictional worlds was presumably undiminished, but its exercise came to seem suspiciously akin to cowardice in the face of the enemy. Throughout Europe—and, for the matter, the entire British Empire and its French and German analogues—the evolution of scientific romance came to an abrupt halt. If the war had not happened, or if it really had been a world war from day one, the subsequent history of speculative fiction might have been quite different. As things were, the catastrophe overwhelmed what had already begun to seem like one of two alternative branches of modern imaginative fiction; the other, which had already begun to diverge from it, was based in the one fully literate, economically dynamic, and forward-looking nation that was not immediately embroiled in the war: the United States of America. Although the United States did become involved in the war in 1916, it did so at a distance; its economy suffered far less disruption than the economies of the European nations and its future economic prospects, far from suffering a fatal depletion, made vast relative gains from the war's aftermath.

The result of the arrival of the Great War in 1914, therefore, so far as the evolution of speculative fiction was concerned, was a dramatic reinforcement of a divergence that had already become apparent. From that date on, America became the forefront of innovation and diversification in imaginative fiction—a position it has retained ever since. Again, the subsequent history of speculative fiction might have been quite different had that process of innovation and diversification not begun—seemingly by virtue of an arbitrary freak of chance— from such a peculiar starting point.

The Advent of Popular Magazine Fiction in America

Just as there were precedents for Wellsian fiction in Britain before Wells became active, so there were works that might have served as precedents for a similar enterprise in the United States. Although recontextualized Vernian fiction was far more prolific, there were several writers in the upper strata of the marketplace interested in Americanizing *contes philosophiques*. Lacking time machines, however, such writers were hamstrung by their reliance on visionary fantasy as a narrative form; the limitations of that device are clearly exposed by the slightly frustrated ambition of such works as Edward Bellamy's *Dr Heidenhoff's Process* (1880) and "The Blindman's World" (1886), Mark Twain's *A Connecticut Yankee in King Arthur's Court* (1889), and Edgar Fawcett's *Solarion* (1889) and *The Ghost of Guy Thyrle* (1895).

Bellamy did overcome this barrier in his bestselling utopian romance *Looking Backward, 2000–1887* (1888), whose last chapter defiantly casts aside the conventional apology that it was all a dream. Twain's other ventures into science fiction remained incomplete at his death. Fawcett was never able to gain significant public acceptance of his ideas, even though he took the trouble to preface *The Ghost of Guy Thyrle* with a defiant manifesto for a new genre of "realistic romances." The heavy emphasis in American fiction of this kind on matters of psychology—also exemplified by the "medicated" novels of Oliver Wendell Holmes and the psychic research fantasies of William Dean Howells—tended to divert attention from the possibility of handling outré material in a less conscientiously compromised fashion.

The commercial success of *Looking Backward* did little to assist the development of more plausible narrative devices, but it did inspire a sudden flood of variants and ideological replies similar to the one that *The Battle of Dorking* had launched in Britain. Novels including Chauncey Thomas's *The Crystal Button* (written 1872; published 1891) crept belatedly into print, and interest was renewed in such works as Ingmar Thiusen's *The Diothas* (1883) and Princess Vera Zaronovitch's *Mizora* (1880–1881; book 1888). Most of the direct replies to Bellamy were of purely political interest, reacting against his evolutionary socialism in various ways; but several took up his notion that the advancement of technology would assist a trend toward greater social equality—a notion compatible with the views of Adam Smith and American socialists including Henry George.

The most interesting replies to Bellamy, in the context of the development of science fiction, were less narrowly focused, especially those that challenged his tacit assumptions by proposing that technological progress would actually create greater inequality. Ignatius Donnelly's spectacular dystopia *Caesar's Column* (1890) was the most extreme of these, making an interesting contrast with William Morris's plea on behalf of the British arts and crafts movement, *News from Nowhere* (1890). J. A. Mitchell's *The Last American* (1889) is similarly cynical about the prospects of progress.

As in Britain, an explosion of new periodicals in the 1890s opened up new market space in the United States for experimental exploitation, but they arrived in a very different cultural context so far as the fashionability of imaginative fiction was concerned, the agenda having been set by Bellamy rather than Chesney. Many of H. G. Wells's novels and stories were reprinted there, and were certainly not without influence, but the American periodicals that took up "scientific romance" most avidly were not middlebrow periodicals such as *Cosmopolitan* and *Harper's* but the descendants of the dime novels, printed on cheap paper made from wood pulp. The pulp magazines took over the commercial genres identified and exploited by the dime novels, and soon began to develop the melodramatic variants of genre fiction as a key element of their marketing strategy. The key exemplar was provided by Frank A. Munsey when he transformed the relatively staid weeklies *The Golden Argosy* (founded in 1888) and *Munsey's Magazine* (founded in 1889) into monthly magazines dominated by fast-paced action-adventure fiction, the former under the abbreviated title *The Argosy*.

In the early 1900s, Munsey expanded his operation in order to occupy more space on newsstands that were being avidly colonized by his competitors, launching *All-Story Magazine* in 1905 and *The Cavalier* in 1908. *The Argosy* reprinted Vernian romances by André Laurie, Frank Atkins, and George Griffith from 1897 to 1902 before cultivating two prolific native writers, "Edgar Franklin" (Edgar F. Stearns)—who carried forward the dime novel tradition of inventor stories in exuberantly comic fashion—and William Wallace Cook, who also adopted a tongue-in-cheek attitude in his more ambitious works. Unlike Franklin, whose series featuring an ingenious inventor—a fraction of which was reprinted as *Mr. Hawkins' Humorous Adventures* (1904)—stuck so close to actual possibility that many of its items hardly qualify as science fiction. For his part, Cook took aboard the lessons of Wellsian fiction, celebrating the potential of the time machine in his flamboyant comedy *A Round Trip to the Year 2000* (1903).

A few home-grown Wellsians were recruited to the pulps, including Jack London—whose Wellsian short stories like "A Thousand Deaths" (1899) and "The Shadow and the Flesh" (1903) paved the way for *The Scarlet Plague* (1912)—and George Allan England, who made his debut there with "The Time Reflector" (1905). Like Wells himself, however, London and England were committed socialists and they soon found that the crowd-pleasing pulps were inhospitable to their more determined political fantasies. London moved on in *The Iron Heel* (1907) and later works, while England capitulated to demand by conspicuously lowering the tone of such pulp fantasies as *Darkness and Dawn* (1914).

Later pulp Wellsians such as Garret Smith, author of "On the Brink of 2000" (1910), retained an element of moral fabulation in a few of their works but compromised to an even greater extent than England. This gradual exclusion of the more serious inclinations of British scientific romance—only fugitively preserved in such books as Vincent Harper's *The Mortgage on the Brain* (1905)— led to the development in the pulp magazines of a very different kind of fantastic fiction, which made far more of the sheer exuberance of invention than the relatively disciplined extrapolations of political fantasy and the *contes philosophiques.*

The most crucial intervention in the development of pulp romance was that of Edgar Rice Burroughs, whose "Under the Moons of Mars" was serialized in *All-Story* in 1912. This was an unashamed dream story, which brazenly refused to establish a plausible mechanism for its hero's abrupt transplantation to Mars; although the image of that planet presented in the story owed something to speculative descriptions offered by the astronomer Percival Lowell in such books as *Mars as the Abode of Life* (1908), Burroughs used the ideas he borrowed as a backdrop for a fantasy of extraordinary derring-do. As the Great War broke out in Europe, the primary template established for American pulp fantasy was neither Vernian nor Wellsian, but Burroughsian. It was Burroughs and his fellow pulp adventurers who imparted the impulse and spin to popular imaginative fiction in America at the crucial moment when it was suddenly isolated by the temporary disappearance of its rival European traditions.

The extent of the gulf that abruptly opened up between the European and American traditions of proto-science fiction is easily illustrated by comparing the most significant works produced on either side of the Atlantic in the years immediately preceding the outbreak of the Great War. In Britain there was J. D. Beresford's disaster novel *Goslings* and his earnest account of a super-intelligent child, *The Hampdenshire Wonder,* as well as William Hope Hodgson's ornate far-future fantasy *The Night Land.* In the United States there was Burroughs's "Under the Moons of Mars" and England's "Darkness and Dawn." A connecting bridge of sorts was maintained by such British melodramas as Conan Doyle's *The Lost World* and *The Poison Belt* and relatively serious American endeavors such as England's *The Golden Blight,* but the link was already becoming tenuous.

That imaginative middle ground might easily have vanished entirely under the strongly contrasted pressures of war in Europe and commercial demand in the United States, but there remained one intermediate site, hardly visible before 1914, that was to come into its own as the gulf widened and deepened, retaining a perverse possibility of future reconnection. The work that raised a fugitive flag over that tiny island was far less widely read than any of the examples listed above, and it was also far less competent as an item of literature. But it sheltered the seed that would eventually grow into modern science fiction: it was Hugo Gernsback's *Ralph 124C41+,* serialized in 1911–1912 in a glorified mail order catalogue called *Modern Electrics.*

CHAPTER 2

Science Fiction Between the Wars: 1915–1939

Brian Stableford

The Origins of Pulp SF

The subgenre of pulp fantasy that Edgar Rice Burroughs founded in "Under the Moons of Mars" (1912) is routinely called interplanetary romance or "planetary romance," but the labels are rather misleading, because the settings employed in Burroughsian fiction are far less important than the kind of melodramatics to which they play host. The relative dearth of earthly settings readily exploitable as stages for Burroughsian romance favored the use of other planets within the solar system—with the tacit possibility of extending the genre beyond the limits of local space to the worlds of other stars—but the extraterrestrial dimension was always a side effect. The success of Burroughs's fiction derived from the fact that he had discovered a new extreme in the spectrum of fantastic voyages: an extreme of escapist self-indulgence.

Burroughs did develop a few earthly settings for his new brand of action-adventure fantasy—most importantly Tarzan's fantasized Africa and Pellucidar, which was on the inner surface of an allegedly hollow world—while A. Merritt adapted dimensional fantasy to a similar purpose in "The Moon Pool" (1918), and Ray Cummings pioneered a Burroughsian subgenre of microcosmic romances in "The Girl in the Golden Atom" (1919). But the point was never to explore those *milieux* in any kind of rationally guided way; it was, instead, to adapt them as playgrounds for escapist exploits of exactly the sort that seemed in Europe, after 1914, to be exercises in intellectual cowardice.

Dozens of writers were recruited to the new pulp genre within 10 years of Burroughs's providing the crucial exemplars. Most of these writers were only marginally relevant to the evolution of SF, but Merritt and Cummings contrived important extensions to the range of escapist fantasy by elaborating different kinds of melodramatics. While Burroughs was an archetypal action-adventure writer, Merritt's imagination was more languorously inclined. Both men paired their heroes with exotically beautiful women, but Burroughs's heroines were there to be threatened with fates worse than death so that the hero could rescue them over and over again; Merritt's were there primarily to be admired and worshiped in the fabulous contexts of their own exotic worlds. Cummings, a woefully inept writer, compensated for his literary inadequacies by extending the range of his settings, thus causing his heroes to move about in a far more hectic fashion, and presenting them with more dizzying challenges than Burroughs could (Burroughs's worst fault as a writer was his overreliance on standardized cliff-hangers).

In general, the most accomplished writers—including Francis Stevens—who followed in the footsteps of these three pulp pioneers followed Merritt's example, while the less accomplished took their lead from Cummings, as Ralph Milne Farley did. Burroughs was, of course, reprinted in Britain—Tarzan made his debut there in 1917 and the Martian series appeared there in 1919—but his works were regarded as strictly juvenile fare, which is why I flagged them as YA. The subgenre of Burroughsian fantasy had no impact at all on the desultory progress made by scientific romance in the 1920s. In the U.S., by contrast, the influence of Burroughsian fantasy spread out to color the entire spectrum of fantastic fiction contained in the pulps, especially Hugo Gernsback's "scientifiction."

Gernsback's earliest magazines were not pulps—they grew out of mail order catalogs advertising technical materials and devices that he imported from Germany from 1905 onward—but they moved by degrees into the pulp marketplace. The first of them, *Modern Electrics* (launched 1908), carried no fiction until Gernsback began serializing his own futuristic utopian melodrama, *Ralph 124C41+*, in 1911. Thereafter, scientifiction became a regular but minor feature in *Modern Electrics'* successor, *The Electrical Experimenter* (founded 1913). In 1920, however, *The Electrical Experimenter* became *Science and Invention*, and scientifiction began to play an increasingly prominent role in its promotion.

Early scientifiction had much more in common with the inventor stories of the old dime novels and the humorous work of Edgar Franklin than it did with Burroughsian romance. Stories were usually short; the format that early writers found most useful was the conversation piece, and much scientifiction consisted of anecdotal tall tales spiced with technically inclined questions. Series of this type, in which zany scientists and inventors would explain their new ventures to curious innocents, included Gernsback's own accounts of "Baron Munchausen's New Scientific Adventures" (1915–1917) and Clement Fézandie's

"Doctor Hackenshaw" series (1921–1925). In 1923, however, Gernsback began reprinting stories by H. G. Wells and recruiting writers from the pulps, beginning with George Allan England and Ray Cummings. The August 1923 issue of *Science and Invention* was an all-scientifiction issue, in preparation for the launch of a reprint-dominated all-scientifiction magazine, *Amazing Stories*, in 1926.

It was at this point that Gernsback went all out to appeal to the pulp fiction audience, commissioning A. Merritt to produce a revised version of the most science-fictional of his fantasies, *The Metal Monster* (1920)—it appeared as *The Metal Emperor* in *Science and Invention* (1927–1928)—and asking Edgar Rice Burroughs to produce a new Martian novel with more emphasis on science-fictional content, *The Master Mind of Mars*, for a 1927 *Amazing Stories Annual*. Neither Burroughs nor Merritt ever worked for Gernsback again, and the flow of reprints by Jules Verne and H. G. Wells that sustained *Amazing Stories* through its first two years also dried up as the copyright holders began to complain about piracy. But the precedents Gernsback put in place in 1926–1927 defined the shape of SF to come. Gernsback insisted that scientifiction was a continuation of Vernian and Wellsian romance, but he had made every effort to adapt it for the pulp magazine audience by means of a lavish injection of Burroughsian and Merrittesque escapist melodramatics.

The Early History of Pulp SF

Most of the stories that appeared in the pulp SF magazines after 1927 were written by new writers, many of whom who became specialists in pulp SF. This was partly because SF turned out to have a unique appeal to teenage boys fascinated by its expansive effect on their vulnerable imaginations; it therefore developed a "cult following" without parallel in other pulp genres. It was, however, also due to the fact that writers already established in the pulps would not tolerate Gernsback's rates of pay and frequent reluctance to part with any money at all. The significance of Gernsback's one-off co-option of Burroughs and Merritt was exaggerated by the fact that he did not attract any contributions—except occasional works that had been universally rejected elsewhere—from the other writers who were now producing speculative fiction for the mainstream pulps.

Homer Eon Flint, Garret Smith, and Fred MacIsaac had all produced works of a more sober and thoughtful quasi-Wellsian stripe for the Munsey pulps between 1914 and 1926, but Flint was the only one to appear in a Gernsback pulp (in 1928), with a story well below his usual standard. The result of this avoidance was that the hectic races through space and time favored by Ray Cummings and other Burroughsian fantasists became more important models for the earliest would-be writers of scientifiction than MacIsaac's political fantasies or Garret Smith's explorations of the potential inherent in remote viewing devices.

The fortunes of the nascent pulp SF genre were soon complicated. Gernsback, who had tried to cash in on the technological boom he had so long anticipated by launching radio stations of his own while *Science and Invention* and its new companion *Radio News* were still in the ascendant, was overtaken by disaster. His radio stations suffered the fate of many pioneering enterprises, losing money on a massive scale in 1927 and 1928 because there were not yet enough radio sets in people's homes to make them financially viable. Gernsback's empire was bankrupted; *Amazing Stories* and its quarterly companion were sold off by the liquidator as a going concern.

Gernsback immediately launched a new series of commercial enterprises, founding two new magazines, *Science Wonder Stories* and *Air Wonder Stories*, in 1929. They were combined into *Wonder Stories* a year later; a third companion, *Science Wonder Quarterly*, became *Wonder Stories Quarterly*. The *Wonder* magazines substituted the term "science fiction" for "scientifiction" in order to distance themselves from their models. Although the replacement term did not take over immediately, it was markedly less cumbersome than its rival; *Amazing*'s new editor, T. O'Conor Sloane, stuck to the term he had inherited for a while, but it was only a matter of time before he changed *Amazing*'s subtitle from "The Magazine of Scientifiction" to "The Magazine of Science Fiction" (in the November 1932 issue).

The *Amazing* and *Wonder* groups both continued to cling, somewhat disingenuously, to the ideological pretense that Hugo Gernsback had maintained, claiming that science fiction was primarily a didactic medium whose virtue lay in its celebration of science and technology rather than its escapist component, the latter being merely a "sugar coat" to help the medicine down. For this reason, Gernsback was eager to recruit writers to his magazines who were scientifically educated and capable of extrapolating scientific hypotheses in various literary formats. The difficulty he had in finding such writers is graphically illustrated by the fact that the one he seized upon most enthusiastically, David H. Keller—who made his debut with "The Revolt of the Pedestrians" in 1928—was a dyed-in-the-wool conservative who took a very pessimistic view of the process of technological development. Miles J. Breuer, who was also an M.D., tended to take a similarly cautionary line (as did his occasional collaborator Clare Winger Harris, who made her first appearance in the same year, 1927). Nor did the boys' book writer A. Hyatt Verrill take aboard Gernsback's optimistic didacticism when he began penning such tales as "The Plague of the Living Dead" (1927), although Gernsback remained perfectly happy to publish his stubbornly xenophobic lost race stories.

The *Amazing* and *Wonder* groups did, however, offer a welcome haven to a number of writers who had already completed typescripts that they had been unable to place with conservatively inclined book publishers. The first to discover the new refuge was Stanton A. Coblentz in 1928, but his addition to the SF stable was far less significant than that of E. E. Smith, who had casually taken Ray Cummings's hectic brand of Burroughsian space fiction beyond the limits of the solar system in *The Skylark of Space* (written 1915–1920; published 1928). Gernsback gladly appended Smith's Ph.D. in food science to his byline, but it was the melodramatic quality of his work that immediately struck a chord with the readers.

Coincidentally, the same issue of *Amazing* that began serialization of *The Sky-lark of Space* also featured Philip Francis Nowlan's "Armageddon—2419 A.D.," a similarly melodramatic tale of an engineer working for the American Radioactive Gas Corporation who wakes up after suffering an accident in the 25th century to find the U.S. oppressively ruled by conquerors from the Far East; the intrepid hero—Anthony "Buck" Rogers—immediately sets about organizing a Second American Revolution. Buck Rogers was to enjoy an even longer and more successful career than "Doc" Smith's Richard Seaton, diversifying into comic books, radio, TV, and movies. In the meantime, the August 1928 issue of *Amazing Stories* became a key determinant of the image that the new genre would soon acquire: as the origin and natural home of "space opera."

The net result of this odd combination of influences and historical accidents was that labeled SF was, from its very inception, a chimerical genre. No matter what Hugo Gernsback might write in his editorials about SF continuing the great tradition of Jules Verne and H. G. Wells, or about its prophetic power to anticipate the ways in which radio, TV, and atomic energy would transform the human world, it was first and foremost an escapist genre. What appealed to the young readers who constituted its core audience—whose burgeoning "fandom" Gernsback attempted to colonize and capture in the *Wonder* magazines by means of the Science Fiction League—was not the prospect of being painlessly educated in science or alerted to things to come, but the experience of being hurtled into amazing adventures on a vast stage that extended into the remote future as well as the distant reaches of the galaxy.

However ill-fitting these two aspects were, though, they remained glued together, not just because the former served as a convenient justificatory apology for the latter but because it really did add something to the escapist utility of wild adventures to insist that they were not idle dreams but conceivable possibilities. The rhetoric shoring up this pretense was shallow and, frankly, deceptive, but the mere fact that it was offered was far more important than its logical substance. The fiction that Hugo Gernsback promoted was a bizarre patchwork of methods, styles, and ambitions—but that was its greatest virtue as well as a cacophony of faults.

The early science fiction magazines presented a vastly broader spectrum of literary methods and literary images to their readers than the other pulp magazines, which carried some speculative fiction alongside more conventional action-adventure fare. By comparison with what most book publishers would tolerate, even the other pulps were adventurous, but by comparison with the other pulps, the early SF pulps were another world. To many readers, that made them look extremely silly—but to those readers whose minds and standards were flexible enough to let them get a grip on the new genre, they exposed imaginative and literary vistas that had never been glimpsed before, whose very absurdity guaranteed that the genre could not be long weighed down by existing assumptions about what could and could not be done, or ought and ought not to, be done.

Faced with a choice between the kinds of imaginative fiction promoted by the SF pulps and the kinds that were grudgingly permitted to creep into the fringes of the upper strata of the American literary marketplace—as exemplified, for instance, by Garet Garrett's *The Blue Wound* (1921), Gertrude Atherton's *Black Oxen* (1923), Hector C. Bywater's *The Great Pacific War* (1925), and Robert M. Coates's *The Eater of Darkness* (1926)—a reader would have to have been dismally narrow-minded and stupidly blind to the actual pace of technological progress to prefer the latter.

British Scientific Romance in the 1920s

The impact that World War I had on the production and nature of imaginative fiction in Britain lingered long after the war had ended. Looking back from the vantage point of 1919, the various hopes expressed in pre-war scientific romance—especially the notion that it might be possible to fight a "war that would end war" whose settlement would pave the way for a utopian reconstruction of global society—seemed worse than naive. Indulgence in flights of fancy had come to seem treasonous while the war was being fought, and hindsight now revealed the dominant ideologies of pre-war scientific romance as parties to a greater treason: the illusion that had tricked the nations of Europe into a futile conflict whose only result had been the mass slaughter of an entire generation of young men. Those who had not died in combat still had to face the epidemic of "Spanish flu" that swept across the debilitated world, piling random misfortune upon self-inflicted catastrophe.

It is hardly surprising, in this intellectual climate, that those writers of scientific romance anxious to take up where they had left off, such as J. D. Beresford, found the marketplace hostile to their new endeavors. Save for two collections of short stories reprinting earlier achievements, Beresford published nothing of note in the genre for two decades; neither did M. P. Shiel. Arthur Conan Doyle, the other major survivor, did not absent himself entirely, but was mostly content to substitute bad occult fiction for scientific romance. The only writer of magazine scientific romance who seems to have been able to take up more or less where he had left off in 1913 was the Australian Coutts Brisbane, whose work for *The Red Magazine* has never been collected. E. Charles Vivian was able to print his own speculative fiction while he was editor of *Flight*—but that, too, was never collected. And Beresford did contrive to assist E. V. Odle's *The Clockwork Man* (1923) into print, but Odle's second scientific romance was never published.

The great majority of the serious futuristic fantasies that did creep into print in Britain during the 1920s were remarkable for the depth of their pessimism, which readily descended through various phases of black irony toward apocalyptic despair. Unprecedentedly extreme disenchantment and cynicism were mapped by Edward Shanks's *The People of the Ruins* (1920), Cicely Hamilton's *Theodore Savage* (1922), P. Anderson Graham's *The Collapse of Homo sapiens* (1923), Osbert Sitwell's "Triple Fugue" (1924), Shaw Desmond's *Ragnarok* (1926), Guy Dent's *Emperor of the If* (1926), S. Fowler Wright's *Deluge* (1927), and Eimar O'Duffy's *The Spacious Adventures of the Man in the Street* (1928). Meanwhile, a plaintive note of hope continued to sound in such various works as George Bernard Shaw's *Back to Methuselah* (1921) and Victor MacClure's *The Ark of the Covenant* (1924). The utopianism stubbornly reiterated in H. G. Wells's *Men Like Gods* (1923) is manifestly fugitive, consigned to the far future and brutally contrasted with the follies of contemporary politics; rival treatments such as Muriel Jaeger's *The Question Mark* (1926) were mostly skeptical and querulous. Two of the most imaginatively ambitious works of the period— Edward Heron-Allen's *The Cheetah Girl* (1923) and S. Fowler Wright's *The Amphibians* (1925)—were self-published, providing further testimony to the inhospitability of the marketplace. David Lindsay's *A Voyage to Arcturus* (1920) received such a poor welcome, in spite of being a masterpiece, that Lindsay spent the rest of his life broken-heartedly moderating the ambition that had produced it.

While scientific romance languished, however, the rival Wellsian "futurology" continued to make progress. When Kegan Paul, Trench and Trubner attracted considerable attention in 1924 with pamphlets reprinting J. B. S. Haldane's lecture *Daedalus; or, Science and the Future* and Bertrand Russell's ideological riposte *Icarus; or, the Future of Science*, they instituted a Today and Tomorrow series that eventually extended to 108 volumes before the series was terminated in 1930. Many of the contributors—including John Gloag, Gerald Heard, J. Leslie Mitchell, and A. M. Low—went on to write scientific romances; some— including Muriel Jaeger, Winifred Holtby, and the American Garet Garrett— had already done so. André Maurois's contribution, *The Next Chapter: The War Against the Moon* (1928), was the only explicit SF story, but several other writers employed fictional devices in the course of their essays. By far the most extravagant item was J. D. Bernal's *The World, the Flesh, and the Devil* (1929), whose matter-of-fact account of the future evolution of humankind and the colonization of the galaxy easily exceeded the visionary reach of pulp space opera.

Many of the contributors to the Today and Tomorrow series belonged to a generalized intelligentsia that had not yet fragmented into the "two cultures" whose separation was to be lamented by C. P. Snow a generation later; scientists such as Haldane and Bernal moved in the same social circles as philosophers including Russell and literary figures including Holtby, Vera Brittain, and Robert Graves. The result of this social overlap was that the ideas set out in Haldane's *Daedalus* were not only satirized in fiction by his friend biologist Julian Huxley in "The Tissue-Culture King" (1926; reprinted in *Amazing Stories* in 1927), but also by Osbert Sitwell in "Triple Fugue" (1924). Muriel Jaeger responded to Haldane's ideas as well as to those of H. G. Wells, and Julian Huxley's younger brother Aldous took up the theme of "The Tissue-Culture King" far more robustly in *Brave New World*. Essays by Haldane and J. D. Bernal were key influences on the works of Olaf Stapledon—who had made his literary debut in a small press magazine owned by S. Fowler Wright and was also a close friend of John Gloag—which spearheaded the renaissance of scientific romance that began in 1930, just as the Today and Tomorrow series reached its end.

Attempts were made in Britain to import pulpish melodrama into scientific romance—G. McLeod Winsor's *Station X* (1919) and Francis Ridley's *The Green Machine* (1926) vulgarized Wellsian themes in a fashion that cleverly anticipated the substance of horror/SF movies to come. But such melodramatics never caught on in Britain, although science-fictional devices retained a marginal role in stereotyped thriller fiction as Frankensteinian threats to be thwarted and put away. Only a few such thrillers—notably E. Charles Vivian's *Star Dust* (1926) and Edmund Snell's *Kontrol* (1928)—ever seriously discussed the possibilities they sketched out.

Scientific Romance in Continental Europe in the 1920s

The situation of scientific romance in other European nations in 1919 was broadly similar to that in Britain. Although French writers picked up the threads of pre-war production more readily than anyone else, the process of liberation after partial occupation and widespread devastation proved more conducive to imaginative recovery than sending troops abroad to die by the million. French writers who were able to resume careers already launched, with no conspicuous diminution of their imaginative power or audience appeal, included J. H. Rosny aîné, with *La grande énigme* [*The Great Enigma*] (1920) and *Les navigateurs de l'infini* [*Navigators of Space*] (1925); Maurice Renard, with *L'homme qui voulait être invisible* [*The Man Who Wanted to Be Invisible*] (1923) and *Le singe* [*The Monkey*; trans. as *Blind Circle*] (1925 with Albert Jean); and "Claude Farrère," with *Les condamnés à mort* [*The Condemned*; trans. as *Useless Hands*] (1920) and *Contes d'outre et d'autres mondes* [*Tales of the Afterlife and Other Worlds*] (1921). Some popular writers working in outlets closer in kind to the U.S. pulps had been able to continue working, with only slight inhibition of their production, throughout the war years, notably José Moselli and Jean la Hire. French writers who took up scientific romance for the first time shortly after the end of the war included Théo Varlet, whose works included a two-part "Martian epic" written in collaboration with Octave Joncquel, consisting of *Les titans du ciel* (1921) and *L'agonie de la terre* (1922).

Ironically, German writers of futuristic fiction were also quicker to rebuild their morale than their equivalents in Britain, perhaps because the Germans knew full well that they would have won the war in France in the summer of 1918 had American troops not arrived in the nick of time to shore up the exhausted British and French divisions. Germany soon forged its own distinctive tradition of the *zukunftsroman* ("futuristic novel"), which celebrated the efficiency and ambition of German engineers and the contribution they would surely make to the revitalization of the nation's fortunes. The genre's key exemplars were established by Hans Dominik (1872–1945), whose first novel was *Die Macht der Drei* (1922)—although its ambitions had been ironically anticipated in Owen Gregory's satirical account of a revitalized Germany, *Meccania* (1918).

One of Dominik's works was translated in Gernsback's *Air Wonder Stories* in 1930, but U.S. pulp readers got a better appreciation of the German genre's concerns and tone from five novels by Otfrid von Hanstein that the German-speaking Gernsback published, including *Elektropolis* [*Electropolis*] (1927; trans. 1930). The *Wonder* magazines also featured two novels by a member of the German rocket society, Otto Willi Gail—more importantly *Der Schuss ins All* [*The Shot into Infinity*] (1925; trans. 1930). Technological enthusiasm was combined with utopian reformism in the philosophy of Weimar Minister of Culture Walter Rathenau—whose ideas are parodied in Aleksandr Moszkowski's satire *Die Inseln der Weisheit* [*The Isles of Wisdom*] (1922)—and extended to embrace biotechnology in Alfred Döblin's *Berge, Meere und Giganten* (1924). It also overflowed into movies, by courtesy of Fritz Lang's *Metropolis* (1926) and *Die Frau im Mond* [*The Girl in the Moon*] (1928), both of which were novelized by his wife Thea von Harbou (and must have been far more widely read in the U.S. than the SF in Gernsback's pulps). By 1930, however, the rise of Nazism had begun to subject such work to a powerful process of political filtration that leached most of the enterprise out of it.

Russia had undergone a more profound political transformation than any other nation while the war was in progress, thanks to the revolutions of 1917, whose immediate results included an increased interest in scientific education and technological progress that was by no means inhospitable to scientific romance. Rocket pioneer Konstantin Tsiolkovsky finally brought to fruition his long-gestating didactic account of extraterrestrial colonization, *Vne zemli* [*Outside the Earth*] (completed 1920), and Aleksandr Beliaev also became a popular writer of educational science fantasies for children. Alexei Tolstoi's *Aelita* (1922) was adapted to the new regime with a strong dose of socialist rhetoric, although the scriptwriters of the pioneering silent movie based on it decided that trips to Mars were not entirely in keeping with the spirit of socialist realism and wrote the whole enterprise off as a dream. For other Russian writers, however, optimism was very rapidly displaced by profound disenchantment, reflected in Yegevny Zamyatin's extreme dystopia *My* [*We*] (1920) and Mikhail Bulgakov's scathing Wellsian satire "Rokovy'e yaitsa" ["The Fatal Eggs"] (1922).

Disenchantment, usually expressed satirically, can also be found in the work of other writers from the ruins of the old Austro-Hungarian Empire, who found themselves citizens of hastily constructed nation-states in the aftermath of World War I. In Czechoslovakia, Karel Čapek reflected pessimistically on the seeming intransigence of political problems in *R.U.R.* (1921) and *Krakatit* (1925). In Hungary, Frigyes Karinthy sent Lemuel Gulliver on the strangest voyage of all in *Capillaria* (1921). A genuinely international perspective, available only to professional diplomats, could hardly help endorsing the ironic pessimism of these works, as evidenced by Salvador de Madariaga's *The Sacred Giraffe* (1925) and Pierrepoint Noyes's *The Pallid Giant* (1927). Some of these works are very amusing, but their comedy is invariably dyed in black, uniting them in bitterness with the darkest British apocalyptic fantasies.

It cannot be said that this kind of work was *entirely* out of keeping with the spirit of the American pulps of 1914–1930, given that a certain cynical alarmism is certainly detectable there—in such works as Victor Rousseau's *Messiah of the*

Cylinder (1917), Milo Hastings' *City of Endless Night* (1920), and the more politically inclined works of George Allan England. But there was very little sign anywhere in Europe of any imaginative counterbalance of the kind provided in the U.S. by Burroughsian escapist fantasy, especially the extension into space of that kind of fiction by Ray Cummings, E. E. Smith, and others. Even German futuristic fiction kept a relatively narrow focus on the future of European society; only in France was there any resounding echo of American pulp SF enterprise. The war of 1914–1918 was, however, only the first profound shock that 20th-century futuristic speculation had to weather, and Europe did not have to wait for a second World War to suffer another significant interruption of progress. In October 1929, the Wall Street crash caused the U.S. to cut financial support to European economies that were still very fragile; the result was the Great Depression, with its worldwide effects.

Pulp SF in the Early 1930s

The Wall Street crash sent the U.S. into economic depression along with Europe, but the U.S. had come through World War I without suffering any kind of domestic devastation, and the general expectation in 1930 was that it would bounce back from the stock market crash with similar alacrity. That expectation eventually proved unrealistic, but the point was that optimism was far better conserved in the U.S. than in Europe. The pulp fiction industry was not badly hit by the crash, and the escapist fervor of its product enabled it to exploit the situation. In fact, the ultra-cheap magazines grew even more popular as other sectors of the economy languished, and their publishers did their very best to exploit the situation by intensifying competition with one another, recklessly expanding the number of titles they produced and inventing more new genres in some profusion.

One of the products of this rapid expansion and diversification was *Astounding Stories of Super-Science,* a periodical launched by William Clayton's pulp chain at the behest of Harry Bates, who became its editor. Unlike the *Amazing* and *Wonder* magazines, *Astounding* was an unashamedly commercial pulp, which paid far higher word rates—with the result that many of the recent recruits to the genre were avid to write for it. Ray Cummings seized the new opportunity, as did the other pioneers of what eventually came to be known as "space opera": E. E. Smith, Edmond Hamilton, and Jack Williamson. *Astounding* also began to recruit pulp professionals who had not deigned to work for the specialist pulps until then, such as Victor Rousseau and Murray Leinster. Although the general pulps continued to feature Burroughsian fantasy set in other worlds in the solar system, and found space flight acceptable as a climactic device in such works as Edwin Balmer and Philip Wylie's *When Worlds Collide* (1933), the kind of extraterrestrial action-adventure fiction pioneered by Cummings and Smith was left almost entirely to the specialist pulps and *Astounding* rapidly became its primary home.

In the meantime, the stubborn persistence in the Gernsback-founded magazines of pretenses to didactic virtue continued to provide a rival incentive that was not unattractive to hobbyist writers for whom professional rates of pay were not a top priority. Gernsback's pulps countered the superior pay rates of *Astounding* by using a great deal of work in translation (for which Gernsback presumably neglected to pay the original authors), but also continued to attract new work that was not formulated according to the customary precepts of pulp action-adventure fiction.

The first managing editor Gernsback hired to handle the day-to-day operation of the *Wonder* magazines was David Lasser, an engineer and technical writer who was also the first president of the American Interplanetary Society. While editing the magazines, Lasser published *The Conquest of Space* (1932), the first English-language work popularizing the notion that space travel using liquid fuel rockets was a real possibility. One of his fellow founder-members of the AIS, Laurence Manning, was one of Lasser's first and best recruits to the genre; Manning made his debut with the graphic dystopian fantasy "The City of the Living Dead" (1930, in collaboration with Fletcher Pratt). Manning then went on to popularize the society's ideas in "The Voyage of the *Asteroid*" and "The Wreck of the *Asteroid*" (1932) before producing the pioneering future-history series *The Man Who Awoke* (1933).

Although Lasser's involvement with SF was brief (he left the *Wonder* group in 1933 and was replaced by the teenage fan Charles D. Hornig), he did lay important foundations for the emergence of "the conquest of space" as *the* central concern of SF. Arthur C. Clarke ultimately became the genre's most outspoken advocate of the myth of the Space Age—the notion that the establishment of artificial satellites and regular traffic between the earth and the moon would be the first step in a rapid and inexorable process of expansive colonization of other worlds. But Clarke credited Lasser's *Conquest of Space* as the revelation that changed his life, while the stories in the early pulp SF magazines played a key supporting role.

Other new writers recruited to the genre by Lasser included several Britons. "Gawain Edwards" (Gavin Pendray) published "A Rescue from Jupiter" in 1930, following it with two more novellas in 1931. Benson Herbert, who would later become a specialist small-press publisher, made his debut with "The World Without" (1931). John Beynon Harris—who would eventually become far better known as John Wyndham—published "Worlds to Barter" (1931) three months later; and the Australian-born J. M. Walsh published *Vandals of the Void* shortly afterward. Festus Pragnell followed them in 1932. Lasser also published the most notable of the female writers recruited to the SF pulps, the pioneering SF poet "Lilith Lorraine" (Mary Maud Wright), whose "Into the 28th Century" (1930) was one of the boldest utopian speculations to appear in the pulps. P. Schuyler Miller and Nathan Schachner (mostly in collaboration with Arthur Leo Zagat) were other significant writers who published much of their early work in the *Wonder* magazines, both beginning in 1930, before moving on. Fletcher Pratt—whose byline had previously appeared in Gernsback's *Amazing* on allegedly collaborative work—also did much of his early work for the group, while Clifford D. Simak made his debut there in 1931.

In the meantime, Lasser's rival T. O'Conor Sloane provided a home for two of the scientific romances that mathematician Eric Temple Bell (who wrote fiction as John Taine) had penned several years before. *White Lily* (1930; book version as *The Crystal Horde*) and *Seeds of Life* (1931) appeared in *Amazing Stories Quarterly*, although the first and most adventurous of them, *The Time Stream* (written in 1921), appeared in *Wonder Stories* in 1931–1932.

Amazing was also the first and preferred market of John W. Campbell, Jr., who was a student at MIT when he made his debut in 1930 and who had a strong interest in the development of atomic power as well as an ambition to use space opera as a vehicle for scientific speculation. Campbell's short story "The Last Evolution" (1932) provided a synoptic future history very different from that set out in Olaf Stapledon's *Last and First Men*, in which the future evolution of man's descendant species is determined by the political priorities of space opera. In fact, this was a dramatic exemplification of the divergence of 1930s SF and scientific romance, and an important prospectus for the subsequent development of SF. Another writer who made his debut in *Amazing* in this period was Neil R. Jones, whose long series with "The Jameson Satellite" (1931) soon set out on a far-reaching exploration of the wonders of the galaxy, which similarly mapped out imaginative territory that was to be standardized by genre SF.

Some of the space fiction that appeared in the *Amazing* and *Wonder* magazines while the Clayton *Astounding* was in competition with them was obviously material that had been rejected by the higher-paying market. But much of it struck a very different attitude, either choosing to combine the action-adventure formula with other materials—as Campbell did—or flatly refusing the dictates of the formula in order to exercise a purer kind of curiosity and to take delight in the invention of bizarre alien life forms for their own sake. A similar difference is evident in the Earth-set stories favored by the rival magazines. *Astounding* preferred the standard crime fiction formula in which a newly emergent threat would be conclusively thwarted by the hero, although it was not entirely averse to horror stories that ended less happily.

Despite the skepticism manifest by so many of their authors, the Gernsback-founded magazines continued to show a much more celebratory interest in the potential of new technologies to transform social life, and to favor *contes philosophiques* whose frequent crudity could not altogether undermine the relevance of their extrapolations or the seriousness of their arguments.

The Diversification of Pulp Fantastic Fiction

There had, of course, been pulps specializing in fantastic fiction before Gernsback founded *Amazing Stories*, but only one of them had lasted for any length of time: the defiantly eccentric *Weird Tales*, established in 1923. *Weird Tales* published some early space opera in the days before the SF magazines took over the subgenre. Edmond Hamilton was one of the magazine's most prolific contributors in the late 1920s, and published "Crashing Suns" there in 1928 while *Amazing* was serializing *The Skylark of Space*—and *Weird Tales* continued to feature a certain amount of similar material in the early 1930s. Its chief contribution to the early development of SF was, however, its nurturing of a number of other nascent subgenres on the thematic and commercial margins of SF.

The most important of these marginal genres was horror/SF, and the most important species of horror/SF that emerged within the pages of *Weird Tales* was the product of a group of writers associated with H. P. Lovecraft who traced their historical inspiration to Edgar Allan Poe and devoted themselves to the development of a form of "cosmic horror" fiction based on the assumption that the vast universe revealed by astronomical science diminished humankind to the status of a mere plaything of vast alien entities. Having resurrected an allegiance to Poe long after the French had grown tired of him, the Lovecraft school became the last refuge of Decadent fantasy, and the most extreme Decadent fantasist of all, Clark Ashton Smith, was one of those whose tales appeared in the Gernsback pulps in the early 1930s, importing rhapsodic prose-poetry whose narrative thrust made a casual mockery of all the moral aspirations of conventional pulp fiction.

Robert E. Howard, the writer from the Lovecraft circle who set the most important precedents of all for the future evolution of imaginative fiction in America, never appeared in the SF pulps and wrote only one marginal SF story (the posthumously published Burroughsian planetary romance *Almuric*), but his contributions to another nascent subgenre require acknowledgement. Howard founded the hyper-Burroughsian subgenre of supernatural fantasy that eventually came to be known as "sword-and-sorcery" fiction, which co-existed with SF as a kind of annex to its marketplace until the 1970s, when it enjoyed a spectacular renaissance. Howardesque sword-and-sorcery exerted a discernible influence on SF from outside the genre, in much the same way that Burroughsian fantasy had done. Like the work of A. Merritt, the ultra-escapist fantasies of Howard and Clark Ashton Smith functioned as magnets, always straining to draw the narrative ambitions of pulp exotica away from Gernsbackian didacticism and the narrowing gaze of scientific rationalism, striving to keep the furthest reaches of time and space free for play of a very different kind.

Even the most conscientious pulp SF writers felt the power of that attraction, although the extent to which they gave in to it varied. SF writers who also dabbled in sword-and-sorcery fiction—C. L. Moore is the most important early example—tended to produce work that was not merely marginal but frankly chimerical, producing a kind of "science-fantasy" that reveled in the internal contradictions generated by the clash of what were, in effect, irreconcilable worldviews. In particular, the subgenre of far-future fantasy became—primarily under the influence of Clark Ashton Smith—a key arena in which magic and other arbitrary exotica could comfortably co-exist with more orthodox science-fictional apparatus.

No other specialist magazine ever had the same cross-fertilizing influence on the SF pulps that *Weird Tales* contrived, but some of the other magazines established during the diversifying craze of the early 1930s did focus on significant marginal subgenres. The most successful was the "vigilante superhero" subgenre pioneered by such pulps as *Doc Savage* and *The Spider* (both launched 1933), which were a further extension into the fantasy of exotic detective pulps like *The Shadow* (launched 1931). This subgenre ultimately became central to the comic book medium. Another variant of the exotic detective pulps was the "exotic secret agent" subgenre typified by *Operator 5* (launched 1934), which gradually edged into futuristic settings as the menaces thwarted by its hero were forced to extremes by the pressure of melodramatic inflation.

One of the most curious subgenres spawned by the diversification was the "weird menace" story, whose formula required seemingly supernatural—and extremely bizarre—phenomena to be ingeniously rationalized. *Dime Mystery* began specializing in such stories in 1933, with enough success to inspire the foundation of *Terror Tales* in 1934 and *Horror Stories* and *Thrilling Mystery* in 1935. The last-named, edited by Leo Margulies, attracted a great many SF writers to its pages, including Ray Cummings, Jack Williamson, and Edmond Hamilton. Although it is now extinct (except in the animated cartoon series *Scooby-Doo*), the weird menace formula remains an interesting example of calculatedly chimerical fiction that is similar in its method to some kinds of SF.

The extravagant diversification of the pulp magazines proved, however, to be an economic error. The recklessly overheated competition to occupy rack space would probably have been mutually destructive even in a healthy economic climate; in the Depression it soon resulted in fatalities. Like Hugo Gernsback before him, William Clayton had allowed his ambitions too free a rein, and his magazine chain went bankrupt in 1933. Like *Amazing*, however, *Astounding* was sold off by the receiver. Acquired by *Doc Savage* publisher Street and Smith, it reappeared after a six-month hiatus, under the editorial management of F. Orlin Tremaine. Tremaine, a more adventurous editor than his predecessor, attempted to steer a middle course between the orthodox action-adventure fiction of Bates's *Astounding* and the didactic ambitions of the Gernsback-founded magazines. In the hope of contriving an eclectic combination, he advertised what he called "thought variant" stories that would develop interesting new ideas in a fashion that was both imaginatively adventurous and intellectually responsible.

The first writer to be thus labeled was Nathan Schachner, but other writers who rallied to the new flag included Jack Williamson, Murray Leinster, and C. L. Moore. John W. Campbell, Jr. invented a new name—"Don A. Stuart"—to which to attribute his ventures in this line. Raymond Z. Gallun was one of several new writers who found thought variant stories attractive, and *Astounding* resumed its poaching of writers whose first entry into pulp SF had been granted by its rivals—most notably the quirkily inventive Stanley G. Weinbaum, who had made his debut in *Wonder*, and British writer John Russell Fearn, who had made his debut in *Amazing*. Two of H. P. Lovecraft's principal works ended up in the Street and Smith *Astounding*, submitted on his behalf by Donald Wandrei, who became a regular contributor of thought variants. Another Lovecraft Circle writer who appeared there was Frank Belknap Long, who contributed some notable far-future fantasies.

While the Street and Smith *Astounding* thrived, its genre rivals went into steep declines. In 1936, the *Wonder* group was sold to the chain that produced *Thrilling Mystery*, who installed Margulies as its supervising editor and brought its central element into line by retitling it *Thrilling Wonder Stories*. Margulies and his assistant, Oscar J. Friend, set out to build up its teenage audience by concentrating on colorful but rigorously orthodox action-adventure fiction. The first two cover illustrations of the new incarnation advertised its new priorities with such startling clarity that fanzine editor Martin Alger cited them in 1939 as the beginning of a dire trend that he proposed to defy by founding a Society for the Prevention of Bug-Eyed Monsters on the Covers of Science Fiction Publications (correspondence relating to the issue often employed the acronym BEM, which became SF fandom's first contribution to fashionable parlance).

In 1938, the *Amazing* group was sold to Ziff-Davis, who likewise discarded everything but the core title, which was similarly remodeled as an action-adventure pulp reminiscent of the Clayton *Astounding*. Within the space of two years, therefore, the spectrum of the SF pulps was inverted, *Astounding* changing places with its former rivals—a tendency that was to be dramatically emphasized when Tremaine was promoted within the Street and Smith organization late in 1937, abandoning editorial responsibility for *Astounding* to his newly hired assistant, John W. Campbell, Jr.

It is Campbell who is credited with ushering in "The Golden Age of [pulp] Science Fiction," and his missionary zeal to transform the genre and increase its sophistication certainly entitles him to the lion's share of that credit. It is, however, worth observing that Orlin Tremaine had laid vital foundations for him, and that all significant opposition was veering sharply in another direction as he assumed his position. It is worth noting, too, that Campbell was responsible for the final experiment in diversification carried out within the pulp arena, when he created a companion magazine for *Astounding* called *Unknown* in 1939. *Unknown* perished in 1943, sacrificed as the price for keeping *Astounding* on a monthly schedule while the U.S. involved itself in World War II. But its brief existence was highly significant in that it created a new kind of fantasy fiction specifically adapted to the outlook and methods of the specialist SF writers who produced the bulk of it—most notably L. Sprague de Camp.

The essence of this new kind of fantasy was that it drew its narrative energy from the confrontation of characters armed with a scientific frame of mind and science-fictional imaginative enterprise with the agents and devices of traditional magic. The consequences were usually, but not necessarily, humorous. Such stories demonstrated, even more powerfully than the kind of science fantasy developed by C. L. Moore, that there was a great deal of narrative energy to be derived from such chimerical combinations of logically irreconcilable motifs. At the time, Campbell was undoubtedly correct to think that protecting *Astounding* was more important than preserving *Unknown*, and it could not have been conceivable to him that such lightweight chimerical enterprises would one day begin to crowd out of the literary marketplace the "hard" science fiction whose evolution he was supervising. Even so, he deserves more credit for anticipating the shape of things to come than he could possibly have guessed or desired.

The Renaissance of British Scientific Romance

The advent of the Depression was felt more sharply in Europe than in the U.S., and its influence on the evolution of speculative fiction was very different. In the U.S., economic troubles intensified the demand for escapism; in Britain, they intensified anxiety about the future. The principal political response in continental Europe to the Depression was the gradual but seemingly inexorable rise of fascism, not merely in opposition to Soviet communism but also in protest against the workings of the emergent global financial system—for whose inadequacies scapegoats were keenly but arbitrarily sought.

Germany was not the first European nation to fall victim to the glamour of fascism, but it rapidly became the most extreme adopter. By denouncing the Versailles Treaty that had ended World War I—as Benito Mussolini had done in Italy four months earlier—the National Socialists won 107 seats in the German election in September 1930, making them the second-largest party. Early the following year, Oswald Mosley broke away from the British Labour Party to found his own party modeled on Mussolini's *Fascisti*. This was the background against which a renaissance of British scientific romance took place, as anxieties about the potential reinstitution of the hostilities abandoned in 1918 intensified.

The writer who became the central figure of 1930s scientific romance, Olaf Stapledon, made a spectacular debut with the far-reaching future history *Last and First Men* (1930), which saw the future as a sequence of phases in an eternal ideological battle between collectivism and individualism, each enhanced by various innovations of physical evolution. In the same year, Neil Bell—who, like his fellow conscientious objector Stapledon, had served as an ambulance driver on the Western Front in World War I—produced a less far-reaching but more scathingly sarcastic future history in *The Seventh Bowl* (initially bylined "Miles"). Both writers went on to more intimate explorations of human nature, Bell in *Precious Porcelain* (1931) and Stapledon in *Odd John* (1934), and to various Wellsian speculative enterprises. S. Fowler Wright followed a similar trajectory in *Dream* (1931) and the stories collected in *The New Gods Lead* (1934). Wells continued to remain conscientiously aloof, despite issuing his own future history *The Shape of Things to Come* (1933) and dabbling in such "sarcastic fantasies" as *The Autocracy of Mr Parham* (1930) and *The Croquet Player* (1936), as well as consenting to his early works' being reprinted as *Scientific Romances* in 1933.

Future-war fiction became increasingly bitter and increasingly melodramatic in the 1930s as attention focused on the possibilities of aerial bombardment using chemical and biological weapons to supplement ever-more-powerful explosives, as exemplified by John Gloag's *To-Morrow's Yesterday* (1932) and *Winter's Youth* (1934), Frank McIlraith and Roy Connolly's *Invasion from the Air* (1934), Fowler Wright's trilogy that began with *Prelude in Prague* (1935), Joseph O'Neill's *Day of Wrath* (1936), and P. G. Chadwick's *The Death Guard* (1939).

The gathering hysteria of these works is further reflected in the desperation of such political fantasies as Harold Nicolson's *Public Faces* (1932), Bell's *The Lord of Life* (1933), Michael Arlen's *Man's Mortality* (1933), C. S. Forester's *The Peacemaker* (1934), and Alun Llewellyn's *The Strange Invaders* (1934). The last-named adopts the ambiguous post-holocaust pastoralism of John Collier's *Tom's a-Cold* (1933), also reflected in J. Leslie Mitchell's *Three Go Back* (1932) and *Gay Hunter* (1934) and—less enthusiastically—in Wayland Smith's *The Machine Stops* (1936) and R. C. Sherriff's *The Hopkins Manuscript* (1939).

The tenor and tension of such works was readily extrapolated into surrealization and caricaturish exaggeration in O'Neill's *Land Under England* (1935), Herbert Read's *The Green Child* (1935), M. P. Shiel's *The Young Men Are Coming!* (1937), Andrew Marvell's *Minimum Man* (1938), and Alfred Gordon Bennett's *The Demigods* (1939). Similar surrealization and exaggeration are evident in such dystopian satires as Aldous Huxley's *Brave New World* (1932) and Fowler Wright's *The Adventure of Wyndham Smith* (1938), and in such psychological fantasias as Claude Houghton's *This Was Ivor Trent* (1935) and Murray Constantine's *Proud Man* (1934)—the latter of which was followed by a startling account of a Nazi-dominated Europe, *Swastika Night* (1937).

Although there was a counterbalancing good-humored sobriety in such painstakingly understated satirical works as E. C. Large's *Sugar in the Air* (1937) and Eden Phillpotts's *Saurus* (1938), and such works as John Hargrave's *The Imitation Man* (1931) and J. Storer Clouston's *Button Brains* (1933) conserved a purely comic note, these had to swim against a tide of pessimism whose bleakness and anger were unprecedented. The only speculative fictions that conserved a semblance of meditative objectivity were those that dealt with matters of a safely abstract kind, such as J. B. Priestley's "time plays," or matters long settled, such as in the essays in alternative history in J. C. Squire's *If* (1931). Pulp melodramatics were very thin on the ground, save for conspicuously downmarket works including Alan Hyder's *Vampires Overhead* (1935) and such juvenilia as A. M. Low's *Adrift in the Stratosphere* (which was serialized in the first boys' paper to approach status as an SF magazine, *Scoops*, in 1934) and John Beynon's *Planet Plane* (1936). C. S. Lewis's attempt to revive the religious cosmic voyage in *Out of the Silent Planet* (1938) could not in the end escape its own tendency to hysteria.

As in the previous decade, the concerns of British scientific romance were not entirely unreflected in the U.S.—Samuel Hopkins Adams's *The World Goes Smash* (1938) is one of several American future-war novels of the period, while William Sloane's *To Walk the Night* (1937) is a meditative mystery closer in spirit to the British tradition than the native one. But the scarcity of such exceptions is scant defiance of an almost total separation of interests and methods.

This "renaissance effect" was, however, virtually confined to Britain. French scientific romance continued to thrive in the 1930s, but the impetus regained in the 1920s was maintained rather than further enhanced. As the older generation of writers became inactive, like J. H. Rosny, or confined their efforts to other genres, like Maurice Renard, new writers emerged to take their place. Notable among them were André Maurois, author of two fine *contes philo-*

sophiques, Le peseur d'âmes [*The Weigher of Souls*] (1931) and *La machine à lire les pensées* [*The Thought-Reading Machine*] (1937), and Henri Proumen, Jacques Spitz, and Régis Messac—but their work diversified at a moderate rate. As the 1930s progressed, the pulp fiction element long preserved by such writers as José Moselli and Jean la Hire flourished to a greater extent than more earnest scientific romances, in the work of such writers as Tancrède Vallerey and the prolific Maurice Limat.

The early promise shown by the expansion of German speculative fiction was soon aborted in the 1930s, for reasons evidenced by one of the last novels Gernsback had translated for *Wonder Stories*, Friedrich Freksa's *Druso* (1932), which foreshadowed a racist and fascist rhetoric that became increasingly prevalent once Hitler was in power. An element of pulpish action-adventure was, however, preserved at the bottom end of the market in a long series of novels by Paul Alfred Müller, who used the pseudonyms Freder van Holk and Lok Myler. Few works of German speculative fiction from the 1930s have been reprinted in postwar Germany, let alone translated; one of the last to appear in English was Fedor Kaul's highly ambivalent apocalyptic fantasy *Die Welt ohne Gedächtnis* [translated as *Contagion to This World*] (1933).

Russian speculative fiction also suffered from increasing political suspicion as the 1930s advanced. The Stalinist notion that all fantastic fiction was a betrayal of the principles of socialist realism became solidly entrenched and became the official policy of the writers' union, condemning anything remotely resembling SF to a near-total eclipse. In other parts of Eastern Europe, such futuristic fiction as was produced possessed the same anxiousness as British scientific romance, as reflected in such political satire as Karel Čapek's *Válka s Mloky* [*War with the Newts*] (1937). When war resumed in 1939, of course, the effect in Europe was much the same as it had been in 1914—and in the U.S., there was hardly any effect at all until 1943.

The Sophistication of Pulp SF

Pulp SF might have remained a colorful subspecies of action-adventure fiction, but the evidence provided by the revamped *Amazing Stories* and *Thrilling Wonder Stories* is that it would have survived and thrived rather than dying along with the weird menace pulps or moving into another medium along with the superheroic vigilantes. Even without the editorial input of John W. Campbell, Jr., it would undoubtedly have undergone a gradual sophistication. The policies Campbell adopted when he took over *Astounding* in September 1937 hastened that sophistication considerably, and began to have dramatic effects from the beginning of 1938. But he could not have wrought such a rapid transformation had certain expectations not been set in place and patiently cultivated by his predecessors.

The environment provided by a specialist magazine allowed writers of labeled science fiction to take far more for granted than their forebears had been able to do. Readers had formerly needed to be carefully introduced to the notion that a story was to be set in the future or an alien world, and the narrative labor required to establish the particular world-within-the-text could easily cripple the pace and economy of a story, especially one geared to the expectations of pulp readers. Examples of stories written before 1926 that begin in the future without any supportive artifice are extremely rare; those that omitted the initial establishment of a present-day scenario from which a narrative bridge to the future is carefully constructed were virtually obliged to begin with a prefatory "essay section" explaining the situation—what would today be condemned as an ungainly "infodump." Readers of specialist magazines, on the other hand, not only expected to be thrust unceremoniously into exotic settings but could be assumed to be familiar with a series of basic templates, thus relieving the genre SF writer of the necessity of starting the business of "world-building" from scratch.

This benefit was, of course, balanced by the cost that much SF written for "connoisseur readers" became quite opaque to readers unfamiliar with the genre's basic templates. It was inevitable that the SF magazines would become isolated, at least for a while, from the remainder of the pulps, becoming a kind of "literary ghetto"—and it was equally inevitable that early science fiction fans would acquire a reputation for weirdness. The pulp SF ghetto did, however, provide an ideal environment for the evolution of the story format that was to become typical of modern science fiction.

From 1926 to 1930 the Gernsback-founded magazines had a monopoly on labeled science fiction. Because the supposed primary concern of the fiction they offered was its scientific content, whose educational value was enthusiastically touted by the editorial matter surrounding the stories, there was no concerted attempt to force science fiction into the same mold as other pulp melodrama. No objection was raised to stories clotted with long passages of explanatory exposition, monologues in which eccentric inventors lectured the hapless young men who wanted to marry their daughters, or dialogues in which scientists amazed one another with their erudition. Such follies seemed absurd to hard-headed pulp professionals, and it is hardly surprising that Harry Bates saw an opportunity to usurp the color and imaginative verve of the fledgling genre for the tried-and-tested narrative frameworks of pulp SF. But he could not have done that had his rivals not trained a population of connoisseur readers to expect the unexpected when they began every story, and he soon began to disappoint a substantial number of them by failing to provide them with sufficient unexpectedness. Even in 1930, science fiction stories could not be reduced to westerns-with-ray-guns; the imp of the perverse was too deeply entrenched.

When *Astounding* came under new management in 1933, Orlin Tremaine's emphasis on "thought variants" was a necessary response to reader demand. If *Astounding* had not become host to *contes philosophiques* and moral fables that were more open-minded and challenging than those featured in its competitors, someone else would have had to take up that slack. Tremaine's thought variants were rough-hewn even by the relaxed standards of pulp fiction, but their crudity should not distract attention from the fact that they represented striking out in new directions, in terms of form as well as content. Even the most wholeheartedly pulpish of the story templates put in place by the early SF magazines, the space opera, moved rapidly away from its pseudo-Burroughsian origins. The pioneering endeavors of Edward E. Smith, Edmond Hamilton, and—most of all—John W. Campbell, Jr. attempted to draw a firm line of separation distancing themselves from the dreamlike qualities of their nearest kin, aspiring to a kind of narrative "hardness" that P. Schuyler Miller was to identify in the early 1950s as the distinctive texture of authentic science fiction.

Like the faster-than-light spaceships of space opera, time machines were rapidly standardized as a stock facilitating device of pulp SF. But their sheer profusion made it necessary for their users to confront an issue that Wells had elected to ignore: that in making the future accessible, a time machine would also make the past precarious, ever-vulnerable to destructive reconstitution. This idea was celebrated in the very first "thought variant," Nathan Schachner's "Ancestral Voices" (1933), and hectically elaborated in one of the most important exemplary works featured in the early issues of Campbell's *Astounding,* Jack Williamson's "The Legion of Time" (1938). The second significant literary invention of the SF pulps was, therefore, the subgenre of the "time paradox story," which performed the ingenious trick of using a device whose ostensible purpose was to make fantasies seem more rationally plausible, even to play games with logic itself. Thus the writer scrupulously extrapolated psychologically plausible premises into the realms of the blithely nonsensical.

The kind of logical game playing that is fundamental to the time paradox story is by no means limited thereto. The same kind of artistry can, in principle, be applied to any story whose method involves extrapolating the further possibilities stemming from a single hypothetical invention. Such extrapolation can still be very surprising even if it stops short of actual paradox. Science fiction writers who were bound to consider time paradox stories as fantasies rather than examples of "real" science fiction quickly became fascinated with the prospect of constructing stories whose pivots were novelties glimpsed through the lens of scientific or technological possibility, to which they applied scrupulous but ingeniously revealing logical extrapolation. In so doing they invented a new variant of the *conte philosophique.*

The ultimate aim of this kind of extrapolation is to produce a conclusion that is both manifestly logical and totally unexpected, which can serve as a neat ending for a narrative. Such stories became increasingly common in the SF pulps of the 1930s, and by the end of that decade they had effectively displaced action-adventure novels at the core of the genre. From then on, every SF novel, no matter how hectic its pace or how gaudy its action, would need what Darko Suvin would one day call a "novum" to provide proof—or at least an illusion— that it was not really an action-adventure story at all, but rather what Kingsley Amis would eventually label an "idea-as-hero story."

The label coined by Amis is apt, but it should not be taken to mean that the idea on which the story pivots replaces the protagonist. In fact, every science fiction story of this kind requires *two* ideas, one being the novelty whose logical extrapolation provides the backbone of its plot and the other being the challenge or opportunity thus presented to its protagonist, which gives the novelty its narrative relevance. In most naturalistic fiction the second kind of idea is, of course, the overriding feature of a story; even in the plot- and puzzle-dominated stories that constitute the various subgenres of crime fiction, the element of "human interest" is an irreducible necessity. In science fiction, however, "human interest" is routinely replaced by a much more general kind of empathic involvement that may well require readers to put themselves in the shoes of aliens, superhumans, or sentient machines, and frequently requires them to discover some sympathy for such individuals. Any such move immediately renders the character-based narrative subservient to the extrapolative process with which it is entwined. Even when all the characters offered for reader identification or presented as petitioners for sympathy *are* human, serious science fiction requires them to be humans who have been detached from the assumption of a fixed or readily understood human nature.

In spite of the fact that most early exponents of the idea-as-hero story tended to write stories that were even cruder, stylistically speaking, than the general run of pulp fiction, such tales had a special imaginative appeal that seemed to many readers to be uniquely fitted to their era. Pioneering examples such as Edmond Hamilton's "Evolution Island" (1927), David H. Keller's "The Revolt of the Pedestrians" (1928), and Miles J. Breuer's "The Captured Cross-Section" (1929) are barely readable today, but they paved the way for the development of more sophisticated variations on their basic themes: the relentlessness and profligacy of progressive change; humankind's increasing dependence on mechanical technology; and the difficulty of negotiating sudden encounters with the unexpected and the alien.

Edmond Hamilton was typical of those early recruits to science fiction whose discovery of the genre had been akin to a religious conversion: a sudden introduction to a whole new way of seeing that would henceforth color the recruits' attitude toward everything. All of his longer works were conventional action-adventure stories, but in his short stories he worked in a very different way, expressing his profound fascination with scientific ideas. His ruminations were always naive and sometimes risible, but even an absurdity like "The Accursed Galaxy" (1935)—which suggests that the universe might be expanding because all the other galaxies are fleeing in disgust from ours, horrified by its infection with the plague of life—offered its readers a Voltairean counterweight to conventional vanity. Such idea-as-hero stories as "The Man Who Saw the Future" (1930), "The Man Who Evolved" (1931), "The Man with X-Ray Eyes" (1933), and "The Island of Unreason" (1933) incorporate a Wellsian spirit of intellectual inquiry that compensates for their garishness, and "A Conquest of Two Worlds" (1932) is a remarkably outspoken fabular condemnation of the politics of colonialism. Where Hamilton and those like him led, many others were to follow, much more productively. Hamilton never contrived to adapt himself to the more rigorous demands of Campbell's *Astounding,* but those who did stood upon his shoulders, and the shoulders of others like him. Early pulp SF was, almost without exception, horribly bad fiction—but it was a kind of bad fiction that was capable of becoming much better, and it created the possibilities of reader expectation that allowed later writers to fulfill its promises.

Pulp SF crossed a very important threshold when its bestselling magazine was delivered into the charge of John W. Campbell, Jr., because Campbell had no doubt at all that SF had the potential to become an important medium for socially valuable thought experiments. He insisted, therefore, that his writers must take much greater care in the future to make certain that their stories were scientifically plausible and internally consistent. That editorial prospectus firmly established the idea-as-hero story as the primary template of science-fictional thought experiment; Campbell insisted that it could and ought to be employed as a means of intellectually disciplined inquiry. His cause was immediately taken up by a stable of ambitious writers whose potential audience had already been pre-schooled by pulp SF. The writers were ready to move the project forward, and so were the readers. Clifford D. Simak, who had made his debut in 1931 but abandoned the field in 1932, returned to it gladly in 1938, and never looked back. Eric Frank Russell and L. Sprague de Camp, recruited in 1937, also became regulars. Lester del Rey joined the stable in 1938. Robert A. Heinlein, Isaac Asimov, A. E. van Vogt, and Theodore Sturgeon followed in 1939, ready to take their leading roles in shaping modern SF.

While it was still gestating in its pulp womb, therefore, American science fiction brought about a zygotic fusion of the fundamental impetus of Wellsian scientific romance and the narrative energy of Burroughsian otherworldly exotica, lightly leavened with casually extravagant tall tales of scientific miracle-making. Without that fusion, the collaborative work of horizon expansion, social extrapolation, and moral re-sophistication that has been the labor and triumph of modern SF could not have begun, let alone proceeded so rapidly. Then, had it not been for the intervention of the Second World War, which began in Europe in 1939 but did not spread to America until the last days of 1941, some such fusion might have begun to take place in France, and perhaps even in Britain. But even if it had, American SF would have been the first and the fastest to develop. Perhaps, if the native European traditions had not been halted in their tracks, scientific romance would not have been so utterly overwhelmed by imported American SF in the late 1940s—but that cannot detract from the remarkable achievements that pulp SF contrived, in spite of all the handicaps imposed upon it by its idiosyncratic marketplace.

CHAPTER 3

From the Golden Age to the Atomic Age: 1940–1963

Paul A. Carter

Life was grim as the decade of the 1930s drew to a close. "The world was numb under the great depression," Frederik Pohl has written. "I remember the cold city streets, gloveless relief workers shovelling snow outside the second-hand magazine store where I browsed through the old copies of *Amazing Stories* before selecting the one in which I would invest my dime."[1] The New Deal, for all its bright promise, had stalled in its tracks; the economy was typically running at no more than 50 percent of plant capacity, with 10 million Americans still unemployed. In Africa, Asia, and Europe, aggressor powers marched with such seeming irresistibility that some in the still-democratic West saw them pessimistically as "the wave of the future." A young person in the United States could look forward, at best, to an uncertain future with the strong possibility of being conscripted for war. Mainstream writer Edna Ferber, who had been turning out popular novels since the end of the previous world war, summed up in despair: "Who now envies youth?"

Nevertheless, in the then-small world of science fiction, some young people in America experienced and remembered the late 1930s and early 1940s as a Golden Age.

A word of caution here. A familiar adage in the SF community is that "the 'Golden Age' in science fiction was—about thirteen," that is, the age at which one began to read SF, whether that happened in 1940, 1960, 1980, or the last few days. Arthur C. Clarke typically testified, in the first sentence of his *Astounding Days: A Science Fictional Autobiography* (1989): "Sometime toward the end of 1930, in my thirteenth year, I acquired my first science fiction magazine—and my life was irrevocably changed." Just as there were many cultural renaissances in European history but only one that earned the name *the* Renaissance, so too, although there have been many generations of youths discovering SF at 13 (or younger), there remains a period still denotable as *the* Golden Age.

It began just before World War II, and it ended with the war or not long after. To enlarge upon that connection would be to belabor the obvious. An economically limping nation in a prewar mode helps to explain its beginning, and Hiroshima helps to explain its end. But there were two developments within American SF that must also be taken into account: the sudden proliferation of pulp science fiction magazines after a long drought, and the advent of John W. Campbell, Jr., as editor of one of them.

Campbell took charge of *Astounding Stories,* as it was then called, in 1937 and promptly softened its pulp-sounding name to *Astounding Science-Fiction.* Thirty-four years later, when he died, still at the magazine's helm, it had become *Analog.* But the taming of pulp sensationalism went far beyond mere renaming of a product. Out went the gassy, semi-metaphysical "thought variant" stories to which his editorial predecessor had been addicted. In came new writers, some crossing over from non-SF pulps (notably L. Ron Hubbard); others were found in their teens and developed under Campbell's stimulating if autocratic tutelage; still others were mature writers who simply had never before found a suitable niche. Lester del Rey's and L. Sprague de Camp's first stories appeared in the magazine in 1938; so did Isaac Asimov's (not counting—as he did not—a slightly earlier sale to *Amazing*), Robert Heinlein's, A. E. van Vogt's, and Theodore Sturgeon's in that *annus mirabilis,* 1939. Older writers who had been a staple of magazine SF earlier in the 1930s learned to speak Campbell's language or were quietly turned out to pasture.

Some of this makeover was simply learning how to write better English. The pulps have been so carefully sifted for anthologies that we mercifully forget just how unspeakably bad so much of the residue was. (See Bleiler's *Science-Fiction: The Gernsback Years* [7-3] for proof of this during the 1926–1936 period.) Campbell usually had no truck with Gernsback's sugar-coated-pill approach to SF, in which the story leaked away while the characters poured forth great gobs of scientific explanation, not always accurate. Campbell's instruction to his writers was refreshing: Write a story that could be published as a contemporary tale in a magazine published in the 25th century.

He also told them he wanted stories about aliens who could think as well as humans, but not *like* humans. In practice, this latter axiom didn't work out. Campbell made it plain that he wanted *Homo sapiens* to triumph all over the galaxy, and writers including Asimov adjusted what they wrote accordingly. E. E. Smith could be indulged in peopling his future universe with bizarre life forms, but otherwise the Stanley Weinbaum tradition of wacky, appealing nonhuman intelligences went into abeyance until long after the Golden Age was over. On the whole, though, the gains under the Campbell regime far outweighed the losses. He fed his writers ideas, worked out concepts with them (such as the "three laws of robotics"), and—so testified Lester del Rey—loved them best when they could stand up to him in argument.

The other herald of the Golden Age was the arrival of a host of new competitors for Campbell's *Astounding*. At the end of the Depression, as at the beginning, there were only three SF magazines; four if we count *Weird Tales* (and perhaps we should include it as a nurturer of writers—Henry Kuttner, Fritz Leiber, and especially Ray Bradbury—who became important in SF as well as fantasy/horror fiction.) Depression-era fears about the survival of businesses still prevailed, however, and when *Astounding*'s June 1938 issue was late turning up at the Asimov family's Brooklyn candy store, young Isaac made a pilgrimage to the magazine's Manhattan office to find out if it had folded. This was how he came to meet Campbell.

The other survivors, although making it financially, had fallen upon hard times in other ways. *Amazing Stories*, the eldest, shorn of its former folio size, had moved to Chicago and become primarily another men's adventure pulp with an SF veneer. *Wonder*, Gernsback's second venture, had metamorphosed into *Thrilling Wonder Stories*, consciously aiming at a more juvenile audience and devoting its cover art to the Eternal Triangle of pulp SF: the jut-jawed young man, the not-quite-dressed young woman, and the Bug-Eyed Monster (BEM), whose size varied from modest to Godzilla.

But if quality suffered, quantitatively SF at the end of the 1930s enjoyed a substantial boom—and eventually that helped the quality also. Older magazines spun off companions: *Fantastic Adventures* from *Amazing*, *Startling Stories* from *Thrilling Wonder*, and the splendidly innovative and impudent *Unknown* from *Astounding*. New ones popped up like dandelions: *Astonishing Stories*, *Super Science*, *Planet*, *Comet*, *Cosmic Stories*, *Stirring Science Stories*, *Science Fiction*, and *Future Fiction*.[2] In economic terms, SF had become an expanding market, and for would-be writers (it being axiomatic that all who regularly read SF sooner or later try to write it), this was a godsend, at least until wartime paper shortages swept most of these newcomers away.

At the same time, this magazine flood reinforced the ghettoizing of SF in the United States; for unless we count the Sunday funnies (Buck Rogers, Flash Gordon) and the emerging "superhero" comic books, for which indeed some SF writers wrote, there wasn't much else to read *but* the magazines. American hardcover publishers rarely touched SF. An occasional sentimental time-travel tale such as Robert Nathan's *Portrait of Jennie* hardly slaked the science fictionists' thirst. Better stuff was being written in Britain, such as Gloag's *99%* and Stapledon's *Sirius*, but, with infrequent exceptions such as C. S. Lewis's lovely Venus tale *Perelandra*, most imprints from British publishers never made it across the U-boat-infested waters of the Atlantic. That a melodrama as bad as Curt Siodmak's *Donovan's Brain* (1943) could become widely popular is a measure of what the seeker after SF was up against, and it is further indicative of the American SF reader's plight that *Donovan* became a grade-B movie. Hollywood, apart from Frank Capra's stylishly filmed *Lost Horizon* (1937), remained pretty much stuck in its Mad Scientist mode: *Black Friday* with Boris Karloff, *Son of Frankenstein* with Karloff and Bela Lugosi, and *Dr. Cyclops,* which the SF writer Henry Kuttner "wrote down" into a novelette for *Thrilling Wonder Stories,* with crudely executed halftone stills from the movie.

If young fans couldn't get enough SF to satisfy their appetites, they would have to make some. After they had read and reread their Verne and Wells and Edgar Rice Burroughs, they had to go back to the pulps' letter columns as "letterhacks," find and feud with one another in fan clubs, serve an apprenticeship in fanzine fiction (usually awful) and criticism (often quite good), and eventually settle into the serious business of becoming writers. Damon Knight, summing up the history of a most significant fans-into-writers club, *The Futurians* [10-171], argued that the necessary conditions for the flourishing of that group were poverty, political intransigence, and the just-described proliferation of the SF magazines.

The scrappy Futurian Society of New York didn't last long; "as soon as the Futurians began to make a little money," Knight concludes, "the group began to dissolve." However, while it lasted it produced, by Knight's count, "10 novellas, a publisher, 2 agents, 4 anthologies, and 5 editors" out of a total membership of only 20; not to mention 7 intragroup marriages and 5 divorces. The names are a roll call of later prominent figures in the SF world: Donald Wollheim, Frederik Pohl, Isaac Asimov, Cyril Kornbluth, Knight himself, Judith Merril, and James Blish. By the end of 1942, they had collectively produced 129 SF stories, mostly as collaborations and almost all under pseudonyms.

Two observations at this point: Most of the Futurians didn't write for *Astounding,* the pacesetter, and much of the early action among emerging writers occurred elsewhere. Indeed, of the entire group, only Asimov regularly published in Campbell's magazine during the Golden Age, and the rest of them, by Knight's account, considered themselves rather countercultural to Campbell: stylistically more innovative (within the more general limits of pulp publication) and considerably more radical. Three of them—Pohl, Wollheim, and Robert W. Lowndes—edited magazines that, if small in circulation, were nonetheless in direct competition with *Astounding.* The political intransigence Knight referred to in his memoir was real; there was overlap between the science fictionists and the sectarian left in New York City, at least until the Stalinist rejoicing at the fall of France in 1940 made that relationship embarrassing.

As writers, the Futurians derived a strategic advantage from living in New York, the capital of American publishing. In the homeliest terms, it was cheaper to spend a nickel on the subway each way to hand-carry a manuscript to a pulp magazine, and the same to retrieve it, than to put postage stamps on the going and return envelopes at the rate of 3 cents per ounce (about six typed pages, or 1,500 words). Besides, a kindhearted editor might buy a kid lunch after rejecting a story in person; such were Depression-era financial calculations. However, other SF writers' centers had emerged from the fan clubs of the earlier 1930s. In the Los Angeles Science Fantasy Society, fans, writers, and wannabes happily mingled in the basement of the grandiloquently named Prince Rupert Hotel; Ray Bradbury came out of that milieu and Leigh Brackett was close to it. Farther up the coast in the Bay Area, writers in the early 1940s congregated in the Mañana Literary Society, so named for the great stories its members talked of writing "mañana." A similar authors' club in Milwaukee nurtured young Robert Bloch, and young Lester del Rey rode the train in from Philadelphia to deliver his manuscripts, sometimes crashing for a weekend on Campbell's couch.

What kind of SF did the Golden Age writers try to write? Campbell's explicit call for contemporary-sounding futures and his implicit demand for a humans-only cosmos were paralleled in a how-to article by *Amazing*'s assistant editor, Jerry Westerfield: "Stories starting in some large U.S. city are better than those starting off in space somewhere. A story starting in the present is better than one starting in the past or the future."[3] So much for Burroughs's Mars or Stapledon's Neptune! All editorial rules are, of course, made to be broken (as Campbell also knew); *Amazing*'s consort, *Fantastic Adventures*, played by looser rules. Some writers blithely disregarded all such structures. "A large U.S. city like New York is concrete and real to the minds of our readers, while a city off on Mars somewhere is vague and indefinite," Westerfield warned; yet in that same period Leigh Brackett had great fun in *Planet Stories*, starting and ending her stories in cities on Mars or elsewhere.

Nonetheless, the limits proposed by Campbell and Westerfield did have an impact. A perceptive reader commented on the difference between E. E. Smith's space opera *Galactic Patrol*, accepted and published in 1937 before the new era had quite begun, and its sequel *Gray Lensman*, which appeared late in 1939. *Galactic Patrol* had given "the thoughtful reader an impression of the unimaginably huge size of our galaxy," Lew Cunningham wrote in a letter to *Astounding*; but "in 'Gray Lensman' you proceed to shrivel this monstrous aggregation of stars and dirty it up, so to speak, with . . . throwbacks to the ancient twentieth-century system." The Wild West frontier, which SF had often paralleled, was becoming the frontier under settlement and domestication.[4]

But the closing of that frontier had opened the way to a revival of social criticism in place of the gadgeteering of Gernsback and the escapism of Burroughs. The option of social commentary had always been latently present; Verne's classic submarine story was not just a future gadget yarn, but embodied in Captain Nemo some serious criticism of historical trends that Verne didn't like, and of course in Wells the social politics were always integral to the story. Campbell, whose antennae were always sensitive to current concerns until his own idiosyncrasies got the better of him, immediately followed the publication of *Gray Lensman* in *Astounding* with two very un-Smith-like serials: "If This Goes On—," Heinlein's first long story (1940; included in *The Past Through Tomorrow*), which described a media-manipulating fundamentalist religious dictatorship in a future United States; and *Final Blackout*, by L. Ron Hubbard (also 1940), a somber forecast of one possible outcome of the European war then raging.

Campbell's magazines were especially hospitable to this kind of social consequences SF, but other magazines from time to time also took aim at American cultural shortcomings, especially the ones edited by the Futurians. It was of course a highly male-focused kind of social consciousness. To be sure, women were given a bit more to do in the stories than they had been in the earlier 1930s, when the typical SF heroine, in Leigh Brackett's words, had done "nothing but have tantrums, shriek, and generally gum up the action." Even "Doc" Smith, that highly conventional Michigan Republican, had learned between the writing of the Skylarks and his Lensman series that, in one *Astounding* reader's words, "a female can, in fact, once in a while, get in there and *do* something." Brackett contended that her own women characters, in contrast to the previous norm, were "gutsy and intelligent"—but she continued to construct almost all her stories with male viewpoint characters. In this respect SF had a long, long way to go.[5]

Furthermore, the acute social forecasting that did appear (to the delight of subsequent anthologists) in Golden Age SF magazines was surrounded and sometimes submerged by conventional pulp fare. Yet even the straight action-adventure story, which was the staple of most of the magazines most of the time, could quite insensibly take on an element of social consciousness. A sociological study by Walter Hirsch, "Image of the Scientist in Science Fiction," based on a random sample of the SF pulps from 1926 to 1950, found that capitalists, by and large, figured in the stories as disreputable characters: "Scientists comprised the major category of both heroes and villains, but businessmen were, proportionately, more villainous than scientists."[6] In Golden Age SF, greedy, rapacious tycoons or stockbrokers seeking to cash in on their hired scientists' labors became almost a cliché. A classic instance is Theodore Sturgeon's "Microcosmic God" (1941) with its maverick scientist hero and its banker villain, although Sturgeon pro forma disclaimed any such intention by writing, "Don't worry, I'm not going political on you."

One subject about which it had become perfectly acceptable to "go political" was the menace of fascism. In near-future, Earth-focused SF, Hitler and the Japanese warlords regularly got their comeuppance. In transgalactic SF, the alien menaces transmuted into hyper-Nazis. But a disquieting note was sounded alongside these justifications of America's 1941–1945 war: that of its sheer physical and social destructiveness. Forecasts of reversion to barbarism after such a war, deriving from mainstream writer Stephen Vincent Benét's "By the Waters of Babylon" (1937), attracted a number of magazine writers and prompted during 1941 a serious debate in "Brass Tacks," *Astounding*'s letters-to-the-editor department, as to just how far and fast such a collapse could go.

Pretty far, it turned out, if one knew of or guessed about the A-bomb, which was then actually lurking in the wings. The pulps' predictive record on this subject is impressive, *Astounding*'s in particular. In 1941, Heinlein's "Solution Unsatisfactory" asked what must happen to politics and foreign policy when a weapon of war is developed against which there can be no defense. In 1942, Lester del Rey's "Nerves" debated the ethics of covering up a potential worse-than-Chernobyl disaster in a nuclear power plant. In 1944, Cleve Cartmill's "Deadline," a weak story, was so precise in detailing how a uranium bomb could be detonated that it prompted Army counterintelligence to investigate whether anyone on the Manhattan Project had been talking. Then in early 1945, before the war in Europe was over, "The Piper's Son," by Henry Kuttner and C. L. Moore, was set in a post-nuclear-war world of independent city-states, each capable of dusting off any one of the others—a smaller-scaled version of the "balance of terror" that would become the actual foundation of post-bomb U.S.-Soviet relations.[7]

When the nightmare actually came to pass, it put science fictionists in an emotional double bind. It showed beyond dispute that the crazy Buck Rogers stuff they had dreamed of for years was real after all, but it was not the kind of dream one would have wanted to actually come true. As Theodore Sturgeon summed up in "Memorial," a short story published less than a year after the war ended (included in his *Without Sorcery*), SF writers who wrote about atomic energy before the end of the war had been "afraid for humanity, but they themselves were not really afraid, except in a delicious drawing room sort of way, because they couldn't conceive of this Buck Rogers event happening to anything but posterity." But the boy cried wolf, and the wolf came.

So the Golden Age writers (and artists) came back from the wars and resumed their work. The Depression impoverishment in which they had started was over, as pent-up demand for civilian goods produced an economic boom instead of the mass unemployment government experts had predicted—a boom in which SF, like other consumer activities, flourished. Nevertheless it may fairly be said that the Golden Age that had begun at the end of the 1930s was already over. The innocence was gone; as physicist J. Robert Oppenheimer said on behalf of the scientists who had developed the bomb, "We have known sin." People did not yet realize that "civilization, the civilization we have been born into, lived in, and indoctrinated with, died on July 16, 1945, and that the Death Notice was published to the world on August 6, 1945," John Campbell editorialized in *Astounding*. "The atomic bomb must, inevitably, force upon us an era of international good manners and tolerance—or vast and sudden death."[8]

The years immediately following the first use of the atomic bomb were hardly an era of international good manners and tolerance. SF, however, prospered. The bomb and the space program, another activity that the general public had relegated to Buck Rogers and company in the prewar years, broke down the walls of the SF ghetto. Robert Heinlein began selling stories to the *Saturday Evening Post*; Ray Bradbury branched out from *Weird Tales* and *Planet Stories* to *Harper's*, the *New Yorker*, and *Mademoiselle*. Although the pulps enjoyed a kind of Indian summer, not fading finally from the scene until 1955—and in the meantime helping to launch some new writing careers, notably that of Philip K. Dick—the real action in the 1950s was in new kinds of SF magazines and in books.

SF book publication began as an exercise in Golden Age nostalgia. One hardcover publisher that devoted itself almost entirely to reprinting work from the pulps, Arkham House, had been in business since 1939, but its output was limited almost entirely to fantasy and horror. In 1946, Arkham published *Slan*, an *Astounding* serial by van Vogt. Arkham was soon joined by half a dozen small-press publishers, started by long-time SF fans who gambled that readers who had spent 15 to 20 cents during the war for copies of SF magazines might be willing to spend $3 or so for hardcover books that reprinted serials or collections of a favorite author's stories.

Venture capital was on the smallest of scales, and press runs by today's trade publisher standards (although not by those of university presses) were modest. Arkham printed 4,000 copies of *Slan* and 3,000 of Ray Bradbury's first collection, *Dark Carnival* (1947). Fantasy Press usually produced 3,000 or 4,000 copies, reaching its peak with 6,600 copies of "Doc" Smith's *Galactic Patrol*. Prime Press, which grew out of a conversation at the Philadelphia SF Society, printed 2,000 copies of Lester del Rey's first book, . . . *And Some Were Human* (1948), and 3,000 of Sturgeon's first, *Without Sorcery*.

These ventures were economically viable for a time, and new small presses entered the field. Shasta Publishers, originating as a Chicago bookseller, published Heinlein, de Camp, and Alfred Bester; Gnome Press offered Asimov, James Blish, Clifford D. Simak, and C. L. Moore. Other specialty publishers joined in, sometimes with a book or two—"and as soon as they had made a success of it," author/critic Algis Budrys angrily wrote, "Doubleday, Simon & Schuster and the others woke up and with one herbivorous snap took it away from them." In 1950, Doubleday started its long-lasting Science Fiction Book Club (see Chapter 6); in the following year Gnome Press, to take but one example, saw a 90 percent drop in sales.[9]

The publishing giants actually had had an eye on this potential market since the end of the war. Random House entered the lists as early as 1946 with *Adventures in Time and Space*, and before the end of the 1940s other mainline publishers had produced omnibus volumes edited by Groff Conklin and August Derleth. So far, these were all reprint anthologies; even Bradbury's history-making *Martian Chronicles* was in essence a "fix-up novel" composed of late 1940s stories primarily from *Planet* and *Thrilling Wonder*. Nonspecialist hardcover publishers remained resistant to new, not magazine-derived, SF until 1949, when Doubleday published Max Ehrlich's *The Big Eye* and followed it up with Asimov's *Pebble in the Sky*, which two magazines had previously rejected. The face of SF was thereby changed forever.

It was not quite the end for the small presses. Arkham and Donald Grant would continue after Fantasy Press and Shasta and Gnome were gone. But the bulk of SF that appeared after 1950 came either from mainstream hardcover publishers or, once the paperback houses got wind of this bonanza, from publishers like Ace and Dell. This was the price, perhaps, of the tumbling down of those ghetto walls; it meant, for example, that new U.K. science fiction, as before the war, would be reprinted at once in the United States, so that American readers got a reasonably early look at works by writers including John Christopher, John Wyndham, and of course Arthur C. Clarke. However, the power shift also subjected SF thereafter to the marketing pressures of large-scale publishing, which eventually, by packaging for specialized submarkets, in effect reestablished the ghetto. Anything science-fictional in which a publisher scented bestseller potential had best be promoted as something else, indeed as *anything* else; whence the advertising copy or even the book review that lied through its teeth, stating that since this book is good, by definition it can't be science fiction.

The mainstream publishers had also discovered another bonanza. The junior novel, designed to appeal to teenagers' needs, proved a profitable vehicle for science fiction. By the 1950s, after the success of Heinlein's *Rocket Ship Galileo*, SF was well on its way to becoming an important subgenre of both American and British children's and YA literature. Its relatively sudden popularity and acceptance can be attributed to many causes: the pioneering work of Heinlein and Asimov; the emergence of a handful of genuinely talented writers such as Andre Norton and Alan Nourse, who wanted to write for young audiences; the continuing development of preteens and teenagers as separate groups requiring their own reading material; and the growing popularity of SF not only in novels and short stories but in film and comics, the two media that developed teenagers and preteens into avid fans.[10]

It could hardly be claimed that most of the SF for young people in the 1950s was well done. Too many publishers were willing to accept any manuscript dealing with a first trip to the Moon, life on Venus, or a visitor from Mars, provided the story had youngsters for its protagonists, eschewed all references to sex, and ostensibly had some educational or moral value. Within these guidelines, however, there was room for young imaginations to soar—and the generation that grew up with atomic power and rocket ships knew intuitively the truth of Hugo Gernsback's editorial adage, "Extravagant fiction today—cold fact tomorrow."

A major contributor to this emerging subgenre was the John C. Winston Company, which published nearly one third (26) of the juvenile SF books released in the 1950s. Many compare quite favorably, in imaginative conception, style, and narrative pace with the typical YA SF novel written today. Usually each of the stories was preceded by an introduction in which the author summarized briefly then-current information about a particular planet or a particular scientific discipline. The narrative was supposed to embody or illustrate the author's speculation as to future developments. In this way, the didacticism expected of juvenile books was incorporated into the Winston novels, and science fiction—"cheapened" in the eyes of librarians, teachers, and concerned parents by its association with lurid pulp magazines—would be elevated and made respectable. Fortunately for the reader, the narratives are usually relatively unencumbered by ill-digested blocks of information, and they succeed or fail primarily as storytelling, not as instruction.

A high proportion of 1950s SF for young readers was produced by already-established authors of SF for adults, including Isaac Asimov, Robert Silverberg, Donald A. Wollheim, Poul Anderson, James Blish, Ben Bova, Arthur C. Clarke, Lester del Rey, Gordon R. Dickson, Murray Leinster, Andre Norton, Jack Vance, and Harry Harrison. Some of these "name" authors might have been forced to cease writing SF were it not for their juvenile books. Some few may not have been above placing hackwork in the juvenile market. But the highly competent work of the cited authors provided direction to and some prestige for children's and YA science fiction until new talent, seriously committed to writing for youth and unwilling to compromise, entered the field in the next four decades.

One caution here: youngsters, then as now, did not have to limit their reading to "young people's books." It was not until the last decades of the 19th century that distinctions between children's books and adult ones began to be drawn with any kind of precision. Many works now considered "children's classics" were originally written as adult books. In the SF field, young and old might be reading Verne, Wells, or Burroughs. Moreover, many youngsters, even when popular children's SF became available, probably skipped it and read adult SF. Asimov, for example, when speaking of his youth, doesn't mention reading children's SF, but he does vividly recall reading copies of *Science Wonder Stories, Amazing Stories,* and *Air Wonder Stories,* which were for sale on his father's newsstand. Indeed, no small part of the lure of the pulps was precisely that they were *not* considered by teachers, parents, and other guardians of respectability to be suitable reading (and looking) for the young.

This particular transition was eased in the 1950s by the greater maturity of the magazines themselves. The ragged-edged, harshly colored pulps were gone from the scene by 1955, albeit fondly remembered. (Chapter 12 discusses books that reproduce much of this pulp art. Clute's "encyclopedia" [7-20] provides an illustrated overview.) Of equal importance with the entrance of general publishers into the SF field in the pivotal year 1950 was the founding of two new magazines, both of which sought to live down the pulp image and at the same time challenge John Campbell's leadership. One of them, *The Magazine of Fantasy and Science Fiction* (*F&SF*), under the cultivated and urbane editorship of Anthony Boucher, appeared in digest size with restrained cover art, discreet typography, a single-column book-type page layout, no interior artwork, and no letter column. Boucher gave readers subtle characterization and a high literary polish, in the process quietly and unsensationally breaking old magazine taboos concerning (among other matters) religion, sex, and race. Although he bought stories from Golden Age figures, he also showcased newer writers such as Brian Aldiss, Margaret St. Clair, Philip José Farmer, and Richard Matheson.

Respectable folk who had been closet readers for years could now own up to this kind of SF. Back-cover subscription ads for *F&SF* during the 1950s carried testimonials from opera singer Gladys Swarthout, bandleader Guy Lombardo, *New York Times* book review editor Orville Prescott, classical scholar Gilbert Highet—and Eva Gabor. Confessing "I have been a fan of science fiction all my life," the *Saturday Review*'s Basil Davenport went a long step further and edited a series of 1957 guest lectures at the University of Chicago by Robert Heinlein, Cyril Kornbluth, Alfred Bester, and Robert Bloch, titled *The Science Fiction Novel: Imagination and Social Criticism* [9-173]. "This book has given me the pleasure, all too rare since my college days, of being a book that I could argue with," said Davenport in his introduction, and from that initial venture grew all the later, extensive involvement of SF with the academic world.

The other new periodical, *Galaxy*, looked more like a traditional SF magazine than did *F&SF*. But its hard-driving editor, Horace Gold, who has been remembered with fondness and fear by writers forced to put manuscripts through four or five drafts, was just as determined as Boucher to abolish what Gold called "retread private eye, western and Congo Sam stories masquerading as science fiction." Sociological and even psychiatric themes were his forte, and much of the social and political satire that was the great glory of 1950s SF, such as *Fahrenheit 451* and *The Space Merchants*, first appeared in *Galaxy*'s pages or in those of its companion, *If*. In a sense it can be said that in *Galaxy* and *If*, the irreverent spirit of the Futurians came into its own at last; indeed, a former Futurian, Frederik Pohl, in due course succeeded Gold as editor.

The 1940s in American SF had emphatically been Campbell's decade; just as the 1950s definitely were not. To be sure, *Astounding* continued to discover and publish important new writers, such as Frank Herbert and Poul Anderson. But its editor had lately taken to riding hobby horses: dowsing, Dianetics (a horse from which he soon dismounted), engines that supposedly violated the conservation of energy and still worked, and especially "psi" powers—precognition, telepathy, psychokinesis, and the rest. He could have been forgiven his increasingly cantankerous, elitist, and long-winded editorials had not a high proportion of the stories begun to sound dull. Some writers figured out how to cater to Campbell's new preferences while still writing good SF, notably Mark Clifton, and "hard" SF writers including Hal Clement continued to thrive and grow, but if the war years had been golden for *Astounding*, the 1950s were at best its Silver Age.

The magazines, including some new ones like *Fantastic Universe* and *Worlds of Tomorrow*, continued to supply the burgeoning paperback field with reprintable material, but the demand was beginning to exceed the supply. It would increasingly become necessary for writers to submit stories directly to the paperback houses for first publication (this also, regrettably, tipped the balance from short stories to novels). Commercially speaking, a paperback seemed at first to have one advantage over a magazine: with no date on its cover, it could be left on the rack longer. But in the late 1970s, the chain bookstores would come into the picture, with relentless absentee owners who ordered that stock be turned over faster than the magazines ever had—as if books left on a shelf, like groceries, would spoil.

Under either regimen, fast or slow, the paperbacks lacked one vital spark that even the sleaziest of magazines had always possessed: reader input. Writers began to complain that they no longer knew what anyone thought of their stories. SF was suffering like any rapidly growing aggregate of individuals: from a small town where everybody knew everybody else, with both the reassurances and the stiflings that go with that kind of life, it was turning into a metropolis, increasingly hard to think of as a community at all.

The Hugo awards, named after SF founding father Hugo Gernsback and comparable to the Oscars, Edgars, Grammys, and Emmys in other media and genres, were in part an effort to restore that vanishing reader input; if you couldn't write a letter about a favorite story, you could at least cast a vote. Perhaps, one could argue, a quantitative method of rewarding writers was fairer than the capriciousness of letters columns, where the criteria for inclusion had always been the editor's. (Campbell pioneered in this direction, as in so much else, by tabulating his reader choices in a department called the "Analytical Laboratory.") However, there was a catch: to vote for the Hugo nominees you had to be an attending or contributing member of that year's World SF Convention, which made convention support a primary electoral qualification—a dubious proposition, some might say. And worldcon participation has steadily grown more expensive.

At least, as long-suffering fans could console themselves, their beloved genre was at last being "noticed" outside its erstwhile ghetto. Futurian veteran Damon Knight viewed this as a mixed blessing: science fictionists, flattered by the notice, were neglecting the issue of quality in "our delight when the slicks began publishing (bad) science fiction stories, the hardcover houses (worse) science fiction books, and Hollywood began to produce (incredibly awful) science fiction movies." Not all the SF films produced prior to *2001* in 1968 were incredibly awful; they included *On the Beach*, which many viewers found an overpowering emotional experience, and *Forbidden Planet*, which retains a kind of gawky charm. But the great bulk of them were either Creature Features—*Them, The Blob, The Thing*—or disaster epics—*When Worlds Collide*, with its absurd spacecraft takeoff—or sometimes both at once, like the English-lip-synched, Tokyo-stomping adventures of Godzilla and his pals. They were little or no advance upon the SF movies of the 1930s.

This situation was a great pity, reinforcing as it did the general reader's or viewer's impression that this was all there was to SF. Unnoticed by Hollywood, magazine and paperback SF in the 1950s racked up a very creditable achievement. It was both literate and socially critical; more, it was courageous. During "that miserable decade we look back on as the era of McCarthyism," Frederik Pohl recalled in 1968, "about the only people speaking up openly to tell it like it was were Edward R. Murrow, one or two Senators, and just about every science fiction writer alive." Of course, its lingering pulp aura may have given it protective coloration; it was, after all, only science fiction.[11]

If it had been no more than political preaching, however, the SF of the 1950s would not now be remembered and respected to the extent that it is. It had developed a richness and subtlety of characterization all but unknown in the Golden Age, and at its best it was ingenious and imaginative, within the assumptions of its times. On occasion, in stories by Sturgeon or Fritz Leiber or Dick, it went far beyond these assumptions; some of Dick's early stories in particular still surprise present-day readers who wonder that they could have been written so long ago.

It must be countered that maturation involves losses as well as gains. Freud said that the pleasure principle has to give place to the reality principle; are pleasure and reality, then, antithetical terms? "When sf writers began taking themselves seriously, they tended to abandon their imaginations," Brian Aldiss cautioned; "the result was a descent into greyness, a loss of the original driving force, an espousal of literalism." Partisans of SF carried into the 1950s the old defensive insistence that SF, far from being crazy, was good for you. Campbell and his writers in particular "liked to justify sf in terms of how accurately its predictions were fulfilled, or how well it served as propaganda for the space race, or how strongly it influenced American kids to become physicists when they grew up." Important though this influence may have been, the genre's schoolteacherish urge to uplift and edify must be offset, Aldiss believed, by the irreverent spirit of *Homo ludens*—the man who knows how to play—and must recapture what Golden Age survivors refer to as the "sense of wonder" in SF. [12]

But entropy moves onward; SF, however much committed to the future, also reflects sideways upon its contemporary present; the SF of the 1950s, no matter how critical of that decade, was also a product of it, and therefore reminds the reader that these writings are now history as well as prophecy. Science fiction writer and professional anthropologist Chad Oliver, writing in 1971 some "Afterthoughts" for a collection of stories (*Another Kind*), the first of which had been written when Harry Truman was president and the last when Dwight Eisenhower was still in office, reflected from across the gulf of the 1960s that "in a very real sense, these are stories from another world." They therefore demanded from the reader the anthropologist's knack for empathizing with other cultures: "To the extent that they are successful, you will still be able to hear what they are trying to say—but you may have to listen at a different volume, with an unamplified ear."

The pivotal year 1963—the year of the Nuclear Test Ban Treaty, the civil rights march on Washington, the fall of the Diem family in Saigon, the assassination of John Kennedy—began a new moment in history, for SF as for everything else. In that smaller world of SF, the premier British science fiction magazine *New Worlds*, as it incubated the work of a new generation of U.K. writers outside the imperial American orbit, was paving the way under editor Edward John Carnell for a revolution in SF writing. In the following decade it would wash across the Atlantic as the New Wave, but that is a subject for another chapter.

Notes

1. Frederik Pohl, "Ragged Claws," in Brian W. Aldiss and Harry Harrison, eds., *Hell's Cartographers* [10-168].
2. The detailed history of all these magazines is found in the authoritative handbook edited by Tymn and Ashley [13-30]. See also Carter, *The Creation of Tomorrow* [9-46, 13-27].
3. Jerry K. Westerfield, "The Sky's No Limit," *Writer's Digest*, January 1940. Magazines for writers are a relatively neglected source of SF history; writers such as Henry Kuttner and Ross Rocklynne augmented their pulp income by sharing their trade secrets with would-be fellow writers, and John W. Campbell, Jr. in *The Writer* (September 1968) unburdened himself on the

subject of "Science Fiction We Can Buy."

4. Lew Cunningham, letter in "Brass Tacks," *Astounding,* June 1940. The theme of Golden Age SF as a closing of the interplanetary frontier after a more wide-open period of exploration is set forth in an article by Alexei and Cory Panshin, "The Domestication of the Future, 1936–1946," *Fantastic,* December 1972.

5. Leigh Brackett, "The Science-Fiction Field," *Writer's Digest,* July 1944; W. B. Hoskins, letter in "Brass Tacks," *Astounding,* April 1942.

6. Walter Hirsch, "Image of the Scientist in Science Fiction: A Content Analysis," *American Journal of Sociology,* 23 (March 1958), pp. 506–12.

7. In fairness it must be conceded that science fictionists were not the only people capable of shrewd guesses, or at least close shots, about nuclear weapons development. In April 1945—three months before the Alamagordo weapons test—Ben Hecht and Alfred Hitchcock settled on a uranium-derived bomb as the "MacGuffin" (gimmick) for the forthcoming Hitchcock film *Notorious.* Legend has it that movie producer David Selznick doubted the plausibility of such a weapon.

8. John W. Campbell, Jr., "The Editor's Page," *Astounding Science-Fiction,* November 1945. The lead time in magazine production then was months long; this editorial was Campbell's earliest voiced reaction to the actual bomb.

9. Algis Budrys, introduction to Lloyd Arthur Eshbach, *Over My Shoulder: Reflections on a Science Fiction Era* [9-75], p. 22. An exhaustive history of hundreds of specialty fantastic fiction publishers is provided by Chalker and Owings in *The Science-Fantasy Publishers* [7-12].

10. This discussion of YA SF draws on Chapter 5 of the fourth edition of *Anatomy of Wonder,* written by Francis J. Molson and Susan G. Miles. Brian Stableford and Michael Levy joined with me in reviewing the books they annotated that fall within my chapter's period. Thus I have retained their initials following the annotation as (FM/SM). My thanks for their pioneering work in recognizing the importance of young adult SF.

11. Frederik Pohl, remarks as a panelist at the 1968 annual meeting of the Modern Language Association—the first formal panel on science fiction sponsored by a mainstream academic society; Pohl was joined by Robert Silverberg and Isaac Asimov.

12. Brian Aldiss, ed., *Galactic Empires,* vol. 1, p. 53; vol. 2, p. vii. To the perennial charge that SF of this playful kind can be dismissed as escapist, Aldiss quoted a devastating retort by J. R. R. Tolkien: "What class of men would you expect to be most preoccupied with, and most hostile to, the idea of escape?" "Jailers."

CHAPTER 4

The New Wave and After, 1964–1983

Michael M. Levy

For those of us born between the end of World War II and the early 1950s, "the sixties," that strange period that ran from approximately 1963 to 1972, *was* science fiction. New technologies such as nuclear power, television, computers, and space flight were changing our lives at an incredible rate. In 1964, after reading Philip Wylie's *Triumph* (1963), I got into a violent argument with my parents over their unwillingness to build an elaborate fallout shelter in our backyard. A few years later, in my high school math class, a teacher flapped a stack of punch cards in our faces, proclaimed that computers were the wave of the future, and ceremonially (and perhaps a little prematurely) tossed his expensive slide rule in the trash can. In my college freshman English class, a university professor made reference to the psychedelic ending of the new Stanley Kubrick film, *2001: A Space Odyssey,* and hinted that he'd been to that bizarre, unearthly place himself under the auspices of a new drug named LSD. An article in the newspaper that year (1968) mentioned that Pan Am was taking reservations for trips to the moon.

On a more serious note, Vietnam was heating up and, although we had as yet no real notion of that war's true horror, we did recognize its strangeness. With no front lines and dazzling new military technology, it seemed to my rather naive mind to have more in common with Heinlein's *Starship Troopers* than it did with World War II or Korea. And then, in 1969, I stayed up all night watching as a human being walked on the moon. Responsible scientists, flushed with what turned out to be misguided optimism, were even promising us Mars in the not-too-distant future.

It can be argued, of course, that the world is always undergoing change and that every generation sees its own time period as standing in some special relationship to the universe. For every generation, the millennium, or its secular equivalent, seems to be just around the corner. How else, after all, do we account for the periodic visits to the bestseller list of the prophecies of Nostradamus or the enormous popularity of end-times fiction by Frank Peretti, Tim LaHaye, and Jerry B. Jenkins, a popularity that continues virtually unabated to this day despite our having successfully made it well past the beginning of the 21st century?

Still, the 1960s seemed different, at least to those of us who came of age during that period. Perhaps it was the influence of Marshall McLuhan, whose *Understanding Media* (1964) argued that the electronic media generally and television specifically were causing an actual and permanent change in the way that humanity comprehended the world. Perhaps it was the somewhat later influence of Alvin Toffler, whose *Future Shock* (1970) emphasized that the rate of change was picking up dramatically. Perhaps it was the high-tech nature of the change: computers, moon landings, and such. Perhaps it was the violence: the war in Vietnam, the student riots, and the assassinations of the Kennedys, Martin Luther King, and Malcolm X. Or maybe it was the music; to a teenager growing up on the South Side of Chicago in the mid-1960s, The Beatles and The Rolling Stones seemed nearly as strange and wonderful as any being from Arcturus or Deneb.

Other equally important changes were occurring in the 1960s. In the United States, the rise of the civil rights movement and then of the women's and gay rights movements altered the way our laws are written and the way decent people think about human interactions. President Lyndon Johnson's Great Society programs, along with similar efforts in Britain and elsewhere, were sparking enormous growth in public welfare with all its attendant advantages and disadvantages. The Soviet Union, after a brief thaw under Khrushchev, was falling back into dark, repressive stagnation that would both prolong the Cold War and lead to the eventual collapse of the Soviet state.

In the mid-1960s, a phenomenon variously called the youth culture and the counterculture forced its way onto the public stage, gaining moral force from anti-Vietnam protests, vague theological underpinnings from watered-down versions of Buddhism and other East and South Asian religions, visibility from media hype, and economic clout from the sheer size of the baby boom generation. Many of the different components of the youth culture were themselves, at least in part, direct outgrowths of technological change. The sexual revolution would have been highly unlikely if not for conveniently timed breakthroughs in birth control technology. Drug use, always common in some parts of American society, did not become a topic of general concern until it entered the middle class, especially when technology once again took a hand, creating new kinds of highs. The explosive growth of the rock 'n roll industry, fueled by the increased buying power of young people, was also made possible, in part, by new developments in sound reproduction technology. Even the anti-war movement was technology-related. World War II and Korea were distant affairs that the voters back home read about in newspapers or saw on carefully edited, invariably patriotic newsreels. Vietnam, on the other hand, occurred on television, in our homes, its horrors less well disguised by distance and government control.

The social, political, economic, and technological changes of the 1960s were diverse, but they all had an effect on science fiction. The genre always had its political differences, of course. John W. Campbell, Jr., the editor of *Astounding SF*, which became *Analog* in 1960, was a technophile and a political conservative; with a few notable exceptions, the stories he published tended to follow his bent. In the 1950s, *Galaxy*, edited by H. L. Gold and later by Frederik Pohl and others, published stories by such writers as Pohl, Damon Knight, Robert Sheckley, and Fritz Leiber that were less highly enamored of technology and that satirized some of the more conservative and established elements in our society, including government, the military, and big business. Although many of the genre's biggest names published in both *Analog* and *Galaxy* throughout the 1950s and 1960s, the ideological rivalry was quite real. It came to a head with the outbreak of the Vietnam War and the eventual growth of the anti-war movement. Much of the political rhetoric of American SF soon centered on the need to either oppose or support U.S. government policy in Southeast Asia.

In June 1968, two groups of SF writers with opposing views on U.S. involvement in Vietnam published angry advertisements in *Galaxy*. Among the signers of the anti-war advertisement were Ursula K. Le Guin, Philip K. Dick, Joanna Russ, Ray Bradbury, and Harlan Ellison. Among those signing the ad supporting U.S. government policy were John W. Campbell, Jr., Robert A. Heinlein, Poul Anderson, Larry Niven, and Jerry Pournelle. This debate was to achieve the ultimate in public irony nearly a decade later at the 1976 World Science Fiction Convention in Kansas City, where Vietnam veteran Joe Haldeman's bitter anti-war story *The Forever War* received the Hugo Award for best novel of the year in the same weekend that the convention's guest of honor, Robert A. Heinlein, was booed for, in essence, arguing that nuclear war was inevitable and might in fact improve the species.

Radical Changes in the Field

The youth culture, with its attendant drug use and alternative lifestyles, had an enormous effect on the genre as well. Philip K. Dick, one of the most influential writers of the period, had demonstrated an interest in altered states of consciousness from his earliest published fiction—see, for example, *Eye in the Sky*—and this interest only intensified as Dick explored more fully the use of mind-altering substances. The result, of course, was an entire body of literary work in which reality is at best a fragile consensus and drugs can be the key to transcendental knowledge. Among the most notable of Dick's drug-related novels are *The Three Stigmata of Palmer Eldritch*, *Now Wait for Last Year* (1966), and the powerful *Flow My Tears, the Policeman Said.* Following Dick's lead and, perhaps, their own contemporary experiences, many SF writers made the drug culture a standard component of their novels to an extent that today comes across as both naïve and dated. Indeed, when David Gerrold rewrote his successful 1972 novel *When HARLIE Was One* in 1988, he went so far as to remove virtually all mention of casual drug use by his scientist protagonist. With or without drug use, characters who lived decidedly alternate lifestyles also became common in science fiction, especially in the work of Samuel R. Delany. See, for example, *Nova* or the somewhat later *Dhalgren.*

In Britain, a nation that had not fully recovered from World War II and that was still coming to terms with the gradual but painful loss of its colonial empire, a new generation of SF writers was creating what came to be called the "New Wave." Reacting in direct opposition to what they saw as the SF establishment— authors such as Arthur C. Clarke, James White, and John Wyndham, perhaps— these New Wave writers had relatively little interest in science and technology *per se* and were frequently technophobic. They tended toward leftist political values and they prized stylistic experimentation above all else. Infected, perhaps, by the general depression left by the loss of empire, their work also tended toward a depiction of disasters and decay, entropy in all its forms. On the brighter side, they were also interested in sex, drugs, and rock 'n roll!

Although some of the writers who later gained fame as part of the New Wave had been publishing since the mid-1950s, most notably Brian Aldiss and J. G. Ballard, the movement found its focus in 1964 when Michael Moorcock became editor of the British magazine *New Worlds.* Moorcock didn't simply publish avant-garde work, however; he also publicized his work widely and produced a series of manifestos in support of what the New Wave writers were doing. Moorcock's own vision of science fiction was both experimental and politically radical. He saw apocalyptic possibilities in contemporary British life and explored them in a series of bitingly satirical stories, most notably the first of the Jerry Cornelius tales (1965) and the award-winning "Behold the Man" (1966).

Ballard and Aldiss are the most estimable authors connected with the British New Wave, but Moorcock helped develop a large roster of talented younger writers, including Langdon Jones, Barrington J. Bayley, M. John Harrison, and David I. Masson. He also published work by a number of Americans, most notably Thomas M. Disch and John Sladek. Despite its literary excellence, it should be noted that *New Worlds* was pretty much a failure from a financial point of view. Still, the magazine's value as a pioneer was enormous. It provided a venue for writers eager to try new and important approaches to the genre and helped found several major careers.

In America, a number of writers were similarly involved in a radical revisioning of science fiction, though they lacked the focal point provided by Moorcock's *New Worlds.* Among these authors were Disch, Samuel R. Delany, and Harlan Ellison, all of whom published some of their best early work in Moorcock's magazine. Two other American writers associated with the New Wave were Roger Zelazny and Robert Silverberg. Disch, Zelazny, and Delany demonstrated high artistic ambitions virtually from their first published stories. Ellison and Silverberg served apprenticeships in writing more standard fare before spreading their wings. Together these five writers produced some of the best American SF of the 1960s.

Both the British and the American New Wave writers were at first roundly criticized by many long-time genre readers and other SF authors, but the gradual acceptance of their work can be seen in the sheer number of awards they received between 1965 and 1969. Zelazny, for example, picked up two Hugos and two Nebulas, as did Harlan Ellison; Aldiss and Moorcock each received a Nebula, while Silverberg was awarded both the Hugo and the Nebula. Samuel R. Delany earned an amazing four Nebulas as well as a Hugo. Lacking a magazine comparable to *New Worlds,* American New Wave writers published much of their best fiction in original anthologies—Damon Knight's Orbit series, for example, and Harlan Ellison's groundbreaking *Dangerous Visions,* which appeared in 1967 and included superb experimental fiction by Philip José Farmer, Silverberg, Delany, Norman Spinrad, Ballard, and R. A. Lafferty, as well as somewhat more traditional work by a number of other major talents.

Although radical changes occurred in the science fiction of the mid- to late 1960s, more traditional writers continued to produce excellent stories throughout the period, as they do to this day. Among the long-time veterans working at the top of their form were Clifford D. Simak, Fritz Leiber, Philip José Farmer (although he also produced some very experimental work when given the chance), and Robert A. Heinlein, all of whom took home Hugo Awards for what may well be their best novels. Simak received the Hugo in 1964 for *Way Station,* a quiet tale of alien–human interaction; Leiber's large-scale disaster novel, *The Wanderer,* took the award in 1965; Farmer's tale of life after death, *To Your Scattered Bodies Go,* saw magazine publication in 1965–1966, and picked up a Hugo after its book publication in 1971; and Heinlein's much-imitated tale of revolution in space, *The Moon Is a Harsh Mistress,* was the 1967 Hugo winner. Another veteran, Frank Herbert, produced one of the most important SF novels of the modern period in *Dune,* which won the Nebula in 1965. Other veterans publishing excellent more-or-less traditional SF in the 1960s included Jack Vance, Poul Anderson, Cordwainer Smith, Arthur C. Clarke, James White, and Gordon R. Dickson.

Nor did all of the newer writers make a complete break with traditional methods and themes. Among the most important SF authors to begin publishing in the mid-1960s was Larry Niven, who was largely responsible for redefining the concept of hard SF for the modern period and who was also instrumental in infusing that subgenre with a strong conservative-libertarian political stance. Niven's first story appeared in 1964; he went on to win a handful of major awards, most notably both the Hugo and Nebula for his influential 1970 novel, *Ringworld.* SF writers have always had a penchant for the gigantic, the tendency to toss planets and stars around as if they were peanuts, but in *Ringworld* Niven went a step further, creating what may well have been at that time the largest inhabitable artifact in the history of the genre, a ring that quite literally circles a star at approximately the same distance that the earth orbits the sun. Niven's influence continues to this day and can be traced in the careers of hard SF writers including his frequent collaborators Jerry Pournelle and Steven Barnes, Charles Sheffield, Robert L. Forward, David Brin, Greg Bear, and even the newer British hard SF writers such as Stephen Baxter and Alastair Reynolds.

The 1960s saw changes not merely in the kind of science fiction that was written, but also in how the genre was marketed, both in the United States and in Britain. Since Hugo Gernsback founded *Amazing Stories* in 1926, the majority of American SF stories had been published in magazines. Although relatively few of them are remembered today, dozens of SF magazines flourished from 1930 to 1960. When paperback fiction began to appear in the late 1930s and 1940s, collections of SF short stories reprinted from magazines soon became popular and, indeed, one of the first paperback volumes issued was a collection of previously published SF stories, *The Pocket Book of Science Fiction*, edited by Donald A. Wollheim in 1943. Throughout the 1950s and early 1960s, magazine reprints continued to be the dominant form of SF in book format. Even the relatively few novels that were printed as often as not saw their first publication in magazines; both Pohl and Kornbluth's *The Space Merchants* and Heinlein's *Double Star*, for example, had previously appeared as serials in *Galaxy* and *Astounding* respectively. This changed gradually, in part as a result of the gutting of the American News Company in the late 1950s and the increased distribution difficulties that resulted.

By the early 1960s, most of the magazines were gone and more and more original and reprint novels were appearing, in part because publishers began to recognize the drawing power of big-name writers with a number of books constantly kept in print. Publishing houses such as Ace and Ballantine led the way, the former being especially remembered for its back-to-back "Ace Double" format: two original short SF novels for just a quarter! Any number of future giants in the field, such as Philip K. Dick, Ursula K. Le Guin, Thomas M. Disch, and Samuel R. Delany, saw either their first or their second book publications in this format. Ballantine and Ace both had considerable success in promoting reprint editions of the work of Edgar Rice Burroughs, and Ace also turned a profit on its original paperback novels by Andre Norton. Heinlein, Clarke, E. E. Smith, Isaac Asimov, Ray Bradbury, and a few other writers began receiving promotion and fairly large print runs.

Then, in 1965, Ace and Ballantine went to war over the publication of an immensely long heroic fantasy novel by a heretofore virtually unknown writer. J. R. R. Tolkien's monumental, three-volume *The Lord of the Rings* had been published in hardcover in Britain in the mid-1950s to a lukewarm reception and modest sales. In 1965, however, Ace brought out a paperback edition in the United States and did so without paying royalties because of a loophole in the copyright law. Within months Ballantine issued a revised edition of the trilogy with a note from the author castigating Ace Books and asking readers to buy only the new version of his novel. Between them the Ace and Ballantine paperback editions of *The Lord of the Rings* sold more than a quarter of a million copies in their first year in print, an unheard-of figure for a work of genre fiction. The major publishers, of course, took notice, and the publication of high-quality original SF and fantasy became a growth industry. By the mid- to late 1970s, the number of original titles published annually had tripled, and works of SF and fantasy by such authors as Tolkien, Frank Herbert, Stephen R. Donaldson, and Terry Brooks were achieving bestseller status. By the early 1980s, Asimov, Heinlein, Clarke, and Piers Anthony had also become fixtures on the bestseller lists.

Among the outgrowths of this mid-1960s boom period were the establishment of the highly successful Ballantine Adult Fantasy series and, of more relevance here, the creation by editor Terry Carr of the Ace Science Fiction Specials series. Carr published original SF novels of considerable literary merit and, perhaps just as importantly, put covers on the books by top-rated illustrators Leo and Diane Dillon that appealed to an adult audience. Between 1968 and 1971, he edited some of the finest novels ever to appear in the genre, among them Le Guin's *The Left Hand of Darkness*, R. A. Lafferty's *Past Master* and *Fourth Mansions*, Keith Roberts's *Pavane*, Joanna Russ's *And Chaos Died*, and Alexei Panshin's *Rite of Passage*. Other publishers in both the United States and Britain soon developed similar quality SF lines with varying results.

The decades following 1963 saw any number of new themes gaining importance within the genre, but two stand out in particular, one largely sociological in nature, the other largely technological. I am referring, of course, to science fiction's increasing interest in feminism and gender issues and the evolving technology of computers, microprocessors, and cybernetics.

An Influx of Women Writers

It has often been written that prior to the 1960s science fiction was essentially a boys' club, both in terms of its readership and its writers. There is some truth to that assertion, although even a brief examination of the magazines of the 1950s will turn up a surprisingly long list of significant female authors, among them C. L. Moore, Leigh Brackett, Judith Merril, Andre Norton, Katherine MacLean, Mildred Clingerman, Zenna Henderson, Marion Zimmer Bradley, and Margaret St. Clair. Some of these writers—Moore, Brackett, Norton, and Bradley, for example—hid behind initials or gender-obscure first names and wrote what was essentially traditional SF and fantasy, utilizing generally male protagonists and catering to an essentially male audience. Others—Merril, Clingerman, and Henderson in particular—were seen in their day, at least in part, as women's writers and published primarily in *The Magazine of Fantasy and Science Fiction*, which, since its founding in 1949, had adhered to a more urbane, polished, and mainstream literary style than other magazines in the field, a style somewhat more calculated, perhaps, to win a female readership.

What changed in the mid-1960s and early 1970s, then, was not just the number of women writers in the field but also the kinds of things they wrote about. The women's movement transformed science fiction, affecting even those writers who were hostile to it or simply uninterested. The careers of Ursula K. Le Guin and Joanna Russ typify the changes that occurred. Le Guin entered the field with a number of well-done but fairly traditional SF and fantasy stories and novels written somewhat in the manner of Andre Norton—for example, *Rocannon's World* (1966). But in 1969, as part of Terry Carr's Ace SF Specials series, she published one of the three or four most influential science fiction novels of the latter half of the 20th century, *The Left Hand of Darkness,* a brilliant examination of, among many other things, gender stereotypes. Similarly, Joanna Russ, although she had begun publishing short fiction as early as 1959, first came to general notice with stories in *Orbit* in the mid- to late 1960s and with two Ace Specials, 1968's *Picnic on Paradise* and 1970's *And Chaos Died.* These later stories generally revolved around strong female protagonists heretofore rare in science fiction. Russ's controversial third novel, *The Female Man,* a much more radical and bitter feminist critique of contemporary gender roles, appeared in 1975. It had been written some years earlier but had considerable trouble finding a publisher.

Other women writers began to establish increasingly high profiles throughout the late 1960s and the 1970s. Kate Wilhelm, who had been publishing with relatively little notice since the mid-1950s, blossomed into one of the genre's finest stylists, first in the pages of *Orbit* and eventually in such novels as the *Where Late the Sweet Birds Sang* and *The Clewiston Test.* Wilhelm's work has rarely addressed gender issues as directly as the works of Le Guin or Russ, but it has always been clear that she writes from a feminist perspective. Alice Sheldon, writing first under the pseudonym James Tiptree, Jr., and later as Raccoona Sheldon, produced beginning in the late 1960s a series of cutting-edge feminist-oriented short stories, including "The Girl Who was Plugged In," "The Women Men Don't See," and "Houston, Houston, Do You Read?" In 1974, Suzy McKee Charnas published *Walk to the End of the World,* which featured what might well be the most hideous patriarchal dystopia ever conceived by an SF writer. In 1976, Marge Piercy, a well-known mainstream novelist and poet, published *Woman on the Edge of Time,* which, like Russ's *The Female Man,* displayed glimpses of a variety of better and worse universes for women.

Other female, feminist-oriented writers who entered, and helped to change, the field in the 1960s and 1970s included Pamela Sargent, Lisa Tuttle, Elizabeth Lynn, Eleanor Arnason, and Octavia Butler. This process has continued throughout the late 20th century and into the 21st with authors such as Sheri S. Tepper, Joan Slonczewski, Pat Murphy, Candas Jane Dorsey, and Nicola Griffith producing increasingly sophisticated fiction that deals meaningfully with, among other things, the relationship between gender and such topics as violence, race, ecology, pacifism, religion, and child abuse.

Also of note has been the increasing number of male authors who write from a feminist perspective—for example, John Varley, Samuel R. Delany, John Kessel, and Kim Stanley Robinson—as well as writers who introduce gay or lesbian characters into their fiction, including Delany, Thomas M. Disch, Lynn, Arnason, Griffith, Melissa Scott and, somewhat unexpectedly, Marion Zimmer

Bradley, whose work underwent a major transformation in the early to mid-1970s, changing gradually from fairly standard science fantasy in the tradition of Leigh Brackett and Andre Norton to a more serious exploration of women's and gay issues. It should be noted perhaps that, as was the case with the New Wave, the emergence of so many strong female and feminist writers in the genre also led to a fair amount of anger. This criticism came primarily, though not entirely, from male writers who either disagreed with the entire feminist message or saw women writers as responsible for publishing fantasy disguised as SF and thus somehow damaging the genre's legitimacy.

Old Themes, New Technologies

In his Skylark of Space series, E. E. Smith could describe gigantic spaceships powered by hundreds of towering vacuum tubes. Even as late as 1966, Robert A. Heinlein in *The Moon Is a Harsh Mistress* and D. F. Jones in *Colossus* could write of computers that took up entire buildings. But with the invention of the microprocessor in 1969, and the marketing of microcomputers in 1971, sheer size was no longer synonymous with computing power, and further enormous breakthroughs in computer technology seemed to be right around the corner. In the 1960s and early 1970s, computers were primarily of interest to SF writers in terms of the quest for artificial intelligence (AI). The Heinlein and Jones novels are examples of this interest, which was often coupled with a fear that AIs might, for better or worse, take control of the human race, a fear that is, of course, traceable as far back as Jack Williamson's *The Humanoids*, Karel Čapek's *R.U.R.*, and perhaps even Mary Shelley's *Frankenstein*.

Other 1970s examples of the interest in artificial intelligence include David Gerrold's *When HARLIE Was One* and, of course, Isaac Asimov's "The Bicentennial Man" (1976). In the 1960s, scientists were fairly sanguine concerning their ability to create true AIs in the near future, but little real progress was made over the next two decades, and genre interest in artificial intelligence gradually declined. AIs, whether housed in stationary computers or configured as robots, became, for the most part, an assumed background element in stories largely about other things. The major exception to this trend would be in film and television, where AIs continued to be popular, most often in the form of highly attractive young "women," brawny "men," and cute robots and most frequently cast as police officers, faithful sidekicks, or villains.

Even in the 1970s, programmers routinely expected to spend hours punching cards and poring over yards of printout before they could run all but the simplest programs. Gradually, however, as programming became easier and turned into a matter of keyboards and screens, direct, tactile connection between user and machine made it increasingly possible to sink into an almost trance-like creative state. The hardware came to be seen as secondary, a mere interface between the user and both the software (the programs themselves) and the networked electronic space in which those programs were increasingly being run (which came to be called cyberspace). Perhaps the first SF author to make use of this concept in its modern form was Vernor Vinge in his fine 1981 novella "True Names." The idea of cyberspace didn't really catch fire, however, until 1984, when science fiction was turned upside down by cyberpunk, its first highly organized, high-profile literary movement since the New Wave. Cyberpunk is discussed more fully in Chapter 5.

From its earliest days, most obviously in *Frankenstein*, science fiction has concerned itself with such Faustian ambitions as the creation of new life forms and the transformation of already existing life into something either superior to or more specialized than what has gone before. Early writers, including Shelley and H. G. Wells in *The Island of Doctor Moreau*, more often than not saw such actions within the context of surgical science, and in the 1970s this concept continued to be popular, especially whenever new advances in transplant techniques or the use of prosthetics attracted SF writers' attention. Notable examples of the use of surgery to keep alive, augment, or simply change the human body include Heinlein's *I Will Fear No Evil* (1970), Clarke's "A Meeting with Medusa" (1972), and Pohl's *Man Plus*. However, the concept of creating some form of *Homo superior* through surgery has, throughout the history of science fiction, been paralleled by the desire to make genetic alterations—alterations that will breed true. The early-modern period is full of superman tales; in some cases, the new form of humanity is seen as a spontaneous mutation, but in others, for example A. E. van Vogt's *Slan*, the changes are the result of what appears to be (van Vogt's language is rather imprecise) an experiment in genetic manipulation.

In the 1950s and 1960s, spurred perhaps by breakthroughs in DNA research, a number of writers produced excellent stories centered on an improved understanding of genetic engineering, most notably James Blish's *The Seedling Stars* and, on a more modest level, Frank Herbert's *Dune* and the Instrumentality of Man stories of Cordwainer Smith. Lacking specifics on how such engineering should be done, however, these stories tended to concentrate on the spectacular, and at times rather unlikely, end products of the process. In the late 1960s and 1970s, the aspect of genetic engineering that was most widely used in science fiction was cloning; see, for example, Le Guin's "Nine Lives" (1969), Pamela Sargent's *Cloned Lives*, Ira Levin's *The Boys from Brazil*, and Kate Wilhelm's *Where Late the Sweet Birds Sang*.

Other venerable genre topics also received periodic updating between 1963 and 1983, among them nuclear war and militarism. The post-nuclear holocaust theme, which was handled so well by Walter M. Miller, Jr., in *A Canticle for Leibowitz* and by Edgar Pangborn in *Davy* in the 1950s and 1960s, reappeared in the early to mid-1980s in powerful new tales such as Russell Hoban's *Riddley Walker* and Neal Barrett, Jr.'s *Through Darkest America*. Given impetus by the Vietnam War and responding to Heinlein's earlier novel *Starship Troopers*, Joe Haldeman explored with great insight the dangers of militarism in his 1975 novel, *The Forever War*. Then, two years later, Orson Scott Card published what was, at least in part, another installment in an ongoing argument about Vietnam, his classic short story "Ender's Game," which eventually evolved into a multiple–award-winning novel of the same name published in 1985.

Science fiction's debate over militarism continued throughout the 1970s and 1980s. In his Mercenary series and his *There Will Be War* anthologies, for example, Jerry Pournelle conducted a campaign against what he saw as the liberal betrayal of the United States in Vietnam and elsewhere. Although it rarely receives much critical attention, similar military SF by David Drake, David Feintuch, David Weber, and others continues to be enormously popular to the present day. Lois McMaster Bujold in the earlier entries in her Miles Vorkosigan series and C. J. Cherryh in some of her Alliance-Union novels have also produced military SF with higher literary ambitions.

A final theme that has become increasingly important in science fiction during the modern period is ecology. Genre warnings of potential ecological disaster go back at least as far as Ward Moore's *Greener Than You Think* (1947) and John Christopher's 1956 *The Death of Grass*. It wasn't until the 1960s, however, that our society's ability to cause overwhelming ecological damage began to gain more general public attention. Nonfiction works such as Rachel Carson's *Silent Spring* (1962) and Paul Ehrlich's *The Population Bomb* (1968) gained enormous readership. Among the earlier works of science fiction that helped promulgate this new environmental awareness were J. G. Ballard's *The Drowned World, The Drought,* and *The Crystal World,* each of which depicted horrifying ecological disasters; Frank Herbert's *Dune,* with its serious discussion of the possibilities for transforming a planetary ecology; John Brunner's two disaster novels, *Stand on Zanzibar,* which concentrates on the population explosion, and *The Sheep Look Up,* which portrays an America collapsing beneath the weight of its own pollution; and Ursula K. Le Guin's 1972 novella, *The Word for World Is Forest,* which depicts the accidental destruction of an alien ecology by colonists from Earth. Environmentalism, like many of the other themes discussed in this chapter, continues to be a topic of great importance in the science fiction of the last 20 years as well, particularly in the work of such writers as Sheri S. Tepper, Bruce Sterling, and Kim Stanley Robinson.

Children's Books and Short Fiction

A number of critics have argued that science fiction, despite the enormous sophistication of some of its more literary texts, is at its heart a form of children's literature and, whether one agrees with this assertion or not, there's no arguing that the genre has always attracted large numbers of young readers. From the Frank Reade and Frank Reade, Jr. stories of the 1870s and later to the Tom Swift and Tom Swift, Jr. books published throughout the 20th century, there have always been a significant number of SF texts specifically published for children. The most important moment in the history of children's or young adult (YA) SF undoubtedly occurred a couple of years after World War II when Robert A. Heinlein decided to write a series of what were then called "juvenile" novels for Scribners, beginning with *Rocket Ship Galileo* in 1947. The juveniles issued by John C. Winston, which featured fiction by Poul Anderson and others, were also significant throughout the 1950s. Heinlein's fiction for young readers still dominated the market in the early to mid-1960s, although other writers—most notably Andre Norton with *Star Man's Son: 2250 A.D.* and later tales, and Madeleine L'Engle with *A Wrinkle in Time* and its sequels—gained a significant readership as well. Writers who published primarily for adults, such as Lester del Rey and Robert Silverberg, also produced a significant number of solid YA novels in this era.

Moving into the 1970s, however, writers who specialized entirely in YA fiction began to take over the market more and more, most notably Robert O'Brien, William Sleator, Monica Hughes, Louise Lawrence, Robert Westall, and, perhaps most importantly, H. M. Hoover. These writers produced a wide range of adventure fiction, some of it serious, some of it humorous. Perhaps reflecting the concerns of the real world of the 1970s, however, many of their books involved dystopian scenarios in which a small number of children rebelled against or escaped from a variety of repressive, often post-holocaust societies.

Edward James has argued persuasively in his *Science Fiction in the Twentieth Century* [9-99] for the centrality of the short story in science fiction. He suggests that critics have tended to over-emphasize the novel. But *Anatomy of Wonder* necessarily emphasizes book-length works, whether novels, single-author collections, or anthologies. It may therefore be the case that the fiction of writers who produced a small number of key stories but failed to publish a major short-story collection is given short shrift here. We have always included entries for the most important short story collections and anthologies.

In the early years of the modern period, the primary purpose of the science fiction anthology was to preserve in a more permanent form the best stories that had previously appeared in the SF magazines. Thus we had anthologies that collected the finest stories published in a given year by a specific magazine; best-of-the-year anthologies that collected fiction from many different sources—for example, Donald A. Wollheim's *World's Best SF* series; anthologies of award-winning stories—for example, *The Hugo Winners*, edited by Isaac Asimov; theme anthologies, such as Leon Stover and Harry Harrison's *Apeman, Spaceman* (1968), which featured short stories centering on the topic of anthropology, or Pamela Sargent's *Women of Wonder*, which collected stories by women writers; and, finally, general reprint anthologies, which might be structured historically or which might contain stories having nothing more in common than the fact that the editor liked them and thought them important—for example, Norman Spinrad's *Modern Science Fiction* (1974). Anthologies of original short fiction, however, were uncommon in the early modern period. Frederik Pohl had edited six volumes of *Star Science Fiction Stories* between 1953 and 1960 with considerable critical success but only passable sales, and there had been few imitators. By the mid-1960s, however, the number of science fiction magazines was at a low point and original anthologies began to appear in greater numbers, among them John Carnell and Kenneth Bulmer's *New Writings in SF* series (beginning in 1964), Damon Knight's *Orbit* series (beginning in 1966), and Harlan Ellison's *Dangerous Visions* (1967).

The original anthologies were perceived as having several advantages over the magazines. First, since the anthologist wasn't trapped within the framework of a monthly publication schedule, it was assumed that he could simply do a better job of finding quality fiction. Second, it was believed that books containing original fiction would both have a longer shelf life than magazines and be more appealing to libraries. Finally, it was hoped that original anthologies would attract a different, perhaps more mature readership, a readership willing to pay somewhat more and interested in a more varied selection of stories than the traditional magazines were willing to publish. Thus Damon Knight was able to include a variety of experimental, sometimes New Wave stories in *Orbit*, which would have seemed entirely out of place in *Analog* or *The Magazine of Fantasy and Science Fiction*. This was even more true of Ellison's *Dangerous Visions*, which included a number of stories that were explicitly sexual in nature, stories no SF magazine would have considered publishing at that time. In 1971, three more important original anthology series began publication, Terry Carr's *Universe*, Robert Silverberg's *New Dimensions*, and Michael Moorcock's *New Worlds*, recently defunct as a magazine but now newly reconstituted as a quarterly paperback series.

Increasingly popular as well were one-shot theme anthologies composed entirely of original stories or of a mixture of classic reprints and original fiction. Among the most successful such anthologies in the late 1960s and 1970s were Joseph Elder's *The Farthest Reaches* (1968), which featured stories set far away in space and time; Harry Harrison's *The Year 2000* (1970); Thomas M. Disch's *The Ruins of Earth*, which concerned itself with ecological disasters; Roger Elwood's *Future City* (1973); and Jack Dann's *Wandering Stars* (1974), which contained stories on Jewish themes. Elwood was by far the most prolific editor of original SF anthologies in the 1970s, publishing an estimated 70 to 80 volumes within a very brief time span. At one point he supposedly controlled some 25 percent of the market for original short science fiction. A number of the volumes he produced were excellent, or at least contained some excellent fiction. *Epoch*, co-edited with Robert Silverberg, and the Continuum series (1974–1975) were particularly notable.

Elwood's theme anthologies were frequently crowded with mediocre fiction and this shortcoming, combined with the sheer number of books he was producing, more than one a month over a two-year period, quickly led to a glut on the market. Elwood left science fiction editing in the late 1970s, made the jump to Christian publishing, and soon found a long-term niche as the author and editor of inspirational books. Unfortunately, he left behind him a near-moribund market for original SF anthologies, and he remains to this day one of the least popular figures in the history of the genre. Very few anthologies of any significance were published in the early 1980s except for best-of-the-year volumes and later volumes in series such as Orbit, one notable exception being Alan Ryan's excellent reprint anthology on religious themes, *Perpetual Light*.

This chapter began with the 1960s. The world was changing in remarkable ways, both for better and for worse. The era of Vietnam, the sexual revolution, student protests, the civil rights and women's rights movements, Johnson's Great Society, Nixon's opening of China, and Watergate was turbulent and exhilarating, a roller-coaster ride. To a very great extent it was an era when a variety of expansive, liberal political ideologies dominated the western world. By the standards of the early 21st century, it might be noted, even Richard Nixon seems in many ways a liberal. And science fiction was also changing, expanding, producing exhilarating new work. The British New Wave may have been thematically downbeat, but its stylistic experiments helped rejuvenate the genre. Writers such as Ballard, Aldiss, Ellison, Delany, Zelazny, Le Guin, Russ, and Silverberg raised the bar for genre work, producing fiction whose literary excellence often exceeded even the best of what had gone before.

By the late 1970s, however, the mood of the nation had changed. We had failed in Southeast Asia, the scars of Watergate had refused to heal, and Jimmy Carter's administration seemed mired in a hopeless malaise. A rising tide of conservatism swept Ronald Reagan into office in 1981. Political initiatives based in liberal ideology, particularly those relating to civil rights, equal opportunity, and environmentalism, frequently ground to a halt or reversed direction. Science fiction itself seemed to fall into a malaise, with some of the field's best writers ceasing to produce much SF after the mid-1970s (Delany, Ballard, Russ), or seeing a distinct drop-off in the quality of their production (Zelazny, Silverberg), or finding themselves unable to sell their work to major publishers in an increasingly conservative publishing climate (Lafferty).

There are always exceptions, of course, and it's worth remembering that Gregory Benford's *Timescape*, Gene Wolfe's magisterial *The Shadow of the Torturer*, and Joan D. Vinge's *The Snow Queen* all appeared in 1980. Still, science fiction needed something new, a change of direction, a jolt of electricity, and a couple of fellows named Bruce Sterling and William Gibson were poised to provide it.

CHAPTER 5

Cyberpunk and Beyond, 1984–2004

Michael M. Levy

The term "cyberpunk" was created by Bruce Bethke in a story of that name that appeared in *Amazing* in 1983; but it was almost immediately appropriated by Gardner Dozois. He used it to label the early fiction of a new literary movement, much of which he was publishing in the magazine he edited, *Isaac Asimov's SF Magazine* (*Asimov's* for short). The cyberpunks fused a strong interest in technology, and particularly in cybernetics and biotechnology, a generally left-wing or libertarian (anti-government, anti-big business) political stance, and down-and-dirty punk attitudes with a literary aesthetic borrowed, at least in part, from Raymond Chandler, Dashiell Hammett, and *film noir*. They also claimed as progenitors writers as diverse as Alfred Bester, Harlan Ellison, William Burroughs, Anthony Burgess, and J. G. Ballard, not to mention Ridley Scott's 1982 film, *Bladerunner*. Their main theorist and author of manifestos was Bruce Sterling, their finest writer William Gibson.

Other writers closely associated with the early days of the cyberpunk movement were John Shirley (though his career dated back to 1973), Lewis Shiner, Pat Cadigan, Marc Laidlaw, and Richard Kadrey. A number of other SF writers have claimed or been claimed to have occasional connections with the cyberpunks, including Samuel R. Delany, K. W. Jeter, Walter Jon Williams, Rudy Rucker, Michael Swanwick, George Alec Effinger, and Greg Bear.

The work that most epitomized cyberpunk was William Gibson's 1984 novel *Neuromancer*, which, fittingly enough, initiated the second group of Ace SF specials edited by Terry Carr. *Neuromancer*, a stylish and complex tale of computer cowboys hacking their way through cyberspace to commit a variety of computer crimes, won the Hugo, Nebula, and Philip K. Dick awards and, even 20 years later, is clearly the most influential (and most imitated) SF novel since Le Guin's *The Left Hand of Darkness*. Although many of the major cyberpunk stories appeared in *Asimov's*, the core cyberpunk anthology was Bruce Sterling's *Mirrorshades*. Although, or perhaps because, the more talented proponents of the movement quickly branched off in a variety of different literary directions, cyberpunk soon became a rather standardized set of tropes to be readily imitated by less ambitious writers and film makers. By 1990, it was fashionable in academic and book review circles to proclaim the subgenre dead. Not surprisingly, however, one or two excellent new cyberpunk or cyberpunk-influenced novels continued to appear throughout the 1990s and into the 21st century—for example, Neal Stephenson's *Snow Crash*, Melissa Scott's *Trouble and Her Friends*, Raphael Carter's *The Fortunate Fall* (1996), and Pat Cadigan's *Tea from an Empty Cup*. Even Jon Courtenay Grimwood's recent and much-praised Pashazade trilogy, which lacks much in the way of cyber, is right at home with punk.

It should be noted that the concept of cyberspace as a place where an artificial or virtual reality can be constructed and where human and machine intelligences can interact and, in effect, live their lives is not limited in its use merely to the cyberpunks. In becoming the common coin of SF, cyberpunk has also lent its tropes to spectacular use by writers as diverse as Dan Simmons in *The Fall of Hyperion*, Charles Platt in *The Silicon Man*, Marge Piercy in *He, She and It*, Greg Egan in *Permutation City* and other works, and Geoff Ryman in *Air*. Even Poul Anderson, a writer closely connected with the Heinlein-Niven-Sheffield tradition of conservative, libertarian space opera, felt comfortable making use of cyberpunk conventions in his *Harvest of Stars* (1993).

Although writers including Robert Heinlein and Frederik Pohl had written extensively about body modification in the 1970s, continuing improvements in microtechnology led to even more emphasis being placed on the concept of large-scale improvements in the human body in the 1980s, especially in the work of the cyberpunks, who often assumed the widespread adoption of implants to create a direct computer/brain interface; see, for example, Walter Jon Williams's *Hardwired*, George Alec Effinger's *When Gravity Fails*, and Pat Cadigan's *Synners*. The potential for surgically altering the human form to build a superior cyborg warrior has been another ongoing interest in SF and was particularly well handled by Gregory Benford in his *Great Sky River* and its sequels. A more recent use of major surgery to create cyborgs can be found in Peter Watts's *Starfish* and its sequels.

Also building on work published in the 1970s, new writers continued to explore the possibilities for genetic engineering. Such stories generally fall into two groups. The first is concerned with relatively limited and entirely possible near-future attempts to create *Homo superior* (some consciously engineered, others occurring as mutations)—for example, Robert Reed's *Black Milk*, Lois

McMaster Bujold's *Falling Free*, George Turner's *Brain Child* (1991), Nancy Kress's *Beggars in Spain* and its sequels, and Greg Bear's *Darwin's Radio*. The other group comprises more spectacular tales of wholesale genetic transformation, including Charles Sheffield's *Sight of Proteus*, Bruce Sterling's *Schismatrix* and his Shaper and Mechanist stories, Geoff Ryman's *The Child Garden*, and Stephen Baxter's *Flux*. Although set in the far future, C. J. Cherryh's *Cyteen* may be the most realistic portrayal we have of the psychological and sociological ramifications of cloning.

Needless to say, the advent of Dolly the cloned sheep in 1996 gave even more impetus to such stories, with one of the best post-Dolly variations on this theme being Nancy Farmer's *House of the Scorpion*, which concerns a little boy who discovers that he's been raised by a rich drug lord for spare parts. At their most extreme, however, recent stories of human transformation have essentially abandoned the organic body or turned it into just one of a number of options. Fusing fantasies of the posthuman with the trope of virtual reality, writers such as Greg Egan in *Diaspora*, Tony Daniel in *Metaplanetary*, and Justina Robson in *Natural History* tell stories set in universes where their near-immortal characters flit back and forth between the real world and the virtual world, and between organic, mechanical, and virtual bodies, essentially at will. In Daniel's novel, it's even common for organic and inorganic intelligences to marry and produce offspring.

In one of his weaker novels, *Fantastic Voyage* (1966), written as a film tie-in, Isaac Asimov told the basically silly story of the miniaturization of a surgical team, which was then sent into the body of a dying man to save his life. In the 1970s, however, a number of scientists, most notably K. Eric Drexler, began writing about the concept of nanotechnology—that is, the creation of machines on a molecular level—and primitive forms of this technology quickly came into existence in our world (see Drexler's *Engines of Creation*, 1987). Interest in nanotechnology within the science fiction community was immediate and, when combined with research in both genetic engineering and microprocessors, resulted in a number of fine new stories such as Greg Bear's *Blood Music*, which involves a scientist who uses genetic engineering techniques to transform a virus into an intelligent nanocomputer. Replicating rapidly, the virus takes over the scientist's body, transforming the body to the virus's own specifications. Within a very few years, nanotechnology has become, like faster-than-light space travel and artificial intelligence, one of the standard tropes of science fiction and a major element in such works as Paul Preuss's *Human Error*, Walter Jon Williams's *Aristoi*, Michael Swanwick's *Stations of the Tide*, Kathleen Ann Goonan's Nanotech Quartet, Linda Nagata's *Limit of Vision*, and Damien Broderick's *Transcension*. It has even been used as a kind of all-purpose bogeyman in Michael Crichton's not-very-well-informed bestseller *Prey* (2003).

New Ways of Seeing the Universe

In the more than 40 years since 1963, new scientific breakthroughs have transformed science fiction, as have the great sociological and political changes of the period. One of the pleasures of the genre, however, involves discovering the ways in which authors can take some of the older ideas, dust them off, do a little genetic manipulation, perhaps, and present them to us in new and exciting forms. The earliest popular tales of Mars, for example—those of Edgar Rice Burroughs and, somewhat later, Leigh Brackett—were gorgeous, generally lightweight romantic romps. Then, in the decade after World War II, we saw a number of more realistic portrayals of the exploration and colonization of Mars—for example, Heinlein's *Red Planet* (1949) and Arthur C. Clarke's *The Sands of Mars* (1951). In the years that followed, however, other kinds of stories became popular. Ray Bradbury, taking his cue in part from Brackett, but with a more serious purpose, published the highly romantic *The Martian Chronicles* in 1950. He in turn was emulated by any number of other writers, most notably Roger Zelazny in his classic "A Rose for Ecclesiastes" (1963). Neither Bradbury nor Zelazny, it should be noted, made any attempt to depict a scientifically accurate Mars; such accuracy was simply irrelevant to their purposes. Still other authors used a not-very-realistically portrayed Mars as a backdrop for stories in which the location was of secondary importance—for example, Philip K. Dick's *Martian Time-Slip* and *The Three Stigmata of Palmer Eldritch.*

The romanticized Mars of Brackett and Bradbury continues to fascinate SF writers, as has been demonstrated by Ian McDonald in his novel *Desolation Road* and its recent sequel, *Ares Express.* Periodically, however, writers armed with new data about the red planet have returned to attempt to describe its exploration and colonization in ever more realistic terms, as, for example, in Pohl's *Man Plus* (1976), Lewis Shiner's *Frontera* (1984), Ben Bova's *Mars,* Kim Stanley Robinson's Mars trilogy, Greg Bear's *Moving Mars,* and Gregory Benford's *The Martian Race* (1999). The updating that goes on when an author returns to one of science fiction's perennial themes, however, is often much more than just technological. Shiner, for example, uses *Frontera* not merely to describe the colonization of Mars, but also to make some of the standard cyberpunk criticisms concerning the inherent corruption of big business and big government. Similarly, Robinson, while presenting perhaps the most detailed and believable description of planetary colonization ever to appear in a work of fiction, is also pursuing a well-thought-out ecological and political agenda.

Other recent and worthwhile attempts to describe the exploration of the solar system in realistic terms include Stephen Baxter's *Titan,* which sends a souped-up space shuttle on what turns out to be a one-way trip to Saturn's moons, and Ben Bova's ongoing planetary grand tour, which began with *Mars* in 1992, and now includes such volumes as *Jupiter* (2001) and *Saturn* (2003).

In the late 1980s and 1990s, the topic of ecology was ubiquitous, appearing as a background issue in virtually all near-future SF and as a major element in such important novels as Le Guin's *Always Coming Home,* George Turner's *Drowning Towers,* Joan Slonczewski's *Door into Ocean* and its sequels, Judith Moffett's *Pennterra,* David Brin's *Earth,* and Kim Stanley Robinson's *Pacific Edge,* as well as his Mars books, and his borderline-SF novel *Antarctica.* A variety of writers have concentrated on depicting Earth in a state of environmental collapse, from John Barnes, whose *Mother of Storms* envisioned the effect of super hurricanes, to Bruce Sterling, who wiped out most of North America under a barrage of tornadoes in *Heavy Weather,* to Peter Watts, whose novels beginning with *Starfish* have imagined an Earth ravaged by an ancient lifeform accidentally released from deep-sea hydrothermal vents by human intervention. The least dramatic of the recent environmental catastrophe novels, however, though it may be the most realistic, is Robinson's *Forty Signs of Rain,* in which global warming melts the Antarctic ice shelf and kills the Gulf Stream. One day, when the tide comes in on Chesapeake Bay, it simply keeps on coming in until Washington, D.C., is essentially under water.

History has been enormously important to science fiction from its beginnings, of course, and most attempts to predict the future have been based, at least in part, on the study of the past. Asimov's *Foundation* novels, for example, had their genesis in Gibbon's *Decline and Fall of the Roman Empire.* Two other ways in which SF writers have worked with history have been through time travel and what is variously called alternate, alternative, and counterfactual history. Both subgenres saw superb work produced in the period between 1984 and 2004, with Connie Willis clearly the queen of the time-travel tale and Harry Turtledove the king of alternate history. Willis's stunning *Doomsday Book,* the grim story of an Oxford graduate student who accidentally gets trapped in the time of the Black Death, was one of the finest novels of the 1990s, while her *To Say Nothing of the Dog* combined madcap humor with a complex time-travel puzzle centered on Coventry Cathedral. Both books were award-winners. Other outstanding recent time-travel fiction includes John Kessel's *Corrupting Dr. Nice,* which combines dinosaurs, Jesus Christ, and its unique brand of humor; Michael Swanwick's *Bones of the Earth,* which also concerns dinosaurs as well as time-travel paradoxes; and Kage Baker's *In the Garden of Iden* and its sequels, which center on a team of immortal cyborgs who actually live through the past one day at a time, while doing the bidding of the Company, a secret organization located far in the future. Sharing honors for the darkest time-travel tale in recent history with Willis's *Doomsday Book* may well be J. R. Dunn's *Days of Cain,* a bitter story set, in part, in Auschwitz.

Turtledove, a Byzantine historian by training, first made a name for himself with the *Videssos* sequence, a series of magical fantasies set in an alternate universe based on his own area of specialization. But he has since gained his greatest fame writing realistic alternate history novels set largely in the recent past. In 1992, his *The Guns of the South* made the assumption that a small group of time-traveling South Africans was able to arm the Confederacy with modern weaponry; it then played out the effects of this small historical change with great rigor. Later, Turtledove's *How Few Remain* began what is now on its way to becoming at least a trilogy of trilogies, extrapolating in enormous detail the history of a North America in which the South won the Civil War by conventional means.

Recent volumes have carried Turtledove's timeline into an alternate version of World War II. His *World War* series, beginning with *In the Balance,* is a bit more conventionally science-fictional, postulating what would have happened if aliens attacked Earth at the height of the Second World War. Other particularly notable alternate universe novels include Bruce Sterling and William Gibson's *The Difference Engine,* which postulates a Victorian era in which Babbage's proto- type computer was actually built, touching off a scientific revolution, and Kim Stanley Robinson's *The Years of Rice and Salt,* which creates a world in which the Black Death of the 14th century killed off 99 percent of Europeans, resulting in a world dominated by China and Islam.

Besides being an alternate history, *The Difference Engine* also qualifies as a bor- derline example of one of the odder and more delightful SF subgenres of the last 20 years: steampunk. Set more often than not in the Victorian age and emphasizing that era's more eccentric and disreputable features, steampunk novels are generally either alternate histories that make the basic assumption that spectacular scientific advances might have occurred during the 19th centu- ry if things had been just a little bit different, or they're secret histories that assume that spectacular scientific events did in fact occur but simply escaped the attention of the historical record. Frequently satirical in their intent, such works often make the assumption that various incorrect or even crackpot scien- tific ideas of the 19th century—the concept of the ether or the hollow Earth, for example—turned out to be true.

In *The Anubis Gates,* Tim Powers helped to popularize the Victorian-era secret history in 1983, but the clear master of steampunk is Powers's good friend James Blaylock, whose *The Digging Leviathan* plays joyfully with a variety of such notions. Other notable works in this tradition are Blaylock's *Homuncu- lus,* K. W. Jeter's *Infernal Devices* (1987), and Paul Di Filippo's *The Steampunk Trilogy.* An interesting Australian variation on steampunk is found in Sean McMullen's *Souls in the Great Machine,* while it can be argued that Neal Stephen- son's *Cryptonomicon* and his monumental *Baroque Cycle* were also influenced by the steampunk writers.

Space Opera Redux

If you were to survey readers about the one thing that comes to mind when you say the words *science fiction,* however, there's little doubt that most people would come up with a spaceship, whether it be some sleek rocket-shaped creation with totally senseless fins, a flying saucer, or a combination of the two, perhaps Cap- tain Kirk's *Enterprise.* Tales of space exploration and exciting adventures on other planets have always been at the center of the genre, from E. E. Smith to the Heinlein and Norton juveniles to Larry Niven's tales of Known Space. Such stories, space operas if you will, have gone in and out of fashion, however. There have been periods when the "serious" writers in the genre mostly ignored outer space. With very few exceptions (Samuel R. Delany comes first to mind), the writers of the New Wave were more interested in inner space than anything "off planet." Nor did the cyberpunks lavish much attention on other worlds, preferring the down and dirty of Earth and near-Earth orbit. Still, the writers of stories set in outer space have always been there, producing good work, not as flashy as Ballard or Zelazny or Gibson, perhaps, but pumping the heart's blood of the genre. Gregory Benford with *In the Ocean of the Night*, Greg Bear in *Eon*, John Varley in his Titan trilogy, C. J. Cherryh in *Downbelow Station* and numerous other novels, Niven with *The Integral Trees*, and David Brin in *Startide Rising* all produced superior space fiction throughout the 1970s and early 1980s.

Then, in 1987, there appeared two superb new novels: Gregory Benford's *Great Sky River* and Iain M. Banks's *Consider Phlebas*. Benford was (and is) a physicist by trade. Banks started out (and remains part-time) a literary novelist, yet their books shared something not often seen in the genre. Chock-full of wild ideas, fascinating technology, colorful characters, startling vistas, and poetic, even experimental prose, they combined the old-fashioned virtues of traditional space opera with unusually high literary standards. Although neither book was written in a vacuum and other candidates could be suggested, I argue that these two novels set a new standard for excellence in space fiction and more specifically in space opera. We hear a lot these days about the British boom, and indeed much of the best space fiction being produced in the early 21st century is British, but Benford and a number of other American writers also stand out.

All of the writers listed above produced solid space fiction into the 1990s and continue to do so in the early 21st century. Also of note is Vernor Vinge, who bookended the 1990s with his superb, award-winning novels *A Fire Upon the Deep* and *A Deepness in the Sky*, tales set in a universe where the laws of physics decree that a civilization's distance from the galactic center governs its evolutionary potential. Lois McMaster Bujold combined diplomacy, military action, and medical technology with a good deal of humor in her Miles Vorkosigan series, most notably in the award-winning *Mirror Dance*. And C. J. Cherryh simply got better and better. In 1994, she produced *Foreigner*, the first book in a superb, ongoing series of what might be called closet space operas because they combine the traditional tropes of space fiction—aliens, violent action, space battles, and intrigue—with superb character development and carefully structured, intensely stressful interior scenes worthy of an Ingmar Bergman.

On the British side, the names that stand out are, again, Iain M. Banks, whose novels of the Culture, including *Excession* and *Look to Windward*, continue to be the standard against which everyone else should be measured; Stephen Baxter, who, influenced perhaps by Larry Niven, loves to set up bizarre environments such as the surface of a neutron star and then figure out ways to inhabit them; Ken MacLeod, the most overtly political of the newer British writers, who uses his novels, whether set on Earth or elsewhere, to provide proving grounds for radical political theories; and M. John Harrison, a former member of the New Wave who, after years of minimal connection to the field, recently made a triumphant return with his wildly innovative novel *Light*. Throw in newer writers on both sides of the Atlantic, including Alastair Reynolds, Neil Asher, Justina Robson, and Tony Daniel, and it's clear that space opera is alive and well in the early 21st century.

Mention of M. John Harrison brings us to what may be the next new thing in science fiction and fantasy—the New Weird. His *Light* has a significant gothic component, as does some of the work of Reynolds, Asher, and others among the newer British writers, with a tendency toward the extreme and the baroque, emotion for emotion's sake, and darkness beyond the norm in traditional SF. One of the hallmarks of the New Weird also appears to be a willingness to move back and forth between SF and dark fantasy with little regard for traditional genre boundaries. Although *Light* is clearly space opera, for example, there are horrific bits in it that one would be unlikely to find in a novel by Gregory Benford or Iain M. Banks. At the center of the New Weird appears to be the young British writer China Miéville, whose novel *Perdido Street Station* and its two sequels are largely very dark fantasy but also include a fair amount of fascinating technology, not to mention what appear to be aliens. Miéville didn't create this wholesale combination of disparate genres—James Blish and Roger Zelazny were past masters of the form—but he's certainly popularized it and has a number of imitators.

Other writers working independently of Miéville over the past decade and creating interesting work that combines dark fantasy with SF have been Michael Swanwick with *The Iron Dragon's Daughter* (1994) and *Faust* (1997), Ian MacLeod with *The Light Ages*, and Jeff VanderMeer with his genuinely creepy *Veniss Underground*. Some may see such works as fantasy rather than SF, but as with Tim Powers's earlier *Anubis Gates*, which was annotated as early as the third (1987) edition of *Anatomy of Wonder*, such works, beyond their innate excellence, often help define the borders of the genre.

Another recent trend, although no one has called it a formal movement, is what might be described as the publication of novels that lack all or most formal SF content, but nonetheless remain connected to the genre due to their subject matter or their outlook on the world. Like the New Weird, this is not an entirely new thing—much of J. G. Ballard's fiction fits here, for example—but it is clearly a trend. In such recent works as *Zeitgeist* and *The Zenith Angle* (2004), Bruce Sterling has written novels set in the present or even the recent past, using exotic current-day settings and technologies to create fiction that feels little different from his SF novels *Distraction* and *Heavy Weather*.

In his 1999 SF novel *All Tomorrow's Parties*, William Gibson created a character named Colin Laney who, due to an experimental drug, had the ability to sift through enormous quantities of data and make predictions concerning future events. A few years later, in *Pattern Recognition*, which is set at the time of the 2001 World Trade Center disaster, Gibson gave his aptly named protagonist, Cayce Pollard, virtually identical powers, defining them as extreme, in part the result of her borderline personality perhaps, but in no sense psychic or science fictional.

What Sterling and Gibson seem to be implying is that the world of today has in some sense caught up with the predictions and projections they were working with back in the 1980s, that there is no longer a real need to write science fiction *per se* because we're now living in the future they've been predicting all along. Kim Stanley Robinson has done similar things in such recent novels as *Antarctica* and *Forty Signs of Rain*, which concern environmental disasters that may already be in the process of occurring.

Perhaps the most extreme example of the non–science fiction SF novel, however, can be found in the recent work of Neal Stephenson. His *Cryptonomicon*, which won the *Locus* Award for the best SF novel of the year in 2000 and was also nominated for both the Hugo and the Arthur C. Clarke Awards, features two time frames, World War II and a future so close to us that, as in the case of Sterling's *The Zenith Angle*, the rather dazzling computer technology portrayed may already exist, at least in prototype. The only clearly fantastic element in the novel is a character named Root who appears to die in the WWII segment of the book but then shows up, unexplained, in the present-day section.

Even more remarkable, Stephenson's novel *Quicksilver*, a prequel to *Cryptonomicon* and the first book in an enormous trilogy called The Baroque Cycle, received the 2004 Clarke Award for outstanding SF, despite the fact that it's set in the 17th century and has even less fantastic material in it than *Cryptonomicon*. This presumably occurred in part because Stephenson is simply seen as an SF writer (despite the fact that the majority of his published fiction falls outside the genre), in part because *Quicksilver* is simply a very fine novel, and in part because of its ties to *Cryptonomicon* and the implication of more obviously fantastic content in later volumes in the trilogy. Despite the fact that there's little in this excellent book that traditionalist readers of Arthur C. Clarke would define as science-fictional, it somehow manages to feel like SF, perhaps because of Stephenson's superb recreation of a 17th-century London with a mostly implicit alternate or secret history, or perhaps because of his ongoing fascination with technology and science, even when primitive by modern standards.

In Chapter 4, I called Robert A. Heinlein's decision to write *Rocket Ship Galileo* the most important moment in the history of young adult science fiction. Undoubtedly the most influential YA SF novel published since Heinlein, however, was written by a woman who actually knew next to nothing about the genre. Lois Lowry, the Newbery Award–winning author of the historical novel *Number the Stars* and other works of mainstream YA fiction, published *The Giver* in 1993, winning a second Newbery for her efforts. This powerful dystopian novel, which, like Huxley's *Brave New World*, depicts a society that is both horrific and seductive (no one is unhappy, everyone has meaningful work), is one of the bestselling YA novels of the past decade. It clearly demonstrated to both readers and writers that YA SF can also be fine literature.

Since Lowry's book, which in the past four years has grown into one of the genre's more fascinating trilogies, YA writers have produced a small but steady stream of superior, often rather dark, award-winning SF. Most notable among these books are M. T. Anderson's *Feed*, a horrific and very funny story set in an out-of-control, consumption-obsessed dystopia; Nancy Farmer's already-mentioned *The House of the Scorpion*, which concerns the life of a clone raised to be spare parts for a drug lord on the Mexican border; and Philip Reeve's *Mortal Engines*, a truly gonzo dystopian tale set in a future world of mobile predatory cities. Although the sheer number of YA fantasy novels, riding the ongoing Harry Potter craze, far surpasses the number of SF novels being published, the quality of the current crop of science fiction for young readers has never been higher.

When I took over the modern science fiction chapter of *Anatomy of Wonder* from Brian Stableford for the fourth edition of this book, I wrote at some length about my debt to his work in the third edition, and about the differences between his taste and mine. Brian's taste and insight are still an important part of what has now become Chapters 4 and 5 of the book. Many entries are still his, although a number of them have been modified from those in the fourth edition. Some books simply don't age as well as they might. Others become less important as typical examples of an author's work as the writer produces new and better fiction. Still others need to be replaced by newer editions or compilations.

I've also become aware, however, that as the field has changed over the past decade, my own tastes have changed with it. In the fourth edition of *Anatomy of Wonder*, I commented on how Brian's interest in hard SF was greater than my own, whereas I seemed to be more interested than he was in both cyberpunk and feminist SF. In the years since, however, I've found myself reading more and more hard SF, not to mention more space opera, perhaps because it has simply gotten better, or at least I'd like to think so. I've also lost much of my interest in cyberpunk; the cyber side of things still fascinates, but the punk attitude gets kind of stale when both the author and the reader have passed the age of 50. Mirrorshade bifocals just don't make it!

I'm still interested in feminist SF, but have found much less explicitly feminist work to read. Some of the field's more didactic voices—Joanna Russ, for example—have fallen silent, or, as in the case of Sheri S. Tepper and Pamela Sargent, moved on, incorporating their continuing feminism into a broader range of topics. Among the major feminist writers of the 1970s, only Suzy McKee Charnas continues to write feminist dystopia in the same vein as her earlier works, although it should be noticed that even in such an angry novel as *The Conquerer's Child* (1999), she has now taken a more nuanced approach to the possibility for successful male–female relationships. Younger feminist writers such as Joan Slonczewski, Maureen McHugh, Elizabeth Hand, Candas Jane Dorsey, and Nicola Griffith have, in their most recent novels, largely abandoned the pure feminist dystopia/utopia scenarios so common at one time.

Lest this lack of strong, explicitly feminist, dystopian SF be seen as merely the perception of one, aging male reader, let me mention a remark that I overheard at the most recent ceremony for the James Tiptree, Jr. Award. The Tiptree, it should be noted, is not exclusively a feminist award nor is it an award limited to women writers—it's given to SF that does original things with gender—but the vast majority of its winners and finalists over the past decade or so have been explicitly feminist works by female writers. Among the most notable winners have been Eleanor Arnason's *A Woman of the Iron People*, Gwyneth Jones's *White Queen*, Nicola Griffith's *Ammonite*, Charnas's *The Conquerer's Child*, and several short stories by Ursula K. Le Guin. In 2003, however, the award was won jointly by John Kessel for "Stories for Men" and by M. John Harrison for *Light*, and in 2004 it was won by Matt Ruff for his dazzling novel concerning multiple personality disorder, *Set This House in Order*. After the ceremony, one of the founding mothers of the James Tiptree, Jr. Award was heard to wonder, somewhat plaintively, if the Tiptree would ever again be won by a woman!

The Current State of Short Fiction

When the third edition of *Anatomy of Wonder* appeared in 1987, Brian Stableford's comments on the contemporary anthology market were basically negative. "When the recession put a brake on the expansion of SF publication and forced a certain pruning, anthologies were cut back much more severely than novels," he stated. "Anthology production has received very little investment in terms of cash or publicity. Reprint anthologies now flourish only in association with the selling power of Isaac Asimov's name." This last comment was still somewhat true in the mid-1990s despite Asimov's death in 1992.

In fact, under the editorship of Martin H. Greenberg and a variety of collaborators, dozens upon dozens of reprint anthologies were produced bearing Asimov's name, many of them theme anthologies covering topics in which Asimov had never showed any previous interest. And one of the growth industries of the mid-1980s and 1990s involved the mass marketing of the names of major authors. Dozens of shared world anthologies appeared during those years featuring stories set in the universe of Asimov's Foundation series or Marion Zimmer Bradley's Darkover series or Fred Saberhagen's Berserker series or, in some cases, a universe created by a famous writer purely for the purpose of publishing a shared-world anthology.

A few of these volumes produced excellent stories, such as Harlan Ellison's *Medea* (1985), but most were decidedly mediocre. Certainly the best of the reprint anthologies of the 1980s were Gardner Dozois's magisterial *Year's Best Science Fiction* volumes, which began in 1984. In the 1990s, however, the quality of reprint anthologies increased significantly, particularly due to the work of David Hartwell. Hartwell, who has also produced an excellent but somewhat more modest *Year's Best SF* since 1996, often working in conjunction with Kathryn Cramer, has published a series of superb reprint anthologies, most notably *The Ascent of Wonder: The Evolution of Hard SF*, but also including *The Science Fiction Century* and, most recently, *The Hard Science Fiction Renaissance*. These enormous anthologies have become part of an ongoing debate in which anthologists and critics, sometimes with considerable ire, have attempted to identify an SF canon and define (some would say re-define) both the past and future of the field.

Perhaps the most controversial such volume was the *The Norton Book of Science Fiction*, edited by Ursula K. Le Guin and Brian Attebery, which in 1993 presented a selection of stories, reinforced by the Norton imprimatur, that leaned heavily away from the kind of politically conservative, hard SF one might associate with *Astounding* or *Analog SF* and toward the sort of leftist, experimental, and social SF often associated with a magazine like *Galaxy* or with Damon Knight's Orbit anthology series. Some reviewers loved *The Norton Book of Science Fiction*; others absolutely hated it. Yet another attempt at constructing an SF short story canon can be seen in James Gunn's *Road to Science Fiction* anthology series, which had reached six volumes by 1998.

The last decade has also seen the publication of a number of excellent reprint anthologies with narrower focuses. Perhaps the most interesting of these have been volumes attempting to define national or ethnic identities in the field—for example, Hartwell and Broderick's *Centaurus: The Best of Australian SF*, Bell and Molina-Gavilán's *Cosmos Latinos: An Anthology of Science Fiction from Latin America and Spain*, and Sheree R. Thomas's *Dark Matter: A Century of Speculative Fiction from the African Diaspora.*

The mid-1980s and 1990s also saw a partial revival of the market for quality original SF anthologies, and several of these deserve to be singled out. Between 1988 and 1995 the five volumes of *Full Spectrum*, edited by Lou Aronica and others, produced any number of award-nominated stories and clearly constituted the best market for original short SF in book form. Gregory Benford and Martin H. Greenberg's *What Might Have Been* series of alternate history stories, produced between 1989 and 1992, also included a considerable quantity of good fiction. Robert Silverberg and Karen Haber's attempt to revive the Universe series, which ran to three volumes in the early 1990s, did not meet with the same success that Terry Carr achieved in the 1970s, but managed to showcase the work of a number of promising new writers.

Among the one-shot original anthologies, the books that most stood out for me were Jeanne Van Buren Dann and Jack Dann's superb *In the Field of Fire*, a collection of Vietnam-related stories; Jen Green and Sarah LeFanu's feminist-oriented *Despatches from the Frontiers of the Female Mind*; and Ellen Datlow's sometimes horrific *Alien Sex*, the first of several such anthologies she produced.

Over the last decade a number of new original anthologies have also achieved excellence. Patrick Nielsen Hayden's rather eclectic mixture of SF and fantasy, *Starlight 1,* began what is undoubtedly the most successful anthology series since the *Full Spectrum* books. The equally eclectic *Conjunctions 39: The New Wave Fabulists*, edited by Peter Straub, was technically an issue of Bard College's literary journal *Conjunctions* but was published in book format and sold widely to sophisticated genre readers. Greg Bear's fine *New Legends* was probably the best original hard SF anthology of the last decade, followed perhaps by Lou Anders's recent *Live Without a Net.*

Among the more narrowly focused anthologies of note have been Jack Dann and Janeen Webb's selection of original Australian fantasy and SF, *Dreaming Down Under*; Robert Silverberg's *Far Horizons*, which features stories set in universes already made famous by their authors; and Nicola Griffith and Stephen Pagel's *Bending the Landscape*, which features gay SF.

When I was writing the entries for the fourth edition, I received help from many people. Brian Stableford's materials, as already mentioned, were essential to my own work, and Rob Latham also provided a number of valuable entries covering books with which I was unfamiliar, entries that have in most cases been carried over into the fifth edition. For this new volume I also enlisted the aid of two of Great Britain's most astute fan critics, Paul Kincaid and Maureen Speller Kincaid, who did a number of excellent entries, primarily on new SF from the U.K.

I am also, once again, indebted to the work of a variety of fine book reviewers and editors from whom I have learned much. Particularly valuable to me in recent years have been the reviews of Gary Wolfe and Russell Letson in *Locus*, the work of the ubiquitous and invariably essential John Clute, and the many fine reviews that have graced the pages of both David Hartwell's *New York Review of Science Fiction* and Edward James and Farah Mendlesohn's *Foundation.*

As was the case with the fourth edition, I have also made use of a variety of publications for background material, most notably the Nicholls/Clute encyclopedia [7-21]. The range of useful Web sites has also increased since the last edition of *Anatomy of Wonder* and I would particularly like to single out the *Locus Online* site, edited by Mark Kelly, with its all-encompassing list of award winners (annotated in Chapter 8); the Fantastic Fiction site at www.fantasticfiction.co.uk, which features a wide array of useful features; and Cheryl Morgan's review and interview site *Emerald City* at www.emcit.com. Once again I would like to thank my wife, Sandra Lindow, for encouragement, superhuman patience, and editorial help.

The Primary
Literature—
Annotated
Bibliography

The Primary Literature— Annotated Bibliography

This section is in two parts. The first and by far the larger part consists of annotations of novels and collections, sequenced alphabetically by author surname, with cross-references from pseudonyms. The much smaller second part includes edited anthologies, sequenced by title. The editors' names are shown and are indexed in the author index.

Many annotations conclude with the initials of one or more contributors. When two sets of initials are shown, the initials of the principal annotator are shown first.

PC: Paul A. Carter (Chapter 3)
PK: Paul Kincaid (Chapters 4 and 5)
ML: Michael Levy (Chapters 4 and 5)
RL: Robert Latham (Chapters 4 and 5)
SM: Susan Miles, YA titles
FM: Francis Molson, YA titles
MKS: Maureen Kincaid Speller (Chapters 4 and 5)
BS: Brian Stableford (Chapters 1, 2, 4, 5)

Abbott, Edwin A(bbott), U.K., 1839–1926

*II-1.   Flatland: A Romance of Many Dimensions. Seeley, 1884 (as by "A Square"). Ian Stewart edited *The Annotated Flatland* (Perseus, 2003).

A mildly satirical description of the social life of an inhabitant of a two-dimensional world, whose education is assisted by a vision of the one-dimensional Lineland and contact with an inhabitant of the three-dimensional Spaceland. A celebration of lateral thinking based in mathematical reasoning, respectfully echoed and elaborated in numerous subsequent works, notably Ian Stewart's *Flatterland: Like Flatland, Only More So* (2001) and Rudy Rucker's *Spaceland: A Novel of the Fourth Dimension.* Norton Juster's *The Dot and the Line: A Romance in Lower Mathematics* (Random, 1963) is the anguished story of a distraught straight line who falls in love with a frivolous dot. The puns are delicious. The short film based on the book won an Oscar. (BS)

Themes: Satirical SF

About, Edmond (François Valentin), France, 1828–1885

II-2.   **The Man with the Broken Ear**. 1861. Trans. of *L'homme à l'oreille cassée* by Henry Holt. Leypoldt & Holt, 1867.

A fervently nationalistic French officer in Napoleon's army, frozen during the ill-fated retreat from Moscow in 1813, is revived more than 40 years later to find his homeland in what seems to him a parlous state. He cannot adapt and eventually becomes reconciled to his obsolescence. The novel has also been translated as *Colonel Fougas' Mistake* and *A New Lease of Life.* Compare Grant Allen's "Pausodyne" (1881; in Derleth's *Beyond Time and Space*). (BS)

Themes: Satirical SF, Time Travel

Adams, Douglas, U.K., 1952–2001

II-3.   **The Hitch Hiker's Guide to the Galaxy**. Pan, 1979. Series: Hitch Hiker.

An adaptation of a much-loved and very funny British radio series. Earth is demolished to make way for a new hyperspatial bypass, but the hero stows away on a starship with a reporter for the eponymous reference book. Their outrageous extraterrestrial adventures are part satire, part slapstick. *The Restaurant at the End of the Universe* (1980) completed the adaptation of the original radio scripts, but Adams then added *Life, the Universe and Everything* (1982), *So Long, and Thanks for All the Fish* (1984), and *Mostly Harmless* (1992). *The Ultimate Hitch Hiker's Guide to the Galaxy* (2002) collects all five novels in one volume. *The Salmon of Doubt* (2002) includes a variety of essays and other materials, plus the fragment of a final Hitch Hiker's novel that Adams left unfinished at his death. Although all of the books in the series sold well, the later volumes seem less inspired and tend increasingly toward dark humor and irony. Readers who can't get enough of this series should investigate Neil Gaiman's *Don't Panic: The Official Hitch Hiker's Guide to the Galaxy Companion* (1988, rev. ed. 2003). Compare Sheckley's *Options* (1975). (BS/ML)

Themes: Aliens, End of the World, Humorous SF

Adams, Samuel Hopkins, U.S., 1871–1958

II-4.   The World Goes Smash. Houghton-Mifflin, 1938.

An alarmist novel about the prospect of a new world war, of a type far rarer in the U.S. than the U.K., written by a seasoned journalist. Compare McIlraith and Connolly's *Invasion from the Air* and Chadwick's *The Death Guard.*
  Themes: War

Aldiss, Brian W., U.K., 1925–

II-5.   Barefoot in the Head: A European Fantasia. Faber, 1969.

The Acid Head War, fought with psychotropic weapons, has left all Europe crazy. The hero journeys back and forth across the continent, becoming a guru in the Gurdjieff tradition and acquiring quasi-messianic status. A Joycean celebration of the vivid eccentricities of the 1960s counterculture, brilliantly phantasmagoric. Based on materials published in *New Worlds;* a fine testament to the stimulus provided by the magazine. (BS)
  Themes: Absurdist SF, New Wave

*II-6.   Best SF Stories of Brian Aldiss. Gollancz, 1988. U.S. title: *Man in His Time: Best SF Stories of Brian W. Aldiss*. Atheneum, 1989.

Aldiss has written many fine stories, far too many to be contained in one collection, but this volume includes some of the best, among them "Who Can Replace a Man," "Poor Little Warrior," and the Nebula Award-winning "The Saliva Tree." Many of the earlier stories, dating from the late 1960s, are superior examples of the New Wave. The later stories, dating from the mid-1980s, such as "My Country 'Tis Not Only of Thee" and "The Gods in Flight," are often intensely political and rather idiosyncratic. Other excellent collections of Aldiss's work, many with overlapping stories, include *The Moment of Eclipse* (1970), *Last Orders, and Other Stories* (1977), *Seasons in Flight* (1984), *A Romance of the Equator: Best Fantasy Stories of Brian W. Aldiss* (1989), and *Supertoys Last All Summer Long and Other Stories of Future Time* (2001). Compare Jones's *The Eye of the Lens*. (ML)

II-7.   Best Science Fiction Stories of Brian W. Aldiss. Faber, 1962. U.S. title: *Who Can Replace a Man?*, Harcourt, 1966. Recommended ed.: Faber, 1971; 2nd rev. ed., 1988 (U.K.); 1989 (U.S., as *Man in His Time*).

Assembling these 16 stories (14 in the earlier editions, 22 in the latest), Aldiss confessed, made him "realise how rapidly change moves," in SF as in everything else. The stories are arranged in rough chronological order, which, the author comments, "seems to represent also an order of complexity." From the straightforwardly told "Who Can Replace a Man?" (included also in *The Canopy of Time*) to the subtlety of "A Kind of Artistry," or from the hero's anguish at his time-trapped predicament in "Not for an Age" (1957) to the startlingly nonchalant outlook of a chap in a somewhat comparable situation in "Man in His Time" (1966), the reader will perceive the evolutionary process to which Aldiss referred. Nonetheless, a reader of a generation still further down the road from this book's publication will find almost all of these stories fresh and contemporary-sounding, regardless of when they were written. (PC)

II-8.   The Canopy of Time. Faber, 1959. U.S. title: **Galaxies Like Grains of Sand**. Signet, 1960 (substantially rewritten).

Eight early stories, published primarily in British SF magazines in 1957–1958, with connecting narrative that weaves them into a history of the galaxy's future. These unifying passages, set in italic type, have the sweep and cosmic poise of Olaf Stapledon, for whom Aldiss acknowledged admiration in his history of SF, *Trillion Year Spree* [9-4]. The stories also have touches of early and later Arthur C. Clarke, while retaining Aldiss's distinctive voice that foreshadows in mood and philosophic outlook the British New Wave of a later decade. They would certainly have struck U.S. readers in 1959 as very different from what writers carrying over from the previous SF generation (for example, Pohl, Asimov, and Heinlein) were doing at that same time. (PC)

Themes: Far Future

II-9.   Frankenstein Unbound. Cape, 1973.

The protagonist timeslips from the 21st century into a past where Mary Shelley coexists with the monster of her imagination. An interesting extrapolation of Aldiss's fascination with Mary Shelley and her book; more successful than his later attempts to reconsider the philosophical import of a Wells novel, *Moreau's Other Island* (1980; U.S. title: *An Island Called Moreau*) or a Stoker novel, *Dracula Unbound* (1990). Compare Theodore Roszak's *The Memoirs of Elizabeth Frankenstein* (1995) for another look at a universe where Mary Shelley and her monster co-exist. (BS/ML)

Themes: Monsters, Time Travel

*II-10.   Graybeard. Faber, 1964.

Unwise experimentation with nuclear devices has led to the sterilization of mankind, and there seems to be no hope for the future. The central characters, waiting for the end, consider the ironies and frustrations of their situation. A key work in the tradition of British disaster stories. Compare F. Wright Moxley's *Red Snow* (1930) for an earlier variation of the theme. (BS)

Themes: Disaster, End of the World

*II-11.   Helliconia Spring. Cape, 1982. Series: Helliconia.

The first volume in a trilogy continued in *Helliconia Summer* (1983) and *Helliconia Winter* (1985). Helliconia is a planet whose sun eccentrically orbits a much brighter star and thus has a "great year" extending over hundreds of generations. Its societies undergo vast changes, interrupted by periodic plagues, and the relationship between humans and the cold-loving phagors also alters dramatically. Observers from Earth watch with interest from an orbital station and relay the story of one great year back to an avid audience on Earth. The dedication states that the trilogy takes up themes from Aldiss's non-SF novel *Life in the West* (1980) in attempting to analyze the "malaise" from which our time is suffering. Superb world-building SF. Compare Paul Park's *Starbridge Chronicles* and Michael Swanwick's *Stations of the Tide.* (BS/ML)

> Awards: John W. Campbell
> Themes: Aliens, Life on Other Worlds, Politics

II-12. **Hothouse**. Faber, 1962. U.S. title: *The Long Afternoon of Earth.* Signet, 1962. Recommended ed.: Gregg, 1976, ed. by Joseph Milicia.

In the very far future, Earth is tidelocked toward a hotter sun on the verge of going nova, and ferocious, mutually warring vegetative life fills every ecological niche except beyond the "timberline" at the edge of the planet's perpetual nightside. Diminutive human beings, their once-high civilization not even a memory, pick their way through this ultimate Darwinian nightmare—yet the story is an odyssey, not a victim's lament. Originating as five connected magazine stories, this was recognized at once as a major work. Unfortunately the first American edition badly butchered the manuscript, leading Aldiss to remark that copy editing is a form of rape. (PC)

> Awards: Hugo
> Themes: Evolution, Far Future

*II-13. **Non-Stop**. Faber, 1958. U.S. title: *Starship.* Criterion, 1959.

The American title unfortunately gives away the game. A tribe of nomadic bowhunters ranges through a "jungle" that has corridors and doors; the jungle is actually a wild overgrowth from the hydroponic tanks of a derelict multigenerational spacecraft. The characters' search for the control room and, ultimately, the stars, is a subtle variant of the similar quest in Heinlein's *Orphans of the Sky.* Several U.K. science fictionists have testified that this was a formative influence in their earlier years. Compare Don Wilcox, "The Voyage That Lasted 600 Years," *Amazing Stories,* October 1940; contrast Robinson's *The Dark Beyond the Stars.* (PC)

> Themes: Space Flight

II-14. **Report on Probability A**. Faber, 1968.

An attempt to write a novel based on Heisenberg's uncertainty principle. A series of observers sustain alternative realities with their unwavering inquisitiveness. An enigmatic work that has affinities with the French antinovel. Compare Robert Anton Wilson's modeling of modern physical theory in narrative, *Shrödinger's Cat.* (BS)

> Themes: Absurdist SF

Allen, (Charles) Grant (Blairfindie), U.K., 1848–1899

II-15.   The British Barbarians: A Hill-Top Novel. John Lane, 1895.

An anthropologist from the 25th century travels back in time to study the rites and customs of the primitive tribes of Victorian England. Making no attempt at unobtrusive participant observation, he offers his neighbors a great deal of unwanted advice on the faults and follies of their society. Like many other time travelers—e.g., the forward-shifted protagonist of Thiusen's *The Diothas*—he is deemed to be mad, bad, and dangerous, and is treated accordingly. (BS)

   Themes: Anthropology, Satirical SF

Ames, Mildred, U.S., 1919–1994

II-16.   Anna to the Infinite Power. Scribner, 1981.

YA. Perfect student, superintelligent, amoral Anna suddenly begins to question her identity when she spots an exact look-alike, and sets out, with the help of her brother, to solve the mystery. Credible characterization and a poignant conclusion enhance a gripping story of cloning experimentation. Compare Lasky's *Star Split*; contrast Farmer's *The House of the Scorpion*. (FM/ML)

   Themes: Clones/Cloning, Crime and Punishment, Intelligence

Amis, Kingsley, U.K., 1922–1995

II-17.   The Alteration. Cape, 1976.

An alternate-world story of Catholic-dominated Europe; the central character is a young singer who faces the possibility of being castrated to preserve his voice. A nice balance is struck between the hard-edged plot and the ironic background. Compare Roberts's *Pavane* and Miller's *A Canticle for Leibowitz*. (BS)

   Awards: John W. Campbell
   Themes: Alternate Worlds, Religion

Anderson, Chester, U.S., 1932–1991

II-18.   The Butterfly Kid. Pyramid, 1967. Series: Greenwich Village.

Psychedelic adventures in Greenwich Village, with aliens intervening to materialize the phantoms of hallucination. An engaging expression of countercultural exuberance. The author and two friends are the main characters; the friends added their own contributions to an unusual trilogy in *The Unicorn Girl* (1969) by Michael Kurland and *The Probability Pad* (1970) by T. A. Waters. (BS)

   Themes: New Wave, Psychology

Anderson, M. T., U.S., 1968–

*II-19.   Feed. Candlewick, 2002.

YA. In this savage, satiric tale set in an American consumerist dystopia of the not-too-distant future, young Titus tries to make sense of the world through a constant thunder of advertising messages that are piped directly into his head via the "feed." Ignoring all the signs that civilization is on the verge of collapse, he, like everyone else, has dedicated his life to compulsive consumption and mindless pleasure. Then he meets Violet, a girl who has decided to fight the feed. Narrated by Titus in often elliptical, frequently incoherent 21st-century slang, this book may be tough going for younger readers, but it more than rewards the effort. Compare Huxley's *Brave New World* and Farmer's *House of the Scorpion*. (ML)

Themes: Children in SF, Coming of Age, Dystopias, Pollution

Anderson, Poul, U.S., 1926–2001

II-20.   The Avatar. Berkley, 1978.

Progress on Earth is being stifled by a paternalistic regime, and the hero must embark on a transgalactic odyssey to find an alien species sufficiently sophisticated to bring him home adequately enriched with knowledge. Compare Charles Sheffield's *Between the Strokes of Night* (1985). (BS)

Themes: Coming of Age, Politics

II-21.   The Boat of a Million Years. Tor, 1989.

Through the ages random genetic mutation has bestowed immortality on a small number of human beings. Beginning in 310 B.C., Anderson chronicles the lives of a number of such immortals, some who partake in society, some who remain aloof from it. Eventually, tiring of an Earth that has grown too tame, the immortals build a starship and go off to explore the universe. Although the novel is a bit rambling, Anderson's historical detail is endlessly fascinating. Compare Zelazny's *This Immortal.* (ML)

Themes: History in SF, Immortality

II-22.   Brain Wave. Ballantine, 1954.

This was Anderson's first major novel, published after seven years of well-received short stories and novelettes. All intelligence on Earth, animal and human, makes a sudden leap forward as the planet moves out of a belt of radiation that has hitherto held them all back. Retarded persons develop what had formerly been average intellect and formerly average people become supergeniuses, but individuals retain their mental positions in relation to others. This gives Anderson the chance for some quiet observation of the relationship and difference between intellect and character. Compare Keyes, *Flowers for Algernon*; contrast Clarke's *Childhood's End.*

Themes: Intelligence

*II-23.   The Enemy Stars. Lippincott, 1959. Recommended ed.: Berkley, 1979.

Serialized in *Astounding* in 1958 as "We Have Fed Our Sea" (a title derived from a Kipling poem that is quoted effectively at the story's conclusion), this is

Anderson at his tragic-heroic best, blending meticulous astrophysics with brooding romanticism. Four astronauts—Japanese, Russian, Australasian, and North European (with the fascinating projected futures of their respective cultures deftly sketched in)—are, in the *Star Trek* sense, "beamed aboard" an ion-drive spacecraft in orbit around a dark star, whose unexpectedly powerful magnetic field cripples both the ship and their means of escape from it. Working against a dwindling stock of rations to make repairs, each crew member, must, in the face of death, come to terms with the universe and with personal fate. The 1979 revision updated the science. Compare Budrys, *Rogue Moon.* (PC)

Themes: Hard SF, Space Flight

II-24.   Flandry of Terra. Chilton, 1965. Series: Technic Civilization.

Three novellas, originally published in1958, 1958, and 1960, detail the adventures of Captain Sir Dominic Flandry of the Terran Space Navy. In his Flandry and van Rijn stories, Anderson assumes that interstellar history will recapitulate Earth history: a new Renaissance and Age of Discovery, a subsequent period of capitalist consolidation, followed by an Earth-centered, Roman-modeled galactic empire doomed to plunge at last into the Long Night. The Flandry stories are set late enough in this future history that their protagonist knows, under his flip sophistication, that his heroic capers are ultimately futile and that the course of history is in essence tragic. The stories are played out on typically well-crafted Andersonian planets with convincingly worked out planetary cultures. Compare his *War of the Wing-Men*; contrast Asimov's Foundation trilogy. (PC)

Themes: Galactic Empires, Space Opera

II-25.   Genesis. Tor, 2000.

Christian Brannock and Laurinda Ashcroft have achieved immortality by having their personalities uploaded into machines. Millions of years later, the galaxy is run by a star-system–spanning artificial intelligence, one small part of which is Gaia, the AI that rules the Earth. Our sun, however, is beginning to fail, and Gaia isn't doing much to stop this from happening. Christian and Laurinda, assigned to investigate the situation, take virtual human form for the first time in eons. One of Anderson's last novels, this book intelligently extrapolates recent thought about the post-human condition about as far as it's possible to go, dealing seriously with issues of free will and what it truly means to be human. (ML)

Awards: John W. Campbell

Themes: Computers, Far Future, Immortality

*II-26.   Tau Zero. Doubleday, 1970.

A malfunctioning starship continues to accelerate as it nears light speed, and its crew observes relativistic effects, ultimately being carried beyond the time frame of the universe. The cruel circumstances force psychological and interpersonal adaptations. An archetypal example of hard SF with a visionary element. Compare Bear's *Eon*. (BS)

Themes: Fantastic Voyages, Hard SF

II-27.   Time Patrol. Tor, 1991.

If Jack Williamson's *The Legion of Time* represents the "liberal" version of alternate history SF and Fritz Leiber's *Change War* a "radical" approach, Anderson's take can be considered "conservative": better the history we know than another that might have been worse. The role of Williamson's timefighters is to change history for the better; of Leiber's to change it, period; of Anderson's, to maintain the status quo ante. Here, together with a new novel *Star of the Sea*, are the alternate pasts published in the 1950s: "Delenda Est" (Carthage might have beaten Rome), "Brave to Be a King" (the Persia of Cyrus might have prevailed over the Alexandrian Greeks), "The Only Game in Town" (Kublai Khan's minions might have discovered America), and "Gibraltar Falls," set in Ice Age Cro-Magnon Europe where Time Patrolmen repair for R&R. The author's impressive knowledge of actual history makes his proposed alternate pasts all the more intriguing. Compare Squire's *If, or History Rewritten* and Moore's *Bring the Jubilee*. (PC)

Themes: Alternate Worlds, Time Travel

II-28.   Vault of the Ages. Winston, 1952.

YA. Five hundred years after the "Doom," the Lann army from the north invades the peaceful Dale country and threatens the vestiges of civilization. Escaping from marauding Lanns, Carl stumbles among the ruins of a city on a time vault, which summarizes in books and containers past scientific and human knowledge for the use of survivors of the nuclear holocaust. Carl determines that this store of knowledge should be open to the people. However, both the Lann army and the people's ignorance must be overcome before the time vault can open its riches. Brisk adventure, well-written, effective in dramatizing human ambivalence before the potential of knowledge. This would make an excellent introduction for younger readers to Anderson's mature work. Contrast Norton's *Star Man's Son*. (FM/SM/PC)

Themes: Holocaust and After

II-29.   War of the Wing-Men. Ace, 1958. Recommended ed.: Gregg, 1976. Series: Technic Civilization.

Serialized in *Astounding* as "The Man Who Counts," this was the first full-length novel about fat, Falstaffian interstellar merchant-trader Nicholas van Rijn, who appears at an earlier, more youthful and upbeat phase of Anderson's future Technic History than *Flandry of Terra*. This shrewd, sly operator, rather than the story's nominal hero-type viewpoint character, is "the man who counts" because by stealth and guile he manipulates others into doing what must be done. The story's Earthborn castaways on one of Anderson's carefully wrought planets must deal with two convincingly described native avian cultures, one land-based, the other seagoing—the "wing-men" of the title. The Gregg edition corrects unauthorized changes in the first edition and includes a detailed chronology by Sandra Miesel of the whole future history, from Near Future to Long Night, with individual stories logged in. This chapter in that history is a joyous romp and would make a terrific movie. (PC)

Themes: Future History, Life on Other Worlds

Anthony, Patricia, U.S., 1947–

II-30.   Cold Allies. Harcourt, 1993.

A fine first novel. The world is in sorry shape because of the climatic changes of the greenhouse effect. Famine is widespread, and just about every nation is at war with another, struggling over the planet's dwindling resources. Then enigmatic aliens appear; they are seen only as cold blue lights, soaring over the battlefields, occasionally kidnapping people. Anthony is a fine prose stylist with a knack for creating believable characters in a small space, evident also in her second novel *Brother Termite* (Harcourt, 1993). Compare Kessel's *Good News from Outer Space* and Slonczewski's *The Wall Around Eden*. (ML)

Themes: Aliens, Ecology, Pollution, War

II-31.   God's Fires. Ace, 1997.

It's the time of the Inquisition, and miracles appear to be occurring in and around a small village in Portugal. Mysterious lights have appeared in the sky. Someone claims to have been impregnated by an angel. Another woman has had a vision of the Blessed Virgin. Father Manoel Pessoa hopes to clear up these mysteries before it becomes necessary to burn someone. Then a spaceship crashes, marooning its child-like alien crew. This is a beautifully written historical novel, full of fascinating characters, that just happens to also qualify as science fiction. For a similarly well-done portrait of a priest whose faith is tested by the truly alien, see Russell's *The Sparrow*. (ML)

Themes: Aliens, History in SF, Religion

Anthony, Piers (pseud. of Piers Anthony Jacob), U.S., 1934–

II-32.   Macroscope. Avon, 1969. Series: Tarot.

The macroscope is an instrument that allows human observers access to the wonders of the universe. When Homo sapiens is relocated in this cosmic perspective, the narrative shifts to a quasi-allegorical mode in which the symbolic significance of astrological lore is reworked. A more extended exercise in the same vein is the trilogy comprising *God of Tarot* (1979), *Vision of Tarot* (1980), and *Faith of Tarot* (1980), which similarly attempts to display a modern philosophy of life by reinterpreting the apparatus of an occult system. Another series of this type, using even more baroque apparatus and taking its pretensions even more seriously, is The Incarnations of Immortality, a seven-volume saga begun with *On a Pale Horse* (1983). (BS/ML)

Themes: Machines, Religion

II-33.   Race Against Time. Hawthorn, 1973.

YA. Six teens, representing "true Caucasians, Negroids, and Mongoloids," suspect that they are being brought up in a zoo-like setting. After they break out and painfully learn the true reason for their segregation, the youths decide to return to the "banks," where they resolve to master their distinctive cultures and prepare to become elite. An exceptionally well-paced opening highlights a provocative look at a possible future grounded in racial purity and cultural equality. Compare Lightner's *The Day of the Drones.* (FM)

Themes: Biology, Far Future, Sociology

Appleton, Victor *see* Garis, Howard

Arlen, Michael (formerly Dikran Kouyoumidjian), Armenia, 1895–1956

II-34.   Man's Mortality. Heinemann, 1933.

A novel inspired by Rudyard Kipling's accounts of a *pax aeronautica*, which describes the collapse of International Aircraft and Airways in 1987 after 50 years of world domination. The novel's political attitude is deeply ambivalent; the seemingly heroic leader of the rebellion who corrupts the establishment's young aeronauts is eventually identified as a kind of antichrist. Compare the account of the Air Dictatorship offered in H. G. Wells's *The Shape of Things to Come.*

Themes: Politics

Armstrong, Jennifer, 1961– and Butcher, Nancy, U.S., ?

II-35.   The Kindling. HarperCollins, 2002. Series: Fire-us.

YA. In Book 1 of the Fire-us trilogy a small group of teenagers and younger children survive on their own in Lazarus, Florida, several years after a terrifying plague has apparently wiped out the world's adult population. Suffering from severe post-traumatic stress disorder, they have almost no memory of their pasts. When several new children appear and their food runs out, they decide to set out for Washington to ask the President what to do. In the sequels, *The Keepers of the Flame* (2002) and *The Kiln* (2003), the children are captured by an end-times cult and discover the true source of the plague that destroyed society. The authors add a touch of humor to this otherwise grim post-holocaust fiction by their ingenious use of malapropisms. Compare Stoutenberg's *Out There.* (ML)

Themes: Children in SF, Coming of Age, Disaster, End of the World

Arnason, Eleanor, U.S., 1942–

II-36.   Ring of Swords. Tor, 1993.

Humanity and the alien *hwarhath* are on the verge of war, and diplomats are working desperately to avoid bloodshed. The key to negotiations may be Nicholas, a human prisoner of war whom the *hwarhath* leader has taken as his lover. Fine anthropological SF. Arnason is one of the most original writers in the field working on gender issues. A number of her short stories have also appeared set within this universe; several were award nominees. Compare Jones's *White Queen*. Contrast Niven and Pournelle's *The Mote in God's Eye*. (ML)
Themes: Aliens, Anthropology, Feminist SF, War

II-37.   A Woman of the Iron People. Morrow, 1991.

Co-winner of the first annual James Tiptree Award for science fiction, which examines problems of gender. An anthropological team from Earth discovers an alien society where women create all culture and technology, while men live in primitive style on the fringes of civilization. Compare Tepper's *The Gate to Women's Country* and Sargent's *Venus of Dreams* for variations on this idea. (ML)
Awards: James Tiptree
Themes: Aliens, Anthropology, Feminist SF, Life on Other Worlds

Arnold, Edwin Lester, U.K., 1857–1935

II-38.   Lieut. Gullivar Jones, His Vacation. Brown, Langham, 1905.

An exuberant fantasy in which an impoverished U.S. naval officer is transported by magic carpet to Mars, where he is rapidly embroiled in hectic romantic adventures that climax in a planet-wide disaster caused by a comet. An odd *jeu d'esprit* that begins as a comedy in the vein of F. Anstey and morphs into an adventure story in the vein of H. Rider Haggard, with a final dash of Camille Flammarion. Having been plausibly touted as a possible source of inspiration for Edgar Rice Burroughs's *A Princess of Mars*, it was reprinted in 1964 as *Gulliver of Mars*. Compare also Hugh MacColl's *Mr Stranger's Sealed Packet*. (BS)
Themes: Fantastic Voyages, Life on Other Worlds, The Planets

Asaro, Catherine, U.S., 1955–

II-39.   The Quantum Rose. Tor, 2000. Series: Skolian Empire.

Asaro has followed in Anne McCaffrey's footsteps by injecting large doses of formula romance into science fiction, but she's a physicist by training and her books also contain a significant hard science content. In this award-winning installment in the popular Skolian Empire series, Kamoj Argali, the young ruler of a poor nation, finds herself torn between two possible husbands: Jax Ironbridge, the unpleasant ruler of a neighboring wealthy nation, and Lionstar, a mysterious off-worlder. Other books in the series include *Primary Inversion* (1995), *Catch the Lightning* (1996), *The Last Hawk* (1997), *The Radiant Seas* (1998), *Ascendant Sun* (2000), *Spherical Harmonic* (2001), *The Moon's Shadow*

(2003), and *Skyfall* (2003). Compare McCaffrey's *The Ship Who Sang* or *The Rowan* (1990). (ML)

> Awards: Nebula
> Themes: Future History, Hard SF, Women in SF

Ash, Fenton (pseudonym of Francis H. Atkins), U.K., 1840–1927

II-40.   A Trip to Mars. Chambers, 1909.

YA. Two boys who save the life of a visitor from Mars (who turns out to be the planet's king) are abducted to that planet, where they have various adventures and help to suppress a revolt. The story is a simple variation on the theme of "A Son of the Stars," which had been serialized in *Young England* in 1907–1908, but it is not a sequel thereto. Its most original feature is the spaceship used to transport the heroes, a compound of the organic and inorganic that qualifies as an early cyborg. Compare Arnold's *Lieut. Gullivar Jones* and Serviss's *A Columbus of Space*. (BS)

> Themes: Life on Other Worlds, Space Flight, The Planets

Asher, Neal, U.K., 1961–

II-41.   The Skinner. Macmillan, 2002. Series: Polity.

Three travelers arrive on the overwhelmingly dangerous planet Splatterjay: the woman Erlin, who is looking for a reason to live; the man Janer, who serves as eyes for a hive of sentient hornets; and Keech, a former police officer who has been dead for hundreds of years but still seeks revenge. The human beings who inhabit this world, infected by a native virus, are incredibly tough and virtually immortal, but Erlin, Janer, and Keech must all take their chances. Meanwhile a brutal leader of the alien Prador, who committed atrocities during a war on the planet several centuries earlier, has returned to wipe out all evidence of his crimes. This is sophisticated space opera by a major new voice in the field. Other novels set in the same future history include *Gridlinked* (2001) and *Line of Polity* (2003). Compare Alastair Reynolds's *Revelation Space* and its sequels. (ML)

> Themes: Crime and Punishment, Future History, Life on Other Worlds, Space Opera

Asimov, Isaac, U.S., 1920–1992

*II-42.   The Caves of Steel. Doubleday, 1954.

The setting is far-future New York City, which has become one immense building, to which its human inhabitants are fully adapted—but who suffer paralyzing fear at the thought of going outdoors. The plot is a murder mystery: how could one of these deeply inhibited humans have killed a "Spacer," that is, an off-planet visitor, when this would necessitate crossing considerable open ground to get to the Spacers' self-segregated compound? The case is cracked by NYPD detective Lije Baley and his robot partner Daneel Olivaw. Asimov's Three Laws of Robotics, first worked out in the stories comprising *I, Robot*, figure prominently. A richly characterized, thoughtfully told story; justifiably a favorite among Asimov's readers. A sequel, *The Naked Sun* (Doubleday, 1957), takes Lije and Daneel to a planet where the social neurosis is exactly the reverse of Earth's: people live in robot-served isolation, unable to bear being in one another's physical presence. Further sequels, *The Robots of Dawn* and *Robots and Empire*, tie these stories to Asimov's *Foundation* universe. (PC)

Themes: Crime and Punishment, Robots

*II-43.   The Complete Stories. Doubleday, 1990–1992.

Volume one assembles 46 stories from three Asimov collections, *Earth Is Room Enough* (1957), *Nine Tomorrows* (1957), and *Nightfall and Other Stories* (1959). Although not everything here is memorable, there are a number of excellent pieces, including two of the author's own favorite short stories, "The Last Question" and "The Ugly Little Boy", plus the classic "Nightfall" and "Dreaming is a Private Thing." Volume two collects an additional 40 stories. Compare *The Collected Stories of Arthur C. Clarke*. (ML)

II-44.   David Starr: Space Ranger (as by Paul French). Doubleday, 1952. Series: Lucky Starr.

YA. To an Earth suffering from overpopulation, its Martian colony is a necessary breadbasket. When poisoned food begins to turn up, David Starr, agent of the Council of Science, is sent to investigate and uncovers an alien conspiracy. Routine adventure story, among the first space operas for children; significant also because of the special status of its author. Followed by five other adventures (see Chapter 16). (FM/SM)

Themes: Space Opera, The Planets

II-45.   The Early Asimov; or, Eleven Years of Trying. Doubleday, 1972.

Writers don't spring full-armored from the brain of Jove; they creep, they toddle and fall, and eventually they succeed in running. Asimov documented this process both with the stories themselves, drawn from Golden Age pulps (notably *Astounding*), and with narrative commentary between the stories. Valuable descriptions of the New York SF scene in which Asimov learned his trade, both from the formidable editor John Campbell of *Astounding* and from his fellow fans-turning-professional, such as Frederik Pohl. The stories have a "workshop" utility; Asimov's accounts of how there were devised and composed can be instructive to would-be SF writers even today. (PC)

*II-46.   The Foundation Trilogy. Doubleday, 1963. Series: Foundation.

Asimov described the gradual fall of a galactic empire and the effort of psychohistorian Hari Seldon to shorten the ensuing Dark Ages by setting up a hidden Foundation in a remote corner of the galaxy, in stories published in *Astounding* in the early 1940s and collected as *Foundation* (Gnome, 1951). Other, longer *Astounding* stories, describing an attempt at reconquest of the Foundation by the last competent imperial general Bel Riose (like Belisarius, who similarly attempted to reconquer the Roman West for the East Roman Emperor Justinian), and an initially more successful capture of the Foundation by "the Mule," a mutant not subject as an individual to the statistical "laws of psychohistory," were collected as *Foundation and Empire* (Gnome, 1952). Finally, two *Astounding* serials in the late 1940s described the Mule's search for a Second Foundation, established by Seldon as a backup in case something went wrong for the First; these became *Second Foundation* (Gnome, 1953). Asimov then laid this theme aside for 30 years until popular demand and his publisher's prodding led him to compose *Foundation's Edge, Foundation and Earth*, and a prequel, *Prelude to Foundation*, describing how Hari Seldon discovered the laws of psychohistory. Four further adventures of Hari Seldon were published posthumously as *Forward the Foundation* (1993). (PC)

Awards: Special Hugo for best all-time series
Themes: Future History, Galactic Empires

II-47.   Foundation's Edge. Doubleday, 1982. Series: Foundation.

The fourth volume of the Foundation series, uncomfortably extending its themes and beginning the work of binding it into a common future history with Asimov's robot stories. In the 1940s, the series seemed sophisticated in introducing political themes into space opera, but SF had evolved so far in the meantime that *Foundation's Edge* seems rather quaint despite its popularity. It is a feast of nostalgia for longtime readers. The story continues in *Foundation and Earth* (1986), with the hero pursuing his quest to track down the origins of mankind and gradually learning the truth about Earth. *Prelude to Foundation* (1988) and *Forward the Foundation* (1993), which Asimov left unfinished at his death, predate the other novels in the series in terms of internal chronology, describing the early life of Hari Seldon. The series has been extended by Gregory Benford, in *Foundation's Fear* (1997), Greg Bear with *Foundation and Chaos* (1998), and David Brin with *Foundation's Triumph* (1999). (BS/ML)

Awards: Hugo
Themes: Future History, Galactic Empires, Politics

*II-48.   The Gods Themselves. Doubleday, 1972.

A novel reflecting Asimov's fascination with the sociology of science, reminiscent in parts of J. D. Watson's *The Double Helix* (1968). The energy crisis is "solved" by pumping energy from a parallel universe, whose alien inhabitants must try to communicate with humans to tell them that both races are in deadly peril. Written with a verve and economy that are missing from Asimov's later novels. Compare Bob Shaw's *A Wreath of Stars* (1976). (BS)

Awards: Hugo, Nebula
Themes: Aliens, Linguistics, Parallel Worlds, Scientists and Engineers

*II-49.   I, Robot. Gnome, 1950. Series: Robots.

Nine stories from early 1940s *Astounding* that illustrate Asimov's (and perhaps John W. Campbell's) "three laws of robotics." With the memorable exception of

Eando Binder's "I, Robot" (*Amazing*, 1939), this was the first major break-away from the robots-as-menace cliché; contrast *Frankenstein*, Čapek's *R.U.R.*, and Miles J. Breuer, "Paradise and Iron" (1930). Asimov broke with another genre cliché in this series by introducing a high-powered scientific thinker who was not male, Susan Calvin. Harlan Ellison wrote a film script from these early robot stories, structurally modeled on *Citizen Kane*, published in *Isaac Asimov's Science Fiction Magazine*, 1985. Asimov continued to write robot stories throughout his life; many were collected in *The Rest of the Robots* (1964). All the robot stories were assembled in *The Complete Robot* (1982). A weakly reviewed film called *I, Robot* was released in 2004. (PC)

Themes: Robots

II-50.   Nightfall, and Other Stories. Doubleday, 1969.

Twenty stories, all from the 1950s and 1960s except the title story. In his introduction, Asimov said he was piqued at having "Nightfall" referred to as his "best" story 25 years after its initial publication and so he decided to publish it with a succession of other stories, from 1950 onward, each with a sprightly Asimov headnote, and let readers decide whether "Nightfall" really *was* his best. A fairer test for today's reader might be *Nine Tomorrows* (1959), which included such outstanding, frequently anthologized pieces as "The Dying Night," "The Last Question," and "The Ugly Little Boy." *The Asimov Chronicles: Fifty Years of Isaac Asimov* (1989) assembled 50 stories and nonfiction pieces, one from each year from 1939 to 1988. *The Complete Stories* (2 vols., 1990, 1992) collects 86 stories. (PC)

II-51.   Pebble in the Sky. Doubleday, 1950.

Asimov's first published novel, rejected by the pulps. An old man from the present is projected into a far future in which Earth is a pariah planet confronting a galactic empire. He finds himself in a culture that euthanizes old people who can't do useful work, and what kind of work can someone with a mere 20th-century education perform in the far future? Loosely connected with the Foundation series, but the true sociohistorical metaphor in the story is that of ancient Judea facing the might of Rome. A sentimental favorite among Asimov's fans, but significant also as a transitional step between the relatively miserly world of Golden Age pulps and the relatively lucrative world of mainstream book publication; in Asimov's case, for his multifarious nonfiction work as well as his fiction. (PC)

Themes: Future History

II-52.   The Robots of Dawn. Phantasia, 1983. Series: Robots.

The heroes of Asimov's earlier robot detective stories, *The Caves of Steel* and *The Naked Sun*, undertake a new investigation on the utopian world of Aurora, where men live in harmony with their machines. The murder mystery becomes a peg on which to hang part of the argument connecting the robot series with the Foundation series. The argument is further extended in *Robots and Empire* (1985), in which robots renegotiate the famous laws of robotics and set humankind on the road to galactic empire. Prolix, but better connected with their antecedents than the new Foundation novels. (BS)

Themes: Crime and Punishment, Future History, Robots

Astor, John Jacob (IV), U.S., 1864–1912

II-53. **A Journey in Other Worlds: A Romance of the Future**. Appleton, 1894.

A patchwork Vernian romance straddling the border between SF and religious fantasy, which borrows the gravity-nullifying device employed in Greg's *Across the Zodiac* as a means of "straightening" the world's axis and mounting expeditions to Jupiter and Saturn. The ecosphere of the former features many species that have become extinct on Earth; the latter is inhabited by the spirits of the dead, who offer the travelers an account of a Flammarionesque cosmic schema. Compare Griffith's *A Honeymoon in Space*. (BS)

Themes: Life on Other Worlds, Space Flight

Atherton, Gertrude, U.S., 1857–1948

II-54. **Black Oxen**. Boni and Liveright, 1923.

A prolix romance in which an artificially rejuvenated woman has difficulty fitting in to the rigidly stratified world of New York high society. An interesting but unsuccessful attempt to introduce a science-fictional motif into a Henry Jamesian novel of manners and mores. Compare Marie Corelli's *The Young Diana* (1918). (BS)

Themes: Biology

Atkins, Francis H. *see* Ash, Fenton

Attanasio, A. A., U.S. 1951–

II-55. **Radix**. Morrow, 1981. Series: Radix.

Earth is much altered by the loss of its magnetic "shield" against cosmic radiation, and the changes are accelerated by a burst of energy from a "collapsar," which brings about a wholesale metamorphosis of Earth's life system. Many beings transcend the limitations of frail flesh in different ways, and the plot follows one such transcendent maturation. Attanasio has published three further novels that he defines as thematic sequels to *Radix*—*In Other Worlds* (1984), *Arc of Dreams* (1986), and *The Last Legends of Earth* (1989)—none of which have received comparable acclaim. Compare Silverberg's *Son of Man* (1971) and Delany's *The Einstein Intersection*. (BS/ML)

Themes: Coming of Age, Disaster

Atterley, Joseph (George Tucker), U.S., 1775–1861

II-56.   **A Voyage to the Moon: With Some Account of the Manners and Customs, Science and Philosophy of the People of Morosofia, and Other Lunarians**. Elam Bliss, 1827.

A sprawling lunar satire in the vein pioneered by Cyrano de Bergerac, more closely related to SF than most by virtue of the manner in which it toys briefly with the ideas of several contemporary scientists and social philosophers, including William Godwin, Erasmus Darwin, and T. R. Malthus. Compare Trueman's *History of a Voyage to the Moon.* (BS)

Themes: Fantastic Voyages, Satirical SF

Atwood, Margaret, Canada, 1939–

*II-57.   **The Handmaid's Tale**. McClelland & Stewart, 1985.

A dystopian novel of a world ruled by militaristic fundamentalism in which sexual pleasure is forbidden. Conception and childbirth have become difficult, and the handmaid of the title belongs to a specialist breeding stock. The story is annotated by a historian in a further future, whose shape is not revealed. The 1990 film was somewhat sterile. Atwood, a major literary novelist, has returned to speculative fiction in *The Blind Assassin* (2000) and *Oryx and Crake* (2003), but her exact relationship to genre science fiction remains problematic. Compare Wyndham's "Consider Her Ways" (1956), Elgin's *Native Tongue*, and Charnas's *Walk to the End of the World.* (BS/ML)

Themes: Dystopias, Feminist SF, Women in SF

Auel, Jean, U.S., 1936–

II-58.   **Clan of the Cave Bear**. Crown, 1980. Series: Earth's Children.

In the first in Auel's best-selling series of prehistoric novels, collectively called Earth's Children, Ayla, a young Cro-Magnon girl, is orphaned in an earthquake and adopted by a more primitive tribe of Neanderthals. Compulsively readable and filled to overflowing with fascinating, generally believable anthropological extrapolation. Other books in the series include *Valley of the Horses* (1982), *The Mammoth Hunters* (1985), *The Plains of Passage* (1990), and *The Shelter of Stones* (2002). For a more science-fictional view of prehistory see Michael Bishop's *No Enemy but Time.* (ML)

Themes: Anthropology, Coming of Age

Bacon, Sir Francis, U.K., 1561–1626

II-59.   **New Atlantis: A Worke Unfinished**. Bound with *Sylva Sylvarum; or, a Natural Historie.* Lee, 1627 [dated 1626].

A depiction of the island kingdom of Bensalem, emphasizing Salomon's House, an institution of scientific research whose specialists have made many significant discoveries and pioneered numerous technological inventions. Seemingly designed as a prospectus for a Royal Society, which Bacon hoped to persuade James I to finance, it was abandoned when that prospect faded; its propaganda for progress establishes it, in retrospect, as a key celebration of the potential of the scientific imagination to transform social life. Compare Campanella's *City of the Sun* and Cavendish's account of the scientists of *The Blazing World*. (BS)

Themes: Scientists and Engineers, Utopias

Baird, Thomas, U.S., 1923–1990

II-60.   Smart Rats. Harper, 1990.

YA. Embittered 17-year-old Laddie, living with his parents and younger sister, learns several of his friends are being terrorized as the Big Brother-like government goes about removing one child from all two-progeny households for "conservation" purposes. Laddie plots to save himself and his parents by pretending to collaborate with the government. Readers of this gripping and suspenseful story will identify with the complaining, sarcastic, yet idealistic hero. Contrast Westall's *Futuretrack 5*. (FM)

Themes: Coming of Age, Dystopias, Sociology

Baker, Kage, U.S., 1952–

II-61.   In the Garden of Iden. Harcourt Brace, 1998. Series: The Company.

There are few original ideas in science fiction, but Baker has found a good one. In a world where time travel is possible but ruinously expensive, the Company sends a small number of its operatives back in time to recruit homeless children and turn them into immortal cyborgs who live down through the centuries, doing the Company's secret business of preserving lost and endangered treasures of various sorts. In 16th-century England, an inexperienced operative named Mendoza, who has been trained as a botanist and sent to recover rare plants for the Company, jeopardizes her mission by falling in love with a mortal man. Later, and equally good, books in the series include *Sky Coyote* (1999), *Mendoza in Hollywood* (2000), *The Graveyard Game* (2001), and *Black Projects, White Knights: The Company Dossiers* (2002). As the series evolves, it becomes gradually clear that the Company is not simply the idealistic preserver of beauty that it makes itself out to be, but that it in fact has a darker and more mysterious agenda. Compare Connie Willis's *Doomsday Book*. (ML)

Themes: Future History, Genetic Engineering, History in SF, Time Travel

Ballard, J(ames) G(raham), U.K., 1930–

II-62.   The Atrocity Exhibition. Cape, 1970. U.S. title: *Love and Napalm: Export U.S.A.,* 1972.

A series of "condensed novels"—collages of images presenting a kaleidoscopic pattern of 20th-century myths and motifs, particularly those that dominated the 1960s. Political assassinations, customized cars, the space program, the arms race, the media as brokers of celebrity—are all juxtaposed here in a nightmarish panorama of a culture out of control, subject to a cancerous malaise. Compare Burroughs's *Nova Express*. (BS)

Themes: Absurdist SF, New Wave

*II-63.   The Complete Short Stories. Flamingo, 2001.

More than a thousand pages covering Ballard's entire career. This volume replaces *Chronopolis and Other Stories* (1971) and *The Best Short Stories of J. G. Ballard* (1978) as the definitive collection. Among the classic pieces included here are "The Sound Sweep" (1960), "The Drowned Giant" (1964), "The Terminal Beach" (1964), "Love and Napalm USA: Export USA" (1969), and "Myths of the Near Future" (1982). In many of these stories alienated protagonists bear witness to the world's descent into a perverse decadence; if they attempt to resist (many do not), they are likely to be maddened by the consciousness of their hopeless entrapment. "The Terminal Beach" marked a turning point in the concerns of British SF and signaled the start of the era of avant-garde methods. In the 1980s, Ballard moved away from science fiction and towards the mainstream, but his work continues to be enormously influential. (ML/BS)

II-64.   Crash. Cape, 1973.

Perhaps Ballard's most controversial novel, the book concerns Vaughan, a scientist who experiments with the sexual possibilities inherent in automobile accidents. Ballard goes out of his way to describe the various injuries that occur in graphic detail. Beautifully written, but not for the squeamish, the book bears some similarities to Brett Easton Ellis's *American Psycho*. Within genre fiction, the closest comparison might be to Richard Calder's *Dead Girls* trilogy. (ML)

Themes: Psychology, Satirical SF

*II-65.   The Crystal World. Cape, 1966.

Completes a quartet of apocalyptic novels begun with *The Wind From Nowhere* (1962) and continued with *The Drowned World* and *The Drought*. Time begins to "crystallize out," causing vast tracts of African rain forest to undergo a metamorphosis that echoes and contrasts with the metamorphosis of human flesh that is leprosy. The hero's symbolic odyssey, like that of the protagonist in Conrad's *Heart of Darkness*, brings him to a more fundamental existential level. Superb imagery. (BS)

Themes: Disaster, New Wave

*II-66.   The Drought. Cape, 1965. U.S. title (of a considerably shorter version): *The Burning World*. Berkley, 1964.

Evaporation from the world's oceans is inhibited by pollutants, and inland areas are devastated by drought. Humans adapt psychologically in various ways, and the protagonist's personal life becomes spiritually desiccated in tune with his surroundings. The narrative is suitably dry and laconic. (BS)

Themes: Disaster, Ecology, Pollution

*II-67.   The Drowned World. Berkley, 1962.

Climatic change reverts Earth's ecosystem to early Triassic; an expedition from what remains of the British government in northern Greenland explores submerged London. The viewpoint character, haunted by dreams of an earlier Earth, battles the leader of looters who land in London, but eventually heads southward into even hotter and wetter realms, "a second Adam searching for the forgotten paradises of the reborn Sun." The theme of capricious natural catastrophe rather than human-caused ecological disaster links this story with *The Wind from Nowhere* (Berkley, 1962), also set in London, in which a world-girdling hurricane, despite all efforts by the military and by a mad, Ahab-like entrepreneur, literally blows everything away, and then for no reason simply stops blowing. The mood of both novels anticipates New Wave SF, of which Ballard was a primary founder and maker. Compare Bowen, *After the Rain*; contrast Serviss, *The Second Deluge*. (PC)

  Themes: Disaster, Evolution

II-68.   High-Rise. Cape, 1975.

An early example of a novel that is not strictly speaking science fiction but nonetheless feels like SF due to its radical outlook, *High-Rise* concerns the collapse of civilization in a 40-story apartment building that is home to some 2,000 tenants. Inhabited almost entirely by well-to-do people, the building becomes a seething hotbed of hatred and violence as various residents react to technological breakdowns, building politics, and the perceived slights of their fellow tenants. Full-scale civil war eventually breaks out. Not as graphically violent as *Crash*, but not for the weak at heart. Compare Gibson's *Pattern Recognition* for a similarly non-SF SF novel. (ML)

  Themes: Satirical SF, Sociology

II-69.   Vermilion Sands. Berkley, 1971.

This collection of stories shows the more colorful and romantic side of Ballard's imagination. In a decadent resort town, avant-garde artists and the jetsam of faded star-cults play out their casual tragedies. Elegantly ironic and overripe; *Sunset Boulevard* transposed into the SF idiom. Compare Lee Killough's *Aventine* (1982). (BS)

  Themes: Psychology

Balmer, Edwin, U.S., 1883–1959

II-70.   When Worlds Collide. Stokes, 1933 (in collaboration with Philip Wylie).

A classic disaster story serialized in *Blue Book* in 1932. The discovery that Earth will be destroyed by a close encounter with one of two stray planets leads to the establishment of a hurried program to build spaceships that might carry a select few survivors. The ships have to be defended against those ambitious to displace the chosen few before they even take off. *After Worlds Collide* (1933 *Blue Book*,

book 1934) carries forward the story of the survivors. John Hawkins's *Ark of Fire* (1937–1938 *American Weekly*) is the most faithful imitation; other science-fictional exercises in hard-headed social Darwinism include J. J. Connington's *Nordenholt's Million* (1923). (BS)

Themes: Disaster

Banks, Iain M(enzies), Scotland, 1954–

II-71.　Against a Dark Background. Orbit, 1993; Bantam Spectra, 1993.

First drafted before his controversial "debut," *The Wasp Factory* (1984), this novel has the most straightforward construction of any of Banks's science fiction. It is basically a chase novel, in which heroine Sharrow, aided and abetted by former military comrades, has to flee for her life from members of an apocalyptic sect. The novel is distinguished by wayward inventiveness (notably the "Lazy Gun" that kills by improbable means such as materializing an anvil above the victim's head) and casual violence (virtually every member of the cast is dead by the end of the book). His first SF novel not set in the "Culture," but it confirmed his reputation as a hip and witty talent. (PK)

Themes: Crime and Punishment, Machines, Politics, Satirical SF

*II-72.　Consider Phlebas. Macmillan, 1987. Series: The Culture.

After publishing a number of highly experimental literary novels, Banks changed gears and produced a series of sophisticated space operas. Horza, an alien shape changer and one of the most feared spies and assassins in the galaxy, is hired by another alien race, the Idirans, to further their religious crusade against the Culture, a technologically advanced, liberal-minded human civilization. Banks combines wit, political acumen, and nonstop action with complete success. Other early volumes in this highly influential future history include *The Player of Games* (1988), *Use of Weapons* (1990), and *The State of the Art* (1991). As Iain Banks, the author has a separate career as one of the U.K.'s most respected mainstream novelists. Compare Vinge's *A Fire Upon the Deep*. (ML)

Themes: Aliens, Future History, Galactic Empires, Politics, Space Opera

*II-73.　Excession. Orbit, Bantam Spectra, 1996. Series: The Culture.

Returning to the Culture, Banks brings to the fore the epic scale that has been a background feature of this series. A vast mysterious object appears in a little-known part of space; like the message from outside in *Feersum Endjinn*, it is what it portends that sets the complex plot in motion. For the first time, the leading characters in this novel are not the humans, aliens, or stored personalities of the Culture but the vast ships as they investigate what this "Excession" might mean. In what is perhaps the best of his Culture novels, Banks begins to question what the Culture is and what it stands for. Compare Harrison's *Light*. Contrast Clarke's *Rendezvous with Rama* or Bear's *Eon*. (PK)

Themes: Future History, Galactic Empires, Space Opera

*II-74.   Feersum Endjinn. Orbit, 1994.

Set within a single building of Gormenghastly size that dwarfs its inhabitants, multiple narrative strands revolve around the possibility of receiving a message from outside. The content of the message matters far less than the fact that it augurs an end of things, a sense that would play an increasing role in Banks's science fiction. One strand of the story is told in a debased form of English (a *jeu d'esprit* made more complex by the fact that several characters in this strand have speech defects), while another is a very early expression of the idea of digital storage of personalities. For the language, compare Hoban's *Riddley Walker*; for the digital storage of personalities, compare Egan's *Permutation City*. (PK)

Themes: Computers, Far Future, Intelligence, Linguistics

*II-75.   Look to Windward. Orbit, 2000. Series: The Culture.

The latest of Banks's Culture novels links back to the climactic moment of his first, *Consider Phlebas* (1987), and in that tying off there is also a sense of closing down. For this Culture is not a brash, aggressive young society but one grown old and decadent, strangely afraid of sublimation, or the move to a higher, other state, that all previous pangalactic societies have taken. Against this thoughtful background, Banks constructs a story as inventive, as rich, as full of such trademark techniques as the domestication of the immense as any of his novels, so although the Culture is losing impetus there is no similar slowing down of Banks's invention. (PK)

Themes: Future History, Galactic Empires, Space Opera

Barnes, John, U.S. 1957–

II-76.   A Million Open Doors. Tor, 1992. Series: The Thousand Cultures.

The Thousand Cultures, once separated by interstellar distances, are now being connected by instantaneous matter transmission, and each formerly isolated planet is going through intense culture shock. Giraut, who comes from a high-tech, pseudo-medieval culture of duels, troubadours, and chivalry, finds himself employed on Caledony, a grim, no-frills world run according to the utilitarian dictates of Rational Christianity. The clash of cultures is fascinating, though too much of the novel's action occurs off stage. Later books in the series include *Earth Made of Glass* (1998) and *The Merchant of Souls* (2001). Compare Heinlein's *Beyond This Horizon*. (ML)

Themes: Coming of Age, Future History, Life on Other Worlds, Sociology

II-77.   Orbital Resonance. Tor, 1991 Series: War of the Memes.

Earth has been half-destroyed by a series of man-made and natural catastrophes. Thirteen-year-old Melpomene Murray, however, who lives on The Flying Dutchman, an asteroid set in Mars-Earth orbit, has what she sees as a pretty good life. Then another teenager arrives, a refugee from Earth, and Mel begins to see her world in a somewhat different and more troubling light. With its teen protagonist, *Orbital Resonance* feels very much like a Heinlein juvenile, but later books in the series become much darker. *Kaleidoscope Century* (1995) details the horrors being perpetrated on an Earth ravaged by rogue memes that brainwash entire nations and turn people into virtual zombies. *Candle* (2000) is set on Earth after one particular meme, One True, has taken over the entire planet. *The Sky So Big and Black* (2002), which features another Heinleinesque girl hero, describes One True's attempt to invade Mars. Barnes deals with some very complex moral issues, and he does so extremely well. (ML)

Themes: Children in SF, Coming of Age, Future History

Barnes, Steven, U.S., 1952–

II-78.   Lion's Blood. Warner Aspect, 2002.

In this well-done work of alternate history, the northern part of what we think of as the United States was colonized by Vikings, while the southern part was colonized by black Africans. It's 1863, and an 11-year-old Irish Druid, Aidan O'Dere, is kidnapped in a slavers' raid, transported to the New World, and sold to a black southern plantation owner, a Moslem named Kai ibn Jallaleddin ibn Rashid. As war looms in Bilalstan, as the New World is called, O'Dere and Rashid, slave and slave owner, must come to terms with their relationship if they are both to survive. The sequel is *Zulu Heart* (2003). For another look at a world where Christian Europe is not a dominant force, compare Robinson's *The Years of Rice and Salt*. (ML)

Themes: Alternate Worlds, Politics, War

Barrett, Neal, Jr., U.S., 1929–

II-79.   Through Darkest America. Congdon and Weed, 1986.

When his isolated farm is destroyed and his family is murdered, young Howie Ryder sets off to seek revenge. As he travels across a continent still recovering from nuclear war, Howie discovers a horrifying world of government-sanctioned cannibalism, slavery, and child abuse. This is one of the bleakest and most powerful post-holocaust novels ever written. *Dawn's Uncertain Light* (1989) is a competent, somewhat less harrowing sequel. Compare Miller's *A Canticle for Leibowitz*, Pangborn's *Davy*, and Charnas's *Walk to the End of the World*. (ML)

Themes: Holocaust and After

Barth, John, U.S. 1930–

II-80.   Giles Goat-Boy: or, The Revised New Syllabus. Doubleday, 1966.

A fabulation in which the world is a university and the hero an experimental embodiment of the theriomorphic image of human nature. A clever satire, very much the product of its time. One of the works that began drawing science fiction ideas into the American literary mainstream. See also Pynchon's *Gravity's Rainbow*. (BS)

Themes: Satirical SF

Batchelor, John Calvin, U.S., 1948–

II-81.   The Birth of the People's Republic of Antarctica. Dial, 1983.

As civilization collapses, an odd assortment of characters sets sail for Sweden in search of a better world. Their journey ultimately takes them into the icy wastes of Antarctica, but even there they find no escape from the troubles that afflict humankind. Compare Vidal's *Kalki*. (BS)

Themes: End of the World

II-82.   The Further Adventures of Halley's Comet. Congdon & Lattes, 1980.

Members of a wealthy bourgeois family plot to extend their empire into space. Their Machiavellian schemes require the kidnapping and incarceration of assorted idealists. Meanwhile, an extraordinary trio of mages associated with Halley's Comet look on. A baroque tale. Compare Pynchon's *Gravity's Rainbow*. (BS)

Themes: Satirical SF

Baxter, Stephen, U.K., 1957–

II-83.   Coalescent. Gollancz, Del Rey, 2003.

George Poole discovers that he has a long-lost twin sister and that she is part of an ancient religious order living underground in Rome. This order, founded by their distant ancestor, Regina, has separated itself from humankind and evolved into a new hive life form whose destiny may be to take over the world. Volume two in the Destiny's Children trilogy, *Exultant* (2004), jumps far into the future to another crux point in human evolution. Volume three will reportedly move even further into the future and will link back to the ancient past, forming a complete circle. Compare Bear's *Darwin's Radio*. (ML)

Themes: Evolution, History in SF, Religion

II-84.   Raft. Grafton, 1991. Series: Xelee.

Generations ago, an interstellar spacecraft from Earth accidentally broke through into another universe, one only 5,000 miles across, where gravity is much more intense than it is in our universe. At its center is the Core, a planetoid some 50 miles in diameter, with a black hole at its center. Surrounding the Core is a nebula of breathable air. With no inhabitable planets available, the survivors live on rock fragments and bits of wreckage from their ship that have been tied together into a ring of sorts about the kernel of a dead star. The nebula, however, is dying, its limited air supply going bad. The bizarre native life forms are preparing to shift to another universe and, if the humans trapped with them are to survive, they will have to move as well. Despite a few typical first-novel problems, *Raft* features some of the most startling hard SF content in recent years. It is the first volume in the author's loosely connected Xelee future history. Other books include *Timelike Infinity* (1992), *Flux* (1993), *Ring* (1994), and the short story collection *Vacuum Diagrams* (1997), which received the Philip K. Dick Award. Compare Niven's *The Integral Trees* and its sequel (ML).

Themes: End of the World, Future History, Hard SF, Parallel Worlds

II-85.   Time: Manifold I. HarperCollins, 1999. U.S. title: *Manifold: Time.* Ballantine Del Rey. Series: Manifold.

The year is 2010 and industrialist Reid Malenfant has a plan to bypass NASA and mine the asteroids using a simplified spaceship design "manned" by genetically modified squids. Then he gets involved with an eccentric mathematician, Cornelius Taine, who convinces him that humankind is on the verge of extinction and can only be saved by a revolutionary new piece of technology that will make it possible to access myriad alternate universes. Although the plotting and character development have weaknesses, this is sense-of-wonder science fiction with a vengeance. In the sequels, *Space: Manifold 2* (2000; U.S. title *Manifold: Space*) and *Origin: Manifold 3* (2001; U.S. title *Manifold: Origin*), two different Reid Malenfants in their own alternate universes once again face the potential destruction of all life on Earth. (ML)

Themes: Hard SF, Parallel Worlds

*II-86.   The Time Ships. HarperCollins, 1995; HarperPrism, 1995.

In this sequel to Wells's *The Time Machine,* the Traveller heads into the future once again to rescue Weena, the Eloi girl he'd befriended on his first journey. However, after an encounter with creatures resembling Wells's Morlocks, he realizes they are different and that he is not exploring the same future. Journeying with Nebogipfel, representative of an intelligent, educated race of Morlocks, the Traveller is obliged to confront the failings of his own species in his own time stream, but is also able to confront the nature of 20th-century scientific theories about the universe. Having traveled far into the future, he finally experiences post-human transcendence before returning to his own body and being reunited with Weena. Baxter's long-standing fascination with cosmology is set against a range of more typically Wellsian preoccupations, as he addresses the ramifications of time travel in permitting the prosecution of a seemingly endless war against the Germans, alongside the Traveller's rapidly developing "long view" of history. One of the best of Baxter's novels, this is also one of the most successful of sequels by another hand. Compare Priest's *The Space Machine* and Wright's *Scientific Romance.* (MKS)

Awards: John W. Campbell, Philip K. Dick
Themes: Alternate Worlds, Time Travel

II-87.   Titan. HarperPrism, 1997.

Baxter, who has degrees in mathematics and engineering and once applied to become a cosmonaut, tells the hyper-realistic tale of a one-way flight to Saturn's largest moon. Astronaut Paula Benacerraf attempts to rescue NASA from collapse after signs of life have been detected on Titan. Using outmoded technology from several generations of spaceflight, including a stripped-down space shuttle, a Skylab module, and a bunch of surplus Soviet nukes, she and her crew of visionaries and space junkies make the greatest flight in the history of the space program, knowing full well that they will probably never return to Earth. Compare Benford's comparably realistic *The Martian Race* (1999) and Landis's *Mars Crossing*. (ML)

Themes: Hard SF, Life on Other Worlds

Bayley, Barrington J(ohn), U.K., 1937–

II-88.   The Fall of Chronopolis. DAW, 1974.

An autocratic empire extends across time, its armies deployed in time-traveling citadels, but its attempts to control change are subverted. A colorful adventure story with metaphysical themes woven into the plot. Compare Harness's *Ring of Ritornel*. (BS)

Themes: Time Travel

II-89.   The Knights of the Limits. Allison & Busby, 1978.

These stories, mostly from the *New Worlds* anthologies, show the versatility of Bayley's fertile imagination. "The Exploration of Space" is a strange dimensional fantasy; "Me and My Antronoscope" is a bizarre exercise in speculative cosmology; "The Cabinet of Oliver Naylor" is a baroque space opera exhibiting the author's fascination with philosophical problems. A 1979 collection, *The Seed of Evil* is slightly less dazzling but has the gruesome "Sporting with the Child" and the fine *conte philosophique* "Man in Transit." Compare Masson's *The Caltraps of Time*. (BS/ML)

Bear, Greg, U.S., 1951–

*II-90.   Blood Music. Arbor House, 1985.

A genetic engineer conducts unauthorized experiments that result in the creation of intelligent microorganisms. Having infected himself, he becomes a "universe" of sentient cells, and when his "disease" becomes epidemic the whole living world undergoes an astonishing transformation. A brilliant novel, expanded from a novelette (Hugo, 1984) that extends the SF imagination to new horizons. Compare Clarke's *Childhood's End* and Slonczewski's *Brain Plague* (2000). (BS/ML)

Themes: Evolution, Genetic Engineering, Nanotechnology

*II-91.   The Collected Stories of Greg Bear. Tor, 2002.

This enormous volume subsumes Bear's earlier collections, *The Wind from a Burning Woman* (1983) and *Tangents* (1989), while also including more recent work. Among the many outstanding pieces, most of them hard SF, are the Hugo- and Nebula Award-winning short story "Tangents," a beautifully understated tale about the relationship between a fugitive scientist and a young refugee from a future war; "Sleepside Story"; "Schrodinger's Plague"; "Sisters";

Bear's Hugo- and Nebula Award-winning novella "Hardfought"; "Scattershot"; "White Horse Child"; and "Dead Run." Bear has also included extensive notes on each story (ML).

Themes: Hard SF

*II-92.   Darwin's Radio. Ballantine Del Rey, 1999.

A new, flu-like disease begins to appear worldwide, causing deaths, miscarriages, and then strange new births. A retrovirus that has slept in humanity's junk DNA for ages has awakened, and the human race is about to be transformed. Soon scientists and politicians are searching desperately for some means of coping with the emergence of *homo superior* in our midst. Two things place this well-done novel a level above the common run of superman tales: Bear's well-developed characters and the fascinating scientific rationale he's worked out for the appearance of the new supermen. *Darwin's Children* (2003) is an equally fascinating sequel. Compare Baxter's *Coalescent* and, of course, Arthur C. Clarke's *Childhood's End*. (ML)

Awards: Nebula

Themes: Biology, Evolution, Hard SF, Supermen/women

II-93.   Eon. Bluejay, 1985. Series: Eon.

World War III looms as an asteroid starship mysteriously orbiting Earth is taken over by Americans, who discover that it is an artifact from the future that offers a gateway to infinite opportunity. Hard SF unfolding into vast realms of possibilities. In the sequel, *Eternity* (1988), humans explore the seemingly endless corridor of the Way and the alternate universes and time periods that lead off it. *Legacy* (1995) is a prequel to *Eon*. Compare Reed's *Down the Bright Way*. (BS/ML)

Themes: Alternate Worlds, Hard SF, Parallel Worlds, Time Travel

II-94.   The Forge of God. Tor, 1987.

Bear has occasionally been compared to the pulp writer Edmond Hamilton because of his propensity for destroying entire worlds during the course of his novels. This book is the ultimate example of the tendency. In the near future, a series of strange events occurs: one of the moons of Jupiter disappears; an exact duplicate of the Ayers rock appears in the Australian desert; strange robots and aliens show up at various sites. One of the aliens explains that a gigantic machine is approaching through space, its sole purpose to destroy all planets that harbor life and thus make the universe safe for those who built it. The machine appears and, as the novel ends, Earth is destroyed. Although lacking the focus provided by strong central characters, this is a powerful novel, with magnificently described scenes of destruction. The sequel, *Anvil of Stars* (1992), details the quest by a small number of human children who were saved from Earth's destruction to uncover those responsible for their planet's death and gain revenge. Compare Clarke's *Childhoods End* and Jack McDevitt's *The Engines of God*. (ML)

Themes: End of the World, Religion

*II-95.   Moving Mars. Tor, 1993.

Charles Franklin is a brilliant young physicist. Casseia Majumdar is the daughter of one of Mars' oldest and most conservative great families. Together they participate in the student protest of 2171 that turns the future of their planet upside down and leads to a permanent split between an overbearing Earth and a Mars that is growing daily more radical. A sophisticated tale of political intrigue that also features well-developed characters and some spectacular hard science speculation, *Moving Mars* makes for interesting comparisons with both Heinlein's *The Moon is a Harsh Mistress* and Robinson's *Red Mars*. (ML)

>   Awards: Nebula
>   Themes: Life on Other Worlds, The Planets, Politics, Women in SF

*II-96.   Queen of Angels. Warner, 1990.

Because of the virtually universal use of therapy to promote mental health and the prosperity brought on by the perfection of nanotechnology, crime is virtually unknown in the 21st century. Then the famous poet Emanuel Goldsmith commits mass murder and flees the country; police investigator Mary Choy is sent to track him down. Psychologist Martin Burke is preparing to enter Goldsmith's mind to uncover the cause of his actions. Meanwhile, out in space, headed for distant worlds, the AXIS probe broods over the nature of its own intelligence. An engrossing story as well as a complex meditation on the nature of intelligence, free will, and sin. *Slant* (1997) is an equally engrossing sequel. Compare Zelazny's *The Dream Master*. (ML)

>   Themes: Crime and Punishment, Intelligence, Psychology, Sociology

Beliaev, Aleksandr (Romanovich), Russia, 1884–1942

II-97.   The Amphibian. 1928. Trans. of *Chelovek amfbiya* by L. Kolesnikov and R. Dixon. Foreign Languages Publishing House, 1959 (as by Alexander Belayev).

YA. The adventures of Icthyander, a young man equipped with gills by an experimental scientist, who is exploited by a piratical pearl-fisher and condemned to death by a churchman before escaping to pursue his own destiny. Interesting for its account of human modification for marine life. (BS)

>   Themes: Biology

II-98.   Professor Dowell's Head. 1925. Trans. of *Golova professora Douela* by Antonia W. Bouis. Macmillan, 1980.

The eponymous head is that of a murdered English scientist, maintained in the absence of its body by an ambitious biological engineer. The heroine serves as the villain's assistant in a head transplant before deciding that he must be stopped. A lurid melodrama anticipating the manner and mode of many horror/SF movies. Compare Curt Siodmak's *Donovan's Brain* (1943). (BS)

>   Themes: Biology

Bell, Clare, U.K./U.S., 1957–

II-99.   Ratha's Creature. Atheneum, 1983. Series: Ratha.

YA. Long ago in an alternate world, a band of intelligent wild cats, the Named, survive because Ratha dares to use fire as a weapon against predatory cat raiders, the UnNamed. In this borderline SF/fantasy novel, believable characterization, vivid, accurate details, and plausible incidents make for a fascinating story. Sequels are *Clan Ground* (1984), in which Ratha faces challenges to her leadership and use of fire, and *Ratha and the Thistle-Chaser* (1990). Contrast O'Brien's *Mrs. Frisby and the Rats of NIMH.* (FM/ML)

Themes: Alternate Worlds, Feminist SF, Pastoral, Science Fantasy

Bell, Eric Temple *see* Taine, John

Bell, Neil (Stephen Southwold) (formerly Stephen Henry Critten), U.K., 1887–1964

II-100.   The Lord of Life. Collins, 1933.

A blackmail story carried through to its conclusion when the scientist who threatens to destroy the world if his terms are not met makes good his promise. A party of survivors aboard a submarine immediately falls to fighting over the one woman in their company, with blackly comic consequences. Compare Sinclair's *The Millennium.* (BS)

Themes: End of the World

II-101.   The Seventh Bowl. Partridge, 1930 (as by Miles).

An immortality serum invented in the wake of a world war is monopolized by the political elite and used to perpetuate their rule, eventually precipitating a revolution whose violence escalates to apocalyptic levels. An episode from the future history sketched out in the novel was more elaborately explored in *The Gas War of 1940* (1931 as by Miles), which was retitled *Valiant Clay* when it was reprinted, along with its predecessor, under the Bell byline. The two novels are a deeply embittered response to the prospect of a second World War; Bell's early short SF, notably "The Mouse" and "The Evanescence of Adrian Fulk" in *Mixed Pickles* (1935), is similarly inventive and bleakly ironic. Compare Potter's *Life—the Jade* and Gloag's *Winter's Youth.* (BS)

Themes: Future History, War

Bellamy, Edward, U.S., 1850–1898

*II-102.   Looking Backward, 2000–1887. Ticknor, 1888.

A Bostonian insomniac who resorts to desperate means wakes up in the year 2000 to find the U.S. transformed by evolutionary socialism and (elliptically glimpsed) technological progress. The book became a huge bestseller, and Bellamy responded to its many critics by further elaborating his political scheme in *Equality* (1897). Technological advancements also remain in the narrative background of the sequel, but their contribution to the comforts of millennial life are more elaborately acknowledged. By far the most influential American euchronian novel, Bellamy's novel stimulated as much debate as to the social role of technology as political controversy about the ideals of socialism, remaining a fugitive but significant influence on domestic science fiction until Mack Reynolds produced transfigurations of both texts in the 1970s. Compare Thiusen's *The Diothas;* contrast Donnelly's *Caesar's Column* and Morris's *News from Nowhere.*

Themes: Utopias

Benford, Gregory, U.S., 1941–

II-103.   Against Infinity. Timescape, 1983.

The first part of this novel set on Ganymede draws its inspiration from Faulkner's novella, "The Bear," with an adolescent and an aging hunter tracking down a strange alien creature. Inevitably, the story moves to new ground when it gives more attention to the nature of the alien and the kind of world into which the hero's rite of passage will take him. An interesting attempt to infuse SF with narrative realism. A related work is *Beyond Infinity* (2004). Compare Clarke's *Rendezvous with Rama.* (BS/ML)

Themes: Coming of Age, Life on Other Worlds

II-104.   Cosm. Avon Eos, 1998.

Physicist Alicia Butterworth conducts an experiment designed to duplicate the conditions that existed just before the big bang, but gets more than she bargained for when she accidentally creates a pocket universe, or cosm. The chance to watch a universe evolve from outside and at an accelerated rate of speed is too much to pass up, and Butterworth steals the sphere, putting herself and conceivably our entire world in danger. For a similar idea carried out on a much larger scale, see Greg Egan's *Schild's Ladder* (2001). (ML)

Themes: Hard SF, Scientists and Engineers, Women in SF

II-105.   Eater. Eos, 2000.

In the very near future, astronomers discover that a black hole is approaching our solar system, apparently under intelligent guidance. The novel features crisp dialogue, three believable and well-developed scientist protagonists, and, despite a rather unlikely premise (the black hole turns out to be self-aware), a realistic look at how modern science is done. One of the major characters is apparently based on Freeman Dyson. (ML)

Themes: Aliens, Hard SF, Scientists and Engineers

*II-106.   Great Sky River. Bantam, 1987. Series: Galactic Center.

Across the galaxy, humanity is on the run from the encroaching Mech civilization. On the planet Snowglade, family Bishop and other bionically enhanced human survivors are treated as vermin by the Mechs, either ignored or "harvested." Killeen, leader of the Bishops, must find some way of defeating, communicating with, or escaping from the Mantis, an advanced artificial intelligence that seems set upon tracking them down. In the sequel, *Tides of Light* (1989), Killeen and family Bishop flee to a new planet where they discover more Mechs who are at war with a race of alien cyborgs. In these fine novels Benford presents a sophisticated and endlessly fascinating portrayal of the multiple forms that intelligence might take. Later and somewhat less successful sequels in the Galactic Center sequence include *Furious Gulf* (1994), and *Sailing Bright Eternity* (1995). Compare Silverberg's *The Alien Years* and Tenn's *Of Men and Monsters*. (ML)

Themes: Future History, Hard SF, Intelligence, Life on Other Worlds, Religion, Robots

II-107.   In the Ocean of Night. Dial, 1977.

A fix-up novel, set in the same universe as the later Galactic Center books, in which the hero looks for evidence of the existence of aliens and ultimately meets one; contact may invigorate a world becoming gradually decadent. In a sequel, *Across the Sea of Suns* (1984), the difficulty of coming to terms with alien beings and the necessity of so doing lie at the heart of a complex plot involving the confrontation of alternative human philosophies of life. Thoughtful hard SF, its visionary element is less wide-eyed than in Anderson's *The Avatar* and other like-minded works. (BS/ML)

Themes: Aliens, Future History, Hard SF

II-108.   Jupiter Project. Nelson, 1975.

YA. What prevents the shutting down of the Astronautical-Biological Laboratory orbiting Jupiter, which has had no luck in finding life and justifying its high cost, is young Matt Bowles's accidental discovery of Jovian bacteria. Expertly and plausibly, the novel weaves together details of the operations of a scientific expedition in space, the problems of a closed-in society, and the challenges and difficulties of growing up. Through additional material—in particular, scenes of explicit sexual activity—the second edition (Berkley, 1980) amplifies the sociological and rite-of-passage dimensions. Compare Williamson's *Trapped in Space*, contrast Stone's *The Mudhead*. (FM)

Themes: Coming of Age, Hard SF, The Planets, Space Flight

*II-109.   Timescape. Simon & Schuster, 1980.

As the world lurches toward disaster, scientists in 1998 try to transmit a warning message to 1962 by means of tachyons. Their story is told in parallel with that of the earlier scientists trying to decode the transmission, and the two plots converge on the possibility of paradox. Unusual for the realism of its depiction of scientists at work; admirably serious in handling the implications of its theme. Compare Carter Scholz and Glen A. Harcourt's *Palimpsests* (1985). (BS/ML)

Awards: John W. Campbell, Nebula

Themes: Hard SF, Scientists and Engineers

Benford, Gregory, U.S., 1941– and Brin, David, U.S., 1950–

II-110.   Heart of the Comet. Bantam, 1986.

Scientists exploring Haley's Comet in 2061 are marooned when plague breaks out and monsters attack, but they survive and thrive in extraordinary fashion. Colorful space adventure that diversifies into speculative metaphysics. Compare Williamson's *Lifeburst*. (BS)

   Themes: Fantastic Voyages, Space Opera

Bennett, Alfred Gordon, U.K., 1901–1962

II-111.   The Demigods. Jarrolds, 1939.

A melodrama in which the world is invaded by a race of giant ants, whose collective intelligence has permitted them to make scientific and technological progress. One of the better variants of a popular theme, introduced by H. G. Wells in *The First Men in the Moon* and addressed with far less restraint in David H. Keller's *The Human Termites* (1929; book 1979). Contrast the ant societies of Hernaman-Johnson's *The Polyphemes* and Ridley's *The Green Machine*. (BS)

   Themes: Invasion

Beresford, J(ohn) D(avys), U.K., 1873–1947

II-112.   Goslings. Heinemann, 1913.

A Wellsian catastrophe novel reprinted in the U.S. as *A World of Women*. A new plague selectively kills off the male of the human species in Europe, leaving only a few specimens alive as involuntary feminists strive to save as much as they can of their crumbling civilization. It turns out that the divinely inspired disease has had different effects in America, thus providing a lame anticlimax, but the careful extrapolation of England's decline is exceptional. Compare Philip Wylie's *The Disappearance*. (BS)

   Themes: Disaster, Women in SF

*II-113.   The Hampdenshire Wonder. Sidgwick and Jackson, 1912.

A classic scientific romance presenting a groundbreaking account of a superhuman child born out of his time who becomes a reluctant but devastating commentator on the current state of human knowledge and aspiration. His revelations are understandably unwelcome, even to the narrator, who is capable of appreciating their underlying argument. Olaf Stapledon's *Odd John* is a calculated reprise; compare also Weinbaum's *The New Adam*. (BS)

   Themes: Supermen/women

II-114.   Signs and Wonders. Golden Cockerel Press, 1921.

A collection of philosophical vignettes including several visionary fantasies that offer tantalizing glimpses of the past and future and several character sketches based in Freudian and Jungian psychoanalytical theory. "A Negligible Experiment" is an account of Earth's destruction by cosmic disaster. In "The Cage" a modern man exchanges perceptions with a prehistoric ancestor. "Young Strickland's Career" features a premonition of World War I whose horrific significance remains unperceived. Some similar visionary fantasies and philosophical allegories had appeared in the author's first collection, *Nineteen Impressions* (1918). (BS)

Bergerac, Cyrano de *see* Cyrano de Bergerac

Besant, Walter, U.K., 1836–1901

*II-115.   The Inner House. Arrowsmith, 1888.

A novella in which a medical treatment preventing aging, discovered in 1890, transforms English society dramatically, necessitating strict population control, socialist economic reorganization, and the evolution of a scientistic religion centered in the House of Life (Canterbury Cathedral). The subsequent loss of all progressive impetus seems permanent, but accidental deaths result in occasional injections of unruly youth. An enterprising *conte philosophique*, the first important British dystopia, unless one counts Besant's earlier account of a female-dominated England, *The Revolt of Man* (1882). Compare Potter's *Life—The Jade*. (BS)

Themes: Biology

Bester, Alfred, U.S., 1913–1987

*II-116.   The Demolished Man. Shasta, 1953.

A Freudian-tinged murder mystery given a science fictional spin: how does one premeditate a murder, knowing that police detectives are all telepaths, and expect to get away with it? A convincing portrait of how a society of mutual mind readers might actually function. Typographic tricks further the impact of this first novel. Written in close consultation with *Galaxy* editor Horace Gold—as much a midwife of ideas, in a different way, as John Campbell—this story richly earned the first Hugo for novel. Compare Silverberg's *Dying Inside*. (PC)

Awards: Hugo
Themes: Crime and Punishment, Paranormal Powers

*II-117.   The Great Short Fiction of Alfred Bester. Berkley, 1976. 2 vols. titled *The Light Fantastic* and *Star Light, Star Bright*.

Sixteen stories from 1941 to 1974 in this author's distinctive style. The earliest is his somber "Adam and No Eve." Significant headnotes to each story describe the circumstances and emotions surrounding its composition, although as a good Freudian Bester warns against drawing causal inferences; at the time of writing, your rational composing mind doesn't know what your unconscious is doing. Time travel especially engaged Bester, as in "Hobson's Choice," "Of Time and Third Avenue," and "The Men Who Murdered Mohammed." But here are also "Time Is the Traitor"—*not* time travel, but a wildly neurotic love story; "Fondly

Fahrenheit" and "They Don't Make Life Like They Used To," which in tone and temper came close to the verge of SF's modern period. Bester concluded with a wry, lively, informative essay, "My Affair With Science Fiction." Many of the same stories were included in *Virtual Unrealities* (1997). (PC)

II-118. **Tiger! Tiger!** Sidgwick, 1956. U.S. title: *The Stars My Destination*. Signet, 1958.

Although the *Galaxy* serial and the U.S. edition were both titled *The Stars My Destination*, the U.K. title, with its allusion to Blake, is far more apt. The character "burning bright/In the forest of the night" is Gully Foyle, the protagonist of an escape-from-prison story Bester said he modeled on *The Count of Monte Cristo*. But this story veers in a different direction; whereas the Count's dominant motive after his prison break is to wreak vengeance on the men who framed him, Foyle's is to undercut the entire rapacious class system that brutalized him, by bringing to all humankind the power to teleport—"jaunt"—anywhere in the universe. Bester called this character an "antihero," contrasted with the clean-cut models of much SF. However, Foyle is perhaps more accurately seen as a *proletarian* hero in the tradition of Victor Hugo. Texts of the U.S. and U.K. editions differ. (PC)

Themes: Crime and Punishment, Paranormal Powers

Bethancourt, T. Ernesto, U.S., 1932–

II-119. **The Mortal Instruments**. Holiday, 1977.

YA. Humanity in the far future is evolving into bodiless energy and sends those few who cannot evolve into the past, where they become geniuses or great leaders, both good and evil. Eddie Rodriguez is revealed as an evil genius who seeks to take over the computers of I.G.O. in order to dominate the world. Suspenseful, quick-moving, well-plotted, and superbly written. The sequel *Instruments of Darkness* (1979) manifests the same high level of craftsmanship and interest. (FM/ML)

Themes: Computers, Intelligence, Paranormal Powers

Beynon, John *see* Wyndham, John

Biemiller, Carl L., U.S., 1912–1979

II-120. **The Hydronauts**. Doubleday, 1970. Series: The Hydronauts.

YA. A post-catastrophe story. Because of great changes brought about by radiation, the seas have become the major source of food. Kim, Toby, Genright, and Tuktu are trainees in the Warden Service, which oversees the harvesting of the oceans. Patrolling the kelp forests, guarding the shark pens, and tracking down a mysterious hostile power provide the four ample adventure and experience. Provocative look at future marine life, harvesting the sea, and water survival techniques; taut writing; credible characterization. Compare Clarke's *Dolphin*

Island. Subsequent adventures of the quartet are found in *Follow the Whales: The Hydronauts Meet the Otter People* (1973) and *Escape from the Crater: More Adventures of the Hydronauts* (1974). (FM)

Themes: Disaster, Pollution

Bilderdijk, Willem, Netherlands, 1756–1831

II-121.   A Short Account of a Remarkable Aerial Voyage and the Discovery of a New Planet. 1813. Trans. of *Kort verhaal van eene aanmerklijke luchtreis en nieuwe planeetokdekking* by Paul Vincent. Wilfion, 1989.

A balloonist is stranded on a small satellite orbiting within the Earth's atmospheric envelope. Although it acknowledges its debt to the satirical tradition of lunar voyages, the story makes a serious attempt to acquire the verisimilitude for which Edgar Allan Poe had not yet made his tongue-in-cheek call in "The Remarkable Adventure of One Hans Pfaall," and is thus more closely related to modern SF. (BS)

Themes: Fantastic Voyages

Bishop, Michael, U.S., 1945–

II-122.   Ancient of Days. Arbor House, 1985.

Expanded from the novella, "Her Habiline Husband," this book continues themes first tackled in *No Enemy But Time* in a more lighthearted vein. A modern woman falls in love with a relic of the prehistoric past, outraging the neighbors. Funny and sentimental. Compare Farmer's "The Alley Man" (1959). (BS)

Themes: Anthropology

II-123.   Blooded on Arachne. Arkham, 1982.

The first of several collections of short stories, followed by *One Winter in Eden* (1984). Bishop claims to be stressing the "palpability" of alien landscapes and transfigured futures in these atmospheric stories, which do indeed seem infatuated with strangeness. The title story draws on anthropological material after the fashion of *Transfigurations*, while the novella "The White Otters of Childhood" has a leading character named after the protagonist of *The Island of Dr. Moreau.* Later collections, *Close Encounters With the Deity* (1986), *At the City Limits of Fate* (1996), *Blue Kansas Sky* (2000), and *Brighten to Incandescence* (2003) are equally strong, but tend much more heavily towards fantasy. (BS/ML).

II-124.   Catacomb Years. Berkley, 1979.

A fix-up novel extrapolating themes from *A Little Knowledge* (1977) and introducing new insights into an elaborate study of the culture of 21st century Atlanta. The diffuse and richly detailed text presents an unusually convincing picture of future life in a period of crisis. Compare Pohl's *Years of the City.* (BS)

Themes: Cities, Sociology

*II-125. No Enemy But Time. Timescape, 1982.

A strange, alienated child has lurid dreams of the Pleistocene era, and discovers their truth when he becomes a time traveler in adulthood. He joins forces with a band of habiline protohumans and fathers a child, which he brings back to the present. Brilliant and memorable, written with great conviction. Compare Vercors's *You Shall Know Them*. (BS)

  Awards: Nebula

  Themes: Anthropology, Time Travel

II-126.   The Secret Ascension; or Philip K. Dick is Dead, Alas. Tor, 1987.

In the late 1980s, Richard Nixon is in the fourth term of his "imperial Presidency," and an obscure but talented mainstream novelist named Philip K. Dick has recently died in California. Soon after his death, however, Dick, apparently suffering from amnesia, makes an appearance in a psychiatrist's office in Georgia. Bishop covers most of Dick's major themes in this well-done pastiche and also does a fine job of copying Dick's somewhat idiosyncratic style. Compare Dick's *Ubik* and other novels. (ML).

  Themes: Alternate Worlds, Politics, Satirical SF

II-127.   Transfigurations. Berkley, 1979.

Expanded from the story "Death and Designation Among the Asadi." One of the more impressive SF novels using perspectives and themes drawn from anthropology to aid depiction of an enigmatic alien culture. Compare Le Guin's *The Word for World Is Forest*. (BS/ML)

  Themes: Aliens, Anthropology

Bisson, Terry, U.S., 1942–

II-128.   Fire on the Mountain. Arbor, 1988.

The Civil War as we know it never occurred in this alternate universe because John Brown, with Harriet Tubman acting as his lieutenant, sparked a successful slave rebellion. The outcome was a divided United States with an African-American-dominated South emerging as a socialist utopia. This somehow led to a Europe that avoided world war and to an Africa that developed free from the worst results of colonial rule. The viewpoint alternates between Yasmin, a successful anthropologist and citizen of the utopian South; her great grandfather Abraham, who, born a slave, took part in the rebellion; and Dr. Hunter, a white abolitionist who served as Abraham's mentor. The novel's basic premise seems a bit farfetched, but Bisson's alternate 20th century is endlessly fascinating and well worth a visit. Compare Harry Turtledove's alternate Civil War novels, particularly *The Guns of the South*. (ML)

  Themes: Alternate Worlds, History in SF, Utopias

II-129.   The Pickup Artist. Tor, 2001.

In this engaging satire on America's throwaway culture, Hank Shapiro makes his living as a Pickup Artist, a government bureaucrat who collects out-of-date works of literature and art, catalogues them, and then destroys them. There's simply too much art in the world, after all, and the new stuff is invariably better than the older stuff, right? The obvious progenitor of this tale, although the mood of Bradbury's novel is radically different, is *Fahrenheit 451.* (ML)

Themes: Dystopias, Politics, Satirical SF

II-130.   Pirates of the Universe. Tor, 1996.

In a 21st-century America grown tired and depleted from too much pollution and too many wars, Gunther Glenn's main goal in life is to win the right to live in the Pirates of the Universe theme park in Orlando, FL with his girlfriend. First, however, he must succeed as a Space Ranger, harvesting the enormously valuable skins of Peteys, gigantic alien creatures who have begun to float through the solar system. Eventually, Gunther discovers that the game is rigged, the Peteys aren't what they seem, and he quite literally has to save the universe. This is a gentle, laid-back satiric novel, not major Bisson, but still good fun. (ML)

Themes: Aliens, Pollution, Satirical SF

II-131.   Voyage to the Red Planet. Morrow, 1990.

A Mars ship was built, but the mission was mothballed at the onset of the world-wide Grand Depression, and all the astronauts were laid off. Years later, an on-the-cheap mission has been commissioned by sleazy Pellucidar Pictures, which plans to use the trip to film a pulp adventure flick about, you guessed it, the first trip to Mars. Bisson manages the difficult job of writing a hilariously funny spoof that still takes the grandeur of Mars seriously. For a more deadpan description of the first exploration of the Red Planet, compare Ben Bova's *Mars.* (ML)

Themes: Life on Other Worlds, The Planets, Satirical SF, Space Flight

Blair, Andrew, U.K., ?–1885

II-132.   Annals of the Twenty-Ninth Century; or, The Autobiography of the Tenth President of the World Republic. Tinsley, 3 vols., 1874 (issued anonymously).

A detailed anticipation of future social and technological progress—resulting in the domestication of Earth's entire ecosphere—including a cosmic tour that depicts the humanoid inhabitants of other species at various levels of spiritual evolution. The quasi-nonfictional format is clumsy, reducing the work's appeal to modern readers, but the story's substance is remarkable in its imaginative extravagance. It makes an interesting contrast with the only other Victorian three-decker SF novel, Maitland's *By and By.* (BS)

Themes: Future History

Blaylock, James P., U.S., 1950–

II-133.   The Digging Leviathan. Ace, 1984.

A complicated adventure story that plays affectionately with supposedly anti-quated pulp ideas, including the hollow Earth. Evil conspirators try to use the imaginative power of a young genius for their own nefarious ends. Breezy homage to the delights and eccentricities of pulp SF, witty and well written. Compare Mark Helprin's *Winter's Tale* (1983). (BS)

Themes: Machines, Satirical SF, Steampunk

II-134.   Homunculus. Ace, 1986.

An intricately plotted tale in the steampunk tradition set in Victorian England, where the natural philosophers of the Trismegistus Club battle a sinister reanimator of corpses and a greedy entrepreneur. Meanwhile, a tiny alien imprisoned in one of four identical boxes is passed unwittingly from hand to hand, causing havoc wherever he goes. A witty and very stylish combination of SF and Victorian melodrama. In the sequel, *Lord Kelvin's Machine* (1992), the Earth is nearly destroyed by a passing comet. Compare other steampunk novels such as Power's *The Anubis Gates* and K. W. Jeter's *Infernal Devices* (1987). (BS/ML)

Awards: Philip K. Dick

Themes: History in SF, Satirical SF, Steampunk

Blayre, Christopher *see* Heron-Allen, Edward

Blish, James, U.S., 1921–1975

II-135.   The Best Science Fiction Stories of James Blish. Faber, 1966. Recommended ed.: Faber, 1973.

Eight stories from 1952–1970 with a brief but highly provocative introduction. Leads off with "Surface Tension," which in reworked form became part of *The Seedling Stars*. Stories include "Testament of Andros," which can be taken either as stages in the disintegration of a paranoid schizophrenic or as a succession of science fictional disasters (or both!); "A Work of Art," in which the mind of Richard Strauss is implanted upon another person 200 years after Strauss's death; and "The Oath," about a post-nuclear holocaust doctor who would rather be a poet. For the 1973 revision, a werewolf story was dropped and two later stories were added. (PC)

*II-136.   A Case of Conscience. Ballantine, 1958.

Except at the simplest level, religion in Golden Age SF was almost as taboo a subject as sex. (This is one more demonstration of the difference between U.S. and U.K. sensibilities; compare the serious theological argument of C. S. Lewis and, in an entirely different way, of Olaf Stapledon.) Blish tackled the subject head-on. Lithia is a newly discovered planet whose intelligent inhabitants have developed a culture that is completely ethical, rational, and without religion.

The very *absence* of visible moral evil in them makes them, in the eyes of Jesuit priest/biologist Ramón Ruiz-Sanchez, creations of the devil. He brings one of them in embryo back to Earth. It grows up traumatized (by Earth's own moral evil?), creates social chaos, flees back to Lithia followed by the priest, who exorcises the planet, which is immediately (coincidentally?) destroyed. A rich, ambiguous, deep-cutting probe into the most ultimate concerns. (PC)

>   Awards: Hugo
>   Themes: Religion

*II-137.   Cities in Flight. Avon, 1970. U.K. title: *A Clash of Symbols*. Series: Cities in Flight.

The stories comprising *Earthman, Come Home* (Putnam, 1955) were the first of the tales in this tetralogy. John Amalfi is mayor of a future New York, which flies through interstellar space trading work for supplies; it, and other such itinerant cities, are "Okies." Two prequels, *They Shall Have Stars* (Faber, 1956) and *A Life for the Stars* (Putnam, 1962) describe respectively the development of the cities' means of propulsion and the subsequent flight of the cities from Earth's dreary totalitarian government. Finally, in *The Triumph of Time* (Avon, 1958; U.K. title *A Clash of Symbols*), Amalfi's can-do New Yorkers are faced with the ultimate challenge of the collapse of the universe and contrive to solve even *that*. An essay by Richard Mullen parallels the youth-maturity-senescence cycle Oswald Spengler charted for the comparative history of civilizations in *The Decline of the West* with a similar cycle for Blish's "Earthmanist" civilization. A major, if ponderous, work. (PC)

>   Themes: Future History, Space Flight

II-138.   The Seedling Stars. Gnome, 1957.

Four stories blended into an account of "pantropy": the genetic alteration of humans in order to colonize radically non-Earthlike planets. This method of planetary settlement is presented as more viable than creating an artificial Earth environment under domes or terraforming the planet to make it resemble Earth. The opening and closing chapters make it clear that Blish was writing not only about biological adaptation in the far future but about racism and social adaptation in the here and now. His characteristic care and craft in revising his own work can be traced through these stories, an example of an author committing a kind of pantropy upon his own literary offspring. Compare Williamson's *Manseed*. (PC)

>   Themes: Colonization of Other Worlds, Genetic Engineering

Blumlein, Michael, U.S., 1948–

II-139.   The Brains of Rats. Scream/Press, 1990.

Twelve stories, three previously unpublished, from the 1984–1990 period. The title story and "Tissue Ablation and Variant Regeneration: A Case Report," both published first in *Interzone*, are corrosively brilliant studies of biotechnology, extrapolating the impact of medical research on sexual and national politics. Though other tales are solid but unexciting, these two clearly mark Blumlein as a major talent. His knowledge and experience as a practicing physician are also evident in *The Movement of Mountains* (1987), an ambitious if uneven novel about genetic engineering and future class warfare. Compare the stories of Tiptree and Ballard. (RL)

Themes: Biology, Medicine

Bond, Nancy, U.S., 1945–

II-140.   The Voyage Begun. Atheneum, 1981.

YA. In a future where pollution, energy shortages, and changes in the climate severely affect the economy, Paul takes part in an apparently harebrained scheme to help old Walter Jepson build a boat. Impressive narrative; distinctive characters, most of whom are rendered to a degree rarely found in YA science fiction; especially sensitive nature description; convincing study of impact of changing environment on human life. Compare Corlett's *Return to the Gate*; contrast Christopher's *Empty World* (1977). (FM)

Themes: Ecology, Far Future, Pollution

Boucher, Anthony (pseud. of William Anthony Parker White), U.S., 1911–1968

II-141.   Far and Away: Eleven Fantasy and Science-Fiction Stories. Ballantine, 1955.

Before Boucher became a distinguished editor, he was an accomplished writer. These stories were published 1941–1954; he took the helm of *The Magazine of Fantasy and Science Fiction* when it began in 1949. He was also a devotee of the mystery story, and one of these stories, "Elsewhen," combines the SF and detective genre using a time machine. Another time-travel piece is "Snulbug." Boucher, a political liberal and practicing Catholic, showed his humane religious concerns in "The Anomaly of the Empty Man" and, especially, in "Balaam." The last story, extrapolating from the politics of the 1950s but unhappily still relevant, is the devastating "The Other Inauguration." *The Compleat Boucher* (NESFA, 1999) contains 45 stories, one original, and a recipe. (PC)

II-142.   Rocket to the Morgue. Duell, Sloan, 1942.

Written under the name "H. H. Holmes," which he used for all his whodunits and some of his book reviews, this book is not SF but a murder mystery, with leading SF writers as principal suspects. The book is also unabashed missionary work for SF: the fictional writers' shop talk in the then-existent Mañana Literary Society (to which the book was dedicated), converts the detective character, who had appeared in a previous Boucher whodunit, into a SF reader. Compare (and contrast!) Malzberg, *Herovit's World* (1973). (PC)

Themes: Crime and Punishment

Boulle, Pierre, France, 1912–1994

II-143.   Planet of the Apes. Vanguard, 1963. Trans. by Xan Fielding of *La planète des singes*.

A good example of the way visual media can dilute a literary work, SF or otherwise. Boulle is a vivid writer and a fine ironist as well as author of *The Bridge Over the River Kwai*, which was not diluted in translation from book to film. Boulle made the Earth astronauts' visit to a far planet where apes are the dominant species and humans a despised underclass a parable of racial and other social failings on Earth, in the grand satiric tradition of *Gulliver's Travels*. Little of the satire came through to the screen and less in each successive film sequel. The one superiority of the movie over the book is that last unforgettable image of the Statue of Liberty. Ignore the film's reputation; the book is really worth your while. (PC)

Themes: Far Future, Satirical SF

Bova, Bova, Ben, U.S., 1932–

II-144.   Colony. Pocket Books, 1978.

Carries forward themes from *Millennium* (1976) and *Kinsman* (1979). With Earth in trouble, the future of humankind seems tied up with the fortunes of orbital space habitats that are stepping stones to the colonization of the solar system and focal points of desperate power struggles. The wide-ranging story takes in many convincing near-future scenarios; an attempt to incorporate the format of mainstream bestsellers into SF. Compare Dickson's *The Far Call*. (BS)

Themes: Hard SF, Life on Other Worlds, Politics, Space Opera

II-145.   Exiled from Earth. Dutton, 1971. Series: Exiles.

YA. A world suffering from overpopulation fears genetic engineering, so the best geneticists and support scientists are banished to an orbiting satellite. Some scientists are mysteriously reprieved but only, as scientist Lou Christopher discovers, to aid unwittingly a revolt that fails. Banished once again, Lou convinces his associates that the only hope for the race's preservation is to aim for the stars, and they depart Earth. Tight, suspenseful writing, especially the description of Lou's escape attempt; thoughtful examination of science's need to be free. Compare Norton's *The Stars Are Ours*. The story of the long flight to the stars and a new home is continued in two subsequent novels—*Flight of Exiles* (1972) and *End of Exile* (1975)—that conclude the trilogy. This is probably the best of Bova's novels for young adults, although *The Winds of Altair* is also excellent. (FM/ML)

Themes: Far Future, Genetic Engineering, Space Flight

II-146.   Mars. Bantam, 1992.

An international mission to Mars is undertaken in this highly realistic novel by one of the leading exponents of the manned exploration of outer space. Bova's characters are not very well developed, but they're secondary to his detailed and at times breathtaking descriptions of the Red Planet. Later books set in this continuing future history include *Return to Mars* (1999), *Jupiter* (2001), *The Rock Rats* (2002), *Saturn* (2003) and others. Compare Kim Stanley Robinson's *Red Mars* for a more literary, but equally hard-science description of the colonization of Mars. Contrast Terry Bisson's *Voyage to the Red Planet* for a somewhat more satirical approach. (ML)

Themes: Future History, Hard SF, Life on Other Worlds, The Planets

Bowen, John (Griffith), U.K., 1924–

II-147.   After the Rain. Faber, 1958.

A second deluge covers the Earth. An "ark" carries survivors after many days to an island, but the catastrophe has not been a purgation; they have brought all of humanity's aggression, irrationality, and pettiness through the flood intact. Even the narrator, nominally the hero, falls into a jealous rage over a believably innocent relationship between his wife, a ballet dancer, and the young male bodybuilder with whom she works out. Published also as a stage play (Faber, 1967), and the theatrical structure is evident in the scene-building for this powerful story. Compare Serviss, *The Second Deluge*, and Ballard, *The Drowned World*. (PC)

Themes: Disaster

Boyd, John (pseud. of Boyd Upchurch), U.S., 1919–

II-148.   The Last Starship from Earth. Weybright & Talley, 1968.

An alternate Earth is ruled by a dictatorship that employs religion and the insights of social science to secure its hegemony, exporting dissidents to the planet Hell. The hero plans to save the world by striking at the very heart of the despised order, preventing Christ's conquest of Rome. Clever development of an interesting premise. Compare Brian Earnshaw's *Planet in the Eye of Time* (1968). (BS)

Themes: Alternate Worlds, Religion

II-149.   The Pollinators of Eden. Weybright & Talley, 1969.

A repressed female scientist is liberated and fulfilled, thanks to alien orchids. Sexual mores and the working of the scientific community are gently satirized. Compare Ronald Fraser's classic fantasy *Flower Phantoms* (1926). (BS)

Themes: Satirical SF, Scientists and Engineers, Sex in SF, Women in SF

Brackett, Leigh (Douglass), U.S., 1915–1978

II-150.   The Best of Leigh Brackett. Ed. by Edmund Hamilton. Nelson Doubleday, 1977.

Ten stories from 1944 to 1957 in Brackett's typical, colorful action-adventure style. Hamilton suggested that one story was Brackett's regretful leave-taking from the imagined Mars that she had been building since she first read Edgar

Rice Burroughs on a California beach at the age of eight, but that science (already, before *Viking*) had denied her the right to believe in. Other stories take place on a similarly defunct Venus; one on Mercury; and three on Earth, with imported aliens. Readers who find such an Earth milieu more plausible may prefer the story selection in Brackett's *The Halfling, and Other Stories* (Ace, 1973); its raw, tough pulp title story describes an earthly carnival, all of whose caged animals and most of whose crew are extraterrestrials. Such readers are warned that the collection contains "The Lake of the Gone Forever," which splendidly lives up to the extravagance of its title. (PC)

II-151.   Eric John Stark: Outlaw of Mars. Ballantine, 1982.

Two novellas from the wondrously lurid pages of *Planet Stories* (1949 and 1951), set in the Mars that Brackett shared with Bradbury and Burroughs: a dry, western U.S. landscape, an ancient but socially archaic civilization, and a breathable atmosphere. Stark, an interplanetary wanderer and womanizer like C. L. Moore's Northwest Smith, but a tad more complex and with a saving note of tragedy, paradoxically would not retire when probes definitively disproved the existence of that kind of Mars. Brackett simply moved him across the galaxy to the planet Skaith, where he roamed in the 1970s. Meanwhile, the outdated Mars of these stories and others remains a compelling mythic landscape, created by a master storyteller. (PC)

Themes: Space Opera, The Planets

*II-152.   The Long Tomorrow. Doubleday, 1955.

After nuclear war, the U.S. Constitution has been amended to limit the size of cities, and the predominant religiously conservative culture persecutes would-be scientific researchers as witches. Unlike its treatment in most SF, however, the small-town society is richly and even sympathetically described, so that the viewpoint character's decision to cut his home ties and exile himself to the citadel where scientists are redeveloping atomic energy is presented as a real personal struggle, with which any young person who has ever had to grow away from a nurturing but confining community can empathize. Very different in its matter-of-fact realism from Brackett's Mars and Venus stories. Compare Wyndham's *Re-Birth*; contrast Miller's *A Canticle for Leibowitz*. (PC)

Themes: Holocaust and After, Pastoral

Bradbury, Ray (Douglas), U.S., 1920–

II-153.   Fahrenheit 451. Ballantine, 1953.

Expanded from a 1951 novella, "The Fireman," in which firemen no longer put out fires but start them to burn books (the title refers to the ignition point of paper). The hero, a fireman but a closet reader, eventually joins an underground of itinerants who have committed the literary classics to memory and recite them orally. The much-admired film made from the novel, by making the firemen into brutal, black-uniformed Nazi types, missed a point made by Bradbury early on: that hostility to books and ideas was generated by ordinary people, not simply imposed upon them by government. Frequently reprinted and often used in the classroom, although I consider the original novella tighter, more vivid, less diffuse—in short a better literary work than the full-length book. (PC)

Themes: Crime and Punishment, Dystopias

*II-154. The Martian Chronicles. Doubleday, 1950. U.K. title: *The Silver Locusts*. Hart-Davis, 1951.

There is still Golden Age magic here as Bradbury transplants his boyhood "Green Town, Illinois" to Mars, and there works out the *two* planets' tragic but ultimately redemptive destiny. The stories in the book were published in the 1940s, some in mainstream magazines, most in the SF pulps. Some were reprinted in *The Stories of Ray Bradbury* (but not " . . . And the Moon Be Still as Bright," which contains the key to Bradbury's entire argument). Expanded versions published in 1963 (Time, Inc.) and 1977 (Doubleday) added stories absent in the 1950 edition. In 1980, a TV miniseries adapted them with Rock Hudson as the spaceship captain; episodic, uneven, but at times highly effective. By any measure, this work is a major landmark, both as SF and as literature. (PC)

Themes: Holocaust and After, The Planets

*II-155. The Stories of Ray Bradbury. Knopf, 1980.

One hundred tales, drawn from his previous collections, including some from 1947's *Dark Carnival*, his first collection (of mostly horror tales), with the horror softened in the reprints. Here are many of his favorites: "The Veldt," "Frost and Fire," "The Fog Horn," "The Pedestrian," "A Sound of Thunder," "The Million-Year Picnic" and many more. The magazine credits remind us of Bradbury's breakout from the pulp ghetto to his appearance in *Harper's*, *Mademoiselle*, *McCall's*, and *Playboy*. Another large collection, *Bradbury Stories: 100 of His Most Celebrated Tales* (Morrow, 2003), selected by the author, draws on similar sources but—a measure of how prolific Bradbury is—does not duplicate any tales in the 1980 collection.

Bradley, Marion Zimmer, U.S., 1930–1999

II-156. The Heirs of Hammerfell. DAW, 1989. Series: Darkover.

A typical novel in the Darkover series, which began with the Ace Double, *The Planet Savers/The Sword of Aldones* (1962). Associated materials include a number of Darkover anthologies, edited by Bradley, with stories by various friends and associates, as well as four collaborative novels, written with Mercedes R. Lackey and Adrienne Martine-Barnes. *The Planet Savers* first appeared in 1958, and the series thus extends across more than 35 years. It has evolved as the changing market situation of SF has altered. The early novels are generally action-adventure stories confronting ordinary humans with the psi-powered descendants of colonists whose world has been long out of touch with galactic civilization, although *Darkover Landfall* (1972) is notable for its early inclusion of homosexuality as a theme. Bradley gradually elaborated the history of Darkover and began to write longer, denser novels that focus more and more on the relationships between characters, diversifying into an elaborate discussion of sexual politics and exploring the ramifications of the intimacy permitted by telepathic communication. In the later novels, therefore, psychological melodrama replaces action-adventure and female protagonists replace male ones. The history cobbled together from the earlier novels eventually proved unsatisfactory, and *The Heritage of Hastur* (1975)—generally considered the best book in the series—became the first novel assuming the fully worked out and coherent history. *Sharra's Exile* (1981) was subsequently rewritten to replace *The Sword of Aldones* in the "official canon." The series is fascinating as an exercise in world building and as a testament to changing fashions in SF during the modern period. Compare McCaffrey's *Dragonflight* and sequels. (BS/ML)

Themes: Future History, Life on Other Worlds, Paranormal Powers

Breuer, Miles J(ohn), U.S., 1889–1947

II-157.   Paradise and Iron. *Amazing Stories Quarterly*, Summer 1930.

A utopia of comforts is established on an island by means of sophisticated machinery operated and coordinated by an artificial brain, but its citizens are plunged into trouble when the brain begins to malfunction. Like Breuer's enterprising short SF, it was never reprinted in book form. An interesting pulp SF variant of the theme of E. M. Forster's "The Machine Stops." (BS)

Themes: Disaster, Utopias

Brin, David, U.S., 1950–

*II-158.   Earth. Bantam, 1990.

This is a big, engrossing novel with half a dozen fully developed plot lines. Fifty years in the future the ozone layer is gone, sea levels are rising and the ecology is on the verge of collapse. An engineer struggles to save the world through large-scale technology. A biologist sets up gigantic indoor refuges to preserve at least a few of the many species that face extinction. Neo-Luddites stage raids on scientific laboratories, making no attempt to differentiate between technologies that will help and those that will damage the environment. Worst of all, scientist Alex Lustig has created a black hole and then lost it—inside the Earth. The end of the world may be at hand. *Earth* has a few structural weaknesses and tends towards the didactic, but it's enormously readable. Compare Brunner's *Stand on Zanzibar*. (ML)

Themes: Disaster, Ecology, Hard SF, Scientists and Engineers

II-159.   Glory Season. Bantam, 1993.

The planet Stratos was founded centuries ago by feminist separatists who set up a matriarchal civilization based on families of female clones. A limited number of noncloned females, called vars, provide genetic variety, and a small number of men are used both to impregnate clonal women with vars and to "spark" clonal reproduction itself. Although neither vars nor men have complete equality, the society of Stratos is generally benign and nonviolent. Tensions grow, however, with the rise of the Perkinites, who would eliminate all men, and with the appearance of a male emissary from human space. Against this background, two young var twins come of age and attempt to make a life for themselves. Compare Tepper's *The Gate to Women's Country*, Sargent's *The Shore of Women*, and Orson Scott Card's *The Memory of Earth* (1992). (ML)

Themes: Clones/Cloning, Coming of Age, Life on Other Worlds, Women in SF

II-160.   Kiln People. Tor, 2002.

Inexplicably retitled *Kil'n People* in the U.K., this is a near-future thriller that posits the idea that people can create short-lived duplicates of themselves, "dittos," to perform routine or dangerous acts. Private detective Al Morris uses a variety of dittos to investigate corruption that centers around the makers of dittos, but in the process Brin questions who is the real Al Morris and, even more interestingly, examines a host of ontological problems raised by ditto technology. For the most part, Brin skillfully balances these philosophical issues with a gripping thriller, bringing a remarkable new dimension to traditional SF stories of golems and robots. Contrast Asimov's *I, Robot*. (PK)

Themes: Androids, Clones/Cloning, Crime and Punishment

II-161.   The Postman. Bantam, 1985.

Expanded from a novella. In post-holocaust America, a scavenger picks up the uniform of a dead postman, triggering the myth that the Post Office still survives and that order might soon be restored to the shattered world. By degrees he is forced reluctantly to accept the responsibility of his peculiar charismatic authority. An antidote to post-holocaust romanticism, but not without a romanticism of it own. Compare and contrast the trilogy beginning with Robinson's *The Wild Shore*. (BS)

Awards: John W. Campbell, *Locus*
Themes: Holocaust and After

*II-162.   Startide Rising. Bantam, 1983. Series: Uplift.

The intelligent species of Earth (men, apes, and dolphins) seem to be highly exceptional in having advanced to technological sophistication without the alien Patrons that generally supervise the "uplift" of sentient species throughout the galactic culture. Now a dolphin-commanded starship has made a significant discovery in deep space, but must take refuge from its rivals in an alien ocean. While the dolphins struggle desperately to survive, the starships of a number of alien races do battle overhead for the prize. Superior space opera of a very high order. Brin's "uplift" universe was first introduced in *Sundiver* (1980). Compare Niven's Known Space series. (BS/ML)

Awards: Hugo, Nebula, *Locus*
Themes: Aliens, Future History, Genetic Engineering, Space Opera

*II-163.   The Uplift War. Phantasia Press, 1987. Series: Uplift.

Whoever owns the secret discovered by the dolphins of *Startide Rising* can gain control of the entire galactic civilization. The planet Garth lies on the other side of the galaxy from the site of that discovery, but the alien Gubru, in a bold move to force humanity to give up the secret, have taken that planet and its population of human beings and neo-chimps hostage. Only a small band of humans and chimps stands between the Gubru and success. The setting here is less exotic than those of the previous two books in the Uplift series, but Brin's character development is particularly good, and the neo-chimps especially are a wonderful creation. Later and somewhat less successful books in the series include *Brightness Reef* (1995), *Infinity's Shore* (1996), and *Heaven's Reach* (1998). (ML)

Awards: Hugo, *Locus*
Themes: Aliens, Future History, Genetic Engineering, War

Broderick, Damien, Australia, 1944–

II-164.   The Dreaming Dragons: A Time Opera. Pocket Books, 1980. Series: Faustus Hexagram.

An aborigine anthropologist and his nephew discover an alien artifact that gives them access to a vault beneath Ayers Rock. The boy is changed by the experience and becomes the key to scientific study of the vault and its builders. An intriguing combination of SF motifs and mythological references. Compare Zelazny's *Eye of the Cat* (1982). (BS/ML)

Themes: Anthropology, Mythology

II-165.   The Judas Mandala. Pocket Books, 1982. Rev. ed., Mandarin, 1990. Series: Faustus Hexagram.

Carries forward themes from *The Dreaming Dragons*; in a far future benevolently ruled by powerful computers, some humans find a way to escape their governance by dimensional side-stepping. They gradually extend their ability to travel in time until they begin trying to alter and control history. A convoluted and effective SF mystery. Related volumes in the Faustus Hexagram series include *Transmitters* (1984), *The Black Grail* (1986), *Striped Holes* (1988), and *The Sea's Furthest End* (1993). Compare van Vogt's *Masters of Time* (1950). (BS/ML)

Themes: Far Future, Time Travel

II-166.   Transcension. Tor, 2002.

In his recent work of nonfiction, *The Spike* (2002), Broderick predicted a variety of post-singularity futures. In this witty novel, he explores one of those possibilities, a world of highly developed AI, rampant nanotechnology, and post-human possibilities. Mathewmark is a relic, an unmodified young man living in the Valley of the God of One's Choice, a place reserved for those who have refused artificial augmentation. Then he meets Amanda, a brilliant post-human mathematician and musician with a chip on her shoulder. Meanwhile, Mohammed Abdel-Malik, a resurrected 21st century man, tries to come to terms with the fact that society is now ruled by Aleph, an artificial intelligence apparently patterned on him, and apparently intent on coaxing humanity into its next evolutionary leap. (ML)

Themes: Computers, Evolution, Intelligence, Nanotechnology

Brown, Eric, U.K., 1960–

II-167.   New York Nights. Gollancz, 2000. Series: Virex.

Volume 1 of the Virex Trilogy, this is a cross-genre novel combining private investigator Hal Holliday with a near-future setting (2040 New York) and a sketchy background of various environmental disasters that do not impinge on the main action of the narrative. Holliday specializes in finding missing persons, and in this and the second volume, *New York Blues* (2001), his cases lead him into the worlds of artificial intelligence and virtual reality, which are assuming ever greater importance in Brown's vision of the future. However, they are little more than science-fictional window dressing for what are otherwise conventional pieces of detective fiction. Even Virex, the shadowy anti-VR group, plays surprisingly little part in the first two volumes, though this may change in *New York Dreams* (2003). These two volumes are a far remove from Brown's earlier work, which centered on a space-faring society, peopled with detached and aloof characters, on far-flung worlds, described with a delicacy and precision often reminiscent of Ballard or Bradbury. (MKS)

Themes: Computers, Crime and Punishment, Intelligence, Virtual Reality

Brown, Fredric, U.S., 1906–1972

II-168.   From These Ashes: The Complete Short Fiction. NESFA, 2001.

All 118 short stories by a talented author who died in 1972. Includes such classic stories as "Armageddon," "Eine Kleine Nachtmusik," "The Star Mouse," "The Waveries," and "Paradox Lost," plus an introduction by Barry Malzberg. Brown's hallmarks are humor combined with a gritty, noirish sensibility. (ML)

II-169.   Space on My Hands. Shasta, 1951.

Nine stories reprinted from 1941 magazines with an introduction on the craft of SF writing. "The Star Mouse" is a funny saga of a mouse fired into space, who returns speaking English with the heavy German accent of the rocket builder. Humor is the dominant note of the tales. Brown was a thoroughly professional writer who could work within the genre and sometimes transcend it. Later, more authoritative collections include *And the Gods Laughed* (1987), 70 fantasy and SF stories, and *From These Ashes: The Complete Short SF of Fredric Brown* (2001), which assembles tales from 1941 through 1965. A 2002 omnibus, *Martians and Madness*, collects *What Mad Universe*, *Martians Go Home* (1955), *Rogue in Space* (1957), *The Mind Thing* (1961), and *The Lights in the Skies Are Stars* (1953). (PC)

II-170.   What Mad Universe. Dutton, 1949.

This was Brown's first SF novel after several well-crafted mysteries. An SF magazine editor is thrown into an alternate universe where space travel was accidentally discovered in 1903 and General Eisenhower is now—1949—leading a space war against invading Arcturans. Every cliché in pulp SF exists here: bug-eyed monsters, young women in see-through space suits, a superhero who is also a scientific genius—and who turns out to be a particularly vapid and obnoxious science fiction fan in "our" universe, who had been writing nasty letters to the editor-hero's magazine. Brown wrote this before the pulps were quite extinct, so the satire still had bite and still does vis-à-vis visual media. Compare Adams, *The Hitchhiker's Guide to the Galaxy;* contrast Harrison's *Bill, the Galactic Hero*. (PC)

Themes: Satirical SF

Bruller, Jean *see* Vercors

Brunner, John, U.K., 1934–1995

II-171.   The Jagged Orbit. Ace, 1969.

A dystopian black comedy of a culturally fragmented near-future United States whose citizens are armed to the teeth and have made fortresses of their homes. As the personal arms race threatens to escalate yet again, an investigative journalist and a psychologist combine forces to strike a blow for sanity. The bitter alarmism, very much a product of the 1960s, makes the novel a striking period piece. Compare Stephen Barnes's *Streetlethal* (1983) and Bunch's *Moderan*. (BS)

Themes: Dystopias, Satirical SF

II-172.   No Future in It. Gollancz, 1962.

Eleven stories, half from the U.K.'s *New Worlds,* most of the remainder from U.S. magazines. The stories in this first collection ranged from hard SF, such as the murder mystery "Puzzle for Spacemen," to psychologically penetrating stories like "Elected Silence" and "Protect Me from My Friends." "The Iron Jackass" is a lovely retelling of the American legend of John Henry. A promising start for a writer who would later be a major force. *The Best of John Brunner* (1988) collects 17 additional stories. (PC)

*II-173.   The Sheep Look Up. Harper, 1972.

The most elaborate alarmist novel about industrial pollution. Uses techniques similar to *Stand on Zanzibar* to present a kaleidoscopic image of future America drowning in its own wastes. Relentlessly angry and anguished. Compare Philip Wylie's *The End of the Dream* (1972). (BS)

Themes: Ecology, Pollution

II-174.   The Shockwave Rider. Harper, 1975.

The third of Brunner's major alarmist fantasies, partly inspired by Alvin Toffler's *Future Shock*, warning against the loss of individual freedom that might result from widespread use of information technology and against the psychological effects of rapid technological change. Brunner complained bitterly about Harper's insensitive editing; the 1976 Ballantine reprint restored the author's text. (BS)

   Themes: Computers, Dystopias, Psychology

*II-175.   Stand on Zanzibar. Doubleday, 1968.

A complex novel borrowing techniques from John Dos Passos and ideas from Marshall McLuhan and other 1960s commentators to provide a multifaceted image of an overpopulated near future. Clever, highly detailed, and frequently very witty, the book is a successful experiment and one of the key works of the period. Compare *A Torrent of Faces* (also 1968) by James Blish and Norman L. Knight and Turner's *The Sea and the Summer*. (BS/ML)

   Awards: Hugo, Prix Apollo
   Themes: Dystopias, Overpopulation

II-176.   The Whole Man. Ballantine, 1964. British title: *Telepathist*, 1965.

Developed from two novellas. A crippled and deformed social outcast is nearly destroyed by his telepathic powers, but learns to use them to create therapeutic dreams for others and eventually to create a new art form. Good characterization and sensitive narration, Compare Silverberg's *Dying Inside* and Zelazny's *The Dream Master*. (BS)

   Themes: Paranormal Powers

Brussof, Valery (Yakovlevich), Russia, 1873–1924

II-177.   "The Republic of the Southern Cross" ("Respublika yuzhnavo kresta"). 1905. Trans. anonymously in *The Republic of the Southern Cross and Other Stories*. Constable, 1918.

A technologically advanced society established in Antarctica prospers until its domed polar capital, Star City, is catastrophically afflicted by a plague of mental illness that transforms intentions into opposite actions. A remarkable *conte philosophique* with roots in Dostoyevskyan pessimism and Gogolesque cynicism, also reprinted in Fetzer's *Pre-Revolutionary Russian Science Fiction*. (BS)

   Themes: Disaster

Bryant, Edward, U.S., 1945–

II-178.   Cinnabar. Macmillan, 1976.

A "mosaic novel" about a decadent far-future city where aesthetic motives are paramount and ennui reigns supreme. Equally well done is the short fiction found in Bryant's several collections, most importantly *Particle Theory* (1980). Compare Harrison's Virconium series and Carr's *Cirque*. (BS/ML)

Themes: Cities, Far Future

Budrys, Algis, U.S., 1931–

II-179.   The Falling Torch. Pyramid, 1959.

Earth, conquered by interstellar invaders, has a government-in-exile on Alpha Centaurus IV, which exists on sufferance of the local regime. The son of the exiled president, who left Earth as an infant, returns to fight and finds a faction-ridden guerilla movement, whose leader aspires to become Earth's dictator. He prefers the Spartan militarism of the invaders at first, but they have the typical character flaws of occupation troops, and he escapes from them. Melodramatic, but nonetheless a bildungsroman of especially acute anguish, since it combines political conflict with the usual confusions of coming-of-age. The parallel with the "captive nations" situation during and after World War II is clear and reflects the author's own ethnic and political heritage. The book also foreshadows Budrys's *Michaelmas*. (PC)

Themes: Coming of Age, Invasion

II-180.   Michaelmas. Berkley, 1977.

The hero and his machine intelligence sidekick secretly rule the world, but their subtle dictatorship is threatened by insidious alien intruders. A slick power fantasy. Compare van Vogt's *The Anarchistic Colossus* (1977). (BS)

Themes: Aliens, Computers, Intelligence

*II-181.   Rogue Moon. Gold Medal, 1960.

This probes a major metaphysical problem with the widely used SF concept of matter transmission. If a person is "scanned," sent in dissociated form to wherever, and then reassembled, does not the scannee (from his/her own point of view) cease to exist? In this instance, a Moon-based receiver merely duplicates the traveler, leaving the original on Earth, resulting eventually in a situation in which the transportee must die so that there will not be two of him. Budrys cuts deeply into some age-old questions about the nature of the self, or soul. But this is no abstract philosophic discourse; the situation is handled with unsparing realism, and the psychic aberrations of the major characters led James Blish to exclaim that they were all certifiably insane. A major work, well meriting its Hugo nomination.

Awards: Nebula (as novella)

Themes: Clones/Cloning, The Moon

II-182.   The Unexpected Dimension. Ballantine, 1960.

The title exactly describes what Budrys was doing in each of these seven stories: giving what in less skilled hands could have been a conventional plot an "unexpected dimension" of insight, irony, or invention. "Go and Behold Them" does this with the age-old theme of love stronger than death; "The End of Summer" with the frequent SF gambit of biological immortality as stagnation; "The Executioner" with the pompous idiocies of legal ritual; "The Burning World" with the ambiguities of political revolution. Except for "First to Serve," a wry satire on the military mind, the tone is uniformly somber. (PC)

II-183.   Who? Pyramid, 1958.

Budrys blends the theme of cyborgs (although the term for cybernetic organisms had not yet been coined) with the competitive dehumanization inherent in the Cold War. A scientist of humble immigrant origins—a status in itself sufficient to make him suspect in some paranoid, subversive-haunted minds—is injured in a laboratory accident and falls into Soviet hands. The Russians equip him with a metal face and other mechanical parts. He returns to the U.S. and is forbidden to continue his research on the ground that nobody can prove who he really is. A strong indictment of the idiocies dignified at that time (and to a great extent still today) as "security," but a parable also of estrangement and alienation more generally. Compare Bernard Wolfe's *Limbo*. (PC)

Themes: Cyborgs

Bujold, Lois McMaster, U.S., 1949–

*****II-184.   Barrayar**. Baen, 1991. Series: Vorkosigan.

Cordelia Naismith and Aral Vorkosigan were once enemies in an interstellar war. Now a fragile peace has been established, and they're a married couple expecting their first child. Cordelia, a liberated woman, is ill at ease among the more conservative, less civilized people of Barrayar and, when her husband is named regent, she realizes that she, Aral, and their unborn baby are in great danger. Traditional space opera at its very best with a mild feminist tone and twist. Bujold's highly competent first novel, *Shards of Honor* (1986), details Cordelia and Aral's first meeting in the midst of war. Compare C. J. Cherryh's *Rimrunners* and other novels. (ML)

Awards: Hugo, *Locus*
Themes: Feminist SF, Future History, Galactic Empires, Space Opera

*****II-185.   Falling Free**. Baen, 1988.

Leo Graf, a welding engineer hired to train workers on a space station, is astonished to discover that his new pupils are "quaddies," genetically engineered living tools with extra arms where normal people have legs. Designed by the GalacTech corporation to be perfect zero-gravity employees, the quaddies have unfortunately failed to turn a profit for their owner/employers. Soon after Graf's arrival, the corporation decides to cut its losses and return the quaddies to Earth, where they will presumably be dumped in nursing homes on a small pension. The quaddies, however, have other ideas, and convince Graf to join them in revolt. Originally published as a serial in *Analog* in 1987–1988, this is an example of old-fashioned, Campbell-style hard SF at its best, but with a fascinating feminist twist. Compare Steele's *Orbital Decay*. (ML)

Awards: Nebula

Themes: Future History, Genetic Engineering, Hard SF, Scientists and Engineers

*II-186.   The Vor Game. Baen, 1990. Series: Vorkosigan.

The culture of the planet Barrayar values men only to the extent that they prove themselves in the military, and Miles Vorkosigan, the disabled son of Lord Aral and Lady Cordelia Vorkosigan, has determined to succeed in such a career despite his disability. Miles proves his worth, first at an isolated weather station and then in space, where he rescues his runaway cousin, the Emperor Gregor, from possible death. This is superior space opera with a touch of humor. Earlier books in the series include *The Warrior's Apprentice* (1986), *Brothers in Arms* (1989), and *Borders of Infinity* (1989), one previously published section of which, "The Mountains of Mourning," won both the Hugo and Nebula awards for best novella in 1990. All the Miles Vorkosigan books make for fine reading. Later volumes in the series—*Mirror Dance* (1994), a Hugo and *Locus* award winner; *Cetaganda* (1996); the remarkable *Memory* (1996); *Komarr* (1998); *A Civil Campaign* (1999); and *Diplomatic Immunity* (2002)—have moved away from military space opera into realms of diplomatic suspense and even sophisticated drawing room comedy as Bujold continues to mature as an artist. The most recent addition to the series is "Winterfair Gifts," a novella that appeared for the first time in *Irresistible Forces* (2004), an anthology of romantic fantasy and science fiction, edited by Catherine Asaro. Compare C. S. Forester's Horatio Hornblower novels and, for the later volumes in the series, the regency romances of Georgette Heyer, a writer who has always had a following among female SF readers. (ML)

Awards: Hugo

Themes: Coming of Age, Future History, Galactic Empires, Space Opera, War

Bulgakov, Mikhail (Afanasievich), Russia, 1891–1940

*II-187.   "The Fatal Eggs" ("Rokovy'e yaitsa"). 1922. Recommended trans. by Carl R. Proffer in *Diaboliad and Other Stories*, Univ. of Indiana Press, 1972.

A fine political satire whose premise is borrowed from H. G. Wells's *The Food of the Gods*. The cooperative farms of Soviet Russia are overrun by giant snakes when a scientist attempting to use a growth-enhancing ray to increase the productivity of poultry receives the wrong batch of eggs. (BS)

Themes: Politics, Satirical SF

Bull, Emma, U.S., 1954–

II-188.   Bone Dance: A Fantasy for Technophiles. Ace, 1991.

Sparrow, a sexless, artificial person who makes a living tracking down and selling videos and other aging technological artifacts in punked-out, post-nuclear-war Minneapolis, accidentally becomes involved with the Horsemen, U.S. government-developed secret agents capable of entering the minds of others. In the past, the Horsemen were secretly used to destabilize foreign governments until their actions triggered the nuclear war; now they serve other masters, and Sparrow is at risk simply for having discovered their existence. To complicate matters, there is evidence that at least some of what's going on is supernatural, rather than merely weird science. Bull's world is gritty, well realized, and a lot of fun. For a variant on the possession motif, see Cadigan's *Fools*. (ML)

Themes: Cyberpunk, Genetic Engineering, Mythology

Bulwer-Lytton, Edward *see* Lytton, Edward Bulyer

Bunch, David, U.S., 1925–2000

II-189.   Moderan. Avon, 1971.

A collection of linked stories of a future world completely altered by the progressive cyborgization of its inhabitants and artificialization of its environments. Humanity is lost with the discarded "flesh-strips," and the nightmare progresses to its inevitable conclusion. A magnificent work full of striking imagery and fine prose. Compare Wright's *The New Gods Lead*. (BS)

Themes: Cyborgs

Burdekin, Katharine P. *see* Constantine, Murray

Burgess, Anthony (pseud. of John Anthony Burgess Wilson), U.K., 1917–1993

*II-190.   A Clockwork Orange. Heinemann, 1962.

In highly inventive future slang based on Russian loan-words, the story's hero tells how casual recreational gang violence, including murder, got him into prison and then into super-Pavlovian therapy; after treatment, even the thought of violence makes him sick. But so, as side effects, do sex and his former love for classical music; the point apparently being that it is better to do bad things as a free person than not to do them as the result of conditioning. Recognized by "mainstream" critics who probably wouldn't call it SF, and filmed effectively by Stanley Kubrick, this is a world as bleak and vicious as that of *Nineteen Eighty-Four*—and disturbingly closer now, than Orwell's, to our own. However, Kubrick's film was based on the incomplete U.S. edition, which omitted the crucial last chapter in which, as Burgess later said, "my young thuggish protagonist grows up . . . and recognizes that human energy is better expended on creation than destruction," which radically changes the meaning of the novel from the way it was received in America. Compare Knight, *Hell's Pavement*; contrast Skinner's *Walden Two*. (PC)

Themes: Dystopias

Burroughs, Edgar Rice, U.S., 1875–1950

II-191.   At the Earth's Core. McClurg, 1922. Series: Pellucidar.

Serialized in *All-Story* in 1914, this was the first of the Pellucidar series, in which Burroughs developed the interior of a hollow Earth as a milieu for the fabulous adventures that were his chief stock-in-trade. Pellucidar is a lush ecosphere in which primitive tribal societies battle for survival against various monstrous species, most notably the intelligent and telepathic reptilian Mayhars, whose civilization is sustained by the labor of human slaves. The two heroes, carried from the surface by a runaway boring machine, launch a revolution against Mayhar domination whose progress is desultorily tracked in subsequent volumes. (BS)
   Themes: Lost Races/Worlds

II-192.   The Land that Time Forgot. McClurg, 1924.

An omnibus of three novellas published in *Blue Book* in 1918. This is the most orthodox of Burroughs's lost world stories, set on the island of Caspak, where survivors from various prehistoric eras coexist. The human situation is complicated by a life-cycle in which post-embryonic ontogeny recapitulates phylogeny. In the third part, the bizarre civilization of the winged Wieroos on the neighboring island of Oo-oh—considerably more interesting than the Mayhars of Pellucidar—provides a satirical contrast to the human noble savages. (BS)
   Themes: Lost Races/Worlds

II-193.   The Moon Maid. McClurg, 1926.

An omnibus of three serials from *Argosy-All-Story* (1923–1925) in which the interior of the Moon adds yet another exotic setting to Burroughs's repertoire. The first part, set in the early 21st century, features the usual adventures—complicated by a healthy dose of political satire—but these give way in the second and third parts to dourly unromantic accounts of America under the domination of the Kalkars—brutal invaders from the Moon who are not overthrown until the 25th century. Compare Nowlan's *Armageddon 2419 A.D.* (BS)
   Themes: Invasion, Life on Other Worlds

*II-194.   A Princess of Mars. McClurg, 1917. Series: Barsoom.

YA. Serialized in *All-Story* in 1912 as "Under the Moons of Mars" by Norman Bean, this pioneering account of John Carter's magical transmission to the planet Mars and his subsequent baroque adventures established a new template for fiction set on other planets, developing such imaginative spaces as arenas for exuberantly uninhibited tales of exotic derring-do. Although the series ran out of steam after seven volumes, it was sustained for a further four, at least one incorporating material by another hand. A similar series set on Venus failed to recover the spirit of the original, and imitations by other hands—including Ralph Milne Farley's *The Radio Man*—never quite replicated Burroughs's imaginative zest. Although it hardly qualifies as science-based speculative fiction, Burroughs's account of Barsoom was enormously influential in pulp SF standing at the head of a rich subgenre of "planetary romances" whose evolution was carried forward by such writers as C. L. Moore, Leigh Brackett, and Ray Bradbury. (BS)

Themes: Life on Other Worlds

Burroughs, William S(eward), U.S., 1914–1997

II-195. **Nova Express**. Grove, 1964.

A novel of future violence and corruption, in which the anarchic Nova Mob descends like the Furies on hapless humankind, while the Nova Police try to match them. Carries forward themes from the famous avant-garde trilogy, *The Naked Lunch* (1959), *The Soft Machine* (1961), and *The Ticket That Exploded* (1962). Burroughs influenced the work of J. G. Ballard, especially *The Atrocity Exhibition*. (BS)

Themes: Crime and Punishment, New Wave

Butler, Octavia E(stelle), U.S., 1947–

II-196. **Blood Child and Other Stories**. Four Walls Eight Windows, 1995.

This small volume includes Butler's five published short stories. Of particular interest is the horrific Hugo- and Nebula Award-winning title story, which concerns a man "pregnant" with an alien's baby. Also outstanding are the Hugo Award-winning "Speech Sounds," and "The Evening and the Morning and the Night." The volume includes two autobiographical essays and a short afterword for each story. (ML).

*II-197. **Dawn**. Warner, 1987. Series: Xenogenesis.

Lilith Iyapo, a contemporary African American and survivor of the recent nuclear war that has destroyed virtually all life on Earth, awakes to find herself one of a small number of human beings "rescued" by aliens. The Oankali, however, are not entirely altruistic. It is part of their genetic imperative that they must mate with other species, thus sharing genetic material. This fine, if at times harrowing novel, like much of Butler's work, can be read as an allegory of sorts for the African American experience in the United States. The two outstanding sequels are *Adulthood Rites* (1988) and *Imago* (1989). Butler explores somewhat similar ideas in *Clay's Ark* (1984).

Themes: Aliens, End of the World, Feminist SF, Life on Other Worlds, Sex in SF

II-198. **Kindred**. Doubleday, 1979.

Dana, a well-educated contemporary African American woman, suddenly finds herself pulled into the past to save the life of a distant ancestor, an early-19th-century southern white boy named Rufus Weylin. Although she returns to the present moments later, she soon finds herself saving Rufus again and again. Although only a short time passes for her between each bout of time travel, years pass for Rufus, who gradually grows into adulthood and becomes a slave owner. This sometimes painful novel features superb character development. By forcing Dana to confront her own white ancestry, Butler points out the necessity of coming to terms with the past without oversimplifying it. Compare Lisa Tuttle's *Lost Futures* (1992) and Jane Yolen's *The Devil's Arithmetic* (1988). (ML)

Themes: Feminist SF, History in SF, Time Travel

*II-199.   Parable of the Sower. Four Walls Eight Windows, 1993.

In a near-future America on the verge of environmental and economic collapse, Lauren Olamina, an African American teenager, finds herself driven from her neighborhood by marauding gangs. Lauren, who suffers from hyperempathy, an obsessive awareness of other's pain, sets out across a lawless landscape, intent on founding a new community based on Earthseed, a revolutionary new philosophy. In 1995, Butler received a MacArthur "Genius" Award. Three years later, she published *Parable of the Talents* (1998), in which Lauren's teachings come to fruition, with complex and unexpected results. *Talents* won the Nebula Award. (ML)

Themes: Feminist SF, Paranormal Powers

II-200.   Wild Seed. Doubleday, 1980. Series: Patternist.

The first story in Butler's Patternist series in terms of internal chronology, though not in terms of publication. In ancient Africa, Doro, an immortal telepath, begins the work of genetic manipulation that will help him create an empire. Doro's work comes to apparent fruition with the creation of his telepathic daughter, Mary, in *Mind of My Mind* (1977). In *Patternmaster* (1976) we see an entire telepathic society. *Survivor* (1978) is another book in this well-done series. Although *Clay's Ark* (1984) is not a Patternist novel, it explores similar themes. Compare Sturgeon's *More Than Human*. (ML)

Themes: Evolution, Immortality, Paranormal Powers

Butler, Samuel, U.K., 1835–1902

II-201.   Erewhon; or, Over the Range. Truebner, 1872.

A scathing utopian satire, whose principal interest as a work ancestral to modern SF is contained in the chapters dealing with the classic Erewhonian text *The Book of Machines*. This offers a quasi-Darwinian account of mechanical evolution whose implication is that intelligent machinery will supplant humankind unless mechanical technology is ruthlessly suppressed. The equally witty sequel, *Erewhon Revisited* (1901), is mostly devoted to assaults on religion, although it does reveal that the Erewhonians have relented in their opposition of mechanical progress. (BS)

Themes: Evolution, Satirical SF

Bywater, Hector C(harles), U.K., 1884–1940

II-202.   The Great Pacific War: A History of the American-Japanese Campaign of 1931–1933. Houghton Mifflin, 1925.

A future-war novel by a naval historian, which employs little innovative technology but acquired a certain belated notoriety when Bywater's biographer William

H. Honan suggested in 1990 that Admiral Yamamoto used it as a blueprint for the 1941 attack on Pearl Harbor. Less cautious accounts of similar future conflicts were featured in various pulp magazines—notably "The Yellow Scourge" (1934) and "The Invasion of the Yellow Warlords" (1935) in *Operator #5*. (BS)

Themes: Politics, War

Cadigan, Pat, U.S., 1953–

*II-203.   Patterns. Ursus Imprints, 1989.

Fourteen stories from the 1980s. Some are horror, but most—including "Angel," "Rock On," and "Pretty Boy Crossover," all award nominees—are hard-edged, ferociously inventive cyberpunk ranking with best of Gibson and Sterling. Cadigan's milieu is a gritty urban zone where funky street life and slick corporate power interact unpredictably. A more recent collection is *Dirty Work* (Ziesing, 1993). Compare Gibson's *Burning Chrome*. (RL)

Themes: Cyberpunk

II-204.   Synners. Bantam, 1991.

In a near-future United States, an obsessed video artist pioneers brain-socket implants that allow electronic "uploading" of consciousness, but the artist suffers a stroke while psychically online, releasing a destructive virus into the worldwide computer network. A loose fraternity of teen hackers, aging rock-and-rollers, and corporate moguls struggles to eradicate the virus and restore the "crashed" system. Tense and complex, brilliantly wedding cyberpunk with the disaster story; along with *Mindplayers* (1987) and the Arthur C. Clarke Award-winning *Fools* (1992), this novel established Cadigan as a visionary explorer of high technology, pop culture, and cyborg consciousness. Compare Spinrad's *Little Heroes* and Laidlaw's *Kalifornia*. (RL)

Awards: Arthur C. Clarke

Themes: Computers, Cyberpunk, Disaster, Intelligence

II-205.   Tea from an Empty Cup. Voyager, Tor, 1998.

In this hard-boiled police procedural, detective Dore Constantin must enter Artificial Reality and explore the virtual streets of post-Apocalyptic Noo Yawk Sitty in search for a serial killer who has done what everyone says is impossible: committed murder while in the virtual world. This is a gripping mystery made even more powerful by Cadigan's detailed and believable descriptions of how virtual reality might really work. Compare Platt's *The Silicon Man* and Williams's *City of Golden Shadow*. The sequel is *Dervish Is Digital* (2000). (ML)

Themes: Crime and Punishment, Cyberpunk, Feminist SF, Virtual Reality

Calder, Richard, U.K., 1956–

II-206.   Dead Girls. HarperCollins, 1992. Series: Dead Girls.

In this intensely decadent and unrelentingly depressing satiric novel, two English teenagers, Ignatz Zwakh and Primavera Bobinski, undergo a series of harrowing, often sexual adventures in Thailand. Primavera, however, is something other than entirely human. She's a Lilim, an artificially created Dead Girl, and her relationship with Ignatz is intensely perverse. Written in a lapidary, surreal style that can be slow going at times, *Dead Girls* and its sequels, *Dead Boys* (1994) and *Dead Things* (1996), are extremely powerful, but should definitely be kept out of the hands of minors. Compare Mark Laidlaw's *Kalifornia*. (ML)

Themes: Satirical SF, Sex in SF

Callenbach, Ernest, U.S., 1929–

II-207.   Ecotopia. Banyan Tree, 1975.

A utopian novel of ecologically sensitive political reorganization. The West Coast states have seceded from the Union and have established a life-style based on small-scale technology and environmental conservation. A visitor from the East is gradually converted to these ideals. The 1981 sequel *Ecotopia Emerging* fills in (and revises) the historical background. This is perhaps the most important modern addition to the tradition of Bellamy's *Looking Backward* and an interesting development of the ideologies that have since been adopted by various European and American "green" parties. Compare Robinson's *Pacific Edge*. (BS)

Themes: Ecology, Utopias

Calvino, Italo, Italy, 1923–1985

II-208.   Cosmicomics. Harcourt, 1968. Trans. by William Weaver of *Le cosmicomiche*, 1965.

The childlike Qfwfq has the entire cosmos and all eternity as his playground, and naively confronts the great mysteries of time and space in 12 bizarre tales. *t zero* (1969) offers more of the same. Zestful modern fabliaux with a unique charm. Weaver won the National Book Award for translation for *Cosmicomics*. (BS)

Themes: Evolution

Campanella, Tommaso, Italy, 1568–1639

II-209.   The City of the Sun; A Poetical Dialogue. 1602. Recommended trans. of *La citta de sole; Dialogo poetico* by Daniel J. Donno. Univ. of California Press, 1981.

Utopian satire first published in Latin as *Civitas Solis* in *Realis Philosophiae Epilogisticae Partes Quatuor* (1623); earlier translations into English—including the one featured in Henry Morley's anthology *Ideal Commonwealths* (1885)—are abridgments of that version. The Italian manuscript of 1602 is one of several that Campanella penned while in prison, and by no means the most elaborate. The eponymous city, situated on the island of Taprobane, is a supposedly rational communistic society whose accumulated wisdom is inscribed on its seven concentric walls for educational purposes. Compare Bacon's *New Atlantis*. (BS)

Themes: Utopias

Campbell, John W(ood), Jr., U.S., 1910–1971

II-210. **The Black Star Passes**. Fantasy Press, 1953. Series: Arcot, Morey and Wade.

A collection of three novellas published in *Amazing Stories* and its quarterly companion in 1930, in which inventive scientists battle air piracy on Earth before extending their heroism into the solar system, which is invaded in the third tale. The series was taken on to a galactic stage in the novels *Islands of Space* (1931; book 1956) and *Invaders from the Infinite* (1932; book 1961). This was Campbell's first venture into the nascent subgenre of space opera, juxtaposing hectic action sequences with long lectures on theoretical physics after a fashion that he was never quite able to perfect in 40 years as an author and editor, but which supplied the raw materials of hard SF. Compare Smith's *Skylark of Space,* Hamilton's *Crashing Suns* and Williamson's *Legion of Space.* (BS)

Themes: Space Opera

*II-211. **A New Dawn: The Don A. Stuart Stories**. NESFA Press, 2003.

An omnibus of the sixteen pseudonymous stories Campbell published in 1934–1939, including the classic elegiac fantasies "Twilight" and "Night"; the trilogy begun with "The Machine", which similarly investigates the possible downside of human reliance on technology; "Forgetfulness," which provides an answer to that problem in the development of new mental powers; and a fine paranoid fantasy about an alien mimic, "Who Goes There?" Far more skillfully wrought than his space operas, these stories laid the groundwork for the editorial philosophy Campbell applied to the sophistication of *Astounding;* "Forgetfulness" is the seed of that project's spoliation in the 1950s psi-boom, but the extrapolative ingenuity of "Who Goes There?" and the curious psychology of the couplet comprising "Out of Night" and "Cloak of Aesir" bore much richer and stranger fruit. (BS)

Čapek, Karel, Czechoslovakia, 1890–1938

II-212. **Krakatit**. 1925. Trans. by Lawrence Hyde. Bles, 1925.

A surreal allegory in which a young scientist who has discovered how to make the eponymous atomic explosive lets the secret slip while delirious and then must try to put the genie back in the bottle, while harassed by A. M. Daimon (the Devil). A variation on the theme of Čapek's previous novel, *Tovarno na absoluto* (1922; trans. as *The Absolute at Large*, 1927), *Krakatit* dispenses with scathing satire in favor of a more intense and intimate study of humankind's dealings with uncontrollable power. (BS)

Themes: Discoveries and Inventions

II-213. **The Makropoulos Secret**. 1922. Trans. of *Vec Makropulos* by Paul Selver. Luce, 1925.

A melodrama in which an awkward legal dispute is settled by the intervention of a woman in search of the secret recipe that has granted her extreme longevity.

When the recipe is found, the *dramatis personae* decide to destroy it, in accordance with their pessimistic philosophy—a remarkable act of intellectual vandalism. Čapek soon became aware of the sharp ideological contrast between his play and George Bernard Shaw's *Back to Methuselah*, stridently denying any direct influence. (BS)

Themes: Immortality

*II-214.   R.U.R. (Rossum's Universal Robots). 1921. Trans. by Paul Selver, Oxford Univ. Press, 1923. Unabridged trans. by Norman Comrada in *Toward the Radical Center: A Karel Čapek Reader.* Catbird Press, 1990.

A classic satirical play set in a factory where sexless artificial humans are mass-produced in order to serve as slave labor. The sophistication these "robots" gain by equipping them with emotions and "souls" leads to a revolution, which meets little resistance from a human race that has become completely sterile. The worldwide success of Fritz Lang's *Metropolis* (1926; novelization) created a link between the word *robot* and mechanical contrivance that gave the word its modern meaning but served to obscure the political and religious significance of Čapek's allegory, leading to its widespread misinterpretation as a critique of mechanization. (BS)

Themes: Politics, Satirical SF

*II-215.   War with the Newts. 1936. Recommended trans. of *Válka s Mloky* by M. and R. Weatherall. Putnam, 1939.

A masterpiece of political satire in which a race of intelligent and imitatively gifted amphibians discovered in the South Pacific are initially enslaved by humankind, but soon find a "newt Hitler" to liberate them; when they flood the planet to increase their *lebensraum* their former conquerors are doomed. Its blackly effervescent humor acquired new depths of horrid irony within two years, establishing it as a uniquely fascinating work in retrospect. Compare Norman Spinrad's *The Iron Dream.* (BS)

Themes: Politics, Satirical SF

Capon, Paul, U.K., 1911–1969

II-216.   Flight of Time. Heinemann, 1960.

YA. A Wellsian time-travel book. Four children accidentally blunder into a UFO and travel to 2260 England. Then follows a glance at futuristic cities, travel and communication, and at alterations to the country's geography. More interesting is the adventure in the past, 1960 B.C. While observing a bloody battle between two Stone Age peoples over the talisman spaceship, the children come under attack and just barely return to the present. Above average in style. (FM/SM)

Themes: Children in SF, Time Travel

Card, Orson Scott, U.S., 1951–

*II-217.   Ender's Game. Tor, 1985. Series: Ender Wiggins.

The child hero is subjected to horrific manipulation by the military in order to make him a perfect commander able to annihilate the insectile aliens who have twice attacked the solar system. Based on a Hugo Award-nominated novelette, the expanded version includes much discussion of moral propriety and undergoes a dramatic ideological shift at the end, but remains in many ways a sophisticated power fantasy. Grimly fascinating. The sequel, *Speaker for the Dead* (1986, a Hugo and Nebula Award-winner), takes off from the climactic shift in perspective to construct a very different story in which Ender becomes a more Christ-like savior. The third book in the series, *Xenocide* (1991), is most notable for a new subplot, the story of a world whose future leaders are genetically engineered for brilliance, but also for a crippling obsessive-compulsive disorder designed to limit their power. The ending of the novel is weak, shifting into wish fulfillment fantasy, The later volumes in the series, *Children of the Mind* (1996), *Ender's Shadow* (1999), *Shadow of the Hegemon* (2001), and *Shadow Puppets* (2002), also failed to achieve the excellence of the first two books, although the Shadow trilogy took the unusual tack of retelling much of Ender's story from the viewpoint of his best friend, another child soldier named Bean. *First Meetings in the Enderverse* (2003) collects the original short story version of "Ender's Game" along with several other shorter works. Another novel in the series is promised. Compare Heinlein's *Starship Troopers,* Haldeman's *Forever War,* and Dave Wolverton's *On My Way to Paradise* (1989). (ML/BS)

> Awards: Hugo, Nebula
> Themes: Coming of Age, Religion, War

*II-218.   Maps in a Mirror: The Short Fiction of Orson Scott Card. Tor, 1990.

This enormous volume, some 46 stories, represents most of Card's short fiction. Included are such well-known pieces as the award-winning "Lost Boys" and "An Eye for an Eye," "Dogwalker," "Unaccompanied Sonata," "Ender's Game," "The Originist," and "Kingsmeat." Some of the early fiction and particularly the non-science fiction is minor, but generally speaking this is an excellent collection from a controversial and important writer, who provides commentary on the stories. (ML)

> Awards: *Locus*

II-219.   Pastwatch: The Redemption of Christopher Columbus. Tor, 1996.

In the 23rd century, using a remarkable new machine called TruSite II, the scientists of Pastwatch look back through time. Focusing on Christopher Columbus, they search for ways to change the past and thus improve their own present.

The Columbus they study and eventually meet turns out to be both more and less than the man we read about in history books. A thoughtful and well-meant book, though some of the historical analysis is less than entirely convincing. Compare Connie Willis's *Doomsday Book* and J. R. Dunn's *Days of Cain*. (ML)

Themes: History in SF, Time Travel

Carmody, Isobelle, Australia, 1958–

II-220.   Obernewtyn. Puffin, 1987. Series: Obernewtyn.

YA. Humanity struggles to survive in an agrarian, post-holocaust world. Mutants called Misfits, many of whom have psychic powers, are persecuted. Elspeth has kept her psychic powers a secret but is eventually found out and taken to Obernewtyn, a legendary place where people like her are supposedly tortured but where she instead finds redemption and discovers a dark secret. With her ability to predict the future and speak with animals, Elspeth could easily be the heroine of a tale by Marion Zimmer Bradley or Andre Norton. Compare Norton's *Star Man's Son: 2250 A.D.* or any of Bradley's Darkover novels. The well-done sequels are *The Farseekers* (1990), *Ashling* (1995), and *The Keeping Place* (1999). (ML)

Themes: Holocaust and After, Mutants, Paranormal Powers

Carr, Terry, U.S., 1937–1987

II-221.   Cirque. Bobbs-Merrill, 1977.

A decadent far-future city faces a crisis that demands heroic action from some of its strange citizens. Clever and colorful, with a rich underlay of moral and metaphysical questions. Compare Bryant's *Cinnabar* for another version of the far-future *civitas solis* and Dick's *Galactic Pot-Healer* for some similar play with metaphysical anxiety. (BS)

Themes: Cities, Far Future

Carter, Angela, U.K., 1940–1992

II-222.   Heroes and Villains. Heinemann, 1969.

After the holocaust, the flame of culture and learning is kept alight by Professors guarded by Soldiers, while barbarians and mutants threaten to extinguish it. The heroine, a Professor's daughter, runs off with a barbarian and enjoys her just desserts. A strange combination of the lyrical, the ironic, and the author's usual flirtation with horrors. (BS)

Themes: Holocaust and After

*II-223.   The Infernal Desire Machines of Doctor Hoffman. Hart-Davis, 1972. U.S. title: *The War of Dreams*. Harcourt, 1974.

The hero, Desiderio, sets out to find and defeat Dr. Hoffman, whose machines are the fountainhead of troublesome illusions. His journey is an odyssey into the unconscious, where he is alternatively (sometimes simultaneously) seduced and threatened in a phantasmagoric variety of ways. A gothic black comedy, elaborating and decoding much of the erotic symbolism of fantastic fiction; a disturbing tour de force. (BS)

Themes: Machines, Psychology

II-224.   The Passion of New Eve. Gollancz, 1977.

The English hero loses himself in a decadent near-future New York, undergoes a forced sex change at the hands of sex war guerrillas, is captured by a brutal masculinist nihilist, and meets the transvestite film star who incarnated in celluloid the perfect image of feminine frailty, before floating away from the California coast as the holocaust destroys America. Wonderfully phantasmagoric. Compare Ballard's *Vermilion Sands* and *Hello America* (1981). (BS)

Themes: Absurdist SF, Sex in SF

Casanova, Giovanni Giacomo, Italy, 1725–1798

II-225.   Casanova's "Icosameron," or The Story of Edward and Elizabeth, Who Spent Eighty-One Years in the Land of the Megamicres, Original Inhabitants of Protocosmos in the Interior of the Globe. 1788. Trans. of *Icosameron ou histoire d'Édouard et d'Élisabeth qui passerent quatre vingt et un ans chez les Mégamicres habitants aborigènes du Protocosme dans l'intérieure de notre globe* by Rachel Zurer. Jenna Press, 1986.

One of the earliest and most sustained attempts to imagine an alien culture; its depiction of the society of the oviparous and hermaphroditic Megamicres—whose sensory range and processes of alimentation are also distinctive—is fascinating, although the author's commentary tends to the prolix even in this abridged version. Obviously influenced by Holberg's *Journey to the World Underground*, it also invites comparison with Foigny's *Southern Land, Known* and Flammarion's *Urania*. (BS)

Themes: Aliens, Fantastic Voyages

Cavendish, Margaret (Lucas), Duchess of Newcastle, U.K., 1623–1673

II-226.   The Description of a New World, Called the Blazing World. Appended to *Observations Upon Experimental Philosophy*. A. Maxwell, 1666. Reprinted in *An Anthology of Seventeenth Century Fiction*. Ed. Paul Salzman, Oxford Univ. Press, 1991.

A remarkable combination of proto-feminist utopia and phantasmagoric fantasy describing a world attached to ours at the pole, published as an appendix to Cavendish's critique of Robert Hooke's *Micrographia* (1666). Its commingled aspects are described by the author as "romantical," "philosophical," and "fantastical"—thus identifying a frankly chimerical nature similar to that of much early SF. The most interesting passage is that in which the Empress of the Blazing World (i.e., the Enlightenment) consults various chimerical races—bird-men, bear-men, fish-men, worm-men, etc.—that stand in for scientific special-ists, about their technologically observations of the world. Her judgments on their revelations—and of the deductions of her logicians—are ambivalent as well as unorthodox, extending into an elaborate discussion of the Cabala. The author enters into her own tale as a character, concluding with a confession of her ambition "not only to be Empress but authoress of a whole world." A unique work, seen at the time as evidence of madness but certainly not devoid of method. (BS)

Themes: Fantastic Voyages, Science Fantasy

Chadwick, P(hilip) G(eorge), U.K., 1893–1955

II-227.   The Death Guard. Hutchinson, 1939.

A vegetable species of humanoid automatons—the "Flesh Guard"—is devel-oped to defend Britain against her enemies, who are similarly developing new armaments. When World War II breaks out, the resultant orgy of destruction soon reaches horrific levels. The original edition seems to have been destroyed, probably deliberately, when the actual world war broke out; it was not reprinted until 1992. An extrapolation of the logic of such texts as Bell's *Seventh Bowl* and McIlraith and Connolly's *Invasion from the Air* to its unpleasant extreme. (BS)

Themes: War

Charnas, Suzy McKee, U.S., 1939–

*II-228.   Walk to the End of the World. Ballantine, 1974. Series: Holdfast.

In a grim, post-holocaust world, the Holdfast is a nightmarish, intensely patriar-chal society where women are treated as no more than subhuman breeders of the next generation of men. The symbolically named Alldera escapes from cap-tivity to the wilderness and a new life. In *Motherlines* (1978), she discovers a number of all-female societies, none of them utopian. Although both novels have occasional weaknesses in style and plot. they serve as a powerful indict-ment of patriarchal attitudes. The later novels in the series—*The Furies* (1994) and the Tiptree Award-winning *The Conqueror's Child* (1999)—are better written and more mature works that move beyond anger and toward tentative reconcili-ation between the sexes. Compare Sally Miller Gearhart's *The Wanderground* (1978) and contrast Tepper's *The Gate to Women's Country*. (ML)

Awards: Retrospective Tiptree
Themes: Feminist SF, Holocaust and After, Women in SF

Chayefsky, Paddy, U.S., 1923–1981

II-229.   Altered States. Hutchinson, 1978.

A first novel by a well-known movie scriptwriter, subsequently filmed. Experi-ments in hallucination induced by sensory deprivation ultimately lead the hero into a psychic and physical regression to the protohuman. An interesting development of theme from the work of John Lilly. Compare Ian Watson's *The Martian Inca* (1977). (BS)

Themes: Psychology

Cherryh, C. J. (pseud. of Carolyn Janice Cherry), U.S., 1942–

II-230.   Cuckoo's Egg. Phantasia, 1985.

A member of a cat-like race rears an unlovable alien child, training him for membership in an elite corps of judges. The child resents his status as a stranger, but ultimately learns the ways and wherefores of his situation, and that he must accept it. The cool, mannered narrative suits the theme. (BS)

Themes: Aliens, Children in SF

*II-231.   Cyteen. Warner, 1988.

The rulers of the planet Cyteen have a monopoly on the creation of Azi, the artificial human beings who have featured so prominently in such earlier Cherryh novels as *Downbelow Station* and the underrated *Forty Thousand in Gehena* (1983). They also have the rarely used ability to clone human beings. When the aging Ariane Emory, ruthless director of the planet's genetic labs and a major political figure, decides to have herself cloned, the resulting child becomes a pawn in a complex series of political manipulations. This powerful psychological study is one of Cherryh's longest novels and may be her most difficult, but there's plenty of meat here to reward the diligent reader. For a very different novel that nonetheless asks similar questions about genetic determinism, compare Levin's *The Boys from Brazil* and, for a more realistic approach, Sargent's *Cloned Lives*. (ML)

Awards: Hugo, *Locus*
Themes: Clones/Cloning, Future History, Women in SF

*II-232.   Downbelow Station. DAW, 1981. Series: Alliance-Union.

A political space opera set on the star station Pell, caught in the middle of the conflict for control of humankind's fragile interstellar empire. Complex and multifaceted, the many-sided conflict provides action and intrigue while the central characters try to construct viable personal relationships and work out careers in a fluid situation. The novel is a key work in the Alliance-Union Universe, an elaborate future history used as a background for many other novels, including *Serpent's Reach* (1980), *Merchanter's Luck* (1982), *Voyager in Night* (1984), *Angel with the Sword* (1985), and a number of other titles mentioned here. (BS/ML)

Awards: Hugo
Themes: Future History, Space Opera

II-233.   The Faded Sun: Kesrith. DAW, 1978.

The first volume in a three-part novel, completed in *The Faded Sun: Shon Jir* (1979) and *The Faded Sun: Kutath* (1980). An alien society organized somewhat in the fashion of an anthill hires out its warriors as mercenaries. But when its clients get into a war with humankind, the warriors and their kin are virtually wiped out. The client species sues for peace, but the survivors go their own way. One human involves himself with their cause and their quest to save their race. Compare Carr's *Leviathan's Deep* (1979). (BS)

Themes: Life on Other Worlds, War

*II-234.   Foreigner. DAW, 1994. Series: Foreigner.

Hundreds of years ago a starship, lost in interstellar space, abandoned its colonists in orbit around an alien world. Eventually the colonists went down to the planet, where they found the atevi, a sentient race who look humanoid but who operate under far different biological imperatives than do homo sapiens. Misunderstandings led to a history of warfare and a long, uneasy truce. Now a charismatic and far-seeing new leader has arisen among the atevi, and Bren Cameron has been chosen to be humanity's sole contact with him. If human beings are to survive on the planet, Bren must prove that he personally can survive in the midst of a violent and complex alien culture. This is superbly written, complexly plotted science fiction for adult readers. Character development is paramount. Taken as a whole the series represents Cherryh at the top of her form. Sequels include *Invader* (1995), *Inheritor* (1996), *Precursor* (1999), *Defender* (2001), and *Explorer* (2002), with more to come. (ML)

Themes: Aliens, Colonization of Other Worlds, Life on Other Worlds, Politics

II-235.   The Pride of Chanur. DAW, 1982. Series: Chanur.

The Chanur books are relatively lightweight when compared to Cherryh's major work, but they are still superior space opera. The series follows the adventures of a female starship commander in a politically corrupt, multispecies interstellar civilization. A fascinating exercise in speculative cultural anthropology, with Cherryh's usual deft and intense plotting. Sequels are *Chanur's Venture* (1984), *The Kif Strike Back* (1985), *Chanur's Homecoming* (1986), and *Chanur's Legacy* (1992). Compare Arnason's *Ring of Swords* and Walter Jon Williams's *Angel Station* (1989). (ML/BS)

Themes: Aliens, Anthropology, Space Opera

II-236.   Rimrunners. Warner, 1989. Series: Alliance-Union.

One of the strongest additions to Cherryh's fine Alliance-Union series, *Rimrunners* is the tale of tough-as-nails Bet Yeager, a soldier separated from her ship and stranded on a dying space station. Out of work, desperate, and close to starvation, Bet takes a berth on the *Loki*, nominally an enemy ship, where she must hide her past. Things turn even more difficult for her, however, when she takes as her lover the ship's scapegoat, an unstable loser with a lot of enemies on board. This is gritty, small-scale hard SF at its best. Cherryh's characters are memorable, and her portrayal of life on a warship seems very real. Other excellent novels in the Alliance-Union series include *Tripoint* (1994) and *Finity's End*

(1997). Compare Heinlein's *Starship Troopers* and Robinson's *The Dark Beyond the Stars*. (ML)

Themes: Future History, Space Opera, War, Women in SF

Chesney, (Sir) George T(omkyns), U.K., 1830–1895

II-237. **The Battle of Dorking: Reminiscences of a Volunteer**. Blackwood, 1871.

An alarmist novella swiftly reprinted as a pamphlet after its appearance in *Blackwood's Magazine*. Once the Royal Navy has been lured away, an invading German army meets as little resistance on the British mainland as Bismarck's Prussians had met when they invaded France in 1870. A strident call for military reform and rearmament, in the service of a political campaign that continued for a generation. Chesney's later contribution to *Blackwood's*, *The New Ordeal* (1879), which proposed that all-out war might be replaced by limited quasi-gladiatorial contests as a means of settling international disputes, proved far less influential. *The Battle of Dorking* is reprinted in both I. F. Clarke's anthologies of futuristic fiction and in Moorcock's similar selection, in which contexts its crucial contribution to the development of British imaginative fiction can be accurately assessed. (BS)

Themes: War

Chesterton, G(ilbert) K(eith), U.K., 1874–1936

II-238. **The Napoleon of Notting Hill**. John Lane, 1904.

An assault on the notion of progress and H. G. Wells's futurological extrapolations. Like Herbert Butterfield, the great assailant of "the Whig interpretation of history," Chesterton thought that all *necessary* progress had been achieved by Christ's crucifixion, and that the world would be better off if it had accepted and retained the goals and ideals of the medieval church. The novel's account of the decivilization of London is funnier than Chesterton's religious-allegory-cum-spy-novel, *The Man Who Was Thursday* (1908), but the tale is no less preposterous. (BS)

Themes: Future History, Satirical SF

Chiang, Ted, U.S., 1967–

II-239. **Stories of Your Life and Others**. Tor, 2002.

Since his debut story "Tower of Babylon" appeared in 1990, Chiang has been one of the most highly regarded and most consistent award-winners among the current generation of SF writers. Yet he is far from prolific; to date he has written no novel and only eight stories, all of them gathered in this collection. The stories are notable less for their style than their careful and inventive working out of complex ideas often inspired by mathematics ("Division By Zero") or the nature of language ("Story of Your Life," "Seventy-Two Letters"). His view of humanity tends to be bleak (consider his examination of prejudice in "Liking

What You See: A Documentary"), but his hopes for what can be achieved through the human intellect appear to be boundless. (PK)

Christopher, John (pseud. of Christopher Samuel Youd), U.K., 1922–

II-240.   The Death of Grass. Michael Joseph, 1956. U.S. title: *No Blade of Grass*. Simon & Schuster, 1957.

A rapidly mutating virus wipes out all of Earth's grasses, including grain crops. As mass starvation sweeps the world, a London architect leads a small family group toward a valley in the north of England where his brother has barricaded the family farm against looters and planted potatoes, which the virus spared. As they journey northward in the growing social chaos, the characters—while preserving a British stiff upper lip!—descend toward murderous savagery themselves. The story is told with convincingly realistic detail. The explicit Cain and Abel parallel at the conclusion implies that the cycle of history will resume. Filmed under its American title. For the exactly opposite situation, of too much rather than too little plant life, compare Ward Moore's *Greener Than You Think* (1947) and, more successfully, Wyndham's *Day of the Triffids*. (PC)

Themes: Disaster

II-241.   Fireball. Gollancz, 1981. Series: Fireball.

YA. Drawn into a parallel world similar to Roman Britain, Brad and Simon participate in the Bishop of London's successful revolt. When the ensuing regime promises to be repressive, the boys and two friends escape to the New World. Vintage Christopher: the terse, plausible story continues the author's investigation of various political systems and their treatment of individual rights. Sequels are *New Found Land* (1983) and *Dragon Dance* (1986), in which the friends journey to California, then China and finally an alternate world. Compare Silverberg's *The Gate of Worlds* (1967); contrast Oliver's *Mists of Dawn*. (FM)

Themes: Coming of Age, Parallel Worlds, Sociology

*II-242.   The Guardians. Hamish Hamilton, 1970.

YA. England of 2052 is divided into two parts: the Conurb, a megalopolis teeming with unrest and pacified by bread and games; and the County, where the gentry pursue a rural lifestyle. Conurban Rob flees, after the mysterious death of his father, to the County, where he is befriended by the Giffords and passed off as gentry. In the course of an uprising, Rob learns the terrifying facts of the guardians' systematic repression of all dissident elements and, giving up an opportunity to become a guardian, leaves for the Conurb to join the revolutionary movement. Tautly written; thoughtful study of the potentially evil implications of behavioral modification and mind control. Contrast Severn's *The Future Took Us*. (FM)

Themes: Coming of Age, Overpopulation, Sociology

II-243.   The Prince in Waiting. Hamish Hamilton, 1970. Series: Luke.

YA. After a series of earthquakes destroys much of civilization, England rebuilds following the pattern of medieval walled cities ruled over by the Spirits as they are interpreted by the seers. Thirteen-year-old Luke suddenly finds himself recognized when his father is selected Prince of Winchester. After his father's sudden death, Luke is forced to flee to the Sanctuary, where science and technology are preserved and augmented and the seers practice trickery to keep the people malleable. Luke also discovers that he is to be groomed to become prince of princes and reunite the cities. The first of a trilogy; the others, *Beyond the Burning Lands* (1971) and *The Sword of the Spirits* (1972), continue Luke's career as he fails at reunification through force and becomes content to wait and use peaceful means. As usual, Christopher's work features dramatic interplay and ample incidents, plus investigation of both proper use of science and technology and individual right versus society's needs. Compare Dickinson's *The Weathermonger*. (FM)

   Themes: Coming of Age, Disaster, Sociology

*II-244.   The White Mountains. Hamish Hamilton, 1967. Series: Tripod.

YA. The first volume in the Tripod trilogy about a successful invasion of Earth by aliens and the eventual triumph by humans over the invaders. The tripods consolidate their control by inserting metal communicators into the heads of all adults; thus, behavior modification is quick and brutal if need be. Will, Henry, and Jean Paul all fear the ceremony of capping that marks rites of passage and set out to join a small band of humans at the White Mountains who resist the tripods. The picture of future life in England after an alien invasion is convincing and troubling; the journey of boys is exciting and suspenseful; tripods are suggestive of Wells. In *The City of Gold and Lead* (1967), Will and Fritz enter the city of the masters to discover the nature of tripods and ascertain their vulnerabilities. *The Pool of Fire* (1968) describes the overthrow of tripods and their masters. However, an ominous note enters at the end when the various nations squabble among themselves. A prequel is *When the Tripods Came* (1988). (FM)

   Themes: Aliens, Invasion, Politics

Clarke, Arthur C., U.K., 1917–

*II-245.   Against the Fall of Night. Gnome, 1949.

Partisans are deeply divided between this early work, which first appeared in the plebeian pages of *Startling Stories*, and the completely revised and expanded version, *The City and the Stars* (Harcourt, 1956). Raw first novel versus smoother, more complex finished work; take your pick. Yes, the initial account of how lonely young Alvin finds his way from the self-satisfied stagnation of the far future city Diaspar to the pastoral community of telepaths known as Lys shows the rough carpentry of its pulp origin. But it also exemplifies in its very simplicity the archetypal quest of a youth for hidden treasure for the regeneration of humanity that is the theme of Joseph Campbell's essay in comparative mythologies, *The Hero With a Thousand Faces*. In the revision, that theme is lost in the plot's van Vogtian complexity. It may be significant that when Clarke and Gregory Benford decided upon a sequel, *Beyond the Fall of Night* (Ace, 1990), they chose to base it upon the earlier version. Note also the profound influence, on both versions, of John W. Campbell's 1934 tale "Twilight." (PC)

Themes: Coming of Age, Far Future

*II-246.   Childhood's End. Ballantine, 1953.

Earth, on the verge of nuclear Mutual Assured Destruction, is saved by the intervention of benevolent aliens who have the form of traditional devils. A calm interregnum prepares the way for the last generation of children, who are telepaths. The adults left behind watch helplessly as the children, outgrowing them as no young generation ever has before, rise up and merge with the spiritual powers of the cosmos. The influence of Olaf Stapledon, who was as formative for Clarke's generation of SF writers, at least in the U.K., as H. G. Wells, is patent. The pedestrian, at times downright static, pace of the novel has apparently not interfered with its immense popularity. Perhaps it has been received not as a story but rather as a scripture: Fallible humanity can't make it without transcendent help. If so, that says a lot about the audience for early nuclear age SF, which would have upset that era's for the most part quite hard-headed writers. (PC)

Themes: Coming of Age, Utopias

*II-247.   The Collected Stories. Tor, 2001.

Among the many classic stories in this career-spanning collection are "Rescue Party," "The Lion of Comarre," "Before Eden," "Earthlight, "The Star," "The Nine Billion Names of God," "The Sentinel," and "A Meeting with Medusa." Compare Asimov's *Complete Stories*. (ML).

II-248.   The Deep Range. Harcourt, 1957.

The Malthusian food/population crunch has been averted by domesticating and herding whales as immense cattle. If you're grounded as a spaceman, as the hero of this story is, you become a submarine-riding cowboy. After numerous vividly told adventures with a sea serpent, a giant squid, and the like, he rises to become Director of the Bureau of Whales, where he is confronted by a Buddhist leader who objects to whale killing. The Director decides that creatures as uncomfortably close to human intelligence as whales really ought not to end their days herded into slaughtering pens, a nicety that apparently did not occur to Melville even after comparable brooding about whales' deep, dark intellect. This novel was later incorporated into an omnibus volume titled *From the Ocean, From the Stars* (Harcourt, 1961), which assembled this work along with *The City and the Stars* and the collection titled *The Other Side of the Sky*. (PC)

Themes: Biology, Coming of Age

II-249. **Dolphin Island**. Holt, 1963.

YA. A story of experiments on Dolphin Island to open up more effective communication with the dolphins. Johnny Clinton, unloved runaway, discovers a special affinity with dolphins when they rescue him from a sinking hovercraft. Later, after a great storm, he uses the dolphins to surf across to the mainland to bring medical aid. Characterization of humans and the incidents are routine; what is above average is the depiction of various experiments, current and future, with dolphins, all of which assume that one day dolphins and humans will communicate freely. Compare Robert Merle's *The Day of the Dolphin* (1967). (FM/SM)

Themes: Biology, Coming of Age

*II-250. **The Fountains of Paradise**. Gollancz, 1979.

An engineer succeeds in building a space elevator connecting a tropical island (modeled on Sri Lanka, where Clarke lives, but moved for geographical convenience) to a space station in geosynchronous orbit. Imposing propaganda for high technology as the means of human progress and salvation. Charles Sheffield's *The Web Between the Worlds* (1979) develops the same premise in a more conventional fashion. (BS)

Awards: Hugo, Nebula

Themes: Hard SF, Space Flight

II-251. **Islands in the Sky**. Winston, 1952.

YA. As his prize for winning a television quiz show in the second half of the 21st century, Roy Malcolm goes to an orbiting space station. There he has adventures involving space pirates, the making of a space film, and a runaway rocket ship. The strength of the book, despite its publication date, is in the details, all plausibly explained, of the procedures of space travel and life on an orbiting station. The same thoroughness later seen in *2001: A Space Odyssey* is clearly evident. As an adventure story, routine; as an investigation into the required technology necessary for space travel, exceptional. (FM/SM)

Themes: Space Flight

II-252. **The Other Side of the Sky**. Harcourt, 1958.

These 24 tales, written between 1947 and 1957, include two series of 1,500-word mini-stories for the London *Evening Standard*, which represent Clarke's response to the challenge of writing good, terse SF for a mass readership at that time unfamiliar with the conventions of SF. Also included are "The Wall of Darkness" (1949), a fascinating variant on the boy's quest theme of *Against the Fall of Night*, with a very different outcome; "Refugee" (1955), which takes on a special poignancy in light of the subsequent history of the British royal family; and such Clarke favorites as "The Star" (Nebula, 1955), "All the Time in the World," and "The Nine Billion Names of God." The final story, "The Songs of Distant Earth," would later be developed into one of Clarke's best novels. *The*

Collected Stories of Arthur C. Clarke (2001) assembles 104 vignettes, stories, and articles published between 1939 and 1999.

*II-253.   Rendezvous with Rama. Gollancz, 1973. Series: Rama.

A vast alien spaceship passes through the solar system, using the sun's gravity to boost its velocity. Human explorers witness the brief blossoming of its artificial life system, but do not meet its makers. Ten years later, in *Rama II* (1989) by Clarke and Gentry Lee, a second spaceship repeats the maneuver and a second group of human explorers is dispatched. When the Raman ship departs the solar system, however, three of the explorers go along for the ride. In Clarke and Lee's *The Garden of Rama* (1991), by far the most successful of the two writers' several collaborations, the three humans aboard the Raman vessel spend 13 years on their journey. Not expecting to see Earth again, they settle in, have babies, and explore in much greater depth. They also meet other alien residents of the vessel, though not the Ramans themselves. Eventually reaching a gigantic space station, they learn much more about the Ramans, though enough mysteries remain to provide material for the final book in the series, *Rama Revealed* (1993). Compare Niven's *Ringworld* and Shaw's *Orbitsville* for similarly charismatic artifacts. (ML/BS)

Awards: Hugo, Nebula, John W. Campbell

Themes: Aliens, Robots, Space Flight

*II-254.   2001: A Space Odyssey. New American Library, 1968. Series: 2001.

A novelization of the Stanley Kubrick film partly based on the short story "The Sentinel." Alien monoliths mysteriously influence human evolution and entice a space mission into the outer solar system, where the computer HAL breaks down and the lone survivor undergoes a psychedelic encounter with strangeness: a symbolic transcendence of the human condition. In the sequel, *2010: Odyssey Two* (1982), a joint Russian/American expedition to Jupiter resurrects HAL and discovers life on Europa; then the intelligence controlling the monoliths of *2001* begins to move in its characteristically mysterious way, sending a messiah to Earth to save humankind and issuing a new commandment forbidding access to Europa. The combination of technological realism and awed mysticism works as well in these novels as anywhere else in Clarke's work, and the religious imagery is even more pronounced than in *Childhood's End*. Significantly less successful are *2061: Odyssey Three* (1988), which describes events after a human spacecraft accidentally crashes on Europa, and *3001: The Final Odyssey* (1997), in which astronaut Frank Poole, who supposedly died in the first volume, is brought back to life and taken on a tour of the future. *Time's Eye* (2004), co-authored with Stephen Baxter, is tangentially related to the Odyssey series. Compare Gregory Benford and Gordon Eklund's *If the Stars Are Gods* (1977) and Wilson's *The Harvest*. (BS/ML)

Themes: Aliens, Computers, Intelligence, Religion

Clarke, Joan B., U.K., 1921–

II-255.   The Happy Planet. Cape, 1963.

YA. A post-catastrophe story. Three future societies are contrasted: the Tuanians, descendants of the Getaways who left before the great destruction, are a technologically advanced, highly regimented people; the Hombods, descending from holocaust survivors, have established a semipastoral life that may make Earth a "happy planet"; and the Dredfooters, descended from cyborgs, attempt to prey on the Hombods. A Tuanian attempt to investigate Earth's utility is thwarted, and the planet is spared the joyless, rationalistic life of Tuan. Although a relatively thoughtful study of possible societies, its excessive length may hamper enjoyment. (FM/SM)

Themes: Holocaust and After, Pastoral

Claudy, Carl H(arry), U.S., 1879–1957

II-256.   The Mystery Men of Mars. Grosset and Dunlap, 1933. Series: Adventures in the Unknown.

YA. A serial from *American Boy*, an abridged reprint of which appeared as "The Master Minds of Mars" in Lester del Rey's anthology *The Year After Tomorrow*, alongside a version of the dimensional fantasy *Land of No Shadow* (1933). The Martian life forms that capture the heroes and their mentor are a curious compound of Wellsian images, fusing the Martians of *The War of the Worlds* with the Selenites of *The First Men in the Moon*, and the pulpish zest of the plot is offset by such motifs as the professor's use of mathematics in proving that humans are intelligent beings. Claudy's series is much better than its model, the Great Marvel series by Howard Garis. (BS)

Themes: Life on Other Worlds, Space Flight

Clemens, Samuel L. *see* Twain, Mark

Clement, Hal (pseud. of Harry Clement Stubbs), U.S., 1922–2003

II-257.   Close to Critical. Ballantine, 1964.

One of the subtlest of Clement's far-out planetary environments, narrated rather dryly but with flashes of understated humor. The title refers to the temperature at which water hovers between liquid and gaseous phases, at 800 atmospheres on the planet's surface. Fire is a gift from an Earth expedition orbiting the planet. The reader will need a smattering of physical chemistry to fully understand this; better to read *Iceworld* before tackling this one. (PC)

Themes: Hard SF, Life on Other Worlds

II-258.   Cycle of Fire. Ballantine, 1957.

Earthman and alien make their way across a planet whose conditions are at the absolute tolerable limits for each. The Earthman wants to rescue the alien, but the alien wishes to die at the ritually appropriate time with its people. They feel and think their way with true Clementian logic toward an understanding of each other's radically different cultural and personal points of view. Compare Forward's *Rocheworld* (1990) and Benford's *Tides of Light* (1989). (PC)

Themes: Hard SF, Life on Other Worlds

II-259.   Iceworld. Gnome, 1953.

YA. "Iceworld" is the Earth, from the viewpoint of a being that breathes gaseous sulfur and occasionally drinks molten copper chloride. Aliens based on the hot side of Mercury trade with terrestrial "savages" worthless chunks of platinum and gold in exchange for the illegal drug "tofacco." An alien survives on the Earth and has adventures with a human family. The explanatory science isn't obtrusive, and this would make an excellent story with which to introduce an inquisitive, science-minded teenager to "hard" SF. (PC)

Themes: Aliens, Hard SF

*II-260.   Mission of Gravity. Doubleday, 1954.

This 1953 serial was accompanied by an article, "Whirligig World," reprinted in some later editions, in which Clement described how he concocted the planet on which the story takes place. It is an accurate description of the way in which writers like Clement work: get the science right and it will drive the plot. But this is also a first-rate story of First Contact between explorers from Earth and a most unhuman sentient native species, to the benefit of both, rejecting the cliché one still sees in movie and TV SF that alienness equals evil. Clement stated that this novel was his personal philosophical bottom line, and the novel deserves a careful reading not only for its scientific ingenuity but also for the working out of that philosophy. A major work. The sequel is *Star Light* (1971). Compare Forward's *Dragon's Egg* and Anderson's *The Enemy Stars*. *The Essential Hal Clement* (NESFA), volume 1: *Trio for Slide Rule and Typewriter* (1999) is an omnibus that collects *Needle* (1950), *Iceworld*, and *Close to Critical*. Volume 2, *Music of Many Spheres* (2000), collects 17 short stories; volume 3, *Variations on a Theme By Isaac Newton* (2000) collects *Mission of Gravity, Star Light*, two stories, and an article; all the "Mesklin" writings. (PC)

Themes: Hard SF, Life on Other Worlds

Clifton, Mark, U.S., 1906–1963

II-261.   The Science Fiction of Mark Clifton. Ed. by Barry Malzberg and Martin H. Greenberg. Southern Illinois Univ. Press, 1980.

In the earliest of these 11 stories, 1952–1962, "What Have I Done?," alien visitors made over to pass as humans are thereby psychically destroyed; in the last, Earth astronauts on Mars, after starting a nuclear experiment that will wipe out the indigenous Martians, leave behind a space suit, "the image of a man stuffed with straw." Between the bleakness of these two, the author's first and last published stories, Clifton more optimistically functioned as one of John Campbell's psi-writers of the 1950s, apparently from a belief that latent paranormal powers exist and might emerge in a new generation, possibly even in SF fans. Compare Clifton and Riley's *They'd Rather Be Right*. (PC)

II-262. **They'd Rather Be Right** with Frank Riley (U.S., ?). Gnome, 1957.

Serialized in *Astounding* at the height of Campbell's emphasis on paranormal powers, at a time when the potential of the computer was just beginning to be grasped, this novel combines these two concepts. "Bossy," the first supercomputer, not only computes but also heals humans (an echo here of Dianetics?) and develops their "psi" powers. Such talents, perceived as evil by the media, trigger a witch hunt. The only solution is to give "Bossy" to the world, rather than the presumable alternative of exploiting it as a private property of its inventor and its financial backer. A subtext of the necessity of freedom for scientific research, as against the Cold War fetish of "security," a favorite target of 1950s SF. Compare Bester's *The Stars My Destination* and Robinson's *The Power*. (PC)

Themes: Discoveries and Inventions, Paranormal Powers

Clingerman, Mildred (McElroy), U.S., 1918–1997

II-263. **A Cupful of Space**. Ballantine, 1961.

Sixteen stories from genre and mainstream sources, all laden with charm, a word not usually descriptive of SF. In the 1950s, they constituted one of the bridges away from the pulp tradition. Aliens mingle happily with kids on Halloween in "The Word," and other aliens decide to spare Earth after interviewing a color-blind elderly lady who doesn't mind their being green. Time-travel stories as deft as "Mr. Sakrison's Halt" and "The Day of the Green Velvet Cloak" certainly deserve to be remembered, and in "A Red Heart and Blue Roses" Clingerman showed she could also write quiet, non-splattering, but quite hair-raising horror. (PC)

Clouston, J(oseph) Storer, U.K., 1870–1944

II-264. **Button Brains**. Jenkins, 1933.

A comedy about a robot that is continually mistaken for its human model, with farcical consequences. It is solidly set in the tradition of F. Anstey's comic fantasies, which Jenkins carried forward steadfastly. Clouston wrote two other marginal SF stories in the same light-hearted vein, but *The Man in Steel* (1939) is a darker and more thoughtful timeslip romance. (BS)

Themes: Humorous SF

Clowes, W(illiam) Laird, U.K., 1856–1905

II-265. **The Great Peril, and How It Was Averted**. Black and White, 1893.

A mild social satire in which a technology of thought control is among various dirty tricks employed to fight a future election campaign. Although calculatedly silly, the plot proved oddly prophetic, not only in its anticipation of the role that advertising would come to play in future politics but also in its description of the technique of "pyramid [multi-level] selling." As was the case with many writers of the period, Clowes was a journalist and military historian recruited to scientific romance via future-war fiction, including the Chesneyesque *The Great Naval War of 1887* (1887) and *The Captain of the "Mary Rose"* (1892). (BS)

Themes: Humorous SF, Politics

Clute, John, Canada/U.K., 1940–

II-266.   Appleseed. Orbit, 2001; Tor, 2002.

The first SF novel by one of the most acute of science fiction's critics, this is a book that revels in the genre's most baroque and amazing space operatic wonders. Written in a complex, allusive prose full of covert and overt references to other works, most notably *The Wizard of Oz*, the legend of King Arthur, and the Book of Genesis, it tells of a space trader hired to take an alien passenger to an unknown planet. In a universe crowded with aliens and artificial intelligences, but under threat from a strange disease, plaque, this journey proves to be the first move in a war against God (who turns out to be a grotesque self-eating alien). A sequel is promised. For the space opera, compare Greenland's *Take Back Plenty* and Harrison's *Light*; for the war against God, compare Pullman's *His Dark Materials* (1995). (PK)

Themes: Aliens, Computers, Intelligence, Linguistics, Religion, Space Opera

Coates, Robert M(yron), U.S., 1897–1973

II-267.   The Eater of Darkness. Contact, 1926.

A conspicuously avant-garde novel executed in accordance with the surrealist manifesto and formulated as a parody of popular thrillers featuring scientific supercriminals (e.g., Holt-White's *The Man Who Stole the Earth* and MacClure's *Ark of the Covenant*). The chapter in which the villain explains his inventions is a merciless parody of pulp science-fictional exposition, while the sequence in which the hero is glad to assist the mad scientist in wiping out New York's literary critics is obviously heartfelt. (BS)

Themes: Humorous SF

Cobban, J(ames) MacLaren, U.K., 1849–1903

II-268.   Master of his Fate. Blackwood, 1890.

A story inspired by Stevenson's *Strange Case of Dr Jekyll and Mr Hyde*, whose tormented central character employs a method of transferring "animal magnetism" between individuals to rejuvenate himself continually at the expense of others. An interesting thriller prefiguring late 20th-century accounts of "vampire existentialism." (BS)

Themes: Discoveries and Inventions

Coblentz, Stanton A(rthur), U.S., 1896–1982

II-269.   The Sunken World. FPCI, 1948.

A utopian satire featuring the submerged civilization of Atlantis, first published in *Amazing Stories Quarterly* in 1928. The protagonist, a castaway submariner, finds Atlantean society congenial but bland; his account of the surface world persuades the local Party of Emergence of the folly of their cause, but the Atlanteans are overtaken by disaster anyway. Coblentz went on to write a great deal more satirical SF, whose quality ebbed away by degrees, eventually attaining abysmal depths; the better examples include *After 12,000 Years* (1929; book 1950) and *In Caverns Below* (1935; 1957 as *Hidden World*; original title restored 1975). (BS)

Themes: Satirical SF, Utopias

Cole, Robert William, U.K., ?

II-270.   The Struggle for Empire: A Story of the Year 2236. Elliot Stock, 1900.

The technologically advanced world of 2236, dominated by the Anglo-Saxon Federal Union, has colonized the worlds of many neighboring stars but comes into conflict with another burgeoning interstellar empire based on the Sirian world of Kairet. War breaks out and the bloody devastation wrought by its battles in space is graphically described. Earth is on the brink of destruction when the tide is turned by the invention of a new superweapon. This pioneering exercise is one of the great lost texts of SF; it attracted no attention at the time and has never been reprinted, although it is recognizable in retrospect as the first space opera. It is much harsher in its outlook and calculations than similar pulp romances of the 1920s and 1930s. Compare and contrast Smith's Skylark and Lensman series and Campbell's Arcot, Morey and Wade series. (BS)

Themes: Future History, Galactic Empires

Collier, John, U.K., 1901–1980

II-271.   Tom's a-Cold. Macmillan, 1933.

A novel of post-catastrophe primitivism, reprinted in the U.S. as *Full Circle*. Although tribal elders are struggling to preserve the last fugitive relics of the heritage of civilization, their attempt is doomed; survival now depends on very different qualities. Less celebratory in its attitude to this prospect than Jefferies's *After London*, this is nevertheless a key item in the British tradition of ambivalent catastrophe novels. Compare Wright's *Deluge* and the final chapters of Cicely Hamilton's *Theodore Savage*. (BS)

Themes: Holocaust and After

Compton, D(avid) G(uy), U.K., 1930–

*II-272.   The Continuous Katherine Mortenhoe. Gollancz, 1974. U.S. title: *The Unsleeping Eye*. DAW, 1974.

In a world from which pain and disease have been banished, the heroine contracts a terminal illness and has to cope with the intense media interest her condition provokes. Her attempts to hide come to nothing when a reporter with cameras implanted in his eyes wins her confidence, but he becomes bitterly disillusioned with his mission. Brilliantly filmed in France as *Death Watch*, under which title it was once reprinted. One of the finest examples of the SF novel. A 1979 sequel, *Windows*, further develops the reporter's crisis of conscience; he has his camera-eyes put out but ironically makes himself the object of the same kind of curiosity to which he once pandered. Contrast Silverberg's more stylized and hyperbolic *Thorns*. (BS)
   Themes: Medicine

II-273.   The Electric Crocodile. Hodder & Stoughton, 1970. U.S. title: *The Steel Crocodile*. Ace, 1970.

Two workers at a secret research institute act as agents for a dissident group, but ultimately cannot oppose the claustrophobic conservatism that has sterilized both scientific and moral progress. Subtle and very convincing. Compare Kate Wilhelm's "April Fool's Day Forever" (1970). (BS)
   Themes: Scientists and Engineers

II-274.   Synthajoy. Hodder & Stoughton, 1968.

A machine is developed that can record emotional experiences for later transmission into the minds of others. Abused by its inventor, it is subsequently used in the psychiatric treatment of his wife and murderer. Intricately constructed, with fine characterization and compelling cynicism. Compare Malzberg's *Cross of Fire*. (BS)
   Themes: Machines, Psychology

Condon, Richard (Thomas), U.S., 1915–

II-275.   The Manchurian Candidate. McGraw-Hill, 1959.

A Korean War Medal of Honor winner is "brainwashed" by his Communist captors into becoming an assassin, with a U.S. presidential election at stake; he is to be activated by post-hypnotic suggestion. The plan backfires as right-wing elements in America contrive that the assassination of a presidential nominee will throw the country into the hands of their own hawkish vice-presidential candidate, whose fiery speech immediately after his running mate's death will, they hope, precipitate World War III. Powerfully and convincingly told. After the assassination of President Kennedy in 1963 and the controversy it generated, the film based on the novel was withdrawn from distribution; one could say that this was a dreadful instance of life imitating science fiction. Compare Knebel and Bailey, *Seven Days in May*. (PC)
   Themes: Politics, Psychology

Conrad, Joseph, Poland/U.K, 1856–1924

II-276.   The Inheritors: An Extravagant Story. Heinemann, 1901 (in collaboration with Ford Madox Hueffer, subsequently known as Ford Madox Ford, U.K., 1873–1939).

A study of moral and political corruption in which two of the quasi-satanic agents claim to be inhabitants of the Fourth Dimension (not so much a parallel world displaced therein as a future with which the present is already pregnant). The Dimensionists are the heirs apparently destined to supplant contemporary humankind. Contrast the ebullience with which Clowes's *The Great Peril* contemplates a similar degeneration of political affairs. (BS)
Themes: Politics

Constantine, Murray (pseudonym of Katharine Penelope Burdekin), U.K., 1896–1963

II-277.   Proud Man. Boriswood, 1934.

Three exemplary individuals in contemporary London are studied and interrogated by a hermaphrodite visitor from the far future who is anxious to understand the mysteries of sexuality and their social corollaries. A fascinating intellectual exercise, more closely akin to Olaf Stapledon's *Last Men in London* than Grant Allen's *The British Barbarians*. It anticipates the use of science fiction as an exploratory medium by modern lesbian feminists. Burdekin probably adopted the new pseudonym because of negative publicity generated by her pacifist novel *The Quiet Ways* (1930), although modern reprints of this and the following item restore her real name. (BS)
Themes: Sex in SF

*II-278.   Swastika Night. Gollancz, 1937.

Burdekin's masterpiece is the most striking of all novels describing a Nazi-dominated Europe—all the more impressive for having been written before the outbreak of World War II—in which the establishment of a mystical religion of fascism associated with a radical differentiation of the social roles of men and women has had drastic physical and political consequences. It has something of the surreal quality of Sarban's *The Sound of His Horn*, although it has a robust plot centered on ideological and actual rebellion. (BS)
Themes: Future History

Constantine, Storm, U.K., 1956–

II-279.   The Enchantments of Flesh and Spirit: The First Book of Wraeththu. Macdonald, 1987. Series: Wraeththu.

Civilization is on the skids and technology is in decline. A spontaneous mutation occurs all over the world producing the Wraeththu, hermaphrodites with psionic powers and an affinity for down-and-dirty, punk lifestyles. Humanity's natural enemy, the Wraeththu soon overcome our species, but then engage in violent confrontations with each other in an attempt to achieve dominance.

There are many logical problems with the Wraeththu books of a sort calculated to annoy the traditional SF reader, but the series succeeds on the strength of Constantine's somewhat decadent prose style, her powerful depiction of character, and her frequent and unusually graphic portrayal of some very strange sex. The Wraeththu trilogy was completed by *The Bewitchments of Love and Hate* (1988) and *The Fulfillments of Fate and Desire* (1989). A new series, the Wraeththu Histories, begins with *The Wraiths of Will and Pleasure* (2003) and continues with *The Shades of Time and Memory* (2004). Compare Hand's *Winterlong* and its sequels; contrast Doris Lessing's *The Fifth Child* (1988). (ML)

   Themes: Mutants, Paranormal Powers, Sex in SF

Cook, William Wallace, U.S., 1867–1933

II-280.   Adrift in the Unknown. Street and Smith, 1908.

A satirical novel serialized in *Argosy* in 1904–1905, featuring an expedition to Mercury undertaken by a party of millionaires and their hireling scientist, as recorded by a criminal stowaway. Cook was an amazingly prolific contributor of tongue-in-cheek SF to the pulp magazines in the 1900s, his work anticipating the more politically inclined SF novels of George Allan England and the satirical SF of Homer Eon Flint and Stanton Coblentz. (BS)

   Themes: Humorous SF, Life on Other Worlds

II-281.   A Round Trip to the Year 2000; or, A Flight Through Time. Street and Smith, 1908.

A mock-Wellsian extravaganza serialized in *Argosy* in 1903 and reprinted in a pioneering paperback format decades ahead of its time. It launched Cook's brief but hectic career in pulp scientific romance, whose abrupt termination before the advent of the SF pulps is regrettable. Miscellaneous time travelers attracted by the roundness of the target date gather in a future New York dominated by Trusts which charge for all the necessities of life, although the edge is taken off their exploitation by the use of humanoid automata ("muglugs") as slave labor. Wonderfully extravagant, anticipating England's *The Air Trust* and Čapek's *R.U.R.* as well as pulp SF "time operas." The belated sequel *Castaways of the Year 2000* (*Argosy* 1912–1913) was never reprinted. (BS)

   Themes: Humorous SF, Time Travel

Cousin de Grainville, Jean-Baptiste François Xavier, France, 1746–1805

II-282.   The Last Man. 1805. Recommended trans. of *Le dernier homme* by I. F. and M. Clarke. Wesleyan Univ. Press, 2002.

A ground-breaking apocalyptic fantasy first translated into English in an unacknowledged version published as *The Last Man; or, Omegarus and Syderia: A Romance in Futurity* (1806). Charles Nodier saw it through to publication when Cousin died. Although primarily a religious fantasy mirroring and transfiguring

Biblical themes—especially the allegory of the Fall—its image of the future takes shrewd account of technological and social progress as well as Malthusian anxieties about their unsustainability and the pessimistic theory of historical cyclicity developed in Volney's *Les ruines, ou Méditations sur les révolutions des empires*, 1791. It is more interesting in this respect than Mary Shelley's *The Last Man* and is intriguingly echoed in the climax of Camille Flammarion's *Omega*. (BS)

Themes: End of the World

Corlett, William, U.K., 1938–

II-283.   Return to the Gate. Bradbury, 1977. Series: Gate.

YA. This conclusion to a trilogy dramatizing growth in self-knowledge and the necessity of risking friendship—the highly praised *The Gate of Eden* (1975) and *The Land Beyond* (1976) being the other segments—takes place in a not-too-distant future of violent social disintegration and painful rebuilding. The focus is on old age and its natural, although often unrealized, alliance with youth. The visionary is subordinate, but the portrait of love's insistence on no conditions is memorable for its lyrical terseness and allusiveness. Compare L'Engle's *A Wrinkle in Time*, where unconditional love is also demanded and the young and old are allies. (FM)

Themes: Coming of Age, Sociology

Cowper, Richard (pseud. of John Middleton Murry, Jr.), U.K., 1926–2002

II-284.   The Custodians, and Other Stories. Gollancz, 1976.

The first of Cowper's collections, followed in Britain by *The Web of the Magi and Other Stories* (1980) and *The Tithonian Factor and Other Stories* (1984); the U.S. collection, *Out There Where the Big Ships Go* (1980), combines materials from the first two. Cowper displays a poetic style and an unusual delicacy of touch in featuring encounters between his characters and the speculative situations in which they are placed. He frequently builds tragic images of people dehumanized by technophilia and the lust for power. "The Custodians" is one such lament for lost sanity. (BS).

II-285.   The Road to Corlay. Gollancz, 1978. Series: Bird of Kinship.

The first of three novel-length sequels to the fine novella, "Piper at the Gates of Dawn," which deals with the revival of a heretical cult in a post-holocaust Britain dominated by oppressive religious orthodoxy. The cult, organized around the symbol of the White Bird of Kinship, enjoys the advantage that its most talented members can invoke and use a paranormal empathy, often associated with music. In *A Dream of Kinship* (1981), the cult has been transformed by the passing of centuries into an alternative orthodoxy, but in *A Tapestry of Time* (1982) it undergoes a further renewal. These lyrical books affirm the author's conviction that it is spiritual rather than technological development that truly constitutes human progress. U.S. editions include "Piper at the Gates of Dawn" as a prelude. Compare Le Guin's *Always Coming Home.* (BS/ML)

Themes: Holocaust and After, Religion

Crichton, Michael, U.S., 1942–

II-286.   The Andromeda Strain. Knopf, 1969.

A satellite returns to Earth harboring a deadly plague, and worldwide catastrophe is narrowly averted. Realistic and suspenseful, this was made into an effective film. *The Terminal Man* (1972) is similar in its convincing handling of technical matters, though a number of Crichton's later novels, such as *Timeline* (1999) and *Prey* (2002), are less effective. (BS/ML)

Themes: Aliens, Invasion, Medicine

II-287.   Jurassic Park. Knopf, 1990.

A wealthy industrialist bankrolls an attempt to re-create dinosaurs using Cray computers, the latest in gene-sequencing technology, and DNA recovered from prehistoric insects trapped in amber. Succeeding, he builds a glorified theme park to house them. But, just as the park is about to open, things begin to go wrong and the dinosaurs break loose. Although somewhat predictable, the novel is tremendous fun. It's also much more intelligent than viewers of the Spielberg film might be led to believe. A sequel, *The Lost World,* appeared in 1995 and was also made into a film. Compare Larry Niven's *Dream Park* (1981). (ML)

Themes: Clones/Cloning, Genetic Engineering

Cromie, Robert, Ireland, 1856–1907

II-288.   A Plunge into Space. Warne, 1890.

A Vernian interplanetary novel—whose second edition carried an introduction by Verne—making use of a gravity-neutralizing technology to effect a trip to Mars. The story is more melodramatic than the general run of Vernian romances, especially in its climax, but the mildly satirical description of Martian society is a conventional utopia. Antigravity technologies had previously been deployed in similar romances by "Chrysostom Trueman" and Percy Greg, but Cromie was incensed when H. G. Wells employed Cavorite in *The First Men in the Moon,* accusing him of theft. (BS)

Themes: Space Flight, Utopias

Cross, John Kier, U.K., 1914–1967

*II-289.   The Angry Planet. Peter Lunn, 1945.

YA. Three children stow away on an experimental rocket ship bound for Mars. There they encounter the Beautiful People, who are mobile plant life, and the Terrible Ones, ugly mushroom-like plants. In spite of their best efforts, the humans and the Beautiful People are overcome in battle, the rocket crew barely managing to escape. Finally, a volcanic explosion seemingly terminates all Martian life. A British book influenced by Wells and one of the very first SF mainstream novels, it precedes even *Rocket Ship Galileo*. Use of journal device for a multiple perspective provides effective change of mood and narrative pace. Careful, speculative discussion of possible life on Mars. Compare Carl Claudy's *The Mystery Men of Mars* (1933). Sequel: *The Red Journey Back* (1954). (FM/SM)

Themes: Space Opera, The Planets

Crowley, John, U.S., 1942–

II-290.   Beasts. Doubleday, 1976.

In a balkanized near-future America, various outsiders, including hybrid beast-men left over from an experiment in genetic engineering, resist the recentralization of authority. Displays the same romantic nostalgia as Crowley's other work but in a less expansive fashion. (BS)

Themes: Genetic Engineering

II-291.   Engine Summer. Doubleday, 1979.

In a far-future America returned to agrarian primitivism by disaster, the hero has recorded for future generations the story of his youthful quest for enlightenment. Beautifully written and eloquently argued; it can be appreciated even by those who lack sympathy with the ideology behind its Arcadian romanticism. Compare Le Guin's *Always Coming Home*. (BS)

Themes: Disaster, Far Future

II-292.   Novelty. Doubleday, 1989.

This collection contains four stories: the novella "Great Work of Time" and three shorter pieces—"In Blue," "Novelty," and "The Nightingales Sing at Night." "Great Work of Time," winner of the 1990 World Fantasy Award and the centerpiece of the book, is an alternate history story in which Cecil Rhodes, founder of Rhodesia, also set up the Otherhood, a secret society of time travelers whose purpose is to preserve the British Empire. Thanks to their meddling, England wins World War I without help and dominates the world to this day. Eventually, however, the Otherhood discovers that its present course will lead to disaster and that, to save the Earth, the Empire must fall. Crowley is one of science fiction's finest stylists and these stories are a delight. *Novelties and Souvenirs* (2004) combines the contents of Crowley's earlier collection with later, uncollected stories. Compare Michael Flynn's *In the Country of the Blind* (1990) and Poul Anderson's *Time Patrol* (1991). (ML)

Themes: Alternate Worlds, Time Travel

Cummings, Ray(mond King), U.S., 1887–1957

II-293.   Brigands of the Moon. McClurg, 1931.

A hectic account of an interplanetary battle for control of the Moon's radium deposits, serialized in *Astounding* in 1930. It poses as a contemporary adventure story written in the late 21st century—one of Cummings's more enterprising devices—but is otherwise typical action-adventure SF. The pretense is abandoned in the sequel, *Wandl, the Invader* (1932; book 1961), which is distinguished by its elaborate use of explanatory footnotes. (BS)

Themes: Space Flight

II-294.   The Girl in the Golden Atom. Methuen, 1922.

A novel that combines the novelette that boldly took microcosmic romance beyond worlds-within-water-drops observed in microscopes into the mysterious spaces within the atom—first published in *All-Story* in 1919—with its sequel, "People of the Golden Atom" (1920). The narrative format is borrowed from H. G. Wells's *The Time Machine*, the Time Traveller being replaced by a Chemist who has developed a drug that will shrink him sufficiently to deliver him into a world contained within an atom in a wedding ring. Once there, his adventures switch into the pattern popularized by Edgar Rice Burroughs. A belated sequel, *The Man Who Mastered Time* (1924; book, 1929), reverted to Wells's original theme, recasting the Time Traveller's adventure in a Burroughsian vein. (BS)

Themes: Fantastic Voyages

Cyrano de Bergerac, Savinien, France, 1619–1655

*II-295.   Other Worlds: The Comic History of the States and Empires of the Moon and the Sun. 1657–1662. Recommended trans. of *L'autre monde* by Geoffrey Strachan. Oxford Univ. Press, 1963.

Although fragmentary translations were made from corrupted French versions in the 17th century, it was not until manuscript versions surfaced in France that Richard Aldington was able to issue the first proper translations of the surviving texts of Cyrano's satires as *Voyages to the Moon and Sun* (Routledge, 1923). Although the author apparently completed a trilogy, the greater part of the second volume and all of the third (*The History of the Spark*) have been lost. Written at a time when it was still dangerous to challenge the authority of the Church on the matter of the Copernican theory of the solar system, Cyrano's bold freethought and scathing satire were sufficiently controversial to invite suppression. The texts are the most exuberant and skeptical contributions to the rich tradition of lunar satires, and significantly influenced the method of Jonathan Swift's *Gulliver's Travels*. (BS)

Themes: Fantastic Voyages, Satirical SF

Daniel, Tony, U.S., 1963–

II-296.   Metaplanetary. Tor, 2001.

In the far future, a gigantic system of cables and space habitats called the Met hangs between the planets of the inner solar system, housing billions of human beings and artificial intelligences, far more than now live on Earth. Society has prospered like never before in history, but the culture of the outer planets has strayed from what the people of the Met consider normal and war seems immi-

nent. This is sophisticated, large-scale space opera with some startling technological innovations. The sequel, *Superluminal* (2004), is taken up almost entirely
with space warfare. Compare Walter Jon Williams's *The Praxis*; contrast Charles
Stross's more ironic take on space warfare in *Singularity Sky*. (ML)

Themes: Computers, Intelligence, The Planets, Space Opera, War

Dann, Jack, U.S./Australia, 1945–

II-297.   The Man Who Melted. Bluejay, 1984.

A man searches for his lost wife in a world where social order has been torn
apart by outbreaks of hysterical collective consciousness, which have spawned a
new religiosity and an epidemic of schizophrenia. An ironic reconstruction of
the voyage of the *Titanic* is featured in the plot. Aggressively decadent, with a
hint of Jacobean tragedy. Compare Zelazny's *Dream Master*. (BS)

II-298.   The Memory Cathedral. Bantam, 1995.

Although he began his career as an SF writer, much of Dann's recent work has
been in the mainstream. *The Memory Cathedral* creates an interesting intersection between his genre and non-genre work. Much of the book is straight and
extraordinarily well-done historical fiction, but it gradually moves into the
realm of secret history, when the protagonist, Leonardo da Vinci, actually
builds and tests a flying machine and other marvelous inventions. Contrast Paul
McAuley's more explicitly science-fictional *Pasquale's Angel*. (ML).

Themes: History in SF, Machines

II-298A.   The Rebel. Morrow, 2004.

In this subtle, beautifully done alternate history, James Dean survives his 1955
automobile accident and goes on to live a rich and varied life. After a major
career as an actor and director, he becomes a liberal activist and eventually runs
for political office. Dann does a wonderful job of developing Dean's character,
never denying the actor's tendency toward self-destructive behavior, but believably extrapolating that behavior into mature adulthood. Marilyn Monroe, Elvis
Presley, Ronald Reagan, and a host of other Hollywood and California characters make cameo appearances, but there's real depth to this novel. Compare
Priest's *The Separation* or Dann's own *The Memory Cathedral*. (ML)

Themes: Alternate worlds, Politics

Danvers, Dennis, U.S., 1947–

II-299.   The Fourth World. Avon Eos, 2000.

Although science fiction writers run a political gamut from left to right wing,
relatively few devote their careers to explicitly didactic fiction, with Mack
Reynolds, Kim Stanley Robinson, Ken MacLeod, and Danvers being the most
obvious exceptions on the left. *The Fourth World* concerns Santee St. John, a
jaded American journalist hired as a living camera for the Web-based NewsReal.
When St. John records the massacre of an Indian town in Chiapas, Mexico, by

disguised government troops, however, he is outraged to discover that his network will not air the story. St. John soon finds himself working for the doomed Zapatistas and eventually learns that far worse secrets are being covered up by corporate America. In another explicitly leftist SF novel, *The Watch* (2002), Danvers transports the great anarchist philosopher Peter Kropotkin to 20th-century America. (ML)

Themes: Fantastic Voyages, Politics, Satirical SF, Sociology

Davidson, Avram, U.S., 1923–1993

II-300.   The Best of Avram Davidson. Ed. by Michael Kurland. Doubleday, 1979.

Eleven stories and a book chapter, from 1956 to 1971. Editor Kurland's short, sarcastic introduction reminds us that academicians seek to "classify" a magnificently unorganized writer like Davidson at their peril. Some tales are conventional SF; as for the others, if they are as good as "King's Evil" and "The Golem," does it really matter whether they are SF or fantasy? Peter Beagle, a student of Davidson during that writer's brief (and quite ungovernable) sojourn as a college professor, testifies in a foreword to Davidson's incredible, casual erudition; Davidson himself wrote a modest afterword. *Or All the Seas With Oysters* (Berkley, 1962) contains the Hugo-winning title story. *The Avram Davidson Treasury* (1998) collects 38 stories, each introduced by a different author. (PC)

II-301.   Joyleg (with Ward Moore, U.S., 1903–1978). Pyramid, 1962.

The recent political exploitation of fraud, real and imagined, in government entitlements is topped by this saga of a war veteran in the Tennessee foothills who has been drawing a government pension for as far back as records exist, and is in fact a veteran of the American Revolutionary War. A congressional committee, media reporters, "revenuers," even the ubiquitous Soviets turn up in the vicinity of Issachar Joyleg's moonshine still, whose product dispenses rejuvenating powers. A trunkful of undeniably authentic Revolution-era papers gives Joyleg the upper hand. Social satire, allied to the best of the "Li'l Abner" comic strip tradition (before its creator went sour and conservative), aimed at targets that perennially deserve ridicule, and good clean fun. (PC)

Themes: Immortality, Satirical SF

Davy, Sir Humphry, U.K., 1778–1829

II-302.   Consolations in Travel; or, The Last Days of a Philosopher. John Murray, 1830.

Davy's last book consists of a series of meditative dialogues reflecting on a cosmic vision that imagines life as a series of incarnations—some of them in radically alien biospheres, including the surface of Saturn and the heads of comets—in which the soul has the opportunity to ascend (or slip back down) a Creationist scale of moral perfection. Possibly influenced by Louis-Sébastien

Mercier's "Nouvelles de la lune" (1768), it certainly had a profound influence on Camille Flammarion, who translated it into French while writing *Lumen* and greatly extrapolated its imagery therein. (BS)

Themes: Life on Other Worlds

de Camp, L. Sprague, U.S., 1907–2000

II-303.   The Continent Makers and Other Tales of the Viagens. Twayne, 1953.

By the 22nd century, Brazil has become the world's greatest power, so that when space exploration gets under way, Viagens Interplanetarias, the agency that manages space transport among the planets of Sol, Tau Ceti, and Procyon, uses Portuguese as its lingua franca. Guided by something like *Star Trek*'s "Prime Directive," Viagens personnel seek to prevent the contamination of not-fully-developed planetary cultures by Earth technology. As several of these breezy action-adventures demonstrate, these efforts are not always successful. Written with the author's characteristic rationality, erudition, and humor. (PC)

Themes: Life on Other Worlds

*II-304.   Lest Darkness Fall. Holt, 1941.

This was one of the earliest pulp stories (1939) to be taken up by a mainstream hardcover publisher. Aware of a problem with the "Connecticut Yankee" theme, namely that not even a supergenius from the modern era could have single-handedly introduced the full panoply of modern industrial technology into antiquity, de Camp gave his hero, stranded in A.D. 535 in the post-Roman inter-regnum, the one indispensable survival skill: he can understand spoken Vulgar Latin! Martin Padway then proceeds to introduce what the primitive technology of the period could actually have absorbed. In his headnote to the *Unknown* version, regrettably omitted from the book, de Camp listed his classical sources. The author's meticulous care in this regard breathes life into what is by all odds de Camp's finest book. (PC)

Themes: History in SF, Time Travel

II-305.   The Wheels of If; and Other Science Fiction. Shasta, 1948.

The title story is one of the most engaging of alternate histories, drawn from the work of philosopher of history Arnold Toynbee. The story is told with de Camp's usual wit and scholarship. Also included are such early de Camp stories as "The Merman" (1938), "The Gnarly Man" (1939), and "The Contraband Cow." (PC)

Themes: Alternate Worlds, History in SF

del Rey, Lester, U.S., 1915–1993

*II-306.   Early del Rey. Doubleday, 1975.

A generous helping of 24 stories by a major Golden Age writer, with connecting autobiographical narrative that throws light on much in SF of the period, especially in wartime. There are fantasies and SF, including such classics as "Though Dreamers Die," but lacking are some of the best tales from his first collection, . . . *And Some Were Human* (1948), such as "The Day Is Done," "Helen O'Loy," and "The Pipes of Pan." Many stories contain unabashed sentimentalism, a not unattractive element in the period's SF. Del Rey also had a somewhat different take on editor John Campbell from that of Asimov; compare *The Early Asimov*. (PC)

II-307.   The Eleventh Commandment. Regency, 1962. Recommended ed: Ballantine, 1970.

In the chaos following nuclear war an American variant of the Catholic church has taken over society and decreed that people be fruitful and multiply without restraint. The result, as seen by an immigrant from Mars—a low-density, rational/scientific society—is a world of wretched overcrowding, pollution, and economic depression. Unlike other population explosion scenarios, however, this one concluded that unlimited proliferation has become *necessary*, in order to grow out of the radiation-induced mutation that has contaminated Earth's entire gene pool. Compare Miller's *A Canticle for Leibowitz*; contrast Harrison's *Make Room! Make Room!,* Brunner's *Stand on Zanzibar,* or George R. R. Martin's Haviland Tuf stories. (PC)

Themes: Overpopulation, Religion

II-308.   Nerves. Ballantine, 1956.

Developed from a 1942 novella in *Astounding* about the time the first experimental nuclear pile went critical, the story deals with an accident in a nuclear power plant and the resulting panic and cover-up. A vivid melodrama in del Rey's characteristic style, told from the point of view of the plant's doctor. Compare Pohl's dramatic, nonfictional account, *Chernobyl*, and Heinlein's 1940 story, "Blowups Happen," which offered a perhaps still valid solution to such problems. (PC)

Themes: Disaster, Machines

II-309.   Step to the Stars. Winston, 1954.

YA. Eschewing space opera gadgetry and employing then-current knowledge and techniques, the book plausibly and convincingly lays out the various stages and dangers of constructing the first space station. The narrative describes the growth of a lonely, skilled mechanic to a confident, poised man who earns his space pilot wings. Compare Heinlein's *Starman Jones* or Norton's *Star Man's Son*. (FM/SM)

Themes: Coming of Age, Space Flight

De Mille, James, Canada, 1833–1880

II-310.   Strange Manuscript Found in a Copper Cylinder. Harper, 1888.

A lost-race novel describing the Antarctic civilization of the troglodytic Kosekin, whose values have been inverted in accordance with their lightless life, so that they abhor wealth and treasure death. A curious narrative, presumably inspired by Poe's *Narrative of Arthur Gordon Pym*. Its romantic subplot—involving the hero's attempt to escape from the Kosekin with an exotic female who is also their captive—prefigures a standard format adopted by many subsequent lost-race stories. (BS)

Themes: Lost Races/Worlds

Defontenay, Charlemagne Ischir, France, 1819–1856

II-311.   Star (Psi Cassiopeia). 1854. Trans. of *Star ou Psi de Cassiopée, histoire merveilleuse de l'un des mondes de l'espace* by P. J. Sokolowski. DAW, 1975.

A pioneering account of life in the vicinity of Star, a world in a solar system that has three principal suns and a miniature sun that orbits Star along with four satellite planets. The multicolored light from these various sources has kaleidoscopic effects on the surface of Star, which is inhabited by variously sized humanoids whose history—involving forced migrations to its inhabited neighbors—is elaborately described. Examples of native literature are included in the text. A Romantic epic with no modern equivalents, although it might be regarded as an intellectual descendant of Casanova's *Icosameron*, it can hardly help but seem alien to contemporary readers but is nevertheless an imaginative tour de force. (BS)

Themes: Life on Other Worlds

Deighton, Len, U.K., 1929–

II-312.   SS-GB: Nazi-Occupied Britain 1941. Cape, 1978.

A best-selling alternate history describing Britain occupied by Nazis in 1941. Compare Martin Hawkin's *When Adolf Came* (1943), Benford and Greenberg's *Hitler Victorious*, and Robert Harris's *Fatherland* (1992). (BS/ML)

Themes: Alternate Worlds

Delany, Samuel R., U.S., 1942–

*II-313.   Aye, and Gomorrah. Vintage, 2003.

This volume replaces *Driftglass* (1971) and *The Complete Nebula Award-Winning Fiction* (1986) as the definitive collection of Delany's shorter work. It includes such masterpieces as the Nebula Award-winning "Time Considered as a Helix of Semi-Precious Stones" and "The Star Pit." (ML)

*II-314.   Babel-17. Ace, 1966.

An unorthodox heroine must come to terms with an artificial language whose constraints on thought and behavior make it an effective weapon of war. Clever, colorful, and highly original; it updates and sophisticates the theme of Vance's *The Language of Pao*. Compare also Watson's *The Embedding*. (BS)

Awards: Nebula

Themes: Linguistics

*II-315.   Dhalgren. Bantam, 1975.

To the depopulated city of Bellona, which is subjected to occasional distortions of time and space, comes a youthful hero hungry for experience and keen to develop his powers as a creative artist. A dense and multilayered novel that alienated some readers who had previously applauded Delany's colorful fantastic romances, but that reached a much wider audience. Convoluted and fascinating, it remains one of the key works of avant-garde SF, by an author determined to extend the limits of the genre. (BS)

Themes: New Wave

*II-316.   The Einstein Intersection. Ace, 1967.

In the far future, the nonhuman inhabitants of Earth mine the mythologies of the ancient past in search of meanings appropriate to their own existence. The hero must undertake an Orphean quest into the underworld of the collective unconscious, confronting its archetypes. A fabulous tour de force of the imagination. Compare Zelazny's *This Immortal* and Carter's *Infernal Desire Machines of Dr. Hoffman*. (BS)

Awards: Nebula

Themes: Far Future, Mythology

*II-317.   Nova. Doubleday, 1968.

A grail epic as space opera, in which the hero must trawl the core of an exploding star for the fabulous element that is the power source of the galactic civilization. The most romantic and action-packed of Delany's novels, but no less sophisticated for that. Beautifully written. (BS)

Themes: Mythology, Space Opera

II-318.   Stars in My Pocket Like Grains of Sand. Bantam, 1984.

The first part of a novel that accepts the impossible task of describing, analyzing, and bringing to life the culture of a galactic civilization, meanwhile telling a story of love and conflict at the individual level. An awesome project, with all the density and richness accompanying Delany's determination to stretch the limits of the genre. Unfortunately, the second half of the novel, *The Splendor and Misery of Bodies, of Cities,* apparently was never completed. (BS/ML)

Themes: Galactic Empires

II-319.   Triton: An Ambiguous Heterotopia. Bantam, 1976.

Republished by Wesleyan University Press as *Trouble on Triton: An Ambiguous Heterotopia* (1996), this complex novel considers the problems that might arise for an individual struggling to orient himself in a culture where people have almost unlimited choice of identity and social role. The uncertainty of the protagonist's life is reflected in the unstable politics of the solar system, which ultimately becomes embroiled in a brief but catastrophic war. A rich, dense dramatization of issues in existential philosophy and sexual politics. Compare Marge Piercy's *Woman on the Edge of Time.* (BS/ML)

Themes: Feminist SF, Politics, Sociology

Dent, Guy (unattributed pseudonym)

II-320. **Emperor of the If**. Heinemann, 1926.

A wonderfully extravagant account of a scientist's experimental use of a disembodied brain to create two new versions of reality: an alternate history in which the dinosaurs never died out, and the future that will emerge two million years hence if present social trends persist. The striking phantasmagoric imagery may owe something to S. Fowler Wright's *The Amphibians*. Heinemann's records were lost during the war, so no clue survives as to the identity of the pseudonymous Dent, but the name might conceivably be a contraction of that of Geoffrey Dennis (1892–1963), who was working for the publisher at that time and subsequently displayed a similar imaginative reach in his speculative survey *The End of the World* (1930).

Themes: Alternate Worlds, Far Future

Denton, Bradley, U.S., 1958–

II-321. **Buddy Holly Is Alive and Well on Ganymede**. Morrow, 1991.

Oliver Vale, in his late 20s and not terribly successful, has spent his entire life acutely aware that his mother conceived him at the very moment in 1959 when rock star Buddy Holly's plane crashed in Iowa. Now, in 1989, the deceased Holly has inexplicably begun to appear "live" on every TV set in the world. Apparently broadcasting from one of Jupiter's moons, he informs the Earth that Oliver is responsible for Holly's usurpation of the airwaves. Needless to say, Vale soon ends up on the run, pursued by the police, angry neighbors, secret agents, his therapist, a cyborg Doberman named Ringo, and some very strange aliens. This is gonzo, absurdist fiction at its best. For similar delights, compare John Kessel's *Good News From Outer Space*. (ML)

Awards: John W. Campbell
Themes: Aliens, Satirical SF

Desmond, Shaw, Ireland, 1877–1960

II-322. **Ragnarok**. Duckworth, 1926.

An extravagant future-war story in which air fleets devastate the cities of the world using a combination of chemical and biological weapons and high explosives—a prospect graphically revisited in McIlraith and Connolly's *Invasion from the Air*, O'Neill's *Day of Wrath*, and the sequels to Wright's *Prelude in Prague*. Desmond went on to produce the more modest *Chaos* (1938) and *Black Dawn* (1944) when he had formed a clearer picture in his mind of what World War II would actually entail. (BS)

Themes: War

Di Filippo, Paul, U.S., 1954–

II-323.   The Steampunk Trilogy. Four Walls Eight Windows, 1995.

This collection of three novellas, all set in the 19th century, represents one of the genre's most original and humorous writers at his raunchy, gonzo best. In "Victoria," the queen takes a lover, and scientists replace her with a newt-human clone stand-in while she's otherwise engaged. In "Walt and Emily," Walt Whitman and Emily Dickinson have their own fling together before getting all mystical. In "Hottentots," the naturalist Louis Agassiz goes in search of the bottled remains of the notorious Hottentot Venus, while Lovecraftian monsters lurk in the shadows. Other particularly worthwhile examples of Di Filippo's work include *Fractal Paisleys* (1992), *Ribofunk* (1996), *Babylon Sisters* (2002), and "A Year in the Linear City" (2002). Compare the work of other steampunk writers; for example, Blaylock's *Homunculus*. (ML)

   Themes: History in SF, Science Fantasy, Steampunk

Dick, Philip K., U.S., 1928–1982

*II-324.   The Collected Stories of Philip K. Dick. Underwood-Miller, 1987. 5 vols.

With introductions to its individual volumes by Roger Zelazny, Norman Spinrad, John Brunner, James Tiptree, Jr., and Thomas M. Disch, this set was a major publishing event in SF. The 118 stories range from his first, from 1952, to a few that were first published here. Dick was so far ahead of his contemporaries in the 1950s that few of these stories are dated. The voluminous discussion of Dick's novels had obscured the author's gifts as a craftsman of shorter tales. Endnotes to individual stories, written by Dick for earlier collections, are informative and wise. Dick said in 1976 that the story "Human Is" (1953) "is my credo. May it be yours." The trade paperback reprint by Citadel Twilight, 1990–1992, shifted two stories and retitled individual volumes. (PC)

II-325.   The Divine Invasion. Timescape, 1981.

The chief characters return to Earth from a space colony, setting in motion a remarkable second coming, which heralds a strange millennium. The religious philosophy interwoven with the plot is idiosyncratic, but Dick's usual fervor of sympathy and anxiety is here strengthened by a powerful injection of faith and hope as well as charity. The religious themes were carried forward into Dick's last (non-SF) novel, *The Transmigration of Timothy Archer* (1982). (BS)

   Themes: Religion

*II-326.   Do Androids Dream of Electric Sheep? Doubleday, 1968.

In a future where technological sophistication has made the ersatz virtually indistinguishable from the real, the hero is a bounty hunter who must track down and eliminate androids passing for human. But android animals are routinely passed off as real by people trying to purge human guilt for having exterminated so many living species, and the new messiah is an artificial construct; so what is the difference between the human and the android? A key novel in Dick's canon. The film, *Blade Runner*, is loosely based on this novel. *We Can Build You* (1972) further explores the ambiguity of such distinctions as human/android and sane/schizophrenic in a haunting story of people who create machines more human than themselves. (BS/ML)

Themes: Androids, Ecology

II-327.   Dr. Bloodmoney; or How We Got Along After the Bomb. Ace, 1965.

A striking post-holocaust novel in which the United States, despite awful devastation, sticks perversely to the same old social ruts. The characters struggle manfully to get by in appalling circumstances, wondering where the blame for it all truly lies. Compare Swanwick's *In the Drift*. (BS)

Themes: Holocaust and After

II-328.   Eye in the Sky. Ace, 1957.

In the security-crazed, McCarthyite, cold-warring U.S. at the time this novel was written, a freak accident projects the psyches of eight people into the private reality of one of them, which becomes not only psychologically but even in a sense physically the entire universe. The worlds imagined by a racist religious fanatic, a repressed Victorian lady, and an American communist are compellingly described and hold up remarkably well for a reader in the post-McCarthy, post-Cold War era. The story also foreshadowed the ambiguity of "reality," which would be a major theme in much of Dick's later work. Compare Dick's *Ubik* and Le Guin's *The Lathe of Heaven*.

Themes: Alternate Worlds, Satirical SF

II-329.   Flow My Tears, the Policeman Said. Doubleday, 1974.

The protagonist is drawn into the reconstructed reality of a woman's drug-induced dream where he has been stripped of his identity and made vulnerable to persecution by her policeman brother. Written with the author's customary fervor, more emotionally charged than the earlier drug story *Now Wait for Last Year* (1966), but less nightmarish than *The Three Stigmata of Palmer Eldritch*. (BS)

Awards: John W. Campbell

Themes: Crime and Punishment, Psychology

II-330.   Galactic Pot-Healer. Berkley, 1969.

A very curious novel in which the hero, a dissatisfied mender of pots, joins a group of misfits assembled by a godlike alien to raise a sunken cathedral, while other aliens read the runes that may indicate the destiny of the universe. A prefiguration of the metaphysical themes of Dick's last novels, developed in a mock-naive fashion slightly reminiscent of Vonnegut's *The Sirens of Titan*. A *Maze of Death* (1970) picked up the theological issues for more earnest development. *Our Friends from Frolix 8* (1970) reassigned them to a throwaway role as an alien god is discovered dead in the void and his human messiah plays an essentially ambiguous role. (BS)

Themes: Aliens, Religion

*II-331.　The Man in the High Castle. Putnam, 1962.

An alternate history in which Germany and Japan won World War II and partitioned the U.S., except for the Rocky Mountain States, where were left in a kind of political limbo. Faction-ridden Nazism oppressively rules the eastern U.S. In the west, the Japanese overlords are reconciling Oriental and American cultural values. In this cosmos, an underground novel circulates, in which the Allies won the war; but, characteristic of Dick's layers-within-layers approach to "reality," it is not quite *our* history. This is Dick's most important early book. Compare Benford and Greenberg's anthology, *Hitler Victorious*. (PC)

Awards: Hugo
Themes: Alternate Worlds, History in SF

*II-332.　Martian Time-Slip. Ballantine, 1964.

On a colonized Mars that largely resembles the Australian Outback or the American West, the Water Worker's Union is one of the most powerful organizations, political and business corruption abound, and primitive aliens haunt the fringes of human civilization. Arnie Kott is a Supreme Good member of the Water Worker's union and has ties with a 10-year-old, seemingly autistic boy named Manfred Steiner who may in fact live in a different time frame from other human beings. *Martian Time-Slip* represents one of Dick's finest early explorations of the transcendent possibilities of schizophrenia. Compare Jonathan Lethem's *Girl in Landscape* and K. W. Jeter's *Madlands*. (ML)

Themes: Paranormal Powers, Psychology

II-333.　A Scanner Darkly. Doubleday, 1977.

The protagonist is, as usual in Dick's novels, gradually enmeshed by a web of circumstance in which he ceases to be able to distinguish between reality and hallucination. The fascination with which the author had previously contemplated such situations is here replaced by horrified revulsion. An affecting, powerful novel. (BS)

Themes: Psychology

II-334.　Solar Lottery. Ace, 1955. Recommended ed.: Gregg, 1976, with introduction by Thomas Disch.

A world supposedly run at the top by the random chances of a great lottery is actually a mix of rival industrial fiefs; would-be Quizmasters seek to rig the odds. The complex plot is driven by games theory (von Neumann and Morgenstern's *Theory of Games* had recently been published). Dick was concerned lest the mathematics of games theory dissolve all political claims of law, tradition, and morality, leaving only the rules of the game: "Minimax is gaining on us all the time," he said in a statement included with the book. Dick's first major work. Contrast van Vogt's *The World of Null-A*. (PC)

Themes: Computers, Dystopias

II-335.   The Three Stigmata of Palmer Eldritch. Doubleday, 1965.

Dick did considerable drug experimentation, and this novel may well be one of the outcomes. Set on a surreal, desiccated Mars that reviewers have compared with a painting by Dali or Picasso, the tale concerns the hallucinogenic drugs that the colonists on Mars must take to maintain some remote semblance of sanity. Problems occur when the sinister Palmer Eldritch attempts to supply the colonists with his own drug, a drug that doesn't simply warp reality but actually changes it in a variety of terrifying and perhaps transcendent ways. A very difficult read, particularly within the context of mid-1960s genre SF, the novel prefigures his later, more explicitly mystical works such as *The Divine Invasion* and *The Transmigration of Timothy Archer*. (ML)

Themes: Psychology, Religion

*II-336.   Ubik. Doubleday, 1969.

The dead can be reactivated into a kind of half-life in which they must construct their own shared realities, competing with one another to impose their own patterns. In this Schopenhaueresque world of will and idea, it is not easy for the characters to formulate a policy of psychological adaptation. Takes up themes from *Eye in the Sky* (1957) and is closely related to his hallucinatory novels but is more tightly plotted than many Dick novels. (BS)

Themes: Psychology

II-337.   VALIS. Bantam, 1981.

A convoluted novel in which the author figures as a character, although his role is subservient to that of his alter ego, Horselover Fat, who achieves miraculous enlightenment courtesy of the godlike Vast Active Living Intelligence System but has difficulty communicating his insight to others. *Radio Free Albemuth* (1985) uses similar materials, apparently being a different draft for the same purpose. (BS)

Themes: Religion

Dickinson, Peter, U.K., 1927–

*II-338.   Eva. Gollancz, 1988.

YA. After a terrible car accident, 13-year-old Eva's neuron memory is transferred into a chimp. The girl adjusts to her new body, so successfully that she learns to live with chimps, mates with them, and becomes their leader. Brilliant in concept and execution, the novel is both emotionally shocking and intellectually provocative: exemplary SF for young readers. Compare Bell's *Ratha's Creature*; contrast Hughes's *The Keeper of the Isis Light*. (FM)

Themes: Biology, Pastoral, Sex in SF

II-339.   The Weathermonger. Gollancz, 1968. Series: Changes.

YA. The first volume in the Changes trilogy. Geoffrey and Sally, brother and sister, abandoned to die as witches, escape to France. There they are urged to return to England and discover the cause of the changes that have thrown the British Isles back into the Middle Ages, where ignorance and superstition again rule, all things mechanical are feared, and even the weather is controlled by incantation. The children find out that Merlin's sleep has been disturbed, and, unhappy with what he sees, Merlin has sent England back to a time he knows. Geoffrey and Sally convince him to relent, and he frees England from its curse. A brilliantly imaginative combination of myth and science fiction. *Heartsease* (1969) recounts the successful rescue of a witch by a group of children. In *The Devil's Children* (1970), Nicky and a band of Sikhs, free of the madness caused by the changes, become allies, settle on a farm, and beat off various threats to their safety. Compare Mayne's *Earthfasts* or Christopher's *The Prince in Waiting*. (FM)

Themes: Disaster, Science Fantasy, Time Travel

Dickson, Gordon R(upert), Canada/U.S., 1913–2001

II-340.   Dorsai! DAW, 1976. Series: Childe Cycle.

A revised version of *The Genetic General* (1960), the first volume in one of the more popular military SF series. Some of the later books in the series are, in whole or in part, revised versions of earlier books. The Dorsai are the greatest soldiers in the galaxy, having developed a mercenary culture in order to gain the capital necessary to survive on a resource-poor planet. In Dickson's universe, humanity has fragmented into three basic genetically determined types— men of faith, of war, and of philosophy—with the Dorsai exemplifying men of war. The three types, however, are destined to come together again to form a new, higher type of human being called the Ethical-Responsible Man. Donal Craeme, Dorsai, military genius, and psychic superman, is the first of this new kind of human being. Dickson outlined an ambitious plan to write a dozen novels describing the evolution of the Ethical-Responsible Man from our past, through the present, and into the future, called the Childe Cycle. At his death, however, none of the novels set in the past or present had appeared; and it seems unlikely that they were ever written. The early Dorsai novels, such as *Soldier, Ask Not* (1967), were primarily action-adventure of a superior sort. The later novels, such as *The Final Encyclopedia* (1984), became increasingly philosophical and perhaps a bit long-winded. Compare David Drake's *Hammer's Slammers* (1979) and its sequels and Jerry Pournelle's *The Mercenary* and sequels. (ML)

Themes: Evolution, Future History, Politics, War

II-341.   The Far Call. Dial, 1978.

A political novel about a mission to Mars that is doomed to fail by the chicanery of its promoters. The book version is much expanded from a 1973 *Analog* serial, the private lives of the characters being mapped out extensively, presumably with the intention of appealing to a wider audience. Interesting for its study of the clash between the ideals of scientific progress and the follies of political pragmatism. Compare Bova's *Colony*. (BS)

Themes: Politics, The Planets

II-342.   Space Winners. Holt, 1965.

YA. Jim, Curt, and Ellen are selected by the Alien Federation for a secret training mission of great moment. They are joined by Atakit, a small, squirrel-like, but strong alien. Crash-landing on Quebahr, a planet closed to technological knowledge, the four have various adventures and then assist in establishing cooperation among the several hostile peoples. They discover that their mission actually was to Quebahr, and the three teenagers become part of an advance cadre for bringing Earth into the federation. Well-paced narrative, competently written, many surprises. Contrast Heinlein's *Tunnel in the Sky* for a less sanguine adult view of teenagers. (FM)

Themes: Aliens, Children in SF, Space Flight

Disch, Thomas M., U.S., 1940–

*II-343.   Camp Concentration. Hart-Davis, 1968.

A political prisoner is a guinea pig in an experiment that uses a syphilis-related spirochete to boost IQ to unparalleled levels. The author boldly presents the story as first-person narrative and carries it off brilliantly. A key work of avant-garde SF, written with its serialization in *New Worlds* in mind. Compare Keyes's *Flowers for Algernon*. (BS)

Themes: Intelligence, New Wave

II-344.   The Man Who Had No Idea. Bantam, 1982.

The most recent collection of Disch's shorter fiction follows *One Hundred and Two H Bombs* (1966; enlarged as *White Fang Goes Dingo and Other Funny SF Stories*, 1971); *Under Compulsion* (1968; U.S. title: *Fun With Your New Head*), *Getting Into Death* (1973; U.K. and U.S. editions differ), and *Fundamental Disch* (1980). Disch is a master of black comedy but can also write with nightmarish intensity or with a cool weltschmertz. This collection has nothing to match the classic "The Asian Shore" (Nebula nominee, in *Getting Into Death* and *Fundamental Disch*) but it has the ironic and satirical title story as well as another novelette, "Concepts," in which people separated by a vast gulf of space fall in love via a hyperspatial link, and the bleakly horrific "The Apartment Next to the War." Disch is one of the best contemporary American short story writers; a new collection of his work is long overdue. Compare Ellison's *Deathbird Stories*. (BS/ML)

II-345.   On Wings of Song. St. Martin's, 1979.

The hero, growing up in the ideologically repressive Midwest, yearns to learn the art of "flying," by which talented individuals can sing their souls out of their bodies. He loses his freedom, his wife, and his dignity to this quest, but in a cruelly ambiguous climax might have achieved an absurd triumph. Clever and compelling; a disturbing satire subverting SF myths of transcendence. Contrast *Stardance* by the Robinsons and Clarke's *Childhood's End.* (BS)

> Awards: John W. Campbell
> Themes: Satirical SF

*II-346.   334. MacGibbon & Kee, 1972.

A dystopian vision of future New York focusing on various residents of a huge apartment house and other parties interested in it. A brilliant work, utterly convincing in its portraits of people trying to get by in a world they are powerless to influence or control. The most eloquent display of the pessimism that became newly acceptable in New Wave SF. Compare Brunner's *Stand on Zanzibar.* (BS)

> Themes: Cities, New Wave

Doctorow, Cory, Canada, 1971–

II-347.   Down and Out in the Magic Kingdom. Tor, 2003.

In a post-human future where people live for hundreds of years and death is simply a minor inconvenience, Jules, a mere youngster at just over a century old, moves to Disney World, that pinnacle of 20th-century art and culture, intent on helping to preserve it. Soon, however, he discovers that dark forces are out to "improve" the attractions in a variety of inappropriate ways, and they won't stop at murder to get what they want. This first novel is satire at its best by one of the genre's hot new writers. For more of Doctorow's deliciously skewed perspective see his first short story collection, *A Place So Foreign and 8 More* (2003). (ML)

> Themes: Immortality, Satirical SF

Donnelly, Ignatius, U.S., 1831–1901

II-348.   Caesar's Column: A Story of the Twentieth Century. Schulte, 1890 (as by Edmund Boisgilbert, MD).

In stark contrast to the egalitarian society of Edward Bellamy's *Looking Backward*, the developed world of the 1990s in Donnelly's groundbreaking American dystopia is a ruthless plutocracy in which capital is concentrated in a few hands while the proletariat suffers extreme misery. A visitor to New York from a Swiss colony in Africa records the progress of a nihilist revolution led by the Brotherhood of Destruction; the eponymous monument being comprised of the skulls of its victims. Escaping to Africa, the narrator establishes a utopian colony run on Christian and socialist principles. The story contains echoes of Griffith's *Angel of the Revolution* as well as inversions of Bellamyesque assumptions. (BS)

> Themes: Dystopias

Dorsey, Candas Jane, Canada, 1952–

II-349.   Black Wine. Tor, 1997.

The lives of three women intertwine in this subtle, quietly complex narrative. An old woman, kept hanging in a cage as punishment for crimes unknown, tells her story to a young girl who cannot remember her own past. An adventurous young woman goes on a quest to find her lost mother. Another woman is on the run from an unwanted husband. At various points in the narrative, the protagonists become waifs, concubines, slaves, princesses, mothers, and lovers, switching roles and identities until the reader is left unsure of exactly how many women the story is really about. But a constant thread is the travel across a stark, unlovely landscape. This beautifully written first novel should appeal to readers of Russ, Le Guin, and Arnason. (ML)

Awards: Tiptree

Themes: Feminist SF

II-350.   Machine Sex and Other Stories. Porcepic, 1988.

A first collection of short fiction by a highly promising new Canadian writer. Dorsey experiments widely and wildly, ranging from cyberpunk to surrealism. Among the better stories in the book are "The Prairie Wanderers," "Machine Sex," "Time Is the School in Which We Learn," "Time Is the Fire in Which We Burn," and "Black Dog." Compare Cadigan's *Patterns*. (ML)

Themes: Feminist SF

Douglass, Ellsworth (pseudonym of Elmer Dwiggins), U.S., ?

II-351.   Pharaoh's Broker: Being the Very Remarkable Experiences in Another World of Isidor Werner (Written by Himself). Pearson, 1899.

An interplanetary novel that follows examples set by Jules Verne and Percy Greg in giving elaborate attention to the voyage through space and its effects. The other planets apparently follow the same scheme of social evolution as Earth, Mars having reached a phase comparable with the famine-prone ancient Egyptian civilization—an idea promptly borrowed by Pearson employee and habitual literary magpie George Griffith for use in *A Honeymoon in Space*. (BS)

Themes: Life on Other Worlds, Space Flight

Dowling, Terry, Australia, 1947–

II-352.   Rynosseros. Aphelion, 1990. Series: Rynosseros.

A collection of linked stories set in a future Australia, which has reverted to Ab'O rule, and featuring Tom Tyson, captain of the immense "sandship" *Rynosseros*, which plies desert wastes separating balkanized tribes. Political background is shadowy and volatile, involving artificial intelligences that meddle in conflicts between clashing principates. Exquisitely detailed, lushly baroque, elliptical to the point of unintelligibility. *Blue Tyson* (1992) and *Twilight Beach* (1993) are sequel collections. *Antique Futures: The Best of Terry Dowling* (1999) is an excellent retrospective collection. Compare Herbert's *Dune* and Wolfe's *Fifth Head of Cerberus.* (RL/ML)

Themes: Far Future

Doyle, Arthur Conan, U.K., 1859–1930

II-353.   The Doings of Raffles Haw. Lovell, 1891.

A scientist who has solved the ancient alchemical problem of turning base metal into gold is disappointed when his philanthropic largesse does not have the immediate beneficial results for which he had hoped, so he reverses the process and destroys the secret. Such pusillanimity was, alas, common among hypothetical scientists of the period. Compare Vivian's *Star Dust.* (BS)

Themes: Discoveries and Inventions

*II-354.   The Lost World. Hodder & Stoughton, 1912. Series: Professor Challenger.

Doyle's finest scientific romance is a robust adventure story that brought a new sophistication to a standard boys' book formula and provided the lost race story with its ultimate flourish. The notion of dinosaurs and other charismatic prehistoric creatures surviving in a remote enclave had been elaborately developed in France by Charles Derennes' *Le peuple de la pôle* (1907), but Doyle leavened his own plot with the vivid character of Professor Challenger, who went on to star in *The Poison Belt* (1913)—based on an idea borrowed from Camille Flammarion—before suffering a tragic decline in the spiritualist fantasy *The Last of Mist* (1926) and the minor melodramas "When the World Screamed" (1928) and "The Disintegration Machine" (1929). (BS)

Themes: Lost Races/Worlds

Dozois, Gardner, U.S., 1947–

II-355.   Geodesic Dreams: The Best Short Fiction of Gardner Dozois. St. Martin's, 1992.

Before he gained renown as one of the finest magazine editors in the field, Dozois was known primarily as a short story writer. This collection includes such "Solace," "Slow Dancing with Jesus," and "A Kingdom by the Sea." Other collections include *Slow Dancing Through Time* (1990), a collection of collaborative stories with Jack C. Haldeman II, Susan Caspar, and Michael Swanwick, and *The Visible Man* (1973). A new Dozois collection is long overdue. (ML)

II-356.   Strangers. Berkley, 1978.

Expansion of a novella (Hugo and Nebula nominee) tracking the love affair between a man and an alien woman whose reproductive biology is exotic. A virtual reprise of Farmer's *The Lovers,* with added depth of characterization. (BS)

Themes: Sex in SF

Du Bois, William Pène, U.S., 1916–1993

*II-357.   The Twenty-One Balloons. Viking, 1947.

YA. Krakatoa in the late 19th century is the site of an amazing civilization that combines outlandish but workable household devices to save labor and a utopian social organization built around eating tastes and financed by a diamond hoard. Professor Sherman, a retired teacher on a balloon tour over the Pacific, is forced down near Krakatoa and invited to join the group. The eruption of the volcano ends the utopian experiment and the professor escapes to inform a curious country why he was found in the ocean amid 21 balloons. A humorous, Jules Verne-like, richly imaginative book that can be enjoyed by all. (FM/SM)

   Awards: Newbery
   Themes: Lost Races/Worlds, Utopias

Dunn, J. R., U.S., ?

II-358.   Days of Cain. Avon, 1997.

Based far in the future, a society of time travelers has dedicated itself to preserving the past, but one of their members, Alma Lewin, goes renegade. Faced with the evil that is Auschwitz in 1943, she decides to take action. Her supervisor, Gaspar James, sympathizes, but realizes that he can't let her succeed. This is an unusually dark and powerful novel. Compare Connie Willis's *Doomsday Book*. (ML)

   Themes: History in SF, Time Travel, War

II-359.   Full Tide of Night. Avon Eos, 1998.

Taking John Webster's bloody 17th-century revenge tragedy, *The Duchess of Malfi*, as his source, Dunn tells a complex tale of political intrigue and out of control passion. Julia Amalfi is the benevolent, nearly immortal ruler of her colony world. Many years ago she fled an Earth on the verge of being taken over by a hostile artificial intelligence. Now, more than a century later, the younger generation of colonists no longer believe in that danger and, having evolved their own political movement, are ready to overthrow her. The leader of the revolutionaries, however, seems unbalanced, obsessed with Julia for more than mere political reasons. Compare Barnes's *The Sky So Big and Black*. (ML)

   Themes: Intelligence, Life on Other Worlds, Politics

Dunn, Katherine, U.S., 1945–

II-360.   Geek Love. Knopf, 1989.

Although widely reviewed as a work of horror, this fine novel clearly qualifies as science fiction. It concerns the Binewski Fabulon freak show, a family-run business in which the father intentionally creates mutants by exposing his frequently pregnant wife to toxic materials. The resulting children include an albino hunchback dwarf (the novel's fascinating protagonist), a flipper boy, and others. At least one child has paranormal powers. *Geek Love* was nominated for the National Book Award and the Bram Stoker Award. Compare Tod Browning's classic film *Freaks* (1932); contrast Tom Reamy's *Blind Voices*. (ML)

Themes: Genetic Engineering, Mutants, Paranormal Powers

Durrell, Lawrence, U.K., 1912–1990

II-361.   The Revolt of Aphrodite. Faber, 1974.

An omnibus edition of *Tunc* (1968) and *Nunquam* (1970). The inventor of a supercomputer is hired by a multinational corporation that wants him to predict the future, but he is corrupted by greed. He reemerges from the madhouse in the second volume in order to make a duplicate of the corporation head's lost love. Mannered and convoluted. Compare Barth's *Giles Goat Boy*. (BS\ML)

Themes: Computers, Intelligence, Scientists and Engineers

Effinger, George Alec, U.S., 1947–2002

II-362.   What Entropy Means to Me. Doubleday, 1972.

A complex set of interwoven stories in which the central character invents the tale of his brother's search for his father, while beset by problems of his own. Highly unusual, reminiscent in some ways of Flann O'Brien's *At Swim Two-Birds* (1939). Effinger's penchant for surrealism and the intricate interweaving of story lines is further demonstrated in *Relatives* (1973) and *The Wolves of Memory* (1981), which exhibit the same sharp imagery and the same conscientious failure to achieve coherency. (BS)

*II-363.   When Gravity Fails. Arbor, 1987. Series: Marid Audran.

Marid, a small-time hood, is a citizen of the Budayeen, the red-light district of an unnamed 21st-century Arabic city. He is also something of an anomaly; virtually all of his friends and acquaintances have had their brains wired to accept "moddies," behavior modules that can be chipped in to give the wearer an entirely different set of skills or personality. One day, someone Marid is conducting business with is murdered and Marid finds himself caught up in a complex web of intrigue and death. This is a fine, gritty, violent novel borrowing equally from the cyberpunks and Raymond Chandler. *A Fire in the Sun* (1989), also a Hugo Award nominee, is an excellent sequel. Somewhat weaker, but still worth reading is the third book in the series, *The Exile Kiss* (1991). A posthumous short story collection with related materials is *Budayeen Nights* (2003). Compare Gibson's *Neuromancer* and, for another take on the future of North Africa, compare McHugh's *Nekropolis*. (ML)

Themes: Coming of Age, Crime and Punishment, Cyberpunk

Egan, Greg, Australia, 1961–

*II-364.   Diaspora. HarperPrism, 1998.

Egan is perhaps the ultimate SF chronicler of the post-human future, and *Diaspora* may well be his most daring exploration. Since the late 21st century, humanity has reconfigured itself into a wide variety of life forms. Many millions of people live entirely digital lives as citizens of a vast network of computers spread across the solar system. Essentially they have become conscious software. Others, called gleisners, have opted to live more fully in our universe, but in robotic bodies. A small number of traditionalists, called fleshers, have chosen to remain organic, although they often vary radically from what the early 21st century would define as normal humanity. Then the stability of this system is threatened by an unforeseen disaster brought about by heretofore unknown astrophysical events and a varied group of humans and post-humans set out to make things right. Egan's novels have occasionally been criticized as lacking in human warmth, but no one has taken hard scientific speculation further. Compare Justina Robson's *Natural History*. (ML)

Themes: Far Future, Hard SF, Virtual Reality

II-365.   Distress. Millennium, 1996.

In the year 2055, SeeNet reporter Andrew Worth is offered the chance to do a documentary on a new form of mental illness—acute clinical anxiety syndrome, popularly known as Distress. Instead he takes an assignment to cover a meeting of physicists where Nobel laureate Violete Mosala is expected to announce her TOE, the much sought after Theory of Everything, which will explain how all of the various forces of the universe are interconnected. Mosala, however, has attracted a raft of anti-science cultists and religious crazies who see her actions as either sacrilegious or as the Aleph Moment, the moment when the entire universe will be fundamentally changed. And somehow, Worth discovers, her TOE is tied into the spread of Distress and, worse yet, the possible destruction of the universe! Well written, scientifically challenging, and exciting, this is a fine example of hard science fiction. Compare Danvers's *The Fourth World* for a similar picture of a future journalist at work. Compare Clarke's "The Nine Billion Names of God" for another example of how small human actions might affect the entire universe. (ML)

Themes: End of the World, Hard SF, Psychology

II-366.   Luminous. Millennium, 1998.

This collection of some of Egan's best short fiction includes such stories, many of them award nominees, as "Reasons to be Cheerful," "Cocoon," "Our Lady of Chernobyl," "Luminous," and "The Planck Dive." Also of interest is his earlier collection, *Axiomatic* (1995). Egan continues to produce excellent short fiction, and a new short story collection is due. (ML)

Themes: Hard SF

*II-367.   Permutation City. Millennium, 1994.

Pursuing his ongoing fascination with different forms of life, Egan explores the ramifications of scanning and downloading the human mind into virtual environments. But while *Permutation City* is partially concerned with the vulnerability of such "Copies," dependent on the stability of the computer systems they inhabit, Egan is also preoccupied with the nature and fluidity of identity. Which is more real, the scan or the person, and can the two co-exist? And having been scanned and then reloaded into a body, is the Copy different from the original? Egan uses a complex, multi-viewpoint narrative to reflect the shifting natures of reality and experience in a world that may be a computer construction or the real thing. In the end, only uncertainty remains, in what is one of Egan's best novels, with tightly structured plotting and coherent storytelling. Compare Banks's *Feersum Endjinn*. (MKS)

  Awards: John W. Campbell
  Themes: Hard SF, Immortality, Virtual Reality

II-368.   Teranessia. Gollancz, HarperPrism, 1999.

An unusual book for Egan in that it is heavily character driven, *Teranessia* recounts the early life of Prabir Suresh, a boy growing up on an Edenic Indonesian island with his little sister and his scientist parents, who are there to study some odd mutations among the local butterfly population. Then Prabir's life is torn apart by civil war. Jump 20 years into the future. Reports are appearing of bizarre, large-scale mutations throughout the region and Prabir's sister, herself now a biologist, returns to their long-lost island, the apparent nexus for the mutations. Prabir, worried for her safety, follows, joining up with another scientist. Together they unravel the scientific mystery and begin to deal with an unparalleled biological revolution. Compare Ian McDonald's *Chaga*. (ML)

  Themes: Biology, Evolution, Hard SF

Elgin, Suzette Haden, U.S., 1936–

II-369.   Communipath Worlds. Pocket Books, 1980. Series: Communipath.

An omnibus containing *The Communipaths* (1970), *Furthest* (1971), and *At the Seventh Level* (1972). The telepathic hero is a reluctant agent for a galactic federal government, but his particular missions remain subservient to the author's interest in general issues of communication and the way in which communication systems and languages are implicated in social stratification. Coyote Jones, the hero of *Communipath Worlds*, also features in *Star Anchored, Star Angered* (1979), which deals with questions of theology, and in *Yonder Comes the Other End of Time* (1986), which links the series to her Ozark trilogy of fantasies. Elgin's plots are rough-hewn, but the ideas in them are intriguing and sometimes challenging. Compare the works of C. J. Cherryh. (BS)

  Themes: Linguistics, Paranormal Powers

II-370.   Native Tongue. DAW, 1984. Series: Native Tongue.

This angry and moving feminist dystopian novel assumes a powerful backlash against women's rights in the 1980s and 1990s, culminating in the loss of the vote and the complete domination of American women by men. Centuries later, living in virtual slavery, women have developed a secret language that allows them to continue the struggle for freedom. When humanity is contacted by aliens, the linguistic facility of women makes them the logical choice to conduct negotiations, under the watchful eyes of their male oppressors. The well-done sequel, *The Judas Rose* (1987), shows the women making some progress toward attaining their freedom. A third, somewhat weaker volume in the series, *Earthsong*, was published in 1994. Compare Atwood's *The Handmaid's Tale* and Helen Collins's *Mutagenesis* (1993). (ML)

Themes: Dystopias, Feminist SF, Linguistics

Ellis, Edward S(ylvester), U.S., 1840–1916

II-371.   The Steam Man of the Prairies. American Novels Publishing, 1868.

YA. A pioneering Western SF novel by the writer who established the basic formula of dime novel publishing, borrowing Zadoc P. Dederick's unsuccessful invention of a humaniform steam engine, as exhibited in Newark, New Jersey, in 1868. The speedier version featured in the novel is the work of a vertically challenged 15-year-old genius, Johnny Brainerd. Some of the many reprints, including the one reproduced in facsimile in Everett F. Bleiler's *Eight Dime Novels* (Dover, 1974), carried the title *The Huge Hunter*. The story, awful as it is, established the template for dime novel series featuring young inventors Frank Reade and Tom Edison Jr. (BS)

Themes: Discoveries and Inventions

Ellis, T(homas) Mullett, U.K., 1850–1919

II-372.   Zalma. Tower, 1895.

A melodramatic political fantasy, somewhat reminiscent of the works of the French *feuilletonist* Eugène Sue, pitting the Catholic Church against anarchists and nihilists. The plot is complicated by themes borrowed from George Griffith's *Angel of the Revolution*; the eponymous anti-heroine formulates a plan to wage biological warfare on the capitals of Europe, using anthrax as an agent of destruction. The narrative is as chaotic as the ideology but has an appealing fervor. (BS)

Themes: Biology, War

Ellison, Harlan, U.S., 1934–

II-373.   Alone Against Tomorrow. Macmillan, 1971.

Short stories dramatizing situations of acute alienation, including many of Ellison's best, among them such award winners as "I Have No Mouth and I Must Scream" and " 'Repent, Harlequin!' Said the Ticktockman." Intense, filled with Sartrian nausea but by no means lacking in caritas. Compare Disch's short fiction. (BS/ML)

II-374.   Angry Candy. Houghton, 1988.

Most of these stories are vintage Ellison, all centering on the theme of death. Among the best are the Hugo Award-winning "Paladin of the Lost Hour," the Edgar Award-winning "Soft Monkey," "With Virgil Oddum at the East Pole,"

"Broken Glass," and the very funny "Prince Myshkin, and Hold the Relish." (ML)

Awards: World Fantasy, *Locus*

*II-375.   Deathbird Stories: A Pantheon of Modern Gods. Harper, 1975.

A collection of stories said to display "a pantheon of modern gods"; angry reactions against aspects of the contemporary world. Outstanding are the Hugo Award-winning "The Deathbird," "Pretty Maggy Moneyeyes," "Shattered Like a Glass Goblin," and "Paingod." Demonstrates Ellison's brilliance as a short story writer able to generate great affective power. Compare Spinrad's *No Direction Home* (1975). (BS/ML)

Themes: Mythology

*II-376.   The Essential Ellison: A 50-Year Retrospective. Ed. by Terry Dowling, Richard Delap, and Gil Lamont. Morpheus, 2000.

A revision of *The Essential Ellison: A 35 Year Retrospective*, this book features more than a thousand pages of Ellison's work as a science fiction and fantasy writer, essayist, screenwriter, television and film critic, and all-purpose social commentator. Most of the classics and award winners are here, including "Pretty Maggie Moneyeyes," "I Have No Mouth and I Must Scream," "'Repent Harlequin!' Said the Ticktockman," "A Boy and His Dog," and "Deathbird." This edition adds major recent fiction such as "With Virgil Oddum at the East Pole," "Paladin of the Lost Hour," and "Mefisto in Onyx." Less well-known are some of Ellison's earlier stories and his nonfiction. Other later Ellison collections of note include *Slippage* (1988), *Mindfields* (1989), and the multi-volume Edgeworks series, published by White Wolf, which plans to reprint 31 titles in 20 omnibus volumes; list at harlanellison.com/newspub.htm. (ML)

II-377.   Shatterday. Houghton Mifflin, 1980.

A collection continuing a trend in Ellison's work toward surrealism and psychological study, including the ironic non-SF novella "All the Lies That Are My Life" and the bitter fable "Count the Clock That Tells the Time." Compare Disch's *The Man Who Had No Idea.* (BS)

Emshwiller, Carol, U.S., 1921–

II-378.   The Mount. Small Beer Press, 2002.

Charley is a Mount. Earth has been conquered by the alien Hoots who have domesticated humanity, breeding us for speed and beauty. Charley's entire world revolves around his alien Little Master and his desire to be a successful racer. This is a beautifully drawn portrait of the complex relationship between slaves and their owners. Compare Butler's short story "Blood Child" and Mike Conner's "Guide Dog" (1991). See also Silverberg's *The Alien Years* for a larger scale look at such relationships. (ML)

Awards: Philip K. Dick

Themes: Aliens, Invasion

II-379.   The Start of the End of It All. Women's Press, 1990.

Perhaps the best of the author's several story collections, following *Joy in Our Cause* (1974) and *Verging on the Pertinent* (1989) and followed by *Report to the Men's Club* (2002); gathers 18 stories from 1960s, 1970s, and 1980s. Some are straight mimetic fiction, but most construct absurdist SF scenarios enabling brilliantly pointed observations of sexual politics, such as the cat-hating aliens of the title story, whose attitudes converge with those of human men toward women. The texts of the 1990 U.K. and 1991 U.S. editions differ. Compare the stories of Russ. (RL/ML)

Awards: World Fantasy

Themes: Absurdist SF, Feminist SF

Engdahl, Sylvia Louise, U.S., 1933–

*II-380.   Enchantress from the Stars. Atheneum, 1970.

YA. A long, detailed novel built around the notion that a traditional fairy tale may actually refer to incidents involving a wise, superior race visiting a younger race and world to spare it contamination. To Georyn, a youngest son, Elana is an enchantress who would help him destroy a ravaging dragon, actually a rock-destroying machine of the Imperial Exploration Corps. Elana and her father instruct Georyn in using his latent psychic power, which frightens the materialistic Imperial colony, who are a Youngling people, into leaving the planet—Earth? Strong features are the working out of correspondences between fairy tale and the mission, the anti-colonizing theme, and the preeminence of Elana; thus, a rare example of an early non-sexist novel. A competent but less successful sequel is *The Far Side of Evil* (1971). Compare L'Engle's *A Wrinkle in Time;* contrast Heinlein's *Tunnel in the Sky.* (FM/ML)

Themes: Feminist SF, Science Fantasy

Engh, M(ary) J(ane), U.S., 1933–

II-381.   Arslan. Warner, 1976. U.K. title: *A Wind from Bukhara,* 1979.

Having already defeated the Soviet Union and the United States in battle, Arslan, a charismatic young Asian conqueror, personally oversees mopping up operations in the American Midwest. Deciding to make a small town in Illinois his temporary headquarters, Arslan at first rapes and terrorizes the citizens, but then seduces them by the force of his personality. This frightening and disconcerting novel features superb character development and fascinating political insights. Compare Sinclair Lewis's *It Can't Happen Here.* Engh's more recent novel, *Rainbow Man* (1993), deals with the theme of personal responsibility in a radically different but equally fascinating manner. (ML)

Themes: Dystopias, Invasion, War

England, George Allan, U.S., 1877–1936

II-382.   The Air Trust. Wagner, 1915.

A political fantasy that—rare for England—went straight to book publication rather than being serialized in the pulps. Although it is essentially a straightforward assault on monopoly capitalism in the vein of Jack London's *The Iron Heel* (it is dedicated to the American socialist leader Eugene Debs), its plot retains too many pulpish clichés to be fully effective. Contrast Cook's *Round Trip to the Year 2000*. (BS)

II-383.   Darkness and Dawn. Small Maynard, 1914.

An omnibus edition of three serials published in *The Cavalier* in 1912–1913, which established England as a key writer of pulp romance. The hero and heroine awake from suspended animation to find the world much altered by the Great Death—a variant of M. P. Shiel's *Purple Cloud*—triggered by an asteroid strike. They battle against degenerate descendants of the poorer specimens of humankind (the story is vilely racist) to restore the rudiments of civilization, but the emotional core of the story is a delight in "noble savagery" which echoes the mythology of Edgar Rice Burroughs' tales of Tarzan and helped to lay the groundwork for the enthusiastic reception in the U.S. of Fowler Wright's *Deluge*. (BS)

Themes: Holocaust and After

II-384.   The Golden Blight. H. K. Fly, 1916.

A political thriller serialized in *The Cavalier* in 1912 (not long after "Darkness and Dawn," whose success presumably opened the window of opportunity) in which a young scientist takes on the world's capitalists, threatening to use his newly discovered zeta ray to turn their gold into ash if they will not outlaw war; they refuse. Entertaining, though somewhat contrived; the central notion had previously been employed by Jules Lermina in a serial in the *Journal des Voyages*, *To-Ho le tueur d'or* (1905). (BS)

Themes: Politics

Eskridge, Kelly, U.S., 1960–

II-385.   Solitaire. Eos, 2002.

Ren "Jackal" Segura has been raised to be a Hope, a symbol of the highest principles of humanity, and to eventually take her place as a representative in the corporate-run government that dominates a future Earth. When her life comes crashing down, Jackal finds herself proclaimed a murderer and is sentenced to solitary confinement in a stripped down virtual environment. Driven nearly mad by her experience, she must use all of her wits to survive. But upon release she finds her reintroduction to society almost as difficult. This is a beautifully written first novel and Eskridge's protagonist is one of the most fully formed characters in recent science fiction. (ML)

Themes: Crime and Punishment, Psychology

Farley, Ralph Milne (pseud. of Roger Sherman Hoar), U.S., 1887–1963

II-386.   The Radio Man. FPCI, 1948. Series: Radio Man.

Burroughsian adventure story serialized in *Argosy-All-Story* in 1924, set on Venus, where the Formians—intelligent giant ants—have co-existed peacefully with the humanoid Cupians for some time. Now, however, hostilities are about to break out again. The human hero's knowledge of guns and explosives proves crucial to the developing contest, which was further developed in *The Radio Beasts* (1925; book 1964), *The Radio Planet* (1926; book 1964), and *The Radio Menace* (1930). The first volume was once reprinted as *An Earthman on Venus*. The adventure aspect is stereotypical but the depiction of the civilized ants is of some interest. Compare Bennett's *The Demigods*. (BS)

    Themes: Life on Other Worlds

Farmer, Nancy, U.S., 1941–

II-387.   The Ear, the Eye and the Arm. Orchard, 1994.

YA. In the year 2194, the children of Zimbabwe's military ruler escape from their over-protected environment to go adventuring as detectives. Confronting the paradox that is Africa, they encounter futuristic technology and horrid poverty. On the run from gangsters, they spend time in a traditional African village that seems by turns Edenic and mired in closed-minded superstition. Farmer, who spent a decade in Africa, obviously loves the world she's created and does a fine job of making it real. The book is both exciting and at times genuinely funny. It is also one of the relatively few YA SF novels with non-white protagonists. (ML)

    Awards: Newbery Honor Book
    Themes: Crime and Punishment, Mythology

*II-388.   The House of the Scorpion. Atheneum, 2002.

YA. Matt is the clone of the fabulously wealthy, 140-year-old drug lord Matteo Alacran and has been raised on his estate in the independent country of Opium, which lies on the border between a future United States and Aztlan, the former Mexico. Alternately pampered and treated as a sub-human by various of Alacran's family and servants, he manages to maintain his basic decency and only gradually realizes the horrific fate in store for him. This is an intelligent and powerfully written look at some of the potential evils of cloning and, as usual, Farmer, who grew up on the U.S./Mexico border, does a masterful job of creating a sense of place. Compare Ames's *Anna to the Infinite Power* and Lasky's *Star Split*. (ML)

    Awards: National Book, Newbery Honor Book, Printz Honor Book
    Themes: Clones/Cloning, Crime and Punishment, Dystopias

Farmer, Philip José, U.S. 1918–

II-389.   A Feast Unknown: Volume IX of the Memoirs of Lord Grandith.
Essex House, 1969.

Superheroic rivals Lord Grandith (that is, Tarzan) and Doc Caliban (that is, Doc Savage) tensely join forces to battle a shadowy cult. Brilliant satire of superhero fantasies, first (despite its subtitle) in a loosely related series including *Lord of the Trees* (1970), *The Mad Goblin* (1970), *Tarzan Alive: A Definitive Biography of Lord Greystoke* (1972), *Doc Savage: His Apocalyptic Life* (1973), and (less certainly) many other texts, elaborating a potent celebration-cum-critique of SF's fascination with supermen. Compare Spinrad's *The Iron Dream*. (RL)

Themes: Satirical SF, Supermen/women

II-390.   The Green Odyssey. Ballantine, 1957.

A picaresque novel about a shipwrecked spaceman on a barbarian planet, who is enslaved and finds himself part of a family, with a strong-minded wife and her five children (some sexist stereotyping here). When he learns of the capture of two other Earthmen, he sets off to rescue them in one of the wind-driven wheeled ships that sail the planet's grassy plains. The "wind roller" lifeways and other aspects of the planet's culture are vividly realized in a fast-paced adventure story laced with humor. Compare de Camp's *The Continent Makers* and Poul Anderson's *War of the Wing-Men*. (PC)

Themes: Life on Other Worlds, Satirical SF

***II-391.   The Lovers.** Ballantine, 1961. Recommended ed.: Ballantine, 1979.

Expanded from a 1952 story that provided controversy at the time for its sexual content. On a wretchedly overpopulated Earth ruled with fiendish ingenuity by an oppressive state church that considers all sex evil except for procreation, Hero and his wife are—understandably—unhappily married. Sent in to help kill off an intelligent insect-like race on a planet slated for colonization, the man falls in love with a female of another alien species, which can mimic human appearance and behavior up to and including sex. But the consequences are tragic and horrible. Films like *Alien* and its sequels may have taken the edge off the raw shock this story would have given some readers a generation ago. Compare Gardner Dozois's *Strangers*; contrast del Rey's *The Eleventh Commandment*. (PC)

Themes: Aliens, Sex in SF

II-392.   Strange Relations. Ballantine, 1960.

Farmer has been praised and reviled as the writer who brought sex into SF. More precisely, he wrote *alien* sex and, like an orthodox Freudian, defined sex to include sibling and parental relationships as well. This comes through most clearly in "Mother," about an earthly "mama's boy" who is trapped within the womb of an alien female monster. Diametrically opposite is the scenario of "Son"; other stories include "Daughter," "Father," and "My Sister's Brother."

Two years later, Naomi Mitchison's *Memoirs of a Spacewoman* casually trumped Farmer's ace on this subject of interspecies sex. (PC)

Themes: Aliens, Sex in SF

II-393.   To Your Scattered Bodies Go. Putnam, 1971. Series: Riverworld.

The entire human race is reincarnated along the banks of a huge river. Sir Richard Francis Burton sets off to find out who accomplished this remarkable feat, and why. In *The Fabulous Riverboat* (1971), Sam Clemens undertakes a similar quest. Both characters, and others who become involved in further books of the series, *The Dark Design* (1977) and *The Magic Labyrinth* (1980), are continually sidetracked by violent conflicts in which characters from various phases of Earth's history are idiosyncratically matched against one another, causing the main issue to be constantly confused, sometimes to the detriment of the story. Associated stories outside the main sequence are "Riverworld" in *Riverworld and Other Stories* (1979) and *The Gods of Riverworld* (1983). An early version of the story, written in the 1950s for an ill-fated competition, was rediscovered and issued as *River of Eternity* (1983). Like a number of authors of successful, long-running series, Farmer eventually franchised out the River World. He edited a shared-universe anthology, *Tales of the Riverworld* (1992), that features a new novella by Farmer, "Crossing the Dark River," plus solid fiction by Phillip C. Jennings, Harry Turtledove, Allen Steele, and others. Compare *Time's Eye* by Arthur C. Clarke and Stephen Baxter (2004). (BS/ML)

Awards: Hugo

Themes: Fantastic Voyages, History in SF

II-394.   The Unreasoning Mask. Putnam, 1981.

A swashbuckling space opera with heavy metaphysical overtones. The ambiguous hero undertakes a fabulous quest despite the suspicions of his crew that he is committing awful crimes and exposing them to great danger. Much more tightly organized than most of Farmer's later works, with a suitably apocalyptic climax. Compare Ian Watson's *The Gardens of Delight*. (BS)

Themes: Space Opera

Farrère, Claude (pseudonym of Charles Pierre Édouard Bargone), France, 1876–1957

II-395.   Useless Hands. 1920. Trans. of *Les condamnés à mort* by Elisabeth Abbott, Dutton, 1926.

A depiction of the society of the 1990s reminiscent of Donnelly's *Caesar's Column*, in which the revolution of the proletariat—prompted when they are made redundant from factories as a result of automation—is ruthlessly put down, according to the dictates of social Darwinism. Similar ideas formed the ideological backdrop to Čapek's *R.U.R.* The 1974 Arno reprint uses Bargone's real name. (BS)

Themes: Politics

Fast, Howard, U.S., 1914–2003

*II-396.   The Edge of Tomorrow. Bantam, 1961.

Seven superbly told stories dealing with such themes as the survival of superhuman children in a human, therefore savage, world ("The First Men"); the faking of three ultra-fashionable stores offering "Martian" goods for sale in order to prompt Earth's nations to unite against the alleged menace; in counterpoint, a grim tale of Martian xenophobia toward Earth, "Cato the Martian," and a pioneering inquiry into the ethics of cryonically freezing terminally ill persons until a cure for their condition can be found, "The Cold, Cold Box." In this first SF collection, a well-known mainstream writer speaks with a distinctive voice of his own. (PC)

Fawcett, Edgar, U.S., 1847–1904

*II-397.   The Ghost of Guy Thyrle. Peter Fenelon Collier, 1895.

The longest and most ambitious of the author's ambiguous hallucinatory fantasies, including an enterprising cosmic voyage undertaken by the astrally projected hero following the cremation of his uninhabited body. An "epistolary proem" sets out a manifesto for a new literary species of "realistic romance" but the story's publication in an ephemeral "semi-monthly" series demonstrates the difficulty Fawcett had in selling such a notion to publishers and the public. Several science fiction manuscripts whose copyright he registered were never published and appear to have been lost. Compare the comic voyage sequence to Flammarion's *Lumen* and Astor's *Journey in Other Worlds.* (BS)
   Themes: Paranormal Powers

II-398.   Solarion. Lippincott's, 1889.

Like the identity-exchange novella *Douglas Duane* (1887), the "book" version of this story is extracted from *Lippincott's Monthly,* which published a short novel in every issue, designed to be thus extracted. Cast in the standard pattern of possibly hallucinatory fantasy that he established for his bolder works, it describes the fraught relationship between its protagonist and a dog with artificially augmented intelligence, anticipating the theme and curious sexual charge of Olaf Stapledon's *Sirius.* (BS)
   Themes: Intelligence

Fawcett, E(dward) Douglas, U.K., 1866–1960

II-399.   Hartmann the Anarchist; or, The Doom of the Great City. Arnold, 1893.

An alarmist novel hastily inspired by George Griffith's *Angel of the Revolution,* in which an airborne anarchist's demolition of London is not viewed with the same cheerful equanimity as the activities of Griffith's Terrorists. The interplay between the hero and the charismatic anti-hero recalls the uneasy contemplation of Captain Nemo in Verne's *Twenty Thousand Leagues Under the Sea* and is

strikingly similar to the relationship featured in Max Pemberton's *The Iron Pirate* (1893), which Fawcett had presumably also read in serial form. (BS)
Themes: War

Fearn, John Russell, U.K., 1908–1960

II-400.   **The Intelligence Gigantic**. World's Work, 1943.

A novel first published in *Amazing Stories* in 1933, in which an artificially created superman takes over the world, but is undone in his turn by Martians who are even more advanced. Fearn revisited the theme in a series of novellas featuring the charismatic "Golden Amazon" (1939–1943), who was transformed into a conventional superhero in a subsequent series of novels. Fearn's pulp SF, sampled in *The Best of John Russell Fearn Volume One; The Man Who Stopped the Dust and Other Stories* and *Volume Two: Outcasts of Eternity and Other Stories* (both 2001), edited by Philip Harbottle, demonstrated the rapidity with which pulp SF's melodramatic imagery became standardized, while retaining a vividly slapdash glamour. Compare Taine's *Seeds of Life*. (BS)
Themes: Supermen/women

Finney, Jack (pseud. of Walter Braden Finney), U.S., 1911–1995

II-401.   **The Body Snatchers**. Dell, 1955. Variant title: *Invasion of the Body Snatchers*.

It pretends to be your best friend, but it's really an invading seed pod from outer space. The entire population of a city is gradually replaced with almost no one noticing. That takeover could be a metaphor for either communism or McCarthyism; it has had ardent partisans on both sides. Other critics find it a metaphor for 20th-century human civilization, without benefit of invasion: we are becoming affectless, loveless pods. Finney's human protagonists eventually prevail, but in two film versions the pods win. The seed for this story was planted in Campbell's "Who Goes There?" (1937). For a superb 1950s rendition, compare Dick's terrifying, Freudian "The Father-Thing" (1954). (PC)
Themes: Aliens, Invasion

*II-402.   **The Third Level**. Rinehart, 1957. U.K. title: *The Clock of Time*. Eyre, 1958.

Most of the dozen stories here deal with time travel, not on a cosmic but a domestic scale, with a dominant theme of escape. People from a threatening future escape to a safer present, but may be unraveling the whole future by doing so ("I'm Scared"); people from an unsafe, or simply dull and unpleasant, present escape into the past; others, as in "Of Missing Persons" and the title story, glimpse such an escape but do not achieve it. Humor, as in "Quit Zoomin' Those Hands Through the Air," alternates with the quiet drama found in "There Is a Tide . . . . " Deceptively well written, with lower-middle-class urban characters reminiscent of O. Henry's; themes anticipate Finney's outstanding novel in this subgenre, *Time and Again*. (PC)

Themes: Time Travel

II-403.   Time and Again. Simon & Schuster, 1970.

A timeslip romance whose plausibility is enhanced by making the time travel part of an experimental project and by unusually scrupulous research. Excellent historical detail and a compelling plot make this a superior example of the subgenre. A collection of related stories, *About Time*, appeared in 1986, and a sequel, *From Time to Time*, was published in 1995. Compare Matheson's *Bid Time Return* (BS/ML).

Themes: History in SF, Time Travel

Fisk, Nicholas, U.K., 1923–

II-404.   A Rag, a Bone and a Hank of Hair. Kestrel, 1982.

YA. Super-intelligent Brin, required to take part in experiments manipulating Reborns (artificially created humans of the 23rd century), are increasingly resentful of their inhumane treatment. Although the impact of this insightful critique of social engineering is muted by point-of-view problems and an inconclusive ending, the story is worthwhile and at times very moving. Compare Ames's *Anna to the Infinite Power*; contrast Sargent's *Alien Child*. (FM)

Themes: Androids, Far Future, Intelligence

II-405.   Trillions. Hamish Hamilton, 1971.

YA. Countless numbers of strange geometric objects, called trillions by the children, fall from the skies onto Earth. Thirteen-year-old Scott Houghton, who has extraordinary ability to observe and think, discovers that the trillions have intelligence, are from a destroyed planet, and have come to Earth seeking work and a new home. General Hartman is the leader of those who see the trillions as invaders seeking to destroy, and he proposes to exterminate them. Scott, however, who communicates with the trillions, has them leave Earth to continue their search. Suspenseful, well-written narrative, political overtones, and ecological orientation. Contrast Finney's *The Body Snatchers* or Wyndham's *The Day of the Triffids*. (FM)

Themes: Aliens, Invasion, Paranormal Powers

Flammarion, (Nicolas) Camille, France, 1842–1925

II-406.   Lumen. 1872. Recommended trans. of *Récits de l'infini* by Brian Stableford. Wesleyan Univ. Press, 2002.

A philosophical dialogue modeled on Mercier's "Nouvelles de la lune" (1768) and strongly influenced by Davy's *Consolations in Travel*. The spirit of a dead man tells his former friend about his adventures in the universe; he can now travel faster than light, enabling him to bear witness to the relativity of time and space and to review his past incarnations on many different worlds, where living organisms are adapted to a wide range of local circumstances. Awkwardly constructed, but brilliantly imaginative. (BS)

Themes: Aliens, Fantastic Voyages

II-407.   Omega: The Last Days of the World. Cosmopolitan, 1894.

Following a sequence in which the Earth is struck a glancing blow by a comet, a sketchy future history extends over hundreds of thousands of years to the death of the Earth's last couple, Omegar and Eva, when the sun has grown cold—but the history of the universe continues. Compare Cousin de Grainville's *The Last Man*, Poe's *Eureka*, and Wells's *Time Machine*. (BS)

Themes: End of the World, Future History

II-408.   Urania. 1889. Recommended trans. of *Uranie* by Augusta Rice Stetson. Estes and Lauriat, 1890.

A patchwork loosely linked together by the presiding figure of the eponymous muse of astronomy. The first part adds a few footnotes to *Lumen*, the second consists of anecdotal ramblings about psychical research (in which Flammarion was intensely interested) and the third is a depiction of life on Mars, where life is morally advanced by comparison with Earth. Compare the final section to Lewis's *Out of the Silent Planet*. (BS)

Themes: Life on Other Worlds

Flint, Homer Eon, U.S., 1888–1924

II-409.   The Lord of Death and The Queen of Life. Ace, 1965.

An omnibus of two novellas published in *All-Story* in 1919, which launched a series of interplanetary adventures concluding with *The Devolutionist and The Emancipatrix* (both 1921; omnibus book 1965). The stories are unusual in extrapolating various aspects of social and political theory; the first couplet examines extraterrestrial manifestations of the principle of the survival of the fittest and Malthusian theory, while the second exaggerates distinctions between the bourgeoisie and the proletariat and examines a society based on that of the social insects. Compare Schachner's Past, Present and Future series. (BS)

Themes: Life on Other Worlds, Politics

Flynn, Michael F., U.S., 1947–

II-410.   Firestar. Tor, 1996. Series: Firestar.

In this well-done but decidedly right-wing near-future novel, misguided liberals have all but destroyed the U.S. economy, the space program, and the public school system. Mariesa van Huyten, a visionary industrialist very much in the Heinlein mold, decides to take things into her own hands by creating her own private space program and school system. She succeeds admirably despite underhanded competitors and governmental attempts to undermine her work, and humanity soon returns to space. The novel excels in its well-developed descriptions of alternate near-space technology, though some of Flynn's suggests for reforming the American education system seem naïve. In succeeding novels in the series, humanity moves further and further into space, and hints of an alien presence in the solar system, first introduced in *Firestar*, begin to take stage center. Sequels are *Rogue Star* (1998), *Lodestar* (2000), *Falling Star* (2001), and *Wreck of the River of Stars* (2003). Compare Heinlein's "The Man Who Sold the Moon" (1950) and Poul Anderson's *Harvest of Stars* (1994) and its several sequels. (ML)

Themes: Future History, Hard SF

Foigny, Gabriel de, France, 1640–1692

II-411.　The Southern Land, Known. 1693. Recommended trans. of *La terre australe connue, c'est à dire la description de ce pays inconnu jusqu'ici de ses moeurs et ses coutumes* by David Fausett. Syracuse Univ. Press, 1993.

A painstaking utopia, written in 1676, that attempts to imagine a rational and egalitarian society, taking as its precept that such perfect organization is incompatible with sexual differentiation. The hermaphrodite Australians, without this disadvantage, have succeeded, but a visitor from the outside world cannot fit in. Compare Sturgeon's *Venus Plus X.*

Themes: Sex in SF, Utopias

Ford, John M., U.S., 1957–

II-412.　Growing Up Weightless. Bantam Spectra, 1993.

YA. Matt Ronay has his heart set on going to space but, as the son of a major Lunar politician, it seems unlikely that he will be allowed a life of adventure. He drifts through his world without much purpose, weightless one might say. Then he finds himself in a position to save the crew of a starship who have been endangered in a riot and, as a reward, they offer him a place aboard their ship. The strength of this novel is Ford's beautifully realized lunar society. Compare Barnes's *Orbital Resonance.* (ML)

Awards: Philip K. Dick

Themes: Life on Other Worlds, The Moon, Space Flight

Forester, C(ecil) S(cott), U.K., 1899–1966

II-413.　The Peacemaker. Heinemann, 1934.

A pacifist schoolteacher invents a machine that disrupts magnetic force, thus disabling machinery. He attempts to blackmail world leaders into accepting an end to war, but they refuse to comply. One of the more thoughtful examples of the subspecies; compare S. Fowler Wright's *Power* (1933) and Bob Shaw's *Ground Zero Man* (1971). (BS)

Themes: Politics

Forster, E(dward) M(organ), U.K., 1879–1970

*II-414. **"The Machine Stops"** in *The Eternal Moment and Other Stories*. Sidgwick and Jackson, 1928.

First published in the *Oxford and Cambridge Review* in 1909 and often reprinted, this *conte philosophique* is an ideological reply to the technological utopianism of H. G. Wells. The human race lives underground; individualism and mechanization have proceeded to their logical limit, but the Machine that sustains this society has become faulty and no one any longer knows how to repair it. A devastating assault on what the similarly skeptical S. Fowler Wright was later to call "the Utopia of Comforts," whose anxieties are echoed in such pulp SF stories as Laurence Manning and Fletcher Pratt's "The City of the Living Dead" (1930) and John W. Campbell, Jr.'s "Twilight" and "The Machine." (BS)

Themes: Utopias

Forward, Robert L(ull), U.S., 1932–2002

II-415. **Dragon's Egg**. Ballantine, 1980.

A race that evolves on the surface of a neutron star lives on a vastly compressed time scale, but nevertheless manages to make contact with human observers. A fascinating and ingenious example of hard SF. Its representation of scientists at work compares with Benford's *Timescape,* although Forward's shortcomings as a stylist may annoy some readers. In the sequel, *Starquake* (1985), the aliens achieve technological sophistication, are returned to primitivism by a "starquake," and rebuild their civilization—a process that takes several of their generations but only 24 hours of our time. *The Flight of the Dragonfly* (1984), first in the Rocheworld series, is a similar example of hard SF. Compare Baxter's *Flux* (1993) for another take on the potential for life on a neutron star. (BS/ML)

Themes: Hard SF, Life on Other Worlds, Scientists and Engineers

Foster, Alan Dean, U.S., 1946–

II-416. **The Tar-Aiym Krang**. Ballantine, 1972. Series: Flinx.

The first part of a trilogy continued in *Orphan Star* (1977) and *The End of the Matter* (1977), which has since turned into an open-ended series following the adventures of a young psi-powered hero who takes on mighty adversaries and wins by ingenuity and audacity. Entertaining picaresque space opera. Other novels in the series include *Bloodhype* (1973), *Nor Crystal Tears* (1982), *For Love of Mother Not* (1983), *Flinx in Flux* (1988), *Mid-Flinx* (1995), *Flinx's Folly* (2003), and *Sliding Scales* (2004). The more recent works move away from pure space opera toward more thoughtful consideration of the relationships between different species in the interstellar commonwealth. (BS/ML)

Themes: Aliens, Space Opera

Foster, M(ichael) A(nthony), U.S., 1939–

II-417.   The Morphodite. DAW, 1981. Series: Morphodite.

On a planet where change is suppressed by a determined totalitarian government, revolution is precipitated by an assassin whose calculation of social stresses tells him where to strike and whose shape-shifting power keeps him one step ahead of his pursuers. In the sequels, *Transformer* (1983) and *Preserver* (1985), the morphodite's mission is carried further, into the wider reaches of interstellar civilization. Action-adventure fiction enlivened by the protagonist's dramatic changes of identity and the problems that ensue. (BS)

Themes: Life on Other Worlds, Politics

Fowler, Karen Joy, U.S., 1950–

*II-418.   Artificial Things. Bantam, 1986.

It's rare for a new SF author's first published book to be a short story collection, but Fowler's polished tales have had a powerful and immediate impact within the genre. Included are the hysterically funny "The Faithful Companion at Forty," which gives us the truth about the Lone Ranger's relationship with Tonto, as well as such fine pieces as "The Gate of Ghosts," "The View From Venus," "Praxis," and "The Lake Is Full of Artificial Things." Fowler is a true slipstream writer who frequently skates the boundaries between genres, so it's frequently difficult to clearly label her stories as science fiction, fantasy, or mainstream. A later, equally superb collection, is *Black Glass* (1998). Compare Wilhelm's *The Infinity Box* and other collections. (ML)

*II-419.   Sarah Canary. Holt, 1991.

In 1873, an apparent madwoman stumbles into a Chinese labor camp in Washington State and is led to a nearby insane asylum. The woman, named Sarah Canary at the asylum, escapes and wanders the Pacific Coast, accompanied by a host of fascinating characters. But who is Sarah: a broken victim of male oppression, the simple madwoman she first appeared to be, or something more sinister, a vampire perhaps, or something not of this planet? We never find out for sure, which has frustrated critics bent on sticking the book into a generic pigeonhole. What is certain, however, is that *Sarah Canary* is a brilliantly conceived, beautifully written book. Compare Robert Charles Wilson's *A Hidden Place* (1986). (ML)

Themes: Absurdist SF, Aliens, Feminist SF, History in SF

France, Anatole (pseudonym of Jacques Anatole François Thibault), France, 1844–1924

II-420.   The White Stone. 1903. Trans. of *Sur la pierre blanche* by Charles E. Roche. John Lane, 1910.

A philosophical novel about the difficulty of anticipating the future, in which two novellas are embedded in a conversation piece. In the first novella, exiled

Romans come to the conclusion that Nero's impending reign will usher in a new era of cultural achievement, while considering a brief encounter with Paul of Tarsus devoid of significance; the second, "Through the Horn or the Ivory Gate," carefully—albeit rather somberly—envisages the Marxist utopia of 2270. The novel's commentary on the manner in which writers employ the future as a canvas for painting their hopes and fears, being quite incapable of imagining future shifts in the moral order because they are prisoners of their own moral consciousness, is very perceptive. Compare the second novella to Bellamy's *Looking Backward*, Tarde's *Underground Man*, and Wells's "A Story of the Days to Come." (BS)

Themes: Utopias

Frank, Pat (pseud. of Harry Hart Frank), U.S., 1907–1964

II-421.   Alas, Babylon. Lippincott, 1959.

This effective novel may be the most widely read of all post-holocaust stories. A small band of people survives a nuclear war by hiding in Manhattan's subway tunnels and emerges to start rebuilding. The key to survival, depressing to those who imagine primitiveness as innocence, is discipline. Compare Christopher's *No Blade of Grass* and Stewart's *Earth Abides*. Frank also wrote *Mr. Adam* (Lippincott, 1946), lighter in tone, about a nuclear accident that sterilizes all Earth males except one. The tale seemed hilarious at the time of pubication but sounds sexist and a bit dated today. (PC)

Themes: Holocaust and After

Franklin, Edgar (pseudonym of Edgar Franklin Stearns), U.S., 1879–1958

II-422.   Mr Hawkins' Humorous Inventions. Dodge, 1904.

Along with William Wallace Cook, Franklin was one of the most prolific contributors of SF to the pulp magazines in the first decade of the 20th century. Mr. Hawkins is an inventor of considerable ingenuity, but lacks common sense, so his plans invariably go awry. The 12 stories from 1903–1904 collected here include a perpetual motion machine and a weird airship, but they also feature humbler innovations such as a mobile dishwasher, a sprinkler system for putting out fires, and a steam-operated elevator. The series continued for a further decade, but no further collections were issued. Franklin wrote a couple of serial novels in the same vein, but the relative modesty of their inventions makes them seem tame in retrospect. Contrast Howard Garis's contributions to the Tom Swift series. (BS)

Themes: Discoveries and Inventions

French, Paul *see* Asimov, Isaac

Gail, Otto Willi, Germany, 1896–1956

II-423.   The Shot into Infinity. 1925. Trans. of *Der Schuss ins All* by Francis Courrier. Garland, 1975.

YA. A German interplanetary novel involving a solid-fuel rocket that becomes stranded in lunar orbit, necessitating a rescue attempt by a rival pioneer. It was translated for *Science Wonder Quarterly* in 1929. The German Interplanetary Society, of which Gail was a member, advised Fritz Lang on the design of a rocket ship for the movie *Die Frau im Mond* (1928; *The Girl in the Moon*), which has a similar, but somewhat less plausible, plot. A sequel, *Der Stein vom Mond* (1926; *The Stone from the Moon*), also appeared in *Science Wonder Quarterly*, but deploys so many dubious ideas (Madame Blavatsky's Theosophy, Hoerbiger's World Ice theory, Atlantis, etc.) that its science-fictional credentials are severely weakened. Compare Wyndham's *Planet Plane*. (BS)

Themes: Space Flight

Gallun, Raymond Z(inke), U.S., 1910–1994

II-424.   The Best of Raymond Z. Gallun. Ballantine, 1978.

A collection of 13 stories from 1934–1954, all of the early examples taken from *Astounding*. It opens with the classic "Old Faithful"—an ideological reply to H. G. Wells's *The War of the Worlds* in which biological differences do not prevent humans and a Martian from recognizing their intellectual kinship; two sequels, "The Son of Old Faithful" (1935) and "Child of the Stars" (1936), are not included. "Derelict" (1935) and "Davy Jones' Ambassador" (1935) are similarly positive in their attitude to problematic first contacts, while "Seeds of the Dusk" (1938) is an interesting elegiac account of the far future. Gallun's best work is similar in tone and thoughtfulness to that of "Don A. Stuart" but he rarely appeared in *Astounding* after John Campbell assumed the editorship, perhaps because the two writers were not in harmony ideologically. (PC)

Galouye, Daniel, U.S., 1920–1976

*II-425.   Dark Universe. Bantam, 1961. Recommended ed.: Gregg, 1976.

A vividly imagined, carefully worked out cultural and material setting: total darkness, in which humans subsist on plants that are thermosynthetic rather than photosynthetic, and find their way about by using "clickstones" or by heat-sensing. At the simplest level, the story is a parable of the fallout shelter obsession of the 1950s, but the author was after bigger game. As Robert Thurston points out in his introduction to the Gregg reprint, the characters are like the inmates of Plato's cave in *The Republic*, with their backs to the outside world and able to describe it only inferentially. Lacking first-hand knowledge of light, they deify it, giving rise to some pointed religious satire. The central character's eventual emergence into sunshine and open sky is one of the great epiphanies in SF. Compare Heinlein's "Universe," Blish's "Surface Tension," and Asimov's "Nightfall." (PC)

Themes: Dystopias, Satirical SF

Gamow, George, Russia/U.S., 1904–1968

II-426.   Mr Tompkins in Wonderland; or, Stories of c, G and h. Cambridge Univ. Press, 1939.

A classic collection of six didactic visionary fantasies in which the eponymous protagonist is inspired by lectures on relativity and quantum theory (contained in an appendix) to visit a series of worlds in which those mysteries become much more easily perceptible. It was combined with its sequel, *Mr Tompkins Explores the Atom* (1944), in *Mr Tompkins in Paperback* (1965) and carefully updated by Russell Stannard in *The New World of Mr Tompkins* (1999). (BS)

Themes: Alternate Worlds

Garis, Howard R(oger), U.S., 1873–1962

II-427.   Through the Air to the North Pole; or, The Wonderful Cruise of the Electric Monarch (as by Roy Rockwood), Cupples and Leon, 1906. Series: Great Marvel.

YA. Garis apparently wrote the first six volumes in the Great Marvel series for the Stratemeyer syndicate between 1906 and 1913. Vernian fantasies of a slightly more sophisticated kind than most dime novel fare, they provided a bridge between that kind of work and Carl H. Claudy's Adventures in the Unknown series. Garis also wrote the first 35 novels featuring boy inventor Tom Swift—beginning with *Tom Swift and his Motor-Cycle* (1910)—as Victor Appleton, similarly carrying forward dime novel themes. A prolific writer in several genres, Garis was an efficient hack who rarely rose above mediocrity, but these works were very popular among young readers, and Tom Swift went on to star in three more series. (BS)

Garrett, Garet, U.S., 1878–1954

II-428.   The Blue Wound. Putnam, 1921.

A surreal philosophical fantasy extending from the remote past to 1950, when a second World War completes the destructive work of the first. A critique of civilization and technology anticipating the work of the Marxist historian Lewis Mumford, author of *Technics and Civilization* (1934) and *The Myth of the Machine* (1974), although Garrett later became a right-wing hero for his opposition to the New Deal. He elaborated his ideas on technological progress in the Today and Tomorrow pamphlet *Ouroboros; or, the Mechanical Extension of Man* (1925). Compare Brussof's "The Republic of the Southern Cross." (BS)

Themes: History in SF

Gentle, Mary, U.K., 1956–

II-429.   Ash: A Secret History. Gollancz, 2000.

Originally published as four separate volumes in the U.S., and in one volume in the U.K., Ash is the story of a female mercenary in late medieval Europe, just at the moment when Burgundy as an independent land was written out of history. Two contemporary researchers uncover the story of Ash, which is initially shocking in its depiction of a female mercenary. Eventually they realize that the story is far more subversive than that. What is eventually presented is a complex alternate history of North African interference in Europe, of previously unsuspected technologies, and, in the end, of the survival of Burgundy. The medieval world is convincingly (if occasionally melodramatically) presented; though the modern sections, presented mostly as an exchange of e-mails, are less satisfactory. Compare Stephenson's *Quicksilver*. (PK)

Themes: Alternate Worlds, History in SF, Science Fantasy, War

II-430.   Golden Witchbreed. Gollancz, 1983.

Lynne Christie, envoy of Earth Dominion, has been sent to Orthe to determine whether its humanoid inhabitants are ready for diplomatic and economic relations. She discovers a complex world with factions both friendly to and hostile to her goal. Gentle's Orthe is a superb example of world building, comparable in many ways to Herbert's *Dune* or Le Guin's *The Left Hand of Darkness*. Compare also Cherryh's *The Faded Sun* and her Foreigner series. The excellent sequel is *Ancient Light* (1987). (ML)

Themes: Aliens, Life on Other Worlds, Politics, Women in SF

Gernsback, Hugo, Luxembourg/U.S., 1884–1964

II-431.   Ralph 124C41+. Stratford, 1925.

A novel serialized in *Modern Electrics* (1911–1912) and revised for book publication in order to augment and update its extraordinary catalogue of technical wonders. The propaganda for technological progress is embedded in a crude plot derivative of the worst of dime novel melodrama, but the essence of the work is its gadgetry. Useful as an insight into the mission statement of Gernsbackian "scientifiction." (BS)

Themes: Discoveries and Inventions

Gerrold, David (pseud. of Jerrold David Friedman), U.S., 1944–

II-432.   The Man Who Folded Himself. Random, 1973.

A time traveler shuttles back and forth, replicating himself many times over and creating practical and existential problems for himselves. A playfully narcissistic treatment of the time paradox theme, developing ideas from Heinlein's "By His Bootstraps" (1941) and "All You Zombies . . . " (1959). (BS)

Themes: Time Travel

II-433. **When HARLIE Was One**. Doubleday, 1972.

The hero supervises the making and education of a sentient computer, which in turn eventually designs an artificial intelligence even more powerful in order to demonstrate its usefulness. *When HARLIE Was One (Release 2.0)* (1988) is a rewrite of the earlier novel, updating the computer technology and jettisoning its early-1970s drug culture milieu. Opinions are mixed as to which version is superior. Compare Thomas J. Ryan's *Adolescence of P-1* (1977) and Tom Maddox's *Halo* (1991). (ML/BS)

Themes: Computers, Intelligence

Geston, Mark S(ymington), U.S., 1946–

II-434. **Lords of the Starship**. Ace, 1967. Series: Starship.

In the far future, a nation whose ancestors once built starships attempts to duplicate their achievement, though the country no longer has the appropriate technology and must expend many generations in the project. *Out of the Mouth of the Dragon* (1969) is set in the same desolate far future and deals with the last of the many wars that have laid it waste. Related novels are *The Day Star* (1972) and *The Siege of Wonder* (1976). Grim and somber stories. with some fine imagery and a uniquely bitter ennui. (BS)

Themes: Far Future

Ghosh, Amitav, India, 1956–

II-435. **The Calcutta Chromosome: A Novel of Fevers, Delirium and Discovery**. Ravi Dayal, New Delhi, 1996; Picador, 1996.

Two parallel stories tell of a search in the near future for a scientist who disappeared in India while investigating a new theory about malaria, and of Ronald Ross's original research into malaria in Calcutta in 1898. Ross remains blissfully ignorant that the local technicians he uses are actually steering his research, while in the near future a secret society is revealed that has kept India technologically more advanced than their colonizers have ever realized. Ghosh, an acclaimed mainstream novelist, here uses science and science fiction skillfully to present a very different perspective on the colonial experience. Compare Jones's *White Queen*. (PK)

Awards: Arthur C. Clarke

Themes: Biology, History in SF, Medicine, Scientists and Engineers

Gibson, William, U.S./Canada, 1948–

*II-436. **Burning Chrome**. Arbor, 1986.

Ten short stories by one of the most innovative new voices to enter the science fiction field in decades. Included here are such superb short fictions as "Burning Chrome," "The Winter Market," "Dogfight" (co-authored with Michael Swanwick), and "Hinterlands," as well as collaborations with Bruce Sterling and

John Shirley. Several are award nominees. Many of the stories are set in the sleazy, cyberpunk future made famous in Gibson's novels. Compare Sterling's *Crystal Express* and *Global Head*. (ML)

Themes: Cyberpunk

II-437.   Count Zero. Arbor House, 1985. Series: Neuromancer.

A complex adventure story set in the same future as *Neuromancer*. The eponymous hero gets into trouble as a result of a weird experience in cyberspace, while two other protagonists follow their own projects to the entangled climax; clever and slick. The same settings also feature in many of Gibson's short stories, collected in *Burning Chrome*. (BS)

Themes: Computers, Cyberpunk, Dystopias, Intelligence, Virtual Reality

II-438.   Mona Lisa Overdrive. Gollancz, 1988. Series: Neuromancer.

Gibson's third cyberpunk novel, following *Neuromancer* and *Count Zero*, features a complex plotline and four separate protagonists: a teenage runaway, an artist who creates kinetic sculpture from scrap, the daughter of a wealthy Japanese industrialist, and a Sense/Net star. A number of characters from the earlier stories also reappear. Although not generally regarded as highly as is *Neuromancer*, *Mona* is engrossing. A novel of dark settings and pointed details, it features Gibson's usual superb style. (ML)

Themes: Computers, Cyberpunk, Dystopias, Intelligence, Virtual Reality

*II-439.   Neuromancer. Ace, 1984. Series: Neuromancer.

In a highly urbanized future dominated by cybernetics and bioengineering, anti-hero Case is rescued from wretchedness and given back the ability to send his persona into the cyberspace of the world's computer networks, where he must carry out a hazardous mission for an enigmatic employer. An adventure story much enlivened by elaborate technical jargon and sleazy, streetwise characters—the pioneering "cyberpunk" novel and arguably the most influential SF novel of the 1980s. Compare Vinge's *True Names*, Sterling's *Islands in the Net*, and the film *Blade Runner*. (BS/ML)

Awards: Hugo, Nebula, Philip K. Dick

Themes: Computers, Cyberpunk, Dystopias, Intelligence, Virtual Reality

*II-440.   Pattern Recognition. Putnam, 2003.

The present has caught up with the future in this first of Gibson's novels set in the current day. Cayce Pollard is a successful but neurotic market researcher with a virtually psychic ability to pick just the right logo and track trends before anyone else has noticed them. Pollard is hired to hunt down the source of a series of ambiguous and mysterious film clips that have been appearing on the internet and that have attracted a cult following. Then she finds herself being followed, and someone hacks her computer. There's evidence of a connection to her late father, a security specialist and probable CIA agent who was supposedly killed in the World Trade Center disaster, though no body was ever recovered. This is Gibson at his most brilliant and elliptical, a novel that qualifies as science fiction due more to its attitude towards the world than any formal genre trappings. Compare Sterling's *Zeitgeist.* (ML).

Themes: Paranormal Powers, Politics

II-441.   Virtual Light. Viking, 1993. Series: Virtual Light.

In post-quake San Francisco, the badly damaged Golden Gate Bridge has become home for hundreds of dropouts and counterculture types. One such, Chevette, while working as a bicycle messenger, steals a pair of virtual reality glasses that contain a secret that a number of people are willing to kill for. Gibson's early-21st-century California is wonderfully well realized, and the action plot is nicely handled. Two later novels set in the same future are *Idoru* (1996) and *All Tomorrow's Parties* (1999). Compare Richard Paul Russo's *Destroying Angel* (1992); contrast Pat Murphy's *The City, Not Long After.* (ML)

Themes: Computers, Crime and Punishment, Cyberpunk, Intelligence

Gibson, William, U.S./Canada, 1948– and Sterling, Bruce, U.S., 1954–

II-442.   The Difference Engine. Gollancz, 1990.

The Victorian scientist Charles Babbage designed a primitive but workable mechanical computer. He never built it, of course, but what if he had? The novel postulates an enormously accelerated Industrial Revolution fueled by construction of gigantic Babbage machines and, as a result, a social revolution as well. Lord Byron, leader of the Industrial Radical party, has become Prime Minister, and the country is largely run by a science-based meritocracy. Against this wonderfully complex backdrop, the authors work a fairly straight-forward mystery plotline: it seems that a valuable deck of programming cards has been stolen and a variety of powerful people are willing to do virtually anything to recover them. One of the joys of this rather erudite novel lies in spotting the many historical personages and figuring out exactly how their lives have changed. Compare Michael Flynn's use of the Babbage machine in *In the Country of the Blind* (1990). (ML)

Themes: Alternate Worlds, Computers, History in SF, Intelligence, Steampunk

Gilman, Charlotte Perkins, U.S., 1860–1935

II-443.   Herland. Pantheon, 1979.

A utopian novel first serialized in Gilman's periodical *The Forerunner* in 1915. Three male explorers stumble upon an all-female society that has attained a kind of pastoral ideal based on mutual cooperation and the sanctification of motherhood. In a sequel, *With Her in Ourland* (1916; book 1997), one of the protagonists escorts an emissary back to the greater world so that she can report on its shortcomings. Gilman had earlier written a futuristic feminist utopia *Mov-*

ing the Mountain (1911); all three novels are in the omnibus *Charlotte Perkins Gilman's Utopian Novels* (1999). *Herland*'s reputation is a trifle over-inflated, but the more imaginative image of an all-female society presented in Zaronovitch's *Mizora* is too tongue-in-cheek to recommend itself to earnest feminists. (BS)

Themes: Feminist SF, Utopias

Gloag, John (Edward), U.K., 1896–1981

II-444.   The New Pleasure. Allen and Unwin, 1933.

The invention of a euphoric drug that stimulates the sense of smell brings its manufacturers into fierce competition with the tobacco industry, presenting its advertisers with a tough challenge, but ultimately allows its users to realize that modern civilization stinks. A politely witty but highly effective satire. (BS)

Themes: Satirical SF

II-445.   99%. Cassell, 1944.

Written (judging from internal evidence) in 1935/1936 at the time of the Italo-Ethiopian War but not published until late in World War II. A physician believes that 99 percent of our consciousness is ancestral and as an experiment he gives each of seven men a pill that will bring up an ancestral memory in dream form. The resulting adventures in earlier, violent centuries shake up the present-day one percent of the minds of these well-characterized conventional Londoners so that each makes a personal life change, with ironic or ambiguous results; one renounces the modern world entirely. The message at least borders on the pessimistic: life is just one damn thing after another and with our one percent minds we just keep doing them over and over. Compare Jack London's *Before Adam*. (PC)

Themes: Pastoral, Psychology

*II-446.   To-Morrow's Yesterday. Allen and Unwin, 1932.

A Wellsian novel based on a film script that was never shot. The movie, shown in London in a new high-tech theatre to an audience that cannot realize its significance, displays the decline of humankind into degenerate savagery after a series of destructive wars. A scathing commentary is provided by our cat-descended successors. The novel's bitter sarcasm is strongly reminiscent of that displayed in Edward Shanks's *People of the Ruins*. (BS)

Themes: Holocaust and After

*II-447.   Winter's Youth. Allen and Unwin, 1934.

A political satire in which a discredited British government tries to recover its popularity by promoting a rejuvenation technology. The ploy works in the short term, but it is only a matter of time before the young react to the realization that they are no longer destined to inherit the Earth; the one sane man at the heart of the government fails to prevent a destructive conflict. Compare Bell's *The Seventh Bowl* and Shiel's *The Young Men Are Coming!* (BS)

Themes: Biology

Gloss, Molly, U.S., 1944–

II-448.   Wild Life. Simon and Schuster, 2000.

A multilayered novel in which the life of the author Charlotte Bridger Drummond, writing in the early 1900s, is pieced together from diary entries, extracts from her stories, and an unpublished account of her experience living in the forests of the Pacific North West with a group of sasquatch-like creatures. Gloss paints a vivid portrait of an unconventional but practical woman, earning a living by writing adventure stories, constantly questioning women's roles in society and society's expectation of them, but also obliged to juggle her own family responsibilities with her need to write. However, throughout, the novel is also hedged with uncertainty; the reader is never entirely clear whether Drummond has told a true story or whether her "diary" is yet another thrilling adventure story, left unfinished. Compare Fowler's *Sarah Canary*. (MKS)

Awards: James Tiptree
Themes: Feminist SF, Women in SF

Godwin, Francis, U.K., 1562–1633

II-449.   The Man in the Moone; or, A Discourse of a Voyage Thither by Domingo Gonsalez, the Speedy Messenger. Kirton and Warre, 1638.

A highly influential lunar voyage story, important in bridging the gap between earlier travelers' tales and such supposedly enlightened satires as Cyrano's (in which Domingo Gonsalez crops up as a minor character). There is some comment on the adaptation of the humanoid Lunarians to the long cycle of day and night, but the story warrants attention mainly because its blithe absurdity is so amusing. (BS)

Themes: Fantastic Voyages

Gold, H(orace) L., U.S., 1914–1982

II-450.   The Old Die Rich and Other Science Fiction Stories: with Working Notes and an Analysis of Each Story. Crown, 1955.

Twelve stories, 1939–1953, by the distinguished editor of *Galaxy* magazine. In "Hero," the modest leading character returns from the first expedition to Mars and receives corrosive media and commercial hype; he flees back to Mars. The vivid title story is a well-plotted time travel-cum-murder mystery. Other stories typify the sardonic medical-meddling SF that was a prominent theme in *Galaxy* under Gold. A choice collection, enhanced by Gold's working notes, that could be profitably studied by anyone interested in how one writer proceeded with a story before doing the actual writing. (PC)

Golding, William, U.K., 1911–

II-451.   The Brass Butterfly. Faber, 1958.

A stage play, adapted from the novella "Envoy Extraordinary" in the anthology, *Sometime, Never* (Ballantine, 1956). A Leonardo-like genius comes to the court of a Roman emperor with models of inventions that could, at that moment, unleash a full-scale industrial revolution. The emperor backs off, ostensibly on the ground that these are toys, but also with the insight that down the road lies the horror of modern industrialism and war. An early instance of the anti-technology SF that became a major emphasis in the 1960s to the distress of "Old Wave" partisans, by the author of *Lord of the Flies* and a Nobel Prize-winner. Contrast de Camp's *Lest Darkness Fall.* (PC)

Themes: History in SF, Satirical SF

Goldstein, Lisa, U.S., 1953–

II-452.   A Mask for the General. Bantam, 1987.

Twenty-first-century America, plunged into a permanent depression by the collapse of computer technology, struggles under the repressive rule of the General, while in Berkeley, California, a group of artists and latter-day hippies do their best to promote revolution. Foremost among them is Livia, a mask maker whose creations appear to have almost mystical powers. This is a subtle, but moving novel, lacking much in the way of action, but making up for it with fine writing. Compare two very similar books, Murphy's *The City, Not Long After* and Russo's *Subterranean Gallery.* (ML)

Themes: Disaster, Dystopias, Science Fantasy

Goodman, Alison, Australia, 1966–

II-453.   Singing the Dogstar Blues. HarperCollins Voyager, 1998; Viking 2002.

YA. Joss, a brilliant but headstrong student of time travel at the prestigious Centre for Neo-Historical Studies, discovers that she's been chosen to be the roommate of Mavkel, the first alien to study at the Centre. This doesn't please her because she's used to living a fairly wild life and the security around the young alien makes this impossible, particularly after an assassination attempt. Joss soon finds something in common with Mavkel, however. They both love music. Then the alien becomes ill and Joss, breaking all of the Centre's rules, resorts to time travel to save Mavkel's life. A well-done cross between science fiction and mystery by a talented new writer. (ML)

Themes: Aliens, Coming of Age, Time Travel

Goonan, Kathleen Ann, U.S., 1952–

II-454.   Queen City Jazz. Tor, 1994. Series: Nanotech Quartet.

Sequentially the second of Goonan's jazz-infused Nanotech Quartet, though the first to be published, followed by *Mississippi Blues* (1997), *Crescent City Rhap-*

sody (2000), and *Light Music* (2002), set in a near-future world afflicted by communications problems brought about by electromagnetic pulses from space, and by nanotech plagues that inflict strange compulsions on sufferers. Goonan portrays a world struggling to come to terms with finding new (or old) ways in which to communicate, and to recover and preserve information, but also explores what happens when civilization breaks down so suddenly, and human beings are obliged to become heavily self-sufficient. In many respects, Goonan is drawing on a long tradition of post-catastrophe novels, stretching back at least to George R. Stewart's *Earth Abides*, in a style also reminiscent of Pat Murphy's *The City, Not Long After* and Lisa Goldstein's *A Mask for The General*. The blend of jazz and organic chemistry is, however, uniquely hers. (MKS)

Themes: Holocaust and After, Nanotechnology

Goto, Hiromi, Japan/Canada, 1966–

II-455.   The Kappa Child. Red Deer Press, 2001.

Hiromi Goto's novel combines Japanese mythology with modern mores to produce a remarkable portrait of a deeply dysfunctional Japanese-Canadian family struggling to survive in a harsh physical and emotional landscape. The eponymous kappa is a water spirit (or could it be an alien?), and the entire novel is informed by drought: a lack of water, a lack of love. The narrator's father's failure to grow rice in one of the driest Canadian provinces mirrors his failure to support his wife and four daughters in other, less material ways. As adults they all struggle with their guilt in having fled but are unable to bring the family together again until the narrator has a mysterious moonlight encounter with a stranger and comes to believe herself pregnant with a kappa. Whether or not the pregnancy is real, its effect on the narrator and her family is to lift the emotional drought and bring new life. (MKS)

Awards: James Tiptree
Themes: Mythology, Science Fantasy

Goulart, Ron, U.S., 1933–

II-456.   After Things Fell Apart. Ace, 1970.

A detective pursues a gang of feminist assassins through the eccentric subcultures of a balkanized future United States. The best of the author's many humorous SF novels, with a genuine satirical element to add to the usual slapstick. Compare Robert Sheckley's *Journey Beyond Tomorrow* (1962). (BS)

Themes: Humorous SF

Graham, P(eter) Anderson, U.K., ?–1925

II-457.   The Collapse of Homo Sapiens. Putnam, 1923.

One of the many apocalyptic future-war novels published in the aftermath of World War I, this envisages the majority of humankind reverting to degenerate animality after another destructive war, while those attempting to keep the flickering flame of civilization alight are doomed by their low birthrate. Its racist rhetoric recalls England's *Darkness and Dawn*, while the images of degeneration anticipate Gloag's *To-Morrow's Yesterday*. (BS)

Themes: Holocaust and After

Grainville, Cousin de *see* Cousin de Grainville

Grant, Richard, U.S., 1952–

II-458.   Rumors of Spring. Bantam, 1987.

A strange blend of satire, fable, science fiction, and fantasy set on a far-future Earth where technology is in a state of collapse, entropy seems to be gaining, and a badly damaged ecology is actively fighting back. The First Biotic Crusade, a group of eccentrics worthy of a Mervyn Peake novel, set out in a huge Rube Goldberg–like vehicle to uncover the truth behind the strange goings-on in the world's last woodland, the Carbon Bank Forest. At once a cutting attack on government bureaucracy, a sprightly and somewhat silly adventure story, and an ecological fable, *Rumors of Spring* is beautifully written and constantly surprising. Compare John Crowley's *Little, Big* (1981). (ML)

Themes: Ecology, Holocaust and After, Humorous SF, Mythology

Gray, Alasdair, Scotland, 1934–

II-459.   A History Maker. Canongate, 1994; Harcourt Brace, 1996.

Gray is a fiercely political writer whose work is always intimately connected with what it is to be Scottish. In this short novel, this theme is at its most overt. Set in the 23rd century on the Scottish Borders, when war is regulated like a football match, it concerns the intriguingly named Wat Dryhope, hero of the Ettrick army who wins the iconic standard through a maneuver he himself believes is a cheat. Through this he becomes the vector for a worldwide wave of militarism manipulated by those who want to end the peaceful status quo; but at the same time he finds himself drawn to those who best represent this rustic peace. Using postmodern devices, including a long section of notes, this is Gray's most straightforward embrace of science fiction themes. (PK)

Themes: Politics, Satirical SF, War

*II-460.   Lanark: A Life in 4 Books. Canongate, 1981; revised 1985.

Although fragments of this monumental novel first appeared as early as 1958, Gray's first novel was only published in 1981, while an expanded "definitive edition" appeared in 1985. In an epilogue, which perversely appears only partway through Book Four, Gray lists his "plagiarisms," which include Borges, Wells, Poe, and Chris Boyce among other SF writers; nevertheless, the novel remains sui generis. It tells of the unsatisfactory (and autobiographical) life of artist Duncan Thaw in contemporary Scotland, and of the odyssey of a parallel character, Lanark, in the posthumous city of Unthank. Mysterious, daring, and breathtakingly original, this was one of the major novels of the 1980s. Compare (at a pinch) Wells's *The Sleeper Awakes*; Millhauser's *In the Realm of Morpheus* (1986). (PK)

Themes: Mythology, Politics, Satirical SF

II-461.   Poor Things. Bloomsbury, 1992.

Presented as the memoirs of "the Early Life of a Scottish Public Health Officer" set in the 1880s, this is a version of the Frankenstein story mixed with elements of Jekyll and Hyde (Stevenson is a notable influence on Gray, who has completed one of Stevenson's unfinished stories). Told by medical student Archie McCandless and set largely in Glasgow, it tells of his rivalry with Duncan Wedderburn for the beautiful Bella Baxter and his gradual discovery that she is the creation of the larger-than-life Godwin Baxter. The character of the spirited Bella and her ambiguous place in life allows Gray to give the novel a very strong feminist theme. Compare Shelley's *Frankenstein*. (PK)

Themes: Feminist SF, History in SF, Monsters

Greenland, Colin, U.K., 1954–

*II-462.   Take Back Plenty. Unwin, 1990. Series: Take Back Plenty.

This sophisticated and enormously funny postmodernist space opera owes a debt not only to the pulp tradition, but also to Lewis Carroll. Tabitha Jute, a freelance space trucker with a penchant for partying and choosing unsuitable lovers, is hired to transport a rather shady troupe of entertainers from the decaying space habitat Plenty to the surface of Titan. The entertainers, however, are not what they claim to be, and Tabitha soon finds herself up to her neck in intrigue. Sequels include *Seasons of Plenty* (1995) and *Mother of Plenty* (1998). Compare Iain M. Banks's *The Player of Games*. (ML)

Awards: Arthur C. Clarke

Themes: Feminist SF, Life on Other Worlds, Satirical SF, Space Opera, Women in SF

Greg, Percy, U.K., 1836–1889

II-463.   Across the Zodiac: The Story of a Wrecked Record. Truebner, 2 vols., 1880.

An interplanetary novel whose hero employs an antigravity technology similar to that devised by "Chrysostom Trueman" to travel to Mars, where he discovers a rational society menaced by the rebellious Children of the Star (who cling to beliefs and folkways more akin to those preserved on Earth). His part in the consequent conflict is minor, but it turns out that he has brought a plague to Mars that might have more apocalyptic consequences; Hugh MacColl and H. G. Wells probably came by the same idea independently. The interplanetary voyage is described with conscientious verisimilitude, and the depiction of Martian society is meticulous, including some account of its exotic language. An ambitious work developing many ideas broached in Greg's rambling nonfiction work *The Devil's Advocate* (1878). (BS)

Themes: Space Flight, The Planets, Utopias

Gregory, Owen (unattributed pseudonym)

II-464.   Meccania the Super-State. Methuen, 1918.

A fine social satire in which a young Chinese visitor visits the technologically advanced European state of Meccania (Germany) in the year 1970. The Meccanians are chauvinistic, pedantic, militaristic, and obsessed with bureaucracy, but their supposedly rational state is a repressive tyranny of whose essential precariousness they are all too well aware. In retrospect, a dramatically prophetic work, written while World War I was still going on. Compare the high-tech utopia in Moszkowski's *Isles of Wisdom* and von Hanstein's account of *Electropolis*. (BS)

Themes: Satirical SF

Griffith, George (Chetwynd), U.K., 1857–1906

II-465.   The Angel of the Revolution. Tower, 1893.

An inventor places his new airship at the disposal of anarchistic Terrorists intent on bringing down the world's tyrannies (especially the Tsar of Russia). After much fighting—more elaborately described in the *Pearson's Weekly* serial version—the Terrorists win, then thwart a revolt of Islam before assuming overall control of the world order from a base in the remote African valley of Aeria. The novel sparked a new boom in future-war stories, but even Griffith could only match its imaginative daring once more, in *Olga Romanoff; or, The Syren of the Skies* (1894). That sequel takes up the story in the mid-21st century, when Aerian dominion is threatened by the eponymous *femme fatale*, reaching the brink of destruction before a stray comet arrives to trash the world. The stories sprawl rather drunkenly, partly because they were made up as they went along, but they were key foundation stones of scientific romance. (BS)

Themes: War

II-466.   A Honeymoon in Space. Pearson, 1901.

A tale of interplanetary tourism borrowing adeptly from previous works that had modified the imagery of religious cosmic visions to correspond more closely with the imaginative tenor of scientific romance. Griffith routinely copied popular imaginative works by other writers, so this exercise was presumably inspired by Astor's *A Journey in Other Worlds*, but the sequence in which the *Astronef* is trapped by the gravity of a dark star in the outer reaches of the solar system is innovative, anticipating the melodramatics of pulp SF. (BS)

Themes: Space Flight

II-467.   The Lord of Labour. F. V. White, 1911.

Griffith's last novel, left incomplete on his death (the final chapters are synoptic and were probably penned by another hand). Since *The Outlaws of the Air* (1895), Griffith had moved away from the far left position of *The Angel of the Revolution*; the hero of this novel is still fighting greedy capitalists, but on behalf of liberal democracy rather than anarchism. In any case, the Citizen's Army he organizes soon has more important work to do in thwarting the Kaiser. The Germans are armed with a ray that destroys steel, but the English fight back with portable atomic weapons. Clearly derivative of M. P. Shiel—especially *The Lord of the Sea*—but interesting in its attempt to recover the imaginative verve of Griffith's earliest novels. (BS)

Themes: War

Griffith, Nicola, U.K./U.S., 1960–

II-468.   Ammonite. Ballantine Del Rey, 1992.

Centuries ago a corporate-owned colony on the planet Jeep met with disaster when a deadly virus killed all of the colony's men and made permanent changes in the genes of its few surviving women. The corporation abandoned the remaining colonists, but now it has returned, ready to make a new attempt to exploit the planet's resources. Anthropologist Marghe Taishan has been sent to test a new defense against the virus and to evaluate the culture that evolved during Jeep's long isolation, but she soon finds herself going native. This is an unusually impressive first novel that deals intelligently with gender issues and same-sex relationships. Compare Russ's *The Female Man* and Charnas's *Motherlines*. (ML)

Awards: James Tiptree
Themes: Feminist SF, Life on Other Worlds

II-469.   Slow River. Ballantine Del Rey, 1995.

In this intense, near-future novel, heiress Lore Van de Oest is kidnapped and left for dead when her family refuses to pay her ransom. Taken in by a woman named Spanner, who makes her living as a thief on the Net, Lore abandons her well-to-do lifestyle, becomes Spanner's lover, and finds a job in a high-tech sewage disposal plant. Transformed by her experiences, she eventually returns to her family in order to uncover some of their more unsavory secrets. Lore and Spanner are extremely well-realized characters. Like *Ammonite*, *Slow River* received the Lamba Award for contributions to gay and lesbian literature. (ML)

Awards: Nebula
Themes: Crime and Punishment, Feminist SF, Psychology

Grimwood, Jon Courtenay, U.K., 1953–

II-470.　Pashazade: The First Arabesk. Earthlight, 2001. Series: Arabesk.

Grimwood has frequently addressed the twin themes of identity and the autonomy of artificial intelligence in his novels, but *Pashazade*, and its sequels, *Effendi: The Second Arabesk* (2002) and *Felaheen: The Third Arabesk* (2003), tackle these issues head-on. Set in a small North African country, in the not-so-distant future, the series follows the fortunes of Ashraf Bey or Rafi, a young man of uncertain parentage and identity, who possesses a body that has been augmented with some sort of AI. His efforts to maintain a stable persona as Rafi, distinct from his AI and from his former identity, ZeeZee, reflect the struggles of El Iskandriya, his newly adopted country, to maintain its own political autonomy in the face of threats from larger powers and from internal political threats that would otherwise tear the country apart. Thus Grimwood explicitly makes the personal political and vice versa, all this set against the backdrop of a vividly realized desert landscape. Compare Effinger, *When Gravity Fails*. (MKS)

　　Themes: Alternate Worlds, Computers, Crime and Punishment, Intelligence, Politics

Guin, Wyman (Woods), U.S., 1915–1989

II-471.　Living Way Out. Avon, 1967.

A superior collection of seven stories, showcasing the writer's ability to create works that are logical and consistent in their details but whose totality is bizarre. "Beyond Bedlam" required three revisions before it was accepted by H. L. Gold; the story remains politically and psychiatrically harrowing in spite of dated elements. "The Delegate from Guapanga" is a deliciously skewed parable of politics. (PC)

Gunn, James E., U.S., 1923–

II-472.　The Dreamers. Simon & Schuster, 1980.

Once the mechanism of memory is known, the business of learning is technologically transformed, but the acquisition of information by ingestion and injection mechanizes the personality. Thoughtful development of fascinating premises; similar in structure and import to the author's *The Joy Makers* (1961). (BS)

　　Themes: Psychology

II-473.　The Listeners. Scribner, 1972.

A fix-up novel about the radio astronomers who pick up and decode a message from an alien civilization, and about the public reaction to the event. The work is heavy with religious symbolism and literary allusion. Compare Clarke's *2010* (1982) and Michael Kube-McDowell's *Emprise* (1985). (BS)

　　Themes: Aliens, Religion

**II-474.	Some Dreams Are Nightmares**. Scribner, 1974.

Strongly believing that "the ideal length for science fiction is the novelette," Gunn excerpted from novels four stories of that length. "The Cave of Night" (1955) is a first-man-in-space story with a wry twist at the end, taken from *Station in Space* (1958). "The Hedonist," from *The Joy Makers* (1961), describes a world dedicated to "happiness," not pursued ad lib à la Jefferson but therapeutically prescribed and coerced, resulting in a peculiarly horrible dystopia. "New Blood" (1955) describes a mutation that renders people virtually immune to death. "Medic" (1957) extrapolates from the then already obscene cost of medical care in America and the corporate insensitivity of hospitals to a really savage future; both tales are from *The Immortals* (1962). He makes his case that such tales can stand alone, a point library users attuned to "the book," that is, the novel, should ponder carefully. Forty years after *The Immortals*, which in the interim had also become a TV series, Gunn produced another powerful novelette in the same future history of medicine, "Elixir" (*Analog*, May 2004). (PC)

Haddix, Margaret Peterson, U.S., 1964–

**II-475.	Among the Hidden**. Simon & Schuster, 1988.

YA. The first in the Shadow Children series, this novel is set in a future world where overpopulation has led to the creation of the Population Police and having more than two children is illegal. Luke, a third child, has spent his life in hiding on his family's isolated farm until their land is taken for new housing and he must retreat to the attic. After meeting another third child, Luke must decide whether to continue in hiding or to openly defy the repressive government. Sequels to this well-done novel for middle school readers are *Among the Imposters* (2001), *Among the Betrayed* (2002), *Among the Barons* (2003), and *Among the Brave* (2004). Compare Christopher's *The Guardians*. (ML)

Themes: Dystopias, Overpopulation

Haggard, H(enry) Rider, U.K., 1856–1925

**II-476.	She: A History of Adventure**. Longmans, 1887.

The best and by far the most influential of Haggard's many exotic romances. It belongs to the subgenre of "karmic romance" that he pioneered, its hero being the reincarnation of a lover for whom the charismatic anti-heroine has been waiting for centuries. It was the inspirational ancestor of a great many modern *femme fatale* stories, including such quasi–science-fictional examples as G. Firth Scott's *The Last Lemurian* (1896; book 1898), Pierre Benoit's *L'Atlantide* (1919; trans. as *The Queen of Atlantis* and *Atlantida*) and numerous tales from the U.S. pulps; Haggard probably had some influence on Edgar Rice Burroughs and certainly influenced A. Merritt. (BS)

Themes: Immortality

Halam, Ann *see* Jones, Gwyneth

Haldeman, Joe, U.S., 1943–

II-477.   The Coming. Ace, 2000.

As the Earth moves towards environmental collapse and an impending nuclear war, astronomer Aurora Bell receives what appears to be a message from the stars heralding the arrival in three months of extraterrestrials. But are the aliens real or is it all an elaborate hoax? Much of the emphasis here is on the effect of the impending visit on a society gone out of control. Unusually thoughtful science fiction. Compare Sagan's *Contact* and Blish's *A Case of Conscience.* (ML)

   Themes: Aliens, Ecology, Sociology

*II-478.   Forever Peace. Ace, 1997.

Julian Class makes his living as a university professor in the United States, but for a week or so each month he goes on duty, fitting himself into a virtual "soldierboy," a telepresence device that links him to a nearly indestructible military robot that allows him to participate in horrendous wars taking place on the other side of the world. His military service is completely safe, from a physical point of view, but it's taking a serious emotional toll. Worse yet, Class and his lover, Dr. Amelia Harding, have discovered that some of the new technology spurred on by the war is getting out of control and has become a danger to the entire world. Like Haldeman's earlier novel, *The Forever War*, this well-written book serves as a powerful indictment of both humanity's greed and its proclivity for fouling its own nest. (ML)

   Awards: Hugo, Nebula, John W. Campbell
   Themes: Psychology, Virtual Reality, War

*II-479.   The Forever War. St. Martin's, 1975.

Fix-up novel of interstellar war against hive-organized aliens. Realistic descriptions of military training and action, with interesting use of relativistic time distortions. A reprise of and ideological counterweight to Heinlein's *Starship Troopers*. *Forever Free* (1999), not to be confused with *Forever Peace* (1997), which is a stand-alone novel, is a solid sequel. *The Forever War* is one of the most important novels to come out of the U.S. experience in Vietnam. Compare also Card's *Ender's Game*. (BS/ML)

   Awards: Hugo, *Locus*
   Themes: Aliens, Psychology, War

II-480.   The Hemingway Hoax. Morrow, 1990.

John Baird, a Hemingway specialist at Boston University with severe financial problems, falls in with some shady characters who persuade him to fake and then claim to have rediscovered a series of stories that Hemingway is known to have lost on a train trip. Unbeknown to Baird or his confederates, however, some very strange people—people not from our world—have a stake in Baird's *not* writing the stories. Haldeman's intimate knowledge and love of Hemingway and his work are highly apparent in this very short, very intense novel based on a Hugo- and Nebula-winning novella of the same name. Compare MacDonald Harris's non-SF novel, *Hemingway's Suitcase* (1990). (ML)

Themes: Alternate Worlds, History in SF, Time Travel

II-481.   None So Blind. Morrow, 1996.

Outstanding collection of stories by this sometimes underrated writer. Among the highlights are the Hugo- and Nebula-winning novella "The Hemingway Hoax," which became the basis for Haldeman's fine novel of the same name; the Nebula- and World Fantasy Award-winning "Graves"; and the Hugo- and *Locus*-winning "None So Blind." Earlier collections include *Infinite Dreams* (1978), *Dealing in Futures* (1985), and *Vietnam and Other Alien Worlds* (1993). (ML)

Awards: *Locus*

II-482.   Worlds. Viking, 1981. Series: Worlds.

The first volume of a trilogy, followed by *Worlds Apart* (1983). Earth lurches toward World War III, after which devastation the future of humankind will become dependent on the society of the "Worlds"—orbital space colonies. Near-future realism combined with loosely knit action-adventure. The long-delayed and very well done concluding volume, *Worlds Enough and Time* (1992), describes the difficult journey of one of those colonies to another star system. Compare Bova's *Colony*. (BS/ML)

Themes: Colonization of Other Worlds, Holocaust and After

Hale, Edward Everett, U.S., 1822–1909

II-483.   "The Brick Moon" in *His Level Best and Other Stories*. Roberts Bros, 1872.

A combination of two novelettes published in *The Atlantic Monthly* in 1869 and 1870. The first, describing a project to build and launch an artificial satellite, whose premature launch isolates a miscellaneous population of tourists in orbit, is a parody of Verne's *From the Earth to the Moon*. The second, which is more satirically inclined, describes the manner in which the brick Moon's involuntary inhabitants buckle down to the job of creating and maintaining a viable ecosystem, while communicating with the inhabitants of the Moon by Morse code. (BS)

Themes: Humorous SF, Space Flight

Hamilton, Cicely (pseudonym of Cicely Mary Hamill), U.K., 1872–1952

II-484.   Theodore Savage: A Story of the Past or the Future. Parsons, 1922.

One of the more graphic future-war novels produced in the immediate aftermath of World War I. The destruction of civilization by aerial bombardment results in a return to barbarism. The eponymous survivor, contemplating the new generation that will carry human history forward, realizes that ancient mythologies must have been a record of a previous cycle in a pattern of eternal recurrence. A new edition published as *Lest Ye Die* (1928) was extensively rewritten. Compare Verne's "Eternal Adam," Shanks's *People of the Ruins*, Stewart's *Earth Abides*, and Hoban's *Riddley Walker*. A less apocalyptic second world war is featured in Hamilton's *Little Arthur's History of the Twentieth Century* (1933), cast as a parody of a popular Victorian educational text. (BS)

Themes: Holocaust and After, War

Hamilton, Edmond (Moore), U.S., 1904–1977

II-485.   Battle for the Stars. Torquil, 1964.

This starts with a threatened space fleet ambush but moves to a dark and folksy village on Earth in which the hero vows to settle; a treasure-finding, self-discovering odyssey, but in the opposite direction from most such quests; contrast Clarke's *Against the Fall of Night*. *Battle* is less flamboyant than the space operas Hamilton had been writing for 30 years. Reissued in 1989 as part of a Tor Double, its companion, *The Nemesis from Terra*, was by Leigh Brackett, his wife. Their respective styles make an instructive contrast and comparison. (PC)

Themes: Pastoral, Space Opera

II-486.   Crashing Suns. Ace, 1965.

A collection of five stories. The serialization of the title story—in *Weird Tales* in 1928—overlapped that of E. E. Smith's *The Skylark of Space*, its rival for the distinction of being the first pulp space opera to take its action onto a galactic playing field. In the remainder, the Canopus-based Interstellar Patrol battles various alien menaces; the sequence skips the series' only full-length novel, *Outside the Universe* (1929), which Ace had reprinted separately in 1964. Hamilton tried hard to cope with the pressure of melodramatic inflation, but used up his ammunition too quickly in ramshackle stories like these, then spent the rest of his career searching fruitlessly for bigger and better special effects. (BS)

II-487.   The Horror on the Asteroid and Other Tales of Planetary Horror. Philip Allan, 1936.

One of the earliest collections of SF stories reprinted from the pulps—including *Weird Tales*, in the days when it featured SF as well as supernatural fiction. The six stories are mostly horror/SF geared for maximum sensationalism, but most of them also have a *conte philosophique* element that placed Hamilton a notch above his fellow space opera pioneer, Ray Cummings. "The Monster-God of Mamurth" (1926), "The Earth-Brain" (1932), and the title story (1933) are monster stories similar in spirit to those that took over movie SF, while "The Man Who Saw Everything" (1930, as "The Man Who Saw the Future") and "The Man Who Evolved" (1931) are extravagant cautionary tales. "The Accursed Galaxy" (1935) reveals that the universe is expanding because the other galaxies are fleeing from the plague (life) that afflicts ours. (BS)

II-488.   What's It Like Out There? And Other Stories. Ace, 1974.

Twelve stories from 1941 to 1962, a better selection than that in *The Best of Edmond Hamilton* (1977). Some of these sensitive, stylistically distinctive tales may reflect changing magazine standards. In "Castaway," Poe meets a time-traveling woman who becomes the inspiration for all his doom-haunted heroines (Ligeia, Eleanora). Other fine pieces include "The Stars My Brothers," "Sunfire!," "Isle of the Sleeper," and stories from *Weird Tales*, where Hamilton had made his debut. (PC)

Hamilton, Peter F., U.K., 1960–

II-489.   The Reality Dysfunction. Macmillan, 1996, Warner Aspect, 1997. Series: Night's Dawn.

An ultra-large scale space opera with an enormous cast of characters and too many subplots to count. At more than 1,000 pages, this novel had to be published in two volumes in the United States and it is still only the first part of the gigantic Night's Dawn trilogy. The two sides in an interstellar war are the Edenists, who practice radical genetic engineering, are telepathic, and live in space, and the Adamists, who are relative Luddites, colonizing new worlds in a more traditional manner. The novel opens on the planet Lalonde, the latest battleground between the two cultures. There are interesting affinities between Hamilton's work and that of such pioneering space opera writers as E. E. Smith and A. E. van Vogt. Oddly enough, there's also a touch of H. P. Lovecraft. Sequels are *The Neutronium Alchemist* (1998) and *The Naked God* (1999). *A Second Chance at Eden* (1998) is a short story collection set in the same universe. *The Confederation Handbook* (2001) is a nonfiction work about the universe of the stories. Compare Daniel's *Metaplanetary*. Contrast MacLeod's *Cosmonaut Keep*. (ML)

Themes: Future History, Space Opera

Hamilton, Virginia, U.S., 1936–2002

*II-490.   Justice and Her Brothers. Greenwillow, 1978. Series: Dustland.

YA. Justice and her older brothers, who are identical twins, along with a fourth child, slowly realize that they are gifted with ESP. Conflict ensues as one brother cruelly manipulates his weaker twin, and Justice senses that she, not the older boys, is to become leader of the linked group and possible progenitor of a new life form. In this exceptionally good book, strong writing and characterization and brooding, convincing atmosphere and setting accompany themes familiar in adult science fiction—for example, Clarke's *Childhood's End* or Sturgeon's *More Than Human*—but even now relatively novel in SF for young readers. Sequels: *Dustland* (1980) and *The Gathering* (1981). (FM/ML)

Themes: Disaster, Evolution, Paranormal Powers

Hand, Elizabeth, U.S., 1957–

II-491.   Glimmering. HarperPrism, 1997.

In the year 1999, the world is going to hell, the result of urban decay, global warming, a series of environmental disasters, economic collapse, and an out-of-control AIDS epidemic. One product of these disasters is the Glimmering, charged particles that are destroying the ozone layer. Dying from AIDS, magazine publisher Jack Finnegan has returned to his collapsing New York mansion to await the millennium. There he will re-connect with his former lover, Leonard Thrope, and meet a drug-addicted rock star named Trip Marlowe. The three men will then act out a strangely affecting end-times drama. Compare to other millennial fiction like John Kessel's *Good News from Outer Space* and James Morrow's *Only Begotten Daughter* (1990). (ML)

   Themes: Ecology, End of the World, Medicine

II-492.   Winterlong. Bantam, 1990. Series: Winterlong.

Hand's first novel features gorgeous prose reminiscent of Gene Wolfe and an exotic and decadent setting, the City of the Trees in the Northeastern Federated Republic of America, in essence a far-future Washington, D.C., half destroyed by global warming, biological warfare, and time. Among the characters are Wendy Wanders, half-mad victim of a government-sponsored parapsychology program, and Margalis Tast'annin, the Mad Aviator, hero of the Archipelago Conflict. Tast'annin has been sent to close down the parapsychology program and execute all those involved in it. When Wendy escapes, he must pursue her through the nightmarish City. Two loose sequels to *Winterlong* are *Aestival Tide* (1992) and *Icarus Descending* (1993). Compare Ryman's *The Child Garden* and Constantine's *The Enchantments of Flesh* and *Spirit*. (ML)

   Themes: Cities, Dystopias, Far Future

Hanstein, Otfrid von *see* von Hanstein, Otfrid

Harbou, Thea von *see* von Harbou, Thea

Hargrave, John (Gordon), U.K., 1894–1982

II-493.   The Imitation Man. Gollancz, 1931.

A scientist creates a homunculus after the fashion of the alchemist Paracelsus (of whom Hargrave wrote a biography). The homunculus grows rapidly to maturity; although his behavior is imitative, his ability to read thoughts causes embarrassment and his inconvenient presence cannot long be tolerated. The novel is more light-hearted and tongue-in-cheek than the author's Wellsian bildungsroman *Harbottle* (1923), but its satirical component makes it an interesting addition to the subspecies of scientific romance that imported "objective" observers to mock the follies of humankind. Compare Odle's *The Clockwork Man* and Phillpotts's *Saurus*. (BS)

   Themes: Humorous SF

Harding, Lee, Australia, 1937–

II-494.   Misplaced Persons. Harper, 1979. Australian title: *Displaced Person*.
YA. Aware that he cannot make contact with people and that the world is turning gray, Graeme soon finds himself alone, except for an alcoholic ex-teacher and a frightened girl, in a terrifying world where food must be scavenged and darkness is becoming total. Suddenly returned to the normal world, the boy retains a few shreds of evidence that the bizarre events did actually happen. Convincing psychological study of timeslip; well plotted and written; fresh characterization. Contrast Engdahl's *The Far Side of Evil.* (FM)
Themes: Disaster, Psychology, Time Travel

Harness, Charles L(eonard), U.S., 1915–

II-495.   The Ring of Ritornel. Gollancz, 1968.
A fine space opera in which a corrupt galactic empire faces apocalyptic destruction as the contending forces of chance and destiny (personalized in rival deities) resolve their conflict. Will the cosmos be reborn and renewed when the cycle ends? The themes echoed here from the earlier *Flight Into Yesterday* (1953) recur again in *Firebird* (1981), and these three works are among the most stylish space operas of their respective eras. Compare Ian Wallace's Croyd series, but contrast Alastair Reynolds's *Revelation Space.* (BS/ML)
Themes: Space Opera

Harper, Vincent (unattributed pseudonym)

II-496.   The Mortgage on the Brain, Being the Confessions of the late Ethelbert Croft, M.D. Doubleday Page, 1905.
A curious philosophical novel exploring the relationship between the mind and the brain by means of a hypothetical experiment in which an electrical apparatus substitutes a new personality for the one that had previously occupied the grey matter of its subject, causing romantic complications. An interesting treatment of the theme of multiple personality; the presumably pseudonymous author also published *The Terrible Truth About Marriage* (1907), which similarly seeks to stoke the fires of controversy. (BS)
Themes: Psychology

Harris, Clare Winger, U.S., 1891–1969

II-497.   Away from Here and Now. Dorrance, 1947.
A collection of 11 stories, including all the author's pulp SF, "A Baby on Neptune" (1929, written with Miles J. Breuer) being run together with its sequel "A Child of Neptune" (1941). One of the few female contributors to the Gernsback pulps, Harris was as inventively slapdash and as conspicuously unfeminist as most of her contemporaries. Interesting items include "A Runaway World" (1926) and "The Diabolical Drug" (1929), both of which feature glimpses of a

macrocosm beyond our universe. "The Ape Cycle" (1930) describes the enslave-ment of other primate species, which leads inexorably to rebellion and a rever-sal of the regime. (BS)

Harris, John Beynon *see* Wyndham, John

Harrison, Harry, U.S., 1925–

II-498.   Captive Universe. Putnam, 1969.

A well-done variation on the concept of the generation ship that spends years, possibly centuries, reaching another star system at sub-light speeds. Many such novels suggest that the society of such a ship will break down over the years, leading to barbarism. Harrison postulates a ship with an artificially constructed, conservative social order patterned on the Aztecs. Most citizens aren't even aware they're on a starship. Only the priests who lead the culture know the true nature of their environment. Compare Heinlein's *Orphans of the Sky* and Aldiss's *Non-Stop.* (ML)

   Themes: Anthropology, Space Flight

II-499.   Deathworld. Bantam, 1960.

Deathworld is a planet whose local life reads the hostile thoughts of Earth settlers and transforms itself into ever more deadly forms. Paradoxically, therefore, the harder the humans fight the more formidable becomes the planetary opposi-tion. The taming of Deathworld didn't lead to peace and quiet but to less suc-cessful sequels, *Deathworld 2* (1964; *The Ethical Engineer* in the U.K. edition); and *Deathworld 3.*

   Themes: Life on Other Worlds, Monsters

II-500.   Make Room! Make Room! Doubleday, 1966.

A classic novel of overpopulation and pollution, which was also made into a bet-ter-than-average science fiction film as *Soylent Green*. An archetypal example of 1960s alarmism. Compare Brunner's *Stand on Zanzibar* and Turner's *The Sea and the Summer.* (BS/ML)

   Themes: Overpopulation, Pollution

II-501.   West of Eden. Bantam, 1984. Series: Eden.

An alternate history story in which the dinosaurs were not killed off and ulti-mately produced sentient, humanoid descendants devoted to biotechnology. Their civilized race is ultimately forced into contact and conflict with savage human beings, adding culture shock to crisis. Inventive, fast-paced narrative. Followed by two sequels, *Winter in Eden* (1986) and *Return to Eden* (1988). (BS/ML)

   Themes: Alternate Worlds

Harrison, M(ichael) John, U.K., 1945–

II-502.   A Storm of Wings. Sphere, 1980. Series: Viriconium.

A sequel to the downbeat sword and sorcery novel, *The Pastel City* (1971). It begins the transformation of the city Viriconium into a milieu for more sophisticated literary exercise, extended in *In Viriconium* (1982; U.S. title: *The Floating Gods*) and *Viriconium Nights* (1984). Images of decadence and exhaustion abound in this series, which contrasts with other images of far-future cities in Bryant's *Cinnabar* and VanderMeer's *City of Saints and Madmen: The Book of Ambergris* (2001) and has strong affinities with certain aspects of Michael Moorcock's work. SF motifs are relatively sparse in what is essentially a fantasy series, but the use of entropic decay as a prevalent metaphor sustains the bridge between genres. (BS/ML)

Themes: Cities, Far Future, Science Fantasy

*II-503.   Light. Gollancz, 2002; Bantam Spectra, 2004.

Harrison's first venture into pure science fiction since *The Centauri Device* (1974) has proved to be one of the most complex and daring novels in recent years. The central strand of the novel is set in the present and concerns a serial killer, Michael Kearney, haunted by a nightmare monster, the Shrander, that takes on the appearance of a horse's skull, yet he is also involved in formulating the equations that will lead to the human conquest of space. The other two strands, concerning Seria Mau, who is directly plugged into her spaceship, and her brother, Ed Chianese, a down-and-outer on the run, might be set in the distant future or could as easily be in the mind of Kearney. Set in the Kefahuchi Tract, where the flotsam of all spacefaring races seems to be swept up, Seria Mau and Ed find themselves on a quest that eventually involves Kearney and the Shrander. Though superficially space opera, as *The Centauri Device* was, this is a work that subverts the genre to Harrison's own particular and challenging ends. Compare Banks's *Excession* and Greenland's *Take Back Plenty*. Contrast McCaffrey's *The Ship Who Sang*. (PK)

Awards: James Tiptree

Themes: Crime and Punishment, Life on Other Worlds, Space Opera, Virtual Reality

Hastings, Milo (Milton), U.S., 1884–1957

II-504.   The City of Endless Night. Dodd Mead, 1920.

A dystopian fantasy serialized in *True Story* in 1919 as "Children of Kultur." After defeats in a series of world wars, Germans have built Berlin into an impregnable fortress-city. An American chemical engineer who finds his way into the city describes its highly organized society while planning its subversion. Like Owen Gregory's *Meccania*, an ominous anticipation of many key features of Nazi ideology, including its preoccupation with "racial purity." (BS)

Themes: Dystopias

Hawthorne, Nathaniel, U.S., 1804–1864

II-505.   Mosses from an Old Manse. Wiley and Putnam, 1846.

A mixed collection including a number of classic *contes philosophiques* employing science-fictional imagery. "The New Adam and Eve" (1843) and "The Hall of Fantasy" (1843) are allegories extrapolating themes from the prophecies of William Miller, who had persuaded many Americans that the end of the world was near. "The Birthmark" (1843), "The Artist of the Beautiful" (1844), and "Rappaccini's Daughter" (1844) are moral tales warning against an obsession with purity, the last-named featuring a girl made poisonous by the environment in which she has been raised. "P's Correspondence" (1845) describes an alternative England whose Romantic poets lived on into ignominious old age instead of dying glamorously young. (BS)

Heinlein, Robert A(nson), U.S., 1907–1988

II-506.   Beyond This Horizon. Fantasy Press, 1948.

A 1942 tale in which society achieves an economy of abundance for all. What do people then do with their time, especially the hero, who no longer has anything to challenge him? Themes that would later occupy Heinlein got a preliminary hearing in this early work, toward which a later generation of criticism has been unfairly condescending. (PC)

Themes: Immortality, Utopias

II-507.   Citizen of the Galaxy. Scribner, 1957.

YA. Serialized for adults in *Astounding*, the Horatio Alger hero is a slave on a far planet of a despotic empire. He escapes into space and eventually returns to Earth, where he assumes the leadership of a giant financial corporation. This is a bildungsroman, except that the young hero never really grows up. Heinlein's knack for creating sociologically plausible cultures is well displayed. Alex Panshin in *Heinlein in Dimension* [10-74] argued that *Citizen*, with a plot revealed at the end to be essentially circular, is normative for all of Heinlein's longer work. (PC)

Themes: Coming of Age, Space Flight

II-508.   Double Star. Doubleday, 1956.

A ham actor is persuaded to impersonate the kidnapped prime minister of Earth's government. The actual politician is rescued but dies, and his double must carry on. *Double Star* offers convincing description of the way a planet-spanning constitutional monarchy (with the *Dutch* sovereign as its titular head!) might actually work. Heinlein's lifelong concern for citizen involvement in politics, shorn of his usual meritocratic elitism, is shown to good advantage. Contrast the 1993 film, *Dave*. (PC)

Awards: Hugo
Themes: Future History, Politics

II-509.   Friday. Holt, 1982.

An artificially created superwoman, courier for a secret organization, has to fend for herself when the decline of the West reaches its climax; she ultimately finds a new raison d'être on the extraterrestrial frontier. Welcomed by Heinlein fans as action-adventure respite from his more introspective works, but actually related very closely to some sections of *Time Enough for Love*, and it refers to much earlier material ("Gulf," 1949). (BS)

   Themes: Supermen/women, Women in SF

II-510.   Have Space Suit—Will Travel. Scribner, 1958.

YA. Fresh from high school, with a summer job making malts at a soda fountain, Kip Russell enters a contest and wins a secondhand space suit which he names Oscar. No sooner has he tinkered it into full space-tightness than he, his undersized but super-smart girl buddy Peewee, and a benevolent motherly nonhuman alien are kidnapped by, and escape from, space pirates. Their subsequent odyssey takes them to the Moon and to Pluto, where Oscar, quite evidently sentient, saves Kip from an icy demise by nagging and cheerleading him to crawl to safety. Then they're off to a planet orbiting Vega, and thence to the Lesser Magallenic Cloud. Whisked back to Earth, Kip, his future as M.I.T. student and eventual spaceman now secure, returns to his soda fountain job. Scientific lore is deftly woven into the narrative, as are potshots at 1950s-style public education (compare Piper's *Crisis in 2140*), but basically this is a wonderful romp, which I would rank with Heinlein's more adult-focused novels.

   Themes: Coming of Age, Space Flight

II-511.   The Menace from Earth. Gnome, 1959.

These eight stories are not part of the future history of *The Past Through Tomorrow*, except for the title story. The stories don't always work but include "By His Bootstraps," "All You Zombies" (1959), and such unique and unduplicable stories as "Year of the Jackpot," "Creation Took Eight Days," and "Columbus Was a Dope," with its lovely punch line. (PC)

*II-512.   The Moon Is a Harsh Mistress. Putnam, 1966.

Colonists of the Moon declare independence from Earth and contrive to win the ensuing battle with the aid of a sentient computer. Action-adventure with some exploration of new possibilities in social organization and fierce assertion of the motto "There Ain't No Such Thing as a Free Lunch." Though not a true sequel, *The Cat Who Walks Through Walls* (1985) is a much weaker novel set in the same universe and with some of the same characters. Compare John Varley's *Steel Beach*. (BS/ML)

   Awards: Hugo
   Themes: Politics, The Moon

II-513.   Orphans of the Sky. Gollancz, 1963.

Based on two 1941 *Astounding* novellas, "Universe" and "Common Sense," *Orphans* is the only major work from his formal future history that isn't in *The Past Through Tomorrow*, perhaps because it's peripheral to that history. This was one of the first serious treatments of the less-than-light-speed multigenerational starship whose actual origin and destination have become lost in legend. It's also a story of the quest for truth, both against organized superstition and against shortsighted, wrong-headed "realism." Compare Aldiss's *Non-Stop* and Robinson's *The Dark Beyond the Stars*. (PC)

Themes: Mutants, Space Flight

*II-514.   The Past Through Tomorrow. Putnam, 1967. Series: Future History.

Most of this omnibus had been previously published in four separate books: *The Man Who Sold the Moon* (Shasta, 1950); *The Green Hills of Earth* (Shasta, 1951); *Revolt in 2100* (Shasta, 1953); and *Methuselah's Children* (Gnome, 1958). These in turn derived from magazines, starting in 1939 and continuing through the 1940s, mainly in *Astounding*, a few in the *Saturday Evening Post*. Collectively they constitute the bulk of Heinlein's detailed forecast for the next two centuries. Other SF writers (Poul Anderson, Isaac Asimov, James Blish, H. Beam Piper, Cordwainer Smith) have undertaken future-building of this kind, but rarely with Heinlein's degree of verisimilitude. The only major omission is "Universe" (in *Orphans of the Sky*). All the other memorable tales are here. (PC)

Themes: Future History

II-515.   Rocket Ship Galileo. Scribner, 1947.

YA. Ross, Art, and Morrie, all amateur rocketeers, become involved with Morrie's uncle, Doctor Cargraves, and his plan to fly to the Moon. Having worked together in building an experimental, atomic-powered rocket, the three boys and Cargraves set off for the Moon. There they are attacked by a few Nazis plotting World War III from a secret lunar base. The boys overcome the Nazis and, having also discovered the ruins of a dead lunar civilization, return to Earth famous. Despite its creaky pulp plot, this was a pioneering novel that began American mainstream SF for children and combined young protagonists, gadgetry, current science, and adventure in such a way that even today the book retains interest. (FM/SM/PC)

Themes: Space Opera, The Moon

II-516.   Starman Jones. Scribner, 1953.

YA. The story of Max Jones's rise from hillbilly runaway to acting captain of a starship. What makes Max's rise possible is a phenomenal memory that retains all the astrogator's tables, needed for navigation, and the cunning of Sam, an older man who befriends the runaway and gets him aboard the *Asgard* with fake credentials. Striking are the detailed, convincing pictures of spaceship operational procedures and the suspense whenever the ship must pass through an anomaly. (FM/SM/PC)

Themes: Coming of Age, Space Flight

II-517.   Starship Troopers. Putnam, 1959.

Heinlein's Annapolis and navy background form the context for the training and baptism-of-fire of future space cadets. A well-told story that later was caught in the crossfire of powerful pro- and anti-Vietnam War feeling, which divided the SF community as it did the "mainstream." The paradox is that Heinlein, with this work, gave aid and comfort to the war supporters, while with *Stranger in a Strange Land* he helped to energize the radical student generation that opposed the war. Compare Smith's Lensmen series; contrast Pangborn's *A Mirror for Observers*. (PC)

Awards: Hugo
Themes: Space Opera, War

*II-518.   Stranger in a Strange Land. Putnam, 1961. Unabridged ed., 1991.

This is the best known of all Heinlein's works. It reached large audiences farther away from his SF roots than anything else he wrote, and inspired insurgencies both right and left. The contradictory libertarian and authoritarian elements in the writer are present in the saga of Valentine Michael Smith, born human, raised Martian, who returns to Earth a religious, political, and sexual messiah. The first third of the novel is well and suspensefully told. Thereafter he ascends into the pulpit where, sadly, this highly creative writer would remain for the next quarter-century, preaching, with unfortunately few lapses into good storytelling (that is, *showing*, not *telling*), such as *The Moon Is a Harsh Mistress*. *Stranger*'s cultural impact on an entire generation is nonetheless undeniable. (PC)

Awards: Hugo
Themes: Religion, Sex in SF

II-519.   Time Enough for Love. Putnam, 1973.

A partial biography of Lazarus Long, the long-lived hero of *Methuselah's Children*, involving the promiscuous multiplication of his genes and a journey into the past that affords him the opportunity to seduce his mother and die a hero's death (not final, of course) in World War I. An extravagant exercise in the production of an idealized fantasy self, drawing on the repertoire of SF ideas to support and sanction an extraordinary form of imaginary self-indulgence. Powerful because of the wish-fulfillment aspect of the composition. Compare Baron Corvo's *Hadrian VII* (1904). (BS)

Themes: Future History, Immortality, Sex in SF

II-520.   Time for the Stars. Scribner, 1956.

YA. Although written and marketed as a YA novel, this book is a mature treatment of the relativistic time-dilation effect in interstellar travel. Identical twin brothers are telepathically linked; one goes into space, the other remains on Earth. The object of the experiment is to determine whether continuing telepathic communication is possible over astronomical distances. It is, up to a point; but the astronaut brother returns, still youthful, to Earth, where the stay-at-home brother has become an old man. And there are other complications. For young readers, a good, graphic introduction to relativity; for older readers, a very readable yarn on its own terms. Compare Anderson's *Tau Zero*. (PC)

　　Themes: Space Flight

Henderson, Zenna, U.S., 1917–1983

II-521.　Pilgrimage: The Book of the People. Doubleday, 1961.

In these short stories with connecting narrative, "The People" are humans in hiding who came to Earth after their sun became a nova. They have telepathy and telekinesis, which they use solely for benevolent purposes and conceal most of the time lest they rouse hysteria against them as "witches." The host culture they live among is southern Appalachian, which Henderson understood and portrayed accurately and sympathetically; reminiscent in that regard of the fantasy (not the SF) of Manly Wade Wellman. Confrontations with Earth folk that endanger their cover drive most of the plots, which are saved from sentimentalism by The People's realization that any revelation of their true nature may endanger their existence. Compare Howard Fast's "The First Men" and Shiras's "In Hiding." *Ingathering: The Complete People Stories* (NESFA, 1995) assembles 17 stories, plus bridging material. (PC)

　　Themes: Aliens, Children in SF

Herbert, Frank, U.S., 1920–1986

II-522.　Destination: Void. Berkley, 1966. Series: Pandora.

The computers guiding a starship en route to a new world fail, and the crew must construct an artificial intelligence to repair the damage, but the intelligence defines itself as God and demands worship as the price of looking after its human cargo. In three sequels written with Bill Ransom, *The Jesus Incident* (1979), *The Lazarus Effect* (1983), and *The Ascension Factor* (1988), this artificial God and its human subjects draw on biblical lore in order to explore the possibilities of worship, trying to figure out how it should be appropriately done. Compare Chris Boyce's *Catchworld* (1975) and Gerrold's *When HARLIE Was One*. (BS/ML)

　　Themes: Colonization of Other Worlds, Computers, Hard SF, Intelligence, Religion

*II-523.　The Dragon in the Sea. Doubleday, 1956. Variant titles: *21st Century Sub* (Avon, 1956); *Under Pressure* (Ballantine, 1974).

Originating as the *Astounding* serial, "Under Pressure," this was Herbert's maiden voyage, so to speak. Far transcending its routine plot—a "subtug" seeks to steal oil deposits from the unspecified enemy's continental shelf, with a crew, one of whom must be a spy (shades of *The Hunt for Red October!*)—the story conflates the deep, closed-in submarine environment with the crew members' psychic stress; they are both materially and mentally "under pressure." The seemingly half-mad captain has echoes of Captain Ahab, and there are also allusions to the Book of Job and Freud. (PC)

Themes: Fantastic Voyages, Psychology

*II-524. Dune. Chilton, 1965. Series: Dune.

The first of a seven-volume best-selling series is the story of a selectively bred messiah who acquires paranormal power by use of the spice that is the main product of the desert planet Arrakis, and uses these powers to prepare for the ecological renewal of the world. Politics and metaphysics are tightly bound into a remarkably detailed and coherent pattern; an imaginative tour de force. The series as a whole is overinflated, the later revisitations of the theme being prompted more by market success than the discovery of new things to do with it. The series demonstrates how a good SF writer's ability to build a coherent and convincing hypothetical world can serve the purpose of making philosophical and sociological questions concrete; the series thus becomes a massive thought experiment in social philosophy, and is more considerable as such than Asimov's Foundation series or Bradley's Darkover series. *House Atreides* (1999) by Frank Herbert's son Brian and Kevin J. Anderson is the first in a surprisingly well-done series of prequels to the original books. It has now reached five volumes, with at least one more planned. Three films have also been made based on the series. (BS/ML)

Awards: Hugo, Nebula

Themes: Ecology, Future History, Life on Other Worlds, Politics

II-525. Whipping Star. Putnam, 1970.

The awesome basic premise of Herbert's novel is that some stars are merely one part of an intelligent, extra-dimensional life form. When a star dies, one of these super-aliens dies. The aliens also manifest themselves physically in our universe as Calebans and, in this form, have introduced humanity to teleportation via jumpdoors. Now, however, the last Caleban is dying and humanity finds out too late that, when it does die, everyone who has ever used a jumpdoor will die with it. The novel's protagonist must find a way to save the Caleban's life, thus saving his own and those of untold millions of other intelligent beings. A lesser, but still worthwhile sequel is *The Dosadi Experiment* (1977). (ML)

Themes: Aliens, End of the World

II-526. The White Plague. Putnam, 1982.

A molecular biologist driven mad by cruel circumstances unleashes a plague that will universalize his personal tragedy and destroy the women of the world. The terrorism that initially provoked him is reproduced on a grand scale: an appalling visitation of a kind of "justice." Compare Christopher Priest's *Fugue for a Darkening Island* (1972). (BS)

Themes: Biology, Disaster, Medicine

Hernaman-Johnson, F(rancis), U.K., 1879–1949

II-527.   The Polyphemes. A Story of Strange Adventures and Strange Beings. Ward Lock, 1906.

An account of intelligent "giant" ants, much more like those featured in H. G. Wells's "The Empire of the Ants" (1905) than the vaster giants deployed in Bennett's *The Demigods*. Despite being no bigger than human fingers, the polyphemes' superior technology lends plausibility to their plans for world conquest, which proceed apace until the corruption at the heart of their own caste-divided society is revealed. A curious offshoot of the jingoistic British future-war genre. (BS)

Themes: Monsters, War

Heron-Allen, Edward, U.K., 1861–1943

II-528.   The Cheetah-Girl (as by Christopher Blayre). Privately circulated, 1923; reprinted by Tartarus Press, 1997.

Ostensibly intended to be published as the concluding item in *The Purple Sapphire and Other Posthumous Papers* (1921) (although the different typesetting suggests that the pretence is a joke), this novella is a remarkably vivid example of biological SF, in which an experiment involving the impregnation of a loose woman by a cheetah produces a remarkable hybrid. Seemingly inspired by Hanns Heinz Ewers' occult novel *Alraune* (1911), "The Cheetah Girl" borrows heavily from Krafft-Ebing's *Psychopathia Sexualis* to produce a calculatedly unpublishable work that qualifies as a bizarre tour de force. After Tartarus Press reprinted it, they reissued it in an omnibus of *The Collected Strange Papers of Dr Blayre* (1998). (BS)

Themes: Biology

Hill, Douglas, U.K./Canada, 1935–

II-529.   Galactic Warlord. Gollancz, 1979. Series: Galactic Warlord.

YA. Shocked to learn that he is the only legionary to survive the destruction of Moros, Keill Randor, assisted by the alien Glr, smashes Thr'un, one of the evil Deathwing, and begins his search for the dreaded Warlord. One of the best examples of space opera for young readers from the 1970s; quick-moving, suspenseful, action-filled. Followed by *Day of the Starwind* (1980), in which Randor contends with bogus legionaries, *Deathwing Over Veynaa* (1980); *Planet of the Warlord* (1981), in which Randor and Glr finally destroy The One, responsible for destroying Moros; and *Young Legionary* (1983). Compare Vance's *Vandals of the Void* (1953). (FM/ML)

Themes: Far Future, Space Opera, War

Hinton, C(harles) H(oward), U.K., 1853–1907

II-530.   Scientific Romances. Swan-Sonneschein, 1884.

A collection of essays including much speculation about the fourth dimension and a curious allegory applying mathematical theory to the logic of Christian sacrifice, "The Persian King." "A Plane World" anticipates Abbott's *Flatland,* and Hinton was to go on to write an account of a rather different two-dimensional world in *An Episode of Flatland* (1907). Later editions of *Scientific Romances* carried the subtitle "first series" because Hinton produced a second volume in 1902, which reprinted two novellas previously published as *Stella and An Unfinished Communication* (1895) along with more essays. "Stella," featuring an invisible girl, may well have been read by H. G. Wells before he wrote *The Invisible Man.* Wells seems to have borrowed the explanatory logic of *The Time Machine* from Hinton, so the use of "scientific romance" to describe Wellsian speculative fiction has a definite propriety. (BS)

Hoban, Russell, U.S., 1925–

II-531.   Riddley Walker. Cape, 1980.

A post-holocaust story in which gunpowder is rediscovered but set aside by the naively wise hero, who believes that humankind must find a new path of progress this time. The first-person narrative is presented in the decayed and transfigured dialect of the day and represents a fascinating linguistic experiment. Compare Aldiss's *Barefoot in the Head.* (BS)

Awards: John W. Campbell
Themes: Holocaust and After, Linguistics

Hodgson, William Hope, U.K., 1877–1918

II-532.   Deep Waters. Arkham House, 1967.

A collection of 13 of Hodgson's sea stories, most of which employ the biological imagination and dimensional theory to generate monsters. "The Voice in the Night" (1907), in which castaways forced to live on a peculiar fungus undergo a remarkable metamorphosis, and "The Stone Ship" (1914), in which an ancient wreck thrust up from the depths by a volcanic eruption bears a weird living cargo, are the best. *Out of the Storm* (1975) collects most of his other fantasies. Hodgson's first published novel, *The Boats of the Glen Carrig* (1907)—in which shipwreck survivors take refuge on an island near a mass of floating seaweed inhabited by bizarre life forms—is a compendium of effects similar to those deployed in the stories in *Deep Waters.* (BS)

*II-533.   The House on the Borderland. Chapman and Hall, 1908.

A remarkable visionary fantasy that includes an allegorical cosmic journey. Like Poe's *Eureka* and Flammarion's *Lumen,* the cosmic voyage sequence draws on recent astronomical discoveries and speculations, presenting a synoptic account of the end of the Earth as the Sun burns out before going on to discover the central sun of Creation, whose nature is allegorical. (BS)

Themes: Fantastic Voyages

*II-534.   The Night Land. Eveleigh Nash, 1912.

A phantasmagoric Orphean fantasy that helped to set a pattern for many subsequent far future fantasies. It appears to have been written before Hodgson's other novels, but must have seemed too risky a proposition until his reputation was established. As the sun wanes, and monsters from other dimensions break through weakening barriers to take up residence on the dying Earth, the hero sets out from the Great Redoubt to rescue the young woman who is the last survivor of the Lesser Redoubt; he is menaced all the way by bizarre life forms. The calculatedly archaic style of the book—it is presented as a vision experienced in the early 18th century—alienates some readers, although others feel that its subject matter warrants exotic presentation. A heavily abridged version was issued as *The Dream of X* (1912). (BS)

Themes: Far Future

Hogan, James P(atrick), U.K., 1941–

II-535.   The Minervan Experiment. Doubleday, 1981. Series: Minervan Experiment.

An omnibus SFBC edition of a trilogy: *Inherit the Stars* (1977), *The Gentle Giants of Ganymede* (1978), and *Giants' Star* (1981). A humanoid corpse discovered on the Moon presents a puzzle that unravels into the story of an ancient civilization whose colonies in the solar system were destroyed by war. The trilogy starts well but deteriorates gradually into unexceptional space opera; in the third volume, humans and alien allies resist absorption into a nasty galactic empire. The strength of the first volume is its portrayal of scientists battling with a mystery, producing and testing hypotheses until the solution is found. Compare Benford's *Timescape.* (BS)

Themes: Aliens, Scientists and Engineers, Space Opera

Holberg, Ludvig, Denmark, 1684–1754

*II-536.   A Journey to the World Under-Ground by Nicholas Klimius. 1741. Trans. anon of *Nicolai Klimii Iter Subterraneum.* Astley and Collins, 1742.

A satirical fantastic voyage first published in Latin, the first to make use of the hollow Earth as a setting. Klim falls through a hole into the world's interior, where he finds miniature planets orbiting a tiny sun. After drifting into orbit about the planet Nazar, he is forced down to its surface by a hungry griffin. He is captured by tree-men, who exploit his mobility by sending him to report on neighboring nations. He also has adventures on the concave inner surface, which is inhabited by even stranger hybrids. Presumably inspired by Swift's *Gulliver's Travels*, it is neither as vivid nor as scathing, but it has its own comedic charm. (BS)

Holdstock, Robert, U.K., 1948–

II-537.   Where Time Winds Blow. Faber, 1981.

Time winds carry objects back and forth in time on an alien planet; the detritus they leave is eagerly investigated during periods of calm. Investigators, though, live in constant peril of being caught up by the winds. The story is heavy on dialogue and philosophical discussion. Although this is an excellent novel, Holdstock went on to do far more important work in fantasy. Compare Priest's *An Infinite Summer*. (BS/ML)

Themes: Fantastic Voyages, Satirical SF, Time Travel

Holmes, Oliver Wendell, U.S., 1809–1894

II-538.   Elsie Venner: A Romance of Destiny. Ticknor and Fields, 1861.

An allegorical exploration of moral responsibility and the notion of "original sin." The eponymous anti-heroine has been corrupted in the womb by a rattlesnake bite, which has imprinted her personality with *femme fatale* characteristics. An interesting ancestor of Heron-Allen's *The Cheetah Girl*, very restrained by comparison. Holmes's other "medicated novels," *The Guardian Angel* (1867) and *A Mortal Antipathy* (1885), are straightforward case studies of psychological aberration. (BS)

Themes: Psychology

Holt-White, William (Edward Braddon), U.K., 1878–?

II-539.   The Man Who Stole the Earth. Fisher Unwin, 1909.

A Ruritanian romance complicated by the introduction of a Griffithesque flying machine, whose destructive power is soon made manifest. Holt-White, a prolific writer of commercial fiction, borrowed elements of scientific romance in half a dozen other potboilers, including *Helen of All Time* (1910), which features a continually reincarnated Helen of Troy as well as another flying machine. As with many make-it-up-as-you-go writers, his interesting beginnings usually faded away into incoherence, but his work provides an apt illustration of the way in which aspects of scientific romance had begun to modify other popular genres before World War I all but obliterated its influence. (BS)

Themes: Discoveries and Inventions

Hoover, H(elen) M(ary), U.S., 1935–

*II-540.   Another Heaven, Another Earth. Viking, 1981.

YA. Discovering that Xilan, presumably ignored by explorers 400 years earlier, has a human colony, a scientific team learns that the planet is genuinely inhospitable to human life. In spite of the fact that they are doomed, the original colonists will not leave. Intriguing concepts, plausible scenario, and rich and sustained characterization add up to an exceptionally interesting and moving novel. Perhaps the best of Hoover's many fine YA SF novels. Contrast Sargent's *Earthseed*. (FM/ML)

   Themes: Colonization of Other Worlds, Ecology, Far Future, Life on Other Worlds

II-541.   The Lost Star. Viking, 1979.

YA. As part of an archaeological team surveying Blathor, Lian Webster realizes that the indigenous Lumpens, apparently fat and stupid animals, are really intelligent. Soon she uncovers their secret—they are an alien race, the Toapa, protected by a powerful computer brain within a mysterious dome—and must decide whether to share her knowledge with other team members. Multi-layered story: mystery, coming of age, and study of racism and xenophobia. Compare Engdahl's *Enchantress from the Stars* and Silverberg's *Across a Billion Years* (1969); contrast Anthony's *Race Against Time*. (FM)

   Themes: Aliens, Coming of Age, Sociology

*II-542.   The Rains of Eridan. Viking, 1977.

YA. The three experimental stations on Eridan are inexplicably infected by unnatural fear. The cause of and antidote to the fear are discovered by Theo Leslie, a biologist, who also learns the challenge and joy of parenting when she befriends an orphan child. Superior science fiction: a plausible alien world, well-paced plotting, and sensitive and tactful characterization—in particular, the growth of love between an older woman and a young girl who share a deep commitment to science. Compare Lightner's *The Space Plague* (1966). (FM)

   Themes: Aliens, Biology, Feminist SF, Scientists and Engineers

II-543.   The Shepherd Moon. Viking, 1984.

YA. Lonely 13-year-old Merry unexpectedly makes friends with her powerful grandfather, and together they stave off an attempt to conquer Earth by an invader from a forgotten artificial Moon. Especially good are the sympathetic insight into the relationship between youth and old age, and the study of the corrosive effects of stagnant social classes. Compare Bond's *The Voyage Begun* or Corlett's *Return to the Gate*. (FM/ML)

   Themes: Coming of Age, Invasion, Sociology

Hopkinson, Nalo, Canada, 1960–

II-544. Midnight Robber. Warner Aspect, 2000.

Drawing on Caribbean folklore, Hopkinson weaves a powerful story of a young girl who follows her father into exile after he is charged with murder. Leaving the planet Toussaint for New Half-way Tree, Tan-Tan finds herself on a primitive pioneer world, bereft of the support of the Nannyweb, where the creatures of her childhood stories are real, living in complex societies, while humans struggle to scratch a living. Sexually abused by her father whom, finally, she murders, Tan-Tan goes to live among the douens, only to find herself torn between two worlds. Masquerading as the Midnight Robber, a carnival character, Tan-Tan is able to confront the demons of her past, while for her unborn child there is the promise of a return to contact with the artificial intelligence of Toussaint, and the hint of a new way of life. Hopkinson's first novel, *Brown Girl in the Ring* (1998), makes similar use of Caribbean folklore. Compare Wolfe, *The Fifth Head of Cerberus*. (MKS)

Themes: Coming of Age, Computers, Feminist SF, Intelligence, Life on Other Worlds, Mythology, Sex in SF

Horowitz, Anthony, U.K., 1955–

II-545. Point Blank. Philomel, 2001. Series: Alex Rider.

YA. One of a number of popular Alex Rider adventures. In this volume, 14-year-old Alex, a reluctant but talented spy for the British government, is sent to investigate an elite boarding school where the troublesome sons of wealthy people are being transformed by a mysterious scientist into perfect gentlemen with what can only be described as fascist tendencies. Is cloning somehow involved? There's a lot of exciting, James Bond-style pyrotechnics in these books. They aren't great literature, but they're great good fun. (ML)

Themes: Clones/Cloning

Houghton, Claude (pseudonym of Claude Houghton Oldfield), U.K., 1889–1961

II-546. This Was Ivor Trent. Heinemann, 1935.

A curious mystery story in which the strange behavior of a writer is ultimately explained as the result of a vision that confronted him with a man of the future. Trent's extreme disillusionment is summed up in a hysterical concluding monologue in which he begs the man from the future to hasten the advent of his species. Compare the more ambivalent attitude of the narrator of Beresford's *Hampdenshire Wonder*. (BS)

Themes: Supermen/women

Howarth, Lesley, U.K., 1952–

II-547.   MapHead. Walker, 1994.

YA. MapHead, a boy from another universe, who can travel in time, erase people's memories and, oddly enough, reproduce maps on his face, has come to our world with his father to find his human mother, Kay, whose memory of her alien family has been wiped out. Moving into a quiet English village, they uncover her whereabouts and gradually reestablish contact. Not much action, but excellent character development. (ML)

   Themes: Parallel Worlds, Paranormal Powers

Hoyle, Fred, U.K., 1915–2001

II-548.   The Black Cloud. Heinemann, 1957.

A cloud of interstellar matter drifts into the solar system, bringing chaos and destruction. The cloud is sentient; contact is established, and it withdraws. Its collective mind is not a wholly original idea but derivative, like so much else in British SF, from Stapledon's *Last and First Men*. What carries it is the jargon and banter, whose authenticity derives from Hoyle's position as the U.K.'s Astronomer Royal (the book has been used in astronomy classes as supplemental reading). (PC)

   Themes: Invasion, Scientists and Engineers

Hubbard, L(afayette) Ron(ald), U.S., 1911–1986

*II-549.   Final Blackout. Hadley, 1948.

Serialized in 1940 just before the Nazi blitzkrieg, this grim novel predicted that World War II would drag on for many more years, reducing Europe to peasant villages and bands of soldier-foragers. Out of this chaos arises a British officer who leads his ragged troops back to England, deposes its government, and at the cost of his own life thwarts an attempt at colonization by the Americans. Very controversial when first published. With the possible exception of *Fear* (*Unknown*, 1940), this is Hubbard's finest work. Its theme was echoed in a 1947 *Astounding* serial, "The End Is Not Yet," which is better than any of the heavily subsidized and promoted Hubbard novels of the 1980s, which are self-parody 40 years too late. This serial is an important and curiously neglected work, finally reprinted by Hubbard's publisher, Author Services, Inc., as part of a limited edition luxury series. Its theme of the ambiguity of all revolutions, even "good" ones, has taken on new meaning since the collapse of the USSR, especially in the Balkan states. (PC)

   Themes: Politics, War

Huddy, Delia, U.K., 1934–

II-550. Time Piper. Hamish Hamilton, 1976.

YA. When Luke goes to work for Humboldt, the brilliant scientist experimenting with a time machine, he meets Hare, a strange young girl disliked by most of her peers. As the machine is tested, he realizes that Hare and her just-as-strange friends have been transported from the past, actually Hamlin, Germany. Fascinating blend of legend and science fiction, mystery and suspense, the well-plotted novel also examines teenagers at odds with their surroundings and reaching out for sympathy. The sequel is *The Humboldt Effect* (1982). Compare Mayne's *Earthfasts*; contrast Engdahl's *Enchantress from the Stars*. (FM/ML)

Themes: Children in SF, Machines, Science Fantasy, Time Travel

Hudson, W(illiam) H(enry), U.K., 1841–1922

*****II-551. A Crystal Age**. Fisher Unwin, 1887 (published anonymously).

A classic work of proto-ecological mysticism, envisaging a pastoral far-future utopia in which humankind lives in harmony with nature, having altered our reproductive arrangements in order to avoid Malthusian problems. When Hudson's second attempt to popularize a similar ideal, *Green Mansions* (1904), became a bestseller, *A Crystal Age* was reissued, this time bearing the author's signature. Few readers would have been able to share Hudson's sentimental regard for his imaginary world, but the story is poignant nevertheless. Compare Jefferies's *After London*. (BS)

Themes: Utopias

Hughes, Monica, U.K./Canada, 1925–2003

II-552. Invitation to the Game. HarperCollins, 1990.

YA. In the year 2154 a group of new high school graduates find themselves permanently unemployed and forced to live in a ghetto called a Designated Area. Then they hear about The Game, a government-run contest supposedly designed to improve their lot in life, but actually intended to send them off-world to a colonial planet. After hardship and hard work, the teens triumph and begin to build a better civilization on their new world. Compare Pournelle's *Starswarm*. (ML)

Themes: Colonization of Other Worlds, Dystopias

II-553. The Keeper of the Isis Light. Hamish Hamilton, 1980. Series: Isis.

YA. Olwen, keeper of the intergalactic lighthouse Isis Light, who has been isolated from humanity except for Guardian, welcomes settlers from Earth only to discover the poignant truth about her capacity to survive on harsh Isis. A likable protagonist, plausible setting, and provocative scenario more than offset the conventional story of lovers' misunderstanding. Sequels are *The Guardian of Isis* (1981), which won the Canadian Council Children's Literature Prize, and *The Isis Peddler* (1982). They continue the story of Olwen's unhappy romance and the fate of the Isis human colony. Contrast Engdahl's *The Far Side of Evil.* (FM/ML)

Themes: Colonization of Other Worlds, Genetic Engineering, Life on Other Worlds

II-554.   The Tomorrow City. Hamish Hamilton, 1978.

YA. C-Three, a computer built to coordinate all power uses in a city, takes literally its charge to do what is best for children, in particular, Caro, daughter of its designer. A reign of terror, instigated by C-Three, is terminated only when the computer, "grief-stricken" at having blinded Caro, blows up. A convincing, plausible scenario and believable characterization. Compare Bethancourt's *The Mortal Instrument* and Jack Williamson's *The Humanoids.* (FM/ML)

Themes: Children in SF, Computers, Far Future, Intelligence

Hunt, Robert, U.K., 1807–1887

II-555.   Panthea, the Spirit of Nature. Reeve, Bentham and Reeve, 1849.

Hunt, the most important British pioneer of the popularization of science, followed up *The Poetry of Science, or Studies of the Physical Phenomena of Nature* (1848)—whose ardent enthusiasm prompted William Wilson to invent the term "science-fiction" in 1851—with his own novel. *Panthea* is a chimerical bildungsroman, seemingly influenced by the romances of Lord Lytton and perhaps by Humphry Davy's *Consolations in Travel*, whose hero experiences two remarkable symbolic cosmic visions courtesy of a Rosicrucian guru, eventually forsaking occultism for the more rewarding vocation of empirical scientific enquiry and technological development. A patchwork, presumably composed in three stages in different phases of the author's life, which tracks his intellectual journey from Romanticism to a fervent scientific vocation. (BS)

Themes: Fantastic Voyages

Hunter, Evan, U.S., 1926–

II-556.   Find the Feathered Serpent. Winston, 1952.

YA. Neil, substituting for his father, the inventor of a time machine, journeys back in time, hoping to find the origin of Quetzalcoatl, the great white god. He meets Eric, who becomes instrumental in assisting the Mayans to resist barbarian invaders and in introducing corn and other agricultural innovations, which become part of later legend and myth. A time travel tale involving a Wellsian time machine and also patterned after books describing long-lost people. More interesting as an archaeological and anthropological reconstruction rather than as hard SF. Compare Oliver's *Mists of Dawn*; contrast Grace Chetwin's *Collidescope* (1990). (FM/SM/PC)

Themes: Anthropology, Time Travel

Huxley, Aldous (Leonard), U.K., 1894–1963

II-557.   Ape and Essence. Harper, 1948.

What *Brave New World* might look like after a nuclear war, told in the form of a prophetic motion picture screenplay. An expedition from New Zealand encounters the denizens of what's left of Los Angeles, who dig up the perfectly preserved bodies in Forest Lawn cemetery (an echo of Huxley's satiric *After Many a Summer Dies the Swan*) and dress in elegant, stolen funeral attire. Humanity's breeding habits have changed to a seasonal rut, with strict celibacy at other times; a dissident minority who can have sex any time are reviled as the "Hots" and pursued as witches. The worst of Dark Ages clericalism combined with social idiocies that could only have been made in America. Not quite the polished polemic of *Brave New World*, but effective on its own satiric terms. Compare del Rey's *The Eleventh Commandment*; contrast Robinson's *The Wild Shore*. (PC)

Themes: Dystopias, Holocaust and After

*II-558.   Brave New World. Chatto and Windus, 1932.

A classic dystopian satire, based on the future history sketched out in J. B. S. Haldane's *Daedalus; or, Science and the Future* (1924) and the moral qualms on that subject featured in "The Tissue-Culture King" (1926), a satire written by Haldane's close friend and Aldous's elder brother, the biologist Julian Huxley. *Brave New World* describes a highly ordered future Britain, where biological and behavioral engineering ensure universal contentment, as viewed with growing horror by a "savage" recovered from the Reservation where he was accidentally cast away. Although it is a vitriolic and very funny black comedy, many of its readers apparently contrive to read it as a straightforward condemnation of biological science. Along with Orwell's *Nineteen Eighty-Four*, it is one of only two futuristic novels to have made a considerable contribution to the social and political rhetoric of the 20th century. (BS)

Themes: Biology, Satirical SF

Hyder, Alan (unattributed pseudonym)

II-559.   Vampires Overhead. Philip Allan, 1935.

A bizarre thriller in which Earth is invaded by vampiric alien life forms carried into its vicinity by a passing comet. They cause a great deal of mayhem. A hectically melodramatic anticipation of one of the standard patterns favored by horror/SF, especially in the movies. Obviously inspired by Wells's *War of the Worlds* but more closely akin to the horror/SF stories in Hamilton's *The Horror on the Asteroid*, issued by the same publisher.

Themes: Invasion, Monsters

Jablokov, Alexander, U.K., 1956–

II-560.   Carve the Sky. Morrow, 1991.

It is the 24th century, and Earth has colonized both the inner planets and the larger moons of the gas giants. In the distant past, our solar system was visited by starfaring aliens, but humanity has not yet developed interstellar travel. The ability to do so lies in the possession of a fabulously rare metal found in artifacts left by the aliens. Now, some of that metal has turned up in a new sculpture by a supposedly long-dead artist. Several powerful organizations are searching for the artist's source of materials and are willing to stop at nothing to find it. Jablokov has created a complex and fascinating culture here, and his knowledge of the art world is considerable. The mannered style and use of anachronistic technology recalls the work of Jack Vance. Jablokov's talent for writing colorful narratives is also on display in such later novels as *River of Dust* (1996) and *Deepdrive* (1998). Compare Simmons' *Hyperion* and Rosenblum's *The Stone Garden*. (ML)

Themes: Religion, Space Opera

II-561.   Deepdrive. Avon Eos, 1998.

In the late-21st century, 11 different extraterrestrial species have settled different parts of our solar system, all having arrived here through the use of faster-than-light "deepdrives," a secret technology they refuse to share with humanity. Now a group of hard-bitten mercenaries has learned that an alien who has crash-landed on Venus and been taken into protective custody may be willing to share the secret of extra-solar flight and they're willing to undergo any hardship to attain it. Well-done, noirish space opera. Compare Brin's *Startide Rising*. (ML)

Themes: Aliens, Crime and Punishment, Life on Other Worlds, The Planets, Space Opera

Jacobs, Paul Samuel, ?

II-562.   Born Into Light. Scholastic, 1988.

YA. When a number of feral children suddenly appear in a New England town 75 years ago, a young boy, his mother, and the local doctor discover the children are aliens come to Earth to find ways to renew their species "back home." The story's strength is not so much concept but narrative point of view, poignant tone, and believable characterization. (FM).

Themes: Aliens, Children in SF, Invasion

Jaeger, Muriel, U.K., 1893–?

II-563.   The Man with Six Senses. Hogarth Press, 1927.

A careful philosophical novel whose young hero is trying to develop and make use of a new mode of sensory perception. Much more thoughtful than previous tales such as Louis Tracy's *Karl Grier: The Strange Story of a Man With a Sixth Sense* (1906) and Stephen McKenna's *The Sixth Sense* (1915), it also contrasts strongly with tales of ESP produced in the genre SF psi-boom, such as James Blish's *Jack of Eagles* (1952) and Wilson Tucker's *Wild Talent* (1954). (BS)

Themes: Paranormal Powers

II-564.   The Question Mark. Hogarth Press, 1926.

A skeptical study of the quality of life in a Wellsian utopia and the folkways that might evolve there, inspired by the conduct of the "bright young things" of the 1920s. The title refers to the question of whether humankind is capable of living a fruitful life in the absence of the spur of necessity. Jaeger's later Wellsian novel, *Retreat from Armageddon* (1936), reverses the scenario, featuring speculative conversations between intellectuals hiding out from a second world war; it treats the prospectus of Haldane's *Daedalus* (1923) far more seriously than Jaeger's fellow Bloomsbury hanger-on Aldous Huxley did in *Brave New World*. Haldane's sister Charlotte published a utopian novel, *Man's World*, in the same year as *The Question Mark*, which makes an interesting comparison. (BS)

Themes: Utopias

Jane, Fred(erick) T(homas), U.K., 1865–1916

II-565.   The Violet Flame: A Story of Armageddon and Afterwards. Ward Lock, 1899.

A tongue-in-cheek novel in the manner of George Griffith, which pioneered the world blackmail theme. Jane's mad scientist demonstrates his power and becomes master of the world; he is ingeniously murdered, but it turns out that he was also protecting the planet from destruction by an exotic comet. Although rather slapdash, the story has some fine imaginative flourishes. Compare the climax of Griffith's *Olga Romanoff* and Bell's *Lord of Life*. (BS)

Themes: End of the World

Jarry, Alfred, France, 1873–1907

II-566.   The Supermale (*Le surmâle*). 1901. Trans. by Barbara Wright, Cape, 1964.

A comic fantasy whose hero, nourished on an experimental superfood, develops extraordinary powers of strength and endurance, which he employs in winning bicycle races (Jarry was a keen cyclist) and extraordinary erotic performances, until he finally meets his match in a brutal machine. Jarry was sufficiently inspired by H. G. Wells to write an article on "How to Construct a Time Machine" (1899), but whether Wells returned the compliment in *The Food of the Gods* is unclear. Compare Philip Wylie's account of a physical superman in *Gladiator*. (BS)

Themes: Supermen/women

Jefferies, (John) Richard, U.K., 1848–1887

*II-567. After London; or, Wild England. Cassell, 1885.

A pastoral romance describing a post-catastrophe England that has reverted to a primitive stage of society that combines elements of the neolithic and medieval. What remains of London is a poisonous marsh. The first, entirely descriptive, part of the story is an extended prose-poem of considerable power, but the second half attempts to tell a story that gradually decays into conventional sentimentality. The probable inspiration of W. H. Hudson's *A Crystal Age*, S. Fowler Wright's *Deluge*, John Collier's *Tom's a-Cold* and many other lyrical depictions of future primitivism.

Themes: Holocaust and After

Jenkins, William Fitzgerald *see* Leinster, Murray

Jeschke, Wolfgang, Germany, 1936–

II-568. The Last Day of Creation. Century, 1982. Trans. of *Der letzte Tag der Schöpfung*, 1981, by Gertrud Mander.

Time travel story in which Americans try to hijack the Middle East's oil from the past; when paradoxes accumulate, the travelers are cut off from futures that no longer exist. A fast-paced adventure story with a touch of weltschmerz that may in some odd way have relevance to the current situation in the Middle East. Compare Silverberg's *Up the Line*. (BS/ML)

Themes: Time Travel

Jeter, K. W., U.S., 1950–

II-569. Dr. Adder. Bluejay, 1984. Series: Dr. Adder.

Violent and overtly sexual novel of a decadent future Los Angeles and the attempt made by a video evangelist to clean it up, with the protagonist caught in the exotic crossfire. Compare Steven Barnes's *Street Lethal* (1983). (BS/ML)

Themes: Cyberpunk, Religion

II-570. Madlands. St. Martin's, 1991.

For reasons unknown—though a government conspiracy is rumored—part of southern California has been warped into the Madlands, a place where dreams, particularly nightmares, come true and where a variety of gruesome diseases run rampant. Identrope, a corrupt televangelist, controls the city from a copy of the Hindenburg, which burns perpetually in the sky above. Then Trayne, a private eye with a bizarre secret, runs afoul of the televangelist and a series of odd and violent events is set in motion. This compelling example of postmodernist SF reads very much like a bad acid trip and owes an obvious debt to both the cyberpunks and Raymond Chandler. A more subtle connection may be with the work of Barry Malzberg, who is Jeter's only equal when it comes to bleakness of the spirit. Compare also Newman's *The Night Mayor*. (ML)

Themes: Alternate Worlds, Crime and Punishment

II-571.   Noir. Bantam Spectra, 1998.

In a decadent future Los Angeles, a detective named McNihil, who hates the dystopian world he lives in, has had his eyes surgically altered so that he sees everything in black and white, and, even more extreme, with a virtual reality overlay that turns the world into a 1930s noir cityscape. When a wealthy young executive is murdered, McNihil is blackmailed into chasing down the dead man's "prowler," a virtual reality simulation of its deceased owner. This is a dark, disturbing, and rather difficult novel by a masterful prose stylist. For a comparably dark vision, see Gibson's *Neuromancer* and Newman's *The Night Mayor*. (ML)

Themes: Crime and Punishment, Cyberpunk, Dystopias, Virtual Reality

Johnson, Annabel, U.S., 1921– and Johnson, Edgar, U.S., 1912–

II-572.   Prisoner of Psi. Atheneum, 1985.

YA. When the famous psychic Emory Morgan is kidnapped, his previously estranged son, Tristan, assembles a team and, using psi, frees Morgan. Oddball characters, unexpected plotting, and a suggestive portrait of a future America suffering from climatic changes result in fresh, contemporary story. (FM)

Themes: Crime and Punishment, Disaster, Paranormal Powers

Jones, Diana Wynne, U.K., 1934–

II-573.   A Tale of Time City. Greenwillow, 1987.

YA. Time City is a marvelous place that exists outside of space and time and in its Time Patrol works to prevent historical events from being changed by time travelers. Now, however, the city is under attack, endangering the entire universe. Vivian Smith, a child being evacuated from London in 1939, is kidnapped by agents from Time City who are under the mistaken impression that she is the Time Lady, a mysterious woman whose aid they need to save the city and the universe. Jones is arguably one of the two or three finest writers of fantasy for children and young adults of the past 50 years. This is her only true SF novel. (ML)

Themes: Children in SF, Time Travel

Jones, Gwyneth, U.K., 1952–

II-574.   Divine Endurance. Allen & Unwin, 1984.

On a far future Earth, in an isolated citadel in central Asia, live the immortal cat Divine Endurance and the last of the manufactured humans, Chosen Among the Beautiful. When the machines that imprison them finally cease functioning, they venture forth into the wasteland to see the world. In Southeast Asia they find what might well be the last human civilization on Earth. Cho was created with the need to fulfill human desires, but the people she meets find her presence to be at best a mixed blessing. A densely written and difficult novel, with a touch of Jack Vance, though lacking his wittiness and exhibiting a radically different political sensibility. A fine sequel, *Flowerdust*, appeared in 1993. Compare Slonczewski's *A Door into Ocean*. (ML)

   Themes: Androids, Far Future, Feminist SF, Immortality

II-575.   Dr. Franklin's Island (as by Anne Halam). Orion Children's Books, 2001; Wendy Lamb, 2002.

YA. A contemporary reworking of Wells's *The Island of Doctor Moreau*, in which teenage survivors of an air crash are turned into transgenic chimeras by the eponymous Dr. Franklin (the name presumably acknowledging Shelley's Frankenstein) and his assistant, Dr. Skinner. There is a strong emphasis on the developing bond between the three young people as they attempt first to survive on a seemingly deserted island, and then endeavour to retain their humanity once they have been captured by Franklin and transformed into animals. By contrast, the doctor, portrayed as a classic mad scientist, is shown to be devoid of any emotional response towards his experimental subjects, and to be entirely unconcerned by ethical standards. Instead, he is driven by a desire to make and profit from scientific breakthroughs. While the novel's ending is a bit weak, it is rescued by the compelling portrayal of the teenagers' experiences as animals. (MKS)

   Themes: Biology, Coming of Age, Mutants

II-576.   White Queen. Gollancz, 1991. Series: Aleutian Trilogy.

This gender-bending story concerns a reporter who, blackballed from his profession and living a hand-to-mouth existence in a second-rate African city, is contacted by an apparently female alien who offers him an interview and later seduces/rapes him. Although the aliens look human, their thought patterns are radically different from ours, and Jones does a particularly good job of portraying them. The Aleutian trilogy is completed by *North Wind* (1994) and *Phoenix Café* (1998). Compare Dozois's *Strangers*. (ML)

   Awards: James Tiptree
   Themes: Aliens, Feminist SF, Paranormal Powers, Sex in SF

Jones, Langdon, U.K., 1942–

II-577.   The Eye of the Lens. Macmillan, 1972.

A collection of New Wave stories by a *New Worlds* writer, including the controversial "I Remember, Anita" and such fine surreal stories as "The Great Clock" and "The Time Machine." (BS)

   Themes: New Wave

Jones, Neil R(onald), U.S., 1909–1988

II-578.   The Planet of the Double Sun. Ace, 1967. Series: Professor Jameson.

A collection of three novelettes in a series begun with "The Jameson Satellite" (1931), which tells of the revival 40 million years hence, by the cyborg Zoromes, of a 20th-century man whose body has been cryonically preserved in Earth orbit. Jameson becomes a Zorome himself, his brain encapsulated in an immortal metal body, and sets off with his new companions to explore the universe. They are nearly wiped out in "The Planet of the Double Sun" (1932) but the survivors replenish their numbers in "The Return of the Tripeds" (1932), after which there is no stopping them. Nine more early stories were collected in *The Sunless World* (1967), *Space War* (1967), and *Twin Worlds* (1967); the series continued into the 1940s and beyond. (BS)

Jones, Raymond F., U.S., 1915–1994

II-579.   The Year When Stardust Fell. Winston, 1958.

YA. Cosmic dust from an approaching comet disturbs the surface tension of all metals, causing them to blend together. The resulting destruction of virtually all machinery breeds violence and chaos. Ken Maddox, his chemist father, and a few other scientists find a remedy. Except for the prominence of young Ken, the picture of social disintegration and scientific antidote is plausible and convincing, but lacks the emotional impact the British post-catastrophe novel began to have for children in the 1960s. Best of the author's three novels in the Winston 1950s series. (FM/SM)

Themes: Disaster

Judd, Cyril *see* Kornbluth, C.M.

Kagan, Janet, U.S., 1946–

II-580.   Mirabile. Tor, 1991.

The designers behind Mirabile colony thought they had developed a foolproof way to guarantee the colonists a wide range of Earth life forms to choose from on their new world. Each Earth species was engineered to carry the genes of other species piggybacked within its own. Thus, under controlled conditions, one species would beget another, daffodils giving birth to bugs, for example. Unfortunately, due to an accident that destroyed many of their records, the colonists never know what they're going to get and often end up with bizarre mutations and unwanted pests. Take, for example, the Loch Moose Monster, Kangaroo Rex, or the ever-dangerous Frankenswine. These enormously popular stories, all originally published in *Asimov's SF*, engagingly combine broad humor and fascinating genetics. Compare Varley's *Titan*. (ML)

Themes: Genetic Engineering, Humorous SF, Life on Other Worlds

Kandel, Michael, U.S., 1941–

II-581.   Strange Invasion. Bantam, 1989.

Shape-shifting alien invaders turn Earth into a tourist site, bizarrely unsettling the global political balance. Wildly funny satire with a sting in its tail from the renowned English translator of Lem. Contrast Fredric Brown's *Martians Go Home!* (RL)

Themes: Aliens, Invasion, Satirical SF

Karinthy, Frigyes, Hungary, 1887–1938

II-582.   Voyage to Faremido/Capillaria. 1916; 1921. Trans. of *Utazás Faremidóba* and *Capillária* by Paul Tabori. Corvina, 1965.

An omnibus of two fine *contes philosophiques* cast as accounts of further voyages made by Swift's Lemuel Gulliver. The first introduces him to a machine society whose language is based on musical notes and finds the notion of organic life rather repulsive; the second features a submarine civilization whose sexual politics are based in a highly exotic biology. Although they are satirical, both stories offer carefully extrapolated accounts of the ways in which societies composed of individuals whose existential circumstances are very different from our own might be organized, bringing them close to the spirit of hard SF. (BS)

Themes: Satirical SF

Karl, Jean E., U.S., 1927–2000

II-583.   The Turning Place: Stories of a Future Past. Dutton, 1976.

YA. A series of loosely related stories concerning a future Earth, defeated by aliens and forced to rebuild, which decides to forgo materialism and imperial expansion and utilize human intelligence and curiosity to form a new society. Aimed explicitly at youth in terms of themes and interest and thoroughly non-sexist in characterization, the stories are genuinely speculative as they imagine a future extrapolated from humanity's "best" traits; hence, hopeful and even inspiring. Compare Bradbury's *The Martian Chronicles*; contrast Simak's *City*. (FM)

Themes: Far Future, Holocaust and After, Sociology

Kaul, Fedor, Germany, ?

II-584.   Contagion to this World. 1933. Trans. of *Die Welt ohne Gedächtnis* by Winifred Ray, Bles, 1933.

A deformed scientist hits back at the world that despises him by releasing a plague whose chief symptom is amnesia, taking a perverse delight in the subsequent collapse of civilization and the eventual emergence of a new human species. Kaul—whose literary efforts include other exotic revenge fantasies—is not unsympathetic to this cause. Thomas Calvert McClary's *Rebirth*, serialized in *Astounding* in 1934, describes a similar project with only slightly less relish, and may have been inspired by it.

Themes: Holocaust and After

Kavan, Anna (pseud. of Helen Woods), U.K., 1901–1968

II-585.   Ice. Owen, 1967.

A dreamlike story whose narrator pursues a fragile girl through increasingly ice-bound war zones while harboring nostalgic feelings about the warm and gentle world of the indri of Madagascar. A classic surreal novel of existential catastrophe. Contrast Ballard's *The Drowned World*. (BS)

Themes: Absurdist SF

Keller, David H(enry), U.S., 1880–1966

II-586.   Life Everlasting and Other Tales of Fantasy and Horror. Avalon, 1947.

This collection includes the title novella and 10 short stories. "Life Everlasting" (1934) is a curious moral fable, typical of Keller's phobic response to all innovation, in which a technology of immortality is represented as a curse rather than a blessing because it renders the body incapable of reproduction as well as immune to all disease. "Unto Us a Child Is Born" (1933) expresses similar convictions; the remainder are horror stories and psychological *contes cruels*. (BS)

II-587.   Tales from Underwood. Arkham House, 1952.

A collection of 23 stories divided into three genre categories; the nine SF stories include "The Revolt of the Pedestrians" (1928), in which dependence on motorized transport causes the limbs of the rich to degenerate (Keller was a country doctor who preferred horse-drawn transport). Other tales extrapolating what Isaac Asimov called "the Frankenstein syndrome"—the conviction that all inventions are fated to frustrate the hopes and ambitions of their makers—include "the Psychophonic Nurse" (1928) and "The Flying Fool" (1929), while "The Worm" (1929) and "The Ivy War" (1930) are monster stories. "A Biological Experiment" (1928) was the earliest of Keller's many ultra-conservative stories about future sexual relations; when Hugo Gernsback abandoned his SF magazines in favor of *Sexology*, Keller accompanied him. (BS)

Kelly, James Patrick, U.S., 1951–

II-588.   Look into the Sun. Tor, 1989.

A talented young American architect suffers a crisis of confidence because he fears he will never be able to equal his masterpiece, a floating sculpture called the Glass Cloud. When the alien Messengers, powerful but not entirely competent evangelists, offer him a job creating a shrine for a dying goddess on another planet, Wing jumps at the chance to escape Earth. Kelly's characters are well developed and his alien religion is extremely interesting. An earlier, relatively minor novel set in the same universe is *Planet of Whispers* (1984). (ML)

Themes: Aliens, Immortality, Religion

*II-589.   Think Like a Dinosaur. Golden Gryphon, 1997.

The 1996 Hugo Award-winning title story concerns a form of teleportation that, like a fax machine, invariably leaves an extra copy of the traveler behind to be disposed of. Other well-done stories include "Pogrom," "The First Law of Thermodynamics," "Breakaway, Breakdown," "Big Guy," and the remarkable "Mister Boy," in which a young man's mother has turned herself into a quarter-size, living copy of the Statue of Liberty. *Strange But Not a Stranger* (2002) is another strong collection. (ML)

Kepler, Johannes, Germany, 1571–1630

II-590.   Somnium. 1634. Recommended trans. by Edward Rosen in *Kepler's "Somnium,"* Univ. of Wisconsin Press, 1967.

Kepler's attempt to dramatize Copernican theory by means of a thought experiment in which Earth would be observed from a standpoint on the Moon was originally presented as a thesis in 1593, but was rejected by the University of Tübingen (the idea was extremely controversial; Galileo Galilei had not yet come into conflict with the church in Italy with respect to his own adherence to the Copernican worldview). In 1609, Kepler reformulated the piece as a visionary fantasy in which his observer is transported to the Moon by a "daemon" summoned by the protagonist's mother; the immediate result of showing the manuscript to others was that Kepler's own mother was arrested and charged with witchcraft, but he continued to add explanatory footnotes so that it could be published posthumously. The final phase of the narrative is a remarkable description of the adaptations forced on lunar life by local conditions—a dramatic anticipation, far in advance of evolutionary theory, of the kind of imaginative exercise undertaken by Camille Flammarion in *Lumen*. (BS)
   Themes: Hard SF

Kessel, John, U.S., 1950–

II-591.   Corrupting Dr. Nice. Tor, 1997.

In this humorous time travel novel that successfully captures the feel of a Preston Sturgis comedy, Dr. Owen Vannice, a wealthy, but innocent amateur paleontologist finds himself in an alternate universe Jerusalem in 40 A.D., trying to deal with a couple of time traveling con artists, a rapidly growing baby dinosaur, and a Jesus Christ who differs considerably from the one in the Bible. Compare Connie Willis's *To Say Nothing of the Dog*. (ML)
   Themes: History in SF, Religion, Satirical SF, Time Travel

*II-592.   Good News from Outer Space. Tor, 1989.

The millennium is at hand and America is in bad economic and spiritual shape. To make matters worse, the aliens have apparently landed, though they refuse to show themselves and their purposes remain highly ambiguous. At once chilling and very funny, this novel is notable for its portrayal of aliens whose motives are beyond our comprehension. For other portraits of millennial fervor, compare James Morrow's *Only Begotten Daughter* (1990), Mark Geston's *Mirror to the Sky* (1992), and Elizabeth Hand's *Glimmering.* (ML)

Themes: Aliens, Religion, Satirical SF

II-593.   The Pure Product. Tor, 1997.

This collection of Kessel's best short fiction largely overlaps the earlier *Meeting in Infinity* (1992). At once erudite and witty, Kessel has a particular genius for literary pastiche. Among his best stories are the Nebula Award-winning "Another Orphan," in which a commodities broker finds himself in the world of *Moby Dick;* the Sturgeon Award-winning "Buffalo," in which the author envisions a meeting between his father and H. G. Wells; and the hilarious "Faustfeathers," which successfully combines the Marx brothers and Christopher Marlowe with truly amazing results. Also highly recommended are the stories "Animals," "The Franchise," "Buddha Nostril Bird," and "Invaders." Compare Swanwick's *Gravity's Angels* and Kelly's *Think Like a Dinosaur.* (ML)

Kesteven, G. R. (pseud. of G. R. Crosher), U.K., 1911–

II-594.   The Pale Invaders. Chatto, 1974.

YA. After the Upheavals, the inhabitants of a peaceful valley who are satisfied with a quiet pastoral life are disturbed by strangers asking for permission to dig "coal." The elders must decide whether the past—what young Gerald has accepted as "make-believe"—can be learned from or must be avoided at all costs. An air of mystery, a sensitive depiction of coming of age, and a probing of the morality of technology result in superior children's science fiction. Compare Hoover's *Children of Morrow* (1973). (FM)

Themes: Coming of Age, Holocaust and After, Pastoral

Key, Alexander, U.S., 1904–1979

II-595.   Escape to Witch Mountain. Westminster, 1968.

YA. Tony and Tia, orphan brother and sister, are placed in a home with no possessions except a star box that suggests a mysterious origin and an equally mysterious destination. When a stranger seeks to adopt them, the children run away. Before they reach the safety of Witch Mountain, they realize that they possess parapsychological powers and remember that they are "Castaways" from a destroyed planet. It is also hinted that the children are sought by forces of satanic evil; thus the book dramatizes the universal struggle between good and evil while its youthful protagonists play active roles. Contrast Jacob's *Born Into Light.* A mediocre Disney film of the same name was released in 1975. Sequel: *Return from Witch Mountain* (1978). (FM)

Themes: Aliens, Children in SF, Paranormal Powers

II-596.   The Forgotten Door. Westminster, 1965.

YA. Little Jon falls through a forgotten door into an alien world—Earth. Temporarily forgetting his past, Jon is befriended by the Bean family, who gradually suspect he is from another, peaceful world. Others, not that perceptive, are frightened by, or want Jon's telepathic power for their own uses. As a mob closes in on him, Jon tries to find the door back; when he does, he takes the Bean family with him. Taut, suspenseful story; firm characterization, with the depiction of Jon's returning memory especially good; ethical commentary never allowed to take over narrative. Compare Winterfield's *Star Girl* (1957); contrast Jacob's *Born into Light*. (FM)

Themes: Invasion, Paranormal Powers

Keyes, Daniel, U.S., 1927–

*II-597.   Flowers for Algernon. Harcourt, 1966.

Developed from a Hugo-winning short story with the same title. A mentally retarded man's intelligence is enhanced to that of a normal adult and then to supergenius. His diary charts his progress with successive changes in diction and spelling as well as intellectual content. As the treatment fails, the reports record his collapse back into subnormality. A sensitively told, low-key masterpiece made into a film that won an acting Oscar for Cliff Robertson. Compare Anderson's *Brain Wave* and Sturgeon's "Maturity"; contrast Fast's "The First Men" and Shiras's *Children of the Atom*. (PC)

Themes: Intelligence, Supermen/women

Kilworth, Garry, U.K., 1941–

II-598.   A Theatre of Timesmiths. Gollancz, 1984.

A closed-world story; the inhabitants of a city completely surrounded by vast walls of ice face crisis as their central computer becomes unreliable and they must rediscover their history in search of a solution. (BS)

King, Stephen, U.S., 1947–

II-599.   Carrie. Doubleday, 1974.

The story of an alienated teenage girl whose latent psychokinetic power bursts forth in an orgy of destruction when she is humiliated at a high school prom. A graphic and satisfying revenge fantasy. Contrast van Vogt's *Slan*. (BS)

Themes: Paranormal Powers

II-600.   The Dead Zone. Viking, 1979.

The juvenile hero acquires the gift of precognition, although his talent is almost entirely limited to disastrous events; but can the holocaust he foresees in connection with the campaign of a presidential candidate be averted? Compare Cherry's "Cassandra" in *Visible Light* (1986). (BS)

Themes: Paranormal Powers

*II-601.   The Stand. Doubleday, 1978. Recommended ed.: Doubleday, 1990.

This new edition not only restores cut material, but updates the book as well, setting it in the 1990s and improving the science content. The basic plot remains unchanged: a killer flu escapes from a bio-weapons facility and 99 percent of the human race dies. In the United States, most of the good people who are left gather in Boulder while most of the evil people end up in Las Vegas. Armageddon follows. The novel's greatest strength lies in King's ability to portray characters who are either highly believable or chillingly twisted. Contrast Brin's *The Postman*. Although a few of King's later novels include science-fictional touches, for example *The Tommyknockers* (1987), most are straight fantasy or psychological horror. (ML)

Themes: Holocaust and After, Mythology

Kingsbury, Donald, U.S., 1929–

II-602.   Courtship Rite. Timescape, 1982. U.K. title: *Geta*, 1984.

A colony on an arid world is in cultural extremis because of its lack of resources, and the central characters become involved with a challenge to its established order. An unusually detailed and complex novel, interesting because of its carefully worked political and anthropological themes. Compare Herbert's *Dune*. (BS)

Themes: Colonization of Other Worlds, Life on Other Worlds

Kipling, (Joseph) Rudyard, U.K., 1865–1936

II-603.   With the Night Mail: A Story of 2000 A.D. Doubleday Page, 1909.

An edition of a Wellsian short story published in *McClure's Magazine* in 1905, augmented with various "extracts from contemporary magazines," including feature articles and advertisements. The future world is dominated by the Aerial Board of Control, which regulates the movement of massive dirigible airships. The story is slight, involving a mail ship caught in a storm, but a more substantial sequel, "As Easy as A.B.C." (1912), set in 2065, offers a more elaborate account of a society anxiously preoccupied with Malthusian problems and Marxian class conflict; in the second story the dictatorial A.B.C. sends a new aircraft to sort out a rebellion in Illinois. Michael Arlen's *Man's Mortality* is, in essence, a further sequel.

Themes: Politics

Klass, Philip *see* Tenn, William

Klein, Gérard, France, 1937–

II-604.   The Day Before Tomorrow. DAW, 1972. Trans. of *Le temps n'a pas d'odeur*, 1967, by P. J. Sokolowski.

Interplanetary peace is secured by transtemporal agents who alter the history of worlds that are likely to prove troublesome, but a team on one such mission finds unexpected problems with paradoxes and a peculiar alien culture. Compare Michael Jeury's *Chronolysis* (1973; trans. 1980). (BS)

Themes: Time Travel

Knebel, Fletcher, U.S., 1911–1993 and Bailey, Charles W., II, U.S., 1929–

II-605.   Seven Days in May. Harper, 1962.

This realistically detailed account by two Washington news professionals of an attempted coup d'état by a chairman of the Joint Chiefs impatient with the president's "softness" toward the Russians, still has a disturbing ring, even though the long U.S.-Soviet superpower confrontation that made such scenarios imaginable is over. The one real implausibility is that both the conspiracy and its foiling could have taken place in flap-mouthed Washington without anybody but the immediate participants knowing about it. The successful film featured strong performances by Burgess Meredith, Kirk Douglas, Ava Gardner, and especially Burt Lancaster as the general. (PC)

Themes: Politics

Knight, Damon F., U.S., 1922–2002

II-606.   The Best of Damon Knight. Nelson Doubleday, 1976.

Twenty-two stories, 1949–1972, "most of the best work I did" during that time, Knight attests. They include "To Serve Man," which became a memorable *Twilight Zone* episode; the sardonic "Not With A Bang"; "Special Delivery," in which a pregnant woman learns she is carrying a fetal supergenius; several time travel tales; and "Mary," a powerful love story with a quite unexpected happy ending. Barry Malzberg's introduction, "Dark of the Knight," is short and laudatory; Knight's own headnotes are disconcertingly frank about his personal life at the time the stories were written, but that has always been his way. (PC)

II-607.   CV. Tor, 1985. Series: CV.

At first *CV* reads much like a Michael Crichton thriller. A gigantic, high tech ocean habitat, on its maiden voyage, hauls an artifact up from the ocean floor, which contains something not of this world, a disease of some sort, or perhaps something worse. Soon many passengers and crew are falling into a coma and the habitat's physician, Dr. McNulty, notices a strange pattern of infection emerging. In the sequels, *The Observers* (1988) and *A Reasonable World* (1991), it becomes clear that those who have survived McNulty's Disease are changed by it forever, made more rational, less violent. When the infection begins to make its way through the general population, doing so in a way that implies conscious intent, radical change occurs throughout the world. Compare Crichton's *Sphere* (1987) and Heinlein's *The Puppet Masters* (1951). (ML)

Themes: Aliens, Paranormal Powers

II-608.   Hell's Pavement. Lion, 1955. Variant title: *Analogue Men,* Berkley, 1962.
The coming of a bland totalitarianism that does not need to resort to the crude tortures of *Nineteen Eighty-Four* was a favorite theme in 1950s SF. This novel also exemplifies a political theme we've heard in mainstream more recently: the unintended consequences of successful action. Disturbed individuals are provided with "analogues" within their own psyches that prevent them from engaging in antisocial or dysfunctional behavior. Then it goes on to mass treatment against crimes of violence and immunization from corruption for all candidates for public office, and it's a short step from there to conditioning against any attempt to overthrow the government. Compare Burgess's *A Clockwork Orange,* contrast Skinner's *Walden Two.* (PC)

Themes: Dystopias

Kornbluth, C(yril) M., U.S., 1923–1958

*II-609.   The Best of C. M. Kornbluth. Ed. by Frederik Pohl. Nelson Double-day, 1976.
Nineteen stories, 1941–1958, attest to the high quality of what Kornbluth wrote in his tragically short career: "The Adventurer," with its devastating punch line; as well as "The Little Black Bag"; "Gomez" (perhaps the first SF story set in a New York City Hispanic milieu); and "Marching Morons." Most have been repeatedly anthologized. Pohl, Kornbluth's frequent collaborator, selected the stories and wrote the introduction. *His Share of Glory: The Complete Short Science Fiction of C. M. Kornbluth* (NESFA, 1997) assembles 56 stories with an introduction by Pohl. (PC)

II-610.   Not This August. Doubleday, 1955. U.K. title: *Christmas Eve.* Michael Joseph, 1956. Recommended ed.: Pinnacle, 1981.
Serialized in *Maclean's,* a Canadian mainstream magazine. For U.S. publication, the Battle of Yellowknife, at which U.S. and Canadian forces surrendered to the victorious Russians and Chinese, became (less plausibly) the Battle of El Paso. One of the few such warnings that showed what rule by Russians under Stalinist principles might actually have been like. An underground resistance triumphs. Widely noticed in the mainstream media, for self-serving purposes, as a Cold War wake-up call. The 1981 revision included a foreword and afterword by Frederik Pohl. (PC)

Themes: War

II-611.　Outpost Mars by Kornbluth and Judith Merril, U.S., 1923–1997 (published as by Cyril Judd). Abelard, 1952.

This well-characterized novel pits a utopia against a dystopia, both of them on Mars. The utopia is a small cooperative commonwealth; its antithesis is a large mining corporation that brings to Mars the same brutality with which such outfits operated in the American West. One focus of the co-op is the first baby born there. Before the story ends, native, non-threatening Martians appear. Mood and conclusion are upbeat, in an old-fashioned American leftist way. Compare Dick's *Martian Time-Slip*; contrast Brackett's *Eric John Stark*. (PC)

　　Themes: The Planets, Utopias

II-612.　The Syndic. Doubleday, 1953.

A very different reading of the New York underworld from that of *The Godfather*. In a future New York, the Syndic has evolved into a free, highly permissive society, with what used to be "protection" functioning as a mild form of taxation. Chicago's mob is quite the opposite, a brutal police state. A U.S. government-in-exile on the Irish coast complicates the picture. Faced with all these menaces, the Syndic is told by the hero that it must prepare for war and, in violation of its permissive principles, institute a military draft. But its genial philosopher-king refuses on the ground that the Syndic would then no longer be the Syndic. Kornbluth at his wickedly fun-poking best. (PC)

　　Themes: Crime and Punishment, Politics

Kress, Nancy, U.S., 1948–

II-613.　An Alien Light. Arbor, 1987.

Humanity is at war with the alien Ged and apparently winning. Unable to understand the human propensity for violence, the Ged conduct an experiment on two isolated and primitive human societies that are hereditary enemies, hoping to uncover the key to defeating a more advanced human foe. They build a gigantic maze-like structure, lure humans from both cultures into it, and then study their interactions. Kress's characters are well developed and sympathetically portrayed. Her ideas on the nature of human violence are thoughtful, though she differs from many of the recent feminist SF writers who have examined the issue. Contrast Tepper's *The Gate to Women's Country* and her *Raising the Stones*. (ML)

　　Themes: Aliens, War, Women in SF

II-614.　Beggars in Spain. Morrow, 1993. Series: Beggars.

Based on a Hugo- and Nebula-winning novella, *Beggars in Spain* concerns the creation of a brilliant new race of genetically enhanced supermen who have no need to sleep. The Sleepless gradually take over the government of the United States, but must deal with increasing hostility from normal human beings. Kress breathes new life into one of the most tired SF plots. In the well-done sequels, *Beggars and Choosers* (1994; Hugo nominee) and *Beggars Ride* (1996), Kress explores the implications of a society in which a very small percentage of the population can do virtually everything that needs to be done to keep things functioning, leaving everyone else essentially idle. Compare van Vogt's *Slan* and Reed's *Black Milk*. (ML)

Themes: Genetic Engineering, Intelligence

II-615.   Probability Moon. Tor, 2000. Series: Probability.

Set on the same world as the Nebula-, Sturgeon-, and *Locus*-winning "The Flowers of Aulit Prison" (1996), *Probability Moon* initially focuses on Enli, who is working through the process of atonement towards achieving reality once again, working as an informant. The human research team she is spying on is endeavoring to understand the curious phenomenon of "shared reality" experienced by the inhabitants of World. However, during the course of the trilogy (sequels are *Probability Sun* [2001] and *Probability Space* [2002]), once it is discovered that this is a property of an alien artifact concealed on the planet, the novels shift towards a more conventional militaristic style of SF, with interest focusing on use of the artifact to defeat the menace of the alien Fallers, with the inhabitants of World becoming a secondary part of the action. The novels are well-written adventure stories but seem to lack the freshness of the original story. (MKS)

Themes: Aliens, Life on Other Worlds, Psychology, Space Opera, War

Kube-McDowell, Michael P., U.S., 1954–

II-616.   The Quiet Pools. Ace, 1990.

The purpose of the Diaspora Project is to send humanity to the stars. One starship has already left and a second, the *Memphis*, is nearly completed. Many people are opposed to the project, however, in part because of the enormous cost and in part because of the ecological damage humanity might do to another planet. Anti-project terrorism has become common. Chris McCutcheon, an archivist working on the *Memphis*'s library, but not himself scheduled to take the journey, must make up his own mind as to the rightness of the Diaspora Project. He must also unravel the frightening biological secret that makes the project a necessity. Compare Vonda McIntyre's *Starfarers* (1989). (ML)

Themes: Biology, Colonization of Other Worlds, Ecology

Kuttner, Henry, U.S., 1914–1958

*II-617.   The Best of Henry Kuttner. Nelson Doubleday, 1975.

Seventeen stories with an acute psychological sensibility, straightforwardly told. Ray Bradbury contributes an appreciative introduction. Here are mordant stories penned under the Lewis Padgett pseudonym, including "The Twonky," "The Proud Robot," and the haunting "Mimsy Were the Borogoves"—the most plausible explanation yet of where Lewis Carroll *really* got that nonsense poem. Other stories were first published under Kuttner's own name, including the powerful "Absalom." There are no stories under "Lawrence O'Donnell" (that is, written with C. L. Moore), although that is always a hard judgment call with that highly symbiotic husband-wife writing team. (PC)

II-618.   Mutant by Kuttner and C(atherine) L. Moore, U.S., 1911–1987 (as by Lewis Padgett). Gnome, 1953.

These are the "Baldy" stories, published 1945–1953. Radiation-induced mutation has begotten a race of telepaths, with a secondary genetic trait of baldness. To wear a wig or go proudly bald signified an ideological division, between living as harmoniously as may be with the nontelepath majority and aggressively asserting superiority on Nazi "superman" lines. The rational working out of this dilemma created a warm, socially and politically thoughtful story. Compare Bester's *The Demolished Man*; contrast Henderson's *Pilgrimage*. (PC)
  Themes: Evolution, Paranormal Powers

II-619.   Tomorrow and Tomorrow; and, The Fairy Chessmen as by Kuttner and Moore. Gnome, 1951.

Two grim short novels, perhaps a reflection of dashed hopes and the beginning of the Cold War. *Tomorrow* (1947) presents the achievement of world government at the cost of suppressing "dangerous" scientific research that might promote war or social instability. This society's underground therefore decides that the only way to reopen the path to progress is by starting a nuclear war. Compare Aldiss's *Earthworks* (1965). *Chessmen* (1946) describes a weird, even psychotic future in which conventional scientists trying to solve a crucial mathematical equation go mad. The only person who can face that challenge is someone who enjoys playing "fairy chess" with different chessmen and boards. The paranormal powers so central in 1950s Campbellian SF are broached, not as a bright promise but as a frightening irreality. (PC)
  Themes: Politics, Psychology

Lafferty, R(aphael) A(loysius), U.S., 1914–2002

II-620.   Annals of Klepsis. Ace, 1983.

A minor historian comes to Klepi but is told that it has no history for him to write, because its existence is merely a prelude to the beginning of time, and the universe to which he belongs is only a figment of the imagination of its founder. Typical wild Lafferty-esque adventure with apocalyptic undertone. Compare Dick's *Galactic Pot-Healer*. (BS)
  Themes: Absurdist SF

*II-621.   Fourth Mansions. Ace, 1969.

An innocent tries to understand the enigmatic events and secret organizations that are symbolic incarnations of the forces embodied in the (highly problematic) moral progress and spiritual evolution of humankind. A bizarre tour de force; one of the finest examples of American avant-garde SF. Compare Zelazny's *This Immortal* and Delany's *The Einstein Intersection*. (BS)

Themes: Absurdist SF

*II-622.   Nine Hundred Grandmothers. Ace, 1970.

The first and best of Lafferty's collections, followed by *Strange Doings* (1971), *Does Anyone Else Have Something Further to Add?* (1974), *Ringing Changes* (1984), and various collections issued by small presses. Lafferty's shorter works tend to be highly distinctive and idiosyncratic, often mixing materials from Celtic or Native American folklore with SF motifs in order to produce tall stories with a philosophical bite. At his most stylized, his work is comparable to Calvino's *Cosmicomics*, but he is rarely so abstracted and his stories have a characteristic warmth as well as a breezy imaginative recklessness and a good deal of wit. (BS)

Themes: Humorous SF

II-623.   Past Master. Ace, 1968.

St. Thomas More is snatched out of the past in order to save a decidedly ambiguous utopia—if its enemies can't prevent him from doing so. A heartfelt but lighthearted exercise in the theater of the absurd: bewildering, funny, and thought-provoking. (BS)

Themes: History in SF, Humorous SF, Utopias

II-624.   Space Chantey. Ace, 1968.

The Odyssey transposed into bizarre space opera, omnivorously devouring bits and pieces from other mythologies, to construct a futuristic mythos open to all possibilities, where the outrageous can only be commonplace and characters who are innocent and worldly-wise at the same time can stroll through the tallest tales ever told. (BS)

Themes: Humorous SF

Laidlaw, Marc, U.S., 1960–

II-625.   Dad's Nuke. Donald Fine, 1985.

A mock soap opera set in a near future where the domestic scene has been transformed by all manner of new technologies and every man's home is a fortress. Clever black comedy, taking themes from such novels as Brunner's *The Jagged Orbit* to absurd extremes. (BS)

Themes: Humorous SF

II-626.   Kalifornia. St. Martin's, 1993.

In the 21st-century United States, where nerve implants allow mass audiences to share the sense perceptions of media stars, a cyborgized baby (who may be an incarnation of the goddess Kali) threatens to become the omnipotent puppet-master of the "livewired" populace. Hilarious satire of media landscape, with a dark undercurrent; carries forward themes from *Neon Lotus* (1988). Compare the "Sense/Net" media of Gibson's *Mona Lisa Overdrive*. (RL)

Themes: Cyberpunk, Cyborgs, Satirical SF

Lake, David J(ohn), Australia, 1929–

II-627.   The Right Hand of Dextra. DAW, 1977.

A New Jerusalem is built in a green and pleasant alien land, where the emigrant pilgrims from Earth face the prospect of mingling and merging with the unfallen telepathic natives. In the sequel, *The Wildings of Westron* (1977), their hopes seem to have come to nothing because the legacy of their earthly existence has not been entirely set aside. Action-adventure SF with considerable metaphorical weight. Compare and contrast Lewis's *Out of the Silent Planet* and *Perelandra*. (BS)

Themes: Colonization of Other Worlds, Life on Other Worlds

Landis, Geoffrey A., U.S., 1955–

II-628.   Impact Parameter: And Other Quantum Realities. Golden Griffin, 2001.

A short story collection by one of the genre's most talented working scientists. Included are the Hugo Award-winning "A Walk in the Sun," in which a marooned astronaut must save herself by walking 11,000 kilometers across the Moon's surface as well as such stories as "Outsider's Chance," "Across the Darkness," "The Singular Habits of Wasps," and "Beneath the Stars of Winter." Landis does a masterful job of combining hard science concepts with a real concern for human beings. (ML)

Themes: Hard SF

II-629.   Mars Crossing. Tor, 2000.

When a spaceship is stranded on the planet's surface, five crew members set off across Mars in search of an abandoned Brazilian ship that can fly them to safety, even though they know the ship can only carry three passengers. The journey is dangerous and it eventually becomes clear that one of the crew members is willing to kill to assure his or her place on the return flight. As a scientist, Landis has been actively involved in the last several missions to Mars, so he knows the planet as well as anyone working in the field and his descriptions of the planetary surface beg for comparison with Robinson's *Red Mars*. Compare also Baxter's *Titan* and Benford's *The Martian Race* (1999). (ML)

Themes: Hard SF, The Planets

Lang, Herrmann (unattributed pseudonym)

II-630.   The Air Battle: A Vision of the Future. William Penny, 1859.

An enterprising novel in which the world 5,000 years hence is dominated by empires based in the Sahara, Madeira, and Brazil (most of Great Britain having sunk at the end of the 19th century). The eponymous conflict is between the

Saharans and the Madeirans, with the trade in European slaves at stake. A remarkable work for its time, anticipating the cavalier future-war genre launched by George Griffith's *Angel of the Revolution* but more ingenious in its treatment of racial issues than Louis Tracy or M. P. Shiel. (BS)

Themes: War

Lanier, Sterling, U.S., 1927–

II-631. Hiero's Journey. Chilton, 1973.

The world, wasted by nuclear war, is dominated by horrid mutants; the protagonist goes questing for the legendary computers that might save humankind. *The Unforsaken Hiero* (1983) presents his further adventures. Boisterous picaresque adventure fiction, comparable to Pier Anthony's Xanth fantasy novels as well as SF post-holocaust romances like Zelazny's *Damnation Alley* (1969). (BS)

Themes: Holocaust and After

Large, E(rnest) C(harles), U.K., ?–1976

II-632. Sugar in the Air. Jonathan Cape, 1937.

A novel by a noted plant physiologist about a scientist who discovers a method of artificial photosynthesis but is frustrated in his attempts to exploit its potential by the crass mismanagement of the company that employs him. A scathing critique of the capitalist mentality and its alleged antipathy to progress. Compare the chapters of John Gloag's *The New Pleasure* that deal with the problems of marketing new technologies. Large's other scientific romances, *Asleep in the Afternoon* (1939) and *Dawn in Andromeda* (1956), are more broadly satirical but considerably less effective. (BS)

Themes: Politics

Lasky, Katherine (pseud. of Kathryn Lasky Knight), U.S., 1944–

II-633. Star Split. Hyperion, 2001.

YA. In the year 3038, Darci Murlowe is a typical teen, privileged, genetically enhanced, and intimately familiar with her own carefully designed DNA. Then Darci's world is turned upside down when she discovers that she has been illegally cloned and that her parents are part of a secret movement aimed at preserving original human DNA and preventing humanity from fracturing into more than one species. Compare Ames's *Anna to the Infinite Power*. Contrast Farmer's *House of the Scorpion*. (ML)

Themes: Children in SF, Clones/Cloning, Coming of Age

Lasswitz, Kurd, Germany, 1848–1910

*****II-634. Two Planets**. 1897. Trans. of *Auf zwei Planeten* by Hans J. Rudnick, Southern Illinois Univ. Press, 1971.

An extraordinarily elaborate political allegory in which a company of German balloonists is abducted by technologically advanced Martians ambitious to open trade relations with Earth. When this project goes awry, the Martians take political control of Earth, but are soon corrupted by the responsibilities of colonial administration. Humans who have spent time on Mars become increasingly involved in campaigns for political reform, which ultimately turn violent. Modern German editions, although abridged, tend to retain more of the original text than the drastically-cut English translation. In the introduction to *Bilder aus der Zukunft* [*Images of the Future*] (1878), Lasswitz had analyzed the philosophical method of his speculative short stories in terms that anticipated many aspects of John W. Campbell, Jr.'s manifesto for SF, and he might have been as important a precursor as Verne and Wells had he been as widely imitated at home and abroad as they were, but his work was always more esoteric. (BS)

Themes: Politics

Laumer, Keith, U.S., 1925–1993

II-635.   Reward for Retief. Baen, 1989. Series: Retief.

Although he wrote a wide variety of SF novels over a career spanning 30 years, including the Bolo military SF series, Laumer will always be best remembered for his stories about the diplomat Jaime Retief. A somewhat smug variation on Heinlein's competent man, Retief invariably finds himself surrounded by stupid fellow diplomats, eccentric aliens, and near-psychotic military men. In this volume Retief is posted to a planet inhabited by xenophobic caterpillars on which is located a "trans-temporal flux," a strange phenomenon that allows reality to be changed by a thought. Other volumes in the series include *Envoy to New Worlds* (1963), *Retief's Ransom* (1971), *Retief: Diplomat at Arms* (1982), *Retief to the Rescue* (1983), and *The Return of Retief* (1985). For equally inspired silliness, compare Ron Goulart's *The Chameleon Corps* (1972) and *Starpirate's Brain* (1987). (ML)

Themes: Aliens, Humorous SF, Politics

Lawrence, Louise (pseud. of Elizabeth Rhoda Wintle), U.K., 1943–

II-636.   Andra. Collins, 1971.

YA. When, far into the future, a brain graft enables Andra both to live and to experience the feelings of a boy who died in 1987 and was frozen, she incites rebellious change among the young. A conventional story of youthful rebellion and challenge to established order is enhanced by engaging characterization, celebration of the worth of the individual, and, most unusually, a tragic ending. Contrast Dickinson's *Eva*. (FM)

Themes: Children in SF, Far Future, Genetic Engineering

II-637.   Children of the Dust. Bodley Head, 1985.

YA. The several Harnden daughters and their children, who survive the terrible first years after a nuclear war, represent contrasting approaches to rebuilding society, and then embody the mutations able to thrive in the reconstructed civilization. A compassionate yet honest tone, coupled with effective use of point of view, enriches a plausible, detailed plot. Compare Hoover's *Children of Morrow* (1973) and Kestaven's *The Pale Invaders*. (FM/ML)

Themes: Children in SF, Holocaust and After, Mutants, Sociology

II-638.   The Warriors of Taan. Bodley Head, 1986.

YA. Struggling to save their planet for their Goddess and restore peace, the Sisterhood on Taan plot by any means necessary to reconcile natives, Outworlders, and Stonewraiths. Plotting and an alien setting vaguely resembling Earth mark a story extolling the advantages of a matriarchy. Contrast Heinlein's *Citizen of the Galaxy*. (FM)

Themes: Feminist SF, Mythology, Science Fantasy

Le Guin, Ursula K., U.S., 1929–

II-639.   Always Coming Home. Harper, 1985.

An elaborate account of the culture of the Kesh—people living in "the Valley" in northern California in a post-industrial future. The main narrative sequence concerns the experience of a girl fathered on a woman of the Valley by an outsider, but there is a great wealth of supplementary detail to set this story in context; the environment, mythology, and arts of the imaginary society are scrupulously described. A fabulously rich work, the most elaborate exercise in imaginary anthropology ever undertaken, even including, in the original edition of the book, a cassette recording of the music of the Kesh. Compare Wright's *Islandia* and Brunner's *Stand on Zanzibar*. (BS/ML)

Themes: Anthropology, Feminist SF

*II-640.   The Dispossessed: An Ambiguous Utopia. Harper, 1974.

This story contrasts the poverty-stricken world of Anarres, whose political order is anarchist and egalitarian, with its rich neighbor Urras, from whose capitalist and competitive system the settlers of Anarres initially fled. A physicist who must travel from one world to the other serves as a self-conscious and anxious-viewpoint character. A dense and very careful work, arguably the best example of how SF can be used for serious discussion of moral and political issues. The quality of the writing is also outstanding. Compare Lessing's Canopus in Argos series and Hermann Hesse's *Magister Ludi* (1943). (BS)

Awards: Hugo, Nebula, John W. Campbell

Themes: Future History, Utopias

*II-641.   Four Ways to Forgiveness. HarperPrism, 1995.

Perhaps the best of the several recent collections that represent Le Guin's superb later short fiction. Four interconnected novellas set in the author's Hainish universe, center on the twin planets of Werel and Yeowe, including "Forgiveness Day," which was a Hugo and Nebula nominee, and won the Sturgeon and *Locus* Awards; and "A Man of the People" and "A Woman's Liberation," both of which were Hugo nominees. Centering primarily but not exclusively on the lot of women, Le Guin brilliantly explores the twin concepts of slavery and freedom. Other later collections of this author's short stories, all excellent, include *Buffalo Gals and Other Animal Presences* (1987), which features her Hugo award-winning fantasy "Buffalo Girls, Won't You Come Out Tonight?"; *Sea Road* (1991); *A Fisherman of the Inland Sea* (1994); *Unlocking the Air* (1996); *The Birthday of the World* (2002); and *Changing Planes* (2003). (ML)

Themes: Feminist SF, Future History

II-642.   The Lathe of Heaven. Scribner, 1971.

A psychiatrist sets out to use a patient whose dreams can alter reality to create utopia, but in usurping this power he is gradually delivered into madness. Compare Dick's *Flow My Tears, the Policeman Said* and *Ubik*. (BS)

Themes: Parallel Worlds, Psychology

*II-643.   The Left Hand of Darkness. Ace, 1969. Recommended edition: Walker, 1994.

Humans on the world of Winter are hermaphrodites, able to develop male or female sexual characteristics during periodic phases of fertility. An envoy from the galactic community becomes embroiled in local politics and is forced by his experiences to reconsider his attitudes toward human relationships. Serious, meticulous, and well written, the book has been much discussed, praised, and taught in university classes because of its timely analytic interest in sexual politics. One of the three or four most influential SF novels of the last half-century. The 1994 Walker reprint includes a new afterward and approximately 60 pages in four appendixes. Compare Sturgeon's *Venus Plus X* (1960). (BS/ML)

Awards: Hugo, Nebula, Retrospective Tiptree

Themes: Feminist SF, Future History, Life on Other Worlds, Sex in SF

II-644.   The Telling. Harcourt, 2000.

In the most recent novel set in her Hainish universe, Le Guin sends Sutty, a young Observer from the Ekumen, to the planet Aka, where she thinks she will be working with a thriving but essentially static culture based on something very much like Taoism. To her dismay, however, she discovers that the traditional culture of Aka has been virtually destroyed by recently imposed corporate communism. Sutty, who is also dealing with tragedy in her own recent past, is hard put to come to terms with the disaster that has befallen the planet. (ML)

Awards: *Locus*

Themes: Crime and Punishment, Future History, Life on Other Worlds, Politics

*II-645.   The Wind's Twelve Quarters. Harper, 1975.

The first of Le Guin's short fiction collections. The stories are various in theme but uniformly well written, ranging from the philosophical "Vaster Than Empires and More Slow" and the moving story of clone siblings, "Nine Lives," to the Nebula Award-winning prelude to *The Dispossessed*, "The Day Before the Revolution," and the dark, Hugo Award-winning fable, "The Ones Who Walk

Away from Omelas." Within the SF field their elegance is matched by some of the work of Thomas Disch and Michael Swanwick, but their earnest seriousness is without parallel. Other excellent early collections include *Orsinian Tales* (1976) and *The Compass Rose* (1982). (BS/ML)

    Awards: *Locus*

II-646.   **The Word for World Is Forest**. Berkley, 1976.

A short novel originally published in *Again, Dangerous Visions*. Human colonists on an alien world cause untold damage to the innocent natives and their environment. A harsh comment on the ethics and politics of colonialism, making good use of anthropological perspectives. Compare Bishop's *Transfigurations*. (ML)

    Awards: Hugo
    Themes: Anthropology, Colonization of Other Worlds

Le Queux, William (Tufnell), U.K., 1864–1927

II-647.   **The Invasion of 1910, with a Full Account of the Siege of London**. Eveleigh Nash, 1906.

Like many other journalists, Le Queux was urged to dabble in the future-war genre in the early 1890s, when he described *The Great War in England in 1897* (serial, 1893; book, 1894); he was instructed to revive the genre when *The Daily Mail*—the upstart pioneer of the British "popular press"—entered into a circulation war against its established rivals in 1906. Fellow journalist H. W. Wilson helped with the writing while the redoubtable Lord Roberts was recruited as military adviser. But the necessity of having the imaginary invasion fit in with Lord Northcliffe's clamorous advertising campaigns took priority over military logic, and the story takes the form of a long series of localized conflicts, climaxing with a heroic defense of London; the ultimate outcome is the ruination of both nations. Compare Chesney's *Battle of Dorking*. (BS)

    Themes: War

Lee, Tanith, U.K., 1947–

II-648.   **The Silver Metal Lover**. Nelson Doubleday, 1981.

A teenage girl finds the perfect soul mate—but how is she going to explain to her mother that he is a robot? An ironic inversion of del Rey's "Helen O'Loy," told in earnest fashion, ultimately facing (as del Rey's story does not) the issues involved in its premise. (BS)

    Themes: Robots

Leiber, Fritz, U.S., 1910–1992

*II-649.   **The Best of Fritz Leiber**. Nelson Doubleday, 1974.

Twenty-two stories, mid-1940s through the 1960s, ranging from fiendish puzzlers ("Sanity," "The Enchanted Forest") through dystopias ("Coming Attraction," "Poor Superman") to atmospheric tales from the late 1950s. Only one story is in Leiber's supernatural horror vein, and there are none of his sword and sorcery tales. (PC)

*II-650.   The Change War. Gregg, 1978.

Serialized in 1957 as "The Big Time," a saga of soldiers who have been recruited as "Spiders" or "Snakes" to battle each other and alter past events to the advantage of their own side, it won the Hugo for that year. That novel (Ace, 1961) and a collection of shorter stories on the same theme, *The Mind Spider* (Ace, 1961), were combined with other related pieces for the Gregg collection. Leiber's vision rejected the good-evil dualism in favor of a relativist view. A major and disturbing work. Contrast Anderson's *Time Patrol* and Leiber's own *Destiny Times Three*. (PC)

Awards: Hugo
Themes: Alternate Worlds, Time Travel

II-651.   Destiny Times Three. Galaxy, 1956.

This 1945 serial was an important precursor to Leiber's change wars but came to an opposite conclusion: don't mess with a world's future. Three future worlds result from a new energy source, leading to a stagnant, complacent utopia, a cruel totalitarianism, and a wrecked landscape ravaged by intelligent cats, each society left to work out its individual destiny. A dark, unduly neglected work of which Leiber was personally fond. (PC)

Themes: Alternate Worlds, Dystopias

II-652.   Gather, Darkness! Pelligrini & Cudahy, 1950.

A 1943 serial built on the religious dictatorship theme pioneered by Heinlein, but the fundamentalist regime here is basically Catholic. A revolutionary underground's goal is the restoration of political and particularly scientific freedom, but which wraps itself in the trappings of Satanism, complete with witches who zap around on jet-propelled broomsticks. A brainwashing of the hero raises darker issues of social control, but the forces of enlightenment prevail. Compare del Rey's *The Eleventh Commandment*. (PC)

Themes: Religion

*II-653.   The Leiber Chronicles: Fifty Years of Fritz Leiber. Ed. by Martin H. Greenberg. Dark Harvest, 1990.

This definitive collection of Fritz Leiber's science fiction and fantasy contains 44 stories that span the author's career, among them such acknowledged classics and award winners as "The Girl With the Hungry Eyes," "Coming Attraction," "A Bad Day for Sales," "The Man Who Made Friends with Electricity," "Gonna Roll Them Bones," "Ship of Shadows," and "Ill Met in Lankhmar." The book gives evidence, if such were needed, that Leiber is one of our very finest short story writers. Another excellent, if somewhat smaller, collection of the author's work is *The Ghost Light* (1964). Compare Ellison's *The Essential Ellison*. (ML)

II-654.   The Wanderer. Ballantine, 1964.

Worldwide disaster occurs when a mysterious, planet-sized spaceship appears out of nowhere, goes into Earth orbit, and begins to take the Moon apart, apparently for fuel. Leiber's characters and dialogue haven't held up all that well over the years, but his description of a large-scale catastrophe still impresses. Compare Wylie and Balmer's *When Worlds Collide* and Greg Bear's *The Forge of God*. (ML)

  Awards: Hugo

  Themes: Aliens, Disaster

Leinster, Murray (pseud. of Will[iam] F[itzgerald] Jenkins), U.S., 1896–1975

II-655.   The Best of Murray Leinster. Ed. by J. J. Pierce. Ballantine, 1978.

Thirteen stories from 1934 to 1956 by one of the most consistent lifetime practitioners of SF. His earliest work had appeared in 1920, before there were any SF magazines, and well reflect transformations in SF's outlook over that time span. "Proxima Centauri" (1935) confronts the first Earth visitors to our nearest stellar neighbor with a race of particularly nasty aliens, whereas "First Contact" (1945) poses and solves the problem of how two mutually suspicious alien species can manage *not* to engage in hostilities; an early, hopeful parable of the Cold War. "Sidewise in Time" (1934) is one of the earliest—and wildest—of alternate histories. *First Contacts: The Essential Murray Leinster* (1998) collects 24 stories, two of them original. (PC)

II-656.   Sidewise in Time and Other Scientific Adventures. Shasta, 1950.

A collection of six stories, including two novellas, from the early SF pulps. "Sidewise in Time" (1934) is the story that introduced alternate histories into pulp SF in flamboyant fashion, featuring a series of slippages that turn the surface of the globe into a historical patchwork; "Proxima Centauri" (1935) is one of Leinster's many first contact stories, this one occurring in the context of humankind's first interstellar expedition. Leinster had begun writing SF before the advent of the SF pulps, with melodramatic tales of timeslips, scientific supercriminals, and miniature humans battling gigantic spiders, but all the collections of his work except this one favor his later, more mature, fiction. (PC)

Lem, Stanislaw, Poland, 1921–

II-657.   The Cyberiad: Fables for the Cybernetic Age. Seabury, 1974. Trans. of *Cyberiada*, 1967, by Michael Kandel.

A series of fables about two robot "constructors" who build marvelous machines that usually fulfill their appointed tasks, but with unforeseen side effects. Futuristic folklore akin to Lafferty's *Space Chantey* but with a satirical element more akin to the work of John Sladek. *Mortal Engines* (1977) is a similar collection of 14 tales. (BS)

Themes: Robots, Satirical SF

II-658.   The Futurological Congress: (From the Memoirs of Ijon Tichy). Seabury, 1974. Trans. of *Ze wspomnien Ljona Tichego, Kongres Futrologiczny*, 1971, by Michael Kandel.

A story of Ijon Tichy, whose adventures can also be found in *The Star Diaries* (trans. 1976; also published as *Memoirs of a Space Traveler*). A convention of futurologists is disrupted by terrorism, and the release of psychotropic chemicals hurls the protagonist into a dream of a violent and decadent dystopian future. Satire of the "no-good-will-come-of-it-all" school pioneered by Karel Čapek. (BS)

Themes: Satirical SF

II-659.   His Master's Voice. Secker, 1983. Trans. of *Glos pana*, 1968, by Michael Kandel.

A stream of "signals" from outer space is the subject of various attempted decodings and an excuse for all kinds of wild hypotheses about who might have sent the message and why, in which are reflected various human hopes and fears. Good satire; contrast Sagan's *Contact.* (BS)

Themes: Satirical SF

II-660.   The Investigation. Seabury, 1974. Trans. by Adele Milch of *'Sledztwo*, 1959.

Scotland Yard investigators are baffled: corpses are disappearing from mortuaries all over Greater London. A brilliant but unstable outside consultant has been called in. But this is not an amateur outsmarts professionals in the tradition of Doyle or Poe, for this is not a closed universe of cause and effect. The sciences in this work of SF are the 20th-century investigative tools of information theory and statistics, about which Lem was very knowledgeable. A stimulating work. (PC)

Themes: Crime and Punishment

*II-661.   Solaris. Walker, 1970. Trans. from a French trans. by Joanna Kilmartin and Steve Cox.

Written in Polish in 1961, this novel combines profound philosophic speculation with the structure of action-adventure SF, embodied in a clear, vivid writing style that somehow survived two translations. A planet under study by Earth scientists is swathed in a world-girdling ocean, which the scientists conclude is sentient. For unknown reasons, the ocean "reads" the deepest memories of the four men and sends each a double of a woman in his past. The mysterious world-ocean, constantly flinging up strange shapes that defy the savants' efforts at classification, may be the first, infantile phase of an emerging "imperfect God." A major work by any measure. The Soviet film version was well received;

the later American version was less successful. Compare Silverberg's *The Face of the Waters* (1991). (PC)

Themes: Life on Other Worlds

L'Engle, Madeleine, U.S., 1918–

*II-662. A Wrinkle in Tiime. Farrar, 1962. Series: Time.

YA. Meg and Charles Wallace Murray, along with Calvin, Meg's classmate, become involved in an attempt to find Dr. Murray, a brilliant scientist who has mysteriously disappeared. Under the direction of Mrs. Who, Mrs. Whatsit, and Mrs. Which, three "angels," they "tesseract" to Camazotz, a distant star, where the children must save Dr. Murray. It's the self-effacing love of Meg, not the brilliant intelligence of Charles, that saves their father. A contemporary fantasy-SF novel that enmeshes young people in planetwide struggles between good and evil. Well written, firm characterization, provocative themes. Companion novels are *A Wind in the Door* (1973), in which Charles Wallace's bloodstream becomes an arena for a clash between good and evil; *A Swiftly Tilting Planet* (1978), in which an older Charles Wallace, aided by Meg and a unicorn, goes back in time to solve several moral crises and avert nuclear catastrophe; *Many Waters* (1986); and *An Acceptable Time* (1989). Contrast Heinlein's *The Rolling Stones* (1952). Manuela Soares wrote a 64-page guide *Scholastic Bookfiles: A Reading Guide to A Wrinkle in Time by Madeleine l'Engle* (Scholastic, 2004), which includes an interview and a list of related reading. (FM/SM)

Awards: Newbery, American Book for *A Swiftly Tilting Planet*
Themes: Space Flight, Time Travel

Lessing, Doris, Iran/U.K., 1919–

II-663.   The Memoirs of a Survivor. Octagon, 1974.

The heroine watches the slow disintegration of civilization while a teenage girl left in her care slowly matures, the two processes of decay and growth being carefully contrasted. Compare and contrast Disch's *334*. (BS)

Themes: Disaster, Psychology

II-664.   Shikasta. Cape, 1979. Series: Canopus in Argos.

First of the Canopus in Argos: Archives five-volume series. Shikasta is Earth, whose history—extended over millions of years—is here put into the cosmic perspective, observed by Canopeans who seem to be in charge of galactic history although responsible to some higher, impersonal authority. The sequels follow the exploits of various human cultures whose affairs are subtly influenced by the Canopeans; all share the remotely detached perspective that transforms the way in which individual endeavors are seen. Thoughtful and painstaking. Compare Stapledon's *Last and First Men* and *Last Men in London* and Pangborn's *A Mirror for Observers*. (BS)

Themes: Far Future, Future History

Lethem, Jonathan, U.S., 1964–

*II-665.   Girl in Landscape. Doubleday Anchor, 1998.

This mildly surreal literary SF novel predates Lethem's soon-to-occur leap to more mainstream fiction, for example the National Book Critics Circle Award-winning *Motherless Brooklyn* (1999). Echoes of John Ford's *The Searchers* and Vladimir Nabokov's *Lolita* add depth to the grim but well-told story of 14-year-old Pella Marsh, whose family has fled a collapsing New York City to become colonists on the newly discovered Planet of the Archbuilders. Left pretty much to her own devices by her mother's death just before their departure, Pella, who finds herself in telepathic communication with the native fauna, soon discovers more than perhaps she should about the dark side of humanity and about her own awakening sexuality. Compare Dick's *Martian Time-Slip* and other novels, as well as K. W. Jeter's *Madlands*. (ML)

Themes: Aliens, Colonization of Other Worlds, Life on Other Worlds, Paranormal Powers

II-666.   Gun, With Occasional Music. Harcourt Brace, 1994.

In this well done, darkly humorous first novel set in a near-future Oakland, California, evolution therapy has made it possible for animals to think and speak rationally. PI Conrad Metcalf finds himself at odds with both the police and the crooks when one of his clients is found murdered, but nothing, not even a tough-guy kangaroo or an evolved baby, will keep him from solving the crime. Other Lethem novels of interest to SF readers include *Amnesia Moon* (1995) and *As She Climbed Across the Table* (1997). For other, somewhat more serious SF takes on the noir detective novel, see K. W. Jeter's *Noir* and Kim Newman's *The Night Mayor*. (ML)

Awards: *Locus*

Themes: Crime and Punishment, Evolution, Satirical SF

II-667.   The Wall of the Sky, the Wall of the Eye. Harcourt Brace, 1996.

Lethem's first short story collection, much of which fits as comfortably within the borders of what might be called surrealism or postmodernism as science fiction, features seven remarkable stories, including "The Hardened Criminals," "Forever, Said the Duck," "Vanilla Dunk," and the Nebula Award-nominated "Five Fucks." Compare the short fiction of Thomas Disch and Harlan Ellison. (ML)

Levin, Ira, U.S., 1929–

II-668.   The Boys From Brazil. Random, 1976.

An aging Nazi hunter discovers Dr. Mengele's plot to produce a series of Hitler clones when the boys' adoptive fathers have to be killed to reproduce the key event in Hitler's upbringing. A thriller that cleverly questions genetic determination. For a more science-fictional variation on this theme, see Cherryh's *Cyteen*. (BS/ML)

Themes: Clones/Cloning

Lewis, C(live) S(taples), U.K., 1898–1963

II-669. **Out of the Silent Planet**. John Lane, 1938. Series: Space Trilogy.

A religious fantasy whose hero is accidentally abducted to Mars by an ambitious scientist (a compound of J. B. S. Haldane and H. G. Wells), where he finds a world whose various intelligent inhabitants live in ecological and spiritual harmony under the guidance of a tutelary spirit. Similar conditions apply elsewhere in the solar system, Earth being an exception because its tutelary spirit has become "bent"—a notion echoing an opinion voiced by Marie Corelli in *A Romance of Two Worlds* (1887). The novel became the first element in a "cosmic trilogy" whose inquisitorial zeal became increasingly strident. (BS)

Themes: Religion

Lewis, (Harry) Sinclair, U.S., 1885–1951

II-670. **It Can't Happen Here**. Doubleday Doran, 1935.

A political fantasy in which the U.S. is taken over by a quasi-fascist dictatorship whose path to power is paved by the populist appeal of Buzz Windrip (a caricature of Huey Long). A sarcastic cautionary tale that ends with a dose of saccharine sentimentality. Compare and contrast Čapek's *War with the Newts*. (BS)

Themes: Politics

Lightner, A(lice) M., U.S., 1904–1988

II-671. **The Day of the Drones**. Norton, 1969.

YA. A post-catastrophe story. Afria (once Africa) seems the only land uncontaminated by radioactivity. An expedition sets out to explore the potentially dangerous nearby lands and discovers in an ancient northern country (once England) the Bee-people, a mutant, dwarfed race descended from the pre-disaster white population, organized around matriarchal principles, and controlled by gigantic mutant bees. A harrowing look at a possible future society adversely affected by radiation, virtually bookless, and unsure of the uses of power and knowledge; a perceptive study of the nature and effects of racial prejudice. Contrast O'Brien's *Z for Zachariah*. (FM)

Themes: Holocaust and After, Pollution, Sociology

II-672. **Doctor to the Galaxy**. Norton, 1965.

YA. Young Dr. Garrison Bart becomes, through a mix-up, a veterinarian instead of a physician on a faraway planet. He discovers that lustra, a local money-making grain, inhibits growth. He announces the discovery to the Assembly of Scientists, but his findings are rejected; he is also charged with illegally practicing medicine. Bart makes another discovery: lustra inhibits cancerous growth. This time he is honored for his discovery and is able to become a physician. Interesting story that aptly represents the author's ability to find subject matter appealing to preteens. Other Lightner novels that show an interest in biology include

The Space Plague (1966) and *The Space Ark* (1968). Compare Norse's *Star Surgeon.* Contrast Heinlein's *Farmer in the Sky.* (FM/ML)

Themes: Biology, Life on Other Worlds, Medicine

Lindsay, David, U.K., 1878–1945

*II-673.   A Voyage to Arcturus. Methuen, 1920.

A classic visionary fantasy in which the ecosphere of the Arcturan planet of Tormance is an allegorical representation of the moral and metaphysical enigmas of the modernist era. Extraordinarily complex, vivid, and—in the end—decisive, it maps out a post-theistic confrontation between the human mind and the natural order by which it was spawned and shaped. It provided a model for C. S. Lewis's much inferior *Out of the Silent Planet* and its ambition is echoed in Olaf Stapledon's *Star Maker*, but it remains a unique tour de force. (BS)

Themes: Life on Other Worlds

Linebarger, Paul Myron Anthony *see* Smith, Cordwainer

Llewellyn, (David William) Alun, U.K., 1903–1988

II-674.   The Strange Invaders. Bell, 1934.

An intriguing political fantasy set during a future Ice Age, describing a quasi-medieval society in which Marx, Lenin, and Stalin are revered mythical figures. Civilization has been all but obliterated by warfare, and its last relics are now under threat from giant lizards. The novel has something of the surrealism of O'Neill's *Land Under England* as well as some of the elegiac pastoralism of Jefferies's *After London* and Collier's *Tom's a-Cold*, but its bleakness is distinctively casual. (BS)

Themes: Holocaust and After

London, Jack (i.e., John) (Griffith), U.S., 1876–1916

II-675.   The Iron Heel. Macmillan, 1907.

A Marxist fantasy describing the development of American capitalism into a brutally repressive regime, and the tragic failure of organized labor to launch a successful revolution. The story is, however, represented as an ancient manuscript recovered in the much happier 27th century, when socialism has triumphed (a device borrowed by Margaret Atwood's *The Handmaid's Tale*). Compare and contrast Farrère's *Useless Hands* and Lewis's *It Can't Happen Here*. (BS)

Themes: Dystopias, Politics

II-676.   The Science Fiction of Jack London. Ed. by Richard Gid Powers. Gregg Press, 1975.

A collection of 11 stories, including the Wellsian fantasy of invisibility "The Shadow and the Flash" (1903), the classic disaster story *The Scarlet Plague* (1912; book 1915), and an account of a mysterious object fallen from the sky among unappreciative savages, "The Red One" (1918). "Goliah" (1908), "A Curious Fragment" (1908), and "The Dream of Debs" (1909) are political fantasies. London's earliest pulp SF stories, "A Thousand Deaths" (1899) and "The Rejuvenation of Major Rathbone" (1899), are omitted, but can be found in the overlapping collection *Curious Fragments: Jack London's Tales of Fantasy Fiction* (1975). (BS)

Long, Frank Belknap, U.S., 1903–1994

II-677.   The Rim of the Unknown. Arkham House, 1972.
A collection of 23 stories including most of Long's contributions to the SF magazines. The most notable early items are three pioneering far future fantasies from *Astounding*, "The Last Men" (1934), its prequel "Green Glory" (1935), and "The Great Cold" (1935), in which humankind has been superseded by various other species. (BS)

Longyear, Barry B(rookes), U.S., 1942–

II-678.   Manifest Destiny. Berkley, 1980.
A collection including "Enemy Mine," the winner of both Hugo and Nebula awards in which an alien and a human stranded on a hostile world must cooperate although their species are at war. "The Jaren" expresses a similar conviction that if different races cannot achieve a proper sympathy for one another, the results must be tragic. *The Tomorrow Testament* (1983) is a novel set against the same background as "Enemy Mine" and similarly deals with the cultivation of understanding; "Enemy Mine" itself was expanded to novel length by David Gerrold, the resultant 1983 book being issued as a collaboration in connection with the film version. (BS/ML)

II-679.   Sea of Glass. St. Martin's, 1987.
Longyear's most powerful novel and one of the grimmest stories of overpopulation ever written. When seven-year-old Thomas Windom's parents are discovered to have committed the crime of having an illegal child in the grossly overpopulated 21st century, they are put to death gruesomely on public television, and Thomas is sent to spend his life in a brutal labor camp. Compare Harrison's *Make Room! Make Room!* and Brunner's *Stand on Zanzibar*. (ML)
   Themes: Coming of Age, Dystopias, Overpopulation, Religion

Lovecraft, H(oward) P(hillips), U.S., 1890–1937

II-680.   The Outsider and Others. Arkham House, 1939.
A collection of 36 stories, including those that filled in the background of what August Derleth was later to call the Cthulhu Mythos—a careful distillation of a sensation of "cosmic horror" in plots that gradually reveal to unwise scholars that all human and scientific ambition is a futile folly because the universe is dominated by malevolent godlike aliens whose apocalyptic re-emergence is inevitable, even though their present dormancy restricts them to relatively ten-

tative abominations. The key novellas embodying this perspective (which connect well enough with several of Lovecraft's earlier horror stories to draw them into an incoherent series) are *The Shadow over Innsmouth* (1936), "The Shadow out of Time" (*Astounding*, 1936), and "At the Mountains of Madness" (*Astounding*, 1936); all of them have been extensively reprinted in other collections, more recently in corrected versions. Lovecraft's enormous influence on American weird fiction is reflected in hundreds of pastiches and sequels—which he encouraged by making his imaginative universe available to his many correspondents—many of which similarly hybridize SF and supernatural fiction. (BS)

Lovelace, Delos W(heeler), U.S., 1884–1967

II-681.   King Kong. Grosset and Dunlap, 1932.

An early film novelization based on a script cobbled together under the supervision of director Merian Cooper from a story line by Edgar Wallace. The story of an expedition to a remote island, where a vast wall separates human tribesmen from a lost world inhabited by prehistoric monsters and the eponymous giant ape, seems preposterous in print, although the movie's spectacular imagery gave birth to a significant modern myth. Compare Burroughs's *The Land That Time Forgot.* (BS)

Themes: Monsters

Low, A(rchibald) M(ontgomery), U.K., 1888–1956

II-682.   Adrift in the Stratosphere. Blackie, 1937.

YA. A novel about the first rocket flight into space, written by a leading member of the British Interplanetary Society; it was serialized in the boys' paper *Scoops* in 1934 as "Space." The narrative becomes wildly improbable when the spacecraft is attacked by a space monster and threatened by Martian rays, whereupon the adventurers seek refuge on a handy "space island." Similar in spirit and intent to Gail's *Shot into Infinity*, but less controlled. (BS)

Themes: Space Flight

Lowry, Lois, U.S., 1937–

II-683.   Gathering Blue. Houghton Mifflin, 2000. Series: The Giver.

YA. In this well-done companion volume to *The Giver*, Kira has grown up in a primitive society dominated by casual cruelty and scarcity. Lame and recently orphaned, she is marked for death but, instead, is sent to live as a slave in the Council Edifice, where the local rulers can make use of her skill in embroidery. Put to work restoring a ceremonial robe, she befriends other child-artists who have been forced to take up ceremonial tasks, all of which involve harnessing their creativity to maintain the community's sterile sense of its own past. Collectively the children struggle to preserve their own individuality and creativity. *The Messenger*, a sequel to both *Gathering Blue* and *The Giver*, appeared in 2004. (ML)

Themes: Children in SF, Coming of Age, Dystopias

*II-684.   The Giver. Houghton Mifflin, 1993. Series: The Giver.

YA. Arguably the most respected YA science fiction novel of the past 20 years and a Newbery Award winner, *The Giver* is set in what at first appears to be a utopia, a society without unemployment or poverty, where everyone is happy. Twelve-year-old Jonas is chosen to be the Receiver of Memories, the only person in his community who will be aware of the history and the emotions that have been forgotten in order to achieve this supposedly utopian state. Gradually other secret evils emerge, particularly the mass euthanasia of less-than-perfect babies and the elderly. Sickened by what he has learned, Jonas flees his society. This grim but overwhelmingly powerful tale, which echoes *Brave New World* and other classic dystopias, ends in a fascinatingly ambiguous manner that has long provoked much serious discussion among teenage readers. (ML)

Awards: Newbery

Themes: Children in SF, Coming of Age, Dystopias

Lundwall, Sam J., Sweden, 1941–

II-685.   2018 A. D.: or, The King Kong Blues. DAW, 1975.

In a polluted future world dominated by crass commercialism, the hero struggles to make a living in the corrupt advertising profession, while a bored oil sheik plays games with the world economy. Satirical black comedy with considerable bite. Compare Pohl and Kornbluth's *The Space Merchants* and Snoo Wilson's *Spaceache* (1984). (BS)

Themes: Pollution, Satirical SF

Lupoff, Richard A., U.S., 1935–

II-686.   Space War Blues. Dell, 1978.

A fix-up novel in which human colonies fight a race war in space, disrupting the lives of the peaceful tribesmen who have adapted to life as spacefaring nomads. A deliberate mingling of the avant-garde and romantic aspects of 1970s SF, based on a short novel that appeared in Ellison's *Dangerous Visions*. (BS)

Lynn, Elizabeth A., U.S., 1946–

II-687.   The Sardonyx Net. Putnam, 1981.

On the one planet in the galactic community where slavery still survives, political adversaries fight over the drug that sustains the system. The chief protagonist is caught in a conflict of loyalties, finding his principles and emotions continually at odds as he moves through the convoluted plot. Colorful action-adventure with pretensions to moral seriousness and a touch of sado-masochism. Compare Jayge Carr's *Navigator's Syndrome* (1983). (BS/ML)

Themes: Life on Other Worlds, Sex in SF

Lytton, Edward George Bulwer-, U.K., 1803–1873

II-688.   The Coming Race. Blackwood, 1871 (issued anonymously).

A utopian satire exploring the underground civilization of the Vril-ya, whose mastery of technology based on the elementary force of vril (which embraces electromagnetism and various other radiations) has allowed them to create an ideal society of sorts. The satirical aspects of the story comment on religion and evolutionary theory, but the main thrust of its argument is that a society whose members were content would lose its artistic and progressive impetus. Although the story idea seems to have arisen by extrapolating the themes of Lytton's earlier Rosicrucian romances, the occult elements are downplayed in favor of philosophical speculations that were carried forward by such works as Butler's *Erewhon* and Besant's *The Inner House*. (BS)
  Themes: Utopias

MacClure, Victor (Thom MacWalter), U.K., 1887–1963

II-689.   The Ark of the Covenant: A Romance of the Air and Science. Harper, 1924.

A political fantasy reprinted in the U.K. as *Ultimatum*, in which a company armed by a scientific Master with airships, narcotic gases, substance-transmuting rays, and atomic energy set out to loot the financial centers of the world, although their ultimate aim is to cure the world of the disease of war by means of benevolent blackmail. Unusually, in a romance of this kind, they succeed. Compare and contrast Griffith's *The Angel of the Revolution* and Forester's *The Peacemaker*. (BS)
  Themes: War

MacColl, Hugh, U.K., 1837–1908

II-690.   Mr Stranger's Sealed Packet. Chatto and Windus, 1889.

An interplanetary romance by a Scottish logician in which a schoolmaster employs a kind of antigravity to travel to Mars, where red and blue humanoid races are in conflict. He falls in love with a blue girl, but she dies when he brings her back to Earth because she has no resistance to Earthly diseases. Interesting for its anticipation of ideas developed in a rather more extravagant fashion by H. G. Wells and Edgar Rice Burroughs, and in a much less extravagant fashion by MacColl's own dour treatise on *Man's Origin, Destiny and Duty* (1909). (BS)
  Themes: Life on Other Worlds

Mace, Elisabeth, U.K., 1933–

II-691.   Out There. Greenwillow, 1978. British title: *Ransome Revisited*, 1975.

YA. Eleven confronts a bleak life after his schooling is finished and he is sent to the quarries. Along with his subnormal older brother and two acquaintances,

Susan and Will, Eleven escapes and sets out for a community where, rumor has it, freedom exists. This post-holocaust survival story is marked by tough-minded honesty in its depiction of the ways supposedly deprived youth manage to survive with self-respect and dignity fundamentally intact and continue to hope for a better life. Compare Maguire's *I Feel Like the Morning Star* and Armstrong and Butcher's *The Kindling*. Contrast Mark's *The Ennead*. (FM)

Themes: Children in SF, Coming of Age, Holocaust and After, Pollution

MacIsaac, Fred(erick John), U.S., 1886–1940

II-692.   The Hothouse World. Avalon, 1965.

A post-catastrophe novel serialized in *Argosy* in 1931, in which the inhabitants of a carefully regulated 21st-century enclave are eventually rescued from their voluntary imprisonment and cultural sterility by a 20th-century man awakened from suspended animation—a notion probably borrowed from Rousseau's *Messiah of the Cylinder* rather than Wells's *When the Sleeper Wakes*. The story retains some of the political combativeness of MacIsaac's anonymous pulp serials "The Seal of Satan" (1926) and "The Great Commander" (1926) and the adventurous "World Brigands" (1928), in which an Anglo-American war waged over unpaid war debts is settled by the threat of an atomic bomb, but makes more concessions to conventional pulp romanticism. (BS)

Themes: Holocaust and After

MacLean, Katherine, U.S., 1925–

II-693.   The Missing Man. Berkley, 1975.

Expanded from a Nebula Award-winning novella. The psychic hero, although a social outcast, uses his powers for the public good but has still to achieve full development of his superhuman nature. Compare Brunner's *The Whole Man* and Sellings's *Telepath* (1962). (BS)

Themes: Paranormal Powers

MacLeod, Ian R., U.K., 1956–

II-694.   The Great Wheel. Harcourt Brace, 1997.

In this angst-ridden, evocative novel, Europe has become a virtual utopia, but Father John, a priest who has lost his faith, spends his time in the squalor of North Africa's Endless City, ministering to the wretched. Gradually the priest realizes that far too many of the people he sees are dying from myeloid leukemia. When he uncovers evidence that these deaths are the result of the koiyl leaf, a popular opiate, he attempts to convince government officials to outlaw it, only to discover that the government is more interested in keeping its citizens docile than in keeping them alive. This is a beautiful and understated character study. Compare McHugh's *Nekropolis*. (ML)

Awards: *Locus*
Themes: Medicine, Politics, Religion, Utopias

II-695.   The Light Ages. Ace, 2003.

This beautifully written novel on the border between science fiction and fantasy describes an England in which the discovery of aether, a magical substance of enormous power, sparked a much earlier industrial revolution. Now, hundreds of years later, in the Third Age of Industry (roughly equivalent to our Victorian Age), great Guilds run the nation, with powerful captains of industry living like nobility while the impoverished masses risk their lives mining and refining the dangerous substance that supports the economy. Society, however, is ripe for change and the novel's well-drawn narrator, Robert Borrows, stands poised to witness the revolution. A sequel is forthcoming. Compare Swanwick's *The Iron Dragon's Daughter* (1994), Walter Jon Williams's *Metropolitan*, and Miéville's *Perdido Street Station*. (ML)

Themes: History in SF, Politics, Science Fantasy

II-696.   Starlight. Arkham, 1997.

MacLeod's first collection combines fantasy, horror, and science fiction, all of them beautifully written. Among the science fiction highlights are "Grownups," which is set in a world where all reproduction requires three sexes, men, women, and uncles, and "Starship Day," in which the jaded citizens of a future Earth await the news that the crew of the first starship have awakened from suspended animation. Other excellent stories include "Papa," "The Giving Mouth," and "The Perfect Stranger." A new collection, *Breathmoss and Other Exhalations*, was published in 2004. Compare Priest's *An Infinite Summer* and *The Dream Archipelago*. (ML)

MacLeod, Ken, Scotland, 1954–

II-697.   Cosmonaut Keep. Orbit 2000, Tor, 2001. Series: Engines of Light.

In volume one of his Engines of Light sequence, MacLeod tells two alternating stories. In the mid-21st century, while a right-wing America is engaged in a cold war with a Russia-dominated European Union, Matt Cairns, a Scottish computer programmer, finds himself on the run and in possession of a mysterious computer disk that may hold the secret to interstellar flight. Meanwhile, far in the future, Gregor Cairns, Matt's descendant, works as a scientist on the planet Mingulay, where human beings co-exist with intelligent dinosaurs and travel in gigantic starships piloted by giant squid. This is intelligent, politically left-leaning space opera of a very sophisticated sort. Sequels are *Dark Light* (2001; U.S. 2002), and *Engine City* (2002; U.S. 2003). (ML)

Themes: Aliens, Life on Other Worlds, Politics, Space Opera

*II-698.   The Star Fraction. Legend, 1995, Tor 2001. Series: Fall Revolution.

In volume one of the Fall Revolution sequence, set in a Balkanized, mid-21st-century England, Moh Kohn, a Trotskyite mercenary with a heart of gold and a self-aware gun, joins forces with a fugitive computer scientist, a runaway evangelical, and a feminist terrorist in an attempt to derail an artificial intelligence on a doomsday mission. MacLeod's invented society (many different societies, actually) and his plot are both incredibly complex. His knowledge of the various flavors of Socialist and Anarchist political philosophy is daunting, as is his willingness to discuss such matters at great length, but he never fails to make things interesting. Other novels in the sequence, each of which explores one or more cultures based on a different leftist political theory, are *The Stone Canal* (1997, U.S. 1999), *The Cassini Division* (1998, U.S. 1999), and *The Sky Road* (1999, U.S. 2000). For some reason the books were published out of order in the United States. Compare McAuley's *Fairyland* and Danver's *The Fourth World*. (ML)

Themes: Computers, Future History, Intelligence, Politics

Madariaga (y Rojo), Salvador de, Spain, 1886–1978

II-699.   The Sacred Giraffe: Being the Second Volume of the Posthumous Works of Julio Arceval. Hopkinson, 1925.

A remarkable futuristic fantasy whose background is curiously similar to that of Herrmann Lang's *The Air Battle*, save that the submergence of Europe has led to the extinction of white men, leaving the dominant race of the seventieth century to wonder whether they ever really existed. The satire is unusually urbane—as might be expected of a career diplomat—and mostly bears on questions of sexual politics and social class; the text is a curious patchwork of miscellaneous fragments. (BS)

Themes: Politics

Maguire, Gregory, U.S., 1954–

II-700.   I Feel Like the Morning Star. Harper, 1989.

YA. Three teens in The Pioneer Colony, a post-holocaust subterranean station that has ironically become virtually a prison, break out, along with the children, to the surface and freedom. Very literate style, rich characterization, and plausibly rendered setting elevate conventional plot to superior status. Contrast Hoover's *Children of Morrow*. (FM)

Themes: Children in SF, Coming of Age, Holocaust and After

Maitland, Edward, U.K., 1824–1897

II-701.   By and By: An Historical Romance of the Future. Bentley, 3 vols., 1873.

One of only two SF three-deckers produced in the Victorian era, when fiction publishing in England was dominated by that format, far more restrained in its manner and content than Blair's *Annals of the Twenty-Ninth Century*. The story is the biography of a balloon-borne foundling in a world more than 200 years in the book's future, whose great achievement is the irrigation of the Sahara. The background is a politically settled world in which religion has declined almost to extinction and the sexes are equal. The second edition included a preface in which the author, seemingly stung by the charge that his account of the future was conspicuously unadventurous, says that his intention was to extrapolate present trends sensibly, unlike the authors of *The Coming Race* and *Erewhon*; modern readers are likely to side with the critics, but Maitland's careful approach is not without virtue. (BS)

Themes: Politics

Malzberg, Barry, U.S., 1939–

*II-702. Beyond Apollo. Random, 1972.

Winner of the first John W. Campbell Memorial Award (1973), causing controversy because it is a wickedly funny undermining of the SF myth of the conquest of space, of which Campbell was one of the principal promoters. The sole survivor of a Venus mission cannot explain what became of his companions. *The Falling Astronauts* (1971) and *Revelations* (1972) also challenge with mockery the values implicit in the space program. (BS)

Themes: Psychology, The Moon, Space Flight

II-703. The Cross of Fire. Ace, 1982.

Expanded from the novella "Le Croix." A dissident in a future totalitarian state undergoes a kind of psychotherapy involving induced illusions, which allow him to play Christ, in which role he ardently but hopelessly seeks meaning through self-sacrifice. Mordant wit and graphic imagery combine in a powerful and disturbing story. Compare Moorcock's *Behold the Man*. (BS)

Themes: Psychology, Religion

II-704. Galaxies. Pyramid, 1975.

Expanded from the novelette "A Galaxy Called Rome." The plot, deliberately designed as a hard SF story, involves a spaceship endangered by a black hole, on whose fate much depends; this is blended with an elaborate commentary on the psychology and sociology of SF writing, using the story as paradigm. It thus becomes a brilliantly self-conscious work of art, more telling in many ways than Malzberg's *Herovit's World* (1973). Compare Eleanor Arnason's "Warlord of Saturn's Moons" in Sargent's *Women of Wonder: The Classic Years*. (BS/ML)

Themes: Hard SF, Psychology, Sociology

II-705. The Man Who Loved the Midnight Lady. Doubleday, 1980.

Perhaps the best of Malzberg's several collections; also outstanding is the earlier *Down Here in the Dream Quarter* (1976). Most of Malzberg's stories contrive to be anguished and witty at the same time—classic examples of ironic weltschmerz. Compare the short fiction of John Sladek and the work of nongenre writers including Bernard Malamud. (BS)

II-706. The Remaking of Sigmund Freud. Ballantine, 1985.

A fix-up novel featuring an alternate world where Freud psychoanalyzes Emily Dickinson from afar and is assassinated by a disappointed patient, and a future where he is reincarnated aboard a spaceship to save its crew members from the kind of extraterrestrial angst that was suffered by the protagonist of *Beyond Apollo*. Lacks the fluency of Malzberg's early novels but gains in complexity by way of compensation. Compare Jeremy Leven's *Satan* (1982). (BS)

Themes: Alternate Worlds, Psychology

Mann, Phillip, U.K./New Zealand, 1942–

II-707.   Wulfsyarn: A Mosaic. Gollancz, 1990.

In this strangely metaphysical and heavily symbolic tale, Captain Jon Wilberfoss, commanding the starship *Nightingale,* is sent on a mission of mercy to return home hundreds of refugees who were scattered across the galaxy by the recently ended War of Ignorance. En route, the *Nightingale* inexplicably vanishes, only to reappear a year later, ruined and devoid of life with the exception of its captain, who has gone mad. Wulf, an artificial intelligence that has devoted itself to Wilberfoss, must try to heal him and discover what really happened. Compare Wallace's *Croyd* and Farmer's *The Unreasoning Mask.* (ML)

Themes: Aliens, Religion, Space Opera

Manning, Laurence (Edward), Canada, 1899–1972

*II-708.   The Man Who Awoke. Ace, 1975.

An omnibus edition of a series of stories published in *Wonder Stories* in 1933, in which a contemporary man employs suspended animation to visit a series of future scenarios ranging from 5,000 to 25,000 A.D. before taking advantage of new technologies to view the more distant future of humankind in the further reaches of the universe, following the death of the sun. Many scenarios standardized by British scientific romance and American pulp SF are glimpsed en route, and this is one of very few works that tries conscientiously to bridge the two traditions; its immediate inspiration was obviously Stapledon's *Last and First Men.* Manning was perhaps the best and most adventurous of the "discoveries" made by Hugo Gernsback's SF pulps, but he quit the field abruptly when Gernsback abandoned it; the advertised sequel to his final pulp story "World of the Mist" (1935) was never published. (BS)

Themes: Future History

Mark, Jan, U.K., 1943–

II-709.   The Ennead. Crowell, 1978.

YA. Three socially deviant characters, Isaac, Eleanor, and Moshe, are destroyed by the rigidly stratified society of Erato, a harsh, stark planet still struggling through to the freedom of spirit its inhabitants have sought. Unusually somber in mood and marked by sharp characterization and a distinctive setting, the novel is a ringing statement of the need for individual freedom and the power of the human spirit. Compare Lowry's *The Giver,* contrast Mace's *Out There.* (FM/ML)

Themes: Anthropology, Coming of Age, Life on Other Worlds

Martel, Suzanne, Canada, 1924–

II-710.   The City Under Ground. Viking, 1964.

YA. A post-catastrophe story. Where old Montreal used to be, Surreal, an underground city, survives because of a highly technological and rigidly organized society. Two sets of brothers, Luke and Paul and Eric and Bernard, showing curiosity and initiative, help the city fight a mysterious, hitherto-unknown underground enemy and stumble on a way to the surface where they discover a cleansed Earth and other survivors, the Lauranians, a free, less repressed, and technologically inferior people. Surreal decides to go above ground and ally itself with the Lauranians. Adequately written and mildly engaging incidents. Compare Silverberg's *Time of the Great Freeze*. (FM)

   Themes: Holocaust and After, Pastoral, Sociology

Martin, George R. R., U.S., 1948–

II-711.   Dying of the Light. Simon & Schuster, 1977.

On a wandering world, briefly brought to light by its temporary association with a sun, several races have built cities for a great festival. The self-pitying protagonist pursues his lost love here and becomes involved with the alien tribe into which she has married as the long night closes in again. Compare Elizabeth Lynn's *A Different Light* (1978). (BS)

   Themes: Aliens, Life on Other Worlds

*II-712.   GRRM: A RRetrospective. Subterranean Press, 2003.

This massive collection brings together nearly 1,300 pages of Martin's short fiction and covers his entire career. It incorporated stories to be found in *A Song for Lya and Other Stories* (1976), *Songs of Stars and Shadows* (1977), *Sandkings* (1981), *Songs the Dead Men Sing* (1983), *Portraits of His Children* (1987), and other collections. Among Martin's many award-winning and nominated stories are "A Song for Lya," which concerns an alien species whose biology is such that their religious faith in life after death has material foundation; "Nightflyers," another story of contact with mysterious aliens; "Sandkings," a memorable account of insectile "pets" learning to see their "owners" in a new light; and "Portraits of His Children" and "The Pear Shaped Man." A superb collection. (ML)

Martin, George R. R., U.S., 1948– and Tuttle, Lisa, U.S., 1952–

II-713.   Windhaven. Timescape, 1981.

A fix-up novel including "One-Wing." On a stormy world humans struggle to survive on the islands of an archipelago, their communications depending on the flyers who use artificial wings. The heroine has a turbulent time on the ground as well as in the air. Compare McCaffrey's Pern series. (BS)

   Themes: Life on Other Worlds

Martin, Valerie, U.S., 1948–

II-714. **Mary Reilly**. Doubleday, 1990.

All the actual science fiction content in this brilliant revisioning of Robert Louis Stevenson's classic novella exists offstage and in the mind of the reader. The title character is Dr. Jekyll's maid, a kind, competent, but sadly damaged young woman who is herself the victim of a monster, her father's alcoholism. Despite their differences in class and education, Mary's background makes her an ideal companion for Dr. Jekyll as he journeys into the heart of evil. This was made into an excellent film. Compare Stevenson's *The Strange Case of Dr. Jekyll and Mr. Hyde*. (ML)

Themes: Biology, History in SF, Women in SF

Marvell, Andrew (pseudonym of Howell Davies), U.K., 1896–1985

II-715. **Minimum Man; or, Time to be Gone**. Gollancz, 1938.

A subtle but sharp political fantasy in which a race of tiny supermen survives initial persecution to win the hearts of right-thinking people by assisting in the overthrow of English fascism. Ultimately, one presumes, they will replace *Homo sapiens* entirely. Davies, a journalist, wrote two other novels during a brief pre-World War II lacuna in his highly successful career, whose tenor is equally sarcastic; *Three Men Make a World* (1939) features an oil-devouring bacterium, while *Congratulate the Devil* (1939) features a euphoric drug that receives a cold welcome in an anxious society. (BS)

Themes: Politics

Masson, David, U.K., 1924–1974

II-716. **The Caltraps of Time**. Faber, 1968.

Notable short stories by a writer associated with Moorcock's *New Worlds*, including the fine "Traveller's Rest," about a war fought on a world where time passes at different rates in different places. Polished and original. Compare Bayley's *The Knights of the Limits* and James Sallis's *A Few Last Words* (1964). (BS)

Mastin, John, U.K., 1865–1932

II-717. **The Stolen Planet: A Scientific Romance**. Welby, 1906.

YA. Two young friends employ the antigravity technology that was by then conventional in British scientific romance to build a spaceship capable of interstellar flight. After watching two planets collide, they visit various other worlds before returning briefly to the solar system, visiting the ideal world of Venus before winging their way to Sirius. The author, a clergyman and amateur naturalist, claims in a preface to be developing a story and scientific ideas given to him by one James Frederick Bennett, but the frequent intrusions of religious material into the text—which are even more obvious in the preposterous sequel, *Through the Sun in an Airship* (1909)—are presumably his own, given that they create such odd juxtapositions. On the other hand, Mastin must have been aware of the residual religious component of such texts as Griffith's *Honeymoon in Space*, from which the Venerians seem to be borrowed. There are also echoes of Cole's *Struggle for Empire*, although the absence of any large-scale conflict reduces the novel's qualification as space opera. (BS)

Themes: Space Flight

Matheson, Richard (Barton), U.S., 1926–

II-718.   Bid Time Return. Viking, 1975.

A timeslip romance in which a young author is allowed to meet (briefly) the actress from the past with whose photographic image he's fallen in love. Compare Finney's *Time and Again*. (BS)

Awards: World Fantasy
Themes: Time Travel

*II-719.   Born of Man and Woman. Chamberlain, 1954. Variant title: *Third From the Sun*, Bantam, 1955.

Seventeen stories, the best of the author's early work, including the horrific title story, whose diction and punctuation help convey an aura of chill alienness. Almost equally terrifying is "Lover When You're Near Me." In a more reflective mood are "Third from the Sun" and "The Traveller." A fresh and distinctive new voice, in whom it was clear that the 1950s would not be simply a continuation of SF's Golden Age. A massive (900-page) collection of Matheson's short fiction was published by Dream/Press in 1989.

Themes: Monsters

II-720.   I Am Legend. Fawcett, 1954.

What Williamson's *Darker than You Think* was to lycanthropy, this novel was to vampirism—an attempt to give what had been considered purely supernatural horror a scientific basis. Since vampires flee from light, the hero goes forth by day to destroy them. Reversing the Dracula theme, *he* becomes an object of terror to *them*. Two attempts to translate it for the screen failed, casualties of Hollywood simple-mindedness, which failed to include the tale's metaphysical and psychological implications.

Themes: Monsters

II-721.   The Shrinking Man. Gold Medal, 1956.

Radioactive fallout causes the hero to shrink. His psychological dilemma is that friends and family start treating him according to his size rather than his personality. A narrow escape from a cuddly kitten leads to a climactic battle with a spider. The physics of size change is ignored as the hero shrinks to oblivion. Effectively filmed as *The Incredible Shrinking Man.*

Themes: Fantastic Voyages

Matson, Norman (Haghejm), U.S., 1893–1965

II-722.   Doctor Fogg. Macmillan, 1929.

An amiable satire in which the eponymous hero achieves undesired fame after building a radio receiver capable of picking up messages from other worlds. The knowledge thus acquired promises a technological revolution, but Fogg and an extraterrestrial refugee wonder whether humankind is quite ready to take its place in the galactic community. An intriguing early development of the theme of SETI fantasies such as Gunn's *The Listeners,* which might have helped to inspire William Sloane's more earnest account of a mysteriously imported female, *To Walk the Night.* (BS)

Matthews, Susan, U.S., 1954–

II-723.   An Exchange of Hostages. AvoNova, 1997. Series: Andrej Koscuisko.

In this disturbing but well-done work of military science fiction, a young doctor named Andrej Koscuisko finds himself assigned to be a Ship's Surgeon, but, as with Bradbury's Fireman in *Fahrenheit 451,* the title is misleading. In actual fact, Koscuisko is trained as a torturer and inquisitor and his job to gain important information from prisoners, no matter what the cost. Interestingly enough, the author is a former security officer assigned to a combat support hospital special-izing in biological and nuclear warfare. The sequels, all equally disturbing and absorbing, are *Prisoner of Conscience* (1998), *Hour of Judgment* (1999), *Angel of Destruction* (2001), and *The Devil and Deep Space* (2002). Compare Lynn's *The Sardonyx Net* for a tale with a similarly powerful sadomasochistic subtext. (ML)

Themes: Medicine, Space Opera, War

Maurois, André (pseudonym of Émile Salomon Wilhelm Herzog), France, 1885–1967

II-724.   The Thought-Reading Machine. 1937. Trans. of *La machine à lire les pensées* by J. Whithall. Jonathan Cape, 1938.

The invention of a machine that records subvocalized thoughts and replays them audibly fails to bring about any dramatic transformation of society. The argument is that our internal monologues do not reflect our profound feelings or intentions, and would therefore prove less revealing than we might fear or suspect—with the result that people would soon recognize them as idle chitchat. The intention is satirical rather than existential. Compare Jaeger's *The Man with Six Senses.* (BS)

Themes: Discoveries and Inventions

II-725.   The Weigher of Souls. 1931. Trans. of *Le peseur d'âmes* by Hamish Miles. Cassell, 1931.

A *conte philosophique* in which science confronts theological supposition, with discomfiting results, as a result of the success of one of the key quests of experimental psychic research—the capture and imprisonment of the soul after death. The premise was further extrapolated, in mercilessly satirical fashion, by Romain Gary in *The Gasp* (1973). (BS)

Themes: Discoveries and Inventions

May, Julian, U.S., 1931–

II-726.   The Many-Colored Land. Houghton, 1981. Series: Saga of the Pliocene Exile.

Misfits flee by time warp from the 22nd century, ending up in the Pliocene, where they and other time travelers are caught up in a conflict between two alien species, members of an interstellar civilization called the Galactic Milieu. Although May's language is occasionally overly elaborate, the rich background is well worked out and her characters are engaging. The four Pliocene novels were followed by *Intervention* (1987), first of a trilogy exploring events on Earth in the 20th and 21st centuries and leading to the Galactic Milieu Trilogy, the first volume of which, *Jack the Bodiless* (1992), deals with contacts between Earth and the Milieu in the near future. (ML/BS)

Themes: Aliens, Paranormal Powers, Time Travel

Mayne, William, U.K., 1928–

*****II-727.   Earthfasts**. Hamish Hamilton, 1966.

YA. David and Keith meet an 18th-century drummer boy emerging from a newly formed grassy mound and carrying a steady, cold, white-flamed candle. Before Keith can return the candle to the past, inexplicable phenomena—"boggarts," heaving ground, moving stones, wild boars, giants, shadowing horsemen, awakening Arthurian knights, and even David's "death"—plague the area. A remarkable combination of fantasy and science fiction; strong characterization; fine depiction of the boys' determination to treat the constantly burning candle scientifically before succumbing to its power; exceptional use of atmosphere; brilliant style. Contrast Huddy's *Time Piper*. (FM)

Themes: Children in SF, Coming of Age, Science Fantasy, Time Travel

McAllister, Bruce, U.S., 1946–

II-728.   Dream Baby. Tor, 1989.

Based on an award-nominated short story, *Dream Baby* is the disturbing tale of Mary Damico, a trauma nurse in Vietnam who, discovered to have psychic powers that appear under extreme stress, finds herself co-opted into a top-secret,

CIA-led experiment in parapsychology. Eventually she becomes one of a team of psychics sent on a grueling and desperate terrorist mission into North Vietnam. At least some of McAllister's material is apparently based on the real experiences of men and women who served in Vietnam. Compare Elizabeth Ann Scarborough's *The Healer's War* (1988) and Lucius Shepard's *Life During Wartime*. (ML)

Themes: Medicine, Paranormal Powers, War

McAuley, Paul J., U.K., 1955–

II-729.   Child of the River. Gollancz, 1997; Avon Eos, 1998. Series: Confluence.

Much like Gene Wolfe's Book of the New Sun sequence, McAuley's Confluence series has the feel of fantasy, but is actually science fiction set in a distant and decadent future. Yama is an orphan of mysterious lineage in a world where everyone else knows their bloodlines. His search for his own roots takes him from one wondrous setting to another, from the enormous necropolis of Aeolis to the teaming city of Ys. Only gradually does he discover the marvelous truth behind his birth and the awe-inspiring secret at the heart of Confluence. The other books in the series are *Ancients of Days* (1998, U.S. 1999) and *Shrine of Stars* (1999, U.S. 2000). Compare Wolfe's *The Shadow of the Torturer*. (ML)

Themes: Far Future, Life on Other Worlds, Mythology, Science Fantasy

*II-730.   Fairyland. Gollancz, 1995, Avon, 1996.

McAuley posits a 21st century in which half of Europe has become rich through nanotechnology and the creation of genetically engineered dolls that provide slave labor, while the rest of the population have been made homeless by war and economic upheaval. When Milena learns how to give the dolls intelligence, a new race comes into being. Through the medium of the dolls, or "fairies," McAuley addresses issues of autonomy, physical and intellectual, for genetically engineered humans, blending these with humanity's age-old belief in fairyfolk and dreams of creating new forms of life. (MKS)

Awards: John W. Campbell, Arthur C. Clarke

Themes: Androids, Genetic Engineering, Nanotechnology

II-731.   Four Hundred Billion Stars. Ballantine, 1988. Series: Four Hundred Billion Stars.

Explorers from Earth discover a planet that doesn't seem old enough geologically to have developed its complex native ecology. Adding to the mystery, abandoned, hive-like cities are discovered, even though the dominant life form, the nomadic herders, seem to be only semi-sentient. Humanity is currently engaged in an interplanetary war elsewhere in the galaxy, and the naval officers in charge of the expedition fear there may be some connection between the primitive herders and humanity's enemy. This seems unlikely until someone notices that the abandoned hive-cities are coming to life and the herders are beginning to change their age-old behavior patterns. McAuley's exploration of the complex herder species is fascinating and his protagonist, the astronomer Dorthy Yoshida, an unwilling psychic, is well developed. *Eternal Light* (1991) is a direct sequel to *Four Hundred Billion Stars* and is every bit as good. *Of the Fall* (1989), titled *Secret Harmonies* (1991) in its British edition, is a solid, but relatively minor tale set in the same universe as the other two novels. All three books, along with McAuley's first short story collection, *The King of the Hill* (1991), demonstrate the author's genius for creating fascinating aliens. Compare Gregory Benford's *Great Sky River* and its sequel. (ML)

Awards: Philip K. Dick

Themes: Aliens, Evolution, Hard SF, Life on Other Worlds

II-732.   Pasquale's Angel. Gollancz, 1994.

An alternate history in which Leonardo da Vinci devoted his life to engineering rather than to art, creating a very different Florence. The skills of the artists and the craftsman are being supplanted by those of the artificer, while the city suffers pollution from the factories that fill the shops with goods. McAuley uses the detective novel genre in order to guide the reader through the alternative universe he has created. It is extremely well-realized, with a wealth of detail that is offered in an unself-conscious manner. While the plot is conventional enough—a series of murders must be solved—McAuley's novel is lifted out of the ordinary by the charm of his main characters, the eponymous Pasquale and Niccolo Macchiaveglia, and the fast (though not breakneck) speed of the narrative. Compare Dann's *Memory Cathedral*. (MKS)

Themes: Alternate Worlds, History in SF

II-733.   The Secret of Life. HarperCollins, 2001.

In the year 2026, the world is still recovering from the Firstborn Crisis, a virus that nearly wiped out humanity. Now, however, a new plague has appeared in the waters of the Pacific, a strange growth called Chi that contains genetic material that originated on Mars. Dr. Mariella Anders is sent to the red planet to unravel the mystery, but soon discovers that one of her fellow scientists, an employee of the genetic engineering firm that helped fund the mission, knows more than he's letting on. Indeed, it eventually becomes clear that the deadly organism may be less of a threat to humanity than the corporate greed that motivates several of the novel's principle characters. Anders is a nicely drawn protagonist. In recent years, McAuley has moved more and more into techno-thriller territory, beginning with this novel and continuing with *Whole Wide World* (2003) and *White Devils* (2004).

Themes: Biology, Hard SF, The Planets

McCaffrey, Anne, U.S., 1926–

*II-734.   Dragonflight. Ballantine, 1968. Series: Pern, Harper Hall.

First of the Pern series, combining the novellas "Weyr Search," which won a Hugo, and "Dragonrider," which won a Nebula. Immediate sequels are *Dragonquest* (1971) and the bestselling *The White Dragon* (1978); these novels appeared in an omnibus as *The Dragonriders of Pern* (1978). An associated and very highly regarded trilogy aimed at YA readers is *Dragonsong* (1976), *Dragonsinger* (1977), and *Dragondrums* (1979), the third volume of which won both the Children's Book Showcase and Balrog Awards. Later novels set on Pern include *Moreta, Dragonlady of Pern* (1983), *Nerika's Story* (1986), *Dragonsdawn* (1988), *The Renegades of Pern* (1989), *All the Weyrs of Pern* (1991), and many others, the most recent, *Dragon's Kin* (2003) being co-authored with her son Todd McCaffrey. Pern is a lost colony where dragons telepathically bonded to male riders breathe fire to burn up the spores of deadly vegetable invaders that appear at long intervals. The dragons can also travel through time whenever the plots require a deus ex machina. Despite the commercial success of later volumes, the quality and originality of the books decline significantly after *All the Weyrs of Pern*. In these novels the author achieved a mode and intensity of feeling that broke new ground in fitting SF to the imaginative needs of teenage girls, thus helping to break the masculine mold of most previous SF. Jody Lynne Nye, who has collaborated with McCaffrey on other books, has also written two volumes in the Crossroads Adventure series set in the world of Pern, *Dragonharper* (1987) and *Dragonfire* (1988). Compare Jacqueline Lichtenberg's Sime/Gen series, beginning with *House of Zeor* (1974), and C. J. Cherryh's Morgaine series, beginning with *Gates of Ivrel* (1976), both of which show McCaffrey's influence. Also compare Bradley's Darkover series. (BS/ML)

Themes: Future History, Life on Other Worlds, Paranormal Powers, Women in SF

II-735.   The Ship Who Sang. Walker, 1969. Series: Ship Who Sang.

A fix-up novel in which the severely disabled heroine is the cyborg guidance system of a spaceship, in which role she can construct more fulfilling relationships with male pilots than she ever could have hoped to have found in her fleshly incarnation. The initial story is genuinely poignant, but the later sections are more strained. McCaffrey has since published a number of sequels, recently dubbed the Brainship series, books largely written by a junior collaborator based on her outlines. These include *PartnerShip* (1992) with Margaret Ball, *The Ship Who Searched* (1992) with Mercedes Lackey, *The City Who Fought* (1993) with S. M. Stirling, *The Ship Who Won* (1994) with Jody Lynn Nye, *The Ship Errant* (1996) with Nye, *The Ship Avenged* (1997) with Stirling, and *The Ship Who Saved the World* (2003) with Nye. The initial collaborations with Ball and Lackey were also reprinted in one volume as *Brain Ships* (2003). Compare McIntyre's *Superluminal*. Contrast M. John Harrison's *Light*, which features a character developed as a response to McCaffrey's original novel. (BS/ML)

Themes: Cyborgs, Women in SF

McCarthy, Wil, U.S., 1966–

II-736.   The Collapsium. Ballantine Del Rey, 2000.

Set in a post-human future of sophisticated technology, this well-done, humorous hard SF tale relates the conflict between two highly talented scientists who are rivals in their love for Her Majesty Tamra Lutui, the Queen of Sol. Bruno de Towaji invented collapsium, a material constructed from black holes, which has made teleportation possible. Marlon Sykes hopes to use Towaji's invention for his own stupendous projects. Then, when a saboteur sends Sykes's gigantic collapsium ring hurtling toward the sun, the two enemies must join forces to prevent the destruction of the solar system. The equally enjoyable sequel is *The Wellstone* (2003). Compare Daniel's *Metaplanetary*. (ML)

Themes: Hard SF, Humorous SF

McDevitt, Jack, U.S., 1935–

II-737.   Ancient Shores. HarperPrism, 1996.

Tom Lasker, a North Dakota farmer, finds a high-tech boat of unimaginably ancient lineage buried on his land. Then an interdimensional transportation device is discovered on nearby land owned by the Sioux, who decide that they want to use the device to reestablish their traditional lifestyle in an alternate universe. Unfortunately, the U.S. government wants to destroy the machine. This is well written, carefully detailed science fiction, but it closes with one of the oddest deus ex machina endings in all of literature as a host of famous people, including Stephen Hawking, Ursula K. Le Guin, and Stephen Jay Gould show up to protect the artifact. Compare Reed's *Down the Bright Way* and Bear's *Eon*. (ML)

Themes: Parallel Worlds

II-738.   The Engines of God. Ace, 1994. Series: Priscilla Hutchins.

In this exciting SF adventure novel, archaeologist Richard Wald and starship pilot Priscilla Hutchins undertake a dangerous archaeological expedition to the planet Quaraqua. A badly damaged Earth desperately needs space and the planet has been scheduled for immediate terraforming despite the incalculably valuable alien ruins that dot its surface. What Wald and Hutchins eventually discover, however, turns out to be far more important to Earth's survival than anyone could have imagined. The further, equally exciting adventures of Priscilla Hutchins are recounted in *Deepsix* (2001), *Chindi* (2002), and *Omega* (2003). These novels highlight McDevitt's talent for portraying large-scale scenes that trigger the reader's sense of wonder. Compare Clarke's *Rendezvous with Rama* and Niven's *Ringworld.* (ML)

Themes: Aliens, Anthropology, Disaster, Life on Other Worlds

II-739.   Infinity Beach. HarperPrism, 2000.

A thousand years in the future, human-settled planets are strung across the galaxy, but we've yet to discover an intelligent alien species; at least that's the official story. Kim Brandywine knows that her older, clone sister disappeared on a space voyage many years earlier, but now she's found evidence that aliens, or perhaps some sort of supernatural phenomenon, may have been involved. And then there's the question of the strange alien presence that has begun to make itself known in the backwoods of her home world. This is a well-done science fiction mystery with nice character development and some genuinely eerie moments. (ML)

Themes: Aliens, Clones/Cloning, Colonization of Other Worlds

McDonald, Ian, Northern Ireland, 1960–

II-740.   The Broken Land. Bantam, 1992. U.K. title: *Hearts, Hand, and Voices.*

The Broken Land is an oppressed colonial nation, ripped apart by strife between its two major religious groups, the Proclaimers and the Confessors. It's a land of amazing biotechnology, where new homes can be grown and where the heads of the newly dead can be planted in pots and continue to offer their wisdom to their families. It's a land of terrible suffering, revolution, mass deportations, and the murder of innocents. *The Broken Land* is also an allegory of sorts for McDonald's homeland, Northern Ireland. This is a beautifully written but at times very painful novel. Compare Geoff Ryman's *The Unconquered Country* (1987) and Paul Park's *Starbridge Chronicles.* (ML)

Themes: Alternate Worlds, Politics, Religion

*II-741.   Chaga. Gollancz, 1995. U.S. title: *Evolution's Shore.* Bantam Spectra, 1995.

McDonald twists the familiar SF trope of invasion by life-changing bugs, representing them as another race's terraforming devices, and also as possibly beneficial. Called Chaga after the first tribe to be swallowed up by it, an alien flora consumes man-made materials, and radically alters the humans it comes into contact with. McDonald juxtaposes the viewpoints of First World nations, reluctant to embrace change when it destabilizes the equilibrium of their capitalist society, with those of African nations for whom a new life, even substantially altered, is better than what they currently have. The novel and its sequel, *Kirinyaga* (1998), are both informed by a strong sense of social justice and compassion towards those willing to take the step into the unknown in search of a better life, however it comes. Compare Wilson's *Darwinia.* (MKS)

Themes: Aliens, Invasion, Mutants, Politics

II-742.   Desolation Road. Bantam, 1988.

Lost in the desert of a terraformed Mars after having met an alien, Dr. Aliman-tando decides to found a settlement. To Desolation Road are attracted many of the red planet's eccentrics, refugees, and dreamers. As the town grows, conflicts arise between those with differing visions of its future. This beautifully written, somewhat mystical, and at times very witty tale has occasionally been criticized as a pastiche of Bradbury, García Márquez, and early Roger Zelazny. A sequel, *Ares Express*, appeared in 2001. Compare Bradbury's *The Martian Chronicles*; contrast Robinson's more realistic *Red Mars*. (ML)

   Awards: *Locus*
   Themes: Colonization of Other Worlds, Life on Other Worlds, The Planets

II-743.   Empire Dreams. Bantam, 1988.

A first collection by one of the most brilliant new stylists to enter the field in years. Included here are "King of Morning, Queen of Day," the basis for McDonald's Philip K. Dick Award-winning fantasy novel of the same name, as well as "Unfinished Portrait of the King of Pain by Van Gogh," "The Catherine Wheel," "The Island of the Dead," and six others. McDonald's second collection, *Speaking in Tongues* (1992), is equally impressive and a collection of his fine later fiction is long overdue. For sheer poetic exuberance, compare the short fiction of Harlan Ellison. (ML)

II-744.   Necroville. Gollancz, 1994. U.S. title: *Terminal Café*. Bantam Spectra, 1994.

McDonald presents a society where nanotechnology has changed everything, including death. A third of the world's population consists of the resurrected dead, forming the majority of the workforce and living in a parallel culture alongside the living, in necrovilles, until the Freedead return from space, having been shipped there as indentured workers, to lead a rebellion. McDonald skilfully evokes many historical precedents while also focusing on the human dimension, as his protagonists venture into Necroville on the Day of the Dead, to find answers to everything which dissatisfies them in their own extremely comfortable and privileged lives. (MKS)

   Themes: Immortality, Nanotechnology

*II-744A. River of Gods. Simon & Schuster U.K., 2004.

In this sprawling, complex masterpiece of a novel, McDonald portrays India in 2047, exactly 100 years after independence. The nation has split into a number of smaller states, but remains a place of both great poverty and enormous advances in information technology, including, just possibly fully sentient artificial intelligence. Nearly a dozen viewpoint characters give us their input on the state of the nation, while, unbeknownst to any of them, a billion-year-old artifact has been discovered in space and the Singularity approaches on Earth. Compare Scott's *Dream Ships* and Broderick's *Transcension*. (ML)

Themes: Computers, Intelligence

McHugh, Maureen F., U.S., 1959–

*II-745. China Mountain Zhang. Tor, 1992.

The title character of McHugh's first novel is a Chinese American living in a United States that has fallen to Third World status just as China has risen, through apparently peaceful means, to dominate the world. In this hierarchical culture, Zhang's ancestry automatically places him above most Caucasians in status (though below native-born Chinese). Zhang, however, has a couple of dirty secrets. First, he's only half-Chinese, though his parents had him genetically adjusted to hide his Hispanic ancestry. Second, he's gay, and both China and Chinese-dominated America are puritanical societies. As the story progresses, we follow Zhang's rise from construction worker to successful architect. The novel's two greatest strengths lie in its depiction of a believable and sympathetic gay character and in its equally believable portrayal of a Chinese-dominated, 21st century. *China Mountain Zhang* won both the Tiptree Award for gender-bending SF and the *Locus* Award for best first novel. Compare Wingrove's Chung Kuo series for a comparable portrayal of a future China. For an equally strong portrayal of a lesbian protagonist, see Griffith's *Slow River*. (ML)

Awards: James Tiptree

Themes: Coming of Age, Sex in SF, Sociology

II-746. Mission Child. Avon Eos, 1998.

A teenager growing up in a peaceful primitivist settlement on a colonial world has her life disrupted when her village is attacked by raiders and nearly everyone is killed. Left to her own resources, she undergoes unbelievable hardships before finding a place for herself in the world. This beautifully written novel features McHugh's trademark superb character development, strong sense of place, and serious exploration of gender issues. Compare Le Guin's *Left Hand of Darkness* or Arnason's *A Woman of the Iron People*. (ML).

Themes: Coming of Age, Feminist SF, Life on Other Worlds

II-747. Nekropolis. Eos, 2001.

In this dark, moving tale of sexual obsession and repression set in a future North Africa, Hariba, a young woman, has been "jessed," permanently bonded to her employer by a black-market chemical process. Somehow, though, she transfers her obsession from him to another servant in the household, a "harni" or genetically engineered man, who may not be entirely human. When they run off together, tragedy and heartbreak seem the likely result. This is a beautifully written meditation on love, self-reliance, and the conflict between the two. Compare MacLeod's *The Great Wheel*. (ML)

Themes: Feminist SF, Genetic Engineering

McIlraith, Frank, U.K., ?

II-748.   Invasion from the Air: A Prophetic Novel (with Roy Connolly). Grayson and Grayson, 1934.

A typical British future-war novel of the 1930s, more convincing than most, with airfleets raining down poison gas, incendiary bombs, and high explosives. Here, the result is a universal loss of support for the national governments that started the war, resulting in coups and revolutions. Compare O'Neill's *Day of Wrath* and Wright's *Prelude in Prague* trilogy. (BS)
   Themes: War

McIntyre, Vonda N(eel), U.S., 1948–

*II-749.   Dreamsnake. Houghton Mifflin, 1978.

A novel based on the Nebula Award-winning short story "Of Mist and Grass and Sand." A healer whose instruments are genetically engineered snakes must journey to a city that has contacts with the star worlds in the hope of replacing the dreamsnake that eases the pain of her clients. A convincing mixture of stoicism and sentimentality, rather highly strung. Compare Tiptree's *Up the Walls of the World.* (BS)
   Awards: Nebula, Hugo, *Locus*
   Themes: Medicine

*II-750.   The Moon and the Sun. Pocket, 1997.

Is this beautifully written tale science fiction or fantasy? It all depends on whether you see the "sea monsters" brought back to the court of Louis XIV as an alternate, aquatic species of humanity or as mythical mer creatures. Marie-Josèphe is a talented young woman doing her best to maintain her virtue, prove her intellectual acumen, and negotiate the treacherous corridors of 17th-century Versailles. The aging king sees the creatures as marvelous but ultimately subhuman things who may hold the secret of immortality, but Marie Josèphe recognizes that the monster who remains alive is intelligent and she chooses to defy both the king and the pope to defend the creature. Beyond its strong characters and its well-conceived fantastic elements, McIntyre's novel is a wonderful historical portrait of the Sun King's world at something just past its prime. Compare Baker's *In the Garden of Iden* and Turtledove's *Ruled Britannia.* (ML)
   Awards: Nebula
   Themes: History in SF, Immortality, Science Fantasy

II-751.   Superluminal. Houghton Mifflin, 1984.

A novel based on the novella "Aztecs." The heroine surrenders her real heart for an artificial one in order to become a starship pilot. Her subsequent struggles against the effects of this voluntary alienation ally her with other social outsiders, but in the end she wins a spectacular victory over the natural and technological handicaps afflicting humankind. Intense to the point of feverishness. Not to be confused with the Tony Daniel novel of the same name. Compare Cordwainer Smith's "Scanners Live in Vain." (BS/ML)

Themes: Space Opera

McKenna, Richard M(ilton), U.S., 1913–1964

II-752.   Casey Agonistes, and Other Science Fiction and Fantasy Stories. Harper, 1975.

Damon Knight's introduction argues that McKenna, eschewing "the trivial puzzles and adventures" of so much SF, "tackled the basic problems of philosophy." These five fine stories bear out that judgment, such as "Fiddler's Green" and the partly autobiographical "The Secret Place." The title story is not SF but a superbly told ghost story. "Hunter, Come Home" and "Mine Own Ways" deal with interplanetary cultural anthropology, as did Le Guin in "The Word for the World Is Forest" from a female viewpoint. McKenna is a superior literary craftsman, author also of non-SF works such as *The Sand Pebbles*. (PC)

McKillip, Patricia A(nne), U.S., 1948–

II-753.   Fool's Run. Warner, 1987.

Cyberpunk SF by a writer better known for her high fantasy. Several years ago Terra Viridian murdered some 1,500 innocent people in response to an overwhelming but unexplained vision. Now, apparently psychotic, she bides her time in the Underground, a grim orbital penal colony. When a high-tech band is brought up to the Underground to give a performance, the stage is set for some very strange goings-on. Although the plot of *Fool's End* is occasionally a bit confusing, this is a beautifully written novel with lots of lush visual imagery. Compare Pat Cadigan's *Synners* and Norman Spinrad's *Little Heroes*. (ML)

Themes: Crime and Punishment, Cyberpunk

II-754.   Moon-Flash. Atheneum, 1984.

YA. Impelled by questions concerning Riverworld and her own dreams, Kyreol, accompanied by Terje, a young man, travels beyond the end of the world and learns the truth: River is a small "primitive" region carefully observed and guarded by the Dome, a technologically developed civilization. A superior story: fascinating application of anthropology; rich, detailed nature description; sustained mystery. A sequel is *The Moon and the Face* (1985), in which Kyreol and Terje bring about the commingling of River and the Dome. Compare Stone's *The Mudhead*; contrast Hunter's *Find the Feathered Serpent*. (FM)

Awards: Parents' Choice
Themes: Anthropology, Ecology, Pastoral

McMullen, Sean, Australia, 1948–

II-755.   Souls in the Great Machine. St. Martin's, 1999. Series: Greatwinter.

Two thousand years in the future, Australia, not yet entirely recovered from a nuclear winter, exists in a quasi-feudal state, essentially ruled by librarians. As Highliber, Zavora controls the Calculor, a gigantic calculating machine made from partially human components. Zavora's society is threatened by both the possibility of a new "Greatwinter" and the Call, a mysterious phenomenon that causes all who hear it to walk into the sea. The Highliber must act to save her world. This fecund, action-packed novel delivers up a rich stew of wild ideas and bizarre technologies somewhat in the manner of the steampunks. An earlier version of this novel appeared as two books, *Voices in the Light* (1994) and *Mirrorsun Rising* (1995), in Australia. Sequels to the current version are *The Miocene Arrow* (2000) and *Eyes of the Calculor* (2001). Compare Gibson and Sterling's *The Difference Engine*. (ML)

Themes: Holocaust and After, Machines, Paranormal Powers, Steampunk, War

McQuay, Mike, U.S., 1949–1995

II-756.   Memories. Bantam, 1987.

David Wolf, a psychiatrist with a troubled personal history, is approached by Silv, a woman from the far future, who asks his help. An experiment in pharmacotherapy has gone wrong in her own age and an aggressive, unstable soldier, Hersh, has escaped into the distant past where, as Napoleon, he is using his knowledge of military tactics to change history. Silv wants Wolf to follow Hersh into the past and convince the soldier to enter therapy with him. Although a bit unwieldy in its construction, this Philip K. Dick Award runner-up is both wise and emotionally satisfying. Compare Willis's *Doomsday Book*, Moorcock's *Behold the Man*, or Michael Crichton's *Timeline* (1998). (ML)

Themes: History in SF, Psychology, Time Travel

Mercier, Louis-Sébastien, France, 1740–1814

*II-757.   Memoirs of the Year Two Thousand Five Hundred. 1771. Trans. of *L'an deux mille quatre cent quarante* by William Hooper. Robinson, 1772.

The first account of an ideal society to be set in a real place (Paris) in the future, thus establishing the image as a goal to be attained rather than a mere standard for comparison. The reforms imagined by Mercier—the extrapolation of Enlightenment ideals, including a keen appreciation of scientific and technical progress, guided by Rousseauesque Romanticism—are instituted by a wise and benevolent king, but the book lent encouragement nevertheless to would-be revolutionaries. It was unlicensed by the government censors, and thus circulated illegally, but became a massive bestseller. Later editions were considerably augmented, mostly by the addition of new footnotes, which eventually expanded to greater length than the main text, making its construction very awkward; even so, it remains a landmark text. Compare and contrast Bellamy's end-of-century bestseller *Looking Backward*. Mercier's earlier *contes philosophiques*, collected in *Songes et visions philosophiques* (1768), include "Nouvelles de la lune," which describes a universe in which the disincarnate souls of the dead are free to roam while making progress (or not) toward further phases of evolution—an obvious precursor of Flammarion's *Lumen*. (BS)

    Themes: Utopias

Merle, Robert, France, 1908–2004

II-758. **Malevil**. Simon & Schuster, 1974. Trans. of *Malevil*, 1972, by Derek Coltman.

Survivors of a nuclear holocaust are drawn to the medieval castle of Malevil where a charismatic leader supervises the progress of their community. Dense and thoughtful. Compare Stewart's *Earth Abides*. (BS)

    Awards: John W. Campbell
    Themes: Holocaust and After

Merril, Judith, U.S., 1923–1997

*II-759. **The Best of Judith Merril**. Warner, 1976.

Nine stories, including "That Only a Mother," the author's first; two poems; and an informative memoir by Virginia Kidd, who once roomed with Merril. (See also *Better to Have Loved* [10-101].) Readers attuned to modern (or postmodern) feminist sensibilities may find these tales somewhat old-fashioned; readers with awareness of SF's prior history will enjoy their dramatic break with earlier male-sexist genre clichés. Indeed, stories like "Whoever You Are" and "Dead Center" carry dramatic tragic power even today. One fine novella, detailing the conflict between venturesome daughters and protective mothers over going into space and exploring, is also the title story of another fine Merril collection, *Daughters of Earth* (Gollancz, 1968, Doubleday, 1969). NESFA Press announced for 2005 *Homecalling and Other Stories: The Complete Short SF of Judith Merril*. (PC)

II-760. **Shadow on the Hearth**. Doubleday, 1950. Recommended ed.: Roberts & Vintner, 1966.

Rejecting the post-nuclear war scenario of bands of survivors stumbling through radioactive rubble, Merril narrows the focus to that of a housewife in suburbia. The imprisoning circle so typical of that 1950s lifestyle is intensified by the outbreak of war. With the "shadow" (radiation sickness) hanging over one of her children, the mother copes as best she can. The banal familiarity of the suburban setting made this book accessible for people who normally would not have been attracted to SF. Compare Shute's *On the Beach*; contrast Frank's *Alas, Babylon*. (PC)

    Themes: Holocaust and After

Merritt, A(braham), U.S., 1884–1943

II-761.   The Face in the Abyss. Liveright, 1931.

A novel compounded out of abridged versions of two pulp serials, "The Face in the Abyss" (*Argosy-All-Story*, 1923) and "The Snake-Mother" (*Argosy*, 1930); the fusion ruins the former text, which is far better in the original, and the abridgement does no favors to the latter. The hidden land of Yu-Atlanchi, where the human Old Race remain in thrall to the last survivors of the serpentine race that enslaved their ancestors, is the most elaborate and compelling of Merritt's lost worlds, with anticipations of H. P. Lovecraft as well as echoes of Edgar Rice Burroughs. (BS)

Themes: Lost Races/Worlds

II-762.   The Moon Pool. Putnam, 1919. Recommended ed.: edited by Michael Levy, Wesleyan Univ. Press, 2004.

A novel compounded out of the short story "The Moon Pool" (*All-Story*, 1918) and its long sequel "Conquest of the Moon Pool" (*All-Story*, 1919). The former item, a perfervid celebration of the ambivalent allure of the exotic, was enormously influential in re-establishing portal fantasy in 20th-century fantastic fiction. The second, which describes the world beyond the portal—a subterranean remnant of the ancient Oceanian continent of Lemuria—is a mere sketch by comparison with the rich evocation of Yu-Atlanchi in *The Face in the Abyss*. A sequel, originally published in *Argosy-All-Story* as *The Metal Monster* in 1920, is set an area of the Hindu Kush transfigured by an alien invasion of inorganic life; Hugo Gernsback persuaded Merritt to beef up its science-fictional component for reprinting in *Science and Invention* as "The Metal Emperor" (1927–1928); the author, still dissatisfied with it, went on to produce a third version in the 1940s, which was slightly abridged for book publication. (BS)

Themes: Lost Races/Worlds

Miéville, China, U.K., 1972–

*II-763.   Perdido Street Station. Macmillan, 2000; Ballantine Del Rey, 2001. Series: New Corobuzon.

The setting for this sprawling novel, the city of New Corobuzon, also provides perhaps the most important character in the book. A strange horror is unleashed upon the city, and the quest for a solution takes us into a Dickensian underworld, including a host of distinctive districts. We meet a wide range of curious and vividly described alien inhabitants, restrictive politicians and bureaucrats, and left-wing insurgents. A sequel, *The Scar* (2002), retains the richness of invention, the love of the curious, the attention to political aspiration, and the overt affection for the variety that a city contains, though this novel moves out of New Corobuzon to Armada, a city made up of a disparate collection of boats lashed together. A third superb entry in the series, *The Iron Council*, appeared in 2004. Compare Harrison's *Viriconium*. (PK)

Awards: Arthur C. Clarke
Themes: Aliens, Crime and Punishment, Politics, Science Fantasy

Miklowitz, Gloria, U.S., 1927–

II-764.   After the Bomb. Scholastic, 1985.

YA. When a Russian nuclear bomb accidentally explodes over Los Angeles, young Philip Singer is forced into the unlikely role of leader for his family. A well-researched and harrowing depiction of immediate aftermath of a nuclear disaster is joined to attractive characterization. Followed by a sequel, *After the Bomb: Week One* (1987). Contrast Swindells's *Brother in the Land*. (FM)

Themes: Coming of Age, Holocaust and After, Sociology

Miller, P(eter) Schuyler, U.S., 1912–1974

II-765.   The Titan. Fantasy Press, 1952.

A collection of eight stories. The title novella, featuring vampiric Martians and a human visitor imprisoned in their zoo, was considered too graphic for the SF pulps of the early 1930s; it began serialization in the small press *Marvel Tales* in 1935, but this first complete publication was unfortunately belated. Also included are two accounts of exotic alien life that were remarkable in their day, "The Arrhenius Horror" (1931) and "Spawn" (1939), and another account of a human castaway on Mars, "Forgotten" (1933, as "The Forgotten Man of Space"), which offers a more direct challenge to the human chauvinism that had been rapidly standardized in the SF pulps. (BS)

Miller, Walter M(ichael), Jr., U.S., 1922–1996

*II-766.   A Canticle for Leibowitz. Lippincott, 1960.

Seamlessly novelized from three 1950s stories. The Earth plunges into a new dark age after nuclear war. Scientists, scapegoats blamed for the war, flee to monasteries, which shelter them. As in the previous downfall, the one coherent surviving social institution is the Catholic Church. A new Renaissance sees the rediscovery of electricity and, as an inescapable consequence, weapons development. The new civilization once again falls into nuclear war, although missionaries on a starship that got away will plant a new, autonomous church on a far planet. Bare-bones criticism cannot do justice to this outstanding work, which must be read, or rather experienced. A long-rumored sequel, *Saint Leibowitz and the Wild Horse Woman*, was left uncompleted by Miller, finished by Terry Bisson, and published by Bantam in 1997. This sprawling novel, full of church politics and military engagements, received generally mixed reviews. Compare Card's *Folk of the Fringe* for a different church as the chrysalis of a new civilization. (PC/ML)

Awards: Hugo
Themes: Holocaust and After, Religion

*II-767.   The Science Fiction Stories of Walter M. Miller, Jr. Gregg, 1978.

The Gregg edition assembles all stories in *Conditionally Human* (Ballantine, 1962) and *View from the Stars* (Ballantine, 1964). Even before *Canticle*, it was apparent from Miller's shorter fiction that in his depth of feeling and character-ization this writer had moved decisively away from the space opera tradition, while retaining the ability to write strongly plotted action stories. Typically, "The Darfsteller" (1954; Hugo) sensitively explores the psychology of occupa-tional obsolescence, in this case an aging actor displaced from the stage by com-puter-programmed androids. When Miller did venture into space, as in "Crucifixus Etiam," his Mars depicts people struggling on the outermost edge. Introduction by David Samuelson. Highly recommended. (PC)

Mitchison, Naomi, Scotland, 1897–1999

*II-768.   Memoirs of a Spacewoman. Gollancz, 1962; Berkley, 1973.

The viewpoint character's scientific specialty is communication with aliens. Women, in this intergalactic future, are by and large better at that than men; they are likelier to perceive the reality of sentience in bizarre life forms, and more adroit at devising ways of making contact. ETs in this novel include a starfish-like, radially symmetrical species whose mathematics and philosophy differ profoundly from Earth's simple yes–no bilateralism, and a caterpillars-and-butterflies race whose adult form abuses the sentient larval stage from which it metamorphoses. This story also explores, more boldly even than Philip Farmer (*The Lovers*), the possibilities of interspecies sex (and parenting). Con-sidered a pioneering proto-feminist work; certainly the female protagonist's outlook differs markedly from that of the extroverted aggressive male heroes of most space opera. (PC)

Themes: Aliens, Feminist SF

Milne, Robert Duncan (Gordon), U.K./U.S., 1844–1899

II-769.   Into the Sun and Other Stories: Science Fiction in Old San Fran-cisco, Volume Two. Grant, 1980.

A collection of 11 stories rescued from East Coast periodicals by Sam Moskowitz; the first volume of the project is a history of 19th-century East Coast fantasists who published in the same media. "Into the Sun" (1888) and its sequel "Plucked from the Burning" (1882) feature a disastrous comet strike and its aftermath. Several of the other stories treat "electricity" as the force underly-ing occult phenomena, applying it in various exotic ways. "Ten Thousand Years in Ice" (1889) is an account of cryonic preservation; the story told by the pre-served individual is told in "The World's Last Cataclysm" (1889). Milne—who published at least a dozen other stories of SF interest—was one of the most interesting writers of his day, and it is unfortunate that his work did not have the opportunity to exert more influence. (BS)

Mitchell, Edward Page, U.S., 1852–1927

II-770.   The Crystal Man: Landmark Science Fiction. Doubleday, 1973.

A collection of 30 stories mingling SF and supernatural fiction, mostly consisting of items rescued from West Coast periodicals—particularly the New York *Sun*, which employed Mitchell for most of his journalistic career—by Sam Moskowitz. The SF stories are mostly light-hearted accounts of absurd inventions, following a pattern set by "The Tachypomp" (1874); the most interesting are "The Ablest Man in the World" (1879), in which an idiot's brain is replaced by a far more powerful mechanical calculator, and "The Crystal Man" (1881), featuring a technology of invisibility. (BS)

Mitchell, J(ames) Leslie, U.K., 1901–1935

II-771.   Gay Hunter. Heinemann, 1934.

A novel whose disaffected heroine is catapulted into the future with two male companions, the more articulate of whom is an ardent fascist. When she discovers that civilization has been obliterated by nuclear wars fought by fascist states, she becomes determined to protect the innocently primitive society of the new world from the ambitions of her rivals. A companion piece to *Three Go Back*, similarly based on the author's conviction that civilization was a terrible mistake (as the descendant of Highland crofters, Mitchell considered himself something of an educated barbarian). A descendant of Jefferies's *After London*, similar in its assumptions to the works of S. Fowler Wright.

Themes: Holocaust and After

*II-772.   Three Go Back. Jarrolds, 1932.

Two men and a women timeslip into the remote past, where they observe the lifestyle of their Cro-Magnon ancestors and the threat posed thereto by brutish Neanderthals. They realize that humankind is not innately aggressive by virtue of our evolutionary heritage, but has been corrupted by the unnatural pressures of civilization. The allegory makes an interesting contrast with William Golding's *The Inheritors* (1955), which imagines the Neanderthals as innocents whose quasi-Edenic existence is fatally disrupted by brutal invaders. (BS)

Themes: Evolution

Mitchell, J(ohn) A(mes), U.S., 1845–1918

II-773.   The Last American: A Fragment from the Journal of Khan-Li, Prince of Dimph-Yoo-Chur and Admiral in the Persian Navy. Stokes, 1889.

A curious satire in which a 30th-century Persian expedition explores the ruins of New York, puzzling over the artifacts they find, before pressing on to Washington, where the last survivors of a once proud people perish in a senseless brawl. The U.S. has been devastated by the persistent feuding of its various imported cultural groups. The "Edition de Luxe" of 1902 is more lavishly illustrated than the first. Compare Verne's "The Eternal Adam," Noyes's *The Pallid Giant*, and Graham's *The Collapse of Homo Sapiens.* (BS)

Themes: Future History, Satirical SF

Moffett, Judith, U.S., 1942–

II-774.   Pennterra. Congdon & Weed, 1987.

The planet Pennterra was originally settled by Quakers who were entirely willing to accept the native *hrossa's* strict rules for the maintenance of their environment. Trouble breaks out, however, when a shipload of non-Quaker colonists arrives and begins tearing up the landscape. Moffett's desire to give a powerful environmental message occasionally overwhelms her artistic sense in this first novel, but her strong character development and poetic style never falter. Compare Slonczewski's *Still Forms On Foxfield* (1980) and *The Wall Around Eden.* (ML)

Themes: Colonization of Other Worlds, Ecology, Life on Other Worlds, Religion

II-775.   The Ragged World: A Novel of the Hefn on Earth. St. Martin's, 1991.

A starship commanded by the alien Gaff, but crewed by a different race, the Hefn, returns to Earth to retrieve Hefn mutineers left behind centuries ago and to stop humanity's destruction of the ecosystem. The aliens decree that no more human babies will be born until we cease polluting. Originally a series of short stories, including two award nominees, this fix-up novel is a powerful indictment of humanity's ability to foul its own nest. In the more unified sequel, *Time, Like an Ever-Rolling Stream* (1992), two young people grow up in the more primitive world that has resulted from the Hefn's stay on Earth. Moffett continues her ecological theme, but also deals movingly with the topic of sexual abuse. Compare Slonczewski's *The Wall Around Eden.* (ML)

Themes: Aliens, Coming of Age, Ecology

Moon, Elizabeth, U.S., 1945–

II-776.   Remnant Population. Baen, 1996.

Ofelia Falfurrias, aging and not worth much to her corporate masters, refuses to leave the colony world where she's lived much of her life when the Company moves its business interests and all of the remaining colonists to another planet. Left alone, she soon discovers that the planet has an indigenous sentient population that had previously gone unnoticed by the human colonists and with which she must now learn to coexist. This is an unusually thoughtful planetary adventure novel, with well-developed aliens and a refreshingly different protagonist. Compare Thomson's *The Color of Distance.* (ML)

Themes: Aliens, Life on Other Worlds

II-777.   Speed of Dark. Orbit, 2002; Ballantine, 2003.

Lou Arrendale, a bioinformatics specialist, is one of a number of well-adjusted autistic people successfully employed by a near-future pharmaceutical company. His well-ordered world comes to an end, however, when the corporation insists that he and his fellow employees undergo an experimental procedure to "cure" their autism. Lou, who doesn't feel the need to be cured of what to him feels normal, must struggle to reestablish his sense of self-worth and his ability to relate to the outside world. A quiet and unusually thoughtful work. Compare Keyes's *Flowers for Algernon* and Matt Ruff's *Set This House in Order* (2003). (ML)

   Awards: Nebula
   Themes: Medicine, Psychology

Moorcock, Michael, U.K./U.S., 1939–

*II-778.   Behold the Man. Allison & Busby, 1969.

Expanded from a Nebula Award-wining novella. The alienated hero travels back to the time of Christ in the hope of enlightenment, but he finds Jesus grotesquely ill-fitted to the role of messiah and must take his place. Darkly ironic; a fascinating exercise in the psychology of martyrdom. Compare Malzberg's *The Cross of Fire* and James Morrow's *Only Begotten Daughter* (1990). (BS/ML)

   Themes: New Wave, Psychology, Religion, Time Travel

II-779.   The Black Corridor. Mayflower, 1969.

A novel actually written in collaboration with Hillary Bailey, whose contribution is acknowledged in some later (revised) editions. A crewman aboard a starship carrying frozen survivors away from a ruined Earth is beset by guilt-stricken dreams and delusions. An innovative work of avant-garde SF. Compare Cherryh's *Voyager in Night* (1984) and Stableford's *Man in a Cage* (1976). (BS)

   Themes: New Wave, Psychology, Space Flight

II-780.   The Cornelius Chronicles. Avon, 1977. Series: Jerry Cornelius Chronicles.

An omnibus containing *The Final Programme* (1969), *A Cure for Cancer* (1971), *The English Assassin* (1972), and *The Condition of Muzak* (1977), the first three in slightly revised form. Jerry Cornelius, the contemporary and near-future avatar of the multifaceted Moorcockian hero, features in the tetralogy in various roles: secret agent, messiah, corpse, dreary teenager, and even a negative image of himself. The first novel begins as a parody of heroic fiction, its events running parallel to two of Moorcock's early Elric stories, but moves on to parody other themes in popular fiction. The middle volumes present a kaleidoscopic display of 20th-century motifs, and the fourth moves on again to subvert the fantasy elements in the first three and add its own theme of tragedy, symbolized with the aid of images drawn from harlequinade. The series is a sprawling masterpiece: a dream story loaded with all the threads of contemporary consciousness and modern mythology, bearing an appropriate burden of nightmare and irony. *The Lives and Times of Jerry Cornelius* (1976) collects short stories in the series. Two later novels are *The Entropy Tango* (1981) and *The Opium General* (1984), and Cornelius makes occasional appearances in a variety of other Moorcock books. (BS/ML)

Themes: New Wave, Satirical SF

II-781.   The Dancers at the End of Time. Granada, 1981. Series: Dancers at the End of Time.

An omnibus containing *An Alien Heat* (1972), *The Hollow Lands* (1974), and *The End of All Songs* (1976). At the end of time, all-powerful immortals have no problems except how to amuse themselves, which they do in exotically contrived fashion, mining the past for its quaint inspirations. Colorful, witty, and boisterously decadent, with a certain distinctive weltschmerz. Later books in the series include *Legends from the End of Time* (1976), *The Transformation of Miss Mavis Ming* (1977), *A Messiah at the End of Time* (1978), and *Elric at the End of Time* (1984), the last book part of Moorcock's ongoing attempt to interconnect all or most of his major work. (BS/ML)

Themes: Far Future, Immortality

Moore, C(atherine) L(ucille), U.S., 1911–1987

*II-782.   The Best of C.L. Moore. Nelson Doubleday, 1975.

Ten stories from 1933 to 1946, selected by long-time admirer Lester del Rey, who wrote a biographical introduction, supplemented by Moore's personal afterword. Outstanding are three stories from *Astounding*: "The Bright Illusion" (1934), a human–alien love story that anticipates issues raised by Le Guin's *Left Hand of Darkness*; "No Woman Born" (1944), about the triumphant return to the stage of a singer-dancer all but destroyed by a fire, whose brain has been transplanted into a robot body; and "Vintage Season" (1946), about time-traveling tourists and the present-day man who rents his house to them with tragic results. From *Weird Tales* comes Moore's first story, "Shambleau" (1933), which introduced her popular interplanetary roamer, Northwest Smith, and two tales of her medieval female knight Jirel of Joiry. A highly satisfying collection. (PC)

II-783.   Doomsday Morning. Doubleday, 1957.

Realistic action-adventure on a near-present Earth, whose underground citizens rebel against an authoritarian state. Moore invigorates this tired theme with a traveling theater company, a milieu she understood well, and her description of it will speak to anyone who's ever been even minimally stage-struck. For the theme of an apparently necessary regime that became corrupt, compare Knight's *Hell's Pavement;* for the lively theater subculture, compare the chapter titled "Pageant Wagon" in Card's *Folk of the Fringe*. (PC)

Themes: Dystopias

II-784.   Judgment Night. Gnome, 1952.

What Moore did in the title story, in effect, was to translate her medieval war-rior-woman Jirel (renamed Juille here) from the *Weird Tales* realm of fantasy to the *Astounding* world of space opera, where this tale ran as a serial in 1943. It works spectacularly; the destruction of a pleasure satellite (a more aesthetic ver-sion of Las Vegas/Disneyland) is made a metaphor for the downfall of an entire galactic civilization. Of the other four stories here, only "The Code" is memo-rable. (PC)

Themes: Galactic Empires

Moore, Ward, U.S., 1903–1978

*II-785.   Bring the Jubilee. Farrar, 1953.

With the possible exception of Churchill's brilliant essay in *If, or History Rewrit-ten*, this is far and away the best story on the theme of the South having won the Civil War. Moore's fine historical sense lead him to describe some perhaps unexpected consequences; in a less affluent North, the presidency is won three times by William Jennings Bryan, and in a backlash against the prewar antislav-ery movement the Grand Army of the Republic, the Union veterans' organiza-tion, becomes a terrorist outfit like the Klan. Imaginative rethinking of real history, highly recommended. (PC)

More, Thomas, U.K., 1478–1535

II-786.   Utopia. 1516 in Latin. Trans. by Ralphe Robynson (expanded). Abraham Vele, 1551. Modern editions include those by H. V. S. Ogden (Apple-ton) and Edward Surtz and J. H. Hexler, *Collected Works*, vol. 4, and *Selected Works*, vol. 2 (both Yale Univ. Press).

The original Latin text is a description by one Ralph Hythloday (whose name is translatable as "nonsense-talker") of the society of the island of Utopia ("nowhere"), whose laws are simple and where labor is strictly regulated within a moneyless communist economy; the political order is, however, hierarchically organized. Utopian religion (unlike More's) is tolerant, although its sexual morality is restrictive. The account is light-hearted and does not represent More's opinions as to how English society ought to be organized. The English version—which adds a long prologue in the form of a Platonic dialogue, in which Hythloday is mildly critical of English politics—is even less clear as to its own moral standpoint. The work is best interpreted as an exploratory text rather than an explanatory one, but its model of social organization has been taken seriously in some modern reformist works, notably *The New Moon* (1918) by Oliver Onions and *The Rebel Passion* (1929) by Katharine Burdekin. (BS)

Themes: Politics, Utopias

Morgan, Richard, U.K., 1965–

II-787.   Altered Carbon. Gollancz, 2002.

Winner of the Philip K. Dick Award for best original paperback SF book of 2003 in its U.S. edition, this violent, fast-paced first novel is a prime example of latter-day cyberpunk. In a world in which everyone's mind is stored in a digitized "cortical stack," making it possible to "resleeve" people into new bodies, natural or accidental death is virtually unknown. Super-agent Takeshi Kovacs is "resleeved" into a cop's body and sent to investigate the murder of a prominent citizen, but if he is to succeed, he must first survive a number of violent attacks by unknown assailants, not to mention an encounter with a police officer who used to love the original owner of his new body. For a comparable noir police novel, see Richard Paul Russo's *Destroying Angel* (1992). For a contrasting look at "resleeving," see John Barnes's *Merchant of Souls*. The sequel is *Broken Angels* (2004). (ML)

   Awards: Philip K. Dick
   Themes: Crime and Punishment, Cyberpunk

Morris, William, U.K., 1834–1896

II-788.   News from Nowhere; or, An Epoch of Rest. Roberts Bros, 1890.

A visionary fantasy promulgating the ideas and ideals of Morris's Crafts Movement, serialized in his own periodical *The Commonweal* before being rushed into print (probably in a more abbreviated form than was originally intended) as a book in the U.S. to cash in on the fashionability of such works in the wake of Bellamy's *Looking Backward*. Although it is, to some extent, an ideological reply to Bellamy, offering a very different vision of a communist society, it is also the culmination of a tradition of English Romantic pastoralism extending from William Cobbett through Richard Jefferies and W. H. Hudson. (BS)

   Themes: Utopias

Morrow, James, U.S., 1947–

II-789.   This Is the Way the World Ends. Holt, 1986.

Satirical apocalyptic fantasy written within a science fiction framework in which the few survivors of the holocaust are put on trial by those who would have lived if only their ancestors had ordered their affairs more reasonably. Clever and elegant. Morrow's later, equally well-done theological fantasies, such as *Only Begotten Daughter* (1990) and the trilogy begun with *Towing Jehovah* (1994), continue to include a small number of science fiction elements. Compare Vonnegut's *Cat's Cradle*. (ML/BS)

   Themes: Holocaust and After, Mythology, Religion, Satirical SF

Moszkowski, Aleksandr, Germany, 1851–1934

*II-790.   The Isles of Wisdom. 1922. Trans. of *Die Inseln der Weisheit* by H. J. Stenning. Routledge, 1924.

A bitingly satirical account of an expedition through an archipelago of islands in which all the classic utopias, from Plato's *Republic* to the visions of Moszkowski's contemporaries, are reproduced. The ideas that were soon to form the basis of the German *zukunftsroman*—whose most successful contributor, Hans Dominik, published his first novel, *Die Macht der Drei*, in 1922—are realized on Sarragalla, the Mechanized Island, a high-tech paradise similar in many respects to the vision of the future promoted by Hugo Gernsback's *Ralph 124C41+*. Sarragalla's technology is, however, entirely dependent on atomic energy fueled by ores that have to be imported from the individualist island of Vorreia, whose Rousseauesque philosophy disapproves of technological development. The novel's eventual climax describes, with blackly comic glee, how two rival pacifist islands are inexorably forced to go to war in defense of their ideals. The author's cynicism probably seemed excessive at the time. Compare Sarragalla to von Hanstein's *Electropolis* and the whole enterprise to Sweven's account of an archipelago of utopias. (BS)

   Themes: Utopias

Munro, John, U.K., 1849–1930

II-791.   A Trip to Venus. Jarrolds, 1897.

An eccentric elaboration of a didactic short story, "A Message from Mars" (1894), by an enthusiastic popularizer of science. The interplanetary romance offers a conventional account of a paradisal Venus (which owes more to Jean-Jacques Rousseau than the quasi-religious imagery adopted by J. J. Astor's *Journey in Other Worlds* and George Griffith's *Honeymoon in Space*). But a fascinating preliminary chapter offers a discussion of various possible ways of achieving space flight, which rejects Vernian space guns in favor of various means of staged propulsion, including linear motors and rockets. (BS)

   Themes: Space Flight

Murakami, Haruki, Japan, 1949–

II-792.   Hard-Boiled Wonderland and the End of the World. Kodansha, 1991. Trans. of *Sekai No Owari to Hado-Boirudo Wandarando* by Alfred Birnbaum.

An unnamed but decidedly hard-boiled detective takes on a strange case involving a brilliant but naive elderly scientist, his beautiful, apparently mute granddaughter, some very strange technology, and what appear to be kappas, traditional Japanese monsters. In alternating chapters a different unnamed narrator visits a town at the end of the world, where things aren't what they seem and unicorns are common. This strange and surrealistic novel by a mainstream writer who occasionally strays into genre territory is heavily influenced by the cyberpunks. Compare Neal Stephenson's *Snow Crash* and Michael Swanwick's *Stations of the Tide*. (ML)

> Themes: Absurdist SF, Crime and Punishment, Cyberpunk, Linguistics

Murphy, Pat, U.S., 1955–

II-793.   The City, Not Long After. Doubleday, 1989.

San Francisco has been decimated by plague and virtually abandoned. Those who remain are mostly artists and counterculture types. Word arrives, however, that a power-mad military officer has determined to retake the city, and a mixed coalition of oddballs, mystics, and artists forms to defeat him. Murphy manages to carry the spirit of the late 1960s into the late 1980s with considerable success. Compare two similar works, Goldstein's *A Mask for the General* and Russo's *Subterranean Gallery*. (ML)

> Themes: Cities, Disaster, Science Fantasy

II-794.   Points of Departure. Bantam, 1990.

Nineteen short stories by a writer whose work ranges widely over the genres of science fiction, fantasy, and horror. Among the best are the Nebula- and *Locus* Award-winning novelette "Rachel in Love," the heartbreaking story of a young girl trapped in a chimpanzee's body; "Dead Men on TV"; "Bones"; and "His Vegetable Wife." Compare Swanwick's *Gravity's Angels* and Fowler's *Artificial Things*. (ML)

> Awards: Philip K. Dick
> Themes: Feminist SF

Murry, John Middleton *see* Cowper, Richard

Nagata, Linda, U.S., 1960–

II-795.   Limit of Vision. Tor, 2001.

In previous novels, Nagata wrote about nanotechnology; in *Limit of Vision*, she creates LoVs, so-called because they live at the limit of human vision. Bioengineered neurons, they are illegal on Earth, but working in space, scientists have discovered their amazing properties, and one group has entered into a symbiotic relationship with the LoVs. Furthermore, and as is now common in this type of science fiction, the artificial life forms have begun to function independently, and have returned to Earth, where they encounter a group of children who are organized by an AI. Nagata explores the implications of the relationship between the AI and the LoVs, and also human attitudes towards these new and rapidly evolving machine-human relationships, posing the stark question: containment or destruction? Compare Slonczewski's *Brain Plague*. (MKS)

> Themes: Computers, Genetic Engineering, Intelligence

II-796.   Memory. Tor, 2003.

Jubilee lives in a strange, artificial world in which human beings can be reborn over and over again. Their needs are met by robotic "kobolds" and each night a mysterious fog called "silver" rises across the world, magically transforming the landscape and the people it touches. Jubilee is heartbroken when her brother Jolly disappears, apparently taken by the silver. Eventually learning that he may still be alive, she sets out on a quest to find him and, incidentally, to discover the secrets of her world. A well-done hard SF novel set in what at first appears to be a fantasy world. Compare McAuley's *Child of the River*. (ML)

Themes: Hard SF, Immortality, Nanotechnology, Virtual Reality

Nasir, Jamil, Palestine/U.S., 1957–

II-797.   Tower of Dreams. Bantam Spectra, 1999.

Blaine Ramsey is a tool of American capitalism. His job is to travel to other countries and live there, absorbing the local culture. An image digger, he has the unique ability to use his dreams to uncover the deepest unconscious desires of a society so that they can be turned into advertising and profits for his employers. Unexpectedly, however, things begin to go very wrong for Ramsey when he visits North Africa and dreams of a young Arab girl in distress. Nasir, who has a propensity for metaphysical speculation, is one of the more interesting new writers in the field. His other worthwhile novels include *Quasar* (1995), *The Higher Space* (1996), and *Distance Haze* (2000). Compare Gibson's *Pattern Recognition*; contrast Sterling's *Zeitgeist*. (ML)

Themes: Paranormal Powers, Psychology, Sociology

Nearing, Homer, Jr., U.S., 1915–

II-798.   The Sinister Researches of C.P. Ransom. Doubleday, 1954.

Eleven stories humorously describing the self-absorbed rivalry of two all-too-typical academicians—Professor Ransom, a mathematician, and Professor Tate, a philosopher. They try to develop inventions that blend the arts and sciences and hilariously fail. Gentle in tone but reflective of a deadly serious quarrel between the sciences and the humanities that was described by C. P. Snow in his 1956 Reith lectures, published as *The Two Cultures*. Some of the humor may be a bit esoteric, but the book's influence could be subtly salutary on university types outside the SF orbit. (PC)

Themes: Humorous SF

Nesvadba, Josef, Czechoslovakia, 1926–

II-799.   The Lost Face: Best Science Fiction from Czechoslovakia. Tapling-er, 1971. Trans. by Iris Urwin.

These Czech magazine stories were translated and first published as *In the Steps of the Abominable Snowman* (Gollancz, 1970). SF with an East European accent, but drawing upon the Anglo-American SF tradition also. "Dr. Moreau's Other

Island" is a variant on one of Wells's grimmer tales, and another owes much to Tarzan-and-Jane. Two—"Expedition in the Opposite Direction," a time travel story, and "The Lost Face," about some startling consequences of plastic surgery—deal in fresh ways with the perennial questions of determinism versus freedom of the will. The stories are told with verve, humanity, and wit. (PC)

Neville, Kris (Ottman), U.S., 1925–1980

II-800.   The Science Fiction of Kris Neville. Ed. by Barry Malzberg and Martin Harry Greenberg. Southern Illinois Univ. Press, 1984.

Eleven stories, 1949–1967, showcasing the variety of styles and themes in Neville's work, from "Cold War" (1949), forecasting an unexpected difficulty in the "balance of terror" nuclear foreign policy, to chilling exposition, in "From the Government Printing Office" (from *Dangerous Visions*, 1967), of what three-and-a-half-year-olds *really* think of adults. The two novellas published as *Bettyann* (1951, 1954 as stories, 1970 as book) are here, in which the estrangement of the lone alien on Earth, common in 1950s SF, receives a warm and winning twist. If, as Malzberg states, Neville became totally frustrated at being unable to sell work that went beyond current SF conventions of his day, that does not speak well for the genre. Contains a useful, accurate bibliography of all of Neville's writings. (PC)

Themes: Children in SF

Newman, Kim, U.K., 1959–

II-801.   The Night Mayor. Simon & Schuster, 1989.

The brilliant but psychopathic criminal Truro Daine, incarcerated for life on 8,921 counts of first-degree murder, has used advanced dream technology to escape into virtual reality, and the government sends two agents in after him. They discover a run-down city like something out of Cornell Woolrich or American *film noir*, populated exclusively by characters from classic gangster films, where it is always 2:30 in the morning, where it's always raining, and where Daine is the all-powerful title character. Newman is an expert on horror movies and *film noir* and it shows in this brilliant tour de force of a first novel. Most of his later work, although equally good, moves more directly into straight horror fiction. Compare Zelazny's *The Dream Master*. (ML)

Themes: Computers, Crime and Punishment, Cyberpunk, Intelligence, Virtual Reality

Nicolson, Harold (George), U.K., 1886–1968

II-802.   Public Faces. Constable, 1932.

A political fantasy detailing the diplomatic chicanery surrounding the development and use (in 1939) of an atomic bomb. As in Gloag's *Winter's Youth* and Chadwick's *The Death Guard*, the hypocrisy and pusillanimity of self-serving statesmen bring about a war that common sense and the logic of deterrence should have prevented. (BS)

Themes: Politics

Niven, Larry, U.S., 1938–

II-803.   The Integral Trees. Ballantine, 1984. Series: Known Space.

The descendants of humans shipwrecked in an alien solar system eke out a difficult living in a bizarre worldless ecosystem. One group, forced into exile, undergoes a series of adventures culminating in their meeting with a strange spacefarer. The plot is mainly a vehicle to display the intricately worked out environment; the book is thus an imaginative exercise comparable to *Ringworld*. The 1987 sequel, *The Smoke Ring*, continues the story and further explores the unusual environment. Compare Baxter's *Raft*. (BS)

Awards: *Locus*
Themes: Ecology, Hard SF, Life on Other Worlds

II-804.   The Long ARM of Gil Hamilton. Ballantine, 1976. Series: Known Space.

A collection of novellas featuring a hero whose amputated and replaced arm is more versatile in spirit than it was in the flesh. Although the series is integrated into the Known Space future history, they are Earthbound mysteries set against the background of the development of organ-bank technology, and they are among the finest examples of the SF detective story. The series continues in *The Patchwork Girl* (1980), an excellent story of futuristic detective work set on the Moon. The criminal activities usually involve "organ legging," which also features in other short stories and in the Known Space novel *A Gift from Earth* (1969). *Flatlander* (1995) includes some later Gil Hamilton stories. (BS/ML)

Themes: Crime and Punishment

II-805.   Neutron Star. Ballantine, 1968. Series: Known Space.

The first collection of Niven's hard SF stories, early works developing the Known Space future history. The Hugo Award-winning title story is one of several in which Beowulf Shaeffer is blackmailed into taking on a dangerous mission in an exotic environment. The bibliography of Niven's collections is complex, stories being recombined into some later selections, but *The Shape of Space* (1969), *All the Myriad Ways* (1971), and *A Hole in Space* (1974) preserve most of the important early fiction. *Tales of Known Space* (1975) is useful for the notes about the future-historical background. The title story of *Inconstant Moon* (1973) (also in *All the Myriad Ways*) is a marvelous, Hugo Award-winning story in which people on the night side of the world realize that the sun has gone nova when the Moon becomes much brighter. *Limits* (1985), a relatively minor collection, includes a number of collaborative stories. *N-Space* (1990) and *Playgrounds of the Mind* (1991) are retrospective collections covering Niven's entire career to date. These volumes include essays, novel excerpts, appreciations by other writers, and bibliographies, but leave out some of Niven's better early stories. *Crashlander* (1994) collects all of the Beowulf Shaeffer stories in one volume. *Scatterbrain* (2003) is a miscellany of mostly minor later short fiction, nonfiction, and novel excerpts. (BS/ML)

Themes: Future History, Hard SF

II-806.   Protector. Ballantine, 1973. Series: Known Space.

Here the Pak Protectors, remote ancestors of humankind and builders of Ringworld, are introduced; the discovery of a Pak ship leads to the creation of a human/alien "hybrid" whose subsequent career threatens to alter the course of human destiny. (BS)

Themes: Future History, Hard SF

*II-807.   Ringworld. Ballantine, 1970. Series: Known Space.

An exploration team consisting of an exotic mix of humans and aliens investigates a huge artifact occupying a planetary orbit around a sun. A novel of imaginary tourism; its real hero is the artifact, whose nature is further explored and explained in *Ringworld Engineers* (1980; Hugo nominee), *The Ringworld Throne* (1996), and *Ringworld's Children* (2004). Compare Clare's *Rendezvous with Rama* and its sequels. (BS/ML)

Awards: Hugo, Nebula
Themes: Future History, Hard SF, Life on Other Worlds

Niven, Larry, U.S., 1938– and Barnes, Steven, U.S., 1952–

II-808.   The Descent of Anansi. Tor, 1982.

Near-future melodrama in which a space shuttle delivering a monomolecular cable from the Moon to the Earth becomes a pawn in a political power play. Taut and suspenseful (in more ways than one). Compare Bova's *Colony*. (BS)

Themes: Politics

Niven, Larry, U.S., 1938– and Pournelle, Jerry, U.S., 1933–

II-809.   Footfall. Ballantine, 1985.

The aliens displaced from the outline of *Lucifer's Hammer* come into their own here, in an invasion story that aspires to be the definitive modern version of the theme, just as *The Mote in God's Eye* attempted to provide a definitive first contact story. Spectacular in scale and detail. Compare Wells's *The War of the Worlds* and Heinlein's *The Puppet Masters* (1951) to put the story in historical perspective. (BS)

Themes: Aliens, Invasion

II-810.   Lucifer's Hammer. Playboy, 1977.

The world is badly damaged by a meteor strike, but the survivors manage to get things going again. An SF book that cashed in on the Hollywood boom in (more localized) disaster stories and became a bestseller, though the aliens who were in the original outline had to be left out. A tough-minded exercise in imaginary social Darwinism. Compare and contrast R. C. Sherriff's *The Hopkins Manuscript* (1939). (BS)

Themes: Disaster

II-811.   The Mote in God's Eye. Simon & Schuster, 1974.

Superior space opera in which Earth's interstellar navy contacts and does battle with an enormously hostile alien race. The scenes of space warfare are well handled, and the alien Moties are fascinating. The sequel, *The Gripping Hand* (1993), is more mundane. Compare C. J. Cherryh's *Downbelow Station* or Vernor Vinge's *A Fire Upon the Deep*. (ML)

Themes: Aliens, Space Opera, War

Nolan, William F(rancis), U.S., 1928– and Johnson, George Clayton, U.S., 1929–

II-812.   Logan's Run. Dial, 1967. Series: Logan's Run.

In a world where population control requires euthanasia at 21, a policeman puts to good use his expertise in hunting down those who won't submit when he becomes a "runner" himself. A slickly written and lively entertainment, horribly mangled in the film version. Inferior sequels by Nolan alone are *Logan's World* (1977) and *Logan's Search* (1980). (BS)

Themes: Crime and Punishment, Overpopulation

Noon, Jeff, U.K., 1957–

*II-813.   Vurt. Ringpull, 1993; Crown, 1994. Series: The Manchester Novels.

Noon's first novel combined a decaying urban landscape (a futuristic version of his native Manchester), a group of disaffected young people, and a society in retreat. Mixed with artificial intelligence, nanotechnology, and bioengineering, this seemed to point to an intention to create a uniquely British style of cyberpunk. However, Noon then applied further spin, presenting his virtual dreamworlds in a mode more immediately identifiable as fantastic, drawing heavily on classic mythology, and, in *Pollen* (1995), British folklore. *Nymphomation* (1997) turned to mathematics for its overarching metaphor. All three novels display an acute understanding of the substrata of English society, combined with a wild joy in the use of words, creating a unique fusion of SF and other literary tropes. (MKS)

Awards: Arthur C. Clarke

Themes: Genetic Engineering, Psychology, Satirical SF

Norton, Andre (pseud. of Alice Mary Norton), U.S., 1912–

II-814.   The Beast Master. Harcourt, 1959.

Hosteen Storm is one of the few survivors of an Earth incinerated by interstellar war. He is also of the *Dineh*—a Navajo—and thus doubly alone. Terrans have, however, spread to other solar systems, and it is to one of these worlds that Storm emigrates, with his team of highly mutated Earth-fighting and -scouting animals. The planetary scene is very like the half-mythical American West, but the story is saved from stereotyping by vivid descriptive and action writing and evident empathy for Navajo folkways, like that of Tony Hillerman in a different genre. Probably the first SF novel in which the viewpoint character was a Native American. Norton featured Storm in *Lord of Thunder* (Ace, 1962) and, less successfully, branched out to a different tribe in *The Sioux Spaceman* (Ace, 1960). (PC)

Themes: Space Opera

II-815.   Catseye. Harcourt, 1961. Series: Janus.

YA. Temporary work in a strange interplanetary pet shop involves Troy Horan, a displaced person, in adventure, intrigue, and mystery, hallmarks of typical Norton work. Surprised to learn that he can communicate with animals, Troy discovers that several pets are being used as secret weapons in a plot against the rulers of Korway. Troy is forced to flee into the wild and a dead, booby-trapped underground city. Only the closest cooperation between Troy and several exotic animals enables him to survive and become a member of the Rangers, who patrol the wild. Skillful narration of SF adventure and sympathetic depiction of animal–human relationships. Followed by two sequels. (FM/SM).

Themes: Space Opera

*II-816.   Operation Time Search. Harcourt, 1967.

YA. Ray Osborne is accidentally sent back into a time when the Atlantean Empire sought to overthrow the Murians, and he becomes the instrument whereby the latter, worshipers of the Flame, are able to annihilate Atlantis, where devotees of the false Poseidon traffic in demonic powers. Osborne wonders why Atlantis lingers in legend while the Murian Empire disappeared, but fails to observe that the religion and kings of Mura provide the basis for the Greek pantheon and mythology. Osborne remains in the past, determined to organize in the Barren Lands a colony, ruins of which are the mounds dotting the central United States. An Atlantis legend story, entertaining, especially stimulating in its speculation concerning origin of myth. A prime example of Norton's SF. Compare Hunter's *Find the Feathered Serpent* and A. Merritt's *The Moon Pool* (1919). (FM/ML)

Themes: Lost Races/Worlds, Time Travel

II-817.   Quest Crosstime. Viking, 1965. British title: *Crosstime Agent.*

YA. In a future when moving "crosstime" to parallel universes is possible, one group on Vroom favors crosstiming so that society can rebuild itself after nuclear devastation by using the resources of other universes. The Rogan sisters and Blake Walker, all with various parapsychological abilities, are swept into a revolt organized by those opposed to crosstiming. Before the revolt is put down, the adventure spills over to E625, a crosstime world embroiled in a tense stalemate modeled on the conflict between the American Plains Indians and the pioneers. An exciting and fast-moving story. Blake Walker first appeared in *The Crossroads of Time*, half of a 1956 Ace Double. Norton has continued to write highly competent science fiction (much of it no longer labeled YA but similar to her YA books in form and content, much of it produced with a co-author) into the 21st century, but most of her best late work has been in series begun in the 1950s and 1960s. (FM/ML)

Themes: Far Future, Parallel Worlds, Paranormal Powers

*II-818.   Star Man's Son: 2250 A.D. Harcourt, 1952. Variant title: *Daybreak 2250 A.D.*

YA. Rejected by his father's clan, young Fors, a mutant, runs away to prove himself a Star Man, or explorer. Along with Arskane, a black youth who befriends him, Fors is successful in uniting the several clans against their common enemy and in instilling in the former the dream of starting over without repeating the mistakes of the Old Ones. The author's first SF novel, one of her best, both a fine study of coming of age and a convincing portrait of a post-holocaust world. (FM/SM)

Themes: Holocaust and After, Mutants

II-819.   The Stars Are Ours! World, 1954.

YA. Even when Earth has embarked on interplanetary flight, old animosities continue and eventually lead to a devastating war. Scientists are proscribed by the Company of Pax, and a handful of Free Scientists escape to the stars. After exploring a new planet, the humans enter an alliance with a race of mermen to take up anew the history of humanity. Well-plotted, filled with incident, and skillfully written. Sequel: *Star Born* (1957). (PC)

Themes: Space Opera

Nourse, Alan E(dward), U.S., 1928–1992

II-820.   The Bladerunner. McKay, 1974.

YA. By the early 21st century, overpopulation has forced sterilization on anyone seeking medical care. A medical black market springs up for those opposed to this kind of medical practice. When a mysterious flu virus threatens a nationwide epidemic, Billy Gimp and other bladerunners—that is, persons who provide black-market physicians with supplies and assistance—are called on to warn the populace. The epidemic is curtailed and humane changes in health care ensue. Suspenseful incidents; fascinating look at future medical care and procedures; responsible handling of overpopulation control problem. Compare Lightner's *Doctor to the Galaxy*. Contrast Nancy Kress's short story "The Mountain to Mohammed" (1992). Nourse sold the title of this novel, but not the plot, to the makers of the film *Blade Runner*. (FM/ML)

Themes: Medicine, Overpopulation

II-821. The Mercy Men. McKay, 1968.

YA. In this novel of narrative twists and surprises, Jeff Mayer feels a compulsion to seek out and kill a man he believes has killed his father. Suspecting that the man has entered a research medical center, Jeff decides to enter also as a mercy man, that is, one who allows medical self-experimentation for money. Before Jeff can leave the center, he is shocked to learn that he, like his father, is triggered to go insane and that this insanity affects the laws of probability. Jeff is a carrier of a disorder that must be eradicated or treated. As in other novels by the author, speculation about future medical practice is stimulating; style and characterization are above average. Expanded from a 1955 Ace Double titled *A Man Obsessed.* Compare the Suttons' *The Programmed Man* (1968). (FM)

Themes: Crime and Punishment, Genetic Engineering, Medicine

*II-822. Star Surgeon. McKay, 1960.

Expert blend of futuristic medicine, its procedures and organization, and the story of Earth's attempt to enter the Galactic Confederation. Earth, hospital center for the entire galaxy, prides itself on its medical skill and begrudgingly allows Dal, a Garvian and first off-Earth medical student, to intern. After several adventures, Dal wins his silver star as a star surgeon, and Earth has passed its probation. Suspenseful in depicting possible future medical technology; especially provocative speculation about possible applications of symbiosis. Compare Lightner's *Doctor to the Galaxy* (1965).

Themes: Medicine, Space Flight

Nowlan, Philip Francis, U.S., 1888–1940

II-823. Armageddon 2419 AD. Avalon, 1962.

A novel compounded out of two novellas published in *Amazing Stories* in 1928 and 1929, whose timeslipped hero helps future Americans rebel against their Oriental conquerors. They are of historical interest as the origin of "Buck" Rogers, who went on to reach a much larger audience in comic strips, radio shows, and movies and helped characterize SF in the public mind as "that Buck Rogers stuff." (BS)

Themes: War

Noyes, Pierrepoint B(urt), U.S., 1870–1959

II-824. The Pallid Giant: A Tale of Yesterday and Tomorrow. Revell, 1927.

A political fantasy written by a diplomat involved in the post-World War I peace settlement, whose father had founded the utopian Oneida community. A book recovered from a cave in the Dordogne reveals that the Earth has given rise to advanced civilization before, but that the race in question waged wars with death rays until extinction was inevitable; humankind—produced by means of genetic engineering by the last survivors of the elder race—is now about to repeat the process. The book was reprinted in 1944, when its expectations seemed to be on the brink of justification, as *Gentlemen, You are Mad!* Compare Hamilton's *Theodore Savage* and Verne's "The Eternal Adam." (BS)

Themes: War

O'Brien, Fitz-James, Ireland/U.S., 1828–1862

II-825. **"The Diamond Lens"** in *The Poems and Stories of Fitz-James O'Brien*, Osgood, 1881.

A short story originally published in *The Atlantic Monthly* in 1858, in which a murderous microscopist discovers a miniature world within a water-drop and becomes entranced by a humanoid female he names Animula; she perishes when the drop evaporates. It is probably best understood as a hallucinatory fantasy, in which respect it is ancestral to the similarly ambiguous SF stories of Edgar Fawcett. It is not impossible that O'Brien had seen a French translation of Vladimir Odoevsky's alchemical fantasy "The Sylph" (1837), which develops a similar motif in a more profound *conte philosphique*. *The Supernatural Tales of Fitz-James O'Brien* (Doubleday, 1988), edited by Jessica Amanda Salmonson, assembled O'Brien's SF tales, including "The Diamond Lens," "What Was It?," "The Last Room," and "The Wordsmith." (BS)

Themes: Psychology

O'Brien, Robert C., U.S., 1922–1973

*II-826. **Mrs. Frisby and the Rats of NIMH**. Atheneum, 1971.

YA. Mrs. Frisby, head of a family of field mice, is told to consult neighboring rats concerning the illness of her son. Justin, a leader of the rats, agrees to help because Mr. Frisby had been of assistance to the rats. On hearing the whole story of the rats as the object of psychological and biological experimentation by the NIMH laboratories and the rats becoming, as a result, superintelligent, Mrs. Frisby also volunteers to aid them. The rats escape from an attempt by the NIMH laboratories to exterminate them and establish a utopian society away from humans. An outstanding combination of beast fable and science fiction; a winning portrait of rats and mice that has little cuteness. *The Secret of NIMH*, a feature film based on the story, was released in 1982, when Scholastic reprinted the book under the film title. (FM)

Awards: Horn Book, Newbery, Lewis Carroll Shelf, Mark Twain

Themes: Intelligence, Paranormal Powers, Science Fantasy, Utopias

*II-827. **Z for Zachariah**. Atheneum, 1975.

YA. A post-catastrophe story. Believing she may be the only survivor of a devastating war, Ann Burden is pleased to see a man enter the Burden valley and decides to befriend him. Shocked when, after all she has done for him, he tries to rape her, Ann is forced to leave the valley, hoping to come across other survivors. Sensitive transformation of trite subject into a tragic story of human behavior in the face of destruction and possible extinction. The use of a journal to record struggle for understanding, carefully paced narrative, and characterization of the protagonist are distinctive. Compare Engdahl's *The Far Side of Evil* and Armstrong and Butcher's *The Kindling.* (FM)

> Awards: Edgar Allen Poe
> Themes: Feminist SF, Holocaust and After, Sociology

Odle, E(dwin) V(incent), U.K., 1890–1942

*II-828.　The Clockwork Man. Heinemann, 1923.

A carefully understated but imaginatively ambitious scientific romance, partly inspired by J. D. Beresford's *The Hampdenshire Wonder.* An English village is briefly visited by a timeslipped cyborg from a future in which some of humankind's descendants have accepted mechanical regulation in return for access to many dimensions, while the "makers" who have perfected this technology remain tantalizingly out of view. One of the outstanding works of its genre; it is a great pity that the other scientific romance Odle is known to have completed was lost. (BS)

> Themes: Evolution

O'Duffy, Eimar, Ireland, 1893–1935

II-829.　The Spacious Adventures of the Man in the Street. Macmillan, 1928.

A flamboyant satire whose hapless hero takes the place of his *alter ego* on the planet Rathe, where they do everything differently but no better. As in Butler's *Erewhon,* there is a considerable component of pure comedy, but the parodic assaults on religion, sexual morality, and capitalism are scathing and the climactic vision presents a cogent plea for humanist values. (BS)

> Themes: Satirical SF

O'Leary, Patrick, U.S., 1952–

II-830.　The Impossible Bird. Tor, 2002.

Two estranged brothers, Michael and Daniel Glynn, who haven't seen each other in years, find their lives changed forever when mysterious gunmen claiming to be from an elite government agency burst in on them, insisting that one brother or the other has a secret code and promising to kill them if they don't produce it. The brothers soon set out on a quest to find each other but end up in a bizarre utopia controlled by aliens. Dense but rewarding literary science fiction. (ML)

> Themes: Aliens, Utopias

Oliver, Chad (pseud. of Chadwick Symmes Oliver), U.S., 1928–1993

II-831.   Another Kind. Ballantine, 1955.

Oliver's first collection, which Anthony Boucher judged the best SF book of the year. The seven stories, written early in Oliver's career as an anthropologist, reflect his training and expertise in that field, which in the 1950s was probably the freshest and most creative of the social sciences. In "Rite of Passage," an apparently primitive culture proves to be a highly advanced society that's deliberately edited itself down to the essentials; in "Artifact," Paleolithic-type flint scrapers turn up in the unlikely sands of Mars. A related collection is Oliver's *The Edge of Forever: Classic Anthropological Science Fiction* (Sherbourne, 1971), whose focus is more on the manipulation of a culture by external agencies unknown to it, as in "Transfusion," a startling revision of conventional wisdom about Earth's own prehistory. Superseding these early collections are two comprehensive collections, *A Star Above It* and *Far From This Earth* (both NESFA, 2003), containing a total of 40 stories. (PC)

Themes: Anthropology

II-832.   Mists of Dawn. Winston, 1952.

YA. A time-travel machine accidentally transports young Mark Nye 50,000 years into the past. Attacked by brutish Neanderthals and befriended by the relatively civilized Cro-Magnons—we now know better about both—Mark learns how to survive by cooperating with nature and with other human beings. The plot is less adventure and more a dramatized and still engrossing presentation of then-current anthropological speculation about primitive people. Compare Hunter's *Find the Feathered Serpent*. (FM/SM/PC)

Themes: Anthropology, Time Travel

*II-833.   Shadows in the Sun. Ballantine, 1954.

A field anthropologist learns that the South Texas community he has been studying is a colony of a galactic civilization; its inhabitants convincingly come on as small-town folk of appropriately diverse ages and conditions, but hold nightly meetings in which they commune with the interstellar home country. The story is in sharp contrast, however, to the popular paranoid "aliens are among us" theme, for the hero has an honest inner conflict between leaving to join the galactic culture and remaining on Earth as, in effect, an "Indian." Oliver used to good advantage his training and his residence in Texas—not the small-town Texas of *The Last Picture Show*, to be sure—in this impressive first novel. Compare Simak's *Way Station*; contrast Finney's *The Body Snatchers*. (PC)

Themes: Anthropology, Galactic Empires

II-834.   The Winds of Time. Doubleday, 1957.

A burned-out M.D. on a fishing trip encounters stranded space visitors, who left their own war-threatened world only to find the same situation on Earth. Our technology can't repair their ship but can synthesize the drug the visitors use for suspended animation and perhaps find salvation in Earth's far future. The doctor, whose wife has taken up with another man in his absence, decides to go with them. The existential resolution for this viewpoint character is thus the diametric opposite of that in Oliver's *Shadows in the Sun*. The story has a mixed mood of estrangement, nostalgic leave-taking, and desperate hope. Contrast Neville's *Bettyann*. (PC)

Themes: Aliens, War

O'Neill, Joseph, Ireland, 1886–1953

II-835.   Day of Wrath. Gollancz, 1936.

An account of a new world war, notable for its chilling description of the devastation of civilian populations by aerial bombardment with poison gases, high explosives, and other advanced weapons. It brings the arguments of McIlraith and Connolly's *Invasion from the Air* much closer to home, echoing the grim conviction of Hamilton's *Theodore Savage* and anticipating the gruesomeness of Chadwick's *The Death Guard*. (BS)

Themes: War

II-836.   Land Under England. Gollancz, 1935.

A surreal political fantasy whose protagonist descends into an underworld in search of his lost father, discovering a totalitarian state where thought control has been greatly advanced by means of telepathy. One of the most nightmarish anti-fascist novels of the period, anticipating such graphic visionary fantasies as Ruthven Todd's *The Lost Traveller* (1943) and J. D. Beresford and Esmé Wynne-Tyson's *The Riddle of the Tower* (1944). (BS)

Themes: Politics

Ore, Rebecca, U.S., 1948–

II-837.   Becoming Alien. Tor, 1987. Series: Tom "Red Clay."

Tom Red Clay, a smart young hillbilly kid with unsavory relatives, is kidnapped/rescued by aliens, emissaries from a galactic federation sent to Earth undercover to judge whether humanity is ready for contact. Tom starts out as a test case and eventually becomes a recruit in the federation's alien contact agency. Ore is a fine stylist and her characters, both human and alien, are well developed and quirky. Two more volumes in the series are *Being Alien* (1989), and the less well-known but equally good *Human to Human* (1990). Compare Brin's *The Uplift War* and James White's *Hospital Station* (1962) and sequels. (ML)

Themes: Aliens, Galactic Empires

Orwell, George (pseud. of Eric Arthur Blair), U.K., 1903–1950

*II-838. Nineteen Eighty-Four. Secker, 1949.

One of the greatest novels of the 20th century, which anti-SF critics still insist is not science fiction. Although British in flavor, this is a universal future projection of the totalitarian state: its nature, purposes and prospects. Plotted like a suspenseful pulp thriller, but with characters with whom the reader empathizes, it carries one along to its last ironic line. And it should be read that way, freshly, even though a substantial cottage industry of criticism had grown up around it. The fact that 1984 came and found not a Big Brother watching in London but an indulgent and inattentive Old Uncle in Washington does not diminish the importance of the warning: eternal vigilance, well before the event, is still the price of liberty. Made into an effective film in which Richard Burton played his last screen role as the inquisitor, O'Brien. Compare Huxley's *Brave New World* and Knight's *Hell's Pavement*. (BS)

Themes: Dystopias

Padgett, Lewis *see* Kuttner, Henry

Palmer, David R., U.S., 1941–

II-839. Emergence. Bantam, 1984.

A juvenile genius is enabled by her superhumanity to survive a nuclear holocaust and sets off across the blasted United States to search for others of her kind. Compare George O. Smith's *The Fourth "R"* (1959) and Armstrong and Butcher's *The Kindling*. (BS/ML)

Themes: Holocaust and After, Supermen/women

Paltock, Robert, U.K., 1697–1767

II-840. The Life and Adventures of Peter Wilkins. Robinson and Dodsley, 2 vols., 1751 (as by R. S.).

A fantastic Robinsonade, which diverges into mild Swiftian satire when the hero finds himself among the Glumms, an Antarctic race whose extra limbs equip them for flight. One of the better examples of English Gulliveriana, buoyed up by an uncommon narrative exuberance.

Themes: Satirical SF

Pangborn, Edgar, U.S., 1909–1976

*II-841. Davy. St. Martin's, 1964. Series: Davy.

Nuclear war is now 300 years in the past, but the world is still a primitive place. The title character begins life as a bondsman and grows to become a great leader. Though his intent is serious, Pangborn's tone is satirical and a bit bawdy throughout. Numerous critics have noticed similarities between *Davy* and Fielding's *Tom Jones*. Set in the same post-holocaust world are *The Judgment of Eve* (1966), *The Company of Glory* (1975), and stories found in the collection *Still I Persist in Wondering* (1978). Compare Miller's *A Canticle for Leibowitz* and Crowley's *Engine Summer*. (ML)

Themes: Coming of Age, Holocaust and After, Satirical SF

*II-842.   A Mirror for Observers. Doubleday, 1954.

Martians in underground cities for thousands of years have manipulated Earth's historical development. Martian Elmis foresees a great new ethical age for Earth under the leadership of a Gandhi/Martin Luther King saint-figure; Martian Namir looks toward a "final solution" for the Earth problem in mutually annihilative war. The conflict between Elmis and Namir has been compared with that of God and Satan in the Book of Job; and beyond that, wrote Peter S. Beagle in an afterword to a later edition of the novel (Bluejay, 1983, p. 228), it reflects "the endless internal battle that everyone fights who cannot quite abandon hope of one day waking from the nightmare of our species' history." Contrast Vonnegut's *The Sirens of Titan*. (PC)

Themes: Aliens, Mythology

II-843.   West of the Sun. Doubleday, 1953.

A spacecraft crash-lands on a planet inhabited by two different sentient humanoid species, intelligent but preliterate. One forceful crew member wishes to "bring them civilization," that is, exploit them; the others, although of necessity becoming involved in fierce intertribal war, envision a harmonious community of all three species. Given a chance to return to Earth rather than remain with their aboriginal friends, they refuse. Convincing description of planetary milieu; good characterization. The last chapter gets a tad didactic, but this first novel still reads well today. Compare Piers Anthony's trilogy, *Omnivore, Orn,* and *Ox* (1968, 1971, 1976). (PC)

Themes: Colonization of Other Worlds

Panshin, Alexei, U.S., 1940–

II-844.   Rite of Passage. Ace, 1968.

The heroine belongs to a starfaring culture, and her rite of passage into adulthood involves her descent into a colony world whose culture is very different. A homage to Heinlein's juveniles but more carefully and painstakingly constructed than most of his models; compare especially his *Tunnel in the Sky* (1955). (BS)

Awards: Nebula

Themes: Coming of Age

Park, Paul, U.S., 1954–

II-845.   Coelestis. HarperCollins, 1993; Tor, 1995.

On a distant world, human colonists have converted the natives to Christianity, molded them into a servant class, and used surgery and drug therapy to transform them into close approximations of human beings. Simon, an aide to the British consul, and Katherine, a talented and beautiful native who can pass for human, are captured by terrorists. Under the press of circumstances they fall in love. Then Katherine, deprived of her regular drug therapy, begins to change and, worse yet, to see things the Earthman can't. Comparisons between Park's aliens and the native peoples of Africa and Australia are obvious, but his superb style and his strong characters make this novel much more than a mere polemic. Compare Robert Silverberg's *Downward to Earth* and Resnick's *Paradise*. (ML)

Themes: Aliens, Colonization of Other Worlds

II-846.   Soldiers of Paradise. Arbor, 1987. Series: Starbridge Chronicles.

On a planet called Earth by its inhabitants, though it and its solar system differ dramatically from our own, the seasons last for lifetimes and, as in Aldiss's Helliconia series, they change with such violence that entire civilizations are in danger of dying or being transformed. Two misfit members of the Starbridge family, the planet's ruling class, wander through the confusion and growing revolution of the oncoming springtime, pondering the ills of their society. *Soldiers of Paradise* is nearly plotless, but its beautifully wrought prose, carefully etched characters, and strong moral sense make it an unforgettable experience. Two fine sequels are *Sugar Rain* (1989) and *The Cult of Loving Kindness* (1991). Compare Aldiss's Helliconia series, Swanwick's *Stations of the Tide*, and Wolfe's *Book of the New Sun*. (ML)

Themes: Ecology, Life on Other Worlds, Religion

Percy, Walker, U.S., 1916–1990

II-847.   Love in the Ruins: The Adventures of a Bad Catholic at a Time Near the End of the World. Farrar, 1971.

Dr. Thomas More invents a device that might cure the world of its chemically induced collective insanity, but things are too far gone. In the sequel, *The Thanatos Syndrome* (1987), More deals with a series of strange phenomena, including female patients who exhibit unusual sexual behavior and a conspiracy to improve humanity by placing drugs in the water supply. Allegorical social comment. Compare Jeremy Leven's *Satan* (1982). (BS/ML)

Themes: Psychology, Satirical SF

Pešek, Luděk, Czechoslovakia, 1919–1999

II-848.   The Earth Is Near. Bradbury, 1974. Trans. of *Die Erde Ist Nah*, 1970, by Anthea Bell.

YA. An engrossing adventure, convincing investigation of what happens to an international crew during a journey to Mars and its exploration. The dramatization of the shifting psychological states of mind on the long trip and during the terrifying dust storms; the explicit and hidden animosities and rivalries that emerge; the loneliness and futility experienced because the crew has depended too much on specialized machines, which fail or prove useless; the frustration resulting from the suspicion that the expedition might have done better if it had attempted to harmonize with Martian ecology; and human courage and endurance all give the novel its distinction. Compare Halacy's *Return From Luna* (1969). (FM)

Themes: Psychology, The Planets, Space Flight

Philbrick, Rodman, U.S., 1951–

II-849.   The Last Book in the Universe. Scholastic, 2000.

YA. Spaz, an epileptic and gang member living in the Urbs in a horrendous post-apocalyptic future, is ordered to murder an old man named Ryter. Instead they become friends, and when Spaz learns that his foster sister Bean is dying, they set out to find her. Eventually Spaz meets Lanaya, a "proov" or genetically engineered girl, who takes them to Eden, a utopian community reserved for a chosen few. Rejected by the citizens of Eden, Spaz and company return to the Urbs, where Ryter is murdered. This is a beautifully written but intensely painful novel. Compare Anderson's *Feed*. (ML)

Themes: Coming of Age, Dystopias, Utopias

Phillpotts, Eden, U.K., 1862–1960

II-850.   Saurus. John Murray, 1938.

A space shot from the asteroid belt carries an egg to Earth, which hatches an intelligent lizard. Raised as a kind of feral child by an English family, the alien becomes a critical observer of contemporary mores, considerably more sympathetic than the anthropologist from the future in Allen's *The British Barbarians* or the superhuman born ahead of his time in Beresford's *The Hampdenshire Wonder*, but not as insightful as Olaf Stapledon's *Sirius*. Phillpotts's later novel *Address Unknown* (1949) is suspicious of the entitlement of a far more conceited alien observer to criticize humankind's folkways. (BS)

Themes: Aliens

Piercy, Marge, U.S., 1936–

II-851.   He, She, and It. Knopf, 1991. U.K. title: *Body of Glass*, 1992.

Scarred by a painful divorce and custody fight, Shira Shipman leaves her 21st-century urban, male-dominated corporation and returns to the egalitarian Jewish enclave of Tikva, where she takes part in the programming of a revolutionary and illegal new cyborg named Yod. As part of Yod's education, Shira's grandmother narrates the story of the 17th-century Prague golem; the lives of the two artificial beings have obvious connections. Piercy uses many techniques borrowed from the cyberpunks and, although her usage is occasionally clumsy, it's fun to watch her put them into the service of ideas radically different from those generally touched on by Gibson and company. Compare Gibson's *Neuromancer* and Asimov's "The Bicentennial Man." (ML)

Awards: Arthur C. Clarke
Themes: Cyberpunk, Cyborgs, Feminist SF, Mythology

II-852.   Woman on the Edge of Time. Knopf, 1976.

A Hispanic-American mother undergoes experimental psychosurgery. She makes psychic contact with the 22nd-century world that has resulted from a feminist revolution whose success may depend on the subversion of the experiments in which she is involved. Outstanding for the elaborate description of the future utopia and the graphic representation of the inhumanity inherent in the way that contemporary people can and do treat one another. Compare Russ's *The Female Man* as well as Sylvia Plath's non-science-fictional *The Bell Jar* (1963). (BS/ML)

Themes: Feminist SF, Utopias

Pinkwater, Daniel M(anus), U.S., 1941–

II-853.   5 Novels. Farrar, Straus & Giroux, 1997.

YA. Omnibus reprinting of two of this author's gonzo SF novels, *Alan Mendelsohn, the Boy from Mars* (1977) and *Slaves of Spiegel* (1982). In *Alan Mendelsohn*, an unpopular fat kid named Leonard enrolls in a new school and is totally miserable until he meets Alan Mendelsohn, who convinces people that he's from Mars and can can visit other dimensions. *Slaves of Spiegel* concerns two boys who are kidnapped by and forced to cook for aliens who love junk food. The other three works, *The Snarkout Boys and the Avocado of Death* (1982), *The Last Guru* (1978), and *Young Adult Novel* (1982) are not science fiction, but are equally funny. (ML)

Themes: Children in SF, Humorous SF

Piper, H(enry) Beam (pseud. of John J. McGuire), U.S., 1904–1964

II-854.   Crisis in 2140. Ace, 1957.

Serialized in *Astounding* in 1953 as "Null-ABC." Idiotic, systematically applied learning theories have resulted in paradox: an advanced high-tech civilization in which the great majority of people are illiterate. Political conflict is between those who support the status quo, in which Literates (like the "scribes" of biblical antiquity) are a licensed, closed guild, and the radicals, who want Socialized Literacy, that is, that the necessary few who can read and write should become government employees. It does not occur to either side that children at large could simply be taught to read. Good satire on the U.S. teacher-training establishment and on other hidebound, self-serving guilds such as the American Medical Association. Published as an Ace Double, paired with an unrelated novel, *Gunner Cade* by Cyril Judd (Cyril Kornbluth and Judith Merril), itself a neglected gem that undercuts the militaristic ideology of such books as Heinlein's *Starship Troopers*. (PC)

Themes: Satirical SF

II-855.   Federation. Ace, 1981.

Five stories by an unduly neglected writer who broke into print in 1947 with the frequently anthologized "Time and Time Again" (not included here) and whose career tragically ended with his suicide in 1964. Human–alien communication is the theme of three of the tales: "Oomphel in the Sky," "Naudsonce," and, most notably, "Omnilingual," about the cracking of a long-dead Martian language by a woman scientist who must also battle an ambitious, sexist male colleague. John F. Carr in his introduction describes how he pieced together from Piper's fiction and from recalled conversations between Piper and Jerry Pournelle a centuries-spanning future history, cyclic in nature like Poul Anderson's with a Terran Federation that eventually thickens into empire. A follow-up collection edited by Carr, *Empire* (Ace, 1981), leads off in the near-present with "The Edge of the Knife," about a history professor who remembers future events and gets into trouble for absentmindedly referring to them in class! Other, longer works in the Federation saga include *Space Viking* (Ace, 1963) and *Junkyard Planet* (Putnam, 1963; variant title, *The Cosmic Computer*). (PC)

Themes: Future History

Platt, Charles, U.K./U.S., 1945–

II-856.   The Silicon Man. Bantam, 1991.

An FBI agent finds himself captured by unscrupulous scientists who download his mind into a computer and murder his body. The scientist who heads the illicit project has set up his own little virtual reality kingdom and the agent at first finds himself a helpless prisoner, but determines to fight back. Platt's depiction of a computer-generated environment comes across as much more believable than William Gibson's cyberspace. Compare Gibson's *Neuromancer* and Philip K. Dick's *Eye in the Sky*. (ML)

Themes: Computers, Crime and Punishment, Intelligence, Virtual Reality

Poe, Edgar Allan, U.S., 1809–1849

*II-857.   The Works of the Late Edgar Allan Poe. Redfield, 4 vols., 1850–1856.

The first comprehensive edition of Poe's works, edited by his executor Rufus W. Griswold (whose reputation was permanently blackened by his seemingly vicious biography damning Poe as a drunken lunatic, although it would not have been out of character for Poe to leave instructions for his own demonization). The addition of such previously unreprinted tales as "A Tale of the Ragged Mountains" (1844), "The Balloon-Hoax" (1844), and "Von Kempelen and His Discovery" (1849) to "MS Found in a Bottle" (1833), "The Unparalleled Adventured of Hans Pfaall" (1835; rev. 1840), *The Narrative of Arthur Gordon Pym* (1838), "The Conversation of Eiros and Charmion" (1839), "The Colloquy of Monos and Una" (1841), "Mesmeric Revelation" (1844), "The Facts in the Case of M. Valdemar" (1845), and *Eureka!* (1848) allowed the whole range of Poe's experiments in speculative fiction to be seen in juxtaposition (alongside his experiments in psychological horror fiction, detective fiction, fabulation, etc.), displaying a whole much greater than its parts despite its nebulosity. No other writer was ever so innovative or so forward-looking; we can only speculate as to what Poe might have achieved had he not died of cruel neglect at the age of 40. Other recommended editions include *The Science Fiction of Edgar Allan Poe*, edited by Harold Beaver (Penguin, 1976), and *The Annotated Tales of Edgar Allan Poe*, edited with notes and bibliography by Stephen Peithman (Doubleday, 1981). (BS)

Pohl, Frederik, U.S., 1919–

*II-858.   The Best of Frederik Pohl. Nelson Doubleday, 1975.

Sixteen stories from 1954 to 1967, selected by Lester del Rey. An afterword by Pohl describes the genesis of some of them. "The Midas Plague" inverts the values of our present consumer society: wealth is defined as the right to consume *less*; as you rise in social rank, you move into a smaller house. "The Census Takers" have the job, in an overcrowded world, of killing off every 300th person; the surplus folk are referred to, in chilling bureaucratese, as Overs. Pohl's mordant wit, masking an old-fashioned moral concern, is shown to advantage in this choice collection. (PC)

II-859.   Drunkard's Walk. Ballantine, 1960.

The hero, a math teacher, repeatedly attempts to kill himself, but with no known motivation of his own. He discovers that a closed corporation of immortal telepaths exists, which seeks to prevent the general spread of telepathy and has been sending suicidal messages to him in particular. A state of drunkenness protects him temporarily against mental control; but the "drunkard's walk" of the title is also a mathematical concept, referring to the irregular motion of small particles under random molecular collision (Brownian movement). Straight-line social progress, which the immortal elite will attempt to carry out if they win, is doomed to peter out, exhausted; for society to continue evolving, uncontrolled randomness—the "drunkard's walk"—is necessary. A thoughtful argument wrapped in an action adventure plot. Compare Robinson's *The Power*. (PC)

*II-860.   Gateway. St. Martin's, 1977. Series: Heechee.

Mankind "inherits" the stars by finding and exploiting (with considerable difficulty) the starships and gadgets left behind by the alien Heechee. The flippant, guilt-ridden hero has greatness thrust upon him by degrees as he picks up his winnings in the game of Russian roulette that men must play in gaining control of the Heechee artifacts. His luck continues to hold in *Beyond the Blue Event Horizon* (1980), which ends with his finding out why the Heechee ran away. This is fine contemporary space opera, with some neatly ironic characterization. Enjoyable, but somewhat less successful are the later volumes in the series, *Heechee Rendezvous* (1984), in which the aliens finally arrive on stage, *Annals of the Heechee* (1987), and *The Gateway Trip: Tales and Vignettes of the Heechee* (1990). A new Heechee novel, *The Boy Who Would Live Forever*, was announced for late 2004. (BS/ML)

   Awards: Hugo, Nebula, John W. Campbell, *Locus*
   Themes: Aliens, Space Flight, Space Opera

II-861.   JEM: The Making of Utopia. St. Martin's, 1979.

A new planet is ripe for exploitation by Earth's three power blocs: food-exporting nations, oil-exporting nations, and people's republics. Three species of intelligent natives enter into appropriate associations with the three colonizing groups, and are thus drawn into the web of conflicts and compromises that reproduces all the evils of earthly politics. A cynical ideological counterweight to stories of human/alien cooperation along the lines of Poul Anderson's *People of the Wind* (1973). (BS)

   Themes: Aliens, Colonization of Other Worlds, Politics, Utopias

*II-862.   Man Plus. Random, 1976.

The protagonist is technologically adapted for life on Mars. The process by which he is made into an alien is revealed, ironically, to be part of a plan to save humanity from the coming self-destruction of a nuclear war. A convincing and critical reexamination of the theme of Bradbury's *The Martian Chronicles*. A less successful sequel, *Mars Plus* (1994), was outlined by Pohl and written by Thomas T. Thomas. (BS)

   Awards: Nebula
   Themes: Colonization of Other Worlds, Cyborgs, The Planets

II-863. **Pohlstars**. Ballantine, 1984.

Twelve short stories, most dating from the late 1970s and early 1980s. Among the best tales here are "Spending a Day at the Lottery Fair," "We Purchase People," and "The Sweet, Sad Queen of the Grazing Isles." Among Pohl's best collections are *Digits and Dastards* (1966), *Day Million* (1970), *The Gold at the Starbow's End* (1972), *The Best of Frederik Pohl* (1975), *In the Problem Pit* (1976), and *Our Best: The Best of Frederik Pohl and C. M. Kornbluth* (1987). Tor brought out a retrospective collection, *Platinum Pohl*, in 2001. In recent years, Pohl has concentrated on novels but has also produced two fine, individually published novellas, *Stopping at Slowyear* (1991) and *Outnumbering the Dead* (1992), both of which deal in a very thoughtful manner with the problems of old age and impending death. (ML)

II-864. **The Space Merchants** (with C. M. Kornbluth). Ballantine, 1953.

Serialized in *Galaxy* as "Gravy Planet," 1952. Between the 1930s and the 1950s, the target of social criticism in America shifted from Wall Street to Madison Avenue. Reflecting that shift, this novel depicts an overcrowded, resources-starved future ruled by two rival advertising agencies. Thematically related to the mainstream novel (and film) *The Hucksters*, but carried out to a satiric *reductio ad absurdem*. Kornbluth later stated that he and Pohl packed into this story everything they hated about advertising, and it came out with Swiftian savagery. One of the first novels by writers with roots in the pulps to make an impact in mainstream circles, and, by mainstream measurements, a bestseller. A sequel by Pohl (after Kornbluth's death) is *The Merchant's War* (St. Martin's, 1984); both were collected as *Venus, Inc.* (Nelson Doubleday, 1985). (PC)

Themes: Dystopias, Satirical SF

II-865. **Wolfbane** (with C. M. Kornbluth). Ballantine, 1959. Recommended ed.: Baen, 1986.

This was regrettably the last collaboration between Pohl and Kornbluth before the latter's too-early death. It's one of their strangest. The Earth has been hauled farther out from the sun by pyramidal, solid-state robots, which from time to time kidnap individual humans and plug them into their control system as, in effect, high-grade computers. Meanwhile the rest of humanity develops a culture (driven essentially by malnutrition!) of ritual speech and gesture and Zen-like meditation. A few, however, are not docile Citizens but Wolves, and some of them end up in the robots' comm net and begin to sabotage it. The largely unintelligible activities of the Pyramids, and the stealthy gnawing at their fortress by the human mice in their midst, strikingly resemble the incomprehensible doings of the "mechs" and the effort of humans to survive among them in Greg Benford's *Great Sky River*. Pohl addressed himself to the problem of a too-compressed second half in the 1986 revision. (PC)

Themes: Robots, Space Flight

II-866.   The Wonder Effect (with C.M. Kornbluth). Ballantine, 1962.

Nine stories from 1940 to 1961; the later ones were completed by Pohl from manuscripts left unfinished at Kornbluth's death in 1958. Of the early ones, "Best Friend" is a touching story of human–canine relationships in an urban, mechanized future, told from the viewpoint of the dog; compare Simak's *City*. The authors' acute political consciousness is apparent in stories like "The Engineer" and "Critical Mass," but they could be cold warriors too, as in "The Quaker Cannon." Pohl's introduction also describes how some of their novel-length collaborations were written. More recently, *Our Best: The Best of Frederik Pohl and C.M. Kornbluth* (1987) collects 12 collaborations with introductions by Pohl. (PC)

II-867.   The Years of the City. Simon & Schuster, 1984.

Five interconnected novellas track the future of New York City as its leading citizens grapple with the problems of armies, urban decay, and pollution, using the electronic media to create a new style of democracy. A fascinating set of extrapolations, determinedly constructive. Compare Niven and Pournelle's *Oath of Fealty* (1981). (BS)

Awards: John W. Campbell
Themes: Cities, Ecology

Potter, Martin H., U.K., ?

II-868.   Life—the Jade. Everett, 1912.

When a newly discovered elixir of life is used to resurrect the prime minister, its inventor is quickly persuaded that the discovery must be reserved to the monopoly of the English ruling class. A hundred years later—after a war that has ended war—the caste of Immortals is challenged by disaffected plotters expelled from its own ranks; they decide to give up their privileges in order to enjoy the privileges of reproduction again. This is a link text between Besant's *The Inner House* and Bell's *The Seventh Bowl*; Martin Swayne's *The Blue Germ* (1918) and H. F. Parkinson's *They Shall Not Die* (1939) offered further variants on the theme. Potter's argument is similar to that of Keller's *Life Everlasting* but is more ingenious in setting out the vulpine argument for the sourness of the relevant grapes. (BS)

Themes: Immortality

Pournelle, Jerry, U.S., 1933–

II-869.   The Mercenary. Pocket, 1977. Series: Falkenberg's Legion.

A fix-up novel about space mercenaries led by a charismatic military genius. Other novels in the series include *West of Honor* (1976, rev. 1980), *Prince of Mercenaries* (1989), *Falkenberg's Legion* (collects *The Mercenary* and *West of Honor*) (1990), *Go Tell the Spartans* (1991; written in collaboration with S. M. Stirling), and *Prince of Sparta* (1993; also written with Stirling). One of the most fascinating things about this series is the way it has merged with the universe of Pournelle and Larry Niven's *The Mote in God's Eye*. Similar works include *Janissaries* (1979), in which involuntary mercenaries serve alien masters, and that novel's two sequels, written in collaboration with Roland Green, *Clan and Crown* (1982) and *Storms of Victory* (1987). These exciting stories present a polemical glorification of militarism and libertarian tough-mindedness. Compare Heinlein's *Starship Troopers*, David Drake's *Hammer's Slammers* (1979) and sequels, and the work of imitators too numerous to mention. (ML/BS)

Themes: Politics

II-870. **Starswarm**. Tor, 1998. Series: The Jupiter Novels.

YA. A genuine throwback to the Heinlein juveniles of the 1950s, this (apparently) final volume in the Jupiter series of YA novels, all of which are set within the same future history, tells the story of Kip, who lives on a colonial planet named Paradise. When the corporation that owns the colony attempts to wipe out two native sentient species, Kip and his friends decide to do everything they can to prevent it. A well-done planetary adventure. Pournelle co-authored the first novel in the series, *Higher Education* (1996), with Charles Sheffield and wrote this, the fifth, on his own. Sheffield's solo contributions to the series are *The Billion Dollar Boy* (1997), *Putting Up Roots* (1997), and *The Cyborg from Earth* (1998). (ML)

Themes: Aliens, Children in SF, Colonization of Other Worlds

Powers, Tim, U.S., 1952–

*II-871. **The Anubis Gates**. Ace, 1983.

An academic interested in a minor Victorian poet named William Ashbless is recruited as a kind of tour guide to a time-traveling expedition whose members expect to hear Coleridge lecturing. When he is marooned in 1810, he has to fight a multitude of enemies, including the man who marooned him. His struggle for survival, which necessitates his becoming Ashbless, makes a fabulous adventure story with some excellent gothic elements. More fantasy than SF, but the ingeniously constructed paradox-avoiding time-tripping draws heavily on the SF tradition. Compare Blaylock's *Homunculus*. (BS)

Awards: Philip K. Dick

Themes: History in SF, Science Fantasy, Time Travel

II-872. **Dinner at Deviant's Palace**. Ace, 1985.

A hardboiled version of the story of Orpheus and Eurydice set in post-holocaust California, with a bizarre alien presiding over an exotic hell. A fast-moving adventure with the author's usual gothic touches; a key example of the new post-holocaust romanticism. Compare Zelazny's *Damnation Alley* (1969). Virtually all of Powers's superb later work has moved into what is clearly the territory of fantasy rather than SF. (BS/ML)

Awards: Philip K. Dick

Themes: Holocaust and After, Mythology

Pratchett, Terry, U.K., 1948–

II-873.   Only You Can Save Mankind. Doubleday, 1992. Series: Johnny Maxwell.

YA. The first in the Johnny Maxwell trilogy, followed by *Johnny and the Dead* (1993) and *Johnny and the Bomb* (1996). The 12-year-old protagonist finds himself involved in a computer game in which the invading aliens, rather than waiting to be blown to bits, insist on surrendering and then give all sorts of other evidence that they're actually quite real and simply want to be allowed to go home! This is excellent humorous SF, quite up to the high standards of Pratchett's adult novels. Contrast Rubinstein's *Space Demons* and Sleator's *Interstellar Pig*. (ML)
   Themes: Aliens, Humorous SF

II-874.   Strata. Colin Smythe, 1981.

The heroine, a "worldbuilder," deserts her work in order to investigate the mysterious works of others (presumably aliens) in the same vein—in particular, a flat Earth enclosed within a crystal sphere, complete with monsters and demons. She sets out with two alien companions to explore it, attempting to find out who built it and why. An absurdist *Ringworld*, subverting SF clichés by a writer who went on to become one of the great comic fantasy writers of the century. (BS/ML)
   Themes: Aliens, Humorous SF

Preuss, Paul, U.S., 1942–

II-875.   Broken Symmetries. Timescape, 1983.

A brilliant theoretical physicist becomes involved in controversy—and ultimately conflict—generated by the discovery of a new subatomic particle. Technically detailed; its fascinating scientific and technological speculations are virtues making up for the rather makeshift plot. Compare Benford's *Timescape*. (BS)
   Themes: Hard SF, Scientists and Engineers

II-876.   Human Error. Tor, 1985.

A biologist and a computer scientist combine their artistry to produce a powerful biochip microcomputer. Inevitably, though, the potential of the new creation extends far beyond the purpose for which it was intended. Not as apocalyptic as Bear's *Blood Music* but very effective in its fashion. (BS)
   Themes: Computers, Hard SF, Intelligence, Scientists and Engineers

Priest, Christopher, U.K., 1943–

II-877.   The Affirmation. Faber, 1981.

The protagonist exists simultaneously in London and the exotic Dream Archipelago. As the state of his affairs in the former deteriorates, he finds new opportunities in the latter, but he does not know whether this represents a viable solution to his predicament. Compare Saxton's *Queen of the States*. (BS)

Themes: Parallel Worlds, Psychology

II-878.   The Extremes. Simon & Schuster, 1998; St. Martin's, 1999.

Twins and doubles have recurred in Priest's work since at least *The Affirmation*, but here they acquire a distinctly sinister character. FBI Agent Teresa visits the site of a massacre in a British seaside town that occurred at exactly the same time as a similar massacre in a Texas shopping mall at which her husband was killed. However, virtual reality re-creations ("Extreme Experience") of the shooting reveal curious gaps in the sequence of events and also unexpected links between the two shootings. This is possibly the most interesting use of virtual reality to question the very nature of our consensus reality. (PK)

Themes: Crime and Punishment, Virtual Reality

II-879.   The Glamour. Cape, 1984.

Outcasts of society, who pass unnoticed in "the hierarchy of visual interest," can make themselves invisible, a talent that is, ironically, the "glamour" of the title. The amnesiac hero gradually relearns the use of this talent and rediscovers his love for the heroine. A delicately ambivalent tale of welcome alienation. The U.S. edition (Doubleday, 1985) is substantially revised. Compare Fritz Leiber's *The Sinful Ones* (1953; revised 1980). (BS)

Themes: Paranormal Powers, Psychology

II-880.   An Infinite Summer. Faber, 1979.

Priest's second collection, superior to *Real-Time World* (1974). The mundane lives of the characters are usually interrupted by fantastic distortions of time and space, whose consequences are seductive but possibly subversive of sanity. Includes two Hugo nominees, "Palely Loitering" and "The Watched." An equally superb, more recent collection is *The Dream Archipelago* (1999). (BS/ML)

II-881.   Inverted World. Faber, 1974.

A city is subject to space-time distortions that force its inhabitants to move it en masse, pursuing a point of stability across a hyperbolic surface, although observers from outside see it progressing across Europe. A fascinating juxtaposition of incompatible worldviews, with some fine imagery in the description of the hero's mission away from the city. Compare Dick's *Martian Time-Slip* and, more recently, Reeve's *Mortal Engines*. (BS/ML)

Themes: Cities, Far Future

*II-882.   The Prestige. Simon & Schuster, 1995.

Though this novel received a major literary award and a fantasy award, it is actually pure science fiction. Around the turn of the 20th century, two stage magicians become caught in a vicious rivalry. As the climax to their act, each has a trick involving apparent instantaneous projection. One uses conventional trickery (though at considerable personal cost), the other uses a device invented by Nikolas Tesla in which his body is destroyed and reconstituted. Their efforts to sabotage each other's acts have horrific consequences, both for themselves and their descendants. Told through the (unreliable) memoirs and diaries of the protagonists, this is a powerful and disturbing examination of themes Priest has made his own, notably involving twins. Compare Budrys's *Rogue Moon*. (PK)

Awards: James Tait Black Memorial Prize, World Fantasy

Themes: History in SF, Machines, Psychology

*II-883.   The Separation. Scribner, 2002.

Priest's only venture into alternate history is a critique of the whole idea of alternate history. Twins with the same initials (J. L. Sawyer) compete for Britain in the Berlin Olympics. By World War II they are estranged; one is an RAF pilot and one a conscientious objector. On the day Rudolf Hess (or a doppelgänger) flies to Britain, one J. L. Sawyer is killed. Depending on which one dies and which survives, Hess's mission fails and history follows a course (roughly) like the one we know, or Hess succeeds and the consequent peace treaty creates a very different world. Building on his familiar obsession with twins and doubles, Priest extends questions of identity to consider the way each individual shapes his own world. Appallingly mishandled and underpromoted by Scribner, the book has since been republished by Gollancz (2003). Contrast Robinson's *The Years of Rice and Salt*. (PK)

Awards: Arthur C. Clarke

Themes: Alternate Worlds, History in SF, Psychology

Priestley, J(ohn) B(oynton), U.K., 1894–1984

II-884.   Three Time Plays. Pan, 1947.

An omnibus edition of previously published items. Few science-fictional themes work well on stage, but timeslips are easily arranged. In *Dangerous Corner* (1932), time is wound back to prevent the accidental triggering of a disastrous series of revelations. *Time and the Conways* (1937) interposes a second act seemingly set in the future (actually taking place in a parallel universe within the kind of "serial universe" imagined by J. W. Dunne) between two acts set in the present, exerting a subtle influence on their development. *I Have Been Here Before* (1938) dramatizes the theory of eternal recurrence as popularized by P. D. Ouspensky. (BS)

Pynchon, Thomas, U.S., 1937–

II-885.   Gravity's Rainbow. Viking, 1973.

A sprawling slipstream novel about a World War II psychological warfare unit full of weird characters, one of whom seems to be determining the pattern of V-2 rocket attacks by his sexual activities but refuses to submit to study and possible control. Extraordinarily elaborate black comedy. Compare the research establishment in Carter Scholz and Glen A. Harcourt's *Palimpsests* (1985). Compare also Stephenson's *Cryptonomicon*. (BS/ML)

Themes: Psychology, War

Rand, Ayn, Russia/U.S., 1905–1982

II-886.   Anthem. Cassell, 1938.

A Promethean fantasy novella whose individualist hero contrives a rebellion against the ultimate collectivist state by rediscovering the proscribed perpendicular pronoun. It carries forward ideas broached in Zamyatin's anti-Soviet dystopia *We* in a more stylized manner than Orwell's *Nineteen Eighty-Four* but dissents stridently from the pessimism of those novels by asserting that egoism will always triumph in the end. Rand went on to write a *Romantic Manifesto* (1971), which assaulted all pessimistic manifestations of modernism on the grounds that faith in oneself is as more-than-adequate replacement for the loss of faith in God. (BS)

Themes: Dystopias

Randall, Florence Engel, U.S., 1917–1997

II-887.   The Watcher in the Woods. Atheneum, 1976.

YA. From the day the Carstairs family inhabits an old house, individual members sense a mysterious, powerful, and potentially dangerous force in the woods watching them. Increasingly bizarre electronic and other disturbances culminate in the discovery of a time-trapped visitor from space in the woods. Stylistic excellence, plausible use of science fiction and ghost story elements, and fresh characterization, especially of warm family life, make for superior storytelling. Compare L'Engle's *A Wrinkle in Time*, contrast Jacob's *Born Into Light*. (FM)

Themes: Invasion, Science Fantasy, Time Travel

Rankin, Robert, U.K., 1949–

II-888.   Armageddon: The Musical. Bloomsbury, 1990. Series: Armageddon.

Truly bizarre aliens have been secretly televising life on Earth for centuries, and intentionally screwing around with human development whenever the ratings have begun to slip. The alien production staff eventually decides to bolster their ratings by sending someone to Earth with a Time Sprout. Elvis is involved in the attempt to avoid world catastrophe. One of the silliest works of science fiction ever published. Sequels include *They Came and Ate Us: The B-Movie* (1991) and *The Suburban Book of the Dead: The Remake* (1992), and Rankin's other novels are pretty much of a piece. Compare Adams's *The Hitchhiker's Guide to the Galaxy* and Denton's *Buddy Holly Is Alive and Well on Ganymede*. (ML)

Themes: Aliens, Humorous SF, Invasion

Read, Herbert (Edward), U.K., 1893–1968

II-889.   The Green Child: A Romance. Heinemann, 1935.

A surreal fantasy, whose subtitle emphasizes that it is deeply steeped in Romanticism, and preoccupied with contradictions between that philosophy and Rationalism. The story is based on an old English folktale, but its latter phases contrast a Latin American utopia with a bizarre underworld inhabited by a green-skinned race whose life cycle culminates in a literal transcendence of the human condition. It makes an interesting juxtaposition with O'Neill's exactly contemporary *Land Under England*, although it has more in common with such visionary fantasies as Vladimir Odoevsky's "The Cosmorama" (1839) and Gerald Warre Cornish's *Beneath the Surface* (1918). (BS)

Reamy, Tom, U.S., 1935–1977

II-890.   Blind Voices. Berkley, 1978.

A small Kansas town is visited during the Depression by a circus whose freaks have been produced by psionic genetic engineering. A moving study of exotic evil vanquished by exotic saintliness, very much in the tradition of Sturgeon's *The Dreaming Jewels*. Contrast Dunn's *Geek Love*. (BS)

Themes: Genetic Engineering, Paranormal Powers, Science Fantasy

Reed, Kit, U.S., 1932–

II-891.   Armed Camps. Faber, 1969.

Warfare is institutionalized as a means of social control and a product of technological imperatives. The two protagonists move from opposite political poles toward a climactic meeting. Reed's forte is the production of SF fabulations in which characters struggle to retain and assert their humanity in a mechanized and devalued world, but she can also be very witty—both aspects of her writing are displayed in her later novel *Fort Privilege* (1986) and in her collections: *The Killer Mice* (1976), *Other Stories and the Attack of the Giant Baby* (1981), *The Revenge of the Senior Citizens, **Plus* (1986), and *Seven for the Apocalypse* (1999). (BS/ML)

Themes: Dystopias, Politics, Sociology, War

Reed, Robert, U.S., 1956–

II-892.   Black Milk. Donald Fine, 1989.

Ryder, Cody, Marshall, and their friends live a happy, pastoral life, hardly aware of the fact that they're different, superior, the result of Dr. Aaron Florida's experiments in genetic engineering. As the children learn more about some of their surrogate father's other experiments, however, they begin to see that not everything is sweetness and light. When Dr. Florida's Sparkhounds escape confinement, all humankind is at risk. Well-developed, complex characters and fascinating scientific concepts are the hallmark of this satisfying novel. Compare Lois McMaster Bujold's *Falling Free* and Nancy Kress's *Beggars in Spain*. (ML)

Themes: Genetic Engineering, Intelligence

II-893.   Down the Bright Way. Bantam, 1991.

In the unimaginably distant past, a departed race of superbeings created the Way, a road of sorts that cuts across a seemingly endless number of parallel worlds. The Founders, distant relatives of ours from one of those worlds, discovered the Way and began a quasi-religious quest to find its creators. These Wanderers have traveled through an enormous number of parallel worlds, recruiting pilgrims as they go. Kyle, who comes from a world that may well be ours, is not sure whether he wants to be a Wanderer, but then finds himself kidnapped by a secret organization out to use the Way for its own dark purposes. This is large-scale sense-of-wonder SF of a rather old-fashioned sort. It is also a meditation on the nature of violence. Compare Greg Bear's *Eon* and *Eternity*. (ML)

Themes: Evolution, Parallel Worlds, War

II-894.   Marrow. Tor, 2000.

In this large-scale space opera, the Ship, a starship the size of a gas giant manned by a virtually immortal human crew and housing thousands of different alien races, travels through space, the reason for its journey long since lost. Then, at the very center of the starship, an amazing discovery is made, an actual planet, Marrow, sustained within the Ship by forces unknown. When a hand-picked team of explorers descends to Marrow's surface, they find a hellish world that is stranger than anything they might have expected. Well-done high-concept SF. The sequel is *The Well of Stars* (2004). Compare Russo's *Ship of Fools*. *Sister Alice* (2003) is another fine recent example of Reed's work in space opera mode. (ML)

Themes: Aliens, Far Future, Space Opera

II-895.   The Remarkables. Bantam, 1992.

When the damaged starship *Pitcairn* makes an emergency landing on a new world, its crew discovers the Remarkables, the only other intelligent species in known space. Unable to digest native foods on their own, the survivors enter into a permanent symbiotic relationship with the Remarkables and create a successful joint civilization. Rediscovered by Earth years later, the Pitcairners have no interest in rejoining the human race, though they periodically invite humans to their planet to contribute genetic material by taking part in a momentous ritual called a passion. Reed has created a fascinating alien species, and one of the most intriguing examples of alien–human symbiosis in recent science fiction. Compare Butler's *Dawn* and its sequels, as well as Thomson's *The Color of Distance*. (ML)

Themes: Aliens, Colonization of Other Worlds

Reeve, Philip, U.K., ?

II-896.   Mortal Engines. Point, 2001; Eos, 1993.

YA. In this wildly inventive novel, a post-holocaust London has been transformed into a mobile, traction city, traveling across Europe, preying on smaller, weaker towns, while desperately trying to avoid the larger, more dangerous traction cities of the continent. Tom, a young orphan, idolizes Valentine, the head of the Historian's guild, and truly believes in the validity of Municipal Darwinism, the pseudo-philosophy used to justify the city's rapacious ways, but eventually discovers the darker truth that underpins his world. The sequel is *Predator's Gold* (2004) and more books are promised in The Hungry Cities Chronicles. Contrast Christopher Priest's *The Inverted World* for a similar concept used very differently. (ML)

Awards: The Smarties Prize
Themes: Cities, Coming of Age, Ecology, Satirical SF

Renard, Maurice, France, 1875–1939

II-897.   Blind Circle (by Renard and Albert Jean). 1925. Trans. of *Le singe* by Florence Crewe-Jones. Dutton, 1928.

A convoluted mystery story; its eventual solution involves a technology of matter duplication whose inventor cannot quite bring it to the level of perfection required to reproduce the phenomena of life. As in many of Renard's works—the best, including *Le péril bleu* (1912) and *Le maître de la lumière* (1933), remain untranslated—enterprising inventions are undermined by the inadequacy of the narrative vehicle selected to display them. (BS)

Themes: Discoveries and Inventions

II-898.   The Flight of the Aerofix. 1909. Anon. trans. of *Le Voyage immobile*. Stellar Publishing Co., 1932.

A novella in which a castaway picked up by a yacht explains certain strange phenomena observed from its decks with a seemingly wild tale of a machine that can hold its position in space relative to the Earth's center while the surface rotates beneath it, thus making it into a speedily orbiting satellite. Perhaps the most interesting of Renard's SF stories to have been translated, certainly the one most closely resembling the inventor stories that formed the core of American SF in the early 1900s. Compare the works of Edgar Franklin. (BS)

Themes: Discoveries and Inventions

Resnick, Mike, U.S., 1942–

II-899.   Ivory: A Legend of Past and Future. Tor, 1988.

The sacred ivory of the Kilimanjaro Elephant, the largest tusks ever recorded, were in the keeping of the Masai for thousands of years until one such keeper, proving himself unworthy, lost them in a card game. Now, 7,000 years after the elephant died, Bukoba Mandaka, the last Masai, wants them back and he hires Duncan Rojas, a computer expert who specializes in authenticating interstellar hunting trophies, to get them back. This is an intelligent tale that treats African culture with considerable respect. Resnick has also written three novels—*Paradise* (1989), *Purgatory* (1993), and *Inferno* (1993)—that take the histories of individual African nations and reinterpret them in SF terms, as well as a series of award-winning short stories set on an artificially created world, Kirinyaga, intended to duplicate pre-colonial East Africa. Compare the stories in the anthology *Future Earths: Under African Skies* (1993), which Resnick co-edited with Gardner Dozois. (ML)

Themes: Anthropology, History in SF

*II-900.   Kirinyaga. Ballantine Del Rey, 1998.

A superb collection of interrelated short stories marketed as a novel. Koriba, a highly educated, 22nd-century Kenyan, decides to create a primitivist Kikuyu utopia on a terraformed asteroid with himself as *mundumugu* or witch doctor. The results are both complex and, occasionally, tragic. This is one of the most honored story cycles in the history of the field. Included are the Hugo Award-winning stories "Kirinyaga" and "The Manamouki" as well as such Hugo- or Nebula-nominated stories as "One Perfect Morning, With Jackals," "For I Have Touched the Sky," "The Lotus and the Spear," "A Little Knowledge," "When the Old Gods Die," and "The Land of Nod." Compare Resnick's other novels set on Africa-like planets as well as his anthology *Future Earths*. (ML)

Themes: Colonization of Other Worlds, History in SF, Politics, Sociology

Reynolds, Alastair, U.K., 1966–

II-901.   Revelation Space. Gollancz, 2000; Ace, 2001. Series: Revelation Space.

A much-admired debut novel from an author, seen as part of the British SF renaissance, who clearly delights in the broad-brush approach of space opera. Reynolds packs his story with numerous SF tropes, from sentient oceans to huge starships, to underground cities – his sources are legion, reflecting his wide knowledge of the genre. The novel tackles a familiar theme, that too much knowledge can be dangerous; at its heart is a mystery as to why many civilizations in the universe are extinct. Dan Sylveste, an archaeologist, is attempting to solve this problem. His attempts to do so lead to him being targeted for assassination by Ana Khouri, who works her passage to his planet on a huge lighthugger spaceship that is in the throes of a bizarre metamorphosis. This novel and its successors—*Chasm City* (2001), *Redemption Ark* (2002), and *Absolution Gap* (2003)—set in the same universe, are inventive and entertaining. Reynolds occasionally comes close to losing control of the narrative, such is its immensity, but never entirely loses his grip. Compare Banks's Culture novels and Greenland's *Take Back Plenty*. (MKS)

Themes: Aliens, Future History, Galactic Empires, Space Opera

Reynolds, Mack, U.S., 1917–1983

II-902.   The Best of Mack Reynolds. Pocket, 1976.

Foreword by Barry Malzberg; introduction and headnotes by the author. Versatility and a knack for the O. Henry surprise ending, which on first reading actually does surprise, mark this collection of 22 stories from 1950 to 1974 featuring, among others, time-travel paradoxes, a Sherlock Holmes pastiche, utopias and dystopias, a parody tourist guide for Mars, and "Fad," which tells what happens when the motivational researchers con the American woman once too often. Reynolds played to his strengths, the social sciences and foreign travel. There isn't a dull story in the bunch. (PC)

II-903.   Lagrange Five. Bantam, 1979. Series: Lagrange.

An O'Neill space colony develops an effective social system, but its key role in the power politics of the solar system makes it the target of subversive conspiracy. The theme is further developed in *The Lagrangists* (1983), *Chaos in Lagrangia* (1984), and *Trojan Orbit* (1985), all edited by Dean Ing from posthumously discovered manuscripts. Compare Haldeman's Worlds series. (BS)

Themes: Life on Other Worlds, Politics, Sociology, Space Flight

Rhodes, W(illiam) H(enry), U.S., 1822–1876

II-904.   Caxton's Book: A Collection of Essays, Tales and Sketches by the Late W. H. Rhodes. Ed. by Daniel O'Connell. Bancroft, 1876.

A mixed collection of items by a journalist who routinely signed himself "Caxton," including an early account of attempted blackmail by a scientist in possession of a destructive new technology, "The Case of Summerfield" (1879), and two tales of exotic optical technology, "Phases in the Life of John Pollexfen" and "The Telescopic Eye." Interesting in juxtaposition with the works of Robert Duncan Milne and Edward Page Mitchell. (BS)

Ridley, Francis H. (his middle name was actually Ambrose), U.K., 1897–1994

II-905.   The Green Machine. Noel Douglas, 1926.

An eccentric interplanetary romance whose hero, equipped with a space vehicle modeled on a bicycle, hitches a ride to Mars on a passing comet. He encounters many monsters there, including humanoid brutes, but eventually makes contact with a race of intelligent ants. Distressed by what he tells them about humankind, they expel him into space again; his new orbit takes him to the outer planets, where he finds Uranus inhabited by superintelligent spiders, before returning him to a splashdown in the South Atlantic. A *jeu d'esprit* that has as much in common with Edgar Rice Burroughs as with H. G. Wells, with more than a dash of John Mastin. Compare the ant civilization in Farley's *The Radio Man*. (BS)

Themes: Life on Other Worlds, Space Flight

Roberts, Keith, U.K., 1935–2000

II-906. **The Chalk Giants**. Hutchinson, 1974.

A fix-up post-holocaust novel in which Britain is rent apart and barbarism reigns. The final sequence, like the final sequence of *Pavane*, is set at Corfe Gate. A brilliant and disturbing book that develops the grimly realistic aspect of British catastrophic fiction. To be sharply contrasted with Cowper's Kinship trilogy. (BS)

Themes: Holocaust and After

II-907. **Kiteworld**. Gollancz, 1985.

A fix-up novel set in a pseudo-medieval world dominated by a religious elite, in which men are carried aloft by giant kites to look out for invading demons. Has affinities with *Pavane* and *The Chalk Giants*, although it sets aside the idea of historical cyclicity that underlies these novels. (BS)

II-908. **The Lordly Ones**. Gollancz, 1986.

Perhaps Roberts's best short story collection, this volume followed *Machines and Men* (1973), *The Grain Kings* (1976), and *Ladies From Hell* (1979). The title story and "The Comfort Station" both deal with the collapse of civilized order—one of Roberts's favorite themes—and do so with much feeling. "Diva" and "Sphairistike" are more playful, as is the author's wont when dealing with the leisurely aspects of life. Later collections are *A Heron Caught in the Weeds* (1987) and *Winterwood* (1989). Compare Richard Cowper's short fiction. (BS/ML)

II-909. **Molly Zero**. Gollancz, 1980.

The adolescent heroine escapes from intense and enigmatic education in "the Blocks," living as a working girl, a gypsy, and ultimately an urban outlaw, but her apparent escape turns out to be simply one more phase in her rite of passage. A grimly earnest version of a common SF theme, exhibiting Roberts's fondness for young female protagonists threatened by the forces of corruption. (BS)

Themes: Coming of Age, Women in SF

*II-910. **Pavane**. Hart-Davis, 1968.

Fix-up novel describing what appears to be an alternate world where the Catholic church retained its hegemony in Europe because of the victory of the Spanish Armada. But this technologically retarded world also harbors fairies who know the real truth, and when progress rears its ugly head again, its value is brought sharply into question. A rich, many-faceted narrative, written with great care and delicacy; one of the finest SF novels of the period. U.S. editions add an extra episode. Compare Miller's *A Canticle for Leibowitz* and Amis's *The Alteration*. (BS)

Themes: Alternate Worlds, Religion

Robinson, Frank M., U.S., 1926–

II-911.   The Dark Beyond the Stars. Tor, 1991.

Robinson's first SF novel in decades concerns the starship *Astron,* which has searched the galaxy for alien life for 2,000 years. The ship is now falling apart and its crew, all born during the voyage, are ripe for mutiny. Unfortunately the *Astron's* immortal captain has been conditioned to refuse to turn back until he finds evidence of life, evidence that apparently does not exist. Sparrow, a 17-year-old crewman who suffers from amnesia, is caught up in the mounting discontent and soon discovers that his lost past may hold a clue to what has gone wrong with the mission. This gritty, moving variation on the generation starship concept features an unusually adept handling of same-sex relationships as well as a well-constructed mystery plotline. Compare Heinlein's *Orphans of the Sky* and Russo's *Ship of Fools*. (ML)

Themes: Coming of Age, Sex in SF, Space Flight

II-912.   The Power. Lippincott, 1956.

An emerging psi powers story, well told as a suspense thriller. A navy research group sees evidence of telekinesis. Several deaths and surprise twists complicate the search for the holder of this power. The story has some similarities to Wells's *The Invisible Man*. (PC)

Themes: Paranormal Powers

Robinson, Kim Stanley, U.S., 1952–

II-913.   Antarctica. HarperCollins, 1997; Bantam, 1998.

In the early 21st century, Wade Norton has been sent on a fact-finding mission to Antarctica by a U.S. senator to chase down rumors that someone been sabotaging governmental, scientific, and industrial concerns on the continent. He discovers a complex political situation that is on the verge of exploding because of radical environmentalists who are willing to do anything to stop the "Gotterdammerung capitalism" at the heart of the impending ecological collapse of both Antarctica and the Earth as a whole. As in his classic Mars trilogy and the recent *Forty Signs of Rain*, Robinson's passionate environmental concerns provide the fuel to make this heavily didactic novel a success. Compare Sage Walker's *Whiteout* (1997). (ML)

Themes: Ecology, Politics

II-914.   Forty Signs of Rain. HarperCollins, Bantam, 2004.

The Antarctic ice shelf is collapsing, the Arctic ice pack is breaking up, and the Gulf Stream may have just stalled out. It's only a few years in the future, but global warming is in full swing and the effects are becoming obvious. Low-lying countries have begun to drown and even Washington, D.C., is about to be inundated. Robinson's portrayal of environmental catastrophe in this first novel in a new trilogy is unusually low-key, but feels very real. His description of scientists at work is highly believable. At least one character from *Antarctica* also appears in this book. For other portrayals of the effects of global warming and environmental collapse, see Sterling's *Heavy Weather* and Spinrad's *Greenhouse Summer*. For an older, but equally believable novel about scientists at work, see Benford's *Timescape*. (ML)

Themes: Ecology, Politics

II-915.   The Memory of Whiteness. Tor, 1985.

An inspired musician tours the solar system with a one-man orchestra designed by a brilliant physicist, whose theory of the universe is strongly linked to the fundamentals of musical aesthetics. The protagonist's friends must try to protect him from threats that appear to come from a strange religious cult, though he seems not unwilling to accept a messianic role in their unfolding psychodrama. A highly original and delicately fashioned novel whose exotic settings are remarkably convincing. (BS)

Themes: Religion, Space Opera

II-916.   The Planet on the Table. Tor, 1986.

A collection of early fiction by one of the genre's finest literary writers, including Robinson's World Fantasy Award-winning story about the Spanish Armada, "Black Air," and the fine alternate history tale, "The Lucky Strike," which is set in a world where the bomb was not dropped on Hiroshima. Robinson's other major collections are *Escape From Kathmandu* (1989), which includes the Hugo- and Nebula Award-nominated title novella; *Remaking History* (1991), which includes "Before I Wake," as well as "Vinland the Dream," "Glacier," and 12 other fine stories; and *The Martians* (1999). Compare Kessel's *The Pure Product*. (ML)

*II-917.   Red Mars. HarperCollins, 1992. Series: Mars.

This novel, taken with its two award-winning sequels, provides, without a doubt, the most detailed and impressive portrayal of the exploration and colonization of another planet ever published. Robinson is in complete control of his materials, whether he is describing the engineering difficulties involved in the building of a large-scale underground habitat or the political wheeling and dealing involved in placating a wide range of political, religious, ethnic, and commercial interests, all of which want a slice of the Martian pie. The novel features a large cast of well-developed characters, breathtaking descriptions of the Martian landscape, and a sophisticated understanding of the complex interplay between technology and politics. *Red Mars* may be the finest hard-science fiction novel of the last decade. Sequels are *Green Mars* (1994; Hugo and *Locus* Award) and *Blue Mars* (1996; Hugo and *Locus* Award). *The Martians* (1999; *Locus* Award) contains short stories set on Robinson's version of Mars, with at least one story taking place in an alternate universe. Robinson's independently published novella *Green Mars* (1985) is a separate story despite sharing a title with the later novel. For a competent, smaller-scale approach to the exploration of the Red Planet, compare Ben Bova's *Mars*. For another excellent take on Martian politics, see Greg Bear's *Moving Mars*. (ML)

Awards: Nebula

Themes: Colonization of Other Worlds, Ecology, Hard SF, Life on Other Worlds, The Planets, Politics

*II-918.   The Wild Shore. Ace, 1984. Series: Orange County.

After the nuclear holocaust, the United States is quarantined by the United Nations, and the survivors must remake their civilization in isolation. The protagonist, his role analogous to that of Huckleberry Finn, explores this new frontier world. The most sophisticated example of contemporary American romantic catastrophism. Compare Powers's *Dinner at Deviant's Palace* and Brin's *The Postman*. Robinson followed *The Wild Shore* with two more novels set in the same location in Southern California, thematic sequels considering alternate historical possibilities. *The Gold Coast* (1988) describes a near-future Orange County of superhighways and designer drugs that is only marginally different from our own. *Pacific Edge* (1990), which won the John W. Campbell Award, is set in a post-disaster, small-scale community where everything is done with an eye toward its effect on the ecology. (ML/BS)

Awards: *Locus*

Themes: Coming of Age, Ecology, Holocaust and After

*II-919.   The Years of Rice and Salt. Bantam, 2002.

In this impressive work of large-scale alternate history, the Black Death of the 14th century killed 99 percent of the inhabitants of Europe rather than just 30 percent, leaving the world free for exploitation by the expanding empires of China, Arabia, and India. As the years pass, various technological and cultural events occur at a pace that is sometimes radically at odds with events in our world. On an unusual note, Robinson provides continuity for his centuries-long tale by running a small cast of recurring characters through a series of lifetimes. Between rebirths, these people exist in what appears to be a variation on the Tibetan concept of the afterlife. During their various stints on Earth, they often interact without knowing anything about their past lives. Robinson uses his enormous canvas to discuss a variety of theories about politics, culture, and religion, with sometimes controversial results. Whether one agrees with him or not, it's clear that this novel has raised the bar for all future authors of serious alternate history. Compare Steven Barnes's *Lion's Blood* and the alternate histories of Harry Turtledove. (ML)

Awards: *Locus*

Themes: Alternate Worlds, History in SF, Religion

Robinson, Spider, U.S./Canada, 1948–

II-920.   Callahan's Con. Tor, 2003. Series: Callahan.

The latest entry in a popular comic SF series that began with *Callahan's Crosstime Saloon* (1977) and that has now reached 11 volumes. Jake Stonebender's bar in

Key West appears to be the natural gathering place for a wild collection of aliens, time travelers, aging hippies, psychics, and other assorted riffraff. In this latest adventure, a Mafioso named Tony Donuts decides to open up a protection racket and makes the mistake of choosing Jake as his first "customer," but Jake's precocious daughter, Erin, intervenes, using time travel to con Tony into believing that she can sell him the fabled Fountain of Youth. This is madcap farce with puns piled on puns. Other volumes in the series include *Callahan's Secret* (1986), *Callahan's Legacy* (1996), and *Time Travelers Strictly Cash* (2001). Compare Terry Pratchett's *Strata* and his Discworld novels. (ML)

Themes: Aliens, Humorous SF, Satirical SF

Robinson, Spider, U.S./Canada, 1948– and Robinson, Jeanne, U.S./Canada, 1948–

II-921.   Stardance. Dial, 1979. Series: Stardance.

Based on a Hugo- and Nebula Award-winning novella. A story of exotic redemption in which a crippled dancer becomes involved in humanity's first contact with aliens, and helps set the stage for a mystical communion between the species. The sequels, *Starseed* (1991) and *Starmind* (1995), are somewhat less successful. Compare Orson Scott Card's *Songmaster* (1980). (BS/ML)

Themes: Aliens

Robson, Justina, U.K., 1968–

II-922.   Mappa Mundi. Macmillan, 2001.

A mappa mundi was intended to be a pictorial summation of available knowledge of the world rather than providing an accurate geographical map. In her novel Robson both exploits and inverts this motif. The Mappa Mundi project, of interest to a number of governments, is working on controlling the minds of groups of people. At the same time, Robson's novel is peopled with characters who are often unsure in their own identities, leaving readers unclear in turn how they are supposed to respond to them. Mappa Mundi brings with it not security and certainty, as its medieval counterpart was intended to do, but instead a destabilizing effect for all those who are not intimately involved. Even those who are part of the project, to whom a new kind of humanity is offered, cannot be certain of the truth of their world. Robson combines the complex uncertainties of a developing science with the verities of an old-fashioned spy plot in which no one can be trusted, to show her readers the fragile nature of the world around them. (MKS)

Themes: Nanotechnology

II-923.   Natural History. Macmillan, 2003.

The sense of unease that pervades Robson's earlier books returns in this novel, here manifested in a bewildering diversity of body types from the conventional to the Forged (genetically engineered for specific tasks), to those who seek to escape even this for a new existence. Voyage Lonestar Isol has possibly discovered the answer to their problems and her own, in the shape of an alien artifact that brings faster-than-light travel, and a potential refuge. However, the slipperiness of existence, particularly for those who have Evolved, and the consequent Unevolved human desire to maintain life within rigid, comprehensible structures and systems drive the narrative inexorably into greater political uncertainty as different factions wrangle over what to do with Isol's discoveries. Robson has created a particularly bleak brand of space opera, focused far more on humanity's problems than on the glories of the open galaxy. Compare Greg Egan's *Diaspora* and Jack McDevitt's *The Engines of God.* (MKS)

Themes: Space Opera

Rocklynne, Ross, U.S., 1913–1988

II-924.   The Men and the Mirror. Ace, 1973.

A collection of six stories from the SF pulps (two of which are accidentally run together), all following the same plot pattern, first set out in "At the Centre of Gravity" (1936), in which rivals locked in conflict become trapped in awkward extraterrestrial predicaments that provide stern challenges to their scientific reasoning and practical ingenuity. Such puzzle stories became a standard feature of *Astounding*, providing a convenient narrative format for "hard SF." (PC)

Rockwood, Roy *see* Garis, Howard

Rosenblum, Mary, U.S., 1953–

II-925.   The Stone Garden. Del Rey, 1994.

One of the rare SF novels that deals intelligently with the fine arts. A new kind of asteroid has been found in deep space that, when sculpted by the proper artist, creates a complex collage of human emotions. Michael Tryon is a Stone sculptor of enormous talent so, when he discovers that artists who work with the asteroids are being murdered, he has good reason to try to get to the bottom of the mystery. Intelligent characters and an art form that, given the Stone's existence, actually makes sense. Compare Jablokov's *Carve the Sky.* (ML)

Themes: Paranormal Powers

Rosny, J. H., aîné (pseudonym of Joseph-Henri Boëx), France, 1856–1940

***II-926.   The Xipehuz and The Death of the Earth** ("Les Xipéhuz" and "La mort de la terre"). 1887; 1910. Trans. by George Slusser. Arno, 1978.

Two novellas. In the former, members of a nomadic tribal society of some 7,000 years ago make uncomfortable contact with exotic, seemingly inorganic aliens and must summon up all their ingenuity to combat them. The latter is a far-future fantasy in which the last surviving humans are similarly harassed by inorganic creatures, although they coexist more amicably with intelligent birds. "The Death of the Earth" is interesting in juxtaposition with Hodgson's *The*

Night Land, which it cannot have influenced, and is also comparable to Wright's *The World Below.* (BS)

Themes: Evolution

Rousseau (Emanuel), Victor, U.K./U.S., 1879–1960

II-927.   The Messiah of the Cylinder. McClurg, 1917.

An ideological reply to H. G. Wells's *When the Sleeper Wakes,* presumably written some time before its publication (the future history sketched out within it does not include the war that began in 1914). Instead of awakening into the oppressive regime that greeted Wells's sleeper, Rousseau's awakes into an alleged Wellsian utopia, atheistic and run according to supposedly scientific principles (including eugenic population control). Although the masters of the new society can offer physical immortality, the hero prefers the kind promised by Christianity and the majority eventually sides with him. In spite of the pulpish plotting that dominated Rousseau's subsequent works, the dystopian vision has several interesting features anticipating Orwell's *Nineteen Eighty-Four* and the fierce critique of Wellsian ideas mounted in Leon Stover's *The Shaving of Karl Marx* (1982). (BS)

Rubinstein, Gillian, Australia, 1942–

*II-928.   Beyond the Labyrinth. Hyland House, 1988.

YA. An extraterrestrial anthropologist, Cal, precipitates and then resolves tension within 14-year-old Breton's family, as the former, shifting her studies from aboriginal to contemporary life and falling ill, invites the youth to come to her home. Intriguing use of alternate points of view and conclusions; provocative investigation of social and cultural issues affecting individuals and families alike. Contrast Engdahl's *The Far Side of Evil.* (FM)

Awards: Children's Book of the Year Award of Australia, National Children's Literature Award of Australia

Themes: Aliens, Anthropology, Women in SF

II-929.   Galax-Arena. Penguin, 1992.

YA. On an overpopulated future Earth, a group of Australian children are kidnapped, supposedly to be transported to a distant planet for the entertainment of aliens. Upon arriving on their new world, they are put through an extensive and grueling course of training to prepare themselves, training that forces them to turn on each other. Eventually, however, Joella, one of the children, notices a common housefly and realizes that they aren't on an alien world at all. They discover that they've been the victims of a hoax, the subjects of a secret gerontological experiment, and the aliens are simply very old human beings. This is a bleak but well-done novel with nicely developed characters. The sequel is *Terra-Farma* (2001). Compare William Sleator's *House of Stairs.* (ML)

Themes: Children in SF, Overpopulation

II-930.   Space Demons. Omnibus, 1986. Series: Space Demons.

YA. Literally caught up in Space Demons, an experimental computer game, four temperamentally and socially ill-suited teens need every skill they possess to win the game and save each other's lives. Brilliant concept; engaging style sensitive to actual teen talk; rounded honest characterization. Compare Sleator's *Interstellar Pig*. Contrast Pratchett's *Only You Can Save Mankind*. A sequel, *Skyway* (1989), which uses the challenges of a second computer game to continue exploring the changes within the four teenagers, is just as well written and exciting as its predecessor. A third sequel is *Shinkei* (1997). (FM/ML)

  Awards: National Children's Literature Award of Australia
  Themes: Children in SF, Coming of Age, Computers

Rucker, Rudy, U.S., 1946–

II-931.   The Hacker and the Ants. Morrow, 1994.

In this wildly funny satire, Jerzy Rugby, a computer scientist who has dedicated his life to the creation of AI robots, finds himself blamed for the unleashing of new and unusually damaging computer viruses called "ants." Investigating, Rugby discovers that he's been set up as the fall guy in a huge conspiracy. At great personal danger, he enters the virtual world of the viral ants hoping to end their invasion and clear his name. Given the explosive growth of spam and hacking in the 10 years since it was published, the novel comes across as rather prophetic. Compare Bruce Sterling's *The Zenith Angle* (2004). (ML)

  Themes: Computers, Intelligence, Satirical SF, Virtual Reality

II-932.   The Hollow Earth. Morrow, 1990.

Edgar Allan Poe and others head out on a mad, sometimes hilarious expedition to seek the polar hole that will allow them to enter the hollow Earth. Succeeding, they find a bizarre interior world, a number of unusual civilizations, some mindbending physical phenomena, flying saucers, and special effects of a sort usually associated with a trip on LSD. Compare Burroughs's *At the Earth's Core*, Poe's *The Narrative of Arthur Gordon Pym*, and Seaborn's *Symzonia: A Voyage of Discovery*. (ML)

  Themes: Alternate Worlds, Fantastic Voyages, History in SF, Satirical SF

II-933.   Software. Ace, 1982. Series: Software.

Artificial intelligence has developed to the point where computers can begin the inevitable power struggle with mankind. Should we be prepared to put aside our frail flesh in favor of inorganic forms that will preserve our personalities in their software? The extravagant plot is well spiced with wit. The equally well-done sequels are *Wetware* (1988; Philip K. Dick Award), *Freeware* (1997), and *Realware* (2000). Compare Piercy's *He, She, and It*. (BS/ML)

  Awards: Philip K. Dick
  Themes: Computers, Cyberpunk, Intelligence, Satirical SF

II-934.   Spaceland: A Novel of the Fourth Dimension. Tor, 2002.

In this wild satire, Rucker borrows from Edwin Abbott's classic *Flatland* to tell the story of a computer techie named Joe Cube whose marriage is on the rocks and who finds himself at the center of a battle between two warring tribes from the fourth dimension, the Kluppers and the Dronners. A mathematician by profession, Rucker combines valid mathematical speculation with a genuinely nasty spoof on the folkways of Silicon Valley. (ML)

    Themes: Parallel Worlds, Satirical SF

II-935.   White Light. Ace, 1980.

A strange fantasy of life after death that has abundant SF interest by virtue of the author's use of "higher dimensions" as a milieu for displaying ideas drawn from number theory and other areas of higher mathematics. The author suggests that this exercise in "transrealism" can be regarded as the first element in a trilogy completed by *The Sex Sphere* (1983), in which a hypersphere trapped in an intersection with our 3-D space obligingly responds to the sexual fantasies of the male characters, and *The Secret of Life* (1985). Rucker's work invites comparison with some very early SF writers, including Camille Flammarion and C. H. Hinton, as well as cyberpunks such as John Shirley and Bruce Sterling. (BS/ML)

    Themes: Parallel Worlds, Satirical SF

Russ, Joanna, U.S., 1937–

II-936.   Alyx. Gregg Press, 1976. Variant title: *The Adventures of Alyx.*

Incorporates the novel *Picnic on Paradise* (1968) with four short stories featuring the same heroine. Alyx's native land is the cradle of civilization, where she is an outlaw because her ideas are so far ahead of her time, but in the novel she is snatched out of context to become a time-traveling agent charged with rescuing a group of tourists trapped on a resort planet where local politics have turned sour. Clever and lively. Another similar novel is *The Two of Them* (1978), in which a female agent is dispatched to a quasi-Islamic world where she rescues a girl from a harem. Compare Baker's *In the Garden of Iden* and other tales of the Company. (BS/ML)

    Themes: Feminist SF, Women in SF

II-937.   And Chaos Died. Ace, 1970.

A castaway on a colony world, whose inhabitants have been taught telepathy by mysterious aliens, picks up the gift himself, but then finds himself alienated from ordinary humans, able to remain sane only among members of what is now his own kind. A determined attempt to examine psi power from a new angle. Compare Silverberg's *Dying Inside*. (BS/ML)

    Themes: Paranormal Powers

II-938.   Extra(ordinary) People. St. Martin's, 1984.

A collection of linked stories, deliberately didactic in form, in which liberated women in different societies challenge the forces of oppression. Includes the Hugo Award-winning "Souls." As with *The Female Man*, the result is multifaceted and the call for a revolution in sexual politics is eloquent even though the stories retain a full appreciation of the difficulty of compiling a manifesto for a nonsexist society. Other, more varied, collections are *The Zanzibar Cat* (1984), which features the Nebula Award-winning "When It Changed," the seed story for *The Female Man*, and *The Hidden Side of the Moon* (1988), which includes such stories as "The Dirty Little Girl" and "Reasonable People." (BS/ML)

   Themes: Feminist SF

*II-939.   The Female Man. Bantam, 1975.

A contemporary woman encounters three "alternative selves," including a version from the feminist utopia Whileaway, a version from a world where patriarchy is more powerful and more brutally imposed, and a version from a world where the sex war has exploded into armed conflict. The juxtaposition of these alternatives, phantasmagoric and very witty, provides an extraordinarily rich and thought-provoking commentary on sexual politics. A key novel of feminist SF. Compare Piercy's *Woman on the Edge of Time* and Saxton's *Queen of the States*. (BS)

   Awards: Retrospective Tiptree
   Themes: Feminist SF, Politics, Satirical SF, Sex in SF

Russell, Eric Frank, U.K., 1905–1978

II-940.   The Best of Eric Frank Russell. Ballantine, 1978.

Thirteen stories, almost all from *Astounding*, starting with the touching far-future tale "Mana" (1937), of the last man on Earth bestowing the gift of fire and technology upon humanity's heirs. Good sampling of Russell, from humor to high drama. Alan Dean Foster contributed an introduction about Russell, who deserves to be remembered more for these thoughtfully worked out shorter pieces than for hokey works such as *Sinister Barrier*. A recent and wider collection is *Major Ingredients: The Selected Short Stories of Eric Frank Russell* (NESFA, 2000). (PC)

II-941.   The Great Explosion. Dobson, 1962.

An expansion of " . . . And Then There Were None" (1951). The "explosion" of the title is that of Earth's mavericks and malcontents carried by faster-than-light drive to other worlds. Earth's military and diplomatic forces go after four such worlds only to find that the colonists' answer to "Take me to your leader" is "What's *that?*" The political economy of such settlements is what we now call libertarian; their psychological condition is a happy anarchy. A fine, government-deflating satirical romp. Would it could be true. (PC)

   Themes: Colonization of Other Worlds, Utopias

II-942.   Sinister Barrier. World's Work, 1943.

A paranoid thriller, based on a casual speculation by Charles Fort that the human race might be mere domestic animals kept by alien intelligence we are incapable of perceiving. It appeared as the lead novel in the first issue of *Astounding*'s companion magazine *Unknown* in 1939. The products harvested from humans like milk from dairy cattle are pain and misery—a notion that struck a chord in a war-threatened world. As soon as the truth is realized, the revolution gets under way. Compare Hyder's *Vampires Overhead*. (BS)

  Themes: Aliens

Russell, Mary Doria, U.S., 1950–

*II-943.   The Sparrow. Villard, 1996.

Marketed as a mainstream bestseller, this rich first novel took the publishing world by storm in 1996, appealing equally to those who generally didn't read science fiction and those who did. In well-crafted prose, Russell tells the story of a Jesuit-led mission to an alien world in the year 2019. The well-meaning members of the expedition make first contact with two alien races and, with the best intentions in the world, manage to totally mishandle the situation, leading to tragedy for everyone involved. The novel's protagonist, Father Emilo Sandoz, is a beautifully drawn character, and Russell's handling of interspecies gender misunderstandings is particularly deft. Although the book involves a few improbable events, it nonetheless stands as one of the finest first-contact novels ever written. The powerful sequel is *Children of God* (1998). Compare Jones's *White Queen* for another take on the relevant gender issues. Compare Blish's *A Case of Conscience*, Miller's *A Canticle for Leibowitz*, and Anthony's *God's Fires* for other science fictional treatments of Catholic priests. (ML)

  Awards: Arthur C. Clarke, James Tiptree
  Themes: Aliens, Life on Other Worlds, Psychology, Religion, Sex in SF

Russo, Richard Paul, U.S., 1954–

II-944.   Ship of Fools. Ace, 2001.

The starship *Argonos* has wandered through space for generations, its mission to search out other life forms. Then it receives a transmission that leads it to a heretofore unknown planet. Landing, the crew find no signs of life on the jungle planet until they happen upon an underground cavern filled to overflowing with the remains of gruesomely slaughtered bodies, each one neatly hung on its own hook. Then another starship appears. Russo tells a dark and powerful tale of horror and existential angst that attempts to come to terms with a variety of religious questions. Compare Robinson's *The Dark Beyond the Stars* and Reed's *Marrow*. (ML)

  Awards: Philip K. Dick
  Themes: Psychology, Space Flight

II-945.   Subterranean Gallery. Tor, 1989.

Rheinhardt, a San Francisco-based sculptor living in a repressive, near-future America, has tried to keep out of politics, but a series of events makes this increasingly difficult. A close friend is drafted to fight in a gruesome South American war. Much of the best work by local artists is systematically destroyed or suppressed. Police helicopters circle overhead nightly. Then a mysterious Vietnam veteran named Justinian persuades Rheinhardt to fight back. This novel is very dark and emotionally powerful. Compare two similar books, Murphy's *The City, Not Long After* and Goldstein's *A Mask for the General*. (ML)

    Awards: Philip K. Dick
    Themes: Cities, Dystopias

Ryman, Geoff, Canada/U.K., 1951–

*II-946.   Air (or Have Not Have). St. Martin's Griffin, 2003.

Ryman's protagonist, Chung Mae, is the local fashion expert in a small village in the backward nation of Karzistan. One day, however, the entire world is changed by the brief testing of Air, an experimental quantum communications system that, in effect, puts the Internet in everyone's mind. Accidentally trapped in the system during the test, Mae is driven nearly insane, but realizes that she must use the unique insight the experience has given her to prepare her village for the impending permanent imposition of Air upon the world. Ryman's new technology is fascinating, but what makes his novel special are his well-drawn characters, his detailed description of the culture of Karzistan, and his understanding of the ways in which western society takes the Third World for granted. Compare Danver's *The Fourth World*. (ML)

    Themes: Anthropology, Feminist SF, Paranormal Powers, Politics, Virtual Reality, Women in SF

*II-947.   The Child Garden: A Low Comedy. Unwin, 1989.

This brilliant postmodernist extravaganza takes place in a tropical future London where genetic engineering has abolished cancer, mastered the art of passing on knowledge through viruses, allowed human beings to photosynthesize, and, tragically, caused an irreversible change in human genetics, which leads most human beings to die in their mid-30s. The complex plot centers on a pair of artist–lovers—Milena, a mediocre actress with a talent for directing, and Rolfa, a huge, genetically engineered Polar Woman who sings opera. For comparably audacious speculation about bioengineering, see Bear's *Blood Music*. For a comparable picture of a city transformed by the greenhouse effect, see Hand's *Winterlong*. (ML)

    Awards: Arthur C. Clarke, John W. Campbell
    Themes: Cities, Disaster, Feminist SF, Genetic Engineering

Saberhagen, Fred, U.S., 1930–

II-948.   Berserker. Ballantine, 1967. Series: Berserker.

A collection, the first book in an extensive series of novels and collections (see series listing). Berserkers are automated war machines programmed to destroy life, whose perennial and inescapable threat unites the life forms of the galaxy and stimulates their collective technological progress. The power of the premise and its fecundity in generating plots is aptly demonstrated by the expansion of the series to take in work by other writers. The series has become an archetypal example of the SF myth that opposes man and machine, and also develops the common assumption of SF writers that, without some kind of challenge, men might use their technology to become lotus eaters, stagnating in evolutionary decadence. The early stories tend to be a little clumsy, but Saberhagen's writing skills have developed. Compare Benford's *Great Sky River* and sequels. (BS/ML)

Themes: Future History, Robots, War

Sagan, Carl, U.S., 1934–1996

II-949.   Contact. Simon & Schuster, 1985.

The much-touted first novel by the noted popularizer of science, concerning the deciphering of a message from the stars and the voyage to a fateful rendezvous. The fervor of the story exceeds that of Gunn's *The Listeners* and Kube-McDowell's *Emprise* (1985). It can also be compared with Clarke's *2010: Odyssey Two*. Made into a successful movie starring Jody Foster. (BS/ML)

Awards: *Locus*
Themes: Aliens, Scientists and Engineers

St. Clair, Margaret, U.S., 1911–1995

II-950.   Agent of the Unknown. Ace, 1956.

On a remote planetoid, beachcomber Don Haig acquires an exquisite doll made by a mysterious artificer, Vulcan, while Mulciber, head of the police, wants the doll, which reputedly heals diseases. A darkly told tale that confutes the Golden Age derring-do tradition. The story's atmosphere and mood sound much like Ballard, with a conclusion that is an echo of Dick. (The other half of this Ace Double is the early Dick novel, *The World Jones Made*, thematically related both to this story and to Dick's *Martian Time-Slip*.) (PC)

*II-951.   Change the Sky, and Other Stories. Ace, 1974.

Eighteen stories, 1951–1961, written with irony, sophistication, and sometimes real bite. "The Wines of Earth" introduces galactic wine tasters to the pleasures of California's Napa Valley. St. Clair had a knack for fresh twists on older SF ideas, such as "Lazarus," a particularly grisly reworking of the original Frankenstein theme. The title story of this superior collection is especially memorable. *The Best of Margaret St. Clair* (1985) collected 20 stories and a new introduction by the author. Contrast Clingerman's *A Cupful of Space.* (PC)

Sand, George (pseudonym of Aurore Dupin), France, 1804–1876

II-952.   Journey Wthin the Crystal. 1865. Trans. of *Laura: Voyage dans le cristal* by Pauline Pearson-Stamps. Peter Lang, 1992.

A visionary fantasy inspired by reading Verne's *Journey to the Centre of the Earth* (in manuscript). The narrator explains how he was driven by frustration in love to accompany his uncle on an exploratory expedition, sailing in the brig *Tantalus* in search of a polar paradise; they discover that the world is a massive geode whose interior structure is elaborately crystalline. A strange fusion of Vernian romance and Romantic allegory, akin to Hunt's *Panthea.* (BS)
    Themes: Fantastic Voyages

Sanders, William, U.S., 1942–

II-953.   Are We Having Fun Yet? Wildside, 2002.

Short stories by a talented Native American SF writer. "The Undiscovered," which concerns William Shakespeare's adventures in North America, won the Sideways Award for alternate history and was a Hugo and Nebula nominee. Other excellent stories include "Words and Music" and "When This World is All on Fire." (ML)
    Themes: Alternate Worlds, History in SF

II-954.   The Wild Blue and the Gray. Warner, 1991.

Alternate history as written by a Native American SF writer. The Confederacy has survived the Civil War, largely as a result of its having allied itself with England and the Indian Nations of Oklahoma. When World War I opens, the Confederates are England's main ally against Germany. Cherokee ace pilot Amos Ninekiller and his good friend Will Faulkner set out to do battle against the Hun. Compare Sargent's *Climb the Wind* and Turtledove's *The Guns of the South* and *How Few Remain.* (ML)
    Themes: Alternate Worlds, History in SF, War

Sarban (pseud. of John W. Wall), U.K., 1910–1989

*II-955.   The Sound of His Horn. Davies, 1952. Recommended ed.: Ballantine, 1960.

A British POW "escapes" from a Nazi prison camp into an alternate future world in which the Nazis have won World War II. The story takes place on a forested estate where feudal barons stage great hunts with humans as prey (hence the story's title). An understated but quite harrowing tale. Compare the even more chilling "Weihnachtsabend" by Keith Roberts, in the Hartwell anthology *World Treasury of Science Fiction*; contrast the Japanese-occupied San Francisco locale in Dick's *The Man in the High Castle*. (PC)

Themes: Alternate Worlds

Sargent, Pamela, U.S., 1948–

II-956.   Alien Child. Harper, 1988.

YA. Having been revived by their alien-guardians from a frozen embryonic status, Nita and Sven, discovering they are the only living human beings on Earth, decide after some misgivings to revive the other frozen human embryos and restore human life to Earth. Provocative concept and plausible depiction of adolescent sexuality, both human and alien. Contrast Hamilton's *Justice and Her Brothers*. (FM)

Themes: Aliens, Children in SF, Sex in SF

II-957.   Climb the Wind: A Novel of Another America. HarperCollins, 1998.

In this alternate history, a charismatic Lakota chief unites the nations of the Great Plains and leads a conquering army east against the post-Civil War United States. Lemuel Rowland, a Seneca Indian, but also a Washington bureaucrat, must make a difficult choice between his adopted culture and the native culture he has abandoned. Compare Sanders's *The Wild Blue and the Gray* and Turtledove's *Guns of the South*. (ML)

Themes: Alternate Worlds, History in SF, Politics

II-958.   Cloned Lives. Fawcett, 1978.

Sargent takes an unusually realistic look at what it might be like to grow up as the "children" of the first successful human cloning experiment. Paul Swenson is a famous astrophysicist, but his five clones each pursue a different career despite facing almost overwhelming public hostility to their very existence. Compare Cherryh's *Cyteen*. (ML)

Themes: Biology, Children in SF, Clones/Cloning

II-959.   Earthseed. Harper, 1983.

YA. Zoheret and her young companions, artificially born and raised aboard ship, struggle to colonize Hollow, contending against their own inner doubts and the hostility of other human colonizers. Attractive characters, unexpected plotting, and perceptive insight into social and political organizations make the narrative superior storytelling. Compare Karl's *But We Are Not of Earth* (1981); contrast Ames's *Anna to the Infinite Power*. (FM)

Themes: Colonization of Other Worlds, Genetic Engineering

II-960.   The Shore of Women. Crown, 1986.

In a post-holocaust world, women live in high-tech cities, while men dwell among ruins and wilderness, worshiping women as gods. Birana is cast out from the city into the wilderness. There she meets Arvil and, eventually, falls in love. *The Shore of Women* differs from most of the separatist novels that have appeared over the past quarter-century in that it sees the separation of men and women as less than desirable and takes strong exception to the concept of the all-female state as utopia. Compare Tepper's *The Gate to Women's Country* and Brin's *Glory Season*. (ML)

Themes: Dystopias, Feminist SF, Religion

II-961.   Venus of Dreams. Bantam, 1986. Series: Venus.

A long novel about the relationship between two people involved in a project to terraform Venus. The book is carefully constructed and delicately handled, with some striking imagery to set off the love story. The political background is complex. In the sequel, *Venus of Shadows* (1988), humans have descended to the partially terraformed surface, living in domed cities. Although the settlers are able to control the planet, they are unable to control themselves, and political and religious rivalries begin to tear the colony apart. A third volume in the series, *Child of Venus*, appeared in 2000. Compare Robinson's *Red Mars*. (ML/BS)

Themes: Colonization of Other Worlds, Politics, Religion

Sawyer, Robert J., Canada, 1960–

II-962.   Calculating God. Tor, 2000.

An alien paleontologist comes to the Royal Ontario Museum to study the five great extinction events that have hit our planet over the ages and offers human paleontologist Tom Jericho evidence that similar events have struck worlds circling other stars at the exact same time. The alien further insists on seeing this synchronicity as proof of God's existence. Sawyer does a fine job of developing both his human and his alien protagonists. This is an unusually thoughtful novel, which finished second for the Hugo Award and features serious discussion of issues not often considered in science fiction. Compare Blish's *A Case of Conscience*. (ML)

Themes: Aliens, Anthropology, Religion

II-963.   Factoring Humanity. Tor, 1998.

In the second decade of the 21st century, Heather is a psychologist who has devoted her life to translating messages from outer space. Her husband Kyle is a computer scientist on the verge of a major breakthrough. Their marriage, however, is a train wreck, due in part to the strain put upon it by the suicide of their oldest daughter. Then things get immensely worse, when their younger daughter accuses Kyle of molesting her. Just as things are about to explode, Heather succeeds in cracking the alien message and discovers that it is a blueprint for a device that, among other things, allows her to read Kyle's thoughts and exonerate him. Sawyer's novel differs from most tales of first contact in that it centers on the important, but small-scale effects such an event might have on individual human beings. Compare Sagan's *Contact.* (ML)

Themes: Aliens, Paranormal Powers, Psychology

*II-964.   Hominids. Tor, 2002. Series: Neanderthal Parallax.

In the first volume of the Neanderthal Parallax trilogy, physicist Ponter Boddit, who comes from an alternate universe where Neanderthals are Earth's dominant life form, accidentally crosses between worlds and ends up in a Canadian physics lab. Neanderthal civilization is radically different from others and Boddit finds himself profoundly confused by humanity, despite the help of paleoanthropologist Mary Vaughan. Meanwhile, back in Boddit's universe, his partner and fellow scientist, Adikor, has been accused of Boddit's murder and Boddit's daughter Jasmel works desperately to reopen the path between worlds so that her father can return and exonerate his friend. Sawyer does a brilliant job of highlighting the differences between human and Neanderthal society. Later, equally well-done volumes in the series are *Humans* (2003) and *Hybrids* (2003), the latter of which won the Hugo Award. (ML)

Themes: Anthropology, Parallel Worlds, Scientists and Engineers, Sociology

*II-965.   The Terminal Experiment. HarperPrism, 1995.

In this well-done thriller, computer scientist Peter Hobson creates three AI versions of himself to test his theories concerning the afterlife. One of them lacks all knowledge of aging or death and is designed to believe itself immortal. The second has no memory of physical life and is designed to simulate life after death. The third is the control; it is, to the extent possible, a clone of Hobson himself. Eventually all three AIs escape onto the Net and one of them proves to be a murderer. More action-oriented than most of his later work, this novel nonetheless features Sawyer's trademark interest in the thoughtful exploration of important ideas. Compare Cadigan's *Synners.* (ML)

Awards: Nebula

Themes: Computers, Immortality, Intelligence

Saxton, Josephine, U.K., 1935–

II-966.   Queen of the States. Women's Press, 1986.

Magdalen is confined in a mental hospital because people think she suffers from delusions; she coexists in several realities, in one of which she is politely studied by aliens interested in the mysteries of human sexuality. Lively and witty, with a profusion of deft ironies. Compare Vonnegut's *Slaughterhouse-Five* and Piercy's *Woman on the Edge of Time.* (BS)

Themes: Feminist SF, Psychology

II-967.   The Travails of Jane Saint and Other Stories. Women's Press, 1986.

In the title short novel (first published separately in 1980) the heroine, imprisoned in a sensory deprivation tank awaiting brainwashing, embarks on a dreamquest in search of her lost children, hoping perhaps also to save the world. The sequel novella, *Jane Saint and the Backlash* (1989), published jointly with the novella *The Consciousness Machine*, concerns Jane's second trip into the Unconscious, which she takes in a quest to counteract renewed hostility toward women. Saxton has stated that both the Jane Saint stories and *The Consciousness Machine* are attempts to explore the Collective Unconscious as if it were an actual physical place. Compare and contrast Russ's *Extra(ordinary) People*. (ML/BS)

   Themes: Feminist SF, Psychology, Women in SF

Schachner, Nat(haniel), U.S., 1895–1955

II-968.   "Past, Present and Future." *Astounding Stories*, September 1937.

The first element of a five-part story series—better regarded as an episodic novel, although it was never reprinted as such—in which three heroes in a fragmented far-future America try to rally opposition to an impending invasion by fascist hordes. Various ideological excuses are offered for refusal to join in the common cause, not only on the perversely extreme "Island of the Individualists" (1938) but in the technologically sophisticated "City of the Cosmic Rays" (1939). The unfortunate but seemingly inevitable result is to leave the necessary opposition to the "City of the Corporate Mind" (1939), whose communistic totalitarianism has the will as well as the means. A precursor of the paranoid political fantasies of the Cold War, this was pulp SF's most extravagant equivalent of such hyped-up British parables as O'Neill's *Land Under England* and Marvell's *Minimum Man*. (BS)

   Themes: War

Schenck, Hilbert, U.S., 1926–

II-969.   At the Eye of the Ocean. Pocket Books/Timescape, 1980.

A novel about individuals whose extraordinary sensitivity to the sea enables them to locate the places and times at which a mystical moment of enlightenment is available to those who ardently desire it. Finely realized background (Cape Cod at widely spaced intervals of history) and effective writing; mystical SF at its best. (BS)

   Themes: Religion

II-970.   A Rose for Armageddon. Pocket Books/Timescape, 1982.

As a new dark age looms, a handful of aging intellectuals race to finish a project in the computer simulation of social relationships in the history of a small island. A mystery emerges whose solution may offer an opportunity for redemption not only to the unhappy characters but also to their unhappy era. Poignant and beautifully written; highly original in its recompilation of the timeslip romance. Compare and contrast Finney's *Time and Again*. (BS)\

Themes: Time Travel

Schlee, Ann, U.K., 1934–

*II-971. The Vandal. Macmillan, 1979.

YA. Placed under psychological care because of his act of vandalism, Paul slowly realizes that the daily Drink, which all must take, no longer is making him immune to the "contamination" of memory, the past, and history. Impressive story: taut narrative pace, Kafkaesque atmosphere, and insightful study of once-benevolent government gone bad. Compare Westall's *Futuretrack 5* and Lowry's *The Giver*. (FM/ML)

Themes: Disaster, Dystopias, Psychology

Schroeder, Karl, Canada, 1962–

II-972. Permanence. Tor, 2002.

Rue Cassels, a young woman living on a decaying, backwater habitat orbiting a brown dwarf star, is on the run, having been threatened with slavery by her brother, when she discovers an abandoned starship filled with advanced technology. Her discovery sets off a firestorm of interstellar intrigue as various factions maneuver for control of the starship and the power its advanced technology represents. Schroeder's Cycler Compact civilization is extremely well-realized and so full of fascinatingly idiosyncratic ideas that the book works as well as *Ventus* (2000), an earlier an equally powerful novel. (ML)

Themes: Far Future, Space Opera

Scott, Melissa, U.S., 1960–

II-973. Dream Ships. Tor, 1992.

Reverdy Jian, a starship pilot, is hired to fly to the planet Refuge and find her employer's brother, but the computer that helps run their ship appears to have achieved artificial intelligence. Reverdy and her crew must decide whether or not the computer should therefore be accorded human rights. Scott's novel is set in a well-thought-out future and sets the stage for its even stronger sequel, *Dreaming Metal* (1997), in which Reverdy and two other protagonists, a stage magician and a musician, have further run-ins with newly aware AIs. Both novels demonstrate Scott's trademark interest in class and class warfare. Compare Gerrold's *When HARLIE Was One*. (ML)

Themes: Computers, Feminist SF, Intelligence, Women in SF

II-974. The Jazz. Tor, 2001.

Tin Lizzy is a hacker/artist who specializes in the "jazz," the Internet's latest art form, a combination of personality journalism, gossip, online pranks, and creative lies. Lizzy senses that one of her collaborators, a boy named Keyz who does work brilliant beyond his years, may not be on the up and up and she eventually discovers that much of his brilliance is due to his use of a stolen and highly illegal expert program. Soon Lizzy and Keyz find themselves on the run from a monomaniacal security agent who wants the program back and them dead. This simple plot line allows Scott to explore a variety of bizarre and occasionally very funny postmodern American pocket cultures. (ML)

Themes: Crime and Punishment, Satirical SF, Sociology, Virtual Reality

II-975.　Shadow Man. Tor, 1995.

As a result of mutations induced by faster-than-light travel, humanity has evolved into five distinct sexes, but the backwards planet of Hara refuses to recognize this fact and forces its citizens to define themselves legally as either male or female. This causes serious tensions between Hara and the rest of human space, but it allows Warreven, a "herm" native to Hara, the opportunity to overcome the gender straitjacket within which he's been forced to spend his entire life. This thoughtful novel received the Lambda Award for outstanding SF with gay content. Compare Stephen Leigh's *Dark Water's Embrace* (1998). (ML)

Themes: Feminist SF, Life on Other Worlds, Mutants, Sex in SF

*II-976.　Trouble and Her Friends. Tor, 1994.

Scott's most popular novel, which might be labeled feminist cyberpunk, tells the story of Cerise and Trouble, two young lesbians who make a living hacking computer networks and stealing industrial secrets. Eventually, like many young hackers, the women go straight and get legitimate jobs in the field. Then they break up. Years later Cerise discovers that someone is impersonating Trouble on the Web, hacking industrial secrets, and intentionally spreading viruses. The two team up again to stop the attacks and clear Trouble's name. Unlike many cyberpunk novels, Scott's book devotes significant space to personality development and interpersonal relationships. Compare Gibson's *Neuromancer* and Cadigan's *Synners*. (ML).

Themes: Crime and Punishment, Cyberpunk, Feminist SF, Women in SF

Seaborn, Adam (unattributed pseudonym)

II-977.　Symzonia: A Voyage of Discovery. Seymour, 1820.

A voyage to the interior of the Earth following a scheme popularized by John Cleve Symmes, now more interesting as an early American image of a utopian society than as a parodic fantastic voyage. J. O. Bailey, overlooking or disregarding the sly sarcasm in the references to his supposed genius, suggested that Symmes might have been the author. The account of the ideal society is also somewhat tongue-in-cheek, in which respect it invites comparison with Zaronovitch's *Mizora*. (BS)

Serviss, Garrett P(utnam), U.S., 1851–1929

II-978.   A Columbus of Space. Appleton, 1911.

YA. An interplanetary novel in the vein of the English Vernians—even to the extent of employing an antigravity technology, albeit an atomic-powered one. It was serialized in *All-Story* in 1909, although it is essentially a boys' book. Its depiction of Venus, featuring hairy anthropoid hordes and other monsters as well as blond telepathic human inhabitants equipped with airfleets, may have given some slight inspiration to Edgar Rice Burroughs. (BS)
    Themes: Life on Other Worlds, Space Flight

II-979.   The Second Deluge. McBride Nast, 1912.

A disaster novel serialized in *The Cavalier* in 1911, in which Noachian scientist Cosmo Versal constructs an ark when he discovers that Earth is about to have a close encounter with a watery nebula. Another party of American survivors employs an experimental airship, while the Frenchmen aboard the submarine *Jules Verne* are also untroubled. The enthusiasm with which Serviss contemplates the disaster and its adventure-rich aftermath proved infectious—the first part of England's *Darkness and Dawn* was deliberately overlapped with it in order to hold its audience a little longer. (BS)
    Themes: Disaster

Severn, David (pseud. of David Unwin), U.K., 1918–

II-980.   The Future Took Us. Bodley Head, 1957.

YA. A timeslip narrative. Two boys, Peter and Dick, are carried forward into a Great Britain of A.D. 3000 via a machine devised by the Calculators, who venerate mathematics and reason and dominate the masses who are growing increasingly restive and seeking liberty under the leadership of a handful of aristocrats. A provocative look at a future England controlled by an elite and devastated by social unrest, which predates similar portraits by both Peter Dickinson (the Changes trilogy, 1968–1970) and John Christopher (the Luke trilogy, 1970–1973). (FM/SM)
    Themes: Dystopias, Time Travel

Shanks, Edward (Richard Buxton), U.K., 1892–1953

*II-981.   The People of the Ruins. Collins, 1920.

The first of many British novels published in the aftermath of World War I that preached the lesson that the next such conflict was bound to institute an irredeemable reversal of social and technological progress. The hero, a Wellsian sleeper, yearns to reverse that trend, but his quest is hopeless in a world where his only value is his knowledge of armaments. Compare Desmond's *Ragnarok* and Gloag's *To-Morrow's Yesterday*. (BS)

Themes: War

Shaw, Bob, Northern Ireland, 1931–1996

II-982.   Orbitsville. Gollancz, 1975. Series: Orbitsville.

The protagonist is forced to flee from Earth when he incurs the wrath of his imperious employer, and discovers a vast artificial sphere surrounding a sun, which offers apparently unlimited opportunities for human colonists. A sequel, *Orbitsville Departure* (1983), is a taut thriller in whose climax the purpose of Orbitsville is revealed. The trilogy concludes with *Orbitsville Judgment* (1990). Inevitably invites comparison with Niven's *Ringworld*, although the books are very different in tone and technique and a more apt comparison is to Simak's *Ring Around the Sun*. (BS)

Themes: Colonization of Other Worlds, Hard SF

II-983.   Other Days, Other Eyes. Gollancz, 1972.

A fix-up novel featuring one of the most ingenious SF inventions, "slow glass," which is quite transparent but lets light through so slowly that the image may take years to emerge. The book presents a marvelous study of the possible applications of the substance and its impact on society, incorporating some fine vignettes (including the brilliant "Light of Other Days"). A thoughtful and painstaking exercise in extrapolation, demonstrating how an apparently trivial and by no means implausible innovation would have dramatic and far-reaching effects; a key thought experiment in the sociology of technology. (BS)

Themes: Machines

II-984.   The Palace of Eternity. Ace, 1969.

A thriller in which it transpires that humans have alien commensals that secure a kind of life after death—but the aliens are under threat of destruction as a side effect of a new technology. Thematically fascinating; compare Simak's *Time and Again* (1951) and Martin's *A Song for Lya* (1976). (BS)

Themes: Aliens, Immortality

II-985.   The Ragged Astronauts. Gollancz, 1980. Series: Land and Overland.

In a planetary system where two worlds share a common atmosphere, the inhabitants of one are forced by circumstance to migrate to the other in hot air balloons. An unusual adventure story in which good characterizations helps to make extraordinary events plausible. The somewhat less successful sequels are *The Wooden Spaceships* (1988) and *The Fugitive Worlds* (1989). (BS/ML)

Themes: Fantastic Voyages, Life on Other Worlds

II-986.   The Two-Timers. Ace, 1968.

The protagonist, traumatized by the death of his wife, transports himself into an alternate world where he saves her, but then faces a problematic confrontation with his other self when the unforeseen side effects of his displacement disrupt the space-time continuum. A tense and dramatic thriller, convincingly handled. (BS).

Themes: Alternate Worlds

Shaw, George Bernard, Ireland/U.K., 1856–1950

II-987. **Back to Methuselah: A Metabiological Pentateuch.** Constable, 1921.

A classic drama, extremely difficult to present on stage, whose first and last acts are Biblical allegory but whose intermediate phases offer snapshots of a future history in which enlightened humans seize the Lamarckian opportunity (whose logic is elaborately defended in the preface) to engineer their own evolution. Their first desire is longevity, but their ultimate destiny is to forsake the flesh altogether to become beings of "pure thought"—one of the alternative images of ultimate evolutionary destiny that became standardized in both scientific romance and pulp SF. Compare and contrast Odle's *The Clockwork Man.* (BS)

Themes: Evolution

Shea, Robert, U.S., 1933–1994 and Wilson, Robert Anton, U.S., 1932–

II-988. **The Illuminatus! Trilogy.** Dell, 1984.

An omnibus edition of a three-decker novel whose separate parts—*The Eye in the Pyramid, The Golden Apple,* and *Leviathan*—first appeared in 1975. A wild extravaganza that hypothesizes that all the secret societies claiming access to a special enlightenment were and are part of huge conspiracy that will take over Earth unless the heroes of the counterculture can stop them. A crazy compendium of contemporary concerns. Compare Pynchon's *Gravity's Rainbow.* (BS)

Themes: Absurdist SF

Sheckley, Robert, U.S., 1933–

II-989. **Dimensions of Miracles.** Dell, 1968.

The winner of a galactic sweepstake finds problems returning home with his prize, passing through various absurd parallel Earths, perennially threatened by imminent death. Less chaotic than the later bizarre odyssey, *Options* (1977), and more imaginative than the convoluted *Dramocles* (1983), but not up to the standard of the earlier *Journey Beyond Tomorrow* (1962). Sadly demonstrates the difficulty that Sheckley has in developing his brilliant comic writing at novel length. This novel was collected in 2001 with *Immortality, Inc, Minotaur Maze, Journey Beyond Tomorrow,* and *Mindswap* in the omnibus volume *Dimensions of Sheckley.* (BS/ML)

Themes: Humorous SF, Parallel Worlds

II-990.   Immortality, Inc. Bantam, 1959. Variant title: *Immortality Delivered.* Avalon, 1958.

"Immortality" in SF has usually meant biological longevity, as in Vance's *To Live Forever* or Anderson's *The Boat of a Million Years*. In Sheckley's variant, science has discovered an actual afterlife complete with real ghosts, and an ever-ingenious capitalism has figured out a way to market it. Dark comedy, of which Sheckley was a master, with serious social commentary underlying the fast-moving surface adventure. Compare Pohl and Kornbluth's *The Space Merchants*; contrast Heinlein's *Stranger in a Strange Land.* (PC)

Themes: Immortality

II-991.   Is *That* What People Do? Holt, 1984.

This collection recombines stories from earlier collections, as did *The Wonderful World of Robert Sheckley* (1979). A five-volume set collected 132 stories, *The Collected Short Stories of Robert Sheckley* (Pulphouse, 1991). His stories are very funny, but the humor is generally underlaid with a dark and serious suspicion of the follies of human vanity. His robot stories are exceptionally fine and should be compared and contrasted with the Asimov stories, whose themes they often subvert and mock. Compare also the short fiction of John Sladek. (BS)

Themes: Humorous SF

II-992.   Notions: Unlimited. Bantam, 1960.

Twelve stories from 1952 to 1957, in which the dangerous folly of quick technological fixes is a common theme, as is the maladaptability of humans to alien planets. Some readers may prefer the tales in *Pilgrim to Earth* (Bantam, 1957), whose title story's basic idea is given a sharp, savage, and, some would say, sexist twist in the end. The stories in this earlier collection have a flavor like that of New York standup comedy routines, but are more coherent and blacker in their humor. (PC)

*II-993.   Untouched by Human Hands. Ballantine, 1954.

Sheckley's first story collection, and a brilliant debut, contains "Seventh Victim," in which an otherwise conventional near-future society sanctions the lethal but apparently stress-reducing game of Hunter and Victim; it was made into an effective film, *Tenth Victim.* "The Monsters," a straight-faced exercise in cultural relativism, has one of the most startling opening lines in all fiction. The U.K. edition (M. Joseph, 1955) drops and replaces two stories. Sheckley represented an early break with, and fresh contrast to, the styles and themes of Golden Age SF. (PC)

Sheffield, Charles, U.K./U.S., 1935–2002

II-994.   Brother to Dragons. Baen, 1992.

In a future America where the Royal Hundred run everything from their luxurious Mall compound, most Americans live in polluted, disintegrating slums. Job

Salk, the deformed child of one such slum dweller, is saved by a nurse in a charity ward and ends up in an orphanage. Father Bonifant, Chief Steward of Cloak House, teaches him the value of hard work and sends the boy, now six years of age, out into the street to borrow, earn, or otherwise acquire the necessities of life for the orphanage. Sheffield has a reputation as a hard SF writer, but this touching novel owes more to Charles Dickens than it does to John W. Campbell. (ML)

Awards: John W. Campbell
Themes: Coming of Age, Dystopias

II-995. Sight of Proteus. Ace, 1978. Series: Proteus.

Tracks the 23rd-century development and eventual application of a technology of transmutation allowing human bodies to be reshaped and augmented. Although treated with great suspicion, the techniques ultimately prove themselves of immense value. In the sequel, *Proteus Unbound* (1989), 30 years have passed and a revolutionary has discovered a way to interfere with the delicate computers that govern human transformation. Behrooz Wolf, the protagonist of the earlier novel, is called out of retirement to stop him. *Proteus Combined* (1994) is a one-volume edition of the first two books in the series. *Proteus in the Underworld* (1995) continues the series. Sheffield isn't strong on character development, but his novels invariably feature superb scientific speculation. (ML/BS)

Themes: Biology, Computers, Intelligence

Sheffield, Charles, U.K./U.S., 1935–2002 and Pournelle, Jerry, U.S., 1933–

II-996. Higher Education. Tor, 1996. Series: The Jupiter Novels.

YA. The first volume in the Jupiter series of novels set in the same future history and reminiscent of the Heinlein juveniles of the 1950s. In the 21st century, American public education is at the point of collapse. Rick, a bright teenager, is expelled from a high school where he's obviously wasting his time anyway and signs up with an asteroid mining company where he not only receives a formal education but also learns to be a man. Well-done hard SF with a decidedly didactic conservative/libertarian message. Volumes two through four in the series—*The Billion Dollar Boy* (1997), *Putting Up Roots* (1997), and *The Cyborg from Earth* (1998)—were written by Sheffield alone, with the (apparently) final volume, *Starswarm*, written by Pournelle. (ML)

Themes: Coming of Age, Future History

Shelley, Mary Wollstonecraft, U.K., 1797–1851

*II-997. Frankenstein; or, The Modern Prometheus. Lackington Hughes, 3 vols., 1818 (published anonymously).

A classic gothic fantasy in which hubris alloyed with scientific method leads the eponymous anti-hero to emulate the Creator. His Adam, cast out of Eden by a bitter look, becomes a resentful Monster. The first SF novel, if "novel" is narrowly defined. Brian Aldiss, in *Billion Year Spree* [9–4], also hailed it as the root text of the entire genre, although enthusiasts for scientific progress tend to resent the implication. Isaac Asimov complained about the development of a "Frankenstein syndrome" whose unthinking assumption is that all inventions are likely to turn destructively on their creators, although the fact that the story arc is so common probably has more to do with its dramatic convenience (and lack of similarly qualified opposition) than with the innate technophobia of its users. Most modern reprints follow the revised text of 1831, to which Mary Shelley added a preface of her own to supplement the one her husband had provided for the first edition. Two editions reprint the 1818 edition: one edited by James Rieger (Bobb-Merrill, 1974), which includes variations and notes, and the other edited by Leonard Wolf (Clarkson Potter, 1977), which includes many illustrations along with notes. (BS)

Themes: Discoveries and Inventions

II-998.   The Last Man. Henry Colburn, 3 vols., 1826.

A lachrymose apocalyptic fantasy whose narrative attitude draws on the inspiration of "graveyard poetry"—Edward Young's *Night Thoughts* (1742–1744) had been reissued in 1817, bundled with a paraphrase of *Job* called *The Grave* and Bishop Porteous's homily on *Death*—to melodramatize the author's mourning of her husband as a requiem for all humankind. The selected method of execution is a great plague. Contrast Cousin de Grainville's *The Last Man* and Thomas Campbell's poem "The Last Man" (1823), which take far more consolation from religion than Mary Shelley could. (BS)

Shepard, Lucius, U.S., 1947–

II-999.   Green Eyes. Ace, 1984.

Scientific researchers reanimate corpses biotechnologically, introducing new personalities. One of these "zombies" escapes in the company of a female doctor and gradually acquires superhuman powers that enable him to find out the truth behind voodoo mythology and the true purpose of the project that created him. Shepard's first novel is powerful combination of horror and SF motifs. Compare Matheson's *I Am Legend*. (BS/ML)

Themes: Biology, Mythology, Science Fantasy

*II-1000. The Jaguar Hunter. Arkham, 1987.

One of the finest collections of fantasy and science fiction published in the 1980s. Probably the best story included is the Nebula- and *Locus* Award-winning "R&R," the tale of an American soldier on leave from a future war in Central America, which was later incorporated into Shepard's second novel, *Life During Wartime*. Other outstanding stories, many of them award nominees, include "The End of Life as We Know It," "A Traveler's Tale," "The Man Who Painted the Dragon Griaule," and "A Spanish Lesson." Shepard's second volume of short stories, *The Ends of the Earth* (1991), a World Fantasy Award nominee, includes such fine pieces as "Delta Sly Honey," "Shades," "The Ends of the Earth," and "Surrender." Later, almost equally good collections, include *Barnacle Bill the Spacer and Other Stories* (1997), *Beast of the Heartland* (1999), and *Two Trains Running* (2004). Compare Tiptree's *Tales of the Quintana Roo* (1986). (ML)

Awards: World Fantasy, *Locus*

*II-1001. Life During Wartime. Bantam, 1987.

Based in part on Shepard's Nebula Award-winning novella, "R&R," and several other short stories, this is the tale of David Mingolla, a psychic drafted to fight in a near-future, Vietnam-style conflict in Central America. Like many fix-up novels, *Life During Wartime* suffers from occasional discontinuities, but the language is brilliant, and Shepard's searing portrayal of the soul-destroying immorality of contemporary warfare rivals that to be found in such films as *Apocalypse Now* and *Platoon*. Compare also McAllister's *Dream Baby*. (ML)

Themes: Paranormal Powers, Politics, Psychology, War

Sherriff, R(obert) C(edric), U.K., 1896–1975

II-1002.   The Hopkins Manuscript. Gollancz, 1939.

A satirical disaster story by the author of the World War I drama *Journey's End* (1929), in which a collision between Earth and the Moon becomes the prelude to a conflict to exploit the fallen Moon's resources, whose deflection of attention away from the possibility of reconstruction completes the ignominious defeat of civilization. The last of the many speculative works produced in Britain between the two world wars that propose that the unlearned lessons of the first will make the next even more terrible. It also prefigures the quintessentially English disaster novels of John Wyndham and his imitators, embodying a similarly ambivalent attitude. (BS)

Themes: Disaster

Shiel, M(atthew) P(hipps), U.K., 1865–1947

II-1003.   The Lord of the Sea. Grant Richards, 1901.

Intended as the second unit of a loosely knit trilogy of novels fusing scientific romance with religious fantasy (although the first, *The Last Miracle*, was not published until 1907), *The Lord of the Sea* offers an elaborate account of the career of a new Jewish messiah. Initially an unwitting outcast from his own people, he takes out his resentment on the entire world by setting up a series of floating forts to control sea traffic before his Judas obligingly redirects him—exiled, along with his people, to Palestine—to his true destiny: using advanced scientific knowledge to make the Promised Land flow with milk and honey. The original version, couched in an elaborately Decadent style, is superior to later abridged editions. (BS)

Themes: Coming of Age

*II-1004. The Purple Cloud. Chatto and Windus, 1901.

The third unit of the trilogy whose second part was *The Lord of the Sea*, this classic apocalyptic fantasy is a fabular transfiguration of the Book of Job. Adam Jeffson, the sole survivor of a polar expedition, returns south to find the human race obliterated by an outrush of cyanogen gas, now dissipated. He lives as a mad emperor among the ruins for many years before finding another survivor: a girl whom he refuses to accept as his Eve until he can come to a proper understanding of humankind's place in the universal evolutionary scheme. The first version—reprinted in 2004 by Tartarus Press—is preferable to the more familiar toned-down abridgement. (BS)

Themes: End of the World

II-1005. The Yellow Danger. Grant Richards, 1898.

Shiel's first scientific romance, a future-war story commissioned for *Short Stories* (1898 as "The Empress of the Earth") as that periodical's contribution to the glut of George Griffith imitations. Here the coming world war is envisaged as a racial conflict between East and West, personalized as a duel for the heroine's affections between English naval officer Jack Hardy and the Chinese genius Yen How. The conflict is ultimately settled by biological warfare. Shiel modified the racist attitude of the text considerably in a conscientiously evenhanded extrapolation of the Russo-Japanese war, *The Yellow Wave*, and a more carefully balanced retread, *The Dragon* (1913; rev. as *The Yellow Peril*), but still lent inspiration to a whole subgenre of "yellow peril" stories, whose most conspicuous examples are Sax Rohmer's series featuring Fu Manchu (launched in 1913). (BS)

Themes: War

*II-1006. The Young Men Are Coming! Allen and Unwin, 1937.

A scientist abducted aboard a passing spaceship is returned to Earth with a rejuvenating serum, with whose aid he founds a revolutionary social movement. The forces of reaction mass against the Young Men, whose rashness tends to obscure and frustrate their progressive ambition; a reckless challenge issued to a religious fundamentalist to compete in the raising of a storm proves too successful when the tempest released by superhuman science devastates the planet. In stark contrast to the vast majority of those who worked in the shadow of Mary Shelley's *Frankenstein*, Shiel does not permit his imaginative exuberance to be entirely undermined by his querulous uncertainties. (BS)

Themes: Evolution

Shiner, Lewis, U.S., 1950–

II-1007. Frontera. Baen, 1984.

Fairly traditional SF novel written by a member of the cyberpunk movement. Frontera, NASA's Mars colony, has been abandoned for 10 years, but the giant corporation Pulsystems has now mounted a dangerous mission hoping to bring back a mysterious treasure from the Red Planet, possibly some form of new technology. Kane, a corporate mercenary hired for the trip, finds himself programmed to do Pulsystems's bidding no matter how strange things get. A well-done, gritty adventure story. Compare Allen Steele's *Labyrinth of Night* (1992) and contrast Terry Bisson's *Voyage to the Red Planet*. (ML)

Themes: Colonization of Other Worlds, Cyberpunk, The Planets

Shiras, Wilmar H., U.S., 1908–1990

II-1008. Children of the Atom. Gnome, 1953.

Originally a series in *Astounding* that began with "In Hiding," whose supergenius young hero carefully conceals his higher intelligence from the normals around him; a situation familiar to anyone who was a bright kid roughly handled by parents, other adults, or peers. Most prodigies do work their way through the problem, and so it is with David and a handful of other supernormal children who were produced as mutants by an atomic power explosion. They are helped out of their isolation by a sympathetic psychiatrist and emerge into society to make the world better; the world's willingness to take their advice is, alas, less plausible. Compare Kuttner and Moore's *Mutant*; contrast Stapledon's *Odd John*. (PC)

Themes: Children in SF, Supermen/women

Shirley, John, U.S., 1953–

II-1009. Eclipse. Bluejay, 1985. Series: A Song Called Youth.

In Shirley's A Song Called Youth series, set in the early 21st century, the United States is bogged down in a non-nuclear war with the Soviet Union while Europe has been taken over by the intensely racist, neo-fascist Second Alliance. Led by a motley crew of rock musicians, anarchists, and counterculture types, the Resistance struggles valiantly to stem the tide of right-wing domination. The second and third volumes, *Eclipse Penumbra* (1988) and *Eclipse Corona* (1990), play down the cyberpunkish special effects of volume one as Shirley concentrates on a more straightforward presentation of guerrilla warfare. Compare Sinclair Lewis's *It Can't Happen Here* and Walter Jon Williams's *Hardwired*. (ML)

Themes: Cyberpunk, War

II-1010. Heatseeker. Scream/Press, 1989.

A mixed collection of reprint and original science fiction, horror, and surrealism, by one of the genre's more radical innovators and a cofounder of the cyberpunk movement. Particularly powerful are the very dark new story "Equilibrium" and the stunning cyberpunk tale, "Wolves of the Plateau." Few writers are capable of getting away with so much over-the-top craziness. Compare Ellison's *Alone Against Tomorrow* and *Shatterday*. (ML)

Shusterman, Neal, U.S., 1962–

II-1011.   The Scorpion Shards. Tor, 1995. Series: Star Shards.

YA. Like a particularly unpleasant group of X-Men, six teenagers with super-powers, terrible attitudes, and serious physical imperfections (we're talking things like killer acne, major obesity, and permanent horniness), first find each other and then chase down the possibly extraterrestrial source of their prob-lems. Although the overwrought action may seem comic book-like at times, and there's enough gratuitous grossness to turn off many adult readers, this intense novel, the first in the Star Shards Trilogy, packs a powerful emotional punch. It also teeters on the borderline between science fiction, fantasy, and horror. The sequels are *Thief of Souls* (1999) and *Shattered Sky* (2002). (ML)

Themes: Children in SF, Humorous SF, Paranormal Powers

Shute, Nevil (pseud. of Nevil Shute Norway), U.K., 1899–1960

*II-1012.   On the Beach. Heinemann, 1957.

A nuclear war has happened. Australia is spared material damage and contin-ues a semblance of normal life, but the radiation level has risen to such a level that all humanity is doomed. A U.S. submarine that survived the war fails to find any survivors and returns to Australia, where the government has prepared euthanasia tablets. An effective warning of an all-too-real possibility; even more effective as a film, with understated images of a civilization shutting down. This novel may have had an indirect impact on foreign policy. (PC)

Themes: Holocaust and After

Silverberg, Robert, U.S., 1935–

II-1013.   The Alien Years. HarperPrism, 1998.

Arguably Silverberg's best novel in a quarter of a century. In the near future, aliens land on Earth, taking over our world with little difficulty, and destroying civilization. As the decades pass, human beings continue to exist on the fringes of the new alien society, hiding when necessary, resisting when possible. Silverberg centers this episodic tale on various members of the Carmichael family, who play important roles in fighting and resisting the alien invasion. The novel had its source in Silverberg's "The Pardoner's Tale" (1986). Compare Tenn's *Of Men and Monsters*, Disch's *The Genocides* (1965), or Benford's *Great Sky River*. (ML)

Themes: Aliens, Invasion

II-1014.   The Book of Skulls. Scribner, 1972.

A student finds an ancient manuscript in the rare books room at the university library, which seems to promise immortality if he and three friends can track down the Brotherhood of the Skull. They travel to Arizona on their quest, only to find that what awaits is not immortality but terror and death. Very much a product of the late-1960s and early-1970s fascination with the occult and hallucinogenic transcendent experience, this novel retains a considerable emotional power. Compare Attanasio's *Radix*. (ML)

Themes: Immortality, Religion

*II-1015. The Collected Stories of Robert Silverberg Volume One: Secret Sharers. Bantam, 1992. In U.K. published as two volumes—*The Collected Stories of Robert Silverberg, Volume One: Pluto in the Morning Light* (Grafton, 1992) and *Volume Two: Secret Sharers* (Grafton, 1993).

There are 24 stories collected here, all published between 1981 and 1988. Approximately half made one or more of the "best of the year" anthologies, and a number were award winners or nominees. Among the most memorable stories included are: "Chip Runner," "The Secret Sharer," "Sailing to Byzantium," "A Sleep and a Forgetting," "Enter a Soldier. Later: Enter Another," "The Pardoner's Tale," and "Homefaring. " Silverberg is one of our finest writers of short fiction and the 1980s may well have been his most fertile period. A variety of "best of" collections of Silverberg's work have appeared in both in the U.S. and the U.K. and their relationship to each other can be rather confusing. Numerous earlier collections are also available, among the best of them *Moonferns and Starsongs* (1971), *The Reality Trip and Other Implausibilities* (1972), *Born with the Dead* (1974), *The Conglomeroid Cocktail Party* (1984), and *Beyond the Safe Zone: Collected Short Fiction of Robert Silverberg* (1986). A more recent collection is *In Another Country and Other Short Novels* (2002). *Roma Eterna* (2003) has been marketed as a novel, but is actually a collection of linked stories all set in an alternate universe where the Empire never fell. A major retrospective volume titled *Phases of the Moon* (2004) assembled stories from a six-decade career and includes extensive biographical and story notes. (ML)

*II-1016. Downward to the Earth. Doubleday, 1970.

The guilt-stricken protagonist returns to the alien world where he was once a colonial officer and where he committed crimes for which he now seeks forgiveness and redemption. To become truly human, he must become alien, sharing the religious rituals of the natives and the related processes of physical metamorphosis. A superb novel; one of the best examples of the use of hypothetical biology and alien culture to symbolize problematic aspects of human existence. Compare Le Guin's *The Word for World Is Forest* and Paul Park's *Coelestis*. (BS/ML)

Themes: Aliens, Biology, Life on Other Worlds

*II-1017. Dying Inside. Scribner, 1972.

The story of a telepath whose powers are fading—a loss that may allow him to overcome his alienation from the human world. Told with great intensity and merciless realism; one of the finest works of the period and one of the best examples of the SF novel. Compare Russ's *And Chaos Died*. *The Stochastic Man* is a similar but less impressive story of ESP-related alienation, this time embodied in a story of the acquisition of precognitive abilities. (BS)

Themes: Paranormal Powers

II-1018.   Hawksbill Station. Doubleday, 1968. U.K. title: *The Anvil of Time*, 1969.

A future government sends dissidents back in time to a Cambrian prison camp; moves for their repatriation are made—but can they really be rescued from their spiritual wasteland? A grim story of exile, told with compassion. (BS)

Themes: Crime and Punishment

II-1019.   Lord Valentine's Castle. HarperCollins, 1980. Series: Majipoor.

In the first volume of his popular Majipoor Cycle, a series that sits on the border between fantasy and science fiction, Silverberg paints an elaborate portrait of a gigantic, quasi-medieval world populated by billions of human beings and several alien races. Valentine, a traveling juggler, dreams that he is in fact Lord Valentine, the Coronal, the second most powerful man on the planet, who has been deposed by a complex conspiracy. He soon sets out across Majipoor to discover the truth. Sequels include *Majipoor Chronicles* (1982), *Valentine Pontifex* (1983), *The Mountains of Majipoor* (1995), *Sorcerers of Majipoor* (1996), *Lord Prestimion* (1999), and *King of Dreams* (2001). *Revolt on Majipoor* (1987), part of the Crossroads of Adventure series, is a novel set on Silverberg's world by Matthew J. Costello.

Themes: Life on Other Worlds, Politics, Science Fantasy

II-1020.   The Masks of Time. Ballantine, 1968. U.K. title: *Vornan-19*, 1970.

As the millennial year 2000 approaches, an enigmatic visitor from the future comes to study 20th-century man and is trapped in a quasi-messianic role. Compare Russell Griffin's *Century's End* (1981). Another enigmatic messiah figure is the industrialist in *Tower of Glass* (1970), who builds a new Tower of Babel and is deified by oppressed androids. (BS)

Themes: Androids, Religion, Time Travel

II-1021.   Nightwings. Avon, 1969.

A fix-up novel (first novella, Hugo, 1969) in which a decadent Earth is taken over by aliens who have old scores to settle, but who might offer humankind a path to salvation too. Lushly romantic and elegiac far-future fantasy. (BS)

Themes: Aliens, Far Future

II-1022.   Thorns. Ballantine, 1967.

Two lonely people, alienated by awful experiences, are brought together by a psychic vampire in order that their anguish might feed his extraordinary lust, but they achieve a remarkable transcendence of their predicament. A highly stylized SF fable, comparable to Charles Harness's *The Rose* (1966). (BS)

Themes: Psychology

II-1023. A Time of Changes. Doubleday, 1971.

A colony world preserves a strange culture based on self-hatred, but the protagonist learns individualism from a visiting Earthman and becomes a revolutionary advocate of a new kind of community. Unlike Ayn Rand's *Anthem*, with which it inevitably invites comparison, it is not a political allegory but an exploration of the value of human relationships. (BS)

Awards: Nebula

Themes: Life on Other Worlds

II-1024. Time of the Great Freeze. Holt, 1964.

YA. By A.D. 2230, because of the fifth ice age, cities were forced underground. Centuries later, the inhabitants of these cities, afraid and suspicious, are content with their living conditions and the lack of communication with each other. Jim Barnes and his father, having made radio contact with London, are as a consequence expelled from New York and determine to reach London over the ice. A fast-moving story that also entertains through suggesting what elements in today's civilization might survive after an ice age. Probably the best of Silverberg's several young adult novels. Others include *The Gate of Worlds* (1967) and *Across a Billion Years* (1969). (FM/ML)

Themes: Anthropology, Disaster, Far Future

II-1025. Up the Line. Ballantine, 1969.

A satirical and sexy extrapolation of the "time patrol" theme, in which the protagonist turns outlaw, trying to alter history instead of protecting it, and is appropriately punished. Compare Poul Anderson's *Guardians of Time* (1961). (BS)

Themes: Satirical SF, Time Travel

*II-1026. The World Inside. Doubleday, 1971.

In a crowded future, populations have to be gathered together in massive Urbmons: compact high-rise cities whose culture has set aside ideas of privacy. For some this is a kind of hell, but there can be no escape from it, even to the world outside. Compare T. J. Bass's *Half Past Human* (1971). (BS)

Themes: Cities, Overpopulation

Simak, Clifford D(onald), U.S., 1904–1988

II-1027. The Best of Clifford D. Simak. Ed. by Angus Wells. Sidgwick & Jackson, 1975.

Ten stories from 1939 to 1971. Simak in a modest introduction noted the newspaper experience that influenced his early (not so much his later) work, and accepted with pleasure the "pastoral" label critics have hung on him; one writes about what one loves. Most of these stories deal with usually benign alien–human encounters in a rural Midwest setting, as in "The Sitters," "A Death in the House," and "Shotgun Cure." Simak's Hugo-winning story, "The Big Front

Yard," was omitted but can be found in *The Worlds of Clifford Simak* (1960). Some readers may prefer the selection in *Strangers in the Universe* (1956) or, more recently, *Over the River and Through the Woods: The Best Short Fiction of Clifford Simak* (1996), which assembles eight stories. (PC)

II-1028.   A Choice of Gods. Putnam, 1971.

In a depopulated post-technological world, robots have taken over man's religious quest. An interesting example of SF mysticism, carrying forward themes from *City*; rather more ambitious, despite its relative orthodoxy, than Schenck's *At the Eye of the Ocean*. (BS)

   Themes: Religion, Robots

*II-1029.   City. Gnome, 1952.

Eight quietly told stories from *Astounding*, 1944 to 1951, which describe the decline and disappearance of humanity once it abandons its most characteristic habitat, the city. Some of the more venturesome leave civilization to imprint their psyches on wild, non–tool-using animals native to Jupiter ("Desertion"); others retreat to automated estates, as in "Huddling Place," a locale that recurs in later stories. In book form the stories are framed as "legends," told around campfires by the dogs, who politely debate whether humans in fact ever existed. A haunting, elegiac tale, diametrically opposed to the "can do" spirit of most Golden Age SF. An additional story, "Epilog," was added for a later edition (Ace, 1981). A major work, which won the International Fantasy Award. (PC)

   Awards: International Fantasy

   Themes: Cities, Pastoral

II-1030.   Time Is the Simplest Thing. Doubleday, 1961.

Humans can travel to the stars only telepathically. Fishhook, the organization that sends its employees out on these mental missions, has acquired great economic and political power through its monopoly of the goodies these agents find in space. Then one of its operatives returns from a far planet with his mind linked to that of a benevolent but very strange alien. Parallels are drawn, implicitly, with the Salem witch craze and with the Nazi *Kristallnacht* in 1934. Simak's message, as in so much of his work: trust the unknown, embrace the strange. Compare Henderson's *Pilgrimage* and van Vogt's *Slan*; contrast Robinson's *The Power*. (PC)

   Themes: Aliens, Paranormal Powers

II-1031.   The Visitors. Ballantine, 1980.

Alien "black boxes" descend on Earth in droves, peacefully reproducing themselves and minding their own business. They pay for what they consume, but their payments threaten to precipitate economic chaos. An ironic story to be compared and contrasted with the Strugatskys' *Roadside Picnic*, and more recently, Charles Stross's *Singularity Sky*. (BS/ML)

   Themes: Aliens, Time Travel

*II-1032. Way Station. Doubleday, 1963.

A Civil War veteran comes home to the family farm, which becomes a station for interstellar travelers. Time passes more slowly inside the disguised farmhouse, so that the stationmaster's longevity in the outside world attracts the attention of hostile neighbors and a CIA agent. The story gets its effect from casual juxtaposition of bizarre alien visitors and artifacts with realistic southwestern Wisconsin locale. It carries Simak's perennial message that all sentient beings can and must get along, or perish; the various galactic races face the same danger from themselves as do Earth's own warring peoples. A sentimental but effective story. (PC)

   Awards: Hugo
   Themes: Aliens, Pastoral

Simmons, Dan, U.S., 1948–

*II-1033. Hyperion. Doubleday, 1989. Series: Hyperion.

Hyperion is the first half of one of the most complex space operas ever written. With a structure based on the *Canterbury Tales,* it tells the story of a pilgrimage of sorts to the planet Hyperion, where the Time Tombs, alien artifacts that run backward through time, are about to open. As in Chaucer, each pilgrim has his or her own story to tell; stories that are individually riveting and contribute thematically to the novel as a whole. The book ends just as the travelers reach their destination. The *Locus* Award-winning *The Fall of Hyperion* (1990) takes its inspiration from Keats's poem of the same name. It continues the narration of events at the tombs, but also opens up into a portrait of a sophisticated interstellar culture where teleportation is so basic that people routinely build homes with rooms on more than one planet. Powerful players are interested in the events on Hyperion, and the individual crises faced by the pilgrims may have galaxy-spanning outcomes. The later books in the series, *Endymion* (1996) and *The Rise of Endymion* (1997), are also excellent. The *Hyperion* books suffer from occasional problems of continuity, but they are beautifully written and have few equals for sheer, large-scale sense of wonder. On a somewhat smaller scale, compare Alexander Jablokov's *Carve the Sky*. Compare also Alaistair Reynolds's *Revelation Space* and its sequels. (ML)

   Awards: Hugo, *Locus*
   Themes: Computers, Galactic Empires, Intelligence, Life on Other Worlds, Space Opera

II-1034. Illium. Bantam, 2003.

Far in the future, a small post-human population leads enjoyable, but drone-like lives on Earth. Meanwhile, somewhere else, the battle for Troy is in its ninth year. The combatants, from Achilles to Priam, follow Homer's script while the Gods, or super-human beings who claim to be the Gods, look on and Thomas Hockenberry, a late-20th-century classics professor in their employment, takes careful notes. Meanwhile, representatives of an AI society centered on the outer planets have noticed that something odd is taking place on the planet Mars and have sent an expedition to investigate. This sprawling book is beautifully written and, as one would expect from a Dan Simmons novel, full of allusions to a wide range of great literary works. The second half of the novel, titled *Olympos* (2005), will presumably explain the many mysteries set forth in this volume. (ML)

Themes: Cyborgs, History in SF, Mythology, The Planets, Space Opera

Sinclair, Upton (Beall), U.S., 1878–1968

II-1035.   The Millennium. Werner Laurie, 1924.

A witty adaptation of a satire originally written as a play in 1909, in which the survivors of a worldwide catastrophe fight for control of a food producing machine, reproducing the various economic phases mapped out in Karl Marx's dialectical theory of history. Sinclair subsequently mobilized his radical ideas in a political campaign to End Poverty in California (EPIC). Robert A. Heinlein's involvement in the campaign created the debt whose clearance led him to take up writing pulp SF. (BS)

Themes: Holocaust and After, Satirical SF

Sitwell, Osbert, U.K., 1892–1969

II-1036.   "Triple Fugue" in *Triple Fugue and Other Stories*. Duckworth, 1924.

A stylistically mannered but cutting satirical novella set in 1948, in which the advancement of "human grafting" in the wake of a third World War has greatly increased the capabilities of medical science. Heroic surgical invention after an airplane crash allows one complete individual to be reassembled from three smashed-up bodies—but which of the three identities should he be allowed, or forced, to assume? A graphic response to J. B. S. Haldane's *Daedalus*, similar in spirit to Huxley's *Brave New World*. (BS)

Themes: Satirical SF

Skinner, B(urrhus) F(rederick), U.S., 1904–1990

II-1037.   Walden Two. Macmillan, 1948.

Most post-World War II SF considered social control by psychological conditioning to be a form of hell on Earth. Skinner presents it grandly as utopian, as the answer to all of society's ills. The choice of title, from that most unconditionable of Americans, Henry David Thoreau, is simply incomprehensible. Unrepentant, Skinner returned to this thesis 23 years later in a nonfiction work, *Beyond Freedom and Dignity*, and again in the third volume of his autobiography, *A Matter of Consequences* (1983). Contrast Huxley's *Brave New World*, Burgess's *A Clockwork Orange*, Knight's *Hell's Pavement*, and Orwell's *Nineteen Eighty-Four*. At the opposite ideological extreme from Skinner, contrast Ayn Rand, *Atlas Shrugged* (1957), which is even more didactic and talky but at least has a plot. (PC)

Themes: Dystopias, Psychology

Sladek, John T(homas), U.S., 1937–2000

II-1038. The Lunatics of Terra. Gollancz, 1984.

Possibly Sladek's best collection, following *The Steam-Driven Boy and Other Strangers* (1973), *Keep the Giraffe Burning* (1977), and *Alien Accounts* (1982). His main theme is the invasion of the human environment and usurpation of human prerogatives by machines, but he also has a strong interest in peculiar logics and creative illogicalities, which often supply him with ideas for short stories. He is a surreal humorist; no one in SF has a finer feeling for the aesthetics of the incongruous. A posthumous volume, *Maps: The Uncollected John Sladek*, appeared in 2001. Compare the short fiction of Robert Sheckley and Kit Reed. (BS/ML)

Themes: Humorous SF, Machines

II-1039. The Müller-Fokker Effect. Hutchinson, 1970.

Computer tapes on which a man's personality is stored are bootlegged about, causing havoc wherever they go, until the millionaire who caused all the trouble reintegrates the personality in a new body. Wild and intricate satire. Compare Russell Griffin's *Century's End* (1981). (BS)

Themes: Satirical SF

II-1040. The Reproductive System. Gollancz, 1968, U.S. title: *Mechasm*, 1969.

Metal-eating, self-replicating robots threaten to destroy the fabric of civilization if they cannot be controlled and contained, although if used responsibly they might pave the way to paradise. A satirical parable of man/machine relationships. Compare and contrast Rucker's *Software*. (BS)

Themes: Machines, Robots, Satirical SF

II-1041. Roderick. Granada, 1980.

Original U.S. edition (1982) was abridged, but 1987 reprint was complete. First part of a two-decker novel completed in *Roderick at Random* (1983). A satirical bildungsroman in which the title character, a robot, slowly develops through eccentric infancy to detached maturity while various enemies attempt to locate and destroy him. Very funny, picking up themes from *The Reproductive System* in presenting its satirical account of man/machine relationships but extrapolating them to new extremes. If Roderick is the epitome of the good robot, his opposite is found in Sladek's *Tik-Tok* (1983). Tik-Tok is a robot whose "asimov circuits" malfunction, allowing him to become as morally defective as the humans who made him and thus enabling him to build a spectacular career for himself. A fine black comedy. *The Complete Roderick* appeared in 2001. Compare Gerrold's *When HARLIE Was One*. (BS/ML)

Themes: Coming of Age, Robots, Satirical SF

Sleator, William, U.S., 1945–

II-1042. The Duplicate. Dutton, 1988.

YA. Coming across an odd-looking machine that he discovers can duplicate living organisms, 16-year-old David decides to duplicate himself, only to find his life at peril when Duplicate A, replicating itself, plots with Duplicate B to eliminate David. Suspenseful, quick-moving, and (after the initial strain on credibility) plausible twist on the *Frankenstein* story. Contrast Ames's *Is There Life on a Plastic Planet?* (1975). (FM)

Themes: Clones/Cloning, Machines, Monsters

*II-1043. House of Stairs. Dutton, 1974.

YA. Five 16-year-old orphans find themselves in a house of stairs with a red machine as the only furniture. When the machine light blinks and sounds are emitted, the teenagers realize they must perform in a certain way or the machine will not spit out food pellets. Three of the young people do what the machine wants, use each other, and become brutal and mechanistic. The other two open to and sustain each other as humans. The young people discover that they have been subjects in a psychological conditioning experiment. The language and attitudes of teenagers are captured; the breaking down of all external, protective devices is plausibly rendered. A chilling and powerful dystopian tale. Compare Anderson's *Feed* and Huxley's *Brave New World*. (FM/ML)

Themes: Children in SF, Coming of Age, Dystopias, Intelligence, Psychology

II-1044. Interstellar Pig. Bantam, 1984.

YA. Pretty much left to his own devices while on vacation at his parents' summer house, Barney discovers that his decidedly odd neighbors are obsessed with a very strange board game. When they convince him to play, however, he soon discovers that he's gotten more than he bargained for. Turns out they're aliens and the prize for winning the game, called Interstellar Pig, is the Earth itself. This is a suspenseful, but humorous, and occasionally somewhat gross novel. The sequel, *Interstellar Parasite* (2002), is also fun, but increases the gross-out factor. Compare Pratchett's *Only You Can Save Mankind*; contrast Rubinstein's *Space Demons*.

Themes: Aliens, Humorous SF, Invasion, Virtual Reality

II-1045. Strange Attractors. Dutton, 1990.

YA. Clever twists on time travel and contemporary chaos theory force Max to choose between identical pairs of Eve and her brilliant scientist father, Sylvan— one set, good and relatively dull, from Max's time; the other, fascinating and amoral from an alternate world. Intriguing story, which forthrightly includes sex among "attractions," should prove attractive to teens. Contrast Bethancourt's *The Mortal Instruments* and O'Brien's *Z for Zachariah*. (FM)

Themes: Alternate Worlds, Time Travel

Sloane, William M(illigan III), U.S., 1906–1974

II-1046. To Walk the Night. Farrar and Rinehart, 1937.

A young college graduate is romantically drawn to the widow of his old teacher, who has died under mysterious circumstances, but she is not what she seems. A cleverly wrought example of a mystery story with a science-fictional solution, which is also an exceptionally poignant example of the subgenre of alien *femme fatale* stories. Contrast Matson's *Doctor Fogg* and Moore's "Shambleau." Sloane's other hybrid mystery, *The Edge of Running Water* (1939), tends more towards occult fiction than SF in featuring a machine for communicating with the dead, but its narrative attitude is very similar to that of *To Walk the Night* (and the construction of such a machine had been a pet project of Thomas Edison's). (PC)

   Themes: Aliens

Slonczewski, Joan, U.S., 1956–

*II-1047. A Door into Ocean. Arbor, 1986. Series: Shora.

The planet Valedon is ruled by a highly militaristic patriarchy. The water world of Shora is all-female, pacifist, lacking any military. When Valedon invades Shora, the women's world seems helpless to stop its advance, but appearances can be deceiving. Slonczewski is one of the best of the second-generation of feminist SF writers who are examining such important issues as pacifism, environmentalism, and the relationship between language and violence. Although somewhat slow-moving, this is a very wise novel with interesting characters and plenty of food for thought. The immediate sequel is *Daughters of Elysium* (1993). In later books in the series, *The Children Star* (1998), and *Brain Plague* (2000), Slonczewski explores the possibility of microscopic intelligent life forms. Compare Moffett's *Pennterra*, Tepper's *The Gate to Women's Country* and, for the later books in the series, Bear's *Blood Music*. (ML)

   Awards: John W. Campbell
   Themes: Feminist SF, Hard SF, Life on Other Worlds, Utopias, War

*II-1048. The Wall Around Eden. Morrow, 1989.

Twenty years ago, full-scale war broke out and the world was plunged into nuclear winter. Simultaneously, aliens appeared and preserved a few scattered towns and cities from destruction by means of force fields. Some think that the aliens, who have made virtually no attempt to communicate with humanity, triggered the war intentionally. In tiny Gwynwood, Pennsylvania, the people go on with their lives, practicing a pacifist, ecologically sound lifestyle heavily influenced by the Quaker faith. But one young woman isn't satisfied with things as they are, and vows to discover the aliens' secrets. One of Slonczewski's purposes here, as in *A Door Into Ocean*, is to suggest practical alternatives to violence. Her novel can be seen as a welcome rejoinder to the current glut of military SF novels. Compare Moffett's *Pennterra*. Contrast Drake's *Hammer's Slammers* (1979). (ML)

   Themes: Aliens, Feminist SF, Holocaust and After, Utopias

Smith, Clark Ashton, U.S., 1893–1961

II-1049.   Out of Space and Time. Arkham House, 1942.

A collection of 20 stories, most of them supernatural. The most important SF inclusions are a fusion of the classic portal fantasy "The City of the Singing Flame" (*Wonder Stories*, 1931) with its sequel "Beyond the Singing Flame (1931); the satirical comedy "The Monster of the Prophecy" (1931); and the Mars-set SF/horror story "The Vaults of Yoh-Vombis" (1932). The collection also features several far-future fantasies set in Zothique, which helped establish a crucial exemplar within that subgenre—four more are in *Lost Worlds* (1944). *Genius Loci and Other Tales* (1948) includes the metaphysical fantasy "The Eternal World" (1931) and the wry first contact story "A Star-Change" (1933 as "The Visitors from Mlok"). Smith wrote a good deal of interplanetary fiction for the Gernsback pulps, including a series comprising "Marooned in Andromeda" (1931), the belatedly rediscovered "Red World of Polaris" (2004), and "The Amazing Planet" (1931), but was never entirely comfortable with the medium, preferring story forms more hospitable to the blithely bizarre invention that was his forte. "The Master of the Asteroid" (1932) and *The Immortals of Mercury* (1932) were reprinted alongside other SF trivia in *Tales of Science and Sorcery* (1964), while the two series stories appeared with "An Adventure in Futurity" (1931), "The Invisible City" (1932), and the interesting dimensional fantasy "The Dimension of Chance" (1932) in *Other Dimensions* (1970). (BS)

Smith, Cordwainer (pseud. of Paul Myron Anthony Linebarger), U.S., 1913–1966

*II-1050. The Rediscovery of Man: The Complete Short Science Fiction of Cordwainer Smith. Ed. by J. J. Pierce. NESFA Press, 1993.

Gathers 33 stories, including two previously unpublished, thus replacing *The Best of Cordwainer Smith* (1975; U.K. title: *The Rediscovery of Man*) and *The Instrumentality of Mankind* (1979). Most tales belong to an elliptical, vaguely allegorical future history, relating colonization of space and achievement of virtual immortality, both purchased at the price of growing class division between Instrumentality and Underpeople, genetically engineered slaves. Most tales can stand alone, and many are classics: "Scanners Live in Vain," "The Dead Lady of Clown Town," "The Ballad of Lost C'Mell," and others. *Norstrilia* (1975), a novel relating the accession of Underpeople to full civil rights, continues the overarching story. The future history is evocative, baroquely brilliant (though at times politically dubious), moving between the early scientific romances of Wells and 1960s New Wave. (RL)

Themes: Colonization of Other Worlds, Future History, Genetic Engineering

Smith, E(dward) E(lmer), U.S., 1890–1965

II-1051. Galactic Patrol. Fantasy Press, 1950. Series: Lensman.

A definitive space opera serialized in *Astounding* (1937–1938) that took up the challenge, temporarily abandoned at the end of *The Skylark of Valeron*, to restore potential for a more ambitious escalation of narrative scale. An archetypal boys' book adventure, employing a hero gifted with superpowers by the lens bestowed on him by pseudoparental Arisians so that he might fight the powers of evil hierarchically stacked behind the pirates of Boskone. The modest *Triplanetary* (1934) was revised to form the first volume of the book publication of the series (collectively billed as "The History of Civilization"), whereupon *Galactic Patrol* became the third item of six. (BS)
  Themes: Space Opera

II-1052. The Lensman Series. Fantasy Press, 1948–1954. Series: Lensman.

The space opera to end all space operas, with humans and aliens arrayed (some on each side) in a cosmic war of Good and Evil, which even George Lucas would be hard put to top. For all its implausibilities, this series represents a vast improvement in Smith's skills of storytelling and character portrayal over his *Skylark of Space*. Reader response to the "Civilization" vs. "Boskonia" theme as an allegory of the "West" vs. "Fascism" during World War II was an important factor in the stories' initial reception. The novels are best read in the order in which they appeared as serials: *Galactic Patrol* (1937–1938), *Gray Lensmen* (1939–1940), *Second-Stage Lensmen* (1942), and *Children of the Lens* (1947–1948). *Triplanetary* is a fix-up novel; this and *First Lensman* were written after the initial tetralogy but preceding its chronology and give away Smith's conceptual scheme, which his Lensman-hero had to puzzle out through four long novels. (PC)
  Themes: Galactic Empires, Space Opera

II-1053. The Skylark of Space. Buffalo, 1946. Series: Skylark.

A pioneering space opera serialized in *Amazing Stories* in 1928 (but written several years earlier, the "love interest" chapters in the first version being provided by Lee Hawkins Garby). This was the story that revealed the potential of the galaxy as a vast playground for action-adventure fiction. Essentially a boys' book, it uses its heroic scientist's contest with a charismatic supervillain as a dramatic frame for encounters with various exotic races and dangerous situations. *Skylark Three* (1930; book 1948) ratchets up the action with an interstellar war and the founding of a galactic empire. *Skylark of Valeron* (1934–1945; book, 1949) continues the story, struggling to cope with the problem of melodramatic inflation by further extrapolating the scale of events. (BS)
  Themes: Space Opera

Smith, Garret, U.S., ca. 1876–1954

II-1054.   Between Worlds. Stellar Publishing Co., 1929.

An interplanetary novel serialized in *Argosy* in 1919, in which explorers from the light side of Venus venture into the dark side, where they encounter a charismatic *femme fatale* reminiscent of Haggard's *She*, before visiting Earth to find that she and a rival have taken control of the German and Russian military machines, intent on the conquest of the world. Smith's other pulp SF is relatively enterprising, including several stories employing remote viewers: "On the Brink of 2000" (1910), "The Treasures of Tantalus" (1920–1921), and "You've Killed Privacy" (1928). (BS)

   Themes: Space Flight

Smith, Wayland (pseudonym of Victor Bayley), U.K., 1880–1972

II-1055.   The Machine Stops. Hale, 1936.

A novel in which modern civilization collapses as a result of a "plague" that consumes all metals. The hero races to discover a resistant alloy while the barbarians gather. The same premise had recently been developed in interestingly different ways by the French writer S. S. Held in *The Death of Iron* (1931; trans. in *Wonder Stories*, 1932) and David H. Keller in *The Metal Doom* (*Amazing Stories*, 1932). (BS)

   Themes: Disaster

Snell, Edmund, U.K., 1889–?

II-1056.   Kontrol. Benn, 1928.

A lurid thriller in which a mad scientist conceives a plan for creating a superrace, involving the transplantation of human brains. The later phases of the plot abandon the conventional thriller plot, switching the scene to an island where the artificial supermen are building a technological utopia, taking the author well out of his natural depth. An interesting instance of idea intoxication. Compare Fearn's *Intelligence Gigantic*. (BS)

   Themes: Supermen/women

Snyder, Zilpha Keatley, U.S., 1927–

*II-1057.   Below the Root. Atheneum, 1975. Series: Green Sky.

YA. In the first part of the Green Sky trilogy, the Kindar are introduced. They live pleasantly in the large branches and trunks of the great trees of Green Sky; the banished Erdlings live below, barely above subsistence level, and are called monsters by the Ol-zhaan, leaders of Green Sky. Young Raamo, destined to be a leader and very curious, descends to the ground and, finding out the truth, sets in motion the rejoining of the two peoples. A low-key, leisurely moving narrative pace does not seriously detract from the impact of the very detailed and ultimately convincing portrait of this unique arboreal society. Compare Williams's *The People of the Ax. And All Between* (1976) focuses on two children, Teera and Pomma (Erdling and Kindar, respectively), who use their telekinetic powers to smooth over the forces working to keep apart the two groups. *Until the Celebration* (1977) details the growing pains of the peoples' rejoining, finally accomplished when Raamo gives his life to cement the union. (FM)

Themes: Life on Other Worlds, Pastoral, Sociology

Spinrad, Norman, U.S., 1940–

II-1058. Bug Jack Barron. Walker, 1969.

A TV personality makes a powerful enemy when he attacks a plutocrat who is trying to develop an immortality treatment. Taboo-breaking in its day because of its sexual frankness and extravagant cynicism; remains significant as an early examination of the growing media and their manipulators. Compare Sterling's *The Artificial Kid* (1980). (BS)

Themes: Immortality, Sex in SF

II-1059. Greenhouse Summer. Tor, 1999.

The ice caps have melted, deserts have expanded, and Siberia has become the most fertile land on Earth. When corporate spy Monique Calhoun attends the latest United Nations conference on global warming, she learns that there's evidence that the environmental balance on Earth has already tipped and that runaway climate change may convert the planet to something very much like Venus with startling rapidity. The novel serves as a powerful warning, but loses some of its power due to a less than entirely successful spy thriller plot. Compare Robinson's *Forty Signs of Rain.* (ML)

Themes: Ecology, Politics

II-1060. The Iron Dream. Avon, 1972.

A futuristic fantasy ostensibly written by Adolf Hitler, who is here said to have become a pulp SF writer after emigrating to the United States in the 1920s. Here the ideas that inspired the Third Reich are rendered harmlessly into a pulp adventure fiction—but how harmless, then, is such fiction? Hitler's *Lord of the Swastika* is similar enough to much real pulp SF to make us look again at the ideologies embedded in the genre. Compare Malzberg's *Herovit's World* (1973). (BS)

Themes: Alternate Worlds, Politics

II-1061. Little Heroes. Bantam, 1987.

In a grim future United States, soulless corporations that manage culture conspire to replace unruly rock stars with computer-generated "Artificial Personalities," but encounter resistance from the "Reality Liberation Front"—not to mention from the ungovernable spirit of rock and roll itself. Energetic and hard-edged; weds *Bug Jack Barron*'s scathing critique of cynical media establishment with cyberpunk. Considering that at least one such artificial rock star has since been created in Japan, this book is particularly prescient. Compare Shirley's *Eclipse* and Gibson's *Idoru*. (RL/ML)

Themes: Cyberpunk, Dystopias, Politics

II-1062. Other Americas. Bantam, 1988.

A collection of four novellas, including "The Lost Continent of America" (1970), "Street Meat" (1983), "World War Last" (1985), and the fine original story "La Vie Continue," which concerns a writer named Spinrad exiled to Paris in the near future as a result of his left-wing political writings and his attempts to gain readmittance into the United States. Spinrad's stories are frequently satiric and often touched by bitterness. Two excellent early collections are *No Direction Home* (1975) and *The Last Hurrah of the Golden Horde* (1970). *The Star-Spangled Future* (1979) combines stories from Spinrad's first two collections. (ML)

II-1063. Russian Spring. Bantam, 1991.

In a 21st century where an intact, liberalized Soviet Union prospers and a United States weighted down by Reagan-era paranoia is on the verge of collapse, a U.S. space scientist tries desperately to maintain a place for himself in an international space program, where Americans are increasingly persona non grata. Although he may have gotten the actual historical events wrong, Spinrad's novel comes across as intensely realistic. He's particularly good on the behind-the-scenes politics. Compare Robinson's *Red Mars* for another realistic portrayal of the near future of the space program. (ML)

Themes: Politics, Space Flight

*II-1064. The Void Captain's Tale. Pocket Books/Timescape, 1983.

Like *The Iron Dream*, this novel delves beneath the surface of SF mythology looking for the psychological drives within—and presents a phallic starship that really does have a psychological drive! A fabulous erotic fantasy deployed in SF dream-symbolism; very clever and written with much verve. Set in the same universe as *The Void Captain's Tale* and a thematic sequel to that novel, *Child of Fortune* (1985) is an exotic bildungsroman whose heroine falls in for a time with the ageless storyteller and philosopher Pater Pan, and undertakes a journey across the psychedelic Bloomenveldt, before attaining her particular enlightenment. A fabulously ornamented and compelling story, carrying forward the erotic themes of its predecessor and developing them in a broader context. Compare Carter's *The Infernal Desire Machines of Doctor Hoffman* and Delany's *Stars in My Pocket Like Grains of Sand*. (BS/ML)

Themes: Psychology, Sex in SF, Space Opera

Spitz, Jacques, France, 1896–1963

II-1065. Sever the Earth. 1935. Trans. of *L'agonie du globe* by Margaret Mitchiner. John Lane, 1936.

A spirited satirical disaster story in which the Earth is split into two halves, one containing the Old World and one containing the New (i.e. the Americas). As they drift progressively farther apart, contact between the two is lost, and when the Moon comes between them the Old World is seemingly doomed. Spitz, who had previously been a naturalistic writer, went on to write several more SF novels, gradually settling into the conscientiously melodramatic but ideatively ambitious vein pioneered by Maurice Renard. (BS)

Themes: Disaster, Satirical SF

Stableford, Brian, U.K., 1948–

II-1066. The Empire of Fear. Simon & Schuster, 1988.

A big, sprawling alternate history novel in which vampirism has a scientific basis and vampires, among them Vlad Dracul and Richard the Lionhearted, have ruled much of the world since the Middle Ages. A 17th-century scholar searches for the cause of vampirism, and his quest takes him to the heart of darkest Africa. Stableford has done a fine job of working out his alternate history, continuing it up to the present day. The African chapters of the novel read like H. Rider Haggard at his best. Compare Haggard's *Allan Quatermain* and Kim Newman's Anno Dracula series. (ML)

Themes: Alternate Worlds, Biology, Mythology

II-1067. Inherit the Earth. St. Martin's, 1998. Series: Emmortality.

This is the first volume in Stableford's intellectually ambitious six-book Emmortality series, which centers on the possibilities for life extension and the effect of nanotechnology on society. Having barely survived a devastating biotech war in the 21st century, humanity has entered an era of plenty. Damon Hart, the son of the scientist who saved the Earth from destruction, has cut himself off from his dead father's heritage, but to no avail. He finds himself attacked by the Eliminators, self-appointed vigilantes who claim that his father, far from a hero, was actually responsible for the runaway plague that he supposedly tamed. Worse still, they claim that Damon *is* his father and must pay for his crimes. Further volumes in the series track a variety of characters into the future as various life-extension breakthroughs lead humanity closer and closer to the possibility of true immortality. Taken as a group, these books may well be the most ambitious attempt ever made to consider the effect of immortality on the human race. The sequels are *Architects of Emmortality* (1999), *The Fountains of Youth* (2000), *The Cassandra Complex* (2001), *Dark Ararat* (2002), and *The Omega Expedition* (2002). Compare Sterling's *Holy Fire* and Turner's *Beloved Son*. (ML)

Themes: Future History, Immortality, Politics

II-1068. Sexual Chemistry: Sardonic Tales of the Genetic Revolution. Simon & Schuster U.K., 1991.

Stableford is by training a biologist and sociologist, and the 10 tales (6 reprinted from *Interzone*) and single essay collected here effectively blend his specialties. Black comedy is the tone, whether he is telling us about a researcher with the unlikely name of Casanova in "A Career in Sexual Chemistry" or about assorted disasters by well-meaning scientists. Stableford has argued that biotechnology will affect our world far more than, say, space travel, and these dryly witty tales make his point well. Three new collections are *Complications: And Other Stories* (2003), *Designer Genes: Tales of the Biotech Revolution* (2004), and *Salome and Other Decadent Fantasies* (2004). (ML)

Stapledon, (William) Olaf, U.K., 1886–1950

*II-1069. Last and First Men. Methuen, 1930.

An "essay in myth creation" detailing the future of humankind's descendant species, culminating with the "eighteenth men" 2 billion years in the future, whose story must come to an end because the sun is dying (previous change in its radiant power having necessitated emigrations to Venus and Neptune). An extraordinary elaboration of a sketch set out in J. B. S. Haldane's philosophical essay "The Last Judgment" (in *Possible Worlds and Other Essays*, 1927), it is somewhat undermined by weak biology and its insistence on remaining within the bounds of the solar system, but it is admirably earnest in its narrative ambition. *Last Men in London* (1932) uses one of the eighteenth men as an objective observer to pass judgment on contemporary human nature, as revealed by early 20th-century history. (BS)

Themes: Future History

II-1070.   Odd John: A Story Between Jest and Earnest. Methuen, 1935.

The story of a superhuman child born ahead of his time, taking up the theme of Beresford's *Hampdenshire Wonder* and extrapolating it by allowing the feral superchild to grow to adulthood and discover others of his kind, operating meanwhile as an uncompromising observer of human failings. It is less charitable in its judgments than the author's *Sirius* or Weinbaum's exactly contemporary *The New Adam*. (BS)

Themes: Supermen/women

II-1071.   Sirius: A Fantasy of Love and Discord. Secker, 1944.

Related to his *Odd John* in its portrayal of the estrangement of a superbeing among limited, unimaginative normals. Here the superbeing is a surgically enhanced dog, Sirius, who also becomes, in effect, an outside observer commenting on the shortcomings of civilization. His ultimately tragic love relationship with a young human woman, which in our own more explicit era might have been simply gross, is tastefully handled. Lacking the cosmic sweep of Stapledon's *Star Maker* and *Last and First Men*, it is far more satisfying—more even than *Odd John*—in the qualities that make a good novel. Compare Neville's *Bettyann*; contrast Shiras's *Children of the Atom*. (PC)

Themes: Supermen/women

*II-1072. Star Maker. Methuen, 1937.

A companion piece to *Last and First Men* that takes the essay in myth creation to the next logical level, embracing the entire history of the cosmos. Formulated as a visionary fantasy rather than a history (an aborted first draft in the alternative format was issued as *Nebula Maker* in 1976), it contrives to endow a human individual with a perceptive power that lays the whole of Creation before him and allows him to formulate an image of its Creator as a journeyman who needs more practice. A masterpiece, undoubtedly the finest scientific romance of the 20th century. Recommended is the edition introduced and edited by Patrick A. McCarthy (Wesleyan Univ. Press, 2004). (BS)

Themes: Evolution

Steele, Allen, U.S., 1958–

II-1073. Coyote. Ace, 2002.

A fix-up novel in which rebels steal a prototype starship from under the nose of a right-wing, fundamentalist American dictatorship. Eventually reaching a new world, which they name Coyote, they colonize and explore the planet. Individual segments of this novel were nominated for the Hugo and Nebula awards. Although necessarily episodic, Steele's tale features some extremely well-done world building and a lot of old-fashioned sense of wonder. The sequel is *Coyote Rising* (2004). Compare Kagan's *Mirabile.* (ML).

Themes: Aliens, Colonization of Other Worlds, Religion

II-1074. Orbital Decay. Ace, 1989.

The first novel by a writer who has quickly established himself as a leading exponent of realistic, near-future hard SF of a sort that harks back to science fiction's golden age. In the year 2016, a group of competent but not very well-mannered construction workers are engaged in the building of a new orbital solar-powered satellite. To succeed they often have to work against both the interference of their superiors and the machinations of various government agents who want to use the satellite as a weapons platform. Steele followed *Orbital Decay* with a number of similar tales, including *Clarke County, Space* (1990), and *Lunar Descent* (1991). Compare Clarke's *A Fall of Moondust* (1961). (ML)

Awards: *Locus*
Themes: Hard SF, Space Flight

Stephenson, Neal, U.S., 1959–

*II-1075. Cryptonomicon. Avon, 1999. Series: The Baroque Cycle.

This complex and ambitious cyber-thriller, which begs comparison with Pynchon's *Gravity's Rainbow*, features half a dozen well-conceived plot lines. During World War II, the mathematical genius and cryptographer Lawrence Waterhouse, a friend of Alan Turing, is instrumental in breaking the Nazi's Enigma code. Some 60 years later, his grandson Randy, a computer hacker, is involved in setting up a small-scale, but high-tech data haven in Southeast Asia, only to find out that his project has attracted the attention of a number of powerful governments, multinational corporations, and secret organizations. Randy also discovers evidence of a secret conspiracy that may be centuries old. Wandering through the various plot lines is the enigmatic, possibly immortal figure of Enoch Root, secret agent for a secret organization. *Cryptonomicon,* as large as it was, was eventually revealed to be merely a prelude to the much more ambitious Baroque Cycle, which consists of *Quicksilver* (2003), *The Confusion* (2004), and *System of the World* (2004). Set in the 18th century and featuring the ancestors of some of the major characters in *Cryptonomicon, Quicksilver* is more a historical novel about science than a work of science fiction, though the shadowy presence of Enoch Root would seem to promise more obviously fantastic events to come in later volumes. (ML)

Awards: *Locus*
Themes: History in SF, Satirical SF, War

*II-1076. The Diamond Age: or, A Young Lady's Illustrated Primer. Bantam Spectra, 1995.

Far in the future, nations have been made superfluous by the creation of "claves" or enclaves of common cultures. Much of humanity is fabulously wealthy although the poor are still with us. John Percival Hackworth is a successful nanotech engineer in the neo-Victorian clave and has been commissioned by one of the world's most powerful leaders to create a Primer, an enormously powerful, high-tech teaching device for the great man's granddaughter. Hackworth illicitly makes a spare copy of the Primer for his own daughter, but, when it accidentally falls into the hands of a working-class girl named Nell, all hell breaks loose and powerful forces are soon arrayed to get it back. This is a complex and challenging novel full of fascinating anthropological and technological extrapolation. It delves deeply into such subjects as information theory and educational theory. *The Diamond Age* is a difficult but rewarding read. (ML)

Awards: Hugo
Themes: Anthropology, Cyberpunk, Nanotechnology, Satirical SF

*II-1077. Snow Crash. Bantam, 1992.

An outrageous combination of cyberpunk tropes, sophisticated linguistics theory, and postmodernist satire, *Snow Crash* is set in a near-future America where government has broken down and just about everything is done by franchise. The main character, Hiro Protagonist, a.k.a. the Deliverator, is a genius hacker and samurai warrior, but he makes his living delivering pizza for the Mafia. When a deadly disease, the snow crash virus, begins to take out hackers and threatens virtual reality itself, Hiro is the man to tame it. The novel is a complex stew of cyberspace high jinks, religion, off-the-wall humor, and action-adventure sequences. It's crammed with delightful throwaway ideas, such as Mafia-enforced, potentially deadly, 30-minute pizza delivery deadlines and semi-intelligent, nuclear-powered watchdogs. Although not calculated to bring pleasure to fans of old-fashioned, meat-and-potatoes hard SF, *Snow Crash* is a genuinely dazzling novel. Compare Gibson's *Neuromancer* and Cadigan's *Synners*. (ML)

Themes: Cyberpunk, Satirical SF, Virtual Reality

Sterling, Bruce, U.S., 1954–

*II-1078. Crystal Express. Arkham, 1989.

Early short fiction by one of the co-founders of the cyberpunk movement. Included is Sterling's entire Shaper/Mechanist series, most importantly "Swarm," as well as such excellent stories as "The Flowers of Edo," "Dinner in Audoghast," "Green Days in Brunei," and "Twenty Evocations." A number of these are award nominees and all are worth reading. Two more recent and equally good collections of Sterling's short fiction are *Globalhead* (1992) and *A Good Old Fashioned Future* (1999). Compare Gibson's *Burning Chrome* and Cadigan's *Patterns*. (ML)

 Themes: Cyberpunk, Future History

*II-1079. Distraction. Bantam Spectra, 1998.

In the mid-21st century, political operative Oscar Valparaiso, himself a clone, investigates a scandal-ridden federal laboratory in East Texas. Meanwhile, Leonard Two Feathers, the newly elected president of the United States, considers declaring war on the rapidly submerging Netherlands, and Green Huey, the corrupt governor of Louisiana, engages in illegal genetic research while establishing his own private biker army. This brilliantly done example of satiric SF shows Sterling at his post-cyberpunk best. (ML)

 Awards: Arthur C. Clarke

 Themes: Clones/Cloning, Ecology, Genetic Engineering, Politics, Satirical SF, Sociology

II-1080. Heavy Weather. Bantam Spectra, 1994.

In the mid-21st century, the world is increasingly bedeviled by "heavy weather"—out-of-control tornadoes, hurricanes, and typhoons fueled by the greenhouse effect. Led by scientist Jerry Mulcahey, a group of storm watchers who call themselves the Storm Troupe chase a series of increasingly violent storms across the heartland of America in search of a never before witnessed "F-6" super-tornado. An exciting adventure, which touches on Sterling's usual political, ecological, and scientific concerns. Compare John Barnes's *Mother of Storms* (1994), Spinrad's *Greenhouse Summer*, and Robinson's *Forty Signs of Rain*. (ML)

 Themes: Cyberpunk, Disaster, Ecology, Politics

II-1081. Holy Fire. Bantam Spectra, 1996.

In the late 21st century, Earth has achieved near-utopia due to advances in cybernetics, medicine, and nanotechnology. Mia Ziemann is 94 years old, but still lives an active, healthy existence as a medical economist. Tired of her life, she undergoes a radical medical procedure that leaves her looking 20 and then drops out of her profession. Taking up the life of a young bohemian, she wanders the streets of Europe looking for meaning and discovers another world, that of the truly young who see themselves as forever powerless and under the thumb of the gerontocracy that rules the world. Serious SF that extrapolates a number of current trends in a believable way. Compare Stableford's *Inherit the Earth*. (ML)

Themes: Biology, Genetic Engineering, Immortality, Medicine, Politics, Sociology, Utopias

*II-1082. Islands in the Net. Arbor, 1988.

There's a perfectly fine plot here, involving data piracy, and some nicely developed characters, including Laura, who goes out and has adventures while her husband takes care of the baby. What stands out in Sterling's novel, however, is the extraordinarily detailed and highly believable world he has created. The almost universal presence of the data Net, the widespread use of creative ecological engineering, the economic and cultural interpenetration of formerly separate societies, the fads and styles, all come together in one of the most fascinating sociological and political SF novels of the past 20 years. Contrast Stephenson's equally good, but much less believable *Snow Crash*. (ML)

Awards: John W. Campbell

Themes: Computers, Cyberpunk, Ecology, Intelligence

*II-1083. Schismatrix. Arbor House, 1985.

The hero, in the course of a long and eventful life, witnesses the political and technological evolution of the solar system after Earth has been devastated. The long struggle between the bio-technologically inclined Shapers and the electronically expert Mechanists is complicated by the arrival of aliens and the eruption of new ideological movements. A marvelous compendium of ideas; an imaginative tour de force. *Schismatrix Plus* (1996) includes the novel plus other stories set in the same universe. Compare Williamson's *Lifeburst*. (BS/ML)

Themes: Colonization of Other Worlds, Cyberpunk, Future History

II-1084.   Zeitgeist. Bantam Spectra, 2000.

Set in 1999, this satiric borderline-SF novel features Leggy Starlitz, entrepreneur extraordinaire and the hero of a number of Sterling short stories. On tour with his ersatz all-girl band G-7, Leggy hatches a plan to popularize the band and start up a major merchandising campaign in the Muslim world. Things begin to go wrong, however, when he alienates some of his former business partners and they come gunning for him and the band members. Compare Sterling's own *Distraction*. Contrast Nasir's *Tower of Dreams*. (ML)

Themes: Satirical SF

Stevens, Francis (pseudonym of Gertrude Barrows Bennett), U.S., 1884–ca. 1939

II-1085.   The Heads of Cerberus. Polaris, 1952.

A portal fantasy first published in *The Thrill Book* in 1919, in which a dimensional hinterland separates our world from a hypothetical future in which Philadelphia has become an isolated city state under totalitarian rule. Stevens was one of the more imaginative pulp fantasy writers, whose interests and methods had much in common with those of A. Merritt; she had previously deployed marginal SF elements in the enterprising thriller *The Citadel of Fear* (1918). (BS)

Themes: Parallel Worlds

Stevenson, Robert Louis (Balfour), U.K., 1850–1894

II-1086. Strange Case of Dr Jekyll and Mr Hyde. Longmans Green, 1886.

A mystery story with a science-fictional solution: as everyone now knows (although it might have come as a delicious surprise to the original readers), the horrid Mr. Hyde is the alter ego of the benevolent Dr. Jekyll, whose experimental dabblings have produced a drug capable of isolating the best and worst elements of a man's personality. A classic moral fantasy, as stubbornly and perversely pusillanimous in its implicit conclusions as such similar classics as *Frankenstein* and *The Island of Dr Moreau*, not to mention Oscar Wilde's *The Picture of Dorian Gray* (1891) and Bram Stoker's *Dracula* (1897). (BS)

Themes: Psychology

Stewart, George R(ippey), U.S. 1895–1960

*II-1087. Earth Abides. Random, 1949.

In a near future, a plague devastates humankind, leaving isolated pockets of survivors. (The 2003 SARS epidemic hinted that such a plague is possible.) One group in the San Francisco Bay area subsists for some time on the bounties of civilization that have remained intact. But the subtler social fabric, formerly held together by the cooperation of large numbers of people, is too much for this handful to sustain. With a mournful backward look at the millions of now-doomed volumes in the University of California library, the protagonist teaches the new children how to make bows and arrows. He lives long enough to see society forming itself anew at the tribal level. He himself is fated to be misremembered as a legendary culture hero. A major work. Compare Stephen King's *The Stand*, Shelley's *The Last Man*, and "The Scarlet Plague" in *The Science Fiction of Jack London*. (PC)

Awards: International Fantasy

Themes: Holocaust and After, Pastoral

Stockton, Frank R(ichard), U.S., 1834–1902

II-1088. The Great Stone of Sardis. Harper, 1898.

A compound of two invention stories, one involving a submarine voyage to the North Pole and the other the use of devices for penetrating solid matter visually and physically, revealing that the Earth's core is a vast diamond. The novel is a dime novel-style Vernian romance adapted for the more sophisticated audience of *Harper's*, where the story was serialized in 1897; it was the first significant popular novel to begin its action in the future without an explanatory preamble—

although the precedent is promptly compromised by having its viewpoint rapidly look "back" to the present. (BS)

Themes: Fantastic Voyages

II-1089. The Great War Syndicate. Scribner, 1889.

A pseudo-documentary account of a future war between the U.S. and Britain, enlivened by the plot device of having the American part in the war outsourced to a syndicate of capitalist industrialists, who take full advantage of the business opportunity. It is interesting historically because it precedes the British boom sparked by George Griffith (who paid homage in his usual fashion by publishing *The Great Pirate Syndicate* in 1899 and *The Great Weather Syndicate* in 1906). (BS)

Themes: War

Stone, Josephine Rector (pseud. of Jeanne Dixon), U.S., 1936–

II-1090. The Mudhead. Atheneum, 1980.

YA. The "purple people-eaters" of Sigma capture Corly when, bored and resentful, the young boy leaves the station established by the terran scientific team. Physically tormented, he is saved by the tribe's shaman, a Mudhead, despised but required by the people, only to realize that he is himself destined to become a Mudhead. Further pain and deprivation must be suffered before Corly and his brother, also captured, can escape. Impressive mingling of anthropology and space exploration; especially effective setting; convincing and moving portrait of a boy's maturation through physical and psychological suffering. Compare Engdahl's *The Far Side of Evil*. (FM)

Themes: Aliens, Anthropology, Coming of Age, Life on Other Worlds, Psychology

Stoutenburg, Adrien, U.S., 1916–1982

II-1091. Out There. Viking, 1971.

YA. Sometime in the 21st century cities lie sterile under steel and plastic domes. Outside is a land so ravaged by waste and pollution that virtually all wildlife is gone. Into this land Zeb and a handful of youngsters travel on an outing to find animal life. The group does locate ample signs of wildlife, but also meets a hunter. An even more ominous note is sounded at the end: the possibility that the restored land may become recreational land, and the cycle of ecological nightmare begin anew. Well-written and believable situation; polemic against human selfishness and exploitation balanced. Contrast Norton's *Star Man's Son: 2250 A.D.* or Anderson's *Feed*. (FM/ML)

Themes: Anthropology, Children in SF, Cities, Coming of Age, Ecology, Holocaust and After

Stratemeyer, Edward (syndicate) *see* Garis, Howard

Strete, Craig, U.S., 1950–

II-1092. The Bleeding Man and Other Science Fiction Stories. Greenwillow, 1977.

YA. One of the relatively rare collections of original science fiction short stories for youth, the book is also superior science fiction. Exceptional among the well-crafted and provocative stories are "The Bleeding Man," about a young Indian male who becomes psychochemically a superman, and "Into Every Rain, A Little Life Must Fall," a portrait of a future city controlled by "wombeops." Added strength is an Amerind dimension that challenges Western logic and reason. Compare William Sanders's *Are We Having Fun Yet?*, a collection of adult SF stories by a Native American writer. Contrast Norton's *The Beast Master* (1959). (FM/ML)

Themes: Far Future, Psychology, Supermen/women

Stross, Charles, Scotland, 1964–

II-1093. Singularity Sky. Ace, 2003.

Stross is currently one of the hottest short-story writers in the field and his first novel shows why. It's chock-full of exciting ideas concerning technological and political change and it moves at a breakneck pace. The New Republic is a repressive, backwater group of planets that has intentionally limited all technology other than that needed for interstellar warfare. When one of the New Republic's colonial worlds comes in contact with the Festival, an enigmatic alien intelligence that is seemingly bent on promoting revolutionary change, the Republic illegally utilizes time travel to put its huge war fleet in position to attack the Festival. Martin Springfield and Rachel Mansour, two officials from Earth, must stop the New Republic from bringing down upon humanity the wrath of the Eschaton, a super-powerful being that has placed strict limits on time travel. The sequel is *Iron Sunrise* (2004). (ML)

Themes: Aliens, Dystopias, Invasion, Politics, Satirical SF, Space Opera, War

Strugatsky, Arkady Natanovich, Russia, 1925–1991 and Strugatsky, Boris Natanovich, Russia, 1931–

II-1094. Definitely Maybe. Macmillan, 1978. Trans. of *Za millird let do konsta sveta*, 1976–1977, by Antonina W. Bouis.

The work of the world's leading scientists is radically disrupted by inexplicable events. Can they mount an investigation of what is happening, or must any such project be disrupted in its turn? As in other Strugatsky works, characters must bring rationality to bear on the irrational, and must accept the probability that it will prove inadequate. (BS)

Themes: Scientists and Engineers

*II-1095. Roadside Picnic and The Tale of the Troika. Macmillan, 1977. Trans. of *Piknik na obochine*, 1972, and *Skazka o troike*, 1968, by Antonina W. Bouis.

Two short novels. In the first, human scavengers try to make capital out of the rubbish left behind by alien tourists, which poses awful dangers as well as promising fabulous rewards. Human vanity is satirized but credit is given where it is due. Filmed as *Stalker*, 1979. The second, which is linked to the novel *Monday Begins on Saturday* (trans. 1977), mixes motifs from SF and folklore in order to satirize the bureaucratic process in scientific research and society. As usual, the scientific method proves no match for the arbitrarily miraculous. (BS)

II-1096.   The Snail on the Slope. Bantam, 1980. Trans. of *Ulitka na sklone*, 1966–1968, by Alan Meyers.

Two interlocked stories offer different views of a strange alien forest, the perspectives embodying contrasting ideologies of intellectual method and social organization. A dense and complex work, comparable in many ways to Lem's *Solaris*. (BS)

II-1097.   The Ugly Swans. Macmillan, 1979. Trans. of *Gadkie lebedi*, 1972, by Alexander Nakhimovsky and Alice Stone Nakhimovsky.

In a decadent future, strange weather conditions bring fantastic changes to a region where children appear to be evolving into superhumanity. Contrast Clarke's *Childhood's End*. (BS)

Themes: Supermen/women

Sturgeon, Theodore, U.S., 1918–1985

II-1098.   The Dreaming Jewels. Greenberg, 1950. Variant title: *The Synthetic Man*, Pyramid, 1957. Recommended ed.: Gregg, 1978.

Sturgeon's first novel was expanded from its magazine format and may have been influenced by Hubbard's introduction of Dianetics. Paul Williams's introduction to the Gregg edition discusses the evolution of the story, useful to anyone interested in a writer's working methods, and points also to the autobiographical elements in the story. (Similar, detailed background information is provided by Williams in the 10-volume set of Sturgeon's complete short stories, North Atlantic, 1995–2005, each volume individually titled; see later annotation). Horty, the young hero, runs away from "home" (and an evil stepfather) and grows up in a carnival, over which presides an even more evil stepfather. The story nevertheless exemplifies Sturgeon's conviction, which would be expressed often in later work, that "a touch of kindness is not cancelled out by all the villainy in the world." (PC)

Themes: Coming of Age

*II-1099. E Pluribus Unicorn. Abelard, 1953.

Thirteen fine, emotionally intense stories, ranging from "The World Well Lost," probably the first serious and sympathetic treatment in magazine SF of homosexuality, to "The Professor's Teddy Bear," in the most horrific *Weird Tales* tradition; from the touching love story "A Saucer of Loneliness" to a celebration of jazz musicianship, "Die, Maestro, Die!" Sturgeon's forte was telling stories about people at the edge, and treating them with compassion and nonjudgmentally even when they acted as shockingly as at the climax of "A Way of Thinking." Compare to his earliest collection, *Without Sorcery.* (PC)

*II-1100. More than Human. Farrar, 1953.

Growing out of the acclaimed novella, "Baby Is Three," this excellent work describes the rise, against all the meanness and bigotries of the surrounding world, of *Homo Gestalt,* an individual composed of the blended intelligences of numerous people, each of whom retains personal identity while contributing a particular special strength or talent to the whole. An emergence-of-the-superhuman story, made more of a struggle than it was for the superchildren in Clarke's *Childhood's End,* but shorn also of the inevitable tragedy forecast for the superhumans in Stapledon's *Odd John.* Arguably Sturgeon's best book. (PC)

    Awards: International Fantasy

    Themes: Coming of Age, Supermen/women

*II-1101. Sturgeon Is Alive and Well . . . . Putnam, 1971.

Among the finest short story writers in America, Sturgeon was never very prolific and is now in danger of being forgotten. This collection, one of his best, includes his Hugo- and Nebula Award-winner "Slow Sculpture," the earlier classic "To Here and the Easel," and a variety of other fine stories. Two other late collections are *Case and the Dreamer* (1974), which includes the title novella, plus "If All Men Were Brothers, Would You Let One Marry Your Sister?" and "When You Care, When You Love," and *The Stars Are the Styx* (1979), which features the title story, "Occam's Scalpel," "Tandy's Story," "Granny Won't Knit," and others. In an attempt to preserve Sturgeon's work between hard covers, the small press North Atlantic Books in 1994 published *The Ultimate Egoist: The Complete Short Stories of Theodore Sturgeon,* Vol. 1, with Vol. 10, *The Man Who Lost the Sea,* scheduled for 2005. Compare Ellison's *Alone Against Tomorrow* and *Deathbird Stories.* (ML)

*II-1102. Without Sorcery. Prime, 1948.

Thirteen of his earliest stories, from 1939 to 1948, including "Microcosmic God"; "Poker Face," one of the earliest stories to portray future-time travelers going native in the present; "It," a truly oppressive horror story; and "The Ultimate Egoist," an exercise in philosophical solipsism with an incredible shaggy dog last line. Introduction by Ray Bradbury. See preceding entry for mention of Sturgeon's collected fiction. (PC)

Sucharitkul, Somtow, Thailand, 1952–

II-1103. Light on the Sound. Pocket Books, 1982. Series: Chronicles of the High Inquest.

First of a series. A galactic civilization is dominated by the all-powerful Inquestors, who cruelly exploit the sentient Windbringers to sustain their hegemony. The Windbringers' only defense is the beauty of light and sound, so the Inquestors use deaf and dumb humans as their agents. The heroes and heroines of the books are rebels against this monstrous tyranny, but their resistance is a complicated business. An understanding of their enemies slowly emerges. Baroque, highly ornamented SF, original in style and outlook. Compare Smith's *Norstrilia* and Delany's *Stars in My Pocket Like Grains of Sand.* (BS)

    Themes: Galactic Empires

II-1104. Starship and Haiku. Pocket Books, 1984.

An extraordinary work in which Earth has suffered ecocatastrophe, men rediscover their kinship with whales, and a dubious messiah urges the entire Japanese nation to expiate their historical sins in seppuku. Compare Watson's *The Jonah Kit* and Bear's *Beyond Heaven's River* (1980). (BS)

    Awards: *Locus*

    Themes: Disaster, Pollution

Suddaby, (William) Donald, U.K., 1900–1964

*II-1105. Village Fanfare. Oxford, 1954.

YA. In 1908, the village of Much Swayford becomes the center of activity for Burton, a man from the future who came to Edwardian England to learn from the past. Through his giant computator and his ability to project images of himself anywhere in the world, he relearns and takes back the human attributes— laughter, courage, and love for music—that he believes will enable his time, the age of great brains, to go on. Clearly indebted to Wells not only for its depiction of scientific apparatus and time travel, but for its sympathetic, gently humorous portrayal of British village life. A book that deserves wider reading. (FM/SM)

    Themes: Pastoral, Time Travel

Sullivan, Tricia, U.S., 1968–

II-1106. Dreaming in Smoke. Bantam Spectra, 1998.

This nightmarish, surreal novel is set on the inimical planet T'nane, where a human scientific colony finds itself at risk when Ganesh, the artificial intelligence that keeps the colony functioning and its inhabitants alive, begins to crash. Kalypso Deed is a shotgun, riding the interface between the AI and the scientists who do their work in cyber-assisted Dreams. Marcsson, a statistician, has gone mad, apparently while Dreaming, and it is his madness that is taking Ganesh down with him. Kalypso must try to persuade Marcsson to save the AI, but soon discovers that there are even stranger beings on the planet who have plans for her and the rest of the colony. This is a powerful and uncomfortable novel. Compare Nagata's *Memory* and *Limit of Vision*. (ML)

Awards: Arthur C. Clarke

Themes: Aliens, Biology, Colonization of Other Worlds, Computers, Cyberpunk, Intelligence, Psychology, Women in SF

II-1107. Maul. Orbit, 2003.

Sullivan's gonzo new novel features two storylines whose connections only become clear at the end of the book. In one plot, a suburban shopping mall is terrorized by over-sexed girl gangs armed with pistols. In the other, women dominate a futuristic world where men have been all but wiped out by a series of plagues and the few who are left are carefully guarded, let out only to compete in hypermasculine competitions by which they gain the right to be sperm donors. The novel is both outrageous and raunchy, enormous fun, but almost guaranteed to offend more conservative readers. Compare Tepper's *The Gate to Women's Country*. (ML)

Themes: Absurdist SF, Biology, Dystopias, Feminist SF, Genetic Engineering, Medicine, Satirical SF, Supermen/women

Sutton, Jeff(erson), U.S., 1913–1979

II-1108. Beyond Apollo. Putnam, 1966.

YA. Delivery of the first lunar permanent station is on schedule when Logan sickens from weightlessness and Apollo II has to return to Earth. Clay, the command pilot, decides to go ahead putting Big Lander on the Moon. The landing is successful, but an off-target landing spot and another injury appear to force abandonment of the project until Clay stays behind alone to man the station. A taut, suspenseful story; vivid, believable rendering of landing procedure; good description of Moon scenery, atmosphere, and travel; theme of human endurance and determination easily comes across. Probably the best of Sutton's several YA SF novels. (FM/ML)

Themes: Space Flight

Swanwick, Michael, U.S., 1950–

II-1109. Bones of the Earth. Eos, 2002.

Expanded from the Hugo Award-winning short story "Scherzo with Tyrannosaur," *Bones of the Earth* tells the tale of paleontologist Richard Leyster, who is approached by a mysterious government operative and offered the chance to travel back in time to the age of dinosaurs. Unfortunately, time proves to be amazingly brittle and time-travel paradoxes, some created by accident, some intentionally, soon begin to do serious damage to the present. This is a thoughtful tale, full of fascinating information about dinosaurs, driven by a solid suspense plot. Compare Crichton's *Jurassic Park* for realistic dinosaurs. Compare Dunn's *Days of Cain* for time-travel paradoxes. (ML)

Themes: Alternate Worlds, Biology, Pastoral, Scientists and Engineers, Time Travel

*II-1110. Gravity's Angels. Arkham, 1991.

This collection of Swanwick's major early short fiction includes such fine stories as "The Feast of St. Janis," "The Transmigration of Philip K, " "Mummer's Kiss," "The Edge of the World," and "Trojan Horse." A number of these stories are award nominees and all are beautifully written. One of the best collections in recent memory. Two other collections containing award-winning stories are *A Geography of Unknown Lands* (1997) and *Moon Dogs* (2000). Compare Sterling's *Crystal Express* and Gibson's *Burning Chrome*. (ML)

*II-1111. Stations of the Tide. Morrow, 1991.

The jubilee tides are coming, and the heavily populated lowlands of the planet Miranda are about to be drowned. Entire cities must relocate to the highlands. Against this chaotic background a government agent known only as the bureaucrat searches for the outlaw Gregorian who, although locally rumored to be a magician, is actually the possessor of stolen and very dangerous nanotechnology. Swanwick presents a marvelously complex world in a very small space, filling it with finely drawn characters, superb stylistic flourishes, tantric sex, literary allusions galore, and fascinating bits of cybernetic technology, including an almost magical artificial intelligence briefcase and a government office complex located exclusively in virtual reality. For similar literary excellence, albeit on a much larger scale, compare Simmons's *Hyperion*. (ML)

Awards: Nebula

Themes: Disaster, Ecology, Life on Other Worlds, Science Fantasy, Virtual Reality

II-1112.   Vacuum Flowers. Arbor, 1987.

Rebel Elizabeth Mudlark is a persona bum; she's addicted to the use of persona wafers, computer chips that, when clipped into the brain, can radically reprogram an individual's personality. Rebel is responsible for the destruction of the master copy of an important new persona wafer, and the mega-corporation, Deutsche Nakasone, which owns rights to the wafer, is after her. Swanwick's venture into cyberpunk is well-written and exciting, though the plot is somewhat on the picaresque side. Compare Effinger's *When Gravity Fails* and Cadigan's *Fools*. (ML)

Themes: Cyberpunk

Sweven, Godfrey (pseudonym of John Macmillan Brown), New Zealand, 1846–1935

*II-1113. Riallaro: The Archipelago of Exiles. Putnam, 1901.

The first part of a couplet concluded with *Limanora: The Island of Progress* (1903). The first volume features a journey though an extraordinarily elaborate chain of islands, whose societies satirize different tendencies in the contemporary human world. Limanora is a scientific utopia reached by the narrator in the final pages, which has established the societies on all the other islands as experimental dumping grounds for its intransigent dissidents. The second volume offers an extraordinarily detailed description and evaluation of Limanora's technological and social achievements, including synopses of several of its key texts, one dealing with the technological transcendence of sex, one with techniques of mental control, and three with broader possibilities of future human evolution. Unfortunately, the island is consumed by a natural disaster before it can export its achievements and ambitions. The couplet is an enormously ambitious work, flawed in some respects but far more imaginative than Bellamy's *Looking Backward,* more constructively inclined than Moszkowski's *The Isles of Wisdom,* and more earnestly profound than Huxley's *Brave New World.* (BS)

Swift, Jonathan, Ireland, 1667–1745

*II-1114. Travels into Several Remote Nations of the World. Benjamin Motte, 2 vols., 1726 (as by Lemuel Gulliver).

The classic four-part imaginary voyage usually known as *Gulliver's Travels,* which defined "Swiftian satire" and spawned an entire subgenre of imitations, including many cast as sequels. Although Gulliver's journeys to Lilliput and Brobdingnag are more familiar, having been given pride of place in the many versions of the text marketed for children, it is the third and fourth parts that are most relevant to SF. The third takes Gulliver to the flying island of Laputa and various nations it overpasses, where the ambitions and methods of contemporary scientists are ruthlessly mocked, while the fourth takes him to the land of the Houyhnhnms, intelligent horses who co-exist with—and strongly disapprove of—bestial human Yahoos. This final voyage obliterates Gulliver's respect for his own kind, making a successful return to his own social sphere impossible. As brilliant and persuasive as it is vitriolic, the pitch-black comedy of the third and fourth voyages establish the book as the greatest work of anti-science fiction and anti-humanism ever penned. The best sequels by other hands include Karinthy's *Voyage to Faremido and Capillaria.* (BS)

Themes: Satirical SF

Swindells, Robert, U.K., 1939–

*II-1115. Brother in the Land. Oxford, 1984.

YA. In the aftermath of nuclear war in Britain, Danny, his younger brother, Ben, and their friend, Kim, can hope to survive only by adopting "Neanderthal" tactics. Ruthlessly honest extrapolation, realistic characterization, and starkly effective style constitute a powerful story. Compare Mace's *Out There;* contrast Lawrence's *Children of the Dust.* (FM)

Themes: Children in SF, Coming of Age, Holocaust and After

Taine, John (pseudonym of Eric Temple Bell), U.K./U.S., 1883–1960

II-1116.   The Greatest Adventure. Dutton, 1929.

The first (written in 1922–1923) of Taine's "mutational romances" crediting dramatic metamorphic power to radioactivity. Cast as a lost world story, it deals with the relics of an experiment in life creation carried out in the Antarctic by an extinct non-human race, including idiosyncratic saurians. The back story is reminiscent of Merritt's *Face in the Abyss,* denuded of its escapist fervor. It was followed by the similarly organized but more complex (and unpleasantly racist) *The Iron Star* (written 1924; published 1930), in which a radioactive meteorite causes bizarre transformations in central Africa; the foregrounding of a character who has "devolved" into a protohuman ape-man makes the novel a companion piece of sorts to *Seeds of Life.* Although *White Lily* (*Amazing Stories Quarterly,* 1930; book, 1952 as *The Crystal Horde*) is an account of alien invasion reminiscent of Merritt's *The Metal Monster* rather than a mutational romance, it emphasizes the same theme of mutability. (BS)

Themes: Evolution

II-1117.   Green Fire. Dutton, 1928.

A thriller written in 1919, inspired by Frederick Soddy's *The Interpretation of Radium* (1909), in which a scientist resentful of his early treatment by his fellow men determines to take revenge when he has the financial and technological means to destroy the world. An early example of Taine's fondness for climactic catastrophes. (BS)

Themes: Scientists and Engineers

II-1118.   Seeds of Life. Fantasy Press, 1951.

A mutational romance first published in *Amazing Stories Quarterly* in 1931, in which an overdose of radiation transforms an ineffectual human into an enterprising superman, whose plans for the future go awry when he comes to count the cost of that kind of accelerated evolution. The probable inspiration of Fearn's *The Intelligence Gigantic* and Weinbaum's *The New Adam,* which assisted it in establishing a stereotypical image of *Homo superior,* not merely for pulp SF but for the comic books that took over the pulp mythology of superhumanity in order to take melodrama to its metalogical extreme. (BS)

Themes: Supermen/women

*II-1119. The Time Stream. Buffalo Book Co., 1946.

One of Bell's earliest experiments in futuristic fiction, written 10 years before it was serialized in *Wonder Stories* in 1931–1932; it draws upon his early experiences of living in California (which he subsequently erased from his official biography) to embed an account of the great San Francisco earthquake in a philosophical romance of time travel. One of the best SF novels of its period; the difficulty Bell had in getting it into print (while he had no trouble publishing a lost race story and modest thrillers that paved the way for the belated publication of *Green Fire*) is illustrative of the inhospitability of the contemporary literary marketplace to intellectually guided speculation. (BS)

Themes: Time Travel

Tarde, (Jean) Gabriel (de), France, 1843–1904

II-1120. Underground Man. 1896. Trans. of *Fragment d'histoire future* by Cloudesley Brereton. Duckworth, 1905.

A novel by an academic sociologist in which a near-ideal society, triumphantly established in the wake of a long series of destructive wars with the aid of advanced science and technology, is forced by the sudden cooling of the sun to move its last survivors underground, where they continue to thrive with the aid of geothermal power. A preface by H. G. Wells comments on the Gallic stubbornness of the author's optimism, although the attitude of the narrative is actually rather dour; Anatole France must have read it before writing the utopian segment of *The White Stone*. (BS)

Themes: Utopias

Temple, William F(rederick), U.S., 1914–1989

II-1121. Four-Sided Triangle. John Long, 1949.

Derived from a 1939 novelette, written at a time when the concept of cloning didn't exist in the non-SF world. The plot sounds mechanical: boy, A, loves girl, B; boy, C, also loves B, but she loves only A; C therefore duplicates B in the laboratory; but alas, since girl, D, is an exact duplicate of B, therefore D also loves only A. (The situation recalls the song from *The Mikado:* "See how the fates their gifts allot/For A is happy, B is not.") But the story, realistically told and richly characterized, far transcends its pulp origin and remains readable today. It can also be read as an interesting variant on Lester del Rey's classic "Helen O'Loy." (PC)

Themes: Clones/Cloning

Tenn, William (pseud. of Philip Klass), U.S., 1920–

II-1122. The Complete Science Fiction of William Tenn: Volume One, Immodest Proposals and **Volume Two: Here Comes Civilization**. NESFA, 2001, 2003.

Classic short fiction from one of the masters of the field. Among the high points are "Down Among the Dead Men," "The Liberation of Earth," "The Masculinist Revolt," "On Venus Have We Got a Rabbi," "Betelgeuse Bridge," and "She Only Goes Out at Night." Although Tenn could write fiction in a serious vein, he was also one of the great satirists of his day. Compare *Our Best: The Best of Frederik Pohl and C. M. Kornbluth* (1987). (ML)

Themes: Satirical SF

*II-1123. Of All Possible Worlds. Ballantine, 1955.

Seven stories and an essay, "On the Fiction in Science Fiction," in this first collection by a writer with an even more savage wit than Sheckley, if that's possible. Memorable items include "Down Among the Dead Men," in which recycled soldiers' corpses are fitted out to fight again because the world is running out of cannon fodder; "The Custodian," a last-person-on Earth story; and "The Liberation of Earth," a sarcastic parable on the hapless fate of small nations invaded and counterinvaded by ideologically well-intentioned superpowers. (PC)

II-1124.   Of Men and Monsters. Ballantine, 1968.

After Earth is invaded and colonized by gigantic aliens, humanity is driven to live a rat-like existence within the walls of the invaders' dwellings. Years later, a few courageous human beings steal an alien spaceship and head for the stars. A fine novel by a talented writer who largely dropped out of the field in the late 1960s and whose work is little remembered today. Compare Disch's *The Genocides* (1965), Benford's *Great Sky River*, and Silverberg's *The Alien Years*. (ML)

Themes: Aliens, Anthropology

II-1125.   Time in Advance. Bantam, 1958.

Highly advanced aliens, in "Firewater" (1952), visit Earth and demoralize humans just by being there. In "Time in Advance" (1956), "pre-criminals" are permitted to do prison time *prior* to committing the crime, which they may then do without interference with the law. In "The Sickness" (1955), a precariously coexistent Russian-American expedition to Mars finds a dead city and is infected with a Martian disease, with unexpected results. Finally, "Winthrop Was Stubborn" (1957) humorously depicts the plight of five ordinary 20th-century people allowed to time travel. A highly satisfactory collection. (PC)

Tepper, Sheri S., U.S., 1929–

II-1126.   The Fresco. Eos, 2000.

The alien Pistach come to Earth and offer us membership in a benevolent interstellar Confederation; the catch is that we have to clean up our act in order to be accepted and the alternative may well be predation by a number of less friendly alien species. The situation becomes even more complex when one of the alien ambassadors to Earth accidentally uncovers information that contradicts ancient Pistach social and religious beliefs as sanctified by the fresco of the title, thus throwing his own heretofore peaceful society into chaos. The novel features Tepper's trademark liberal social criticism and caustic humor at its most powerful, though some may disagree with her faith in the power of social engineering. Compare Moffett's *The Ragged World* (ML).

Themes: Aliens, Galactic Empires, Politics, Satirical SF, Sociology

*II-1127. The Gate to Women's Country. Doubleday, 1988.

After the nuclear war, women rebuilt society with themselves in control of all government, commerce, agriculture, and art. The men live in garrisons outside the city walls, devoting themselves to games, parades, military training, and occasional, strictly controlled, small-scale wars. When they come of age, boys are given the choice of leaving the city to join the men or remaining as servants. One young woman takes exception to this system and runs away with her male lover. Although Tepper has occasionally been criticized for the stridency of her message, *The Gate to Women's Country* is in reality a subtle and sophisticated novel. Compare Slonczewski's *A Door Into Ocean* and Arnason's *A Woman of the Iron People*. Contrast David Brin's *Glory Season* (1993) and Orson Scott Card's *The Memory of Earth* (1992). (ML)

    Themes: Feminist SF, Holocaust and After, Utopias

*II-1128. Grass. Doubleday, 1989.

Diplomats are dispatched to the planet Grass in search of the cure for a deadly disease that is spreading throughout inhabited space. The human settlers, xenophobic and conservative landed gentry, lead an existence tightly structured around the Hunt, a complex and violent ritual involving the use of alien mounts that seem nearly demonic in their malevolence. The presence of a number of not particularly sympathetic religious groups adds complexity to the situation. This is a beautifully written novel with well-developed characters and a number of very interesting aliens. It's also a serious study of the relationship between gender and violence. Two other fine novels set in the same universe and examining similar themes are *Raising the Stones* (1990) and *Sideshow* (1992). Compare Butler's *Dawn* and its sequels and Robert Reed's *The Remarkables*. (ML)

    Themes: Aliens, Colonization of Other Worlds, Feminist SF, Sex in SF

II-1129. A Plague of Angels. Bantam, 1993.

The story opens in what appears to be a village from a typical fantasy novel, but eventually is revealed to be something much stranger. A farm boy named Abasio sets out on an adventure to the wicked big city where a supposed witch is assembling an army of androids equipped with high-tech weapons from a long-abandoned space station. Tepper has mixed fantasy and science fiction tropes before, and she does it particularly well here. Compare Wolfe's *The Book of the New Sun*. (ML)

    Themes: Coming of Age, Science Fantasy

Tevis, Walter S(tone), U.S., 1928–1984

II-1130. Mockingbird. Doubleday, 1980.

In a decadent future whose inhabitants have abandoned literacy, the alienated hero becomes a rebel, while one of the robots that keep things going acquires human sensibilities (to his cost). A further study of alienation using SF motifs is his *The Steps of the Sun* (1983). (BS)

Themes: Psychology, Robots

Thiusen, Ismar (pseudonym of John Macnie), U.K./U.S., 1836–1909

II-1131.   The Diothas; or, A Far Look Ahead. Putnam, 1883.

A utopian novel in which an experiment in mesmerism transports the narrator to 96th-century Niorc (New York). It is a kind of companion piece to Bellamy's *Looking Backward*; the two writers corresponded in advance of writing their novels, so Bellamy's is a parallel text rather than a response. Macnie's has more emphasis on technology and the regulation of sexual relations, and features social reform within a capitalist framework rather than socialist reorganization. (BS)

Themes: Utopias

Thomas, Chauncey, U.S., 1822–1898

II-1132.   The Crystal Button; or, The Adventures of Paul Prognosis in the 25th Century. Houghton Mifflin, 1891.

A hallucinatory fantasy featuring visions of the utopian city of Boston in 4872 A.D. (the novel was written in 1872 but remained unpublished until the success of Bellamy's *Looking Backward* cleared the way for a version edited for publication by George Houghton). Its description of a rationally organized future society—featuring airships, monorail trains, huge pyramidal tower blocks, and the widespread use of solar energy—and its climactic destruction by a comet was a remarkable achievement in 1872, but must have seemed slightly more run-of-the-mill in 1891. (BS)

Themes: Utopias

Thomson, Amy, U.S., 1958–

II-1133.   The Color of Distance. Ace, 1995.

In this planetary adventure tale with strong environmentalist tendencies, Juna, the only human survivor of an exploratory team on a dangerous alien planet, finds that she must totally transform herself to survive, in effect becoming one of the Tendu, the amphibian native species. In the sequel *Through Alien Eyes* (1999), Juna returns to Earth, bringing some of the Tendu with her. Thomson creates a very well-realized rainforest environment. Compare Moon's *Remnant Population* and Reed's *The Remarkables*. (ML)

Themes: Aliens, Biology, Ecology, Genetic Engineering, Life on Other Worlds, Pastoral

Tiptree, James, Jr. (pseud. of Alice Sheldon), U.S., 1915–1987

II-1134. Brightness Falls from the Air. Tor, 1985.

A thriller in which a lonely outpost of galactic civilization is taken over by gangsters while the debris of a nova comes ever closer. The violent oppression recalls old sins committed and old hurts sustained by the human and alien characters. Seemingly modeled on the 1948 film *Key Largo*. Compare Cherryh's *Downbelow Station*. *The Starry Rift* (1986), although billed as a sequel, is actually a collection of three novellas with the same background, including the Hugo-nominated "The Only Neat Thing to Do." (BS)

*II-1135. Her Smoke Rose Up Forever: The Great Years of James Tiptree, Jr. Arkham, 1990.

More than 500 pages of the best fiction of one of the best short story writers in the genre, including such award winners as "The Women Men Don't See," "Love Is the Plan, the Plan Is Death," "The Screwfly Solution," and "Houston, Houston, Do You Read?" Among Tiptree's other fine collections are *Ten Thousand Light Years from Home* (1973), *Warm Worlds and Otherwise* (1975), *Star Songs of an Old Primate* (1978), *Out of the Everywhere and Other Extraordinary Visions* (1981), the World Fantasy Award-winning *Tales of the Quintana Roo* (1986), *The Starry Rift* (1986), *Crown of Stars* (1988), and *Meet Me at Infinity* (2000). Her most effective stories seem motivated by outrage, using SF motifs to set up situations in which the injustices and tragedies of our world are magnified. Scientism, cruelty, and sexism are all attacked. Among those writers currently publishing, the closest in spirit to Tiptree may well be Sheri Tepper. Compare her *Grass* and its sequels. Compare also Russ's *Extra(ordinary) People*. (ML/BS)
  Themes: Feminist SF

II-1136. Up the Walls of the World. Berkley, 1978.

Airborne aliens who enjoy a utopian existence are threatened with extinction when a sun-destroying entity nears their home. Telepathic explorers set up a psychic pipeline to Earth, which might allow some of them to escape by appropriating human bodies. Meanwhile, the human contactees have problems of their own. Compare Jeffrey Carver's *The Infinity Link* (1984). (BS)
  Themes: Aliens, Paranormal Powers

Tolstoi, Alexei, Russia, 1882–1945

II-1137. Aelita. 1922; revised 1937. Recommended trans. (of the revised version) by Antonina W. Bouis. Macmillan, 1981.

An interplanetary romance about a trip to Mars, whose decadent inhabitants are descended from emigrants from Atlantis. The idealistic scientist who builds the rocket ship that makes the journey is entranced by the eponymous Martian princess, but his proletarian assistant is more interested in fomenting revolution. Some strident political propaganda may have been belatedly grafted onto a text that began as a pastiche of Western scientific romance; the story is reminiscent of Robert Cromie's *A Plunge into Space* although it is more likely to have been inspired by Alexander Bogdanov's *Red Star* (1908), an English version of which can be found in Fetzer's *Pre-Revolutionary Russian Science Fiction*. Tolstoi's other scientific romance, published in 1926 and translated as *The Death Box* or *The Garin Death Ray*, adds similar propagandistic elements to a stereotyped thriller about a megalomaniac scientist. (BS)

Themes: Politics, Space Flight

Townsend, John Rowe, U.K., 1922–

II-1138.   Noah's Castle. Oxford Univ. Press, 1975.

YA. The Mortimer family, led by its stubborn father, battens down through hoarding to live out a catastrophe of inflation and scarcity befalling England in the near future. Strains within the family and without force several members to break with the father's plan, and the "castle" is invaded and destroyed. Relentlessly honest in its picture of strong personalities clashing and vivid in depicting society's disintegration, the novel is superior post-catastrophe fiction. Compare Christopher's *The Guardians*; contrast Corlett's *Return to the Gate*. (FM)

Themes: Disaster, Sociology, War

II-1139.   The Visitors. Lippincott, 1977. British title: *The Xanadu Manuscript*.

YA. While jotting down his rapidly fading memories of the Wyatts and their daughter, ostensibly foreign and very mysterious visitors to Cambridge, young John Dunham is forced to admit that the latter are actually visitors from the future and can bring only grief to those whose lives they touch. The time-travel motif is handled freshly and poignantly; characterization is deft and insightful. Compare Suddaby's *Village Fanfare*. (FM)

Themes: Aliens

Tracy, Louis, U.K., 1863–1928

II-1140.   The Final War. Pearson, 1896.

A future-war story from the British boom, stereotypical in most respects but of some historical importance for its outspoken championship of the notion of a "war to end war" that would secure Anglo-Saxon hegemony over the world in perpetuity; the last chapter is a rhapsodic celebration of this notion, which was later employed as a slogan to recruit the cannon fodder profligately wasted on the battlefields of World War I. Tracy's other novels in the same genre were *An American Emperor* (1897), some chapters of which were written by M. P. Shiel when Tracy fell ill during its serialization, and its sequel *The Lost Provinces* (1898); they employ technological innovations very sparingly. (BS)

Themes: War

Trueman, Chrysostom (unattributed pseudonym)

II-1141.   The History of a Voyage to the Moon, with an Account of the Adventurers' Subsequent Discoveries. Lockwood, 1864.

An interplanetary fantasy whose protagonists employ a force of "repulsion" to convey an "island earth" to the Moon. They discover a communistic utopian society of miniature humans, who are unwitting reincarnations of souls who have previously lived on Earth (the latter notion had yet to be featured in Flammarion's *Lumen*, although it had been broached in previous lunar romances and cosmic voyages). A fascinating philosophical romance, intermediate between satirical lunar voyages and scientific romances, which carries forward the kind of bridging work begun by Atterley's *Voyage to the Moon*. (BS)

Themes: Space Flight, Utopias

Tsiolkovsky, Konstantin (Eduardovich), Russia, 1857–1935

II-1142.   Outside the Earth. 1920. Trans. of *Vne zemli* by V. Talmy in *The Call of the Cosmos*. Foreign Languages Publishing House, 1963.

YA. A novel begun in 1896, intended to popularize Tsiolkovsky's ideas about the possibility of employing liquid fueled multistage rockets as a means of space travel. The one featured in the story carries four men into orbit, where space suits enable them to work on the construction of a greenhouse-like satellite that becomes the model for a large-scale colonization enterprise. They spend some time on the Moon and visit Mars, but return without landing there. The story's anticipations are remarkable, although its narrative is clumsy. The collection also contains Tsiolkovsky's pioneering papers on rocketry and several other didactic fantasies, and is therefore preferable to the earlier translation of the novel published as *Beyond the Planet Earth* (1960). (BS)

Themes: Space Flight

Tucker, Wilson, U.S., 1914–

II-1143.   The Long Loud Silence. Rinehart, 1952.

The U.S. east of the Mississippi has been devastated by nuclear and biological weapons. A few surviving immunes are quarantined and refused reentry to civilization because they are carriers of disease. Returning to the wasteland, the narrator becomes reconciled to a life of savagery. Cannibalism, deleted from the initial edition, reappears in a 1970 Lancer revised edition. Even without that denouement, this is a grim, unsparing post-holocaust scenario. Compare Christopher's *The Death of Grass*; contrast Frank's *Alas, Babylon*. (PC)

Themes: Holocaust and After

II-1144.   The Time Masters. Rinehart, 1953.

Derived from a well-told short story, "The Job Is Ended," this is an effective presentation of a taken-for-granted sexual chauvinism and a document of the prejudice that SF shared with other literature and with the "real world" in the early 1950s. Followed by a sequel, *Time Bomb* (1955). The 1971 Nelson Doubleday (SF Book Club) edition restored missing text. Contrast Mitchison's *Memoirs of a Space-woman*, Le Guin's *The Dispossessed*, and anything by Joanna Russ, Vonda McIntyre, Pamela Sargent, or indeed by most *male* SF writers since about 1970. (PC)

  Themes: Supermen/women, Women in SF

II-1145.   The Year of the Quiet Sun. Ace, 1970.

Time travelers trying to figure out a way to subvert the future Armageddon that their research may actually be initiating. Their research also stirs up, ironically, controversy regarding the authenticity of the biblical Book of Revelations. A grimly realistic and cleverly constructed story, unusual in its subtlety. Compare Silverberg's *The Masks of Time*; contrast Kessel's *Corrupting Dr. Nice*. (BS/ML)

  Awards: John W. Campbell (retrospective)
  Themes: Time Travel

Turner, George, Australia, 1916–1997

II-1146.   Beloved Son. Faber, 1978. Series: Ethical Culture.

The first part of a trilogy also including *Vaneglory* (1981) and *Yesterday's Men* (1983). Social reconstruction has followed ecocatastrophe and international relations are being conducted on the basis of a strict ethic of noninterference, but order and control are threatened by the results of experiments in biotechnology and research into the possibility of immortality (already possessed by the mutants who are the main characters of *Vaneglory*). Cynical and downbeat, convinced of the imperfectability of humankind. Compare Compton's *The Electric Crocodile*. (BS/ML)

  Themes: Ecology, Immortality, Pollution

*II-1147. The Sea and the Summer. Faber, 1987. U.S. title: *Drowning Towers*, Arbor House, 1988.

A boy grows up in a future Australia where global warming has raised the level of the sea, drowning most of the coastline, and where out-of-control population growth has led to mass starvation. Despite the hellishness of the situation, we're told that Australia is better off than most places. This is a powerful, depressing, and intensely didactic novel. Compare Harrison's *Make Room! Make Room!* and Brunner's *Stand on Zanzibar*. (ML)

  Awards: Arthur C. Clarke
  Themes: Coming of Age, Ecology, Overpopulation

Turtledove, Harry, U.S., 1949–

*II-1148. The Guns of the South. Ballantine Del Rey, 1992.

On the eve of the Battle of the Wilderness (1864), time-traveling South Africans who are anxious to keep apartheid alive deliver Kalashnikov rifles to General Lee's Confederate army. This vastly improved firepower gives Lee a decisive victory and Lincoln is forced to the negotiating table. Installed as President of the newly independent Confederacy, Lee finds himself having to confront the racist policies of the South Africans and their ally, Nathan Bedford Forrest, until he discovers how the war should "really" have turned out. Informed by a thorough knowledge of the history of the Civil War and also of the politics of the age, this is probably the most interesting and the most insightful of all attempts to rewrite the Civil War. Compare Kantor's *If the South had Won the Civil War* (1961) and Moore's *Bring the Jubilee*. (PK)

Themes: Alternate Worlds, History in SF, Time Travel

*II-1149. How Few Remain. Ballantine Del Rey, 1997. Series: The Great War, American Empire.

This is the opening volume in what may well be the most extensive and detailed work of alternate history ever written. Approximately 20 years before, the Confederacy won the Civil War. When the South purchases parts of bankrupt Mexico from the Emperor, James G. Blaine, President of the United States, uses this as a pretext to launch a war of reunification. Various other famous Americans live their lives and react to these events. Lincoln, for example, has become a socialist while Samuel Clemens edits a newspaper in San Francisco. Following *How Few Remain*, in two trilogies, history continues on its complex, alternate path through the equivalent of World War I and edges towards an American confrontation with a fascist Europe. The first trilogy, The Great War, consists of the volumes *American Front* (1998), *Walk in Hell* (1999), and *Breakthroughs* (2000); the second trilogy, American Empire, consists of *Blood and Iron* (2001), *The Center Cannot Hold* (2002), and *The Victorious Opposition* (2003). A third trilogy is promised. For something comparably ambitious, see Robinson's *The Years of Rice and Salt*. (ML)

Themes: Alternate Worlds, History in SF, War

II-1150.   Ruled Britannia. NAL, 2002.

Turtledove takes one of the standard alternate history "what ifs," what would have happened if the Spanish Armada had defeated Queen Elizabeth's fleet and reimposed Roman Catholicism on England, and somewhat improbably but with great aplomb makes William Shakespeare the hero of an attempt to restore Elizabeth to her throne. All of the great names play their roles, from Christopher Marlowe to Robert Cecil. Turtledove's historical detail is superbly rendered as is his faux Elizabethan language. For the period setting, compare Baker's *In the Garden of Iden* and McIntyre's *The Moon and the Sun*. (ML)

Themes: Alternate Worlds, History in SF, Politics

II-1151. World War: In the Balance. Ballantine Del Rey, 1994. Series: World War, Colonization.

Together with its immediate sequels, *World War: Tilting the Balance* (1995), *World War: Upsetting the Balance* (1996), and *World War: Striking the Balance* (1996), this tells the story of an invasion of Earth by lizard-like aliens in the middle of World War II. With a huge cast of characters and settings that range from China and Russia to Poland and the U.S., Turtledove combines pulp SF action with a nuanced story of shifting loyalties (Jews in German-occupied Poland, for instance, find it preferable to throw in their lot with the aliens). A subsequent series, set some years after an uneasy truce when the alien colonization fleet starts to arrive, *Colonization: Second Contact* (1999), *Colonization: Down to Earth* (2000), *Colonization: Aftershocks* (2001), and *Colonization: Homeward Bound* (2005), is less successful, dragging real historical figures clumsily into the narrative and with a huge cast that has a soap operatic feel. (PK)

Themes: Alternate Worlds, History in SF, Invasion, War

Twain, Mark (pseudonym of Samuel Langhorne Clemens), U.S., 1835–1910

*****II-1152. A Connecticut Yankee in King Arthur's Court**. Webster, 1889.

A classic timeslip romance and allegorical political fantasy, in which a modern man armed with liberal ideals and considerable technological know-how sets out to reform King Arthur's court, but ultimately finds the retardant force of historical inertia too powerful. Very witty, but also very serious and remarkably even-handed, more thought-experiment than exercise in propaganda. Twain never managed to complete any of the other ambitious exercises in satirical SF that he began, although the bizarre microcosmic romances "Three Thousand Years Among the Microbes" and "The Great Dark" were published in 1966 along with other manuscript material. SF scholar David Ketterer usefully collected and edited 15 shorter pieces in *The Science Fiction of Mark Twain* (Archon, 1984). Compare de Camp's more optimistic *Lest Darkness Fall*. (BS)

Themes: Politics, Time Travel

Ure, Jean, U.K., 1943–

*****II-1153. Plague**. Harcourt, 1991. British title: *Plague 99*, 1989.

YA. Three teenagers—Harriet, Fran, and Shahid—struggle to survive when a plague devastates the cities of England. Plausible study of both the pathology of disease and the unpredictability of human response to tragedy is further enhanced by skillful use of multiple points of view. Compare Christopher's *Empty World* (1977) and Armstrong and Butcher's *The Kindling*. (FM/ML)

Themes: Disaster, Medicine, Psychology

van Vogt, A(lfred) E(lton), Canada/U.S., 1912–2000

II-1154. Away and Beyond. Pelligrini, 1952.

Nine stories, 1940–1948, primarily from *Astounding.* Includes his first-written story, "Vault of the Beast," an alien monster from the monster's viewpoint story, "Asylum," in which a newspaper reporter must deal with high-IQ, energy-stealing interstellar vampires, and "Secret Unattainable," told in the form of interoffice memos among the Nazi bureaucracy, which offers a novel explanation for Hitler's suicidal invasion of Russia. *Destination Universe* (Pelligrini, 1952) selects from more sources. Most balanced is *Transfinite: The Essential A. E. van Vogt* (NESFA, 2003), which collects 25 stories from throughout the writer's career. (PC)

II-1155. Slan. Arkham, 1946.

The author's first novel-length work, serialized in 1940, which cast as a superbeing a 9-year-old boy on the lam from the cops and was told in a breathless style. van Vogt later claimed he took the interstellar alien monster viewpoint character he'd previously used, made it sympathetic and installed it in a human body. It worked then; today's readers will have to judge. Simon & Schuster published a revised edition in 1951, but the first edition is preferred. Compare Weinbaum's *The New Adam* and Stapledon's *Odd John.* (PC)

Themes: Paranormal Powers, Supermen/women

II-1156. The Voyage of the Space Beagle. Simon & Schuster, 1950.

The fearsome interstellar beasts encountered by the crew of the future *Beagle* might have made Darwin give it all up as a bad job. The novel, a "fix-up" of unified short tales, may be better as the original stories. The academic emphasis on novels tends to slight shorter, better-written pieces; see the argument by James Gunn in his introduction to his *Some Dreams Are Nightmares.* The viewpoint character is one of van Vogt's obnoxious know-it-all superheroes, who lacks the appeal of young Jommy Cross in *Slan.* (PC)

Themes: Aliens, Space Opera

II-1157. The Weapon Shops of Isher. Greenberg, 1951.

The publishing history of this work is as intricate as some of van Vogt's plots. The NRA should love this series about the Weapon Shops with their slogan, "The right to buy weapons is the right to be free." The story continued in a sequel, *The Weapon Makers,* 1952.

Themes: Supermen/women

*II-1158. The World of Null-A. Simon & Schuster, 1948. Recommended ed.: Berkley, 1970.

"Null-A"—non-Aristotelianism—was supposed to be a new way of thinking that would permeate humankind with the acceptance of General Semantics, popular among many SF readers in the 1940s. But the novel exemplifies what psychologists today call "magical thinking"—not scientific and not, except superficially, semanticist. Gilbert Gosseyn acts for most of the story like a pawn in the hands of vast unknown forces. His superman qualities emerged more clearly in the sequels: *The Pawns of Null-A* (Ace, 1948; as *The Players of Null-A*, Berkley, 1966) and *Null-A Three* (DAW, 1985). (PC)

Themes: Supermen/women

Vance, Jack (pseud. of John Holbrook Vance), U.S., 1916–

II-1159.   Araminta Station. Tor, 1987. Series: Cadwal Chronicles.

Araminta Station on the planet Cadwal was founded as a nature preserve with a strictly limited population of conservationists and research scientists. Over the centuries, however, using a series of legal subterfuges, its now hereditary administrators have allowed enormous population growth, and society has taken on an almost Byzantine complexity. As social unrest begins to spread across the planet, one young police officer attempts to solve a murder. Vance is one of science fiction's premier stylists, though his often wayward plotting and cynical characters aren't to everyone's taste. Sequels include *Ecce and Old Earth* (1991) and *Throy* (1992). (ML)

Themes: Crime and Punishment, Life on Other Worlds, Politics

II-1160.   The Demon Princes, Vol. 1, *The Star King, The Killing Machine, The Palace of Love*, Vol. 2, *The Face, The Book of Dreams*. Orb, 1997.

Originally published between 1964 and 1981 and reprinted in two volumes, these five picaresque novels are vintage Jack Vance, crammed to the brim with sardonic wit and beautiful, slightly understated prose. Five aliens, the Demon Princes of the title, were responsible for the Mount Pleasant Massacre, which destroyed an entire world. Kirth Gersen, whose entire family died in the massacre, has dedicated his life to hunting down and avenging himself upon the princes, one per volume. (ML)

Themes: Aliens, Crime and Punishment

II-1161.   The Dragon Masters. Ace, 1963. Recommended ed.: Gregg, 1976.

At the edge of the galaxy, what is possibly the last human-controlled world is periodically invaded by aliens. The human defenders deploy dragons, of several sizes and degrees of ferocity. However, no summary can do justice to the richness of Vance's atmospherics, which critics often label "baroque." A landmark in the transformation of SF away from both Golden Age and 1950s themes, yet in a different direction from the emerging New Wave. The advent of the dragon foreshadowed its use in other works, such as Anne McCaffrey's popular series with dragons. The Gregg edition features an introduction by Norman Spinrad. (PC)

Themes: Aliens, Invasion

II-1162.   The Dying Earth. Hillman, 1950. Series: Dying Earth.

A hauntingly beautiful story of a far-future Earth "steeped in magic born of rotting history," as Norman Spinrad put it. Scientific experiment has given place to charms and enchantments that really work in these six loosely connected episodes, derived not from technophile Golden Age SF but from a quite antithetical tradition, the world-ends-in-magic milieu explored in the 1930s by Clark Ashton Smith, and picaresque sword and sorcery, such as Leiber's early-1940s Fafhrd and Gray Mouser tales. The hope of a scientific renaissance was not realized in this novel's several sequels. This work launched a whole subgenre of fictional futures in which magic replaces science, a development not altogether healthy for SF or implicitly for the place of science in modern civilization. (PC)

Themes: Science Fantasy

II-1163. Emphyrio. Doubleday, 1969.

The protagonist must travel to Earth to recover the knowledge necessary to free his world from the cultural rigidity imposed on it by alien rulers. Picks up themes from earlier Vance novels, including *The Languages of Pao*, to further illustrate the author's fascination with colorful, exotic cultures and messianic rebels against their stagnation. (BS)

Themes: Aliens

II-1164. The Languages of Pao. Avalon, 1958.

The planet Pao's 15 billion inhabitants have developed a stagnant, passive culture under hereditary rule through an omnipresent civil service, with a language having no formal comparatives and no verbs. By developing entire new languages, with grammars and vocabularies appropriate to particular vocations (soldiers, scholars, technicians), the way is paved for breaking the cultural mold. Relying on the work of Whorf and Sapir, this is the first full-scale use in SF of linguistics as a "hard" science. Compare Delany's *Babel-17*; contrast Piper's "Omnilingual" in *Federation*. (PC)

Themes: Linguistics

II-1165. The Last Castle. Ace, 1967.

A novella in which far-future Earth is recolonized by humans who establish themselves as an aristocracy supported by alien underclasses, but become vulnerable to revolution. Elegant exoticism with an underlying political message. Compare Smith's *Norstrilia*. (BS)

Awards: Hugo, Nebula
Themes: Far Future

II-1166. Night Lamp. Tor, 1996.

Vance's picaresque tale, his last major novel, follows the adventures of Jaro, a young orphan who has lost his early life to brain damage but still looks for answers. The story features the author's trademark leisurely pacing, intense use of irony, complex verbal interplay, and outlandishly constructed societies. (ML)

Themes: Crime and Punishment, Satirical SF

*II-1167. To Live Forever. Ballantine, 1956.

Biological immortality is possible but has to be earned. One rises in rank, with a set number of years added to life, by civic participation, productive employment, or some spectacular public achievement. People who fail to rise are visited by their assassins at the end of their allotted time. One may also choose not to participate and live out one's natural, probably short, life unmolested. Vance works all this out and much more, in terms of a stratified society driven by a covertly vicious form of social climbing. A logical, imaginative work; very possibly Vance's best book. Compare Heinlein's "Methuselah's Children" (in *The Past Through Tomorrow*) and Anderson's *The Boat of a Million Years*. (PC)

Themes: Dystopias, Immortality

VanderMeer, Jeff, U.S., 1968–

II-1168.   Veniss Underground. Nightshade, 2003.

In this dark and intensely allegorical tale, VanderMeer portrays a complex and decadent far-future city populated by Living Artists who create monsters from human flesh, sentient meercats who plot the end of the human race, and doomed lovers who wander the streets of the city and its capacious underworld in black despair. Shadrach, a man of dubious morality, must travel deep into the bowels of Veniss Underground, in search of Nicola, his former lover. Allusions abound to Dante, Orpheus and Eurydice, Hieronymus Bosch, Cordwainer Smith, and Edward Whittemore. For a comparable use of allegory, see James Morrow's *Towing Jehovah* and its sequels. For comparable urban landscapes, see Miéville's *Perdido Street Station*. (ML)

Themes: Cities, Clones/Cloning, Crime and Punishment, Genetic Engineering, Monsters, Mythology

Varley, John, U.S., 1947–

*II-1169. Millennium. Berkley, 1983.

A slick time-travel story based on the award-nominated short story "Air Raid" in which the damaged citizens of a ruined future Earth try to save humankind by kidnapping people from the past whose disappearance cannot create paradoxes. While they are snatching passengers from a doomed jumbo jet, an object is left behind, sparking off changes that may destroy the universe if the time stream is not healed. Clever and tightly constructed, acknowledging its debt to the long tradition of time paradox stories by using famous titles as chapter headings. Made into an adequate film. (BS/ML)

Themes: Time Travel

II-1170.   The Ophiuchi Hotline. Dial, 1977.

Contact with aliens at first brings new opportunities, but then come the Invaders, determined to take over the solar system and expel humankind. What future can there be for displaced persons in the galactic civilization? Compare Brin's *Startide Rising*. (BS)

Themes: Aliens, Future History, Invasion

*II-1171. The Persistence of Vision. Dial, 1978. U.K. title: *In the Hall of the Martian Kings*, 1978.

The first of Varley's short story collections, followed by *The Barbie Murders and Other Stories* (1980) and *Blue Champagne* (1986). The title story, a Nebula- and Hugo award-winner, is a parable in which men are so alienated that the path of true enlightenment is reserved for the handicapped. "In the Hall of the Martian Kings" has castaways on Mars saved by the advent of miraculous life forms. Varley almost always deals in extremes, and the fervent inventiveness of his early stories made them very striking. Compare the short fiction of James Tiptree, Jr. (BS/ML)

II-1172.   Steel Beach. Ace/Putnam, 1992.

Innovations in nanotechnology and medicine have turned the Moon into a near utopia, but our protagonist, the flippant, angst-ridden Hildy Johnson, 100-year-old ace reporter for *The News Nipple*, is onto a hot story. Suicide rates are way up (Hildy himself has committed suicide several times recently) and Luna's Central Computer is afraid that it too may be on the verge of killing itself, permanently. Hildy, who undergoes sex change surgery during the story, must, in effect, track down the Meaning of It All in order to save his/her own life, the life of the Central Computer, and, perhaps, the entire Lunar civilization. What stands out in *Steel Beach*, however, is not the plot or the somewhat arch characters, but rather the amazingly complex society of the Moon. The plot is in effect Varley's excuse to give the reader a guided tour of a marvel-filled new world. Compare Heinlein's *The Moon is a Harsh Mistress* and *Time Enough for Love*. Contrast Bear's *Queen of Angels*. (ML)

Themes: Satirical SF, The Moon, Utopias

II-1173.   Titan. Putnam, 1979. Series: Gaea.

The multiple–award-nominated first volume of a trilogy completed in *Wizard* (1981) and *Demon* (1984). The female protagonist finds an artificial world among the satellites of Saturn and becomes an agent of its resident intelligence, the godlike Gaea, before being forced to turn against "her." Conscientiously nonsexist action-adventure SF. Compare Doris Piserchia's *Earthchild* (1977). (BS)

Awards: *Locus*
Themes: Feminist SF, Satirical SF

Vercors (pseud. of Jean Bruller), France, 1902–1992

II-1174.   You Shall Know Them. Little, Brown, 1953. Trans. by Rita Barisse of *Les animaux dénaturés*, 1952. Variant titles: *Borderline*, Macmillan, 1954; *The Murder of the Missing Link*, Pocket, 1958.

A tribe of "missing links" between ape and human is discovered in a remote corner of New Guinea. Transported to London, one of them is artificially inseminated with human sperm and gives birth. Is *he* a baby boy, or *it* a little ape? Can it be christened according to the rites of the Church of England? When it is killed, was that act a murder? To the growing dismay of the characters, all dwellers at one or another level of the British Establishment, no generally accepted legal, scientific or philosophical definition of "man" exists. A court of law, Parliament, and the U.K.'s famous penny-dreadful press all grapple with the problem. Perhaps only a French writer could so keenly have dissected the ways of his cousins in a matter both witty and wise. Scientific knowledge of pre-human hominids has grown considerably since 1952, but this book still raises some fundamental questions as to who and what we are. The author intensely disliked the 1970 American film version, *Skullduggery*, and had his name removed from the credits. Compare Sawyer's *Hominids*. (PC)

   Themes: Anthropology, Biology

Verne, Jules (Gabriel), France, 1828–1905

II-1175.   The Begum's Fortune. 1879 (with Paschal Grousset). Trans. of *Les cinq cents millions de la bégum* by W. H. G. Kingston. Sampson Low, 1880.

Verne rewrote this political fantasy by Paschal Grousset at the request of his publisher, P. J. Hetzel, and went on to adapt several more manuscripts by the same author; the later ones were identified as collaborations with "André Laurie"—the pseudonym Grousset went on to use on his solo works. The story explains how rival heirs employ vast inheritances to built the rival cities of Frankville (embodying the utopian ideals of French social philosophy) and Stahlstadt (representing the worst aspects of German culture). The story is a reprisal of sorts for France's defeat in the Franco-Prussian War, remarkable for its early description of a proto-fascist dystopia. It is surprising that Hetzel, who used the pseudonym P.-J. Stahl on his own fiction, allowed the name of the dystopian city to stand. (BS)

   Themes: Politics

II-1176.   The Clipper of the Clouds. 1886. Anon. trans. of *Robur le conquérant*. Sampson Low, 1887.

A virtual reprise of *Twenty Thousand Leagues Under the Sea*, featuring an airship in place of the earlier novel's submarine. Nemo's replacement, the arrogant and overbearing Robur, is explicitly presented as an allegory of scientific progress, reflecting the increasing conservatism of Verne's attitude in his later years. Seen in the same light, the sequel, *The Master of the World* (1904; trans. 1914), marches relentlessly towards a conventional technophobia. (BS)

   Themes: Discoveries and Inventions

II-1177.   Dr Ox's Experiment. 1872. Recommended trans. of *Une fantaisie du Docteur Ox* by George M. Towle (originally made in 1874 but here usefully supplemented). Macmillan, 1963.

A novella in which a staid Flemish town accepts an offer by the eponymous philanthropist to equip its streets with a lighting system fueled by the mixing and burning of oxygen and hydrogen; while the pipes are being laid, however, remarkable personality changes begin to afflict the town's inhabitants. An interesting parable; compare David H. Keller's account of a similarly disinhibiting experiment in "The Abyss" (1947). (BS)

Themes: Scientists and Engineers

II-1178. "The Eternal Adam" ("L'eternel Adam"). 1910 (with Michel Verne). Trans. by I. O. Evans in *Yesterday and Tomorrow*. Arco, 1965.

A novella allegedly found among Verne's posthumous papers, probably the work of his son Michel, although the pessimistic ideology is not out of keeping with such late Jules Verne works as *Master of the World*. In the distant future, a historian contrives to decipher a manuscript detailing the destruction of our civilization by a great flood, thus discovering that history is cyclic and progress non-linear. Compare Mitchell's *The Last American*. (BS)

Themes: History in SF

II-1179. Floating Island; or, The Pearl of the Pacific. 1895. Trans. of *L'île à hélice* by William J. Gordon. Sampson Low, 1896.

A quirky political fantasy in which a syndicate constructs a nation-in-miniature, Standard Island, in order to rent its space to millionaires desirous of evading taxes and cruising the world. Their petty rivalries lead them inexorably to disaster. The later translation published as *Propellor Island* is drastically abridged. (BS)

Themes: Fantastic Voyages, Politics

*II-1180. From the Earth to the Moon. 1865. Recommended trans. of *De la terre à la lune* by Jacqueline and Robert Baldick. Dent, 1970.

The first interplanetary novel to focus on the technical and organizational preparations for the voyage, using the actual blast-off as a climax—introducing thereby a new narrative realism whose importance remains unsullied by the unfortunate observation that the envisaged giant cannon would have been fatal to anyone attempting to use it as a means of travel. The inevitable sequel, *Autour de la lune* (1869; uniform with its predecessor as *Around the Moon* in the Baldicks' translation of 1970), continues the story by describing the experiences of the intrepid voyagers as they observe the Moon *en passant* before a slingshot effect hurls them earthward again. The couplet is one of the definitive foundation stones of the SF genre. (BS)

Themes: Hard SF, Space Flight

II-1181. Hector Servadac; or, The Career of a Comet. 1877. Trans. of *Hector Servadac* by Ellen E. Frewer. Sampson Low, 1878.

One of the most ambitious (but least plausible) of Verne's SF novels, whose intriguing first half is framed as a mystery in which a series of puzzling scientific observations are eventually explained by the fact that a fragment of the Earth's surface has been dislodged by a comet—after which the survivors must seek refuge from the rapidly falling temperature in the comet's warm core. Later translations tend to be drastically abridged and very free, reflecting the fact that

Verne seemed to lose confidence while writing the novel and failed to contrive a satisfactory conclusion. Ridley's *The Green Machine* borrows from it, tentatively but even less convincingly. (BS)

Themes: Fantastic Voyages

*II-1182. A Journey to the Centre of the Earth. 1863. Recommended trans. of *Voyage au centre de la terre* by William Butcher. Oxford Univ. Press, 1992.

YA. A classic novel of exploration, whose use of a juvenile protagonist encouraged its earliest (1872) translator to produce a heavily abridged and insultingly dumbed down version, in which young Axel becomes "Harry" and Otto Lidenbrock "Professor Hardwigg"—thus setting an appalling precedent for subsequent adaptors of Verne's work. The original is a classic adventure story about a careful scientific expedition into an underworld inhabited by survivals from various eras of prehistory. It is a key foundation stone of the SF genre, in terms of its careful narrative method and its imaginative ambition. It set the pattern for "Vernian romance" and helped inspire similarly adventurous works by other writers, including George Sand's *Journey Within the Crystal*—which almost beat it into print, so rapid was Sand's response when Hetzel sent her a manuscript copy. (BS)

Themes: Fantastic Voyages, Scientists and Engineers

*II-1183. Twenty Thousand Leagues Under the Sea. 1870. Recommended trans. of *Vingt milles lieues sous les mers* by Walter J. Miller as *The Annotated Jules Verne, Twenty Thousand Leagues Under the Sea*, Crowell, 1976. Also trans. by Emanuel J. Mickel, Indiana Univ. Press, 1992.

A mystery novel in which investigators of a reported monster discover that it is, in fact, a fabulous submarine designed and operated by the misanthropic Captain Nemo. The protagonists, kidnapped aboard the vessel, share in its submarine adventures until they can escape, leaving it to apparent destruction by the maelstrom (although Verne had to rescue it from that fate in order to employ Nemo as a *deus ex machina* in the languorous Robinsonade *The Mysterious Island*, 1874–1875). This was the most popular of Verne's *voyages extraordinaires*, the charismatic figure of Captain Nemo becoming a model for dozens of other characters and cropping up in numerous metafictional pastiches, including Albert Robida's *Voyages très extraordinaires de Saturnin Farandoul* (1879). (BS)

Themes: Fantastic Voyages

Vidal, Gore, U.S., 1925–

II-1184.   Kalki. Random, 1978.

A would-be avatar of the eponymous deity annihilates humankind save for a chosen few, but the New Order quickly founders in betrayal and cruel circumstance. Bleakly ironic. Compare Neil Bell's *The Lord of Life*. (BS)

Themes: End of the World, Religion

II-1185. Messiah. Dutton, 1954.

A mainstream writer's most impressive venture into SF. A new religion pro-claims the worship of death, with suicide the ultimate sacrament. The faith spreads across America, then the world. The story is told by the founder's unbe-lieving PR man, who eventually flees to Egypt, where a stern Muslim fundamen-talism bars the entrance of any infidel notions. A chilling, plausible novel; it anatomizes in particular the amoral, for hire potential of the mass media at the service of an unscrupulous fanatic. Revised in 1965. *Kalki* (1978) is another attack on organized religion. Compare Heinlein's *Revolt in 2100* (in *The Past Through Tomorrow*) and Leiber's *Gather Darkness!* (PC)

Themes: Religion

Villiers de l'Isle, Adam (Jean-Marie-Matthias-Philippe-Auguste, Comte de), France, 1840–1889

II-1186. Tomorrow's Eve. 1886. Recommended trans. of *L'Ève future* by Robert M. Adams. Univ. of Illinois Press, 1982.

A remarkable satirical novel in the same misanthropically Idealist spirit as Vil-liers' early fantasy novella "Claire Lenoir" (1867; recommended trans. by Brian Stableford in *Claire Lenoir and Other Stories*, Tartarus, 2004). A deeply disen-chanted nobleman prevails upon Thomas Edison to manufacture an android who will reproduce the appearance of his mistress without the personality flaws that force him to despise her. The resultant ideal lives up to all his hopes, mak-ing her eventual destruction all the more tragic. A badly mangled translation by Florence Crewe-Jones was serialized in *Argosy-All-Story* in 1926–1927, presumably in response to the release of the novelization of Fritz Lang's movie *Metropolis*, where it may have been read—not quite in the spirit that the author intend-ed—by Lester del Rey, whose "Helen O'Loy" (1938) is a crassly sentimentalized version of the plot. (BS)

Themes: Androids

Vinge, Joan D(ennison), U.S., 1948–

II-1187. Eyes of Amber and Other Stories. Signet, 1979.

A collection whose title novella (Hugo, 1978) is the story of communication between a human linguist and a strange female alien. "To Bell the Cat" also revolves around problems of human–alien communication, while "Tin Soldier" is a curious tale of alienation in which the hero falls out of touch with those around him by aging more slowly. Vinge's short fiction is also found in *Fireship* (1978) and *Phoenix in the Ashes* (1985). (BS)

Themes: Linguistics

II-1188. Psion. Delacorte, 1982. Series: Psion.

YA. Centuries in the future, Cat, an illiterate slum child, reluctantly undergoes training to utilize his telepathic powers and becomes involved in the struggle both to outwit Robiy, an evil telepath, and to aid the wise telepaths, the Hydrans. Fine characterization, detailed setting, provocative study of psi, and suspenseful plotting; engrossing narrative. The sequels, which were marketed as and feel more like adult novels due to their level of violence, are *Catspaw* (1988) and *Dreamfall* (1996). Compare the Johnsons' *Prisoner of Psi*; contrast Norton's *Quest Crosstime*. (FM/ML)

Themes: Children in SF, Far Future, Paranormal Powers

*II-1189. The Snow Queen. Dial, 1980. Series: Snow Queen.

A colorful amalgam of SF and heroic fantasy borrowing the structure of Hans Christian Andersen's famous story, set on a barbarian world exploited by technologically superior outworlders, against the background of a fallen galactic empire. The convoluted plot makes heavy use of ideas drawn from Robert Graves's classic *The White Goddess*. *World's End* (1984), a more modest sequel, relates the adventures of an important secondary character from the first book. The Hugo Award-nominated *The Summer Queen* (1991) ties together plot threads from both of the previous novels. Lacking the fairytale-like qualities of *The Snow Queen,* it is a well done but somewhat more conventional story of planetary intrigue and interstellar politics. *Tangled Up in Blue* (2000) is another competent but modest sequel. Compare Herbert's *Dune* and Mary Gentle's *Golden Witchbreed*. (ML/BS)

Awards: Hugo
Themes: Future History, Life on Other Worlds, Mythology, Paranormal Powers

Vinge, Vernor, U.S., 1944–

*II-1190. A Deepness in the Sky. Tor, 1999.

In this independent prequel to *A Fire Upon the Deep,* the Queng Ho, a company of human interstellar traders, have made a rare discovery, the Spiders, an intelligent alien species whose technological progress has heretofore been limited by the erratic fluctuations of their sun, which forces them into long periods of suspended animation. The aliens, however, now seem poised for a rapid period of growth that could include a dangerous nuclear arms race. Making things even more difficult is the presence of the Emergents, a much less beneficent human culture, bent on enslaving both the Queng Ho and the Spiders. This is one of the best of the recent crop of intellectually challenging, well-written space operas. It features finely drawn characters and a number of well-done action sequences. Compare Brin's *The Uplift War* and Bank's *Excession*. (ML)

Awards: Hugo, John W. Campbell
Themes: Aliens, Future History, Hard SF, Space Opera

*II-1191. A Fire upon the Deep. Tor, 1992.

The Milky Way is divided into four concentric zones: the Unthinking Depths, the Slow Zone, the Beyond, and the Transcend. Inherent in the basic physics of these zones are limitations to intelligence; intellect increases as one moves outward. Humanity, originally from the Slow Zone, is merely one of uncounted races on the Known Net. It is a mark of our success, however, that we have planted thriving colonies well into the Beyond. A human research team exploring the edge of the Transcend accidentally releases a Power, a malevolent superbeing that begins laying waste to the galaxy, wiping out entire intelligent species in a matter of days. Two human children, survivors of the accidental release of the Power, hold the key to its defeat, but they have been shipwrecked on a distant planet on the edge of the Slow Zone and their rescue will be difficult. Vinge's plot is big and bold, almost in the manner of E. E. Smith, but his scientific content is quite sophisticated and his character development is solid. His doglike aliens, with their limited group minds, are endlessly fascinating. Compare Brin's *Startide Rising.* (ML)

Awards: Hugo

Themes: Aliens, Future History, Hard SF, Intelligence, Life on Other Worlds, Space Opera

II-1192. The Peace War. Bluejay, 1984.

The superhuman protagonist can augment his talents even further by interfacing with computers, and must exploit such advantages to the full in order to survive in a future transformed (and wrecked) by the exploitation of elaborate information technology, new biotechnologies, and "bobbles"—stasis fields. Bobbles offer a means of suspended animation, and this becomes the starting point of a sequel, *Marooned in Realtime* (1986), which features an Earth abandoned save for those committed, voluntarily or involuntarily, to such imprisonment. The books combine interesting extrapolations with lively plotting. (BS)

Themes: Computers, Intelligence, Supermen/women

II-1193. True Names. Bluejay, 1984.

A novella first published in 1981. Clever computer hackers have established their own fantasy world within the data matrix of the world's computers, where they can work mischief and enjoy themselves—until someone (or maybe something) tries to take over the world and the hero, blackmailed into cooperating with the FBI, has to stop the rot. A lively and fascinating extrapolation of the idea that advanced technology opens up the opportunities traditionally associated with wizardry. A precursor of Gibson's *Neuromancer.* (BS)

Themes: Computers, Intelligence

Vivian, E(velyn) Charles, U.K., 1882–1947

II-1194. Star Dust. Hutchinson, 1926.

A hopeful scientist perfects a method of making gold, but the discovery brings such complications in its wake that he is quickly disenchanted with its potential to do good. An interesting and more convincing reprise of Doyle's *The Doings of Raffles Haw.* (BS)

Themes: Discoveries and Inventions

Voltaire (Pseudonym of François-Marie Arouet), France, 1694–1778

*II-1195. Micromegas (*Micromégas*). 1752. Recommended trans. by H. Bruce Roswell in *The Romances of Voltaire*, Lincoln MacVeagh, 1928.

A classic *conte philosophique* that assaults the religiously sanctioned notion that humankind is the center of the universe and the pinnacle of creation by bringing a visitor to the solar system from a planet orbiting Sirius; he makes contact with a Saturnian of much smaller dimensions and accomplishments (only a mile tall, possessed of only 72 senses and a lifespan of only 15,000 years) before traveling with him to Earth, where he is understandably surprised to find that creatures who can only be perceived with a microscope are possessed of rudimentary intelligence and ridiculous delusions of grandeur. One of the chief candidates for consideration as the first authentic SF story, though few of its many successors—the best of which include Wells's *The First Men in the Moon*, Beresford's *The Hampdenshire Wonder*, Odle's *The Clockwork Man*, and Phillpotts's *Saurus*—replicate the full extent of its modesty, and few American examples make any such effort at all. (BS)

Themes: Satirical SF

von Hanstein, Otfrid, Germany, 1869–1959

II-1196. Electropolis. 1927. Trans. of *Elektropolis* by Francis Currier in *Wonder Stories Quarterly*, Summer 1930.

A typical German *zukunftsroman* of the 1920s, which reacts to the humiliation of defeat in World War I by imagining a future in which the superior skill and determination of German engineers will enable a phoenix-like regeneration of a high-tech superstate. Here, the exploitation of radium deposits in Australia facilitate the building of a futuristic city by a Teuton industrialist, which he must then defend when the relic of the decadent British Empire attempts to take it over. The other von Hanstein novels featured in the *Wonder* magazines— "Between Earth and Moon" (1930), "Utopia Island" (1931), "In the Year 8000" (1932), and "The Hidden Colony" (1935)—display a considerable imaginative range as well as political attitudes likely to discomfit modern readers. Compare Hastings's *City of Endless Night* and the sequels to Schachner's "Past, Present and Future." (BS)

von Harbou, Thea, Germany, 1888–1954

II-1197. Metropolis. (*Metropolis*). 1926. Anon. trans. Hutchinson, 1927.

A novelization of the famous silent film by the director's wife, which has no opportunity to reproduce the visual imagery that made the movie so successful and therefore reads as lamely as Lovelace's novelization of *King Kong*. The plot is a woefully unconvincing political fantasy about the attempted subversion of a labor dispute by a magically disguised robotic *femme fatale*. *The Rocket to the Moon* (1930), von Harbou's novelization of Lang's other SF film—the interplanetary romance *Die Frau im Mond* (1929)—is similarly depleted in print. (BS)

Themes: Politics

Vonarburg, Élisabeth, Canada, 1947–

II-1198. Reluctant Voyagers. Bantam Spectra, 1995. Trans. of *Les voyageurs malgré eux* by Jane Brierley.

Catherine Rhymer begins to notice odd and subtle differences between the world around her and the world she remembers. The streets of her native Montreal have changed in small ways. The dates in and details in history books aren't what they used to be. She doubts her own sanity at first, but when she discovers information concerning a secret revolutionary movement, she realizes that the world itself has gotten very strange indeed. (ML)

Themes: Alternate Worlds, Crime and Punishment

II-1199. The Silent City. Press Porcepic, 1988. Trans. of *Le silence de la cité*, 1981, by Jane Brierley.

In this award-winning novel, life on Earth has nearly been destroyed by a massive ecological collapse. Elisa has grown up in a high-tech underground city under her father's tight control. Utilizing the city's technology to change herself into a man and to create children who can change sex at will, Elisa attempts to end patriarchal control of the remaining human enclaves on the planet's surface. Vonarburg's Tiptree Award-nominated *In the Mother's Land* (1992; republished in 2001 as *The Maerlande Chronicles*) is set in the same world, but many years later, after the establishment of a matriarchal society. Both novels are rather slow-moving; but their examination of gender issues is both earnest and intelligent. Compare Wilhelm's *When Late the Sweet Bird Sang*, Charnas's *Walk to the End of the World*, and Louise Lawrence's *Children of Dust*. (ML)

Themes: Ecology, Feminist SF, Genetic Engineering, Holocaust and After

Vonnegut, Kurt, U.S., 1923–

II-1200. Cat's Cradle. Holt, 1963.

The absurdist vision, going beyond mere satire, that had been subtly implicit even in straightforwardly extrapolative SF by Vonnegut such as *Player Piano* is unabashed in this novel. Not that his earlier satiric targets escape unscathed here, including both organized religion and the organized corporate idiocies of "Ilium." But here Vonnegut has more in common with Ballard and Dick than with, say, Pohl and Kornbluth. Like other Vonnegut works, the story also has traceable roots in traditional American folk humor, especially the southwestern tall tale. (PC)

Themes: Absurdist SF

II-1201.   Galapagos. Delacorte, 1985.

A group of tourists on a cruise survive the end of the world, settling on a small Galapagos island and beginning a new evolutionary sequence. The ghostly narrator looks back on things from a perspective of a million years later. Compare Bernard Malamud's *God's Grace* (1982). (BS)

   Themes: End of the World, Evolution

*II-1202.   Player Piano. Scribner, 1952. Variant title: *Utopia 14*, Bantam, 1954.

In this first novel, Vonnegut realistically traced the personal and political consequences of what used to be called "technological unemployment," then "automation," now "job displacement." Most working people have been forced into a future WPA while the technocratic upper class languishes in a stifling corporate culture. In his opposition to replacing people with machines, the rebellious hero identifies with the Luddites of the 19th-century Industrial Revolution and with the Native Americans' last Ghost Dance uprising: quixotic, but necessary "for the record." The story has touches of the absurd that would be evident in later work, but it is increasingly prescient as globalism triumphs. Compare Pohl and Kornbluth's *The Space Merchants*. (PC)

   Themes: Satirical SF

II-1203.   The Sirens of Titan. Dell, 1959 (paper); Houghton, 1961 (hardcover).

In this second novel, Vonnegut put a reverse-English spin on some standard gambits of SF, such as time and space travel, and this is less a straight SF novel than a jazz variation on/takeoff from the genre, anticipating the work of Douglas Adams. Monuments on Earth and on Saturn's satellite Titan exist only to convey an utterly banal message from one galactic civilization to another. Elements of this plot reappear in Vonnegut's most bitterly autobiographical novel, *Slaughterhouse-Five*. The journeyings here aren't jaunty pulp adventures but are darkly disturbing, which may be a reason why SF fans were slow to respond to this work. (PC)

   Themes: Absurdist SF

*II-1204. Slaughterhouse-Five; or, The Children's Crusade. Delacorte, 1969.

Billy Pilgrim survives the Dresden firestorm as a POW during World War II but subsequently becomes unstuck in time after being kidnapped by Tralfamadorians and caged with a pornographic film star. Thus he learns that everything is fixed and unalterable, and that one simply has to make the best of the few good times one has. A masterpiece, in which Vonnegut penetrated to the heart of the issues developed in his earlier absurdist fabulations. A key work of modern SF. (BS/ML)

   Themes: Time Travel, War

Waldrop, Howard, U.S., 1946–

*II-1205. Night of the Cooters: More Neat Stories. Ursus, 1990.

One of Waldrop's better collections, following *Howard Who?* (1986) and *All About Strange Monsters of the Recent Past* (1987; U.S. paperback, *Strange Monsters of the Recent Past* (1991) adds the novella "A Dozen Tough Jobs"), gathering 10 stories from the 1980s. All are outrageously imagined and narrated with scathingly deadpan humor. The title story retells Wells's *War of the Worlds* in a Texas setting; "Thirty Minutes Over Broadway" re-creates the atmosphere of early comic books; "French Scenes" hilariously applies sampling/mixing technologies to film. The three collections are filled with deceptively lightweight but ingeniously crafted gems, marking Waldrop as one of best short story writers of the 1980s. Many are alternate histories. *Strange Things in Close-up: The Nearly Complete Howard Waldrop* (1989) mixes stories from the earlier volumes. Two more recent collections are *Dream Factories and Radio Pictures* (2001) and *Custer's Last Jump and Other Collaborations* (2003), which includes stories co-authored with George R. R. Martin, Bruce Sterling, and others. Compare the stories of Lafferty. (RL/ML)

> Themes: Humorous SF, Satirical SF

Wallace, Ian (pseud. of John W. Pritchard), U.S., 1912–1998

II-1206.   Croyd. Putnam, 1967. Series: Croyd.

First of a series of sophisticated van Vogtian superman stories, in which the eponymous hero must continually save the galaxy. *Dr. Orpheus* (1968) is a particularly fine blend of SF and quasi-mythological themes, strongly recalling Charles Harness's casually embellished van Vogtian adventure stories. (BS)

> Themes: Supermen/women

Walton, Bryce, U.S., 1918–1988

II-1207.   Sons of the Ocean Deeps. Winston, 1952.

YA. Chagrined at having been washed out of the rocket program, Jon West hopes to hide away in the underseas service. Gradually learning underwater survival techniques, suffering patiently the taunts of Sprague, who resents his family, and acquiring self-knowledge, Jon proves himself a man. Depiction of aquatic life, real and imagined, and of possible living quarters is extensive and interesting; style is competent; and the hero's maturation is plausible and convincing. One of the better 1950s Winston novels. Compare Norton's *Star Man's Son: 2250 A.D.* (FM/SM)

> Themes: Coming of Age

Wandrei, Donald, U.S., 1908–1987

II-1208.   Colossus: The Collected Science Fiction of Donald Wandrei.
Fedogan and Bremer, 1989.

An omnibus edition of 21 SF stories, mostly written in a conspicuously slapdash fashion for the pulps. They are of some significance because of the gloriously uninhibited temper of Wandrei's imagination, which revels in exotic cataclysms and extremes of scale. "Colossus" and its sequel "Colossus Eternal" (both 1934) are colorful macrocosmic fantasies, while "Finality Unlimited" and "Infinity Zero" (both 1936) describe ironic apocalypses with ghoulish glee, as does the far-future couplet consisting of "The Red Brain" (1927) and "On the Threshold of Eternity" (1937). (BS)

Watson, Ian, U.K., 1943–

II-1209.   The Book of the River. Gollancz, 1984. Series: Black Current.

The first part of a trilogy completed in *The Book of the Stars* (1985) and *The Book of Being* (1985). Societies on the two banks of a vast river are kept apart by the living "black current," which also intervenes to make females dominant in the economic life of one shore. The protagonist manages to cross to the other side, where she finds a cruelly oppressive male-dominated society, and then must play crucial role in the events following the withdrawal of the alien divider. In the later volumes she gradually learns the truth behind the enigmatic mythology of her world and must join in a cosmic conflict between the Worm and the Godmind, suffering death and rebirth in her quest to save humankind from the fate planned for it by the latter. Echoes themes from Watson's earlier work, but the tone is much lighter and the plotting more easily paced; the central character is appealing. Compare Varley's Titan trilogy and McAuley's Confluence sequence. (BS/ML)

Themes: Mythology, Science Fantasy, Women in SF

*II-1210.   The Embedding. Gollancz, 1973.

An intricately constructed novel about the power of language to contain and delimit "reality." It features an experiment in which children are taught an artificial language to alter their perception of the world; a Native American tribe whose use of psychotropic drugs is associated with transformations of their native tongue; and alien visitors who seek to understand humans via their communicative artifacts. Original and mind-stretching, something of an imaginative tour de force. Compare Delany's *Babel-17*. (BS)

Themes: Linguistics, Psychology

II-1211.   The Flies of Memory. Gollancz, 1990.

Aliens who look very much like human-sized flies visit the Earth and spend most of their time viewing our great works of art and architecture, as well as our natural wonders. They say their purpose is simply to record what they're seeing, but then some of the objects begin to disappear, including a significant part of the city of Munich. Compare Mark S. Geston's *Mirror to the Sky* (1992). (ML)

Themes: Aliens, Linguistics

*II-1212. The Gardens of Delight. Gollancz, 1980.

A colony world visited after many years by a starship from Earth is found to have been remade in the image of the Bosch triptych, whose centerpiece is the famous "Garden of Earthly Delights"; here the characters (human, nonhuman, and mechanical) undergo continual metamorphic reincarnations, apparently striving to ascend an evolutionary ladder to transcendental enlightenment. Despite the fabulous trappings and the use of alchemical metaphors, the story is provided with a sound SF explanation and has the sense of discipline that is (or ought to be) characteristic of SF. Marvelous imaginative and intellectual showmanship, unparalleled in its exoticism. Compare and contrast Silverberg's *Son of Man* (1971). (BS)

Themes: Evolution, Life on Other Worlds

II-1213.   The Jonah Kit. Gollancz, 1975.

Men open communication with whales by imprinting a human thought pattern on the brain of a sperm whale, but when the whales learn what we have to tell them—including an astronomer's recent discovery that ours is only an echo of the "true" universe—their worldview is devastated. A highly original novel with some effective description of nonhuman consciousness. Compare Sucharitkul's *Starship and Haiku*. (BS)

Themes: Linguistics

II-1214.   Miracle Visitors. Gollancz, 1978.

A novel developing the hypothesis that UFO experiences are altered states of consciousness that tantalize rationality and beckon humankind to further mental evolution. Some fine imagery displayed in a careful and orderly narrative. Picks up themes from the earlier novels, *The Martian Inca* (1977) and *Alien Embassy* (1977), which feature more melodramatic images of emerging metahumanity. (BS)

Themes: Psychology

II-1215.   The Very Slow Time Machine. Gollancz, 1979.

Watson's first collection, followed by *Sunstroke and Other Stories* (1982), *Slow Birds and Other Stories* (1985), *Salvage Rites and Other Stories* (1989), *Stalin's Teardrops and Other Stories* (1991), and *The Great Escape* (2002), among others. The stories display his delight in novel and startling ideas, filling a spectrum from the flippant "My Soul Swims in a Goldfish Bowl" to the extravagant title story about a most unusual journey through time. The versatility of Watson's imagination is well suited to short fictions of the "idea as hero" variety, and all of his short story collections are worth exploring. Compare Bayley's *The Knights of the Limits*. (BS/ML)

Watson, Simon, U.K., 1975–

II-1216.   No Man's Land. Gollancz, 1975.

YA. Set in a future England where progress rules and the countryside is "rationalized" through technology, the story concerns Alan's fight, aided by another youth, Jay, and the 65-year-old general, to prevent the demolition of an ancient keep by a gigantic robot. Although the fight is successful, the victory over rationalizing is just local. A bit slow-moving, the novel impresses because of its plausible scenario and its sympathetic portrait of old age and love of the countryside. Compare Corlett's *Return to the Gate*, contrast Christopher's *The Prince in Waiting*. (FM)

   Themes: Far Future, Pastoral

Watts, Peter, Canada, 1958–

II-1217.   Starfish. Tor, 1999. Series: Starfish.

In the 21st century, the maintenance workers doing long duty tours at a geothermal power plant in deep ocean off the northwest coast of Canada are intentionally chosen for their psychotic tendencies on the theory that they're already adapted to a high-stress lifestyle and unlikely to want to return to their former lives in any case. They've also been surgically altered to live under water at intense pressures. Life at the plant is pretty awful, but quickly gets much worse when the workers uncover a dangerous and archaic, bacterial life form that, if it makes it to the surface, could destroy all life on Earth. Watts starts with a hoary pulp premise reminiscent of Campbell's "Who Goes There?" (1938) and several bad SF films of the 1990s, but turns it into a fine piece of noir SF through his well-developed underwater setting, fascinating use of technology, excellent pacing, and powerfully developed sense of horror and paranoia. *Maelstrom* (2001) is an equally strong, but radically different cyberpunkish sequel. The third tale in the series, *Behemoth* (2004), was arbitrarily divided into two volumes, subtitled *β-max* and *Seppuku*. Compare Herbert's *The Dragon in the Sea*. (ML)

   Themes: Biology, Hard SF, Psychology

Webb, Jane (later Mrs. John Claudius Loudon), U.K., 1807–1858

II-1218.   The Mummy! A Tale of the Twenty-Second Century. Colburn, 3 vols., 1827 (published anonymously).

A futuristic romance inspired by Mary Shelley's *Frankenstein*, in which the place of the monster as a critical observer of human affairs is taken by the revived mummy of Cheops. The mummy takes a hand in the political affairs of the day, but the motivation and objectives of its machinations remain unclear; in the meantime, the characters pursue their own amatory ends with mixed results. The novel's proto-feminism is more conspicuous than Mary Shelley's, though far less assertive than Mary Wollstonecraft's; nothing anywhere near as bold appeared for 50 years after Victoria—a queen far less akin to Elizabeth I than the one featured in the novel—ascended to the British throne in 1837. The version reprinted in 1994 is heavily and rather arbitrarily abridged. (BS)

Webb, Sharon, U.S., 1936–

II-1219. Earthchild. Atheneum, 1982. Series: Earthchild.

YA. Young people who can become immortal because of the Mouat-Gari process must be protected from their envious elders. Since immortality is no guarantee of creativity, a select few, chosen by Kurt Kraus, one of the immortal leaders, are asked to decide between immortality and creative mortality. Engrossing reading, provocative speculation, and poignant and believable situations. Sequels are *Earth Song* (1983), which focuses on David Defour, a gifted young composer who chooses music over immortality, and *Ram Song* (1984), in which Kurt again intervenes to preserve balance between demands for immortality and society's need for creativity. Compare Bonham's *The Forever Formula* (1979); contrast Bethancourt's *The Mortal Instruments.* (FM)

Themes: Far Future, Genetic Engineering, Immortality

Weber, David, U.S., 1952–

II-1220. On Basilisk Station. Baen, 1993. Series: Honor Harrington.

The first volume in an enormously popular series. This is decidedly old-fashioned space opera with a female hero, Honor Harrington, who is reminiscent of both C. S. Forester's Horatio Hornblower and Lois Bujold's Miles Vorkosigan. Commander Harrington's joy at having received command of her first Manticoran navy starship, *HMS Fearless*, is tempered by the fact that some fairly idiotic naval politics has saddled her ship with an experimental weapons system that simply doesn't work the way it's supposed to. By succeeding despite this impediment, she unintentionally makes some powerful enemies. Then, exiled to what appears to be a minor post in the back of the beyond, Harrington saves the day when Manticore's primary enemy, the Haven Republic, attacks unexpectedly. Sequels to date include *The Honor of the Queen* (1993), *The Short Victorious War* (1994), *Field of Dishonor* (1994), *Flag in Exile* (1995), *Honor Among Enemies* (1996), *In Enemy Hands* (1997), *Echoes of Honor* (1998), *Ashes of Victory* (2000), and *War of Honor* (2002), plus a number of shared-world novels and collections set in the Honor universe. Compare Bujold's Vorkosigan books and Cherryh's Union-Alliance novels, although the latter two series have higher literary ambitions. (ML)

Themes: Politics, Space Opera, War

Weinbaum, Stanley G(rauman), U.S., 1902–1935

II-1221. The Black Flame. Fantasy Press, 1948.

Omnibus of two novellas (actually two drafts of the same story) in which Weinbaum attempted to fuse the conventions of pulp SF and the "love story" in order to express his Haggardesque fascination with *femmes fatales* figures. Neither sold while he was alive, although both were picked up for posthumous publication, the former as "Dawn of Flame" (1936) and the latter (1939) in the somewhat abbreviated form reproduced here. The full-length version of *The Black Flame* reissued by Tachyon in 1995 is the preferable text of that element. It is more reminiscent of A. Merritt's purple-dyed pastiches of Haggard than of *She* itself. (BS)

Themes: Women in SF

*II-1222. A Martian Odyssey and Other Science Fiction Tales: The Collected Short Stories of Stanley G. Weinbaum. Ed. by Sam Moskowitz. Hyperion, 1974.

An omnibus edition of Weinbaum's short fiction, including the contents of two earlier collections, *A Martian Odyssey and Others* (1949) and *The Red Peri* (1952). Weinbaum set important precedents with his blithely exotic accounts of alien life, the first in the pulp magazines to exhibit a rudimentary awareness of ecological issues; the best are "A Martian Odyssey" (1934), "Flight on Titan" (1935), "Parasite Planet" (1935), "The Mad Moon" (1935), and "The Lotus Eaters" (1935). Other notable inclusions are "The Adaptive Ultimate" (1935), a superwoman story more closely akin to *The Black Flame* than *The New Adam*, and "Proteus Island" (1936), a pastiche of Wells's *Island of Dr Moreau* recast as a mutational romance. (BS)

II-1223. The New Adam. Ziff-Davis, 1939.

Weinbaum's best novel is a thoughtful account of a superhuman growing up as a "feral child" in ordinary human society. Insufficiently melodramatic for the pulp magazines of the 1930s, its neglect illustrates the marketing problems faced by writers of that era who desired to take their story ideas more seriously. Although somewhat less polished than Stapledon's *Odd John*, its extrapolation of its central premise is equally conscientious; it contrasts strongly with the first outstandingly successful pulp superman story, van Vogt's *Slan*, which appeared in *Astounding* a year later. (BS)

Themes: Supermen/women

Wells, H(erbert) G(eorge), U.K., 1866–1946

II-1224. The Croquet Player. Chatto and Windus, 1936.

A satirical novella presenting an allegory of evolution in the story of a young socialite haunted by "ghosts" of a brutal past. This was the best of the *contes philosophiques* that Wells produced towards the end of his life, which he classified as "sarcastic fantasies." The others include an account of a critical alien observer, *The Camford Visitation* (1937); the Lamarckian fantasy *Star-Begotten* (1937); and the biblical fantasy *All Aboard for Ararat* (1940). (BS)

Themes: Evolution

*II-1225. The First Men in the Moon. Newnes, 1901.

The last of Wells's classic scientific romances, which carefully bridges the gap between his scientifically inspired *contes philosophiques* and his comic studies of late Victorian social life, pushing the speculative material to the sidelines of the narrative (where Wells hoped that it might be just about tolerable to arrogantly narrow-minded champions of "the novel of character" who thought "the novel of ideas" essentially despicable). The standard 19th-century British method of imaginary space travel, antigravity, is here recast as Cavorite. The two ill-matched protagonists put on a spirited comedy double act for the greater part of the novel, whose serious aspect is carefully reserved for the epilogue in which the stranded Cavor transmits his account of the hyper-organized Selenite society back to Earth. (BS)

Themes: Life on Other Worlds, Space Flight

II-1226.   The Food of the Gods and How It Came to Earth. Macmillan, 1904.

A satire in which a biotechnology promoting accelerated growth during the earliest phases of life is briefly promoted as "boomfood"—the downside being that it works just as well on pests (and humans) as it does on meat-producing animals. After 20 years, the population of human giants, though small and exploitable, begins to generate hostility among their ordinary kin; now growing to adulthood, the giants formulate a society of their own and decide that their superior race will inherit the Earth. The story is an uneasy combination of scientific romance and satire, neither aspect of the story being extrapolated with sufficient force; Bulgakov got more mileage from the idea when he borrowed it for "The Fatal Eggs." (BS)

Themes: Discoveries and Inventions

II-1227.   The Invisible Man: A Grotesque Romance. Pearson, 1897.

A mystery story whose enigmatic anti-hero, initially a fugitive, is finally provoked by the prying of others into revealing that he has made himself invisible. As he despairs of finding a remedy for his condition, his initially trivial exploitations of his condition become increasingly anti-social, until he goes mad and has to be put down. The U.S. edition added an epilogue in which the secret is inherited by a tramp, which became a fixture in all editions after 1906. The inspiration of dozens of dramatizations—because it offers a perfect testing ground for theatrical special effects—the story became a modern myth in the same conspicuously paranoid vein as Mary Shelley's *Frankenstein*, although it has not generated the same interest in the peculiarities of its underlying psychology; John Sutherland's analysis of a key element in the story's dubious logic, "Why Is Griffin Cold?" (an essay in his *Is Heathcliff A Murderer? Puzzles in Nineteenth-Century Fiction*, Oxford, 1996), is a useful signpost for such analysis. (BS)

Themes: Discoveries and Inventions

*II-1228.   The Island of Doctor Moreau: A Possibility. Heinemann, 1896. Variorum ed. by Robert Philmus. Univ. of Georgia, 1993.

A highly significant literary experiment, partly inspired by Victor Hugo's paradigm example of a philosophical satire cast in the form of a popular melodrama, *L'homme qui rit* [*The Man Who Laughed*; trans. as *The Laughing Man*] (1869). Essentially a satirical allegory in which Moreau stands in for God and his gruesome methods of surgical adaptation model Darwinian processes of evolution, it is also a graphic horror/SF story. The hybridization seemed shocking at the time but served to reveal the potential of SF to couch serious questions in a melodramatic matrix—a potential that garish pulp fiction was, however ironically, ideally placed to exploit. The many revisitations of its theme include several homages, notably Brian Aldiss's *Moreau's Other Island* (1980) and *Dr. Franklin's Island* (2002) by "Ann Halam" (Gwyneth Jones). (BS)

Themes: Evolution

II-1229.   Men like Gods. Cassell, 1923.

A utopian novel in which a group of contemporary observers (all based on contemporary figures, including Winston Churchill and the then prime minister Arthur Balfour) are catapulted into a distant future inhabited by scientifically advanced telepathic supermen. They import disease, dissent, and other contemporary brutalities, thus deserving the contempt lavishly heaped upon them by the author, his alter ego within the story, and the affronted utopians. The story is as waspish as contemporary future-war novels in the vein of Shanks's *People of the Ruins*; it makes an interesting contrast with Odle's meditatively laid-back *Clockwork Man.*

Themes: Utopias

II-1230.   The Shape of Things to Come. Hutchinson, 1933.

A hybrid of scientific romance and futurology that summed up Wells's conclusions—considerably revised since *Anticipations* (1901)—regarding the *via dolorosa* that his contemporaries were doomed to follow because they refused to listen to all his good advice. The images of a new world war and the emergence thereafter of a fascist air dictatorship are in keeping with the general tenor of contemporary scientific romance, but the detail is impressive. Compare the more narrowly horizoned of Olaf Stapledon's future histories, especially *Darkness and the Light* (1942).

Themes: Future History

*II-1231. The Complete Short Stories of H. G. Wells. Ed. by John Hammond. Dent, 1998.

An omnibus of all the stories Wells thought worthy of reprinting was issued by Ernest Benn in 1927 and frequently reprinted; this belatedly updated edition includes items excluded therefrom and a handful of stories written after that date. The most notable SF inclusions, in addition to *The Time Machine*, are those from *Tales of Space and Time* (1899), which include a visionary account of life on Mars, "The Crystal Egg" (1897), the disaster story "The Star" (1897), and the elaborate futuristic novella "A Story of the Days to Come" (1899). Also of considerable interest are several stories about exotic life forms, including "In the Abyss" (1896), "The Sea Raiders" (1896), and "The Empire of the Ants" (1905);

several about ingenious inventions, including "The New Accelerator" (1901) and a prophetic account of tank warfare, "The Land Ironclads" (1903); and a few visionary fantasies, including the brief cosmic extravaganza "Under the Knife" (1896). (BS)

*II-1232. The Time Machine. Heinemann, 1895. *The Definitive Time Machine,* ed. by Harry M. Geduld. Indiana Univ. Press, 1987.

The definitive version of a far-future fantasy first conceived as a series of *contes philosophiques* whose earliest manifestation was a three-part series, "The Chronic Argonauts," in the *Science Schools Journal* in 1888. This was redeveloped in seven episodes in the *National Observer* in 1894 before being more elaborately fictionalized in a serial published in the *New Review* in 1895; the Heinemann version omits two episodes from the *New Review* serial but retains more of its text than the near-simultaneous edition published in the U.S. by Holt. The opening sequence—in which a character identified only as the Time Traveller, explains the theory of his time machine to a skeptical audience, before recounting the story of his first exploratory journey into the far future—may seem clumsy to modern readers, but was crucial in establishing the narrative status of an extremely precious literary device. The account of future evolution offered by the novella—in which the social classes of Victorian England fragment into separate species, one effetely degenerate and the other brutally predatory, followed by a long and terminal decline of the biosphere as the sun cools—was soon outdated, but it offered a crucial signpost and precedent for subsequent explorers of the future. It is the most important foundation stone of British scientific romance and the SF genre in general. (BS)

Themes: Far Future, Time Travel

II-1233. The War in the Air, and Particularly How Mr Bert Smallways Fared While it Lasted. Bell, 1908.

Wells stayed away from the future-war subgenre pioneered by George Griffith (whose works are wryly acknowledged herein) because he did not want to be associated with it, and when he finally condescended to join in—on the grounds that no serious futuristic speculator could evade the conclusion that a war was looming—he took up a standpoint directly opposed to the enthusiastic jingoism of such journalistic contributors as le Queux and Tracy. He adopts the viewpoint of a hapless bicycle repairman and busker, who is carried off by a stray balloon and swept up by the violent tide of aerial warfare, surviving not as a heroic combatant but as an improvisatory scavenger. As in so many of Wells's later novels, the fusion of comedy and satirical melodrama is awkwardly chimerical, but the novel is a useful admonitory antidote to the general run of future-war stories. (BS)

Themes: War

*II-1234. The War of the Worlds. Heinemann, 1898. *A Critical Edition of The War of the Worlds*, ed. by David Y. Hughes and Harry M. Gedult. Indiana Univ. Press, 1993.

A hybrid satirical melodrama in much the same spirit as *The Island of Dr Moreau*, save that the allegory is political rather than religious. The inhabitants of Mars, whose own planetary resources are on the point of exhaustion, decide to colonize Earth, adopting the same attitude and methods as the British colonists of Tasmania. They arrive with guns blazing to plant their crops, treating humankind as vermin to be exterminated. Unlike the colonists of the Americas, however—who imported diseases that wiped out almost all the native Americans—the Martians are stopped in their tracks by Earthly bacteria, which provide a deeply ironic *deus ex machina*. The novel is a tour de force whose innumerable fictional offspring include numerous adaptations and homages, by far the most effective of which was Orson Welles's Mercury Theater radio broadcast of 1938. It is not Wells's fault that the story was copied so profusely and so slavishly that alien beings were firmly established in the public eye as monstrous invaders, thus giving rise to a new kind of xenophobia. (BS)
Themes: Invasion, Life on Other Worlds

II-1235.   When the Sleeper Wakes. Harper, 1899.

A classic dystopian novel ironically modeled on Bellamy's *Looking Backward* but more closely akin to Donnelly's *Caesar's Column*, in which a young liberal who goes to sleep in 1897 wakes to find that the scientifically advanced world of 2100 is still dominated by oppressive capitalists. Fortunately, his invested wealth has accumulated so vastly over the years that his trust fund now controls half the world's capital and his own reputation has become messianic; gladly accepting his destiny, he sets about putting the social order to rights but finds the task extremely difficult. A revised version published as *The Sleeper Awakes* (Nelson, 1910) corrects the story's provenly mistaken view of future air transport, and makes the hero's tragic failure more explicit. A product of one of Wells's pessimistic moods—although his equipment of such subsequent utopian romances as *In the Days of the Comet* (1906) with flagrantly miraculous generative devices implies that he never really escaped the mood in question. (BS)
Themes: Dystopias

II-1236.   The World Set Free: A Story of Mankind. Macmillan, 1914.

Wells's second future-war novel provides a striking contrast with *The War in the Air*, substituting an earnest quasi-documentary style for the social comedy of the earlier novel, and taking the view that no matter how destructive a world war might be—this one is fought with atomic bombs, albeit of a peculiar kind—it might perform the invaluable service of obliterating the present petrified social order, thus clearing the way for a new and better one. Like Mercier in *Memoirs of the Year Two Thousand Five Hundred*, Wells appoints a wise king as the primary agent of his social reforms, although he concedes a crucial role to revolutionary rhetoric (which is treated, in the final section of the text, with deep ambivalence). Although it is more closely in tune with post-World War I scientific romance than with its jingoistic predecessors, the story retains an optimism in respect of technological development that the actual war obliterated—as evidenced by such cynical atom bomb stories as Nicolson's *Public Faces*. (BS)

Themes: Politics, War

Westall, Robert, U.K., 1929–1993

*II-1237. Futuretrack 5. Kestrel, 1983.

YA. A young computer genius, Kitson, goes "razzle," running away from tending Laura, the master computer, and joining up with Keri, a master cyclist. The couple set out to discover the secret of Scott-Astbury, responsible for much that explains tightly controlled 21st-century England. A powerful novel: nightmarish depiction of future life, especially in the cities; intriguing plot; distinctive, richly allusive, yet colloquial style. Compare Burgess's *A Clockwork Orange* and Anderson's *Feed*. (FM/ML)

Themes: Cities, Computers, Dystopias, Intelligence

II-1238. Urn Burial. Viking, 1987.

YA. Ralph's accidental discovery of an ancient burial site involves him in a conflict between two alien peoples—an evil one seeking to establish a new home on Earth, and a good one wishing to prevent it. In spite of the common plot situation, the tale is marked by suspense, deft characterization, wit, and a richly allusive style. Contrast L'Engle's *A Wrinkle in Time*. (FM)

Themes: Aliens, Invasion, War

White, James, U.K., 1928–1999

II-1239. The Dream Millennium. Michael Joseph, 1974.

Colonists in suspended animation aboard a generation starship experience dreams that unlock a way into the collective unconscious and allow them to obtain new insights into their past lives and their human nature. Painstaking and neatly understated. Contrast Michael Moorcock's *The Black Corridor*. (BS)

Themes: Space Flight

II-1240. Hospital Station. Ballantine, 1962.

This collection brought together White's early Sector General short stories about a multi-environmental galactic hospital whose doctors use special Educator tapes that allow them to absorb the medical knowledge and sometimes the cultural peculiarities of a wide range of alien races. The series features a host of memorable characters, including the gruff Chief Psychologist O'Mara, young Dr. Conway, who will stop at nothing to save a patient regardless of its species, and the brilliant alien physician Prilicla, who looks for all the world like a giant mosquito. Other volumes in this much-beloved series—some of them collected short stories, others novels on which White worked for some 40 years—include

Star Surgeon (1963), *Major Operation* (1971), *Ambulance Ship* (1979), *Star Healer* (1985), and *Final Diagnosis* (1997). The early volumes of the series are most easily available in omnibus editions published in recent years by Orb. (ML)
   Themes: Aliens, Medicine

II-1241.   The Watch Below. Ballantine, 1966.

Descendants of people trapped in the hold of a sunken cargo ship have developed a worldview that makes them suitable contactees of aquatic aliens in search of a new home. Intriguing development of an unusual premise, showing White's preoccupation with the idea of establishing harmonious relationships between species with very different biologies. Another extrapolation of the theme can be found in *All Judgement Fled* (1968). (BS)
   Themes: Aliens, Psychology

White, T(erence) H(ansbury), U.K., 1906–1964

II-1242.   The Master. Cape, 1957.

YA. Exploring the supposedly barren island of Rockall, Nicky and Judy accidentally fall into the water and into the secret headquarters of the Master, a 157-year-old ESP adept who is plotting to conquer the world via powerful vibrators he has invented. Another accident, when the Master slips into the ocean after being bitten by the children's dog, finally saves the world. Offbeat characterization and psychological probing are revealed through the extensive dialogue; hence, a bit talky for many young readers. Still, the acerbic wit and charm characteristic of the author are present. (FM/SM)
   Themes: Paranormal Powers

White, William Anthony Parker *see* Boucher, Anthony

Wilder, Cherry (pseud. of Cherry Barbara Grimm), New Zealand, 1930–2002

II-1243.   The Luck of Brin's Five. Atheneum, 1977. Series: Torin.

YA. Scott Gale, the navigator of a terran bio-survey team on Torin, crash lands and is found and befriended by Dorn, a member of the family called Brin's Five. According to custom, the family considers Scott a Diver and their new "luck." Through the ensuing adventures—in particular, those involving flying machines and air races—and the dangerous intrigue of those opposed to change, Scott proves he is indeed a "luck" and precipitates a new openness to change among the people. Although the narrative pace flags occasionally, the novel creates an original world and a vaguely oriental culture. Sequels are *The Nearest Fire* (1980), which just as engagingly continues to detail Torin, and *The Tapestry Warriors* (1983). Compare Yep's *Sweetwater*. (FM)
   Themes: Colonization of Other Worlds

Wilhelm, Kate, U.S., 1928–

*II-1244. The Clewiston Test. Farrar, 1976.

The protagonist, recovering from a serious accident, throws herself into her scientific work but becomes increasingly frustrated by the personal and professional problems that develop as her experiments with behavior-controlling drugs produce ambiguous results. A first-rate novel presenting an excellent picture of scientists at work, developing a compelling argument about the conflict that can arise between the objectivity of the scientific outlook and the need for warmth and concern within human relationships. Compare Benford's *Timescape* for a comparably realistic look into the laboratory. (BS/ML)

Themes: Scientists and Engineers

*II-1245. The Infinity Box. Harper, 1975.

Perhaps Wilhelm's best early short story collection, including the fine title novella and "April Fool's Day Forever," both Nebula nominees, the latter presenting a characteristic Wilhelm theme: a new and promising discovery with tragic side effects. The earlier collections, *The Downstairs Room* (1968) and *Abyss* (1971), also have some strong material; the former includes "The Planners," a Nebula winner, one of many convincing stories of scientists at work in the forefront of genetic and behavioral research. Other collections are *Somerset Dreams and Other Fictions* (1978); *Listen, Listen* (1981); *Children of the Wind* (1989), which includes the Nebula Award-winning "The Girl Who Fell into the Sky" and the Nebula-nominated "The Gorgon Field"; and *And the Angels Sing* (1992), which features the Nebula-winning "Forever Yours, Anna." Wilhelm has no peer as a writer of realistic near-future SF stories examining the human implications of possible biological discoveries. Unfortunately, for SF genre readers at least, she has in recent years largely abandoned the field in favor of mystery novels. Compare Fowler's *Artificial Things*. (BS/ML)

II-1246. Juniper Time. Harper, 1979.

The protagonist is a linguist sought by the authorities because they need her to help translate an alien message, but she has fled decaying civilization for the simpler life of the Indians, who have again come into their own in the returning wilderness. Compare Crowley's *Engine Summer* for a similar celebration of the pastoral. (BS)

Themes: Linguistics, Pastoral

II-1247. Welcome Chaos. Houghton Mifflin, 1983.

A serum that immunizes against all disease and stops aging is kept secret by a group of scientists because many people cannot survive the initial administration. Their hopes of increasing its success rate and overcoming the sterility that is its main side effect are dashed when the world comes to the brink of nuclear war because the Soviet government apparently has the secret, and they must decide whether to make public what they know. A gripping account of individuals wrestling with a novel moral dilemma; excellent characterization. H. F. Parkinson's *They Shall Not Die* (1939) provides an interesting contrast of perspectives. (BS)

Themes: Immortality, Medicine

*II-1248.   Where Late the Sweet Birds Sang. Harper, 1976.

Ecocatastrophe destroys the United States, but a family of survivalists comes through the crisis, using cloning techniques to combat a plague of sterility. But are their descendants really victors in the struggle for existence, or has their artificial selection simply delivered them into a different kind of existential sterility? Compare Herbert's *Hellstrom Five* (1973) and Pamela Sargent's *Cloned Lives* (1976). (BS)

Awards: Hugo
Themes: Clones/Cloning, Disaster

Williams, Jay, U.S., 1914–1978

II-1249.   The People of the Ax. Walck, 1974.

YA. A post-catastrophe story. Two societies have survived: human beings, or the ax people, who have souls and no longer kill except for food, and the "crom," a human-like people hated by the humans. Arne realizes he possesses "tendo," the ability to sense the spirit of harmony in all, and hence is destined to become a leader of the humans. Arne's first, and revolutionary, intuition is a suspicion that the crom may also be human, and he successfully awakens soul in one of their leaders. A competently written, plausible look at possible future societies, except that author becomes too tendentious when contemporary civilization is blamed for all human failures. Compare Norton's *Star Man's Son: 2250 A.D.* (FM)

Themes: Anthropology, Holocaust and After, Paranormal Powers

Williams, Liz (Elizabeth Helen Laura Williams), U.K., 1965–

II-1250.   Empire of Bones. Bantam, 2002.

Set in a near-future India, in which the caste system has been restored and is rigorously enforced, the novel addresses the problems of the oppressed, first on Earth and then within a wider, interstellar setting. Jaya Nihalani is a freedom fighter, working for those who have been forced back to their traditional roles and are struggling in poverty. At the point when it seems her campaign has failed, aliens return to Earth, having long since seeded it, wanting to draw the planet into their empire. A society that also possesses a rigorous caste system, it's difficult to ignore this similarity, particularly when some alien factions wish to exclude humanity; and indeed, it's difficult to avoid the analogy with earlier colonial influences in India. Williams's indebtedness to Ursula Le Guin invites a comparison with the latter's Hainish novels, but Williams provides little in the way of utopian possibilities. Compare Jones's Aleutian Trilogy. (MKS)

Themes: Aliens, Far Future, Invasion, Sociology

Williams, Tad, U.S., 1957–

II-1251. City of Golden Shadow. DAW, 1996. Series: Otherlands.

Williams is primarily a fantasy writer and much of *Otherlands,* his massive four-volume novel, reads like a well-done quest fantasy, but since most of the work is set inside of a virtual reality environment it qualifies as science fiction. Renie Sulaweyo, a computer scientist, becomes worried when she discovers that her younger brother has been visiting some unsavory places in the virtual world and, when he winds up in a coma, she decides to do something about it. Soon, however, she finds herself enmeshed in a complex and terrifying conspiracy, not to mention a quest to find a mysterious golden city that apparently only exists in the virtual world. After a powerful start, later volumes in the novel occasionally bog down in a bewilderingly complex plot, but Williams is invariably inventive and the novel has some powerful "sense of wonder" moments. The tale continues in *River of Blue Fire* (1998), *Mountain of Black Glass* (1999), and *Sea of Silver Light* (2001). Compare Cadigan's *Tea from an Empty Cup* and Stephenson's *Snow Crash.* (ML)

Themes: Virtual Reality

Williams, Walter Jon, U.S., 1953–

II-1252. Aristoi. Tor, 1992.

In the far future, a galaxy-spanning human empire is ruled by the Aristoi, super-competent geniuses with vast psychic powers and sophisticated technological support. Although the rule of the Aristoi is far from democratic, humanity has achieved unprecedented comfort and harmony under them. When the Aristo Gabriel uncovers a plot to overthrow the system from within, he takes it upon himself to defeat the traitors. This is a beautifully written, morally complex novel, that explores the nature of personal power and its ability to corrupt. Compare Moorcock's *The Dancers at the End of Times* and Banks's Culture novels. (ML)

Themes: Far Future, Galactic Empires, Paranormal Powers

II-1253. Hardwired. Tor, 1986. Series: Hardwired.

Earth's surface has been devastated in a war against orbiting space stations; the survivors live in a violent world of petty tyrants and black marketeers. The tough hero, who can enter into cyborg symbiosis with his high-tech transport, and the equally tough heroine are outlaws caught up in renewed world conflict. The novella *Solip:System* (1989) is a direct sequel, recounting the last part of *Hardwired*'s plot from another character's perspective. *Voice of the Whirlwind* (1987) is an indirect sequel. All three volumes are excellent examples of the fusion of military SF with cyberpunk. Compare John Shirley's *Eclipse* and sequels. (BS/ML)

Themes: Cyberpunk, War

II-1254.   **Metropolitan**. HarperPrism, 1995.

In this beautifully realized science fantasy novel, the world runs on a powerful, dangerous, and very possibly magical energy source called plasm. One day Aiah, a minor government employee, is sent to discover the source of a plasm leak and winds up smack in the middle of a revolution. The political machinations here are extremely complex and the action unflagging, but what raises this novel far above the average are Williams's baroque, world-encompassing city and his enormously inventive use of plasm. The strong sequel is *City on Fire* (1996). For Williams's depiction of a city, compare Miéville's *Perdido Street Station*. For his depiction of a seemingly magical energy source, compare MacLeod's *The Light Ages*. (ML)

Themes: Cities, Dystopias, Far Future, Politics, Science Fantasy

II-1255.   **Praxis**. Harper, 2002.

The alien Shaa, who have ruled the galaxy for millennia, have gone extinct and several species are willing to wage war to fill the power vacuum thus created. This upscale diplomatic and military space opera, volume one of the Dread Empire's Fall series, features well-developed, if not entirely likable characters, a human society analogous to Great Britain at the time of Napoleon, and some smashing space battles. Volume two is *The Sundering* (2003). Compare David Weber's Honor Harrington series and Tony Daniel's *Metaplanetary* and its sequel *Superluminal*. Contrast Charles Stross's more ironic take on space warfare in *Singularity Sky*. (ML)

Themes: Aliens, Space Opera, War

Williamson, Jack, U.S., 1908–

II-1256.   **Darker than You Think**. Fantasy, 1948.

This 1940 work may be Williamson's finest work, a pioneering effort to give "supernatural" phenomena, in this case lycanthropy, a scientific rationale. The science is a bit shaky from today's perspective, but the felt response of the viewpoint character as a werewolf and in his other shape changes is vivid and convincing. The experience also converts his purpose from a stock pulp-heroic defense of humanity to a Nietzschean "beyond good and evil" embrace of his antihuman role, reminiscent of the change in the way the young giants are perceived in Wells's *The Food of the Gods*. In this sense this is a variation on the Superman theme, except that it does not depict the superbeings as benevolent toward humanity; their coming regime truly will be "darker than you think." Compare Matheson's *I Am Legend*; contrast Stapledon's *Odd John*. (PC)

Themes: Supermen/women

*II-1257. The Humanoids. Simon & Schuster, 1949. Recommended ed.: Avon, 1980.

"To serve and obey, and guard men from harm." This slogan of the highly efficient humanoids sounds at first like Asimov's Three Laws of Robotics; the catch is that these robots interpret "guarding" as preventing humans from doing anything that could possibly harm themselves; in short, anything at all. John Campbell was so upset by the downbeat ending of the first humanoids story, "With Folded Hands" (1947), that he insisted Williamson write a happy-ending sequel, " . . . And Searching Mind," from which this novel grew. Williamson balked at this, and in later stories on the humanoid theme persisted in regarding the robots as inimical. The story can also be taken as a parable about the effect of ever-increasing mechanization in our civilization. The 1980 edition includes "With Folded Hands" and a new introduction by the author. Compare Čapek's *R.U.R.* and Vonnegut's *Player Piano*. Note: *The Collected Stories of Jack Williamson* are being published by Haffner Press (1999–) (www.haffnerpress.com), each volume reproducing a pulp magazine cover in color, each individually titled. See *The Metal Man* below. *Seventy-Five: The Diamond Anniversary of a Science Fiction Pioneer* (Haffner, 2003) assembled fiction, essays, speeches, and other materials. (PC)

Themes: Dystopias, Robots

II-1258.　The Legion of Space. Fantasy Press, 1947. Series: Legion of Space.

Williamson's second space opera, serialized in *Astounding* in 1934, unites characters based on Alexandre Dumas' *Three Musketeers* and William Shakespeare's Falstaff in a quest to recover the beautiful guardian of the ultimate superweapon when she is abducted by alien Medusae. A straightforward adaptation of swashbuckling adventure fiction for a galactic stage, it was followed by the more inventive sequel "The Cometeers" (1936); the series was further extended in "One Against the Legion" (1939) and "Nowhere Near" (1967). Compare Smith's *Galactic Patrol*. (BS)

Themes: Space Opera

II-1259.　Lifeburst. Ballantine, 1984.

Intelligent space opera in which the human conquest of the solar system is inhibited by violent political disputes and interrupted by the arrival of a gravid alien queen of a powerful and rapacious species, while gentler aliens stand on the sidelines. An illustration of the way in which Williamson's work has become gradually more sophisticated with the evolution of the genre; compare the author's *The Legion of Space* and *The Reefs of Space* (1964). (BS)

Themes: Aliens, Space Opera

II-1260.　The Metal Man and Others: The Collected Stories of Jack Williamson, Vol. 1. Haffner, 1999.

A collection of nine pulp stories, the first in a series intended to provide a uniform edition of all Williamson's short stories, novellas, and previously unreprinted serial novels. This volume includes two collaborations with Miles J.

Breuer, including a novel transfiguring the American War of Independence into an account of a lunar colony's bid for freedom, *The Birth of a New Republic* (1931). Other novellas include the Merrittesque "The Alien Intelligence" (1929) and *The Green Girl* (1930), which begins with the uncompromisingly melodramatic first line: "At high noon on May 4, 1999, the sun went out." The 10 stories in Volume Two, *Wolves of Darkness* (1999), include Williamson's first space opera, *The Stone from the Green Star* (1931), as well as the horror/SF portal fantasy "Wolves of Darkness" (1932) and an exotic interplanetary novella inspired by S. Fowler Wright's *The World Below*, "The Moon Era" (1932). Volume Three, *Wizard's Isle* (2000), features 16 stories, including the macrocosmic romance "The Galactic Circle" (1935). Volume Four, *Spider Island* (2002), has 12 stories, concluding with the classic "time opera" *The Legion of Time* (1938), in which alternative futures championed by rival *femmes fatales* recruit soldiers from the battlefields of the past in order to fight for the privilege of existence. When complete, the set will provide a remarkable compendium of work spanning the entire history of genre SF, by the only writer who contrived to adapt himself—with unfailing inventiveness and energy—to the requirements of every phase of its evolution. (BS)

II-1261.   Seetee Ship (as by Will Stewart). Gnome, 1951.

The earliest SF to deal systematically with the concept of antimatter, then called contraterrene matter—C.T.—hence, "seetee." One of the early 1940s *Astounding* stories combined into this work was titled "Opposites—React!"; oppositions not only of matter–antimatter but of human beings and governments. Stereotyped gender relationships and national traits, but an absorbing story; the pulp tradition at its best. The sequel, *Seetee Shock*, was paradoxically published by Simon & Schuster in 1950. (BS)

Themes: Hard SF, Space Flight

II-1262.   Terraforming Earth. Tor, 2001.

In his nineties and still going strong, Williamson produced his best novel in decades in *Terraforming Earth*. An eccentric billionaire, Calvin DeFort, sets up an automated moonbase, complete with frozen specimens of all of the Earth's important plant and animal species as a protection against the planet being wiped out by an asteroid strike. When an asteroid does indeed hit the Earth, the planet is eventually restocked by clones of the few human survivors. Millions of years pass and new civilizations rise and fall, all of them descended from the original cloned stock. Although somewhat slow-moving, this is big-picture, Stapledonian SF of a rare sort. Compare Wright's *The Golden Age*. (ML)

Awards: John W. Campbell

Themes: Clones/Cloning, Disaster, Far Future

II-1263.   Trapped in Space. Doubleday, 1968.

YA. Although resenting Ben, his older and more talented brother, Jeff Stone still volunteers to search for him, missing while exploring Topaz. Accompanied by Lupe Flor, a fellow starman, and a fuzzy alien, Buzzy Dozen-Dozen, Jeff locates his brother among the hostile rock hoppers of Topaz. Before a rescue can be effected, the humans must convince the hoppers to trust Earth and join the galaxy-wide family. Written economically without sacrificing detail or variety, the story effectively combines adventure, space technology, and the theme of growing up. (FM)

Themes: Aliens, Coming of Age

II-1264. Undersea Quest. Gnome, 1954. **Undersea Fleet**. Gnome, 1956. **Undersea City**. Gnome, 1958, by Williamson and Frederik Pohl. Collected as *The Undersea Trilogy*, Baen, 1992. Series: Undersea Trilogy.

YA. Colonization of the ocean deeps, seriously discussed beyond SF circles in the 1950s as a possible solution to mineral shortages and overpopulation, but then displaced by the growing interest in space exploration, inspired this series. The authors forecast no U.S./Soviet rivalry under the sea, with the UN controlling all weapons. In spite of an often creaky plot and awkward dialogue, the seismology that drives the plot of *Undersea City* (which is much the best of the stories), is meticulously set forth and convincingly explained. The sheer sweep of the entire series, punctuated by varied plot elements, carries the reader along. It could certainly help present-day youth understand what two and more prior generations saw and cherished in pulp SF. Compare Arthur C. Clarke's *The Deep Range*; for an even sharper contrast, see Peter Watts, *Starfish* (1999). (PC)

Themes: Coming of Age, Discoveries and Inventions

Willis, Connie, U.S., 1945–

*****II-1265. Doomsday Book**. Bantam, 1992.

Kivrin, a time traveling history student from 21st-century Oxford is sent back to the 14th century for her Practicum. It's supposed to be a routine trip, but everything seems to go wrong at once. Kivrin is accidentally set down in the heart of the Black Plague and soon falls ill. Worse still, 21st-century Oxford is also hit by some sort of plague, making her immediate retrieval impossible. This is a grim but beautifully written novel, full of carefully drawn characters and fascinating historical detail. It's one of the best time-travel stories ever written. The title piece from Willis's collection *Fire Watch* is set in the same universe as *Doomsday Book*, as is her award-winning comic novel *To Say Nothing of the Dog*. Compare McQuay's *Memories* and Bishop's *No Enemy but Time*. (ML)

Awards: Hugo, Nebula, *Locus*
Themes: Disaster, History in SF, Time Travel

II-1266. Fire Watch. Bluejay, 1985.

The title story of this collection, a Hugo- and Nebula Award-winner, has time-traveling students discovering the real texture of history and shows off the author's main strength: her ability to import warmth and intimacy into classic SF themes. Other collections are the equally well-done *Impossible Things* (1993) and the relatively minor *Miracle and Other Christmas Stories* (1999). Compare C. J. Cherryh's *Visible Light* (1986). (BS/ML)

Themes: Time Travel

*II-1267. Passage. Bantam, 2001.

While *Passage* starts out in Willis's familiar screwball comic territory, as it progresses the novel suddenly becomes unexpectedly dark; with the death of one of the major characters partway through, Willis sacrifices the perfect romantic ending such comedies usually demand and returns to the emotionally taxing arena she evoked so successfully in *Doomsday Book*. Joanna Lander is researching near-death experiences, trying to establish their physiological and biochemical sources; obliged to become her own research subject, in collaboration with Richard Wright, using a drug that simulates NDEs, she realizes her own experience is a memory of the sinking of the *Titanic*, but one at variance with known historical facts. Willis's attempt to explore the nature of death and to portray what happens in a dying mind is a literary tour de force, profoundly moving and yet, at the end, also startlingly life-affirming. (MKS)

Awards: Hugo, *Locus*

Themes: Immortality, Paranormal Powers, Psychology, Religion

II-1268.   To Say Nothing of the Dog. Bantam Spectra, 1998.

The title indicates Willis's debt to Jerome K. Jerome's *Three Men in a Boat* (1889) (it is the subtitle of that book) but other influences are apparent throughout this novel, not least the detective fiction of Dorothy L. Sayers (constantly invoked by Verity Kimble, one of the main characters) and Agatha Christie, not to mention Willis's well-documented liking for romantic comedy. Set once again in the Oxford history department of the future, first seen in *Doomsday Book* and *Fire Watch*, this time we meet Ned Henry, who is despatched to Coventry during the Blitz to discover the nature of a mysterious artifact, the Bishop's bird stump, for a detailed reconstruction of the cathedral being undertaken by a wealthy American. Recuperating from this during the 19th century, Ned finds that he has unwittingly set events in train that will disrupt history unless he can resolve matters. Willis, as usual, combines a deft handling of the multi-stranded plot with a keen eye for historical detail. It is an affectionate evocation of 19th-century literary England as well as being a successful blend of SF and light comedy. (MKS)

Awards: Hugo, *Locus*

Themes: Time Travel

Wilson, Robert Anton, U.S., 1932–

II-1269.   Schrödinger's Cat: The Universe Next Door. Pocket Books, 1979. Series: Schrodinger's Cat.

First part of a three-decker novel continued in *The Trick Top Hat* (1981) and *The Homing Pigeons* (1981). The three stories run more or less in parallel, and the workings of their convoluted plots model alternative interpretations of the strange world of subatomic physics. Funny and clever, carrying forward some of the countercultural fascination of *The Illuminatus! Trilogy*. Compare Aldiss's *Report on Probability A* and Wilhelm's *Huysman's Pets* (1986). (BS)

Wilson, Robert Charles, Canada, 1953–

II-1270. Blind Lake. Tor, 2003.

In the mid-21st century, a revolutionary new technology makes it possible for Marguerite Hauser, a scientist working at the Blind Lake research installation on Earth, to make close-up observations of aliens living on a planet circling another star. Without warning, however, the installation suddenly finds itself locked down, cut off from all contact with the outside world, although automated trucks continue to provide supplies. Gradually, after months of total isolation, evidence begins to accumulate that Hauser's emotionally disturbed daughter, Tessa, may herself be in contact with the aliens in some unexplainable way. Wilson's trademark well-developed, emotionally insecure characters and his fine style make this a superior example of thoughtful SF. (ML)

Themes: Aliens, Discoveries and Inventions, Life on Other Worlds, Paranormal Powers, Scientists and Engineers, Women in SF

II-1271. The Chronoliths. Tor, 2001.

Scott Warden, an emotionally unstable computer programmer with a teetering marriage and a desperately ill daughter, takes a job in Thailand where he is witness to the arrival of the first Chronolith, an enormous, high-tech monument sent from 20 years in the future to commemorate a military victory by Kuin, a heretofore unheard-of Asian tyrant. Soon thereafter more Chronoliths appear, often with devastating results, each commemorating another of the tyrant's victories. As the years pass and Kuin's era comes closer, society as we know it begins to collapse. Scott is recruited to help uncover the identity of the mysterious tyrant and stop him. He must also put his own life back together and come to terms with his failures as a husband and father. This is a beautifully written book, full of well-drawn characters and fascinating, high-tech physics. (ML)

Themes: Disaster, Invasion, Machines, Sociology, Time Travel

II-1272. Darwinia. Tor, 1998.

In the year 1912, with no prior warning, Europe disappears, to be replaced by Darwinia, an alien landscape empty of human beings, but filled with dangerous creatures. Darwinia soon becomes the subject of exploration and colonization by the remaining nations of the Earth. Guilford Law, a photographer, accompanies one such expedition to the bizarre new continent and eventually discovers that the appearance of Darwinia is in fact a result of an intergalactic war being fought between forces too vast for humanity to fully comprehend. Reviewers have compared *Darwinia* to works by authors as diverse as Stephen King,

Michael Moorcock, Philip K. Dick, and H. P. Lovecraft; particularly compare Ian McDonald's *Chaga*. (ML).

Themes: Aliens, Alternate Worlds, Biology, Ecology, End of the World, Invasion, Parallel Worlds

II-1273. The Divide. Doubleday, 1990.

Benjamin appears to be a normal man, trying to lead a normal life, but appearances are deceiving. He's also John Shaw, a gene-engineered superman created by an unscrupulous scientist. The division between the two personalities is extensive; each is only vaguely aware of the other's existence, and each has a life of his own. When the scientist who created Shaw and then abandoned him when funding ran out sends Susan, a graduate student, to reestablish contact, both personalities are in crisis. Wilson's trademark strong and sympathetic character development is very much in evidence in this well-done tale of a crippled superman. Compare Stevenson's *Strange Case of Dr. Jekyll and Mr. Hyde* and Keyes's *Flowers for Algernon*. (ML)

Themes: Genetic Engineering, Psychology, Supermen/women

II-1274. The Harvest. Bantam, 1993.

The Alien Travelers have arrived in a planet-sized spaceship and they bring with them god-like possibilities. Humanity is invited to join them on their journey through the universe; all that is required is that we give up our material bodies, merge with the group mind, and achieve immortality. Within a short time, most people accept the Travelers' offer. Wilson concentrates, however, on the one in ten thousand who turn the offer down and who must watch their world gradually fall to pieces. This is a somber, almost elegiac tale, filled with interesting characters. Comparisons with Clarke's *Childhood's End* are almost inevitable, and it is to Wilson's credit that he holds his own when that comparison is made. (ML)

Themes: Aliens, End of the World, Immortality

II-1275. Mysterium. Bantam Spectra, 1994.

The small town of Two Rivers, Michigan, site of a top-secret government lab, suddenly finds itself transported into an alternate universe ruled by a repressive government dominated by a dark version of Gnostic Christianity. Howard Poole, a physicist from the lab, teams up with local history teacher Dex Graham and Linneth Stone, an anthropologist from the parallel world, to figure out what happened and to put things right. Wilson's Gnostic culture is well developed and the bizarre physics he invokes to explain events is fascinating. His characters, as usual, are also very well developed.

Awards: Philip K. Dick

Themes: Parallel Worlds, Religion, Scientists and Engineers

Wingrove, David, U.K., 1954–

II-1276.   The Middle Kingdom. New English Library, 1989. Series: Chung Kuo.

The Middle Kingdom is the first installment in the eight-volume Chung Kuo series. Later books include *The Broken Wheel* (1990), *White Moon, Red Dragon* (1994), and *The Marriage of the Living Dark* (1996). It is the 22nd century and China rules the Earth. In many ways the great mass of humanity has never had it better; poverty and civil strife are virtually eliminated, though at the cost of limited personal freedom and progress. A mixed group of younger Chinese and Europeans want change and are willing to start the War of Two Directions to get it. The series' greatest strength lies in its detailed depiction of a complex and fascinating culture, though some readers will find the plot a bit slow. Compare McHugh's *China Mountain Zhan*. (ML)

Themes: Alternate Worlds, Politics

Winsor, G. McLeod (unattributed pseudonym)

II-1277.   Station X. Jenkins, 1919.

An experimental radio station on a Pacific island picks up messages from Venus warning of an imminent invasion of Earth by Martians, who can project their disembodied minds through space to possess new bodies. The warning comes too late. A compound of Wells's *War of the Worlds* and French SF based on Flammarion's notions of interplanetary reincarnation, similar in some respects to a two-volume "Martian Epic" (1920–1921) penned by Théo Varlet and Octave Jonquel. Hugo Gernsback reprinted it in *Amazing Stories* in 1926, and its plot is echoed in numerous paranoid horror/SF movies. Compare Hyder's *Vampires Overhead*. (BS)

Themes: Invasion

Winter, Laurel, U.S., 1959–

II-1278.   Growing Wings. Houghton Mifflin, 2000.

YA. At the age of 11, Linnet suddenly discovers that she's growing wings. Her mother reacts with understandable distress, but later reveals that she too had wings as a child, only to have them cut off by her own mother, Linnet's estranged grandmother. The girl eventually winds up at a secret compound where winged people like herself are nurtured and trained. There she must learn to use her wings, come to terms with the difficult choices made by her mother and grandmother, and deal with the normal problems of adolescence as well. This is a delicate and beautifully written book. (ML)

Themes: Children in SF, Coming of Age, Paranormal Powers

Wolfe, Bernard, U.S., 1915–1985

*II-1279. Limbo. Random, 1952. U.K. title: *Limbo 90*. Secker, 1953. Recommended ed.: Carroll & Graf, 1987.

Hailed as America's answer to the two greatest British dystopias, *Brave New World* and *Nineteen Eighty-Four*, this remarkable novel blends satire, Freudian psychoanalysis, outrageous puns, literary allusions, and scientific and technical extrapolation. After World War III, allegedly pacifist regimes come to power in what is left of the U.S. and USSR, based on voluntary quadruple amputation—literal dis-armament. A doctor returns to this mad culture 18 years later and finds that all that was dysfunctional in Wolfe's 1950 has been carried forward 40 years into an appalling future. Although sometimes lapsing into didacticism, especially toward the conclusion, the narrative is hard-driving and dramatic. The author described in the 1987 reprint the intellectual influences upon him when he composed the story, including Norbert Wiener and A. E. van Vogt. By any measure, including that of "mainstream" literature, this is a major achievement. (PC)

Themes: Dystopias

Wolfe, Gene, U.S., 1931–

*II-1280. The Fifth Head of Cerberus. Scribner, 1972.

Three exquisite linked novellas forming a coherent whole. The key issue is the identity of the main characters. One is a boy who is the latest in a series of clones whose failure to achieve success in life has become the focal point of obsessive "self"-examination; the other is apparently an anthropologist who offers a strange "reconstruction" of the life of the alien aborigines that were supposedly wiped out by human colonists but actually used their shape-shifting powers to mimic and displace the humans (including the anthropologist). A supremely delicate exercise in narrative construction; not easy to follow, but one of the true classics of SF. (BS/ML)

Themes: Aliens, Clones/Cloning

II-1281. The Island of Doctor Death and Other Stories and Other Stories. Pocket Books, 1980.

A collection including the award-nominated title story and a novella that inverts its themes, the Nebula Award-winning "The Death of Doctor Island." They deal with the subtle interaction of "private" fictional worlds and "public" real ones. Wolfe is playing, as in *The Fifth Head of Cerberus*, with relationships between appearance and reality more subtle and mystifying than those to be found in such Philip Dick novels as *Martian Time-Slip* and *Do Androids Dream of Electric Sheep?* This preoccupation occurs in many of his other stories. Later Wolfe collections, all of them excellent, include *Gene Wolfe's Book of Days* (1981), *Storeys From the Old Hotel* (1988), *Endangered Species* (1989), *Castle of Days* (1992), *Strange Travelers* (1999), and *Innocents Aboard* (2004). (BS/ML)

*II-1282. The Shadow of the Torturer. Simon & Schuster, 1980. Series: Book of the Long Sun, Book of the New Sun, Book of the Short Sun.

The first volume of The Book the New Sun, a superb four-volume novel completed in the Hugo Award-winning *The Claw of the Conciliator* (1981), *The Sword of the Lictor* (1982), and the John W. Campbell Award-winning *The Citadel of the Autarch*. SF and fantasy motifs are combined here in a far-future scenario akin to Vance's *The Dying Earth*, but much more ambitious; planetary resources are exhausted and civilization is in the final stages of decline. The hero, Severian, is a disgraced torturer who embarks on a long journey, becoming involved with a religious order that preserves a relic of a long-gone redeemer, and eventually with a plan to renew the sun. A rich, many-layered story; the detail and integrity of the imagined world invite comparison with Herbert's *Dune* and Tolkien's Middle Earth, but it is a unique literary work that transcends issues of categorization. *The Urth of the New Sun* (1987), a separate novel detailing Severian's later, off-Urth quest for transcendence, is a lesser, but still worthwhile story. *Nightside the Long Sun* (1993), first volume of The Book of the Long Sun, is set on an extremely baroque generation starship and has connections to the earlier series that become gradually apparent in the later volumes: *Lake of the Long Sun* (1994); *Caldé of the Long Sun* (1994), and *Exodus from the Long Sun* (1996). A final trilogy, The Book of the Short Sun—*On Blue's Waters* (1999), *In Green's Jungles* (2000), and *Return to the Whorl* (2001)—apparently completes the sequence. Taken as a whole, the entire 12-book sequence is a stunning accomplishment. Compare Zelazny's *Lord of Light*. (BS/ML)

Themes: Far Future, Future History, Life on Other worlds, Science Fantasy

Wollheim, Donald A., U.S., 1914–1990

II-1283. The Secret of Saturn's Rings. Winston, 1954.

YA. Young Bruce Rhodes accompanies his famous scientist father on a UN mission to prove that Saturn's rings were artificially caused. The expedition is successful, and evidence of life on Saturn is uncovered. The scenes describing father and son marooned in the rings and devising ways to travel are still imaginative. One of the better 1950s Winston books, even though we now know this isn't the way the rings were formed. (FM/SM/PC).

Themes: Space Flight, The Planets

Womack, Jack, U.S., 1956–

II-1284. Ambient. Weidenfield, 1987. Series: Terraplane.

In a future milieu as gritty and dark as that of the cyberpunks, but minus their ubiquitous computer technology, the Dryco Corporation dominates the world through its control of the recreational drug market. The various members of the Dryden family, owners of Dryco, seem to be involved in endless, borderline-psychotic plots to increase their power over the world around them. Later books in the series, not all of which are tightly connected to *Ambient*, include *Terraplane*

(1988), *Heathern* (1990), the Philip K. Dick Award-winning *Elvissey* (1993), and *Going, Going, Gone* (2000). Womack's books are difficult because he writes in a futuristic slang, much as Anthony Burgess did in *A Clockwork Orange*. (ML)

Themes: Crime and Punishment, Dystopias

*II-1285. Random Acts of Senseless Violence. Atlantic Monthly, 1994.

In the near future, New York City is in a state of collapse. Unemployment is rampant and the National Guard patrols large segments of the city. When 12-year-old Lola Hart's parents lose their white-collar jobs, they are forced to move to a poorer part of town and Lola gradually becomes accustomed to the mean streets of her new environment. The novel is her diary. Written in a brilliant street slang that becomes more extreme as Lola acclimatizes to the radical change in her life, *Random Acts* is a brilliant portrayal of an all-too-believable future that lacks any of science fiction's traditional high-tech glitz. For a similar and comparably brilliant book, see Butler's *Parable of the Sower*. (ML)

Themes: Children in SF, Cities, Coming of Age, Crime and Punishment, Dystopias, Linguistics, Sociology

Woods, Helen *see* Kavan, Anna

Wright, Austin Tappan, U.S., 1883–1931

II-1286.   Islandia. Farrar, 1942.

This is a worthy conclusion to the "lost continent" literary tradition, which became excluded from SF by geographic exploration and satellite mapping. The Islandians, after a long history of isolation (like Tokugawa, Japan), are debating the extent to which they should allow relations with the (real) nations of the modern world. The story unfolds in leisurely fashion, with dense discussions of Islandia's culture; the novel is a posthumous abridgement of a 400,000-word original. It thus compares in scope and texture with Tolkien's Middle Earth and Herbert's Arrakis, but is more conventionally realistic than either. A unique work likely to always find readers. *Islandia* earned the compliment of semi-sequels, all by Mark Saxton: *The Islar* (1969), *The Two Kingdoms* (1979), and *Havoc in Islandia* (1982), all from Houghton Mifflin. (PC)

Themes: Lost Races/Worlds

Wright, John C., U.S., 1961–

II-1287.   The Golden Age. Tor, 2002. Series: The Golden Transcendence.

The first third of what is essentially a three-volume novel, this far-future tale tells the story of Phaethon, who has challenged the Golden Oecumene, the utopian society into which he was born. Utilizing a pulp plot (Phaethon must go on a quest to regain his lost memory and reach the stars), a wide range of mythological and genre references, and an ornate prose style, Wright explores a variety of philosophically difficult concepts. There's still some clumsiness here—*The Golden Age* is a first novel, after all—but no one can fault Wright's soaring ambition. Phaethon's quest continues in *The Phoenix Exultant* (2003) and *The Golden Transcendence* (2003). Compare Williamson's *Terraforming Earth* and the fiction of Greg Egan. (ML)

Themes: Coming of Age, Computers, Far Future, Intelligence, Mythology, Space Opera

Wright, S(ydney) Fowler, U.K., 1874–1965

II-1288. The Adventure of Wyndham Smith. Jenkins, 1938.

A compound of satire and Romanticism in which the inhabitants of a future "Utopia of comforts" decide to commit mass suicide, on the grounds that their lives are pointless; a dissenting couple ambitious to become a new Adam and Eve must first dispose of the killer machines sent to hunt them down. A graphic expansion of an unsold short story that was eventually published as "Original Sin" (1946). Compare Forster's "The Machine Stops." (BS)

Themes: Dystopias

II-1289. Deluge. Fowler Wright, 1927.

A self-published disaster novel improvised from a much longer manuscript, which was critically praised in the U.K. before William Randolph Hearst's Cosmopolitan Book Company boosted it to bestseller status in the U.S.—partly by making it an early book club selection—in anticipation of a movie (which did not materialize until 1934 and was then lost when its special effects footage was separately sold; it was recently rediscovered). The remainder of the manuscript was decanted into a sequel, *Dawn* (1929), whose text mostly runs in parallel, but a projected third volume was never completed. It is more polished than pulp disaster stories of a similarly neo-Romantic stripe—notably England's *Darkness and Dawn* and Serviss's *The Second Deluge*. It proved an influential work, inspiring a "sequel" by another hand in *The World Ends* (1937) by "William Lamb" (Storm Jameson) and coloring the attitudes of many subsequent British disaster stories, from Collier's *Tom's a-Cold* to the works of John Wyndham and J. G. Ballard. The Wesleyan University Press edition of 2003 has a definitive text and a long introduction that sets the book in its historical and literary context. (BS)

Themes: Disaster

II-1290. Dream: or, The Simian Maid. Harrap, 1931. Series: Dream.

The first of a trilogy of stories in which a socialite disenchanted with the safety of modern civilization escapes through time into more challenging eras, pursued by an enthusiastic wooer and his sister. The present volume is a feverish prehistoric romance, as is its successor *The Vengeance of Gwa* (1935), which was shorn of its frame narrative when it had to be sold to another publisher (who released it under the pseudonym Anthony Wingrave). The long-delayed *Spiders' War* (1954) takes the characters into an equally strife-ridden future, in which the joyous challenge of the bloody struggle for existence has been restored to humankind's descendants. Compare Mitchell's *Three Go Back* and *Gay Hunter*. (BS)

Themes: Evolution

*II-1291. The New Gods Lead. Jarrolds, 1932.

A collection of 10 stories, 7 of which are fitted into a loosely knit future history intended to display the logical outcomes of present social trends, including the dystopian "P.N.40" (1930) and a tripartite *conte philosophique* describing the gradual replacement of humankind by machinery, "Automata." The others include a scathing account of the unfortunate discovery of an immortality serum, "The Rat" (1929). Two stories, including "Original Sin," were added to the contents in the Arkham House collection *The Throne of Saturn* (1949) and two more to make up *S. Fowler Wright's Short Stories* (1996). (BS)

II-1292.   Prelude in Prague. Newnes, 1935.

A future-war novel written as a newspaper serial in a belated attempt to recover the circulation boosting appeal of le Queux's *The Invasion of 1910*, although the first volume is more spy story than future-war novel. It narrowly missed out on being prophetic, imagining World War II beginning in 1938 with a German invasion of Czechoslovakia; the U.S. edition was equipped with a different ending for diplomatic reasons. Two sequels, *Four Days War* (1936) and *Megiddo's Ridge* (1937), extend the story into an apocalyptic fantasy; the description of the results of aerial bombing in the second volume is even more horrific than the similar imagery of O'Neill's *Day of Wrath*. (BS)

Themes: War

*II-1293. The World Below. Collins, 1929.

A novel hastily improvised from an incomplete manuscript from which Fowler Wright had earlier abstracted his first Wellsian romance, *The Amphibians* (1925). He had originally intended that volume as the first in a trilogy, but the later chapters of the second part are crudely synoptic—a great pity, given that the vision of the far future presented in the earlier narrative is imaginatively enterprising and wonderfully phantasmagoric. Even in its aborted form, the story is a masterpiece of sorts, drawing on the inspiration of Wright's translations-in-progress of Dante's *Divine Comedy* to provide a new commentary on the ecospheric context and progressive impetus of Earthly life, more in keeping with the implications of Darwin's theory of evolution. It addresses philosophical issues that are also tackled, in similarly bold fashion, in Shiel's *The Purple Cloud* and Stapledon's *Star Maker*. (BS)

Themes: Far Future

Wylie, Philip (Gordon), U.S., 1902–1971

II-1294.   The Disappearance. Rinehart, 1951.

For unexplained reasons, all of Earth's men and women suddenly disappear from each other's worlds. With his own critical agenda, Wylie traces the evolution of these two single-sex societies; the deterioration of the men, the necessary empowerment of the women, and the creative consequences of their eventual, equally unexplained reunion. There are a few miscalls from today's perspective; Wylie was basically an anti-feminist who criticized Simone de Beauvoir, for example, as admittedly brilliant but totally wrongheaded. But on the whole this was, *for the time*, a compassionate commentary on what used to be called the "battle of the sexes" and on the prurient, hung-up society that made the rules by which the battle had traditionally been fought. Compare Le Guin's *The Left Hand of Darkness*; contrast Russ's *The Female Man* and Michaela Roessner's *Vanishing Point* (1993). (PC)

Themes: Women in SF

II-1295. Gladiator. Knopf, 1930.

A novel describing the childhood and early adulthood of a physical superman, whose intellectual prowess is quite ordinary. It is more sympathetic than such accounts of mental superhumanity as Beresford's *Hampdenshire Wonder* because the hero is representative of a commonplace power fantasy daydream. But it is equally pessimistic about the prospect of his successful integration into human society—in which respect it hoisted an invaluable signpost for later designers of comic book superheroes. (BS)

Themes: Supermen/women

Wyndham, John (pseud. of John Beynon Harris), U.K., 1903–1969

II-1296.   The Day of the Triffids. Doubleday, 1951. Variant title: *Revolt of the Triffids*. Popular Library, 1952.

Expanded from a serial in *Collier's*, this tale of monsters from a botched experiment marching over the world is a superior example of its breed. Triffids are sentient plants that walk, sting, and feast on carrion. To even the odds, a shower from space, probably from one of the erstwhile dominant species' own secret military satellites, has rendered most of humanity blind. What raises this novel far above almost others in the subgenre is the quality of the writing and characterization. Details unfold with leisurely novelistic richness and the characters' actions make logical and psychological sense. The sequel by Simon Clark, *Night of the Triffids* (Hodder, 2001), isn't nearly as good as the original. (PC)

Themes: Disaster, Monsters

II-1297.   Planet Plane (as by John Beynon). Newnes, 1936.

YA. An account of humankind's first flights to Mars, where the adventurers meet a stern response from the last survivors of the dominant species and the machines destined to succeed them; its conclusion was daring by the standards of the day (and was censored from the second serial version in the boys' paper *Modern Wonder*, 1937). The novel is also known as *Stowaway to Mars*; the final version published under that title carried the author's more familiar pseudonym John Wyndham, although it has more in common with the pulp SF he published as John Beynon Harris, carrying forward a key motif from "The Lost

Machine" (1932). A sequel novella "Sleepers of Mars" (1938) was reprinted as the title story of a Wyndham collection in 1973. Compare Raymond Z. Gallun's "Old Faithful" series (1934–1936). (BS)

   Themes: Life on Other Worlds, Space Flight

II-1298.   Re-Birth. Ballantine, 1955. U.K. title (with altered text): *The Chrysalids*. Michael Joseph, 1955.

Nuclear warfare has not only reverted civilization to a Dark Age village culture but unleashed a flood of mutations, which a revived religious bigotry curses as the fruit of sin. The mutants, however, are not sub- but superhuman, since they are telepaths. Two mutant children make contact with a distant community, high-tech as well as telepathic, which triggers a climactic rescue scene, strongly reminiscent of *Things to Come*, the SF film for which Wells wrote the screenplay, very loosely adapting it from his *The Shape of Things to Come*. The message is the same as with Wells: old ways, no matter how comfortably familiar, must give way to the rational new. Compare Brackett's *The Long Tomorrow* and Clarke's *Childhood's End*; contrast Miller's *A Canticle for Leibowitz*, in which mutation has an entirely different social function and theological meaning. (PC)

   Themes: Holocaust and After, Mutants

Yep, Laurence, U.S., 1948–

*II-1299.   Sweetwater. Harper, 1973.

YA. Young Tyree is torn between pursuing an interest in music encouraged by Amadeus, an Argan (the oldest race on the planet Harmony), and obeying his father, elected captain of the Silkies, descendants of the starship crews from Earth, who are fighting for a life in harmony with the dominant sea. A distinctive narrative that unexpectedly and winningly combines a richly imagined world and its ecology, a boy's rite of passage, and wide-ranging allusions to music and the Old Testament. Compare Norton's *Star Man's Son: 2250 A.D.* (FM)

   Themes: Colonization of Other Worlds, Coming of Age, Mythology

Yolen, Jane, U.S., 1939–

II-1300.   Dragon's Blood. Delacorte, 1982. Series: Pit Dragon Trilogy.

YA. Book 1 in the Pit Dragon Trilogy, followed by *Heart's Blood* (1984) and *A Sending of Dragons* (1987). Human beings on the former penal colony Austar IV raise the planet's top predators, which they call dragons, to fight in pits. Jakkin, a young bond servant, buys his freedom by raising a prime fighting dragon. Compare McCaffrey's dragon novels. (ML).

   Themes: Children in SF, Coming of Age, Life on Other Worlds

Yolen, Jane, U.S., 1939– and Coville, Bruce, U.S., 1950–

II-1301.   Armaggedon Summer. Harcourt Brace, 1998.

YA. Two children are dragged to the top of a mountain by their evangelical parents and become part of an end-times group reminiscent of the Jonestown or

Heaven's Gate cults. This is tautly written, genuinely frightening near-future SF. (ML)
Themes: Children in SF, Coming of Age, End of the World, Religion

Youd, Christopher Samuel *see* Christopher, John

Zamyatin, Yegevny (Ivanovich), Russia, 1884–1937

*II-1302. We. 1920. Trans. of *My* by Gregory Zilboorg. Dutton, 1924.
The ultimate dystopian novel, presenting a vision of the United States: a society whose suppression of individuality in the cause of order proceeds to the logical limit of eliminating the imagination. Its origin, and the fact that it circulated surreptitiously in Russia as a samizdat publication, encourages a reading that construes it as an attack on Soviet communism, but it actually refers to a much more fundamental tendency in human nature towards conformity and automatism. Not published in the USSR until 1988. Other notable literary offspring of the same process of extrapolation include O'Neill's *Land Under England*, Rand's *Anthem*, Orwell's *Nineteen Eighty-Four*, and J. D. Beresford and Esmé Wynne-Tyson's *The Riddle of the Tower* (1944). (BS)
Themes: Dystopias

Zaronovich, Princess Vera (unattributed pseudonym)

II-1303.   Mizora: A Prophecy. Dillingham, 1890.
A satirical novel describing an all-female society, serialized in the *Cincinnati Commercial* in 1880–1881. The copyright notice of the Dillingham edition is in the name of Mary E. Bradley, who is identified by the National Union Catalogue as Mary E. (Bradley) Lane—a byline reproduced on recent reprints—but the basis of the attribution is tenuous and the tongue-in-cheek nature of the text makes it seem unlikely to some readers that it is actually the proto-feminist parable it pretends to be (comments about the innate troublesomeness of brunettes are especially suspicious). The book carries a preface by Murat Halstead, the editor of the *Cincinnati Commercial*, who seems a likely contender to be the author of the work, but in the absence of further evidence judgment is best withheld. Arguably, the most interesting aspect of Mizoran society is not the absence of men but the way in which the biotechnology recruited to compensate for their lack is also deployed to facilitate food supply, exhibiting an open-mindedness in respect to biological engineering that was not to be replicated for nearly a century. Compare Thomas's *Crystal Button*. (BS)
Themes: Satirical SF, Utopias

Zebrowski, George, U.S., 1945–

II-1304.   Brute Orbits. HarperPrism, 1998.
Heavily didactic, but intellectually provocative, this novel concerns the incarceration of criminals on prison asteroids, supposedly for the length of their sentences. In fact, however, the governments in charge have "accidentally"

miscalculated the orbits, guaranteeing that the asteroids will never return to near-Earth orbit. The novel follows the fates of several of these permanently lost asteroids as their inhabitants gradually evolve a variety of different societies, some of them far better than the world they left. (ML)

Awards: John W. Campbell

Themes: Crime and Punishment, Dystopias, Sociology, Utopias

II-1305. Macrolife. Harper, 1979.

Humans are forced by cosmic catastrophe to quit Earth, dispersing into the galaxy in space habitats hollowed out of asteroids. As much essay as story, providing a sociology of these quasi-Utopian "macroworlds" as they continue the human story across vast reaches of future time. Comparable in scope to Stapledon's *Last and First Men* and very impressive in the breadth of its vision despite being a bit of a stylistic patchwork. (BS)

Themes: Colonization of Other Worlds

II-1306. Sunspacer. Harper, 1984. Series: Sunspacer.

YA. Unsure if he wants a career in theoretical physics but aware that he needs adventure and the challenge of hardship and danger, Joe Sorby, a high school student of the future, forgoes college on Bernal to become a maintenance apprentice. Very detailed scenario of possible solar system exploration and convincing portrait of youth unsure of himself and his options. Followed by *The Stars Will Speak* (1985) and *Behind the Stars* (1996). Compare Heinlein's *Starman Jones*. (FM/ML)

Themes: Coming of Age, Scientists and Engineers

Zelazny, Roger, U.S., 1937–1995

*II-1307. The Doors of His Face, The Lamps of His Mouth and Other Stories. Doubleday, 1971.

A fine collection; the Nebula Award-winning title story concerns a man facing up to his fears in the shape of a Venerian sea monster, and "A Rose for Ecclesiastes" is a poignant story about a man who unwittingly brings faith to a Martian race on the brink of extinction. The earlier collection, *Four for Tomorrow* (1967), is equally good, but two subsequent short story volumes, *My Name Is Legion* (1976) and *The Last Defender of Camelot* (1980), are weaker, although the former does feature the Hugo Award-winning "Home Is the Hangman," a suspenseful story about an enigmatic robot executioner. Zelazny's later collections are *Unicorn Variations* (1983), which features "Unicorn Variation," and *Frost and Fire* (1989), which contains "Permafrost" and "24 Views of Mt. Fuji by Hokusai," all of which were Hugo Award winners. (BS/ML)

*II-1308. The Dream Master. Ace, 1966.

Expanded from the Nebula Award-winning novella "He Who Shapes." A psychiatrist links minds with disturbed patients to construct therapeutic dream experiences. He tries to train a blind woman in the relevant techniques, despite opposition from her intellectually augmented guide dog, and finds his own balance of mind threatened. Compare Le Guin's *The Lathe of Heaven* and Bear's *Queen of Angels*. (BS)

Themes: Psychology

II-1309.   Isle of the Dead. Ace, 1969.

The human hero has learned the alien power of "worldscaping," embracing a new religion along with his godlike powers, but a resentful alien sets out to destroy him. The hero's psychological hang-ups are incarnated in one of his creations, and his inner and outer conflicts are fused. (BS)

Themes: Mythology, Psychology, Religion

*II-1310.   Lord of Light. Doubleday, 1967.

A colony world has used its powerful technology to recreate Hindu culture, its elite assuming the roles of the gods. The hero first rebels against these "gods" on their own terms, but then opposes them more successfully with a new faith. Pyrotechnically dramatic and imaginatively fascinating. The similar *Creatures of Light and Darkness* (1969), which draws heavily on Egyptian mythology, is less successful. Compare Gene Wolfe's Book of the New Sun. (BS)

Awards: Hugo

Themes: Mythology

*II-1311.   This Immortal. Ace, 1966.

Expanded from a shorter version, the Hugo Award-winning ". . . And Call Me Conrad." The superhuman hero must defend an extraterrestrial visitor against the many dangers of a wrecked Earth where mutation has reformulated many mythical entities. A fascinating interweaving of motifs from SF and mythology—perhaps the most successful of Zelazny's several exercises in that vein. Compare Delany's *The Einstein Intersection*. (BS)

Themes: Immortality, Mythology, Supermen/women

Živković, Zoran, Serbia, 1948–

II-1312.   The Fourth Circle. Trans. by Mary Popovic. Night Shade/Ministry of Whimsy, 2004.

Zivkovic writes from a unique viewpoint that lies somewhere equidistant between Borges, Lem, surrealism, and genre SF. His first full-fledged novel, after a series of highly praised short story collections, features an astonishing mixture of themes, settings, and characters that defy easy categorization or summary. The story moves from a medieval cathedral to a Buddhist temple to the edge of a black hole and features Nikola Tesla, Stephen Hawking, and Sherlock Holmes among its varied cast of characters. A literary tour de force. (ML)

Themes: History in SF, Satirical SF

Zoline, Pamela, U.K., 1941–

II-1313. Busy About the Tree of Life. Women's Press, 1988, U.S. title: *The Heat Death of the Universe and Other Stories*, 1988.

Zoline hasn't written very much, but what she has produced is superb. Her first story, "The Heat Death of the Universe," was hailed as a masterpiece when it appeared in *New Worlds* in 1967. In the following decades, however, she published only three more stories. This first collection includes five stories, all of Zoline's previously published fiction plus the new title story, a cutting satire on evolution. Compare Langdon Jones's *The Eye of the Lens* and Pat Cadigan's *Patterns*. (ML)

Anthologies

Sequenced by title. Consult the author index for access by editor.

*II-1314. Adventures in Time and Space. Ed. by Raymond J. Healy and J. Francis McComas. Random, 1946. Retitled *Famous Science-Fiction Stories*, 1957.

Long part of the Modern Library series, this hefty 33-story anthology, quarried entirely from genre magazines, represents one of the earliest breakouts from SF's pulp ghetto. To general readers and to libraries that might not have purchased any other SF, it introduced such memorable tales as Asimov's "Nightfall," Bester's "Adam and No Eve," Heinlein's "Requiem" and "By His Bootstraps," van Vogt's "Black Destroyer," P. Schuyler Miller's "As Never Was," del Rey's "Nerves," Campbell's "Who Goes There?," Raymond Z. Gallun's dark Darwinist parable, "Seeds of the Dusk," and many more, together with two non-fiction pieces. The selections were overwhelmingly from Campbell's *Astounding*, further reinforcing the reputation of that editor and magazine as founders and shapers of SF's Golden Age. A Golden Age selection drawn entirely from *Astounding*'s rivals would have read very differently from this one and usually to the other magazines' and stories' credit. (PC)

II-1315. Afterlives. Ed. by Pamela Sargent and Ian Watson. Vintage, 1986.

A theme anthology mixing a few reprints with mostly original stories of life after death. SF and fantasy approaches mingle in many of the tales, demonstrating again the fascination many SF writers have with questions of metaphysics and with the possibility that technology might one day provide opportunities that humans have long yearned for in the context of the theological imagination. Compare Ryan's *Perpetual Light*. (BS/ML)

Themes: Religion

II-1316. Alien Sex. Ed. by Ellen Datlow. Dutton, 1990.

Nineteen science fiction and horror stories about sex with the alien. The most memorable story in the book is undoubtedly Pat Murphy's Nebula Award-nominated "Love and Sex Among the Invertebrates." Other fine pieces include

Leigh Kennedy's "Her Furry Face," Harlan Ellison's "How's the Night Life on Cissalda?," Larry Niven's bizarre "Man of Steel, Woman of Kleenex," Edward Bryant's "Dancing Chickens," and Connie Willis's extremely controversial "All My Darling Daughters." Datlow has done other sex-related anthologies over the past decade, for example *Little Deaths* (1995) and *Off Limits* (1996). Compare *Strange Bedfellows: Sex and Science Fiction*, edited by Thomas N. Scortia (1972). (ML)

    Themes: Sex in SF

II-1317. Alternate Empires. Ed. by Gregory Benford and Martin H. Greenberg. Bantam, 1989.

Each volume of the What Might Have Been? original short fiction series focuses on a different aspect of alternate history. The stories in Volume One are designed to explore the changed world that would have occurred as the result of some "grand event that did not come about." Two stories from the book received Hugo Award nominations, George Alec Effinger's "Everything but Honor" and Larry Niven's "The Return of William Proxmire." The impressive list of contributors also includes Poul Anderson, Kim Stanley Robinson, Harry Turtledove, Gregory Benford, Robert Silverberg, Karen Joy Fowler, and Frederik Pohl. Later volumes in the series are *Alternate Heroes* (1990), *Alternate Wars* (1991), and *Alternate Americas* (1992). (ML)

    Themes: Alternate Worlds, History in SF

II-1318. Ancestral Voices. Ed. by R. Reginald and Douglas Menville. Arno, 1974.

An anthology of 10 early SF stories, including Jack London's "The Red One" and George Griffith's "A Corner in Lightning" (1898). The rest are minor, and mostly marginal, but two interesting idiosyncratic items featuring modest inventions include "The Space Annihilator" (1901) by Harle Oren Cummins and "Beyond the Spectrum" (1914) by Morgan Robertson. (BS)

*II-1319. The Ascent of Wonder: The Evolution of Hard SF. Ed. by David G. Hartwell and Kathryn Cramer. Tor, 1994.

A massive but controversial anthology that brings together 67 stories by a total of 57 authors, plus introductions by the two editors and Gregory Benford, an afterword by Cramer, and extensive notes on each story. The anthology claims to chart the development of hard SF from its prehistory ("Rappaccini's Daughter" by Nathaniel Hawthorne) to the 1990s ("Chromatic Aberration" by John M. Ford). The collection does represent the subgenre solidly with notable stories from Tom Godwin ("The Cold Equations"), Arthur C. Clarke, Isaac Asimov, and Vernor Vinge among others, but gives weight to authors not generally associated with hard SF, including J. G. Ballard, Gene Wolfe, and Philip K. Dick. The anthology is marked by an intellectual confusion that makes it impossible to tell from the material collected exactly how hard SF differs from any other part of the genre, but the book still stands as an important collection of short

SF. See also the listing for the companion volume, *The Hard Science Fiction Renaissance*. (PK)

Themes: Hard SF

II-1320. The Battle of the Monsters and Other American Science Fiction Stories. Ed. by David G. Hartwell and L. W. Currey. Gregg Press, 1976.

Eight early SF stories; a more interesting selection than Reginald and Menville's *Ancestral Voices*. It leads off with Leonard Kip's enterprising evolutionary fantasy novella "The Secret of Apollonius Septrio" from *Hannibal's Man and Other Tales* (1878). Also featured are W. C. Morrow's gruesome horror/SF story "The Monster Maker" (1887), Morgan Robertson's microcosmic romance "The Battle of the Monsters" (1899), and Simon Newcomb's far-future account of "The End of the World" (1903). (BS)

II-1321. Before Armageddon: An Anthology of Victorian and Edwardian Imaginative Fiction Published Before 1914. Ed. by Michael Moorcock. W. H. Allen, 1975.

The first volume of a two-part anthology of antique SF, whose second volume was issued as *England Invaded* (1977). The most substantial of its six items are future-war fictions—Chesney's *The Battle of Dorking*, George Griffith's "The Raid of *Le Vengeur*" (1901), and an excerpt from le Queux's *The Great War in England in 1897*—but E. Nesbit's horror/SF story "The Three Drugs" (1910) is also included. The second volume is mostly taken up with a political fantasy depicting England under the Kaiser's rule, *When William Came* (1914) by H. H. Munro (better known as "Saki"); the most interesting of the five minor items included is "The Abduction of Alexandra Smale: A Tale of the Twentieth Century" (1900) by Fred C. Smale. (BS)

*II-1322. Before the Golden Age: A Science Fiction Anthology of the 1930s. Ed. by Isaac Asimov. Doubleday, 1974.

A showcase anthology of 26 stories from 1931–1938, arranged year by year so as to provide a sketch of pulp SF's evolution from the Gernsbackian era through the various phases of *Astounding*'s early evolution. Notable inclusions are "The Jameson Satellite" by Neil R. Jones, "The Moon Era" by Jack Williamson, "The Man Who Awoke" by Laurence Manning, "Colossus" by Donald Wandrei, "Sidewise in Time" by Murray Leinster, "Old Faithful" by Raymond Z. Gallun, "The Parasite Planet" by Stanley G. Weinbaum, "Past, Present and Future" by Nathan Schachner, and "The Men and the Mirror" by Ross Rocklynne. The most substantial contributions by less famous hands include two microcosmic romances by Capt. S. P. Meek and one by Henry Hasse, and two futuristic adventure stories by Charles R. Tanner. The stories were actually selected by Sam Moskowitz, a prolific ghoster of anthologies, but Asimov contributed useful nostalgic and context-setting introductions. (BS)

II-1323. Bending the Landscape: Science Fiction. Ed. by Nicola Griffith and Stephen Pagel. Overlook, 1998.

A well-done anthology of gay- and lesbian-themed science fiction, part of a three-book set that also includes volumes centered on fantasy and horror. Among the better known writers included in the volume, not all of whom are gay, are Stephen Baxter, Ellen Klages, L. Timmel Duchamp, Charles Sheffield, Nancy Kress, Jim Grimsley, Élizabeth Vonarburg, and Mark W. Tiedmann. For other anthologies of gay and lesbian science fiction and fantasy, see Eric Garber and Jewelle Gomez's *Swords of the Rainbow* (1996) and Garber, Camilla Decarnin, and Lyn Paleo's *Worlds Apart: An Anthology of Lesbian and Gay Science Fiction and Fantasy* (1999). For novels featuring gay and lesbian characters, see the fiction of Griffith, Thomas Disch, Melissa Scott, Samuel Delany, and Maureen McHugh. (ML)

   Awards: World Fantasy
   Themes: Feminist SF, Sex in SF

II-1324. The Best of Interzone. Ed. by David Pringle. Voyager, St. Martin's, 1997.

For nearly two decades. *Interzone* has been the U.K.'s premier science fiction magazine. This outstanding reprint anthology collects stories by such luminaries as Mary Gentle, Thomas M. Disch, J. G. Ballard, Greg Egan, Brian Aldiss, Nicola Griffith, Stephen Baxter, and Cherry Wilder. (ML)

II-1325. The Best of Science Fiction. Ed. by Groff Conklin. Crown, 1946.

Intended to introduce previous nonreaders of SF to the genre, this 40-story reprint anthology opened with an essay, "Concerning Science Fiction," by *Astounding* editor John W. Campbell, and included notable mainstream writers such as Wells, Poe, Conan Doyle, Julian Huxley, and Frank R. Stockton, as well as pulp stalwarts like Leinster ("First Contact"), Sturgeon ("Killdozer"), Heinlein ("Solution Unsatisfactory"), and Kuttner/Moore ("The Piper's Son"). The stories were divided into thematic categories, a format he repeated in *A Treasury of Science Fiction, The Big Book of Science Fiction* (1950), and *The Omnibus of Science Fiction* (1952), comprising with this volume 2,400 pages, well covering the short story field prior to the 1950s. These large books, together with some 30 smaller (often theme) anthologies, made Conklin the leading reprint anthologist in the field prior to the advent of Martin H. Greenberg. (PC)

*II-1326. The Best Science Fiction of the Year. Ed. by Terry Carr. Ballantine, Holt, Pocket Books, Timescape, Baen, Tor, 1965–1987.

Carr first began editing this peripatetic series with Donald Wollheim. He struck a good balance between big names and not-yet-established writers and was always sensitive to originality of approach. When published by Ballantine, a supplemental volume was issued, *Best Science Fiction Novellas of the Year*, 1979–1980. (BS)

II-1327.   The Best Science Fiction Stories. Ed. by Everett F. Bleiler and T. E. Dikty. Fell, 1949–1958.

The pioneering "year's best" series, mainly from U.S. genre sources but, within that limitation, well-selected. Conventional choices are interspersed with a few offbeat items. Outstanding stories include J. J. Coupling's "Period Piece" and a virtuoso tale by Kuttner, "Happy Ending," both in Volume 1; and Sturgeon's jolly "The Hurkle Is a Happy Beast" and Simak's darkly ironic "Eternity Lost" in Volume 2. Bleiler dropped out as editor after 1954, but the series continued into 1956, with a final volume (from Advent) in 1958, thus overlapping with Judith Merril's competing volume, *SF: The Year's Greatest*. Dikty's solo editions included yearly review essays, a practice taken up by many other editors of annual anthologies. (PC)

II-1328.   Beyond Time and Space: A Compendium of SF Through the Ages. Ed. by August Derleth. Pellegrini and Cudahy, 1950.

A showcase anthology whose 32 items—mostly excerpts—attempt to construct and exemplify the history of SF as a literary species ultimately descendant from Plato's invention of Atlantis and Lucian's *True History*, which evolved via More, Campanella, Godwin, Swift, Kepler, Bacon, and Holberg to the modern era launched by Poe, Verne, and Wells—also represented by Grant Allen's "Pausodyne" (1881), Frank Stockton's "A Tale of Negative Gravity" (1884), Edward Bellamy's "The Blindman's World" (1886), and others. The pulp writers represented include David H. Keller, Stanley G. Weinbaum, Clark Ashton Smith, and Donald Wandrei; William Hope Hodgson, Olaf Stapledon, and H. F. Heard represent the later development of scientific romance. It was a very useful compendium in its day, especially in the assembly of early texts (many of which were virtually unknown in 1950), and it remains a useful overview. (BS)

II-1329.   British Future Fiction 1700–1914 (8 vols.). Ed. by I. F. Clarke. Pickering and Chatto, 2001.

A massive 4,413-page sampler compiled for the publisher who had earlier issued Gregory Claeys's 8-volume compendium of *Modern British Utopias 1700–1850* (1997). The featured texts juxtaposes a few "lost" works, such as William Grove's revolt-of-the-machines story *The Wreck of a World* (1889) and two works by William DeLisle Hay—the disaster story *The Doom of the Great City* (1880) and the futuristic utopia *Three Hundred Years Hence* (1881)—with more commonplace ones, including such standards as Chesney's *The Battle of Dorking* and Hudson's *A Crystal Age*. As might be expected from Clarke, the collection is particularly rich in future-war fiction (albeit of a rather restrained stripe), although several works dealing with the suffragette movement are included, most notably A. C. Fox-Davies's *The Sex Triumphant* (1909). A mixed bag that contrives to present a remarkably unrepresentative cross-section of its already-limited field (all interplanetary fiction is excluded, no matter how futuristic its setting) by omitting longer works and works by such familiar but central writers as Wells, Griffith, Doyle, and Shiel. (BS)

II-1330. Centaurus: The Best of Australian Science Fiction. Ed. by David G. Hartwell and Damien Broderick. Tor, 1999.

An excellent reprint anthology featuring stories by such major Australian writers as George Turner, A. Bertram Chandler, Greg Egan, Sean McMullen, Terry Downing, Cherry Wilder, Damien Broderick, and Peter Carey. Compare Broderick's *Strange Attractors* and Dann and Webb's *Dreaming Down-Under*. (ML)

II-1331. A Century of Science Fiction. Ed. by Damon F. Knight. Simon & Schuster, 1962.

Only the three stories by Bierce, Wells, and Fitz-James O'Brien are actually a century old; nearly half fall within the 1950s. Stories are grouped thematically, then chronologically, supplemented with incisive and informative commentary. Although most of the stories appear in author collections, this way of looking at them provides fresh insight. A companion volume, *One Hundred Years of Science Fiction* (Simon & Schuster, 1968), is similarly organized but lacks commentary. Only three go back about a hundred years; one is Kipling's "With the Night Mail," happily published here with the ads from the magazine of the year 2000 in which it purportedly appeared. Other, less familiar tales included Sturgeon's creepy "The Other Celia," Anderson's powerful and tragic "The Man Who Came Early," Leinster's sentimental but effective "The Other Now," Kornbluth's chilling "The Mindworm," and Budrys's melancholy "Nobody Bothers Gus." (ML)

II-1332. Cities. Ed. by Peter Crowther. Gollancz, 2003.

Four novellas, most on the borderline between science fiction and fantasy, all set in fascinating and disturbing urban environments. The talented contributors to this superb anthology are China Miéville, Michael Moorcock, Paul di Filippo, and Geoff Ryman. (ML)

Themes: Cities, Science Fantasy

*II-1333. Conjunctions: 39, The New Wave Fabulists. Ed. by Peter Straub. Bard College, 2002.

Technically an issue of Bard College's creative-writing journal *Conjunctions*, *The New Wave Fabulists* looks like and essentially is a meaty trade paperback. Many of the stories here are generically unclassifiable or would fit more comfortably under the label of literary fantasy than that of science fiction, but enough of the work found between the covers of this incredibly well-done volume qualifies as SF to justify its inclusion here. The all-star cast of authors includes John Crowley, Kelly Link, M. John Harrison, Peter Straub, James Morrow, Nalo Hopkinson, Jonathan Lethem, Joe Haldeman, China Miéville, Andy Duncan, Gene Wolfe, Patrick O'Leary, Jonathan Carroll, John Kessel, Karen Joy Fowler, Paul Park, Elizabeth Hand, and Neil Gaiman. The book concludes with essays by Gary Wolfe and John Clute. (ML)

II-1334.   Cosmos Latinos: An Anthology of Science Fiction from Latin America and Spain. Ed. by Andrea L. Bell and Yolanda Molina-Gavilán. Wesleyan UP, 2003.

This groundbreaking anthology features well-done translations of fiction by a wide range of talented Spanish and Portuguese-speaking writers, most of whom will be totally unfamiliar to English-language readers. Several stories date from the 19th century but many are quite recent. Most of the fiction is rather dark and the stories often work with political or religious themes. (ML)

Themes: Politics, Religion

*II-1335.   Dangerous Visions. Ed. by Harlan Ellison. Doubleday, 1967.

The first big hardcover anthology of original SF stories—a classic that launched a publishing vogue as well as providing a manifesto for the American New Wave. Ellison's combative introductions set off the stories superbly, though some of the efforts at "taboo-breaking" now seem a little sophomoric. A very influential book, followed by the even bigger and equally fine *Again, Dangerous Visions* (1972). An endlessly promised third volume, *The Last Dangerous Visions*, was the subject of a scathing pamphlet by Christopher Priest, *The Last Deadloss Visions* (1987), reprinted with revisions as *The Book on the Edge of Forever* (Fantagraphic Books, 1994). (BS)

Themes: New Wave

II-1336.   Dark Matter: A Century of Speculative Fiction from the African Diaspora. Ed. by Sheree R. Thomas. Warner Aspect, 2000.

Fine anthology of African-American science fiction and fantasy, mixing original fiction with reprints. Among the earlier writers included are Charles W. Chesnutt and W. E. B. Dubois. Well-known contemporary voices include Samuel Delany, Octavia Butler, Amiri Baraka, Ishmael Reed, Walter Mosley, Tananarive Due, Jewelle Gomez, Steven Barnes, and Nalo Hopkinson. The sequel, *Dark Matter: Reading the Bones* (2004), received somewhat less positive reviews. (ML)

II-1337.   Decade: The 1940s. Ed. by Brian W. Aldiss and Harry Harrison. Macmillan, 1975.

Eight stories, all from *Astounding*, which in the 1940s, the editors argue, was all we had. In the same editors' *Decade: The 1950s* (Macmillan, 1976) there were no stories from *Astounding*. A characteristic choice was Cordwainer Smith's "Scanners Live in Vain." *Decade: The 1960s* (Macmillan, 1977) carried their selections on into the New Wave, although the editors didn't use that term. An excellent series, foreshadowing other retrospective "decade" collections such as Pohl, Greenberg, and Olander's *Science Fiction of the Forties* (Avon, 1978), which in contrast to Aldiss and Harrison chose less than half its 21 stories from *Astounding*; Barry Malzberg and Bill Pronzini's *The End of Summer: Science Fiction of the Fifties* (Ace, 1979); and Terry Carr's *Classic Science Fiction: The First Golden Age* (Harper, 1978). The judicious, but idiosyncratic, choices of all these editors bring to life the *Zeitgeist* of the periods they anthologized; and their own diversity of temperaments and tastes assure that those periods are presented with appropriate variety. (PC)

II-1338. Despatches from the Frontiers of the Female Mind. Ed. by Jen Green and Sarah Lefanu. Women's Press, 1985.

An original anthology of feminist SF including American as well as British writers. The stories range from the heavily didactic to the sensitively sentimental. Russ, Tiptree, and Tanith Lee are among those featured. This feminist anthology was preceded by those of Sargent (*Women of Wonder*), *Aurora: Beyond Equality* (edited by Vonda N. McIntyre and Susan Janice Anderson, 1976), and *Cassandra Rising* (edited by Alice Laurance, 1978). (BS)
Themes: Feminist SF

II-1339. Dreaming Down-Under. Ed. by Jack Dann and Janeen Webb. Voyager-Australia, 1998.

There have been several outstanding collections of Australian science fiction and fantasy in recent years, but most have been reprint anthologies. This all-original volume, which reviewers have compared to Ellison's *Dangerous Visions*, features excellent fiction by Stephen Dedman, Isabelle Carmody, Sean McMullen, Rosaleen Love, Terry Dowling, Russell Blackford, George Turner, Jane Routley, Sean Williams, Cherry Wilder, David J. Lake, Damien Broderick, and a host of other writers from down under. Compare Broderick's *Strange Attractors* and Hartwell and Broderick's *Centaurus*. (ML)
Awards: World Fantasy

II-1340. Epoch. Ed. by Roger Elwood and Robert Silverberg. Berkley, 1975.

Elwood was one of the most prolific SF anthologists of all time, but few of the books he produced were memorable. *Epoch*, by far the best of his anthologies, included excellent original stories by Niven, Pohl, Wilhelm, Martin, Russ, Attanasio, Bishop, Malzberg, Benford, Aldiss, Vance, Le Guin, and others. (ML)
Awards: *Locus*

II-1341. The Expert Dreamers. Ed. by Frederik Pohl. Doubleday, 1962.

Sixteen SF stories by scientists, some of them regular SF writers: Asimov, Clarke, R. S. Richardson (Philip Latham), Hoyle, and George R. Smith; plus others who have published SF only occasionally, such as George Gamow, Leo Szilard, and Norbert Wiener. A cognate anthology is Groff Conklin's *Science Fiction by Scientists* (Collier, 1962), with stories by some of the same authors as in Pohl, as well as Eric Temple Bell (John Taine), J. B. S. Haldane, Julian Huxley, and Chad Oliver. Both anthologies contain helpful biographical and story notes. (PC)

II-1342. Far Horizons. Ed. by Robert Silverberg. Avon Eos, 1999.
In this generally well-done theme anthology, each story takes place in a universe already made famous by its author. For example, Ursula K. Le Guin contributed a piece set in her Hainish universe while Anne McCaffrey's story takes place in

the world of Helva, the Ship Who Sang. Other contributors include Orson Scott Card, Dan Simmons, Joe Haldeman, David Brin, Nancy Kress, Frederik Pohl, Greg Bear, Gregory Benford, and Silverberg himself. (ML)

II-1343.   Flying Cups and Saucers: Gender Explorations in Science Fiction and Fantasy. Ed. by Debbie Notkin and the secret feminist cabal. Edgewood, 1998.

The James Tiptree Award, established in 1991, and named for Alice Sheldon, who wrote under the pseudonym of James Tiptree, Jr., honors science fiction and fantasy, long or short form, that explores and expands gender roles, male and female. This reprint collection of short stories is drawn from those short stories singled out for mention by judges during the first five years of the award. It offers a remarkably heterogeneous set of views and attitudes about the nature of gender, drawn from the work of a wide range of authors, some of whom might not ordinarily be regarded as addressing gender issues. Like the award itself, the anthology has been widely influential in bringing gender issues forward for discussion. (MKS)

Themes: Feminist SF

II-1344.   From Off This World: Gems of Science Fiction Chosen from "Hall of Fame Classics." Ed. by Leo Margulies and Oscar J. Friend. Merlin, 1949.

Margulies and Friend were the creators and initial editorial supervisors of *Startling Stories*, a companion to *Thrilling Wonder Stories*, whose predecessor they had acquired from Hugo Gernsback. *Startling* instituted a "Hall of Fame" that mostly reprinted stories from the Gernsback era. The 18 items reproduced here include Clark Ashton Smith's "The City of the Singing Flame" and its sequel, and Stanley G. Weinbaum's "A Martian Odyssey" and its sequel. Other notable inclusions are Benson Herbert's innovative parallel-worlds story "The World Without" (1931) and Thomas Gardner's ironic far-future fantasy "The Last Woman" (1932). (PC)

*II-1345. Full Spectrum. Ed. by Lou Aronica and Shawna McCarthy. Bantam, 1988–1995.

A fine continuing series of original science fiction and fantasy stories. James Morrow's "Bible Stories for Adults, No. 17: The Deluge" won the 1988 Nebula Award, while Norman Spinrad's "Journals of the Plague Years," Pat Murphy's "Dead Men on TV," Jack McDevitt's "The Fort Moxie Branch," and Thomas M. Disch's "Voices of the Kill" were also award nominees. *Full Spectrum* itself won the 1989 *Locus* Award for best SF anthology. Five volumes had appeared by 1995, each containing a number of excellent stories. (ML)

*II-1346. Future Perfect: American Science Fiction of the Nineteenth Century. Ed. by H. Bruce Franklin. Rev. ed. Oxford Univ. Press, 1978.

Easily the best showcase anthology of its field, with useful commentaries by the editor, this anthology samples the pioneering short SF of Hawthorne and Poe before going on to summarize and exemplify the contributions made by such familiar icons of 19th-century American literature as Herman Melville, Jack London, Ambrose Bierce, Edward Bellamy, Washington Irving, Fitz-James O'Brien, and Mark Twain. The more esoteric items include J. D. Whelpley's intriguingly prophetic tale of invention "The Atoms of Chladni" (1860), Thomas Wentworth Higginson's visionary fantasy "The Monarch of Dreams" (1886), and William Harben's brief future history "In the Year Ten Thousand" (1892). (BS)

II-1347. Gulliveriana. Ed. by Jeanne Welcher and George E. Bush, Jr. 6 vols. Scholars' Facsimiles and Reprints, 1970–1976.

A useful collection of photographic reproductions of various sequels to and works inspired by Swift's *Gulliver's Travels*. The most notable inclusions relevant to the history of SF are Murtagh McDermot's *A Trip to the Moon* (1728) in Volume One; Samuel Brunt's *A Voyage to Cacklogallinia* (1727) and Holberg's *Journey to the World Underground* in Volume Three; and Voltaire's *Micromegas* in Volume Five. (BS)

Themes: Satirical SF

*II-1348. The Hard Science Fiction Renaissance. Ed. by David G. Hartwell and Kathryn Cramer. Tor, 2002.

A companion volume to *The Ascent of Wonder* which purports to bring the story up to date. With 41 stories by 34 authors (but less critical material, only one introduction plus long introductions to each story), it covers the period from 1987 ("A Career in Sexual Chemistry" by Brian Stableford) to 2001 ("Fast Times at Fairmont High" by Vernor Vinge). Like its predecessor, it seems to suffer a strange schizophrenia about what actually constitutes hard SF, including writers and stories (Bruce Sterling, Joe Haldeman, "A Good Rat" by Allen Steele) that are associated only tangentially at best with the subgenre. The anthology nevertheless represents an interesting overview of science fiction in the 1990s, notable particularly for the high number of British writers represented (a much higher proportion than in the previous volume). (PK)

Themes: Hard SF

II-1349. Hitler Victorious: Eleven Stories of the German Victory in World War II. Ed. by Gregory Benford and Martin H. Greenberg. Garland, 1986.

A theme anthology mixing reprints and originals dealing with the most popular of all alternate history premises. (BS)

Themes: Alternate Worlds, War

*II-1350. The Hugo Winners. Ed. by Isaac Asimov. Doubleday, 1962 (vol. 1), 1971 (vol. 2).

Short stories and novelettes that won the Hugo, based on ballots of delegates to the annual World SF Convention (worldcon). A guide to what was well-received in the SF community in particular years, most of it of enduring value and often noted in annotations of collections. Asimov provided introductions. Volume 1, covering 1955 through 1961, omitted 1957, when the worldcon was in London. Winners included Walter Miller's "The Darfstellar," Clarke's "The Star," Davidson's "Or All the Seas With Oysters," Simak's "The Big Front Yard," and the novelette version of Keyes's *Flowers for Algernon*. Volume 2 covered 1963 through 1970, when the field was undergoing rapid change, as reflected in titles like "Repent, Harlequin! Said the Ticktockman" (Ellison) and "Time Considered as a Helix of Semi-precious Stones" (Delany). The series continued with Volume 3, 1977, 1971–1975; Volume 4, 1985, 1976–1979; and Volume 5, 1986, 1980–1982. Martin H. Greenberg joined Asimov as co-editor and the title changed to *The New Hugo Winners* (see below). Four volumes have been published since, collecting stories published 1983–1985, 1986–1988, 1989–1991 and 1992–1994, edited by Greenberg and changing co-editors. (PC)

II-1351.   If; or, History Rewritten. Ed. by J. C. Squire. Viking, 1931.

A classic anthology of 11 essays in alternative history; the contributors include G. K. Chesterton, André Maurois, and Winston Churchill, whose "If Lee Had Not Won the Battle of Gettysburg" ingeniously employs the alternative world as the essayist's viewpoint. An expanded edition was issued in 1972. (BS)

  Themes: Alternate Worlds

II-1352.   Imagination Unlimited: Science-Fiction and Science. Ed. by Everett F. Bleiler and T. E. Dikty. Farrar, 1952.

Thirteen stories grouped under specific scientific disciplines, good, strong, well-told tales whose science in most cases is surprisingly undated. Under mathematics we get Sturgeon's "What Dead Men Tell"; under psychology, Peter Phillips's "Dreams Are Sacred"; under anthropology, Frank Robinson's quietly melancholy "The Fire and the Sword"; and under biochemistry, Julian May's quite marvelous and too-little-known "Dune Roller." A good book for a humanities-oriented reader who's skittish about the science in SF. (PC)

II-1353.   In the Field of Fire. Ed. by Jeanne Van Buren Dann and Jack Dann. Tor, 1987.

This well-done collection of short science fiction stories about the war in Vietnam includes the Hugo- and Nebula Award-nominated novelette "Dream Baby" by Bruce McAllister, which was later expanded into a successful novel, and the World Fantasy Award-nominated "Shades" by Lucius Shepard, as well as stories by Kim Stanley Robinson, Karen Joy Fowler, Kate Wilhelm, Harlan Ellison, Joe

Haldeman, Brian Aldiss, and others. Compare Joe Haldeman's *The Forever War* and Lucius Shepard's *Life During Wartime*. (ML)

Themes: War

*II-1354. Isaac Asimov Presents the Great Science Fiction Stories. Ed. by Isaac Asimov and Martin H. Greenberg. DAW, 1979–1992.

Differs from all previous "year's best" anthologies, which typically selected from the previous year. Asimov and Greenberg began their series *40* years after the stories' initial appearance, giving plenty of time for reflection and recall. Each story is supplied with helpful critical and biographical notes. The initial year covers the pivotal year 1939, noteworthy for several debut stories in *Astounding* by van Vogt, Asimov, Heinlein, and Sturgeon, and early work by de Camp and del Rey. Later volumes chronicled the Golden Age SF of the 1940s, the shift to social criticism and satire in the 1950s, and by the final volume (vol. 25, 1992, 1963 stories) were including the U.S. and U.K. writers who were about to launch SF's perceptual revolution. A must purchase for any library. (PC)

II-1355.   The James Tiptree Anthology 1: Sex, the Future and Chocolate Chip Cookies. Ed. by Karen Joy Fowler, Pat Murphy, Debbie Notkin, and Jeffrey Smith. Tachyon, 2004.

The first in a series of anthologies that will collect short stories and novel excerpts short-listed for the annual Tiptree Award for gender-bending SF. (ML)

II-1356.   The Light Fantastic. Ed. by Harry Harrison. Scribner, 1971.

Thirteen stories, mostly from the 1950s and early 1960s, by authors not commonly thought of as genre SF writers. Avoiding most frequently anthologized works, Harrison chose tales like "The Muse" by Anthony Burgess, "The End of the Party" by Graham Greene, "Something Strange" by Kingsley Amis, "The Shout" by Robert Graves, and the quietly unsettling "The Shoddy Lands" by C. S. Lewis. Kipling's "The Finest Story in the World" will strike a responsive chord in any author who has ever been accosted by a would-be writer purporting to have some great story ideas: you write 'em down and we'll split fifty-fifty. James Blish's introduction offered persuasive explanation of the ghettoization of American SF; Harrison's afterword argued that the situation was about to change.

II-1357.   Light Years and Dark: Science Fiction and Fantasy of and for Our Time. Ed. by Michael Bishop. Berkley, 1984.

A large anthology mixing reprints and originals and providing a good cross-section of the concerns and modes of imaginative fiction up until the early 1980s. Authors featured include Spinrad, Niven, Tiptree, Wolfe, Ballard, and Dozois. (BS/ML)

Awards: *Locus*

II-1358.   Live Without a Net. Ed. by Lou Aronica. Roc, 2003.

Original SF centered on cutting-edge technology by such authors as Charles Stross, Michael Swanwick, Rudy Rucker, Paul Di Filippo, Stephen Baxter, David Brin, and John Meany. (ML)

   Themes: Hard SF

II-1359.   The Locus Awards. Ed. by Charles N. Brown and Jonathon Strahan. Eos, 2004.

This fine reprint anthology collects 18 novelettes and short stories that were voted the best in the field in an annual poll of its readers conducted by *Locus*, the most influential trade magazine in the field for more than 30 years. Among the many classics contained herein are Gene Wolfe's "The Death of Doctor Island," Harlan Ellison's "Jeffty Is Five," Ursula K. Le Guin's "The Day Before the Revolution," John Varley's "The Persistence of Vision," Joanna Russ's "Souls," Octavia Butler's "Bloodchild," John Kessel's "Buffalo," and Connie Willis's "Even the Queen," along with other stories by Neil Gaiman, Ted Chiang, Greg Egan, Bruce Sterling, John Crowley, Terry Bisson, Lucius Shepard, Pat Murphy, James Tiptree, Jr., and George R. R. Martin. (ML)

II-1360.   Machines That Think: The Best Science Fiction Stories About Robots and Computers. Ed. by Isaac Asimov, Patricia Warrick, and Martin H. Greenberg. Holt, 1984.

Perhaps the best of the retrospective theme anthologies using Asimov's name as a selling point. The contents span the entire history of SF, and although many of the stories have also appeared in earlier theme anthologies, this large volume (29 stories, 627 pages) offered the best historical overview in its day. (BS/ML)

   Themes: Computers, Intelligence, Robots

II-1361.   The Man in the Moone: An Anthology of Antique Science Fiction and Fantasy. Ed. by Faith K. Pizor and T. Allan Comp. Praeger, 1971.

Anthology of nine items, mostly excerpts from longer works, tracking the evolution of lunar fantasy through its later satirical phases, extending from Godwin and Cyrano to the 1835 version of Poe's "Hans Phaal," the hoax newspaper articles by Richard Adams Locke published in the same year and obviously inspired by it, and a parodic account of "The Great Steam Duck" (1841) signed by "A Member of the L.L.B.B." (i.e., the Louisville Literary Brass Band). Far more varied and inclusive is the four-volume boxed set edited by John Miller and Tim Smith, *The Moon Box* (Chronicle Books, 1995), with each volume having its own title. (BS)

   Themes: The Moon, Space Flight

II-1362.   Masterpieces: The Best Science Fiction of the Twentieth Century. Ed. by Orson Scott Card. Ace, 2004.

An intelligent reprint anthology featuring such classics as "Call Me Joe" by Poul Anderson, "A Saucer of Loneliness" by Theodore Sturgeon, "The Nine Billion

Names of God" by Arthur C. Clarke, as well as newer work by Harlan Ellison, Brian W. Aldiss, George R. R. Martin, William Gibson, Ursula K. Le Guin, John Kessel, and others. (ML)

*II-1363. Mirrorshades: The Cyberpunk Anthology. Ed. by Bruce Sterling. Arbor, 1986.

A reprint anthology of what was in 1986 the cutting edge of American SF, edited by one of the major proponents and theorists for "cyberpunk," which features a streetwise and cynical assessment of future possibilities generated by innovations in computer and biotechnology. Other leading figures in the movement—William Gibson, Pat Cadigan, and John Shirley prominent among them—are of course represented. (BS/ML)

Themes: Cyberpunk

*II-1364. Nebula Awards Showcase. Ed. by Nancy Kress. Roc, 2003.

This is the most recent volume in a series stretching back to 1966 that features the winners and runners-up for the annual Nebula Awards, given by the Science Fiction and Fantasy Writers of America (SFWA). For many years called simply *The Nebula Awards*, the series has had several publishers and many different editors. Besides the award-winning stories and runners-up, various volumes of the series have included excerpts from the winning novel, the winners of the Rhysling Award for outstanding SF poetry, essays of varying quality on a variety of subjects, including SF film, stories by early giants of the field, and bibliographies of past winners and runners-up. There is also a *Best of the Nebulas* (1989). (ML)

II-1365. New Dimensions. Ed. by Robert Silverberg and Marta Randall. Doubleday, Signet, Harper, Pocket Books, 1971–1981.

The early volumes of this series helped establish the careers of Barry Malzberg, James Tiptree, Jr., and Gardner Dozois, and the series continued to promote new writers to the end, much as did Terry Carr in his *Universe* series. Randall co-edited the last two of the dozen volumes. (BS)

*II-1366. The New Hugo Winners. Ed. by Isaac Asimov and Martin H. Greenberg. Wynwood (vol. 1), Baen (vol. 2), 1989, 1991.

First two volumes in the second series of anthologies collecting Hugo award winners in the novella, novelette, and short story categories, assembling stories published 1983–1985 and 1986–1988. Volume 3 in the series, edited by Greenberg, but "presented" by Connie Willis, appeared in 1994 and covered stories published in 1989–1991. Volume 4 in the series, edited by Greenberg, but "presented" by Gregory Benford, appeared in 1997 and included stories published in 1992–1994. Preceded by the series edited by Asimov alone, *The Hugo Winners*, discussed above. Together with the annual Nebula Awards anthologies, these two series provide a valuable record of the best short SF to appear in the United States. Note that both Hugo and Nebula awards have a history of ignoring stories published outside the United States. (ML)

II-1367.   New Legends. Ed. by Greg Bear and Martin H. Greenberg. Tor, 1995.

A well-done original anthology designed to prove that rigorous hard SF can also demonstrate "great soul." Among the highlights are Ursula K. Le Guin's "Coming of Age in Karhide," Gregory Benford's "High Abyss," Carter Scholz's "Radiance," and Greg Egan's "Wang's Carpets." Other contributors are Paul J. McAuley, Robert Sheckley, Geoffrey A. Landis, Robert Silverberg, George Alec Effinger, and Poul Anderson. (ML)

   Themes: Hard SF

II-1368.   New Soviet Science Fiction. Ed. by Theodore Sturgeon. Macmillan, 1979.

A representative anthology of mid-20th-century Soviet SF, featuring most of the major writers from the USSR with the exception of the Strugatskys, whose work was independently featured in the collection, *Noon: 22nd Century* (1978). Other early anthologies along the same lines include *Russian Science Fiction*, edited by Robert Magidoff; *The Ultimate Threshold* (1970), edited by Mirra Ginsburg; and Darko Suvin's *Other Worlds, Other Seas* (1970), which also features considerable Soviet SF alongside stories from Eastern Europe. These anthologies provide an interesting contrast of perspectives with American SF. (BS/ML)

II-1369.   New Tales of Space and Time. Ed. by Raymond J. Healy. Holt, 1951.

The first venture by a major hardcover publisher into anthologizing *original* SF stories, reprint anthologies having become fairly common by 1951. Neville's lovely, bittersweet "Bettyann" might never have seen publication otherwise. In contrast, R. Bretnor's "Little Anton" introduced the great-nephew of that other great comic creation by Bretnor, Papa Schimmelhorn. P. Schuyler Miller, *Astounding*'s veteran book reviewer, made his first fiction appearance in five years. Anthony Boucher's "The Quest of Saint Aquin," reprinted several times since its initial appearance here, rounds out an excellent collection. Introduction by Boucher. Compare Pohl's *Star Science Fiction Stories*. (PC)

II-1370.   New Voices in Science Fiction: Stories by Campbell Award Nominees. Ed. by George R. R. Martin. Macmillan (no. 1), Jove/Berkley (nos. 2–4), Bluejay (no. 5), 1977–1984.

Each volume featured long stories by the authors nominated for the John W. Campbell Award for the best new writer in the years 1973 to 1976. The final volume in the series was titled *The John W. Campbell Award Volume 5*. The award is still given. (BS)

II-1371.   New Writings in SF. Ed. by Kenneth Bulmer. Dobson & Corgi; Sidgwick & Jackson, 1964–1977.

Begun under the editorship of E. J. Carnell (nos. 1–21, 1964–1972) and continued by Bulmer (nos. 22–30, 1973–1977). The series was an important market for many British SF writers, especially those whose careers were launched after the demise of *New Worlds* and those who were more traditionally inclined. (BS)

II-1372. Northern Stars: The Anthology of Canadian Science Fiction. Ed. by David G. Hartwell and Glenn Grant. Tor, 1994.

Twenty-five short stories, including hard-to-find translated pieces by talented French Canadians Yves Meynard and Jean-Louis Trudel, as well as more familiar fiction by Phyllis Gotlieb, Robert J. Sawyer, Candas Jane Dorsey, William Gibson, A. E. van Vogt, Spider Robinson, and Charles de Lint. Dorsey and Judith Merril also contribute worthwhile essays on Canadian SF. A well-done sequel is *Northern Suns* (1999). (ML)

*II-1373. The Norton Book of Science Fiction. Ed. by Ursula K. Le Guin and Brian Attebery. Norton, 1993.

Unlike the usual Norton anthology, this enormous, 67-story, 864-page volume makes no pretense of establishing a canon of standard classics. The selection, although excellent, is somewhat idiosyncratic, excluding such expected names as Bradbury, Asimov, Heinlein, and Clarke (only North American authors are included), with coverage limited to the 1960–1990 period. Many of the genre's acknowledged masters are here, however, among them Sturgeon, Blish, Dick, Benford, Butler, Gibson, and Le Guin herself, but also included are stories by less well-known writers such as Eleanor Arnason, Molly Gloss, Andrew Weiner, and Diane Glancy. The book places an unusually strong emphasis on women, minority, and, oddly, Canadian writers. The 129-page paperback teacher's guide, by Attebery alone, provides one-page commentaries on each story and short chapters on teaching SF, SF history and marketing, critical approaches to SF, primary and secondary bibliographies, and a list of resources. The book was something of a late-20th-century lightning rod for disagreements over the essential nature of the genre. Contrast the 1946 golden age Healy/McComas classic, *Adventures in Time and Space*, and Hartwell and Cramer's more recent *The Ascent of Wonder*. (ML)

*II-1374. Orbit. Ed. by Damon E. Knight. Putnam (nos. 1–12), Berkley (no. 13), Harper (nos. 14–21),1966–1980.

The last of the pioneering original anthology series. Knight's relationship with the Clarion workshops ensured that he was often in a position to find talented new writers as their careers were just getting under way, and the series played a major role in establishing the careers of several major writers, inducing Kate Wilhelm and Gene Wolfe. R. A. Lafferty was also extensively featured. An early preference for material with particularly polished literary style gradually gave way to an interest in esoteric material, sometimes without much discernible speculative content, but the series was a worthy experiment whose volumes feature some very fine material. (BS)

II-1375. Other Edens. Ed. by Christopher Evans and Robert Holdstock. Unwin, 1987.

An excellent British all-original anthology. Among the best stories included are Tanith Lee's "Crying in the Rain," Brian Aldiss's The Price of Cabbages,"

Michael Moorcock's "The Frozen Cardinal," and Lisa Tuttle's "The Wound." *Other Edens II* (1988) was equally strong, though *Other Edens III* (1989) tailed off somewhat in quality. (ML)

II-1376.   The Other Side of the Moon. Ed. by August Derleth. Pelligrini, 1949.

Twenty stories selected by the founder of Arkham House. A few stories are horror, such as Bradbury's "Pillar of Fire" or, in a different fashion, van Vogt's "Vault of the Beast." But there is also straightforward SF including Wells's "The Star," keen satire as in S. Fowler Wright's "Original Sin," and post-A-bomb social criticism in Sturgeon's "Memorial." Clark Ashton Smith's poetic "City of the Singing Flame," F. B. Long's wondrously deranged robot story, "The World of Wulkins," and Nelson S. Bond's "Conqueror's Isle" help to round out a balanced collection. (PC)

II-1377.   The Other Worlds. Ed. by Phil(ip Duffield) Stong. Wilfred Funk, 1941. Variant title: *25 Modern Stories of Mystery and Imagination*, Garden City, 1942.

A pioneering attempt by a mainstream publisher to draw upon the pulps for hardcover publication. Stong's conviction that "the first requirement of a good fantastic story . . . is that it should not be even remotely possible" weights the anthology toward fantasy and ghost stories, some of them excellent, by writers such as Sturgeon, del Rey, Wellman, Kuttner, and Lovecraft. The selection of SF stories is capricious; a truly representative *science fiction* anthology was yet to come. Contrast Wollheim's *The Pocket Book of Science Fiction*. (PC)

II-1378.   Oxford Book of Science Fiction Stories. Ed. by Tom Shippey. Oxford, 1992.

This large selection of 30 classic American and British SF stories stands up well against other attempts to establish a canon. Among the authors represented are Aldiss, Ballard, Blish, Brin, Clarke, Disch, Gibson, Kipling, Le Guin, McAuley, Miller, Niven, Pohl, Sterling, Tiptree, van Vogt, Wells, and Wolfe. The volume includes a useful introduction by Shippey. Compare Gunn's *The Road to Science Fiction*. (ML)

II-1379.   The Penguin World Omnibus of Science Fiction. Ed. by Brian W. Aldiss and Sam J. Lundwall. Penguin, 1986.

An anthology of stories from many nations, assembled in connection with the World SF organization founded in 1976. Most of the material is fairly recent, though some dates back to the 1950s. Notable for featuring material from South America and Southeast Asia as well as more familiar points of origin, and fascinating in its diversity. (BS)

II-1380. Perpetual Light. Ed. by Alan Ryan. Warner, 1982.

A theme anthology offering 23 original stories dealing with aspects of "religious experience." Modern SF writers have been curiously fascinated by the phenomena of religious observation and questions of theology and metaphysics. This anthology revisits the themes of some of the better anthologies of the 1970s, including Mayo Moh's *Other Worlds, Other Gods* (1971; reprints) and Terry Carr's *An Exaltation of Stars* (1973; original novellas). Ryan includes particularly fine stories by Silverberg, Benford, and Schenck. (BS)

Themes: Religion

II-1381. The Pocket Book of Science Fiction. Ed. by Donald A. Wollheim. Pocket, 1943.

The first modern pulp-derived SF anthology, not fantasy or horror. Hedging his bet with work by mainstreamers Stephen Vincent Benét, Ambrose Bierce, John Collier, and Wells, Wollheim included Weinbaum's "A Martian Odyssey," Campbell's "Twilight," and Sturgeon's "Microcosmic God," as well as Heinlein's lighthearted ". . . And He Built a Crooked House." Only one of the stories is a dud. Two years later, Wollheim edited *The Portable Novels of Science* (Viking, 1945), which reprinted four longer works: Stapledon's *Odd John*, Wells's *First Men in the Moon*, Taine's *Before the Dawn* (1934), and *The Shadow out of Time*, one of two Lovecraft novellas to have first appeared in *Astounding*. These works anticipated Wollheim's later best-of-the-year anthologizing. (PC)

*II-1382. Pre-Revolutionary Russian Science Fiction: An Anthology (Seven Utopias and a Dream). Ed. by Leland Fetzer. Ardis, 1982.

Eight stories ranging from Faddei Bulgarin's "Plausible Fantasies of a Journey in the 29th Century" (1824) and Vladimir Odoevski's "The Year 4338: Letters from St Petersburg" (1838–1840) to two ironic fantasies by Alexander Kuprin (1906; 1913) and two by Valeri Briusov, including "The Republic of the Southern Cross." The longest story is an abridgment of the novel *Red Star* (1908) by "Alexander Bogdanov" (Alexander Malinowski), a Bolshevik vision of a socialist Mars that outshines Tolstoi's *Aelita*. A fascinating collection, whose contents may be interestingly contrasted with scientific romances in Western Europe. (BS)

II-1383. Redshift: Extreme Visions of Speculative Fiction. Ed. by Al Sarrantonio. Roc, 2001.

Sarrantonio wanted to pull off something akin to a 21st-century equivalent of Ellison's *Dangerous Visions* in this fat anthology of original speculative fiction. He doesn't really succeed—few of the stories are all that extreme by contemporary standards, or even by the standards set by Ellison's breakthrough anthology—but there's still a lot of good fiction here by such writers as Harry Turtledove, Gregory Benford, Dan Simmons, Stephen Baxter, Rudy Rucker, and, surprisingly, Joyce Carol Oates. (ML)

II-1384.   The Road to Science Fiction from Gilgamesh to Wells. Ed. by James E. Gunn. New American Library, 1977.

The first element of a series of showcase anthologies that eventually extended to six volumes, including 20 items; the earlier ones, all excerpted from longer works, overlap very considerably with Derleth's *Beyond Time and Space*—for which this is a useful substitute—but those from the late 19th century mostly provide different exemplars by the same authors. Also annotated as [14-23]. (BS)

II-1385.   The Road to Science Fiction Vol. 5: The British Way. Ed. by James Gunn. White Wolf, 1998; **The Road to Science Fiction Vol. 6: Around the World**. White Wolf, 1998.

These are the most recent volumes in Gunn's well done series of reprint anthologies designed largely for the university market. Volume 5 includes excerpts from such novels as Chesney's *The Battle of Dorking* (1871), Abbott's *Flatland* (1884), and Stapledon's *Star Maker* (1937), as well as classic stories by Kipling, Conan Doyle, Clarke, Wyndham, Ballard, Aldiss, Brunner, Priest, and others. As always, Gunn's introductions are one of the highlights of the volume. Volume 6 collects stories from more than a dozen countries, including stories by Verne, Čapek, Calvino, García Márquez, Lem, and others. Volumes 1 to 4 are discussed in [14-23]. (ML)

II-1386.   The Ruins of Earth. Ed. by Thomas M. Disch. Putnam, 1971.

First of a series of theme anthologies edited by Disch in the 1970s. The others are *Bad Moon Rising* (1975), *The New Improved Sun* (1975), *New Constellations* (1976), and *Strangeness* (1977), the last two in collaboration with Charles Naylor. The books mix original and reprinted material, focusing on themes of contemporary concern and fashion. They are interesting because they operate on the boundary between SF and the literary mainstream, juxtaposing SF with more conventional avant-garde items. The material is high in quality, heavy on irony, and (despite the title of the third volume) bleak in outlook. (BS)

Themes: Disaster, Ecology

II-1387.   Russian Science Fiction. Ed. by Robert Magidoff. Allen & Unwin, 1963. Trans. by Doris Johnson (except three stories).

Eleven stories, ranging from an archaic piece by Konstantin Tsiolkovsky, the father of astronautics in the USSR and, indirectly, in the West, to Vladimir Dudintsev's allegory, fable, or whatever, "A New Year's Fairy Tale." Ivan Yefremov's "Cor Serpentis" challenged the plot of Leinster's "First Contact" (1945), which argued that starships from different civilizations meeting in space would be motivated to destroy each other to safeguard the home world from invasion.

Soviet SF was in even more rapid flux in the 1960s than in the West, as Judith Merril discovered when editing *Path Into the Unknown: The Best of Soviet Science Fiction* (MacGibbon & Kee, 1966; Dell, 1968). (PC)

II-1388. Science Fiction by Gaslight: A History and Anthology of Science Fiction in the Popular Magazines, 1891–1911. Ed. by Sam Moskowitz. World, 1968.

A thematically organized representative anthology of 26 stories with a useful historical introduction. The best of five "Catastrophes" is Frank Lillie Pollock's "Finis" (1906), while the most interesting of four accounts of "Marvelous Inventions" is "The Ray of Displacement" (1903) by veteran fantasist Harriet Prescott Spofford and the more enterprising of two "Adventures in Psychology" is "Citizen 504" (1896) by Charles H. Palmer. A useful overview of the spectrum of relevant magazine material of the time. Moskowitz continued the enterprise in the more narrowly focused *Under the Moons of Mars: A History and Anthology of "The Scientific Romance" in the Munsey Magazines, 1912–1920* (1970). The anthology element is less useful than its predecessor, in that it mostly consists of excerpts—including samples from Burroughs's "Under the Moons of Mars" and England's "Darkness and Dawn"—and such familiar texts as Merritt's "The Moon Pool" and Cummings's "The Girl in the Golden Atom." But the supportive text provides a useful overview of the emergence of escapist fantasy in the pulps. (BS)

*II-1389. Science Fiction by the Rivals of H. G. Wells. Ed. by Alan K. Russell (pseudonym of Lionel Leventhal). Castle, 1979.

A photographically reproduced collection of 31 stories culled from the middle-brow British magazines from 1895 to 1906—the formative years of scientific romance. It includes six comprising the serial version of George Griffith's *A Honeymoon in Space* and two other stories by Griffith; three stories by Cutcliffe Hyne—including the Atlantean fantasy novel *The Lost Continent* (1899); and an eccentric series of six catastrophe stories by Fred M. White (1899–1904). Other interesting inclusions are the far-future fantasy "The Last Days of Earth" (1901) by George C. Wallis; a humorous account of "The Lady Automaton" (1901) by E. E. Kellett; and the cautionary melodramas "The Man Who Meddled with Eternity" (1901) by E. Tickner-Edwards and "The Black Shadow" (1903) by Owen Oliver. The paranoid attitude of the vast majority of the stories toward any and all change and innovation emphasizes by contrast the exceptional openness of H. G. Wells's mind before its ambitions were ground down by the dismal expectations of his conservative audience. (BS)

*II-1390. The Science Fiction Century. Ed. by David G. Hartwell. Tor, 1997.

A monumental anthology that purports to chart a century of science fiction from 1895 ("Another World" by J. H. Rosny aîné) to 1991 ("Beggars in Spain" by Nancy Kress), though it excludes many major figures (Asimov, Heinlein, Le Guin, and British writers later than John Wyndham). The stories are not arranged chronologically and several are not dated. And though Hartwell insists that science fiction is overwhelmingly American, he includes more non–English-language SF than any comparable anthology. Nevertheless, with nearly 1,000 pages of small type, Hartwell has been able to assemble an invaluable collection of stories and (often) novellas important to the history of the genre that are not often anthologized, including Kipling's "As Easy as ABC," London's "The Scarlet Plague," and Harness's "The Rose." (PK)

*II-1391. Science Fiction Hall of Fame, vol. 1, ed. by Robert Silverberg, Doubleday, 1971; vols. 2A and 2B, ed. by Ben Bova, Doubleday, 1974.

Volume 1 consisted of 26 short stories and novelettes chosen by ballot of the SF Writers of America as the best shorter works in the field to have been published before 1965. The range is from Weinbaum's "A Martian Odyssey" (1934) to Zelazny's "A Rose for Ecclesiastes" (1963). The decision to limit selection to one story from each author may have slightly skewed the selection. On the whole, however, the selection is near-definitive. Ben Bova edited 22 novellas, 11 in each volume, chosen the same way. They range from Wells's *The Time Machine* through such Golden Age classics as Heinlein's "Universe" and Campbell's "Who Goes There?" to strong works from the early 1960s, such as Vance's "The Moon Moth." There is surprisingly little overlap with the stories in *The Hugo Winners*: one short story, "Flowers for Algernon" and one novella, "The Big Front Yard," which may say something about the differences between fans' and writers' literary tastes. (PC)

II-1392.   Science Fiction of the Thirties. Ed. by Damon Knight. Bobbs-Merrill, 1975.

A showcase anthology of the period, whose contents do not overlap with Asimov's more wide-ranging *Before the Golden Age*, although many of the same authors are sampled. The most interesting inclusions are Murray Leinster's dimensional fantasy "The Fifth-Dimension Catapult" (1931), Harry Bates's far-future fantasy "Alas, All Thinking!" (1935), and "Seeker of Tomorrow" (1937) by Eric Frank Russell and Leslie Johnson. (BS)

II-1393.   Science Fiction: The Best of 2002. Ed. by Robert Silverberg and Karen Haber. ibooks, 2003.

A reprint anthology designed to compete with Dozois and Hartwell, this "best of" selection premiered to generally mixed reviews; features stories by Charles Stross, Brian Aldiss, Christopher Priest, and Geoffrey Landis, among others. The second volume in the series, *Science Fiction: The Best of 2003* (2004), was edited exclusively by Haber. (ML)

*II-1394. SF: The Year's Greatest. Ed. by Judith Merril. Dell, 1956–1966, 1968.

Merril's care for balance between genre and nongenre sources and U.S. and U.K. writers is evident in her selection: Shirley Jackson, Steve Allen, Bertrand

Russell, and Conrad Aiken among the latter; Davidson's "The Golem," Knight's "The Country of the Kind," Sturgeon's "The Man Who Lost the Sea," and Cordwainer Smith's "A Planet Named Shayol" among the former. Merril also included "honorable mention" listings and wrote provocative, well-founded essays on the state of the art (and the world). The title changed in 1960 to *The (5th) Annual of the Year's Best SF*. The series continued through number 11, 1966; the final volume, *SF 12*, appeared from Delacorte in 1968. Worthy successors took up the annual anthology format in more recent years. (PC)

II-1395.   So Long Been Dreaming: Postcolonial Science Fiction and Fantasy. Ed. by Uppinder Mehan and Nalo Hopkinson. Arsenal Pulp Press, 2004.

This original anthology looks at the future from the point of view of writers of color. It features SF by Nisi Shawl, Sheree R. Thomas, Larissa Lai, Karin Lowachee, Vandana Singh, and Tamai Kobayashi. Compare Thomas's *Dark Matter*. (ML)

II-1396.   Space Opera: An Anthology of Way-Back-When Futures. Ed. by Brian W. Aldiss. Weidenfeld, 1974.

Long-term science fictionists do not forget their roots. Aldiss, in this and successor volumes, remembered the excesses of youth with affection rather than disdain. Although including conventional space opera items like an excerpt from Edmond Hamilton's *The Star of Life* (1947; revised 1959), he also sought out good stories not already over-anthologized, such as Vance's brief, beautiful, heartbreaking "The Mitr." *Space Odysseys* (1975) included both Clarke's "The Sentinel" (the germ of *2001*) and Leigh Brackett's unashamedly romantic-nostalgic "The Lake of the Gone Forever." *Evil Earths* (1975) turned to the dark side of the Force, as exemplified in Campbell's "Night." *Galactic Empires* (1976) ranged in its two volumes from the technocratic optimism of Asimov's "Foundation"—and, in an entirely different way, of Blish's cogently argued "Beep"—to the quiet sadness of Budrys's "To Civilize" and Clarke's "The Possessed." An outstanding and distinctive series, boldly arguing that SF was at its best when least respectable. (PC)

Themes: Space Opera

II-1397.   Spectrum. Ed. by Kingsley Amis and Robert Conquest. Gollancz, 1961–1966.

Designed to introduce U.K. readers to SF, primarily from U.S. magazines and authors, as an acceptable literary medium. Contrary to notions of fundamental Anglo-American cultural divergences, this British-selected fiction meshed with the U.S. genre consensus: items like Pohl's "The Midas Plague," Kuttner and Moore's "Vintage Season," Anderson's "Call Me Joe," Bester's "Fondly Fahrenheit," and Kornbluth's "The Marching Morons" all made it into the SFWA's own *Science Fiction Hall of Fame* anthologies. The stories that did not—such as Sheckley's "Pilgrimage to Earth," Wyman Guin's "Beyond Bedlam," and Sturgeon's "Killdozer"—were very much in the American grain. By the third volume, evidence of the British New Wave, such as Ballard's "Voices of Time," were beginning to appear. A special departure in *Spectrum 4* was "Unreal Estates," a debate on SF among Amis, Aldiss, and C. S. Lewis, the last in effect renewing his old feud with Wells. (PC)

*II-1398. Star Science Fiction Stories. Ed. by Frederik Pohl. Doubleday, 1962–1960.

The first of six original anthologies by Pohl, which well epitomized the state of 1950s SF. Stories included Clarke's "The Nine Billion Names of God" and Kuttner/Moore's "A Wild Surmise" in number 1; Bixby's "It's a *Good* Life" and Richard Wilson's "Friend of the Family" in number 2; Clarke's "The Deep Range" and Dick's depressing "Foster, You're Dead" in number 3. Concerned for the viability in the SF marketplace of works that fell between short story and book length, Pohl also launched *Star Short Novels* (Ballantine, 1954), which showcased three new novellas: a sprightly thought experiment, "Little Men," by Jessmyn West; "To Here and the Easel," by Sturgeon; and a powerful and memorable statement on religion, "For I Am a Jealous People," by Lester del Rey. (PC)

*II-1399. Starlight 1. Ed. by Patrick Nielsen Hayden. Tor, 1996.

Arguably the best original SF anthology series since the days of *Orbit*, assembled by one of the most knowledgeable SF editors currently working in the field. Nielsen Hayden describes short fiction as "the R&D laboratory in which SF constantly reinvents itself," and, like Damon Knight before him, sets out to show the wealth of good material available within the form, deliberately sidestepping any attempt to aim the series at a specific niche market. Nielsen Hayden has assembled a formidable stable of writers, spanning every aspect of the fantasy and science fiction genres, presenting new voices such as Andy Duncan and Susanna Clarke alongside more familiar names like Maureen McHugh and Jonathan Lethem, Jane Yolen, and D. G. Compton. Three volumes as of 2004. (MKS)

II-1400.   Strange Attractors: Original Australian Speculative Fiction. Ed. by Damien Broderick. Hale & Iremonger, 1985.

One of several collections of SF stories by Australian writers. Such collections provide a significant market for writers whose domestic opportunities for publication are limited. Broderick's material is rather more avant-garde than that featured in the trio edited by Paul Collins, *Envisaged Worlds* (1978), *Distant Worlds* (1981), and *Frontier Worlds* (1983). (BS)

II-1401.   Strange Ports of Call. Ed. by August Derleth. Pellegrini, 1948.

Derleth was already recognized as a major anthologist of ghost and horror stories when he turned his attention to SF in this still eminently readable selection of 20 stories, of which the centerpiece is Lovecraft's longest tale, "At the Mountains of Madness." He also included Bradbury's "The Million Year Picnic," Heinlein's "The Green Hills of Earth," Kuttner/Moore's disturbing "Call Him Demon," and Sturgeon's powerful plea against the nations' mutual nuclear suicide, "Thunder and Roses." Derleth also picked worthy stories other editors had overlooked. (PC)

*II-1402. The Tale of the Next Great War, 1871–1914: Fictions of Future Warfare and of Battles Still-to-Come. Ed. by I. F. Clarke. Liverpool Univ. Press, 1995.

The first of two anthologies of future-war stories, followed by *The Great War with Germany, 1890–1914: Fictions and Fantasies of the War-to-Come* (1997). The first volume kicks off, inevitably, with Chesney's *Battle of Dorking* and its 15 items include many brief items in a similar vein. By far the most notable inclusion is a translation of the text of Albert Robida's *La guerre au vingtième siècle*, although it makes little sense without the illustrations it was designed to support (only a few samples of which are included here). Also included are a rare essay in future history by Jack London, "The Unparalleled Invasion: Excerpt from Walt Nevin's *Certain Essays in History*" (1910), and Arthur Conan Doyle's all-too-prophetic account of U-boat attacks, "Danger! Being the Log of Captain John Sirius" (1914). The 35 items in the companion volume are mostly extracts from novels, the most interesting of which are translations from the German, offering the other side of the anticipatory story. A few parodies are featured, including one by W. Heath Robinson and an extract from P. G. Wodehouse's novel *The Swoop! or, How Clarence Saved England* (1909). The couplet provides a useful overview of the subgenre's development and ideology. (BS)

II-1403.   Terra SF: The Year's Best European SF. Ed. by. Richard D. Nolane. DAW, 1981, 1983.

DAW's head, Donald A. Wollheim, read French, and his was the only mass market imprint to occasionally publish translations. Most of these stories are from France and Germany, although the net is cast wide enough to include Finland and Italy. Although not all published in a single year, the stories were all newly translated. The *Terra SF* anthologies followed Wollheim's earlier *The Best from the Rest of the World* (1976). Franz Rottensteiner, a Viennese attorney active in European SF (he was Lem's agent), edited *View From Another Shore* (1973), which included some East European SF. Compare also Aldiss and Lundwall's *Penguin World Omnibus*. (BS/ML)

II-1404.   Tesseracts. Ed. by Judith Merril. Press Porcépic, 1985.

A representative anthology of stories by Canadian writers, mixing originals and reprints. More-famous names include William Gibson, Spider Robinson, and Phyllis Gotlieb, but the main interest is in the juxtaposition of unusual genre material with speculative work by mainstream writers—a mix similar to that which distinguished Merril's famous best-of-the-year anthologies of the 1950s and early 1960s, which were renowned for their eclecticism and favoring of avant-garde material. Some stories here have been translated from French. The series appears irregularly but has now reached at least eight volumes, edited by a variety of people, and it is currently published by Tesseract books. Compare

Hartwell and Grant's *Northern Stars*; contrast Dann and Webb's *Dreaming Down-Under.* (BS/ML).

II-1405.   There Will Be War. Ed. by Jerry Pournelle and John F. Carr. Tor, 1983–1990.

A theme anthology series that reached nine volumes, each with a distinctive subtitle, mixing original and reprint stories with poems and essays. Reflected a strong commitment to militarism and its associated codes of behavior; featured what some might consider propaganda for the Strategic Defense Initiative and similar political/military programs. Comparable to British future-war fiction of the sort produced in the wake of Chesney's *The Battle of Dorking* until the outbreak of World War I. Compare Reginald Bretnor's less didactic three-volume series *The Future of War* (1979–1980). Contrast Harry Harrison and Bruce McAllister's *There Won't Be War* (1991), 19 mostly anti-war stories, and Lewis Shiner's *When the Music's Over* (1991), 18 original anti-war stories, proceeds from which were to be donated to Greenpeace. (BS/ML)
    Themes: Holocaust and After, War

II-1406.   Thirteen French Science Fiction Stories. Ed. by Damon Knight. Bantam, 1965.

Since Verne's time, France has had an independent SF tradition that is largely unknown in the English-speaking world. In 1959, Knight found these stories in *Fiction: La revue littéraire de l'étrange*, the Paris affiliate of *The Magazine of Fantasy and Science Fiction*. The oldest is Pierre Mille's "After Three Hundred Years," a believable portrait of a far-future French society that has regressed to barbarism, which dates from 1922. Gérard Klein, a Bradbury-influenced prodigy in the 1950s and a major mover and shaker of French SF of that period, contributed the suspenseful "The Monster." (PC)

II-1407.   A Treasury of Great Science Fiction. Ed. by Anthony Boucher. Doubleday, 1959. 2 vols.

This generous selection by the long-time editor of *The Magazine of Fantasy and Science Fiction* reprints four book-length works (Wyndham's *Re-Birth*, van Vogt's *The Weapon Shops of Isher*, Anderson's *Brain Wave*, and Bester's *The Stars My Destination*), along with 21 shorter works, most overlooked by other anthologists. Offered repeatedly as a bonus for book club enrollment, this anthology has given many readers their first in-depth introduction to SF. (PC)

*II-1408. A Treasury of Science Fiction. Ed. by Groff Conklin. Crown, 1948.

Much better than his 1946 effort, *The Best of Science Fiction*, with only one concession to "mainstream" writing, H. F. Heard's thoughtful and haunting "The Great Fog." Many of the 30 stories come from *Astounding*, including Chan Davis's "The Nightmare," Poul Anderson's debut story (with F. N. Waldrop) "Tomorrow's Children," Williamson's "With Folded Hands," C. L. Moore's "No Woman Born," and Moore/Kuttner's "Mimsy Were the Borogoves." The popularity of this anthology is shown by the additional printings as late as the 1980s. (PC)

*II-1409. Universe. Ed. by Terry Carr. Doubleday, 1971–1987.

Terry Carr's *Universe* series of original SF anthologies began publication in 1971 and, along with Damon Knight's somewhat more experimental *Orbit* series, helped redefine the science fiction short story. The last volume in the series features a number of excellent tales, including Marta Randall's "Lapidary Nights," James Tiptree, Jr.'s "Second Going," and Jack McDevitt's "In the Tower." Carr tended to shy away from both highly experimental fiction and hard SF, preferring stories that featured traditional storytelling techniques and fine style. Writers identified with the later volumes in the series include Howard Waldrop, Lucius Shepard, and Kim Stanley Robinson. Carr died in 1987, but the series was revived in 1990 with a renumbered *Universe 1* (Doubleday), edited by Robert Silverberg and Karen Haber. New volumes followed from Bantam in 1992 and 1993. Silverberg stated that his goal was to publish stories similar to those that appeared when Carr was editor, but the new *Universe* never achieved comparable critical acclaim. (ML)

II-1410. What If: Stories that Should Have Won the Hugo. Ed. by Richard A. Lupoff. Pocket, 1980 (vol. 1), 1981 (vol. 2).

Lupoff's introduction describes the history of the movement toward annual awards in SF culminating in the Hugo, which is conferred by vote of the members of each year's World Science Fiction Convention (see description in Chapter 16). He cautions that the selection process is subject to fads, sentimentalism, electioneering, and slow response to avant-garde writing. That stories as good as Sturgeon's "Golden Helix," Anderson's "The Man Who Came Early," and Kornbluth's "Two Dooms" were overlooked gives credibility to Lupoff's thesis. Volume 1 tracked the years 1952 to 1958, Volume 2, 1959 to 1965; the latter made the point that the U.K. and other non-U.S. sources were slighted by the conventions' mostly American attendees. This condition has been somewhat alleviated in more recent years by holding the worldcons in Canada or overseas, with awards going to writers including the Strugatsky brothers from the former USSR. (PC)

II-1411. Women of Other Worlds: Excursions Through Science Fiction and Feminism. Ed. by Helen Merrick and Tess Williams. Univ. of Western Australia Press, 1999.

A well-done anthology mixing fiction and nonfiction on feminist themes. Among the strongest stories included are Eleanor Arnason's "The Small Black Box of Morality," Kelly Eskridge's "And Salome Danced," Élisabeth Vonarburg's "Home by the Sea," Nalo Hopkinson's "A Habit of Waste," and Karen Joy Fowler's "The Marianas Islands." Compare *Despatches from the Frontiers of the Female Mind* and other feminist anthologies listed here. Among the essays are pieces by Ursula K. Le Guin, Pat Murphy, Nicola Griffith, and Lois McMaster Bujold. (ML)

Themes: Feminist SF, Women in SF

*II-1412. Women of Wonder: Science Fiction Stories by Women About Women. Ed. by Pamela Sargent. Vintage, 1974.

Twelve reprinted short stories by women writers, all devoted to the examination of sex roles. Included are a number of classics, among them Judith Merril's "That Only a Mother," Anne McCaffrey's "The Ship Who Sang," Sonya Dorman's "When I Was Miss Dow," Kate Wilhelm's "Baby, You Were Great," Carol Emshwiller's "Sex and/or Mr. Morrison," Ursula K. Le Guin's "Vaster Than Empires and More Slow," and Vonda N. McIntyre's "Of Mist, and Grass, and Sand." Sargent's long introductory essay is particularly valuable. A second reprint volume, *More Women of Wonder* (1976), featured another introduction by Sargent and seven novelettes, including C. L. Moore's "Jirel Meets Magic," Joanna Russ's "The Second Inquisition," and Le Guin's "The Day Before the Revolution." A collection of original fiction, *The New Women of Wonder* (1978), included Dorman's "Building Block," Eleanor Arnason's "Warlord of Saturn's Moons," and others. Two new *Women of Wonder* reprint anthologies, subtitled *The Classic Years* and *The Contemporary Years*, appeared in 1995. Compare *Cassandra Rising* (1978), edited by Alice Laurance; *Millennial Women* (1978), edited by Virginia Kidd; and *Aurora: Beyond Equality* (1976), edited by Vonda N. McIntyre and Susan J. Anderson. (ML)

Themes: Feminist SF, Women in SF

II-1413.   Worlds Apart: An Anthology of Interplanetary Fiction. Ed. by George Locke. Cornmarket, 1972.

An anthology of nine items photographically reproduced from British magazines, two of which are series: W. S. Lach-Szyrma's nine-part "Letters from the Planets" (1887–1893) and George Griffith's six-part "Stories of Other Worlds" (the serial version of *A Honeymoon in Space*). The latter, along with two other items, is also reproduced in Russell's *Science Fiction by the Rivals of H. G. Wells*, but its combination here with the Lach-Szyrma series (as a pair of parenthetical "book-ends" contextualizing the other stories) offers useful insight into the development of interplanetary fiction as it moved from the context of religious fantasy to that of commercial scientific romance. Other interesting items include George C. Wallis's "The Great Sacrifice" (1903) and George Allan England's early account of "A Message from the Moon" (1907). (BS)

II-1414.   World's Best Science Fiction. Ed. by Donald A. Wollheim, Terry Carr, and Arthur W. Saha. Ace, DAW, 1970–1990.

A long running best-of-the-year anthology, with Saha replacing Carr with the 1972 annual, and DAW taking over with 1973. The title varied slightly over the years. Despite Wollheim's reputation for favoring traditional material, he was reasonably eclectic in selecting stories for these anthologies, and although he was slightly inclined to favor DAW authors, he was a reliable spotter of stories that subsequently won awards. Compare the best-of anthologies edited by Dozois. (BS)

*II-1415. The World Treasury of Science Fiction. Ed. by David G. Hartwell. Little Brown, 1989.

The first in a series of large and masterful reprint anthologies by one of the genre's finest editors. Most of the best-known American writers are represented among these 52 classic stories, many of which are available elsewhere. What makes this anthology important is Hartwell's inclusion of so much work from outside the English-language tradition. Among the authors present in translation who have reached an American audience previously are Borges, Calvino, the Strugatsky brothers, Gérard Klein, and Kiril Bulychev, but a number of less well-known and highly talented authors are also included. Compare Aldiss and Lundwall's *The Penguin World Omnibus of SF*. A Book of the Month Club selection. (ML)

*II-1416. The Year After Tomorrow: An Anthology of Science Fiction Stories. Ed. by Lester del Rey, Cecile Matschatt, and Carl Carmer. Winston, 1954.

YA. A pioneering collection of short SF for youth. Important because most stories were actually written for young readers, unlike the vast majority of subsequent anthologies for the juvenile market, whose contents were written for adults and then deemed, on perfunctory editing, "suitable" for youth. Special features are four stories reprinted from the *American Boy*, three by Carl Claudy (1879–1957), who was one of two writers of SF for younger readers prior to Heinlein (the other is Roy Rockwood, a house pseudonym used for the Great Marvel series; see Howard Garis entries) and one by P. van Dresser. (FM/SM)

*II-1417. The Year's Best Science Fiction. Ed. by Gardner Dozois. St. Martin's, 1984–.

Dozois's enormous best-of-the-year collections have dominated the field virtually since their inception. The editor's taste is impeccable, as reflected in his Hugo awards, and he simply has more room than anyone else around to include a wide range of outstanding fiction, some of which might more accurately be labeled fantasy or magic realism. The 2003 volume features the editor's usual detailed and valuable summation of the year in SF, plus outstanding fiction by Gregory Benford, John Kessel, Molly Gloss, Nancy Kress, Eleanor Arnason, Bruce Sterling, Geoff Ryman, Walter Jon Williams, Ian McDonald, Ian MacLeod, Greg Egan, Maureen McHugh, and others. (ML)

II-1418. Year's Best SF. Ed. by David G. Hartwell. Eos, 1996–.

Hartwell simply doesn't have the space Dozois has in his own *Year's Best Science Fiction*, but his choices are invariably intelligent and, given the limitations under which he works, the book stands as a worthy companion to Dozois. Unlike Dozois, Hartwell also tends to stick with straight science fiction, rather than wandering off into fantasy. The most recent anthology in the series, which is co-edited by Hartwell's wife Kathryn Cramer (though her name doesn't appear on the cover), features excellent stories by such giants of the field as Ursula K. Le Guin, Greg Egan, Nancy Kress, Michael Swanwick, Bruce Sterling, and Gene Wolfe. (ML)

The Secondary Literature— Annotated Bibliography

CHAPTER 6

Science Fiction: Publishing, Reviewing, Readers, and Libraries

Neil Barron

Few people, including many librarians, are aware of the number of books published in the United States each year. The principal publisher for the book trade, R. R. Bowker, has compiled industry statistics for many years, formerly tabulated in *Publishers Weekly*, now found in detail in the hardcover *Bowker Annual and Book Trade Almanac* (published by Information Today Inc.). In 1991, having received increasing complaints from libraries and bookstores, Bowker recognized the growing inadequacy of its former database, *American Book Publishing Record* (monthly, with an annual cumulation), as a source for book publishing statistics. It therefore shifted to the much more inclusive *Books in Print*, published annually as a hardcover set and available by subscription online (www.booksinprint.com), which has links to reviews and other features.

Preliminary figures for 2003 indicated that approximately 175,000 titles were published in the United States, approximately 17,000 adult fiction, of which perhaps 10 percent to 15 percent were reprints, reissues, or new editions of previously published books. Figures for popular fiction genres were cited in the Nov. 13, 2000, *Publishers Weekly*, on page 42. Romance led with 38.2 percent of popular fiction sales (no surprise), followed by mystery/detective with 25.7 percent, general fiction 12.1 percent, and SF and fantasy combined at 7.3 percent.

Locus [13-17] annually tabulates in detail publication of fantastic fiction (SF, fantasy, horror). For 2003, the magazine counted 2,429 American books—hardcovers (860), trade paperbacks (754), and mass market paperbacks (815)—57 percent originals, the balance reprints and reissues. The 2,429 figure, which includes some nonfiction (see Table 6-1), is about 14 percent of the 17,000 figure. For the United Kingdom, the corresponding figures were 674 titles (the lowest figure since 1988; 2002 totaled 908), 55 percent originals, many of which were later (or simultaneously) published in the United States, and vice versa. Table 6-1 shows the distribution by type of original books published in 2003.

Table 6-1.   Types of Original Fantastic Literature
Published in the U.S. and U.K. in 2003

	US	UK	
SF novels	236	48	Adult and YA for U.S. books; see below for YA U.K. books
Fantasy novels	340	97	Ditto
Horror novels	171	23	Ditto
Anthologies	97	11	
Collections	113	14	
Media-related	213	60	Mostly film and TV tie-ins
YA fiction		77	Not analyzed by SF/fantasy/horror
Nonfiction	80	15	Reference, history, criticism

The figures above are reasonably accurate. Historical figures are far more conjectural. Peter Nicholls, co-editor of *The Encyclopedia of Science Fiction* [7-21], provided an "informed guess" that the total number of English-language SF/fantasy/horror books, using an inclusive definition, "would be in the region of 90,000" (foreword to *The MUP Encyclopaedia of Australian Science Fiction* [7-22]). The figure for SF only is much smaller. Reginald says he listed about 38,000 books published between 1700 and 1991 in English [7-8]. The *Locus* totals for original books have varied over the years, but about 400 SF novels, collections, and anthologies were published annually from 1992 to 2003, a bit less in the earlier years, a bit more today. That's an additional 4,800; giving a total of 42,800 original SF works. This guide is necessarily selective and annotates about 3 percent of the total original fiction, much of it published in the last half-century.

Each issue of *Locus* has bestseller information (by binding and whether media- or gaming-related) for both specialty and general bookstores and provides brief annotations of 12 to 15 "new and notable" books, in addition to more reviews than any other publication. SF routinely appears on hardcover and mass-market paperback bestseller lists, most commonly tie-ins to TV and film series such as *Star Trek* and *Star Wars*, undemanding costume dramas in space that appeal to a younger, less sophisticated audience.

Demographic data for SF readers are sketchy; some data may be proprietary and are therefore not published. For more than 30 years, *Locus* has conducted an annual survey of its readers, who are probably more knowledgeable and older than the typical fan/reader. The 2003 survey results, published in the September 2003 issue, are based on replies representing about 7.2 percent of the approximately 8,000 paid circulation (subscribers and stores), or 12 percent of the average subscription-only sales of 4,700. SF is still a "guy" thing. In 1971, the split was about 80/20 male/female; it's about 74/26 today. *Locus* readers are well educated (80 percent college grads, 38 percent have advanced degrees), with family incomes averaging $50,000+. A June 2002 survey of the subscribers to *The Magazine of Fantasy and Science Fiction* [13-4], which had a paid circulation in 2003 of about 21,000 readers, revealed figures similar to *Locus*: 67.5 percent male, 55 percent of readers ages 26 to 45 with a mean age of 40, and about 41 percent college grads. Scott Edelman of www.scifi.com [8-9], a media-oriented site, said in July 2003 his audience was 66 percent male, 68 percent were ages 24 to 49, and 62 percent college graduates, some with advanced degrees. Ellen Asher, head of the Science Fiction Book Club, which was founded in 1950, said the club had approximately 200,000 members in September 2003 (more than twice the total paid circulation of the three major SF magazines), 60 percent male, 55 percent married, median age 44.7 years, 45 percent with some college or more, median income about $50,000. The SF fan culture is explored in Bacon-Smith's *Science Fiction Culture* [9-14] and in Chapter 13 of this guide. Hall's online research database [7-17] cites many articles under the headings "fans" and "sociology of SF," which may provide other demographic information.

Publishing of SF books as a specific genre began following World War II when fans founded specialty presses to put into hardcovers fiction they'd read in the pulp magazines. Only Arkham House survives from this early period (it predates World War II). Several dozen specialty presses, some specializing in one type of fantastic fiction, exist today, but few survive as long as a decade. (For details about such publishers, see Chalker & Owings [7-12], Eshbach [9-75], and Harbottle [9-89].) See also Chapter 3.

Librarians who select SF should pay particular attention to the major publishers of SF, listed in the February issue of *Locus*. The top dozen in 2003, by total number of books, were Tor/St. Martin's, Penguin Group, SF Book Club, Simon & Schuster/Pocket Books, Random/Ballantine, HarperCollins, iBooks, Baen, Bantam/Doubleday/Dell, DAW, Wizards of the Coast (role-playing game books), and Warner/Little Brown. The Science Fiction Book Club makes available hardcover reprints of original paperbacks as well as printing various omnibus editions, most under the Nelson Doubleday imprint. Libraries should consider joining because of the low prices and the more durable hardcover editions of mass-market paperbacks.

The sheer number of books published each year, discussed above, means that no magazine or newspaper can review more than a very small selection, many of them simply the most heavily hyped. This fact alone means that little SF will be reviewed in general review media. Library and book trade journals review more, and a few specialty magazines more still, as Table 6-2 shows. Reviews range from one-paragraph book notes to very detailed. The table's figures mostly represent SF but include some fantasy. Library and book trade journals and *Locus* usually provide pre- or on-publication reviews. Readers and librarians who are knowledgeable about SF can also use the comprehensive lists of forthcoming books published quarterly in *Locus*, as well as the monthly lists of U.S. and British books received, for selection purposes. Also very valuable are the recommended reading lists by the knowledgeable reviewers for *Locus*, published in the February issue, and the best books reader poll published in the August issue. The academic magazines (see Chapter 13) review some fiction and a moderate amount of nonfiction about fantastic literature.

Table 6-2.   Science Fiction Book Reviewing

Magazine	Issues/Year	No. Reviewed/Year
General		
New York Times Book Review (Gerald Jonas)	52	45
Booklist	26	150
Kirkus Reviews	24	120–170
Kliatt	6	120
Library Journal	20	170
Publishers Weekly	52	150
Voice of Youth Advocates (VOYA)	6	30–40
Specialty (see Chapter 13)		
Analog Science Fiction and Fact	10	90
Asimov's Science Fiction Magazine	10	60
Chronicle	12	240
Foundation	3	30
Interzone	10	90
Locus	12	130
Magazine of Fantasy and Science Fiction	11	30
New York Review of Science Fiction	12	122 + 40 essays

Anatomy of Wonder has always been a critical guide to the best or better works. Scarcity, rarity, or collectibility were not and are not among the selection criteria, as I stated in the preface. SF has been collected almost since its inception as a distinct genre, and over the years various price guides have been issued, some of them indexing specialty dealer catalogs, such as *The Inter-Galactic Price Guide to Science Fiction, Fantasy (and Horror)*, compiled by Stephanie Howlett-West (1996, 1997, 1999), an inevitable victim of the the many Internet-based used-book Web sites (www.bookfinder.com provides convenient access to many such sites). Collectors should acquire a copy of *Science Fiction and Fantasy Authors*

[7-6], which provides the essential points for thousands of editions issued through mid-1977 by 215 of the major authors.

Academic libraries usually catalog both hardcovers and paperbacks, but paperbacks in many public libraries are apparently judged as something close to expendable supplies, based on replies I received. Some libraries simply place SF paperbacks on shelves or spinner racks, tagged with a spine label; they do not catalog them. Since a user has no way of accessing the library's holdings of such paperbacks, simple chance determines what is found. These volumes cannot be used effectively for interbranch or interlibrary lending, nor are they listed in the online library catalogs.

Although the Library of Congress receives most American SF books in the form of copyright copies, only in 1992 did it begin to catalog SF mass market collections and anthologies, with novels—by far the largest segment—still going to a warehouse unsorted and uncataloged. LC's catalog department bulletin specifically says to exclude from all mass market originals or reprints the cataloging in publication (CIP) information typically found on the copyright page of hardcovers and trade paperbacks. However, some of the libraries with the largest fantastic fiction collections (see Chapter 15) contribute cataloging information to the OCLC WorldCat database, making LC's practices largely irrelevant.

Science fiction as a subject heading in libraries came into use around 1950, roughly 20 years after Hugo Gernsback popularized the term and about the time that larger publishers including Doubleday began to publish books clearly identified as SF. Today the Library of Congress, which uses a regularly revised multi-volume list of subject headings, uses a multitude of headings dealing with SF. The term itself is subdivided into awards, collectibles, history and criticism, psychological and religious aspects, and women authors. Other divisions are by nationality, not only the expected, such as Science Fiction, American/Australian/French, but the unexpected, such as New Caledonia (French), Salvadoran, and Uzbek. Other phrase headings include science fiction followed by comic books, strips, etc./fans/films/illustrators/in art/plays/poetry/radio programs/television programs. Many of the other headings are identical or similar to those used in this guide's theme index.

Within SF, theme indexing has long been common. The section devoted to subject [theme] bibliographies in Burgess [7-11] describes 39 works, from adventure fiction to women writers, almost all long out of print (OP). This guide annotates several, including Bleiler [7-1 and 7-2]. The general encyclopedias [7-20, 7-21] are often the best source for basic information about hundreds of themes. *What Do I Read Next?* (Gale, annual, 1990–1999, semi-annual, 2000–) is a guide to popular fiction in nine (formerly six) categories, including SF, fantasy, and horror. One of the multiple indexes is by theme (called subgenre). The three fantastic fiction categories for 1990–1998 were cumulated in the second edition of *What Fantastic Fiction Do I Read Next?* (1999), which has almost 6,100 entries, approximately equally divided among the three genres. In this new edition of *Anatomy of Wonder*, contributors made a concerted effort to assign one, and often several, theme headings to most novels, theme anthologies, and many nonfiction works (see especially Chapter 9).

CHAPTER 7

General Reference Works

Neil Barron

This chapter discusses books that are referred to but not read continuously and that do not fall within the other chapters: film and TV (11), the Weinberg directory (12), magazines (13), and the biocritical works and author bibliographies in Chapter 10. Theme indexing is discussed in Chapter 6. See also the online resources in Chapter 8. The coverage here is restricted to works limited to SF, to fantastic fiction generally, or to utopian studies.

As science fiction began to be recognized as a distinct type of fiction in the late 1920s, when the specialty pulps began, it wasn't long before fans started listing books and authors, indexing magazines, and engaging in similar hobbyist efforts. Some of this work appeared in the fanzines of the time, others as amateurishly "printed" booklets. It was the efforts of these fans that laid the foundations for the more authoritative works of recent years, themselves usually created by fans, some turned academics. Hundreds of these early efforts are described in detail in the Burgess and Bartle guide [7-11].

For convenience, these several dozen works are grouped in these categories:

- General Fiction Bibliographies
- Specialized Bibliographies
- Encyclopedias
- Other Works (works that don't fit into the other categories)
- Fantasy and Horror Reference Works

502

General Fiction Bibliographies

7-1. Bleiler, Everett F. **The Checklist of Science-Fiction and Supernatural Fiction**. Firebell Books, 1978.

The Checklist of Fantastic Literature (1948), or "Bleiler" as it soon became known to collectors and enthusiasts, was for many years the standard bibliography of English-language fantastic fiction. This revised edition deletes 600 presumably marginal or improper titles and adds 1,150 to the original and extends the coverage through 1948. The 5,600 titles are listed by author with a title index. Although Bleiler attempted to list only the first edition, his citations sometimes differ from those of Reginald [7-8], who Bleiler thinks improperly omits approximately a thousand titles. New to this edition are approximately 90 codes used to denote the dominant theme or motif of the book, one of the earlier theme indexes (see also Chapter 6). See also Bleiler's masterful annotated bibliography of early SF [7-2].

*7-2. Bleiler, Everett F., and Richard J. Bleiler. **Science-Fiction, the Early Years: A Full Description of More Than 3,000 Science-Fiction Stories From Earliest Times to the Appearance of the Genre Magazines in 1930 with Author, Title, and Motif Indexes**. Kent State Univ. Press, 1991.

Although fans such as Moskowitz had explored the early development of SF in various histories and anthologies, the most comprehensive and detailed work by far is this massive reference work, a crowning achievement of his long association with the field. What is perhaps most remarkable is that Bleiler read or reread all the stories, many annotated in great detail and many previously undiscovered in many rare sources. The arrangement is by author, with novels and short fiction in collections or magazines sequenced by title, with abundant cross-references. The annotations are descriptive and provide a historical context as well as full bibliographic details. But almost every annotation ends with a one-line evaluation, often acerbic. Supplementing the author, title, and motif indexes, keyed to the numbered entries, is a chronological index from Plato to Thomas More to about 1930, with later reprints shown as well, and an index by magazine, most entries predating the founding of *Amazing Stories* in 1926, which shows how widely SF was published in the popular magazines of yesteryear. The only weakness of this work, offset from a clear two-column typescript, is the lack of running heads, slowing quick look-up of desired entries. An essential work for the scholar and for the largest libraries. Also annotated as [9-31].

Awards: *Locus*

*7-3. Bleiler, Everett F., and Richard J. Bleiler. **Science-Fiction: The Gernsback Years, a Complete Coverage of the Genre Magazines Amazing, Astounding, Wonder, and Others from 1926 through 1936**. Kent State Univ. Press, 1998.

An extraordinarily thorough bibliography and critical analysis of more than 1,800 stories, plus poetry and letters, whose work by 500+ authors appeared in

13 early American SF magazines, plus the minor British *Scoops*. The story descriptions and evaluations (usually dismissive) occupy 75 percent of the text. The 20-page introduction provides an invaluable synoptic overview of the historical background that led to the pulps and the stories themselves. An essential companion to the author's equally authoritative *Science-Fiction, the Early Years* [7-2]. Also annotated as [13-26].

7-4.   Contento, William G. **Index to Science Fiction Anthologies and Collections, Combined Edition**. http://users.evl/net/~/homeville/isfac/0start.htm. Combined on a CD-ROM (Locus Publications, 2004) with *The Locus Index to Science Fiction (1984–2004)*, www.locusmag.com/index.

Contento compiled the first index and its supplement as books (1978, 1984). The combined edition provides access to more than 38,000 English-language stories by 3,886 authors in 3,921 collections and anthologies published through 1983. Access is by author and title of both book and individual story, including poetry, articles, etc. An author must have had three or more stories to be indexed. Chronology and series lists and statistical data are also included. Beginning with 1984 books, *The Locus Index* continued the indexing, not only of anthologies and collections but of all U.S. and U.K. books listed in the monthly issues and in the professional fiction magazines. *The Locus Index* is also available online but only in several chronological parts: 1984–1998, and 1999–2003 as annuals. New material is added to the online indexes several times yearly, and is merged annually to produce the *Locus Index* on CD-ROM. Valuable not only for those few libraries that have a substantial collection of anthologies and collections but for any library trying to locate a source for an elusive short story. This is vastly more comprehensive than the *Short Story Index* found in many libraries, and it supersedes several similar earlier, less comprehensive indexes. A companion index to supernatural and weird fiction was published in 1995 [7-30].

7-5.   Cottrill, Tim, Martin H. Greenberg, and Charles G. Waugh. **Science Fiction and Fantasy Series and Sequels: A Bibliography. Volume 1: Books**. Garland, 1986.

Series and sequels have become increasingly common in recent years, reflecting publisher preferences for guaranteed sales and reader preferences for more of the same. This compilation lists approximately 1,160 series and more than 6,900 books, many paperback originals, mostly published in the 20th century. Author, title, year, publisher, and sequence in series are shown through 1985 works. Series and book title indexes enhance the books' usefulness. (A planned second volume indexing short fiction series and sequels was never published.) Series have continued to proliferate. Much more complete and current is [Pat] *Hawk's Science Fiction, Fantasy and Horror: Series and Sequels* (compiler, 2001), which indexes approximately 8,800 series and 17,000 book titles by 5,000+ authors, both adult and juvenile, published in the U.S., U.K., Australasia, and Canada. Details from hawk@koyote.com. Both listings are suitable only for large libraries, plus some dealers and fans. See this guide's list of series in Chapter 16.

7-6. Currey, L. W. **Science Fiction and Fantasy Authors: A Bibliography of First Printings of Their Fiction and Selected Nonfiction.** G. K. Hall, 1979.

A comprehensive listing of more than 6,200 printings and editions through June 1977 of books by 215 authors, from Wells to authors prominent by the mid-1970s. Multiple copies of a title were carefully compared to determine first and variant editions, and all essential points are included for collectors, for whom this is an indispensable guide. The original book had to be proofed under a tight deadline, and many errors and omissions slipped through. The revised edition, on CD-ROM, incorporates more than a thousand corrections and some additions, including more information about variant states, issues, and printings, as well as dustjacket points. The CD-ROM is available from the compiler, Box 187, Elizabethtown, NY 12932; lloyd@lwcurrey.com. Non-SF books by the authors are included, along with significant reference material (notably bibliographies) about them published through June 1979, some of it fugitive fan press items rarely recorded elsewhere. As authoritative as Currey but much more personal is *A Spectrum of Fantasy: The Bibliography and Biography of a Collection of Fantastic Literature* (Ferret Fantasy, 1980) by the British dealer/collector, George Locke, who describes in detail his personal collection of more than 3,100 books. These guides are valuable to collectors and would be useful to any special collections librarian whose holdings include substantial fantastic fiction.

7-7. Miller, Stephen T., and William G. Contento. **Science Fiction, Fantasy, and Weird Fiction Magazines: 1890–2003.** Locus Press, 2004.

An annually updated CD-ROM that indexes more than a thousand professional and semi-professional magazines, including major fanzines. More than 100,000 stories by 25,000 authors in 15,000+ individual issues, each personally examined by Miller or occasionally by the owners of rare magazines not owned by Miller. One can access items by author, story title, cover artist, or issue contents. Because many writers wrote several types of stories, the broad coverage of this index picks up all the crossovers. By far the most complete index of its type and essential for libraries or collectors with large fantastic magazine holdings (see Chapter 15).

*7-8. Reginald, R(obert). **Science Fiction and Fantasy Literature: A Checklist, 1700–1974, with Contemporary Science Fiction Authors II.** Gale Research, 1979. 2 vols.

Volume 1 lists the first editions of 15,884 books published in English, which were examined and, if necessary, read to determine if they fell within the work's broad scope. Arrangement is by author, with thorough cross-references among pseudonyms, many newly identified, followed by a title index and several supplemental indexes. Volume 2 replaces the compiler's *Stella Nova* (1970), reprinted as *Contemporary Science Fiction Authors* (1974), and is a now-dated directory of 1,443 modern SF and fantasy writers, including editors and critics, compiled from questionnaires completed by the authors or their estates. The supplement, *Science Fiction and Fantasy Literature 1975–1991* . . .(Gale, 1992), lists more than 22,000 English-language works, fiction and related nonfiction, a small percentage omitted from the original bibliography. Note that half again as many books are listed in the supplement, which covers only 17 years. Easily the most authoritative and comprehensive general bibliography of English-language fantastic literature and essential for larger libraries. Collectors will need Currey [7-6] for points. See also the pioneering works by Bleiler [7-1/2/3].

7-9.   Tuck, Donald H(enry). **The Encyclopedia of Science Fiction and Fantasy Through 1968**. Advent, 1977, 1978, 1983. 3 vols.

One of the most important earlier bibliographies, complementing Bleiler's checklist [7-1], this has grown increasingly dated. The first two volumes include a who's who and works, with a 52-page book title index. Volume 3 provides magazine checklists, extensive paperback information, pseudonyms, series, sequels, and other information. Brief biographical information is included for almost all authors, some of them only peripherally linked to fantastic literature. Primarily descriptive with some evaluative comment. Largely superseded by Reginald [7-8] and Contento [7-4].

Awards: Hugo

Specialized Bibliographies

7-10.   Brians, Paul. **Nuclear Holocausts: Atomic War in Fiction, 1895–1984**. Kent State Univ. Press, 1987. Still being updated with additional entries at www.wsu.edu/~/brians/nuclear/index/htm.

A reflection of an age of anxiety, Brians provides the most comprehensive overview of this sobering literature. The initial fourth of the 400-page guide provides a history of nuclear warfare in five chapters, followed by a 250-page annotated bibliography of novels and shorter fiction, with entries ranging from a sentence to very full coverage, with 100 words about average. A chronological checklist, lists of closely related works of fiction (near-war narratives, doubtful cases, reactor disasters, and so on), and title and subject indexes complete this authoritative survey. Brians is much more comprehensive than John Newman and Michael Unsworth in *Future War Novels: An Annotated Bibliography of Works in English Published Since 1956* (Oryx Press, 1985), which chronologically lists (with annotations) 191 novels, 1946–1983, with author and title indexes. The selection criteria are different from those used by Brians, and the book therefore includes some books not in Brians. The book is based on the Imaginary Wars Collection at the Colorado State Univ. Library [15-50]. Brians continued his work in *Nuclear Texts and Contexts,* an irregular newsletter, 12 issues of which were published 1988–1995; the first 8 are available as pdf files from his Web site. Compare Clarke's *Voices Prophesying War* [9-56], Dowling's *Fictions of Nuclear Disaster* [9-71], and Bartter's *The Way to Ground Zero* [9-25]. Also annotated as [9-36].

7-11. Burgess, Michael, and Lisa R. Bartle. **Reference Guide to Science Fiction, Fantasy, and Horror**. 2nd ed. Libraries Unlimited, 2002.

Writing under his real name, cataloger/bibliographer R. Reginald and a fellow librarian have compiled an authoritative guide to hundreds of encyclopedias, dictionaries, bibliographies/indexes (subject, national, magazine, publisher, author), and similar "reference" works published through 2001. Entries provide very full annotations—far lengthier than space permits in this guide—of all the standard works, as well as the many fan productions unavailable for years or decades. The detailed annotations include full pagination and comparative cross-references and evaluations of the relative value of each work. These evaluations are reflected in his core collection choices for large and smaller academic and public libraries as well as personal libraries. Because most of these works are long out of print and relatively specialized, the audience for this guide remains large university and public libraries and the devoted scholar. Author, title, and subject indexes, plus an attractive layout, make the book very easy to consult.

7-12. Chalker, Jack L., and Mark Owings. **The Science-Fantasy Publishers: A Bibliographic History**. 3rd ed., rev. and enlarged. Mirage Press, 1991.

This edition was almost ten times the length of its two 1966 predecessors, reflecting the rapid growth in specialty publishing since the founding of Arkham House in 1939. The main sequence profiles 148 publishers in almost 500 pages, with books listed alphabetically by publisher, then chronologically. A 135-page appendix lists the work of 48 smaller publishers. There are author-artist and title indexes. Various appendixes provide additional information. Although this compilation provides far more detail about specialty publications than any other source, the text mixes purely factual information—some of it based on the imperfect memories of individuals associated with the publishers—with considerable unsupported opinion, sometimes masquerading as dispassionate fact. Annual supplements have been issued, available as free pdf files from the publisher, or for $10 each in printed format. An annually revised CD-ROM merges the base listing and all the supplements. The Web site www.jackchalker.com/mirage.htp provides the latest information, including how to order the CD-ROM.

7-13. Clareson, Thomas D. **Science Fiction in America, 1870s–1930s: An Annotated Bibliography of Primary Sources**. Greenwood, 1984.

Provides descriptive, occasionally evaluative annotations of 838 books, mostly by American writers, although British and some European writers are represented (for example, Haggard, Wells, Verne). Intended as a companion to Clareson's narrative history, *Some Kind of Paradise* [9-50]. Compare Bleiler [7-2]. Contrast Suvin [9-191] and Stableford [9-184], whose focus is on British writers.

7-14.   Clarke, I. F. **Tale of the Future from the Beginning to the Present Day: An Annotated Bibliography**. 3rd ed. Library Association, 1978.

A chronological and briefly annotated listing by year from 1744 to 1976 of about 3,900 utopian, political, and scientific romance tales of the future published in Britain, excluding juveniles and serial publications. Clarke's definition excludes alternate histories or parallel world tales unless set in the future. Since books had to be published in the U.K., hundreds or perhaps thousands of American works were excluded. The annotations are often too brief to be of much value. There are author and title indexes and a brief bibliography. Clarke's narrative survey of the subject, *The Pattern of Expectation: 1644–2001* [9-55], usefully complements this bibliography.

7-15.   Garber, Eric, and Lynn Paleo. **Uranian Worlds: A Reader's Guide to Alternative Sexuality in Science Fiction and Fantasy**. 2nd ed. G. K. Hall, 1990.

Sexuality was taboo in the pages of most SF pulps, although sometimes it was present in books, a heritage partly derived from the social and literary conventions of the 1920–1960 period, partly because of the heavily male-adolescent readership of pulp magazines. If sexuality was taboo, homosexuality was almost unthinkable until recent years. The second edition includes 935 numbered entries containing "images of and attitudes toward homosexuality," suggesting the greater social acceptance of such fiction. (The stance of the compilers is dismissive of those who find homosexual themes in fiction distasteful.) The second edition also adds films and a list of fan organizations. Arranged by author with title and chronological indexes, the annotations are both descriptive and evaluative, not only of the fiction but of the authors. See also the 33-page annotated bibliography in Palumbo's *Erotic Universe* [9-142], which includes both fiction and nonfiction and is not limited to homosexuality.

7-16.   Hall, H. W. **Science Fiction and Fantasy Book Review Index 1923–1973; 1974–1979; 1980–1984**. Gale, 1975, 1981, 1985. Annuals, vol. 16, 1985–vol. 21, 1990, issued by the indexer.

Indexes almost 68,000 reviews appearing in the dozens of pulp SF magazines since 1923, including many fanzines, and in general reviewing sources since 1970. All these review citations will be cumulated on a CD-ROM to be published by Locus Press. Access is by author of the book reviewed, with a title index. Hall began adding post-1990 citations in 2003 and hopes to bring the indexing current for the CD-ROM. Until that occurs, indexing of some reviews will be found in *What Do I Read Next?*, a guide to popular fiction, annual 1990–1999, semi-annual 2000+. Also useful is the index to reviews published in *Locus*, 1984–date, accessible at www.locusmag.com/indexes/Page0.html. This is far more inclusive than the library tools *Book Review Index* and *Book Review Digest*.

*7-17. Hall, H. W. **Science Fiction and Fantasy Research Database**.
http://lib-oldweb.tamu.edu/cushing/SFFRD/.

Originally published in book form as *Science Fiction and Fantasy Reference Index, 1878–1985: An International Author and Subject Index to History and Criticism* (2 vols., 1981; one vol., 1985–1991 [1993]; and one vol., 1992–1995 [1996], the citations were computerized and now are part of easily the largest such database, with more than 65,000 entries as of summer 2004. New entries are added quarterly. Approximately 90 percent are in English. Particularly valuable is his indexing of the principal fan news magazines (fanzines) from the 1940s on. Fanzines have for decades served as an informal, unrefereed but valuable forum. A major achievement, Hall's indexes provide scholars a comprehensive index to the secondary literature. A template permits users to submit additional citations. Linked to the large SF collection at Texas A&M [15-30]. Hall received the Pilgrim award from the SF Research Association in 2000 for his bibliographic efforts.

7-18. Sargent, Lyman Tower. **British and American Utopian Literature 1516–1986: An Annotated Chronological Bibliography**. Garland, 1988.

SF and utopian literature have a parallel and overlapping history, and many of the cited books are SF. Sargent's bibliography was originally published in 1979 and included a 124-page secondary multilingual unannotated bibliography of about 600 books and dissertations and 1,600 articles that was unfortunately dropped for the enlarged edition, which chronologically lists close to 2,600 entries. Very brief descriptive annotations are provided, along with a code denoting a holding library, or Sargent's, or another private collection. There are author and title indexes. A partial replacement for the dropped bibliography is Paul G. Haschak, *Utopian/Dystopian Literature: A Bibliography of Literary Criticism* (Scarecrow, 1994). The approximately 3,600 citations are to articles discussing utopian and dystopian novels, plays, and short stories by authors from ancient to modern. Also helpful is Erika Gottlieb, *Dystopian Fiction East and West: Universe of Terror and Trial* (McGill-Queens Univ. Press, 2001), whose special strength is its coverage of Eastern, especially Soviet, dystopias.

7-19. Saricks, Joyce G. **The Readers' Advisory Guide to Genre Fiction**. American Library Association, 2001.

Fifteen chapters, each about 25 pages and with a similar structure, explore 15 literary genres, including SF, fantasy, and horror. Each genre is argued to have four elements as part of its appeal: pacing, characterization, story line (plot), and frame. SF has two distinct types of stories, plot-centered with action/adventure prominent, and literary/philosophical, with more emphasis on ideas and character and with a slower pace. Each chapter has a section on reference sources that provide biographical information, plot summaries, background information/history, and best books lists. Although aimed at librarians providing reader advisory services, and necessarily limited in its coverage of each field, this is a well-balanced guide that almost anyone could learn from. Much better than the uneven and often dated *Genreflecting: A Guide to Reading Interests in Genre Fiction* (4th ed., 1995 [5th ed., 2000, not seen]) by Diana Tixier Herald.

Encyclopedias

7-20.   Clute, John. **Science Fiction: The Illustrated Encyclopedia**. Dorling Kindersley, 1995.

Although this survey has a lot of factual information, it's not an encyclopedia, i.e., a series of alphabetical entries with cross-references. Six of the eight chapters are chronological: *future visions* explores futures as seen in past and contemporary works; *historical context* is arranged thematically; *influential magazines* provides a short (10-page) survey, from *Argosy* to mid-1990s English- and foreign-language magazines; *major authors* provides short profiles and bibliographies, with some discussion of thematic shifts; *classic titles* not only discusses many such works, but the jackets in the photos are often worn and thus more believable; and *genre film* provides both narrative history and decade-long filmographies. *Graphic works* briefly surveys the work of some classic illustrations, with the balance devoted to European, American, and Japanese comics. *International television* draws on American, British, European, and Japanese examples. As in all DK books, the illustrations are well selected, and the layout is very inviting. Clute's text is well-informed and accessible to anyone and competes well with the illustrations. A one-page glossary and a five-page index enhance use and make this much more than a coffee table book. A colorful companion to the Clute-Nicholls encyclopedia, well suited to public and school libraries. Also annotated as [12-5].

*7-21.   Clute, John, Peter Nicholls, and Brian Stableford, eds. **The Encyclopedia of Science Fiction**. 2nd ed., rev. and enlarged. St. Martin's, 1993.

The 1979 edition (titled *The Science Fiction Encyclopedia* in the American edition) was the first true English-language encyclopedia, in spite of other books having used *Encyclopedia* in their titles. What made it particularly valuable was its reliance on original research and primary sources, thus correcting much spurious information contained in less carefully compiled works. This new edition retains the virtues of the old and adds many new ones, most notably currency (through 1992) and scope (approximately 1.4 million words versus 730,000 in the first edition versus 475,000 in Gunn [7-23]). In terms of text, it's the lengthiest single work ever devoted to SF. Approximately 85 percent of the text was written by the three editors, assisted by about 80 other contributors in specialized areas, such as non-English SF (300 author entries, close to 40,000 words). The more than 4,000 entries are linked by 2,100 cross-references in the main text plus thousands of *see also* references. The entries mix description and evaluation. There are more theme entries, plus 65 shorter terminology entries, plus more than 2,900 entries for authors, editors, critics, and other individuals. In short, there is much more of everything, including much broader coverage of borderline areas such as game worlds, film and TV spinoffs, graphic novels, YA fiction, and science fantasy. All this has led to a 1,400-page, six-pound volume, very well-designed and made. The updated trade paperback reprint makes it readily affordable. The most essential work for any library. A CD-ROM version was issued in 1994 by Grolier Electronic Publishing.

Awards: Hugo, *Locus*

7-22.　　Collins, Paul, Steven Paulsen, and Sean McMullen, eds. **The MUP Encyclopaedia of Australian Science Fiction**. Melbourne Univ. Press, 1998.

The largest number of entries by far in this work is for authors, few familiar to North American readers and many probably unfamiliar even to fellow Australians. Coverage of children's and young adult SF is commendably thorough, and there's an entry that explores the folklore of the aboriginal Australians. Coverage includes SF and fantasy, including dark fantasy, but straight horror is excluded. The author entries cite short fiction and show original sources and later reprints. Most libraries will find this too specialized and can rely on the Clute/Nicholls SF encyclopedia and its fantasy counterpart.

7-23.　　Gunn, James E., ed. **The New Encyclopedia of Science Fiction**. Viking, 1988.

Gunn is about 60 percent the length of the Clute/Nicholls encyclopedia, with about a third as many entries. (Both include far too many entries on wretched films.) Clute had 1,817 entries for authors, editors, and critics; Gunn had 516. Encyclopedia entries should direct users to sources of additional information; Clute does, Gunn doesn't. The 175 theme entries in Clute are generally much better than their 96 counterparts in Gunn, a few of which deal with modern topics such as cyberpunk. On the other hand, the coated stock in Gunn results in better if fewer illustrations, and the book is well designed. Its value is the consensus American view of SF, quite different from the notably eclectic coverage of the Clute/Nicholls encyclopedia, and it may be retained for that reason.

7-24.　　Mann, George, ed. **The Mammoth Encyclopedia of Science Fiction**. Carroll and Graf, 2001.

The seven sections of this non-encyclopedia include a potted history of SF (26 pp.), an alphabetical guide to authors/editors/artists/magazines (297 pp.), the 100 "most influential" films and the 20 most important/popular U.S./U.K. TV series (128 pp.); terms, themes, and devices (64 entries, 60 pp.); societies, Web sites, and awards (17 pp.); a title index linked to the authors (68 pp.); and a six-page, mostly redundant index to authors, film, and magazine titles and themes. Mann's selection is heavily skewed to more recent authors, especially British, with little recognition of non–English-speaking authors. Many major authors are omitted altogether. Its price is 40 percent of the trade paperback reprint of *The Encyclopedia of Science Fiction*, but with only about a quarter of its text, it is a much poorer value.

7-25.   Stableford, Brian. **Historical Dictionary of Science Fiction Literature**. Scarecrow, 2004.

Brian Stableford is perhaps the best-qualified scholar to compile a work like this. His extensive scientific and literary knowledge is evident in the 16-page chronology and even more evident in the carefully argued 24-page introduction, in which he explores the problems of defining SF and how it differs in content, narrative strategies, and as a commercial product from mimetic/conventional fiction. The approximately 800 entries were selected on the basis of their historical importance. About 85 percent cover authors and include years, nationality, and key works, with terse critical/descriptive information. Other entries explain terms (sense of wonder, space opera, sharecropping, etc.), a few coined by Stableford. Major magazines have entries as do academic and a few fan organizations. His coverage of YA fiction and European SF is commendable. All words/phrases in boldface have their own entries, an easy form of cross-referencing. The dictionary concludes with a detailed and current bibliography of secondary literature, divided into 13 categories, from general reference works to writing guides. Stableford was a major contributor to the Nicholls/Clute *Encyclopedia of Science Fiction* [7-21], which every library should own (it's now o.p.). There is inevitably a lot of overlap in the coverage; Stableford's entries are much more succinct and a dozen years more current. Libraries with the encyclopedia's second edition can probably skip this overpriced volume, but it would be a good choice for libraries lacking the encyclopedia or other recent SF biographical guides.

Other Works

7-26.   Magill, Frank N., ed. **Survey of Science Fiction Literature**. Salem Press, 1979. 5 vols.

A major reference and critical source, containing 513 essays averaging 2,000 words each. Novels and short fiction by 280 authors, a fourth of them foreign, are analyzed by about 130 contributors, whose work was coordinated by the actual editor, Keith Neilson. Each essay is preceded by basic information: year of first book publication, type of work (novel, and so on), time, locale, one-line summary, and principal characters. Essays are arranged by title with an author index. The references following the essays are mostly to book reviews, an oversight corrected with a 1982 bibliographical supplement compiled by Marshall B. Tymn and included with the set. A useful but expensive tool for larger libraries, with a companion set devoted to fantasy.

7-27.   Shippey, T. A., and A. J. Sobczak, eds. **Magill's Guide to Science Fiction and Fantasy Literature**. Salem Press, 1996. 4 vols.

An updating of the two earlier SF and fantasy sets, but not a replacement for them. The 791 entries are arranged by title, with 363 solo books receiving about 1,000 words each, and 155 sequels and series receiving about 1,500 words each, divided about equally between plot summary and critical analysis. The final pages of volume 4 include an annotated bibliography of book-length secondary literature (107 entries), a list of award winners, a list of all books in the 37 subgenres defined in volume 1, a book/series title index, and an author/title index. Less than half the works in the earlier sets are discussed in this new set, and all entries are by different critics, often at shorter length. Suitable for very large libraries, especially those owning the earlier sets. A junior version of this set, with 180 mostly duplicated entries, is *Classics of Science Fiction and Fantasy Literature,* edited by Fiona Kelleghan (Salem, 2002). All the books discussed in both sets are listed by title at www.salempress.com.

7-28. Stableford, Brian. **The Dictionary of Science Fiction Places**. Fireside, 1999.

Milieu has always been important in SF, sometimes at the expense of individual character. Traditional fiction is also shaped by environment—think of Joyce's Dublin or Hardy's Wessex. The index lists 293 authors, and the place log lists more than 700 places, or about half a letter-size page per entry. Each entry is followed by the author, title, and year of publication of the source story (mostly novels, some short stories) and references to three other places. An author index lists the source title and the name of the place, and a place index lists the place, story title, author, and year. The coverage is from Hale's "The Brick Moon" (in 1869–1970) to a Stableford trilogy (1995–1997). Barsoom and Caspar are here, but why not Pellucidar and Venus? No utopias are present, but some dystopias are. Mildly recommended for larger public libraries and geographically challenged readers. A much better similar compilation is *The Dictionary of Imaginary Places* (rev. ed., 1987), by Alberto Manguel and Gianni Guadalupi, whose 1,250 entries omit SF locales.

*7-29. Wolfe, Gary K. **Critical Terms for Science Fiction and Fantasy: A Glossary and Guide to Scholarship**. Greenwood, 1986.

A valuable introduction traces the historical development of fantasy and SF critical discourse. Approximately three-fourths of the book is composed of a glossary of almost 500 terms and concepts, ranging from brief definitions to short essays, keyed to a secondary bibliography and to authors of cited fiction. Clear, concise, and most welcome, it's current enough to include trendy terms such as cyberpunk and postmodern. A useful companion to more general works like *A Glossary of Literary Terms* by M. H. Abrams (7th ed., Harcourt, 1999). The *Oxford English Dictionary* is making a concerted effort to include terminology related to SF from the fiction, criticism, and fandom. For more details, see www.jessesword.com/SF/sf_citations.shtml.

Fantasy and Horror Reference Works

The readership for SF, fantasy, and (to a lesser extent) horror fiction heavily overlaps, and many authors write in multiple fields. Science fantasy is a popular hybrid. Annotated below are a few key works likely to be of value to this guide's users. Since they are outside SF, they haven't been included in the best books listing, but they are recommended for medium and larger libraries. Some of the books annotated in Chapters 9 to 14 are also of interest to readers of fantasy and horror fiction.

7-30.   Ashley, Mike, and William E. Contento. **The Supernatural Index: A Listing of Fantasy, Supernatural, Occult, Weird and Horror Anthologies**. Greenwood, 1995.

A massive index to more than 3,100 English-language anthologies (but excluding individually authored collections) published since 1813. Access by editor, author (by far the lengthiest part of the index), story title, and anthology title, with complete contents shown, including pagination, listed by editor. Original sources of publication are shown, when known, for all 21,300 stories. Representative of the best in fan scholarship.

7-31.   Barron, Neil, ed. **Fantasy and Horror Literature: A Critical and Historical Guide to Literature, Illustration, Film, TV, Radio, and the Internet**. Scarecrow, 1999.

A companion to *Anatomy of Wonder*, this supersedes the separate fantasy and horror guides issued by Garland in 1990. More than 2,300 works of fiction and poetry are annotated, along with more than 800 nonfiction works and other sources of information.

7-32.   Bleiler, Everett F. **The Guide to Supernatural Fiction: A Full Description of 1,775 Books from 1750 to 1960, Including Ghost Stories, Weird Fiction, Stories of Supernatural Horror, Fantasy, Gothic Novels, Occult Fiction, and Similar Literature with Author, Title, and Motif Indexes**. Kent State Univ. Press, 1983.

This is as authoritative as Bleiler's later guide to early SF [7-2], and the subtitle indicates its wide scope. About 7,000 stories are individually described, several thousand from collections and anthologies. The motif index alone has more than 40,000 entries. A remarkable feat of scholarship.

7-33.   Clute, John, and John Grant, eds. **The Encyclopedia of Fantasy**. St. Martin's, 1997.

A companion to *The Encyclopedia of Science Fiction* [7-21], this is the most comprehensive single work devoted to the fantastic in fiction, film, radio, TV, illustration/art, comics, and music. Dark fantasy, supernatural, and weird fiction are discussed, but the treatment of horror that lacks fantasy elements is slight.

7-34.   Magill, Frank N., ed. **Survey of Modern Fantasy Literature**. Salem Press, 1983. 5 vols.

A companion to Magill's SF set, this contains about 500 essays devoted to 341 authors of fantasy and horror literature. Lesser titles receive about 1,000 words, most titles about 2,000, with series, trilogies, and major works receiving 3,000 to

10,000 words. Volume 5 contains 19 topical essays, a chronological listing from 1764 to 1981, an annotated bibliography of secondary literature, a list of major anthologies, and a detailed index.

7-35. Parnell, Frank H., and Mike Ashley. **Monthly Terrors: An Index to the Weird Fantasy Magazines Published in the United States and Great Britain**. Greenwood, 1985.

A total of 1,733 issues of magazines containing at least 50 percent weird fantasy are indexed by issue, author (but not title), artist, and editor. Small press publications are included, with their fiction, poetry, and other contents indexed.

7-36. Sullivan, Jack, ed. **The Penguin Encyclopedia of Horror and the Supernatural**. Viking, 1986.

An attractively designed work for the layperson, with approximately 600 entries. The biographical profiles emphasize the works, not the lives, of authors, artists, directors, actors, composers, and so on. Approximately 150 films have entries, along with 54 essays on topics such as "B" movies, ghosts, graveyard poetry, opera, sex, writers of today (a lengthy and difficult-to-use hodgepodge), and zombies. Approximately 300 monochrome illustrations accompany the text, which is thoroughly cross-referenced. Compare Wolf's much more personal work [7-37].

7-37. Wolf, Leonard. **Horror: A Connoisseur's Guide to Literature and Film**. Facts on File, 1989.

Unlike Sullivan's multiply authored reference work, Wolf provides "a partial record of my own listening" chosen for "historical spread, thematic variety, and fun." Just under 400 entries are arranged by title and include novels, short fiction, some poetry, and films. Ranging from 100 to 1,000 words, the knowledgeable and gracefully written entries reveal an intelligently enthusiastic guide. A useful companion to Sullivan [7-36].

CHAPTER 8

Online Resources

Neil Barron and William Contento

When the fourth edition of *Anatomy of Wonder* was compiled in 1992–1993, the World Wide Web (www) was far less developed than today. As even the most casual searcher of the Web is aware, the information on the Web is not organized in any way, unlike this book or, say, a library of any sort, which depends on organization for its usefulness—a classification scheme (Dewey, Library of Congress, etc.) and an index to the holdings, formerly a card file but now a more versatile online catalog.

To gain access to the contents of the millions of Web sites, search engines have developed over the years, of which Google is often regarded as the most versatile and comprehensive. It permits searching by natural language (a word, phrase, or lengthier text) or by using a classified site directory. This directory (click on *more* on the right-hand side of the home page to gain access) allows a general search or more focused access by selecting successively Arts, Literature, Science fiction, and then one of the more than 20 SF categories. However, the 2,539 individual sites (as of July 2004) represent only a vanishingly small percentage of the sites that would be retrieved by simply entering "science fiction,"

Note: The "I" in this chapter is Neil Barron, who wrote the text and made the judgments. William Contento provided valuable technical support throughout the guide and compiled the lists of sites of authors (Chapter 10), artists/illustrators (Chapter 12), and online magazines (Chapter 13). He does not necessarily share my sometimes harsh judgments on the online world generally or on individual sites.

516

which results in more than 6 million hits, almost all of which would be judged utterly trivial by almost any searcher. When I searched under "Neil Barron" in July 2004, I had more than 2,100 hits. Some of them—a fairly small percentage from some sampling—referred to a namesake who's a Scottish musician. Based on a random sample of sites that referred to me, I can assure you that almost all provided little of substance. Most simply mentioned without comment one or more books I've edited since 1976, when the first edition of this guide was published. My guess is that most such searches, even by more experienced Web users, will generate mountains of trivia and only a few valuable nuggets.

There are almost no barriers to anyone putting up a Web site, which is why I referred to the World Wide Web in the chronology following the preface as the world's largest vanity press. SF fans long ago developed an apt bit of jargon to refer to this tendency for self-promotion: egoboo. Boosting one's ego by having a letter or story printed in a magazine or fanzine was the name of the game. But even then there were gatekeepers, the editors of the magazines, who could and usually did screen out the worst submissions. Given the awful stuff that filled the pulps, to say nothing of the fanzines, one wonders how bad the rejected material was. But the Web has no editors; individual sites may have their own editors, but even then standards are often extremely lax. Ignorance and exhibitionism are rampant, unapologetic, and largely unchecked. Several years ago, Robert Wilensky of the University of California, Berkeley, described this situation very wittily: "We've all heard that a million monkeys banging on a million typewriters would eventually reproduce the works of Shakespeare. Now, thanks to the Internet, we know this is not true."

One of the principal potential advantages of Web sites over printed sources is currency. Updating a book is complex and time-consuming, and the new edition is always slightly out of date on publication and becomes progressively more so. However, as any Web user knows, the potential advantage of a Web site, currency, requires regular updating, checking links for validity, etc. For large Web sites—and some sites contain thousands of pages—the effort required to keep everything current is enormous. Since many Web sites are little more than hobbies of (or advertisements for) individuals, who (one hopes) have other lives to live, the hobby is often neglected for periods ranging from weeks to years. In addition to conventional Web sites, there are also many SF interest groups on usenet, Web logs (blogs), etc., outside the scope of this chapter. More-thoughtful readers who rely on the Web would find very useful the detailed discussion of evaluating information on Web sites at a Johns Hopkins site, www.library.jhu.edu/useit/evaluate/, recommended by Abby Kratz, librarian/wife of Dennis Kratz, author of Chapter 14.

A December 2003 article syndicated by the *Washington Post* provided evidence regarding the ephemeral nature of the Web. Researchers looked at footnotes to Web sites from articles in three major scientific journals at 3, 15, and 27 months after publication. Inactive sites totaled 3.8, 10, and 13 percent, respectively. Another recent study of a Web-based high school science curriculum found that 20 percent of the sites had vanished after a year. Forty percent to fifty percent of the URLs (Web addresses) cited in two computer journals were inaccessible within four years. Of 2,483 British government Web sites, where one might expect greater stability, 25 percent changed their URLs every year. Other studies would reveal similar problems, which are inherent in an electronic medium.

But even with all these limitations there are valuable online resources devoted to SF, and this guide lists some of the best sites in English whose track records suggest greater stability and longevity and usefulness to more serious readers or scholars. Sites are grouped according to their subject emphases, even though this unavoidably results in scattering of sites among chapters, as follows:

Chapter	Content
8	General (multi-subject) sites, bibliographies, and utopias
10	Authors (collective and individual)
11	Film/TV/radio
12	Art/illustration
13	Magazines
14	Teaching SF
15	Libraries
16	Organizations, Awards

Abundant cross-references are included to link print and online resources. And all named Web sites regardless of chapter are indexed in the title index. Because Web sites often vanish abruptly or change in major ways over time (not necessarily for the better), no attempt was made to flag sites as "best," meaning none are listed in Chapter 16's best books listing.

The online sites described and recommended had to have several characteristics: 1) ease in navigating the site, which requires careful Web design and layout; 2) frequent updating (preferably including a line specifically saying "last updated ___"), with systematic elimination of non-working links; 3) reasonably balanced and intelligently edited and accurate text (the absence of which was a major flaw in rejected sites); 4) offering material of general interest to the more experienced reader of SF and often to scholars as well; 5) absence of clutter and limited (preferably zero) advertising on the site; and 6) an e-mail address for the Webmaster or someone having primary responsibility for the site, permitting feedback from site users. Most sites we investigated lacked one or several of these characteristics. And given the number of potential sites, we do not pretend to have identified all of the best or better sites, even those of likely interest to users of this guide.

It was inevitable that an award would be given to the best science fiction Internet site, and in 2003 the first Wooden Rocket awards were given (www. woodenrocket.com). With 17 categories (online-only magazine, online/print magazine, author, artist, art gallery, print and e-book publishers, etc.), it's a little like the Alice in Wonderland race where everybody wins. That there are far too many categories is suggested by the 2004 voting: more than 12,000 voters and 68,000 nominations. The site is sponsored by Sfcrowsnest.com and the WRA organizing committee.

8-1. **Center for the Study of Science Fiction**, www.ku.edu/~sfcenter

James Gunn, jgunn@ku.edu or Chris McKitterick, cmckit@ku.edu.

Founded in 1982 at the University of Kansas as a focus for programs in SF that began in 1970 when Gunn offered his first SF courses and the libraries began serious acquisition of SF materials (see [15-12] for a summary of holdings). The center is associated with the English Department. Areas of this Web site include news, especially about the SF summer programs (on writing SF, Campbell conference at which the Campbell Memorial award is given, and the two-week Intensive Institute in SF); a 1971 interview with John W. Campbell, Harry Harrison, and Gordon Dickson; other interviews with major SF authors (Aldiss, Asimov, Bear, Delany, Silverberg, Sterling, etc.); an SF youth program with many links to activities; links to SF teaching sites; Gunn's A Basic SF Library; and an annotated A–Z list, current through 1995 (compare with the best books listing in Chapter 16 of this guide). Links to writing, teaching, current magazines, forthcoming conferences. Easy to navigate; ad-free. More briefly discussed in Chapter 14.

8-2. **Information Database—The Cyberpunk Project**, http://project. cyberpunk.ru/idb/

rodeo@cyberpunk.ru.

A Russia-based site whose English is very good. Sections include history, definitions, essentials, cyber SF (divided into history, style, literature, movies, TV, games, and the arts), subculture, technology, zones and zines, international. Reprints useful documents in the history of cyberpunk, in and outside SF. Argues that cyberpunk in SF has mutated, but as a subculture is more varied, "the grafting of high-technology onto underground, street and avant pop culture." Text is white on black. Many links to alternative sites, magazines, hacker publications (some links inactive). Regularly updated. A useful site for an already committed audience.

8-3. **Locus Online**, www.locusmag.com

Mark R. Kelly, online@locusmag.com.

This online companion to the most comprehensive magazine devoted to news about fantastic literature began in April 1997 and has steadily increased its scope. Its current subtitle is "news, reviews, resources, and perspectives of science fiction, fantasy and horror." Webmaster Kelly casts a very wide net, providing links to reviews, interviews, and all types of news. The home page links to news, monitor (new books and magazines, reprints), reviews and features (including letters), lists of recent and forthcoming books, often with links to reviews; author events, conventions, film reviews. Although the online version draws on the print monthly, little full text is imported but summaries are provided. Supplementing the news is the comprehensive and invaluable awards listing, www.locusmag.com/SFAwards/index.html, 1971–date, to which this guide refers in Chapter 16. The Web sites of many dozens of print and Web-only magazines, mostly fanzines, can be found at www.locusmag.com/Links/Mags.html, with each briefly described. They include fiction, criticism, etc., and SF, fantasy, and horror. Another useful section is www.locusmag.com/Links/Bibliographies.html, which describes five *Locus* indexes and databases, most also available on CD-ROMs (several are described in Chapter 7), plus nine other online bibliographies, some of them foreign-language, and a few of which are annotated in this guide. Updated daily or every few days. The links to amazon.com are the only ads of consequence and are unobtrusive. Full details on the Locus Press CD-ROM bibliographies are provided. Easily navigated, well-designed, this is an essential site for the latest news and information, emphasizing North America but not neglecting overseas news.

8-4.   Science Fiction and Fantasy Research Database, http://lib-oldweb. tamu.edu/cushing/SFFRD/H. W. Hall, hal-hall@tamu.edu.

A major scholarly database, annotated as [7-17]. Indexes contents of nonfiction books more thoroughly than in Chapter 9 and of course is not limited by the selective criteria of this guide (i.e., best or better books only).

8-5.   Science Fiction Studies, www.depauw.edu/sfs/

Istvan Csicsery-Ronay, Jr., icrongy@depauw.edu.

One of the best sites for scholars, supplementing the three-times-yearly journal [13-20], which for many years included a hyphen (*Science-Fiction Studies*). The home page has links to a search engine for the site, contents pages of recent issues, full-text featured essays, a list of special issues with links to contents pages, contents pages of all past issues (1973–date), with links to articles and reviews, a reviews index by author and issue, abstracts of all articles by author and issue, a major bibliography of SF criticism (www.depauw.edu/sfs/biblio. htm), documents in SF history appearing in earlier issues, and a carefully compiled list of links, amusingly called wormholes, to other useful sites (www. depauw.edu/sfs/links.htm), including scholarly journals and organizations, library collections, a list of universities offering degrees in SF, 29 recommended Internet sites, groups whose focus is SF, topical resources, SF magazines and e-zines of critical interest, "interesting" author sites, SF in film/TV, mainstream and "edge" science, and five sites "in the zone" (i.e., focusing on pseudoscience such as alien abductions). Some of these sites are annotated in this guide. Superior design, excellent internal and external linkages, and ad free. An essential site for the serious reader or scholar.

8-6.   Uchronia: The Alternate History List, www.uchronia.net/

Robert B. Schmunk, submit03@uchronia.net.

An annotated bibliography of approximately 2,500 novels, stories, essays and other materials (figure as of June 2004; steadily growing) dealing with "counterfactual" or "allohistorical" narratives, commonly if ungrammatically called alternate (rather than alternative) history. Access by author, keyword, divergence point (e.g., 1863, during the American Civil War), anthologies, series, reference sources, materials in foreign languages. Notes annual Sidewise awards and lists new and forthcoming books. Useful list of links. An accessible site for both the casual reader and the scholar. Linked to amazon.com.

8-7. **Utopus Discovered**, www2.coloradocollege.edu/Dept/EN/Utopus.

This newsletter describes itself as "a most informal newsletter . . . " and is the Web version of a print newsletter sent to members of the Society of Utopian Studies (see Chapter 16). Brenda Cooley of Colorado College is responsible for the Web version. A typical issue includes these sections: from the editors; calls for papers; scholarship (referring to a print bibliography available to society members); reviews of fiction and nonfiction; and perhaps the most useful section, a series of links that group the sites in these categories: general utopian sites (4 sites, including Utopia on the Internet, which itself has 11 subdivisions, with each site within a subdivision having a one-line phrase or sentence description); organizations and communities (19); utopian texts and authors (12); utopian politics and theory (7); utopian art (1); syllabi (3); personal Web sites (9); SF and utopia (2); and related sites (12). A good starting point for anyone interested in utopias, although of more value to someone moderately knowledgeable about utopias.

8-8. **SF Site**, www.sfsite.com/

Rodger Turner, editor, editor@sfsite.com.

An Ottawa-based site that apparently began about 1997. Updated twice monthly, the coverage includes SF, fantasy, and horror, both in print and on film and TV. Many reviews but of widely varying quality, with an apparent emphasis on small press publications. Most reviews, all signed, had too much plot summary and not enough critical analysis and comparisons to similar works. Many pages with links to organizations, authors, publishers, awards, etc., which require a lot of regular updating (some links checked at random were dead). A large site, with more than 2,000 pages, apparently aimed mostly at fans. General news is assembled by Steve Silver but appears only once monthly; the daily coverage of Locus Online is far superior, as are the other features.

8-9. **SF Weekly**, www.scifi.com/sfw/

Scott Edelman, editor, scifiweekly@scifi.com.

Sponsored by the SciFi cable channel, this weekly webzine is predictably a popular site (the masthead claims 340,000 registered readers). A monthly column by John Clute is one of the highlights. There are other columns, about two book reviews in each issue, and reader letters. The emphasis is on general news with a strong media emphasis (or bias): films, TV, games, etc. Relatively thin fare if you're book rather than media oriented.

8-10.   The Ultimate Science Fiction Web Guide, www.magicdragon.com/UltimateSF/SF-Index.html

Jonathan Post, jpost@earthlink.net.

The masthead of this hyperbolically named site claims it provides more than 6,000 links to SF "resources," listed alphabetically—aliens, authors, books, genres, movies, TV, time travel, etc. The author site is said to have 3,284 hot links, with an additional 6,108 authors lacking links. Random searches revealed a lot of dated material, not very well organized, with blocs of unattractive text. The last updating was almost a year prior to the date of our search. Post says the site is nine years old and gets more than 40,000 hits daily. To be used cautiously, with the information checked against sources known to be reliable.

8-11.   The Internet Speculative Fiction Database, http://isfdb.tamu.edu

Al von Ruff, Webmaster, avanruff@isfdb.com.

The home page says this site, hosted by Texas A&M's Cushing Library, catalogs (lists) works of SF, fantasy, and horror in five clickable categories: authors/editors, magazines, forthcoming books, publisher listings, and lists derived from the other categories (e.g., most-reviewed books, oldest/youngest authors, and similar essential information). The information is provided by many named people and occupies several thousand pages; how carefully it is checked for accuracy, completeness, and consistency by von Ruff or others is impossible to say. Errors are common in such a large number of listings, e.g., typos like Maltzberg and Malzberg; listings under variant names, e.g., C. N. Manlove and Colin Manlove, or George R. Stewart and George Rippey Stewart. Currency is spotty, with the listings of forthcoming books most current. The magazine section provides very lengthy listings of contents from the entire publication period, such as 20 years of *Thrilling Wonder Stories*. The listing of 21 publishers includes all imprints, arranged by year, including ISBN, original price, cover illustrator, but many older publishers are missing. There's a huge amount of information here, but it should be verified with other sources known to be reliable.

8-12.   Fantastic Fiction, www.fantasticfiction.co.uk

Dave Wands, Webmaster, dave@fantasticfiction.co.uk.

This British site claims to provide bibliographies of more than 5,000 authors of fantastic fiction, plus mysteries, thrillers, and romances, with information on 100,000 books, published and forthcoming, plus links to booksellers, somewhat dated award listings, brief biographies for most authors, a few paragraphs for the more important, a curious list of the most visited author pages (in July 2004 they were Roald Dahl, J. K. Rowling, Stephen King, Shirley Jackson, and George R. R. Martin). Its British emphasis is clear in the series listing, 341 titles for *Doctor Who* alone, far ahead of *Star Wars* and *Star Trek* books. I was unable to judge the error/omission rate on such a large site. Like the ISFDB (above), this site can be useful but users should try to verify the information in another source.

CHAPTER 9

History and Criticism

Gary K. Wolfe

Anyone first approaching the now-considerable body of SF criticism and history might reasonably be daunted by the plethora of conflicting voices and traditions. The works discussed in this chapter range from the relatively uncritical zeal of devoted fans to the most abstruse postmodern theorizing, and it is evidence of the genre's vitality and broad appeal that nearly all of them have something useful to add to the ongoing discourse. Like SF itself, scholarship and criticism of the field have had their own ghettos, their own warring camps, their own struggle for respectability, and their own ambivalence about whether they really want to be "respectable." Complicating matters further is the fact that critical discourse about SF has evolved out of three distinct traditions, and that only in the last couple of decades have these traditions begun to talk to each other at all.

The earliest of these traditions began in the letter columns of the pulp magazines and the hectographed "fanzines" of the 1920s and 1930s. The founder of *Amazing Stories*, Hugo Gernsback, encouraged such feedback and did much to help create the sense of extended community among SF readers that came to be known as fandom (one scholar, Gary Westfahl, even argues that Gernsback was the genre's first literary theorist [9-199]). While much of this early commentary was simply a listing of story preferences, it also often touched upon questions of what SF ought to be. Although most of these early fan writings are now inaccessible to all but the most devoted scholars (some of whom, such as

Justine Larbalestier in *The Battle of the Sexes in Science Fiction* [9-113], make effective use of them), they helped to establish a tradition of resolutely informal populist criticism that may well have helped shape the genre, and that still informs much that is written about it.

Some of the most enthusiastic of these fan scholars, such as Sam Moskowitz, later organized their commentary into books, and scholars approaching SF in the 1960s found that almost the only source of information about authors was in such titles as Moskowitz's *Explorers of the Infinite* (1963) and *Seekers of Tomorrow* (1966), although a certain amount of that information has since proved of dubious provenance. Still, Moskowitz in 1981 became fandom's first recipient of the Science Fiction Research Association's Pilgrim Award. (It should be noted that some well-known academic critics of SF, such as Thomas D. Clareson, also began their work in fandom.)

A second tradition of SF criticism, related to but not quite congruent with the fan tradition, evolved during the 1940s as professional writers began publishing commentaries on each other, on the nature of SF, and on various matters of technique and professional strategy. By then, with the rise of anthologies and specialty presses (and the attendant promise of hardbound immortality), it was becoming apparent to many of these authors that SF was more than one pulp market among many, and that it was a genre or mode that had developed its own techniques and themes and an increasingly sophisticated audience. Often appearing side by side with fan letters in the same publications, this kind of commentary often took the form of tips to aspiring writers; what may have been the first book about modern SF, Lloyd Arthur Eshbach's *Of Other Worlds* [9-74], consisted mostly of a variety of authors doing just that.

But the tradition of authors-as-critics took on a new dimension of sophistication in the early 1950s when James Blish and Damon Knight began seeking to establish critical standards for the field in their various essays and reviews. (Both Blish and Knight later collected these essays in the books listed in this chapter.) This tradition of writer-critics—later carried on by Algis Budrys, Norman Spinrad, Samuel R. Delany, Gwyneth Jones, Damien Broderick, Elizabeth Hand, and others—added to the fannish discourse a concern with craft and technique, as well as a realistic awareness of the market forces and editorial practices that are crucial to any meaningful discussion of popular fiction. These latter concerns are nowhere more evident than in the various letters and essays that went to make up Theodore Cogswell's "professional fanzine" *Proceedings of the Institute for Twenty-First Century Studies* from 1959 to 1962 [9-60]. This is still the most extensive source for a wide variety of authors' thoughts about the field during that period.

A third tradition of discourse came into play as academically trained scholars—and the occasional commentator from the literary "mainstream"—began to pay increasing attention to popular fantastic literature, sometimes to the chagrin and irritation of the writers and fans. Older writers and fans may have remembered—and resented—such early mainstream attacks on the genre as a 1939 *Harper's* essay by Bernard De Voto titled "Doom Beyond Jupiter" (many of these "mainstream" responses are chronicled in Fred Lerner's *Science Fiction and the American Literary Community* [9-120]). But many of them also came to admit that the first academic study of SF history, J. O. Bailey's *Pilgrims Through Space and Time* (1947) [9-15], helped give the genre its own archaeology and at least something of a pedigree. (Ever since Bailey, some advocates of SF have claimed Plato, Lucian, and Kepler as ancestors.) This pedigree was solidified further by the publication, a year after Bailey's book, of Everett Bleiler's historical bibliography, *The Checklist of Fantastic Literature* [7-1], now long superseded but enormously significant at the time.

Both the Bailey and Bleiler books were published by specialty presses, and were available pretty much only to those who sought them out through fan community channels. Commercial presses published a couple of general studies of SF during the 1950s, including Reginald Bretnor's *Modern Science Fiction: Its Meaning and Future* [9-35] and Basil Davenport's brief *Inquiry Into Science Fiction* (1955), but it wasn't until Kingsley Amis's *New Maps of Hell* [9-7] appeared in 1960 that the SF field began to suspect it was having a substantial impact beyond its own borders. Even though the book was based on lectures given at Princeton, Amis was hardly an academic. But he was at the height of his reputation as one of England's "Angry Young Men," and the attention he paid to SF almost certainly helped to open what would eventually seem the floodgates of academe. (In part because of SF's hunger for respectability, the impact of Amis's book far exceeded its actual contributions to SF scholarship or criticism, and this pattern would be repeated each time a writer or scholar with a substantial mainstream reputation—Leslie Fiedler, Robert Scholes, Harold Bloom— wrote sympathetically of the field.)

SF had never been entirely alien to the academic establishment; Bailey's study was based on his own 1934 dissertation, and James Gunn—in a move that seems emblematic of the whole history of SF scholarship—published substantial parts of his master's thesis in the pulp magazine *Dynamic Science Fiction* in 1953 and 1954. In 1958, the Modern Language Association convention featured the first of what would become annual sessions on SF, and the seminars gave rise to the first academic journal on SF (*Extrapolation,* founded 1959) and eventually to the formation of the Science Fiction Research Association in 1970. Soon after, other journals began to appear, most notably the British *Foundation* in 1972, the Canadian–American *Science-Fiction Studies* in 1973, and *The Journal of the Fantastic in the Arts* in 1988. Nineteen-seventy also saw what was probably the first history of SF to appear with the imprimatur of a university press: Robert M. Philmus's *Into the Unknown* (although Oxford had published H. Bruce Franklin's critical anthology *Future Perfect* in 1966). By 1972, enough books and articles about SF had appeared to fill a book-length bibliography by Thomas D. Clareson, *Science Fiction Criticism: An Annotated Checklist* (Kent State Univ. Press), and from 1972 through 1988 Marshall B. Tymn and Roger Schlobin compiled annual "year's scholarship" bibliographies in the journal *Extrapolation* (and later, briefly, *The Journal of the Fantastic in the Arts*). Similar bibliographies have appeared with some regularity since then, the most comprehensive being Hal W. Hall's *Science Fiction and Fantasy Reference Index* [7-17].

The 1970s saw the flowering of SF scholarship. Major histories of the field appeared from Aldiss ([9-4]; the first edition, titled *Billion Year Spree,* appeared in 1973) and Gunn [9-86], and more personal histories came from Wollheim [9-203] and del Rey [9-63]. More theoretical works appeared from Suvin [9-189], Ketterer [9-104], Wolfe [9-202], and Rose [9-162]. Essay collections, beginning with Clareson's *SF: The Other Side of Realism* [9-49] vied with and at times outpaced the journals as sources of critical essays, and a string of reference books featuring critical assessments often outpaced the essay collections. (One of the most ambitious of these books, Salem Press's *Survey of Science Fiction Literature* [7-26], is not a reference work at all, but a collection of no fewer than 500 essays on key works in the genre.) Several university presses instituted series of studies on SF and fantasy, most notably Oxford, Indiana, Southern Illinois, Kent State, and Bowling Green. (Later the University of Georgia joined this list.) By 1984, UMI Research Press, in a series called Studies in Speculative Fiction, was mining unpublished doctoral dissertations, with mixed results. Other presses with series devoted to the genre included Taplinger, Ungar, Borgo, Starmont House, and most notably Greenwood, whose series Contributions to the Study of Science Fiction and Fantasy, begun under the editorship of Marshall Tymn in 1982, numbered more than 100 titles by early 2003 (shifting in 2004 to Greenwood's Praeger imprint).

It has been suggested that this boom in SF scholarship was partly opportunistic, the result of college English departments cynically trying to attract students by permitting a once-despised genre a place in the curriculum and thus condoning research in the field. The argument makes sense only to a point: certainly the earlier exclusion from the curriculum was accompanied by exclusion from standard reference works and library collections of criticism. The sudden interest in SF among students and teachers revealed an enormous gap in available resources—a gap that was quickly filled to overflowing. Fandom had never provided a substantial market for serious critical commentary (and still does so rarely), so there is little doubt that the academic "discovery" of SF permitted a great many works to be published that otherwise might never have seen the light of day.

But other forces besides academia were at work as well. The more traditional universities in England, for example, participated very little in this "academic awakening," and yet England saw a significant rise in SF studies and even gave birth in 1971 to the Science Fiction Foundation, for which there is still no comparable organization in the United States. (The closest candidate, the Science Fiction Research Association, lacks a central location and research collection.) Elsewhere in Europe—in France and Germany especially—SF studies developed without the benefit of serving as a recruitment strategy for undergraduate students.

Some of the growth in SF studies, then, must be attributed to the growth in stature and the maturation of the genre itself. The mainstream reputation of a Vonnegut; the literary sophistication of a Le Guin (who may still be the most written-about of all modern SF authors); the forays into SF by revered writers such as Doris Lessing and John Updike; the posthumous cult of Philip K. Dick in film as well as literature; the national bestseller status achieved initially by Heinlein, Clarke, Asimov, and Farmer and later by Orson Scott Card and Neal Stephenson; and the substantial share of the overall fiction market garnered by SF and its related genres of fantasy and horror—all these helped make SF difficult to ignore in the literary community. In the academic world, the influence of structuralism, feminism, deconstructionism, Marxism, cultural studies, cybertheory, postcolonialism, and various other postmodern approaches—all with their emphasis on methodology over canonization—have opened up critical discourse to a far wider range of texts than might have been discussed a decade or two earlier.

While SF criticism and history remain wildly eclectic, it has become possible to identify a number of emerging schools of thought, few of which have self-consciously identified themselves as such. For example, what I have termed the "consensus" view of SF history represented in works by Gunn, Asimov, Wollheim, and del Rey refers to a rough consensus of American writers and fans of a certain age group who tend to argue that "real" SF began with the publication of *Amazing Stories* in 1926 despite a lineage dating back to Plato. A radically different view can be found in Aldiss and Wingrove's *Trillion Year Spree* [9-4], which views the genre as descended from the Gothic novel, and in the histories of British SF by Stableford [9-184] and Ruddick [9-164], which trace a clear path of evolution independent of the American magazines. Other writers, such as Lundwall and Rottensteiner, see a much more international pattern of development; while still others, including Kumar, Berger, and Moylan, trace the genre to origins in utopian impulses.

Critical theory, too, has developed in a number of different directions. The journal *Science Fiction Studies* introduced structuralist, narratological, and Marxist approaches to SF, championing authors—Le Guin, Lem, Dick—whose works yielded most readily to such analyses. This trend in SF criticism paved the way for major theoretical studies by Suvin, Malmgren, and others. A somewhat less formalistic but equally theory-oriented attempt to grapple with major themes and problems grew up around California's J. Lloyd Eaton conferences and is reflected in the several volumes of papers drawn from those conferences listed here, edited by George E. Slusser, Gary Westfahl, and others.

The British journal *Foundation*, on the other hand, has often favored a more historical approach and closer connections with the community of writers and publishers. Feminist criticism of SF has grown into a virtual subspecialty of its own, and its variety of approaches is represented by Lefanu, Barr, Bartkowski, Armitt, Donawerth, Russ, Larbalestier, and others. Finally, the cyberpunk movement has drawn SF to the attention of a considerable number of scholars who view aspects of the genre as a symptomatic expression of postmodernism; see, for example, Bukatman, McCaffrey, Hayles, and Slusser and Shippey. Other works listed in this section may treat SF in terms of myth, popular culture, religion, politics, and philosophy.

The body of critical and historical writing on the genre is now substantial enough to sustain internal debates; gone are the days when an author such as Amis could attempt a brief overview of the genre with reference to virtually no prior scholarship—and gone also is the "consensus" that once enabled long-time SF writers and fans to claim virtual ownership of the genre. Much of what passes for academic scholarship is still surprisingly shoddy and piecemeal, often failing to acknowledge earlier scholarship, but the best of it reflects a deep understanding of the field, its most important texts, and its role in the culture at large.

This chapter lists most of the book-length studies of the genre that have appeared in English, eliminating some of those listed in earlier editions that have become dated, but retaining those whose very age has lent them historical significance for the scholar. For the most part, studies of utopian fiction (which has nearly grown into a separate discipline) are included only when they are of particular relevance to SF, and a number of published but unrevised (or barely revised) doctoral dissertations, most of them now all but inaccessible, have been omitted. The listing is alphabetical by author or editor, with proceedings of specific conferences grouped at the end of the chapter.

Bibliography

9-1.   Aldiss, Brian W. **The Detached Retina: Aspects of SF and Fantasy**. Liverpool Univ. Press, 1995.

A collection of 23 essays, eight of which are revised or expanded from pieces originally in *The Pale Shadow of Science* [9-2] and . . . *And the Lurid Glare of the Comet*, the rest new or previously uncollected. More than half the essays are reconsiderations of authors whom Aldiss knew or was influenced by—Mary Shelley, Huxley, Stapledon, Dick, Sturgeon, Orwell, Blish, Amis, Wells, Stevenson, Anna Kavan, and John W. Campbell, Jr. There are also humorous pieces on Lovecraft and utopias, and discussions of differences between American and British fantasy, early voyage-to-the-moon tales, the evolution of SF during the 1960s, and the importance of appropriate prose in SF. The final two pieces, "The Veiled World" and "A Personal Parabola," are of particular interest to Aldiss scholars, since they focus on his own work and his ideas of "discontinuous personality."

9-2.   Aldiss, Brian W. **The Pale Shadow of Science**. Serconia, 1985.

A collection of 13 essays covering Orwell, Shelley, Stapledon, and other topics; some of them autobiographical, including one on his Helliconia novels. Six of the essays are revised and expanded in *The Detached Retina*. The book was a Hugo nominee. A second volume from Serconia, . . . *And the Lurid Glare of the Comet*, appeared in 1986, with essays on Wells, Sturgeon, and Aldiss's own work, including his phantasmagorical *Barefoot in the Head*. "The Glass Forest," an autobiographical piece expanded from his contribution to *Hell's Cartographers*, is of particular interest to readers of Aldiss's excellent non-SF novel, *Forgotten Life*.

9-3. Aldiss, Brian W. **This World and Nearer Ones: Essays Exploring the Familiar**. Weidenfield & Nicolson, 1979.

A collection of 30 essays revised from various sources and including a number of SF writers and topics, including Blish, Dick, Sheckley, Nesvadba, Verne, Vonnegut, British SF, SF art, and SF film. Aldiss, who received the Pilgrim Award in 1978, and the James Blish Award for SF criticism in 1978 is among the most literate and astute of writer-critics in the field, and his essays explore at a more leisurely pace many of the topics covered in his more famous *Trillion Year Spree*.

*9-4. Aldiss, Brian W., and David Wingrove. **Trillion Year Spree: The History of Science Fiction**. Atheneum, 1986.

A thorough revision and expansion of Aldiss's *Billion Year Spree: The True History of Science Fiction* (1973), which was the first attempt at a coherent critical literary history of the field. Unlike works by Gunn, del Rey, and Wollheim, which tend to view SF history as a prologue to the development of the commercial American genre market, *Trillion Year Spree* sets out to be a comprehensive survey of the evolution of a literary form, with a distinctly personal viewpoint. Some of Aldiss's arguments, such as the contention that SF is a "post-Gothic" genre descended largely from Mary Shelley's *Frankenstein*, have gained wide currency and some controversy, while others, such as his comparative treatment of the British and American "New Wave" movements, have also generated debate. Generally, however, the account is balanced and evenhanded. Perhaps in response to complaints that his earlier history slighted more recent SF, Aldiss worked with David Wingrove to assure that extensive coverage increased currency; fully two fifths of the book is devoted to SF after 1960 and includes discussions of films, feminist SF, cyberpunk, mainstream writers such as Doris Lessing, and the growth of SF scholarship, as well as an impressive number of younger writers. Some more recent writers are treated in a kind of headlong rush, and some inaccuracies result, but most of the judgments have held up well, and the book remains the definitive single-volume history of the field. Sixteen pages of photos, detailed reference and explanatory endnotes, a critical bibliography, and a thorough index add to the book's value as a scholarly reference as well as the most graceful and witty account of the genre to date.

Awards: Hugo, *Locus*, Eaton

*9-5. Alkon, Paul K. **Origins of Futuristic Fiction**. Univ. of Georgia Press, 1987.

A literate and scholarly analysis of the early history of prose works set in the future, beginning with Jacques Guttin's *Epigone* (1659) and including useful discussions of works little known even to SF historians, by such authors as David Russen, Thomas Burnet, Samuel Madden, Louis Geoffroy, Louis Sebastien

Mercier, Jean-Baptiste Cousin de Grainville, Restif de la Bretonne, and Jane Webb, whose 1827 *The Mummy!* represents the latter end of the chronological period covered. Especially interesting is Alkon's discussion of early theorists of future fiction, most notably Félix Bodin, whose 1834 *Le roman de l'avenir* anticipates many later defenses of SF. Alkon consistently relates his material to current SF scholarship and literary theory, giving his study a degree of relevance that is unusual among such protohistorical studies, which often focus on social theory more than literary form. Compare I. F. Clarke's *The Pattern of Expectation: 1644–2001.*

Awards: Eaton

9-6.   Alkon, Paul K. **Science Fiction Before 1900: Imagination Discovers Technology**. Twayne, 1994.

A more truncated (138 pages) and general treatment of some of the material found in Alkon's earlier *Origins of Futuristic Fiction* [9-5], this overview is constrained by the publisher's format, which includes a rather quirky chronology, a bibliographic essay on secondary literature, and a list of recommended titles that includes many works and writers not mentioned in the text. Rather than attempting to be comprehensive, Alkon focuses on a few key works and seminal concepts, devoting one chapter each to developments in England, France, and America. He cites Defoe and Swift as two early models for SF narratives, but his chapter on England focuses almost entirely on Shelley and Wells. His treatment of French SF, which he sees as essentially technophilic, is more original and interesting; the centerpiece here is his analysis of Verne's *20,000 Leagues Under the Sea*. Twain's *A Connecticut Yankee in King Arthur's Court* is a similar centerpiece in the American chapter. More useful as a general overview of major works in the genre's pre-1900 evolution than as a comprehensive history.

9-7.   Amis, Kingsley. **New Maps of Hell: A Survey of Science Fiction**. Harcourt, 1960.

Amis's early study, based on his Christian Gauss lectures at Princeton in 1959, is now of more historical than critical interest. It was the first serious treatment of SF by a reputable mainstream novelist and, thanks to a Ballantine mass-market paperback published in 1960, the first critical work on SF to reach a wide audience. Amis sees SF largely as a vehicle for satire, and thus his discussion of contemporaneous writers leans heavily on the work of Pohl and Kornbluth. Though there are clear gaps in his knowledge of the field, Amis does not look down on genre writers, his style remains sharp and acerbic, and his book is justifiably cited as one of the landmarks in gaining broad recognition for the genre. Amis's later *The Alteration* is an alternate-world SF novel, and he edited a number of anthologies, some with Robert Conquest.

9-8.   Armitt, Lucie. **Theorising the Fantastic**. St. Martin's, 1996.

Organized in two parts, "Reading Theory" and "Reading Texts," this rather densely written study attempts to offer an overview of previous theoretical models of the fantastic (which the author views as a mode of writing rather than a genre). Then it gives Armitt's own view of the "metamorphic body" as a central conceit, which Armitt then elaborates on in discussions of particular texts by Carroll, Gilman, Iain M. Banks, and others. Her notion of the "cyborg body" is of particular relevance to SF and its role in the broader spectrum of fantastic literature. With its emphasis on psychoanalytic and poststructuralist models, Armitt's often provocative discussions bear comparison to Rosemary Jackson's *Fantasy: The Literature of Subversion* (1981) and Christine Brooke-Rose's *A Rhetoric of the Unreal* (1981).

9-9.   Armitt, Lucie, ed. **Where No Man Has Gone Before: Women and Science Fiction**. Routledge, 1991.

Thirteen original essays by British women writers and academics offer a variety of perspectives on various writers, women characters, and problems of genre writing. The first section, on individual authors, includes a rare discussion of works by Charlotte Haldane and Katherine Burdekin (by Elizabeth Russell), plus essays on C. L. Moore, Ursula Le Guin, and Doris Lessing. The second section offers perspectives on the Frankenstein tradition, the metamorphosis theme in recent SF, the role of language in SF, and film. The final section considers relations between SF and young adult fiction, horror fiction, and Arthurian romance, and concludes with a lively autobiographical piece by Josephine Saxton. An important collection, which should be consulted together with Lefanu [9-117], Donawerth [9-69], and Barr [9-20].

Themes: Women in SF

*9-10.   Ashley, Mike. **The Time Machines: The Story of the Science Fiction Pulp Magazines from the Beginning to 1950: The History of the Science Fiction Magazine, Vol. I**. Liverpool Univ. Press, 2001.

A substantial expansion and reworking of material that appeared in Ashley's four-volume anthology *History of the Science Fiction Magazine* and in the reference work *Science Fiction, Fantasy, and Weird Fiction Magazines* (co-edited with Marshall Tymn) [13-30]. This study, the first of three proposed volumes, aims to provide the first single coherent narrative history of SF magazines. While Ashley recounts many familiar stories and anecdotes—Gernsback's legendary tightfistedness, the teenagers who ended up editing magazines, the Army intelligence brouhaha over a Cleve Cartmill story, the Shaver "mystery," and the rise of dianetics—he also demonstrates that SF had been a regular, and recognized, feature of popular fiction magazines for decades before Gernsback launched *Amazing Stories*, even finding examples dating back to early 19th-century England. His style is generally clear and crisp, his research authoritative, and his judgments reasonable, even when he discusses stories that, once regarded as major breakthroughs, sound appalling by contemporary standards. This is perhaps the most informed and bibliographically sound study of the pulp magazine era, and if the proposed second and third volumes match the density of information and insight in this one, Ashley will have produced one of the central contributions to English and (especially) American SF. Compare Carter [9-46]. Also annotated as [13-23].

9-11.   Asimov, Isaac. Asimov on Science Fiction. Avon, 1981.

A collection of 55 short pieces—22 of them editorials from *Isaac Asimov's Science Fiction Magazine* and others from sources as varied as *TV Guide* and liner notes from recordings—that offer provocative glimpses into Asimov's attitudes toward the field, writers, fans, and the process of writing. Written with Asimov's familiar chatty wit, the pieces are mostly directed toward wide, popular audiences and thus offer little in the way of extended critical arguments or information unfamiliar to SF readers. Taken together, however, they provide a useful overview of the opinions of one of the most prolific and popular authors of this century. A second collection, *Asimov's Galaxy: Reflections on Science Fiction* (Doubleday, 1989), assembles 66 short editorials that were originally published in *Isaac Asimov's Science Fiction Magazine* between 1980 and 1985, and is of more interest to students of Asimov than to students of SF in general.

*9-12.   Atheling, William, Jr. (pseud. of James Blish). The Issue at Hand: Studies in Contemporary Magazine Science Fiction. Advent, 1964.

From 1952 through 1963, Blish published an ongoing critical commentary on magazine SF, with occasional comments on major novels of the period. His essays, which originally appeared in a variety of fanzines, are collected here together with two convention speeches, and make clear why Blish, along with Damon Knight, is counted as a pioneer in establishing critical standards for the field. While his discussions of stories that have since become famous are of obvious interest, his demolition of less successful stories is often more informative from a technical standpoint. This volume is useful not only to those interested in the history of SF during the 1950s, but to anyone interested in the technique and construction of SF stories. A second volume, *More Issues at Hand*, appeared from Advent in 1970, emphasizing novels more than magazine fiction and covering works by Heinlein, Sturgeon, and Budrys as well as such earlier authors as A. Merritt. Of particular interest are his early discussions of SF criticism, SF in translation, and the "New Wave" debate. Similar collections by writers as critics include Knight's *In Search of Wonder* [9-107], Budrys's *Benchmarks* [9-42], Spinrad's *Science Fiction in the Real World* [9-180], and several volumes by Samuel R. Delany and Damien Broderick.

*9-13.   Attebery, Brian W. Decoding Gender in Science Fiction. Routledge, 2002.

Attebery is a major critic whose earlier studies (*Strategies of Fantasy*, 1992; *The Fantasy Tradition in American Literature*, 1980) primarily concerned fantasy, but with substantial relevance to SF and "science fantasy." His interest in gender issues in SF was evident in *The Norton Book of Science Fiction* (co-edited with Ursula K. Le Guin, 1993), which generated enough controversy that Attebery spends several pages defending it in the present volume. Following an introductory chapter that discusses gender coding in general, Attebery examines the role of gender in Gothic fiction, the "Golden Age" of pulp fiction, the rise of feminist SF in the 1970s, and "postmodern" SF (which focuses largely on novels by Gwyneth Jones and James Morrow). Interspersed with this historical survey are chapters on the superman theme, the response to it of women writers (what he calls the "wonder woman" theme), single-sex societies, and androgynous societies. Essentially a series of essays on gender themes rather than a history of women's or feminist SF, the book offers provocative and sometimes highly original readings of works not only by women authors such as Le Guin, Octavia Butler, Suzy McKee Charnas, Joanna Russ, C. L. Moore, and Alice Sheldon, but also by Melville, Hawthorne, Poe, Heinlein, Tom Godwin, van Vogt, and Sturgeon.

Themes: Feminist SF

9-14. Bacon-Smith, Camille. **Science Fiction Culture**. Univ. of Pennsylvania Press, 2000.

Intended as an ethnographic study of the various communities of SF, this survey begins with a discussion of "cultural capital" and the formation of conceptual spaces and communities and proceeds to discussions of fan conventions and networks (including online discussion groups); the role of women and gays in such communities (the book is part of a Feminist Cultural Studies series); and the mechanics of the SF publishing and bookselling industry. While Bacon-Smith's brief discussions of the literature itself are sketchy and not always accurate, and her industry material is sometimes dated even at the time of publication, the study draws notable value from its extensive use of interviews and primary sources, particularly in reference to the inner workings of fan conventions and networks and its general overview of SF as an industry. Compare Sanders's *Science Fiction Fandom* [9-168].

9-15. Bailey, J(ames) O(sler). **Pilgrims Through Space and Time: Trends and Patterns in Scientific and Utopian Fiction**. Argus, 1947.

Although largely superseded by more recent scholarship, Bailey's adaptation of his own 1934 doctoral dissertation was the first scholarly study of the roots of the genre, and thus exerted a profound influence on later historians and anthologists—as evidenced by the name of the Pilgrim Award, given annually by the Science Fiction Research Association to distinguished scholars in the field. This influence extends not only to establishing a pedigree for modern SF but also to helping to develop, through its taxonomic organization, a kind of consensus motif-list used by many later scholars. Despite its almost exclusive focus on pre-World War I works, Bailey's study remains readable and useful, if not always reliable in the light of later evidence.

9-16. Bainbridge, William Sims. **Dimensions of Science Fiction**. Harvard, 1986.

Like many attempts at sociological descriptions of the genre, Bainbridge's study—based on surveys of some 600 registrants at the 1978 world SF convention in Phoenix plus follow-up surveys—offers few new insights, but provides statistical data to support what is already common knowledge among, at least, editors and publishers. The main "dimensions" that Bainbridge isolates are hard SF, New Wave, and fantasy. A similar survey taken a few years earlier or later might, of course, have yielded quite different results. Written with jargon-free clarity, Bainbridge's study offers little in the way of literary theory but provides a useful statistical snapshot of the genre at one point in its history. Compare Brian Stableford's *The Sociology of Science Fiction* [9-185].

9-17.   Balsamo, Anne. **Technologies of the Gendered Body: Reading Cyborg Women**. Duke Univ. Pr., 1996.

Drawing on concepts from earlier postmodern theorists such as Donna Haraway, Balsamo's feminist study considers a broad range of body constructions (including bodybuilding and cosmetic surgery) in trying to identify ways in which gender roles are enforced despite the apparently liberating influences of biotechnology and information technology. She examines these tensions in part through readings of SF texts by authors such as Margaret Atwood and Pat Cadigan, but is generally less concerned with SF as literature than as part of a broad range of contemporary cultural expression. Compare Featherstone and Burrows [9-76], Hayles [9-92], and Wolmark [9-204].

Themes: Feminist SF

9-18.   Barr, Marleen S. **Alien to Femininity: Speculative Fiction and Feminist Theory**. Greenwood, 1987.

Barr's first extended attempt to link feminist theory with SF suffers from a tendency to quote rather than elucidate her theoretical sources, and then to rather mechanically apply these quotations to selected texts—although the texts she has chosen to discuss are often quite interesting. The book is divided into three sections, "Community," "Heroism," and "Sexuality and Reproduction," and authors covered include Tiptree, Wilhelm, and Charnas. Both Barr's own *Feminist Fabulation* [9-20] and Lefanu [9-117] are more consistent.

Themes: Feminist SF

9-19.   Barr, Marleen S., ed. **Envisioning the Future: SF and the Next Millennium**. Wesleyan Univ. Press, 2003.

An odd amalgam of five stories, six essays, and two "reviews" of imaginary books, all intended to reflect post-millennial and post-9/11 anxieties. Of the five nonfiction pieces that touch upon SF, the most substantial are Darko Suvin's reconsideration of Zamyatin's *We* in light of later 20th-century history and Patrick Parrinder's examination of past visions of future history. Marge Piercy discusses sex and gender roles, Rosi Braidotti the meanings of "female monsters," and Walter Mosley blacks and science fiction. The two fictional "reviews" by Eric S. Rabkin and Kim Stanley Robinson touch upon SF ideas, Rabkin in particular speculating on how the SF "movement" might be viewed a thousand years hence. Despite some useful insights in these pieces, the collection as a whole is wildly uneven in tone, approach, and intended audience.

*9-20. Barr, Marleen S. **Feminist Fabulation: Space/Postmodern Fiction**. Univ. of Iowa Press, 1992.

An impassioned and energetic study of speculative feminist works that "unmask patriarchal master narratives" but that, Barr claims, are excluded from the postmodern canon because of their genre origins. The first section, "Reclaiming Canonical Space," defines "feminist fabulation" and relates it to earlier traditions of women's literature. The second, "Redefining Gendered Space," includes chapters on flying as portrayed in literature, houses and "domestic spaces," and imaginary societies. The third, "Reconceiving Narrative Space," examines female characters and feminist revisions of traditional "male-centered" stories. A broad range of authors is covered, including Lynn Abbey, Marion Zimmer Bradley, Octavia Butler, Isak Dineson, Gail Godwin, Carol Hill, Doris Lessing, Marge Piercy, Pamela Sargent, and Christa Wolf. Barr's contentious style and overgeneralizations may irritate some, but she succeeds in raising a number of provocative issues, and this remains her major work in this field. A more general application of her ideas to cultural studies, literary criticism, and genre theory is Barr's *Genre Fission: A New Discourse Practice for Cultural Studies* (Univ. of Iowa Press, 2000), though it is not particularly focused on science fiction. Compare Lefanu [9-117] and Wolmark [9-204].

Themes: Feminist SF

9-21. Barr, Marleen S., ed. **Future Females: A Critical Anthology**. Bowling Green, 1981.

Like many topics of SF scholarship, the role of women authors and characters was first explored in individual essays and then in collections like this one before giving rise to more extended studies, such as Barr's own *Feminist Fabulation*. The contributors of these 15 essays—13 of them original—include Joanna Russ, Robert Scholes, and Eric Rabkin; a bibliography by Roger Schlobin was later expanded and published separately as *Urania's Daughters*. Although superseded by later feminist criticism, the book contains useful insights.

Themes: Feminist SF

9-22. Barr, Marleen S., ed. **Future Females, The Next Generation: New Voices and Velocities in Feminist Science Fiction Criticism**. Rowman and Littlefield, 2000.

As its title suggests, this collection of essays by 19 contributors is intended to provide an overview of the state of feminist SF criticism nearly two decades after Barr's pioneering *Future Females* [9-21], and for the most part it succeeds in demonstrating not only the vastly increased breadth of the field but also its increasing turn from literary history toward theory. While the earlier collection focused largely on developing a usable canon, these essays tend to be more intensely culture-oriented. Contributors include a number of major feminist critics, including Joan Gordon, Veronica Hollinger, Robin Roberts, Jane Donawerth, Anne Cranny-Francis, and Barr herself, and the topics reflect the growing influence of "cyberfeminism," cyborg theory, cyberpunk, queer theory, and other postmodern approaches. While such classic authors as Le Guin, Russ, Marge Piercy, Octavia Butler, and Alice Sheldon are inevitably discussed, there are also useful insights on less critically examined writers such as Pat Cadigan, Eleanor Arnason, and Katherine Burdekin, as well as on film and television.

Themes: Feminist SF

9-23.   Barr, Marleen S. **Lost in Space: Probing Feminist Science Fiction and Beyond**. Univ. of North Carolina Press, 1993.

A collection of 13 essays that return to the major themes and writers of Barr's earlier work, notably *Feminist Fabulation* [9-20], but that sometimes broaden the scope to consider such authors as Salman Rushdie and Saul Bellow. The central focus of the book, however, seems to be less on efforts to expand her theoretical framework (which she here tends to take as a given) than to portray herself as a courageous "swordswoman" almost single-handedly bent on rescuing feminist SF from oblivion. This concern with reinventing her autobiography in unironically heroic terms has become increasingly evident in Barr's later work, including her introductory material to *Envisioning the Future* [9-19] and her autobiographical novel *Oy Pioneer!* (2003).

Themes: Feminist SF

9-24.   Bartkowski, Frances. **Feminist Utopias**. Univ. of Nebraska Press, 1989.

Bartkowski discusses 10 American, Canadian, and French novels by pairing them off in five chapters, sometimes almost arbitrarily. The works discussed are Gilman's *Herland* and Monique Wittig's *Les guerelleres*, Russ's *The Female Man* and Marge Piercy's *Woman on the Edge of Time*, Charnas's *Walk to the End of the World* and *Motherlines*, Christian Rochefort's *Archaos, ou le jardin étincelant* and E. M. Broner's *Weave of Women*, and Louky Bersianik's *The Eugelionne* and Margaret Atwood's *The Handmaid's Tale*. Although Bartkowski's familiarity with other scholarship in the field seems limited, her readings of specific texts are valuable.

Themes: Feminist SF

9-25.   Bartter, Martha A. **The Way to Ground Zero: The Atomic Bomb in American Science Fiction**. Greenwood, 1988.

In one of the most thoroughly researched and extensive studies of a single theme in American science fiction, Bartter traces the image of the bomb (and related themes of the scientist, future wars, and the return to barbarism) in works ranging from pre-World War I "superweapon" stories through some novels of the 1980s; coverage is strongest in the 1940s and 1950s. Although the breadth of coverage limits extended treatment of significant works (short shrift is given to *A Canticle for Leibowitz*, for example), a chapter comparing 20 stories by Heinlein with 27 by Sturgeon is especially revealing. Although comparisons with Brians [9-36] are inevitable, Bartter's study is more than twice as long as the essay portion of Brians and more narrowly focused. Compare also Seed, *American Science Fiction and the Cold War* [9-174].

Themes: War

9-26. Baxter, Stephen. **Omegatropic: Non-Fiction and Fiction**. British Science Fiction Society, 2001.

Eighteen short essays (plus two short stories) are particularly interesting for revealing the degree of research that Baxter undertakes, not only on the scientific backgrounds of his own work but also on prior science fiction on topics including machines for viewing the past, alien environments in Blish and Clement, fictions set on the moon or on Titan, sequels or companions to Wells's *The Time Machine*, alternate visions of the space race, eschatology in SF, the portrayal of scientists, and "gadget stories." There are also brief obituaries of Gene Shoemaker, Bob Shaw, and Carl Sagan. Mostly of interest as background for Baxter's fiction, but containing some useful insights about various themes.

Awards: British Science Fiction Association

9-27. Becker, Allienne R. **The Lost Worlds Romance: From Dawn Till Dusk**. Greenwood, 1992.

Becker attempts to trace the history of one of SF's most popular early subgenres from its development late in the 19th century to modern echoes in the work of Andrew M. Greeley (who also provides an appreciative introduction). While Becker makes use of almost none of the existing scholarship in this field, and sometimes seems unclear whether she wants to write a literary history or an indictment of sexist and racist themes (her index includes such odd items as "bare-breasted women"), her lively discussions of the plots of works by Verne, Haggard, Burroughs, and others make this a convenient if incomplete reference. A clearer definition of the form and what it implies can be found in Thomas Clareson's "Lost Lands, Lost Races: A Pagan Princess of Their Very Own" in *Many Futures, Many Worlds* [9-48].

Themes: Lost Races/Worlds

9-28. Ben-Tov, Sharona. **The Artificial Paradise: Science Fiction and American Reality**. Univ. of Michigan Press, 1995.

An examination of how science fiction, in the wake of the transformed view of nature following the Enlightenment, paradoxically attempts to recapture a vision of an American Eden through technology. Ben-Tov's efforts to contextualize the genre in terms of broader technological anxieties and Cartesian ideas are sometimes insightful, but her grasp of the history of the genre itself is somewhat inconsistent and her style sometimes simplistic. Among the works discussed are Asimov's Foundation series (which she claims was "first printed" in 1951), Twain's *A Connecticut Yankee in King Arthur's Court*, Herbert's *Dune*, Cherryh's *The Faded Sun*, Vonnegut's *Player Piano* and *Slaughterhouse-Five*, and Gibson's *Neuromancer*; the Cherryh discussion is perhaps the most valuable.

9-29.   Berger, Harold. **Science Fiction and the New Dark Age**. Bowling Green, 1976.

A relatively early study of some 300 works showing the growing dystopian trend in SF. Berger groups the works into 12 categories (such as Man vs. Machine, the Totalitarian State of the Future, the Revolt of Youth, Race War in America, Nuclear War, the Population Explosion), but offers little detailed analysis of specific works and not much more in the way of theoretical or historical context. Useful as a source of some lesser-known texts. Compare Walsh's more thoughtful *From Utopia to Nightmare* [9-194].

Themes: Dystopias

9-30.   Blackford, Russell, Van Ikin, and Sean McMullen. **Strange Constellations: A History of Australian Science Fiction**. Greenwood, 1999.

Like many histories of SF, this first important study of the genre in Australia breaks into two discontinuous parts, one tracing a pattern of fantastic and utopian works scattered throughout 19th and early-20th-century literature, the other exploring the pulp and post-pulp eras. Beginning with 19th-century writers such as Marcus Clarke, the authors cover a variety of utopian, dystopian, and imaginary war novels (many of which seemed to be paranoid fantasies of racial invasion); the early development of genre SF from 1926 to 1959 (with individual chapters on A. Bertram Chandler and Wynne Whiteford); the influence of the New Wave (with subchapters on David Rome, Lee Harding, John Baxter, and Jack Wodhams); the growing importance of small presses, critical fanzines, worldcons, and workshops in the 1970s and 1980s (with full chapters on George Turner and Damien Broderick); and broad international recognition following Aussiecon II in 1985 (with a full chapter on Greg Egan). While discussions of individual writers tend toward plot summary, there is a fair amount of history of Australian SF publishing, fan activity, and criticism and scholarship, lending the book somewhat greater value as a reference than as a thematically coherent literary history.

*9-31.   Bleiler, Everett F. **Science-Fiction, the Early Years**. Kent State Univ. Press, 1991.

With some 2,475 entries, this massive compilation describes more than 3,000 novels, stories, plays, dime novels, boys' books, utopian fictions, future-war tales, and the like (as well as influential works of nonfiction such as Henry George's *Progress and Poverty* and Madame Blavatsky's *The Secret Doctrine*), which define the prehistory of science fiction from ancient Greece through the 1930s. Amazingly, Bleiler does not rely on secondary sources, as have so many historians of early SF, but has actually read the titles he describes and is able to relate them to one another and to later trends in SF, while identifying a number of themes that have long since died out. Covering a wide variety of texts, Bleiler's study is one of the most impressive achievements of SF scholarship to date, and is both definitive and indispensable. Also annotated as [7-2].

Awards: *Locus*

*9-32. Bleiler, Everett F., and Richard J. Bleiler. **Science-Fiction: The Gernsback Years**. Kent State Univ. Press, 1998.

In their second monumental reference work following [9-31], the Bleilers set out to read, describe, and catalog by topic every single story, editorial, poem, and letter to the editor that appeared in the collective 345 issues of *Amazing* and its dozen or so chief rivals from 1926 through 1936—some 1,834 pieces in all, most of them fairly appalling, but which collectively provide as detailed and unvarnished a picture of modern SF's formative years as has been produced to date. To get a sense of what a vast and forgotten body of work this represents, consider the fact that fewer than 15 percent of the stories discussed here have *ever* been reprinted. A list of anthologizations is included, as is a "Motif and Theme Index"; author and story indexes; a number of charts that try (with limited success) to track the major motifs and formulas in the stories; a section on magazine histories that lists complete issue-by-issue contents (including letters and nonfiction pieces); separate listings for poetry, author's letters, and the original sources of stories that the pulps reprinted; a section on pulp art with discussions of a half-dozen major artists and a few black-and-white illustrations; a useful bibliography; and even an odd description of the science-fictional solar system of the 1930s. Some may argue that Bleiler's critical approach—a mixture of plot summary and structuralist motif-hunting—is inappropriately reductive to the kinds of discourse involved in these tales, and some pulp nostalgists may wince at the often blunt dismissals of most stories, but this remains one of the major indispensable works of SF scholarship. Also annotated as [7-3] and [13-26].

9-33. Blish, James. **The Tale That Wags the God**. Ed. by Cy Chauvin. Advent, 1987.

A posthumous collection of essays on a wide variety of topics, together with an extensive bibliography of Blish's work prepared by his widow, Judith L. Blish. Generally more thoughtful and theoretical than the commentary collected in his *Issue at Hand* volumes [9-12], the topics include the definition of SF, science and the arts in SF, modern music, James Branch Cabell, James Joyce, and Poul Anderson. Of particular interest are a long autobiographical piece and a conversation between Blish and Brian W. Aldiss.

9-34. Booker, M. Keith. **Monsters, Mushroom Clouds, and the Cold War: American Science Fiction and the Roots of Postmodernism, 1946–1964**. Greenwood, 2001.

Although largely concerned with SF films of the 1950s, Booker's Marxist-influenced analysis of several major authors of this period is often insightful and trenchant, arguing that such authors as Bester, Pohl and Kornbluth, Vonnegut, and especially Dick engaged major cultural issues in a manner that prefigured postmodernist approaches of the 1970s and later. He also offers an intelligent assessment of the more conventional conservative and liberal politics evident in the fiction of Heinlein and Asimov. The second half of the book deals primarily with SF films, including nuclear war movies, alien invasion stories, and monster movies, although little convincing effort is made to link these with the same cultural matrix that produced the far more interesting writers he discusses in the first two chapters.

9-35.   Bretnor, Reginald, ed. **Modern Science Fiction: Its Meaning and Its Future**. Coward-McCann, 1953. Recommended ed.: Advent, 1979 (2nd ed.).

Primarily of historical interest (as the first critical overview of SF to come from a mainstream publisher), Bretnor's collection includes pieces on the state of science fiction a half-century ago (by John W. Campbell, Jr., Anthony Boucher, and Don Fabun), its literary merit (by Fletcher Pratt, Rosalie Moore, and L. Sprague de Camp), and various philosophical issues (by Isaac Asimov, Arthur C. Clarke, Philip Wylie, Gerald Heard, and Bretnor himself). Of particular interest are Asimov's essay defining "social science fiction" and Boucher's account of SF's "ghettoization," a term that has remained common since. Bretnor edited a similar follow-up anthology in 1974, *Science Fiction, Today and Tomorrow* (Harper), with 15 essays by authors including Poul Anderson, Hal Clement, Anne McCaffrey, and Gordon R. Dickson on techniques of SF writing; Ben Bova, Frederik Pohl, and George Zebrowski on the state of the field; and Frank Herbert, Theodore Sturgeon, Alan E. Nourse, Thomas N. Scortia, and Bretnor on more philosophical matters. This second book is in many ways as dated as its predecessor, but is also of historical interest.

*9-36.   Brians, Paul. **Nuclear Holocausts: Atomic War in Fiction, 1895–1984**. Kent State Univ. Press, 1987.

Brians's definitive study includes a long essay on the theme of nuclear war in fiction (including mainstream works as well as SF), followed by an annotated bibliography of more than 800 stories and novels, together with a chronology, checklists, and detailed title and subject indexes. Brians's essay traces major themes associated with nuclear war fiction, but is necessarily rather synoptic in its treatment of individual works and is essentially a work of literary history rather than theory. His bibliography, which includes ephemeral works of survivalist fiction as well as SF and mainstream works, features admirably succinct and balanced annotations, and has been regularly updated on Brians's Web site, http://www.wsu.edu/~brians/nuclear/, which contains other related material as well. For more detailed treatment of the theme in American SF, see Martha Bartter, *The Way to Ground Zero: The Atomic Bomb in American Science Fiction* [9-25]; also Seed [9-174]. Also annotated as [7-10].

  Themes: War

9-37.   Brigg, Peter. **The Span of Mainstream and Science Fiction: A Critical Study of a New Literary Genre**. McFarland, 2002.

Brigg proposes a new term, "span fiction," to describe the growing number of works that seem to represent an intersection of science fiction and "mainstream" fiction, although his argument that such works constitute a separate genre is not always convincing and his emphasis is clearly more on mainstream writers using

SF tropes than on SF writers approaching the mainstream. Following an introductory chapter in which he develops his theory, Brigg devotes substantial chapters to Doris Lessing and Thomas Pynchon, followed by a chapter discussing works by Nadine Gordimer, Julian Barnes, John Fowles, John Updike, Lawrence Durrell, Don DeLillo, Margaret Atwood, and others; a shorter chapter touching upon more genre-based writers such as Christopher Priest, Ursula K. Le Guin, Philip K. Dick, J. G. Ballard, Samuel R. Delany, and Joanna Russ; and a brief conclusion reiterating his "proposal for the creation of a new genre." In general, Brigg's discussion of individual writers is more illuminating than his theoretical arguments. Compare Broderick, *Transrealist Fiction* [9-4], for a quite different view of what has sometimes been called "slipstream" fiction.

9-38. Broderick, Damien, ed. **Earth Is but a Star: Excursions Through Science Fiction to the Far Future**. Univ. of Western Australia Press, 2001.

A critical collection of 15 essays and 14 reprinted works of fiction by various authors, intended to illustrate and examine the theme of far-future societies in science fiction. Brian Stableford's characteristically encyclopedic overview of this theme provides a useful context for often very insightful critical essays by John Clute, Alice K. Turner, Yvonne Rousseau, Stanislaw Lem, Russell Blackford, and George Zebrowski on authors such as H. G. Wells, Cordwainer Smith, Gene Wolfe, Octavia Butler, Greg Egan, Dan Simmons, David Zindell, Jack Vance, and Broderick himself. Especially useful for its treatment of authors such as Egan and Simmons, who have almost certainly earned more critical attention than they have received.

Themes: Far Future

*9-39. Broderick, Damien. **Reading by Starlight: Postmodern Science Fiction**. Routledge, 1995.

A series of essays, some of which originally appeared in journals such as *Foundation* and *The New York Review of Science Fiction*, focusing largely on the postmodern theory and practice of SF. Broderick begins with a brief discussion of SF history and early definitions, then turns to theoretical attempts to delimit SF as a genre, as a mode, and finally as a kind of megatext or modal system. The latter suggests certain of Delany's critical positions, and Delany becomes the primary focus of the second part of the book. Broderick offers informed critiques of Delany's theories, connecting them with Delany's multileveled fictions, though detailed discussions of other SF works are rare. SF is not a genre, according to Broderick, but a "species of storytelling native to a culture undergoing the epistemic changes implicated in the rise and supersession of technical-industrial modes of production, distribution, consumption and disposal." The most useful part of Broderick's definition is a list of SF characteristics—"metaphoric strategies" and "metonymic tactics," the foregrounding of objects and icons from a communal "mega-text," and a de-emphasis on "fine writing" and subjectivity. Though sometimes densely written, this is a key work by one of the genre's most accomplished writer-theorists to emerge since Delany, to whose critical work Broderick invites comparison.

9-40.   Broderick, Damien. **Transrealist Fiction: Writing in the Slipstream of Science**. Greenwood, 2000.

Borrowing the term "transrealism" from Rudy Rucker, who defines it as "writing about your immediate perceptions in a fantastic way," Broderick broadens the term to include "writing the fantastic from the standpoint of your richly personalized reality," then further expands the scope of his inquiry to include more traditional works of SF (to establish context) and "alternatives" to the transrealist or "slipstream" option (such as the work of Greg Egan). For the most part, though, Broderick offers intelligent and insightful readings of major authors who have come to be associated with "slipstream" writing from both sides of the SF–mainstream divide, such as Rucker, Philip K. Dick, J. G. Ballard, John Barth, and Kurt Vonnegut, Jr., as well as less-commonly discussed writers such as Mary Doria Russell and Michael Swanwick. Arguing against what he views as an antihumanist trend in SF, Broderick builds a compelling case for this mode of writing as something distinct from either traditional SF or traditional fictions of character and perception. Compare Brigg [9-37].

9-41.   Broderick, Damien. **x, y, z, t: Dimensions of Science Fiction**. Borgo/Wildside, 2004.

Perhaps Broderick's most informal and eclectic book of essays and reviews (although it is organized into chapters to give the appearance of a monograph), this wide-ranging collection includes original and revised pieces ranging from general rhetorical defenses of science fiction and examinations of seldom-discussed themes (such as the fractured self) to individual pieces on works by less-discussed or recent writers including Michael Marshall Smith, Jamil Nasser, John Barnes, Wil McCarthy, John C. Wright, Cory Doctorow, George Turner, and John Clute. Broderick's approach here is less rigorously theoretical than in his earlier critical works, and includes some entertainingly acerbic comments on "classic" SF as well as appreciations of what he regards as the more intriguing recent developments in the field.

9-42.   Budrys, Algis. **Benchmarks: Galaxy Bookshelf**. Southern Illinois Univ. Press, 1985.

As reviewer for *Galaxy* magazine from 1965 to 1971, Budrys established himself as one of the field's most perceptive and influential "in-house critics," as he described himself. His reviews, covering some 161 books, not only provide an overview of a volatile period in SF history but also contribute an important chapter to an informal documentary history of the field that includes review collections by Knight, Blish, and Spinrad. Though some of the reviews or judgments seem dated—which Budrys acknowledges in occasional notes added to this edition—the comments on the techniques and ideas of the genre are still valid. An introduction by Catherine McClenehan provides a perceptive overview of Budrys's criticism, and Frederik Pohl, Budrys's former editor, adds a brief memoir. An index has also been added.

Awards: *Locus*

9-43.   Budrys, Algis. **Outposts: Literatures of Milieux**. Borgo, 1997.

Five essays, one quite long, from sources as diverse as university quarterlies and a neighborhood gathering in Budrys's hometown of Evanston, consider such questions as definitions of science fiction, its relation to the mainstream, the importance of setting, the influences of production processes on SF texts, and Asimov (proposing *Pebble in the Sky* as his best novel). The two most important pieces are "Nonliterary Influences on Science Fiction," arguing the need for close bibliographical criticism of magazine SF, and "Paradise Charted," a lively overview of SF history that, although somewhat dated (it originally appeared in 1980 and ends with the advent of the New Wave), proposes a view of SF as largely a set of writing strategies. Together with another essay, "Literatures of Milieux," it provides a coherent and witty writer's view of the field.

9-44.   Bukatman, Scott. **Terminal Identity: The Virtual Subject in Post-modern Science Fiction**. Duke Univ. Press, 1993.

An ambitious, broadly interdisciplinary, and sometimes densely theoretical attempt to trace the disappearance of the traditional narrative "subject" in the face of new technologies. "Terminal identity" (a term borrowed from William S. Burroughs) is defined as "a transitional state produced at the intersection of technology and narration," and is discussed in terms of works by Gibson, Sterling, Ballard, Dick, Tiptree, Zelazny, Bernard Wolfe, Greg Bear, Vernor Vinge, Neal Stephenson, and others. Bukatman draws heavily on theorists from McLuhan to Baudrillard, and devotes somewhat less attention to fiction than to a variety of postmodern expressions in media: film, TV music, comics, video art, computer games and simulations, virtual reality, and alternative journalism. A professor of film, he seems most comfortable in that arena. Although he provides few extended readings of specific SF works, the complex cultural context in which he locates them is provocatively presented and well-documented. Compare McCaffrey's *Storming the Reality Studio* [9-127].

9-45.   Butler, Andrew M. **The Pocket Essential Cyberpunk**. Pocket Essentials, 2000.

A quite brief introduction and guide to cyberpunk fiction (with a chapter on film), beginning with an overview of the movement's literary antecedents (ranging from Raymond Chandler to William Burroughs to Philip K. Dick), its "core" authors (William Gibson and Bruce Sterling), other authors long associated with the movement (such as Pat Cadigan and Rudy Rucker), and later writers related in varying degrees to the movement (such as Neal Stephenson and Gwyneth Jones). Less a theoretical study than a general guidebook, the volume offers relatively few dramatic insights, but is a competent and evenhanded overview that offers a reasonable view of the parameters of the movement and helpful comments on individual texts. A bibliography is included.

Themes: Cyberpunk

9-46.   Carter, Paul A. **The Creation of Tomorrow: Fifty Years of Magazine Science Fiction**. Columbia Univ. Press, 1977.

A historian as well as an occasional SF author, Carter provides a knowledgeable and witty overview of the major themes and preoccupations of magazine SF from 1919 through the 1950s, including such topics as moon rockets, interplanetary romances, time machines, Hitler and fascism, evolution, dystopia and utopia, post-holocaust tales, and the role of women in SF. By focusing on magazine fiction—which defined the genre much more than novels did during most of this period—and by treating the historical background with informed sophistication, Carter has produced a highly readable and essential counterpoint to the more novel-based histories of the field. His treatment of the World War II period is especially informative. Compare Mike Ashley's *The Time Machines* [9-10].

Awards: Eaton

9-47.   Chapman, Edgar L., and Carl B. Yoke, eds. **Classic and Iconoclastic Alternate History Science Fiction**. Edwin Mellen Press, 2003.

Thirteen original essays, plus an introduction and bibliography, originally planned as a special issue of a journal. Chapman's introduction provides the only theoretical or taxonomic overview of the alternate history motif, and the general focus of the collection is on literary history rather than theory. Essays include Joe Sanders on Murray Leinster and John Taine, Yoke on "Sarban" (John Wall), William Hardesty on the recurrent theme of Nazis in alternate history fiction, Howard Canaan on Philip K. Dick, Olena Saciuk on Robert Silverberg, Martha Bartter on Robert Coover, Thomas Shippey on Kingsley Amis, Karen Hellekson on Joanna Russ, Steven Kagle on Orson Scott Card, Claire-Antoinette Lindenlaub on Pierre Thullier, Chapman on Heinlein and John Crowley, and Darren Harris-Fain on comics and graphic novels. As is almost inevitable in such collections by a variety of contributors, the coverage is somewhat piecemeal and the quality of the contributions uneven, but several of the essays, such as Shippey's and Hardesty's, offer useful general observations on the appeal of this theme as well as trenchant analyses of individual works. A selective bibliography includes both fiction and nonfiction, but is far from definitive. Compare Hellekson [9-93].

Themes: Alternate Worlds

9-48.   Clareson, Thomas D. **Many Futures, Many Worlds: Theme and Form in Science Fiction**. Kent State Univ. Press, 1977.

One of the first books of SF criticism to be reviewed in *The New York Times,* this collection of 14 essays (12 by academic critics and one each by Stanley Schmidt and Samuel R. Delany) helped define some of the major issues that accompanied academic criticism's "discovery" of the genre. Delany's essay also appears in his *The Jewel-Hinged Jaw* [9-65], and three of the academic essays discuss topics that were later expanded into books by their authors: S. C. Fredericks, Gary K. Wolfe, and Patricia Warrick. Other essays still of interest are those by Thomas L. Wymer, Thomas D. Clareson, Robert Canary, and Beverly Friend.

9-49. Clareson, Thomas D., ed. **SF: The Other Side of Realism: Essays on Modern Fantasy and Science Fiction**. Bowling Green, 1972.

Produced in recognition of the first 10 years of the MLA Seminar on Science Fiction and the founding of the Science Fiction Research Association, this collection of 26 essays still retains much of its interest. Problems of definition are addressed by Judith Merril, Julius Kagarlitski, Samuel R. Delany, and Lionel Stevenson; individual works or authors are discussed by Brian Aldiss, Norman Spinrad, Willis McNelly, Bruce Franklin, Richard D. Mullen, and Franz Rottensteiner; themes are explored by Stanislaw Lem and I. F. Clarke; and film is covered by Richard Hodgens, Robert Plank, and Alex Eisenstein. Further evidence of the collection's substance is that no fewer than seven of the contributors went on to receive Pilgrim Awards.

*9-50. Clareson, Thomas D. **Some Kind of Paradise: The Emergence of American Science Fiction**. Greenwood, 1985.

The most comprehensive narrative history of American science fiction of the period 1870–1930, this well-documented study is a companion piece to Clareson's bibliography *Science Fiction in America, 1870s–1930s* [7-13]. Beginning with an overview of the Gothic influence in American SF, Clareson devotes chapters to the future-war motif, the growing celebration of science and scientists, utopianism and catastrophism, the imaginary voyage, and the interplanetary romance. Throughout, he remains sensitive to issues of interest to contemporary readers, such as portrayals of women and Native Americans, and often cites the relationships of texts under discussion with relevant European fiction and modern descendants. Though occasionally simplistic in its treatment of historical contexts, the books fills a useful chapter in American literary history.

    Awards: Eaton

9-51. Clareson, Thomas D. **Understanding Contemporary American Science Fiction: The Formative Period (1926–1970)**. Univ. of South Carolina Press, 1990.

A popular survey prepared as part of a series of monographs on "Understanding Contemporary American Literature." Except for a cursory overview of the period from 1926 to 1950 in the first chapter, the book is entirely a history of American SF of the 1950s and 1960s. The authors covered in greatest detail are Simak, Bradbury, Vonnegut, Pohl, Bester, Sturgeon, Clement, Anderson, Blish, Asimov, Leiber, Dick, Herbert, Pangborn, Disch, Spinrad, Vance, Cordwainer Smith, Delany, Zelazny, and Silverberg. Women's SF is treated almost peremptorily, and some publishing history is offered by way of context. A competent account, with notes and bibliography, of the more-or-less standard view of the period; an interesting contrast is Malzberg's more opinionated *The Engines of the Night* [9-123].

9-52.   Clareson, Thomas D., and Thomas L. Wymer (Vol. 3 only), eds. **Voices for the Future: Essays on Major Science Fiction Writers**. Bowling Green, Vol. 1, 1976; Vol. 2, 1979; Vol. 3, 1983.

Intended as a more detailed follow-up to *SF: The Other Side of Realism*, this series consists of original essays covering major writers whose work is frequently assigned in classrooms. In the first volume, all the authors covered except Vonnegut began their careers before World War II: Williamson, Stapledon, Simak, Asimov, Heinlein, Sturgeon, Bradbury, Kuttner, Moore, and Clarke. The second volume covers eight authors who began in the 1950s and 1960s: Reynolds, Farmer, Ballard, Silverberg, Walter Miller, Le Guin, Brunner, and Zelazny. The third volume broadens its scope to include fantasy and covers Knight, Cordwainer Smith, Gene Wolfe, Mervyn Peake, Frederik Pohl, C. S. Lewis, Delany, and Disch. Though some material is superseded by more extensive studies of the authors covered, much remains valuable.

9-53.   Clark, Stephen R. **How to Live Forever: Science Fiction and Philosophy**. Routledge, 1995.

Oriented more as a guide to science fiction for philosophers and students rather than the other way round, this study focuses particularly on the immortality theme, arguing that SF can provide an arena for experimental thought without the constraints of formal philosophical procedure. "Immortality" here includes resurrection, disembodiment, mind transmission, reincarnation, and technological or medical means of life extension. Among the authors discussed are Arthur C. Clarke, Frank Herbert, Algis Budrys, Frederick Pohl, Jack Williamson, Larry Niven, William Gibson, and Colin Wilson, though in most cases the works are treated as dramatized thought experiments, and more thorough critical discussions of the works as literature, or as part of the broader science fictional dialogue on these issues, are limited. Still, the book provides a more sustained argument than the much earlier eclectic essay collections edited by Fred Miller and Nicholas D. Smith (*Thought Probes: Philosophy Through Science Fiction*, 1981), Robert E. Myers (*The Intersection of Science Fiction and Philosophy*, 1983), and Michael Philips (*Philosophy and Science Fiction*, 1984). Compare Yoke and Hassler, *Death and the Serpent* [9-207], and Slusser, Rabkin, and Westfahl, *Immortal Engines* [9-228].

Themes: Immortality

9-54.   Clarke, Arthur C. **Greetings, Carbon-Based Bipeds! Collected Essays, 1934–1998**. Ed. by Ian T. Macauley. St. Martin's, 1999.

A misleadingly titled (the earliest piece dates from 1942, the last from 1999, and the selection is far from comprehensive) collection of some 110 short essays—many less than a page in length, and some of which are actually expository passages from novels or excerpts from Clarke's 1989 autobiography

Astounding Days [10-43/46]. Another two dozen appeared in earlier nonfiction collections. Readers seeking significant insights into Clarke's fiction or SF in general are likely to be disappointed, although as a primary source for Clarke's famous prognostications (such as his 1945 paper on communications satellites) and apothegms ("When a distinguished but elderly scientist states that something is possible he is almost certainly right. When he states that something is impossible, he is very probably wrong."), it is of some value to researchers.

9-55.   Clarke, I. F. **The Pattern of Expectation: 1644–2001**. Basic Books, 1979.

An informed and well-illustrated scholarly study of future speculation from the 18th century to modern SF. Like Berger and Walsh, Clarke traces the shift from technological and scientific optimism to utopian visions, but his real strength is in portraying earlier historical visions of tomorrow. A comparable study, less focused on fictional texts, is Fred Polak's *The Image of the Future* (1961); more similar is W. H. G. Armytage's *Yesterday's Tomorrows: A Historical Survey of Future Societies* (1968). Clarke's *Tale of the Future* [7-14] is a companion bibliography.

*9-56.   Clarke, I. F. **Voices Prophesying War: Future Wars, 1763–3749**. Oxford Univ. Press, 1992.

A revision and updating of Clarke's classic 1966 *Voices Prophesying War: 1763–1984*, this work remains the standard history of future-war literature, although Clarke's coverage of more recent material is spotty compared with the authoritative treatment of pre-World War I works. Beginning with a survey of the period 1763–1871, Clarke then devotes a chapter to *The Battle of Dorking*, which he convincingly establishes as a benchmark text for this subgenre, and treats science and politics from 1880 to 1914 in the next two chapters. A heavily revised fifth chapter and a new sixth chapter attempt to bring coverage to the present, and a chronological checklist and index round out the volume (though both prove to be somewhat unreliable when dealing with more recent texts). While Clarke's treatment of nuclear war adds little to that of Brians [9-36] or Bartter [9-25], his work as a whole remains one of the core texts of SF historical scholarship.

   Themes: War

9-57.   Clute, John. **Look at the Evidence: Essays and Reviews**. Serconia, 1995.

At nearly three times the length of Clute's earlier collection *Strokes*, which covered 20 years of criticism, this volume covers only the five years 1987–1992, and includes nearly all of Clute's critical writing of this period, virtually unedited except for occasional chronological rearrangements and later interpolations. An introductory section (including Clute's Pilgrim Award Acceptance speech) is followed by a year-by-year survey and a final chapter on individual writers. Each year's chapter begins with a roundup essay followed by reviews from venues as various as *Interzone*, the *Washington Post*, the *New York Review of Science Fic-*

tion, and the *Times Literary Supplement.* But the book can't really be approached as a simple chronicle of the years in SF, since coverage depends on review assignments, and a fair amount of non-SF is discussed as well. Clute is the field's most provocative critic, and a demanding scholar as well; his review, for example, of the Panshins' *The World Beyond the Hill* [9-144], which he describes as a "Whig history" of SF, elegantly dismantles the book's callowness while recognizing its value as raw scholarship on important texts.

Awards: *Locus*

9-58.   Clute, John. **Scores: Reviews, 1993–2003**. Beccon, 2003.

Clute's third collection includes 127 reviews and essays covering nearly 200 books. As with his earlier collections, the intent is less to provide a comprehensive overview of SF or fantasy during the decade covered than to explore ideas occasioned by those reviews, some of which concern comparatively minor works. Clute was perhaps the first reviewer to gain a substantial critical reputation *as a reader* of SF, not as a fan, author, or academic, yet he is a meticulous scholar and he reserves his impatience for work that appears to him sloppy or misguided, such as a flawed scholarly edition of Wells's *Island of Dr. Moreau.* When he does deal with a writer through several reviews—Peter Ackroyd, Gene Wolfe, William Gibson, and a few others—he can offer a clearer definition of an author's cultural space than almost any other critic. The book also helps illuminate some of the highly original critical terms—"instauration fantasy," "face of story," and "polder"—that Clute invented for his *Encyclopedia of Fantasy* [7-33].

9-59.   Clute, John. **Strokes: Essays and Reviews, 1966–1986**. Serconia Press, 1988. Introduction by Thomas M. Disch.

With the exception of an essay on Robert Aickman written for a reference book and a short piece on the film *Them,* all 19 pieces collected here originally appeared as reviews. Clute is among the most acerbic and widely read of SF critics, and his strong opinions and energetic prose make this a stimulating update to a somewhat similar collection from an earlier era, Knight's *In Search of Wonder* [9-107]. The pieces collected here, with introductions and occasional interpolations added for this edition, cover some 60 authors, with somewhat more extended treatment given to Blish, Aldiss, and Gene Wolfe. An insightful and highly readable overview of the period covered.

9-60.   Cogswell, Theodore R., ed. **PITFCS: Proceedings of the Institute for Twenty-First Century Studies**. Advent, 1992. Introduction by Algis Budrys.

From April 1959 through December 1962, SF writer Cogswell used this mock-pretentious title (there was no Institute, and these are not "proceedings") for his "fanzine for professionals," designed initially to encourage debate about forming an SF writers' organization. This large, well-indexed volume assembles the entire run of the magazine (except for one apparently scurrilous issue), and features often lengthy contributions from most of the major SF figures of the day—including Kurt Vonnegut, Kingsley Amis, and Hugo Gernsback—on topics ranging from problems with editors to controversial books such as Heinlein's *Starship Troopers*. As a clearinghouse for writers, PITFCS offered a wealth of critical comment, as well as a detailed history of the issues that eventually led to the founding of the Science Fiction Writers of America. A final 1979 issue—17 years late, long after the SFWA had been formed—lends poignancy to the lost era portrayed here. An invaluable resource in SF history, and a useful companion piece to Blish's *The Issue at Hand* [9-12] and Knight's *In Search of Wonder* [9-107].

9-61.   Davies, Philip John, ed. **Science Fiction, Social Conflict and War**. Manchester Univ. Press, 1990.

A collection of intelligent and informed essays exploring the ways in which SF has examined—and might examine—major contemporary issues of social conflict and international relations. Contributors include Jacqueline Pearson on sexual politics, Edward James (with two essays) on racism and violent revolution as portrayed in American SF, Alasdair Spark on SF and the Vietnam War, H. Bruce Franklin on the ideology of the American superweapon (explored more fully in his *War Stars* [9-80]), and Martha Bartter and Paul Brians on aspects of nuclear war fiction (also treated in more detail in their books). Many of the essays focus on fictional strategies and methods, and all demonstrate a firm grasp not only of relevant fiction, but of the broader social issues as well.

Themes: War

9-62.   De Paolo, Charles. **Human Prehistory in Fiction**. McFarland, 2003.

Despite its title, this is not a monograph on fictional works depicting prehuman or prehistoric societies, but rather an examination of how a number of authors, mostly SF, have expressed or reacted to then-current scientific theories on evolution and paleoanthropology. The study is organized according to evolutionary stages of human development rather than according to any thematic or chronological arrangement of the works discussed, and thus although a wide variety of texts are discussed, often with insight concerning the authors' attitudes toward science, the intellectual context of these works is sometimes unclear. Among the authors prominently discussed are Wells, Verne, Edgar Rice Burroughs, William Golding, Pierre Boulle, Jean Auel, and Rosny aîné.

Themes: Evolution

9-63.   del Rey, Lester. **The World of Science Fiction, 1926–1976: The History of a Subculture**. Ballantine and Garland, 1979.

Despite its title, this history of American commercial SF does not focus in any significant way on the "subculture" of fans and writers during SF's formative years, but instead is an opinionated and very informal survey, divided into 12-year periods, of what the author regards as key works from the periods in question. Offering little in the way of context, broader critical perspective, or discussion of international science fiction, the book is of primary interest when viewed as an example of a significant insider's view of the field's development. As a more or less "official" representation of the perspective of that generation of writers who helped shape American popular SF, it is generally less balanced and comprehensive than James Gunn's *Alternate Worlds* [9-86], which covers much of the same territory, and is far less complete as a general history than Aldiss and Wingrove's *Trillion Year Spree* [9-4] or James's *Science Fiction in the Twentieth Century* [9-99].

9-64.   Delany, Samuel R. **The American Shore: Meditations on a Tale of Science Fiction by Thomas M. Disch—Angouleme**. Dragon Press, 1978.

By devoting more than 200 pages of close analysis to a 20-page story (which appears as part of Disch's novel *334*), Delany has produced the most detailed deconstruction of a single SF text to date. Written at the height of Delany's pre-occupation with European structuralism and semiotics, the analysis attempts to identify the varying "discourses" of the story by dividing it into some 287 lexical units; some, but not all, of these discourses reflect Delany's notion that SF can be characterized by its unique use of language. Of interest primarily to scholars of critical theory, the book represents an extreme application of techniques apparent in some of Delany's other criticism and in Christine Brooke-Rose's *A Rhetoric of the Unreal* (1981).

*9-65.   Delany, Samuel R. **The Jewel-Hinged Jaw: Notes on the Language of Science Fiction**. Dragon Press, 1977.

Thirteen essays, revised from their appearances in various anthologies and journals between 1966 and 1976, plus one original essay on reading Le Guin's *The Dispossessed*. After an opening "Letter to a Critic," Delany describes his language-based approach to SF in three general essays (one more in the form of an extended meditation), then deals with technical concerns of plot, character, and storytelling, and focuses in individual pieces on works by Disch, Zelazny, Russ, and Le Guin. An "autobiographical postscript" provides a context for his experience with SF, anticipating the more extended autobiographical material in *The Motion of Light on Water* (1988; rev. ed. 1990).

9-66.   Delany, Samuel R. **Silent Interviews: On Language, Race, Sex, Science Fiction, and Some Comics**. Wesleyan Univ. Press, 1994.

A collection of 10 written interviews (that is, written responses to written questions, or reworked from transcripts) plus one interview by Delany of composer Anthony Davis and one "conducted" by Delany's own critical alter ego K. Leslie Steiner), covering the decade 1983–1993. When the interviewer is a perceptive critic familiar with Delany's work, such as Takayuki Tatsumi (who has two interviews) or a joint interview by Larry McCaffrey and Sinda Gregory, there is a sense of real engagement, but there is also some repetition—for example, Delany's familiar argument that SF is a way of reading rather than a genre in the traditional sense recurs a number of times. Delany offers a cutting critique of "true" versus "academic" versions of SF history; argues persuasively that SF criticism has been sidetracked into debates over unattainable definitions or catalogues of generic conventions; makes trenchant observations about the New

Wave (which he regards as "anti-theoretical" and in many ways conservative), feminist SF, and cyberpunk; and offers some telling personal reminiscences.

9-67.   Delany, Samuel R. **Starboard Wine: More Notes on the Language of Science Fiction**. Dragon Press, 1984.

Ten essays, plus an introduction and three letters to *Science-Fiction Studies*, deal with major writers and theoretical questions. Two of the author essays, "Heinlein" and "Sturgeon," originally appeared as introductions to Gregg Press reprints of novels by these authors; the others concern Russ and Disch. Of the more theoretical essays, the most important are *"Dichtung* and Science Fiction," which proposes an ideal SF class; "Science Fiction and 'Literature,'" which continues Delany's exploration of the unique use of language in the genre; and "Reflections on Historical Models," which concerns problems in writing SF history. An influential and provocative book, far more accessible than *The American Shore* [9-64].

9-68.   Disch, Thomas M. **The Dreams Our Stuff is Made Of: How Science Fiction Conquered the World**. Free Press, 1998.

In a personal, free-ranging, and acerbic commentary, quite controversial at the time of its publication, Disch says he "provides a key to the allegories of science fiction and chronicles the genre's impact on American and, eventually, global, culture," though many readers might find that impact broadly overstated. In his opening chapter alone, Disch touches upon Oliver North, Reagan, the UFO cult, ancient astronauts, and Afrocentrism, and later connects the genre to Japanese terrorism, Scientology, Newt Gingrich, and white supremacist movements. Arguing that SF relates to a long American tradition of tall tales and that Poe is its true precursor, Disch devotes chapters to space travel, nuclear war fiction, *Star Trek* and media, feminist SF, religion, military SF, and aliens—though each of these chapters segues into unexpected directions. Cast in a deliberately polemical tone that often seems to echo familiar literary arguments against SF, the book is nevertheless fiercely intelligent, and offers insightful commentary on a range of works and authors, including Wells, Dick, Heinlein, Haldeman, Russ, Card, and *The Norton Book of Science Fiction*. Compare Malzberg's *Engines of the Night* [9-123].
    Awards: Hugo, *Locus*

9-69.   Donawerth, Jane L. **Frankenstein's Daughters: Women Writing Science Fiction**. Syracuse Univ. Press, 1997.

Rather than attempting a general history or seeking to build a canon, Donawerth draws on the work of earlier feminist historians (Wolmark, Le Fanu, Barr) in a study focusing on the means by which women writers have responded to the constraints of the male-centered genre, which she sees as prefigured in Mary Shelley's novel. A section on "Utopian Science" examines how authors such as Octavia Butler, Joan Slonczewski, and Naomi Mitchison have questioned traditional notions of science, while a second section, "Beautiful Alien

Monster-Women—BAMs," deals with the women-as-aliens theme as addressed by a wide variety of authors including Marge Piercy, Rebecca Ore, C. J. Cherryh, and Phyllis Gotlieb. The final and most original section, "Cross-Dressing as a Male Narrator," argues that women writers have used male narrative voices for subversive ends; authors discussed include Cherry Wilder, Emma Bull, Suzette Haden Elgin, Cynthia Felice, and others. Donawerth's wide reading, her inclusion of less-discussed authors, and her focus on narrative strategies rather than general overviews make this one of the more insightful and focused second-generation studies of women SF writers.

Themes: Women in SF

9-70.   Donawerth, Jane L., and Carol Kolmerten, eds. **Utopian and Science Fiction by Women: Worlds of Difference**. Syracuse Univ. Press, 1994.

Twelve essays trace the development of utopian writing by women since the 17th century, including discussions and descriptions of relatively little-known texts by Louisa May Alcott, Margaret Cavendish, Elizabeth Gaskell, and Rebecca Harding Davis. While the more historical essays offer a wealth of information on the earlier history of women writers of the fantastic, of particular relevance to science fiction studies are Donawerth's own contribution concerning women writers in the early pulp era, discussions of Naomi Mitchison by Sara Lefanu and of Octavia Butler by Michelle Erica Green, and the "frozen landscape" theme by Naomi Jacobs.

Themes: Utopias

9-71.   Dowling, David C. **Fictions of Nuclear Disaster**. Univ. of Iowa Press, 1987.

This is an informative study, broader in scope than Bartter [9-25] in that it covers international fiction, fiction not specifically concerned with the bomb, and such nongenre oddities as Raymond Briggs's *When the Wind Blows* and Yorick Blumenfeld's *Jenny: My Diary*. Dowling even finds anticipations of nuclear war in the work of Zola. Following six chapters in which he considers the bomb in fiction, the role of the scientist, depictions of nuclear war, postcatastrophe societies, and eschatological issues, Dowling sets up *A Canticle for Leibowitz* and *Riddley Walker* as "exemplary fictions" notable for their focus on language and signs. Well researched and annotated, although the bibliography lists only primary works and the index omits titles.

Themes: War

9-72.   Dunn, Thomas P., and Richard D. Erlich, ed. **The Mechanical God: Machines in Science Fiction**. Greenwood, 1982.

The inaugural volume in Greenwood's Contributions to the Study of Science Fiction and Fantasy series contains 18 essays grouped rather confusingly according to "Authors" (seven essays), "Children's Science Fiction" (one essay), "Attributes" (seven essays), and "Cyborgs" (three essays). Some of the individual essays are quite good, but the breadth of the topic and the spottiness of coverage limits the book's usefulness as an overview. Erlich and Dunn's *Clockwork Worlds: Mechanized Environments in Science Fiction* (Greenwood, 1983) is a companion volume featuring essays that focus on technological or machine-dominated environments more than on individual robots or computers. Erlich and Dunn also compiled *Clockworks: A Multimedia Bibliography of Works Useful for the Study of the Human/Machine Interface in SF* (Greenwood, 1993).

Themes: Machines

9-73. Easton, Tom. **Periodic Stars: An Overview of Science Fiction Literature in the 1980's and '90's.** Borgo, 1997.

Easton became the reviewer for *Analog* magazine in 1982, and here assembles some 250 short reviews from 1986 to 1992, with little subsequent editing and little in the way of the "overview" that the title promises. Since Easton's unpretentious reviews have never been intended as much more than purchasing guides for the magazine's readers, the book offers little serious critical commentary or thorough coverage, while featuring many reviews of minor or forgotten novels. As such, its value is primarily indirect and historical; *Analog* has long been one of the highest-circulating but little-honored magazines in the field, and to the extent to which Easton's reviews might reflect the interests of that readership, they can be of some interest to those wishing to trace the day-to-day history of science fiction during this period as chronicled in one of its most popular magazines.

9-74. Eshbach, Lloyd Arthur, ed. **Of Worlds Beyond: The Science of Science Fiction Writing.** Advent, 1964.

Originally published in 1947, this symposium on SF technique by the leading writers of that era is badly dated as a guidebook for aspiring writers, but is included here as a historic document of how the field viewed itself in the immediate postwar period, and of the compositional methods of some of its major writers. Heinlein offers the earliest argument for the term "speculative fiction"; Jack Williamson argues for the necessity of internal logic in fantasy; van Vogt gives advice on plot complications; de Camp discusses the use of humor; Edward E. Smith discusses the genesis of his space operas; and John Taine and John W. Campbell, Jr., discuss science in SF. Researchers on any of these writers should not overlook this absorbing—and oddly innocent—volume of "advice." (*The Science of Science Fiction Writing* is also the title of a writer's handbook published in 2000 by James Gunn [14-18], one of a number of far more timely such books for aspiring writers.)

9-75. Eshbach, Lloyd Arthur. **Over My Shoulder: Reflections on a Science Fiction Era.** Oswald Train, 1983.

The founder of the important early specialty publisher Fantasy Press and editor of *Of Worlds Beyond* recounts a personal history of SF book publishing from the 1930s to the 1950s, and includes a bibliography of books issued by the fan presses that dominated the field until the 1950s. A useful resource for the collector and the historian of SF publishing, but with little commentary on the literature.

An interesting contrast is the situation in England recounted in Harbottle and Holland [9-89].

9-76.   Featherstone, Mike, and Roger Burrows, eds. **Cyberspace/Cyberbodies/Cyberpunk: Cultures of Technological Embodiment**. Sage Publications, 1995.

This collection of 14 essays, which also appeared as a special issue of the journal *Body & Society,* may be of more interest as an indication of the impact of cyberpunk on general culture studies than as a series of discussions about SF literature, since only a few contributors show much awareness of prior SF scholarship. Although most of the essays make some reference to SF writers—most notably William Gibson, but also Bruce Sterling, Pat Cadigan, Rudy Rucker, and others—literature is not the central focus of the collection. Of particular note are David Tomas's essay on cyborg images in recent culture, Sadie Plant's essay on gender and cybernetics, and essays on film by Samantha Holland and Alison Landsberg. Compare Heuser [9-94], Wolmark's *Cybersexualities* [9-205].

Themes: Cyberpunk

9-77.   Fischer, William B. **The Empire Strikes Out: Kurd Lasswitz, Hans Dominik, and the Development of German Science Fiction**. Bowling Green, 1984.

A revised doctoral dissertation that provided one of the first accounts in English of the early history of German SF. Lasswitz's major novel, *Two Planets,* appeared in 1897; Dominik gained popularity following World War I and remained popular through the Nazi era. Dominik is probably rightly regarded by Fischer as the lesser SF writer, but his glorification of technology and Germany gives his works an ominous edge. A more complete view of pre-Nazi German SF can be found in Fisher [9-78].

9-78.   Fisher, Peter S. **Fantasy and Politics: Visions of the Future in the Weimar Republic**. Univ. of Wisconsin Press, 1991.

An informed and well-documented examination of 30 writers of Weimar Germany, grouped under "radical nationalists," "technological visionaries," and "socialist and pacifist visions." The first section reveals the growing nationalism of the pre-Nazi era, with swastikas appearing on book covers as early as 1921, while the second deals with fiction that most resembles conventional SF (including an extensive discussion of Thea Von Harbou, author of *Metropolis*). The third section concerns leftist writers who never achieved the popularity of the nationalists. Though few of the writers discussed are familiar to English-language readers, Fisher's is an important study of the potential misuses of SF, a rare view of a little-known chapter in its history. Compare Fischer.

9-79.   Foote, Bud. **The Connecticut Yankee in the Twentieth Century: Travel to the Past in Science Fiction**. Greenwood, 1990.

Foote argues that Twain's *Connecticut Yankee in King Arthur's Court,* by focusing on a traveler to the past who is determined to change it through technology, established a paradigm for a whole subgenre of SF. Foote does an excellent job of showing the importance of history to SF in general, and discusses a wide variety of works in chapters that are more substantial than their coy titles would indicate (for example, "Dear Old Dad and His Girl," "These Curious Strangers," "Innocents Abroad"). Although Foote does not claim to be definitive either in his text or his bibliography (there are some surprising omissions), he offers insightful treatments of familiar works by Bradbury and Jack Finney, as well as lesser-known texts by Haiblum and Kirk Mitchell. A clearly written and engrossing thematic study. Compare Westfahl, Slusser, and Leiby, *Worlds Enough and Time* [9-232].

Themes: Alternate Worlds

9-80. Franklin, H. Bruce. **War Stars: The Superweapon and the American Imagination**. Oxford Univ. Press, 1988.

Franklin is one of the few scholars to succeed in raising SF criticism to the level of political and social commentary, and in demonstrating that SF modes of thought have formed as well as reflected American social attitudes and policy. *War Stars is* a general cultural history of superweapon ideology, beginning with Robert Fulton and Thomas Edison and ending with Reagan's "Star Wars" campaign. He describes the rise of paranoid future-war stories between 1880 and 1917, the developing tradition of nuclear war fiction and film, the contribution of SF writers such as Bova and Pournelle to Reagan's "Star Wars" ideology, and even such works as Joseph Heller's *Catch-22* and Vonnegut's *Slaughterhouse-Five*. Although Bartter [9-25], Brians [9-36], and Seed [9-174] provide more extensive discussions of fiction, Franklin's book is crucial to understanding the historical impact of what might be called "science-fictional" thinking.

Themes: War

9-81. Fredericks, Casey. **The Future of Eternity: Mythologies of Science Fiction and Fantasy**. Indiana Univ. Press, 1982.

Familiar with both classical scholarship and SF, Fredericks offers a disciplined and coherent account of the frequently claimed relationships between SF, fantasy, and mythology. Following a discussion of the role of myths in major historical works—*Frankenstein, Dr. Jekyll and Mr. Hyde, The Time Machine, Last and First Men*—he explores creation myths, echoes of Norse mythology, the superman theme, and the "return to the primitive." The three major myths of SF are identified as man–machine, man–superman, and human–alien encounters. Fredericks offers unusual insights into authors as varied as Poul Anderson, de Camp, Dick, Delany, Farmer, Ellison, Leiber, van Vogt, Weinbaum, and Zelazny.

Themes: Mythology

*9-82. Freedman, Carl. **Critical Theory and Science Fiction**. Wesleyan Univ. Press, 2000.

Freedman's widely discussed and sometimes dense study is less an application of particular critical theories to works of science fiction than an argument that critical theory itself, as viewed from a largely Marxist perspective, bears significant rhetorical affinities with SF texts. He begins by developing definitions of both critical theory and science fiction, devotes his most heavily theoretical chapter to outlining what he regards as crucial relationships between them, and ends with extensive illustrative discussions of five prominent novels by Lem, Le Guin, Dick, Russ, and Delany, all published between 1961 and 1984. As this selection of texts might indicate, Freedman's view of science fiction is largely confined to the postmodernist canon, and he devotes some argument to dismissing from his definition a considerable body of work commonly regarded as significant to the genre's history, as well as to demonstrating how most other fiction fails to examine social and economic issues with the critical rigor of the best SF. Revisiting and to some extent revising Suvin's notions of "cognitive estrangement," Freedman offers meticulous and highly structured readings of the novels he has selected, and overall his study is perhaps the most significant Marxist heir to Suvin's original formulations in *Metamorphoses of Science Fiction* [9-189] even as it relies on a limited range of texts, a prescriptive tone, and a relatively narrow set of definitions to sustain itself.

9-83.   Garnett, Rhys, and R. J. Ellis, eds. **Science Fiction Roots and Branches: Contemporary Critical Approaches**. St. Martin's, 1990.

Eleven essays intended to show a variety of then-current critical approaches to SF. The historical section includes Darko Suvin on Morris's *News From Nowhere*, Stanislaw Lem on Wells's *The Time Machine*, and Garnett on *Dracula*. A second section includes Patrick Parrinder on scientists in SF, Jerzy Jarzebski on Lem, Tom and Alice Clareson on Wyndham, R. J. Ellis on Herbert's *Dune*, and Robert Philmus on Le Guin's *The Dispossessed*. The final section, on feminist criticism, includes Marleen Barr on Marge Piercy and Thomas Berger, Jenny Wolmark on Vonda McIntyre, and Anne Cranny-Francis on Suzy McKee Charnas. Individual essays are quite useful, but the book as a whole lacks structure or focus.

9-84.   Grayson, Sandra. **Visions of the Third Millennium: Black Science Fiction Novels**. Africa World Press, 2003.

One of the more significant developments in science fiction over the last couple of decades has been the emergence of an identifiable group of "African diaspora" writers (as identified in Sheree Thomas's two anthologies) and the concomitant introduction of African mythologies, themes, and narrative techniques into the genre. In the first sustained monograph on these topics, Grayson focuses on the lives and work of Octavia Butler, Tananarive Due (better known for her fantasy and horror fiction), Nalo Hopkinson, Samuel R. Delany, Steven Barnes, Charles R. Saunders, and even *Star Trek* alumnus LeVar Burton. Her focus is to introduce these authors and trace African, African American, and Caribbean themes in their work, rather than to construct a consistent theoretical argument about the nature of African diaspora speculative fiction. By far her most detailed analysis covers the work of Butler (who occupies four chapters); her treatment of the other best-known black SF writer, Delany, is by comparison slight, while writers such as Walter Mosley are not analyzed at all, though Barnes and Saunders receive more extended treatment than they have generally received. An important introductory work; compare Leonard's collection *Into Darkness Peering* [9-119].

*9-85. Greenland, Colin. **The Entropy Exhibition: Michael Moorcock and the British "New Wave" in Science Fiction**. Routledge, 1983.

A history of SF's most famous avant-garde movement, based on the author's 1980 Oxford doctoral dissertation. Moorcock is the central figure because it was his editorship of the British magazine *New Worlds* from 1964 to 1970 that defined the "New Wave," but Greenland also includes substantial discussions of two other key writers, Brian Aldiss and J. G. Ballard (all three authors are the subjects of more thorough book-length studies; see Chapter 10). In addition to a history of the magazine and these author studies, Greenland includes chapters on sex in SF, "anti-space" and "inner space" fiction, and stylistic theory and practice. He relates the topics knowledgeably to literary, psychological, and anthropological history, and provides what is close to the standard history of the topic.

Awards: Eaton

Themes: New Wave

9-86. Gunn, James E. **Alternate Worlds: The Illustrated History of Science Fiction**. Prentice-Hall, 1975.

A readable and concise popular history, lavishly illustrated with magazine covers (many in color) and photographs of authors and including lists of Hugo and Nebula awards through 1974, a short list of major themes and representative works, and a chronology. Like del Rey's *The World of Science Fiction* [9-63], the book reflects a kind of consensus view of the field held by many American writers of the postwar period, but Gunn is far more politic and balanced than del Rey. Nearly half the text recounts SF history prior to 1926, with individual chapters on Verne and Wells; later chapters focus on the pulps (with a predictable emphasis on Campbell's *Astounding*) and the 1950s SF boom. Coverage of post-1965 SF is slight. Since Gunn's avowed purpose is not a critical history such as that of Aldiss and Wingrove [9-4], relatively few texts are discussed in depth, and judgments tend to be bland and noncontroversial. Nevertheless, this is the closest thing the SF community of Gunn's generation has to an "official" history.

Awards: Special Hugo

9-87. Gunn, James E. **Inside Science Fiction: Essays on Fantastic Literature**. Borgo, 1992.

The only person to serve as president of both the Science Fiction Writers of America and the Science Fiction Research Association, Gunn consistently brings his dual perspective to these 18 essays, which originally appeared between 1971 and 1989. The first five essays deal with historical and autobiographical matters, the next four with academic questions and the teaching of SF, the next four with SF film and television (including an account of the TV movie and series adaptation of Gunn's *The Immortals*), and the final five with social and economic issues related to SF. Gunn's style is informal and reasonable, and his perspective is much the same as that of *Alternate Worlds* [9-86]. Also annotated as [13-7].

9-88.   Guthke, Karl S. **The Last Frontier: Imagining Other Worlds from the Copernican Revolution to Modern Science Fiction**. Cornell Univ. Press, 1990. Trans. of *Der Mythos der Neuzeit* (Bern, 1983) by Helen Atkins.

An ambitious attempt to trace the "plurality of worlds" theme—the idea that there may be other inhabited planets—from its origins in the Renaissance through late 19th-century SF. (The final chapter is on Lasswitz and Wells.) Despite the title, most of the "modern" SF Guthke discusses is treated somewhat cursorily in his introduction. Nevertheless, he views SF as the principal literary and popular expression of a pattern of mythical belief, which has at various times taken the form of theological, scientific, and philosophical debate. Thus he deals with a number of figures not directly connected with the history of SF narrative, as well as with familiar ancestors such as Campanella, Wilkins, Godwin, Cyrano de Bergerac, and Voltaire. Guthke's European perspective provides a broader context for the relevant chapters of Bailey [9-15], Philmus [9-148], and Alkon [9-5].
     Awards: Eaton

9-89.   Harbottle, Philip, and Stephen Holland. **Vultures of the Void: A History of British Science Fiction Publishing, 1946–1956**. Borgo, 1993.

A fascinating account of an appalling and relatively unexplored chapter in SF history: the postwar British pulp industry, which took advantage of the shortage of popular fiction brought on by paper rationing by issuing large amounts of subliterary genre paperbacks and magazines, usually based on American models and commissioned from poorly paid hack writers working under ridiculous deadlines. A few writers, such as John Russell Fearn, produced considerable bodies of work under these conditions, while more familiar names such as Clarke and Wyndham wrote for the American magazines of the time. Interpolated memoirs from Ted Carnell, Gordon Landsborough, E. C. Tubb, Kenneth Bulmer, and others lend authenticity to this strange history, which focuses more on the industry than on individual works. A valuable complement to more standard histories of the genre.

9-90.   Hartwell, David G. **Age of Wonders: Exploring the World of Science Fiction**. Walker, 1984. Recommended rev. ed.: Tor, 1996.

Hartwell is arguably the most influential SF book editor of the 1970s and 1980s, and his chatty general introduction to the field mixes a sophisticated insider's understanding with astute critical and academic judgments. Although occasionally self-indulgent, Hartwell's is one of the few guidebooks that does not get weighed down in a mechanical recitation of SF history. Following three chapters on aspects of SF's appeal and readership, he explores common myths about the genre (escapism, predictions of the future) and devotes individual chapters to fandom, the New Wave, and academic criticism. The 1996 edition updates the volume to the 1990s, and includes reading lists, a bibliography, a glossary of fan language, suggestions for developing a course in SF, and essays on hard SF, commercial fantasy, and editing the science fiction novel. More academic treatments of similar material may be found in Stableford's *Sociology of Science Fiction* [9-185] and Bacon-Smith's *Science Fiction Culture* [9-14], but Hartwell is more knowledgeable than either in his firsthand awareness of the American fan, writer, and publishing communities.

9-91. Hassler, Donald M., and Clyde Wilcox, eds. **Political Science Fiction**. Univ. of South Carolina Press, 1997.

A collection of 14 essays growing out of a special 1993 issue of the journal *Extrapolation*, in which four of the essays originally appeared, including Frederik Pohl's witty and acerbic lead essay on "The Politics of Prophecy." The rest of the volume is divided between more broadly theoretical pieces and essays focusing on particular works or political situations. The former include Neal Easterbrook's examination of rebellious colonies in works by Heinlein, Le Guin, and Delany; Clyde Wilcox's comparative political science analysis of several novels; Patrick Novotny's consideration of the politics of cyberpunk; Hassler's comparison of Swift's circle with that of the Futurians; and pieces on Wells, Le Guin, Piercy, and Herbert. In the more "applied" section, Ingrid Kreksch examines Latin American politics reflected in its SF; Everett Carl Dolman analyzes Heinlein's *Starship Troopers*; and three essays discuss political aspects of the various *Star Trek* series. Although uneven—both ideologically and historically—and heavily centered on American SF, the collection offers a number of useful perspectives and analyses.

Themes: Politics

*9-92. Hayles, N. Katherine. **How We Became Posthuman: Virtual Bodies in Cybernetics, Literature, and Informatics**. Univ. of Chicago Press, 1999.

Of the various trends in postmodernist cultural studies, the one that became most closely associated with SF scholarship during the 1990s involved the intersection of information theory and cultural expression. This intersection was pioneered in Donna Haraway's 1985 essay "A Cyborg Manifesto: Science, Technology, and Socialist-Feminism in the Late Twentieth Century." Hayles develops this exploration more thoroughly—and with a more thorough mastery of SF texts—than most other scholars in this area through her notion of "posthumanism," the complex of technological, social, and information science trends that in her view precipitates a radical rethinking of the nature of what it means to be human. In earlier works, she examined the literary and cultural impact of such scientific notions as field theory (*The Cosmic Web: Scientific Field Theories and Literary Strategies in the Twentieth Century*) and chaos theory (*Chaos Bound: Orderly Disorder in Contemporary Literature and Science*), but seldom dealt directly with SF. In *How We Became Posthuman*, she traces what she describes as the problem of "disembodiment" through cybernetic theory and through key SF texts, including Bernard Wolfe's *Limbo,* William Burroughs's *The Ticket that Exploded,* and novels by Greg Bear, Cole Perriman, Neal Stephenson, and Richard Powers. Of particular interest is her valuable and insightful treatment of Philip K. Dick's major novels of the 1960s, to which she devotes an entire chapter. Though conceptually dense and sometimes weak on the contextualization of the fiction under discussion, this is one of the more provocative and influential of the postmodernist discussions of SF as an expression of cultural anxieties. Compare Balsamo [9-17] and Featherstone and Burrows [9-76].

9-93.   Hellekson, Karen L. **The Alternate History: Refiguring Historical Time**. Kent State Univ. Press, 2001.

One of the first sustained studies of the alternate history theme, Hellekson's relatively brief work makes extensive use of historiographical theory in discussing works that range from story series (such as H. Beam Piper's "paratime police" and Poul Anderson's "Time Patrol") to more extended works ranging from Ward Moore's *Bring the Jubilee* to Gibson and Sterling's *The Difference Engine,* organized according to what Hellekson views as various subcategories of alternate history. While her insights on individual works in the light of such theorists as Hayden White and Paul Ricouer are often solid, there is little discussion of the contexts of the works in question, or of science fiction's developing internal dialogue concerning alternate history as a narrative technique. Nevertheless, in its own modest way, this is a pioneering study. Compare some of the essays in Westfahl, Slusser, and Leiby's *Worlds Enough and Time* [9-232].

Themes: Alternate Worlds

9-94.   Heuser, Sabine. **Virtual Geographies: Cyberpunk at the Intersection of the Postmodern and Science Fiction**. Editions Rodolpi, 2002.

One of a series of "postmodern studies" from the publisher, Heuser's well-researched study seems more comfortable with postmodern theorists (especially Lyotard) than with science fiction, although she has carefully buttressed her arguments with reference to a variety of early SF critical studies and standard histories. Following a lengthy introduction and chapters in which she seeks to trace the origins and provenance of the cyberpunk movement in popular culture, she offers extended discussions of the work of William Gibson, Pat Cadigan, and Neal Stephenson (though the latter is confined to *Snow Crash,* which Heuser views as "the last throes of cyberpunk"), leading to a series of concluding chapters in which she sees the movement as aspiring to "the virtual sublime" and prefiguring the cyborgian and posthuman concerns of "postmodern science." As with many such heavily theoretical studies, Heuser's readings of individual texts are more compelling than her broader generalizations, although her overview of cyberpunk history is useful. Oddly, the book lacks an index, but contains a timeline of cyberpunk history and an extensive bibliography. Compare Butler's *Pocket Essential Cyberpunk* [9-45].

Themes: Cyberpunk

9-95. Hillegas, Mark R(obert). **The Future as Nightmare: H. G. Wells and the Anti-Utopians**. Oxford Univ. Press, 1967.

Despite the considerable body of more recent scholarship on the topics he covers, Hillegas's pioneering text remains significant for having cogently defined the anti-utopian tradition and its connections to SF. In addition to Wells, Forster, Čapek, Zamiatin, Huxley, Orwell, and Lewis, Hillegas discusses Bradbury, Pohl and Kornbluth, Clarke, and Vonnegut. Compare Walsh [9-194].

Themes: Dystopias

9-96. Hollinger, Veronica, and Joan Gordon, eds. **Edging into the Future: Science Fiction and Contemporary Cultural Transformation**. Univ. of Pennsylvania Press, 2002.

Thirteen original essays (plus an introduction) intended to "examine science fiction's complex intersections with this transitory present moment," which the editors identify as postmodernism. The essays themselves are divided into three sections: "Genre Implosion," which includes Gary K. Wolfe on genre instability, Lance Olsen on rock 'n roll and SF, and Brooks Landon on "post-SF" film; "Imploded Subjects and Reinscripted Bodies," which includes essays by Jenny Wolmark and Rob Latham on posthuman themes, Wendy Pearson on hermaphroditic figures, Brian Attebery on Gwyneth Jones and James Morrow, and Roger Luckhurst on rage in SF; and "Reimagined Apocalypses and Exploded Communities," with examinations of apocalyptic, eschatological, and political themes by Veronica Hollinger, Joan Gordon, Gwyneth Jones, Brian Stableford, and Istvan Csicsery-Ronay. While the essays vary widely in approach and style, the collection provides a valuable overview of critical issues in the genre, and touches on a number of works and authors (Morrow, Stableford, Jones, Tepper) not usually addressed in academic studies of the genre.

9-97. Hume, Kathryn. **Fantasy and Mimesis: Responses to Reality in Western Literature**. Methuen, 1984.

A broad-ranging and highly intelligent argument for the proposition that the fantastic—including SF—represents a historically significant "countertradition" to mimesis in literature from the Icelandic sagas to the present. Rejecting the notion that fantasy constitutes a simple genre, Hume makes such a compelling case that the book should be consulted by anyone interested in SF theory and history, or the relation of SF to other modes of the fantastic. The authors discussed range from John Barth, Jorge Luis Borges, Thomas Pynchon, and Franz Kafka to Vonnegut, Calvino, Le Guin, Herbert, Heinlein, and Wells.

Awards: Eaton

*9-98. Huntington, John. **Rationalizing Genius: Ideological Strategies in the Classic American Science Fiction Short Story**. Rutgers Univ. Press, 1989.

Huntington's ambitious attempt to outline the fundamental ideologies of three decades of American SF by analyzing the stories in a single anthology—Volume I of *The Science Fiction Hall of Fame* edited by Robert Silverberg—is valuable chiefly for his intelligent and perceptive readings of such relatively unexamined "classics" as Tom Godwin's "The Cold Equations" or Kornbluth's "The Marching Morons." The implicit argument that an anthology tabulated by a single vote of SFWA members in 1968 can serve as a touchstone for the genre raises a number of problems, however, since the final selection was further skewed by choices made by the editor and since it necessarily ignores historical, editorial, and literary contexts. Huntington is aware of this, however, and relates each story to other relevant texts. His chapter on "Reading Popular Genres" is especially valuable. Informed readers will find Huntington's analyses often illuminating, although novices may occasionally be misled.

*9-99.   James, Edward. **Science Fiction in the Twentieth Century**. Oxford Univ. Press, 1994.

A clearly organized and written overview that displays the kind of broad-based international perspective we might expect from one of the leading British academic scholars of the field. James, winner of the 2004 Pilgrim Award, begins with an acute discussion of labels and categories, and moves on to two chapters of historical survey beginning in 1895 and taking us roughly through the end of the Campbell period in 1960. He makes the persuasive point that American and British SF diverged following the radically different experiences of the two nations in the First World War, and details what he calls the "victory" of American SF under Campbell. Using Clarke and Wyndham as examples, he shows how British SF of the fifties managed to respond to, and yet remain separate from, the American tradition. Before continuing his historical survey through the New Wave and the cyberpunks, James pauses to add two chapters on "Reading Science Fiction"—which addresses SF's relation with the mainstream, accusations of escapism, the sense of wonder, the satirical and romantic poles of SF, and reading strategies—and "The SF Community." Following a penultimate chapter on SF fandom and its fringe cults, James concludes with a discussion of the 1960s and after. He treats the rise of subgenres such as hard SF, fantasy, feminist SF, and of course cyberpunk. A final section on current trends notes the recent popularity of alternative histories and the recent spate of Mars novels. James is consistently even-tempered, and his coverage more balanced than that of Landon [9-110].

Awards: Eaton

9-100.   James, Edward, and Maxim Jakubowski, eds. **The Profession of Science Fiction**. Macmillan U.K., 1992.

A collection of 16 essays from a long series published originally in the journal *Foundation*, offering authors' own overviews of their work and careers. While a few are dated (five originally appeared before 1981) or were subsequently reprinted elsewhere (Jack Williamson's in his autobiography, and James Blish's in his *The Tale that Wags the God*), some are of unique historical value, such as Naomi Mitchison's account of her friendships with Olaf Stapledon and H. G. Wells. Other authors included are J. G. Ballard, Ursula Le Guin, David Brin,

Richard Cowper, D. G. Compton, Gene Wolfe, Richard Cowper, Michael Coney, M. John Harrison (who produces an odd mixture of autobiography and sophisticated literary theory), Gwyneth Jones, Richard Grant, and Pamela Sargent. Compare to Knight's *Hell's Cartographers* [10-168].

*9-101. James, Edward, and Farah Mendlesohn, eds. **The Cambridge Companion to Science Fiction**. Cambridge, 2003.

A collection of 20 essays, many by leading scholars and writers in the field, intended as a near-comprehensive overview of SF scholarship and critical theory, mostly English-language, at the beginning of the century. The essays are divided into three sections: History (with contributions by Brian Stableford, Brian Attebery, Damien Broderick, John Clute, Mark Bould, and Gary K. Wolfe); Critical Approaches (essays by Istvan Csiscery-Ronay, Veronica Hollinger, Andrew Butler, and Wendy Pearson); and Sub-Genres and Themes (essays by Gwyneth Jones, Joan Slonczewski and Michael Levy, Kathryn Cramer, Gary Westfahl, Andy Duncan, Edward James, Ken MacLeod, Helen Merrick, Elisabeth Anne Leonard, and Farah Mendlesohn). The History section includes not only chronological chapters, but a chapter on film and TV and one on SF editors; the Critical Approaches section covers Marxism, feminism, postmodernism, and queer theory; and the Sub-Genre section includes SF iconography, life sciences, hard SF, space opera, alternate history, utopias and dystopias, politics, gender, race and ethnicity, and religion. Most of the essays are well conceived and substantial, for the most part avoiding catalogues of titles and showing little sign of being written to fulfill a preconceived template. While this inevitably leads to some gaps, it also permits a wealth of original and individual insights, as in Mendlesohn's introduction and the essays by Clute, MacLeod, and Butler. An essential collection, supplemented by a selective chronology and bibliography, and a foreword by James Gunn.

*9-102. Jones, Gwyneth. **Deconstructing the Starships: Science, Fiction, and Reality**. Liverpool Univ. Press, 1999.

Eight essays and lectures and 20 reviews by one of the more astute author-critics to emerge from British SF in the 1990s. Jones's detailed and incisive reviews may be somewhat familiar to readers of *Foundation* and *The New York Review of Science Fiction*, but most of the essays here originally were delivered as papers at various conferences in England and constitute what is essentially a new work, approaching SF and fantasy from a refreshing angle that combines the working author's concern over the field's more arbitrary conventions with the views of an incisive feminist critic. Jones takes on topics such as language in SF and fantasy, what she calls the "science procedural" narrative, aesthetic problems in creating artificial worlds and alien beings, various epistemological problems involved in cyberspace fiction, and her abiding affection for Tolkien and Lewis despite their conservative ideologies. As a feminist writer, Jones devotes a good deal of attention to issues of gender and to women writers, but is far from an uncritical celebrant, pointing out the thinness of central characters in key works by Russ, Le Guin, and Charnas. Some of the essays, such as a projection of future leisure activities prepared for a British Telecom project, seem to wander away from the book's general focus, but most are rich with unexpected and original insights.

9-103. Ketterer, David. **Canadian Science Fiction and Fantasy**. Indiana Univ. Press, 1992.

In what is perhaps the definitive monograph on its subject, Ketterer offers a broad overview of English and French Canadian authors who have written SF or fantasy, although many of them (such as A. E. van Vogt and Gordon Dickson) spent much of their careers elsewhere, and Ketterer finally acknowledges that "Canadian-ness" is marginal to most of the major authors he discusses, which include Margaret Atwood, Phyllis Gotlieb, and Charles de Lint. The avowedly narrow focus of the study disguises some broadly useful insights—such as a distinction between "hermetic" and "consequential" imaginary worlds—and the treatment of French Canadian SF uncovers a surprisingly rich and little-known tradition. A very informative study, which is one of the first national histories of SF. (Another is Robert Mathews's *Japanese Science Fiction* [9-126].) A related essay collection is Andrea Paradis, ed., *Out of This World: Canadian Science Fiction and Fantasy Literature* (Quarry Press and National Library of Canada, 1995), a companion volume to an exhibiton at the National Library of Canada.

9-104. Ketterer, David. **New Worlds for Old: The Apocalyptic Imagination, Science Fiction, and American Literature**. Indiana Univ. Press, 1974.

In one of the first rigorous attempts to establish a theoretical context for science fiction, Ketterer argues that "apocalyptic" literature differs from both mimetic and fantastic literature by creating credible imaginary worlds that lead to the "metaphorical destruction" of the reader's real world. He sees this as a broad tradition in American literature (Poe, Melville, Charles Brockden Brown, Mark Twain), whose most significant modern manifestation is SF. Individual chapters treat Le Guin, Lem, Vonnegut, and several SF themes, with substantial discussion of works by Aldiss, Balmer and Wylie, John Boyd, Bradbury, Dick, Heinlein, Sturgeon, Jack London, Edward Bellamy, Walter M. Miller, Jr., and others. An influential work whose theoretical approach bears some comparison with that of Kathryn Hume [9-97].

9-105. Kilgore, De Witt Douglas. **Astrofuturism: Science, Race, and Visions of Utopia in Space**. Univ. of Pennsylvania Press, 2003.

"Astrofuturism" is essentially the familiar American dream of creating a better society through space exploration—as expressed in fiction, nonfiction, and popular media—but Kilgore, an African American English professor, finds in the movement a reflection of social, racial, and gender concerns as well. While this exceptionally well-written and well-researched study does not focus exclusively on science fiction, it provides a valuable context in which to approach authors concerned with promoting the space movement. Following a provocative introduction, Kilgore devotes a chapter each to David Lasser (an activist and an early editor of pulp SF magazines); such 1950s popularizers as Wernher von Braun and Willy Ley; Robert Heinlein (focusing heavily on his juveniles); Arthur C. Clarke; Gerard K. O'Neill; and Ben Bova (in what is certainly the most important critical discussion of this author to date). There is a final chapter touching upon such authors as Kim Stanley Robinson, Allan Steele, and Vonda McIntyre. Kilgore's exposition of the popular ideology of space flight as developed in the 1950s and earlier is fascinating, and his discussion of relevant fiction by the authors he cites is often insightful and original, as is his overall treatment of the themes of racial tolerance and technological utopianism. An unusual and worthwhile study.

Themes: Space Flight

9-106. Kitchin, Rob, and James Kneale, eds. **Lost in Space: Geographies of Science Fiction**. Continuum, 2002.

Twelve original essays, mostly by academic geographers, that seek to explore the uses of space (both geographical and figurative) in SF texts, and to inaugurate an academic dialogue between the disciplines of geography and science fiction studies. While the essays often cover territory familiar to SF scholars, they offer a number of useful new perspectives on the field. An interesting chapter by Barney Warf on the "contingent geographies" of alternate history is followed by essays focusing on the work of Neal Stephenson, J. G. Ballard, Marge Piercy, Kim Stanley Robinson, and science fiction film. Two of the most unusual and original approaches are those of Marcus A. Doel and David B. Clarke (titled "Motor Pirates, Time Machines, and Drunkenness on the Screen") and Sheila Hones, both of which expand considerably the notion of science fiction as a mode of cultural imagination. A rather odd collection, but one of the more interesting interdisciplinary engagements with the genre from an alternate academic perspective. (Similar collections of essays on SF by scholars from other disciplines have appeared—chemists, philosophers, political scientists, organizational theorists—but seldom with insights particularly useful to the SF literary scholar.)

*9-107. Knight, Damon F. **In Search of Wonder: Essays on Modern Science Fiction**. Advent, 1967. 2nd ed., rev. and enlarged.

A collection of 27 essays, almost all book reviews that appeared in fanzines and *The Magazine of Fantasy and Science Fiction* between 1951 and 1960. Along with James Blish, Knight was among the most influential of writer-critics who sought to impose rigorous and coherent critical standards on the field during one of its most formative decades, often using a review as a platform for broader issues. His piece on van Vogt, for example, led to a serious reassessment of that author's entire reputation. While many of the works he discusses are now nearly forgotten, his insights often remain striking, and these essays helped establish a tradition that has since been continued by Budrys and Spinrad.

9-108.   Knight, Damon F., ed. **Turning Points: Essays on the Art of Science Fiction**. Harper, 1977.

Until the 1970s, SF theory and criticism was largely confined to occasional essays and lectures by practicing authors. Knight's worthwhile intention here was to preserve the most significant of these critical pieces in a historical anthology of SF criticism. He has assembled 21 essays originally published between 1947 and 1973 and added two of his own, on SF definitions and the writing and selling of SF. Other contributors are a mix of familiar SF names (Heinlein, Asimov, Aldiss, Campbell, Poul Anderson, Keith Laumer, Bester, Sturgeon, Clarke, McKenna, Russ), mainstream writers on SF (Huxley, Amis, C. S. Lewis), and critics (H. Bruce Franklin, Pierre Versins). Primarily of historical interest; Nicholls's *Science Fiction at Large* [9-139] and Bretnor's *Science Fiction, Today and Tomorrow* [9-35] are similar collections.

9-109.   Kumar, Krishan. **Utopia and Anti-Utopia in Modern Times**. Basil Blackwell, 1987.

This lengthy work by a respected scholar is the most thorough social and cultural analysis of modern utopian literature to date. Following in the tradition of Frank and Fritzie Manuel's monumental *Utopian Thought in the Western World* (1979), Kumar focuses more on social and political philosophy than on literary form and value, often citing such thinkers as Herbert Marcuse and David Riesman to provide a context for discussions of individual texts. The first section of the book offers a historical overview of the development of utopian and anti-utopian traditions through the 19th century; the second section examines Bellamy's *Looking Backward*, Wells's *A Modern Utopia*, Huxley's *Brave New World*, Orwell's *Nineteen Eighty-Four*, and Skinner's *Walden Two*; and the concluding section includes discussions of Huxley's *Island*, Vonnegut's *Player Piano*, and Le Guin's *The Dispossessed*. A briefer summary of Kumar's ideas on utopianism, with less reference to SF, is his *Utopianism* (1991).

Themes: Dystopias, Utopias

9-110.   Landon, Brooks. **Science Fiction After 1900**. Twayne, 1997.

Landon's overview begins with the notion of SF as a "literature of change," then proceeds to consider the characteristics of "science fiction thinking" as reflected not only in various texts but in the culture at large. The first chapter, which focuses largely on how we know when to read a text as SF, discusses works by Forster, Campbell, and Pamela Zoline. His historical chapters are unexceptional, beginning with Gernsback, skipping over most of the 1930s to focus on Campbell and Heinlein—especially Heinlein's *Starship Troopers*—but eliding most SF of the 1940s and 1950s as well. A chapter on European and Russian SF traditions follows, with the Strugatskys and Lem earning the longest sustained critical discussions of any novels in the book. In his final two chapters, Landon turns his attention toward writers such as Dick, Russ, Le Guin, and Tiptree; Landon's discussion of feminist SF is longer than his account of all SF history from 1926 to the 1970s. A final chapter, focusing on self-reflexive SF, the New Wave, and cyberpunk, draws its main texts from Dozois's 12th *Year's Best Science Fiction*. Includes a bibliographic essay on critical and historical works and an annotated bibliography of recommended titles. Although Landon's approach is skewed away from traditional SF history—he barely mentions such writers as Bradbury, Clarke, or Sturgeon—his insights are useful on those texts he does choose to discuss. Compare James [9-99].

9-111. Langford, David. **The Complete Critical Assembly: The Collected White Dwarf (and GM, and GMI) SF Review Columns**. Cosmos, 2002.

David Langford's long string of Hugo Awards as best fan writer (mostly for his long-running *Ansible*, though the present collection draws mostly on *White Dwarf*) is both deserved and misleading; despite his breezy and witty style, his concerns are those of a serious critic. These reviews and essays, covering 1983–1991, tend to be short and functional, but repeatedly raise issues of central concern to the field, including the plethora of awards, sequels, media-related fiction, and fringe cults, and provide a solid and skeptical overview of the field during that decade.

9-112. Langford, David. **Up Through an Empty House of Stars: Reviews and Essays, 1980–2002**. Cosmos, 2003.

A hundred essays and reviews from two decades, which should be viewed as a companion piece to *The Complete Critical Assembly*. Langford is often at its best when at his most querulous, and here his skeptical responses to the overextended Dune series and the late novels of Asimov and Heinlein are especially sharp. But his best pieces often are those in which he seeks to revive interest in favorite authors such as Chesterton, Ernest Bramah, Rex Stout, Anthony Boucher, and Jack Vance. Langford is a consistently entertaining stylist who takes his material seriously, but not too seriously, and who after nearly three decades remains a valuable and eminently sane voice in the field.

*9-113. Larbalestier, Justine. **The Battle of the Sexes in Science Fiction**. Wesleyan Univ. Press, 2002.

In this fascinating and well-researched study, Larbalestier becomes the first feminist scholar of SF to draw heavily on primary historical research, beginning with the letter columns of the pulp magazines. She argues that feminist SF is less the result of a sudden revolution than an outgrowth of a debate that had been a lively feature of SF fiction and fandom in the period 1926 to 1973. The broad purview of her title enables her to discuss not only little-known pulp tales, but also such authors as Philip Wylie, "feminist utopias" by Russ and other "feminist utopians," and of course Le Guin and Tiptree, whose dramatic unveiling as Alice Sheldon constitutes a kind of definitive test-case on the question of the differences (or lack thereof) between men and women writing SF. Larbalestier approaches her material more in the manner of a cultural historian than of a literary critic, and traces changes in attitudes not only in the fiction and in fan debates, but even in magazine cover art; her final chapter is more involved with the politics of the Tiptree Award than with any of the texts it honors. Larbalestier's study is far from definitive, but its thorough research and wealth of historical detail serve to contextualize women's and feminist SF in a manner not seen before. Compare Attebery [9-13], LeFanu [9-117], and Barr [9-20].

Themes: Feminist SF

9-114.   Le Guin, Ursula K. Dancing at the Edge of the World: Thoughts on Words, Women, Places. Grove Press, 1989.

In a more broad-ranging collection than *The Language of the Night*, Le Guin assembles 32 essays and speeches and 17 book reviews on topics such as literature, travel, feminism, and social responsibility. While relatively few essays are obviously about SF, Le Guin offers insights into utopianism ("A Non-Euclidean View of California as a Cold Place to Be"), narrative theory ("The Carrier Bag Theory of Fiction," "Some Thoughts on Narrative"), her role as an SF writer ("The Space Crone"), and the TV movie version of her novel *The Lathe of Heaven* (1971). Among the authors treated in her reviews are Calvino, C. S. Lewis, Doris Lessing, and Mervyn Peake. Le Guin is as graceful an essayist as novelist, and this collection offers a great deal of wisdom and insight, acknowledged by its Hugo nomination.

9-115.   Le Guin, Ursula K. The Language of the Night: Essays on Fantasy and Science Fiction. Harper, 1992. Rev. ed.

Originally published in 1979 and reissued with corrections and notes in England in 1989 (the 1992 edition adds a useful Le Guin bibliography by L. W. Currey), this collection of essays, speeches, and introductions contains some of the most widely discussed commentary by a modern SF writer, such as "Dreams Must Explain Themselves," "From Elfland to Poughkeepsie," "Science Fiction and Mrs. Brown," and "Is Gender Necessary?" (to which Le Guin adds an extensive gloss for this edition). Le Guin is as elegant in her essays as in her fiction, and the volume is useful to all SF scholars, and indispensable to students of Le Guin; a Hugo nominee.

9-116.   Le Guin, Ursula K. The Wave in the Mind: Talks and Essays on the Writer, the Reader, and the Imagination. Shambhala, 2004.

An engaging and informal collection of essays, talks, readings, and poems, including a section of six short autobiographical or personal essays, seven essays on aspects of the writing process, and various other pieces mentioning topics ranging from the gender biases of various literary awards to the discomfort of women's shoes. While only a few of the essays touch critically on authors or works of science fiction and fantasy (Borges, Cordwainer Smith, Tolkien, and her own story "The Poacher"), Le Guin's wit and clarity of thought lend the volume interest to students not only of her own work but of writing in general.

*9-117. Lefanu, Sarah. **In The Chinks of the World Machine: Feminism and Science Fiction**. Women's Press, 1988. U.S. title: *Feminism and Science Fiction*.

Informed by both current feminist theory and a broad familiarity with both U.S. and European SF by women, Lefanu's study has gained considerable influence as perhaps the most coherent exposition of feminist themes in SF. The first section explores such themes as amazon heroines, feminist utopias and dystopias, romantic love, and treatments of authority in women's SF; the second consists of more extended discussions of the work of Tiptree, Le Guin, Charnas, and Russ. Although her theoretical observations are persuasive, Lefanu's greatest strength is in her readings of individual texts, including rarely discussed works by Marion Zimmer Bradley, Jayge Carr, Angela Carter, Sally Miller Gearhart, Gwyneth Jones, Vonda McIntyre, Marge Piercy, Josephine Saxton, and Pamela Zoline. Compare Barr's *Feminist Fabulation* [9-20].

Themes: Feminist SF

9-118. Lem, Stanislaw. **Microworlds: Writings on Science Fiction and Fantasy**. Ed. by Franz Rottensteiner. Harcourt, 1985.

Ten essays by Poland's leading SF writer include an autobiographical piece (which also discusses Lem's writing methods); individual discussions of Dick, Borges, the Strugatsky brothers, and Todorov's theory of the fantastic; and SF themes and structures. As a critic, Lem is best known for his often stringent treatments of SF tropes; his most important pieces here cover time travel, cosmology, structuralism and SF, and the possibilities of the genre (which Lem sees as often betrayed or unrealized). Lem makes a passionate case for the social and philosophical responsibilities of literature, and his perspective is a valuable one. In his introduction, Rottensteiner relates these essays to Lem's other writings in literary theory.

9-119. Leonard, Elizabeth Anne, ed. **Into Darkness Peering: Race and Color in the Fantastic**. Greenwood, 1997.

A collection of 13 original essays (including Leonard's introduction) exploring racial themes and attitudes, mostly in SF (which is the focus of 10 of the essays). Among the authors discussed are Delany (by Donald M. Hassler), Octavia Butler (Teri Ann Doerksen), Le Guin (Lisbeth Gant-Britton), the pulp writer Leslie F. Stone (Batya Weinbaum), Heinlein (Gary Westfahl), Bradbury and Dick (Ellen Bishop), Neal Stephenson (Philip E. Baruth), Robert Silverberg (John Flodstrom), Elizabeth A. Lynn (Leonard), Stephen King (Samantha Figliola), and Maryse Condé (Faye Ringel). An additional essay by Neal Baker concerns *Star Trek: Voyager*. While the collection suffers from the usual unevenness of quality, spottiness of coverage, and lack of clear focus (there is nowhere an attempted overview of the theme in SF or a clearly established theoretical context), there are nevertheless some excellent insights; especially notable are the essays by Bishop, Baruth, and Westfahl. Compare Grayson, *Visions of the Third Millennium* [9-84].

9-120.   Lerner, Fred. **Modern Science Fiction and the American Literary Community**. Scarecrow, 1985.

Essentially a history of science fiction's reputation in American mainstream culture from 1926 to 1976, Lerner's meticulously documented essay (more than half the book consists of notes, bibliographies, and indexes!) begins by identifying what he views as a representative sample of 94 "substantial" writers active during the period, plus eight additional award-winning authors after 1971. He then tracks references to or reviews of these authors in the mainstream press (using standard library indexes), traces the early development of scholarship and criticism specific to science fiction (including academic meetings and seminars), and discusses the growth of science fiction in school and college curricula, its reception by librarians, and its reception by "futurologists." While there are evident compromises in such a methodology, and while Lerner does not attempt to focus on his own assessments of the literary evolution of the genre, his chronicle (which often takes on the aspect of an annotated bibliography rather than a continuous argument) provides a very useful guide to often-overlooked (and often-dismissive) accounts of SF and SF writers in the literary and mainstream press during this period.

9-121.   Lundwall, Sam J. **Science Fiction: An Illustrated History**. Grosset, 1978.

One of Europe's most knowledgeable critics and historians of SF offers a popular international survey that, because of its coverage of untranslated European SF, serves as a useful supplement to Gunn's *Alternate Worlds* [9-96] and Aldiss and Wingrove [9-4]. Sometimes Lundwall's claims for early European SF are a bit exaggerated, however, and a chapter of this book reprinted in *Foundation* 34 (Autumn 1985) brought a stinging rebuttal from Sam Moskowitz in *Foundation* 36 (Summer 1986). Some of the material here is included in Lundwall's earlier brief survey, *Science Fiction: What It's All About* (1971).

*9-122.   Malmgren, Carl. **Worlds Apart: Narratology of Science Fiction**. Indiana Univ. Press, 1991.

Arguing that SF is better defined by the worlds it creates than by its narrative conventions, Malmgren first divides SF into "speculative" or "extrapolative" modes, then shows how representative texts of each mode treat four major types of SF narrative: the alien encounter, the alternate society (utopian or dystopian works in which society, but not the world, is changed), the gadget story, and the alternate world. A separate chapter discusses science fantasy, which doesn't really fit into the scheme. Like all typologies, Malmgren's is debatable, but he offers insightful readings of works by Wells, Lem, Silverberg, Ian Watson, Wilhelm, Russ, Clarke, Ballard, the Strugatskys, Leiber, Benford and Brin, and Gene Wolfe.

9-123. Malzberg, Barry. **The Engines of the Night: Science Fiction in the Eighties**. Doubleday, 1982.

Malzberg's reputation as SF's most articulate depressive is borne out by many of the 36 essays collected here, a number of them revised from earlier appearances and none having to do with SF in the 1980s. Although he covers a varied list of topics (sex in SF, SF of the 1950s, academia and SF, SF stories *about* SF) and includes tributes to John W. Campbell, Jr., Cornell Woolrich, and Mark Clifton, his recurrent theme is the plight of the writer and the often destructive effects of the SF industry. Malzberg's iconoclastic wit has often gotten him in trouble, but in retrospect his portrait of the profession of SF, and how it often managed to produce masterworks under the most unlikely conditions, is invaluable and often brilliant. An interesting contrast is Gunn's *Inside Science Fiction* [9-87].

9-124. Manlove, Colin. **Science Fiction: Ten Explorations**. Kent State Univ. Press, 1986.

Manlove is a Scottish scholar best known for a series of penetrating studies of fantasy (*Modern Fantasy: Five Studies*, 1975; *The Impulse of Fantasy Literature*, 1983; *Christian Fantasy*, 1992). He sees in SF a unique kind of energy, which he describes as a desire for "more life," and explores this through thoughtful but not always well-informed readings of 10 representative texts. Some are recognized classics—Asimov's Foundation series, Herbert's *Dune*, Farmer's first Riverworld novel, Clarke's *Rendezvous With Rama*—but the selections from Pohl, Aldiss, Silverberg, and Simak are not among the authors' best-known works. The most recent works discussed are Attanasio's *Radix* and Wolfe's *Book of the New Sun*; Manlove sees questions of identity and self in all these books. But while this gives his readings some thematic coherence, he does not offer an overall theory of the genre, claiming that in the face of such inventiveness, all criticism can do is describe.

9-125. Martin, Graham Dunston. **An Inquiry into the Purposes of Speculative Fiction—Fantasy and Truth**. Edwin Mellen, 2003.

Proposing the term "ultrafiction" for modern fantasy and science fiction (intending to suggest its broader purview than mainstream fiction and its secondary remove from experience), novelist Martin here collects a series of essays ranging from folk and fairy tales to Kipling to utopian fiction to more recent authors including Stanislaw Lem, Michel Tournier, Iain M. Banks, and Jonathan Carroll. Although more concerned with fantasy and folklore than with science fiction texts, Martin's approach is useful because of the broad theoretical base of its central argument, which subsumes a variety of types of fantastic narrative. Compare Brigg's *The Span of Mainstream and Science Fiction* [9-37].

9-126. Matthew, Robert. **Japanese Science Fiction**. Routledge, 1989.

The first book-length study in English of an extensive, and largely independent, tradition of Japanese SF dating back to the 19th century. Matthew, an Australian professor and translator, shows little familiarity with other SF scholarship and depends heavily on plot summaries, but such summaries are valuable since many of the works discussed are not available in English. After a historical survey of both fiction and critical attitudes, six chapters deal with characteristic themes of Japanese SF. The themes themselves demonstrate some key ways in which Japanese SF is different: boredom and satiety, advertising and media, economics and trade, "human concerns and values," relations between generations, and sex. Additional chapters discuss religious and ethical concerns and such current anxieties as regimentation, alienation, and the aftermath of the bomb. An extremely useful national-literature study.

9-127.   McCaffery, Larry, ed. **Storming the Reality Studio: A Casebook of Cyberpunk and Postmodern Science Fiction**. Duke Univ. Press, 1992.

An amalgam of 29 stories or novel excerpts and 20 critical or theoretical essays, some of which appeared in a special cyberpunk issue of *Mississippi Review* in 1988. The collection's main value is as a work of criticism, since many of the brief fictional selections illustrate particular points in the essays. The overall goal is to provide an ambitious theoretical, cultural, and historical context for the then-current cyberpunk movement, ranging from Mary Shelley to MTV. The nonfiction includes excerpts from Jacques Derrida, Fredric Jameson, and Jean François Lyotard; essays by Joan Gordon, Veronica Hollinger, Brooks Landon, Bruce Sterling, and Tom Maddox; an interview with William Gibson; and a very strange piece by Timothy Leary. Compare with Slusser and Shippey's somewhat more focused *Fiction 2000* [9-179] and Butler's *Pocket Essential Cyberpunk* [9-45].

Themes: Cyberpunk

9-128.   McGuire, Patrick. **Red Stars: Political Aspects of Soviet Science Fiction**. UMI Research Press, 1985.

This brief study, revised from a 1977 dissertation, focuses on the political and social context of Soviet science fiction published between 1923 and 1976, complete with extensive bibliographies and six tables showing such things as the number of works published over the years and SF preferences among various population groups. Although McGuire does not focus on literary theory or offer much evaluative commentary on individual works (the only authors treated in much detail are the Strugatskys and Ivan Efremov), he makes useful connections with relevant American SF in his extensive notes. His study is generally more informative and current than John Glad's *Extrapolations from Dystopia: A Critical Study of Soviet Science Fiction* (Kingston, 1982), a dated revision of a 1970 dissertation. Compare Zebrowski [9-209].

Themes: Politics

9-129.   Meyers, Walter E. **Aliens and Linguists: Language Study and Science Fiction**. Univ. of Georgia Press, 1980.

A witty and informed study of languages and linguistic evolution as portrayed in SF, with substantial treatment of fantasy languages such as Tolkien's elvish. Meyers is widely familiar with popular Anglo-American SF as well as with linguistics, and his study demonstrates the crucial importance of communication to many SF narratives. Some of the more enjoyable chapters excoriate famous dumb ideas such as implanted knowledge and automatic translators, while others deal with SF's notions of linguistic change. Compare Stockwell, *The Poetics of Science Fiction* [9-186].

Themes: Linguistics

9-130. Mogen, David. **Wilderness Visions: The Western Theme in Science Fiction Literature**. 2nd ed. Borgo, 1993.

A brief but important discussion of the frontier theme in SF—not of westerns with SF elements—based on the author's 1977 dissertation and an earlier 1982 edition, to which this edition adds three chapters covering works by Bradbury, Le Guin, Simak, Brackett, Ellison, and a few others. Following two chapters that summarize the history and prophetic aspects of the frontier myth, Mogen examines works by Heinlein, Asimov, and Pohl and Kornbluth. Though Mogen's was the first extended study of this major SF theme, it is far from definitive, and this second edition adds material without really updating the earlier one; none of Mogen's primary texts come from later than 1974, and (except for books of his own) none of the secondary texts are later than 1976. Compare Westfahl, *Space and Beyond* [9-229].

9-131. Moskowitz, Sam. **The Immortal Storm: A History of Science Fiction Fandom**. Atlanta Science Fiction Organization Press, 1954. Recommended ed.: Hyperion, 1974.

Famous for its hyperbolic title, Moskowitz's largely personal and autobiographical account (originally serialized in *Fantasy Commentator* beginning in 1945) is in fact largely confined to the meetings and squabbles of a handful of 1930s East Coast fans whose efforts eventually led to the first World Science Fiction Convention of 1939. Obsessively detailed and deadly serious, Moskowitz's book reveals almost nothing about SF literature, but is an important source for the study of the origins of that passionate and more-or-less organized body of SF readership that calls itself "fandom." An equally anecdotal but far more complete account is Warner's *All Our Yesterdays*. Also annotated as [13-33].

Awards: Special Hugo plaque

9-132. Moskowitz, Sam. **Science Fiction in Old San Francisco, Vol. 1: History of the Movement from 1854 to 1890**. Donald M. Grant, 1980.

Moskowitz, a devoted fan historian whose early collections of author profiles and theme essays (*Explorers of the Infinite*, 1963; *Seekers of Tomorrow*, 1966) for a time served as almost the only widely available references on SF history, also pioneered in resurrecting little-known aspects of early SF history in anthologies such as *Under the Moons of Mars, Science Fiction by Gaslight*, and the collection of stories by Robert Duncan Milne that is the companion volume to this history. Milne was the chief figure in a group of writers who contributed hundreds of fantastic tales, many of them SF, to San Francisco newspapers in the late 19th century, influencing Ambrose Bierce, among others. While Moskowitz's enthusiasm occasionally gets out of hand, his original research here uncovers a genuinely forgotten chapter in SF history.

9-133.   Moskowitz, Sam. **Strange Horizons: The Spectrum of Science Fiction**. Scribner, 1976.

Eleven essays, 10 revised from earlier magazine appearances, tracing a variety of themes and movements in SF. Although Moskowitz characteristically disdained theory, his broad knowledge of lesser-known works of early SF gives considerable reference value to his treatment of such topics as anti-Semitism, civil rights, religion, matriarchal societies, crime, psychiatry, war, and birth control. Other essays discuss Charles Fort, Virgil Finlay, and juvenile SF. Some of these themes are also treated in Carter [9-46].

9-134.   Moylan, Tom. **Demand the Impossible: Science Fiction and the Utopian Imagination**. Methuen, 1986.

A thoughtful and intelligent analysis of what Moylan calls the "critical utopia," which he sees as having emerged in the 1970s to lend new life to a tradition earlier characterized by "totalizing blueprints" and dystopias. Critical utopias, represented by extended discussions of Russ's *The Female Man*, Le Guin's *The Dispossessed*, Piercy's *Woman on the Edge of Time*, and Delany's *Triton*, question both the utopian tradition and their own assumptions. Moylan's readings of these works in the context of a Marxist-feminist approach, and his general conclusions, constitute a provocative attempt to link modern SF to the utopian tradition.

Themes: Utopias

*9-135.   Moylan, Tom. **Scraps of the Untainted Sky: Science Fiction, Utopia, Dystopia**. Westview, 2000.

While some utopian scholarship of the last few decades has veered away from critical discourses about science fiction, Moylan has consistently explored the connections between these traditions, and is one of the leading scholars of both. Here he begins with a detailed overview of recent scholarship in utopian and science fiction studies, initially organized around discussions of two stories by Joanna Russ and James Tiptree, Jr. The second part of the book explores the history and social contexts of classic dystopian fiction (including Forster's "The Machine Stops," Zamyatin, Huxley, Orwell, Pohl and Korbluth, Dick, and Pamela Zoline) before moving on, in his third section, to often detailed readings of "critical dystopias" by Kim Stanley Robinson, Octavia Butler, and Marge Piercy. While Moylan's theoretical approach is visibly influenced by earlier Marxist critics from Frederic Jameson to Darko Suvin, this book represents a significant extension and updating of ideas originally developed in his *Demand the Impossible*, and is one of the more important studies of the relationship of utopian or dystopian ideas and science fictional narrative strategies.

Themes: Dystopias, Utopias

9-136. Moylan, Tom, and Raffaella Baccolini, eds. **Dark Horizons: Science Fiction and the Utopian Imagination**. Routledge, 2003.

A collection of 12 essays, many by major scholars of science fiction and utopian literature, intending to trace the literary and political growth of the "critical dystopia" (a concept detailed in Moylan's *Scraps of the Untainted Sky*) since the 1980s, and to relate this development to recent global and political events. Among the essays are theoretical pieces by Darko Suvin, Lyman Tower Sargent, Maria Varsam, Ruth Levitas and Lucy Sargisson, and editors Moylan and Baccolini; Jane Donawerth on gender and critical dystopia; Ildney Cavalcanti on Suzy McKee Charnas; Naomi Jacobs on Octavia Butler; Baccolini on Le Guin; Moylan on Le Guin and Kim Stanley Robinson; and Peter Fitting on films and related non-SF literature. For the most part, the contributions are quite strong, and collectively constitute an effective case that the dystopian impulse has reasserted itself noticeably in the fiction of the last three decades.

Themes: Dystopias

9-137. Myers, Robert E., ed. **The Intersection of Science Fiction and Philosophy: Critical Studies**. Greenwood, 1983.

A collection of 17 essays, arranged in eight thematic sections (for example, "Space-Time and Time Travel"), in which philosophers and scholars of other disciplines seek to explore various philosophical issues as treated in SF. Each piece is followed by a list of recommended readings, and in all some 50 SF authors are touched upon. Most of the essays provide little meaningful criticism, although those by William Schuyler, Adam Frisch, Joann Cob, and Bart Thurber are especially insightful. Nicholas D. Smith's *Philosophers Look at Science Fiction* (Nelson-Hall, 1982), a similar collection, is more heavily oriented toward academic philosophy. Compare Clark [9-53].

9-138. Nicholls, Stan. **Wordsmiths of Wonder: Fifty Interviews with Writers of the Fantastic**. Orbit, 1993.

Generally well-informed interviews with a wide variety of famous and less-famous SF and fantasy writers, offering some new insights, as well as familiar concerns. Among younger fantasy writers, for example, the influence of Moorcock seems almost to rival that of Tolkien. Slightly more than half the interviews (26) are classified as SF, 13 as fantasy, and 11 as horror—although there is obvious overlap with authors such as Moorcock, Ray Bradbury, Robert Holdstock, Dan Simmons, and Brian Stableford, who are all included in the SF section. Many focus heavily on the authors' most recent books at the time of interview. Among familiar subjects are Pohl, Aldiss, Moorcock, Sheckley, Silverberg, Bear, Ballard, Donaldson, Barker, Haldeman, Kim Stanley Robinson, Larry Niven and Steven Barnes (interviewed together), James Herbert, and Tanith Lee. But Nicholls doesn't ignore commercial or cult writers such as Brooks, Asprin, and Douglas Adams, and includes writers seen less often in such venues, such as Howard Waldrop, Michael Swanwick, Iain M. Banks, Lisa Tuttle, and David Wingrove.

9-139. Nicholls, Peter, ed. **Science Fiction at Large**. Gollancz, 1976. U.K. title: *Explorations of the Marvelous* (1978). Recommended ed.: Harper, 1977.

Eleven essays derived from a series of lectures delivered at London's Institute of Contemporary Arts in 1975. Some, such as Le Guin's "Science Fiction and Mrs. Brown," have become classics, while others, notably Dick's "Man, Android, and Machine," are indispensable for students of the author involved. Other contributors include SF and fantasy authors Brunner, Harrison, Disch, Alan Garner, and Robert Sheckley, and scholars of SF or related fields Edward de Bono, John Taylor, Alvin Toffler, and Nicholls himself. An excellent overview of major concerns in SF for the general reader, which makes for an interesting comparison with the similar (but much earlier) collection of public lectures *The Science Fiction Novel: Imagination and Social Criticism* [9-173].

9-140. Nicolson, Marjorie Hope. **Voyages to the Moon**. Macmillan, 1948.

An influential early study of SF prehistory, roughly contemporary with Bailey [9-15] but more oriented toward traditional literary history and far more narrowly focused. Nicolson treats principally English-language works of the 17th and 18th centuries and adds a final chapter touching on Poe, Verne, Wells, and Lewis. Illustrated, with primary and secondary bibliographies (the latter now badly dated). A comparable, but more popular early work is Roger Lancelyn Green's *Into Other Worlds: Space Flight in Fiction From Lucian to Lewis* (1958).

Themes: The Moon

9-141. Palumbo, Donald. **Chaos, Theory, Asimov's Foundations and Robots, and Herbert's Dune: The Fractal Aesthetic of Epic Science Fiction**. Greenwood, 2002.

An extended analysis of three novel series, two by Asimov and one by Herbert, that seeks to discover evidence of scientific chaos theory in the "fractal" narrative structures developed by these two authors. While this thesis inevitably involves a certain degree of retrofitting (though Palumbo does demonstrate that late in his career Asimov was interested in such theories), it also provides a useful model for detailed readings of the later works in these series. The discussion of Asimov (which takes up about two thirds of the book) is generally more persuasive than that of Herbert (in which Palumbo digresses into Joseph Campbell's idea of the monomyth), and Palumbo makes little effort to argue persuasively for the ways in which his model might provide a broader theoretical approach to "epic" SF in general. It is worthwhile to contrast this approach with that of Hayles [9-92], although Hayles's use of chaos theory in terms of broad cultural trends is quite different.

9-142. Palumbo, Donald, ed. **Erotic Universe: Sexuality and Fantastic Literature**. Greenwood, 1986.

Fifteen essays, most originally delivered at various conferences, organized according to theory, themes, feminist views, and fanzines. (This last category consists of only one essay, on *Star Trek* fanzines.) Most of the topics covered are relatively unexplored; James Riemer's essay on homosexuality and Judith Bogert's on sexual comedy are especially unusual, if now somewhat dated. Among the authors treated at some length are Angela Carter, Russ, Le Guin, McCaffrey, Farmer, and Sturgeon. A seven-part bibliography and filmography includes a useful annotated section of primary texts. A companion volume on film and the arts is *Eros in the Mind's Eye: Sexuality and the Fantastic in Art and Film* (Greenwood, 1986), containing 11 essays.

Themes: Sex in SF

9-143. Panshin, Alexei. **SF in Dimension: A Book of Explorations**. Advent, 1980. Rev. and enlarged ed.

A collection of 22 essays from 1969 to 1980, ranging from broadly ruminative pieces on the nature of SF to somewhat dated book reviews. Authors or editors discussed in some detail include Heinlein, Anderson, Aldiss, Asimov, Clarke, Campbell, Gernsback, Leiber, Cordwainer Smith, van Vogt, Weinbaum, and Zelazny. Mostly of historical interest, since Panshin's major ideas are developed at much greater length in *The World Beyond the Hill* [9-144].

9-144. Panshin, Alexei, and Cory Panshin. **The World Beyond the Hill: Science Fiction and the Quest for Transcendence**. Jeremy L. Tarcher, 1989.

The authors set out to trace a history of SF as a modern myth of transcendence, from the end of witchcraft trials in England in 1685 through the publication of Asimov's "The Mule" in 1945. They provide little scholarship on myth or intellectual history, citing only Joseph Campbell and two books on Sufism in a tiny bibliography; no secondary sources are indexed. But if their scholarly thesis is finally weak and unconvincing, their contribution to the history of "golden age" SF is invaluable. Fully two thirds of this huge book is virtually a story-by-story analysis of the development of modern magazine SF, mostly through John W. Campbell's editorship of *Astounding*. The Panshins discuss the stories in almost obsessive detail, showing Campbell's role in working with such authors as Heinlein, Asimov, van Vogt, and Williamson. But as a general history, this is far less complete than Aldiss and Wingrove [9-4], and is often eccentric and provincial in its judgments. As a microhistorical portrait of a key period in SF's development, it is quite useful.

Awards: Hugo

9-145. Parrinder, Patrick, ed. **Learning from Other Worlds: Estrangement, Cognition, and the Politics of Science Fiction and Utopia**. Liverpool Univ. Press, 2001.

As the title implies, this collection of 11 essays in honor of science fiction theorist Darko Suvin also intends to re-examine and extend his key notions of cognition and estrangement (see *Metamorphoses of Science Fiction* [9-189]). The first section on science fiction, politics, and utopia includes a useful brief overview of early SF criticism by Edward James, essays by Parrinder and Tom Moylan re-examining Suvin's ideas in light of later theory, and more broadly theoretical pieces on utopianism by Carl Freedman and Marc Angenot. In the second section of more applied criticism, Gerard Klein, Peter Fitting, David Ketterer, Marleen Barr, Rafael Nudelman, and Fredric Jameson explore a range of texts and themes including imagery drawn from science, cloning, and works by Wells, Lem, Wyndham, and Kim Stanley Robinson. In an informal afterword, Suvin offers his own responses to the issues raised by the essayists. The essentially Marxist approach reflected in the essays by Moylan, Freedman, Angenot, and Jameson provides the book with a kind of theoretical focus not always reflected in the other, more eclectic essays.

9-146.   Parrinder, Patrick. **Science Fiction: A Critical Guide**. Longmans, 1979.

Twelve academic essays, with notes and bibliographies, focusing mostly on British and European science fiction and covering such topics as early SF history, Verne, Wells, the utopian tradition, SF editors, the scientific worldview, the Cold War, religion, characterization, and post-1960 American SF. The essays are generally of high quality and some—such as the Raymond Williams essay on utopian themes—reflect a broad understanding of social and political theory as well as SF, although the volume as a whole is dated. Compare Clareson's *Many Futures, Many Worlds* [9-48] and Garnett and Ellis [9-83].

9-147.   Parrinder, Patrick. **Science Fiction: Its Criticism and Teaching**. Methuen, 1980.

A brief and cogent introduction to SF for the student and teacher. An introductory chapter discusses various definitions and types of SF, from the scientific romance to the New Wave. Subsequent chapters discuss the sociology of SF; SF as romance, fable, or epic; the language of SF; and a possible SF course, with valuable insights on the issue of canon-formation. Particular attention is given to Clarke, Delany, Dick (long before he became a critical favorite), Heinlein, Lem, Vonnegut, and Wells. Neither oversimplified nor arcane, this was an excellent text of its time, with notes and annotated bibliography, for the beginning student or teacher of the genre. Also annotated as [14-9].

9-148.   Philmus, Robert. **Into the Unknown: The Evolution of Science Fiction from Francis Godwin to H. G. Wells**. Univ. of California Press, 1970.

A more scholarly survey of the English prehistory of SF treated more synoptically in Bailey [9-15], and the first general study of SF history to come from a university press. Following a long introductory chapter discussing SF as myth and as rhetorical strategy, Philmus covers important works by Godwin, Swift, Aphra Behn, Samuel Butler, Defoe, Bulwer-Lytton, Robert Louis Stevenson, Verne, and Wells. A partially annotated bibliography is now superseded by Bleiler, and an introduction added to the 1983 paperback notes the growth of scholarship after 1970. Compare the broader and more current European perspective in Alkon [9-6].

9-149. Pierce, John J(eremy). **Foundations of Science Fiction: A Study in Imagination and Evolution**. Greenwood, 1987.

Pierce, a critic and professional editor, originally intended his massive study of SF to be published in one volume titled *Imagination and Evolution*. The volumes that eventually emerged constitute an ambitious attempt to write a popular but well-documented history of the genre organized along thematic rather than strictly chronological lines. The overall thesis seems to be intended as an answer to Aldiss and Wingrove's gothic-based history of the genre. Pierce sees SF instead as an evolving fictional portrayal of the scientific worldview. The first volume covers the familiar territory of Plato, Lucian, early utopianists, Verne, Robida, Victorian future-war tales and interplanetary voyages, Rosny, Wells, and Lasswitz. It also offers useful discussions of imaginary worlds from Burroughs to Herbert, space opera from Hamilton to *Star Wars,* and anti-utopian and dystopian traditions. Although he relies heavily on secondary sources, his study is a far more complete version of "official" SF history than, for example, that of Gunn [9-86].

9-150. Pierce, John J(eremy). **Great Themes of Science Fiction: A Study in Imagination and Evolution**. Greenwood, 1987.

The second volume of Pierce's study identifies eight key themes in SF: aliens and alien worlds, supermen and mutations, eternal or extended life, men like gods (and vice versa), artificial intelligence and robots, future cities, future wars, and disasters. A final chapter concerns works at the margins of SF, in Pierce's view, such as parallel universe tales or tales with satirical or allegorical intent. A wide variety of texts and films is invoked, with particularly good discussions of works by Anderson, Asimov, Aleksandr Belyayev, Clement, Farmer, Heinlein, Leinster, Niven, and Wells.

9-151. Pierce, John J(eremy). **Odd Genre: A Study in Imagination and Evolution**. Greenwood, 1994.

Pierce's focus here is on the question of how SF relates to other genres and to mainstream literature in general, and this study, a follow-up to his other volumes on SF history, offers more breadth than depth, touching upon more than 600 separate works. Theoretical questions occupy the first two chapters, in which Pierce considers the "genrefication" of SF, mentioning such theorists as Suvin. Later he explores various subgenres of SF that cross over to other genres: romances, detective stories, juveniles, family sagas, and problem-solving tales. A third section examines such related genres as lost-race stories, superheroes (mainly Doc Savage), horror, and satire, and such gender-directed specialties as men's adventure fiction, technothrillers, and women's romance; and a fourth covers writers who have escaped the SF "ghetto" and mainstream writers who have "invaded" it. A final section deals with problems of story construction, style, publishing constraints, and ideational content. Largely conservative and conventional in his approach, and sometimes hastily ill-considered in his treatment of individual works, Pierce nevertheless offers the worthwhile perspective of a long-time reader.

9-152. Pierce, John J(eremy). **When World Views Collide: A Study in Imagination and Evolution**. Greenwood, 1989.

The third volume of Pierce's ambitious overview sets out to explore "science fiction as a way of defining and delimiting humanity and human values." It begins with a discussion of the Wellsian tradition in Clarke and Asimov, then treats such "anti-Wellsians" as C. S. Lewis, Walter M. Miller, and (surprisingly) Brian Aldiss. Subsequent chapters cover Simak and Sturgeon, social Darwinism in Heinlein and Budrys, the literary experiments of the New Wave and Delany, the protest fiction of Ellison and some feminist writers, Soviet writers, the ideological fiction of Brunner and Ayn Rand, and the "synthetists" Cordwainer Smith and Le Guin. Pierce's odd juxtapositions are often enlightening, but this volume reveals more clearly than the others the consistent "Wellsian" rationalist bias of his overall study, and his impatience with literary matters or works that he sees as betraying the essential mission of SF. A brief afterword touches upon cyberpunk. As in all his volumes, the notes, bibliographies, and filmographies are extensive.

9-153. Pinsky, Michael. **Future Present: Ethics and/as Science Fiction**. Fairleigh Dickinson Univ. Press, 2003.

After an introductory chapter offering a background overview of philosophical notions of space and time as developed principally by Derrida and Heidegger, Pinsky examines a number of science -fictional works as expressions of particular ethical concerns or problems, focusing initially on three novels by H. G. Wells but soon broadening his discussion to include film, television, anime, and even Disneyland and Epcot Center, before turning to a more focused consideration of works by Philip K. Dick. While he offers few surprises or radically new interpretations in his readings of individual works of fiction, Pinsky's locating these works in a broader social context and under the general umbrella of ethical philosophy lends his overall analysis a degree of coherence that is at times compelling. Contrast Clark [9-53] and Myers [9-137] for discussions of other philosophical themes in science fiction.

9-154. Pringle, David. **Science Fiction: The 100 Best Novels—An English Language Selection, 1949–1984**. Xanadu, 1985.

A series of two-page essays on works the author considers to be seminal to modern SF, from Orwell's *Nineteen Eighty-Four* to Gibson's *Neuromancer*. Pringle often mentions other works—including short stories and collections—in annotating his selections, and the selections themselves are intelligent and provocative. The guide is especially useful for libraries and those new to the genre, but is likely to be more fully enjoyed by knowledgeable readers who might quibble with some of Pringle's more unexpected selections, such as novels by Harness, Pat Frank, Bob Shaw, Mack Reynolds, Damien Broderick, and John Calvin

Batchelor. A companion volume is *Modern Fantasy: The Hundred Best Novels, an English-Language Selection,* 1946–1987 (1988).

9-155. Rabkin, Eric S. **The Fantastic in Literature**. Princeton Univ. Press, 1976.

A lucid early theory of the fantastic that arranges relevant genres, including SF, along a continuum according to the extent to which basic "ground rules" are reversed in the fictional world. Rabkin's study is useful for the manner in which it provides a theoretical and historical context for fantastic works, and even though it does not exclusively concern SF and focuses more on theory than analysis of individual texts, it includes insightful discussions of works by Clarke, Asimov, Moorcock, Sturgeon, Wells, and others.

9-156. Rabkin, Eric S., Martin H. Greenberg, and Joseph D. Olander, eds. **The End of the World**. Southern Illinois Univ. Press, 1983.

A collection of six original essays, with notes and a brief overall bibliography, on the various ways SF writers have handled this subject. Contributors are Gary K. Wolfe, Robert Plank, Robert Galbreath, Brian Stableford, and W. Warren Wagar, whose two contributions appear in somewhat shorter form in his *Terminal Visions* [9-193], which in general is a more sustained and coherent approach to the same topic. Nevertheless, these essays offer many useful insights and discussions of works by Clarke, Blish, Wylie, Wyndham, Shiel, Coppel, George R. Stewart, Edmund Cooper, and others.

Themes: Disaster

9-157. Rabkin, Eric S., Martin H. Greenberg, and Joseph D. Olander, eds. **No Place Else: Explorations in Utopian and Dystopian Fiction**. Southern Illinois Univ. Press, 1983.

This publisher's ambitious Alternatives series included collections of fiction, reprints of famous magazine issues, papers from various Eaton Conferences (see "Conference Proceedings"), and occasional volumes of original essays, including this one and *The End of the World*. Most of the essays here consider individual works: *The Coming Race, Erewhon, We, Last and First Men, Brave New World, Nineteen Eighty-Four, The Shape of Things to Come,* and *Lord of the Flies*. Notable are Merrit Abrash on Silverberg's *The World Inside,* James Bittner on *The Dispossessed,* and Jack Zipes on *Fahrenheit 451*. Little overall theory or context is provided, and the essays are of uneven quality. More coherent studies of the topic include those of Moylan [9-134] and Kumar [9-109].

Themes: Dystopias, Utopias

9-158. Reilly, Robert, ed. **The Transcendent Adventure: Studies of Religion in Science Fiction/Fantasy**. Greenwood, 1984.

An uneven but useful collection of 15 essays, together with primary and secondary bibliographies, on the ways in which SF and fantasy writers use religious themes. Four essays attempt to draw general conclusions about religious and ethical themes in SF; the rest focus on such individual authors as Blish, Lewis, Dick, Farmer, Herbert, Miller, Lessing, Tolkien, Zelazny, and Walter Tevis. Although the essays offer little continuity in terms of a developing argument, they cover a far broader range of texts than the more focused studies of Martha Sammons (*A Better Country: The Worlds of Religious Fantasy and Science Fiction*, 1998) or Colin Manlove (*Christian Fantasy*, 1992), both of which focus much more heavily on fantasy than SF.

Themes: Religion

9-159.   Roberts, Adam. **Science Fiction**. Routledge, 2000.

Intended as an overview of the genre for the general reader, Roberts's uneven study devotes only a chapter each to definitions and the history of science fiction before launching into the somewhat more arbitrary topics of race, gender, and "technology and metaphor," with extended discussions of only a handful of texts and films to serve as illustrations (among these are Le Guin's *The Left Hand of Darkness*, Herbert's *Dune*, and Gibson's *Neuromancer*, along with the films *Star Wars* and *Men in Black*). While Roberts offers some original and even provocative arguments, his historical and theoretical material often borrows heavily on the work of earlier scholars, sometimes with inadequate acknowledgment, and his overall approach to the genre is both less comprehensive and less balanced than some other available introductions, such as Edward James's *Science Fiction in the Twentieth Century* [9-99].

9-160.   Roberts, Robin. **A New Species: Gender and Science in Science Fiction**. Univ. of Illinois Press, 1993.

While acknowledging the work of earlier scholars, Roberts promises to add a significant new dimension to feminist studies of SF by covering both 19th-century SF and the pulp era. In fact, her coverage of these periods is slight, including only two novels by Mary Shelley and one each by Bulwer-Lytton, Walter Besant, and H. G. Wells for the 19th century and only Philip José Farmer's "The Lovers" and four very minor stories from the early 1950s (apparently chosen on the basis of their cover illustrations) for the "pulp era," which Roberts misidentifies as the post-World War II period. Subsequent chapters discuss feminist utopias, feminist SF, Doris Lessing, and postmodernism (which focuses on Slonczewski, Finch, Atwood, and Le Guin). Roberts offers some useful insights, despite her tendency to make generalizations based on an inadequate sampling of texts. Eleven illustrations complement the text, which is hampered by a very incomplete and unreliable index, not prepared by the author. Compare Attebery [9-13].

Themes: Feminist SF

9-161.   Roberts, Thomas J. **An Aesthetics of Junk Fiction**. Univ. of Georgia Press, 1990.

In one of the first general theories of popular fiction to appear since John Cawelti's *Adventure, Mystery, and Romance* (1976), Roberts divides literature into canonical, serious, "plain," and "junk," with observations about the readership and authorship of each. "Junk" readers, for example—who include SF readers—engage in "thick reading," in which each new text is measured against a wide familiarity with the genre, and in fact redefines the genre. Although his selection of terminology is unfortunate, his discussion of market and editorial forces weak, and his knowledge of SF critical theory deficient even for its time, Roberts shows a greater sympathetic awareness of the genre than most general-purpose theorists of popular fiction. Recommended for those interested in exploring SF in the broader context of commercial literature.

*9-162.   Rose, Mark. **Alien Encounters: Anatomy of Science Fiction**. Harvard Univ. Press, 1981.

A brief but cogent theory of SF, which argues that the human–nonhuman encounter is the central paradigm of the genre. Following two introductory chapters that delimit the genre and identify this paradigm, Rose explores how it is developed in various ways in chapters titled "Space," "Time," "Machine," and "Monster." Few texts are analyzed in detail, although particular attention is paid to works by Asimov, Clarke, Dick, Heinlein, Lem, Stapledon, Verne, and Wells. Rose's theory is more provocative than definitive, but is elegantly developed, and bears comparison with Wolfe's *The Known and the Unknown* [9-202] and Malmgren's *Worlds Apart* [9-122].

Awards: Eaton

9-163.   Rose, Mark, ed. **Science Fiction: A Collection of Critical Essays**. Prentice-Hall, 1976.

A pioneering but now dated collection of 11 essays, originally published in various sources between 1960 and 1975 and intended to provide an overview of academic SF criticism in much the same way that Knight's *Turning Points* [9-108] provides an overview of criticism by SF writers. The pieces by Amis, Scholes, Suvin, Lem, Rabkin, and Ketterer are all included in books by these authors separately annotated in this chapter. Two other influential essays, by Susan Sontag and C. S. Lewis, are also available in books by those authors. Only the pieces by Robert Conquest, Michael Holmquist, and John Huntington are not widely available elsewhere, and the book's chief value is now as a source of early critical writing by some major figures.

*9-164.   Ruddick, Nicholas. **Ultimate Island: On the Nature of British Science Fiction**. Greenwood, 1993.

Ruddick sets out to contest the notion that British SF is either an offspring of the American tradition or purely a development of the "scientific romance" as described by Stableford [9-184]. Following introductory chapters in which he tries to outline the unique characteristics of British SF, he argues that Wells represented a synthesis of various literary traditions and that later authors self-consciously built upon Wells's work, particularly upon the motif of the island. Subsequent chapters focus on disaster fiction before and after World War II, modern British SF, and apparent future trends. Ruddick offers persuasive and sometimes brilliant readings of works by 14 key authors: Wells, S. Fowler Wright, Golding, Jacquetta Hawkes, Shiel, Doyle, Edward Shanks, J. J. Connington, John Collier, Alun Llewellyn, R. C. Sherriff, Wyndham, Christopher, and Ballard. This valuable study is a companion to Ruddick's *British Science Fiction: A Chronology, 1478–1990* (Greenwood, 1992).

*9-165.   Russ, Joanna. To Write Like a Woman: Essays in Feminism and Science Fiction. Indiana Univ. Press, 1995.

A collection of essays, most of them on SF or related fantastic literature, dating from 1971 to 1988. Although not a complete collection of Russ's SF criticism (none of her reviews from *The Magazine of Fantasy and Science Fiction* are here, for example), this is more directly focused on SF than the material in either of her two previous critical volumes. The two main theoretical pieces, "Towards an Aesthetic of Science Fiction" and "Speculations: The Subjunctivity of Science Fiction," both from the early 1970s, reveal some of that era's hope for the possibilities of SF. She argues that SF, like medieval literature, is essentially didactic, that it deals in collective heroes and dramatized ideas, that it is unique in modern literature for taking "work as its central and characteristic concern." The second half of the book covers some of the same material as her 1983 book *How to Suppress Women's Writing*, offering detailed discussions of Mary Shelley, contemporary women's gothics, feminist utopias, Willa Cather, and lesbian literature. Along with Samuel L. Delany, Russ was among the leading writer-theorists of SF in the 1970s, and in the absence of an extended theoretical statement, this contains the most important critical work relating to SF of one of the most important critics of that period.

Themes: Feminist SF

9-166.   Samuelson, David. Visions of Tomorrow: Six Journeys from Outer to Inner Space. Arno, 1974.

A detailed analysis, based on the author's 1969 dissertation, of six modern novels representing different theoretical aspects of SF: Clarke's *Childhood's End*, Asimov's *The Caves of Steel*, Sturgeon's *More Than Human*, Walter M. Miller's *A Canticle for Leibowitz*, Budrys' *Rogue Moon*, and Ballard's *The Crystal World*. Although a relatively early work, this retains much of its value because of Samuelson's sensitive readings; his discussion of Budrys in particular remains the most cogent extended critical treatment of that novel. A similar "representative novel" approach is taken by Manlove [9-124] and Scholes and Rabkin [9-171].

9-167.   Sands, Karen, and Marietta Frank, eds. Back in the Spaceship Again: Juvenile Science Fiction Series Since 1945. Greenwood, 1999.

In nine short chapters, the authors approach a variety of children's and young adult SF series from various angles: robots and artificial intelligence, utopias and dystopias, aliens, the role of science, humor, and the problematical role of females in books traditionally addressed to an audience of boys. The authors, a children's literature scholar and a librarian, have done a fair amount of research in prior SF criticism. Although they limit their survey to post-1945, primarily American works, coverage is still spotty, as is their annotated bibliography: series that began prior to 1945 but continued afterward are not mentioned, nor are series that may include only one juvenile title (as with Benford and Blish). Heinlein is barely discussed at all, presumably because his juveniles were not really a series, but the bibliography lists them as though they were. Still, this is one of the few critical studies to treat such titles as Joanna Cole's Magic School Bus stories or Jane Yolen's Commander Toad series as SF. Compare Sullivan's *Young Adult Science Fiction* [9-188] and *Science Fiction for Young Readers* [9-187].

Themes: Children in SF

9-168. Sanders, Joe, ed. **Science Fiction Fandom**. Greenwood, 1995.

A collection of 24 essays by various hands, mostly quite short, together with a bibliography and glossary of fannish terms. Much of the material is anecdotal or speculative rather than analytical—Sam Moskowitz arguing that the Roman Emperor Tiberius was an early SF fan; Robert and Juanita Coulson on why people become fans; Harry Warner on how Hiroshima seemed to validate fandom; John and Bjo Trimble on such fringe groups as Trekkies and the Society for Creative Anachronism; Hank Luttrell, Debbie Notkin, and Tom Whitmore on how "cons" are organized; Jack Gaughan on fan artists; Robert Weinberg on fan presses; Howard DeVore on collecting; Sandra Miesel on fan criticism; Russell Letson on fans versus academics. Some of the essays were already dated at the time of publication, and there is virtually no discussion of computer-based discussion groups. International fandom is covered in pieces by Terry Jeeves, Pascal Thomas, Roelof Goudriaan, Wu Dingbo, and Masamichi Osako. The book is more useful as a kind of guide to what fans think of themselves than as a disciplined analysis of the phenomenon. Compare Bacon-Smith's *Science Fiction Culture* [9-14]. Also annotated as [13-33].

9-169. Sandison, Alan, and Robert Dingley, eds. **Histories of the Future: Studies in Fact, Fantasy, and Science Fiction**. Palgrave, 2001.

This collection of essays by Australian, British, and American scholars seeks to explore visions of future history in science fiction and other venues, but covers such a range of texts that its focus sometimes becomes diffuse (an essay by Bruce Basington, for example, deals with the cult of the Navy in early juvenile fiction, while Roslynn D. Haynes discusses scientists in movies and Ken MacLeod discusses alternate history as developed in his own fiction). The issue of science fiction and prediction is a tantalizingly problematic one, but is nowhere systematically addressed. There are nonetheless significant contributions by major scholars, including Tom Shippey on Heinlein, Damien Broderick on the futility of prediction in the shadow of a Vingean "singularity," Charles Gannon on weaponry in SF, Dingley himself on tales of travelers from the future, David Seed on future-war novels, and Robert Crossley on the evolution of the Martian novel. Also of interest are Brian Baker's discussion of nuclear war fiction and Alasdair Sparks on recent failed predictions. An introduction by Harry Harrison on the development of SF scholarship is woefully incomplete, but the volume as a whole contains much that is of substance.

Themes: History in SF

9-170.   Scholes, Robert. **Structural Fabulation: An Essay on Fiction of the Future**. Univ. of Notre Dame Press, 1975.

Scholes, an influential literary theorist, finds in SF fertile ground for exploring ideas he earlier developed in *The Fabulators* (1967) and *Structuralism in Literature* (1974). This brief study, revised from four lectures delivered in 1974, first outlines a general defense of the study of SF in a postmodern context, followed by two chapters of definition with examples drawn from Sturgeon, Keyes, Stapledon, and Herbert; the final chapter is a more extended discussion of Le Guin's Earthsea and *The Left Hand of Darkness*. Despite his limited familiarity with the field, Scholes's theory has been influential. A much more detailed and knowledgeable approach, using some of the same methods, is Suvin's *Metamorphoses of Science Fiction* [9-189].

9-171.   Scholes, Robert, and Eric S. Rabkin. **Science Fiction: History/Science/Vision**. Oxford Univ. Press, 1977.

Intended as an introductory text for the general reader, this clearly written and organized study begins with a general history of SF, followed by a rather weak chapter on SF in nonliterary media. The "science" section offers fairly basic explanations of the scientific method and commonly used concepts from physics, astronomy, computer science, thermodynamics, biology, and psychology, with a brief discussion of pseudosciences. The "vision" section includes discussions of major SF themes and brief analyses of 10 representative novels by Shelley, Verne, Wells, Zamiatin, Lindsay, Stapledon, Clarke, Miller, Le Guin, and Brunner. Annotated nonfiction bibliographies and a list of award-winning novels follow. Although it offers little new for the serious student of SF, this served as a lucid brief overview in its time.

9-172.   Schweitzer, Darrell, ed. **Speaking of the Fantastic**. Wildside Press, 2002.

A collection of 11 interviews (some as much as a decade old at the time of publication) with authors such as Jonathan Carroll, Marion Zimmer Bradley, Terry Bisson, John Brunner, Robert Holdstock, Ellen Kushner, Ursula K. Le Guin, Fritz Leiber, Frederik Pohl, Dan Simmons, Lawrence Watt-Evans, Ray Faraday Nelson, and Jack Williamson. The collection suffers from a lack of discernable focus and carelessness (an interview with Gene Wolfe promised on the cover is not included), but offers useful insights in those interviews with authors not widely covered elsewhere.

9-173. **The Science Fiction Novel: Imagination as Social Criticism**. Advent, 1959.

A series of four lectures—by Heinlein, Kornbluth, Bloch, and Bester—originally delivered at the University of Chicago in 1957, and introduced by Basil Davenport. While the book in general is dated, Heinlein's essay remains of particular interest by developing at length his definition of science fiction; and Kornbluth's is a still-vivid attack on the failure of SF of the day to grapple meaningfully with social issues.

9-174. Seed, David. **American Science Fiction and the Cold War: Literature and Film**. Fitzroy Dearborn, 1999.

Revisiting the once-prominent science fiction of the Cold War era from the perspective of the post-Reagan "Star Wars" debates, Seed presents a reasoned and wide-ranging taxonomy of such texts, devoting chapters to the cautionary fables of Philip Wylie and Leo Szilard and the work of influential science fiction writers Robert Heinlein, Poul Anderson, Bernard Wolfe, Walter M. Miller, Russell Hoban, Frederik Pohl, and C. M. Kornbluth. Other chapters examine differing narrative strategies such as the domestic melodrama (in Judith Merril, Pat Frank, and others), "cultures of surveillance" in the wake of Orwell's *1984*, tales of Russian conquest, computer nightmares, "conspiracy narratives" (focusing largely on Philip K. Dick), the absurdist comedy of *Dr. Strangelove*, post-catastrophe narratives, and the relationship between science fiction and the Star Wars debate. Seed is widely read in this area, discussing some rarely mentioned minor novels, and his insights seem sound if not always original. Much of the bibliographical material could be compared with that in Paul Brians's *Nuclear Holocausts* [9-36], while some of the political and ideological ideas might be compared with H. Bruce Franklin's *War Stars* [9-80].

Themes: War

9-175. Seed, David, ed. **Anticipations: Essays on Early Science Fiction and Its Precursors**. Liverpool Univ. Press, 1995.

All of these 11 essays on SF prehistory—although only one concerns a work earlier than *Frankenstein*— offer at least some new insights on material usually discussed cursorily in SF histories, and usually relate their topics to the later development of the genre. Paul Baines discusses Robert Paltock's *The Life and Adventures of Peter Wilkins;* Edward James presents a largely statistical overview of 19th-century SF (drawing on the work of Darko Suvin and Thomas Clareson), while Brian Stableford undertakes a detailed defense of *Frankenstein* as SF. Patrick Parrinder discusses the important of the Thames Valley as a setting for "topographical romances" from Mary Shelley to Brian Aldiss; and David Seed explores Poe's fascination with exploration. M. Hammerton appreciatively examines Verne's sometimes misguided attempts to get his engineering details right; and Tony Barley regards London's *The Iron Heel* as pioneering the SF notion of a non-deterministic future created by specific social choices. Other contributors include Brian Nellist, on 19th-century predictive fictions, Simon Dentith on utopian fiction, Stephen R. L. Clark on Kipling (in one of the best discussions of his impact on the field), and Val Keith on Charlotte Perkins Gilman. Although far from definitive, none of the essays simply rehashes familiar material, and most are clearly written and persuasive.

9-176.   Seed, David. **Imagining Apocalypse: Studies in Cultural Crisis.** St. Martin's, 2000.

Fifteen original essays covering a variety of approaches to apocalyptic literature, thought, and film, ranging from Veronica Hollinger's discussion of the relevance of postmodern theorists Baudrillard and James, to George Slusser's approach to survivalist writing from the perspective of Thoreau's *Walden*, to Edward James's argument of the importance of the Book of Revelations to SF narratives. Seed himself discusses contemporary accounts of Hiroshima, while Marleen Barr finds evidence of sexism and anti-Semitism in the film *Independence Day*. Other contributors compare American and British nuclear war fiction, the rhetoric of apocalypse in African American texts, the punk and Goth movements, and Ballard's "concrete" trilogy. Like many such collections on broad themes, the essays are inconsistent in both focus and quality; some offer genuinely important insights into the understanding of the theme, while others are of far narrower interest.

9-177.   Shaw, Debra Benita. **Women and Science Fiction: The Frankenstein Inheritance.** Palgrave, 2001.

A revised doctoral dissertation that, despite its title, focuses less on Mary Shelley's novel than on later works by Charlotte Perkins Gilman, Katherine Burdekin, C. L. Moore, Margaret St. Clair, James Tiptree, Jr., Sally Gearhart, Carolyn Forbes, and Marge Piercy. Drawing on scholarship ranging from Freudian theory to the Kinsey reports to Donna Haraway, Shaw seeks to explore ways in which women writers have developed strategies "to imagine new female identities and social orders" within the sometimes confining contexts of science fiction's common ideologies and particular scientific theories. For the most part clearly written, it is of greatest value in discussing such texts as Burdekin and Forbes. Compare Donawerth's *Frankenstein's Daughters* [9-69].

   Themes: Feminist SF, Women in SF

9-178.   Shinn, Thelma J. **Worlds Within Women: Myth and Mythmaking in Fantastic Literature by Women.** Greenwood, 1986.

Shinn sets out to demonstrate how modern male writers, mostly of SF, have redefined and reinvented traditional "patriarchal" myths, as well as creating original myth systems and transforming female archetypes. The first chapter explores works based on familiar myths (such as Bradley's reworking of Arthurian material), and discusses Jean Auel, Doris Lessing, and Octavia Butler. The second chapter shows how Norton, Van Scyoc, Susan Coon, Vinge, Charnas, Elgin, and others reinvent these myths in SF settings. Mythmaking in Lessing, Le Guin, Van Scyoc, Sargent, Butler, Piercy, and others is covered in Chapter 3. Chapter 4 concerns new or transformed female archetypes in Tanith Lee, Russ, Butler, Wilhelm, and others. Shinn's work is persuasive without being polemical, and is of particular value because of the detailed attention she devotes to writers such as Butler or Vinge. Compare Barr's *Feminist Fabulation* [9-20].

Themes: Feminist SF

9-179. Shippey, Tom, ed. **Fictional Space: Essays on Contemporary Science Fiction**. Humanities Press International, 1991.

Eight essays on significant topics and texts in modern SF. Shippey's introductory piece on SF language and neologisms bears comparison with Delany's approach in *The Jewel-Hinged Jaw* [9-65] while Walter E. Meyers' discussion of SF language expands points made in his *Aliens and Linguists* [9-129]. John R. Christie and John Huntington each explore postmodern aspects of SF, emphasizing Gibson's *Neuromancer;* Robert Crossley examines SF museum artifacts; Alasdair Spark compares Heinlein's *Starship Troopers* with Haldeman's *Forever War;* Alan C. Elms explores the biographical sources of Cordwainer Smith's SF; and Shippey's second essay examines the iconography of America in decline. An excellent general collection.

9-180. Spinrad, Norman. **Science Fiction in the Real World**. Southern Illinois Univ. Press, 1990.

Assembled mostly from columns written for *Isaac Asimov's Science Fiction Magazine* from 1985 to 1988, these 14 essays by a major SF novelist show far more coherence than most such collections, since Spinrad used his column to explore ideas rather than merely review books. The three essays in his first section explore SF's relation to the mainstream and to its own easy formulas, which Spinrad terms sci-fi. The second covers SF in graphic novels and films and the third various "modes" such as cyberpunk, hard SF, and space colonies (the only specific theme treated as such). A fourth section discusses power fantasies in SF, including an account of Spinrad's experiences with his *The Iron Dream*. The highly personal final group of essays treats individual writers—Sturgeon, Vonnegut, Ballard, and Dick. The Sturgeon and Dick pieces are passionate and moving, and Spinrad's treatment of cyberpunk is among the best early accounts available. Despite his reputation for being contentious, his arguments are reasonable, balanced, and sound. Compare Budrys's *Benchmarks* [9-42], which offers similar coverage of an earlier period.

9-181. Stableford, Brian. **Algebraic Fantasies and Realistic Romances: More Masters of Science Fiction**. Borgo, 1995.

9-182. Stableford, Brian. **Opening Minds: Essays on Fantastic Literature**. Borgo, 1995.

9-183.   Stableford, Brian. **Outside the Human Aquarium: Masters of Science Fiction**, 2nd ed. Borgo, 1995.

Three short volumes of wide-ranging essays by one of the field's most knowledgeable critics and historians. Of the three, *Opening Minds* is the most broadly theoretical and the most interesting in terms of SF themes, theory, and history, including such topics as a quite original comparison of H. G. Wells with the French absurdist Alfred Jarry; an early 1851 coinage of the term "science fiction"; fictions of manmade catastrophe; the ideas of progress and of mind in SF; narrative tricks and illusions; the failure of prophecy in both SF and Marxism; and SF as medium rather than genre. The other two volumes, a revision and continuation of Stableford's 1981 *Masters of Science Fiction*, consider individual authors. *Outside the Human Aquarium* includes 10 pieces on Vonnegut, Dick, Silverberg, Sturgeon, and such critically underexplored figures as David H. Keller, Stanley G. Weinbaum, Clark Ashton Smith, Edmond Hamilton, Leigh Brackett, Barry Malzberg, and Mack Reynolds (the Vonnegut, Malzberg, and Silverberg essays date from 1976). *Algebraic Fantasies and Realistic Romances* contains seven essays ranging from 19th-century American novelist and poet Edgar Fawcett to bestselling writers Douglas Adams and Stephen R. Donaldson, to Michael Jackson's "Thriller" video. The best essays here are on Fawcett, John Gloag (a British novelist whose major work appeared in the 1930s and 1940s), M. P. Shiel, and Bob Shaw. Stableford's near-encyclopedic knowledge, especially of lesser-known writers and their contexts, is invaluable, as is his sociologist's perspective, although at times he tends to fall into a sociologist's dry style as well.

*9-184.   Stableford, Brian. **Scientific Romance in Britain 1890–1950**. Fourth Estate/St. Martin's, 1985.

One of the major works on SF history, and one of the first to establish a British tradition of fantastic literature clearly independent of American pulp history and, in fact, different from SF itself (although Stableford sees the traditions merging by the 1950s). Following two chapters of definition and background, he proceeds chronologically, first discussing the major preoccupations and writers of the pre-World War I period (George Griffith, Wells, Shiel, Doyle, Hodgson, and J. D. Beresford). Economic and cultural changes after the war altered the nature of works published; inter-war writers discussed include S. Fowler Wright, E. V. Odle, Stapledon, Neil Bell, and John Gloag. The final chapters trace the decline of scientific romance following World War II, discussing C. S. Lewis, Gerald Heard, and the heritage of the tradition in Clarke, Aldiss, and Ballard. As a sociologist as well as novelist, Stableford not only discusses a great many works with insight, but outlines the changing publishing and market conditions as well. Compare Suvin's *Victorian Science Fiction in the UK* [9-191] and Ruddick's *Ultimate Island* [9-164].

   Awards: Eaton

9-185. Stableford, Brian. **The Sociology of Science Fiction**. Borgo, 1987.

Stableford's doctoral thesis in sociology, originally completed in 1978 and reprinted here with a new introduction and index. Following two general chapters on the sociology of literature and communication, he briefly traces the development of the SF market, then devotes the heart of his discussion to chapters on what SF readers expect—which Stableford sees as more emotional than cognitive—and on significant themes (machines, aliens, societies, supermen) and trends. His conclusion is that SF doesn't work well as didactic literature, but serves important "directive," "maintenance," and "restorative" functions for its readership. Though not without its academic jargon, this is far more clearly written than most dissertations and offers solid insights into how SF is "used" by its readers. Compare Bainbridge [9-16], though this is generally superior. A final chapter, written in 1995 and planned for an unpublished revised edition, was published in *Foundation* 79, summer 2000, pp. 41–58, titled "The Economic Context of Contemporary Science Fiction."

9-186. Stockwell, Peter. **The Poetics of Science Fiction**. Longman, 2000.

Basing his approach on theories of cognitive rhetoric, Stockwell examines the complex relationships between linguistics and SF, arguing (in what is a good example of his sometimes specialized language) that the genre is characterized by "constitutive *isomorphisms*" and "architexts." By focusing heavily on the sentences and implied worlds of SF narratives, Stockwell shows little patience with questions of authorial intent or historical contextualization, preferring instead to focus on the experiences of the reader in encountering characteristically science-fictional sentences. While this provides little opportunity for extended discussions of individual works of fiction, it does serve to bring more recent theories of cognitive linguistics into the ongoing discussion of SF style. Compare Meyers's *Aliens and Linguists* [9-129], Delany's *The Jewel-Hinged Jaw* [9-65], and Suvin's *Metamorphoses of Science Fiction* [9-189].

Themes: Linguistics

9-187. Sullivan, C. W., III, ed. **Science Fiction for Young Readers**. Greenwood, 1993.

One of the earliest efforts to provide coverage of an aspect of science fiction often disregarded in the critical literature, this assembly of 16 essays is organized into three sections: "Shapers of Science Fiction for Young Readers," "Specific Authors and Their Works," and "Science Fiction as a Vehicle for Ideas." Most of the essays, however, focus on single authors. Among the authors and books covered are the Tom Swift series; major figures such as Asimov, Heinlein, Anne McCaffrey, Andre Norton, John Christopher, and Alan E. Nourse; and authors better known for children's or young adult fiction, such as Madeleine L'Engle, Russell Hoban, Monica Hughes, Raymond Briggs, Louise Lawrence,

Sylvia Engdahl, and H. M. Hoover. While there is occasionally a sense of over-packing, as though the book has too much catching up to do in an understudied area, and while some essays depend too heavily on descriptions or plot summaries, the collection as a whole is admirably balanced and surprisingly full in its coverage.

Themes: Children in SF

9-188.   Sullivan, C. W., III, ed. **Young Adult Science Fiction**. Greenwood, 1999.

A thematic companion to the editor's earlier author-centered *Science Fiction for Young Readers*, this collection of 12 essays is carefully shaped and organized to cover its topic in the manner of a focused monograph. Its first section includes historical surveys covering young adult fiction in America from 1900 to 1940 (by Francis J. Molson) and since 1947 (by Sullivan himself; it's not clear what happened to 1940–1947); in Canada (Greer Watson); in Britain (K. V. Bailey and Andy Sawyer); in Germany (Franz Rottensteiner); and in Australia (John Foster). A second section includes topical essays by Michael M. Levy (on SF bildungsroman), Marietta Frank (on Heinlein juveniles), Martha Bartter (on war in young adult SF), James Craig Holte (on SF film), and Donald Palumbo (on comics). Sullivan has done an excellent job of rounding up some of the major scholars in the field, and the historical chapters alone make this book a valuable reference and a pioneering critical study, despite some unevenness of approach among the individual essays, which are supplemented by an extensive and useful bibliography of secondary materials by Michael M. Levy.

Themes: Children in SF

*9-189.   Suvin, Darko. **Metamorphoses of Science Fiction: On the Poetics and History of a Literary Genre**. Yale Univ. Press, 1979.

Revised and expanded from the author's *Pour une poetique de la science-fiction* (Montreal, 1977), this has proved to be one of the most influential theoretical studies of SF to date, although many find the style dense and abstract. Suvin begins by proposing his widely cited notions of "cognitive estrangement" and the "novum," and the differences between SF and utopian literature. The second two thirds of the book, focusing on SF history, discuss More's *Utopia*, Shelley's *Frankenstein*, Morris's *News From Nowhere*, Wells's *The Time Machine*, and works by Bellamy, Twain, Poe, Čapek, and Russian SF writers. Suvin's strong opinions are always supported by relentless logic and solid scholarship, and even though some view his approach to SF to be narrow and prescriptive, this remains one of the most serious, scholarly, and important attempts to place the genre in a coherent context of intellectual and cultural history and sociology. Further reconsiderations of Suvin's ideas may be found in Parrinder, *Learning from Other Worlds* [9-145].

9-190. Suvin, Darko. **Positions and Presuppositions in Science Fiction**. Kent State Univ. Press, 1988.

A collection of 13 essays originally published between 1973 and 1984. Two essays provide an overview of Suvin's general ideas on social theories of literature, five deal with SF theory in particular, one with teaching SF, and five with various writers (Asimov, Yefremov, Lem, Dick, Le Guin, the Strugatskys, and Johanna and Gunter Braun). As always, Suvin's criticism is rigorous and theoretically sophisticated, and some readers may find this book a more accessible introduction to his work than his *Metamorphoses of Science Fiction*.

9-191. Suvin, Darko. **Victorian Science Fiction in the UK: The Discourses of Knowledge and of Power**. G. K. Hall, 1983.

In what is perhaps the most detailed and systematic study of a particular period in early SF history, Suvin attempts to expand upon ideas developed in *Metamorphoses of Science Fiction* by investigating in great detail the period 1848 to 1900 in England. He begins with an annotated bibliography of 360 books, then discusses which should and should not be counted as SF; an essay by John Sutherland on the Victorian book trade supplements this. He then offers biographical information on 270 writers and discusses them in terms of social origin, profession, social position, and even longevity. Having thus laid out his data, Suvin devotes the second part of his study to a long essay on the audiences (or "social addressees") of the works discussed and the major themes of knowledge, ideology, and power. An invaluable source for students of Victorian literature, SF history, and the sociology of SF. Contrast Stableford [9-184].

9-192. Tolley, Michael J., and Kirpal Singh, eds. **The Stellar Gauge: Essays on Science Fiction Authors**. Norstrilia Press, 1980.

An international group of contributors (from Australia, Britain, the United States, and Singapore) cover a variety of SF authors and works in an unusually readable and literate collection that features a number of novelists discussing other novelists: George Turner on Pohl, John Sladek on Disch, Brian Aldiss on Blish, and Christopher Priest on Ballard. Other writers covered include Verne, Orwell, Bester, Clarke, Aldiss, Dick, and Silverberg. Only two of the essays (Aldiss and Priest) were previously published. Compare with Clareson's *Voices for the Future* series [9-52].

*9-193. Wagar, W. Warren. **Terminal Visions: The Literature of Last Things**. Indiana Univ. Press, 1982.

Wagar, a historian who has also published SF stories, traces the history of secular eschatological fiction through some 300 works, from Mary Shelley's *The Last Man* through the work of Ballard. Wagar is adept at showing how such works reflect the spirit of the times, and makes some unusual but important discoveries: that most doomsday fiction is actually rather upbeat, and that World War I marked a dramatic turning point between fictions predominantly of natural disaster and those predominantly of disasters of human origin. He is also unusually knowledgeable among cultural historians about SF. Although there are few extended analyses of individual works, this is the most comprehensive analysis of this major SF theme. Compare with Rabkin, Greenberg, and Olander's *The End of the World* [9-156] (with which there is some overlap in Wagar's two contributions to that volume).

Themes: End of the World

9-194. Walsh, Chad. **From Utopia to Nightmare**. Harper, 1982.

From an essentially Christian perspective, Walsh discusses the shift from utopian to dystopian literature (his work was the first to popularize the term *dystopia)* in the 19th and 20th centuries. Among the authors he covers are Bellamy, Huxley, Orwell, Vonnegut, Zamiatin, Wells, Bernard Wolfe, E. M. Forster, and Vladimir Nabokov. Although much of the material is dated, this is still a wide-ranging and elegantly written study.

Themes: Dystopias, Utopias

9-195. Warner, Harry, Jr. **All Our Yesterdays: An Informal History of Science Fiction Fandom in the Forties**. Advent, 1969. Introduction by Wilson Tucker.

A somewhat rambling anecdotal history of fandom, focusing principally on the 1930s and 1940s, and liberally supplemented with photographs, a glossary, profiles of major fans and important conventions, and summaries of regional and international fan activities. Far more thorough than Moskowitz's *The Immortal Storm* [9-131] and probably the most complete compilation of information anywhere about SF's organized readership during this period. (Warner even uncovers information on possible 19th-century fans.) Of limited interest in terms of literary history, but an important ancillary resource for those interested in the culture of SF. Warner continues his history into the 1950s in the generally inaccessible fan-published *Wealth of Fable: The History of Science Fiction Fandom in the 1950s* (Fanhistorica Press, 1976 [13-36]), which was belatedly awarded the Hugo in 1993. Compare Sanders [9-168] and Bacon-Smith [9-14]. Also annotated as [13-35].

9-196. Warrick, Patricia S. **The Cybernetic Imagination in Science Fiction**. MIT Press, 1980.

Warrick surveyed some 225 stories and novels published between 1930 and 1977, all dealing with some aspect of intelligent machines. She discovers two models of the human/machine relationship: the "closed-system" model, focusing on the opposition between humans and machines; and the "open-system" model, suggesting a potentially creative symbiosis of humans and machines. Warrick focuses more on questions of scientific verisimilitude than of literary merit, and her theoretical approach is rather vague, permitting her to cite as the two "giants" of this kind of fiction authors as dissimilar as Asimov and Dick. Although now dated in its use of information theory, literary theory, and the fiction itself, Warrick's broad sampling and often cogent discussions of individual works make this a significant study of its time.

Themes: Computers, Machines

9-197. Westfahl, Gary. **Cosmic Engineers: A Study of Hard Science Fiction**. Greenwood, 1996.

Characteristically supporting his claims with painstaking bibliographical research, Westfahl's overview of the subgenre of hard SF begins by tracing the etymology of the term, which he ascribes to P. Schuyler Miller. This is perhaps indicative of his approach, which seeks less to develop a theory of hard SF than to track the etiology of the concept within the SF community. He derives two broad classes of hard SF: "microcosmic," set in the near-future and extrapolating known science and technology; and "macrocosmic," which leaps far into the future and builds bizarre worlds based on broad scientific principles. He argues that adherence to known science was seldom a major concern of SF prior to the 1950s (Verne repeatedly violated the known physics of his day, Westfahl claims), and that the New Wave represented less a revolution than a return to this laxity. He offers detailed technical discussions of novels by Clarke, Clement, and Charles Sheffield. Westfahl's essentially constructionist and conservative approach to SF leads to some intemperate claims, particularly in regard to literary concerns, but his assiduous attention to detail lends his work considerable research value.

Themes: Hard SF

9-198. Westfahl, Gary. **Islands in the Sky**. Borgo, 1996.

Contending persuasively that SF has not really exploited the space station theme in challenging ways, Westfahl sets out to examine these failures by offering a detailed survey of recurrent motifs and concerns. While there are few extended discussions of individual works in literary terms, Westfahl is skilled at cataloging specific ideas over a broad range of stories—contemptuous attitudes of space dwellers toward Earthlings, for example (he lists 15 different insulting terms for Earth-dwellers drawn from as many different stories), or the dangers of cabin fever. Westfahl tends to champion the Gernsback school of SF as an instrument of education and speculation, and while his sometimes contentious tone may be off-putting, he is a passionate believer in the social worth of SF, arguing that a study such as his "will have significant implications regarding the future of humanity in space, in life, and in literature."

Themes: Space Flight

9-199. Westfahl, Gary. **The Mechanics of Wonder: The Creation of the Idea of Science Fiction**. Liverpool Univ. Press, 1998.

One of the most broadly polemical of this prolific author's several studies of aspects of science fiction history sets out to demonstrate that Hugo Gernsback not only created almost single-handedly the notion of science fiction as a genre, but that his various editorials and commentaries in *Amazing Stories* constituted a coherent and consistent literary theory of paramount importance to modern literature. He develops this notion after castigating many prior historians and critics who find the genre's origins in the 19th century or earlier, or who award what he sees as undue credit to later editors, particularly John W. Campbell, Jr. While his argument that a genre does not truly exist until authors see themselves writing it is necessary to his central thesis, it constitutes a rather unusual view of genre theory, and Westfahl's own efforts at developing a definition of science fiction late in the book are often fuzzy. Nevertheless, as with all Westfahl's studies, his detailed attention to the minutiae of the pulp era lends the volume particular interest to historians and strives to validate many commonly held beliefs among fans.

9-200.   Westfahl, Gary. **Science Fiction, Children's Literature, and Popular Culture: Coming of Age in Fantasyland**. Greenwood, 2000.

Although its title might seem to suggest an exploration of the connections between children's literature and science fiction, this is in fact a *pot pourri* of 11 disparate essays, only three of which focus on children's literature and none in particular on children's SF (instead, they treat juvenile series fiction, the Hardy boys, and a 1920s series of books for young readers). Other essays cover topics as diverse as MTV, science fiction film and television, Hollywood novels, and Superman. Only two are of particular relevance to science fiction literature: an essay on SF attitudes toward information technologies and another on "misinterpretations" of Wells's *The Time Machine*, focusing not on literary analyses so much as on the part of various adapters and marketers of the tale. Of limited value compared with Westfahl's other studies of aspects of the genre.

9-201.   Willingham, Ralph. **Science Fiction and the Theatre**. Greenwood, 1993.

While Willingham devotes a fair amount of his study to pondering the reasons why science fiction and the stage have come to seem almost incompatible, he nevertheless identifies and discusses more than 300 theatricals that could reasonably be regarded as SF or containing SF elements, from Offenbach's opera *The Tales of Hoffman* and adaptations of *Frankenstein* to Čapek's *R.U.R.* and Shaw's *Back to Methuselah*, to more recent operatic works by Philip Glass, dramas by SF writers such as Ray Bradbury, and pulp redactions such as Stuart Gordon's *Warp!* The book is useful as a reference source and as a critical discussion of the possibilities of SF theater. Two earlier books, *Staging the Impossible* (Greenwood, 1992), a collection of essays edited by Patrick Murphy, and *The Plot of the Future: Utopia and Dystopia in Modern Drama* by Dragan Klaic (Michigan, 1992), also deal with SF drama, the latter focusing on 50 works the author views as expressing utopian concerns.

*9-202.   Wolfe, Gary K. **The Known and the Unknown: The Iconography of Science Fiction**. Kent State Univ. Press, 1979.

In this fascinating and exceptionally perceptive study, Wolfe explores the recurrent iconic images that SF writers have used with varying degrees of subtlety, complexity, and power. He suggests that the "sense of wonder" so often talked of is generated by the juxtaposition of the known and the unknown, separated by a barrier. Among the iconic images explored in a wide-ranging selection of American and British stories are those of the spaceship, the city, the wasteland, the robot, and the monster. Wolfe transcends a purely formulaic analysis of SF to show how many works blend traditional images and sophisticated development that engage the reader on many levels. The novice will not have sufficient knowledge of SF to appreciate the breadth and subtlety of Wolfe's analysis, but fans and scholars cannot fail to have their insights enriched. A major study worthy of the widest readership. (NB)

Awards: Eaton

9-203.   Wollheim, Donald A. **The Universe Makers: Science Fiction Today**. Harper, 1971.

A personal and anecdotal brief survey by an influential editor and author, notable for its outline of a "consensus cosmogony" of future history drawn from the works of "Golden Age" writers and later picked up by James Gunn and others. Wollheim's approach is both conservative and commercial, and the book is of greater value as a record of his ideas and experiences than as a general survey. A similar personal history is del Rey [9-63].

*9-204.   Wolmark, Jenny. **Aliens and Others: Science Fiction, Feminism, and Postmodernism**. Univ. of Iowa Press, 1994.

Wolmark sets out to show how feminist SF undercuts traditional hierarchical notions of self and other as expressed not only through the metaphor of the alien, but through other metaphorical strategies as well. Following an introductory chapter on the postmodern theories of Fredric Jameson, Jean Baudrillard, Teresa de Lauretis, Marleen Barr, Donna Haraway, and others, she begins her analyses of specific writers by showing how Octavia Butler and Gwyneth Jones undercut traditional SF assumptions about gender and race. Subsequent chapters deal with the subversion of power structures in C. J. Cherryh and Vonda McIntyre; feminist utopias and dystopias in Suzy McKee Charnas, Sally Miller Gearhart, Sheri Tepper, Pamela Sargent, and Margaret Atwood; the impact of feminist SF on the cyberpunk of William Gibson and Pat Cadigan; and the cyborg metaphor in novels by Rebecca Ore, Marge Piercy, and Elisabeth Vonarburg. Wolmark sees the cyborg image as holding the potential for redefining gender and power roles in a way that the "cyberspace" of cyberpunk only approximates. Although her prose is sometimes stiffly academic, Wolmark's thought is clear and precise. Compare Balsamo [9-17] and Hayles [9-92].

Themes: Aliens, Feminist SF

9-205.   Wolmark, Jenny, ed. **Cybersexualities: A Reader on Feminist Theory, Cyborgs, and Cyberspace**. Edinburgh Univ. Press, 1999.

A collection of 17 essays, originally published between 1988 and 1995, intended to provide an overview of feminist "cybertheory" in terms that are both broadly theoretical and specific to individual texts, particularly of the cyberpunk movement. The first, more theoretical section ("Technology, Embodiment, and Cyberspace") includes pieces by Zoë Sophia, Sadie Plant, Alluquère Rosanne Stone, Mary Ann Doane, Claudia Springer, and Elizabeth Grosz, which explore in various ways the implications of information and cyborg theory for feminist scholars. The second section ("Cybersubjects: Cyborgs and Cyberpunks") includes essays by Anne Balsamo (on pop culture cyborgs), N. Katherine Hayles (who discusses works by Bernard Wolfe, John Varley, and C. J. Cherryh), Veronica Hollinger (on cyberpunk and postmodernism), Nicola Nixon (largely on feminist SF as a precursor to cyberpunk), Thomas Foster (who discusses such writers as Delany and Laura Mixon), and Jenny Wolmark (on feminist SF romances). A final section ("Cyborg Future") expands the discussion more broadly into issues of gender and race and includes essays by Chela Sandoval, Jennifer Gonzalez, Kathleen Woodward, Donald Morton, and Donna Haraway (whose earlier essay "A Cyborg Manifesto" is clearly one of the foundational theoretical texts underlying the entire collection). Often densely theoretical and sometimes polemical, these essays offer a useful overview of a significant trend in science fiction and cultural criticism of the 1990s.

Themes: Feminist SF

9-206.   Yanarella, Ernest J. **The Cross, The Plow, and the Skyline: Contemporary Science Fiction and the Ecological Imagination**. Brown Walker, 2001.

Taking the three images of his title as metaphors for what he views as three distinct strains of American SF—apocalyptic, pastoral, and urban—Yanarella proceeds to examine these traditions in light of their expressions of ecological consciousness. Following a section in which he argues that religious apocalypticism informed much of early America's sense of its own destiny, he turns frankly polemical in his discussions of the Gaia hypothesis (of which he roundly disapproves) and the work of such SF writers as Asimov, Benford, Brin, and Kim Stanley Robinson. With its focus less on literary analysis than on social and ecological critiques of SF ideologies, the study is often more provocative than illuminating. Compare Ben-Tov [9-28].

Add Themes: Ecology

9-207.   Yoke, Carl B., and Donald M. Hassler, eds. **Death and the Serpent: Immortality in Science Fiction and Fantasy**. Greenwood, 1985.

Intended to cover the theme of immortality in much the same way that Erlich and Dunn's books in the same series covered machines, this collection of 19 essays focuses on fantasy, myth, and horror as well as SF. Of interest are Marleen Barr on feminist communities, Nick O'Donohue on Shelley and Leiber, Curtis Smith on Stapledon, C. W. Sullivan, III on Heinlein, Joseph Sanders on

Zelazny, Mark Siegel on Tiptree, and essays on Herbert, Niven, Gunn, and Vance. A useful bibliography covers fiction, nonfiction, and anthologies. Compare Clark [9-53] and Slusser, Rabkin, and Westfahl [9-228].

Themes: Immortality

9-208. Yoke, Carl B., and Donald M. Hassler, eds. **Phoenix from the Ashes: The Literature of the Remade World**. Greenwood, 1987.

Like most such symposia, this collection of 19 mostly short essays on the theme of renewal following catastrophe suffers both from gaps in coverage and overlap among the contributors. Five essays deal with general topics, and 14 on particular writers, texts, or films. Among the more provocative are Yoke's introduction, Paul Brians on the rediscovery of learning as a theme, and Wyn Wachhorst on films. Others cover such authors as Walter M. Miller, Jr., Ballard, Pat Frank, Nevil Shute, Piers Anthony, Wells, Weinbaum, Poul Anderson, Russell Hoban, and Bernard Malamud. A comparable, but somewhat more theoretically oriented volume is Rabkin, Greenberg, and Olander's *The End of the World* [9-156]. See also Wagar, *Terminal Visions* [9-193].

Themes: Holocaust and After

9-209. Zebrowski, George. **Beneath the Red Star: Studies on International Science Fiction**. Borgo, 1996.

A collection of nine essays, mostly on Russian and Polish SF (but with some Japanese as well), based largely on review-essays published in *The Magazine of Fantasy and Science Fiction* and elsewhere between 1974 and 1991. Zebrowski's extensive discussion of the work of Lem and the Strugatskys is especially useful, as is a checklist of some 111 English translations of foreign-language SF. Compare McGuire, *Red Stars* [9-128].

Conference Proceedings

Two major academic conferences have regularly published collections of papers derived from their annual meetings. The International Association for the Fantastic in the Arts (IAFA)—originally called the International Conference on the Fantastic in Literature and Film—has met annually since 1980 (in Fort Lauderdale, Florida, since 1988) and is the largest such academic conference, with registered attendance averaging in the 300 range. Selections of this conference's papers (usually about 10 percent of those delivered at any given conference) began to be published by Greenwood Press in 1985, and additional conference papers sometimes appear in the association's *Journal of the Fantastic in the Arts,* begun in 1988. The J. Lloyd Eaton Conference on Science Fiction and Fantasy Literature, held annually at the University of California–Riverside and a few other venues since 1979, began publishing essays from its conferences with Southern Illinois University Press in 1980, moving to the University of Georgia Press in 1993 and later to Greenwood Press.

In addition, several other conferences have regularly produced papers that eventually saw print in journals, essay collections, or irregular volumes of proceedings. For example, the University of Nice's Colloque International de Science-Fiction de Nice published the proceedings of its biennial meetings as special issues of the journal *Metaphores*. The Science Fiction Research Association (SFRA) holds an annual summer conference at various locations, usually attracting 75 to 150 registrants; it published a volume of *Selected Proceedings* in 1979. The Popular Culture Association has met annually at various location since 1971 and usually features a substantial selection of papers dealing with SF literature and film, as, occasionally, does the Modern Language Association and its regional counterparts.

The largest of the fan conventions, the World Science Fiction Convention, has been held annually since 1939, and has on occasion published proceedings of individual meetings. Since 1982, it has featured a track of academic programming, which has also produced two small volumes of essays. Numerous other "one-shot" conferences on SF topics have also led to essay collections. Most of the collections annotated here and earlier in this chapter are indexed by Hall [7-17]. Since the Eaton Conference and International Conference on the Fantastic in the Arts have produced so many volumes, those series are listed separately here following a general listing of other conference proceedings.

I. General Conferences

9-210.   Emelina, Jean, and Denise Terrel, eds. **Actes du premier colloque international de science-fiction de Nice: Images de l'ailleurs-espace interieur**. Centre d'etude de la Metaphore, 1984.

Eighteen essays and a roundtable discussion from the University of Nice's first biennial conference on SF in 1983; nine of the essays are in English, the rest in French. The English-language essays include significant theoretical and thematic pieces by major scholars and writers such as Robert Scholes, Darko Suvin, John Dean, Brian Stableford, Peter Fitting, Patrick Parrinder, Moria Monteith, David Ketterer, and John Shirley. The proceedings of the fourth Nice conference, with all papers in both French and English versions, were published in a massive two-volume collection, *Science et science-fiction: Actes du 4eme colloque international de science-fiction de Nice* in 1992.

9-211.   Hassler, Donald M., ed. **Patterns of the Fantastic: Academic Programming at Chicon IV**. Starmont, 1983.

A selection of 12 short papers from the first formally organized track of worldcon academic programming, at the 1982 Chicon (the complete track is listed in an appendix). Five essays deal with women writers or characters; others cover Delany, Ellison, King, Robin Cook, and *2001: A Space Odyssey*. Those most relevant to the convention itself discuss the Moebius Theatre Company and the sociology of conventions (based on some 700 questionnaires distributed at various midwestern cons). A second selection, *Patterns of the Fantastic II: Academic Proceedings at Constellation* (Starmont, 1984), from the 1983 Baltimore worldcon, includes ten essays, the best of which is Jan Bogstad's analysis of cross-genre fiction. Two essays compare the film *Blade Runner* with its source, and others cover Wells, mathematics in SF, computers, and Le Guin.

9-212. Merrick, Helen, and Tess Williams, eds. **Women of Other Worlds: Excursions Through Science Fiction and Feminism**. Univ. of Western Australia Press, 1999.

A large collection of essays, fiction, correspondence, interviews, and online discussion transcripts drawn from or otherwise associated with the 1996 WisCon, arguably the world's preeminent annual feminist science fiction convention. By including such a variety of material, some of it generated after the conference itself and some previously published, the editors set out to create a *"virtual* WisCon," and to some extent they succeed, while at the same time they inevitably reproduce some of the chaotic and highly uneven ambience of a con weekend, and relatively little editorial discipline is in evidence. Only some of the material is clearly fannish in nature, however, and the volume includes provocative pieces by Nicola Griffith, Jeanne Gomoll, Sylvia Kelso, and others. Also annotated as II-1411.

Themes: Feminist SF

9-213. Pastourmatzi, Domna, ed. **Biotechnological and Medical Themes in Science Fiction**. University Studio Press, 2003.

A lavish illustrated collection of 32 pieces drawn from a conference on the theme held in Thessaloniki, Greece, in 2001, generally focusing on the ambivalence toward medicine as a potential threat and a promise. The international perspective (two of the essays are printed in Greek) lends the collection an unusual breadth of coverage, including pieces on Indian dramatist Manjula Padmanabhan, French writer Jacques Testart, Greek authors Diamantis Florakis and Kira Sinou, and several Australian authors, most notably Greg Egan. A section on cloning includes significant essays by Darko Suvin and Janeen Webb, while other sections include discussions of Joan Slonczewsi, David Zindell, Octavia Butler, Greg Bear, Rebecca Ore, Pat Cadigan, Paul di Filippo, Philip K. Dick, thriller writers Philip Kerr and Michael Cordy, and science fiction films. Authors Candas Jane Dorsey, Timothy J. Anderson, and Joan Slonczewski provide introductory overviews. While it is almost impossible to maintain a clear focus in a collection of this size, the attractive volume contains a fair amount of original criticism and information. Compare Westfahl and Slusser, *No Cure for the Future* [9-231].

Themes: Medicine

9-214.   Remington, Thomas J., ed. **Selected Proceedings of the 1978 Science Fiction Research Association National Conference**. Univ. of Northern Iowa, 1979.

The only published proceedings volume of the SFRA (except for Westfahl's *Space and Beyond*, the results of a joint Eaton/SFRA conference annotated under the Eaton series) includes 17 essays plus Brian Aldiss's Pilgrim acceptance speech; a dialogue between Gordon Dickson and Joe Haldeman; a roundtable discussion with Le Guin, Robert Scholes, Eric Rabkin, Gene Wolfe, and Darko Suvin; and even transcripts of Le Guin's interaction with the audience. Essayists include Marshall Tymn, Andrew Gordon, Patricia Warrick, Jane Weedman, William Hardesty, Natalie Rosinski, Richard Erlich, Darko Suvin, and Gary K. Wolfe. Though much of the material was later published in various books, this remains valuable as an unfortunately scarce record of one of SFRA's most important conferences.

9-215.   Sawyer, Andy, and David Seed, eds. **Speaking Science Fiction: Dialogues and Interpretations**. Liverpool Univ. Press, 2000.

A wide-ranging collection of 18 pieces from a 1996 conference accompanying the relocation to the University of Liverpool of the substantial collection of the Science Fiction Foundation, and intended to celebrate the diversity of science fiction studies. Of particular interest are the contributions from participating writers such as Gwyneth Jones, Josef Nesvabada, and Candas Jane Dorsey, while the more interesting academic contributions include pieces on Heinlein by Farah Mendlesohn, David Seed on the SF megastory, and Bronwen Calvert and Sue Walsh on cyberpunk and feminist SF (which they argue are quite different). While almost deliberately lacking in focus, the volume contains some quite worthwhile essays and reflections.

9-216.   Sayer, Karen, and John Moore, eds. **Science Fiction: Critical Frontiers**. St. Martin's, 2000.

This collection of 12 essays, from a 1996 conference at England's University of Luton titled "Envisioning Alternatives: The Literature of Science Fiction," is divided into two parts. In the first, critics Darko Suvin, Patrick Parrinder, Gregory Paschalidis, and Tom Moylan present broadly theoretical pieces that serve to describe current social and economic contexts in which to "position" both science fiction and science fiction criticism. In the more uneven second part, generally younger critics examine specific works and authors more or less in the light of these contexts. Authors covered in these pieces include Delany, William Burroughs, Mary Shelley, C. L. Moore, Marge Piercy, Kim Stanley Robinson, Pat Cadigan, William Gibson, Bruce Sterling, Gudrun Pausewang, and Neal Stephenson. One of several essay collections focusing largely on an emerging canon of postmodernist writers of the last several decades, it offers occasionally provocative ideas (especially in the pieces by Suvin and Moylan, although much of the material in the latter is incorporated in Moylan's *Scraps of the Untainted Sky*) but relatively few groundbreaking discussions of individual texts.

9-217. Slusser, George E., and Tom Shippey, eds. **Fiction 2000: Cyberpunk and the Future of Narrative**. Univ. of Georgia Press, 1992.

Seventeen essays and one roundtable discussion drawn from the proceedings of the 1989 "Fiction 2000" conference held in Leeds, England. Gibson's Neuromancer trilogy is a central text for more than half the contributions, which are divided into five sections. The first, on cyberpunk, includes pieces by Lewis Shiner, Istvan Csicsery-Ronay, and George Slusser. The second, on SF traditions related to cyberpunk, features Paul Alkon, Gary Westfahl, and Carol McGuirk. The third section looks outside SF with essays by Lance Olsen, John Huntington, and Brooks Landon. Individual writers, including Shiner, Sterling, and Gibson, are treated in section four, along with film and TV. The final section on the future of narrative includes a refreshingly debunking piece by Gregory Benford as well as more-theoretical essays by David Porush and Eric S. Rabkin. As a whole, the volume is somewhat more focused and less polemical than McCaffery's comparable *Storming the Reality Studio* [9-127].

Themes: Cyberpunk

9-218. Weedman, Jane, ed. **Women Worldwalkers: New Dimensions of Science Fiction and Fantasy**. Texas Tech Press, 1985.

Sixteen papers originally delivered at a comparative literature symposium at Texas Tech 1983 and revised for publication, including two by guest writers Marion Zimmer Bradley (on the responsibilities of women SF writers) and Samuel R. Delany (on Joanna Russ). Others cover a variety of topics from film and SF illustration to Dick, Aldiss, Lessing, Herbert, Christa Reinig, Elgin, and Bradley. The collection has little overall focus and lacks an index, although the abstracts of each paper are helpful. More recent studies by Barr, Armitt, LeFanu, and Larbalestier are more current and less diffuse.

Themes: Women in SF

9-219. Weldes, Jutta, ed. **To Seek Out New Worlds: Exploring Links Between Science Fiction and World Politics**. Palgrave Macmillan, 2003.

This collection of eight essays (plus an introduction by the editor) is intended to offer perspectives on science fiction from political scientists and international relations scholars, but despite its title, it focuses heavily on film and television, with only the introduction and one essay (by Geoffrey Whitehall) discussing literary texts with any substance. For the most part, contributors seem unfamiliar with both SF literature and SF scholarship, resulting in significant lacunae, even while the application of some theoretical models to SF films may provide useful starting points.

Themes: Politics

II. The J. Lloyd Eaton Conference on Science Fiction and Fantasy

9-220.   Slusser, George E., Colin Greenland, and Eric S. Rabkin, eds. **Storm Warnings: Science Fiction Confronts the Future**. Southern Illinois Univ. Press, 1987.

Papers from the 1984 Eaton Conference, which was held in two parts in California and London. Predictably, the major topic of discussion that year was Orwell's most famous novel and its influence. Frederik Pohl's "Coming Up on *1984*" debunks the novel as among Orwell's worst, while other contributors, including John Huntington, Elizabeth Maslen, T. A. Shippey, Colin Greenland, and Frank McConnell discuss the work and its successors more favorably.

9-221.   Slusser, George E., George R. Guffey, and Mark Rose, eds. **Bridges to Science Fiction**. Southern Illinois Univ. Press, 1980.

The inaugural volume in the Eaton series features papers from the first conference, held in 1979. Of particular interest are Gregory Benford's essay on aliens and Patrick Parrinder's on SF as "truncated epic." Eric S. Rabkin compares SF to fairy tales, Harry Levin (in the keynote address) discusses various literary responses to science, and other contributors discuss Dick, SF's treatment of historical time, SF and Gothic, medieval SF, visionary SF, and philosophical empiricism and SF. The second Eaton Conference volume, *Bridges to Fantasy*, concerns itself almost exclusively with definitions and parameters of fantasy fiction rather than SF, although some of the essays are useful for their theoretical genre distinctions.

9-222.   Slusser, George E., and Eric S. Rabkin, eds. **Aliens: The Anthropology of Science Fiction**. Southern Illinois Univ. Press, 1987.

The papers from the 1986 Eaton Conference focus less on anthropology than on a common SF theme that sometimes involves anthropological speculation. Larry Niven and Gregory Benford reveal their different approaches to the topic (and to SF) as Niven considers why aliens haven't visited Earth and Benford considers stylistic problems of dealing with aliens. Other essays discuss friendly aliens, "illegal" aliens, robots, telepaths, and even Barbie dolls. One of the livelier volumes in this series.

Themes: Aliens

9-223.   Slusser, George E., and Eric S. Rabkin, eds. **Fights of Fancy: Armed Conflict in Science Fiction and Fantasy**. Univ. of Georgia Press, 1993.

Fifteen essays chosen from those presented at the 1988 Eaton Conference, many of which define the theme "armed conflict" pretty loosely. Eric S. Rabkin's essay tracing the internalization of warfare in SF is the only piece to offer a substantial overview of the topic. Reginald Bretnor and Gary Westfahl focus on problems of semantics and language; four essays deal with earlier imaginary wars; other topics include film, comics, nuclear war, and Third World issues. Of particular interest are Joe Haldeman's account of his own fiction dealing with Vietnam, Louis Pedrotti's discussion of an 1833 Russian SF novel by Osip Senkovsky, and Martha Bartter's treatment of M. J. Engh's *Arslan*.

Themes: War

9-224. Slusser, George E., and Eric S. Rabkin, eds. **Hard Science Fiction**. Southern Illinois Univ. Press, 1986.

One of the most focused of the Eaton collections, this selection of 16 essays addresses issues of hard SF, which is seldom discussed separately as a form. Four SF writers among the contributors—Brin, Benford, Gunn, and Forward—make a persuasive case for hard SF as a particular kind of craft. Two of the essays, by Alkon and Huntington, are versions of what would become chapters from their books. Slusser's own essay is among the most provocative. Compare Westfahl's *Cosmic Engineers* [9-197] and the introduction to Hartwell and Cramer's anthology, *The Ascent of Wonder*.

Themes: Hard SF

9-225. Slusser, George E., and Eric S. Rabkin, eds. **Intersections: Fantasy and Science Fiction**. Southern Illinois Univ. Press, 1987.

The 1985 Eaton Conference volume collects 17 essays focusing generally on genre theory as it applies to SF and fantasy. The first group of essays, which tries to make distinctions between SF and fantasy, includes Robert Scholes on science fantasy, Michael Collings on horror, Joseph Miller on parallel universes, and a short essay by Zelazny. The second group looks at origins of the forms, and is highlighted by essays by Kathleen Spencer and Frank McConnell. The final section contains essays that seek to make a synthesis, and includes contributions from Slusser, Brian Attebery, and Kathryn Flume.

9-226. Slusser, George E., and Eric S. Rabkin, eds. **Styles of Creation: Aesthetic Technique and the Creation of Fictional Worlds**. Univ. of Georgia Press, 1993.

Aesthetic and stylistic discussions are surprisingly rare in SF studies, and this volume from the 11th Eaton Conference, in 1989, attempts to redress the balance. Benford, a regular at the conference, discusses his own experiments with style, and Paul Carter offers a rare discussion of pulp writer Nat Schachner; other authors covered include Heinlein, Dick, King, and Malzberg. Other provocative essays include Joseph D. Miller on the role of ambiguity in portraying alien mental states, Gary Westfahl on SF neologisms, Patrick Parrinder on landscapes in British SF, Brooks Landon on invisibility, and Robert Crossley on museums in SF narratives. One of the best of the Eaton volumes.

9-227. Slusser, George E., Eric S. Rabkin, and Robert Scholes, eds. **Coordinates: Placing Science Fiction and Fantasy**. Southern Illinois Univ. Press, 1983.

The third Eaton Conference, in 1981, addressed the question of appropriate standards or norms by which to judge SF and fantasy, and this group of 13 essays begins with a lively argument by Leslie Fiedler against the usefulness of traditional elitist versus popular standards. Rabkin offers a philosophical, almost biological theory of the origins of fantasy, and later essays cover specific texts by Verne, Delany, Heinlein, Simak, Ayn Rand, Bradbury, Haggard, and Charlotte Perkins Gilman. H. Bruce Franklin's "America as Science Fiction: 1939" is an especially valuable contribution to SF as cultural history, and Gary K. Wolfe discusses themes of bodily transformation.

9-228.　　Slusser, George E., Gary Westfahl, and Eric S. Rabkin. **Immortal Engines: Life Extension and Immortality in Science Fiction and Fantasy.** Univ. of Georgia Press, 1996.

Essays drawn from the 1992 Eaton Conference focusing on extended-life themes are organized into three sections. In "Approaches to Immortality," John Martin Fischer and Ruth Curl examine the philosophical significance of the theme and Frederick Jameson its cultural implications; the "Science and Immortality" essays focus on more specific methods such as cryonics, neurobiology, genetics, and disembodiment, with a particularly insightful contribution by N. Katherine Hayles. The final 10 essays, on "Literature and Immortality," focus on individual and historical texts, with contributions by Robin Roberts on feminist SF, S. L. Rosen on alienation in immortality narratives, and Terri Frongia on Italian SF. The presence of major scholars Jameson and Hayles lends an unusual weight to this volume. Compare Hassler and Yoke, *Death and the Serpent* [9-207] and Clark, *How to Live Forever* [9-53].

　Themes: Immortality

9-229.　　Westfahl, Gary, ed. **Space and Beyond: The Frontier Theme in Science Fiction.** Greenwood, 2000.

Drawn largely from a joint Eaton/SFRA conference in 1997, this collection of 20 essays, together with an introduction, brief answers to a question posed to a handful of writers, and a transcript of a telephone conversation with Arthur C. Clarke, begins with a section on the wonder of space with two short pieces by Jack Williamson and essays by Peter Nicholls, Danièle Chatelain and George Slusser, and David Pringle; a section on film with contributions by Westfahl, Ira Konigsberg, Susan A. George, and Michael Cassutt; a section on historical texts with Batya Weinbaum (on Leslie F. Stone), William Hardesty (on Iain M. Banks), Robert Gorsch (on C. S. Lewis and Cordwainer Smith), Alan Elms (on Smith and James Tiptree, Jr.), and Jeffrey M. Wallman and Patrice Caldwell on more general themes. The final section, "Other Frontiers," ranges from cyberspace (Janeen Webb) to gender issues (Lynn F. Williams) and the Cold War (Patrick B. Sharp), with other contributions by Clyde Wilcox and Donald M. Hassler. The collection never achieves a consistent focus on or overview of its theme, despite valuable insights in some pieces. Compare Mogen, *Wilderness Visions* [9-130].

9-230. Westfahl, Gary, and George E. Slusser, eds. **Science Fiction, Canonization, Marginalization, and the Academy**. Greenwood, 2002.

The collection of essays, some updated from the 1994 Eaton Conference (which is not directly mentioned in the book itself), is intended to address the sometimes controversial issues suggested by the title, and is divided into three sections: "Overviews," "Mechanisms of Canonization," and "Case Studies in Marginalization." The first section includes compelling pieces by Tom Shippey on Wells and Frank McConnell on Wells and Clarke; Susan Kray discusses Marge Piercy's *He, She, and It*; and Jonathan Langford critiques theories of the fantastic proposed by Todorov, Rabkin, Jackson, Hume, and Attebery. The second section includes Edward James's account of the early years of the Arthur C. Clarke award in England; Joseph D. Miller's almost statistical critique of Le Guin and Attebery's *Norton Book of Science Fiction*; and case histories of the journals *SF Eye* (Stephen Brown) and *Science-Fiction Studies* (Arthur B. Evans). The final five essays include Slusser on multiculturalism in Heinlein and Sterling; Farah Mendlesohn on a historian's approach to SF; Elyce Rae Helford on women of color; and pieces by Howard V. Hendrix and Joseph Childers, Townsend Carr, and Regna Meenk. Somewhat dated even by the time of its appearance, the volume nevertheless raises important but seldom-addressed issues.

9-231. Westfahl, Gary, and George E. Slusser, eds. **No Cure for the Future: Disease and Medicine in Science Fiction and Fantasy**. Greenwood, 2002.

A collection of essays covering a wide range of historical and literary territory, despite the fact that Westfahl acknowledges in his introduction that the theme appeared fairly rarely in SF until recent decades. The book is divided into two parts, "Population Studies" and "Case Histories," and includes H. Bruce Franklin's examination of medical history and its relation to SF, and analyses of doctors in SF by Kirk Hampton and Carol McKay and Joseph D. Miller (and a rather strange piece by Frank McConnell). There are also a discussion by Greg Bear of his own fiction, Westfahl's discussion of James White's "Sector General" stories, and Robert van Cleave on *1984*. A useful bibliography on the topic is appended. Compare Pastourmatzi.

Themes: Medicine

9-232. Westfahl, Gary, George E. Slusser, and David Leiby. **Worlds Enough and Time: Explorations of Time in Science Fiction and Fantasy**. Greenwood, 2002.

Fourteen essays on the broad theme of time in fiction, although many inevitably concern narratives and mechanisms of time travel, which provide the focus in the first section of essays by Slusser and Robert Heath, Richard Saint-Gelais, and David Leiby, although Andrew Sawyer's contribution to this section intriguingly considers narratives in which time runs backwards. A second section is more diffuse, with far-future narratives considered by Carol McKay and

Kirk Hampton, tales of psychic powers analyzed by Susan Stratton, an odd piece on Jewish characters by Susan Kray, and a piece on Japanese manga by Jefferson M. Peters. The final section covers specific works ranging from Dante and *1984* to Stephen Baxter, Diana Gabaldon, and films. Compare Foote's *The Connecticut Yankee in the Twentieth Century* [9-79].

Themes: Time Travel

9-233. Westfahl, Gary, George E. Slusser, and Eric S. Rabkin, eds. **Science Fiction and Market Realities**. Univ. of Georgia Press, 1996.

Fifteen essays, 10 originally delivered at the 1990 Eaton conference, which aim to correct the perceived failure of much contemporary criticism and scholarship to take into account the realities of SF production, publishing, and marketing. The introductory "Overviews" section includes essays by David G. Hartwell, Kathryn Cramer, Norman Spinrad, and George Slusser, most bemoaning the homogenization and verticalization of bookselling. Individual case studies include essays on *Omni*, comics, SF film, and computer games. While the mix of contributors—academics, writers, and editors—provides a useful variety of perspectives and anecdotes, some of the material was dated even by the time of the book's publication, and with the possible exception of the Slusser essay, little effort is evident to examine the broader implications of the concerns expressed. Compare Spinrad [9-180] and Bacon-Smith [9-14].

9-234. Westfahl, Gary, George E. Slusser, and Kathleen Church Plummer, eds. **Unearthly Visions: Approaches to Science Fiction and Fantasy Art**. 2002.

Included here as an Eaton volume, this collection of 12 essays focuses almost exclusively on the visual arts, although several pieces, such as those by Westfahl, Gregory Benford, John Clute, and David Hinckley, make useful ancillary observations on literature as well. Also annotated as [12-37].

III. The International Conference on the Fantastic in the Arts

9-235. Bartter, Martha A., ed. **The Utopian Fantastic: Selected Essays from the Twentieth International Conference on the Fantastic in the Arts**. Greenwood, 2004.

The conference's 20th anniversary took as its general topic utopian and dystopian literature, and this provides the focus of most of the essays in this volume, which includes general essays by Thomas Morrissey, Roger Schlobin, and John C. Hawley, as well as pieces on authors as diverse as Kurt Vonnegut, Jr. (by Donald Morse), David Mamet (by Jeanne Beckwith), Kim Stanley Robinson (by Carl Swindorski), Suzy McKee Charnas (by Bill Clemente), Mike Resnick (by Lynn Williams and Martha Bartter), Sheri Tepper (by Robin Reid and Tamara Wilson), David Brin and Octavia Butler (by Oscar de los Santos), and various other authors treated by Cherilyn Lacey, Dennis Weiss, Sharon Stevenson, and Kelly Searsmith.

Themes: Dystopias, Utopias

9-236. Becker, Allienne R., ed. **Visions of the Fantastic: Selected Essays from the Fifteenth International Conference on the Fantastic in the Arts.** Greenwood, 1996.

Of limited interest to SF scholars (only three of the 22 essays deal directly with genre SF), this collection focuses largely on fantastic elements in "mainstream" authors such as Nathanael West, Katherine Anne Porter, and Shakespeare (whose *Hamlet* is the subject of a witty speculative piece by Brian Aldiss).

9-237. Collings, Michael R., ed. **Reflections on the Fantastic: Selected Essays from the Fourth International Conference on the Fantastic in the Arts.** Greenwood, 1986.

The slimmest of the ICFA volumes also reflects the highest proportion of essays on SF. Twelve papers from the 1983 conference include a provocative short piece by Brian Attebery on fantasy and anti-utopia, two on Brian Aldiss, one on Delany, one on Le Guin and Pohl, and one on Zelazny and Saberhagen's *Coils.*

9-238. Collins, Robert A., and Howard D. Pearce, eds. **The Scope of the Fantastic—Theory, Technique, Major Authors: Selected Essays from the First International Conference on the Fantastic in Literature and Film.** Greenwood, 1985.

The first of two volumes of papers from the inaugural ICFA, held in 1980, establishes the characteristic pattern of the series. The relative brevity of many of the essays, the broadly diffuse focus on almost anything that could be called "fantastic," and the frequency with which the proceedings have appeared suggest a hardbound periodical rather than a series of independently conceived volumes. In this volume, a useful introduction by Eric Rabkin is followed by 30 essays divided into theory, techniques, and author studies. The few essays that deal with SF touch upon works by Golding, Verne, Zelazny, and Piers Anthony.

9-239. Collins, Robert A., and Howard D. Pearce, eds. **The Scope of the Fantastic—Culture, Biography, Themes, Children's Literature: Selected Essays from the First International Conference on the Fantastic in Literature and Film.** Greenwood Press, 1985.

A second selection of 27 essays from the first ICFA includes an interesting essay by Charles Elkins on the social functions of SF and fantasy, Olena Saciuk on the little-known Ukrainian SF writer Oles Berdnyk, Joseph Sanders on filmmaker Willis O'Brien, and pieces on Zelazny and Le Guin.

9-240. Coyle, William, ed. **Aspects of Fantasy: Selected Essays from the Second International Conference on the Fantastic in Literature and Film.** Greenwood, 1986.

Coyle organizes 25 papers from the 1981 conference into five broad categories: creators of fantasy, fantastic creatures, fantasy and the media, fantasy and literary tradition, and fantasy and contemporary concerns. Of particular interest are Rosemary Jackson's psychoanalytic reading of *Frankenstein,* Robert Collins on

Thomas Burnett Swann, and Roger C. Schlobin on the figure of the fool in modern fantasy. Only four essays deal significantly with SF, covering Herbert, Clarke, Shelley, and language.

9-241.   Hokenson, Jan, and Howard D. Pearce, eds. **Forms of the Fantastic: Selected Essays from the Third International Conference on the Fantastic in Literature and Film**. Greenwood, 1986.

A selection of 26 essays from the 1982 ICFA, reflecting the usual variety of approaches and topics. SF topics are covered in essays on Lewis, Delany, Le Guin, and Lessing.

9-242.   Langford, Michele, ed. **Contours of the Fantastic: Selected Essays from the Eighth International Conference on the Fantastic in the Arts**. Greenwood, 1990.

An unusually strong volume in this series contains 22 essays, including speeches by conference guests Brian Aldiss, Brian Stableford, Nancy Willard, and Vivian Sobchak. Other strong essays are by David Miller, Michael Clifton, and especially Peter Malekin, who lucidly applies poststructuralist theory to works by Lem and Delany. (Malekin has not published widely elsewhere in the field, and may be regarded as one of the hidden treasures of these ICFA volumes.)

9-243.   Latham, Rob, and Robert A. Collins, eds. **Modes of the Fantastic: Selected Essays from the Twelfth International Conference on the Fantastic in the Arts**. Greenwood, 1995.

The 1991 conference volume contains 25 essays organized into such broad categories as "technique," "race and gender," and "religion," but reflecting the usual *pot pourri*, with pieces on Pynchon, William Burroughs and Kathy Acker, Louis Aragon, William Gibson, Boris Vian, Nathanael West, Pauline Hopkins, Joanna Russ, Ursula K. Le Guin, Manuel Puig, E. T. A. Hoffmann, Novalis, George Sand, Shakespeare, Charles Williams, Gene Wolfe, Mark Twain, George Pal, and Roger Corman. Brian Attebery's guest scholar address "The Politics (if Any) of Fantasy" is especially insightful, as is a short piece by Brian Aldiss on distinctions between American and British modes of fantasy.

9-244.   Morrison, Michael A., ed. **Trajectories of the Fantastic: Selected Essays from the Fourteenth Annual Conference on the Fantastic in the Arts**. Greenwood, 1997.

Morrison's collection of papers from the 1993 conference include Le Guin's guest of honor speech from that year, plus 18 essays organized according to the headings "Myth and Gender in Science Fiction and the Gothic," "Fantastic Rock," "Cinema Fantastique," and "Fantasy, Genre, and the Mainstream." While much of the volume concerns non-print media, a few essays of interest to SF scholars are included.

9-245. Morse, Donald E., ed. **The Fantastic in World Literature and the Arts: Selected Essays from the Fifth International Conference on the Fantastic in the Arts**. Greenwood, 1987.

Morse tries to give a more coherent comparative cultural focus to this collection of 16 papers from the 1984 ICFA, and it is one of the few volumes to contain illustrations (particularly valuable for Steven Earl Forry's analysis of 20th-century versions of *Frankenstein*). Other relevant pieces include Donald Palumbo on SF film, Peter Malekin on Wolfe's *Book of the New Sun*, and Gregory Shreve on Joan Vinge.

9-246. Morse, Donald E., Csilla Bertha, and Marshall B. Tymn, eds. **The Celebration of the Fantastic: Selected Papers from the Tenth Anniversary International Conference on the Fantastic in the Arts**. Greenwood, 1992.

This volume follows the selected papers of the eighth ICFA (the selection from the ninth conference, in 1988, did not appear until 1997), and includes 26 essays. Of particular SF interest are Joan Gordon on Haldeman, Len Hatfield on Greg Bear, H. Bruce Franklin on superweapon fantasies, Robert Latham on SF and modernism, Barbara Mabee on German fantastic literature, and Judith Kerman on "virtual space" in SF film and television.

9-247. Palumbo, Donald, ed. **Spectrum of the Fantastic: Selected Essays from the Sixth International Conference on the Fantastic in the Arts**. Greenwood, 1988.

Palumbo's selection of 24 papers from the 1985 conference includes a specific section on SF, with papers exploring Platonism in Heinlein and Le Guin, the Foundation and Dune series, Aldiss, and Tiptree. Other essays touch on Vonnegut, King, Lem, and *Star Trek*.

9-248. Ruddick, Nicholas, ed. **State of the Fantastic—Studies in the Theory and Practice of Fantastic Literature and Film: Selected Essays from the Eleventh International Conference on the Fantastic in the Arts, 1990**. Greenwood, 1992.

Ruddick's selection from the 1990 conference is among the most carefully edited and thematically unified volumes in this series, and may be of greatest value to SF scholars. In addition to contributions from writers Jane Yolen and Élisabeth Vonarburg, substantial theoretical approaches are offered by Peter Malekin, Brian Attebery, and Veronica Hollinger. Other topics covered include gnostic SF, SF film, and works by Dick, Zelazny, Russ, Farmer, Ballard, Greg Bear, and Kathy Acker.

9-249.　　Saciuk, Olena, ed. **The Shape of Fantasy: Selected Essays from the Seventh International Conference on the Fantastic in the Arts**. Greenwood, 1990.

Papers from the 1986 conference are highlighted by Brian Aldiss's cogent "What Should a SF Novel Be About?" and C. N. Manlove's "The Elusiveness of Fantasy." Of the 23 other essays, those of particular interest include Leo Daugherty on SF's still-weak academic reputation, Brooks Landon on SF film, and Carl Shaffer on Brunner's *Stand on Zanzibar.*

9-250.　　Sanders, Joe, ed. **Functions of the Fantastic: Selected Essays from the Thirteenth International Conference on the Fantastic in the Arts**. Greenwood, 1995.

Eschewing any attempt to impose a shape on his volume, Sanders simply numbers these essays 1 to 23, beginning with a useful survey of recent American fairy tales by Jack Zipes and closing with Brian Attebery's argument that SF underwent a fundamental change in 1960 or so, an argument amplified in his editorship (with Ursula K. Le Guin) of *The Norton Book of Science Fiction*. Among other interesting pieces of relevance to SF are Veronica Hollinger's comparison of ideas of America in Baudrillard and Ballard and a survey by Rob Latham of America as portrayed in New Wave SF. As usual, the quality varies, and many essays deal with fantasy, horror, or other aspects of the fantastic besides SF, though some of the fantasy essays (such as the one by Bill Senior here) also have relevance for SF scholars.

9-251.　　Sullivan, C. W., III, ed. **The Dark Fantastic: Selected Essays from the Ninth International Conference on the Fantastic in the Arts**. Greenwood, 1997.

This much-delayed volume from the 1988 ICFA conference focuses heavily on dark fantasy and horror, but includes useful pieces on Vonnegut (by Donald Morse) and Lessing (by Carol Franko), as well as a solid theoretical piece by Kathryn Hume.

CHAPTER 10

Author Studies

Richard L. McKinney, Neil Barron, and Michael A. Morrison

Anatomy of Wonder has always been primarily a guide to books and related materials, not to their authors. But the link between SF readers and SF writers is strong, as a work like Hartwell's *Age of Wonders* [9-90] makes very clear. Articles about SF writers appeared in the earliest pulp magazines. Many of these profiles excessively praised their subjects, but some provided both biographical material and varying amounts of critical evaluation, as in the relatively early magazine profiles by Sam Moskowitz, collected in his *Explorers of the Infinite* (1963) and *Seekers of Tomorrow* (1966). As SF's popularity increased, genre writers were the subject of book-length studies, such as Panshin's 1968 study, *Heinlein in Dimension* [10-74], derived from fanzine articles. Along with the growing number of single-author studies, multiple-author biocritical works began to appear, in which biographical, bibliographic, and critical information was included. The most comprehensive earlier work of this type was Tuck [7-9], although it is primarily bibliographic in nature and was therefore annotated in Chapter 7. SF writers, as distinct from writers of occasional SF, are now routinely included in literary and other reference works.

This chapter discusses two types of works: multi-author reference works and books devoted to individual authors, including some collective biographies and interviews. Many other authors and their works are, of course, discussed in the works of history and criticism annotated in Chapter 9. Hal Hall's comprehensive reference index [7-17], now online, provides access to much of the periodical literature. Library users should become familiar with the print and online versions of *Contemporary Authors* and the *Dictionary of Literary Biography* series.

Individual Author Web Sites

The basis for inclusion here is the relative importance of the author, as judged by this guide's contributors and outside readers in the best books listing in Chapter 16. Many significant genre authors lack Web sites, while many minor authors have them, a measure of how easy it is to create a Web site (see the introduction to Chapter 8). Because of the large number of sites, detailed information about each is not provided. The sites vary in their inclusiveness, but most include a biography, a bibliography, current news, often critical writings, sometimes book reviews, and often links to other sites. Currency also varies, with active writers' sites the most up to date. The URL follows the author's surname. William Contento assembled and verified these sites.

Aldiss	www.brianwaldiss.com
Anderson	www.catch22.com/SF/ARB/SFA/Anderson, Poul.php3
Asimov	www.asimovonline.com
Ballard	www.jgballard.com
Iain Banks	www.iainbanks.net/
Baxter	www.cix.co.uk/~sjbradshaw/baxterium/ baxterium.html
Bear	www.gregbear.com
Bellamy	www.sjsu.edu/faculty/wooda/bellamy.html
Benford	www.catch22.com/SF/ARB/SFB/Benford,Gregory. php3
	www.wikipedia.org/wiki/Gregory_Benford
	isfdb.tamu.edu/cgi-bin/ea.cgi?Gregory_Benford
Bester	info.wordsworth.com/www/spresent/besterbio2/ nyt
	www.hycyber.com/SF/bester_alfred.html
Bishop	www.michaelbishop-writer.com/
Blish	www.oivas.com/blish
Brackett	www.kirjasto.sci.fi/brackett.htm
Bradbury	www.raybradbury.com
Brin	www.davidbrin.com
Brunner	www.skypoint.com/members/gimonca/brunner. html
Budrys	www.catch22.com/~espana/SFAuthors/SFB/ Budrys,Algis.php3

Bujold	www.dendarii.com/
Burgess	beifaust.tripod.com/AnthonyBurgess.htm
Burroughs	home.westman.wave.ca/~hillmans/erbkaor.html
Butler	www.feministsf.org/femsf/authors/butler.html
	www.geocities.com/sela_towanda/
Cadigan	users.wmin.ac.uk/~fowlerc/patcadigan.html
Čapek	capek.misto.cz/english/
Card	www.hatrack.com/
Charnas	www.suzymckeecharnas.com/
Cherryh	www.cherryh.com/
Christopher	www.gnelson.demon.co.uk/tripage/jc.html
Clarke	www.lsi.usp.br/~rbianchi/clarke/
Clement	www.geocities.com/gamgeephile/hal/
Crowley	www.michaelscycles.freeserve.co.uk/crowl1.htm
de Camp	www.lspraguedecamp.com/
Delany	www.pcc.com/~jay/delany/
Dick	www.philipkdick.com/
Dickinson, Peter	www.peterdickinson.com/
Disch	www.michaelscycles.freeserve.co.uk/tmd.htm
Doyle	www.ash-tree.bc.ca/acdsocy.html
	www.sherlockholmesonline.org/
Egan	gregegan.customer.netspace.net.au/
Ellison	harlanellison.com/home.htm
Farmer	www.pjfarmer.com
	www.philipjosefarmer.tk
Finney	members.aol.com/leahj/finney.htm
Gibson	www.williamgibsonbooks.com/
Gilman	www.womenwriters.net/domesticgoddess/gilman1. html
	www.cortland.edu/gilman/
Haggard	www.kirjasto.sci.fi/haggard.htm
Haldeman	home.earthlink.net/~haldeman/
Hamilton, Peter	www.sandm.co.uk/mary/sfjournm/Peter_Hamilton/ peter_hamilton.html
Hamilton, Virginia	www.virginiahamilton.com/home.htm
Heinlein	www.nitrosyncretic.com/rah/
Herbert	www.kirjasto.sci.fi/fherbert.htm
Hoover, H(elen) M(ary)	www.ohioreadingroadtrip.org/hoover/
Hubbard	www.lronhubbard.org/
Huxley	somaweb.org/
Jeter, K. W.	www.kwjeter.com/

Kessel, John	www4.ncsu.edu/~tenshi/
Keyes	www.danielkeyesauthor.com/
Knight	www.sfwa.org/news/knight.htm
	www.catch22.com/~espana/SFAuthors/SFK/ Knight,Damon.html
Kornbluth	home.t-online.de/home/herbsev/cmk.htm
Kress	www.sff.net/people/nankress/
Kuttner	www.gwillick.com/Spacelight/kuttner.html
Lafferty	www.mulle-kybernetik.com/RAL/
Le Guin	www.ursulakleguin.com/
	hem.passagen.se/peson42/lgw/
	www.levity.com/corduroy/leguin.htm
Leiber	www.lankhmar.demon.co.uk/
Lem	www.lem.pl/
L'Engle	www.madeleinelengle.com/
Lethem, J.	www.sinc.sunysb.edu/Stu/dmyers/
Lewis	cslewis.drzeus.net/
Lindsay	www.slainte.org.uk/scotauth/lindsdsw.htm
London	sunsite.berkeley.edu/London/
MacLeod, Ken	www.ugcs.caltech.edu/~phoenix/macleod/
Malzberg	www.geocities.com/Area51/Stargate/9022/ bmalzberg.html
McAuley	www.omegacom.demon.co.uk/
McCaffrey	www.annemccaffrey.org/
McDevitt	www.sfwa.org/members/McDevitt/
McDonald, Ian	www.lysator.liu.se/~unicorn/mcdonald/
McHugh	my.en.com/~mcq/
Martin, George R. R.	www.georgerrmartin.com/
Miéville	www.panmacmillan.com/Features/China/
Miller, P. Schuyler	www.gwillick.com/Spacelight/miller_p.html
Miller, Walter M.	www.kirjasto.sci.fi/wmiller.htm
Moorcock	www.multiverse.org/
Neville	www.scifi.com/scifiction/classics/classics_archive/ neville/neville_bio.html
Niven	www.larryniven.org/
Noon	unwound.livid.com/noon.html
Norton, Andre	www.andre-norton.org/
O'Brien, Robert C.	falcon.jmu.edu/~ramseyil/obrien.htm
Oliver	www.gwillick.com/Spacelight/oliver.html
Orwell	www.k-1.com/Orwell/

Pangborn	members.tripod.com/templetongate/pangborn.htm
Piercy	hubcap.clemson.edu/~sparks/piercy/mpindex.html
Poe	www.eapoe.org/
Pohl	www.fantasticfiction.co.uk/authors/Frederik_Pohl.htm
Powers	www.theworksoftimpowers.com
Priest	www.christopher-priest.co.uk
Reynolds, Alastair	members.tripod.com/~voxish/home.html
Reynolds, Mack	www.gwillick.com/Spacelight/reynolds.html
Roberts, Keith	www.solaris-books.co.uk/Roberts
Robinson	www.kimstanleyrobinson.net/
Rubinstein, Gillian	www.gillianrubinstein.com/
Rucker, Rudy	www.cs.sjsu.edu/faculty/rucker
Russ	en.wikipedia.org/wiki/Joanna_Russ
Sargent, Pamela	www.engel-cox.org/sargent/
Sawyer, Robert J.	www.sfwriter.com/
Sheckley	members.tripod.com/~sheckley/
Shelley	www.rc.umd.edu/reference/mschronology/mws.html
Shepard	www.lucius-shepard.com/
Shiel	www.creative.net/~alang/lit/horror/shiel.sht
Shute	www.nevilshute.org/
Silverberg	www.majipoor.com/
Simak	www.tc.umn.edu/~brams007/simak/default.htm
Simmons	www.dansimmons.com/
Slonczewski	www.math.uwaterloo.ca/~dmswitze/slonczewski/
Smith, Cordwainer	www.cordwainer-smith.com/
Smith, E. E.	freespace.virgin.net/johna.fairhurst/Books/EESmith/index.htm
Snyder, Zilpha Keatley	www.zksnyder.com/
Spinrad	ourworld.compuserve.com/homepages/normanspinrad
Stableford	freespace.virgin.net/diri.gini/brian.htm
Stapledon	www.popsubculture.com/pop/bio_project/olaf_stapledon.html
Stephenson	www.nealstephenson.com/
Sterling	www.chriswaltrip.com/sterling/
Stevenson	wwwesterni.unibg.it/rls/rls.htm
Strugatsky	www.rusf.ru/abs/english/

Sturgeon	www.physics.emory.edu/~weeks/misc/sturgeon. html
Swanwick	www.michaelswanwick.com/
Swift	www.victorianweb.org/previctorian/swift/swiftov. html
Taine	encyclopedia.thefreedictionary.com/John%20 Taine
Tepper	www.feministsf.org/femsf/authors/tepper.html
Tiptree	mtsu32.mtsu.edu:11072/Tiptree/
Turtledove	www.sfsite.com/~silverag/turtledove.html
van Vogt	vanvogt.www4.mmedia.is/
Vance	www.massmedia.com/~mikeb/jvm/
Varley	www.geocities.com/Area51/Rampart/3870/
Verne	jv.gilead.org.il/
Vinge, V.	www.ugcs.caltech.edu/~phoenix/vinge/
Vonnegut	www.vonnegut.com/
Waldrop	www.sff.net/people/waldrop/
Watson, I.	www.ianwatson.info/
Weinbaum	www.gwillick.com/Spacelight/weinbaum.html
Wells	www.hgwellsusa.50megs.com/
Westall, Robert	www.norham.n-tyneside.sch.uk/westall/
Wilhelm	www.katewilhelm.com/
Williams, Walter Jon	www.thuntek.net/~walter/
Williamson, Jack	www.fantasticfiction.co.uk/authors/Jack_ Williamson.htm
Willis	www.geocities.com/wellesley/5595/willis/willis.html
Wilson, Robert Charles	www.robertcharleswilson.com
Wolfe	mysite.verizon.net/~vze2tmhh/wolfe.html
	www.urth.net
Wright, S. F.	www.sfw.org/
Wyndham	www.liv.ac.uk/~asawyer/wyndham.html
Zamiatin	www.geocities.com/Athens/Delphi/1634/
Zelazny	www.roger-zelazny.com/

SF author portals, links to author Web sites:

Locus online	www.locusmag.com/Links/Authors.html
SF Site	www.sfsite.com/scribe/scribe01.htm
Links to Literature	www.linkstoliterature.com/

SF author directories, brief encyclopedia-like entries for many authors:

Alpha Ralpha Blvd.	www.catch22.com/SF/ARB/
CyberSpace Spinner	www.hycyber.com/SF/sf_authors.html
The Templeton Gate	members.tripod.com/templetongate/authors.htm
Books and Writers	www.kirjasto.sci.fi/indeksi.htm#a
Spacelight	www.gwillick.com/Spacelight/

Multi-Author Reference Works

The general encyclopedias [notably 7-21] may provide all the material many library users need. Annotated here are works providing more detailed information.

*10-1.   Bleiler, Richard J., ed. **Science Fiction Writers: Critical Studies of the Major Authors from the Early Nineteenth Century to the Present Day.** 2nd ed. Scribner's, 1999.

This is a revised enlargement of the 1982 first edition by Everett Bleiler, the father. This new edition has 98 articles by 42 critics, 23 of them entirely new, with most of the others revised to varying degrees. Each carefully edited essay, averaging about 10 pages, provides biographical information, a critical analysis of the fiction, an assessment of the author's historical importance in the development of SF, a basic primary and secondary bibliography, and a photograph. Both SF writers and writers of occasional SF (Huxley, Orwell, Lovecraft) are discussed, with Čapek, Lem, and Verne the only non–Anglo-American writers. This new edition sequences the authors alphabetically, a feature much easier to use than the chronological periods of the first edition. Although the essays are on average shorter than those in the DLB volumes [10-3 to 10-7], they are more critically acute. Libraries with the first edition should seriously consider acquiring the second. The quality evident here is also seen in the companion two-volume sets by father and son devoted to supernatural, horror, and fantasy writers (1985 and 2002). (NB)

10-2.   Pederson, Jay P., ed. **St. James Guide to Science Fiction Writers.** 4th ed. St. James Press, 1996.

The St. James guides were originally titled *Twentieth-Century [genre] Writers* and now include SF, fantasy, horror, crime/mystery, and similar volumes. The fourth edition profiles 640 writers, dropping 44 from the 1991 third edition and adding 51. The editor was assisted by 21 advisers and 200 contributors, which guarantees wide variation in the quality of entries. The standardized entries provide birth/death dates, nationality, pseudonyms, education, family, career, and awards. Many entries have comments by the author. SF books are listed chronologically. Non-SF books are also listed (pages of Asimov's non-SF, for example), which adds little save bulk and cost to an already expensive book. There are far too many typos. The ratio of plot summary to critical analysis varies widely among entries. The Clute/Nicholls encyclopedia [7-21] has 42 of the 51 new writers, along with at least 2,500 others, whose shorter entries are more balanced, often cross-referencing theme entries and similar authors, and whose length is proportional to the relative importance of the author. While all the "significant" or "major" authors are here, fully three fourths are minor by even a relaxed standard. The encyclopedia is much preferable if breadth is required, while the Bleiler guide provides far better critical guidance to 98 of the truly important writers. (NB)

10-3.   Cowart, David, and Thomas L. Wymer, eds. **Twentieth-Century American Science-Fiction Writers**. Gale, 1981. 2 vols. DLB 8.

10-4.   Harris-Fain, Darren, ed. **British Fantasy and Science-Fiction Writers Before World War I**. Gale, 1997. DLB 178.

10-5.   Harris-Fain, Darren, ed. **British Fantasy and Science-Fiction Writers, 1918–1960**. Gale, 2002. DLB 255.

10-6.   Harris-Fain, Darren, ed. **British Fantasy and Science-Fiction Writers Since 1960**. Gale, 2002. DLB 261.

10-7.   Ivison, Douglas, ed. **Canadian Fantasy and Science-Fiction Writers**. Gale, 2002. DLB 251.

The *Dictionary of Literary Biography* (DLB) began in 1978 and by mid-2004 was approaching Volume 300. Each 8½ x 11-inch volume is edited by a specialist, with the entries written by other experts. The entries vary in length from three pages for writers of occasional SF to 20 pages for prolific or more important authors, averaging 8 to 12 pages. Each essay includes biographical information, critical evaluation of major works, and a bibliography of books and other writings, including a brief secondary bibliography. Photographs of the authors and sometimes pages of manuscript are reproduced.

SF was the subject of a two-volume set early in the series. The 90 essays by 41 contributors treat authors (11 women) who began writing after 1900 and mostly before 1970. A large number have died or become inactive since publication. Some choices are questionable, such as George R. Stewart solely for *Earth Abides*. Six appendixes have grown dated, treating topics such as the New Wave, which long since crested, films, fandom, fanzines, awards, etc. This set retains historical value but is long overdue for extensive updating.

Few writers before World War I, British or American, could be considered SF writers, and most of the 28 subjects in DLB 178 are accordingly fantasy writers, such as Anstey, Blackwood, Haggard, and Stoker. Beresford, Doyle, Shelley, and Wells are the principal authors of SF. As SF evolved into a distinct genre by the 1930s, more writers were attracted to it, although the tradition of the scientific romance persisted in the U.K. Of the 30 subjects in DLB 255, 13 could be considered either writers of occasional SF (Golding, Orwell, Shute) or SF writers (Christopher, E. F. Russell, Stapledon, S. Fowler Wright, Wyndham). The period covered by DLB 261 includes 38 entries, a bit more than half mostly SF writers, from the popular Douglas Adams to the versatile Aldiss and Ballard to the late James White.

DLB 251 provides the first comprehensive survey of Canadian SF authors, some of the 38 writing only in French, and 9 of them (mostly the youngest) not having entries in the *Encyclopedia of Science Fiction* or *Encyclopedia of Fantasy*. Some were merely born in Canada, then lived elsewhere (e.g., van Vogt) or vice versa (e.g., Judith Merril).

The DLB provides the most complete essay-length assessments of its subjects, but Bleiler's *Science Fiction Writers* [10-1] has the edge in scope, critical rigor, and acumen. The DLB essays and the entries in Gale's *Contemporary Authors* series are also available online through many libraries. Far broader but less detailed coverage of SF and fantasy authors is provided in the two cited encyclopedias, whose entries may suffice for many readers. (NB)

10-8. Server, Lee. **Encyclopedia of Pulp Fiction Writers**. Checkmark/ Facts on File, 2002.

An expert in pulp fiction contributes 202 profiles of authors, some of whom he's met. His personal taste is evident in the mix of genres: detective/mystery/ crime/espionage/etc. includes about 40 percent of the authors; there are 12 horror, 9 SF, and 6 fantasy authors. The entries mix description and analysis and are more readable, if informal, than the other biocritical guides annotated here. About three fourths of the authors are found in either the DLB series or *Contemporary Authors*, and the authors of fantastic fiction have entries in the SF and fantasy encyclopedias. The appeal of this breezy but energetic guide will be mostly to pulp freaks. Few libraries own the books he discusses with enthusiasm. (NB)

Individual Authors

This section surveys books devoted to single authors, followed by a discussion of collective biographies and interviews. Coverage is limited to SF writers and to others who wrote at least one work important in the history of SF, such as Orwell and C. S. Lewis. In the latter case, we have annotated primarily those books that focus on the writer's works relevant to SF; general biographies or studies were deliberately not annotated. We also largely excluded purely bibliographic works, which are exhaustively described in the author bibliographies section (227 entries) of Burgess [7-11].

Many single-author studies have appeared as part of discontinued series from publishers such as Oxford, Ungar, and Taplinger, and fan presses such as Starmont House and Borgo Press. Many of the studies share a potential weakness: they were often published while their subjects were still active, sometimes relatively early in their careers, and are therefore dated and sometimes unbalanced. That should be understood as an implicit comment in many of the evaluations. Some of the studies in the fourth edition of this guide were dropped as too dated, although they retain some historical value. The attentive reader will note that many authors who were judged most distinguished lack studies, while less distinguished authors have them, an unfortunate result of the taste of critics and the vagaries of the marketplace. Usefully supplementing these author studies are the author interviews published since the mid-1980s in *Locus* [13-17], more than 250 interviews of SF, fantasy, and horror fiction writers, both established and promising. Copies of the issues are still available or, in a few cases, copies of only the interviews when the original issues are out of print.

The initials (NB, MAM, and/or RLM) found in the entries below indicate the authors of those entries. When more than one set of initials are given, as is the case in several of the entries, the initials of the author who has made the greatest contribution to that entry is given first. Entries with minor revisions retain only the initials of their original authors.

Brian W. Aldiss, U.K., 1925–

*10-9.   Aldiss, Brian W. **The Twinkling of An Eye, Or, My Life as an Englishman**. Little, Brown, U.K., 1998; St. Martin's, 1999.

10-10.   Aldiss, Margaret. **The Work of Brian W. Aldiss: An Annotated Bibliography and Guide**. Borgo, 1992.

10-11.   Henighan, Tom. **Brian W. Aldiss**. Twayne, 1999.

With his prodigious output in numerous genres, Brian Aldiss challenges biographer, bibliographer, and critic alike. The events of his life are often reflected in his fiction, sometimes directly so, a fact that too few of his critics have taken into consideration. Aldiss's most substantial and valuable autobiographical text, which provides considerable insight into his fiction, is *The Twinkling of An Eye*, although the student of Aldiss should also be aware of the earlier autobiographical volumes *Bury My Heart at W. H. Smith's: A Writing Life* (enlarged ed., 1990) and *The Shape of Further Things* (Faber & Faber, 1970), and diverse shorter essays, especially the one in *Hell's Cartographers* [10-168]. The late Margaret Aldiss's well-organized volume is the most complete and accurate bibliography up to the time of its publication, including annotations by Brian Aldiss, a detailed chronology, indexes of titles, and an exhaustive indexed list of secondary sources along with selected excerpts from reviews and critical commentaries.

Two early studies still of interest to students of Aldiss are Richard Mathews's short (64-page) booklet *Aldiss Unbound* (Borgo, 1977) and Michael R. Collins's *Brian W. Aldiss* (Starmont, 1986), which largely supersedes the Mathews title. *Apertures: A Study of the Writings of Brian W. Aldiss* (Greenwood, 1984) by Brian Griffin and David Wingrove has relevant and insightful things to say about its subject, although it is now dated and tends to be overly adulatory and at times somewhat incoherent in its argumentation. The most up-to-date book-length study is Henighan's contribution to the Twayne English Authors series, an adequate but not exceptional volume, prey to the usual limitations of its format. It contains a chronology, notes and references, selected bibliography, and index. Colin Greenland's *The Entropy Exhibition* [9-85] also devotes serious attention to Aldiss's role in relation to the British New Wave in SF. A *festschrift* presented to Aldiss, *A Is for Brian: A 65th Birthday Present for Brian W. Aldiss from His Family, Friends, Colleagues, and Admirers*, edited by Frank Hatherley, Margaret Aldiss, and Malcolm Edwards (Avernus, 1990), unfortunately given extremely limited distribution, also contains useful contributions for the Aldiss scholar. Despite the recognition he has been shown, Aldiss has yet to receive the in-depth critical attention he clearly deserves. (RLM)

Poul Anderson, U.S., 1926–2001

10-12. Miesel, Sandra. **Against Time's Arrow: The High Crusade of Poul Anderson**. Borgo, 1978.

Between 1947, when his first story was published, and his death in 2001, at age 74, Anderson was one of the more prolific writers of SF and fantasy and had won or been nominated for many of the field's most prestigious awards. His undergraduate degree was in physics and a key concept in that field is entropy, which Miesel, following James Blish, argues is the organizing principle of much if not all of Anderson's fiction. Entropy is defined here as the inexorable tendency of systems to become increasingly disordered, leading to the death of individuals and the "heat death" of the universe. But individuals can create, bring order to life, can thus oppose time's arrow, even if only temporarily, and Miesel selects stories published through 1977 that illustrate Anderson's credo that, as Faulkner put it in his 1949 Nobel Prize speech, "I believe that man will not merely endure: he will prevail." A useful, brief (64 pages), if too admiring study—now unfortunately very dated—of one of the field's more important authors. (NB)

Piers Anthony, U.S., 1934–

10-13. Anthony, Piers. **How Precious Was That While: An Autobiography**. Tor, 2001.

Piers Anthony Jacob, for whom Piers Anthony is a pseudonym, produced his first attempt at autobiography in *Bio of an Ogre* (Ace, 1989), which covered his life to the age of 50. This later volume summarizes much of the contents of that first book by reprinting an autobiographical essay originally written for Gale Research before dealing with the author's more recent experiences. In what appears to be a candid review of his life, we learn a good deal, usually via anecdote, about Anthony's (occasionally quite acrimonious) interactions with other authors, publishers, fans, and readers. Anthony makes clear his own opinions and viewpoints, ideals, and beliefs, and is not afraid to take positions that are controversial. The book is most valuable to the student of Anthony's work, but contains some interesting background material on the worlds of science fiction and fantasy writing and publishing. It lacks all scholarly apparatus and an index. (RLM)

Isaac Asimov, U.S., 1920–1992

*10-14.   Asimov, Isaac. **I, Asimov: A Memoir**. Doubleday, 1994.

*10-15.   Gunn, James E. **Isaac Asimov: The Foundations of Science Fiction**. Rev. ed. Scarecrow, 1996.

10-16.   Hassler, Donald M. **Isaac Asimov**. Starmont, 1991.

10-17.   Palumbo, Donald. **Chaos Theory, Asimov's Foundations and Robots, and Herbert's Dune: The Fractal Aesthetics of Epic Science Fiction**. Greenwood, 2002.

10-18.   Touponce, William F. **Isaac Asimov**. Twayne, 1991.

Biographical details of Isaac Asimov's life exist scattered throughout much of his nonfiction, but are to be found primarily in four books. The first two were huge, detail-rich volumes, both Hugo nominees: *In Memory Yet Green: The Autobiography of Isaac Asimov, 1920–1954* (Doubleday, 1979) and *In Joy Still Felt: The Autobiography of Isaac Asimov, 1954–1978.* (Doubleday, 1980). The posthumously published *I, Asimov* (winner of a nonfiction Hugo) retells Asimov's entire life in much less detail and more impressionistically than the earlier books, bringing his story up to 1990 (an epilogue by his widow, Janet Jeppson Asimov, briefly recounts what happened in the final two years of his life). Finally, there is a collection of selected articles, letters, essays, and fiction titled *Isaac Asimov: It's Been a Good Life* (Prometheus, 2002), edited by his widow. In this latter volume (a good portion of which has been condensed from the three previous autobiographical books), it was publicly revealed for the first time that Asimov died of complications from AIDS, which he most likely contracted during blood transfusions in connection with heart bypass surgery in 1983. The enormous amount of raw data collected in the first two of these books make them invaluable for the serious student of Asimov's life and work, but *I, Asimov* will likely be the most readily useful of these autobiographical titles, because of its more manageable size, its more judicious choice of material, and its coverage of the important final years of Asimov's life. Also of some biographical interest is a selection of Asimov's letters compiled and edited by his brother, Stanley, under the title *Yours, Isaac Asimov: A Lifetime of Letters* (Doubleday, 1995). Two collections of essays that provide examples of Asimov's opinions on various aspects of science fiction are *Asimov on Science Fiction* (Doubleday, 1981) and *Asimov's Galaxy: Reflections on Science Fiction* (Doubleday, 1989). Many of the essays in the first of these, and those in the second, were originally published as editorials in *Isaac Asimov's Science Fiction Magazine*.

James Gunn's study of Asimov's science fiction is undoubtedly the best single introduction and critical guide to this author's SF, especially since its revision in 1996. Originally published by Oxford University Press in 1982, the first edition received a Hugo award. The new edition is one third longer than the first, and has been substantially revised and updated to include fiction published after Asimov's return to SF in 1982 with a fourth Foundation novel, *Foundation's Edge*. Also included is a long interview with its subject, from 1979. Gunn was a contemporary of Asimov, a friend of many years, and numerous of his own stories were published at about the same time. He also likes the kind of SF Asimov wrote, and is good at analyzing its appeal, although this study may be considered weak by some observers because of a relative lack of contemporary theoretical sophistication. Gunn discusses both series and non-series novels, and short fiction, providing quite detailed plot summaries for the major works. He also presents biographical information concerning Asimov's dealings with the marketplace. The new edition examines Asimov's return to SF after a nearly quarter-century hiatus, and the controversial and not entirely successful attempts he made at the end of his career to link the Foundation and positronic robot stories into a single future history.

Both the Hassler (Eaton award) and the Touponce books are intended to be introductory works, but they are quite different in structure. Hassler discusses Asimov's works by category, such as short fiction, series novels, and juveniles, and examines how they are derived from Enlightenment sources and rationalist philosophy, and how they are anti-literary in style. Touponce's emphasis is on the influence on Asimov's fiction of his scientific training. Relying heavily on the work of Thomas Kuhn, Touponce argues that the paradigms of science are present throughout Asimov's many writings, and are especially evident in the robot and psychohistory stories. The detailed plot summaries in Touponce will help the novice, although they sometimes reveal too much.

Palumbo's study is an attempt to apply ideas from chaos research to the literary analysis of SF texts, focusing specifically not only on Asimov's Foundation and robot series but also, less successfully, on Frank Herbert's Dune books [for Palumbo's treatment of Herbert, see the entry for Herbert, below]. Palumbo's understanding, interpretation, and communication of chaos theory to the reader is on the whole adequately done (although it appears to be built almost exclusively on popular scientific explanations of the field, such as James Gleick's *Chaos*, [Viking, 1987]), and his application of it to SF is original and promising. Though not always completely successful, this monograph is nonetheless a laudable experiment that has valuable and interesting things to say about both Asimov and Herbert, as well as about science fiction in general, and it is worth examination by the serious SF scholar. (RLM, NB)

J. G. Ballard, U.K., 1930–

10-19. Luckhurst, Roger. **"The Angle Between Two Walls": The Fiction of J. G. Ballard**. Liverpool Univ. Press, 1998.

10-20. Pringle, David. **Earth Is the Alien Planet: J. G. Ballard's Four-Dimensional Nightmare**. Borgo, 1979.

10-21. Stephenson, Gregory. **Out of the Night and Into the Dream: A Thematic Study of the Fiction of J. G. Ballard**. Greenwood, 1991.

Despite his central position in the development of science fiction in Britain after the end of the Second World War, the provocative and often controversial J. G. Ballard still awaits an entirely successful study of his work. Notwithstanding their age and length, among the more important early analyses that do exist are Brian Aldiss's seminal 1965 essay, "The Wounded Land: J. G. Ballard," David Pringle's still quite relevant *Earth Is the Alien Planet*, and Chapter 7 of Colin Greenland's *The Atrocity Exhibition*, which discusses its subject in the context of the British New Wave of the 1960s. Pringle also produced a valuable bibliography and critical introduction, *J. G. Ballard: A Primary and Secondary Bibliography* (G. K. Hall, 1984), which includes a long interview but which is now several years out of date. Peter Brigg's Starmont study, *J. G. Ballard* (1985), is also dated, too short, and too limited by its format to deal in depth with the complexities and paradoxes of Ballard's fiction. The more current but still too limited *J. G. Ballard* (Northcote House, 1998) by Michel Delville suffers similar problems.

Stephenson applies to his analyses what he calls a "combination of elements of New Critical methodology with elements of Archetypal criticism," and, although the study is logically coherent and strongly argued, it is also reductive, missing important aspects of the work of its subject. Ballard cannot be so easily categorized and neatly shelved as Stephenson seems to wish, although there are worthwhile observations in this book, which contains notes, a selected bibliography, and index.

Roger Luckhurst has produced what is clearly intended as a major study, drawing on a very large number of theoretical and analytic perspectives, both to question the authority of the exclusiveness of earlier analyses and to establish the indeterminacy and what he calls the "unreadableness" of Ballard's central texts. Unfortunately, Luckhurst's own monograph is marred by impenetrable prose and an excessively intrusive theoretical apparatus, which is more often displayed than fruitfully applied to his subject matter. The result, despite some fascinating isolated insights into Ballard's work, is itself difficult to read and understand, ultimately producing a largely unsatisfactory study.

Ballard's 1996 collection, *A User's Guide to the Millennium* (Picador), a compilation of three decades' worth of short essays and reviews on various subjects, can also be usefully consulted. (RLM)

Alfred Bester, U.S., 1913–1987

10-22.   Wendell, Carolyn. **Alfred Bester**. Starmont, 1982.

Although his first story was published in a 1939 pulp, Bester had written relatively little SF by the time of his death in 1987. But two of the novels he did write are highly regarded, *The Demolished Man* and *The Stars My Destination*. Wendell devotes a chapter to each of these novels, one to his weak 1975 novel, *The Computer Connection*, and another to his short stories. Wendell favors plot summary over extended analysis, making her short study primarily of use to someone relatively unfamiliar with Bester's fiction. Annotated bibliography of primary and secondary materials. Bester's 30-page autobiographical essay in *Hell's Cartographers* [10-168] provides more insight into the author's work. (NB)

James Blish, U.S., 1921–1975

*10-23. Ketterer, David. **Imprisoned in a Tesseract: The Life and Work of James Blish**. Kent State Univ. Press, 1987.

10-24. Stableford, Brian. **A Clash of Symbols: The Triumph of James Blish**. Borgo, 1979.

Both Ketterer and Stableford skillfully position Blish in the pre- and postwar American SF scenes and show his evolution from a disciple of John W. Campbell to a meticulous craftsman determined through his fiction and criticism (collected in *The Issue at Hand* and *More Issues at Hand*) to drag his chosen literary mode out of the gutter of pulp conventions. Although highly selective, Stableford's fine, brief introduction to the major themes of Blish's work suggests that his central contribution was an emphasis on moral and philosophical (rather than technological) concerns. Ketterer, whose book is almost seven times as long, draws upon exhaustive research in archival materials and extensive interviews with Blish's acquaintances to paint one of the most detailed portraits available of a 20th-century SF author. Ketterer gives due attention to Blish's life and views, but the greatest strength of this remarkable book is its detailed analyses of key texts, ranging from (selected) early short stories Blish published in the pulps through his future history *Cities in Flight* to the book that is his greatest work, *A Case of Conscience*. Adumbrating Blish's major themes, motifs, and image patterns, Ketterer reveals the Spenglerian historical consciousness and fundamentally religious sensibility (one at odds with Blish's scientifically informed skepticism) behind this somewhat paradoxical but unarguably important figure in American science fiction. Extensive notes; primary bibliography of fiction, dramatic work, edited books, criticism, and nonfiction; selected secondary bibliography; index and chronology. (MAM)

Ray Bradbury, U.S., 1920–

10-25. Eller, Jonathan R., and William F. Touponce, eds. **Ray Bradbury: The Life of Fiction**. Kent State Univ. Press, 2004.

10-26. Greenberg, Martin H., and Joseph D. Olander, eds. **Ray Bradbury**. Taplinger, 1980.

10-27. Mengeling, Marvin E. **Red Planet, Flaming Phoenix, Green Town: Some Early Bradbury Revisited**. 1st Books, 2003.

10-28. Mogen, David. **Ray Bradbury**. Twayne, 1986.

10-29. Slusser, George E. **The Bradbury Chronicles**. Borgo, 1977.

10-30. Weist, Jerry. **Bradbury: An Illustrated Life**. Morrow, 2002.

As David Mogen shows in his excellent Twayne overview, Ray Bradbury's position vis-à-vis SF is ambiguous. Despite the antitechnological stance of his best-known early work and his later retreat from the genre, Bradbury is still considered by many mainstream critics and readers as a premier exponent of science fiction. Mogen draws on lengthy interviews (conducted for this book) to present Bradbury as a man, as a stylist, and as a member of the SF and mainstream literary communities. With uncommon skill, Mogen combines biographical, philosophical, and critical insights in discussions organized around the diverse genres in which Bradbury has published: the weird tale, science fiction, etc. Chronology, index, and primary and annotated secondary bibliography.

Like Mogen, Slusser argues that Bradbury attained the pinnacle of his artistry in the 1960s, making less important the fact that both these studies are dated. Slusser, in two extended essays devoted to Bradbury's short fiction and "fix-up" novels, persuasively positions him as a "tenaciously regional" American writer, primarily of short stories. Noting that throughout his career Bradbury has written "essentially the same kind of story," Slusser dates his artistic decline from his abandonment of the "toughminded optimism" of his early and mid-career prose works. Greenberg and Olander's collection of essays is one of the best in the Taplinger series, offering particularly useful examinations of the structural aspects of Bradbury's fiction and of the themes of religion, science and technology, and the frontier myth.

Mengeling's recent study, intended for a general audience rather than for academic specialists, uses a rather old-fashioned approach, as he himself admits, with a significant emphasis on the psychological and autobiographical components of selected examples of Bradbury's early fiction, attempting to answer the question of why Bradbury "has been so deeply involved with certain themes, or why he takes the particular stances that he does in relation to these themes." Despite its relatively unsophisticated theoretical approach, and its not always entirely convincing arguments, the book nevertheless manages to find some suggestive links between Bradbury's life and his fiction, and is largely a positive addition to the critical literature on the early works of its subject.

Drawing on my many conversations with Bradbury plus correspondence and archival manuscripts, Eller and Touponce have written the lengthiest study to date (510 pp.) of its subject. Using carnival in the broadest sense as an organizing metaphor, they explore the evolution of his fiction (not limited to his SF) and how he moved from the marginal field of SF to the literary mainstream. The eight chronological chapters provide a detailed, carefully argued analysis of Bradbury's varied writings. A 78-page appendix, 1938–2003, lists original and reprint appearances of his books (100+) and short fiction (400+ short stories). Another appendix lists his many unpublished works, long and short. Notes, a selected bibliography, and an index complete this study, which is a valuable starting point for any serious student of Bradbury. Touponce has published earlier work on Bradbury, including a revision of his 1981 doctoral thesis, under the title *Ray Bradbury and the Poetics of Reverie: Fantasy, Science Fiction, and the*

Reader (UMI Research, 1984), a specialized work that utilizes reader-response theory extensively. The same author's Starmont guide, *Ray Bradbury* (1989), is far from introductory, being an extended essay on the influence of Friedrich Nietzsche's aesthetics of tragedy on Bradbury's thought and art. (MAM, RLM)

Fredric Brown, U.S., 1906–1972

10-31. Seabrook, Jack. **Martians and Misplaced Clues: The Life and Work of Fredric Brown**. Bowling Green Popular Press, 1993.

Even though he publicly claimed to prefer writing science fiction to mysteries, Fredric Brown is better known today for his crime fiction than for his SF, where his principle contributions were a large number of (often humorous and frequently very short) short stories and five novels, published mainly in the 1940s and 1950s. Following a brief, introductory biographical chapter (there is much that is not known of Brown's life), Seabrook proceeds to discuss (with much reliance on plot summary and in theoretically unsophisticated terms) Brown's writing, including his poetry and mainstream fiction, although the mysteries, appropriately enough, are given the greatest emphasis (and the better analyses). Two chapters focus on Brown's SF: one on shorter works, the other on novels. Many critics think Brown produced his best SF in the shorter format, but his best novel, *The Lights in the Sky Are Stars* (*Project Jupiter* in the U.K.), is a book with surprisingly rich characterization in comparison to most SF of its time, which—even more unusually for its day—portrayed a future America (of 1997) that has largely turned its back on space exploration. Seabrook's monograph, likely to be the only one we will see devoted to Brown, concludes with a list, organized by genre, of its subject's writings, a secondary bibliography of works cited, and an index. (RLM)

John Brunner, U.K., 1934–1995

10-32. De Bolt, Joe, ed. **The Happening Worlds of John Brunner**. Kennikat, 1975.

John Brunner's novels are a good deal more interesting and important than the paucity of critical attention given them would suggest—a case of neglect not excused by a sharp decline in his productivity from the mid-1970s to his death in 1995. The best introductions to his work and his place in modern SF are John R. Pfeiffer's essay in Bleiler's *Science Fiction Writers* and De Bolt's biocritical introduction to this uneven collection. Its strengths include James Blish's brief introduction, a survey of Brunner's now inaccessible poetry, a long concluding essay by Brunner that combines autobiographical remarks with reflections on SF, and a bibliography that was thorough at its time of publication. The volume's weaknesses, regrettably, are its critical apparatus: too many of these essays are undercut by pretentious or downright awkward writing, often in the service of pointless or obvious observations. Nevertheless, this book will be of value to readers focusing on Brunner's most significant and controversial work, the dystopian novels *Stand on Zanzibar, The Sheep Look Up,* and *The Shockwave Rider.* Index of works and persons. (MAM)

Edgar Rice Burroughs, U.S., 1875–1950

10-33.   Holtsmark, Erling B. **Edgar Rice Burroughs**. Twayne, 1986.

10-34.   Porges, Irwin. **Edgar Rice Burroughs: The Man who Created Tarzan**. Brigham Young, 1975.

10-35.   Taliafarro, John. **Tarzan Forever: The Life of Edgar Rice Burroughs, Creator of Tarzan**. Scribner, 1999.

In *Trillion Year Spree* Brian Aldiss comments: "Wells is teaching us to think. Burroughs and his lesser imitators are teaching us not to think. Of course, Burroughs is teaching us to wonder. The sense of wonder is in essence a religious state, blanketing our criticism." Burroughs wrote 70 novels, which have sold well over 100 million copies. Yet, as Aldiss also says, "All Burroughs novels are vaguely similar, wherever they are set, heroes and incidents often transposable, as clips of crocodile fights were transposed from one Tarzan movie to the next."

Published on the 100th anniversary of Burrough's birth, Porges is the authorized and definitive biography, more than 800 pages long, including more than 250 photographs and illustrations. The sources of Burroughs's popularity and the entire scope of his works and life are discussed in detail by Porges, who has relied on many primary sources not previously available. Readers should find Holtsmark, in the Twayne author series, a readily available and convenient survey. He includes a short biography and a discussion of the Mars, Tarzan, Pellucidar, and Venus series; discusses literary background and themes; and offers a balanced final assessment.

John Taliafarro's newer biography, though shorter and less detailed than that of Porges, was also able to draw on additional and more recent resources (including thousands of papers originally extracted by Porges and his wife from Burroughs's warehouse). This volume is quite likely sufficient for most readers searching for a reliable introduction to Burroughs and his life. In fact, its brevity (achieved without neglecting the most important aspects of its subject's life)—and a more popular and lively style of writing—will probably make this book more appropriate (and enjoyable to read) for many than Porges's huge tome. Acknowledgments, bibliographical notes, index. (NB, RLM)

John W. Campbell, Jr., U.S., 1910–1971

*10-36.   Berger, Albert I. **The Magic That Works: John W. Campbell and the American Response to Technology**. Borgo, 1993.

John W. Campbell, Jr. was long considered, by wide agreement among historians and scholars of SF, the most influential single editor the genre has seen in his more than 30 years at *Astounding*, now *Analog*. His importance is discussed in Aldiss's *Trillion Year Spree*, Carter's *The Creation of Tomorrow*, and Panshin's *The World Beyond the Hill*, among other sources. In 1998, however, in *The Mechanics of Wonder* [9-199], a history arguing for the origins of science fiction in the magazines and theories of Hugo Gernsback, Gary Westfahl provides in some detail a reevaluation of Campbell as author and editor, especially in relation to Gernsback, discussing at length Campbell's role in defining American SF and claiming that his importance and impact have been misunderstood and inadequately evaluated. Future discussions of Campbell will need to address Westfahl's controversial and revisionist claims. Somewhat surprisingly, Westfahl does not mention Berger's book.

Berger, a history professor, has provided the first detailed assessment of Campbell, the historical context in which he worked, the commercial pressures to which he was subject, and the influence he and his magazine had on SF. Although published as part of Borgo's Popular Writers of Today series, the work is a case study in American intellectual history derived from a then-despised branch of popular literature. Berger has drawn on his master's and doctoral theses, his published articles, and Campbell's letters to create this detailed and balanced analysis. Berger explores how the writers, editor, and readers of *Astounding* interacted with one another and how they were shaped by the shift from the 19th-century tradition of the inventor/tinkerer (recall Tom Swift and similar boy heroes) to corporate and university laboratories of today, where large budgets and teams dominate. Berger is especially good at dissecting the "amateur" scientist, and even more specifically, the problems Campbell had in distinguishing between "unorthodox" science and outright quackery. (There is considerable discussion of Hubbard's Dianetics and Scientology, and other Campbell enthusiasms such as the Dean Drive and parapsychology generally.) An admirable study, transcending the narrowly literary, well-written, exceptionally well-documented, and well-indexed, and easily the best in this Borgo series. A selection of Campbell's letters was published as *The John W. Campbell Letters*, vol. 1, ineptly edited by Perry A. Chapdelaine, Sr., and others (AC Projects, 1985), upon which Berger draws. A second volume of letters to/from Asimov and van Vogt was published in 1993. (NB, RLM)

Karel Čapek, Czechoslovakia, 1890–1938

10-37. Klima, Ivan. **Karel Čapek: Life and Work**. Catbird Press, 2002.

Karel Čapek, perhaps most well-known in the West for his coinage of the word "robot" in his 1920 play *R.U.R.*, is an important name in Czech literary history who deserves a central place in the history of science fiction, having written several works that belong to the SF genre, the most famous being *The Absolute at Large*, *Krakatit*, and *War with the Newts*. Ivan Klima, himself a prominent and well-respected Czech author, appears to have been an excellent choice to write this engaging and insightful biography. Klima has long been fascinated by Čapek, and indeed is the author of an earlier master's thesis on him. This book, especially commissioned in English with a foreign audience in mind, provides a fascinating and well-written examination of Čapek's life and his work, giving the historical and social background necessary to enable non-Czech readers to understand both Čapek the man and the writer, with due attention paid to his SF-relevant texts. Includes notes, a list of Čapek's works in English translation, and an index. (RLM)

Orson Scott Card, U.S., 1951–

10-38.   Collings, Michael R. **In the Image of God: Theme, Characterization, and Landscape in the Fiction of Orson Scott Card**. Greenwood, 1990.

10-39.   Collings, Michael R. **Storyteller: The Official Orson Scott Card Bibliography and Guide**. Overlook Connection Press, 2001.

A phenomenally diverse and prolific writer, Orson Scott Card has produced a host of novels, collections, stories, poetry, plays, video and tape presentations, nonfiction books, and articles. Michael R. Collings's accessible, intelligent advocacy of Card's work rests on a parallel with C. S. Lewis—another author who fervently affirms the primacy of story, is concerned with theological issues, and whose works manifest an (apparently) deep-seated sense of estrangement. Clearly deeply affected by Card's work, Collings portrays him as "a consummate storyteller whose stories happen to be . . . [about] a world composed of the spiritual as well as the material." Collings examines that world via a singularly perceptive account of Card's analogical use of interior and exterior landscapes and an explication of the structural role played by the monomyth in his construction of heroes. Collings further identifies "the need to identify and define community" as Card's dominant theme and deals with such dicey and important issues as his use of the Bible, Mormonism, and violence. For anyone with more than a passing interest in this author, *In the Image of God* is essential, although it is marred by the exclusionary implication that only those sympathetic to the Mormon worldview can meaningfully interpret Card's fiction. The study is also now quite dated, thanks to significant new work by Card since its original publication. (MAM)

More up-to-date is Collings's *Storyteller*, from 2001, an exhaustive bibliography that covers not only Card's fiction, with (sometimes insufficient) plot summaries, but more or less everything else he has ever had a hand in producing. Also included is a highly useful guide to Card's reception among critics, both popular and academic. Even references to Card's work in languages other than English, and to online resources of relevance are provided. Unfortunately, the non-bibliographic portions of this book are critically questionable and far too extreme in their praise of Card's work, bordering at worst on the hagiographic. (RLM)

Angela Carter, U.K., 1940–1992

10-40.   Day, Aidan. **Angela Carter: The Rational Glass**. Manchester Univ. Press, 1998.

10-41.   Gamble, Sarah, ed. **The Fiction of Angela Carter: A Reader's Guide to Essential Criticism**. Icon, 2001.

10-42. Sage, Lorna, ed. **Flesh and the Mirror: Essays on the Art of Angela Carter**. Virago, 1994.

Angela Carter, who died of cancer at the age of 51 in 1992, was one of the most original, interesting, and controversial of late 20th-century British authors. In her fiction and nonfiction Carter tackled serious contemporary issues, including, prominently, feminism, violence, postmodernity, politics, pornography, mythology, and sexuality. At one point, according to academic legend, grant applications in Britain to study her work were more numerous than were all those focusing on the whole of the 18th century, or on Virginia Woolf. Despite her prominence, and the fact that she cast three of her novels in the science fiction mode (*Heroes and Villains*, *The Infernal Desire Machines of Doctor Hoffman* [retitled *The War of Dreams* in its U.S. edition, a significant de-sexualization of the work's title], and *The Passion of New Eve*), Carter's work has been repeatedly ignored or undervalued in (especially American) academic SF scholarship. She also made extensive use of Gothic, horror, and other fantastic elements in her fiction. The stories in *The Bloody Chamber and Other Adult Tales* (Gollancz, 1979) are classic fairy tales revisited with feminist, erotic, postmodern, and often violent sensibilities.

An excellent, intelligent, up-to-date, and relatively comprehensive overview of major critical material on Carter is Sarah Gamble's *The Fiction of Angela Carter*. In addition to comparative comments on, and appropriate excerpts from, a large number of studies covering Carter's entire oeuvre, this book contains a good selected (and partially annotated) bibliography of Carter's own work and secondary sources. Gamble is also author of a book-length study, *Angela Carter: Writing from the Front Line*, published in 1997 by Edinburgh University Press. Lorna Sage's *Flesh and the Mirror* is another useful collection on Carter, containing an essay by Roz Kaveny of particular interest: "New New World Dreams: Angela Carter and Science Fiction." Kaveny explores Carter's relationships to the British New Wave writers of the 1960s (including Ballard, Moorcock, and Sladek), and argues convincingly for her influence on later British SF authors such as Tanith Lee, Colin Greenland, Geoff Ryman, and Mary Gentle. Sage has also written a short, 77-page booklet, titled *Angela Carter* (Northcote House, 1994). Aidan Day, in *Angela Carter: The Rational Glass*, provides an intriguing discussion of the entanglement of reason, rationality, reality, and desire in Carter's work, including her SF titles. Finally, it can be noted that Lucie Armitt, in *Theorizing the Fantastic* [9-8], discusses at some length *The Passion of New Eve* and contemporary technotheory, reaching conclusions about the novel largely in tune with those of Gamble, but at odds with certain interpretations suggested by Day. (RLM)

Arthur C. Clarke, U.K., 1917–

10-43. Clarke, Arthur C. **Greetings, Carbon-Based Bipeds! Collected Essays 1934–1998**. St. Martin's, 1999.

10-44.   Hollow, John. **Against the Night, the Stars: The Science Fiction of Arthur C. Clarke.** Ohio Univ. Press, 1987.

10-45.   McAleer, Neil. **Arthur C. Clarke: The Authorised Biography.** Contemporary, 1992.

10-46.   Olander, Joseph D., and Martin H. Greenberg, eds. **Arthur C. Clarke.** Taplinger, 1977.

Infused with optimism about the future of humanity, enthusiasm for technology, and a sense of wonder at the universe, Sir Arthur C. Clarke's fiction is a touchstone of 20th-century SF. Unfortunately, there does not currently exist an adequate single-volume study of his science fiction. An important, early, short (64 pages) study from Borgo Press, *The Space Odysseys of Arthur C. Clarke,* by George Edgar Slusser, which strives for a unified perspective on Clarke's fiction using the structural sociology of Lucien Goldmann, is still of interest, but this badly dated booklet can hardly be considered sufficient. John Hollow identifies as a unifying theme Clarke's optimistic view of the potential of the human race for understanding the cosmos. Unfortunately, he overemphasizes this rather obvious point to the exclusion of other important aspects of Clarke's fiction and fails to define a context for Clarke as a major modern SF writer. Hollow took the opportunity, in a 1987 reprint of his book (first published in 1983), to add a chapter on Peter Hyams's film of *2010: Odyssey Two* and various incarnations of *Songs of Distant Earth* (short story, movie outline, novel). The volume is also now quite dated. Nor did Hollow remedy the defects in his book's scholarly apparatus, which offers only a list of Clarke's fiction and a bibliography of selected criticism.

Additional early, but still relevant, criticism of Clarke can be found in the Olander and Greenberg collection, especially the essays by Thomas Clareson on Clarke's vision, by Betsy Harfst on the mythical content of his major novels, and by David N. Samuelson and John Huntington on *Childhood's End.* Even Samuelson's insightful essay in Bleiler's *Science Fiction Writers* should be consulted. Robin Anne Reid's relatively recent *Arthur C. Clarke: A Critical Companion* (Greenwood, 1997) is aimed at a high school, rather than university, audience.

In general, readers seeking biographical information on Clarke face something of a problem. His engaging, somewhat eccentric autobiography, *Astounding Days* (Bantam, 1989), adopts the clever strategy of using the issues of *Astounding Science Fiction* that Clarke read from March 1930 through 1945 as triggers for reflections on his life and stories. The result, though fragmentary, is fascinatingly chatty and usefully complements the equally fragmentary information in *The View from Serendip* (1977). In 1999, Clarke published a large volume that has several essays of biocritical interest to the Clarke scholar: the ingeniously and humorously titled *Greetings, Carbon-Based Bipeds!,* a chronologically arranged collection of diverse, largely previously published (but not necessarily readily available), "representative" nonfiction, containing short sectional introductions to the work of each decade and scattered comments on events that have occurred since the original publication of the pieces.

Most disappointingly, Neil McAleer's well-intentioned but numbing "authorized biography" offers endless details about Clarke's travels, book contracts, and projects, but little insight into his intellectual life or his fiction. Note that the updated U.S. edition, which is the author's preferred text, has a foreword by Ray Bradbury and differs textually by about 10 percent from the British edition, published by Gollancz as *Odyssey: The Authorised Biography of Arthur C. Clarke*. List of sources, index. Two recent books that reprint Clarke's correspondence with, respectively, Lord Dunsany (Daniels, Keith Allen, ed. *Arthur C. Clarke and Lord Dunsany: A Correspondence*. Anamnesis Press, 2002) and C. S. Lewis (Clarke, Arthur C. and C. S. Lewis *From Narnia to A Space Odyssey: The War of Letters Between Arthur C. Clarke and C. S. Lewis*. iBooks/Simon & Schuster, 2003), while of some biographical and historical interest, represent relatively minor contributions to Clarke scholarship. (MAM, RLM)

Hal Clement, U.S., 1922–2003

10-47. Hassler, Donald M. **Hal Clement**. Starmont, 1982.

Clement attended technical high school, earned an undergraduate degree in astronomy from Harvard, and taught science in a private school from 1949, the year before the publication of his first novel, *Needle*, until his retirement. His fiction predictably reflected his interest in and extensive knowledge of "hard" science, from his most famous work, *Mission of Gravity*, to his final novel, *Noise*. Hassler surveys Clement's fiction through *The Nitrogen Fix*, emphasizing his skill in depicting alien intelligences. Using such outsiders to provide an ironic perspective on humanity is a centuries-old literary device. Hassler's is a competent account, if now severely dated, and one that should have been more rigorously edited to improve the often awkward prose. (NB)

John Crowley, U.S., 1942–

10-48. Andre-Driussi, Michael, and Alice K. Turner, eds. **Snake's-Hands: The Fiction of John Crowley**. Wildside, 2001.

Despite having published more than a half-dozen novels, all of which have been well received, and the best of which (*Little, Big*, a fantasy from 1981, generally considered his major work so far) have been very highly praised, John Crowley is an author who is still relatively unknown in many academic and popular contexts. This collection of diverse essays (versions of some of which saw earlier publication in *The New York Review of Science Fiction*), with contributions by Brian Attebery, John Clute, Thomas M. Disch, and Gene Wolfe, among others, is intended to help alter that situation. Crowley, both fascinating to read and worthy of serious critical attention, has proven difficult to categorize in terms of genre, and has consequently sometimes fallen between the cracks of scholarly scrutiny. His writing is characterized by exquisite prose, elaborate plots, complex textual strategies, and sometimes relatively obscure extra-textual points of reference, as this volume demonstrates. *The Deep*, for instance, his first novel, is built literally around the game of chess, with the characters replaying the events of the 15th-century War of the Roses. The initial chapters in *Snake's-Hands* provide discussions and explications of each of Crowley's major novels, while the latter portions of the book address general questions concerning his writing as a whole. As is too often the case with such collections, several of the essays demand further development and greater depth. Furthermore, an attempt to draw attention to Crowley also implicitly supports a tendency to lavish praise without always providing the requisite argumentation necessary to support the words of commendation. Nevertheless, this volume is clearly a worthwhile and useful introduction to the work of an unduly underappreciated author. (RLM)

L. Sprague de Camp, U.S., 1907–2000

10-49.   de Camp, L. Sprague. **Time and Chance. An Autobiography**. Donald M. Grant, 1996.

L. Sprague de Camp's basically traditional autobiography stretches from the author's roots in Europe in the 16th century through the 1990s, providing an adequate, relatively complete, and apparently honest picture (he isn't afraid to characterize himself in unflattering terms when he deems it appropriate) of himself and his life. Unfortunately, although the book is quite readable, de Camp offers far too little insight into his writing, aside from a number of practical details. There is some interesting material on who and what he eventually incorporated into his fiction, and information on his relationship to various people in the SF and fantasy worlds, but even when discussing the likes of Robert Heinlein and Isaac Asimov, whom he had occasion to work with during World War II, his focus is on connections between them other than science fiction. Nevertheless, this book is clearly of significant value to all students of de Camp. (RLM)
   Awards: Hugo

Samuel R. Delany, U.S., 1942–

*10-50.   Barbour, Douglas. **Worlds Out of Words: The SF Novels of Samuel R. Delany**. Bran's Head Books, 1979.

*10-51.   Delany, Samuel R. **1984**. Voyant, 2000.

10-52.   Sallis, James, ed. **Ash of Stars: On the Writing of Samuel R. Delany**. Univ. of Mississippi Press, 1996.

Samuel Delany's paramount contributions to the evolving poetics of SF through his critical writings and multiplex experimental fictions demand critical attention in greater depth than has yet been provided in any single, book-length study. Although now severely dated, Douglas Barbour's study remains the best overall introduction to Delany's early works; in particular his insights into *Dhalgren* are sure to benefit perplexed readers. Barbour leads up to this novel with four chapters that approach Delany's novels of the 1960s from diverse perspectives: his use of the quest pattern as spatial metaphor, his creation of a self-contained system of allusions, his construction of alien cultures, and his style and structure, although Barbour is least successful in dealing with the last of these topics. Barbour's study also offers valuable perspectives on *Triton*, a central novel in Delany's total oeuvre.

1984 is a selection of letters—whose criteria for inclusion are not indicated—written and sent by Delany to diverse persons between June 1983 and January 1985. Like much of Delany's writing, the text is dense (the book contains 351 pages of very small print), expressive, and literarily impressive—amazingly so considering the personal circumstances and limitations of time under which these letters were written. The content of the letters varies from the humdrum and everyday to the literary and philosophical, covering everything from the intimate and often sexually explicit details of Delany's private life to thoughts on major social, political, and philosophical issues. A birthday party for Delany's daughter shares the text with the author's humorous recounting of his encounter with Umberto Eco, reflections on the state of SF publishing, and opinions about the ideas of Walter Benjamin. This is an incredibly rich book, impossible to briefly summarize or easily categorize, filled with the minutiae of daily existence, the drama of political involvement, and the grandeur of intellectual adventure. But, to gain access to its deepest depths, this volume needs to be read (as does most of Delany's prose) carefully, perhaps even savored, with great attention paid to language and detail and nuance. And it should reward such readings with significant insight into Delany's life, his ideas and ideals, and his writing, including, scattered throughout the book, many intriguing comments on science fiction. Unfortunately, the volume does not contain an index, which is sorely needed for anyone studying a text as complex and intricate.

The collection of 10 essays edited by James Sallis is a mixed bag, many of which are available elsewhere, and some of which make worthwhile contributions to Delany studies. In the individual essays, particular attention is focused on SF titles such as *Babel-17*, *Stars in My Pocket Like Grains of Sand*, *Dhalgren*, and *Triton*, as well as on Delany's fantasy and his erotica.

Readers interested in Delany should also consult the autobiographical volumes *Heavenly Breakfast: An Essay on the Winter of Love* (1979) and *The Motion of Light in Water* (1988; rev. ed. 1990), as well as his numerous collections of critical essays. In addition to the four books mentioned in Chapter 9 of this guide, these include *Longer Views: Extended Essays* (Wesleyan, 1996) and *Shorter Views: Queer Thoughts and the Politics of the Paraliterary* (Wesleyan, 1999). (RLM, MAM)

Philip K. Dick, U.S., 1928–1982

10-53. Dick, Philip K. **The Selected Letters of Philip K. Dick, Vols. 1–4.** Underwood Miller, 1991–1993.

10-54. Greenberg, Martin H., and Joseph D. Olander, eds. **Philip K. Dick.** Taplinger, 1983.

10-55. Mackey, Douglas A. **Philip K. Dick.** Twayne, 1988.

*10-56.   Mullen, R. D., Istvan Csicerny-Ronay, Jr., and Arthur B. Evans. **On Philip K. Dick: 40 Articles from Science-Fiction Studies**. SF-TH, Inc., 1992.

*10-57.   Palmer, Christopher. **Philip K. Dick: Exhilaration and Terror of the Postmodern**. Liverpool Univ. Press, 2003.

10-58.   Robinson, Kim Stanley. **The Novels of Philip K. Dick**. UMI Research Press, 1984.

*10-59.   Sutin, Lawrence. **Divine Invasions: A Life of Philip K. Dick**. Harmony, 1989.

10-60.   Umland, Samuel J., ed. **Philip K. Dick: Contemporary Critical Interpretations**. Greenwood, 1995.

10-61.   Warrick, Patricia S. **Mind in Motion: The Fiction of Philip K. Dick**. Southern Illinois Univ. Press, 1987.

Dick is an author popular with readers and academic critics alike, the latter fact attested to by the large number of critical works that examine his life, ideas, and works. A good place to start among these many works is the collection of articles from *Science Fiction Studies* edited by R. D. Mullen, Istvan Csicerny-Ronay, Jr., and Arthur B. Evans. Prefaced by a perceptive introduction on Dick's posthumous reception by critics and its consequences for SF's interpenetration into the mainstream. There are also lists of the manuscript collection at California State University, Fullerton, and of Dick's books in chronological order in this essential volume that maps the development of a critical consensus that is still in flux. Index.

The best introduction to Dick's huge oeuvre is Douglas Mackey's Twayne volume. In chapters arranged chronologically by decade, Mackey presents accurate summaries of Dick's mainstream novels and of many of his short stories, accompanied by brief but sensible critical insights that often parallel (or quote) the work of previous studies. He falters only when confronted with the complexity of the novels of the 1970s. By careful organization and identification of thematic interconnections between various works (primarily Dick's concern for the nature of reality), Mackey brings uncommon coherence to this necessarily brief overview. Chronology, primary and annotated secondary bibliography, index.

Also valuable to newcomers to Dick's fiction are the largely empirical essays collected by Greenberg and Olander. Of special interest are stimulating essays by three contemporaries of Dick: Brian Aldiss, Michael Bishop, and Thomas Disch. Although this collection suffers from the exclusion of novels published after 1974, its 10 accessible, thematically oriented, largely theoretical essays compose a valuable if fragmented survey of Dick's fiction. Biography, index.

Like Mackey and other critics who followed him, Warrick contextualizes Dick's works by presenting his turbulent, troubled life and the mid-century American culture in which he lived and wrote. Drawing heavily on personal interviews and correspondence with Dick, Warrick considers his works chronologically in chapters, each of which addresses a primary theme of the period. Her lucid attempt to resolve the considerable ambiguities of Dick's works through the notion of a "dynamic four-chambered metaphor" and to present his "strange, mutant science fiction" as "quantum-reality fiction" generates myriad insights, especially into the eight major novels on which she focuses. But her study is marred by apparent lack of use of and lack of reference to secondary literature and, more seriously, by the absence of any discussion of Dick's relationship to and views on American SF, its publishers, and its readership. Chronology, primary bibliography, index.

Robinson's brief study of Dick's SF and mainstream novels, based on his 1992 doctoral thesis, complements Warrick's book. Robinson is particularly strong on Dick's challenge to the conventions of traditional American SF, and on the self-referential and broadly metaphorical character of his later works. In spite of a few minor errors, lack of depth in the treatment of some novels, and uneven reference to the secondary literature, Robinson should be read in conjunction with Warrick or after Mackey. Notes, bibliography, index.

Umland's relatively recent collection of essays contains various contributions of interest, several of which attempt to reinterpret Dick's fiction in the light of new critical stances and analytic perspectives. Primary and secondary bibliographies, index.

The most significant recent addition to Dick scholarship is to be found in Christopher Palmer's book-length study. In it Palmer examines at some length selected examples of Dick's novels and his shorter fiction, using both historical and formal criteria to assess them. On historical grounds, Palmer sees the "fiction as a depiction of and a response to postmodernity, and investigates a clash between humanism and postmodernism." With respect to formal issues, he claims that Dick "exploits the conventions of genre rather than obeying them." This study is a theoretically sophisticated, well-reasoned exploration of an author whose works seem especially well-suited to the kind of analyses Palmer is applying. List of works cited and index.

The troubled, turbulent nature of Dick's life and its clear importance to his later fiction has provoked several biographical studies. The best of these is Sutin's, which weaves a compelling, compassionate account of Dick and those who knew him with a narrative of his intellectual life and evolving fictional concerns. Sutin concludes with a very useful "Chronological Survey and Guide," which annotates and rates (on a scale from 1 to 10) every book Dick wrote. Index.

Sutin also edited *The Shifting Realities of Philip K. Dick: Selected Literary and Philosophical Writings* (Pantheon, 1995), a useful book accurately described by its title. Also quite valuable for Dick scholars are the four volumes of Dick's correspondence published by Underwood-Miller, although their usefulness could be improved significantly by the addition of indexes. Emmanuele Carrère is a French novelist and screenplay writer who talked to people who knew Dick and has read about him, but his *I Am Alive and You Are Dead: A Journey into the Mind of Philip K. Dick* (Metropolitan Books, 2004, translated from the 1993 French original) is neither a biography nor literary criticism, but an unsatisfactory secondhand account, far inferior to Sutin's biography. (MAM, RLM)

Gardner Dozois, U.S., 1947–

10-62. Swanwick, Michael. **Being Gardner Dozois**. Old Earth Books, 2001.

Although Gardner Dozois is best known in the science fiction field as an editor (e.g., *Asimov's Science Fiction,* 1986–2004; an annual *The Year's Best Science Fiction* anthology series since 1984), he is also an accomplished writer of fiction, whose work has won or been nominated for several major awards. *Being Gardner Dozois* consists of a single, long, 243-page interview of Dozois conducted by Michael Swanwick, discussing in turn each of the former's published works of fiction, in chronological order of original publication from his first published story (1966) to the novelette "A Knight of Ghosts and Shadows" (1999). The book is often entertaining and it provides some fascinating and valuable—if unevenly and somewhat haphazardly distributed—insights into to both Dozois's life and his fiction. An index would have made the book considerably more accessible for both general reader and scholar. The volume includes an alphabetical list of first publication information for the stories discussed. (RLM)

Harlan Ellison, U.S., 1934–

*10-63. Weil, Ellen, and Gary K. Wolfe. **Harlan Ellison: The Edge of Forever**. Ohio State Univ. Press, 2002.

Ellen Weil and Gary K. Wolfe have at last provided Harlan Ellison with the scholarly attention he has long deserved as a major American author. Their excellent monograph, largely (but not slavishly) chronological in structure, places Ellison's work in the context of the times in which it was written and the life of its author, arguing, quite correctly, that these contexts are vital for understanding the writings of their subject. Although not a literary biography, this book supplies a considerable amount of biographical information about Ellison's life ("autobiographical material is so pervasive in Ellison's work that it cannot be ignored"—which Weil and Wolfe effectively demonstrate) to ground many of the analyses presented. The import for the development, style, and content of Ellison's work of having written for the crime and science fiction digests of the 1950s, the men's magazines of the 1960s, the paperback market, and Hollywood movies and (especially) television—all the while attempting to establish an independent and personal voice—is emphasized and explored in what will likely long remain the standard study of Ellison, easily superseding the interesting but brief and now-dated Borgo Press book by George Slusser, *Harlan Ellison* (1977). Of particular interest is the examination of Ellison's relationship to the various literary, professional, and personal worlds of science fiction. In a book that never claims to be exhaustive in its coverage of the work of an author of more than 60 novels, 1,200 stories, and articles, as well as numerous other items—screenplays, journalism, opinion, comment, etc.—the texts chosen for discussion manage to be representative and/or central enough to illuminate strengths and weaknesses of Ellison's work. Furthermore, Weil and Wolfe write well, and they have produced a book whose prose is a pleasure to read and whose analyses are clearly, logically, and intelligently presented, facilitating enormously for its readers an evaluation of the book's perspectives and claims.

Not seen was a work scheduled for late 2004, Tim Richmond's *Fingerprints on the Sky: The Authorized Harlan Ellison Bibliography and Reader's Guide* (Overlook Connection Press), prepared with the cooperation of its subject. (RLM)

Philip José Farmer, U.S., 1918–

10-64. Brizzi, Mary T. **Philip José Farmer**. Starmont, 1980.

10-65. Chapman, Edgar L. **The Magic Labyrinth of Philip José Farmer**. Borgo, 1985.

Farmer is fond of the picaresque and the playful and has over the years linked his fictions to those of others, such as Edgar Rice Burroughs, Arthur Conan Doyle, and L. Frank Baum. These elements are explored in both books. Brizzi examines Farmer's technique and images in works published through mid-1978. Chapman is slightly more current, though both studies are now severely dated. Chapman is also the more detailed, although he omits the Brizzi from his bibliography. He is strongest in his exploration of Farmer's use of parody and satire. (NB)

Hugo Gernsback, Luxembourg/U.S., 1884–1964

10-65A. Ashley, Mike, and Robert A. W. Lowndes. **The Gernsback Days: A Study of the Evolution of Modern Science Fiction**. Wildside Press, 2004.

Born in Luxembourg in 1884, Gernsback immigrated to the United States in 1904 and founded and edited several electronic hobbyist magazines. In 1926, he founded and edited *Amazing Stories*, the first all-SF magazine, was soon forced into bankruptcy, and later founded several other SF pulps. (See Chapter 2 for details.) Historians of SF recognize the importance of Gernsback but differ sharply on his influence. The dominant view is that he was a disaster, untalented as both an editor and writer of SF, who imposed a crippling philosophy on the early development of SF. Ashley thinks more highly of Gernsback, and over two decades wrote this detailed study (250 of the book's 499 pages). His research provides much detail not previously revealed or placed in context. Lowndes (1916–1998), an early pulp magazine editor, provides 132 pages of numbing summaries of the dreary fiction in Gernsback's magazines from 1926 to 1936. Most of the remaining pages list issue-by-issue contents of SF in Gernsback magazines published from 1908 to 1936. Gernsback has been the subject of many articles and books (the selected bibliography runs 8 pages), including Westfahl's favorable *The Mechanics of Wonder* [9-199]. But the final judgment is likely to be that of Bleiler in *Science-Fiction: The Gernsback Years* [7-3], who concludes: "In general, apart from an occasional story, one must look back at the authors of 1926–1936 mostly as predecessors, rather than as authors to be read today apart from historical reasons."

William Gibson, U.S./Canada, 1948–

10-66.   Cavallaro, Dani. **Cyberpunk and Cyberculture: Science Fiction and the Work of William Gibson**. Athlone, 2000.

10-67.   Olsen, Lance. **William Gibson**. Starmont, 1992.

Despite his central importance to the development of cyberpunk in particular and cyberculture more generally, there exists as yet no completely satisfactory single-volume examination of the work of William Gibson, even though the number of shorter studies that deal at least in part with his writing is quite large. Like Brian McHale in *Constructing Postmodernism* (Routledge, 1993) and several critics who contributed essays to Larry McCaffrey's *Storming the Reality Studio*, Lance Olsen situates Gibson in two overlapping literary schools: SF and postmodernism. Drawing in part on perspectives elaborated in his *Eclipse of Uncertainty* (1987), Olsen explores Gibson's intertextuality, globalism, and eclectic use of genre materials and motifs, particularizing his insights with discussions of style and structure, the dominant aspects of Gibson's art. Best of all, Olsen is balanced; he demonstrates the strengths of several short stories and *Neuromancer*, but also notes the progressive weakening of Gibson's later novels, excluding *The Difference Engine*, which is mentioned only in passing. Readers seeking a broader view of the cyberpunk phenomenon should supplement this essential guide with the aforementioned books by McHale and McCaffrey.

Dani Cavallaro attempts to place Gibson into a much broader cyberpunk context, making her volume more a study of the cyberpunk phenomenon—with Gibson serving as the main example—rather than a study of Gibson and his work per se. Nonetheless, she has some interesting and relevant, but not especially original (she seems to depend quite heavily on McCaffrey's *Storming the Reality Studio*, for instance), things to say about both him and the SF genre. Unfortunately, her book is plagued throughout by sloppiness with respect to its scientific and philosophical foundations, making it often more current than correct. And, although Cavallaro can be quick with direct or implicit references to larger social or scientific contexts, she frequently does not sufficiently explain or justify the deeper significance of her claims or the validity of her connections. Too often Cavallaro presents a superficial and postmodernly popular rehash of certain trendy theoretical positions instead of undertaking original or deeper investigations of her own. References, short annotated guide to further reading, bibliography, and index. (MAM, RLM)

Joe Haldeman, U.S., 1943–

10-68.   Gordon, Joan. **Joe Haldeman**. Starmont, 1980.

In February 1968, at the age of 24, Joe Haldeman was sent to Vietnam where he was seriously wounded in September of the same year. This experience significantly shaped his subsequent writings, especially the semi-autobiographical novel, *War Year* (1972), and particularly *The Forever War*, which won both Hugo and Nebula awards. Joan Gordon's brief study of Haldeman, now seriously out of date, discusses his work and life through the 1978 collection, *Infinite Dreams*. (NB)

Harry Harrison, U.S., 1925–

10-69.   Stover, Leon. **Harry Harrison**. Twayne, 1991.

Harry Harrison's friend and collaborator Leon Stover argues forcefully, in this now somewhat dated contribution to the Twayne's United States Authors series, that Harrison is not merely a fine and prolific SF author but "a significant American writer"—part of the tradition of classic American adventure fiction that includes the likes of Cooper, Melville, Twain, and Mailer. While acknowledging Harrison's reliance on the traditional Gernsbackian mode of technophilic adventure narratives imbued with scientific rationalism and shaped by pulp forms and conventions, Stover successfully situates Harrison's major works, such as *Make Room! Make Room!* and *Captive Universe*, in the stream of social science fiction whose modern incarnations derive from the works of H. G. Wells. Stover argues that Harrison's fiction is rich, mature, and sophisticated, but he makes his case through advocacy and asides rather than analysis: for example, his skimpy discussion of Harrison's epic alternative history, the West of Eden trilogy, arguably the best evidence for his claims concerning Harrison's stature. Stover draws extensively on interviews with Harrison, and his book contains an excellent biographical sketch and provocative asides on Harrison's philosophy. Chronology, notes, primary and (briefly annotated) secondary bibliography, index. (MAM)

Robert A. Heinlein, U.S., 1907–1988

10-70.   Franklin, H. Bruce. **Robert A. Heinlein: America as Science Fiction**. Oxford Univ. Press, 1980.

*10-71.   Gifford, James. **Robert A. Heinlein: A Reader's Companion**. Nitrosyncretic Press, 2000.

10-72.   Heinlein, Robert A. **Grumbles from the Grave**. Ed. by Virginia Heinlein. Del Rey, 1990.

10-73.   Olander, Joseph D., and Martin H. Greenberg, eds. **Robert A. Heinlein**. Taplinger, 1978.

10-74.   Panshin, Alexei. **Heinlein in Dimension**. Advent, 1968.

10-75.   Patterson, William H., Jr., and Andrew Thornton. **The Martian Named Smith: Critical Perspectives on Robert A. Heinlein's Stranger in a Strange Land**. Nitrosyncretic Press, 2001.

10-76.   Slusser, George E. **The Classic Years of Robert A. Heinlein**. Borgo, 1977.

10-77.   Slusser, George E. **Robert A. Heinlein: Stranger in His Own Land**. 2nd ed. Borgo, 1977.

Heinlein began to publish SF in 1939 and for the next 20 years he unquestionably dominated the field, as he moved from the genre magazines to the "slicks" and to book publication of his YA novels by Scribner's and to bestsellerdom in the years preceding his death in 1988. He may have been the first genre author to have a book devoted to him: Panshin's study, which won a nonfiction Hugo award and was revised from its piecemeal appearance in *Riverside Quarterly*. Although limited to the study of Heinlein's earlier works, Panshin's assessment of his plots, subject matter, literary quality, and influence anticipates the later works and themes.

Slusser examines Heinlein's first two decades in his first study, while the second focuses on later work through the mid-1970s. Both studies explore the central dynamics underlying the surface themes, conventions, and doctrines and how they generate the formal structure of the stories. They are especially valuable for their close readings and their heterodox interpretations. The Taplinger collection assembles nine original essays treating the YA novels, Heinlein's future-history series, *Stranger in a Strange Land* and *Time Enough for Love*, and the human sexuality and social Darwinism in his fiction. Primary and secondary bibliography and index. This is a useful synoptic survey and starting point for Heinlein studies.

Franklin approaches Heinlein from a Marxist standpoint and divides the tales into five periods, relating them to contemporary American history. He is effective in showing how the contradictions in a capitalist American society are reflected and refracted in the stories, examining in detail the familiar Heinlein dualism of authoritarianism/anarchism, futuristic realism/nostalgia, and hardheaded rationalism/mysticism. Like many Marxists, Franklin can be a trifle dogmatic, and his study almost wholly neglects the SF genre in which most of Heinlein's work—certainly his most important (though not most popular)—appeared. Nevertheless, this is an important study of a seminal and influential writer (Eaton award).

James Gifford's reader's companion to Heinlein is a well-structured, well-made, easy-to-use, and genuinely valuable guide in the format of an annotated bibliography. Introductory material includes a listing of all published titles, followed by a division of the individual works into shorter lists, with separate chronological breakdowns of those works considered part of Heinlein's future history, short fiction, novels for adults, novels for young people, non-SF stories, nonfiction, and anthologies. There is also a chronology that includes personal events in Heinlein's life and details of publications by year. The centerpiece of the book is an alphabetically arranged, annotated listing of every work published by Heinlein. Full bibliographical information is provided at the top of each entry, and the opening paragraph of each sketches the plot. The next section considers each work in the context of Heinlein's writing in general. Various bits of diverse information are given in what is not seldom the most fascinating portion of each entry, a section entitled "Curiosities and Anomalies." A selected Heinlein bibliography and title and general indexes conclude the volume. No attempt is made to cover the voluminous critical literature on Heinlein.

Patterson and Thornton's book is a detailed examination of what is Heinlein's best-known novel, *Stranger in a Strange Land*. Unfortunately, its authors cannot begin to live up to the high claims made for them on the back cover of this book. The analysis presented is said to focus on *Stranger*'s satire and social criticism, with the intention of demonstrating the masterpiece status of Heinlein's novel. At this task, the volume fails completely, not least because of its eclectic and unconvincing methodological approach. In something of an analytic hodgepodge, the authors shun discussions of Heinlein's style, characterization, or plot to give attention to what they claim are the novel's satiric and mythological aspects. Alas, their often clumsy and sometimes incoherent use of various poorly coordinated historical, philosophical, and theological references provides little insight into Heinlein's fiction. Patterson and Thornton do manage to say a few interesting and valid things about their subject in this book, but they are difficult to discover amid so much of questionable value. Bibliography, glossary, and index.

The central document in J. Neil Schulman's *The Robert Heinlein Interview and Other Heinleiniana* (Pulpless.Com, 1999; also available in a digital edition) is a long interview Schulman conducted with Heinlein in 1973, of greatest interest to those seeking material on Heinlein's thoughts on political issues, especially libertarianism.

Grumbles from the Grave contains a selection of Heinlein's correspondence, notably with his agent Lurton Blassingame and John W. Campbell, thematically organized and edited by his late widow, Virginia. There are also appendixes containing cuts from the novels *Red Planet* and *Podkayne of Mars*. The book is illustrated with a large number of photographs, and includes a chronologically arranged bibliography of Heinlein's work and an index. (RLM, NB)

Frank Herbert, U.S., 1920–1986

10-78. Herbert, Brian. **Dreamer of Dune: The Biography of Frank Herbert**. Tor, 2003.

10-79. O'Reilly, Timothy. **Frank Herbert**. Ungar, 1981.

A journalist for many years, Herbert incorporated many of his interests (e.g., ecology, free will, messianic movements) into *Dune* and the six sequels to it published during his lifetime. In 1999, Herbert's son Brian, working together with Kevin J. Anderson, returned to Herbert's fictional future to produce *Dune: House Atreides*, the first of a new series of novels (at least eight have been published or announced) set in the Dune universe and based in part on notes written by Frank Herbert. *The Dune Encyclopedia*, edited by Willis E. McNelly (Berkeley, 1984), fleshes out and adds multitudinous and various details to Herbert's complex future—although it can now probably best be read as an alternative history of the Dune universe, since no attempt was ever made to correlate the internal details found in any of the Dune books published after 1984 with the contents of the McNelly volume.

O'Reilly's study explores the philosophical ideas underlying and linking most of Herbert's fiction, not just the Dune series, and it remains the most significant book-length study devoted exclusively to Herbert's work. Unfortunately, it is badly outdated in light not only of Herbert's own later Dune novels (and possibly the Herbert/Anderson collaborations, not to mention the film and television mini-series versions of the saga), but also of subsequent scholarship.

Brian Herbert's biography of his father, though understandably subjective and personal, is a useful compendium of much information previously unavailable about the life of Frank Herbert. The book contains 16 pages of photographs and an extensive bibliography covering the published and unpublished works of Frank Herbert, Beverly Herbert (Frank's wife, who is given a central role in this biography), and Brian Herbert, as well as secondary sources. There is also a detailed index.

Finally, mention can be made of Donald Palumbo's *Chaos Theory, Asimov's Foundations and Robots, and Herbert's Dune* [10-17]. Palumbo's study of Asimov's and Herbert's SF from the perspective of chaos theory begins promisingly, but, unfortunately, Palumbo's desire to link Herbert's work to the monomyth of Joseph Campbell deteriorates significantly in quality (and accessibility) from his earlier chapters on Asimov, at times seemingly losing sight of its author's own self-professed focus on a chaos theory perspective, making the book much less valuable to Herbert scholars than to those interested in Asimov. There are still useful insights into Herbert's fiction to be found here, but deciphering them makes considerable demands on the reader. (RLM, NB)

Daniel Keyes, U.S., 1927–

*10-80.   Keyes, Daniel. **Algernon, Charlie and I: A Writer's Journey**. Challenge Press, 2000.

Daniel Keyes's literary reputation rests almost exclusively on two variations of a single work, both justifiably considered modern classics of the science fiction genre: the novelette "Flowers for Algernon," which originally appeared in *The Magazine of Fantasy and Science Fiction* in 1959, and its subsequent expansion into a novel (with the same title), published in 1966. The novelette was given a Hugo award and the novel won a Nebula. This autobiographical book, *Algernon, Charlie and I*, perhaps most accurately labeled a memoir, tells us a good deal about how and why Keyes came to write what was destined to become one of the most famous of all short science fiction works, as well as describing Keyes's relationships to various incarnations the tale was to have in later years, including not just the novel but also TV, dramatic, musical, and film versions, the latter of which, *Charly*, garnered Cliff Robertson an Oscar for his cinematic portrayal of the title character. Particularly illuminating are the descriptions of the unexpected (and sometimes unwanted) consequences of having written a modern literary classic. Among the most fascinating parts of the book are glimpses of the creative writing process itself, although Keyes strenuously and deliberately avoids all attempts at explaining, explicating, or interpreting his own fiction, believing that "once the writer explains or analyzes, he trivializes his own work." This memoir is required reading for any scholar of Keyes or his masterpiece; it is easy to read and insightful, and contains useful and interesting background material about both the author's life (he had a successful career teaching literature and creative writing) and his writing. The book reprints the original novelette, but lacks scholarly apparatus or an index. (RLM)

Ursula K. Le Guin, U.S., 1929–

*10-81. Cummins, Elizabeth. **Understanding Ursula K. Le Guin**. South Carolina Univ. Press. Rev. paperback ed., 1993.

10-82. De Bolt, Joe, ed. **Ursula K. Le Guin: Voyager to Inner Lands and Outer Space**. Kennikat, 1979.

10-83. Rochelle, Warren G. **Communities of the Heart: The Rhetoric of Myth in the Fiction of Ursula K. Le Guin**. Liverpool Univ. Press, 2000.

*10-84. White, Donna R. **Dancing with Dragons. Ursula K. Le Guin and the Critics**. Camden House, 1999.

Among modern SF writers, Ursula K. Le Guin may well be the subject of more published critical commentary than any other single author. One reason for this extensive secondary literature is the fact that her popularity and prolificacy stretches well beyond the confines of genre SF—most obviously into literature for children and young adults, and fantasy, but also including literary criticism, picture books, and poetry. Donna White's volume provides a useful and relatively thorough overview of the major outlines of critical and scholarly work about Le Guin. One of the book's most valuable aspects is its refusal to limit itself to a particular genre (e.g., children's literature, science fiction, fantasy). White instead surveys the entire scope of Le Guin criticism, describing and annotating the main trends and thrusts found therein. She can thus introduce and compare ideas and opinions of specialists on SF, for instance, to those of experts on children's literature, to the intellectual benefit of all.

In 1975, a special issue of *Science Fiction Studies* (No. 7, November) was devoted to essays about Le Guin and her work. Books about her began with George Slusser's 1976 essay, *The Farthest Shores of Ursula K. Le Guin* (Borgo), which provides a careful analysis of her earlier works. Another interesting early, still useful—but severely dated—overview of her achievement can be found in the De Bolt collection of essays. Aside from Le Guin's own nonfictional texts, Cummins's book, in its revised paperback version from 1993 (which adds a chapter and updates the bibliography), is the best single introduction to Le Guin's work, easily superior to both of the two volumes from Twayne: the early, now-dated *Ursula K. Le Guin* (1984) by Charlotte Spivack and the more recent *Presenting Ursula K. Le Guin* (1997) by Suzanne Elizabeth Reid—although Cummins's text also needs further revision. Nonetheless, the relative recency of Cummins's survey, which is part of the Understanding Contemporary American Literature series, gives it a decided advantage as a study of a writer, such as Le Guin, whose ideas have evolved and changed considerably over the years. Cummins is especially good in her analyses of more recent works, such as *Always Coming Home*, and how they are related to Le Guin's earlier fiction.

Warren G. Rochelle's book approaches Le Guin through the perspectives of myth and rhetoric, and his interest in the teaching of composition to American students shapes both his theoretical perspectives and his methodological tools. Consequently, Aristotle, Plato, Kenneth Burke, Suzanne Langer, and, centrally, C. S. Peirce, Carl Jung, and Joseph Campbell feature prominently among the sources of his approach, as do the ideas of Le Guin herself, especially in her emphasis on the importance of language. The result is an original, conceptually unified analysis of Le Guin's oeuvre, which can be questioned in some of its contentions but is nonetheless a thoughtful and valuable contribution to scholarship on this important author. (RLM, NB)

Tanith Lee, U.K., 1947–

10-85.   Haut, Mavis. **The Hidden Library of Tanith Lee: Themes and Subtexts from Dionysos to the Immortal Gene**. McFarland, 2001.

Mavis Haut's study is an attempt to discover recurring "themes and subtexts" (terms that Haut uses in an eclectic, nonstandard manner) in Tanith Lee's work and it focuses, reasonably enough, mainly on the fantasy works for which she is best known. One chapter is devoted to four of Lee's science fiction novels, however, and a short later chapter discusses the early-written *Eva Fairdeath*. Haut's book, as she herself puts it, does not deal centrally with issues of "language, humor, character and plot structure," concentrating instead on "Lee's more esoteric preoccupations." The analyses, which do not treat Lee's shorter fiction, stop with books from the mid-1990s, even though Haut notes that a dozen additional novels have been published since that time. There are some valid observations concerning recurring imagery in, and links between, various texts in Lee's oeuvre, and some useful comments on the importance of myth for her subject, but Haut's own prose is often clumsy, and her arguments are frequently amateurish, poorly structured, inadequately supported, and difficult to follow. Furthermore, the book's discussions assume a familiarity with the structure of Lee's texts and the content of her fiction that many readers may not share. Although detailed plot summaries are not necessarily required, more information concerning the fictional worlds Haut analyzes often is, especially in support of some of her own claims. In short, this monograph (which also includes an interview with Lee conducted via correspondence, "biographical notes" by her subject, notes, a bibliography of novels and secondary sources, and an incomplete and woefully inadequate index) is of strictly limited value, useful at best perhaps to Lee specialists. (RLM)

Fritz Leiber, U.S., 1910–1992

*10-86.   Byfield, Bruce. **Witches of the Mind: A Critical Study of Fritz Leiber**. Necronomicon, 1991.

Although Fritz Leiber won six Hugos, four Nebulas, and myriad other awards, and was one of the pioneers of American sociological fiction, his importance has been underemphasized by many chroniclers of the field. As Bruce Byfield shows in his splendid critical study, "[Leiber] has paced developments in science fiction as no other writer has done," and "his development is a microcosm of the field's." Byfield's book is a bracing corrective to the vacuity of the first two books on Leiber: an overreliance on plot summary, a paucity of analysis, and an excess of errors mar both Jeff Frame's Starmont House guide (1980) and Tom Staircar's entry in the Ungar Recognitions series (1983). Byfield, however, is excellent. He explicates Leiber's oeuvre (which also includes supernatural horror, fantasy, and sword-and-sorcery yarns) via its use of symbols and the influence of three major figures—H. P. Lovecraft, Robert Graves (the novels, not the poetry), and Carl Jung—and several secondary ones (for example, Thomas De Quincy, Henrik Ibsen, and Joseph Campbell). This schema fits Leiber's career almost perfectly, since each stage in his development was influenced by encounters with the works of these three men. Byfield further illuminates the absolutely central place of personal experience in Leiber's later works. Rich with insights into Leiber's life and works, this is an exemplary critical biography. Primary and secondary biography, index. (MAM)

Stanislaw Lem, Poland, 1921–

10-87. Swirski, Peter. **A Stanislaw Lem Reader**. Northwestern Univ. Press, 1997.

Critics tackling the writings of Stanislaw Lem face major obstacles. For one thing, the play of commentary in Lem's fiction undermines most critical approaches as effectively as the better-known tactics of Thomas Pynchon or Umberto Eco. For another, some of Lem's most important works—notably the futurological treatise *Summa Technologiae* (1964) and his critical analysis *Science Fiction and Futurology* (1971)—remain largely untranslated into English, while existing translations of important novels (such as *The Invincible*) are seriously flawed. To date, the best critical work on Lem, by critics such as Jerzy Jarzebski and Andrzej Stoff, is available only in monographs and essay collections published in Germany or Lem's native Poland.

Swirski is a long-time scholar of Lem and has also produced a well-argued but specialized comparative study of Lem and Edgar Allan Poe in the context of the relationship between literature and science titled *Between Literature and Science: Poe, Lem, and Explorations in Aesthetics, Cognitive Science, and Literary Knowledge* (McGill-Queen's University, 2000).

A Stanislaw Lem Reader consists of an introductory essay by Swirski about Lem, two interviews with him, an article by Lem, and bibliographies of Lem's works in English and critical works about him. Considering the relative dearth of autobiographical and critical material by Lem in English, the contents of this volume, which provide valuable background for Lem scholars, should be welcomed by all students of the Polish author. Lem's article, "Thirty Years Later," originally written to commemorate the writing of *Summa Technologiae*, is an especially fascinating and important document.

Lem's *Highcastle: A Remembrance* (Harcourt, 1995) is quite accurately described by its subtitle, being a subjective description of a period of time in Lem's early childhood. It is in its own way a fascinating book, illuminating aspects of Lem's personal development, but of relatively meager value to the student of his science fiction. Lem scholars should also consult the special issue of *Science-Fiction Studies* (No. 40, November 1986) devoted to Lem, and the long review of critical work on him by Peter Swirski in *Science-Fiction Studies* (No. 58, November 1992). As Swirski wryly notes, "we are still waiting for an English volume of interpretation and criticism that will set a standard for all subsequent Lem scholars." (RLM, MAM)

Doris Lessing, Iran/U.K., 1919–

10-88.   Fishburn, Katherine. **The Unexpected Universe of Doris Lessing: A Study in Narrative Technique**. Greenwood, 1985.

10-89.   Greene, Gayle. **Doris Lessing: The Poetics of Change**. Michigan Univ. Press, 1994.

10-90.   Sprague, Claire, and Virginia Tiger, eds. **Critical Essays on Doris Lessing**. G. K. Hall, 1986.

10-91.   Whitaker, Ruth. **Doris Lessing**. St. Martin's, 1988.

Doris Lessing's main contribution to science fiction is her five-volume Canopus in Argos series, although few of her mainstream academic critics appear to have much knowledge of the genre (referring, as Lessing herself prefers to, to her science fiction as "space fiction"), and SF readers have paid her relatively little attention. She has generated somewhat more interest in the academic SF world, and in 1990 *The Journal of the Fantastic in the Arts* devoted a special issue to her work.

Katherine Fishburn allows one chapter each for Lessing's "fantastic" fiction, beginning with the 1971 novel, *Briefing for a Descent into Hell*. Fishburn writes clearly, and her study isn't clogged with the theoretical posturings that disfigure too much literary criticism. Since she provides fairly detailed plot summaries, her account will be of more use to someone who has read little of Lessing's work. She is particularly good at clarifying Lessing's ideas of individuality versus collectivity and how they are embedded in the fiction. Ruth Whitaker's volume in the Modern Novelists series provides a balanced analysis of all of Lessing's fiction, from the relatively straightforward realism of her earlier works to the metaphysical concerns of *The Memoirs of a Survivor*, to the conscious use of a galactic empire structure for the Canopus series. Whitaker devotes 9 pages to *Memoirs* and 20 pages (one chapter) to the Canopus novels, which she regards as "an extraordinary achievement . . . more than an esoteric work of fiction; read aright it may be, quite literally, a handbook for survival." The Sprague and Tiger collection of essays provides an eclectic overview of Lessing's career, and includes several contributions dealing with the Canopus series and *Memoirs* from various perspectives, many of them from nonacademic sources and therefore more readable.

Finally, Gayle Greene's study, as its subtitle indicates, emphasizes the importance of change for Lessing, providing a chronologically arranged analysis of selections of her fiction, with detailed comments on *Memoirs* and two of the Canopus novels, which Greene is not afraid to admit are SF. Greene competently examines Lessing's work not only in an interestingly developed autobiographical context, but also against a broader literary landscape containing Shakespeare, Milton, and T. S. Eliot. Students of Lessing should also consult her two autobiographical volumes—*Under My Skin: Volume One of My Autobiography, to 1949* (HarperCollins, 1994) and *Walking in the Shade: Volume Two of My Autobiography, 1949–1962* (HarperCollins, 1997)—which provide a better introduction to her life than any currently available biography. (NB, RLM)

C. S. Lewis, U.K., 1898–1963

*10-92. Dowling, David C. **Planets in Peril: A Critical Study of C. S. Lewis' Ransom Trilogy**. Univ. of Massachusetts Press, 1992.

10-93. Edwards, Bruce L., ed. **The Taste of the Pineapple: Essays on C. S. Lewis as Reader, Critic, and Imaginative Writer**. Bowling Green State Univ. Press, 1988.

10-94. Murphy, Brian. **C. S. Lewis**. Starmont, 1983.

10-95. Myers, Doris T. **C. S. Lewis in Context**. Kent State Univ. Press, 1998.

Medievalist, Christian apologist, and fantasist and mythmaker second only to fellow Inkling J. R. R. Tolkien, C. S. Lewis remains a problematic if cherished figure in the history of SF. In the mountain of biographical and critical writings on Lewis are a handful that contain either direct explications of or essential background to his fantasies, and only the most relevant of these are mentioned here. The best available general biography of Lewis is probably that by A. N. Wilson: *C. S. Lewis: A Biography* (Norton, 1990). A broad context for the consideration of Lewis's SF can be found in Bruce Edwards's collection of essays on how Lewis's premises as a scholar inform his fiction. This collection features examinations of Lewis's critical practice, the rhetorical strategies he used in writing criticism, the intellectual context in which he wrote, and a fascinating section on how Lewis's critical principles relate to his own fiction, including his interplanetary fantasies. Index.

Into his brief but tightly written Starmont guide, Brian Murphy manages to cram an amazing amount of information, insights, and thoughtful assessments without ever becoming opaque or confusing. After a competent sketch of Lewis's life and principal philosophical beliefs, Murphy concentrates on the Ransom trilogy and Lewis's last works, concluding with a useful, but now dated, primary and secondary bibliography. Dowling focuses even more narrowly on Lewis's space trilogy, showing how religion and fantasy interpenetrate in these three novels. Dowling's fine, thoughtful study is valuable both for its careful background on Lewis's life and scholarship as it informs the trilogy, and for its careful explication of the influences and content of each novel and their critical reception. An appendix on "The Dark Tower," a fragment Lewis apparently began as a dystopian sequel to *Out of the Silent Planet* but then abandoned, rounds out this essential guide to reading or study of Lewis's primary contribution to SF. Notes, bibliography, index.

Doris Myers manages to illuminate several hitherto unexplored aspects of Lewis's work in the context of his contemporaries, arguing strongly and generally convincingly that his work was well-grounded in the philosophy of language as he understood it. In her discussion of the Ransom trilogy, she draws clearly interesting comparisons (albeit with sometimes not entirely convincing conclusions) to the SF of H. G. Wells. Otherwise, on Lewis's place in the history of British SF, see Brian Stableford's *Scientific Romance in Britain 1890–1950* [9-184]. (MAM, RLM)

Jack London, U.S., 1876–1916

10-96.   Beauchamp, Gorman. **Jack London**. Starmont, 1986.

10-97.   Labor, Earle. **Jack London**. Twayne, 1974.

Like Mark Twain, Jack London produced a huge corpus of writing only a small fraction of which is SF. But the considerable influence of London's social and political extrapolations continues to the present: thus *Before Adam* anticipates the series of anthropological novels by Jean M. Auel (1980–1990), and the novella "The Scarlet Plague" (1915) anticipates (among myriad other disaster tales) Stephen King's *The Stand*. Regrettably, the finest critical book to date on London, Charles N. Watson's *The Novels of Jack London: A Reappraisal* (Wisconsin, 1983), excludes all of London's fantasies except the dystopia *The Iron Heel*. Happily, both Beauchamp's guide and Labor's Twayne study are excellent. Beauchamp focuses exclusively on London's SF works and combines plot summary and accessible critical commentary to elaborate their historical, political, and social themes. Of particular value are his contextual connections, such as parallels to Wells's scientific romances and links to the revolutionary theories of the Russian Anarchist Petr Kropotkin and, more generally, to the dominant Social Darwinist intellectual atmosphere of London's *fin de siècle* times. Chronology, annotated primary and secondary bibliography, index.

Labor's balanced overview of London's intensely creative output successively seeks to recuperate him as "a major figure in American literature." Following a sketch of London's irresistibly American life and an excellent synopsis of the state of American popular fiction at the turn of the century, Labor examines all of London's major works, treating his fantasies as "a symbolic path into the deeper, inchoate reality of the unconscious mind." Even for readers interested only in London's SF, Labor defines an essential context for Beauchamp's more narrowly focused book. Chronology, notes and references, selected primary and annotated secondary bibliography, index. (MAM)

Ken MacLeod, Scotland, 1954–

10-98. Butler, Andrew M., and Farah Mendlesohn, eds. **The True Knowledge of Ken MacLeod**. Science Fiction Foundation, 2003.

Ken MacLeod's first novel, *The Star Faction*, called by one reviewer "a successful comic Trotskyist science fiction novel," was published in 1995 to immediate critical acclaim, including a nomination for the Arthur C. Clarke Award. Since then, he has published a new novel almost every year, to generally good reviews and several awards and award nominations. Therefore, and unusually, this book presents a series of reviews, interviews, and critical essays on the work of a writer still at the relative beginning of his career. This means that many of the evaluations and interpretations found here must be considered tentative. That said, this volume, which is the third in the Foundation Studies in Science Fiction series, is a good introduction to the original, politically intense, and conceptually eclectic work of a writer who may well be one of the major voices in British SF in the early 21st century. Contains primary and secondary bibliographies, including Web sites, and an index. (RLM)

Anne McCaffrey, U.S., 1926–

10-99. Hargreaves, Mathew D. **Anne McCaffrey**. Starmont, 1992. Supplement 1994.

10-100. McCaffrey, Todd. **Dragonholder: The Life and Dreams (So Far) of Anne McCaffrey**. Ballantine Del Rey, 1999.

McCaffrey is best known for a series of connected novels and stories set on a lost Earth colony called Pern, whose humans are linked symbiotically with tame, telepathic dragons. This sounds like fantasy, but the dragons are given a bioengineering rationale, and most of her work, while relatively undemanding adventure with wide appeal to younger and older women, is still SF, although she has won awards for both SF and fantasy.

Hargreaves provides a somewhat detailed short biography and an exhaustive listing of published and unpublished works, secondary literature, and reproductions of 350 book jackets or covers, published throughout the world. Despite being marred by many typos, this is still essential for true McCaffrey buffs. A 42-page supplement was issued in 1994. Todd McCaffrey is Anne McCaffrey's son, and his lightweight, easy-to-read, and sometimes overly adulatory biography, filled with numerous personal anecdotes and family photographs, nevertheless provides some useful perspectives on McCaffrey's background and highlights connections between events in her life and her work. Not required reading, but an interesting supplementary text. (NB, RLM)

Judith Merril, U.S., 1923–1997

*10-101. Merril, Judith, and Emily Pohl-Weary. **Better to Have Loved: The Life of Judith Merril**. Between the Lines, 2002.

Judith Merril had an important impact on the field of science fiction: as an author (one of the first significant women writers in the genre); as an editor (with a series of path-breaking and innovative annual "best SF of the year" anthologies in the 1960s, and, later, with *Tesseracts*, the first anthology series devoted especially to Canadian SF authors); as a critic (via comments in her anthologies and in her monthly book review column in *The Magazine of Fantasy and Science Fiction*); and by donating her private SF collection to the Toronto Public Library to form what subsequently became one of the world's leading SF research collections, now known as the Merril Collection of Science Fiction, Speculation, and Fantasy [15-39]. Nor should the personal influence she had through her many contacts—not all of which were affable—with major figures in the science fiction world be forgotten. This autobiographical volume, compiled and edited posthumously by her granddaughter Emily Pohl-Weary, largely following the wishes and instructions of her grandmother, was constructed primarily from notes made by Merril over a period of several years, interview tapes from the last year of her life, and correspondence. Unfortunately, through no fault of the editor, there are gaps in the material, since Merril herself never attempted to fill in these lacunae, or to collate her whole life story in a coherent manner. The result, because of its patchy and incomplete nature, is not entirely successful as traditional autobiography. The volume remains a valuable and useful resource, however, providing a number of fascinating, candid, insightful, and readable snapshots of selected portions and aspects of the life and thought of a major, not seldom controversial, figure in 20th-century science fiction. The book contains a chronology of Merril's life, a bibliography of her works, a list of some important people in her life, and an index. (RLM)

A. Merritt, U.S., 1884–1943

10-102. Foust, Ronald. **A. Merritt**. Starmont, 1989.

A Munsey writer of the first rank and, according to Ronald Foust, "the last great writer of scientific romances," Merritt was one of the most popular writers of the pulp era (1930–1950), and his novels have reappeared intermittently ever since. Foust's well-written guide supplements but does not quite displace Sam Moskowitz's exasperating *A. Merritt: Reflections in the Moon Pool* (Oswald Train, 1985) as an introduction and overview. Except for its long, awkwardly presented biographical introduction, Moskowitz's mosaic of primary materials concerning Merritt's rise to reader acclaim remains essential to scholars. Foust draws upon Freudian and Jungian psychoanalytic concepts in his examination of the protagonists and rhetorical strategies of each of Merritt's major novels and several incidental pieces. This approach, within the context of Foust's mythic and archetypal critical stance, is certainly appropriate to Merritt's supersaturated lost race fantasies and produces interesting readings, especially of *Dwellers in the Mirage* (1932). Ultimately, however, it fails to earn for Merritt a place in the pantheon of significant SF writers; like Moskowitz's book, Foust's will be of more value to scholars of the pulp era than those of SF. For a counterbalancing perspective on Merritt, see E. F. Bleiler's essay in *Science Fiction Writers.* Chronology, annotated primary and secondary bibliographies, index. (MAM)

Walter M. Miller, Jr., U.S., 1922–1996

10-103. Secrest, Rose. **Glorificemus: A Study of the Fiction of Walter M. Miller, Jr.** University Press of America, 2002.

Walter M. Miller is known primarily for his 1959 post-apocalyptic novel, *A Canticle for Leibowitz.* Secrest has undertaken in this monograph to provide a literary analysis of that work, which she says is her favorite SF novel. Unfortunately, her book is a failure on almost all counts: it is badly written, its claims are insufficiently and poorly argued, and it generally falls well short of the standards to which academic criticism should be held. Her conclusions are often either trite or questionable, and she appears to have insufficient knowledge in several of the areas about which she expresses opinions, including, significantly, history, Roman Catholicism, and science fiction scholarship. The book is theoretically and critically unsophisticated, offering very little to scholars or even serious fans of Miller. (RLM)

Michael Moorcock, U.K./U.S., 1939–

10-104. Davey, John. **Michael Moorcock: A Reader's Guide**. Author (U.K.), 1992.

10-105. Gardiner, Jeff. **The Age of Chaos: The Multiverse of Michael Moorcock**. British Fantasy Society, 2002.

10-106. Greenland, Colin. **Michael Moorcock: Death Is No Obstacle**. Savoy, 1992.

Michael Moorcock is nothing if not prolific. His huge, intricately coupled canon includes SF, fantasy, sword-and-sorcery, suspense and adventure stories, pastiches and satires, and unclassifiable "mainstream" novels. Faced with this literary cornucopia, readers urgently need bibliographical and critical help. Davey considers British and American editions and excludes all but one of Moorcock's edited anthologies and all of his short fiction and nonfiction. Still, with its engaging descriptions of the intricate publication histories of Moorcock's self-contained interconnecting series of novels (including variant titles and often bewildering omnibus collections) and its phenomenal list (containing 85 entries!) recommending an eminently sensible sequence for reading Moorcock's entire output, Davey's guide is an essential map through Moorcock's multiverse.

Jeff Gardiner is selective in his short study of Moorcock's output, but he is also systematic, and his short book provides a good first overview of Moorcock's multiverse. After an initial look at his subject's life, early work, stint at *New Worlds*, and the Jerry Cornelius stories, Gardiner proceeds to examine in chronological order, one chapter at a time, a number of major Moorcock novels or series. There is little room for in-depth analysis in these pages, but there are some insightful comments on individual works and series, and the reader is given a useful orientation to the structure and content of several of Moorcock's central works of fantasy. A selected bibliography (but no index) rounds off the volume.

Colin Greenland's book is, unexpectedly, a 143-page interview with Moorcock about the craft of fiction. Greenland is the ideal interviewer—his book *The Entropy Exhibition* [9-85] contains the most extended discussion to date of Moorcock's seminal leadership of the New Wave movement—and Moorcock as interviewee is open and engaging. Reading their dialogue sometimes feels like eavesdropping on a conversation that has been under way for some time. But Moorcock's fiction nevertheless encompasses so many forms—various chapters consider heroic fantasy, comedy and SF, comic strips and commedia dell'arte, didactic fiction, non-linear fiction, pastiches, and more—that this book amounts to a short course on writing techniques compounded with an overview of Moorcock's career. It contains sufficient nuggets of insight to fascinate readers familiar with Moorcock's works. Others should begin with *The Entropy Exhibition* and the somewhat narrower perspectives offered by Brian W. Aldiss in *Trillion Year Spree*, Warren Wager in *Terminal Visions*, and John J. Pierce in *When World Views Collide*. As treatments of Moorcock's oeuvre, however, all these suffer from brevity and narrowness of focus. (MAM, RLM)

George Orwell, U.K., 1903–1950

10-107.   Howe, Irving, ed. **Orwell's Nineteen Eighty-Four: Text, Sources, Criticism**. 2nd ed. Harcourt, 1963.

*10-108.   Reilly, Patrick. **Nineteen Eighty-Four: Past, Present, and Future**. Twayne, 1989.

*10-109.   Sheldon, Michael. **Orwell: The Authorized Biography**. Harper, 1991.

10-110.   Stansky, Peter, ed. **On Nineteen Eighty-Four**. W. H. Freeman, 1983.

Eric Blair, better known under his literary pseudonym of George Orwell, was one of the most famous and influential of British writers and intellectuals of the first half of the 20th century, most prominently, but not exclusively, for the dystopian science fiction novel *Nineteen Eighty-Four*. Consequently, the amount of material published on Orwell and his masterpiece is enormous, and steadily increasing. *Nineteen Eighty-Four* is a warning, not a prophecy, and has explicitly and by influence energized much discussion of its literary and especially its political meanings. The works annotated here are but a handful of the many studies available that focus on and illuminate that novel or that provide a context in which it can be most fully understood.

The first authorized biography was *George Orwell: A Life* (Little, Brown, 1980) by Bernard Crick of the University of London, who was given permission by Orwell's second wife to consult Orwell's papers and to quote freely. According to Michael Sheldon (later authorized by Orwell's literary executor), Sonia Orwell "was disappointed. She condemned it as too political, too dry, and too unsympathetic and tried to stop it from being published," but died of cancer before it was published in late 1980. (It was slightly revised for the Penguin edition of 1982.) Sheldon agrees that Crick's biography is a large collection of facts, and faults it for not attempting to deal with Orwell's personal character, since he argues that facts don't speak for themselves. Crick is still worth the time of anyone seriously interested in Orwell, but the additional information available to Sheldon in the 11 years after Crick was published resulted in a better, much more readable biography, which remains the best currently available. Two recent Orwell biographies that may also be of interest are Gordon Bowker's *Inside George Orwell: A Biography* (Palgrave Macmillan, 2003) and B. J. Taylor's *Orwell: A Life* (Holt, 2003).

Reilly's study in Twayne's Masterwork series vigorously argues that *Nineteen Eighty-Four* be judged by literary not political criteria, even while recognizing that Orwell was an inherently didactic writer. Reilly says Crick argues that Orwell's dystopia stands to the 20th century as Hobbes's *Leviathan* does to the 17th. Reilly also provides a useful summary of the widely varied critical reception it received showing how many critics, then as now, used the novel for political purposes, to defend what Orwell dismissed as "smelly little orthodoxies." Reilly devotes approximately 100 pages to a very close and intelligent reading of the novel, sometimes challenging other readings, such as that of Isaac Deutscher, whose essay Irving Howe reprints. Reilly is especially good in his analysis of the novel as "a love story, conducted against the background of a rebellion against God," which appalls rather than inspires. The novel is contrasted with *Paradise Lost* and Christian doctrine generally, with Ingsoc a perversion and repudiation of such doctrine. Reilly also illuminates the novel by showing parallels with Gulliver's travels. Swift is an obvious influence on Orwell, who discussed Swift in his essays, but it is the bleak pessimism of Swift that permeates the novel, which Reilly aptly calls "the death certificate of Renaissance man." He concludes that *Nineteen Eighty-Four* "is a conditional prophecy, a summons to preventive action, a tocsin to rouse his sleeping fellows." The crystal spirit, argued Orwell, can and must be preserved. Excellent annotated bibliography, now somewhat dated.

The late Irving Howe assembled for his Harbrace Sourcebook the text of the novel, 7 pieces on sources, 13 essays on the novel proper, and 2 essays on the politics of totalitarianism; most of the essays are reprints. The contributors include such influential figures as Lionel Trilling, Isaac Deutscher, Hannah Arendt, and Michael Harrington. Suggestions for papers and further reading conclude the paperback. Howe recognizes that the novel "has become a major document of contemporary politics," and the emphasis of the essays is on the political rather than the purely literary dimensions of the book. An especially well chosen collection of important and insightful essays, fortunately still in print.

Stansky, a professor of history and biographer of Orwell, assembled 22 essays for his book, originally published as part of a series issued by the alumni association of Stanford University. All the contributors were then associated with Stanford. The range of concern among the essays is wide, and anyone would gain a deepened and broadened understanding of the novel from this book. The text is enriched with reproductions of appropriate paintings and cartoons. (NB)

Frederik Pohl, U.S., 1919–

10-111.   Clareson, Thomas D. **Frederik Pohl**. Starmont, 1987.

10-112.   Pohl, Frederik. **The Way the Future Was**. Ballantine, 1978.

Pohl has been involved with SF since his teens as an editor, writer, and agent. His earlier years, including his life spent outside SF proper, are discussed in detail in his memoir, and more briefly in his chapter in *Hell's Cartographers* [10-168] and in his 16-page sketch in *Contemporary Authors Autobiographical Series*, vol. 1. He has written much and won every important award, including the Grand Master Nebula awarded by his fellow writers in 1993. Clareson's 183-page study is one of the best and most detailed of the Starmont guides. He discusses Pohl's works chronologically from the 1940s through 1987, exploring their principal ideas and themes and relating them to the larger world of SF. His influential work as an editor and agent is not neglected. Clareson's friendship for and admiration of Pohl, however, sometimes undercuts the critical distance readers expect him to maintain, with the result that some works are praised excessively. Still, a valuable portrait of a prolific writer who has continued to develop throughout his life. (NB)

Christopher Priest, U.K., 1943–

10-113.   Ruddick, Nicholas. **Christopher Priest**. Starmont, 1990.

After a public break in 1980 with science fiction as a genre and an institution, and his continuing critical attack on the stories and writers of traditional Campbellian mass market SF, American readers deserted Christopher Priest in droves. Although Priest is a writer of integrity, courage, and gifts both visionary and stylistic, his novels—philosophical in intent and (mildly) experimental in execution—are critical and popular successes mainly in Europe, especially in France. His recent novel, *The Separation*, won both major annual British awards, the Arthur C. Clarke Award and the British Science Fiction Association Award. Nicholas Ruddick's exceptional guide should help to retrieve Priest for U.S. readers. In a brief biocritical introduction and separate chapters for Priest's short fiction and each of his seven novels through 1985, when this study was completed, Ruddick offers a balanced perspective on Priest's program, begun in his early New Wave fiction and continued in later metafictional novels, of critiquing "the history and politics of literary genre in general and science fiction in particular." Ruddick's insightful, detailed readings clarify how Priest elaborates (in massively recomplicated, organic plots) a universe constructed out of the private interior worlds of his characters, worlds that remain isolated by their creators' incomprehension and misperceptions. Ruddick and Colin Greenland have further situated Priest within broader contexts of British SF and the New Wave in *Ultimate Island* and *The Entropy Exhibition*, respectively. Together with those books, Ruddick's guide, with its thoroughly annotated (if now dated) bibliography, will serve as an essential starting point for American readers and scholars interested in this unjustly neglected writer. Index. (MAM, RLM)

Mack Reynolds, U.S., 1917–1983

10-114. Smith, Curtis C. **Welcome to the Revolution: The Literary Legacy of Mack Reynolds**. Borgo, 1995.

Mack Reynolds will be remembered mainly for his considerably left-of-center (in American terms) ideas concerning political economy and future socioeconomic developments, rather than for his scientific or technological speculations. Although his novels did indeed deal with interesting and important issues from original perspectives, they are far too often preachy and can be quite tedious, producing works that are more appropriate as pedagogic tools to awaken discussion than as successful or enjoyable fiction. In this short book, Curtis C. Smith provides an acceptable overview of the life and examination of the work of an interesting but decidedly minor 20th-century SF writer. (RLM)

Keith Roberts, U.K., 1935–2000

10-115. Roberts, Keith. **Lemady: Episodes of a Writer's Life**. Wildside, 1999.

Keith Roberts was one of the most highly praised of 20th-century British SF authors, especially for his alternate history classic *Pavane*. The autobiographical *Lemady* is an entertaining, unusual, original, and very subjectively told memoir of various events in Roberts's life that provides interesting and valuable insights into his literate, character-driven science fiction, his strongly held opinions, and his person. The title refers to a woman—perhaps Roberts's muse, although he has "no wish to identify her more closely"—who has, Roberts tells us, "informed all but a couple of my books." *Lemady* touches on its author's experiences as a writer, as an artist, and in publishing, all areas in which he was active. There are also accounts of his travels with Lemady to various places in Europe. Several of the vignettes that make up the book are simultaneously humorous and illuminating, and the volume should clearly be of use to students of Roberts, although its non-chronological, seemingly random internal organization takes some getting used to. Index. (RLM)

Joanna Russ, U.S., 1937–

*10-116. Cortiel, Jeanne. **Demand My Writing: Joanna Russ/Feminism/Science Fiction**. Liverpool Univ. Press, 1999.

10-117.   Russ, Joanna. **To Write Like a Woman: Essays in Feminism and Science Fiction**. Indiana Univ. Press, 1995.

In *Demand My Writing*, Jeanne Cortiel has provided us with a major study of the intersections of feminism and science fiction, exemplified via the writings of Joanna Russ. Building her theoretical foundation on the ideas of French feminist Julia Kristeva, Cortiel examines what she terms three inseparable "moments" in Russ's fiction: "(1) women's agency, (2) female sexuality, and (3) the indeterminacy of both these categories." Even though she structures her study around these "major thematic clusters," rather than basing it on the chronology of Russ's life, Cortiel finds that the three major concerns she has identified nevertheless correspond roughly to the three phases of Russ's career as a writer. Her readings of Russ are well-informed, intelligent, often detailed, and original—and she is quite adept at placing the author's work in the larger context of contemporary feminist (and poststructuralist) thought. Theoretically sophisticated and intellectually demanding, but not impossible to read or understand, this is an important study of a writer crucial to the development of 20th-century speculative fiction. The book contains notes, a primary bibliography of Russ, a secondary bibliography, and indexes of names and Russ's novels and short stories.

Vital to an understanding of Russ and SF are her own comments on the genre, and particularly useful are the essays in the collection *To Write Like a Woman* [also annotated as 9-165], which contains some of her most important and influential essays, including "Towards an Aesthetics of Science Fiction" (1975), "Speculations: The Subjunctivity of Science Fiction" (1978), "*Amor Vincet Foeminam*: The Battle of the Sexes in Science Fiction" (1980), and "Recent Feminist Utopias" (1981). Introduction by Sarah Lefanu; index. (RLM)

Robert Sheckley, U.S., 1928–

10-118.   Stephenson, Gregory. **Comic Inferno: The Satirical World of Robert Sheckley**. Borgo, 1997.

The title of Stephenson's study of Robert Sheckley, which he strangely doesn't explain until near the end of the book, comes from Kingsley Amis, who introduced it in *New Maps of Hell* to describe Sheckley and certain other authors whom he believed captured the kind of satirical, sociologically acute science fiction that characterized some of the most interesting American SF of the period. Stephenson covers Sheckley's work from the 1950s through the 1990s and makes some interesting and useful observations about a seriously undervalued author who has not been given the critical attention he deserves. Unfortunately, the study, though welcome in its focus on Sheckley and valuable for some of its individual close readings of his work, lacks a larger cohesion and unifying thesis or argument; it should have been considerably better. Notes, chronology, annotated bibliographies, and index. (RLM)

Mary Wollstonecraft Shelley, U.K., 1797–1851

10-119. Baldick, Chris. **In Frankenstein's Shadow: Myth, Monstrosity, and Nineteenth-Century Writing**. Oxford Univ. Press, 1987.

*10-120. Mellor, Ann K. **Mary Shelley: Her Life, Her Fiction, Her Monsters**. Routledge, 1987.

*10-121. Schor, Esther, ed. **The Cambridge Companion to Mary Shelley**. Cambridge Univ. Press, 2003.

10-122. Seymour, Miranda. **Mary Shelley**. Grove, 2001.

*10-123. Sunstein, Emily W. **Mary Shelley: Romance and Reality**. Little, Brown, 1989.

*10-124. Tropp, Martin. **Mary Shelley's Monster: The Story of Frankenstein**. Houghton Mifflin, 1976.

10-125. Vasbinder, S. H. **Scientific Attitudes in Mary Shelley's Frankenstein**. UMI Research Press, 1984.

The explosion of critical and biographical interest in Mary Shelley that began in the 1980s presents formidable problems to readers seeking a focus on her contributions to science fiction. The place to start is with Brian W. Aldiss's spirited (widely but not universally accepted) defense in *Trillion Year Spree* and in the essays in *The Pale Shadow of Science* on the progenitive role of *Frankenstein*. Ann K. Mellor also credits Mary Shelley with "[initiating] a new literary genre, what we now call science fiction." Mellor's skillful blend of biography and criticism, most of which focuses on *Frankenstein*, is an especially rewarding approach to her subject, for, as became apparent in earlier studies such as Elizabeth Nitchie's critical biography, *Mary Shelley: Author of Frankenstein* (Rutgers, 1953), Mary Shelley's life informed her fiction in complex, essential ways. To prove the revisionist thesis that Shelley's fiction is an extended attempt to conjure the (idealized) loving bourgeois family she never had, Mellor recounts in detail her troubled life prior to the composition of *Frankenstein*, then brings a variety of critical approaches to bear on the novel. Of special importance to scholars is her detailed study of Percy Bysshe Shelley's editorial changes to the original manuscript. Chronology, eight pages of plates, notes, primary and secondary bibliography, index.

Emily W. Sunstein emphasizes biography over criticism, although her fascinating final chapter shows how Mary Shelley's posthumous reputation was "bent out of shape by admirers and, more lastingly, by traducers." Most important, Sunstein successfully individuates Mary Shelley, removing her once and for all from the shadow of her famous parents and husband and letting her emerge as "a major literary figure of the first half of the nineteenth century." Engaging, well-written, and drawing heavily on her subject's letters, journals, and other writings, Sunstein's "revisionary" biography is the standard for readers more interested in Mary Shelley's life than her fiction. Extensive primary bibliography, notes, index.

More directly focused on *Frankenstein* is Vasbinder's brief monograph, developed from his doctoral thesis. Unfortunately, in his analysis of the novel's structure, setting, and science content, Vasbinder exaggerates his thesis concerning the role of the latter, distorting his representation both of the novel and its place in 19th-century fiction. Also worthy of note is Miranda Seymour's recent, major biography, which takes into consideration much newer feminist and other scholarship to tell Mary Shelley's life in great and tragic detail, although it does not surpass Sunstein's earlier efforts. The book includes two sections of illustrations, three brief appendixes (containing hitherto unpublished letters and comments on portraits of Mary Shelley), notes, bibliography, and index. See also Robert M. Philmus's *Into the Unknown* and Christopher Small's *Ariel Like a Harpy: Shelley, Mary and Frankenstein* (Gollancz, 1972; U.S. title: *Mary Shelley's Frankenstein: Tracing the Myth*; Pittsburgh, 1972).

The enormous and continuing influence of *Frankenstein* is the topic of Martin Tropp's study of the novel's mutation and evolution in the rich media of modern culture. After a discussion of the novel's background (considerably more cursory than Mellor's), Tropp first explicates its dream imagery, technological significance, and use of the *doppelgänger* motif, then turns to stage and film adaptations. Notes, chronology of Frankenstein films, index, and bibliography. Chris Baldick's fine book about "adaptations, allusions, accretions, analogues, parodies, and plain misreadings" in works from 1789 to 1917 also contains a fascinating application of the myth theories of Claude Lévi-Strauss to Mary Shelley's novel.

Finally, the 16 essays in *The Cambridge Companion* constitute an important, major addition to Mary Shelley scholarship, and fully 5 of them, the entire first section of the book, deal with *Frankenstein*, including its cinematic incarnations. One contributor concentrates on *The Last Man*, and other essays examine Shelley as a biographer, cultural critic, and travel writer. The volume is illustrated and contains a chronology, a selection of further reading, a select filmography, and an index. (MAM, RLM)

Robert Silverberg, U.S., 1935–

10-126.   Chapman, Edgar L. **The Road to Castle Mount: The Science Fiction of Robert Silverberg**. Greenwood, 1999.

10-127.   Elkins, Charles L., and Martin H. Greenberg. **Robert Silverberg's Many Trapdoors: Critical Essays on His Science Fiction**. Greenwood, 1992.

10-128.   Silverberg, Robert. **Reflections and Refractions: Thoughts on Science-Fiction, Science, and Other Matters**. Underwood, 1997.

The Elkins and Greenberg volume collects seven original essays introduced by Thomas Clareson, who has himself written about Silverberg in several essays and produced an earlier, short, introductory volume, *Robert Silverberg* (Starmont, 1983), and a detailed bibliography from G. K. Hall the same year, both now seriously out of date. Russell Letson's overview is especially valuable, although it is now also somewhat dated. Other essays discuss various individual novels, while one investigates short fiction from various phases of Silverberg's career. This collection will be especially valuable to those who have read many of Silverberg's works.

Chapman's study deals with Silverberg's major fiction and provides a reliable guide to important recurring themes in his work and to the development of his ideas over the years. Chapman's readings and interpretations of Silverberg's individual novels and shorter fiction is well-presented, interesting, and enlightening. Unfortunately, as Rob Latham pointed out in a review of this book in the July 2000 issue of *Science Fiction Studies*, there is something of an internal discrepancy between Chapman's claiming extra-genre literary genius for his subject and yet presenting a defense of Silverberg as a solid craftsman in the science fiction genre. Nonetheless, this is clearly a worthwhile volume on a central figure in the development of science fiction in the 20th century.

Reflections and Refractions is a collection of thematically organized essays and columns from the SF magazines *Galileo*, *Amazing Stories*, and *Asimov's*, offering Silverberg's personal and often insightful views of the world of science fiction and its practitioners, among other subjects, and it should be of some interest to students of his work. (RLM, NB)

Cordwainer Smith, U.S., 1913–1966

10-129. Hellekson, Karen L. **The Science Fiction of Cordwainer Smith**. McFarland, 2001.

10-130. Lewis, Anthony R. **Concordance to Cordwainer Smith**. 3rd ed. NESFA, 2000.

Cordwainer Smith was the pseudonym used by American academic Paul Myron Anthony Linebarger for his science fiction. Karen Hellekson's study of Smith's SF began as a master's thesis and has grown into a valuable and useful examination of the work of a fascinating and very original, if not absolutely central, genre author. While writing this book, Hellekson had access to Smith's manuscripts held by the Spencer Research Library at the University of Kansas, and she has made good and extensive use of this material. By examining Linebarger's his three published non-SF novels, his three unpublished works, and fragments and alternative versions of various of his texts, and comparing these with the published works, Hellekson has been able to draw and support some interesting conclusions concerning Smith's major SF. The book contains, as an appendix, a glossary of Smith's terms that also includes characters, places, and plot summaries; a bibliography; a partial list of manuscripts held by the Spencer Research Library; and an index. Lewis's *Concordance*, now in its third edition, provides the most complete and detailed practical guide available to the terms and concepts found in Smith's SF, and should be of considerable use to scholars and students of his work. (RLM)

E. E. Smith, U.S., 1890–1965

10-131.   Sanders, Joe. **E. E. "Doc" Smith**. Starmont, 1986.

Smith was a food chemist, and Gernsback's addition of Ph.D. to his name generated his nickname. Smith's space operas were popular from the 1930s through the 1950s, and even today spinoffs appear that hitchhike on his reputation. Sanders's guide, the first critical study, "is intended to explain Smith's popularity while countering some of the unthinking aversion Smith's work has received," such as Brian Stableford's assessment, which Sanders quotes: "aesthetically and intellectually vacuous." Such vacuity has never precluded popularity, and Sanders makes a good case for his subject. Fans of the Lensman and Skylark series may want to investigate *The Universes of E. E. Smith* by Ron Ellik and Bill Evans (Advent, 1966), a concordance and bibliography. (NB)

Olaf Stapledon, U.K., 1886–1950

10-132.   Kinnaird, John. **Olaf Stapledon**. Starmont, 1986.

*10-133.   McCarthy, Patrick A. **Olaf Stapledon**. Twayne, 1982.

10-134.   McCarthy, Patrick A., Martin H. Greenberg, and Charles L. Elkins, eds. **The Legacy of Olaf Stapledon: Critical Essays and an Unpublished Manuscript**. Greenwood, 1989.

One of the many paradoxes of Olaf Stapledon is the fact that this author of philosophical SF on one of the most expansive scales of space and time yet attempted, whom Brian W. Aldiss called "the ultimate SF writer," remained for so long, as Patrick McCarthy notes in his introduction to *The Legacy of Olaf Stapledon*, "a marginal figure in his own field." This excellent and important collection of six well-researched, well-written contextual essays covers Stapledon's nonfiction as well as the religious, mythic, historical, political, and, of course, philosophical dimensions of his SF novels. Perhaps most important, it includes a hitherto unpublished philosophical work by Stapledon: a series of letters written to his great-grandson concerning "the spiritual crisis he saw in his own civilization."

McCarthy's Twayne volume is the best overall introduction to Stapledon's work, although John Kinnaird's guide runs a close second. McCarthy's overview emphasizes the rich matrix of themes and techniques to be found in Stapledon's novels, and, in a somewhat less satisfactory concluding chapter, explores their influence on subsequent American and British authors. McCarthy's thorough biocritical introduction and chronological chapters devoted to thematic, philosophical, ethical, and literary issues admirably fulfill his goals of "[introducing] general readers to the beauty and subtlety of Stapledon's art" and "[laying] a foundation for more specialized studies." Chronology, notes and references, selected bibliography, index.

Kinnaird's book clarifies Stapledon's development as a writer and thinker and convincingly renders him as "a mythopoetic writer—one who not only created myth but thought in terms of myth." Kinnaird elaborates this view with respect to various aspects of Stapledon's fiction, including his central themes and his symbolism of "abstract configurations." While somewhat uneven, Kinnaird's book offers much both to newcomers and to those with Stapledon's novels—including a singularly fine reading of *Last and First Men*. Chronology, annotated primary and secondary bibliography, index.

Robert Crossley's biography, *Olaf Stapledon: Speaking of the Future* (Syracuse, 1994) is thoroughly researched and well-written, and includes notes and a selected bibliography. Readers may also wish to consult Crossley's fascinating collection of Stapledon's letters to his fiancée, *Talking Across the World: The Love Letters of Olaf Stapledon and Agnes Miller, 1913–1919* (University Press of New England, 1987). Finally, none of these books clarifies Stapledon's importance to British SF as well as Brian Stableford's essential *Scientific Romance in Britain 1890–1950*. The November 1982 issue of the journal *Science-Fiction Studies* was a special issue devoted to Stapledon's science fiction. (MAM)

Arkady (Russia, 1925–1991) and Boris (Russia, 1933–) Strugatsky

10-135. Howell, Yvonne. **Apocalyptic Realism: The Science Fiction of Arkady and Boris Strugatsky**. Peter Lang, 1994.

10-136. Potts, Stephen W. **The Second Martian Invasion: The Fiction of the Strugatsky Brothers**. Borgo, 1991.

In the first book-length study of the best-known and most significant Soviet SF writers, which won the Eaton award, Stephen Potts seeks to shift attention away from the ideological controversies that have swarmed about the works of Arkady and Boris Strugatsky (transliteration of the surname differs) toward a middle ground that "plac[es] political and artistic matters in perspective relative to one another." In this he is largely successful. The Strugatskys, whose polemical, often witty novels range from idealistic hard SF to strange absurdist satires that straddle SF and fantasy, exemplify the "warm school" of Soviet writers, a group of less conservative writers who are more concerned with moral issues and literary quality than with technological prediction, and who became prominent during the post-Stalinist thaw in the mid-1950s. Potts lucidly introduces and limns the themes of the Strugatskys' major works and fairly discusses the "esthetic malaise" and "creative exhaustion" of their most recent efforts; but his view of the political, ideological, and global literary contexts of their works is somewhat narrow. Bibliographical notes, index.

Yvonne Howell's study (Russian and East European Studies in Aesthetics and Philosophy of Culture #1) is an attempt to place the Strugatsky brothers in the context of both Soviet and larger Russian literary and intellectual history. She prefers to label their work as "apocalyptic realism" rather than science fiction, linking them with ideas and works from the Russian Silver Age of culture (roughly: the last decade of the 19th century through the first two of the 20th), and with the "millennarian literature" of the 1920s. Analyzing examples drawn from the Strugatskys' entire oeuvre, from the earliest SF through work from the late 1980s, Howell discusses issues of genre, plot, structure, and characterization, displaying an interest in both how the Strugatskys write as well as their "message." She finds evidence for recurring themes and patterns, and a general coherence of thought that helps explain the popularity and strength of the Strugatskys' work. Her knowledge of the Russian and Soviet historical, cultural, and social background make for insights otherwise unavailable to Western readers. Diverse intertextual references, Russian and more general, which would have been evident to the intelligentsia who read the texts when they originally appeared, are suggested and explicated. Several works not yet translated into English are examined, sometimes with relatively long quotations that are especially helpful to non-Russian readers. Chapter notes, chronological overview of the Strugatskys' prose fiction, selected bibliography, and index.

Readers should also see *Red Stars: Political Aspects of Soviet Science Fiction* [9-128] and the shorter but excellent introduction to the chapter on Russian SF in *Anatomy of Wonder*, third edition, 1987, both by Patrick McGuire, and the entry by Gina Macdonald and Darko Suvin in *St. James Guide to Science Fiction Writers* [10-2]. (RLM, MAM)

Theodore Sturgeon, U.S., 1918–1985

10-137.   Menger, Lucy. **Theodore Sturgeon**. Ungar, 1981.

For approximately two decades prior to his death in 1985, Sturgeon produced little. His major work appeared in the late 1940s and 1950s. Menger's account, at approximately 145 pages, provides a short biography, then examines the fiction chronologically, emphasizing four novels and about 25 short stories. (The rationale for selection isn't explained.) Sturgeon is a writer important enough to justify a better assessment than is supplied in this book, or in the shorter, much weaker Starmont booklet by Lahna Diskin. (NB)

James Tiptree, Jr., U.S., 1915–1987

10-138.   Siegel, Mark. **James Tiptree, Jr**. Starmont, 1985.

10-139.   Tiptree, James, Jr. **Meet Me at Infinity**. Tor, 2000.

Alice Sheldon—whose pen name was James Tiptree—came late to science fiction, her first SF story having been published at age 53, under her well-known pseudonym. She will be remembered especially for her short fiction, which won or was nominated for many awards. The first relatively detailed study of Tiptree was the introduction by Gardner Dozois to the 1976 Gregg Press reprint edition of *10,000 Light-Years From Home*. This was later reprinted separately as a 36-page booklet, *The Fiction of James Tiptree, Jr.*, in 1977. Dozois approaches the stories chronologically and stylistically, whereas Siegel, a college instructor when he wrote this study, "examines Tiptree's works thematically in the order in which they appeared in book-length publications, partly as a matter of convenience." Siegel interviewed Tiptree in mid-1982, and his introduction, presumably written later, says of her marriage, "they continue together happily to this day." Siegel's study, while useful, does not emphasize sufficiently Tiptree's preoccupation with death. Her husband was already suffering from Alzheimer's disease and her own health was poor when he interviewed her. Five years after the interview, she shot her husband and killed herself.

A more recent study of Tiptree's work, Inez van der Spek's *Alien Plots: Female Subjectivity and the Divine in the Light of James Tiptree's "A Momentary Taste of Being"* (Liverpool, 1999), is a reworking of a doctoral thesis that, in its theoretical and theological specialization, as well as in its intense focus on a single Tiptree story, will likely be of interest to a limited number of readers.

Edited by Tiptree's friend and long-time editor, Jeffrey D. Smith (but begun long before Tiptree's death and largely steered by her wishes), the posthumously published collection *Meet Me at Infinity* contains a selection of Tiptree's fiction, essays, public letters, poetry, and interviews, stretching "from her first published story in 1946 to her first science fiction story in 1955 to her last long novella in 1986, and includes the letters and informal essays she wrote for publication." The fiction in this book, some of which is published for the first time here, is not major Tiptree, however, with the possible exception of "The Color of Neanderthal Eyes." The nonfiction section, however, is of considerably greater interest, intended "to produce a volume of Alice Sheldon's complete public nonfiction." Taken as a whole, the often sharply written and strongly felt texts in this book provide valuable perspectives on Tiptree's life and work. Among topics of particular interest are Alice Sheldon's thoughts on "James Tiptree, Jr.," on being a woman, on writing as a woman, on writing science fiction, and on writing science fiction as a woman. (RLM, NB)

George Turner, Australia, 1916–1997

10-140. Buckrich, Judith Raphael. **George Turner: A Life**. Melbourne, 1999.

Critic and author George Turner, it has been suggested by more than one observer, may be the most distinguished Australian science fiction author of the 20th century, even though his first SF novel was not published until 1978, when he was over 60. Less well known in the U.S. than the U.K., where he won an Arthur C. Clarke Award for *The Sea and the Summer*, Turner also had an important impact on SF criticism in his homeland, where he received numerous awards and award nominations for both his fiction and his criticism. This biography provides an adequate overview of what was at times an extremely troubled and controversial life and career. Notes, bibliography, and index. Turner's own earlier autobiographical *In the Heart or in the Head: An Essay in Time Travel* (Norstrilia Press, 1984), which was nominated for a nonfiction Hugo award, is also of interest. (RLM)

Jack Vance, U.S., 1916–

*10-141. Cunningham, A. E., ed. **Jack Vance: Critical Appreciations and a Bibliography**. The British Library, 2000.

10-142. Mead, David G. **An Encyclopedia of Jack Vance, 20th Century Science Fiction Writer**. 3 vols. Edwin Mellon, 2002.

10-143.   Rawlins, Jack. **Demon Prince: The Dissonant Worlds of Jack Vance**. Borgo, 1986.

10-144.   Underwood, Tim, and Chuck Miller, eds. **Jack Vance**. Taplinger, 1980.

Vance is one of the more popular writers of SF and fantasy, his fiction expertly blending elements from each. Rawlins, in a competent but unexceptional study, quotes Vance as thinking of himself as a "writer of adventure stories," which is accurate but incomplete. Rawlins suggests that Vance's career can be divided into three periods: from 1945 to the mid-1950s, with a hard science emphasis; a later period emphasizing alien worlds and their cultures; and a post-1973 period. Within about a hundred pages, Rawlins squeezes in a brief sketch, three chapters dealing with Vance's worlds, words, and plots, a two-page update of the 1981 version of this study, a 1985 interview, a selective secondary bibliography, and an index.

The eight reprinted essays in the Taplinger collection treat various aspects of Vance's SF and fantasy, and include an updated version of Richard Tiedmann's *Jack Vance: Science Fiction Stylist*, published separately in 1965, whose 44 pages provide a detailed look at Vance's somewhat mannered diction. The latter is the subject of a dictionary of Vance-coined words, *The Jack Vance Lexicon: From Ahulph to Zipangote* by Dan Temianka (Underwood-Miller, 1992).

Mead, in his three volumes, has extracted from Vance's prolific SF, fantasy, and detective fiction (excluding works bylined Ellery Queen) more than 15,600 terms along with brief (20 to 100 words) definitions, indexing "all the people, places, and things invented by Jack Vance for his fiction in English." Each story or novel abbreviation is followed by the page number of the first appearance of the word. This is an exhaustive and expensive index of primary interest to Vance enthusiasts and a few scholars, but only to the largest libraries.

If a single book about Vance must be selected, the most appropriate would be the Cunningham volume. Cunningham's collection of essays includes quite diverse contributions by, among others, Tom Shippey (who argues that Vance, far from being simply a stylist, is in his work "centrally preoccupied with one of the most acute moral dilemmas and major intellectual developments of our age"), Gene Wolfe (who supplies a reading of *The Dying Earth*), Dan Simmons (who speaks of reading protocols and Vance's use of language), and Vance himself (who provides a brief autobiographical sketch of his life). The quality and content of the essays vary, and sometimes the praise is perhaps slightly over-the-top, but all have something to offer and the best are especially illuminating of Vance's work. The volume's long and well-organized bibliography, compiled by the editor, though not quite exhaustive, is relatively complete and will be sufficient for the needs of most students of Vance. (RLM, NB)

Jules Verne, France, 1828–1905

*10-145.   Butcher, William. **Verne's Journey to the Centre of the Self: Space and Time in the Voyages Extraordinaires**. St. Martin's, 1990.

10-146. Costello, Peter. **Jules Verne: Inventor of Science Fiction**. Scribner, 1990.

*10-147. Evans, Arthur B. **Jules Verne Rediscovered: Didacticism and the Scientific Novel**. Greenwood, 1988.

*10-148. Martin, Andrew. **The Mask of the Prophet: The Extraordinary Fictions of Jules Verne**. Oxford Univ. Press, 1990.

*10-149. Smyth, Edmund J., ed. **Jules Verne: Narratives of Modernity**. Liverpool Univ. Press, 1999.

10-150. Taves, Brian, and Stephen Michaluk, Jr. **The Jules Verne Encyclopedia**. Scarecrow, 1996.

The best critical work in English on Verne is Arthur Evans's study (Eaton award) of scientific and moral didacticism in the *Voyages Extraordinaires*. In separate sections devoted to the pedagogical intent, ideological and intellectual content, and narrative and textual mechanics of Verne's works, Evans applies multiple critical strategies to reveal the *Voyages* as "a unique narrative (and social) configuration in the history of nineteenth-century literary prose." Bristling with first-rate scholarship—including notes, a relatively exhaustive bibliography (though less complete than *Jules Verne: A Primary and Secondary Bibliography* by Edward J. Gallagher, Judith A. Misticelli, and John A. Van Eerde [G. K. Hall, 1980])—and a very detailed index—Evans's book is so well organized that much of it will be accessible even to nonspecialists. Readers as well as scholars will be especially interested in Evans's commentary on the dreadfully distorted English translations—which, he argues, are largely responsible for the lack of attention given Verne by English-language critics and for his comparatively low standing among adult readers—and his clarification of the primary role played by Verne's major publisher, Pierre-Jules Hetzel, in shaping the vast pedagogical project of the *Voyages*. Winner of the Eaton Award.

Like Evans's exemplary study, the monographs by Butcher and Martin show the degree of critical imagination and sophistication Verne's works can call forth. Both are densely argued, highly specialized analyses that draw on recent works by French critics. Butcher uses structuralist and phenomenological criticism to explore "the key questions of dimensionality" in Verne's *Voyages* in space and time. Using often abstruse arguments supplemented by graphs, he illuminates narrative patterns, details of grammar and style, and relevant thematic issues, always carefully contextualizing his discussions within the naturalistic genre in which Verne wrote. Martin's witty deconstructive book seems at first capricious in its plan to "read Verne as if it had been written by Napoleon Bonaparte or [Jorge Luis] Borges," and, "by way of compensating for the historical errors thus committed, [to] read Napoleon and Borges as though they had been written by Verne." But the unexpected nexus Martin establishes between these three disparate writers is a shared, archetypal ideological narrative: the story of a Masked Prophet who rebels against an Empire "to reveal what is concealed." Surprisingly, this strange strategy leads Martin to fascinating insights into the subtext of imperialism in Verne's works. Like Butcher's study, Martin's can be recommended to specialized collections and to readers well-versed in contemporary theory. Bibliography, index.

Readers seeking a less theoretically formidable introduction to Verne as man and writer will find comparatively slim pickings. Costello's is still the best extant English-language biography, but it suffers from an excess of trivial details about Verne's rather sober life and inadequate attention to his novels—particularly unfortunate in light of Costello's intent to present Verne as "the inventor of science fiction." Like Evans, Costello tracks Verne's increasing pessimism and waning faith in science and technology; unlike Evans, he fails to follow through when his thesis takes him close to Verne's writings. Although agreeable and readable, Costello's biography leaves one with the inaccurate impression that Verne was a severely limited writer of escapist adventure stories for children. Eight pages of plates, chronological list of Verne's novels, index.

The 10 theoretically and analytically various essays in Edmund J. Smyth's collection tackle the problems of Verne's relationships to modernity and to science fiction, providing several excellent examples of the "diversity of approaches being brought to bear on the work of Jules Verne." The essays are original, insightful, well researched, well argued, and up to date (including one of the first sustained studies of *Paris au XXe siècle*), and the volume is a significant contribution to Verne scholarship. Index.

Taves and Michaluk's *The Jules Verne Encyclopedia*, despite an unacceptably large number of typographical and similar errors, is of special value to English-speaking scholars, containing, as it does, the first reliable and comprehensive guide to all the English-language editions of Verne's works published in the U.K. and America from the 1860s to the present day. There is also a wealth of other useful incidental information about Verne and his impact—particularly on the Anglophone world; but it is neither primarily intended for, nor written with, the literary scholar in mind. It should nonetheless be of significant value to all students of Verne. (MAM, RLM)

Kurt Vonnegut, U.S., 1922–

*10-151. Boon, Kevin A., ed. **At Millennium's End: New Essays on the Work of Kurt Vonnegut**. SUNY, 2001.

*10-152. Klinkowitz, Jerome. **The Vonnegut Effect**. South Carolina Univ. Press, 2004.

10-153. Klinkowitz, Jerome, and John Somer, eds. **The Vonnegut Statement**. Delacorte, 1972.

10-154. Merrill, Robert, ed. **Critical Essays on Kurt Vonnegut**. G. K. Hall, 1990.

10-155. Morse, Donald E. **The Novels of Kurt Vonnegut: Imagining Being an American**. Greenwood, 2003.

Although Kurt Vonnegut (the Jr. was dropped some years ago) prefers not to be considered a writer of science fiction, and some critics have followed his lead, any sensible study of his career reveals that he has often written SF or used its techniques and tropes for his dark fables. (Robert Scholes has persuasively argued that black humorists like Vonnegut are fabulators who lack "the rhetoric of moral certainty" claimed by satirists.)

Vonnegut was largely ignored for the first two decades of his literary career, tainted perhaps by his association with SF, but by the 1970s he was the subject of extensive criticism. *The Vonnegut Statement* assembles 13 pieces, some revised from earlier publication, mostly by academics. It is valuable for its perspective at a relatively early point in Vonnegut's career. By 1990, when the Merrill collection appeared, Vonnegut, though still popular, was not being ground as actively by the scholarly mills. (So it goes.) Merrill contains a balanced collection of reviews, essays on individual works, and general essays, four of them specially commissioned for this collection. Merrill's own introduction provides a valuable and well-documented, although now dated, 27-page survey of Vonnegut criticism to the time of its publication, which is exhaustively recorded in the bibliography, a revision and expansion of its 1974 predecessor. A slightly later collection of essays on Vonnegut also of interest is *The Critical Response to Kurt Vonnegut* (Greenwood, 1994), edited by Leonard Mustazza. Boon's book provides interesting and valuable points of comparison and contrast to the earlier collections, presenting evidence of the still further evolution of both Vonnegut's fiction and, not least, the critical reactions to it. The 11 essays in this volume also allow for a long-term retrospective over Vonnegut's entire writing life, a perspective not available to critics of a writer at the beginning or midpoint of a career.

Jerome Klinkowitz, who has edited several collections and written much himself on Vonnegut over the years, has also produced what are probably the most knowledgeable studies of both Vonnegut's nonfiction, *Vonnegut in Fact: The Public Spokesmanship of Personal Fiction* (South Carolina, 1998) and his fiction, *The Vonnegut Effect.* The latter, which its author quite accurately characterizes as "a chronological investigation of Kurt Vonnegut's writing as reflected by the social and critical contexts in which it has developed," clearly supersedes his earlier, brief *Kurt Vonnegut* (Routledge, 1982), and will probably remain a standard work on its subject for some time to come. Bibliography, index. The main argument of Donald Morse's study of Vonnegut's novels is that Vonnegut, whom Morse sees as the representative 20th-century American writer, should be placed at the center of America's social and historical concerns and firmly in the American literary and philosophical (i.e., pragmatist) traditions. Bibliography, index. (RLM, NB)

Herbert George Wells, U.K., 1866–1946

10-156. Crossley, Robert. **H. G. Wells**. Starmont, 1986.

*10-157. Huntington, John. **Logic of Fantasy: H. G. Wells and Science Fiction**. Columbia Univ. Press, 1982.

10-158. McConnell, Frank. **The Science Fiction of H. G. Wells**. Oxford Univ. Press, 1981.

*10-159. Parrinder, Patrick. **Shadows of the Future: H. G. Wells, SF and Prophecy**. Syracuse Univ. Press, 1995.

10-160. Scheick, William J., and J. Randolph Cox. **H. G. Wells: A Reference Guide**. G. K. Hall, 1988.

*10-161. Smith, David. **H. G. Wells: Desperately Mortal**. Yale Univ. Press, 1986. Wells, as "the Shakespeare of science fiction," left behind a vast oeuvre of fiction and nonfiction, including several novels written around the turn of the century—the scientific romances—that proved generative to the subsequent evolution of science fiction. Biographies abound and no attempt will be made here to consider them all. The best to date is probably that of historian David Smith. With Wellsian pacing and energy, Smith draws upon the vast paper trail Wells left behind to chronicle his subject's endlessly active life and involvement in a bewildering variety of progressive causes. Smith deals with a number of literary matters, including the argument between Wells and Henry James over the purpose of art, the role of class and social development in his writings, the potential for human betterment he saw inherent in the future, and (briefly) his use of science in the scientific romances—a topic far more thoroughly examined in Roslynn D. Haynes's *H. G. Wells: Discoverer of the Future: The Influence of Science on His Thought* (New York University, 1980). But Smith's exhaustively researched and documented thematic biography is less concerned with explicating Wells's fiction (and not at all with its posthumous critical reception) than with tracking his intellectual development and personal, sexual, and professional involvement in diverse social contexts. Appendix, notes, index.

Best among introductory books that emphasize Wells's SF is Crossley's historically acute Starmont guide. Crossley analyses the motifs, characters, and style of five major early SF novels and a few short stories. The narrowness of focus inevitable in a book of this brevity is compensated for by a particularly fine introductory sketch of Wells's early years and of works written after the five novels he discusses in the chapters that follow. Chronology, annotated primary and secondary bibliography, index. McConnell introduces Wells's life and deftly situates him within well-defined historical and social contexts from the turn of the century through the First World War. He then turns to issues raised by seven key SF works organized into such clusters as evolutionary fables, realistic fantasies, and oneiric extrapolations. If McConnell fails to illuminate the scope of Wells's scientific views, he nonetheless offers perceptive readings of the scientific romances and illuminates Wells's influence, especially on Olaf Stapledon. Chronology, checklist of publications from 1895 to 1945, selected bibliography, index.

Studies since the 1960s that emphasize Wells's science fiction build on earlier scholarship by Bernard Bergonzi, whose *The Early H. G. Wells: A Study of the Scientific Romance* (Manchester, 1961) contextualizes Wells's early SF within the intellectual instability of the late 19th century; Mark Hillegas, whose seminal *The Future as Nightmare: H. G. Wells and the Anti-utopians* [9-95] examines Wells's impact on 20th-century dystopian thought; Patrick Parrinder, whose *H. G. Wells* (Oliver & Boyd, 1970) offers a succinct overview of the thematic and intellectual concerns of Wells's fiction, including the scientific romances; and Robert Philmus, whose *Into the Unknown: The Evolution of Science Fiction from Francis Godwin to H. G. Wells* [9-148] tracks the origins of major themes in Wells's SF in British fiction of the 18th and 19th centuries.

Notable among more recent critical work on Wells's science fiction is Huntington's monograph (Eaton award), which essentially supplants the aforementioned book by Bergonzi as the best formal study of the scientific romances. Central to Huntington's argument is his emphasis on the tension in Wells between opposition and ethics established by the "two world structure" of these works. Huntington appropriately identifies *The Time Machine* as the exemplar of "Wells's use of balanced opposition and symbolic mediation as a way of thinking," then develops analyses of the structures and rhetorical devices in scientific romances, concluding with a chapter on Wells's anti-utopias in conjunction with works by such writers as Zamiatin, Bradbury, and Orwell. Extensive notes, index.

Parrinder's main contention in his excellent *Shadows of the Future* is that *The Time Machine*, upon which this critical volume concentrates, is "one of the Prophetic Books of the late nineteenth century, casting its shadow over futurity." He then proceeds to demonstrate this thesis in a series of independent but conceptually linked essays that focus not on Wells alone, but on the "shadow" that his work has cast on those who have come after him, intending to "show how Wells developed and explored the literary potential of prophecy in new ways." The result is a serious, fascinating, and subtle argument for the significance of Wells, his novel, and the development of the science fiction genre for the evolution of modernity in the 20th century.

Consideration of all the collections of essays about Wells that have been published is not possible here, although three worthwhile compilations can be mentioned and recommended: Bernard Bergonzi, ed., *H. G. Wells: A Collection of Critical Essays* (Prentice-Hall, 1976); Darko Suvin and Robert M. Philmus, eds., *H. G. Wells and Modern Science Fiction* (Bucknell, 1977); and George E. Slusser, Patrick Parrinder, and Danièle Chatelain, eds., *H. G. Wells's Perennial Time Machine: Selected Essays from the Centenary Conference "The Time Machine: Past, Present, and Future," Imperial College, London, July 26–29, 1995* (Georgia, 2001).

Further guidance to the critical literature on Wells can be found in the Scheick and Cox volume, which has unfortunately become quite dated. Impaired only by lack of an adequate index, a somewhat misleading introduction, and a few omissions and deficient annotations, this book follows a list of Wells's fiction and nonfiction books with a 3,019-item annotated secondary bibliography, which includes nearly all salient English-language reviews, essays, and books published through 1986, as well as a selection of foreign pieces. (MAM, RLM)

Jack Williamson, U.S., 1908–

10-162. Hauptmann, Richard A. **The Works of Jack Williamson: An Annotated Bibliography and Guide**. NESFA, 1998.

*10-163. Williamson, Jack. **Wonder's Child: My Life in Science Fiction**. Bluejay, 1984. Expanded version forthcoming from BenBella Books.

Jack Williamson's aptly titled, very personal autobiography reveals a life begun in poverty in the Southwest that led to a doctorate in English in 1974 and his election as a Grand Master by fellow SF writers in 1976. Williamson triumphed over poverty, inadequate education, and emotional problems, and has continued to publish, sometimes in collaboration with Frederik Pohl. A remarkable and moving odyssey more self-reflective than Pohl's *The Way the Future Was* and much less detailed than Asimov's massive two-volume autobiography. Hugo winner, 1985. Hauptmann's volume (also a Hugo finalist), which contains a foreword by Pohl, an afterword by Williamson himself, and a year-by-year chronology of Williamson's life, lists all of his books, shorter fiction, nonfiction, and non-print media material, as well numerous secondary sources. Awards, degrees, honors, pseudonyms, collaborators, and Williamson's SF terms that have passed into the English language are listed and categorized. There are title and general indexes. (NB, RLM)

Gene Wolfe, U.S., 1931–

10-164. Andre-Driussi, Michael. **Lexicon Urthus**. Sirius Fiction, 1994.

*10-165. Wright, Peter. **Attending Daedalus: Gene Wolfe, Artifice and the Reader**. Liverpool Univ. Press, 2003.

Peter Wright's volume is a significant and original study of Gene Wolfe, concentrating on the author's most important work, the multivolume *The Book of the New Sun*, and its single-volume coda, *The Urth of the New Sun*. Building on an extensive knowledge of the totality of Wolfe's fiction, as well as solid familiarity with the critical reactions to which it has given birth, Wright has produced a long overdue exploration of what is undoubtedly a seminal work in 20th-century science fiction, perhaps also in American fiction generally. While admitting that Wolfe is a "complex and wily writer, ambiguous, subtle, and playful," whose fiction "encourages misreadings, demands thoughtful reflection, and is able to involve the reader in labyrinthine possibilities for interpretation," Wright nonetheless manages to lead his own readers skillfully and expertly through sophisticated, detailed—and sometimes controversial—interpretations of the writings of his subject. Well-written, well-researched, carefully argued, and not afraid to challenge what he argues are the flawed analyses of previous commentators, Wright's book, which developed from his doctoral thesis, will likely remain the major academic exploration of Wolfe's masterpiece for some time to come. It clearly supersedes Joan Gordon's brief 1986 Starmont guide *Gene Wolfe*, whose brevity and format mediate against an otherwise valuable, if limited, introduction to Wolfe's fiction. Notes, primary and secondary bibliographies, and index. Also of practical value to the student of the New Sun series is Andre-Driussi's *Lexicon Urthus*, an extensive and detailed glossary and guide to numerous terms and names from Wolfe's fictional world. (RLM)

Roger Zelazny, U.S., 1937–1995

10-166. Lindskold, Jane M. **Roger Zelazny**. Twayne, 1993.

10-167. Yoke, Carl B. **Roger Zelazny**. Starmont, 1979.

Although Roger Zelazny was a central figure in the development of 20th-century science fiction, he is as yet poorly served in the critical literature. Carl Yoke's volume is still the best available study, although it is now very severely dated, is far too brief, and does not provide the depth of analysis Zelazny demands and deserves. Lindskold's book, much more recent and written (as was Yoke's) with Zelazny's cooperation, is rich in useful background material, including relatively extensive quotations from Zelazny's correspondence, but it is also, alas, quite weak analytically, offering little insight into her subject's stylistic strengths or thematic concerns. We still await a major study of Roger Zelazny. (RLM)

Collective Biography

*10-168. Aldiss, Brian W., and Harry Harrison. **Hell's Cartographers: Some Personal Histories of Science Fiction Writers**. Harper, 1976.

10-169. Greenberg, Martin H., ed. **Fantastic Lives: Autobiographical Essays by Notable Science Fiction Writers**. Southern Illinois Univ. Press, 1981.

*10-170. Jakubowski, Maxim, and Edward James, eds. **The Profession of Science Fiction: SF Writers on their Craft and Ideas**. St. Martin's, 1993.

10-171. Knight, Damon F. **The Futurians: The Story of the Science Fiction "Family" of the 30s That Produced Today's Top SF Writers and Editors**. John Day, 1977.

Taking its title from Kingsley Amis's seminal study of SF, *New Maps of Hell*, Aldiss and Harrison's collection gives free rein to six contemporary SF writers, all of whose works, according to Aldiss, share the "unspoken topic" that "the individual's role in society is eroded as society itself becomes wealthier and more powerful." Writing about themselves and their participation in the world of SF, Aldiss, Harrison, Robert Silverberg, Alfred Bester, Damon Knight, and Frederik Pohl produce largely thoughtful pieces supplemented by brief accounts of their working habits and now-dated lists of their writings. See also Aldiss's *The Twinkling of An Eye, Bury My Heart at W. H. Smith's: A Writing Life*, and *The Shape of Further Things*; Pohl's *The Way the Future Was*; and Silverberg's *Reflections and Refractions: Thoughts on Science-Fiction, Science, and Other Matters*. Knight, whose *In*

Search of Wonder: Essays on Modern Science Fiction contains some of the most acute early SF criticism, has also published *The Futurians*, an uncomfortably personal account of his involvement in the Futurian Society of New York, which included such important writers of American pulp SF as Isaac Asimov, James Blish, Judith Merril, and Cyril Kornbluth; therefore, Asimov's numerous autobiographical writings and Merril's posthumous autobiography, *Better to Have Loved: The Life of Judith Merril*, should also be consulted.

Greenberg's sequel to *Hell's Cartographers* gives even more latitude to a wider range of writers. Although a few circle tediously around the perennial question (What is SF?), some like Philip José Farmer offer straightforward autobiography while others articulate their attitudes toward SF as a genre, as a field of commercial writing, as a compact with a highly interactive readership, and as a locus of critical attention. Of particular note are Barry Malzberg's characteristically bitter reflections on the viability of SF—thoughts he has further embellished in *The Engines of Night: Science Fiction in the Eighties* [9-123]; R. A. Lafferty's caustic assault on John W. Campbell and most of the writers of the "Golden Age"; Harlan Ellison's fervid attack on academic critics; and Norman Spinrad's inadvertently complimentary defense of their worth. Like several of the essays in *Hell's Cartographers*, many in Greenberg's collection suggest a disjunction between SF and the mainstream that was more pertinent to the 1980s than to the first decade of the 21st century, lending the whole enterprise a clearly dated tone. Moreover, several of the authors in Greenberg's roster (Katherine MacLean, Mack Reynolds, A. E. van Vogt, Margaret St. Clair) are deceased and their work is generally considered of less than central importance by today's critics; nevertheless, their subjective ruminations remain of interest to scholars. Appended to each essay is a brief biography of primary works.

By far the most interesting and useful of these volumes is the collection edited by Jakubowski and James, containing 16 essays and reminiscences selected from the more than 40 published from 1972 to 1990 under the rubric "The Profession of Science Fiction" in *Foundation*, the premier British journal *about* science fiction. The open-ended invitation offered to the contributors to this series allows them to focus on whatever aspect of SF seems most important; the result is a (necessarily somewhat dated) collection that, because of its breadth, presents a unique snapshot of late-20th-century English-language science fiction. Its contents embrace autobiographical concerns, the origins of key SF works, the experience of being an SF writer, and, most interestingly, the trials and tribulations of SF during the latter half of the last century. Index, notes. (MAM)

Interviews

*10-172. McCaffrey, Larry. **Across the Wounded Galaxies: Interviews with Contemporary American Science Fiction Writers**. Univ. of Illinois Press, 1990.

*10-173. Platt, Charles. **Dream Makers: Science Fiction and Fantasy Writers at Work**. Ungar, 1987.

Larry McCaffrey is an interviewer with an agenda. As clarified in his controversial pronouncements in the *Columbia History of the United States* (1988), he considers science fiction the preeminent literature of our age. More specifically, he considers SF the essence of postmodernism. Unfortunately, McCaffrey carries this thesis, which parallels the thinking of Brian McHale and other contemporary critics, into each of these nine interviews (conducted between 1983 and 1988), where it proceeds to throw several askew. Perhaps in consequence, the most fruitful interactions occur between McCaffrey and William Gibson, Bruce Sterling, and Samuel R. Delany, all of whom seem in sympathy with McCaffrey's argument. Still, except for an uncharacteristically dull encounter with Gene Wolfe and an incoherent one with William Burroughs, the other interviews in this book offer a wealth of insights for readers and scholars as, unleashed from McCaffrey's thesis, Ursula K. Le Guin, Octavia Butler, Thomas Disch, and Gregory Benford discourse on their perspectives on SF and allied matters. As in his previous books of interviews with American writers, *Anything Can Happen* (Illinois, 1983) and *Alive and Writing* (Illinois, 1987), the latter of which included early versions of the interviews with Le Guin and Delany printed here, McCaffrey's questions evince in-depth preparation, a quick intelligence, and a willingness to give his interviewees space. These qualities raise these conversations to a level of sophistication rarely approached in earlier fannish interview series such as the *Science Fiction Voices* series conducted by Jeffrey M. Elliot and Darrell Schweitzer (Borgo). Index.

If McCaffrey's book constitutes a glimpse of the state of SF in the late 1980s, Charles Platt's offers snapshots from previous decades. Ungar's hardcover omnibus reprints (with modest revision) 25 of the 56 profiles previously published in *Dream Makers* (Berkley, 1980) and *Dream Makers II* (Berkley, 1983). Instead of using the conventional question-and-answer format, Platt constructs essays out of material gathered during long taped interviews with his subjects, which include such luminaries as Isaac Asimov, Arthur C. Clarke, Frank Herbert, Stephen King, and A. E. van Vogt. Platt's deep knowledge of SF, his sense of balance and fairness, and his sensitivity to his subject's concerns inform each of these witty, penetrating profiles, making this volume indispensable for readers, libraries, and scholars.

More recent interviews of 50 SF and fantasy writers, conducted by Stan Nicholls, can be found in his *Wordsmiths of Wonder* [9-138]. (MAM)

CHAPTER 11

Science Fiction in Film, Television, and Radio

Joseph Milicia and Michael Klossner

SF in Films

A number of prominent SF writers, editors, and critics have argued that there is no such thing as "genuine" science fiction cinema, at least beyond a very few isolated examples. Rather, there is only something called Sci-Fi, a juvenile fantasy entertainment with motifs appropriated from SF. A number of arguments have been used to support this position, which in its extreme form sees SF cinema as not having gotten much more mature since Georges Méliès's 1902 *Le voyage dans la lune*, except in the superiority of its special effects. For example, it is has often been said that true SF never wantonly disregards established laws of physics (say the speed of light), though it may trump them (say with some mode of faster-than-light travel), while most movie producers, screenwriters, and directors haven't the slightest interest in, or perhaps grasp of, science. (Flouting of the laws of gravity in *Armageddon*, 1998, would be a case in point.)

It has also been claimed that only the written word can provide the discourse necessary for both a grounding in reality—assuming SF is indeed a realist mode of sorts—and extrapolations from it. Naturally, good SF needn't have long paragraphs of scientific explanation, but there should be a spirit of testing hypotheses that is inimical to storytelling in the motion picture (it is said). Some critics have even argued that to the extent that SF movies foreground special effects, they depart from what is truly science fiction, entering instead a world of pure (meaning trivial) spectacle. Here the original *Star Wars* and *Close Encounters of the Third Kind* (both 1977) have been favorite targets. (One critic who makes this argument is Carl Freedman in "Kubrick's *2001* and the Possibility of a Science-Fiction Cinema," *Science Fiction Studies*, 25:2 [July 1998], pp. 300–318.) One could even toss in another argument: that despite the existence of a reference book called *Science Fiction Film Directors* [11-28], there is only marginally a type of film auteur comparable to an "SF writer." Perhaps John Carpenter, James Cameron, and a few "B"-movie directors come very close, but the careers of Stanley Kubrick, Steven Spielberg, and Ridley Scott show us that they are certainly not "SF film directors," despite an affinity for the genre.

Still, there are observations to be made in support of welcoming SF film (and television) as a valid branch of science fiction. First, while some filmmakers do wantonly disregard laws of science (as they do dates in history), this is a tendency, not a principle. Second, even if 90 percent of SF cinema is trash, one might claim the same for literary SF, as Theodore Sturgeon once proposed. In any case, works of "bad" SF in any medium are cultural artifacts from which we can learn a great deal and even get considerable pleasure. As for plausibility, a reasonable definition of literary science fiction cannot limit the field to the hardest of hard SF. There is a continuity stretching from hard SF to the most extravagant intergalactic space opera; or, tracing a different trajectory, to the mind-bending conundrums of Philip K. Dick; or, following a third path of departure, to stories featuring what Kingsley Amis once called "pseudo-science"—time machines and the like. Most of us have a sense of an outer limit, beyond which is "fantasy"; some draw the line this side of comic-book superheroes, some just beyond, while others recognize a "third thing," science-fantasy or whatever. All this is equally true of SF cinema, just as, in both media, when the science of an SF story comes to be proven false by later developments, the story doesn't cease to be SF: the discourse of "scientific possibility" is what counts. It might be added that some of us are of a forgiving nature: we may regret the appearance of the impossible asteroid dragon in *The Empire Strikes Back* (1980) but take it as a minor flaw (or a standard Jungian archetype) in light of the dramatic and visual splendors of the Sky City climax.

As for the "excess" of special effects in SF films, there are several points to be made. Those who dislike *Star Wars* and *Close Encounters* for foregrounding special effects ignore the fact that spectacle alone could not account for those films' enduring popularity—or else they would be as ephemeral as IMAX films. Moreover, determining the point at which special effects subsume narrative and theme is inevitably subjective. We may mention in passing that at least a few of the most important SF films feature hardly any "special effects" beyond creations of the prop shop—the 1956 *Invasion of the Body Snatchers* being a case in point—and that other film genres besides SF and fantasy give welcome prominence to spectacle, notably the historical film and the musical. We will not ask what is wrong with pure spectacle anyway, though we might question whether it could exist without narrative elements, even in non-kinetic art such as book and magazine covers.

Consider a classic case where the film arguably comes to a narrative halt in favor of an "effects-fest." *Forbidden Planet* (1956) has such a scene halfway through the film: the tour of the underground 20-cubic-mile Krell mind-into-matter machine. But this spectacle is utterly subservient to the narrative. Both symbolically and literally, the machine is connected to the "superior" attitude of the tour leader, Dr. Morbius, who has had a Krell I.Q. boost via a link to it. And the scene is necessary to the dramatic climax, in which the power of this very machine is being tapped to enable the monster from Morbius's id to melt the door of Krell steel. We cannot forget the thematic import of the spectacle as well: the automated Krell domain is as melancholy a sign of the mighty having fallen as Shelley's shattered visage of Ozymandius's statue.

Comparable points could be made about other spectacles, including the final sequence of *Close Encounters*: far from a gratuitous fireworks display, it is the quasi-religious "vision" toward which the entire film has been building, not only dramatically but rhythmically through several night-sky sequences. Narrative and theme aside, it can be claimed that visual (and auditory) spectacle in SF film legitimately takes the place of descriptive and explanatory passages in literary SF. "This could be!" can as easily be stated by the image as by the word.

Of course, film scholars, many of whom have no particular interest or expertise in literary SF, are likely to find much of this debate irrelevant when they approach the category "science fiction" from the perspective of their own discipline. Those in genre studies don't normally ask whether or not the objects at hand extrapolate from real-world science and technology; for them a film may be determined to be SF, as distinct from fantasy and horror, not by the rigor of its science but by its foregrounding of "science" through themes and motifs. If there are ray guns, spaceships, robots or androids, time machines, labs with scientists (mad or otherwise), creatures from other planets, and the like— or themes of the glories or dangers of scientific experiment, or efforts to define the human against the lab-created or extraterrestrial Other—it's science fiction. This approach has led at least one critic to list *Teenage Mutant Ninja Turtles* and *The Matrix* in the same sentence, as two martial-arts-inflected SF films of the 1990s: an enlightening grouping in some ways, but dispiriting to anyone who feels that the differences are more significant. Film scholars and theorists who take a more ideological, psychoanalytic, feminist, or even Jungian approach (among others) may be likewise unconcerned with traditional efforts to define SF, though much the same could be said about literary theorists in those fields.

Those in genre studies are also likely to take into account the fact that film genres historically shift and overlap, resulting in hybrids of various sorts. Most commonly, SF films share the genre conventions of horror—compare *Alien* (1979) and countless others. Many of the books annotated in this chapter go to some pains to make distinctions between SF and horror, though a solid line may be impossible to draw, especially if we recall Brian Aldiss's suggestion that the Gothic or post-Gothic mode is characteristic of SF. More recently, many SF films have been action-adventure hybrids (e.g., *The Terminator 2*, 1991), and there have been more unusual mixes: an SF musical (*Just Imagine*, 1930), an SF western (*The Wild, Wild West*, 1999), and an SF screwball-comedy/action-adventure film with elements of horror (*Twister*, 1996).

A number of our annotated books are primarily genre studies, exploring ways that particular conventions, via repetition and variation, express meanings or convey cultural concerns. Occasionally, writers on film have doubted that SF is really separable from the broader category of the fantastic, just as some have asked whether there is really such a thing as "film noir" distinct from "the crime film." Whatever the arguments, the facts remain that dozens of books on "SF films" (and "film noir") are in print and that at least the term "Sci-Fi" (like "noir") has a meaning to a wide public. Most of the writers mentioned in this chapter either argue or assume that there is something that may be fairly singled out as science fiction cinema, however much their definitions and methodologies differ.

Historical surveys of SF film often begin with Georges Méliès's 1902 *Voyage to the Moon*, partly because copies are so readily available and the film is so outrageous in its comic spectacle: most famously, the Man in the Moon getting a spaceship in his eye. But if one allows an extremely broad definition of SF, there are other early short films that may be classified as SF, featuring wondrous forms of advanced transportation, automatons, and the like, often derived from Jules Verne adventures or from *Frankenstein*. Film scholar Tom Gunning famously described the films of the pre-World War I era as the "cinema of attractions," as much akin to circus attractions as to the later feature films made possible by the development of techniques of photography and editing to generate narrative suspense, supremely seen in the works of D. W. Griffith. Gunning's term, of course, has important resonance for those who find special effects central to the SF film. In any case, after the feature film became the dominant mode of the motion picture, SF remained a marginal film genre. During the silent era, only isolated examples stand out, such as the French *Paris qui dort* (*The Crazy Ray*) (1923), the Soviet curiosity *Aelita—Queen of Mars* (1924), and a landmark pair of German films directed by Fritz Lang.

Metropolis (premiered 1927) remains the ur-text for later generations of SF filmmakers. This delirious tale, with a visual design combining Gothic, German Expressionist, and Art Deco elements, featured a futuristic city, a mad scientist with a laboratory that would set the standard for decades to come, and a metallic robot transformed into the likeness of a seductive female. Dismissed by no less an authority than H. G. Wells as being wildly melodramatic and scientifically preposterous, it was nonetheless quite reasonable for its time in extrapolating from the present the triumph of modernist architecture and the continuance of exploitation of labor. A film very much of the Machine Age, as J. P. Telotte has described it [11-59; see also 11-26, 11-27], it remains an endlessly rich source of both pop cultural imagery (e.g., in music videos) and topics for postmodernist study: "the Body," gender and technology, the human and the post-human, and much else. Lang's second SF film, *Die Frau im Mond* (*The Woman in the Moon*,

1929), has not yet proven to be a treasure house for retro-fashions and fore-shadowings of 21st-century preoccupations, but it did set the trend for relatively realistic SF, in this case documenting a first trip to the moon. It was a direct influence on *Destination Moon* (1950), which in turn influenced not only the space station and moon visit portions of *2001: A Space Odyssey* but very likely the American space program itself and our astronauts' lunar-surface frolics.

The first two decades of sound in the motion picture were not marked by a significant increase in the number of SF films, except in two categories: horror-related mad scientist movies like *Frankenstein* (1931), *Island of Lost Souls* (1932), and *Dr. Cyclops* (1940); and comic strip-derived serials like *Flash Gordon* (1936) and *Buck Rogers* (1939). In a class by itself (if a bit creaky today) was H. G. Wells's answer to *Metropolis*, *Things to Come* (1936), with its future history of three generations during and after a world war. *King Kong* (1933), part of the "lost world" tradition continuing from the silent era, is also of note. Through-out the 1940s, when the Golden Age of early Asimov, Heinlein, Clarke, and company was in full literary flower, there was virtually no SF on the screen, for reasons that have long been speculated upon but are doubtless connected to the fact that literary SF was still a niche rather than a mass market. Whatever the reasons, the first recognizable wave of SF films, beyond those mad scientists and Saturday matinees, arrived only in the 1950s.

Many books have been written about the anxieties of the 1950s in an effort to explain such an outpouring of memorable films about invading aliens, nuclear disasters, and occasionally the peaceful (if tacitly militaristic) "conquest of space." In 1951, a pair of films established the models for visitations of god-like and godless aliens, respectively: *The Day the Earth Stood Still*, directed by Robert Wise (who would later make *The Andromeda Strain*, 1970, and *Star Trek—The Motion Picture*, 1979), and *The Thing (from Another World)*, produced by Howard Hawks. A different pair of oppositions might be noted in two 1956 fea-tures, Don Siegel's low-budget *Invasion of the Body Snatchers* and MGM's lavish first foray into the SF field, *Forbidden Planet*. The former with its sparse use of special effects remains a haunting tale of mind control (hotly debated even today as to whether its allegory warns of rampant McCarthyism or communist takeover); the latter may now seem campy for its acting and its heroine (howev-er derived from Shakespeare's Miranda she may be), but it remains a monu-ment of SF cinema for its Robby the Robot and the aforementioned underground Krell complex and "monster from the id."

A 1950s cycle of films about oversized marauding creatures, usually nuclear radiation mutations, was initiated by *Them!* (1954) and epitomized by the Japan-ese *Gojira* (1954) and its dubbed and partly reshot American version, *Godzilla*. Meanwhile, at least two auteurs produced distinctive cycles of their own. The first was producer George Pal, with his quartet of Technicolor spectacles: the independent *Destination Moon*, with contributions from Robert E. Heinlein, and, for Paramount, *When Worlds Collide* (1951), *The War of the Worlds* (1954)—as memorable for the sounds of the alien war machines as for their sleek designs—and *Conquest of Space* (1955). The second was director Jack Arnold, whose modestly budgeted features for Universal-International, several of them in 3-D, had their moments of poetic grace, true eeriness, and a deeper mythic resonance: *It Came from Outer Space* (1953); *The Creature from the Black Lagoon* (1954, with sequels to come), *Tarantula* (1955), and supremely, *The Incredible Shrinking Man* (1957). It should be noted that from a box-office perspective, all of these films were but modest successes: out of 253 films that, according to *Variety* (February 22, 1993), made more than $3 million in rentals during the decade, the only SF films were two Jules Verne romances: Disney's *20,000 Leagues Under the Sea* (1954, in 20th place with $11,267,000) and Fox's *Journey to the Center of the Earth* (1959, in 98th place with $4,777,000).

The cycle of 1950s films didn't exactly end in 1960, for the low-budget monster movies continued unabated. But otherwise we find fewer SF films in the early 1960s: more big-studio Verne and Wells adaptations; a few British films with dark, disturbing uses made of children (*Village of the Damned*, 1960, and *The Damned*, 1961); some highly experimental French films (Chris Marker's short *La jetée*, 1962, remade as *12 Monkeys*, 1995; Jean-Luc Godard's *Alphaville*, 1965; Francois Truffaut's English-language *Fahrenheit 451*, 1966; Alain Resnais' time-traveling *Je t'aime, je t'aime*; and Roger Vadim's international comic strip *Barbarella*, 1967); and isolated masterpieces, chiefly Stanley Kubrick's dark comedy of nuclear madness, *Dr. Strangelove* (1964).

But unquestionably 1968 was a landmark year—for *2001: A Space Odyssey* but also for the grim vision of *Planet of the Apes*. The Stanley Kubrick/Arthur C. Clarke collaboration is one of the few films admired unequivocally by the SF literary community, and was a mind-expanding event for many who saw it upon its first release [see 11-16]. But *Planet of the Apes* [11-31] was more directly influential on later films in certain ways: not only because it spawned four sequels, other media products, and a remake, but because its very pessimistic view of racial relations and, more broadly, human group irrationality, cast a shadow on films of the decade to follow. Incidentally, out of 146 films that made $6 million or more in rentals in the 1960s, these were the only two SF films (*2001*, 12th place, $25,522,000; *Planet of the Apes*, 39th place, $15,000,000), aside from several James Bond pictures and two SF-themed Disney comedies, *The Love Bug* (1969, 14th place, $23,150,000) and *The Absent-Minded Professor* (1961, 56th place, $11,426,000). See Table 11-3 for more box-office listings.

Many of the most prominent SF films of the 1970s and 1980s were dystopian: George Lucas' freshman effort *THX 1138* (1970), Kubrick's *A Clockwork Orange* (1971), *Soylent Green* (1973), *A Boy and His Dog* (1975) from the Harlan Ellison story, *Rollerball* (1975), *Logan's Run* (1976), the *Mad Max* trilogy (1979–1985), *Escape from New York* (1981), *Blade Runner* (1982), and *Brazil* (1985), in addition to the *Apes* sequels. Another trend might be said to have been initiated by 1971's *The Andromeda Strain*: perhaps not a major film in itself, it does mark the screen debut of Michael Crichton, a seldom studied but perennially successful auteur—novelist and scenarist, producer, and sometimes director—whose particular brand of techno-thriller has had an important impact on SF cinema (e.g., *Coma*, 1978; *Looker*, 1981; *Jurassic Park*, 1993; *Sphere*, 1998).

The next landmark year after 1968 is surely 1977, with its double whammy of *Star Wars* and *Close Encounters of the Third Kind*. Of importance here is not simply the (not universally acknowledged) artistic excellence of the films but several more factors: their simultaneously tongue-in-cheek and awestruck tone as they update their subgenres (respectively, galactic space opera/1930s serial and good-alien visitation); their contribution to a "blockbuster mentality" that is still central to the film industry; and their setting the bar higher for spectacular special effects. One might say that contemporary SF film begins with these two works: they are only starting to be perceived as "dated" by younger viewers, while their directors continue to be sensationally popular and have made controversial but inarguably significant contributions to SF film well into the first decade of this century.

A few other important dates must be mentioned. In 1979, two other franchises began: the first of the *Star Trek* films and the first of the *Alien* series, the latter unique in that a strong director for each sequel took the series in a different direction. The year 1982 saw Spielberg's phenomenally successful *E.T., the Extra-Terrestrial*, an old-fashioned if skillfully paced "family entertainment"; but it was also the year of several films now seen as markers of postmodernism, films about disturbing interfaces of the human and "the other," whether extraterrestrial, android (synthesized), or digitally constructed: *Blade Runner,* John Carpenter's version of *The Thing, Liquid Sky,* and *TRON*. One might also mark 1989, the year of John Cameron's *The Abyss* (1989), one of the first films to make conspicuous use of computer graphics imagery (CGI), and 1999, for *The Matrix*'s display of a "second generation" of digital effects.

From the mid-1990s to the present, the number of SF films given wide American theatrical release (if only for a week or two) has remained about a dozen a year—far more than in the 1950s if one excludes "grade Z" drive-in fare. A search of the Internet Movie Database (http://us.imdb.com) in early 2004 found yet more in their category "Sci-Fi": an astonishing 66 a year since 1991, although this includes foreign films, shorts, and animation while excluding made-for-TV and direct-to-video titles. Of 866 titles, 577 were American, 85 Japanese, and 49 British. (The same IMDb search, specifying 100 users' ratings, yields 399 films, or about 31 a year. These would be the most popular titles, and this figure is used in Table 11-2.) Clearly, SF themes have become a standard commodity for filmmakers all over the world, recognized universally by audiences, and a significant source of revenue for the industry, even if only the films of George Lucas and Steven Spielberg have truly been box-office phenomena (with a few other contenders such as the *Matrix* trilogy).

Reasons have been proposed for the ongoing box-office success of SF cinema since the late 1970s: for example, the increasing public awareness of advancements in biological and computer science—notably in matters of "replication," from cloning to virtual realities—and all the elation and anxieties accompanying such awareness. As a number of our annotated books indicate, theories of "post-humanity" dovetail rather neatly with the preoccupations of many recent SF movies—conspicuously the nightmarish films of David Cronenberg, for example. Furthermore, the development of digital technology seems not only perfectly suited to represent SF worlds but is itself the thematic focus of a significant number of films, starting with *Dark City* (1998), *The Thirteenth Floor* (1999), and the *Matrix* trilogy (1999–2003).

SF films have won many Academy Awards for special effects and other technical work but only three major Oscars. Fredric March won Best Actor for *Dr. Jekyll and Mr. Hyde* (1932), Cliff Robertson Best Actor for *Charly* (1968), and Don Ameche Best Supporting Actor for *Cocoon* (1985). Major nominations went to *Jekyll/Hyde* (1932) for Best Screenplay; *The Man in the White Suit* (1952), Screenplay; *Dr. Strangelove* (1964), Best Picture, Director, Screenplay, and Actor; *2001* (1969), Director and Screenplay; *A Clockwork Orange* (1971), Picture and Director; *Young Frankenstein* (1974), Screenplay; *Star Wars* (1977), Picture, Director, Screenplay, and Supporting Actor; *Close Encounters* (1977), Director and Supporting Actress; *The Boys from Brazil* (1978), Actor; *The China Syndrome* (1978), Actor, Actress, and Screenplay; *E.T.* (1982), Picture, Director, and Screenplay; *Testament* (1983), Actress; *War Games* (1983), Screenplay; *Starman* (1984), Actor; *Brazil* (1985), Screenplay; *Back to the Future* (1985), Screenplay; *Aliens* (1986), Actress; the science fact drama *Apollo 13* (1995), Picture, Supporting Actor, Supporting Actress, and Screenplay; and *The Truman Show* (1998), Director, Supporting Actor, and Screenplay.

SF on Television

SF television has typically had some of the same preoccupations as SF cinema, but in turning briefly to TV we must recognize that the predominant subgenres—in regard to both format and subject matter—have been quite different. One distinctive TV format is the anthology series: both the weird tale show with some episodes qualifying as SF—*The Twilight Zone* (1959–1964, 1985–1986) is of course the leading example—and the more strictly SF anthology series. The latter is more rare, but such programs have had an important place in SF TV history, beginning with *Tales of Tomorrow* (1951–1953) and the "harder" science of *Science Fiction Theatre* (1955–1957) and continuing with various incarnations of *The Outer Limits* (1963–1965, 1995–2001). For shows with a continuing cast of characters, one can distinguish between those with discrete episodes that can be replayed in any order (like the original *Star Trek*) and those that are more like an ongoing saga, i.e., leaning toward soap opera, with not only evolving character relationships but sometimes "arcs" of several episodes (such as *Star Trek: Deep Space 9*). The latter type is more typical of contemporary television series. (For more on the subject, see the introduction to Tulloch/Alvarado [11-78].)

Taking an alternative approach to SF TV categories, we can first look across the hazy border separating SF and fantasy to the perennially popular comedies of visiting aliens, from *My Favorite Martian* (1963–1966) through *Third Rock from the Sun* (1996–2001). In the category of animation we cannot overlook *The Jetsons* (1963–1968) and *Futurama* (1999–2003), along with Japanese or Japanese-style Saturday-morning and cable animes. The British fondly remember several

SF puppet shows of the 1960s. Among live-figure serious dramas we can find the occasional show derived from a recent trend in SF literature and film, though these rarely last more than a few episodes: for example, the cyberpunk *Max Headroom* (1987, based on a 1985 British TV movie); the virtual reality/conspiracy theory *VR5* (1995); and the longer-lived James Cameron project *Dark Angel* (2000–2002), which featured illicit government genetic engineering within a dystopia. Alien invasion shows have sometimes been successful: examples include *V* (a miniseries in 1983, then a series in 1984–1985) and *The X-Files* (1993–2002), a hybrid narrative with linked SF episodes alternating with the weird tale or paranormal discrete episode, especially in the early seasons. Time-travel stories show up from time to time, if only because producers save money on special effects once the hero reaches the historical era of the week. These have varied from the mostly forgotten *The Time Tunnel* (1966–1967) to the very successful *Quantum Leap* (1989–1993) and to the unique phenomenon of *Doctor Who* (1963–1989), though the whimsical vehicle in the latter allowed as much space adventuring as time travel.

This brings us to what many consider the supreme category of SF TV, the space adventure saga. Such programs can be traced back to some of the earliest TV in any genre, *Captain Video* (1949–1955) and *Tom Corbett, Space Cadet* (1950–1952) and forward to *Babylon 5* (1993–1998) and the over-the-top *Farscape* (1999–2003), with the various *Star Trek* series dominating the whole category. Doubtless the episodic nature of the weekly series has suited the narrative of explorations, while the more "stationary" shows (*Babylon 5, Deep Space 9*) have some of the story patterns of soap opera.

As the longest-lived TV cult phenomenon in any genre, topping even *Doctor Who, Star Trek* deserves special attention—and indeed, has received it, from academics [11-64 ff.], the popular press with its guides [11-70] and spinoff novels, the motion picture industry (10 features to date), other media, and of course fans, whose conventions and Web sites are legendary. Any one of the five series to date provides a compendium of SF themes, from alternate universes to virtual realities, with each spinoff through *Star Trek: Voyager* (1995–2001) becoming increasingly self-conscious of its place not only in the *Star Trek* universe but in the history of SF. The word "saga" is often bandied about, but the *Star Trek* shows are genuinely comparable to those interlinking Norse cycles of familial, cosmological, and military drama.

SF has always been a commercially weak genre on network television, which until recently has required very large audiences for success. The number of people who could make a film a big hit was inadequate to keep a TV show alive. With the exception of Britain's *Doctor Who*, most SF TV shows have been short-lived. It is worth remembering that the original *Star Trek* series lasted only three years on NBC; its very successful reincarnation *Star Trek: The Next Generation* (1987–1994), flourished not on network TV but in the syndication market, less demanding of the highest ratings. In a sense *Next Generation* blazed a trail for new venues for TV shows, the smaller network (like UPN) and the cable channel (like TNT, which picked up the struggling *Babylon 5*). Today the Sci-Fi

Channel, though some SF enthusiasts still grimace at the name, serves an important function, premiering series such as *Farscape* and mini-series including *Dune* (2001), along with providing a haven for older shows in reruns and a very eclectic mix of SF, fantasy, and horror since it began in 1991.

In the introduction to their *Science Fiction Television Series* [11-77], Mark Philips and Frank Garcia noted that SF TV programs usually had "mediocre" ratings in their original runs but achieved a sort of afterlife denied to most other TV shows in fan clubs, conventions, video releases, and reruns on cable channels. Videorecordings and the insatiable need for programming on cable TV have given young fans the opportunity to become familiar with older genre films and TV programs. In 2002, Americans paid $20.3 billion to rent and buy DVDs and videocassettes and only $9.5 billion for film tickets. (They spent $6.9 billion on video games and computer games, which often have SF themes but are beyond the scope of this chapter.)

Today TV audiences are divided among dozens of cable channels (not to mention online diversions) and shows can survive with far fewer viewers than in the past. Of the recent SF cult series, *The X-Files* (1993–2002) was on Fox, the "fourth network"; *Babylon 5* (1994–1998) was in syndication; and *Farscape* (1999–2003) was on cable TV's Sci-Fi Channel.

SF on Radio and Audio Recordings

In our survey of SF media we should not neglect radio. In the 1930s and 1940s, radio programs such as *Buck Rogers, Flash Gordon,* and *Superman* helped to introduce the basic concepts of SF to both juvenile and adult audiences. However, in his *Tune In Yesterday* (1976), John Dunning notes that "Until the premiere of *Dimension X* (1950)—a full two decades after network radio was established—there were no major science fiction series of broad appeal to adults." Table 11-5 is a list of U.S. SF radio programs. Radio Spirits (www.radiospirits.com) sells recordings of vintage radio programs, including *The Adventures of Superman, Tom Corbett Space Cadet, Dimension X, X Minus One,* and the 1938 Orson Welles broadcast of *War of the Worlds.* Today SF is popular on "audiobooks," spoken recordings on audiocassettes, and increasingly on compact discs. These works are reviewed in *Library Journal* and *Booklist.* Bowker's new *Books Out Loud* (2004–) lists all current spoken tapes and CDs (105,000 in the 2004 edition), both fiction and nonfiction. The subject–genre index lists hundreds of tapes in the fantasy and science fiction category.

The Study of SF in the Media

Considering the prominence of SF cinema ever since the late 1970s, and the continuing fascination that certain TV shows hold for both fans and academics, it is hardly surprising that the number of books on these subjects has greatly increased since the fourth (1995) edition of *Anatomy of Wonder.* Earlier books on SF films, such as John Baxter's *Science Fiction in the Cinema* (1970), tended to be illustrated histories for a popular audience; *Focus on the Science Fiction Film* (1972) [11-39] was one of the earliest collections designed primarily for the college student. It is significant that these works appeared in the years following the success of *2001: A Space Odyssey*, a film whose sophistication in theme, narrative, and special effects artistry made SF movies of less than a decade earlier seem "historical." *Star Wars* and *Close Encounters* created yet another "distancing" from the past, and there soon followed a pioneering academic study, Vivian Sobchak's *The Limits of Infinity: The American Science Fiction Film* (1980), with its focus on genre conventions—visual and auditory—of the SF film. A measure of developments in SF film studies was the fact that only seven years later, Sobchak published a second edition, now called *Screening Space* [11-12], which featured a lengthy new chapter making use of Fredric Jameson's celebrated 1984 article "Postmodernism, or the Cultural Logic of Late Capitalism." Around the same time, influential articles on *Blade Runner, Star Trek*, and certain other works were appearing in *Science Fiction Studies*; some of these and others were collected in Annette Kuhn's *Alien Zone* [11-41], the next academic volume to set a standard for later studies. Since the mid-1990s the field has greatly proliferated, as even a cursory glance at our annotations will indicate. Curiously, there have been fewer popular general illustrated histories comparable to those of the 1970s. Perhaps potential buyers of coffee table books are more interested in their particular favorites, whether *Star Wars*, James Bond [see 11-24], or *The Matrix* [11-37], or in the ever-more-sophisticated techniques of special effects [11-21], rather than in SF cinema or television as a whole. In any case, the wide variety of new books for many SF niches—along with the insatiable need for programming on cable TV and the easy availability on DVD of not only the latest hits but older films dating back to the silents, foreign films, serials, representative episodes of old TV shows, and deluxe editions of complete series—indicates that SF in the media is thriving as never before.

Our thanks go to Rob Latham, who contributed five annotations (11-12, 41, 43, 54, and 57, marked "RL") to this chapter.

Table 11-1.   Best and/or Most Significant SF Films,
TV, and Radio Programs

All are U.S. feature films unless another nationality or form is stated.

Abbreviations—BA: Brian Aldiss; WA: Walter Albert; AC: Arthur C. Clarke; RC: Ramsey Campbell; NF: Nigel Floyd; DG: Denis Gifford; JG: James Gunn; PH: Phil Hardy; IMDb: ratings of 7.5+ by 1,000+ users on Internet Movie Database; AJ: Alan Jones; JJ: top 5 TV series picked by large jury in Javna [11-74], p. 7; SJ: Stefan Jaworzyn; SJo: Stephen Jones; MK: Michael Klossner; JM: Joe Milicia; TM: Tony Masters; TMi: Tom Milne; KN: Kim Newman; PN: Peter Nichols; DP: David Pirie; S/J: rated 8–10 by Senn/Johnson [11-4]; PT: Phil Taylor; BW: Bill Warren; WFF: World of Fantastic Films, ed. Nicholls [11-11], top three ratings (4, 4.5, 5) by jury

of Nicholls, Philip Strick, Tom Milne, Ramsey Campbell. All but JM, MK, JG, WA and those explained above are from the best-films list in Hardy [11-1], p. 461.
H: Hugo Award. This award is not shown for every year since its inception because no awards were made in some years, some Hugos went to non-SF titles, and some SF TV series received the Hugo more than one year.
Anim.: animated.

La lune à un mètre (alt. An Astronomer's Dream, France, short film, 1898) (JG)
Le voyage dans la lune (France, short film, 1902) (MK, JM, WFF)
She (short film, 1908) (JG)
A Trip to Mars (short film, 1910) (JG)
Aelita (USSR, 1924) (MK, JM)
The Lost World (1925) (S/J)
Metropolis (Germany, 1926) (BA, AC, NF, DG, IMDb, PH, MK, JM, S/J, WFF)
Die Frau im Mond (Germany, 1929) (JM)
Just Imagine (1930) (JG)
Frankenstein (1931) (AC, IMDb, SJ, JM, S/J, WFF)
Dr. Jekyll and Mr. Hyde (1932) (MK)
Island of Lost Souls (1932) (MK, S/J)
The Invisible Man (1933) (DG, IMDb, JM, KN, S/J, BW, WFF)
King Kong (1933) (AC, JM, PN)
Bride of Frankenstein (1935) (IMDb, MK, JM, S/J, PT, WFF)
She (1935) (JG)
Flash Gordon (serial film, 1936) (DG, PH, MK, JM)
Things to Come (U.K., 1936) (BA, AC, RC, DG, JM, SJ, SJo)
Lost Horizon (1937) (IMDb, JG)
War of the Worlds (radio broadcast, 1938) (MK, JM)
Buck Rogers (serial film, 1939) (JG)
Son of Frankenstein (1939) (S/J)
Superman (series of anim. shorts, 1941–1943) (MK)
Destination Moon (1950) (JM) (H)
Dimension X (radio series, 1950–1951) (MK)
Seven Days to Noon (U.K., 1950) (MK)
The Day the Earth Stood Still (1951) (AC, NF, IMDb, JM, S/J)
The Man in the White Suit (U.K., 1951) (WFF)
Tales of Tomorrow (TV series, 1951–1953) (MK, JM)
The Thing from Another World (1951) (AC, RC, PH, IMDb, MK, JM, KN, DP, S/J, WFF)
The Adventures of Superman (TV series, 1953–1957) (MK)
The Beast from 20,000 Fathoms (1953) (JM)
Duck Dodgers in the 24½ Century (anim. short, 1953) (IMDb, MK, JM)
Invaders from Mars (1953) (SJo, JM, PT)
It Came from Outer Space (1953) (SJ/JM)
War of the Worlds (1953) (DG, MK, JM, S/J, BW)
Gojira (alt. Godzilla, King of the Monsters) (Japan, 1954) (MK, JM)
1984 (U.K., TV film, 1954) (MK)
Them! (1954) (MK, DP, S/J)
20,000 Leagues Under the Sea (1954) (MK, JM)
Kiss Me Deadly (1955) (SJ, KN)
The Quatermass Experiment (U.K., 1955) (BW)
This Island Earth (1955) (JM, S/J)
Forbidden Planet (1956) (AC, RC, IMDb, MK, JM, TMi, PN, S/J, BW, WFF)

Invasion of the Body Snatchers (1956) (RC, NF, DG, IMDb, MK, JM, TMi, KN, DP, S/J, PT, BW, WFF)

Plan 9 from Outer Space (1956) (SJ)

The Curse of Frankenstein (U.K., 1957) (MK)

The Incredible Shrinking Man (1957) (RC, NF, IMDb, MK, JM, TMi, DP, S/J, PT, WFF) (H)

Not of This Earth (1957) (PH, PT)

Quatermass II (U.K., 1957) (NF, PH, MK, DP, BW)

The Fabulous World of Jules Verne (Czech, anim., 1958) (MK)

The Fly (1958) (JM, S/J)

Journey to the Center of the Earth (1959) (J/S)

On the Beach (1959) (TM)

The Twilight Zone (TV series, 1959–1964) (JJ, MK, JM) (H)

The Time Machine (1960) (MK)

Village of the Damned (U.K., 1960) (MK)

L'année dernière à Marienbad (France, 1961) (BA)

The Avengers (U.K., TV series, 1961–1969) (MK)

The Damned (U.K., 1961) (KN, WFF)

The Day the Earth Caught Fire (U.K., 1962) (MK)

Dr. No (U.K., 1962) (MK)

The Manchurian Candidate (1962) (KN)

Mothra (Japan, 1962) (MK)

The Birds (1963) (TM, S/J)

The Day of the Triffids (U.K., 1963) (JG)

Doctor Who (U.K., TV series, 1963–1989) (JJ, MK, JM)

La jetée (France, short film, 1963) (IMDb, JM, TMi)

The Nutty Professor (1963) (WFF)

The Outer Limits (TV series, 1963–1965) (JJ, MK, JM)

Dr. Strangelove (U.K., 1964) (BA, JM, KM, BW, WFF) (H)

Fail-Safe (1964) (IMDb, S/J)

Alphaville (France, 1965) (WFF, PH, TMi, DP)

Frankenstein Meets the Space Monster (Japan, 1965) (JH)

The War Game (U.K., 1965) (MK)

Fahrenheit 451 (U.K., 1966) (JM, TM, TMi)

Seconds (1966) (IMDb)

Star Trek (TV series, 1966–1969) (JJ, JM) (H)

Danger: Diabolik (Italy, 1967) (AJ)

Je t'aime, je t'aime (France, 1967) (TMi, WFF)

The Prisoner (U.K., TV series, 1967) (MK)

Quatermass and the Pit (U.K., 1967) (SJ, SJo, MK, JM, TM, BW)

Weekend (France, 1967) (WFF)

Barbarella (France/Italy, 1968) (WFF)

Charly (1968) (MK)

The Illustrated Man (1968) (TM)

Night of the Living Dead (1968) (IMDb, MK, S/J)

Planet of the Apes (1968) (IMDb, JM, TM, MK, S/J, WFF)

2001: A Space Odyssey (1968) (AC, RC, NF, DG, IMDb, AJ, MK, JM, TM, PN, DP, S/J, BW, WFF) (H)

Gladiatorerna (Sweden, 1969) (BA)

Gas-s-s-s (1970) (WFF)

Der Grosse Verhau (West Germany, 1970) (BA)

THX 1138 (1970) (JM, WFF)

A Clockwork Orange (U.K., 1971) (BA, IMDb, AJ, SJ, SJo, JM, TM, S/J, WFF) (H)

Silent Running (1971) (PH)
Solaris (USSR, 1971) (BA, IMDb, PN, WFF)
Slaughterhouse-Five (1972) (H)
Fantastic Planet (France, anim., 1973) (MK)
Sleeper (1973) (JM) (H)
The Submersion of Japan (Japan, 1973) (WFF)
Westworld (1973) (BA, DP, WFF)
Zardoz (1973) (JM, WFF)
Dark Star (1974) (RC, PH, TMi, PT, WFF)
The Parasite Murders (Canada, 1974) (PH, PN, PT)
Young Frankenstein (1974) (IMDb, S/J) (H)
A Boy and His Dog (1975) (WFF) (H)
Rollerball (1975) (S/J)
The Man Who Fell to Earth (U.K., 1976) (NF, PH, JM, TMi, KN, PN, BW)
Capricorn One (1977) (BW)
Close Encounters of the Third Kind (1977) (AC, RC, DG, IMDb, JM, TM, PN, DP,
    S/J, BW, WFF)
Demon Seed (1977) (AJ)
Star Wars (1977) (DG, IMDb, AJ, SJo, MK, JM, S/J, BW, WFF) (H)
Dawn of the Dead (1978) (IMDb, MK)
Eraserhead (1978) (MK)
The Hitchhiker's Guide to the Galaxy (U.K., radio series, 1978) (JM)
Invasion of the Body Snatchers (1978) (BW)
Superman: The Movie (1978) (DG, DP) (H)
Alien (1979) (BA, AC, IMDb, AJ, MK, JM, TM, DP, S/J, WFF) (H)
The Brood (Canada, 1979) (PN, WFF)
Mad Max (Australia, 1979) (WFF)
Quintet (1979) (TMi, WFF)
Stalker (USSR, 1979) (IMDb, RC)
Star Trek: The Motion Picture (1979) (JM)
Altered States (1980) (JM)
Star Wars: The Empire Strikes Back (1980) (IMDb, JM, S/J, BW, WFF) (H)
Superman II (1980) (WFF)
The Hitch Hiker's Guide to the Galaxy (U.K., TV series, 1981) (JJ) (BSFA)
Mad Max II: The Road Warrior (Australia, 1981) (AJ, SJ, MK, JM, S/J, PT, WFF)
Time Bandits (1981) (U.K., 1981) (MK, JM)
Android (1982) (PT, WFF)
Blade Runner (1982) (AC, NF, IMDb, AJ, SJ, SJo, JM, PN, BW, WFF) (H)
E.T., the Extra-Terrestrial (1982) (IMDb, JM, WFF)
Star Trek: The Wrath of Khan (1982) (IMDb)
The Thing (1982) (IMDb, SJ, SJo, PN, S/J, WFF)
Tron (1982) (JM)
Videodrome (Canada, 1982) (AJ, SJ, PN, WFF)
The Day After (TV film, 1983) (JG)
The Dead Zone (1983) (JG)
Star Wars: Return of the Jedi (1983) (IMDb, S/J, BW) (H)
Strange Invaders (1983) (JM, PN, WFF)
V (TV miniseries, 1983) (IMDb)
Dune (1984) (SJo, JM)
Iceman (1984) (JG)
Nausicaä (alt. Warriors of the Wind) (Japan, anim., 1984) (IMDb, MK)
1984 (U.K., 1984) (S/J)
Repo Man (1984) (JG, JM)

The Terminator (1984) (IMDb, MK, JM, KN, S/J)
Trancers (1984) (KN)
2010 (1984) (H)
Back to the Future (1985) (IMDb, SJo, JM) (H)
Brazil (U.K., 1985) (IMDb, NF, JM)
Cocoon (1985) (JG)
Aliens (1986) (NF, IMDb, SJo, MK, JM) (H)
The Fly (1986) (RC, S/J)
Invaders from Mars (1986) (JG)
Peggy Sue Got Married (1986) (JG)
InnerSpace (1987) (JG)
Predator (1987) (JG)
Robocop (1987) (AJ, JM, S/J)
Star Trek: The Next Generation (TV series, 1987–1994) (JM) (H)
Akira (Japan, anim., 1988) (IMDb, MK, JM)
Alien Nation (1988) (JG)
The Navigator (New Zealand, 1988) (MK)
Abyss (1989) (JG)
Honey, I Shrunk the Kids (1989) (JG)
Quantum Leap: Genesis (TV film, 1989) (IMDb)
Red Dwarf (U.K., TV series, 1989) (MK, JM)
Edward Scissorhands (1990) (H)
Night of the Living Dead (1990) (S/J)
Delicatessen (France, 1991) (IMDb)
Terminator 2: Judgment Day (1991) (IMDb, JM) (H)
Jurassic Park (1993) (JM) (H)
Star Trek: Deep Space 9 (TV series, 1993–1999) (JM)
The X-Files (TV series, 1993–2002) (IMDb, JM)
Babylon 5 (TV series, 1994–1998) (JM) (H)
La cité des enfants perdus (France, 1995) (IMDb, MK)
Star Trek: Voyager (TV series, 1995–2001) (JM)
Twelve Monkeys (1995) (IMDb, JM)
Ghost in the Shell (Japan, anim., 1996) (IMDb)
Star Trek: First Contact (1996) (JM)
Abre los Ojos [alt. Open Your Eyes] (Spain, 1997) (IMDb)
Contact (1997) (H)
Gattaca (1997) (IMDb, JM)
Dark City (1998) (IMDb, JM)
Pi (1998) (IMDb)
The Truman Show (1998) (IMDb, JM) (H)
Farscape (TV series, 1999–2003) (JM)
Galaxy Quest (1999) (JM) (H)
The Iron Giant (anim., 1999) (IMDb, MK)
The Matrix (1999) (IMDb, JM)
Vampire Hunter D: Bloodlust (Japan, anim., 2000) (IMDb)
Cowboy Bebop: The Movie (Japan, anim., 2001) (IMDb)
Donnie Darko (2001) (IMDb)
Samurai Jack (anim. TV series, 2001–) (WA)
The Adventures of Jimmie Neutron, Boy Genius (anim. TV series, 2002–) (WA)
Equilibrium (2002) (IMDb)
Lilo & Stitch (anim., 2002) (MK)
Minority Report (2002) (IMDb, JM)

Neon Genesis Evangelion (alt. The End of Evangelion, Japan, anim., 2002)
(IMDb)
Spider-Man (2002) (IMDb)
Taken (TV miniseries, 2002) (IMDb)
28 Days Later (U.K., 2002) (MK)
Animatrix: The Final Flight of the Osiris (anim., 2003) (IMDb)
X-2 (2003) (IMDb)

Table 11-2. SF Film Production, 1895–2003

	1895–1949	1950–1957	1958–1967	1968–1976	1977–1990	1991–2003	Total
Years	55	8	10	9	14	13	109
Films (a)	365	150	334	220	415	399 (d)	1,883
Films/year	6.64	18.75	33.4	24.44	29.64	30.69	17.27
11-1 U.S. Films (b)	16	17	8	16	44	19	120
11-1 U.K. films (b)	1	5	9	2	3	1	21
11-1 other films (b)	5	1	9	7	8	7	37
11-1 all films (b)	22	23	26	25	55	27	178
11-1 TV (b)	—	3	6	—	6	8	23
11-1 radio (b)	1	1	—	—	1	—	3
11-1 all titles (b)	23	27	32	25	62	35	204
11-1 4+ titles (c)	6	7	4	6	12	0	35

(a) all films listed in Hardy [11-1].
(b) from Table 11-1.
(c) 11-1 4+ = titles from Table 11-1 with four or more votes or awards.
(d) See introduction for explanation of 1991–2003 IMDb search.

Table 11-3. Top SF Box-Office Films

Title, Year	Box-Office $ (thousands)	Rank
Star Wars, 1977	460,935	2
E.T., the Extra-Terrestrial, 1982	434,949	3
Star Wars, The Phantom Menace, 1999	431,065	4
Spider-Man, 2002	403,706	5
Jurassic Park, 1993	356,763	7
Star Wars, Attack of the Clones, 2002	310,675	14
Star Wars, Return of the Jedi, 1983	309,064	15
Independence Day, 1996	306,200	16
Star Wars, The Empire Strikes Back, 1980	290,158	19
The Matrix Reloaded, 2003	281,492	21
Batman, 1989	251,188	27
Men in Black, 1997	250,147	28
The Lost World, Jurassic Park, 1997	229,074	37
Signs, 2002	227,965	38

Title, Year	Box-Office $ (thousands)	Rank
X2, 2003	214,948	45
Back to the Future, 1985	210,609	47
Terminator 2: Judgment Day, 1991	204,843	49
Armageddon, 1998	201,600	52
Men in Black II, 2002	190,418	57
Batman Forever, 1995	184,013	61
Jurassic Park III, 2001	181,166	68
Planet of the Apes, 2001	180,011	70
Apollo 13, 1995	172,100	82
The Matrix, 1999	171,383	83
Batman Returns, 1992	162,831	95
Die Another Day, 2002	160,201	98
X-Men, 2000	157,175	101
Terminator 3: Rise of the Machines, 2003	150,350	113
Lilo & Stitch, 2002	145,771	118
Deep Impact, 1998	140,387	132
The Matrix Revolutions, 2003	139,224	137
Godzilla, 1998	136,142	144
Teenage Mutant Ninja Turtles, 1990	135,265	146
Superman, 1978	134,218	150
Hulk, 2003	132,122	155
Minority Report, 2002	132,014	156
Honey, I Shrunk the Kids, 1989	130,724	159
The Nutty Professor, 1996	128,769	164
Close Encounters of the Third Kind, 1977	128,290	166
The World Is Not Enough, 1999	126,930	172
The Truman Show, 1998	126,466	176
Tomorrow Never Dies, 1997	125,332	180
Nutty Professor II: The Klumps, 2000	123,307	186
Total Recall, 1990	119,394	199
Back to the Future Part II, 1989	118,500	202
Big, 1988	114,968	217
Wild Wild West, 1999	113,745	218
Spy Kids, 2001	112,692	222
Spy Kids 3-D: Game Over, 2003	111,760	227
Star Trek IV, The Voyage Home, 1986	109,713	233
Superman II, 1980	108,185	241
Batman & Robin, 1997	107,285	244
Golden Eye, 1995	106,635	247
Phenomenon, 1996	104,632	260
Daredevil, 2003	102,543	271
Contact, 1997	100,850	285

Source: *Internet Movie Database*, Feb. 23, 2004. The figures are box-office receipts, not rentals to studios, for the U.S. and Canada only, not adjusted for inflation. Rank is the film's ranking among box-office champions of all genres.

Table 11-3 reminds us that several of the most popular films ever made have been SF. However, a list in the Feb. 22, 1993, issue of *Variety*, which breaks down film rentals by decade, shows that SF was far less popular than other genres during the supposed golden age of SF films in the 1950s. Of 253 films that made $3 million or more in rentals during the 1950s, only two (both based on a Jules Verne romance) were SF—Disney's *20,000 Leagues Under the Sea* (1952, in 20th place for the decade with $11,267,000) and *Journey to the Center of the Earth* (1959, in 98th place with $4,777,000). *20,000 Leagues* and *Forbidden Planet* (1956) were the two big-budget SF films of the decade. In the 1960s, of 146 films that made $6 million or more in rentals, the only SF films (aside from several James Bond movies) were *2001* (1968, 12th place, $25,522,000), *Planet of the Apes* (1968, 39th place, $15,000,000), and two Disney comedies, *The Love Bug* (1969, 14th place, $23,150,000) and *The Absent-Minded Professor* (1961, 56th place, $11,426,000). SF films were commercially important only after 1975.

Table 11-4. SF Films and Their Literary Sources

Film title, Year	*Author, title (if different)*
The Absent-Minded Professor, 1961	Taylor, Samuel W. "A Situation of Gravity"
Aelita, 1924	Tolstoy, Alexei
AI: Artificial Intelligence, 2001	Aldiss, Brian, "Supertoys Last All Summer Long"
Alien, 1979	(see note A below)
Alraune, 1928, 1930, 1952	Ewers, Hans Heinz
Altered States, 1980	Chayefsky, Paddy
The Amphibious Man, 1961	Belyayev, Alexander
The Andromeda Nebula, 1968	Efremov, Ivan
The Andromeda Strain, 1970	Crichton, Michael
At the Earth's Core, 1976	Burroughs, Edgar Rice. *Pellucidar*
L'Atlantide, 1932, 1961	Benoit, Pierre
Atlantis the Lost Continent, 1960	Hargreaves, Gerald. *Atalanta* (play)
The Awful Dr. Orloff, 1962	Kuhne, David
Battlefield Earth, 2000	Hubbard, L. Ron
The Beast from 20,000 Fathoms, 1953	Bradbury, Ray. "The Foghorn"
The Bed Sitting Room, 1969	Antrobus, John, and Spike Milligan (play)
Below the Belt, 2004	Dresser, Richard (play)
Bicentennial Man, 1999	Asimov, Isaac
Biggles, 1986	Johns, W. E. (several *Biggles* novels)
Billion Dollar Brain, 1967	Deighton, Len
The Birds, 1963	Du Maurier, Daphne
The Black Oxen, 1924	Atherton, Gertrude
Blade Runner, 1982	Dick, Philip K. *Do Androids Dream of Electric Sheep?*
A Blind Bargain, 1922	Pain, Barry. *Octave of Claudius*
Body Snatchers, 1993	Finney, Jack
A Boy and His Dog, 1975	Ellison, Harlan
The Boys from Brazil, 1978	Levin, Ira
The Brain, 1962	Siodmak, Curt. *Donovan's Brain*
The Brain Eaters, 1958	Heinlein, Robert. *The Puppet Masters*
Bug, 1975	Page, Thomas. *The Hephaestus Plague*

Film title, Year	Author, title (if different)
Carnosaur, 1993	Knight, Harry Adam (pseud. of John Brosnan)
The Chairman, 1969	Kennedy, Jay Richard
Charly, 1969	Keyes, Daniel. *Flowers for Algernon*
Children of the Damned, 1963	Wyndham, John. *The Midwich Cuckoos*
A Clockwork Orange, 1971	Burgess, Anthony
Colossus, the Forbin Project, 1971	Jones, D. F. *Colossus*
Coma, 1978	Cook, Robin
Communion, 1989	Strieber, Whitley (nonfiction)
Condorman, 1981	Sheckley, Robert. *The Game of X*
Congo, 1995	Crichton, Michael
A Connecticut Yankee, 1931	Twain, Mark
A Connecticut Yankee in King Arthur's Court, 1949	Twain, Mark
The Conquest of Space, 1955	Ley, Willy, and Chesley Bonestell (nonfiction)
Contact, 1997	Sagan, Carl
Countdown, 1968	Searls, Hank. *The Pilgrim Project*
The Curse of Frankenstein, 1957	Shelley, Mary. *Shelley*
Damnation Alley, 1977	Zelazny, Roger
The Damned, 1961	Lawrence, H. L. *The Children of Light*
Day of the Dolphin, 1973	Merle, Robert
Day of the Triffids, 1963	Wyndham, John
The Day the Earth Stood Still, 1951	Bates, Harry. "Farewell to the Master"
Dead-End Drive-In, 1986	Carey, Peter. "Crabs"
The Dead Mountaineer Hotel, 1979	Strugatsky, Boris and Arkady
The Dead Zone, 1983	King, Stephen
Death Race 2000, 1975	Melchior, Ib. "The Racer"
Deluge, 1933	Wright, S. Fowler
Demon Seed, 1977	Koontz, Dean S.
Destination Moon, 1950	Heinlein, Robert. *Rocket Ship Galileo*
The Devil Commands, 1941	Sloane, William. *The Edge of Running Water*
Devil Girl from Mars, 1954	Maher, John H., and James Eastwood (play)
Diamonds Are Forever, 1971	Fleming, Ian
Die, Monster, Die, 1965	Lovecraft, H. P. "The Colour out of Space"
Doc Savage, the Man of Bronze, 1975	Robeson, Kenneth
Dr. Jekyll and Mr. Hyde, 1920, 1932, 1941	Stevenson, Robert Louis
Dr. Jekyll and Sister Hyde, 1972	Stevenson, Robert Louis. *Dr. Jekyll and Mr. Hyde*
Dr. Mabuse, the Gambler, 1922	Jacques, Norbert
Dr. No, 1962	Fleming, Ian
Dr. Strangelove, 1964	George, Peter. *Red Alert*
Donovan's Brain, 1953	Siodmak, Curt
Don't Play with the Martians, 1967	Labry, Michel. *Les Sextuplets de Loqmaria*
Dreamcatcher, 2003	King, Stephen
Dune, 1984	Herbert, Frank

Film title, Year	Author, title (if different)
Earth vs. the Flying Saucers, 1956	Keyhoe, Donald. *Flying Saucers from Outer Space* (nonfiction)
The Electronic Monster, 1957	Maine, Charles Eric. *Escapement*
Empire of the Ants, 1977	Wells, H. G.
Enemy Mine, 1985	Longyear, Barry
Engineer Garin's Death Ray, 1965	Tolstoy, Alexei. *The Garin Death Ray*
Escape to Witch Mountain, 1975	Key, Alexander
The Eye Creatures, 1965	Fairman, Paul W. "The Cosmic Frame"
The Fabulous World of Jules Verne, 1958	Verne, Jules. *Facing the Flag*
The Face of Fu Manchu, 1965	Rohmer, Sax
Fahrenheit 451, 1966	Bradbury, Ray
Fail-Safe, 1964	Burdick, Eugene, and Harvey Wheeler
Fantastic Planet, 1973	Wul, Stefan. *Oms en Serie*
Fiend Without a Face, 1958	Long, Amelia Reynolds. "The Thought Monster"
The Final Programme, 1973	Moorcock, Michael
Firefox, 1982	Thomas, Craig
Firestarter, 1984	King, Stephen
The First Men in the Moon, 1964	Wells, H. G.
First Spaceship on Venus, 1960	Lem, Stanislaw. *The Astronauts*
The Fly, 1958, 1986	Langelaan, George
Food of the Gods, 1976	Wells, H. G.
Forbidden Planet, 1956	Shakespeare, William. *The Tempest* (play)
Four-Sided Triangle, 1953	Temple, William F.
F.P.1 Doesn't Answer, 1932	Siodmak, Curt
Frankenstein, 1931, 1994	Shelley, Mary
Frankenstein Unbound, 1990	Aldiss, Brian; Shelley, Mary. *Frankenstein*
Freejack, 1992	Sheckley, Robert. *Immortality Inc.*
Friendship's Death, 1987	Wollen, Peter
From the Earth to the Moon, 1958	Verne, Jules
Give Us the Moon, 1944	Brahms, Caryl, and S. J. Simon. *The Elephant Is White*
The Gladiator, 1938	Wylie, Philip
Goldfinger, 1964	Fleming, Ian
The Handmaid's Tale, 1990	Atwood, Margaret
The Hands of Orlac, 1925	Renard, Maurice
Hard to Be a God, 1989	Strugatsky, Boris and Arkady
High Crusade, 1994	Anderson, Poul
High Treason, 1929	Pemberton-Billing, Noel (play)
Homunculus, 1916	Reinert, Robert
I, Monster, 1971	Stevenson, R. L. *Dr. Jekyll and Mr. Hyde*
I, Robot, 2004	Asimov, Isaac
The Illustrated Man, 1969	Bradbury, Ray
Impostor, 2002	Dick, Philip K.
The Incredible Shrinking Man, 1957	Matheson, Richard. *The Shrinking Man*
The Incredible Shrinking Woman, 1981	Matheson, Richard. *The Shrinking Man*
Invasion of the Body Snatchers, 1956, 1978	Finney, Jack. *The Body Snatchers*

Film title, Year	Author, title (if different)
Invasion of the Saucermen, 1957	Fairman, Paul W. "The Cosmic Frame"
The Invisible Boy, 1957	Cooper, Edmund
The Invisible Man, 1933	Wells, H. G.
The Iron Giant, 1999	Hughes, Ted
The Island at the Top of the World, 1974	Cameron, Ian. *The Lost Ones*
The Island of Dr. Moreau, 1977, 1996	Wells, H. G.
The Island of Lost Souls, 1932	Wells, H. G. *The Island of Dr. Moreau*
Island of the Burning Damned, 1967	Lymington, John. *Night of the Big Heat*
It's Alive, 1968	Matheson, Richard. *Being*
It's Great to Be Alive, 1933	Swain, John D.
Johnny Mnemonic, 1995	Gibson, William
Journey to the Center of the Earth, 1959	Verne, Jules
Jurassic Park, 1993	Crichton, Michael
K-PAX, 2001	Brewer, Gene
Kiss Me Deadly, 1955	Spillane, Mickey
Krakatit, 1948	Čapek, Karel
The Lady and the Monster, 1944	Siodmak, Curt. *Donovan's Brain*
The Last Man on Earth, 1923	Swain, John D.
The Last Man on Earth, 1964	Matheson, Richard. *I Am Legend*
The Lawnmower Man, 1992	King, Stephen
Lifeforce, 1985	Wilson, Colin. *The Space Vampire*
Light Years, 1968	Andrevan, Jean-Pierre. *Robots Against Gandahar*
Logan's Run, 1976	Nolan, William F., and George Clayton Johnson
Lord of the Flies, 1963, 1990	Golding, William
The Lost Continent, 1968	Wheatley, Dennis. *Uncharted Seas*
Lost Horizon, 1937, 1973	Hilton, James
The Lost World, 1925, 1960	Doyle, Arthur Conan
Mad Love, 1935	Renard, Maurice. *The Hands of Orlac*
Malevil, 1981	Merle, Robert
The Man and the Beast, 1951	Stevenson, Robert Louis. *Dr. Jekyll and Mr. Hyde*
The Man in the White Suit, 1951	MacDougall, Roger (play)
The Man Who Could Work Miracles, 1936	Wells, H. G. "The Man Who Had to Sing"
The Man Who Fell to Earth, 1976	Tevis, Walter
The Man Who Thought Life, 1969	Holst, Valdemar
The Man with the Golden Gun, 1974	Fleming, Ian
The Manchurian Candidate, 1962	Condon, Richard
Marooned, 1969	Caidin, Martin
Martians Go Home, 1990	Brown, Fredric
Mary Shelley's Frankenstein, 1994	Shelley, Mary. *Frankenstein*
The Mask of Fu Manchu, 1932	Rohmer, Sax
Master of the World, 1961	Verne, Jules. *Master of the World* and *Robur the Conqueror*
The Masters of Time, 1982	Wul, Stefan. *L'Orphelin de Perdide*
Maximum Overdrive, 1986	King, Stephen. "Trucks"

Film title, Year	Author, title (if different)
The Maze, 1953	Sandoz, Maurice
Memoirs of a Survivor, 1981	Lessing, Doris
The Memoirs of an Invisible Man, 1992	Saint, H. F.
A Message from Mars, 1913, 1921	Ganthony, Richard (play)
Metropolis, 1926	Von Harbou, Thea
Millennium, 1989	Varley, John. "Air Raid"
Mimic, 1997	Wollheim, Donald A.
The Mind of Mr. Soames, 1970	Maine, Charles Eric
Minority Report, 2002	Dick, Philip K.
Moebius, 1996	Deutsch, A. J., "A Subway Named Möbius"
La mort en direct (alt. Deathwatch), 1980	Compton, David. *Unsleeping Eye*
The Most Dangerous Man Alive, 1958	Rock, Philip, and Michael Pate, "The Steel Monster"
The Mysterians, 1957	Okami, Jojiro
Mysterious Island, 1929, 1961	Verne, Jules
Naked Lunch, 1991	Burroughs, William S.
The Navy vs. the Night Monsters, 1965	Leister, Murray. *The Monsters from Earth's End*
Never Say Never Again, 1983	Fleming, Ian
Nightfall, 1988	Asimov, Isaac
Nightflyers, 1987	Martin, George R. R.
1984, 1956, 1984	Orwell, George
No Blade of Grass, 1970	Christopher, John. *The Death of Grass*
No Escape, 1994	Herley, Richard
The Nutty Professor, 1963	Stevenson, R. L. *Dr. Jekyll and Mr. Hyde*
The Omega Man, 1971	Matheson, Richard. *I Am Legend*
On Her Majesty's Secret Service, 1969	Fleming, Ian
On the Beach, 1959	Shute, Nevil
On the Comet, 1970	Verne, Jules. *Hector Servadac*
Panic in Year Zero, 1962	Moore, Ward. "Lot," "Lot's Daughter"
Parasite Eve, 1997	Sena, Hideaki
Paycheck, 2004	Dick, Philip K.
The Perfect Woman, 1949	Geoffrey, Wallace, and Basil Mitchell (play)
Perry Rhodan-SOS, 1967	Ernsting, Walter
The Philadelphia Experiment, 1984	Moore, William I., and Charles Berlitz (nonfiction)
Planet of the Apes, 1968, 2001	Boulle, Pierre
The Postman, 1997	Brin, David
The Power, 1967	Robinson, Frank M.
Project X, 1967	Davies, Leslie P. *The Artificial Man* and *Psychogeist*
Proteus, 1995	Brosnan, John
The Puppet Masters, 1994	Heinlein, Robert A.
Quest for Fire, 1981	Rosny, J. H.
Quest for Love, 1971	Wyndham, John. "Random Quest"
The Quiet Earth, 1985	Harrison, Craig
The Ravagers, 1979	Alter, Robert E. *Path to Savagery*
Red Planet Mars, 1952	Balderson, John L., and John Hoare.

Film title, Year	Author, title (if different)
	Red Planet (play)
The Return of Dr. X, 1939	Makin, William J. "The Doctor's Secret"
The Riddle of the Sands, 1979	Childers, Erskine
Robinson Crusoe on Mars, 1964	Defoe, Daniel. *Robinson Crusoe*
Rollerball, 1975, 2002	Harrison, William. "Rollerball Murders"
The Running Man, 1987	King, Stephen
The Satan Bug, 1965	MacLean, Alistair
Saturn 3, 1980	Barry, John
Scream and Scream Again, 1969	Saxon, Peter. *The Disoriented Man*
Screamers, 1995	Dick, Philip K. "Second Variety"
Seconds, 1966	Ely, David
The Secret of NIMH, 1982	O'Brien, Robert C. *Mrs. Frisby and the Rats of NIMH*
She, 1908, 1917, 1926, 1935, 1965	Haggard, H. Rider
She Devil, 1957	Weinbaum, Stanley G. "The Adaptive Ultimate"
Sinners in Silk, 1924	Glazer, Benjamin
Siren of Atlantis, 1949	Benoit, Pierre. *L'Atlantide*
Six Hours to Live, 1932	Morris, Gordon, and Morton Barteaux, "Auf Wiedersehen"
Skeleton on Horseback, 1937	Čapek, Karel. *The White Disease* (play)
Slapstick of Another Kind, 1984	Vonnegut, Kurt. *Slapstick*
Slaughterhouse-Five, 1972	Vonnegut, Kurt
Solaris, 1971, 2001	Lem, Stanislaw
Solo, 1996	Mason, Robert
Somewhere in Time, 1980	Matheson, Richard
Soylent Green, 1973	Harrison, Harry. *Make Room, Make Room*
Sphere, 1998	Crichton, Michael
The Spy Who Loved Me, 1977	Fleming, Ian
Stalker, 1979	Strugatsky, Boris and Arkady. *Roadside Picnic*
Starship Troopers, 1997	Heinlein, Robert A.
The Stepford Wives, 1974	Levin, Ira
The Submersion of Japan, 1973	Komatsu, Sakyo. *Japan Sinks*
The Swarm, 1978	Herzog, Arthur
Target Earth!, 1954	Fairman, Paul W. "Deadly City"
The Tenth Victim, 1965	Sheckley, Robert. "The Seventh Victim"
The Terminal Man, 1974	Crichton, Michael
The Terminator, 1984	(see note B below)
The Terronauts, 1967	Leinster, Murray. *The Wailing Asteroid*
Test Pilot Pirx, 1978	Lem, Stanislaw. "Inquiry"
Testament, 1983	Amen, Carol. "The Last Testament"
Them!, 1954	Yates, George W.
They Came from Beyond Space, 1967	Millard, Joseph. *The Gods Hate Kansas*
They Live, 1988	Nelson, Ray. "Eight O'Clock in the Morning"
The Thing, 1951, 1982	Campbell, John W. "Who Goes There?"
Things to Come, 1936	Wells, H. G.
The Thirteenth Floor, 1999	Galouye, Daniel F.
This Island Earth, 1955	Jones, Raymond F.

Film title, Year	Author, title (if different)
Thunderball, 1965	Fleming, Ian
The Time Machine, 1960, 2002	Wells, H. G.
Timeline, 2003	Crichton, Michael
Timeslip, 1956	Maine, Charles Eric. *The Isotope Man*
Total Recall, 1990	Dick, Philip K. "We Can Remember It for You Wholesale"
Transatlantic Tunnel, 1935	Kellermann, Bernhard. *Der Tunnel*
Treasure Planet, 2002	Stevenson, R. L. *Treasure Island*
The 27th Day, 1957	Mantley, John
20,000 Leagues Under the Sea, 1916	Verne, Jules. *20,000 Leagues* and *Mysterious Island*
20,000 Leagues Under the Sea, 1954	Verne, Jules
The Two Faces of Dr. Jekyll, 1961	Stevenson, R. L. *Dr. Jekyll and Mr. Hyde*
2001: A Space Odyssey, 1968	Clarke, Arthur C. "The Sentinel"
2010, 1984	Clarke, Arthur C. *2010: Odyssey Two*
The Twonky, 1955	Kuttner, Henry
Unidentified Flying Oddball, 1979	Twain, Mark. *A Connecticut Yankee in King Arthur's Court*
Valley of the Dragons, 1961	Verne Jules. *Hector Servadac/Off on a Comet*
Vampire Hunter D, 1985, 2000	Kikuchi, Hideyuki
Village of the Damned, 1960, 1995	Wyndham, John. *The Midwich Cuckoos*
Village of the Giants, 1965	Wells, H. G. *Food of the Gods*
Virus, 1980	Komatsu, Sakyo
War of the Worlds, 1953	Wells, H. G.
Watchers, 1988	Koontz, Dean R.
When the Wind Blows, 1986	Briggs, Raymond
When Worlds Collide, 1951	Wylie, Philip, and Edwin Balmer
Who?, 1974	Budrys, Algis
Wild in the Streets, 1968	Thom, Robert. "The Day It All Happened Baby"
Woman in the Moon, 1929	Von Harbou, Thea. *By Rocket to the Moon*
The World, the Flesh and the Devil, 1959	Shiel, Matthew P. *The Purple Cloud*
The World Will Shake, 1939	Dumas, C. R., and R. F. Didelot. *La machine à predire la mort*
You Only Live Twice, 1967	Fleming, Ian
The Young Diana, 1922	Corelli, Maria

A. The producers of *Alien* made an out-of-court settlement with A. E. van Vogt for his story "The Black Destroyer," incorporated in his *The Voyage of the Space Beagle*. B. The makers of *The Terminator* were forced to "acknowledge the work of Harlan Ellison," including the story "I Have No Mouth and I Must Scream."

Anthology films, made-for-TV films and miniseries, films based on comic books and graphic novels, short films, and most sequels are excluded from this list. Most sources are "official." A few were established only by legal action after a film's release. Titles of novels are in italics; titles of shorter fiction are in quotes. Consult author index for annotated fiction.

Table 11-5. SF Radio Programs

1932–1940	Fu Manchu (supercriminal)
1932–1947	Buck Rogers in the Twenty-Fifth Century (& TV) *
1933–1950	Jack Armstrong, the All-American Boy (adventure, with some SF episodes)
1935–1936	Flash Gordon
1938	The War of the Worlds, episode of Mercury Theatre of the Air (the Mars panic broadcast) *
1938–1951	The Adventures of Superman (& TV) *
1938–1952	The Green Hornet (superhero)
1940–1941	Peter Quill (detective with SF gadgets)
1940–1949	Captain Midnight (adventure, with some SF episodes) (& TV)
1941	Latitude Zero
1945–1946	The Avenger (crime-fighting superhero)
1945–1947	Exploring the Unknown ("informative drama" about science)
1947–1954	Escape (adventure, with supernatural and SF episodes)
1950–1951	Dimension X *
1950–1951	2000 Plus
1950–1955	Space Patrol (& TV)
1951	Tom Corbett, Space Cadet (& TV)
1952–1953	The Space Adventures of Super Noodle (juvenile SF comedy)
1953	Tales of Tomorrow (& TV)
1954	Starr of Space
1955–1958	X Minus One
1957–1958	Exploring Tomorrow
1974–1977	CBS Mystery Theater (with SF, supernatural episodes)
1981	Star Wars (on National Public Radio) *
1989	Sci Fi Radio (NPR) *

U.S. programs only. This probably incomplete list is derived from Dunning, Lackmann, and Swartz/Reinehr [all under 11-69] and Clute/Nicholls's *Encyclopedia of Science Fiction* [7-21].

An asterisk (*) indicates a major program.

"(& TV)" means that a television series with the same or nearly the same title and premise existed, often many years later.

Bibliography

This section is divided into five groups: Reference Works on Films; General Studies of Films; Specialized Studies of Films; TV and Radio; and Periodicals.

Reference Works on Films

*11-1.   Hardy, Phil, ed. **The Overlook Film Encyclopedia: Science Fiction**. Overlook Press, 1994. 3rd ed.

Almost 1,500 entries arranged chronologically from 1895 to 1990 cover almost all English-language SF feature films and hundreds of silents (including short films) and foreign films. Annotations are unsigned; besides Hardy, contributors and their areas of expertise are Denis Gifford on silents; Anthony Masters, the 1950s; Paul Taylor, the 1970s and early 1980s; Paul Willemen, foreign films; and Kim Newman, 1985–1990. Entries include variant titles, running time, color or black-and-white, principal credits, and from 100 to 1,000 words of terse, highly erudite criticism. The title index, in tiny print, includes variant titles. More than 500 well-chosen black-and-white and a few dozen color illustrations supplement the text. Appendixes include box-office champions, best film lists by 17 experts (used in Tables 11-1 and 11-2), Oscar nominees and winners, and a selective bibliography. The most sophisticated critical reference work on the subject. [This note was based on the 1991 2nd edition. The 1994 3rd edition was not seen.] *The Encyclopedia of Science Fiction Movies* by C. J. Henderson (2001) updates Hardy's coverage but omits many foreign films found in Hardy; Henderson's annotations are often longer than those in Hardy but much less authoritative. Two books not primarily about films, *The Encyclopedia of Science Fiction*, edited by John Clute and others [7-21], and James Gunn's *New Encyclopedia of Science Fiction* [7-23], both include short articles surveying the history of SF on film, TV, and radio and brief critical notes on individual titles. Most of the more than 500 film entries in the *Encyclopedia* are by Clute and Peter Nicholls; most of the more than 200 film annotations in Gunn are by Bill Warren or Don Willis.

Online, the Internet Movie Database (http://us.imdb.com) is very complete and up to date and permits searching by date, nationality, genre, ratings, and numbers of users who rated a film, as well as cast members and other film workers. It is possible, for instance, to find all U.S. SF films released in 2003 that attracted 1,000 users' votes and were rated 7 or more on a scale of 1 to 10. The Encyclopedia of Fantastic Film and Television (www.eofftv.com), the result of more than 20 years' work by Kevin Lyons and Chris James, has very complete credits and, most valuably, references to magazines and books that discuss the films. The SF Site (www.sfsite.com) [8-8] and Magic Dragon Multimedia (www.magicdragon.com) cover both fiction and film/TV. The Science Fiction, Horror and Fantasy Film Review (www.roogulator.esmartweb.com) contains popular but respectable reviews of hundreds of films by Richard Scheib. (MK)

11-2. Lee, Walt. **Reference Guide to Fantastic Films: Science Fiction, Fantasy and Horror**. Chelsea-Lee Books, 1972–1974. 3 vols.

Many years of fan scholarship lie behind this compilation, the most complete filmography of fantastic films made before the 1970s. This reference includes many obscure, marginal, silent, short, foreign, animated, and juvenile titles not in other sources. About 15,000 films are arranged by title in three sturdy, 8½ x 11 inch paperbacks. Many entries are incomplete; complete entries provide date, country, length, and credits (including casts but not names of characters); a brief, non-evaluative note describing the film's fantastic elements (not a complete synopsis); and references to information (not necessarily reviews) found in hundreds of sources listed in the bibliography. About 5,000 more films are listed briefly as "exclusions" (films that appear to have fantastic elements but do not) and "problems" (for which sufficient information could not be found). The approximately 150 illustrations are mainly unfamiliar and interesting. (MK)

Awards: Special Hugo plaque

11-3. Lentz, Harris M. **Science Fiction, Horror and Fantasy Film and Television Credits**. McFarland, 2001. 2nd ed. 3 vols.

Volume 1 lists credits in genre films and TV programs for more than 10,000 actors, directors, producers, writers, cinematographers, special effects and makeup artists, and composers of film scores. Entries for actors include the names of characters portrayed. Volume 2 lists films, providing date, country, alternate titles, and casts. Volume 3 has titles, actors, character names, and broadcast dates for each episode of every fantastic TV series. This very complete work updates the 1983 first edition and 1989 and 1994 supplements. Anime (Japanese animation) is the only major omission. (MK)

11-4. Senn, Bryan, and John Johnson. **Fantastic Cinema Subject Guide: A Topical Index to 2,500 Horror, Science Fiction and Fantasy Films**. McFarland, 1992.

This much-needed guide arranges 2,500 films under 81 subject areas, such as Alien Invaders, Frankenstein, the Future, Mars, and Robots. Titles are listed alphabetically under each subject; chronological order would have been more illuminating. Entries include the film's principal credits and cast, a description emphasizing subject rather than plot, often ludicrous quotes from dialogue and film ads, and "interesting information" about the film's production and participants. The authors' often harsh critical opinions are relegated to a numerical rating system in the title index. Includes serial films, TV films and miniseries, and foreign films that have been dubbed or subtitled in English. The *Subject Guide* is less complete than other reference books in the field; Senn and Johnson list hundreds of obscure films, but many "B" films and a few notable films are missing. (MK)

11-5. Stanley, John. **Creature Features: The Science Fiction, Fantasy and Horror Movie Guide**. Berkeley Boulevard, 2000. Updated ed.

Stanley covers major and minor SF, fantasy, and horror films including foreign, made-for-TV, and direct-to-video titles. For most films, Stanley provides date, country, director, writer, and principal cast but not length. His evaluative/descriptive notes vary from a few lines to half a page and are fannish and usually sensible but only occasionally insightful. Relatively minor films from the 1990s get longer notes than major, earlier films. Stanley's introduction to the unnumbered 2000 edition says that the fourth edition, *The Creature Features Movie Guide Strikes Again* (1994), had 5,614 titles. The 2000 version has fewer entries; Stanley does not say how many but it appears to be fewer than 4,000. At least one significant film, Fritz Lang's *Die Frau im Mond*, is among the titles dropped. Libraries should keep the fourth, most complete edition, as well as the 2000 and subsequent editions. (MK)

11-6. Weldon, Michael. **The Psychotronic Encyclopedia of Film**. Ballantine, 1983.

Weldon includes expensive SF, horror, and fantasy productions and ranges from the 1930s to the 1980s, but "B" movies of the 1950s and 1960s are his first love. Many of the more than 3,000 films listed are nonfantastic exploitation movies, such as juvenile delinquent and prison films. Except for the very good and the very bad, Weldon describes but does not evaluate most films, recognizing that "B"-movie fans are attracted by plot elements, not by conventional dramatic and cinematic values. He has something interesting to say about almost every film. Weldon's *Psychotronic Video Guide* (1996) includes films made after 1983 as well as older marginal and obscure films not in the *Encyclopedia.* (MK)

11-7. Willis, Donald. **Horror and Science Fiction Films**. Scarecrow, 1972–1997. 4 vols.

Entries include year, country, running times, credits, cast, variant titles, and citations to reviews and sources of more complete information. Volume I (1972) has about 4,400 films, Volume II (1981) about 2,350, and Volume III (1984) 760, but many entries in Volumes II and III are critical commentaries for films listed briefly in a previous volume. As the number of films in each volume decreased, the length of Willis's commentaries increased. His Volume I is comparable to but less complete than Lee's *Reference Guide* [11-2]. Willis's critical annotations are respectable but less authoritative than those in Hardy [11-1]. (MK)

11-8. Willis, Donald, ed. **Variety's Complete Science Fiction Reviews**. Garland, 1985.

In the 1950s, many genre films, even major ones such as *Invasion of the Body Snatchers* (1956), received few reviews in the mainstream press, but almost all were reviewed in *Variety*, the weekly trade paper of the entertainment industry. The approximately 1,000 reviews reprinted here cover films from 1907 to 1984. Most are terse, shrewd, punchy, and extremely knowledgeable about the film industry of their time. *Variety*'s reviewers were primarily interested in a film's commercial prospects, but they also carefully discussed writing, direction, acting, and what they called "technical credits." Some reviews, such as an unfavorable notice on *2001* (1968), are dated but many have stood the test of time and all are of historical interest. Reviews include more detailed credits than most other sources and give character names as well as the names of actors. Many little-known foreign films are covered. Reviews published since 1984 are collected in biennial volumes of *Variety's Film Reviews*, published by Bowker, and in Variety.com, a database free to subscribers to *Variety*. (MK)

General Studies of Films

*11-9. Brosnan, John. **The Primal Screen: A History of Science Fiction Film**. Orbit, 1991.

Primal Screen is greatly expanded from Brosnan's previous history of SF films, *Future Tense* (1978), and, according to the author, is "much more personal" and "should in no way be regarded as a serious reference book." Nonetheless his wit, irreverence, and common sense, laced with Australian colloquialisms, make this the best general history of the genre (through 1990) despite the omission of a few notable films. An ideal critic of popular entertainment, Brosnan holds films to a high standard that few of them meet, but he is fair to the many mediocre films and understands their appeal. He overthrows some icons, unearths some obscure gems, and concludes that SF films are "equally delighting and irritating." With quotes from filmmakers and many well-chosen illustrations. (MK)

11-10. King, Geoff, and Tanya Krzwinska. **Science Fiction Cinema: From Outerspace to Cyberspace**. Wallflower, 2000.

This slender book is part of the Short Cuts film series from the U.K., available in the U.S. through Columbia University Press. The audience is likely to be someone with a little grounding in cultural studies, but the book could serve as a useful supplement to a college SF film course. It is not as in-depth as Vivian Sobchak's *Screening Space* [11-12] or J. P. Telotte's *Science Fiction Film* [11-13], and not free of errors, but in its efforts to define what makes a film "science fiction," it covers a lot of material concisely and with a wide range of film examples. The emphasis tends to be on Hollywood as an industry, but there are sections on typical SF themes (e.g., utopias and dystopias, "travels in time, space, and scale," gender issues, good and evil scientists) and more specifically cinematic matters (the blockbuster phenomenon, special effects, iconic props, and costumes). Books in this series end with a detailed analysis of one film, and here the choice is *Star Wars Episode 1, The Phantom Menace* (1999)—very appropriate considering the authors' interest in cultural products. A glossary of terms is included ("chaos theory," "gaze," "New Hollywood," "queer"), plus a short but decent bibliography; frustratingly, there is no index. (JM)

*11-11. Nicholls, Peter. **The World of Fantastic Films: An Illustrated Survey**. Dodd, Mead, 1984. U.K. title: *Fantastic Cinema*, Ebury, 1984.

Nicholls's survey of SF, horror, and fantasy films has an exceptional critical text, carefully selected illustrations representing many periods and types of films, and reference information. The latter is found in a filmography of 700 titles; each entry includes country, date, length, color or black-and-white, production company, principal credits and cast, and a rating based on the average of four critics' opinions. Three hundred films are briefly annotated in the filmography; the other 400 are discussed at length in the well-organized text. Nicholls includes almost all significant titles and no trivia. He can be faulted for rushing through several decades; 44 pages cover films from the 1890s to 1967 while 120 pages describe movies from 1968 to 1983. Coverage of foreign films is strong. Nicholls concludes that film is better suited to fantasy and horror than SF. *The World of Fantastic Films* remains the best one-volume critical work covering all kinds of fantastic cinema. (MK)

*11-12. Sobchak, Vivian. **Screening Space: The American Science Fiction Film**. Ungar, 1987. 2nd, enlarged ed.

Reprints the first three chapters of *The Limits of Infinity: The American Science Fiction Film 1950–1975* (Barnes, 1980) and adds a long fourth chapter, "Postfuturism," extending the coverage to the 1980s (the "Second Golden Age," in Sobchak's view). The original chapters systematically dissect visual and sound aesthetics, debate competing genre definitions, analyze iconography (especially the "alien"), and assess the significance of sound effects. Chapter 4 is heavily based on Fredric Jameson's Marxian views of "the cultural logic of late capitalism" and discusses the impact of electronic technology and a commodity culture's values on the aesthetics of films both mainstream (for example, *Star Wars*) and marginal (for example, *Repo Man, Buckaroo Banzai*). Her insights, though couched in a demanding critical vocabulary, are important and provide the most sophisticated treatment of contemporary SF film, strongly influencing Landon [11-43]. [RL]

Three selections by Sobchak are included in an important new anthology, *Liquid Metal: The Science Fiction Film Reader*, edited by Sean Redmond (Columbia Univ. Press, 2004), along with 27 other reprinted essays, some highly influential in film scholarship, including Donna Haraway's often-quoted "A Manifesto for Cyborgs" and pieces by Sontag, Bukatman, and Telotte. Another new anthology, aimed for a somewhat broader audience, is Gregg Rickman's *The Science Fiction Film Reader* (Limelight, 2004), illustrated and featuring articles ranging from a 1907 piece by Georges Méliès to a new essay by Rickman on movies derived from Philip K. Dick, plus comments by SF writers on adaptations of their books. (JM)

11-13. Telotte, J. P. **Science Fiction Film**. Cambridge Univ. Press, 2001.

Part of Cambridge University Press's Genres in American Cinema series, *Science Fiction Film* follows a format established by that press. An "Approaches" section examines genre theory as well as other critical approaches; a necessarily brief "Historical Overview" touches upon literature and the pulps in the course of surveying the films; and the rest of the volume features detailed analyses of representative films. Borrowing terms from Tzvetan Todorov, Telotte chooses *THX 1138* as an example of a "fantastic text," *Close Encounters* as a "marvelous text," *RoboCop* as an "uncanny text," and Cronenberg's *The Fly* as a generic hybrid. Painstaking and thought-provoking in its analyses, if a bit dry in style, and useful in its overview of approaches to SF film (Telotte seems to favor ideological and postmodernist readings, though he is fair to currently unfashionable discourses like the Jungian), the book could be a good choice for an upper-division college SF film course. [JM]

Specialized Studies of Films

11-14.   Benson, Michael. **Vintage Science Fiction Films, 1896–1949**. McFarland, 1985.

11-15.   Strickland, A. W., and Forrest J. Ackerman. **Reference Guide to American Science Fiction Films**. TIS Publications, 1981. Vol. 1, 1897–1929.

Benson's examination of the decades before SF became a real film genre strays deep into fantasy, horror, and other marginal material. His commentaries are anecdotal and only occasionally critical, but quite informative about hundreds of little-known silent and sound films and serials. Includes a good selection of illustrations, detailed credits and cast lists, synopses, information on many foreign films not in Strickland/Ackerman, and a very complete index. Strickland's and Ackerman's *Reference Guide* is the most detailed survey of very early SF films, presenting a unique view of a time when both audiences and filmmakers were almost totally ignorant of SF (although several films were based on *Frankenstein, Jekyll-Hyde*, and Verne romances) but were clearly disturbed by rapid technological change. Of the 222 films listed (many of them short films or serials), about one third are comedies and most of the rest thrillers; most deal with the ludicrous or dangerous effects of futuristic inventions. Strickland is listed in Hardy's [11-1] bibliography, but of Strickland's 222 films, 130 are not in Hardy, indicating how many of these titles are quite marginal SF. The *Reference Guide* has more complete filmographic information than Hardy, including character names; much longer, largely uncritical synopses; references to and quotes from contemporary reviews; and dozens of illustrations, many full-page. Only the first volume of Strickland's planned set was published. John Frazer's *Méliès* (1979) recounts the career of the earliest maker of notable SF films and describes his surviving films in detail. (MK)

*11-16.   Bizony, Piers. **2001: Filming the Future**. Aurum Press, 2000.

11-17.   Chion, Michel. **Kubrick's Cinema Odyssey**. Trans. by Claudia Gorbman. British Film Institute, 2001.

Of the several books on *2001: A Space Odyssey* (a number of them rushed out in time for the real 2001), Piers Bizony's book is the best in the "Making of . . . " category, while Michel Chion's volume serves a more academic market. *2001: Filming the Future* is profusely illustrated (especially with production drawings), much of it in color, and features a synopsis that includes all the dialogue, plus Penelope Gilliatt's famous *New Yorker* review. The meat of the book is chapters on the making of the film, with much anecdotal information about what it was like to work with Stanley Kubrick. *The Making of 2001: A Space Odyssey* (Modern Library, 2000), a collection of essays edited by Stephanie Schwam, contains similar information (including some pieces by Bizony) and no illustrations, but is still valuable for additional interviews and more of the original reviews; it is essentially an update of *The Making of Kubrick's 2001* (edited by Jerome Agel; Signet, 1970), reprinting many of the articles from that volume. Chion, an editor of *Cahiers du Cinéma*, does offer basic information on the making of the film, but is more interested in speculations about *2001*'s use of sound and silence, among other cinematic matters. His book is for readers who like close analysis, are intrigued by chapter titles such as "Towards the Absolute Film," and appreciate interpretations that are refreshingly different from the standard American academic approaches. (JM)

11-18. Borst, Ronald V., Keith Burns, and Leith Adams, eds. **Graven Images: The Best of Horror, Fantasy and Science Fiction Film Art from the Collection of Ronald V. Borst**. Grove, 1992.

11-19. Nourmand, Tony, and Graham Marsh, eds. **Science Fiction Poster Art**. Aurum, 2003.

The work of a film poster artist is restricted only by the film's premise and the artist's imagination, not by budgets or physical impossibilities. Not surprisingly, many posters for SF films were more striking than anything in the films they advertised, especially in the early days of limited budgets and primitive special effects. Borst beautifully reproduces about 500 posters from the silents through the 1960s; most are American but many of the best are foreign. Nourmand and Marsh have more foreign posters, from Europe and Japan, than any rival book. They offer a superb selection of art (224 posters) and informative annotations on the artists. Alan Adler's *Science Fiction and Horror Movie Posters in Full Color* (1977) has only 46 posters, most of which promoted schlock films of the 1950s, but his reproductions are large (most a generous 9 by 13 inches) and his brief annotations informative. *Yesterday's Tomorrows: The Golden Age of Science Fiction Movie Posters, 1950–1964*, by Bruce L. Wright (1993), reproduces 75 posters, many 8 by 11 inches. Wright's annotations are fannish and superficial. (MK)

11-20. Brosnan, John. **Movie Magic: The Story of Special Effects in the Cinema**. St. Martin's, 1974.

11-21. Rickett, Richard. **Special Effects: The History and Technique**. Watson-Guptill, 2000.

No other film genre has been more influenced by advances in filmmaking technology than SF films. Brosnan's *Movie Magic* is the most detailed history of effects prior to the mid-1970s, with valuable interviews with veteran technicians; it is of course outdated, but it still provides entertaining reading. Rickett's *Special Effects* is thorough, quite technical but not daunting, and profusely, and handsomely illustrated. Though the focus is not SF in particular, there are inevitably many illustrations from SF films, and of the 40 "Special Effects Landmarks" annotated in the final chapter, 26 of the films are SF, from *Metropolis* and *King Kong* to *The Matrix*. The organization is not chronological but by topic, with chapters on "optical illusions," models, animation, matte painting, makeup, "physical effects" (weather and explosions), and sound effects; a disadvantage of the arrangement is that related techniques such as digital composition and digital matte painting are covered in widely separated chapters.

Patricia D. Netzley's *Encyclopedia of Movie Special Effects* (1999) has entries for effects artists and techniques and major films; some films of significance in the field are omitted. *Cheap Tricks and Class Acts: Special Effects, Makeup and Stunts from the Films of the Fantastic Fifties* by John J. J. Johnson (1995) describes the effects of the first, low-budget period of steady SF filmmaking. *Ray Harryhausen: An Animated Life*, by Harryhausen and Tony Dalton (Billboard Books, 2004), is the definitive volume on the most famous effects artist to date. It is a coffee-table book with many illustrations and data on all of the master's projects—including SF monsters and dinosaurs as well as fantasy creatures—plus biography and "how-we-did-it" explanations. An insightful chapter on Harryhausen's films is found in Paul M. Jensen's *The Men Who Made the Monsters* (1996). Christopher Finch's *Special Effects: Creating Movie Magic* (1984) covers the whole history of the subject to the early 1980s and is more lavishly illustrated but less detailed than Brosnan's book. Thomas C. Smith's *Industrial Light & Magic: The Art of Special Effects* (1986) concentrates on the work of the most famous effects company from 1977 to the mid-1980s. *Cinefex* [11-81] is a valuable magazine covering current effects work. Many "Making of" books on major recent films, such as *The Making of Jurassic Park* (1983) by *Cinefex* editors Don Shay and Jody Duncan, provide abundant information on effects. All these books thoroughly convince the reader of the truth of an effects artist's boast: "We can do anything. It's just a question of how much it's going to cost."

Note also R. M. Hayes's *3-D Movies: A History and Filmography of Stereoscopic Cinema* (1989) for a technique frequently associated with SF. *Hollywood and History: Costume Design in Films*, edited by Edward Maeder (1987), a heavily illustrated survey of costumes in historical films, includes a 16-page chapter by Elois Jensen, "Visions of the Future: Costume in Science Fiction Films."

Finally, for a more theoretical approach, Michele Pierson's *Special Effects: Still in Search of Wonder* (Columbia Univ. Press, 2002) studies the cultural reception of "marvels," from pre-modern stage effects to the Computer Graphics Imagery celebrated by both technical and fan publications. Most cinema examples are taken from SF films. (MK, JM)

*11-22.   Bukatman, Scott. **Blade Runner**. British Film Institute, 1997.

*11-23.   Sammon, Paul M. **Future Noir: The Making of Blade Runner**. HarperPrism, 1996.

One of the most important SF films receives two excellent treatments here. Sammon's book is a kind of ultimate fan's approach to *Blade Runner*. The author was on the set and interviewing the filmmakers from 1980 to 1982, in preparation for a two-part *Cinefantastique* article. His reporting covers the optioning of the Philip K. Dick source novel, pre-production hassles, the shoot itself, post-production, disastrous sneak previews, reception of the 1982 film, and the events that led to the release of the significantly different Director's

Cut in 1992, all with extensive commentary from producers and writers, set and effects designers, and especially from director Ridley Scott. Written for a popular audience, the book provides the scholar with truly exhaustive comparisons between the various versions (including pre-DVD electronic ones), telling interviews, and other data (but no color illustrations). Bukatman's slender book, part of BFI's Modern Classics series of monographs, is more for the academic reader, but conveys a genuine excitement about the film and is packed with insightful comments. Providing material from Sammon's book, Bukatman also offers a definition of SF film and examines *Blade Runner* in relation to topics such as the city in film; androids, memory, and the Body; and postmodernism in general. (For other SF films in the BFI series, see Sean French's *The Terminator* (1996) and Anne Billson's *The Thing* (i.e., the 1982 version; 1998): these are more superficial treatments but do offer valuable material plus a fannish enthusiasm for their films' perversely comic violence.) Two broader studies by Bukatman (both from Duke Univ. Press) offer comments on several other SF films—*Terminal Identity: The Virtual Subject in Postmodern Science Fiction* (1993) [9-44] and *Matters of Gravity: Special Effects and Supermen in the 20th Century* (2003).

A third important book on *Blade Runner* is the anthology of 19 essays *Retrofitting Blade Runner: Issues in Ridley Scott's Blade Runner and Philip K. Dick's Do Androids Dream of Electric Sheep?*, edited by Judith B. Kerman (Bowling Green State Univ. Popular Press, 1991). Somewhat dated because it precedes the release of the Director's Cut, the book is still valuable for the best of its essays (including some feminist and genre-studies approaches); for an interview with Dick and an annotated list of original reviews; and for its overall display of the power the film has had to dazzle even the most staid of academics. (JM)

11-24. Chapman, James. **Licence to Thrill: A Cultural History of the James Bond Films.** Columbia Univ. Press, 2000.

The James Bond films as a series are only marginally SF, though certain ones qualify to the extent that they feature gadgetry, underground cities, and the techno-menace of would-be world rulers (or a space-station battle in *Moonraker*). Chapman's book is a serious film-by-film study of the series through *Tomorrow Never Dies* (1997), written in a style suitable for a popular audience. It sees the films overall as very much about British sensitivity to loss of Empire and individually in relation to the times, from Swinging London through the Thatcher 1980s and the end of the Cold War. An enthusiast, Chapman still offers impartial analysis of the films' sexism and racism, as well as genre patterns and audience reception. For a coffee-table book with the proverbial lavish illustrations and also an informative history, see John Cork and Bruce Sciavally's *James Bond: The Legacy* (Abrams, 2002), an "official" publication that includes *Die Another Day* (2002). For an A-to-Z topics approach, with endless trivia and strong opinions on the merit of each film, see Stephen Jay Rubin's *The Complete James Bond Movie Encyclopedia* (McGraw-Hill, latest edition 2002). For a book comparable to Chapman's on a TV series with major resemblances to the Bond series (British spy adventure, tongue-in-cheek, debuting in 1962, occasional strong SF component), see Toby Miller's *The Avengers* (BFI, 1997), which does not take a historical approach, but is well researched and has provocative comments on the show's relations to pop fashions, gender issues, and the postmodern. (JM)

11-25.   Clements, Jonathan, and Helen McCarthy. **The Anime Encyclopedia: A Guide to Japanese Animation Since 1917**. Stone Bridge Press, 2001.

Japan produces more animation ("anime" in Japanese) than any other country; the authors estimate that the 2,000 feature films, TV films and series, and direct-to-video cartoons they cover are only half the total. Anime productions include almost all genres (including pornography), but SF and fantasy predominate. Clements/McCarthy have short essays on films made from 1917 to 1945 ("Early Anime" and "Wartime Anime"), as well as entries on the most important productions since the war. Entries range from a few column inches to most of a page and include credits, synopsis, and critical commentary. The *Encyclopedia* is a huge (462 three-column pages of text, 80 pages of index), immensely erudite guide to this vast body of work. The few dozen pictures are very small and, oddly, located far from the entries on the films they illustrate. McCarthy's much shorter *Anime!: A Beginner's Guide to Japanese Animation* (1993) is heavily illustrated. Javna [11-74] covers Japanese animated TV series that were shown in the U.S. *Animerica* (1993–), is the major U.S. magazine on anime. The Anime Café Web site (www.abcb.com) has serious fan-written reviews of dozens of films. *Video Watchdog* [11-83] frequently reviews anime videos. For Japanese live-action SF films, see Galbraith [11-29]. [MK]

*11-26.   Elsaesser, Thomas. **Metropolis**. British Film Institute, 2000.

*11-27.   Minden, Michael, and Holger Bachmann, eds. **Fritz Lang's Metropolis: Cinematic Visions of Technology and Fear**. Camden House, 2000.

In combination, these books offer near-definitive coverage of the seminal and still astounding SF classic—i.e., in regard to archival knowledge and critical perspectives as of 1999. Elsaesser's monograph, a volume in the British Film Institute's Film Classics series (see 11-22 for mention of three books in their Modern Classics series), offers detailed, documented commentary on the film's production, reception, variant prints, and contradictory interpretations; unusually favorable attention is given to Giorgio Moroder's 1984 "disco" version, which Elsaesser claims mediates between the "film history classic" and the "cult classic." The Minden/Bachmann anthology provides yet more material on the making of the film and its critical reception (17 contemporary reports and reviews are reprinted, one by Luis Buñuel), plus three articles on the various prints and restorations (at least half an hour of the original film has never been recovered). There are also three new critical studies and four older ones, among the latter Andreas Huyssen's engaging 1988 "The Vamp and the Machine." One could wish for a second edition of either book, taking into account the new Kino International version of the film, probably the standard for some years to come, with its additional footage and newly recorded original orchestral music. (And let's add to our wish-list a screenplay transcribed from the Kino version, with variant texts noted.) All the same, both books are essential to any study of *Metropolis*. [JM]

11-28. Fischer, Dennis. **Science Fiction Film Directors, 1895–1998.** McFarland, 2000.

Fischer's book is one of the longest in the field (759 11-inch pages, even bigger than Hardy [11-1]), an immense compilation of biographical and filmographic information on 83 directors. Many of the directors profiled are obscure. Most are American; several Japanese, British, Italian, Soviet, and Australian filmmakers are included. The five Japanese directors in Fischer do not include Inoshiro Honda, maker of *Godzilla* films, and Hayao Miyazaki, Japan's most celebrated director of animated SF. Silent directors (Fritz Lang, George Méliès) are omitted. Each essay (up to 35 pages long) surveys the director's whole career, with synopses, production information, and Fischer's sharp-eyed, usually sensible comments on each major SF film. With many quotes from filmmakers, a 47-page appendix on "Classic science fiction films from non-genre directors," several dozen black-and-white illustrations, and a large bibliography. For books on specific directors, see Hickman [11-32], Reemes [11-55], Joe Adamson's *Byron Haskin* (1984), John Baxter's *Stanley Kubrick* (1997), Michel Ciment's *Kubrick* (1983), Christopher Heard's *Dreaming Aloud* (1997, on James Cameron), Joseph McBride's *Steven Spielberg* (1997), Dale Pollock's *Skywalking* (1983, on George Lucas), and Rob Van Scheers' *Paul Verhoeven* (1996), among many others. Gary Westfahl's Biographical Encyclopedia of Science Fiction Film (www.sfsite.com/interzone/gary/intro.htm) offers Westfahl's opinionated and often acerbic appraisals of dozens of directors and actors. (MK)

11-29. Galbraith, Stuart, IV. **Japanese Science Fiction, Fantasy and Horror Films: A Critical Analysis of 103 Features Released in the United States.** McFarland, 1994.

Galbraith notes that "in Japan, the so-called realism of a film's story and special effects mattered little, so long as the story was worth telling and the special effects work was visually appealing." He finds that many Japanese SF films were much better in their original form than in the butchered versions seen on U.S. television. Galbraith covers six art film fantasies (three by Akira Kurosawa), 42 *keiju eiga* (the giant monster films that began with *Gojira* (alt. *Godzilla*, 1954)) and 55 other films involving aliens, ghosts, vampires, and even the Frankenstein monster. For each film, Galbraith provides credits, synopsis, a critical assessment, information on directors and other workers, and quotes from U.S. critics. An erudite survey of an underappreciated body of films. Galbraith covers live-action films only; for the huge output of Japanese animated SF films, see Clements/McCarthy [11-25]. (MK)

11-30. Glassy, Mark C. **The Biology of Science Fiction Cinema**. McFarland, 2001.

Great fun for readers who like to ponder what is scientifically possible in SF films and what is not—and who have taken at least a high school or preferably a college biology course. The author is a professional scientist and SF film fan, with seemingly bottomless knowledge of the cheesiest drive-in fodder as well as big-budget spectacles. Each of his 15 chapters singles out a branch of biology, either real ones such as endocrinology and entomology or movie ones such as "shrinkology," then takes a close look at selected films, examining them for "What Is Right with the Biological Science Presented," "What Is Wrong," "Could It Actually Happen," and so forth. One might imagine that almost all biology in SF films is "beyond ludicrous" (as Glassy says of the ability of giant bugs to "mimic" humans in *Mimic*), but the author is generous in explaining what such films as *Fantastic Voyage* got right, though noting that the lab's "radioactive decay detectors" probably couldn't "be sensitive enough to pick up the miniaturized decay particles" of the tiny sub and thus trace its journey. For book browsers who love details and speculation, and don't mind the author mentioning his teenage lust for Raquel Welch, the book is a gold mine, though Glassy's film choices are representative rather than exhaustive, and while writers of each film are listed, actors and directors are not. An appendix on "Accuracy of Laboratory Sets" in 65 films is especially fascinating. (JM)

*11-31. Greene, Eric. **Planet of the Apes as American Myth: Race, Politics, and Popular Culture**. Wesleyan Univ. Press, 1998.

The mythic power of the 1968 film *Planet of the Apes*, inspiring four sequels and numerous media spinoffs in the 1970s, seems unabated, considering not only Tim Burton's 2001 "reimagining" but a considerable number of recent books on the phenomenon. Eric Greene's prize-winning volume, originally published in 1996 by McFarland, may occasionally belabor its point that the entire cycle has a great deal to say about American racial conflict in the 1960s and 1970s, but it is insightful and convincing. Addressed to a serious general reader—neither the film-studies academic nor the fan particularly—the book closely examines each film for its connection to the racial politics of the time. Those seeking more of a "Making Of" book will find satisfaction in *Planet of the Apes Revisited: The Behind-the-Scenes Story of the Classic Science Fiction Saga* (Joe Russo and Larry Landsman with Edward Gross; Thomas Dunne Books, 2001), with much quotation from cast and crew members, some good illustrations, and an overall emphasis on the contribution of producer Arthur P. Jacobs. For a British but equally fannish perspective, see Brian Pendreigh's *Planet of the Apes, or How Hollywood Turned Darwin Upside Down* (Boxtree, 2001); it has a shorter text and fewer illustrations but some points of its own and several references to Greene's book. Both the newer books incorporate a little advance material on the Burton film, but for the script, photos, and background material on the latter, readers must turn to *Planet of the Apes* (2001), a Newmarket Pictorial Moviebook. (JM)

11-32. Hickman, Gail Morgan. **The Films of George Pal**. A. S. Barnes, 1977.
George Pal produced *Destination Moon* (1950), *When Worlds Collide* (1951), and
War of the Worlds (1953) and directed *The Time Machine* (1960). The 14 features
and many innovative short films he produced or directed also included several
fantasy titles. Hickman's discussion is fannish and only mildly critical. She tends
to exonerate Pal and blame screenwriters and studio executives for whatever
faults she finds in the films. Her book is useful for its biographical information
and for the many illustrations. The documentary film *The Fantasy Film Worlds of
George Pal* (1983), by Arnold Leibovitz, is also informative but uncritical and
includes the most spectacular scenes from Pal's movies. (MK)

11-33. Hunter, I. Q., ed. **British Science Fiction Cinema**. Routledge, 1999.
The essays in this collection cover not only the likes of *Things to Come*, the
Quatermass films, *A Clockwork Orange*, and *Brazil* but cult films like *Devil Girl from
Mars* (1954) and such topics as "the British colossal creature film" (in an article
called "Trashing London"). Hunter's introduction offers a reasonable, quali-
fied case for there being a distinctively British SF cinema, at least in recurring
themes and occasional cycles. A different approach is taken in *SF:UK: How
British Science Fiction Changed the World* (Reynolds and Hearn, 2000) by Daniel
O'Brien with a long "Prologue" by Kim Newman. The book enthusiastically
cites movies and TV shows (some American) influenced by British writers from
Shakespeare (*The Tempest*) and Mary Shelley to Wells and Orwell, as well as
looking at fully U.K. productions, even a fondly remembered decade
(1958–1968) of children's SF puppet TV shows. Excellent black-and-white publicity photos and some other illustrations. [JM]. For the record of another European SF tradition, see Jean-Marc Lofficier's *French Science Fiction, Fantasy, Horror
and Pulp Fiction: A Guide to Cinema, Television, Radio, Animation, Comic Books and
Literature* (2000). (MK)

11-34. Iaccino, James F. **Jungian Reflections Within the Cinema: A Psychological Analysis of Sci-Fi and Fantasy Archetypes**. Praeger, 1998.

11-35. Lucanio, Patrick. **Them or Us: Archetypal Interpretations of
Fifties Alien Invasion Films**. Indiana Univ. Press, 1987.
Lucanio examines not only films about aliens but also 1950s movies about terrestrial monsters such as giant spiders, seeking to show that SF is fundamentally
distinct from horror, that the 1950s monster films are SF and not horror, and
that SF films are best studied by Jungian analysis. Three films considered in
detail are *It Came from Outer Space*, and *Invaders from Mars* (both 1953), and
Britain's *Fiend Without a Face* (1958). *Them or Us* is illustrated by frame enlarge-
ments, which are necessary to follow Lucanio's arguments but which are too
tiny and sometimes printed too darkly. The text contains a good deal of theory
but also perceptive observations on the films and such issues as the use of genre
actors, special effects, stock footage, titles, and posters. [MK].

Iaccino looks at the original *Star Wars* trilogy for its "Space-Father Archetype" and the *Planet of the Apes* cycle for its "Shadow Species"; more surprisingly, we get a detailed analysis of *Logan's Run* (not just the film but the TV series!) and *Battlestar: Galactica*. Categories seem loose: some TV shows are covered in the unit on "Science-Fiction Films," others in a separate chapter; the *Back to the Future* trilogy is studied (for its "Alchemic Travelers") in the unit on "Fantasy Films," along with chapters on adventure and horror films. In any case, most critics nowadays look at Jungian readings with a raised eyebrow, if not with a downright scowl, but heroic fantasies do follow ancient patterns that can profitably be studied, and certain filmmakers, most famously George Lucas and George Miller (three *Mad Max* films, 1979–1985), have made conscious use of archetypes. (JM)

11-36.   Irwin, William, ed. **The Matrix and Philosophy: Welcome to the Desert of the Real**. Open Court, 2002.

11-37.   Lamm, Spenser, ed. **The Art of The Matrix**. Newmarket, 2000.

11-38.   Yeffeth, Glenn, ed. **Taking the Red Pill: Science, Philosophy and Religion in The Matrix**. Benbella Books, 2003.

The Matrix (1999) spawned not only two sequels and other media products but a number of fan and scholarly books. *The Art of The Matrix*, something of a coffee-table extravaganza, offers the shooting script, an afterword by William Gibson, the complete storyboards, and a great many other illustrations. The film had a special appeal to a legion of philosophy and theology professors, attracted to its epistemological concerns and hints of religious allegory. The Irwin and Yeffeth essay collections, best among several titles, are suited for lower-level college courses. Irwin, who has edited other books in a popular culture series (*Seinfeld and Philosophy*, *Buffy the Vampire Slayer and Philosophy*), provides 20 articles on knowability and ethics, Buddhist and Christian interpretations, and postmodernism; approaches vary from easy-for-freshmen style to the challenges of the lengthy Slavoj Zizek piece that rounds off the volume. Yeffeth's book covers some of the same ground, but several of its 14 essays, by well-known SF writers and critics, discuss the film as SF. Whether the widely felt disappointment in the two *Matrix* sequels of 2003 will quickly send these and lesser books to the bargain shelves remains to be seen, but more studies, notably *Jacking In to the Matrix Franchise: Cultural Reception and Interpretation* (Matthew Kapell, William G. Doty, eds., 2004) are on the way. (JM)

11-39.   Johnson, William, ed. **Focus on the Science Fiction Film**. Prentice-Hall, 1972.

Johnson's is one of the earliest important books on SF films. The mostly short pieces collected here include contemporary reviews (some of them quaint); screenplay excerpts; articles on the production of five films; thoughtful comments by directors François Truffaut, Don Siegel, and Stanley Kubrick and authors Brian Aldiss and Kingsley Amis; academic film criticism; a report on one of the first SF film festivals (Trieste, 1963); and a remarkably old-fashioned 1959 *Film Quarterly* article denouncing almost all 1950s SF films as absurd and "perverse." Some contributors differ interestingly; Siegel and a European critic see *Invasion of the Body Snatchers* very differently. A useful overview of informed opinion on the genre two decades after production accelerated in 1950. Other early books in the field still of interest are John Baxter's *Science Fiction in the Cinema* (1970), Frederik Pohl and Frederik Pohl IV's *Science Fiction Studies in Film* (1981), and Philip Strick's *Science Fiction Movies* (1976). (MK)

11-40.　Kinnard, Roy. **Science Fiction Serials: A Critical Filmography of the 31 Hard SF Cliffhangers, with an Appendix of the 37 Serials with Slight SF Content**. McFarland, 1998.

A total of 231 sound serials were made in Hollywood, aimed squarely at juvenile audiences. (Silent serials were made for adults.) The "chapter-plays" were ignored by critics but were usually profitable. SF serials such as *Flash Gordon* (three serials, 1936–1940), *Buck Rogers* (1943), and *Superman* (1948) were usually the most lavish and often had good cinematography, stunt work, and (for their time) special effects. They were almost the only SF made in Hollywood in the 1930s and 1940s. The serials were killed by TV in the 1950s, just as SF feature films flourished. Thirty of the 31 serials Kinnard describes still exist; several were syndicated on TV in the 1950s. In both theaters and TV they introduced audiences to primitive SF; in time they influenced Lucas and Spielberg. For each of 31 "hard SF" talking serials (1934–1955), Kinnard provides credits, chapter titles, detailed synopses, and erudite critical commentaries. (MK)

11-41.　Kuhn, Annette, ed. **Alien Zone: Cultural Theory and Contemporary Science Fiction Cinema**. Verso/Routledge, 1990.

Eighteen essays devoted to sociopolitical analysis, ideological critiques, psychoanalytic diagnoses, reader-response investigations, and intertextual explorations. Six discuss *Alien*, a touchstone for feminist issues, and *Blade Runner*, which displays themes and techniques associated with postmodern culture. Excellent essays on *The Thing* (1982) and *Videodrome* and by H. Bruce Franklin on SF films of the 1970s and by Vivian Sobchak on the sexual politics of the genre, the last two reprinted from Slusser [11-57], which provides a broader perspective. For large film collections. (RL)

11-42.　Kuhn, Annette. **Alien Zone II: The Spaces of Science-Fiction Cinema**. Verso, 1999.

It is a sign of the proliferation of academic SF film studies that the original *Alien Zone*—several of whose essays have become "classics," or at least great influences on later writings—spawned a "sequel" only nine years later. The newer volume offers only 11 essays (mostly revised versions of previously published work), but it has a detailed index that was lacking in the original and a bibliography that has quadrupled in length. Only one article is a study of a single film (or rather series in this case), the *Alien* cycle, but there are valuable comments on, for example, *Things to Come* and *Total Recall* as well as the inevitable *Metropolis* and *Blade Runner*. The essays of *AZII* are grouped (with a little shoehorning) in terms of four kinds of "space," really discourses: cultural studies (but mainly genre and fandom issues), the City, the Body, and special effects. Among the best essays are the two on special effects, a difficult but rewarding study of the "photographic trace" by Garrett Stewart, and a connecting by Scott Bukatman of the 19th-century "sublime" to modern SF spectacles. (JM)

11-43.   Landon, Brooks. **The Aesthetics of Ambivalence: Rethinking Science Fiction Film in the Age of Electronic (Re)Production.** Greenwood, 1992.

Collects earlier pieces to create a suggestive if diffuse study. The focus is on the relationship of SF film to SF literature and effectively defends the former against detractors who view it as a second-rate echo of the latter. One part considers adaptations, using *The Thing* and *Blade Runner* as examples. Another treats special effects, arguing for their centrality in historically defining SF as a film genre; a third discusses the influence of electronic technology in transforming SF film's parameters and possibilities. Clearly written and well informed about film, literary, and technical details, but the pieces are not fully integrated into a coherent whole. (RL)

11-44.   Larson, Randall. **Musique Fantastique: A Survey of Film Music in the Fantastic Cinema.** Scarecrow, 1985.

Larson describes the scores of hundreds of SF, fantasy, and horror films from the earliest sound films to the 1980s, with special chapters on TV scoring, use of electronic and classical music, foreign films, and four major composers. He provides many quotations from composers and critics and more than 200 pages of filmography and discography. Larson has gathered an enormous amount of information. He is enthusiastic about the large majority of the scores, in keeping with his conclusion that "music has always seemed to be at its best in fantastic films." (MK)

*11-45.   LaValley, Al. **Invasion of the Body Snatchers.** Rutgers, 1989.

Ignored by most mainstream critics when it was released in 1956, Don Siegel's *Invasion of the Body Snatchers* is now widely regarded as the best SF film of the 1950s. LaValley's collection includes the screenplay, heavily annotated with notes about changes in successive versions; memos and correspondence from Siegel and the film's producer; two interviews with Siegel; a few contemporary reviews; and eight current essays and excerpts from other books. LaValley's 20-page introduction refutes some of the other contributors, demonstrating that investigation of a film's production process and of the backgrounds and intentions of the filmmakers is likely to yield better insights than a theoretical reading of the film. Several pieces consider the long-debated question of *Invasion's* place in Cold War politics; considerably fresher is Nancy Steffen-Fluhr's feminist treatment. LaValley has gathered essential information and a wide variety of critical views about a seminal film. Note also *"They're Here—": Invasion of the Body Snatchers: A Tribute* (1999), a collection of essays edited by Kevin McCarthy (the star of the film) and Ed Gorman. (MK)

11-46. Mank, Gregory William. **It's Alive! The Classic Cinema of Frankenstein**. A. S. Barnes, 1981.

Mank's detailed accounts of the production of the eight Frankenstein films made by Universal from 1931 to 1948 may focus too much on studio politics, but the fascinating anecdotes, hundreds of quotations from veterans of the films, and dozens of illustrations make *It's Alive!* essential for the study of the Universal series, despite the lack of an index. Note also *Universal Horrors: The Studio's Classic Films, 1932–1946* (1990) by Michael Brunas, John Brunas, and Tom Weaver, which includes information on censorship of the Universal series. The Universal Frankenstein movies were only the most famous of many film versions of the Shelley story. More analytical than Mank are four chapters on film and TV versions from 1910 to 1974 in *Mary Shelley's Monster* [10-124] by Martin Tropp. *The Endurance of Frankenstein* (1979), edited by George Levine and U. C. Knoepflmacher, includes a useful survey of "The Stage and Film Children of Frankenstein" by Albert LaValley. Donald Glut's *Frankenstein Catalog* (1984) and Stephen Jones's *The Illustrated Frankenstein Catalog* (1994) gather data on every film and TV version. Leslie Halliwell's *The Dead That Walk* (1988) compares the Universal and Hammer (1957–1974) cycles of Frankenstein films, always to Hammer's disadvantage. David Pirie's *A Heritage of Horror: The English Gothic Cinema, 1946–1972* (1973) defends the Hammer films. (MK)

11-47. Mathews, Jack. **The Battle of Brazil**. Crown, 1987.

Terry Gilliam's dystopian *Brazil* (1985), like *Blade Runner,* failed at the box office but has been championed by many in the SF community; Harlan Ellison called it "the best SF film ever made and very likely one of the ten greatest films of any kind ever made." Mathews's *Battle* includes the annotated screenplay; a relatively brief recounting of the film's production; and a detailed, knowledgeable, persuasively fair account of the struggle between Gilliam and MCA/Universal executives over the final cut of the film. Mathews sees the conflict as a clash of lifestyles and principles as well as egos. (MK)

11-48. McDougal, Stuart, ed. **Stanley Kubrick's A Clockwork Orange**. Cambridge Univ. Press, 2003.

A volume in the Cambridge Film Handbook series, the work at hand features five new essays on *A Clockwork Orange,* plus the editor's introduction and the polar-opposites 1972 reviews of Robert Hughes and Pauline Kael. None of the essays has much to say about the film's relation to SF: the chief topics include the film's ultraviolence and its cultural contexts; the relation of the film to Anthony Burgess's novel; misogyny and homoerotic representations; and distinctive uses of music (with Peter J. Rabinowitz contributing a valuable comparison between Burgess's and Kubrick's musical allusions). (JM)

11-49.   Mulhall, Stephen. **On Film**. Routledge, 2002.

11-50.   Thomson, David. **The Alien Quartet**. Bloomsbury, 1998.

Both these British books are studies of the four *Alien* films, regardless of the bizarrely broad title of Mulhall's work (part of a Thinking in Action series by philosophers, with other titles including *On Belief* and *On the Internet*). Their approaches to the tetralogy—unique among Hollywood cycles for having four strong directors at the helm, each leaving a personal stamp on "his" film despite the continuity of producers and star—are extremely different. Mulhall is a professor of philosophy, with Stanley Cavell his greatest influence in film studies. He admires all four films, is unabashedly an auteurist (with extensive commentary on other films by each director), and takes each "text" as knowing what it is doing, telling us things about identity and the body in particular, through uniquely cinematic means. The analyses are close, the style often difficult, even if not jargonish. In contrast, the prolific David Thomson writes in a breezy personal style, sees each film steadily deteriorating in artistic quality, and gives much more attention to the influence of the producers and Sigourney Weaver (to whose body and signs of aging he gives almost obsessive attention). The book, part of a Bloomsbury Movie Guide Series, offers entertainingly combative opinions, typical of the author; some readers might be impatient with his method of describing each film scene by scene, with digressions about the cast and crew and the making of the film. A forthcoming feminist study, *Alien Woman: The Making of Lt. Ellen Ripley*, by Ximena Gallardo C. and C. Jason Smith (Continuum, 2004), may also be of interest. (JM)

11-51.   Neumann, Dietrich, ed. **Film Architecture: Set Designs from Metropolis to Blade Runner**. Prestel, 1999.

Designed to accompany a traveling art exhibit, this book features valuable short essays, filmographies, and, most important, a great many handsome, very well reproduced production designs, photographs, and posters, some in color. The selected films are not exclusively SF: they include Weimar Expressionist and "Street" films, Jacques Tati's *Mon Oncle* (1958, marginally SF) and *Playtime* (1967), and the 1990 *Dick Tracy*. In addition to quite a few pages on *Metropolis* and *Blade Runner*, we get beautiful material on *Aelita—Queen of Mars* (1924), *Just Imagine* (1930), and *Things to Come*. (JM)

11-52.   Newman, Kim. **Apocalypse Movies: End of the World Cinema**. St. Martin's Griffin, 1999.

With wit, exceptional erudition, and a sharp eye for significant detail (and from a firmly anti-military position), Newman surveys U.S. and foreign films depicting nuclear war, post-nuclear survivors, and radiation-created monsters (including the Japanese giant monster films). TV films are included. Hundreds of obscure films are categorized and dozens of major films discussed in detail. Mick Broderick's *Nuclear Movies* (1991) is even more complete and lists about 850 films from 30 countries. Galbraith [11-29] covers many Japanese films about nuclear issues. Also note Jerome F. Shapiro's *Atomic Bomb Cinema: The Apocalyptic Imagination on Film* (2001) and Charles P. Mitchell's *A Guide to Apocalyptic Cinema* (2001). (MK)

Themes: End of the World

11-53. Newman, Kim, ed. **Science Fiction/Horror: A Sight and Sound Reader**. British Film Institute, 2002.

In his introduction to this collection of reviews and retrospective essays from the British film magazine *Sight and Sound* (most dated between 1992 and 2001), editor Newman has some witty remarks about SF fans who refuse to acknowledge the strong generic connections between SF and horror cinema. Actually, Newman challenges the limits of both genres, by including pieces on *It's a Wonderful Life* and *Groundhog Day* among the more usual suspects. Only 29 out of 80 pieces can really be considered to be about SF films, but the level of writing for these is often high, there are provocative reviews (like J. Hoberman's of *A.I.*), and one of the longest pieces, an appreciation of *2001* by Mark Crispin Miller, is particularly worth seeking out. (JM)

11-54. Penley, Constance, Elizabeth Lyon, and Lynn Spiegel. **Close Encounters: Film, Feminism and Science Fiction**. Univ. of Minnesota Press, 1991.

An expanded version of a special issue of *Camera Obscura* (no. 15, Fall 1986), with nine essays and a film script devoted to feminist analyses and critiques, heavily dependent on psychoanalytic methods. Two essays each on *Metropolis* and *The Terminator* reflect the importance of feminist issues in those films. Coverage of TV includes good essays on 1960s fantastic sitcoms and *Star Trek* fandoms. The script for *Friendship's Death* (1987) is fascinating if out of place. Like Kuhn [11-41], this work focuses on a limited canon, and within a feminist context. Compare the broader treatment in Slusser [11-57]. (RL)

11-55. Reemes, Dana M. **Directed by Jack Arnold**. McFarland, 1988.

Arnold was perhaps the most influential genre director of the 1950s. One of the few directors who actually read SF, he made eight SF films from 1953 to 1959, among them one much imitated film (*It Came from Outer Space*, 1953), one cult movie (*Creature from the Black Lagoon*, 1954), and one highly regarded film (*The Incredible Shrinking Man*, 1957). Reemes's book is informative, with detailed biographical information and many long excerpts from interviews with Arnold, but also excessively adulatory. John Baxter also expresses admiration for Arnold in his *Science Fiction in the Cinema* (1970). (MK)

11-56. Sardar, Ziauddin, and Sean Cubitt, eds. **Aliens R US: The Other in SF Cinema**. Pluto Press, 2002.

This essay collection, basically British but with a range of international contributors, is strongly political, with emphasis on how SF tends to valorize Western techno-imperialism and Orientalist views of the Other. Readers may or may not agree with some of the writers' assertions—e.g., Sardar's argument that *The War of the Worlds'* view of the Martians can be traced right back to the western world's demonization of Muslims after the medieval battles of Tours and Roncesvalles—but the book provides plenty of food for thought. Topics of the nine essays plus introduction include differing notions of "the natural world" in films of Jean-Pierre Jeunet (*Delicatessen, City of Lost Children*) and Luc Besson (*The Fifth Element*); *Independence Day* as "the apotheosis of the American Dream"; the Borg in *Star Trek: First Contact*; "techno-orientalism" and rave culture in Japanese anime; Hong Kong SF cinema; race in *The Matrix*; Wim Wenders's *Until the End of the World*; and two essays on SF TV, *Space: Above and Beyond* and *Star Trek: Deep Space Nine* (the latter with some nice observations, though with a dispensable opening section on Descartes and Burke). (JM)

*11-57. Slusser, George E., and Eric S. Rabkin, eds. **Shadows of the Magic Lamp: Fantasy and Science Fiction in Film**. Southern Illinois Univ. Press, 1985. Fourteen essays from the 1982 Eaton Conference, ranging from structural analyses of form to special effects to sexual politics and political ideology, with some of the best essays considering the cross-pollination of genres, especially SF and horror. The chronological and geographic scope is broad and the general level is high. The first and in many ways still the best collection to display the full range and sophistication of contemporary critical methods, from semiotic analyses to feminist critique, anticipating the later works of Kuhn [11-41, -42] and Penley [11-54]. (RL)

11-58. Stover, Leon. **The Prophetic Soul: A Reading of H. G. Wells's Things to Come**. McFarland, 1987.
H. G. Wells believed in the power of film to effect fundamental social and political change. According to actor Raymond Massey, "No writer for the screen ever had or will have such authority as H. G. Wells possessed in the making of *Things to Come*," produced from Wells's screenplay in 1936. The movie is the only major English-language futuristic film made before the 1950s and one of the most didactic, openly political SF films ever made in the West. Stover reprints the screenplay and Wells's film treatment "Whither Mankind?" and scours Wells's previous writings, both famous and obscure, to paint a devastating picture of a "candidly antidemocratic mind at work." A scholarly tour-de-force and a damning indictment of the politics of a major SF author. Thomas C. Renzi's *H. G. Wells: Six Scientific Romances Adapted for Film* (1992) examines 10 films based on Wells's fiction but with screenplays by others. The significant films are *Island of Lost Souls* (1932), *The Invisible Man* (1933), *War of the Worlds* (1953), *The Time Machine* (1960), and *Time After Time* (1979). Renzi is mainly interested in the process of adaptation. Note also *H. G. Wells on Film: The Utopian Nightmare* by Don R. Smith (2002), which surveys every Wells film from 1909 to 1997. (MK)

*11-59.   Telotte, J. P. **A Distant Technology: Science Fiction and the Machine Age**. Wesleyan Univ. Press, 1999.

*11-60.   Telotte, J. P. **Replications: A Robotic History of the Science Fiction Film**. Univ. of Illinois Press, 1995.

Replications is not only about robots, androids, and other simulacra (like *Blade Runner*'s replicants) but about ways in which the modern and postmodern human feels "reconstructible," as Telotte puts it—lacking a sense of identity and so drawn (in dread or admiration or both) to spectacles of "human artifice." Taking a historical approach, Telotte traces this "fantasy of robotism" back to the mechanical automata of the pre-industrial age, then devotes a chapter each to *Metropolis*; lab creations in 1930s films (*Frankenstein, Island of Lost Souls*); 1930s serials; *Forbidden Planet*'s Robby the Robot; *Westworld* and *Futureworld*; several 1980s films; and the *Terminator* films. *A Distant Technology* is more centrally a historical study, its subject international SF films between the wars and their "dreams" of distance (space flight, trans-atlantic tunnels) and detachment (in emotional and Marxist senses). There are chapters on the Soviet *Aelita*, Fritz Lang's German films, French and British SF, and American features and serials, and a concluding chapter on the 1939 New York World's Fair. Telotte finds differing attitudes toward technological advancement in each national cinema, and foregrounds the apparatus of cinema itself in creating sensations of distance and closeness. (JM)

   Themes: Robots, Androids

11-61.   Vieth, Errol. **Screening Space: Contexts, Texts and Science in Fifties Science Fiction Film**. Scarecrow, 2001.

Vieth, an Australian academic, has made an important attempt to define SF film, notably in terms of its representations of scientists. Films of the 1950s—including a considerable number of "B" and lower-grade pictures—provide examples from the "founding" era, but most of Vieth's points can easily be applied to films of later decades. He studies 1950s products not at all for their nostalgia value or as camp, but because they reveal significant American attitudes toward science and scientists, regardless of the implausibility of their science or lack of artistic merit. The opening chapters attempt to define SF film as a distinct genre, with some attention to the film industry (including some interesting pages on drive-ins); later chapters provide valuable analysis of portrayals of women scientists (with extensive quotation of dialogue), and single out biological and health scientists as well as astronomers and weapons experts. A section on social/political contexts of the 1950s covers ground that many will find overly familiar, but otherwise the book provides fresh insights while synthesizing other critical work. Filmographies, bibliography, and index. (JM)

   Themes: Scientists and Engineers

*11-62.   Warren, Bill. **Keep Watching the Skies! American Science Fiction Films of the Fifties.** McFarland, 1982, 1986. 2 vols.

Warren's two volumes (1,300 pages) are the longest, most detailed books on 1950s SF films. Volume 1 covers 134 films of 1950-1957; volume 2, 153 films of 1958–1962. Warren concludes that the quality of the films declined sharply during the second period. For every SF film released in the United Stares, including several British and a few Japanese movies, Warren provides credits, a synopsis, and an "intensely personal" discussion. For major films, he discusses production history, careers of filmmakers, design, music, acting, camera work, and all other important aspects. These commentaries are chatty and colloquial but perceptive and hugely erudite. Warren is definitive on the minor and middle-quality films of the period and well worth reading on the major titles. In his *Science Fiction in the Cinema* (1970), John Baxter praises the films of the 1950s. (MK)

11-63.   Weaver, Tom. **Double Feature Creature Attack: A Monster Merger of Two More Volumes of Classic Interviews.** McFarland, 2003.

Reprints two volumes (*Attack of the Movie Monster Makers*, 1994, and *They Fought in the Creature Features*, 1995) of 43 interviews with producers, directors, writers, and actors who worked in "B" horror and SF films of the 1940s to the 1960s. Some of the interviewees are known only for genre work (Ann Robinson), some had broader careers (director Val Guest), and a few are famous (Vincent Price). Most of the films are individually obscure, but as a body they had a substantial impact on public perception of SF. Weaver's very well-informed questions elicit anecdotal but usually informative reminiscences about the colorful world of low-budget genre filmmaking. Weaver's other interview books are *Return of the B Science Fiction and Horror Movie Makers* (1999, 57 interviews, reprinting *Interviews with B Science Fiction and Horror Movie Makers* [1988] and *Science Fiction Stars and Horror Heroes* [1991]); *It Came from Weaver Five* (20 interviews, 1996); *Science Fiction and Fantasy Film Flashbacks* (24 interviews, 1998); *I Was a Monster Movie Maker* (22 interviews, 2001); *Monsters, Mutants and Heavenly Creatures* (14 interviews, 2001); *Science Fiction Confidential* (23 interviews, 2002); and *Eye on Science Fiction* (20 interviews, 2003). [MK]

Lee Goldberg's *Science Fiction Filmmaking in the 1980s: Interviews with Actors, Directors, Producers and Writers* (1995) collects interviews from *Starlog* [11-82], covering about a dozen films. (JM)

Television and Radio

11-64.   Barrett, Michèle, and Duncan Barrett. **Star Trek: The Human Frontier.** Routledge, 2001.

11-65.   Bernardi, Daniel Leonard. **Star Trek and History: Race-ing Toward a White Future.** Rutgers Univ. Press, 1998.

11-66.   Harrison, Taylor, et al. **Enterprise Zone: Critical Positions on Star Trek.** Westview Press, 1996.

11-67. Pounds, Micheal [*sic*] C. **Race in Space: The Representation of Ethnicity in Star Trek and Star Trek: The Next Generation**. Scarecrow, 1999.

11-68. Roberts, Robin. **Sexual Generations: "Star Trek: The Next Generation" and Gender**. Univ. of Illinois Press, 1999.

Of the huge number of books on the various *Star Trek* series, some are primarily informational (e.g., Bjo Trimble's *The Star Trek Concordance*, rev. ed., 1995; David Gerrold's *The World of Star Trek*, rev. ed., 1984); some debate the merits of each series and episode; several, designed mainly for the classroom, explore the physics or metaphysics (for example) of *Star Trek*; and a number are more broadly academic, offering various kinds of ideological or cultural studies. Of the last group, the five listed above are among the most noteworthy to date. The essays of *Enterprise Zone* set the agenda, with such topics as "hegemony, utopias, militarism, colonialism, gender, violence, race, class, sexuality, and liminality" (to quote from the afterword), close analysis of particular episodes, and for the most part lack of awareness of SF beyond *Star Trek*. Typically for recent scholarship, nine of the 12 essays are on *Next Generation* (*NG*), with only two on the original series and one on a *Star Trek* film; there is also an interview with Henry Jenkins on his study of fan communities, *Textual Poachers* (see 11-78).

Bernardi and Pounds come independently to the same conclusion: that whiteness is always dominant in both series, though "classic Trek" was perhaps for its time more progressive than *NG*. Bernardi includes chapters on the earlier films and an Internet fan group, while Pounds (who tells of growing up with *Star Trek* as an African American, and relies heavily on semiotic methods) sticks with the two series but offers more on network broadcasting contexts. Unfortunately, neither book gives attention to *Deep Space 9*, arguably far more multicultural and complex in "racial" perspectives than the earlier series.

Roberts, acknowledging Bernardi and other *Trek* critics, and applying French feminist theories, offers close analysis of selected *NG* episodes featuring female aliens and rulers, topics such as abortion and rape, and issues relatable to feminism, including race, sexual orientation, and machine/human interfaces. Finally, the Barretts (she a professor of Literary and Cultural Theory in London, he her teenage son) take what might be called an anti–anti-humanist position. An unusual focus in the first third of the book is a comparison of the shows to classic literary naval voyages of Melville, Verne, Conrad, and C. S. Forrester. Part Two explores the shows' tendency to debate, "consistently, even relentlessly," the nature of humanity, notably in trial scenes and hearings. The final and perhaps most valuable part proposes that *Deep Space 9* and *Voyager* are much more postmodern than the "high-minded" *NG* in their self-referentiality, turn from scientific rationalism toward religion, and focus on destabilized identities. (JM)

11-69. Cantril, Hadley. **The Invasion from Mars: A Study in the Psychology of Panic**. Princeton Univ. Press, 1940.

Radio drama was extremely popular in Depression-era America. Cantril estimates that about 6 million people heard Orson Welles's 1938 *Mercury Theatre of the Air* broadcast of H. G. Wells's *War of the Worlds* and that at least 1 million were frightened. The panic caused many commentators to conclude that SF fans were of feeble mind, but Cantril, who interviewed 135 people in depth, found that listeners who had some familiarity with SF (mainly from magazines, comic strips, radio programs, and serial films) were likely to dismiss the broadcast as "that crazy Buck Rogers stuff" while most listeners who panicked were completely ignorant of SF. Many interviewees' accounts of absolute terror are far from funny. Cantril reprints the script of the broadcast by Howard Koch. In his 1992 book of interviews with Peter Bogdanovich, *This Is Orson Welles,* Welles finally admitted that the broadcast was intended to frighten listeners. *The Complete War of the Worlds: Mars' Invasion of Earth from H. G. Wells to Orson Welles* (Sourcebooks, 2001), by Brian Holmsten and Alex Lubertozzi, discusses Wells's novel and its adaptations and includes a CD of the radio broadcast and other audio documents. Patrick Lucanio and Gary Coville's *Smokin' Rockets: The Romance of Technology in American Film, Radio and Television, 1945–1962* (2002) has a 20-page chapter on the *War of the Worlds* radio broadcast.

Handbook of Old-Time Radio by Jon D. Swartz and Robert C. Reinehr (1993) is one of the most complete guides to U.S. radio series, including several SF programs. John Dunning's *Tune in Yesterday* (1976) and Ronald W. Lackmann's *Encyclopedia of American Radio* (2000) provide more detailed commentaries on the more significant series than Swartz/Reinehr. The most detailed examination of the subject is probably *Science Fiction—on Radio: A Revised Look at 1950–1975* by James F. Widner and Meade Frierson III. Burgess and Bartle's *Reference Guide to Science Fiction, Fantasy and Horror* [7-11] found Widner/Frierson "complete and useful"; it was not seen for this chapter. Also see Table 11-5.

The 1978 British radio series *The Hitchhiker's Guide to the Galaxy* has been immortalized by a series of novels by Douglas Adams (1979–1992) and by Neil Gaiman's *Don't Panic: The Official Hitchhiker's Guide to the Galaxy Companion* (1988, rev. 2003). (MK)

*11-70.   Erdmann, Terry J., and Paula M. Block. **Star Trek: Deep Space Nine Companion**. Pocket Books, 2000.

A model for what any TV-series "companion" book should be, this hefty volume, fitting no imaginable pocket, is simple in its layout but provides enough information for all but the most fanatic fan (if the redundancy may be permitted) or scholar. Each of the 176 episodes is given an entry featuring writer and director credits, a guest cast list, Stardate if known, detailed synopsis, and—the longest section—a thoughtful essay on the making of the episode, its themes and character development, and its place in the overall scheme of the show, with many quotations from producers and writers. Good black-and-white production stills or excellent line drawings of sets and props are found on nearly every page.

In comparison, the commentaries in the *Star Trek: Voyager Companion* (2003) and other "official" Pocket Books *Trek* guides are less informative and less well written, while the great many "unofficial" guides to the various series—though they provide stimulation by rating "best" and "worst" episodes—lack the illustrations and history. For "insider" narratives, *The World of Star Trek* (rev. ed., 1984) by David Gerrold, who wrote one episode of the original series, is still readable, while the more recent *Inside Star Trek: The Real Story* (Pocket, 1996) gives us the perspectives of two of the original producers, Herbert F. Solow and Robert H. Justman. [JM]

See also Tulloch/Jenkins [11-79] on *Trek* audiences. Bjo Trimble's *The Star Trek Concordance* (rev. ed., 1995) is a guide to episodes of the original series. Fine books on two other classic U.S. SF TV series are David J. Schow's and Jeffrey Frentzen's *The Outer Limits: The Official Companion* (1986) and Marc Scott Zicree's *The Twilight Zone Companion* (1989). (MK)

11-71. Fulton, Roger, and John Betancourt. **The Sci-Fi Channel Encyclopedia of TV Science Fiction**. Warner, 1998.

Fulton (without Betancourt) wrote *The Encyclopedia of TV Science Fiction*, a British publication (rev. ed., 1997) that covered U.S. and British programs seen on British TV from 1951 to 1996. The 1998 American version (with Betancourt) adds information on some U.S. programs not seen in the U.K. A total of 239 series are covered in some detail; an appendix provides minimal information for 41 British series that were seen only in the U.K.; these are covered more thoroughly in the 1997 edition. For most series the authors provide a brief, often tart critical note and the regular cast, as well as synopsis, guest actors, writer, and director for each episode. Some series lack data on episodes. See Morton [11-76] for comparisons between his book and this one. (MK)

11-72. Gerani, Gary, and Paul H. Schulman. **Fantastic Television**. Harmony, 1977.

For each of 16 series, some of which they admit are far from good, Gerani and Schulman provide one to seven pages of history and commentary (identifying outstanding episodes), several black-and-white illustrations, and credits and terse synopses for each episode. Each of several dozen other series and TV movies is described in a single paragraph. Largely complete through 1977, except for selective coverage of British and children's shows, Gerani/Schulman differ interestingly with Javna [11-74] on some series, such as *Doctor Who*, which Javna rates highly but Gerani/Schulman relegate to one dismissive paragraph. (MK)

11-73. Helford, Elyce Rae, ed. **Fantasy Girls: Gender in the New Universe of Science Fiction and Fantasy Television**. Rowman & Littlefield, 2000.

Five of the 11 essays collected here are about SF series, or seven if one counts *Third Rock from the Sun* and *Lois and Clark*. The majority of the authors find that recent shows with power heroines are not as progressive as they may seem, with white, heterosexual, and sometimes patriarchal norms prevailing. Two of the best essays are by Linda Badley, on *The X-Files'* Agent Scully, and Robin Roberts (see 11-68), on the women of *Star Trek: Voyager*. (JM)

Themes: Women in SF

11-74.   Javna, John. **The Best of Science Fiction TV**. Harmony, 1987.

Javna solicited comments on SF TV series from a jury of 113 critics, fans, and SF authors. Four pages are devoted to each of 15 "best" shows and two pages to each of the 10 "worst" series. Entries include each program's dates, number of episodes, actors, character names, descriptive and critical notes by Javna, brief comments by jurors, small black-and-white illustrations, "trivia," and some well-chosen quotes from the show (for example, from *Doctor Who*, "I'm a citizen of the Universe and a gentleman to boot"). The terse comments by Javna and jurors are often perceptive. Unlike Gerani/Schulman [11-72], Javna has no episode synopses. Shorter entries describe 38 additional series of special interest—British, Japanese, 1950s, anthology, and animated programs. Bibliography. Javna's book is more fannish than Gerani/Schulman's, more up to date, and more in sympathy with its subject. (MK)

11-75.   Lucanio, Patrick, and Gary Coville. **American Science Fiction Television Series of the 1950s**. McFarland, 1998.

Lucanio and Coville provide detailed, affectionate, but critical accounts of 20 U.S. SF TV series from 1949 to 1959, advancing from the early, primitive, juvenile space operas (*Captain Video and His Video Rangers; Space Patrol; Tom Corbett, Space Cadet*) to later attempts at adult SF (*Science Fiction Theatre; Men into Space; The Man and the Challenge*). The series reflected the values of the 1950s—optimistic, patriotic, and pro-science, but some series indulged in mild satire. Some SF writers contributed stories or scripts to the better programs; SF film director Jack Arnold directed episodes of *Science Fiction Theatre*. For each series, the authors provide a thoughtful discussion; for the best-documented series, they have gathered credits, casts, and episode synopses. Less complete information is available for some series. (One suspects the authors were secretly relieved that very little is known of the approximately 1,500 (!) episodes of *Captain Video*.) Almost a third of the book is devoted to *The Adventures of Superman*. The book contains several wonderful illustrations, but some pictures are of poor quality. A number of desirable illustrations are missing; for instance, there are no pictures of the hand-puppet characters from *Johnny Jupiter* (1953–1954). Morton [11-76] has more information than Lucanio/Coville on a few of the series. *Variety Television Reviews* (1990) reprints terse contemporary reviews of episodes from many of the series, including 47 episodes of *Science Fiction Theatre*. George W. Woolery's *Children's Television* (2 vols., 1983, 1985), Donald F. Glut and Jim Harmon's *The Great Television Heroes* (1975), and Gary H. Grossman's *Saturday Morning TV* (1987) all have additional discussions of the juvenile space series. [MK]

Lucanio and Coville offer a broader but uneven survey in *Smokin' Rockets: The Romance of Technology in American Film, Radio and Television, 1945–1962* (2002). (JM)

11-76.   Morton, Alan. **The Complete Directory to Science Fiction, Fantasy and Horror Television Series: A Comprehensive Guide to the First 50 Years 1946 to 1996**. Other Worlds Books, 1997.

Morton and Lentz [11-3] are the two largest sources of information on SF TV series. Both list the stars of each series and the names of their characters as well as titles, broadcast dates, and guest stars for each episode. Lentz includes TV films and miniseries, which Morton omits. Morton's immense (982 pages of too-small print) *Directory* covers 389 series and about 15,000 episodes. Lentz and Fulton/Betancourt [11-71] have (and Morton lacks) the names of characters portrayed by guest stars in individual episodes. Morton has (and Lentz lacks) terse synopses for each episode. Morton has several series not in Fulton/Betancourt, who have a few British puppet animation series (*Terrahawks, Thunderbirds*) not in Morton. Fulton/Betancourt's *Encyclopedia* lacks episode information for some series for which Morton has that information, but the *Encyclopedia* has more detailed episode synopses than Morton and larger print. Morton is stronger than Fulton/Betancourt on 1950s series. The index of George W. Woolery's *Children's Television: The First Thirty-Five Years, 1946–1981* (2 vols., 1983–1985) lists 50 juvenile SF series; Woolery provides credits and description for each series. John Baxter's *Science Fiction in the Cinema* (1970) has a chapter on SF on TV. Larson's *Musique Fantastique* [11-44] covers music in SF TV. Penley/Lyon/Spiegel's *Close Encounters* [11-54] considers some SF series from a feminist perspective. *Starlog* magazine [11-82] and recent issues of *CFQ* [11-80] cover current and older TV series. (MK)

11-77.   Philips, Mark, and Frank Garcia. **Science Fiction Television Series: Episode Guides, Histories, and Casts and Credits for 62 Prime Time Shows, 1959 Through 1989**. McFarland, 1996.

Philips and Garcia interviewed about 250 TV producers, directors, writers, actors, and other personnel and sprinkled their recollections through this large (691 pp.) survey of 31 years of genre TV. Each show gets an essay (2 to 8 pp.) on its development and success or failure, as well as episode synopses and credits for episode writers, directors, and guest actors. The authors do not give critical judgments, but some of the quoted comments by TV veterans are critical. Comedy shows (e.g., *Mork and Mindy*), marginal SF (*The Man from U.N.C.L.E.*), foreign shows (*Doctor Who, The Avengers*), and horror, animation, and juvenile Saturday-morning series are omitted. It is remarkable that even with all these omissions, 61 series were made in 31 years; the 62nd series included was *Science Fiction Theatre* (1955–1957), which the authors considered too important to omit even though it fell outside their time period. Appendixes list unsold pilots, omitted programs, and Emmy winners and nominees. (MK)

11-78. Tulloch, John, and Manuel Alvarado. **Doctor Who: The Unfolding Text**. St. Martin's, 1983.

11-79. Tulloch, John, and Henry Jenkins. **Science Fiction Audiences: Watching Doctor Who and Star Trek**. Routledge, 1995.

Doctor Who (1963–1989), one of the longest-lived TV series in any genre, attempted with considerable success to entertain both adults and children. For a while, its worldwide popularity rivaled that of *Star Trek*. As seven actors succeeded each other in the leading role, the tone and quality of episodes varied tremendously. Tulloch and Alvarado's *Unfolding Text* is serious and analytic, so much so that casual fans may find it heavy going. The authors explore the show's roots in British pulp fiction, the differences among the first four Doctors, and conflicts among writers, producers, and actors over the proper balance of the show's SF, comic, and adventure elements. The production of "Kinda," an unusually ambitious episode, is examined in detail. There is a large bibliography but few illustrations. In his *Textual Poachers: Television Fans and Participatory Culture* (Routledge, 1992), Jenkins, who is both a scholar and a fan, offers a well-informed and highly laudatory account of activist fans of many cult TV shows, most of them SF or fantasy, showing that committed fans are not passive consumers of their favorite shows but use the shows as raw material for their own creative efforts. Tulloch and Jenkins combine forces in *Science Fiction Audiences* (though only one of their names is assigned to most chapters). *Science Fiction Audiences* examines how fan groups have changed in the 1990s—less "didactic," more playfully ironic. The 1995 book covers some of the same ground as *Textual Poachers* and *Doctor Who: The Unfolding Text*, but there are benefits to comparing fan involvements in such distinctly different series.

The *Doctor Who Programme Guide* by Jean-Marc Lofficier (1989, 2 vols.) furnishes the dates, writer, director, cast, and character names for each episode. Lofficier's episode synopses are a little too terse. Volume one of Lofficier's set is the episode guide; volume two is a reference guide to characters, places, species, and other names from the series. Many heavily illustrated *Doctor Who* books have appeared in Britain, several written by Peter Haining.

Two other major British series with SF elements are chronicled in two books by Dave Rogers: *The Complete Avengers* (1989) and *The Prisoner & Danger Man* (1989). (*The Prisoner* was a futuristic thriller, while *Danger Man* was a spy series without SF content.) Fulton/Betancourt [11-71] is strong on British SF TV. (MK, JM)

Periodicals

*11-80. **CFQ** [formerly **Cinefantastique**]. ISSN 0145-6032. 1970–. Bimonthly. David E. Williams, ed. (P.O. Box 34425, Los Angeles, CA 90034-0425.) Circ.: 30,000. Indexed: *Film Literature Index, Media Review Digest*. Web site: www.cfq.com.

Cinefantastique and *Video Watchdog* [11-83] have long been the highest quality English-language magazines on SF, fantasy, and horror films. After the death of long-time editor Frederick S. Clarke in 2000, the magazine acquired a new title, a new editor, and a "new look." Issues of *CFQ* range from 60 to 90 pages, with in-depth articles and excellent illustrations. Short pieces profile forthcoming productions. Current films are reviewed with independence and sophistication. In the 1990s, *Cinefantastique* began to take a more popular approach, without sacrificing quality. After years of paying scant attention to television, *CFQ* now provides selective coverage of both old and new TV shows, as well as video games and comics.

Locus, Chronicle and *Magazine of Fantasy and Science Fiction* (see Chapter 12) all have frequent but not comprehensive coverage of films and TV. *Harlan Ellison's Watching* (1989) collected Ellison's rambling film columns for the *Magazine of Fantasy and Science Fiction*. Two periodicals, *International Index to Film Periodicals* (1972–) and *Film Literature Index* (1973–), index reviews and articles in film magazines. *Film Review Index* (2 vols., 1986, 1987), edited by Patricia King Hanson and Stephen L. Hanson, indexes both reviews in periodicals and discussions in hundreds of books of more than 7,000 significant films from the silents to 1985. Lee [11-2], Willis [11-7] and the online Encyclopedia of Fantastic Film and Television (www.eofftv.com) all provide citations to periodical reviews. (MK)

11-81.   Cinefex. ISSN 0198-1056. 1980–. Quarterly. Don Shay, ed. (P.O. Box 20027, Riverside, CA 92516.) Circ.: 36,000. Indexed: *Film Literature Index; International Index to Film Periodicals*. Web site: www.cinefex.com.

Cinefex is the magazine of record for special effects. Each issue contains lengthy technical reports on effects work in one to three current productions. *Cinefex* is dependent on the cooperation of filmmakers and does not criticize effects or other aspects of films, but the technical information provided is invaluable. *American Cinematographer* magazine also often has articles on technical work in major genre films. (MK)

11-82.   Starlog. ISSN 0191-4626. 1976–. Monthly. David McDonnell, ed. (475 Park Ave. S., New York, N.Y. 10016.) Circ: 267,000. Web site: www.starlog.com.

The most popular magazine in the field, *Starlog* covers SF and fantasy films and TV—all fantastic media except horror, which is the subject of its sister publication, *Fangoria*. Issues are 80 to 90 pages, with informative but uncritical, heavily illustrated articles and interviews. *Starlog* maintains friendly relations with studios by not reviewing current films. Stronger than *CFQ* [11-80] in coverage of TV series, *Starlog* also includes interviews with fiction authors and reviews of videodiscs, novels, comic books, and computer games. While not as essential as *CFQ*, *Starlog* with its abundance of facts and paucity of analysis is useful for large collections. Interviews from *Starlog* are collected in Lee Goldberg's *Science Fiction Filmmaking in the 1980s*. (MK)

11-83.   Video Watchdog. ISSN 1070-9991. 1990–. Monthly (formerly bimonthly). Tim Lucas, ed. (P.O. Box 5283, Cincinnati, OH 45205-0283.) Circ.: not reported. Reviews only indexed at its Web site: www.videowatchdog.com.

The *Watchdog*'s excellent articles and reviews cover SF, horror, and fantasy films (as well as such cult categories as Italian muscleman movies, Chinese martial arts movies, and Italian Westerns) on videocassette and videodisc. Each issue of about 80 pages has a wealth of information on obscure, low-budget, and foreign films that have been made available by the insatiable video industry. Reviews of big-budget films often provide insights not found in mainstream reviews. Books in the field and soundtrack recordings are also reviewed. A model of fan scholarship, combining industry, accuracy, enthusiasm, and extraordinary erudition. (MK)

Science Fiction Film and Television on the Internet

Brian Stableford has argued that the locus of SF was magazines for approximately 30 years, beginning about 1930, followed by paperback and hardcover books for the next 30 years, and has increasingly been influenced by film and TV since. Whether you accept his argument is less important than that you recognize the growing importance of filmed and televised SF, which is increasingly the entry point for fans, many of whom don't "progress" to written SF.

Not surprisingly, the Internet also reflects these shifts. Listed below are a selection of the better Web sites suggested by Chapter 11's authors. Just as most printed SF is undistinguished, only a few dozen SF films or TV programs have much interest or merit or reward sustained analysis in the judgment of knowledgeable film/TV buffs. The sites listed range from those appealing mostly to fans to more academic fare, with considerable variation in quality. The listing is alphabetical by topic. See also the mentions elsewhere in this chapter of other SF film/TV/radio Internet sites, such as the very large and valuable Internet Movie Database (IMDb), which isn't restricted to fantastic cinema.

Babylon 5
Babylon 5 Lurker's Guide
www.midwinter.com/lurk/lurker.html

Blade Runner
BRmovie.com, the home of Blade Runner
   www.brmovie.com/
2019: Off-world (Blade Runner page)
   scribble.com/uwi/br/off-world.html

Brazil
Brazil film FAQs
   www.faqs.org/faqs/movies/brazil-faq/

Doctor Who
Bevis-Duncan Doctor Who Guide
 www.ee.surrey.ac.uk/Contrib/SciFi/DrWho/

Forbidden Planet
Robby the Robot fan site
 www.100megsfree3.com/glaw/robby/
Fred Barton Productions
 www.the-robotman.com/nv_fs.html
Unofficial Forbidden Planet Home Page
 sfstation.members.easyspace.com/fbhome.htm

Lost in Space
Lost in Space Classic TV
 www.theouterlimits.com/home.html

The Matrix
Matrix: Revolutions
 whatisthematrix.warnerbros.com/
 whatisthematrix.warnerbros.com/rl_cmp/phi.html

The Outer Limits
The Outer Limits Home
 www.theouterlimits.com/home.html

Star Trek (TV series and films)
Star Trek: Deep Space Nine
 www.ee.surrey.ac.uk/Contrib/SciFi/StarTrek/STDS9/welcome.html
Star Trek: Next Generation
 www.ee.surrey.ac.uk/Contrib/SciFi/StarTrek/STTNG/
World of Star Trek
 www.ee.surrey.ac.uk/Contrib/SciFi/StarTrek/
Startrek.com
 www.startrek.com/startrek/view/index.html

2001
2001: A Space Odyssey Internet Resources Archive
 www.palantir.net/2001/

SF on Television

Science fiction on television, from Wikipedia
 en.wikipedia.org/wiki/Science_fiction_television

SF on Film (general sites, filmographies)

List of science fiction films, from Wikipedia
  en.wikipedia.org/wiki/List_of_science_fiction_films
Science Fiction movies of the 60s
  www.sixtiescity.com/SciFilm/Scifilm.htm
Science Fiction, Fantasy, Horror: Media Resources Center
  www.lib.berkeley.edu/MRC/scififilm.html
  and its bibliography:
  www.lib.berkeley.edu/MRC/scifibib.html
Open Directory—Arts: Genres: Science Fiction and Fantasy—links to many sites
  dmoz.org/Arts/Genres/Science_Fiction_and_Fantasy/
Science Fiction Research Bibliography—A Bibliography of Science Fiction
  Secondary Materials
  www.wsu.edu:8080/~brians/science_fiction/sfresearch.html
Science Fiction in Film and Television: A Bibliography of Resources in Print
  www.geocities.com/Hollywood/Lot/2976/SF2-intro.html
Slacker's Sci-Fi Source
  www.whataslacker.com/scifi/html/sgp5.shtml
Science Fiction Film—Clemson University
  hubcap.clemson.edu/~sparks/sffilm/indexsff.html
Gary Westphal's Biographical Encyclopedia of Science Fiction Film
  www.sfsite.com/interzone/gary/intro.htm
Science Fiction Films, long essay by Tim Dirks
  www.filmsite.org/sci-fifilms.html/

CHAPTER 12

Science Fiction Illustration

Walter Albert and Neil Barron

Most historians of science fiction consider Frank R. Paul (1884–1963) to be the father of modern SF illustration. This fits neatly with the importance of the American pulp magazine in popularizing the fiction, but it ignores the tradition that precedes the pulp era, many of whose works were republished in 1920s pulps and in such magazines as *Fantastic Novels* and *Famous Fantastic Mysteries* as late as the 1940s.

Both Robert Weinberg in his *Biographical Dictionary* [12-36] and Gary K. Wolfe in "The Iconography of Science-Fiction Art" in Volume 2 of Coward and Wymer [10-3] place it at the end of the 19th century, in the futuristic drawings of Frenchman Albert Robida and in magazine and book illustrations for Verne (Wolfe) and Wells (Weinberg). They can't, however, agree on the important illustrators. Weinberg identifies Warwick Goble (illustrator of Wells's *War of the Worlds*), Fred Jane, and Henri Lanos as the "three finest artists" specializing in science fiction, while Wolfe refers to Hildibrand (illustrator of Verne) and several other artists (including Jane but not Lanos), but ignores Goble. Vincent di Fate in his chapter, "Science Fiction Art: Some Contemporary Illustrators," in Marshall Tymn's *Science Fiction Reference Book* (1981), avoids the issue and begins his discussion with Frank R. Paul's work for *Amazing Stories* in 1926, with the brief comment that science fiction art is as old as the literature. However, with the recent publication of his important history of SF illustration *Infinite Worlds* [12-8], Di Fate redresses his earlier cursory treatment with coverage of French artists Grandville (1803–1847) and Albert Robida (1848–1926), and British artists Goble (1862–1943), Paul Hardy (1862–194?), and Jane (1865–1916), although he does not include any examples of the work of the three British illustrators. Examples of these artists' works (along with other illustrators of the period) can be found in Frewin [12-12], but treatment of the 19th-century illustrators in the standard histories is generally cursory at best.

The science fiction magazine tradition may have come into prominence in 1926 with the publication of Gernsback's *Amazing Stories,* but it did not inaugurate a new style in fiction but rather continued and made available to a more diverse audience the scientific romance popularized by Wells in England and by Edgar Rice Burroughs in this country.

Burroughs's Mars and Venus stories were illustrated by J. Allen St. John (1872–1957), whose romantic style featured dark-haired women in peril and muscular heroes in conflict with fantastic beasts and alien beings. Wolfe sees him as the "figure who most clearly epitomizes the transition from earlier book and magazine illustrations to the pulp era." Yet even Wolfe considers St. John's style "dated" by 1926. This style was, in the early years of the pulps, bypassed in favor of "gadget" or hardware art, in which spaceships and towering cities of intricate architecture took precedence over character- and situation-based art.

Paul and his contemporaries have not always enjoyed critical appreciation of their work, with their covers characterized by Brian Aldiss in his *Trillion Year Spree* as "gaudy but gorgeous." The stereotypical image of moldering pulp magazines hoarded by aging fans has translated into a dismissal of much of the art and fiction of the 1930s as chiefly of antiquarian interest. This is a point of view promoted not only by academic critics whose disdain of Burroughs and early pulp fiction style is well documented but also recently by the contemporary illustrator Boris Vallejo.

Vallejo, in his foreword to *The Fantasy Art Techniques of Tim Hildebrandt* (Paper Tiger, 1991), comments that only artists of "limited talent" worked in the field in the early years, in a market that was "woefully underpaid." Then, in the 1960s and 1970s, artists often possessing "prodigious talent . . . opened the doors for an art form that now has millions of faithfully following fans all over the world." It is ironic that Boris—as he is known professionally—rose to popularity imitating the style of his gifted colleague Frank Frazetta, who first came to notice in the field illustrating covers for Ace editions of novels by Edgar Rice Burroughs, a task he shared initially with Roy Krenkel, whose covers were very much in the tradition of J. Allen St. John. And the popular sword-and-sorcery genre with which both Frazetta and Boris came to be identified was squarely in the tradition of early pulp fiction.

The first era of the science fiction pulps (1926–1953) is dominated by two men, publisher Hugo Gernsback (*Amazing Stories, Air Wonder Stories,* and other pulps) and John W. Campbell, Jr., editor of *Astounding Science Fiction* from 1937 to 1971. Although their magazines and editorial policies were widely divergent, their artwork, particularly that of the covers, was largely devoted to machine art, with human figures either primitively rendered (Gernsback) or featured as enigmatic or symbolic fixtures in a technocratic society (Campbell). Paul's colorful covers with their impressive alien and futuristic architectures have come to be synonymous with the early years of the pulps. His influence can be seen in the work of Hans Wessolowsky ("Wesso") on covers for the Clayton *Astounding* and even later in the work of Robert Fuqua for the Campbell-edited *Astounding*. Leo Morey was particularly skillful at capturing alien life forms in his work, while Howard V. Brown is often considered to have perfected the first space art style in his gleaming, austere projectiles.

Campbell favored a less imaginative, more "authentic" hardware style. However, when the Gernsback era waned in the mid-1930s, in spite of the importance of the *Astounding* "look," some of the most striking covers were those done for *Startling Stories, Planet Stories,* and *Startling Wonder Stories.* These depicted Flash Gordon space hunks and superbly endowed females threatened by and struggling with Bug-Eyed Monsters (BEMs), a style brought to perfection by Earle K. Bergey, later a notable illustrator of paperback covers. This style, the aesthetic culmination of the space adventure pulp story, would later be updated and modernized in films (the *Star Wars* trilogy) and in the popular and enduring TV and film *Star Trek* series.

However, the most popular artist of the late 1930s and 1940s, equally gifted at fantasy and science fiction, was the prolific Virgil Finlay, whose early work was featured on the covers and interiors of *Weird Tales,* and whose work, along with that of Hannes Bok, Paul, and Lawrence, made the companion magazines *Famous Fantastic Mysteries* and *Fantastic Novels* among the finest repositories of notable pulp art in the 1940s.

As the first generation of pulp magazines went the way of the dinosaur in the early 1950s, it was succeeded by the digest pulps and by an explosion of paperback reprints and original fiction and small-press imprints. Here one found illustrators such as Kelly Freas, Ed Emsh, Edd Cartier, and Edward Valigursky, most of whom had begun their careers in the pulps. The most innovative artist during this period may have been Richard Powers, whose surrealist-inspired paperback covers brought a new level of sophistication to pulp art, preparing the way for a generation of artists, many of them British, with affiliations with European art movements.

The more austere *Astounding* style found its most important legacy in the astronomical space art of Chesley Bonestell, prefiguring the artwork that would celebrate the achievements of American and Soviet space programs. The merging of futuristic science fiction with the reality of a new era of actual space voyages has been a dominant strain in the science fiction illustration of the post-WWII era, but tempered by the popularity of heroic fantasy and sword-and-sorcery art. This was fueled by the resurgent popularity of Burroughs in the 1960s and the rediscovery of Robert E. Howard's pulp fiction. No new icon of the stature of Frank Frazetta appears to have surfaced in the past quarter century, but a continuing infusion of talented American and British artists in the field has kept the quality of new work at a high level. If British illustrators have seemed more influenced by the hardware tradition, American illustrators have often turned to a more fantasy-oriented art, with their models not in the earlier pulp generation but in the work of such notable illustrators as Howard Pyle and Maxfield Parrish. This is especially true in the late 1970s and 1980s in the work of Michael Whelan and, more recently, in the highly decorative work of Don Maitz.

It is often difficult to separate fantasy from science fiction in the work of these illustrators. Both Whelan and Maitz move easily from one to the other, or combine the two in their work. The most influential postwar pulp magazine, *The Magazine of Fantasy and Science Fiction*, can be considered as the model for a genre in which crossover elements are the norm rather than the exception, although the New Wave writers of the 1960s attempted to focus the genre on "hard" science wedded to stories of great technical skill that used fictional techniques usually associated with non-genre fiction, turning away from the colorful, action-filled pulp universe.

If the fiction has managed to escape what it sees as its "humble" adventure epic beginnings and to produce writers who rival non-genre prose writers in their techniques and sophistication, the artists, also refusing to accept traditional categories, have increasingly explored the graphic novel, worked as storyboard illustrators for films, and returned to traditional book illustration. Their recognition has usually come from within the field, most commonly in the form of the Hugo to the best professional artist, awarded each year at the world science fiction convention, but more recently from the Chesleys, named in honor of Chesley Bonestell and recognizing both SF and fantasy artists. In addition, the artists now have exhibitions at art galleries, publish limited-edition prints and portfolios, and are collected by knowledgeable fans for whom illustration is not a second-rate category.

The rise of interest in SF illustration has also resulted in the publication of volumes on individual artists. The British publisher Paper Tiger has been most active in this area, although its focus tends to be on the current generation. Gerry de la Ree was active in the 1960s and 1970s in the publication of books on Virgil Finlay, Hannes Bok, and other illustrators of the pulp era, but even with the increasing recognition of the importance of Frank R. Paul, there has been no comprehensive study of his work. However, an enterprising fan, Frank Wu, has created an impressive Web site (www.frankwu.com/paul.html) devoted to the artist that features an extensive gallery of his color and black-and-white work as well as a bibliography-in-progress.

Wu's well-maintained site is by far the most research-oriented resource for a major SF illustrator. The individual Web sites usually provide only brief biographies and representative examples of the artists' work, generally oriented toward the potential purchaser of reproductions and, occasionally, original artwork. The site devoted to Don Maitz is the most attractive and includes a statement on "what" he's about that furnishes some insight into his working methods, with the gallery of illustrations cataloged by subject. The most useful of the general sites is FANAC's Professional Artists' Index (http://fanac.org/ProArt/index.html), which, in addition to very brief "profiles" of the work of a

Table 12-1. Hugo Professional Artist Winners and Nominees, 1955–2004
Chesley Artistic Achievement Winners, 1985–2004

Illustrator	Entry	Wins	Noms. only	Rank	Chesley
*Michael Whelan, 1950–	E, W	13	9	35	1
*Frank Kelly Freas, 1922–	E, W	10	15	34	2
*Bob Eggleton, 1960–	W	8	8	22	0
*Don Maitz, 1953–	E, W	2	17	21	3
Jack Gaughan, 1930–1985	E, W	3	8	14	0
John Schoenherr, 1935–	E, W	1	10	12	0
*Vincent Di Fate, 1945–	E, W	1	10	12	1
*James Burns, 1948–	E, W	2	9	12	0
Ed Emshwiller (Emsh), 1925–1990	E, W	4	2	10	0
David A. Cherry, 1949–	E, W	0	10	10	0
Stephen E. Fabian, 1930–	E, W	0	7	7	0
*Virgil Finlay, 1914–1971	E, W	0	6	6	0
*Rick Sternbach, 1951–	E, W	2	2	6	0
*Frank Frazetta, 1928–	E, W	1	5	6	2
*Barclay Shaw, 1949–	E, W	0	5	5	0
Donato Giancola, 1967–		0	6	5	1
Thomas Canty, 1952–	E, W	0	4	4	0
Thomas Kidd, 1955–	E, W	0	4	4	1
Leo & Diane Dillon, both 1933–	E, W	1	2	4	1
Mel Hunter, 1929–2004	W	0	3	3	0
Roy Krenkel, 1918–1983	E, W	1	1	3	0
*Gray Morrow, 1934–2001	E, W	0	3	3	0
Jeff Jones, 1944–	W	0	3	3	0
Boris Vallejo (Boris), 1941–	E, W	0	2	2	0
Wally Wood, 1927–1981	E, W	0	2	2	0
Vaughan Bodé, 1941–1975	E	0	2	2	0
Eddie Jones, 1935–1999	E, W	0	2	2	0
*George Barr, 1937–	E, W	0	2	2	0
Paul Lehr, 1930–98	E, W	0	2	2	0
Val Lakey (Lindahn), 1951–	W	0	2	2	0
J(effrey) K(night) Potter, 1956–	E	0	2	2	0
James Gurney, 1958–	E, W	0	2	2	2
H. R. Van Dongen, 1920–	E, W	0	1	1	0
*Alex Schomburg, 1905–1998	E, W	0	1	1	1
*Chesley Bonestell, 1888–1986	E, W	0	1	1	0
Mike Hinge, 1931–2003	W	0	1	1	0
Tim Kirk, 1947–	W	0	1	1	0
*David Hardy, 1936–	E, W	0	1	1	0
Carl Lundgren, 1947–	W	0	1	1	1
Darrell Sweet, 1934–	E, W	0	1	1	0
Nick Stathopoulos, 1959–		0	1	1	1
Todd Lockwood		0	0	0	1

E=*Encyclopedia of Science Fiction* [7-21]; W=Weinberg [12-36]
Rank equals wins times two plus nominations.
* Denotes an illustrator who is the subject of a book annotated in this chapter; see
also the accompanying list of online resources devoted to these SF illustrators.

number of illustrators, also provides links to illustrator sites. However, it's clear that this potentially rich resource has yet to be seen as much more than a showcase for illustrators and illustration.

The most important change in the field has been in the way in which the art is produced, with computer-generated paintings favored by many artists. In films, traditional animation has largely been abandoned by the industry. It's difficult to imagine that oils and watercolors will be completely superseded by new technologies, but artists are, by their very nature, restless, refusing to be bound by the past. What directions that restlessness may take them in can only be guessed at, since the best artists always surprise us with their work, but the results will surely be as rich and exciting as the rapid developments of the past hundred years have been.

Art/Illustration on the Web

Because the Web can show illustration/art, both still and moving images, it is a potentially valuable supplement to printed resources. It is also useful to illustrators wishing to market originals or reproductions and to buyers seeking such work. Artists listed below were selected from the 41 Hugo and Chesley winners included in Table 12-1 who focus more on SF than fantasy (about half of those listed) plus the 24 additional artists whose work is the subject of books annotated in this chapter. All such artists are identified by asterisks in the following list. (The books are obviously the first choice, but the Web sites are sometimes more current.) Not all listed individuals had Web sites. The sites varied considerably in the amount of information provided, with "official" Web sites providing the most information. Both text and images were included on most sites. William Contento identified and verified these sites.

*Artzybasheff	falcon.jmu.edu/~ramseyil/artzybasheff.htm
*Barlowe	www.waynebarlowe.com [under construction May 2004]
*Belarski	www.illustration-house.com/bios/belarski_bio.html
*Berkey	members.fortunecity.com/lioncourt77/berkey.html
*Bonestell	www.bonestell.org
	www.bonestell.com
*Burns	camarila.www.50megs.com/jimburns.html
*Cartier	www.meskin.net/influences/cartier/cartier.html
Cherry	www.davidcherryart.com/
*Dean	www.rogerdean.com/
*Di Fate	www.vincentdifate.com/
*Eggleton	www.bobeggleton.com/
*Elson	hugues.namur.free.fr/images_autres_HD/vaisseaux/illus/ peter-elson_gallery/
Emshwiller	fanac.org/ProArt/Emsh-1.html

	www.eai.org/eai/artist.jsp?artistID=471
*Finlay	www.bpib.com/illustrat/finlay.htm
*Foss	www.altanen.dk/Gallery-main.htm
	www.altanen.dk/ChrisFossBio.htm
*Foster	www.jonfoster.com
*Frazetta	frazettaartgallery.com/ff/index.html
*Freas	www.kellyfreas.com/
*Gambino	www.users.globalnet.co.uk/~fredgamb
Gaughan	www.askart.com/artist/G/jack_gaughan.asp?ID=126742
Giancola	www.donatoart.com/
*Giger	www.hrgiger.com/
*Hardy	www.hardyart.demon.co.uk
*Harris	www.fantasiaonline.com/harris/index.html
Hildebrandt	www.brothershildebrandt.com/
Hinge	www.sfwa.org/News/mhinge.htm
Hunter	www.imagemakers.mb.ca/hunter/hunter1/huntbio.html
Jones	www.ulster.net/~jonesart/
	www.bpib.com/illustrat/jonesjf.htm
Kidd	www.spellcaster.com/tomkidd/
*Kirby	www.abandonart.co.uk/artists/biog_jk.html
Lakey	www.fantasygallery.com, select Lindahn, Val Lakey
Lehr	isfdb.tamu.edu/cgi-bin/ea.cgi?Paul_Lehr
Lundgren	www.carllundgren.com/
*Maitz	www.paravia.com/DonMaitz/
*Manchu	www.planete-art.com/manchu0.htm
*Matthews	www.rodneymatthews.com
*McCall	oncampus.richmond.edu/cultural/museums/maginfo/mccall.html
	www.underview.com/2001/mccall.html
*Mead	www.sydmead.com
*Moore	www.illust.demon.co.uk/
*Pennington	freehost06.websamba.com/fantasy2003/jabba/bpennington1.htm
*Powers	home.earthlink.net/~cjk5/
	www.panix.com/~dgh/Powers.html
*Robida	www.depauw.edu/sfs/reviews_pages/r30.htm#a30
	www.remyc.com/robida.html
*St. John	www.sierra-arts.net/Mar04FHFStJohn.html
Schoenherr	www.embracingthechild.org/aschoenherr.html
*Schomburg	www.ess.comics.org/ess/schomburg/scscanmn.html

*Shaw	www.barclayshaw.com/
Stathopoulos	www.geocities.com/nickpaint/
Sternbach	www.ricksternbach.com/
Van Dongen	fanac.org/ProArt/Dongen-1.html
*Walotsky	www.crescentblues.com/3_2issue/walotsky.shtml
*Whelan	www.michaelwhelan.com
*White	www.tim-white.co.uk

Contento also compiled this list of sites with artist biographies and/or sample artwork, whose subjects are not limited to those whose Web sites appear above. Not all the sites are limited to illustrators of the fantastic.

www.illustration-house.com/

www.askart.com/

www.fantasiaonline.com/

fanac.org/ProArt/index.html

These are directories of SF art sites:

www.spacejetters.co.uk/html/sf_galleries.html

www.wwar.com

Bibliography

I wish to thank Neil Barron and Robert E. Briney for their assistance in the preparation of this bibliography. Contributions are identified by their initials—(NB), (REB)—and by mine (WA).

General and Multi-Artist Studies

12-1.   Aldiss, Brian W. **Science Fiction Art**. Crown, 1975.

An oversized (10½ x 14¾ inches) 128-page softcover book, which showcases the work of 30 American and British magazine illustrators from the 1920s to the 1970s, while providing examples of cover and interior artwork by another 50 or so artists. The subtitle of the book (The Fantasies of SF) expresses the difficulty historians of the field have in distinguishing between science fiction and fantasy illustration. Aldiss's introduction concisely points up the isolation of the illustrators of the 1930s and 1940s from artistic currents such as Surrealism and Expressionism that were themselves dealing in imaginative ways with some of the themes of both science fiction and fantasy illustration. The showcase for the

30 artists is followed by a longer section organized by thematic materials, drawing on a wider range of artists. One of the strong points of the book is that much of the color work is reproduced in color and the striking black-and-white interiors are cleanly and usually sharply reproduced. A gallery of covers (in color and in black-and-white) of 79 magazine titles shows changing styles of both British and American titles. Index of artists and magazines. Compare Frewin [12-12], whose historical scope is broader, the more anecdotal work of Sadoul [12-32], and, most recently, the more comprehensive work of Di Fate [12-8]. (NB/WA)

12-2. Barnett, Paul, ed. **The Fantasy Art Gallery**. Paper Tiger, 2002.
A collection of interviews with 25 fantasy and science fiction artists first published in *Paper Snarl*, a fanzine associated with Paper Tiger and edited by Paul Barnett (a.k.a. John Grant). The science fiction artists include Jim Burns, Vince Di Fate, Bob Eggleton, Frank Kelly Freas, Fred Gambino, John Harris, Ron Miller, Chris Moore, and Ron Walotsky. The artists talk about their current and earlier work, influences, and techniques. Barnett is a good interviewer and the subjects seem to respond frankly to his questions. (WA)

12-3. Brosterman, Norman. **Out of Time: Designs for the Twentieth-Century Future**. Abrams, 2000.

12-4. Corn, Joseph J., and Brian Horrigan. **Yesterday's Tomorrows: Past Visions of the American Future**. Summit, 1984; Johns Hopkins, 1996.
Yesterday's Tomorrows was designed to serve as a narrative and pictorial companion to a traveling Smithsonian exhibition of advertising materials, film lobby cards, books, magazines, toys, and industrial models. The materials were chosen to illustrate "America's visions of the future" but are also "nostalgic bridges to the past" as "futuristic fantasies" are embedded in such earlier concepts as the mythology of the Western novel and film. After a broadly based, if necessarily selective, history of futuristic visions from turn-of-the-century periodicals through the pulp magazine era to the era of manned space exploration, the authors discuss the city, home, and transportation of the "near" future, concluding rather grimly with the "weapons and warfare of tomorrow." The book, which includes a catalog of the exhibition, suggested reading, and an index, is copiously, and often strikingly, illustrated with materials from the exhibition.

Brosterman's *Out of Time* was also written and published to accompany a traveling Smithsonian exhibition (2000–2003). While it touches on many of the same subjects as *Yesterday's Tomorrows* (pulp and magazine art, city of the future, and space exploration), the use of science fiction illustrations is more extensive, there is discussion of artists (with particular emphasis on the pioneering architectural fantasies of Frank R. Paul), and capsule biographies of some 30 artists. Brosterman also includes more examples of turn-of-the-century illustrators (Albert Robida, E. Janos, Hildibrand), as well as several examples of dime novel cover illustrations. In general, the text is subordinated to the impressive gallery of illustrations, but its generous selection of magazine illustrations makes it an ideal complement to the more technological, academically oriented earlier volume. (WA)

12-5.   Clute, John. **Science Fiction: The Illustrated Encyclopedia.** Dorling Kindersley, 1995.

Although Clute's encyclopedia is copiously illustrated, the artists of the many magazine, hardcover, and paperback covers reproduced are not identified, and the book is of marginal interest for this bibliography. Chapter Six ("Graphic Works") is identified as a "gallery of the major illustration trends, comics, and graphic novels," but it is less than 10 pages in length, with only a 2-page spread of "great illustrators," consisting of 10 artists. Of more interest (although it is long out of print) is Brian Ash's *The Visual Encyclopedia of Science Fiction* (Harmony Books, 1977). It contains relatively few color illustrations, but it is generously illustrated with black-and-white interior art, with the artists and source of the illustrations identified. There seems to be little, if any, interest in the great heritage of interior illustrations, a field that largely died with the demise of the pulps, but some of the best work of the pulp era was done in that medium, and Ash's book gives some sense of its quality. Also annotated as [7-20]. (WA)

12-6.   Dean, Martyn. **Dream Makers: Six Fantasy Artists at Work.** Paper Tiger, 1988.

These interviews with six American and British illustrators include Julek Heller, Michael Kaluta, and Chris Moore, who often incorporate science fiction iconography in their work. Their lives, ideas, and attitudes are clearly brought out by Dean's interviews, effectively rewritten by Chris Evans. Although Evans in his brief introduction claims that all the artists "work in an area which can be loosely called fantasy art," Evan describes the heroes of today's generation—and presumably the artists'—as "starship captains, warriors with magical weapons, bizarre but cuddly aliens," and refers to the artists' "soaring visions of human progress—gleaming spacecraft carrying a triumphant human race across the universe." This suggests the extent to which modern illustrators work in a universe of "dreams, nightmares and imagined futures," where fantasy and science fiction are not hostile or indifferent neighbors but co-inhabitants of a vast landscape of the imagination. Profusely illustrated in color and in black-and-white. (NB/WA)

12-7.   Dean, Martyn. **The Guide to Fantasy Art Techniques.** Paper Tiger, 1984.

Like *Dream Makers* [12-6], this *Guide* consists of interviews with several contemporary illustrators, among them Jim Burns, Syd Mead, and Chris Foss, some of whose work is often science fiction rather than fantasy. Also among the artists interviewed are Philip Castle, who works principally in car and airplane advertising art, but who earlier did promotional art for Kubrick's *A Clockwork Orange* and incorporated *Star Trek* elements into billboard art, and Martin Bower, a maker of models for science fiction television shows and feature films. With numerous color and black-and-white illustrations and photographs. (NB/WA)

*12-8. Di Fate, Vincent. **Infinite Worlds: The Fantastic Visions of Science Fiction Art.** Penguin, 1997.

Di Fate's superbly illustrated study of science fiction art provides the detailed historical overview, and biographical and critical coverage of individual artists that the field has long needed. The "Masters of the Infinite," a gallery of some 95 artists, organized alphabetically, with concise biographical and critical commentary, is accompanied by representative examples of artists' work, mostly in color but with some fine black-and-white reproductions that demonstrate the acute eye of Di Fate, himself a noted science fiction artist, for the best in his colleagues' work. The earliest of the artists represented is Joseph Clement Coll (1881–1921), a gifted book and magazine illustrator, probably best known for his illustrations for Arthur Conan Doyle's *The Lost World.* Although Coll died before the era inaugurated by *Amazing Stories* and the seminal influence of Frank R. Paul, his work was an important influence on pulp artists of the 1920s and 1930s, and it is a sign of Di Fate's sense of historical patterns that he includes Coll. The introduction is important not only for its historical charting but for the discussion of many artists not included in the main gallery, as well as providing additional information on artists who are profiled there. Although Di Fate rightly insists on the importance of science in distinguishing between fantasy and science fiction art, the distinctions are not always that easy to make, and the fantastic (particularly in the pre-Space Age artists) is not absent from his history. This is a coffee-table book with a text that redefines that often berated category and makes it, with Weinberg's *Biographical Dictionary* [12-36], one of the two general essential reference books. (WA)

*12-9. Fenner, Cathy, and Arnie Fenner, eds. **Spectrum: The Best in Contemporary Fantastic Art.** Underwood Books, Vols. 1–10, 1994–2003.

The Spectrum Award for fantastic art was established in 1994 by Arnie Fenner and Cathy Burnett (later Fenner). It is an annual juried competition open to all practitioners of fantastic art in all media. The panel of judges, which changes from year to year, is composed of artists, illustrators, art directors, designers, and other professionals in the field. Since 1994, Underwood Books has published an annual volume, edited by the Fenners, with contents drawn from that year's competition. (The first three volumes were co-edited with Jim Loehr.) Each volume contains approximately 200 works, divided into categories: editorial, advertising, book, comics, posters, institutional, and unpublished. The majority of works included are in color, with only occasional black-and-white entries. Three-dimensional works are represented by color photographs. Each volume presents a wide variety of subjects, styles, and uses for science-fictional and fantastic art. Technical details (size, media) for each entry are included, and the works are left to stand on their own merits: no evaluative or comparative commentary is included, other than that implied by identifying the various award winners.

From *Spectrum 2* onward, there has been an annual Grand Master Award, accompanied by representative works of the recipient. The recipients through 2003 have been Frank Frazetta, Don Ivan Punchatz, Leo and Diane Dillon, James E. Bama, John Berkey, Alan Lee, Jean Giraud, Kinuko Y. Craft, and Michael William Kaluta. And from Volume 3 onward, Arnie Fenner has contributed a lengthy survey essay, "The Year in Review," dealing with important events, high points, and trends in fantastic art. Volumes 1 through 4 also contained the winning entries for the Chesley Award, presented annually by the Association of Science Fiction and Fantasy Artists. (REB)

*12-10.   Frank, Jane, and Howard Frank. **The Frank Collection: A Showcase of the World's Finest Fantastic Art**. Paper Tiger, 2000.

Jane and Howard Frank, who have been collecting original SF and fantasy art for more than 30 years, have amassed a collection that "spans almost seventy years of science fiction art and consists of more than six hundred artworks by over one hundred different artists, [with] more than a quarter of the works . . . created in the last twenty years." In *The Frank Collection*, the couple gives an anecdotal account of their impressive odyssey, which moved from their cautious early purchases on a very limited budget to a memorable day at the 1986 World Science Fiction Convention when they bought a dozen paintings on Sunday morning, packed and flew them as air baggage in the afternoon, and hung them on Sunday night. Their account is organized as a tour of their house, and the numerous color reproductions document the range of their interests. I was especially taken with the "Pulp Hall and Staircase," hung with paintings by such artists as Margaret Brundage, J. Allen St. John, Lawrence Sterne Stevens, Hannes Bok, and Virgil Finlay, and by the commissioned paintings for "The Haggard Room," a room-in-progress, which already holds paintings by Jeff Jones, Gary Ruddell, and Don Maitz. A foreword by John C. Berkey and an afterword by Don Maitz, both favorite artists of the Franks, attest to the artists' appreciation of the Franks' interest and support. There is an index of artists and works, and the reproductions include information on the size of the works, their medium, and original place of publication, where appropriate. (WA)

12-11.   Frank, Jane, and Howard Frank. **Great Fantasy Art Themes from the Frank Collection**. Paper Tiger, 2003.

A follow-up to *The Frank Collection* that showcases a number of works from the Franks' extensive collection of original science fiction and fantasy art. Many of the works are fantasy rather than science fiction, but the chapter "Grand Visions: Space, Spaceships and Destiny" features works by John Berkey, Bonestell, Alex Schomburg, and Edward Valigursky (among others), concluding with a particularly impressive two-page reproduction of Tim White's cover for Asimov's *Foundation and Empire* (1985). The artists represented range over the span of the 20th century, with works by Finlay, Lawrence, Bok, Roy Krenkel, Michael Whelan, and Leo and Diane Dillon, to mention only a few of the many fine artists the Franks have collected. The anecdotal text comments on the paintings, on the artists, and on the reasons the Franks chose particular works and is an entertaining and intimate look at the collecting agenda and processes of two remarkable people. The reproductions are captioned with relevant information on the size and medium, and there is an index of artists and works. (WA)

*12-12.   Frewin, Anthony. **One Hundred Years of Science-Fiction Illustration, 1840–1940**. Pyramid, 1975.

Because the early pulps are seldom seen today by many people, this work provides a useful survey of SF illustration. The fascinating work of Grandville and Robida, two prolific 19th-century French artists, begins the book followed by selected illustrations from editions of Verne and Wells. The emphasis is, however, on illustrations from the SF pulps of the 1920s and 1930s. More than 40 covers are reproduced in color, some full-sized, some reduced. All illustrations have captions, and the remaining text, while succinct, is intelligent and helpful, putting SF illustration in a wider historical context. A very good introduction to the early years of SF illustration. Better coverage of the 19th century than the Aldiss survey [12-1], and preferable to Sadoul [12-32]. (NB)

12-13.   Grant, John, and Ron Tiner. **The Encyclopedia of Fantasy and Science Fiction Art Techniques**. Running Press, 1996.

The *Encyclopedia* is directed at the aspiring artist and professional rather than a lay audience, but the well-illustrated discussions of such subjects as "tools and materials," and techniques (including computer enhancement, spatial perspectives, and lighting) will be useful to anyone with an interest in the graphic arts and the mechanics of the artist's trade. The final section ("Themes") is a gallery of paintings with comments on the materials used to produce the works and some analysis of the paintings' techniques and their relationship with the "content." The Introduction, a mini-survey of fantastic art, contains the very arguable premise that "American artists were slower to leap into fantasy" than British and Continental artists. This statement ignores the rich vein of fantasy in illustrations of such magazines as the long-running *St. Nicholas* (first published in 1877), and the work of turn-of-the-century children's book and magazine illustrators including W. W. Denslow, John R. Neill, Fanny Y. Cory, John Gruelle, Jessie Wilcox Smith, and Harrison Cady. (WA)

*12-14.   Grant, John, Elizabeth Humphrey, and Pamela D. Scoville. **The Chesley Awards for Science Fiction and Fantasy: A Retrospective**. Artists' and Photographers' Press Ltd., 2003.

The Chesley Awards, named in honor of Chesley Bonestell, have been given by the Association of Science Fiction and Fantasy Artists (ASFA) since 1985, although they were only officially renamed for the veteran astronomical artist after his death in 1986. The categories include hardcover, magazine, and paperback cover illustrations, interior illustrations, three-dimensional work, and artistic achievement. This volume covers the awards from 1985 (when they were initiated) through 2002, with reproductions of the award-winning illustrations in most of the categories. The award for artistic achievement has gone to science fiction illustrators Carl Lundgren, Alex Schomburg, Frank Frazetta, Don Maitz, Michael Whelan, Frank Kelly Freas, Vincent Di Fate, Bob Eggleton, Thomas Kidd, and Donato Giancola, each of whom is recognized with four to six pages of reproductions. The volume also documents continuing excellence in monochromatic or black-and-white illustration, but it is the beautifully reproduced color work that will attract most readers. The textual material includes an introduction by Ron Miller that consists of a tribute to Bonestell, artists' comments in the captions for many of the works, a history of the awards by ASFA President Elizabeth Humphrey, biographical sketches of the artists, a checklist of the nominations from 1985 to 2002, and an index of artists and works. A well-edited, handsomely produced reference work that belongs in any library purchasing books on contemporary science fiction and fantasy art. (WA)

Awards: Hugo

12-15.   Haining, Peter. **The Classic Era of American Pulp Magazines**. Chicago Review Press, 2000.

Haining has a chapter on the British pulps in which there is some discussion of the science fiction magazines, but this is a fairly sketchy history that does seem to feature more reproductions of spicy and good (and bad) girl pulp covers than Robinson [12-30] and Lesser [12-23]. Many of the covers are chosen not for their quality but for the lurid style that fits the impression many people have had of the pulps. The chapters reflect this aspect, with such tantalizing titles as "All Undressed and Somewhere To Go," "The Spice of Life and Lust," and "The Chilling of Hotsy." The chapter on the science fiction pulps (subtitled "The Sci-Fi Pulps") reflects the basic dumbing-down of the approach to the field with "Knobheads and Other B. E. M.s." Oh, and did I say that I love the breezy style and unashamed kitschiness that may very well be closer to the contemporary reason for the success of the pulp magazines than the glossier, more artistically conceived Robinson and Lesser? (WA)

*12-16.   Hardy, David A. **Visions of Space: Artists Journey Through the Cosmos**. Paper Tiger, 1989.

In his foreword, Arthur C. Clarke notes that the pulp-magazine artists first gave space art a "popular audience," even as he comments that they were concerned with entertainment rather than accuracy. He credits Chesley Bonestell with inspiring a new generation of space artists, characterized by a blend in which entertainment and accuracy were "combined." However, although Hardy's introduction on the "old masters" lists astronomical artists who do not figure in the usual histories of SF illustration, he also includes Alex Schomburg, Frank Tinsley, and Ed Valigursky, who do, and these artists, along with the obligatory Bonestell, suggest the links between the magazine illustrators and the so-called space artists who do not generally illustrate fiction. In addition, Hardy includes capsule career summaries of a number of the space artists, several of whom have illustrated fictional narratives. These biographies, along with the rich assortment of color reproductions (often indicating original size and medium), make *Visions of Space* a highly recommendable resource source for both space and SF art. It should be, along with Ordway's *Vision of Spaceflight* [12-28], the choice among several similar books, such as Miller [12-26], Hartmann [12-17], and Ordway's *Blueprint for Space* [12-17]. Robin Kerrod's *NASA: Visions of Space* (Courage, 1990) is a more conventional tribute to space art and the NASA program in which artists are often not identified and the concerns are more parochial. (WA)

*12-17.   Hartmann, William K., Andrei Sokolov, Ron Miller, and Vitaly Myagkov, eds. **In the Stream of Stars: The Soviet-American Space Art Book.** Chronicle, 1990.

At first glance, Ray Bradbury's very personal, visionary "historical" introduction may seem out of place in a volume ostensibly devoted to recording, with attention to scientific fact, man's obsession with the universe. But three of the editors are artists, and *Stream* is also a celebration of the artist's ability to transform scientific data into soaring works of the imagination. Ron Miller's chapter on space art is a record of a field, science "fact," that is as often imbued with a "sense of wonder" as the work of the illustrators of science fiction. Miller evokes a historical continuum in which the American Hudson River School and the British pre-Raphaelites are seen as major influences, and certainly his grandiose "Within Jupiter's Atmosphere" (p. 68) clearly demonstrates that lineage. Many of the illustrations would not be out of place on the covers of SF magazines, landscapes that lift the soul to the horizon and beyond. With numerous illustrations by artists including Robert McCall, Wayne Barlowe, Vincent Di Fate, and Chesley Bonestell, and several 19th-century illustrators who open up an entire field of investigation and should challenge the standard histories with their focus on the pulp magazine illustrations. Many examples of Russian work are included, along with artist biographies. (WA)

12-18.   Heller, Steven, and Seymour Chwast. **Jackets Required: An Illustrated History of American Book Jacket Design, 1920–1950.** Chronicle, 1995.

The pulps are included in this short but well-illustrated history, with four or five pages of covers of science fiction and adventure pulps. The brief introduction to this section is devoted to Bernarr MacFadden's *True Story* magazine, which began publishing in 1919, and which the authors appear to think initiated the pulp era. Another flimsy Chronicle potted history, notable more for its design than for a substantial treatment of its subject. With an index of artists and magazines, and a brief bibliography of secondary sources. (WA)

12-19.   Heller, Steven, and Louise Fili. **Cover Story: The Art of American Magazine Covers, 1900–1950.** Chronicle, 1996.

The only science fiction/fantasy covers pictured here are Artzybasheff's striking wraparound dust wrapper for Charles G. Finney's *The Circus of Dr. Lao* (inappropriately included in a section on "humor"), and Arthur Hawkins, Jr.'s front panel for Olaf Stapledon's *Last and First Men* jacket, although a number of jackets for mystery novels are reproduced. There's a brief introduction to the subject, a section with basic information on six designers and examples of their work, and an index of names and titles. (WA)

12-20.   Jude, Dick. **Fantasy Art Masters: The Best in Fantasy and SF Art Worldwide**. Watson-Guptill, 1999. Published also as **Fantasy Art of the New Millennium**. Voyager (HarperCollins, London), 1999.

Ten fantasy illustrators talk about their work and in particular their techniques, which range from traditional oils, airbrush, and acrylics to computers and digitally manipulated imagery. Among the group, Don Maitz, Jim Burns, Chris Moore, and Fred Gambino have all done significant science fiction work. The essay/interviews are well illustrated and the volume is a good introduction to contemporary traditionalists and experimenters. It's unfortunate that Jude, in his introduction, refers to the "limited medium" of black-and-white line illustrations and the "garishly colored paintings," which he considers characteristic of the pulp era and which he feels still "appear frequently, particularly on American publications." Color is not inherently superior to black-and-white and I'm sure he's aware of the great tradition of magazine illustrators known for their pencil work (Virgil Finlay, J. C. Coll, and Edd Cartier immediately come to mind), while the tradition of the "pulp ghetto" to which he refers has, I think, been shown to be populated by illustrators every bit as talented as those of the contemporary field. (WA)

12-21.   Jude, Dick. **More Fantasy Art Masters**. Watson-Guptill, 2002.

In this follow-up volume to *Fantasy Art Masters* [12-20], Jude again profiles 10 artists, of whom John Harris and Dave Seeley, with Ian Miller and Darrel Anderson, while in no sense to be taken as traditionalists, create disturbing creatures and architectures that suggest alien cultures and worlds. (WA)

12-22.   Lehkmuhl, Donald. **The Flights of Icarus**. Ed. by Martyn and Roger Dean. Paper Tiger, 1977.

This oversize compilation features the work of 32 illustrators, mostly young Britons, much of which appeared on book covers and record jackets. The text is minimal and banal. Similar to but not nearly as good as the Summers compilation [12-35]. (NB)

*12-23.   Lesser, Robert. **Pulp Art: Original Cover Paintings for the Great American Pulp Magazines**. Gramercy Books, 1997.

With the help of a number of collaborators, Lesser, a major collector of original pulp art, has compiled a survey of pulp art with reproductions of the original art that are as dazzling as, if less numerous than, the reproductions in Robinson/Davidson [12-30]. There is an overview of "populist culture and pulp art," chapters devoted to science fiction illustration and illustrators, the masked crime fighters, Edgar Rice Burroughs and pulp illustration, depictions of women in pulp art, and umbrella coverage of aviation, war, and Western art. An appendix provides profiles of a handful of leading illustrators, and a selection from letter columns in the pulps gives input from contemporary readers. And, finally, there are both an index and a bibliography of secondary sources. The book is a well-written, informative introduction to the subject, and if it seems smaller in scope than *Pulp Culture*, the essays and accompanying materials make the book a more substantial foundation for future studies. (WA)

*12-24. Lupoff, Richard A. **The Great American Paperback**. Collectors Press, 2001.

With the demise of the pulp magazine, the popularity of modern science fiction illustration (and the livelihood of a cottage industry of artists) is largely due to the colorful covers of paperback fiction designed, like those of the pulps, to attract a mass market audience. Richard Lupoff has chronicled the history of the paperback industry, from its barely recognizable beginnings in the early 19th century to its present major role in book publishing. Like all Collectors Press volumes, the book is lavishly illustrated. But it is the text, the product of the dogged instincts of the scholar wedded to a sense of the drama of the history, that makes it an entertaining and informative reference. Lupoff keys the books that are pictured and captioned to give some sense of their value to collectors (without indicating a specific dollar amount). The bibliography of secondary sources is knowledgeable and well annotated, although the index of titles and authors is very selective, so that the majority of the covers pictured remain unindexed. This is probably a marginal purchase for a research library with holdings in genre illustrators and illustration, but it nonetheless provides an impressive gallery of popular illustration that demonstrates the vitality and, often, artistic excellence of the field. (WA)

12-25. Miller, Ron. **The Dream Machines: An Illustrated History of the Spaceship in Art, Science and Literature**. Krieger, 1993.

Miller is well-qualified to write this fascinating history. With a BFA in illustration, he was director of the Smithsonian's Air and Space Museum's Einstein Planetarium, has worked with NASA, won the Frank R. Paul award for outstanding achievement in SF art in 1988, and designed a 10-stamp set of commemorative space postage stamps for the U.S. Postal Service in 1991. The six parts chronologically trace attempts—both in imagination and fact—to reach worlds other than ours, the text supplemented by a large variety of well-chosen illustrations, some of them in color, including schematic drawings of the many spaceships and rockets, fanciful and actual. Of interest to SF readers, aviation and astronautical historians, and model builders. It is about as accessible as one of the Jane's volumes devoted to aircraft, and its high price will limit it to larger collections. Compare the works of Hardy [12-16], Hartmann [12-17], and Ordway [12-27]. (NB)

12-26.   Miller, Ron. **Space Art**. Starlog Magazine, 1978.

The former art director of the Smithsonian's National Air and Space museum provides a comprehensive collection of astronomical art from the 19th century to the present, featuring the work of about 60 artists. The work is semi-photographic in most cases, but the best pieces share the same central concern as traditional religious art–mystery. As landscape and religious paintings are recognized genres, so space art in a secular age may take its place. The Hartmann/Miller *Stream* [12-17] makes an even stronger case for the genre. See also the collections of work by Bonestell [12-46] and by McCall [12-78, 12-79]. (NB)

12-27.   Ordway, Frederick I., III, and Randy Lieberman, eds. **Blueprint for Space: Science Fiction to Science Fact**. Smithsonian, 1992.

A tribute to the development of space illustration with the by-now-obligatory chapter by Ron Miller on space art. Sam Moskowitz traces the history of the American pulp magazine, an essay illustrated by some striking pulp covers and book jacket illustrations that depart from the usual selections, although artists are not always identified. There are several illustrations by Camille Flammarion from *Les terres du ciel* (Paris, 1884) in Ben Bova's chapter on "The Vision of Spaceflight," while a potentially interesting chapter on "The *Collier's* and Disney Series" is diminished by the absence of any reproductions of artwork from Disney's *Man in Space, Man and the Moon,* and *Mars and Beyond,* aired on the Disney program in 1955 and 1956. Less useful as a reference on space art than Miller [12-26] and Hartmann [12-17], but still a handsome volume on man's attempts to conquer space. (WA)

*12-28.   Ordway, Frederick I., III, ed. **Visions of Spaceflight: Images from the Ordway Collection**. Four Walls Eight Windows, 2001.

Ordway worked with Wernher von Braun from the 1950s to the 1970s, is a member of the National Academy of Science, and is a former director of the National Space Society and the National Space Institute. His childhood fascination with space travel, fueled by the pulps and juvenile and adult science fiction, eventually led him to a career in the space industry. He is also a lifelong collector of books, magazines, and prints, anything relating to man's fascination with space and space travel, and *Visions* is a visual treat composed of illustrative material from what appears to be a vast collection, with the chapters tracing the illustrated record from the 16th to the 20th centuries. In the final chapter, the artwork for influential articles that appeared in *Collier's* and *This Week* magazines is reproduced. The book is especially of interest for its illustrations from books and other printed materials predating the 20th century, imaginative attempts to picture what could only be conjectured from a primitive scientific base. The introduction is an absorbing account of Ordway as a collector and scientist, detailing a career and hobby that parallel the gigantic leaps in space science that have occurred during his lifetime. With an annotated bibliography for "companion reading and viewing" that includes many of the standard references on SF illustration and illustrators. (WA)

*12-29. Powers, Alan. **Front Cover: Great Book Jacket and Cover Design**. Mitchell Beazley, 2001.

Superior to *Jackets Required* [12-18], both for the more comprehensive coverage of the period that Heller surveys (1920–1950) and for the more developed text and commentaries. (For example, the captions for the jackets pictured include concise critical summaries of the relationship between the jacket's design and the book's content that are sometimes overviews of the designer's work.) Unfortunately, there is little discussion of science fiction (largely restricted to pp. 50–51), although mystery fiction has some rather significant coverage. Like Heller, coverage begins with the 1920s and although one Burroughs jacket is pictured (the unimpressive *Tarzan and the Foreign Legion*), there is no mention of the far superior early McClurg jackets, illustrated by J. Allen St. John, which appear to be outside the parameters of the discussion. Powers is very good on mainstream and avant-garde fiction jacket design, but the striking genre work (except for the limited coverage of mystery fiction) seems of no interest to him. Still, the book is recommended as an intelligent, general introduction to a subject that has received relatively little critical treatment. (WA)

*12-30. Robinson, Frank M., and Lawrence Davidson. **Pulp Culture**. Collectors Press, 1998.

Tony Goodstone's *The Pulps* (Chelsea House, 1970), an anthology of fiction from the pulps, included reproductions of some of the covers, but it is Robinson and Davidson's *Pulp Culture* that, with its color reproductions of scores of covers, will probably remain the most eye-opening testament to the artistry of the pulp era. With the technical assistance of John Gunnison, the authors have filled the pages with (and subordinated the informative text to) dazzling examples of the work of illustrators whose job it was to sell the magazines with tantalizing pictorial representations of the lead stories, sometimes less tantalizing than the cover art. There is coverage of the wide range of magazines specializing in the weird, exciting adventure, romantic action, and the allegedly scientific, the subject of a chapter titled "The Rocketeers Have Shaggy Ears." The authors may treat their subject with some sense that many of the wonders promised by the covers are not to be fulfilled, but their affection for the pulps is never in doubt. However appealing the covers may have been (and still are), the magazines were purchased to be read, and the large sales of the most popular magazines and the letter columns with their enthusiastic commentaries attest to the love of the readers for the fiction. The volume was, unfortunately, published without an index, but one was later compiled by Rex W. Layton, and published as "The Index to Pulp Culture: The Art of Fiction Magazines" by Paul McCall (5801 West Henry Street, Indianapolis, IN 46241), who was at that time publisher of *Aces*, a fanzine devoted to the pulps. (WA)

12-31.   Robinson, Frank M. **Science Fiction of the 20th Century: An Illustrated History**. Collectors Press, 1999.

Robinson, a well-known SF writer and collector, has written and compiled a history of 20th-century science fiction that is, like all Collectors Press books, a beautiful artifact, filled with color reproductions of magazine, book, and paperback covers. Robinson sees the publication history of the field as dominated by the pulp magazines, and much of the book is a tracing of their rise and fall as the author discusses the contributions of the publishers, editors, writers, and illustrators to their successful, if erratic history. There is some discussion of the pre-Gernsback era but Robinson properly underlines the importance of *Amazing Stories* as the phenomenon that launched a thousand (or so) paper ships. A brief treatment of the British science fiction pulps is appended to a chapter on the American digest pulps (Robinson does not follow a strict chronology), and there are, as well, chapters on hardcover and paperback publications, and science fiction films. The illustrations are captioned and include brief comments, in addition to the identification of the source, date, and illustrator. The illustrators are indexed, along with all other names, and magazine entries. The magazine references are largely to the accompanying text, but where a caption comments on the magazine, that, too, is noted. This is not, perhaps, an essential purchase for a graduate reference library, but the volume will undoubtedly be much consulted by patrons of public libraries, and high school and undergraduate libraries, where the graphics may be the primary appeal but the well-informed and well-written text will expand the horizons of the mind as well as the eye. (WA)

12-32.   Sadoul, Jacques. **2000 A.D.: Illustrations from the Golden Age of Science Fiction Pulps**. Regnery, 1975. Trans. of **Hier, l'an 2000** (Denoël, 1973).

This affectionate study clearly reproduces several hundred black-and-white interior illustrations as well as many covers in full color, all with artist and issue indicated, from the 1926–1953 pulps. All the names familiar to fans and collectors are here. The illustrations are grouped in eight theme chapters, each introduced by a brief commentary. Frewin [12-12], although his coverage stops at 1940, has better-quality illustrations, more in color, and a livelier text. (NB)

12-33.   Sherwin, Mary, Ellen Asher, and Joe Miller, eds. **The New Visions: A Collection of Modern Science Fiction Art**. Doubleday, 1982.

Reproduces jacket paintings commissioned for SF Book Club editions: 46 images without the overprinted text, by 23 contemporary illustrators, who provide biographical notes often linked to the specific painting reproduced, which is always identified by the author and title of the book. (NB)

12-34. Singer, Leslie. **Zap! Ray Gun Classics**. Chronicle, 1991.

Readers old enough to remember the phrase "two boxtops and a dime" will love this book, although in most cases the ray guns were bought in stores, not by mail. Singer, an advertising creative director and copywriter, has collected toys and nostalgic Americana for years, and when you see his beautifully designed and photographed (by Dixie Knight) collection, you may think about becoming a collector yourself. The condition of the pieces varies enormously, from the first, a Buck Rogers Disintegrator from the 1930s that looks as if it had been in the Martian deserts for a few centuries, to pristine multicolored specimens from the 1980s. The 97 pieces lovingly shown are keyed to a price guide. If Singer's book sounds appealing, you'll also enjoy *Ray Gun* by Eugene W. Metcalf and Frank Maresca (Fotofolio, 1999). The photos by Charles Bechtold are equally brilliant and make *Star Trek* phasers look like the garage door openers they really are. Both books include photos of rocket ships, pins, wrist compasses, helmets, movie posters, and advertisements. If you can't find copies of the books, or even if you can, don't miss Metcalf's delightful site, www.toyraygun.com, which is timeless. (NB)

12-35. Summers, Ian, ed. **Tomorrow and Beyond: Masterpieces of Science Fiction Art**. Workman, 1978.

The former art director of Ballantine has assembled more than 300 color reproductions from 67 primarily American illustrators. Much of the work depicted appeared on mass market paperback covers of the 1970s, as well as on LP jackets, in articles, and the like. There is no biographical information on the illustrators, nor are media and size of the original shown. Yet the survey is a broad one and valuable for larger collections devoted to contemporary book illustration. (NB)

*12-36. Weinberg, Robert. **A Biographical Dictionary of Science Fiction and Fantasy Artists**. Greenwood, 1988.

The 279 biographical entries, with bibliographical information on magazine, paperback, and hardcover publication, are the heart of this impressive compilation. Although the entries emphasize the pulp era, 1926–1953, Weinberg's major interest, they include French and British artists, and a substantial number of entries from 1950 through the early 1980s. The lengthy introduction, which Weinberg calls "Science Fiction Art: A Historical Overview," surveys the changing market, tracing changes in the field as it shifts from magazine to book and paperback publication. Weinberg's commentary is strongest in the biographical and historical elements, and less satisfactory in the thumbnail characterizations of style. Thus, the characterization of Bok's work as distinctive for its "style" and Finlay's for its "beauty" is tenuous at best. Nothing of this scope has since been attempted, although Di Fate's handsomely illustrated *Infinite Worlds* [12-8] covers many of the same artists, with Di Fate's critical commentary superior to Weinberg's. Still, by virtue of its comprehensiveness and with its detailed bibliographical information, this remains a major reference tool. (WA)

12-37.   Westfahl, Gary, George E. Slusser, and Kathleen Church Plummer, eds. **Unearthly Visions: Approaches to Science Fiction and Fantasy Art**. Greenwood, 2002.

In his introduction, "The Iconology of Science Fiction and Fantasy Art," George Slusser argues for an iconography, an "exhaustive catalog of all the covers, illustrations, dust jackets" that might be found in a "comprehensive" SF collection, but preceded by an iconology or "interpretive system" of organization of images. It might be argued that the iconography would logically precede the iconology but it is, in any event, a daunting proposal. Slusser admits that this volume of essays by various hands is only a beginning of the process, which consists of two sections, the first of essays on SF art. The most ambitious is Gary Westfahl's "Artists in Wonderland: Toward a True History of Science Fiction Art," in which he identifies six "eras" of SF art, corresponding to the eras of SF literature, from the Gernsback era of the 1920s and 1930s to the cyberpunk era of the 1980s and 1990s. Westfahl lists a representative artist or artists for each of the six periods, but the article largely consists of an attempt to establish a critical perspective and discussion of individual artists is negligible. The other essays in this section are largely brief and unexceptional, offering little in the way of commentary on SF illustration, except for an appreciative essay on the seminal work of Richard M. Powers. With an index and a selective bibliography. (WA) Also annotated as [9-234].

12-38.   Yaron, Dorit, ed. **Possible Futures: Science Fiction Art from the Frank Collection**. The Art Gallery, Univ. of Maryland, 2000.

Possible Futures was published in conjunction with an exhibition of works from the Frank art collection [12-10] and consists of essays on SF art, prefaced by the Franks, who give an abbreviated version of their collecting history. Small reproductions appear to include all of the works in the exhibition. While these make it possible to follow the essays, details are often obscured by the reduction (Richard Powers's paintings suffer most), and it is helpful to have the larger reproductions in the Franks' book to turn to. Dorit Yaron, a graduate student in art history, worked with the gallery staff on the exhibition, and her succinct historical overview gives the reader some perspective for the specialized essays that follow. At least two of the essayists (Greg Metcalf and Dabrina Taylor) have taught courses in popular culture (including science fiction), but the other contributors came from a variety of disciplines and appear to have had little previous contact with the field. Elizabeth Tobey's essay on alien architectures is well argued, but Greg Metcalf's premise that "American science fiction arose from pulp fiction, which was originally a delivery system for cheap westerns," is a historically specious argument. The remaining essays are on topics such as pulp fiction spacecraft and gender in SF art. Supplementary material includes a checklist of the exhibition and author and artist biographies. There is no general bibliography, but the essays are copiously footnoted, with bibliographical information, and there is a short, additional bibliography of books on science fiction art and literature on p. 30. However, references to the Franks' extensive reference collection and a tantalizing photograph (on p. 81 in *The Frank Collection*) of the Master Library make one wish that a bibliographic essay on the library could have been included. (WA)

Individual Artists

Boris Artzybasheff, Russia/U.S., 1899–1965

*12-39.   Artzybasheff, Boris. **As I See**. Dodd, Mead, 1954.

This, the only collection devoted to a survey of Artzybasheff's enormous body of work, was a personal selection by the artist (mostly in black-and-white, but with three color plates) that show his humor (especially in a series of witty but trenchant drawings titled "Neurotica"), his frequent satire of machines and the mechanistic devices of contemporary America, and an ever-present fantasy that seems close to surrealist playfulness. Two plates—"Exploration of Space" and "Origin of the Flying Saucers"—begin to suggest his interest in science and space exploration, a subject that was a recurrent theme in many of the more than 200 covers he illustrated for *Time* from June 16, 1941 to April 2, 1965. The subject of this last cover, "the computer in society," featured a multi-armed computer, sprouting a human brain, performing a multitude of tasks as a group of much smaller men pore over the reams of data he's generating. The artist's few drawings of alien life forms are probably typified by a late 1940s or early 1950s Casco ad in which a Venusian family, human-like but with Artzybasheff's familiar multi-arm motif as well as three eyes, two noses, and two mouths, represents the new market that will open up "just as soon as the atom-drive puts Venus practically in your lap." Artzybasheff understood the contradiction between space age aspirations and the uses to which they might be put, and his art still seems as contemporary as it was during his lifetime. (WA)

Wayne Barlowe, U.S., 1958–

12-40.   Barlowe, Wayne Douglas, and Ian Summers. **Barlowe's Guide to Extraterrestrials**. Workman, 1979.

12-41.   Barlowe, Wayne Douglas. **Expedition**. Workman, 1990.

12-42.   Barlowe, Wayne Douglas. **The Alien Life of Wayne Barlowe**. Text by the artist. Foreword by Vincent Di Fate. Morpheus International, 1995.

Artists as dissimilar as Frederick Church, Howard Pyle, and Jean-Léon Gérôme seem to have figured in Wayne Barlowe's artistic development, but it is of special note that he is, as Vincent di Fate points out, a "second-generation illustrator." Both of his parents are illustrators and have worked in the field of natural history illustration. A portrait of an alien figure with a lobster head graces the front cover of *Alien Life,* and his acrylic paintings of dinosaurs and the exotic life forms encountered in his book *Expedition* (1990) show Barlowe's ability "to create images which seem undeniably real." Barlowe brings photographic clarity to his visions of the past and a potential future. And in addition to the completed paintings, the book abounds in sketches and preliminary drawings, many of them of an anatomical accuracy that shows the very real skeletons on which even his most fantastic creations are based. (WA)

George Barr, U.S., 1937–

12-43. Barr, George. **Upon the Winds of Yesterday and Other Explorations.** Donald Grant, 1976.

Barr began as a commercial illustrator in Utah, had work published in fanzines, and won the 1968 Hugo for best fan artist. His professional SF art was first published in the early 1960s and he has had much work published since. More than 50 pieces are reproduced on glossy stock, a number of them first published here. Most are ballpoint pen, and watercolor, a technique explained by Stuart Schiff in his introduction. Barr's illustrations favor fantasy more than SF and tend toward whimsy. (NB)

Rudolph Belarski, U.S., 1900–1983

12-44. Gunnison, John. **Belarski: Pulp Art Masters.** Adventure House, 2003.

The first in a series of volumes scheduled to be devoted to pulp illustrators, *Belarski* consists largely of a gallery of pulp covers documenting the artist's notable work during the 1930s and 1940s. His SF illustration was much less extensive than his work for the detective, adventure, and air pulps, but it is just as distinctive. He illustrated about 15 covers for *Startling Stories* (1941–1947) and *Thrilling Wonder Stories* (1941–1944), and several covers for Burroughs's Mars and Venus novels for *Argosy* in the late 1930s. The eight covers reproduced on pp. 96–97 show Belarski's familiar decorative but dramatic style, with space heroes, protective of their female companions, blasting away at reptilian and octopus-like aliens. Belarski made a successful transition to paperback covers in the 1950s before retiring from commercial illustration in the late 1950s. The strong suit of this tribute is the well-reproduced cover illustrations. The text is minimal but there is a bibliography of Belarski's pulp work, compiled by Tom Roberts with the assistance of Albert Tonik. (WA)

John Berkey, U.S., 1932–

***12-45.** Frank, Jane. **The Art of John Berkey.** Paper Tiger, 2003.

John Berkey, whose long and varied career includes extensive calendar, magazine, and movie promotional work, is known to SF fans for his dynamic paintings of space vehicles. Where other hardware artists attempt to capture the image with photographic accuracy, Berkey's images remind the viewer of imprecise reflections in a mirror. Thus, the effect shifts from detail to mass and color, with an impression of great energy in momentarily arrested movement. Jane Frank, in her extensive text, surveys all of Berkey's career and, with access to what she describes as "hundreds" of his works, published and unpublished, she has probably produced a near-definitive study of his career. For some reason, she was not able to include any reproductions of his movie work (she claims it is because the artist does not own the rights), but with this exception her coverage appears to be comprehensive. Frank, a noted collector of original science fiction and fantasy art, is also the proprietor of Worlds of Wonder, an agency representing a number of contemporary illustrators, with Berkey one of the clients. While this might raise some question about her impartiality, it has undoubtedly given her access to the artist and to his private collection, and if her text is at times too admiring, it is also detailed in its analysis. "Checklists," pp. 119–125, which Frank does not claim to be complete, is a "best attempt" at a record of his book and magazine work, and the paintings reproduced in the volume are indexed by title and, occasionally, by subject. For a more personal look at the artist, *John Berkey, Painted Space* (Michael Friedlander, 1991) is still to be recommended, especially for Berkey's discussion of his working methods (which involve the use of mirrors as reflecting and imaging devices). In addition to a representative selection of his SF illustrations, the volume also includes examples of his movie work for *Star Wars* and the Di Laurentis *King Kong*. (WA)

Chesley Bonestell, U.S., 1888–1986

*12-46. Miller, Ron, and Frederick C. Durant, III. **The Art of Chesley Bonestell**. Paper Tiger, 2001.

This may well be the most comprehensive volume Paper Tiger has yet published on a science fiction illustrator, but then Chesley Bonestell is probably the most influential artist in the field in the last 50 years, with his first book, *The Conquest of Space* (1948), inaugurating a new wave in astronomical painting. He had already established himself as an internationally known architect and, moving on in his restless, exploratory fashion, re-established himself as a Hollywood matte painter, working on such productions as *Citizen Kane* and *The Magnificent Ambersons*. However, with the publication of his *Conquest*, he easily eclipsed his earlier successes, painting the distinctive, instantly recognizable planetary landscapes that changed the nature of space art, largely leaving behind the more imaginative visions of earlier popular illustrators as inspirations for contemporary artists. In the first part of the book, "Chesley Bonestell: A Life in Art," the authors have provided a detailed account of his life and work, accompanied by photographs and examples of his work at various stages in his several careers. The second section is a gallery of illustrations, largely representing his astronomical paintings, but finding room for the classically serene "Scene and Endymion" (1974) and two examples painted in a style that resembles Japanese woodcuts. It may be somewhat indicative of the importance that he attached to his astronomical work that his favorite painting was "The Engulfed Cathedral"

(1974), a poetic mood study based on a Debussy prélude. The volume also includes a brief checklist of books and magazine articles with illustrations by Bonestell, a list of the motion pictures on which he worked, and a bibliography of secondary sources, as well as an index of names and titles. (WA)

Jim Burns, Wales, 1948–

12-47. Burns, Jim. **Lightship**. Text by Chris Evans. Paper Tiger, 1986.

12-48. Burns, Jim. **The Jim Burns Portfolio**. Paper Tiger, 1990.

12-49. Burns, Jim. **Transluminal**. Paper Tiger, 1999.

Burns, in his short introduction to *Transluminal*, writes that it's been almost 15 years since his "last" publication by Paper Tiger, forgetting that it's been less than 10 years since Paper Tiger published his *Portfolio*. In any event, it appears that much of the work reproduced here dates from the 1990s, although there are no dates, size of originals, or medium included. He refers to "abandoning the traditional tools," in his case the airbrush, and creating his pictures graphically, although he also says there's only one "digitally realized image" in the collection. The paintings/images are grouped by the author for whose books they were commissioned and several of the writers have prefaced the groupings with short introductions. Where they have not, Burns has captioned the pictures with comments on the novels or short stories on which they are based and what he was attempting to achieve in his pictorial transcriptions. Burns has always used the airbrush with great flair and with his frequent references to that medium, it's more than likely that these are airbrush paintings, predating his "millennium" conversion to digital graphics. One of the authors, Kate Elliott, speaks of Burns's "slick futuristic" style and Burns himself elsewhere says that it's in "surfaces that [his] ideals largely find expression," seeing himself as a "kind of purveyor of exotic patinas." (WA)

Edd Cartier, U.S., 1914–

*12-50. Cartier, Edd. **Edd Cartier: The Known and the Unknown**. Gerry de la Ree, 1977.

One of the most popular illustrators for *Unknown* and *Astounding* in the 1940s and early 1950s was Cartier, whose work with brush and lithographic pencil is immediately recognizable. Much of his work has a whimsical quality, and he was especially skilled at depicting gnomes and aliens. This is one of de la Ree's out-of-print series of limited editions devoted mostly to artists specializing in fantasy subjects, such as Finlay and Fabian. (NB)

Roger Dean, U.K., 1944–

12-51. Dean, Roger. **Views**. Paper Tiger, 1975.

12-52. Dean, Roger, and Martyn Dean. **Magnetic Storm**. Paper Tiger, 1984.

Dean's work in a variety of media is showcased here. *Views* shows his varied interests and methods, and the reproductions range from preliminary sketches to finished work. Book and record jackets and architectural and stage designs are among the types of work shown, with the emphasis more on fantasy than SF. The text is by Dominy Hamilton and Carl Capalbo. *Magnetic Storm* shows the work of the brothers during the past decade in architecture, film, TV album covers, posters, and even video games. The interesting text is by Colin Greenland. (NB)

Vincent Di Fate, U.S., 1945–

*12-53.   Di Fate, Vincent. **The Science Fiction Art of Vincent Di Fate**. Paper Tiger, 2002.

In addition to being a fine illustrator, Vincent Di Fate is also a skillful writer, and the more than 100 illustrations are accompanied by three essays that detail his apprenticeship at *Analog* during the Campbell years, Di Fate's typecasting as a "gadget" artist, and his love affair with the science fiction movies of the 1950s and 1960s, on which he writes knowledgeably in the most extended essay in the book. Four "Galleries" provide numerous examples of his work in the "real" future of space exploration, fantasy, and horror, the early flying saucer era (a gallery and essay that oddly are not listed in the table of contents), and the "future imagined," which he describes as his "personal journey of the imagination." Di Fate is modest about his achievements and describes himself as an illustrator whose "job is to create artwork to order and to do so on deadline," but the color palette that enriches his dramatic canvases is something more than the work of an illustrator-for-hire. This overdue survey of his career (in an era when less talented artists seem to publish updated tributes to their work every few years) may still be usefully supplemented by *Di Fate's Catalog of Science Fiction Hardware*, which reproduces approximately 50 works from the 1974 period, along with engineering drawings, grouped by subject (transportation, environments, weapons, and so on). (WA/NB)

Bob Eggleton, U.S., 1960–

12-54.   Eggleton, Bob. **Alien Horizons: The Fantastic Art of Bob Eggleton**. Text by Nigel Suckling. Introduction by Gregory Benford. Paper Tiger, 1995.

12-55.   Eggleton, Bob. **Greetings from Earth: The Art of Bob Eggleton**. Textual "narration" by Nigel Suckling. Paper Tiger, 2000.

Eggleton was first recognized, in the 1980s, for his hard science art as he illustrated both fiction and nonfiction. The art may appear fantastic, but, as Benford points out in his introduction to *Alien Horizons*, Eggleton keeps abreast of scientific developments and incorporates the "latest data" into his work. Chesley Bonestell was a strong influence on his early work, although the drama of Eggleton's acrylic landscapes distinguishes them from the now classic, serene oils of Bonestell. This first collection of Eggleton's work includes some of his early paintings, but is largely devoted to his book covers of the early 1990s, where humans and aliens invade the space and planetary settings of his previous work. By the time he published *Greetings from Earth*, an early interest in dinosaurs had led him to paint both dragons and prehistoric dinosaurs, with the front cover of the collection featuring a flying dragon who circles back to a man standing on the roof of a still-burning house. A series of impressionistic oils and watercolors recalls the seascapes of Turner and the American Hudson Valley painters, while a panoramic "planetscape" ("The Spirit of Science Fiction," 1997) evokes the lunar landscapes of Chesley Bonestell. Eggleton's richly colored vibrant paintings are also marked by humor, and in another panorama, a space-suited alien enters a room from a prehistoric landscape, heading for a door that opens out onto infinity. This wide-ranging artist continues to expand his horizons and his eight Hugos are an impressive testimony to his stature. (WA)

Peter Elson, U.K., 1941– ; and Chris Moore, U.K., 1947–

12-56.   Elson, Peter, and Chris Moore. **Parallel Lines: The Science Fiction Illustrations of Peter Elson and Chris Moore**. Paper Tiger, 1981.

Two British illustrators working in the tradition of Chris Foss [12-59, 12-60, 12-61], largely limited to space hardware. Pat Vincent's introduction suggests Elson is the more romantic of the two, but I found their work almost indistinguishable. Many similar books emphasizing space hardware have been published in the last few years, almost all designed as instant remainders and largely interchangeable. (NB)

Virgil Finlay, U.S., 1914–1971

12-57.   Finlay, Virgil. **Virgil Finlay's Women of the Ages**. Underwood-Miller, 1992.

*12-58.   Finlay, Virgil. **Virgil Finlay's Strange Science**. Underwood-Miller, 1993.

These compilations of Finlay's illustrations for the pulps are the first volumes dedicated to his work since the extensive series of books edited and published by Gerry de la Ree in the 1970s. Like the de la Ree series, all the interior artwork consists of Finlay's black-and-white illustrations, although each of the dust jackets features an attractive color illustration. Finlay was perhaps the most popular and influential pulp artist of the 1930s and 1940s, and he continued to work in the field until his death in 1971. The works are usually dated, but the arrangement appears to be haphazard, and much of the material was originally published by de la Ree or Don Grant (1971). (WA)

Chris Foss, U.K., 1946–

12-59.   Foss, Chris. **Science Fiction Art**. Text by Brian Aldiss. Hart-Davis, 1976.

12-60.   Foss, Chris. **21st Century Foss**. Paper Tiger, 1978.

12-61.   Foss, Chris. **The Chris Foss Portfolio**. Paper Tiger, 1990.

21st Century Foss provides an extensive selection of work by one of the most popular British artists, who has done production sketches for films such as *Dune*,

Superman, and *Alien*. His colorful space vehicles and other machines—humans rarely appear—have influenced the work of many contemporary British illustrators. Much of the work reproduced here originally appeared on the covers of British books, which are identified. The 1976 collection has 10 11 x 18-inch plates, while the 1990 collection has 28 11¼ x 16½-inch plates. In addition to the gleaming metallic ships of the earlier work, the more recent paintings often feature machines that are deadly juggernauts or are themselves threatened by gigantic creatures from some alien film set. (NB/WA)

Frank Frazetta, U.S., 1928–

*12-62. Fenner, Cathy, and Arnie Fenner, eds. **Testament: The Life and Art of Frank Frazetta**. Underwood, 2001.

Frazetta admits that he's not "much of a fan of nuts-and-bolts science fiction," needing, he adds, "a hint of fantasy" to sustain his interest. He's probably best described as a fantasy artist, but his style is so distinctive, his influence so pervasive in both science fiction and fantasy, that he demands to be included in any compilation of major SF artists. This handsome tribute, published in both a limited edition (with additional plates) and a trade edition, includes autobiographical notes (first published in 1972 but updated for this book) and tributes by fellow artists Michael W. Kaluta, Dave Stevens, Bernie Wrightson, and Kenneth Smith. The captions for the paintings and drawings give the medium, size of the original, and date, with additional information often furnished by the artist. In the 1970s and 1980s, Frazetta painted jacket covers and furnished interior drawings for books published by Doubleday's Science Fiction Book Club, although relatively little of this work is reproduced here. The Fenners have also edited two other books on Frazetta and his work (*Icon*, 1998; and *Legacy*, 1999), both of which have introductions that furnish some additional information on Frazetta's biography and career. However, *Testament* has the most representative selection of his science fiction art and would be the first choice for collectors, fans, and libraries looking for a one-volume survey. (WA)

Frank Kelly Freas, U.S., 1922–

*12-63. Freas, Frank Kelly. **As He Sees It**. Text by Frank Kelly Freas and Laura Brodian Freas. Paper Tiger, 2000.

Frank Kelly Freas is undoubtedly the best known contemporary SF illustrator, with a total of 10 Hugos that is only surpassed by Michael Whelan's 13. He has been active since the 1950s, when he illustrated more than 160 stories in *Astounding Science-Fiction*, and is still much in demand. This is the fifth book to be devoted to Freas's work, but it is the first in almost two decades. The earliest, a portfolio, was published by Advent in 1957, followed by three books compiled by Freas (*The Astounding Fifties* [1971], *The Art of Science Fiction* [1977], and, in 1984, *A Separate Star*). These document his prolific output, with *The Astounding Fifties* particularly impressive for its emphasis on his black-and-white interior illustrations, demonstrating his mastery of a skill that is certainly the foundation of any solid technique but that is much less prized in the contemporary illustration field. There are a few examples of this aspect of his work in *As He Sees It*, with a 1996 example on p. 51 showing that his pen has lost none of its magic, but most of the illustrations are in color and concentrate on the work published since *A Separate Star*. There's perhaps less of the whimsical humor than formerly, although it surfaces with delicious pungency in the 1993 *Famous Monsters of Filmland* Convention Poster, dominated by a portrait of Forrest J. Ackerman gazing benignly upon a crowd of movie monsters climbing out of the pages of a pile of issues of *FMF*. The text provides a running commentary on specific works and Freas's working methods, as well as his lively opinions on a variety of topics. (WA)

Fred Gambino, U.K., 1956–

12-64.   Gambino, Fred. **Ground Zero**. Paper Tiger, 2001.

Gambino is a British illustrator who has been active for the past two decades. As fellow British illustrator Tim Burns notes, Gambino embraced digital art early and has become very skilled in its use. The sources are British and American books (credited, but without dates), plus a handful for the U.S. Postal Service celebrating the space program. Although Gambino renders humans capably, and sometimes as the central image, his focus is more on hardware with detailed, intricate surfaces. Like most digital art I've seen (I don't pretend to have seen a lot), it has a sterile perfection much like an architectural rendering or a blueprint. His cities are more detailed than those of Paul (see his panoramic view of Asimov's *Trantor*), courtesy of sophisticated software, but fractals lack that indefinable personal touch. There's a bit of humor now and again, as in the cover for the British edition of Sawyer's *Illegal Alien*. Several writers—Elizabeth Moon, Brin, and Sawyer—explain why they like his illustrations for their works. My guess is that if you liked *The Matrix* you'll like this, which is for pixel buffs, but not for the pixilated like me. (NB)

H. R. Giger, Switzerland, 1940–

12-65.   **H. R. Giger's Necronomicon**. Big O, 1978.

12-66.   **N.Y. City**. Ugly Publishing, 1981.

12-67.   **H. R. Giger's Necronomicon 2**. Editions C, 1985.

12-68.   **Giger's Alien**. Morpheus, 1989. Trans. by Hugh Young of the Swiss ed. Big O, 1979.

12-69.   **H. R. Giger's Biomechanics**. Morpheus, 1990. Trans. by Clara Höricht Frame of Swiss ed. Editions C, 1988.

12-70.   **HR Giger ARh+**. Taschen, 1991.

12-71.   **Posterbook**. Taschen, 1991.

12-72.   H. R. Giger's Retrospective: 1964–1984. Morpheus, 1997. Trans. of Swiss ed. by Clara Höricht Frame and others. ABC Verlag, 1984.

12-73.   www HR Giger com. Trans. by Sandra Hathaway. Taschen, 1997.

Giger is a Swiss artist and illustrator, probably best known for his set designs for the 1978 film *Alien*, for which he and others won an Oscar for visual effects. The autobiographical account in the 1978 volume reveals a preoccupation with death, the fantastic, and the morbid, evident in all his work. He strikingly juxtaposes or blends the human figure with mechanical structures to create biomechanoid images of great power, in which a menacing eroticism is prevalent, unsettling, and visceral in its impact.

The New York oversize volume (11 x 15½ inches) is based on five visits to the city, including photos taken when he was in Hollywood to attend the Academy Award ceremonies. The 48 images were created using watercolors and acrylic and an airbrush (Giger was trained in industrial design) and are reduced to about 40 percent of their 28 x 40-inch original size. Some suggest aerial views of Manhattan's canyon-like avenues, desolate in grey and black, images enhanced through his effective use of stencils.

HR Giger ARh+ takes its name from Abdul Alhazred, H. P. Lovecraft's mad Arab author of a mythical book of spells, *The Necronomicon*. Giger's text is mostly chronological, from his Swiss childhood to 1990, interspersed with reproductions of his paintings (some for *Alien*) and sculpture as well as photos. *Giger's Alien* provides 75 pages of his work at Shepperton studios, England, where he worked on the film. The retrospective volume includes chronological comments by Giger and a page by James Cowan, Giger's primary publisher in the U.S. (see www.morpheusint.com). The reproductions in this 8 x 11-inch volume are far smaller than their originals. The posterbook includes six 12 x 17-inch reproductions and accompanying text in English, French, and German. The posters are borderless and could be removed and framed. Taschen also published a postcard-size edition of these images.

The volume titled with Giger's URL may be the best single work to start with. The 241 9½ x 12-inch pages reproduce sketches as well as finished work, showing both paintings and furniture, with helpful text. If you're ever in Chur, Giger's birthplace, you can visit the Giger bar, whose decor, I guarantee you, is unlike that of any other bar you've visited (you may become a teetotaler after a visit).

The *Biomechanics* volume, almost 12 x 17 inches, includes his work on *Alien*, *Poltergeist II*, and an unproduced version of *Dune*. In his introduction, Harlan Ellison calls Giger "a latter-day Hieronymus Bosch, the Dutch fabulist come again, demonic and erotic, exalting the more Baudelairean elements of the dark human psyche and affirming our now almost totally committed embrace with rust, stainless steel, the malevolent servo-mechanism, and the inescapability of clockwork destiny. He is Bosch adamantime."

Giger is one of the more important artists working in nongenre fantastic art, and libraries with large art collections should consider at least one of these collections. (NB)

David A. Hardy, U.K., 1936–

12-74.   Hardy, David A., and Chris Morgan. **Hardyware: The Art of David A. Hardy**. Text by Chris Morgan. Paper Tiger, 2001.

In his foreword, writer Stephen Baxter speaks warmly of the way in which his discovery of Hardy's astronomical artwork in *Challenge of the Stars* (Michael Beazley, 1972) changed his life with their beauty and "expression of scientific truth." The idea for the book was actually conceived in 1954, at a time when there was no interest on the part of publishers in a "British rival" to Bonestell's *Conquest of Space*, but by the early 1970s it was felt that an "updated version" of the Bonestell book was viable. Although Hardy (as the title *Hardyware* suggests) is probably best known as a "hardware" artist, following in the tradition of Bonestell's astronomical paintings, he is also widely known as an illustrator of science fiction, primarily for his covers for magazines such as *The Magazine of Fantasy and Science Fiction* and *Analog*. *Hardyware*, ably supported by a text compiled from extensive interviews with the artist, is a comprehensive, well-illustrated study of Hardy's career. His early work was done in gouache, while more recently he has used Chroma Colour, a "matte form of acrylic," and digital technology. The date and medium are given in accompanying captions, along with contextual comments, but the dimensions of the original work are less commonly indicated. Hardy, in a preliminary note, says that he kept few records and many of his originals have been sold. (WA)

John Harris, U.K., 1948–

12-75.   Tiner, Ron. **Mass: The Art of John Harris**. Paper Tiger, 2000.

Harris, probably more of a fine art artist than an illustrator, has, as Tiner points out, produced more landscapes than science fiction works, but the centerpiece of this slim, attractive volume is a series of 25 paintings, previously exhibited in one-man shows but here published as a group for the first time, which he calls *Mass*. Tiner traces the artistic and spiritual odyssey that led to the creation of a world with skyscapes dominated by giant ships, celestial fireworks displays, and, in one striking painting, a disintegrating moon falling toward the earth. Below, massive blocks suggest the impenetrable structures of forbidding cityscapes, while, in a view reminiscent of the architecture of the film *Blade Runner*, lightning strikes a cathedral that seems to explode in a maelstrom of blueish, icy light. The dimensions (the largest is 6 x 15 feet, a triptych; the smallest, 10 x 15 inches) often contradict the sense of size that the intense close-ups and medium-shot perspectives create. The style, with the artist's fluid use of inks and oils, ranges from an occasional precisely rendered image to a dreamlike impressionism. The inclusion of covers for novels by Asimov, Larry Niven, and Frederik Pohl indicate some penetration of the illustration market by this talented artist. The book would have benefitted from more mundane (but always useful) data such as information on his commercial work and dates of publication or composition, but this is still an impressive introduction to Harris's work. (WA)

Don Maitz, U.S., 1953–

*12-76.   Maitz, Don. **First Maitz: Selected Works by Don Maitz**. Ursus Imprints, 1988.

In the 1980s and 1990s, Maitz was, with Michael Whelan [12-92, 12-93, 12-94], one of the most talented and influential of the new generation of illustrators. SF motifs are dominated by fantasy treatments of subjects such as battling heroes, exotic heroines, and fey children accompanied by supernatural creatures. The settings are notable for their striking color palette and decorative detail. Color illustrations are centered on the page with white borders, with textual material—often by Maitz—on a facing page. Most of the facing pages include a black-and-white drawing, as well as the medium, dimensions of the original, the author and title of the work illustrated, and publisher, but—a major shortcoming—there are no dates. In *Dreamquests: The Art of Don Maitz* (Underwood-Miller, 1993), which includes more recent work, the illustrations, with few exceptions (pp. 12, 21, 54–65, which have black borders), have no border and instead fill the page, and the relevant information—including, happily, the date of the illustration—is given in a glossary, pp. 96–98. Since there is no border, the pagination is printed on the illustration, an invasive choice that is regrettable. *Dreamquests* is a fine showcase for Maitz's work, but I prefer *First Maitz* for its format and for a larger number of illustrations that seem to me to be less bound to contemporary SF and fantasy conventions. (WA)

Manchu, France, 1956–

12-77.   Manchu. **Manchu: Science Fiction**. Guy Delacourt, 2002.

The artist chose the pseudonym "Manchu" as a tribute to Boris Karloff in the film *The Mask of Fu Manchu*. He has published some 400 illustrations in the past two decades, and is best known for his covers for the French Livre de Poche SF imprint. Manchu cites British artist Chris Foss as his most important influence (along with American artist Robert McCall), and it's not difficult to see the relationship in the sleek spaceships and intricately articulated robots that appear frequently in Manchu's paintings. However, where the human figure is infrequently depicted in Foss's work, Manchu's futuristic world is well populated, with suited astronauts, children (alien and human), and tiny figures dwarfed by massive buildings, ships, and alien flora. Manchu uses acrylics, brushes, and pencils, with only an occasional light "overlay" with the airbrush. He is a frequent contributor to space and astronomical journals, and the second section is devoted to this aspect of his work. In an appendix, Manchu's working methods, career, and biography are detailed, and a bibliography lists his posters, appearances in scientific journals, book cover artwork, and such diverse media as animated film, record covers, and comic books. The reproductions give only the title, with no information on the medium or the size of the original work, and the dates can only be confirmed by referring to the bibliography. Still, this is a handsome, often beautiful survey of the work of an extremely talented and versatile artist. The text is in both French and English. (WA)

Robert McCall, U.S., 1919–

12-78.   Bova, Ben. **Visions of the Future: Art of Robert McCall**. Abrams, 1982.

*12-79.   McCall, Robert. **The Art of Robert McCall**. Captions by Tappan King. Bantam, 1992.

McCall has had his work published in popular magazines for many years, with aviation and aerospace almost his sole subjects. His work is in the Johnson Space Center and the National Air and Space Museum. Included in the 1982 collection are sketches, rough drafts, watercolors, oils, and acrylics, to which Bova—a long-time space booster—contributes a laudatory text. Although his work is resolutely high-tech, the Bantam collection also includes concept art for films, and the work celebrating America's space program casts an optimistic eye toward a future in which science has created a mechanistic context in support of mankind's work and play. While the paintings may lack any sense of mystery, they are often quite beautiful, in particular a series of serene, floating cities. McCall's art may in itself be a kind of futuristic fiction, ignoring the dark side of technology but capturing with great skill science's utopian conquest of the future. The Bantam edition has the advantage of a larger number of color illustrations, but both volumes are fine tributes to McCall's work. (NB/WA)

Syd Mead, U.S., 1933–

12-80.   Mead, Syd. **Sentinel**. Text by Strother MacMinn. Paper Tiger, 1979.

12-81.   Mead, Syd. **Sentinel II**. Kodansha, 1987.

Syd Mead is an industrial designer specializing in transportation. After graduating from the Art Center School in Los Angeles in 1958, he joined the staff of the Ford Advanced Vehicles Center, then published a series of books and portfolios of his designs, and in 1970 formed Syd Mead Incorporated. The two *Sentinel* books are "visualizations of the American dream, taking the year A.D. 2000 as [their] time and place reference." At the time of the publication of the first edition (1979), Mead considered his work to be fantasy only in the sense that the designs had not yet been realized. Now, however, in the brief foreword to the second edition (for which he wrote all the text), he describes it as a "visual encyclopedia of possible fantasies." A number of illustrations have been dropped from the second edition, in particular a series of pencil sketches of alien beings in "ceremonial" dress. Science fiction is not a term that appears in either text, but the illustrations could function as designs for a science fiction film of the near future, and the comments on and sketches for alien beings and—in one painting—mutated horses clearly show some interest in alien cultures. The human figures are, not surprisingly, idealized advertising icons. These are both beautifully produced volumes (the second edition has one foldout painting) and a tribute to a gifted illustrator in the lineage of the hardware and Bonestell space art tradition. (WA)

Chris Moore, U.K., 1947–

12-82. Moore, Chris. **Journeyman: The Art of Chris Moore**. Paper Tiger, 2000.

Chris Moore is probably relatively unfamiliar, at least in this country, although his appearances at a number of American science fiction and fantasy conventions have begun to correct that. *Journeyman* is a fine introduction to a career that spans a quarter of a century (and is a more comprehensive one than *Parallel Lines* [12-56]), with an informative text consisting of a transcription of an interview with Moore by writer Stephen Gallagher. He comes across as a modest, hard-working, talented illustrator, and the layout of the book, with the pages filled with double-page, full-page, and spot drawings that often demonstrate the evolution of a particular painting, presents an attractive portrait of the man and his work. The handsome endpapers are a collage of book covers illustrated by Moore, many of them showing his ability to use a small drawing adroitly combined with a strikingly designed text, in contrast to the current style, which seems intent on crowding as much visual detail as possible into a small area. Moore's sense of drama is always in evidence, with massive ships, planes, and automobiles, and a sense of arrested motion that's palpable in its intensity. A small drawing ("Agent of Destruction," p. 71), in which a fist pushes up forcefully, scattering in all directions what appear to be a group of tiny spaceships, is particularly effective in showing his precision, strength, and economy of style. (WA)

Gray Morrow, U.S., 1934–2001

12-83. Wheatley, Mark, and Allan Gross, eds. **Gray Morrow Visionary**. Insight Studios Group, 2001.

Morrow's last significant work before his untimely death was on the *Tarzan* Sunday strip, but his long and varied career included the illustration of more than 100 covers for the Perry Rhodan English-language paperbacks and prolific contributions of cover and interior illustrations for science fiction digests such as *Galaxy*, *The Magazine of Fantasy and Science Fiction*, and *Analog*. He worked on comic books, illustrated Warren publications (*Creepy* and *Eerie*), did promotional work for movies, created presentation art for projects of animator Ralph Bakshi, and ghosted on numerous comic strips. His SF work is probably closest in spirit to the prewar pulp illustrators and to strips like *Flash Gordon* and *Buck Rogers*. His major strengths were his versatility and his striking use of color, and the tributes from colleagues like Frazetta, Al Williamson, and Jim Steranko show the respect and affection his fellow artists had for him. (WA)

Bruce Pennington, U.K., 1944–

12-84. Pennington, Bruce. **Eschatus**. Paper Tiger, 1976.

12-85. Pennington, Bruce. **The Bruce Pennington Portfolio**. Paper Tiger, 1990.

Some of Pennington's work shares with that of Rodney Matthews a use of biblical and religious imagery. In *Eschatus,* Pennington's mystical nature found expression in illustrations for the prophecies of Nostradamus. In his *Portfolio,* cowled monk-like figures filing into a spiraling tower or alien figures of commanding power dominating ravaged landscapes seem to mediate between the setting and the viewer. Elsewhere, Frazetta-like warriors and horsemen brood over skeletal cities, while a relative of the ancient kraken guards the entrance to an island castle. Pennington's future is haunted by a barbaric past, and cities rise precariously from sandy deserts. In addition to commissioned works, the latest collection contains unpublished paintings based on his increasing interest in the paranormal. (WA)

Richard Powers, U.S., 1921–1996

*12-86.   Frank, Jane. **The Art of Richard Powers**. Paper Tiger, 2001.

Richard Powers was a prolific illustrator and artist. Frank quotes a figure of 1,400 commercial illustrations plus a considerable amount of "fine" art. A chronological checklist of book covers tabulates about half of those, 42 of which have postage-stamp-size reproductions (which are not indexed). The science fiction specialty publishers of the late 1940s relied on pulp illustrators like Bok, Cartier, or Finlay. But major publishers such as Doubleday and Simon & Schuster, which sold more to libraries than to fans, wanted more "respectable" cover art, not the formulaic pulp art. Ian Ballantine commissioned many Powers covers for his new line of original paperbacks aimed at an audience more sophisticated than that for, say, Avon Books. Powers's influences were both classical painters and the European Surrealists, such as Matta, Miró, and especially Yves Tanguy, who was the artist I immediately thought of when I first saw Powers's work in the early 1950s. The abstract, nonrepresentational nature of most of his paintings (and his fine art) is called by Frank abstract surrealism in a valuable 61-page chapter, while Powers's life is profiled by the eldest of his four children, Richard Gid Powers, in an enlightening and balanced chapter. Art directors thought highly of Powers's work, but fans presumably did not. He was never nominated for a Hugo or a Chesley, although he was an artist guest of honor at the 1991 worldcon. Strongly recommended to any library with strength in book illustration and to fans whose tastes transcend the conventional. (NB)

Albert Robida, France, 1848–1926

*12-87.   Robida, Albert. **The Twentieth Century**. English translation of **Le vingtième siècle** (Paris, 1882); ed. by Arthur B. Evans; translation, introduction, and critical materials by Philippe Willems. Wesleyan Univ. Press, 2004.

This first English translation of Albert Robida's futuristic novel, set in the France of the 1950s, includes Robida's original illustrations and finally makes available in an inexpensive edition one of the early landmarks of modern science fiction. The numerous in-text black-and-white illustrations, which are generally well reproduced, highlight Robida's witty, often astonishing depiction of a France in which flying machines, telephones, televisions, and other 20th-century features are commonplace but could only seem fanciful creations of the artist's imagination in the 1880s. Willems, in his introduction, favorably compares Robida's drawings to the work of Daumier and Doré, noting that Gauguin was especially appreciative of Robida's illustrations. Any reader will surely have his own favorites among the illustrations, but a drop of ink flowing out of an inkwell and crowded with books and characters and artifacts prefigures the innovative "Out of the Inkwell" cartoons of the Fleischer brothers in the 1920s, while a revolutionary scene of fighters on the battlements posing for a battery of cameras is an uncomfortable and prophetic look at the way in which major news events were to be increasingly recycled as entertainment by 20th-century media. Robida's Parisian landscape may be crowded with air machines, ground vehicles of transport, and telephone and electric wires and poles, but the portraits of its inhabitants are an engaging mix of a real and an imagined France that record the look and habits of a 19th-century France only marginally altered by Robida's futuristic projections. The novel is extremely well presented in this academic format, with a substantial introduction, notes, bibliography, and index. (WA)

J. Allen St. John, U.S., 1852–1957

*12-88. Richardson, Darrell C. **J. Allen St. John: An Illustrated Bibliography**. Mid-America Publishers (571 S. Highland Ave., Memphis, TN 38111), 1991.

Although Richardson does not include many examples of St. John's SF illustrations, this checklist of his book and magazine illustrations is important as the first such compendium of St. John's work. Although St. John's work was largely absent from the covers of the early years of the American pulp era, in 1933–1934 he painted a series of striking covers for *Weird Tales*, for Kline's *Buccaneers of Venus*, and for Jack Williamson's *Golden Blood*, while in the early 1940s he did a number of cover and interior illustrations for *Amazing Stories* and *Fantastic Adventures*. The most substantial representation of his SF work can be found in volume one of the three-volume *Edgar Rice Burroughs Library of Illustration* (Russ Cochran, 1976, 1977, 1984). This also includes examples of the work of Frank Schoonover in volume one and of Ed Emsch, Frank Frazetta, Reed Crandall, and Roy Krenkel in volume three. For corrections and additions to Richardson's ground-breaking work, see *Addenda and Errata* by Robert R. Barrett and Henry Hardy Heins, privately printed, 1991 (2040 Salina, Wichita, KS 67203). (WA)

Alex Schomburg, U.S., 1905–1998

12-89. Gustafson, Jon. **Chroma: The Art of Alex Schomburg**. Father Tree Press (5 Reno Road, Poughkeepsie, NY 12603), 1986.

Schomburg, at the time of his death probably the oldest illustrator still active in SF, worked for, corresponded with, and dealt with Hugo Gernsback for almost 40 years, from the 1920s to the 1950s. His airbrushed work appeared on the covers of many pulps in the 1950s and 1960s as well as in comics, notably the

Marvel line. Appreciations as offered by Harlan Ellison, Stan Lee, Vincent Di Fate, Brian Aldiss, George Barr, and Frank Kelly Freas. Schomburg has received various awards but not a Hugo, for which he was nominated in 1962. (NB)

Barclay Shaw, U.S., 1949–

12-90.   Shaw, Barclay. **Electric Dreams**. Introduction by Harlan Ellison. Paper Tiger, 1995.

Winner of a Chesley Award in 1996 for best three-dimensional work and nominated five times for a Hugo award, Shaw's work took off in the early 1980s with commissions for the covers for a series of paperback editions of works by Harlan Ellison. Since then, he has illustrated several hundred paperback editions of both fantasy and SF titles. He paints with acrylics and airbrush and, in recent years, has increasingly used the computer for the production of his illustrations. The title of his collection aptly characterizes the vibrant quality of his work, with its striking design and color. He prefers mood to action in rendering a scene, and his influences range from Bosch, Rubens, and Dürer to Maxfield Parrish, with a strong infusion of surrealist fantasy. (WA)

Ron Walotsky, U.S., 1943–

*12-91.   Walotsky, Ron. **Inner Visions: The Art of Ron Walotsky**. Paper Tiger, 2000.

Inner Visions presents examples of Walotsky's work from the 1960s to the 1990s. His style is usually thought to be characterized by a heightened, almost hallucinatory sense of color, but one of his most familiar pieces is the 1981 cover for Thomas Harris's *Red Dragon*, a silvery rendition of William Blake's "Red Dragon" starkly and dramatically posed against an angry, menacing background. And a cover for a recent anthology, *The Crow: Shattered Lives, Broken Dreams* (1998), catches a crow in guarded flight, doubled by a shadowed reflection, posed in the midst of a creamy background that shades into a blue that repeats the color of the crow's shadow. And there are the innumerable canvases teeming with elaborately designed spaceships, alien sculptures, landscapes, and creatures, phantasmagoric cornucopias that seem to spill from Walotsky's restless yet poised imagination. The book also includes a checklist of covers (pp. 111–12), and brief, appreciative comments by fellow artists (among them, Jim Burns, Bob Eggleton, Don Maitz, and Vincent Maitz) and collectors including Jane and Howard Frank, as well as commentaries by the artist. (WA)

Michael Whelan. U.S., 1950–

12-92.   Whelan, Michael. **The Art of Michael Whelan: Scenes/Visions**. Bantam, 1993.

*12-93.   Whelan, Michael. **Michael Whelan's Works of Wonder**. Ballantine, 1987.

12-94. Whelan, Michael. **Wonderworks: Science Fiction and Fantasy Art**. Ed. by Polly Freas and Kelly Freas. Downing, 1979.

Whelan is one of the best of today's illustrators, winner of 13 Hugos as best SF artist and an additional one for his 1987 book. He is possibly the most influential illustrator of the 1980s and dominated the Hugo voting during that decade. *Wonderworks* reproduces working sketches and the finished art, usually much larger than the American paperback covers it adorned. Comments by six writers he illustrated praise his skill in capturing key aspects of their works. *Works of Wonder* reproduces works done for Ballantine covers and features his comments, along with preliminary sketches. Fantasy illustrations predominate, but the stylistic unity of Whelan's work makes this of lesser importance than it might in another artist's work.

The Bantam hardcover (*Locus* award) rivals the art books of Abrams and Abbeville in quality. More than 100 color reproductions are included, along with many sketches for the finished work, whose medium and size are shown. The larger part, "Scenes," reproduces many of his cover illustrations for DAW and Ace. *Visions* is more personal, reproducing for the first time paintings he did for himself, not commissioned by others. Whelan's comments accompany each illustration, and he is the subject of three short interviews. The most expensive by far; libraries may prefer the Ballantine edition. (NB/WA)

Tim White, U.K., 1952–

12-95. White, Tim. **Chiaroscuro**. Paper Tiger, 1988.

Chiaroscuro presents 105 full-color illustrations that showcase White's work since about 1980, thus documenting the period since the publication of *The Science Fiction and Fantasy World of Tim White* (New English Library, 1981; Paper Tiger, 1988). As the introduction points out, White's work has changed very little, although he worked briefly in a medium known as "decalcomania." Fantasy dominates in more recent years, but the volume includes a number of SF landscapes, and spaceship and alien art. There is use of photography, and the perspectives and color may remind the viewer of the work of Maxfield Parrish (1870–1966). The paintings are usually devoid of drama, and the human figures present untroubled profiles as empty of emotion as the ships. (NB/WA)

Stephen Youll, U.K., 1965–

12-96. Youll, Stephen. **The Art of Stephen Youll: Paradox**. Paper Tiger, 2001.

Much of Youll's early work was done in collaboration with his twin brother, Paul. However, when Stephen married and moved to the United States in 1989, the collaboration ended. He continued to work in acrylics after his move, but in 1992, in working on what has become his best-known and favorite image ("Speaking in Tongues," reproduced on the jacket and in the book), he came to feel that acrylics did not "achieve" what he was attempting and thus he experimented with oils, applying layers that sound very much like the glazing that Maxfield Parrish used. Although Youll does not mention Parrish as one of his influences (he cites the 19th-century "masters" J. W. Waterhouse and Jean-Léon Gérôme as sources of inspiration), the background of "Into the Labyrinth" (1993, p. 35) is almost quintessential Parrish. His early interest in science fiction films is reflected in his work, which he calls "movie-istic" in its use of lighting effects to give his "art a more three-dimensional and modern look." Youll's posed human figures (based on models but not "faithful" to them) sometimes seem at odds with his settings—they are actors uncertain of their relationship to other figures, unconnected to them or even to the setting. His work is interesting, technically proficient, and beautifully colored and lighted; yet it is clearly still a work-in-progress, with his willingness to experiment a hopeful augur for further development. (WA)

CHAPTER 13

Science Fiction Magazines and Fandom

Joe Sanders

In earlier editions of *Anatomy of Wonder*, this chapter discussed the magazines' honored role in the continuing development of SF. Now combined with a discussion of SF fandom, the magazines may seem largely of historical interest since short fiction is such a minor part of commercial publishing (just as the antics of a few extreme fans are of little interest to most consumers). Both seem worthy only of a passing glance. But not quite. SF magazines and fandom were born together, and they somehow survive beyond practical considerations. (The development of the SF pulps is discussed in Chapters 2 and 3 of this book. SF reader demographics are discussed in Chapter 6. See also Brian Stableford's "The Economic Context of Contemporary Science Fiction" [*Foundation*, 79 (Summer 2000), pp. 41–58], written as the last chapter in a never-published revision of his valuable 1987 study, *The Sociology of Science Fiction* [9-185].)

The first SF magazines appeared early in the 20th century when a substantial part of the reading public was willing to at least glimpse fictional innovations that extended the rapid, real-life changes that were attracting and bothering them. For the better part of a century, readers had been exposed to samples of SF in a context of mainstream, mass entertainment. It was the magazines specializing in SF, however, that for decades both defined the genre and permitted the development of specialized writers and of a self-aware, continuing readership.

In America, Edgar Allan Poe and Fitz-James O'Brien wrote for pre-Civil War literary periodicals. Later, an assortment of West Coast writers published SF in more ephemeral newspapers, and still later it became one of the subcategories—"different stories"—of adventure fiction in pulp magazines. In Britain, publication of the anonymous future-war tale "The Battle of Dorking" in the May 1871 issue of *Blackwood's Magazine* led writers to do more truly extrapolative fiction so that SF became a popular vein of magazine fiction. In fact, by the turn of the century, H. G. Wells was only the foremost of many writers of the "scientific romance." Even if they found such stories especially resonant, however, readers had to seek them out wherever they appeared in mundane sources.

Modern readers, therefore, notice a certain timidity in these early stories. For one thing, though the stories involve a disruption in the status quo, things usually are put back into place as each tale concludes; most readers of general periodicals wanted to consider the prospect of change, but only from a safe, easily retreatable distance. Also, SF written for a general audience had to take time to ease readers into accepting the anomaly around which the story was built. Such restrictions are no handicap to a writer as gifted as Wells, who plays ironically with the first and slides nimbly past the second. Moreover, it can be argued that fiction *should* strive to connect its truths to readers' mundane experience. In any event, these concerns eased considerably with the 1926 appearance of *Amazing Stories*, the first magazine whose entire contents were presented as science fiction.

Although he produced *Amazing* as part of a career in electronics/gadgeteering publishing, Hugo Gernsback knew that enough readers existed to support the magazine and that enough fiction had been written to fill issues with reprints until he could attract new writers. However, the older fiction that Gernsback gleaned from various periodicals felt different when gathered together. Reading one SF story after another, both readers and writers saw new possibilities. For example, E. E. Smith had completed the manuscript of *The Skylark of Space* in 1919 but had been unable to find any market for it. Although editors such as Bob Davis of *Argosy* liked the novel, they were worried that readers couldn't accept a story that jumped so abruptly from one super-scientific invention to the next and that ventured so far from Earth. When Smith saw an issue of *Amazing* in 1927, he knew he had found his ideal audience, and when the delighted Gernsback serialized *Skylark* in 1928, he was confident that he had found a story that would satisfy his readers by stretching the range of SF imagination. Both men were right.

As Gernsback noted in his editorial for the third issue of *Amazing* (June 1926), "scientifiction" contains more scientific imagination than mundane readers can accept, but "one of our greatest surprises . . . is the tremendous amount of mail we receive from—shall we call them 'Scientifiction Fans'?—who seem to be pretty well oriented in this sort of literature. From the suggestions for reprints that are coming in, these 'fans' seem to have a hobby all their own of hunting up scientifiction stories." SF fans evidently were able not only to relate fictional constructions to their personal lives but also were willing to imagine radical changes in the ways humans lived. This open imagination set such SF readers apart from the people around them, and naturally most chose not to advertise their eccentricity (frequently equated with being out of touch with reality, more socially inhibited than outgoing, generally nerdy, etc.). In fact, an SF fan can be *anyone* who reads/collects/thinks about SF and who needs to participate in its creation, either vicariously or actually. After the birth of *Amazing*, seeing a magazine that presented one vision of radical change after another and also seeing letter columns full of names and addresses of other such readers, potential fans realized they weren't alone. As they began contacting each other through the mails and in person, SF fandom was born.

Not all SF readers were so devoted. However, writers who submitted stories to an SF magazine could be sure that readers willingly would accept notions that would have been more difficult for a general audience, such as the possibility of space flight and the existence of intelligent, nonhuman beings. In fact, such ideas became almost given, as much a part of an SF story's background as railroads and sorority girls in a non-SF story. A few years later, as editor of *Astounding*, John W. Campbell, Jr., would describe the kind of story he was looking for as general fiction—from a magazine published in the next century. This attitude and body of shared conventions made possible such works as Stanley G. Weinbaum's "A Martian Odyssey" (*Wonder Stories*, July 1934), which *begins* on Mars and describes a marooned human's encounters with native beings. It is impossible to imagine this impressive story, which leads off *The Science Fiction Hall of Fame* selected by the Science Fiction Writers of America, being published anywhere except an SF magazine, even assuming it could have been imagined and written otherwise.

Another measure of accomplishment is the commercial viability of the SF magazines. When *Amazing* was hijacked away from him by rival publisher Bernarr MacFadden in early 1929, Gernsback was back two months later with *Science Wonder Stories*, the first of several periodicals that were combined by mid-1930 into *Wonder Stories*. In the meantime, *Astounding Stories of Super-Science* (ancestor of today's *Analog*) began offering the fast-paced storytelling of purer pulp fiction.

Though these magazines competed for somewhat different readers during the Great Depression, their divergent editorial policies also encouraged a dialogue about the nature of this newly recognized type of fiction. Fans took part in the discussion in the magazines' letter columns where, for example, readers nagged E. E. Smith to write more Skylark stories and where Smith and younger writer John W. Campbell, Jr., debated the scientific accuracy of space adventures. Some readers wanted the magazines to offer more of the same; some wanted more polished writing and more elaborate speculation. Fans contributed to the ferment of ideas in their own amateur magazines (fanzines) too, sharing news and opinions, trying out their own efforts at fiction and art, and getting experience in editing and publishing, so that over the decades SF fandom has been important to commercial SF out of proportion to its minuscule size. Self-aware SF fandom soon sprang up in Britain too, but publishers saw that the market was well supplied by imported back issues of American magazines and consequently failed to bring out a home-grown periodical. British SF writers could either send their work to the specialized American magazines or write stories that would reach a general audience. The result was that British SF, for decades, was more "literary" and "serious" than the American variety. Rather than startling ideas, it stressed smooth writing and complex characterization, and while exploring character it depicted personal frailty more frequently than did its brasher, more self-confident American relative. Escaping the "SF" label, it did some things genre SF evaded, while also accepting a niche closer to the mainstream.

During the mid-1930s, however, American SF continued to develop along its independent path. *Astounding Stories* had risen to dominance, partly because of its competitors' weakness but also because editor Orlin F. Tremaine was pushing his writers to try wilder ideas in the "thought-variant" stories he began to feature in each issue. Jack Williamson's "Born of the Sun" (March 1934), for example, considers the question, What if the planets actually are eggs laid by our sun—and what happens when they hatch?

Whether it was successful missionary work by the existing SF magazines or external forces—the interest generated by Orson Welles's radio broadcast of *War of the Worlds*, the futuristic theme of the 1939 World's Fair, or spreading uneasiness as the world political situation slid toward World War II—SF went through a brief boom in the late 1930s and early 1940s. There is little point in enumerating the magazines that fluttered about like mayflies during that time. They did give some valuable professional editing and writing experience to members of New York fandom such as Donald A. Wollheim, Frederik Pohl, C. M. Kornbluth, Robert A. W. Lowndes, and James Blish. However, they were imitative, underfinanced, poorly distributed, or all three, and those that had not expired naturally by 1942 soon disappeared because of wartime paper and ink rationing.

Even after the publishing boomlet had subsided, through most of the 1940s, there remained a full range of magazines for SF readers. At the top, Campbell's *Astounding* published the most sophisticated fiction, including serialized novels. A step below were *Thrilling Wonder Stories* (descendant of *Wonder Stories* after Gernsback left the field) and its younger sister, *Startling Stories*, which featured a complete short novel each issue. A few steps below was *Planet Stories*, whose wild space opera fiction was uninhibited by scientific plausibility but which published many of Ray Bradbury's early stories, including parts of what later became *The Martian Chronicles*. A special case was *Famous Fantastic Mysteries*, which at the time reprinted "classic" novels that had appeared decades earlier in book form (many of them British). And the largest but most juvenile SF magazine was Ray Palmer's *Amazing Stories*.

Another way to look at this period is to see it as a contest between the types of SF represented by the two leading editors. When Ray Palmer became editor of *Amazing* in mid-1938, he turned it into a lively and widely circulated magazine. In the process, he became the least understood person in SF. Palmer was an extremely canny editor, and a decade or so later (in magazines he both owned and edited) he showed that he could publish sophisticated, modern SF when he thought there was a market for it. He also was a fan with a genuine taste for slam-bang adventure, and he shared adolescent frustrations and compulsions even while he exploited them in *Amazing*. In addition, he was a rogue who delighted in seeing how much mischief he could get away with. If outsiders sometimes had difficulty figuring out which role or combination or roles Palmer was filling at a given moment, it appears that Palmer didn't know either. Palmer didn't care about how SF might grow up, and he certainly felt no responsibility to aid that development. He was too busy having fun.

John W. Campbell, Jr., had become editor of *Astounding* about half a year earlier, late in 1937. Besides the momentum established by Tremaine and the growing number of writers ready to try more mature, polished SF, the basis of Campbell's success was his skeptical, probing intelligence. After establishing himself as one of the most skillful writers of planet-hurling interstellar stories, Campbell began exploring a more restrained, reflective, and melancholy attitude under the pen-name Don A. Stuart. As Campbell, he wrote approvingly of "The Mightiest Machine" (*Astounding*, December 1934–May 1935); however, Stuart's "The Machine" (*Astounding*, February 1935) questions whether a human civilization—or a human race itself—dependent on machines can survive. Dissatisfied with easy answers, Campbell gave up his own writing when he became an editor, but he became expert at pushing others to test the limits of their own talents and to explore the implications of new ideas. He was uncomfortable with SF's juvenile image, but since he couldn't change *Astounding*'s name right away, he went about reshaping the genre from the inside. He insisted not only on scientific verisimilitude but also on attention being paid to the social consequences of discoveries; rather than lecturing about how a device worked, characters should show what difference it made to people. Almost immediately, this challenge both attracted thoughtful readers and drew together a recognizable school of writers. If sometimes, as with the prickly Robert A. Heinlein, Campbell benefited from being at the right place at the right time to publish a largely self-developed writer's work, he also encouraged established writers such as Henry Kuttner and Clifford D. Simak to go on expanding their range. He worked especially hard with beginners. Isaac Asimov in particular described in detail how Campbell helped make him a writer by doing things like tossing him the idea for "Nightfall" or insisting that the idea that led to the Foundation series was too big for one short story. Overall, *Astounding* in those days was an exciting place to be; the mood prevailing throughout editorials, fiction, and letter column was a pleasantly surprised "Hey, we can do almost *anything!*"

Though *Amazing* was the bestselling SF magazine at the height of Palmer's exploitation of juvenile adventure, Campbell and *Astounding* won the contest to shape SF's future: SF would keep growing up, utilizing but extending the storytelling and thinking that evolved within the magazines.

It would be a mistake to imagine that all writers were desperate to win Campbell's imprimatur or that all the magazines were imitation *Astounding*s. Nevertheless, throughout the range of SF magazines, the standard of writing and thinking did improve. When, selecting more or less at random, I pick up the November 1948 *Startling Stories*, I see a typically gaudy pulp magazine cover, with a skimpily clad blonde grimacing while a young man struggles with a monster that looks like a cross between a hydra and a trash compactor. But the fiction that cover allegedly illustrates is Arthur C. Clarke's first novel, *Against the Fall of Night*, and five more stories (out of the seven shorter pieces in the issue) have been reprinted either in anthologies or in single-author collections such as Bradbury's *The Illustrated Man*.

In the late 1940s, SF again experienced a publishing boom. As with the earlier boom, the causes may have been both external—as in public concern about the atom bomb or the V-2 rocket (which, German scientist Wernher von Braun blithely commented, really had been designed as a spaceship but unfortunately had landed on the wrong planet)—and internal, since the successful magazines had prepared readers for even more magazines. Whatever the cause, the boom that began in the late 1940s was larger than the 1938–1942 one, but like the earlier one it contained many imitative and poorly financed titles that couldn't survive. By the early to mid-1950s, this boom was over, killed by difficulties with national newsstand distribution and by the popularity of television, which virtually wiped out specialized fiction magazines, including the established SF pulps.

Astounding already had gone to the more compact digest size, and two new digest-sized magazines that appeared early in the boom managed to establish readerships and survive the general collapse: *The Magazine of Fantasy and Science Fiction* and *Galaxy*. *F&SF* began life in late 1949 as *The Magazine of Fantasy*. It featured stories with more polish and depth than most pulp-derived SF; in its early years, it used many reprints from non-genre magazines and books. No other magazine was doing what *F&SF* set out to do, and it established a secure, if not exactly dominant, place for itself. Most characteristically, as in Richard Matheson's "Born of Man and Woman" and Daniel Keyes's "Flowers for Algernon," *F&SF* focused on human responses to strange experience rather than fully analyzing the strangeness. *Galaxy*'s first issue, dated October 1950, was a more direct challenge to *Astounding*. Editor H. L. Gold filled his first issues with stories by some of Campbell's favorite authors. Rather than extrapolation in hard sciences such as chemistry or physics, Gold encouraged writers to deal with soft sciences such as sociology, and he was especially fond of social criticism and satire. The most characteristic story from *Galaxy*'s early years is Frederik Pohl and C. M. Kornbluth's "Gravy Planet," published in book form as *The Space Merchants*. The high quality of its fiction, the fact that it was exploring fresh territory, and Campbell's temporary distraction from SF by Dianetics (a pseudo-scientific cult created by SF writer L. Ron Hubbard) helped *Galaxy* make a big initial splash.

If problems with distribution—getting magazines to where they could be purchased—killed many SF titles in the 1950s, the situation has worsened in recent decades as local newsstands have continued to disappear. My own admittedly anecdotal experience suggests that college students in an SF course don't even know there *are* SF magazines. Without newsstand exposure, magazines have little chance to attract new readers, so they rely on older readers, who subscribe to the magazines they can't locate at newsstands readily, in a declining spiral.

At the same time that neighborhood newsstands were disappearing in the 1950s, another development began affecting the survival of SF magazines: large-scale, commercial SF book publishing. Until after World War II, the SF that appeared in magazines stayed there, not just short stories but all the novels by Smith, Williamson, Leiber, and others. All of Heinlein's *adult* fiction was contained in back issues of pulp magazines; he began writing juvenile novels at least partly because they would be published in hardcover editions. When amateur, SF-fan book publishers began to produce—and to sell out—small editions of their favorite reading, however, major publishers began to see possible profits in SF. In addition to mining the back issues of magazines, they started publishing original books by recognized SF writers, and this new market in turn attracted writers who had not served an apprenticeship in the SF magazines. Thus SF's aesthetic focus and (especially) its economic base shifted.

People who want to understand SF through the 1950s must start with the magazines. That is where SF writers worked. Seeing the stories in context gives a clearer picture than does reading collections or anthologies—even those drawn from individual magazines or representing some particular year or period. But the situation in recent decades is more complicated. The influence of commercial book publishing changed what SF was written and how it was written. For one thing, the magazines were not designed to publish full-length novels, so writers tended to concentrate on shorter works. Now they could think of writing much longer stories, even *groups* of novels. In addition, where formerly only a few people could support themselves as professional writers (and very few as writers of SF only), it now became possible to sign enough contracts for novels to ensure an income for years to come. But with all the factors encouraging longer fiction, there was less incentive to write the shorter works that magazines needed. Instead of dominating the field, magazines sometimes began to look like an afterthought. As one bizarre example, Frederik Pohl's *JEM* was serialized during the last, tottering issues of *Galaxy*, long after the novel had appeared in hardcover and had been read, discussed, and voted awards by anyone interested.

As of early 2004, only a few large-circulation, regularly published SF magazines survive: *Analog: Science Fiction and Fact* (*Astounding* as eventually retitled by Campbell for the sake of respectability), *F&SF*, and two discussed below.

One survivor, *Interzone*, is the only professional SF magazine produced in Britain. It sometimes is suspected of being the successor to *New Worlds*, instigator of the angry and ultra-experimental New Wave in SF, since its name is taken from the fiction of William Burroughs rather than Edgar Rice Burroughs. It sometimes justifies that suspicion by publishing stories like Blumlein's "Tissue Ablation and Variant Regeneration." Generally defining its focus as "radical, hard sf," *Interzone* squints skeptically at the speculations of physical science, especially in stories by Paul McCauley, Stephen Baxter, and Greg Egan. Overall, however, it is an eclectic mix of stories, interviews, and features.

Another innovative magazine began by taking a less confrontational approach that has let it survive in the marketplace. Beginning in 1977, *Isaac Asimov's Science Fiction Magazine* (now simply called *Asimov's Science Fiction*) cannily used Asimov's genial, rather conservative image as an umbrella sheltering a diverse body of fiction, including disturbing stories by such writers as Lucius Shepard, John Shirley, Bruce Sterling, and Michael Swanwick.

While the number of SF magazines was shrinking drastically, the magazines ended their direct support of SF fandom. They no longer published fanzine reviews or fannish news, and letter columns omitted full names and addresses that facilitated contact. Newer magazines such as *F&SF* or *Galaxy* didn't even have letter columns. Rather than disappearing, however, fandom mutated into a numerous (and sometimes problematical) swarm of specially focused groups.

Many fans have established Internet Web sites or communicate through usenet sites. Since fans were seldom interested *only* in SF, fandom always had reflected various sometimes distantly related hobbies. Now, however, there were enough prosperous and committed fans to pursue those divergent interests. The only aspect of these increasingly fragmented fandoms still recognized by the SF magazines (to the extent of brief listings in *Analog* and *Asimov's*) is conventions.

After they recognized that they were members of a distinct group, fans usually wanted to get together for a visit so that the first World Science Fiction Convention was held in 1939, with an attendance of about 200. After World War II, the worldcons resumed, and they now draw thousands of attendees in a combination of social gathering and trade show spread over several days of multiple-track programming. Conventions in limited regions or on specialized subjects proliferated too. Traditional fans frequently are ambivalent about this runaway growth. What they especially abhor are commercially produced "cons" promoted to showcase products or media celebrities, rigidly policed affairs where ticket buyers are discouraged from informal contact with their idols. On the other hand, some SF conventions have become so large that overstuffed panel sessions overflow into the halls and professionals are forced to ride freight elevators to avoid crowds. Looking at the list of upcoming conventions, however, one can pick and choose which *kind* of convention is attractive: one focused on written SF, on a particular writer, on masquerade costuming, or just on relaxing without an extensive program.

One particularly interesting type of convention is the academic SF conference. Against considerable resistance, SF *is* being taken seriously by more and more academic critics, so (like other fans) they want to get together and talk. Oldest of the organizations and conferences is the Science Fiction Research Association (SFRA) annual conference, which is held during mid-summer in a different location each year; this lack of continuity ensures that the conference usually is somewhat unpolished, but it offers local people an excellent chance to meet writers and academics. The International Association for the Fantastic in the Arts (IAFA) existed as a convention before it was an organization; the International Conference on the Fantastic in the Arts (ICFA) grew out of a conference devoted to fantasy writer Thomas Burnett Swann. Held late in March in a warm location (usually in Fort Lauderdale), it attracts large crowds. This academic interest in SF has provoked the wry objection "Get SF out of the classroom and back in the gutter where it belongs," but it may be seen as part of the irreversible sprawl that has made SF so difficult to appreciate overall.

One reason magazines occupy a relatively minor niche in today's SF is that the overall field has become so huge. The later part of the 20th century saw an odd rapprochement between SF and the mainstream. At one time, SF looked like such an obviously subliterary genre that almost no one in a responsible position paid attention to it. Mass media, in particular, usually avoided it. After World War II, general magazines such as *The Saturday Evening Post* ran a few SF stories, and movies discovered the genre during the 1950s with (largely moronic) gusto. Apparently the many real-life echoes of genre gadgets—and the very presence of genre SF for decades even as an officially scorned subliterature—had acclimated a mass audience to SF images. SF fans went from being defensive/offended at how their reading matter was ignored to cynical dismay at how the trappings of SF had been appropriated by mainstream culture. Even if the first *Star Trek* series was not a network TV success, it became a cult franchise, then an even more commercially lucrative TV, movie, and proprietary fiction conglomerate. At first, SF fans expected that Trekkers would move on to contemporarily written, non-Trek SF, since the original series seemed stuck in a late 1940s–mid-1950s groove. It didn't happen. Trekkers didn't want fresh, unfamiliar SF; they wanted more *Star Trek*. Still later, fans waited for a flood of new SF readers to appear when Stephen Spielberg's anthology TV series *Amazing Stories* ran for two years. Certainly people would discover the identically titled magazine and transfer their allegiance to written SF! That didn't happen, either. Apparently, the level of sophistication and the fundamental attitude toward imaginative participation in reading are so different between SF fans and people in the general audience that SF magazines can expect little benefit from SF's mass popularity. To put it another way, many SF fans dislike the label "Sci-Fi" (coined by fan Forry Ackerman to cash in on the recording industry's one-time promotion of high fidelity sound as "hi-fi"), but cable TV's Sci-Fi Channel probably never worried about that when it chose its name or when it put the name on its own magazine of media news and reviews.

SF fans are used to being ignored, but the fading influence of the magazines is changing the ambience of SF. At the same time, fewer commercially oriented magazines are being hatched all the time, despite considerable die-off. *Locus* runs a monthly column listing "Magazines Received" with the titles and mailing addresses of mayfly periodicals, including the tenacious swarm of DNA Publications. The situation is paradoxical. As *Locus* notes in the conclusion to its "2003 Magazine Summary":

> We didn't lose any major magazines, but most have significantly cut back on their print schedules. . . . [But] The smaller magazines are showing great enthusiasm and proving their mettle by printing good fiction. . . . While the downturn in professional magazine numbers is sad—they are our

best and most consistent source of quality stories—it's good to know the smaller magazines are there to provide additional venues for good fiction.

To paraphrase Samuel Beckett, the SF magazines can't continue; they won't continue; they continue.

Evidently, SF magazines somehow *will* continue as long as they have even the bare minimum of commercial viability. Even if they don't, new means of production may make survival possible. One type of survival, which *Locus* considers a step down from "Semi-Professional Magazines," is the "Minuscule Press," a recent development stemming from two writers' production of "a magazine that didn't look like much, but had quality fiction and non-fiction by mostly professional-level writers. It was more a literary newsletter for a small audience with no attempt to sell a lot of copies or to go semi-professional." In other words, the idea of fanzines has been rediscovered.

The other potentially hopeful delivery system for short SF is the e-zine, such as *SciFiction*, which was number 4 in terms of placing stories on *Locus*'s short fiction Recommended Reading List for 2003. This Web site was created in 2000 as a prestige object for the Sci-Fi Network, and it has survived and thrived under the editorship of Ellen Datlow. Another prime e-zine is *Infinite Matrix*, created in 2000 and edited by Eileen Gunn. Still another interesting site is StrangeHorizons.com, run by volunteers. E-zines are cheap to produce (and preserve on the Web), they give writers flexible space, and they *can* make better artwork possible; *Infinite Matrix*, for example, was able to illustrate a series of Michael Swanswick stories based on Goya prints by including copies of the prints themselves. So far, though, no one has developed an economic base for e-publication, beyond private donations or the desire of a commercial organization to advertise itself. As with the other types of public production, the question is whether enough money can be brought in to keep a particular source of SF alive by maintaining the publisher's interest in a marginal publication. At the same time, many fans are able to finance amateur Web sites or communicate through usenet sites such as recarts.sf.fandom.

William Contento recommended these as his top three fiction e-zines:

SciFiction, www.scifi.com/scifiction/
Ellen Datlow, sfeditor@www.scifi.com
The fiction companion to the SciFi Channel Web site (www.scifi.com/), this site features new and reprint fiction by many major authors. Editor Eileen Datlow, who won the Hugo Award for Best Professional Editor in 2002, has previously served as fiction editor of *Omni* magazine and the Omni Online Web site, and is the editor of many SF and fantasy anthologies. New fiction is added every week, and the archive contains material published on the site since May 2000. In 2003, SciFiction stories won Nebula Awards for Best Short Story and Best Novelette, and many of them have appeared in best-of-the-year anthologies. Other features include a bulletin board, list of all SciFiction award-winning and nominated fiction, and links to the other sections of the SciFi Channel Web site.

Strange Horizons, www.strangehorizons.com/

Susan Marie Groppi, editor@strangehorizons.com

A fiction Web site publishing original stories and poetry by professional and semi-professional authors. New material is added weekly. Other regular features include editorials, articles, book reviews, and artwork. The site also contains a Reader's Forum, bookstore and other merchandise, and links portal. The archive provides access to material published since September 2000.

Infinity Plus, www.infinityplus.co.uk/

Keith Brooke, sf@infinityplus.co.uk

A science fiction, fantasy, and horror Web site, updated several times a month. Contains mostly reprint stories and novel extracts by well-known authors, with some original fiction. Submissions are only accepted from previously published authors. Other features include articles, interviews, and reviews. The archive has links to material published since June 1997. Some of the entries include extra material by the authors, giving insights into the story's background, its publishing history, and so on.

One reason the SF magazines will continue to exist in some form is that writers want to write short fiction whether or not it pays them well. There are, besides, some writers whose talents fit the intensity and limited length of short fiction, even when commercial considerations might encourage them to concentrate on novels. Harlan Ellison is a prime example, but recently Ted Chiang has built a brilliant reputation on a handful of short pieces; Chiang's stories are so packed with ideas that if they were any longer, they'd make his readers' brains explode.

Beyond that, however, it appears that people will go on producing SF magazines because they need to. Anyone who has heard Scott Edelman describe his extreme efforts to keep the magazine *Science Fiction Age* alive realizes that SF people are a unique breed. It would be nice, of course, if they could earn money as well as satisfaction by doing SF; however, they are willing to struggle with the mechanics of publication in order to get the satisfaction. SF and fandom can be both ways of life.

Bibliography

This bibliography is arranged in five sections: current fiction magazines featuring SF; notable SF magazines from the past; major nonfiction magazines focused on SF; books about the history and content of SF magazines; and books about SF fandom. See, in particular, the authoritative handbook edited by Tymn and Ashley [13-30] for more thorough histories of the magazines briefly annotated below. Addresses for currently published magazines are accurate as of mid-2004. Circulation figures are for 2003 as tabulated in the February 2004 *Locus*, showing a decline since 1990 of more than 50 percent for the top three magazines.

Current SF Magazines

13-1. **Analog: Science Fiction and Fact**. Dell Magazines, P.O. Box 54625, Boulder, CO 80323. Eleven issues (one double-length) per year. Stanley Schmidt, Ed. Circulation: 40,598. www.analogsf.com.

Discussed extensively above under its earlier name, *Astounding*. The last bastion of "hard" SF, stories whose problems can be stated in quantifiable terms and solved by characters who can control their emotions.

13-2. **Asimov's Science Fiction**. Dell Magazines, P.O. Box 54033, Boulder, CO 80323. Eleven issues (one double-length) per year. Sheila Williams, Ed. Circulation: 30,601. www.asimovs.com.

Currently the most consistently innovative and exciting SF magazine. Gardner Dozois, editor from 1984 until he resigned in April 2004, usually won the Hugo Award for Best Professional Editor. No serialized novels but frequent longer stories ("short novels" or "novellas") that can be converted easily into coherent (though somewhat episodic) fix-up books such as Alan Steele's *Coyote*.

13-3. **Interzone**. TTA Press, 5 Martins Lane, Witcham, Ely, Cambs CB6 2LB, England. Bimonthly. Andy Cox, Ed., replacing David Pringle in spring 2004. Circulation: roughly 3,000.

Successor to *New Worlds* but less radical than its parentage would indicate.

13-4. **The Magazine of Fantasy and Science Fiction**. Spilogale, Inc., P.O. Box 3477, Hoboken, NJ 07030. Gordon van Gelder, Ed./Publisher. Circulation: 21,443. www.sfsite.com/fsf/.

Founding discussed in the introductory essay. Long regarded as the most "literary" SF magazine for its polished prose and emphasis on characterization. This standard was established by first editor Anthony Boucher (1949–1958) and has lasted through a series of editors, supported by the Ferman family as owners. New owner and editor van Gelder continues the tradition.

Significant Magazines No Longer Published

13-5. **Amazing Stories**. 1926–2000.

Discussed in the introductory essay. In addition to the tenures of Hugo Gernsback (1926–1929; important for showing the formation of a conscious SF reading and writing nexus) and Ray Palmer (1938–1949; fascinating in the same way as a major traffic accident), two other editors have made distinctive contributions to the magazine: Cele Goldsmith (1957–1965, notable for encouragement of talented newcomers) and Ted White (1969–1979, who single-handedly and miraculously turned the magazine from a reprint zombie into a lively, cutting-edge periodical). Eventually, however, the first science fiction magazine passed into the hands of gaming publishers who didn't know what to do with it, so it faded pitifully away.

13-6.   Famous Fantastic Mysteries and **Fantastic Novels**. *FFM* 1939–1953; *FN* 1940–1941, 1948–1951.

FFM was created to reprint fiction from the Frank A. Munsey's pulp magazines (*Argosy*, *All-Story*, etc.), and its mixture of short fiction and serialized novels was popular enough to spawn *FN* shortly thereafter. When *FN* ceased publication and *FFM* was sold to another publisher, the policy changed to reprinting novels that never had appeared in a magazine and to more frequent use of new short stories such as Clarke's "Guardian Angel" (April 1950), the seed of *Childhood's End*. The magazines are important for making contemporary American readers aware of other varieties of SF—older tales from the Munsey pulps and hardcover novels that essentially were unavailable otherwise.

13-7.   Galaxy. 1950–1980.

Galaxy's explosive debut is discussed in the introductory essay. H. L. Gold (editor 1950–1961), especially at the beginning, demanded lively, dynamic writing (even when it meant intrusive editorial rewriting; see the opening chapter of the magazine and book [restored text, 1990] versions of Heinlein's *The Puppet Masters*, for example) and strongly preferred stories that emphasized wit and social awareness. Frederik Pohl (editor 1961–1969), whose own writing epitomized these qualities, worked hard to regain the magazine's preeminence, and James Baen (editor 1974–1977) also produced a solid, seriously hopeful magazine.

13-8.   If/Worlds of If. 1952–1974.

Under publisher-editor James L. Quinn (1952–1958), *If* was always readable and sometimes more than that (it was, for example, the only magazine willing to publish "A Case of Conscience," the first section of James Blish's novel). When it was acquired by the publisher of *Galaxy*, however, it became especially interesting, notably under Frederik Pohl (editor 1961–1969). Pohl thought of *Galaxy* as his prestige magazine and filled *If* with what he considered lighter-weight pieces; his playful attitude can be seen in an "All-Smith" issue, the contents of which ranged from adventure by E. E. Smith to surrealism by Cordwainer Smith. The public preferred the lighter fare, and *If* won three Hugo Awards as best SF magazine during those years, while *Galaxy* won none.

13-9.   New Worlds.

After World War II, British fan E. J. (Ted) Carnell tried to convert his 1939 fanzine *New Worlds* into a professional periodical, eventually getting financing from a group of fans in 1949. Carnell was able to draw on many British SF writers so that, without being a pastiche, *New Worlds* during the 1950s had something of the feel of *Astounding* in the late 1930s and 1940s. By the early 1960s, however, Carnell turned away from magazines, and the editorship of *New Worlds* was taken over by Michael Moorcock. An explosion of talent and acrimony followed, as Moorcock led the New Wave movement with the magazine as an extremely visible rallying point. Not all fans are ready for all changes, especially when change involves questioning SF's basic premise that the universe is or will be susceptible to human understanding and control. Rather than simply trashing SF, however, *New Worlds* tried to liberate SF from restrictions that magazine editors previously had accepted unquestioningly—especially in America, where SF's readership sometimes was pictured as adolescent males. Besides less inhibited language, the New Wave featured experimentation with structure and exploration of anomalies in consciousness—journeys into inner rather than outer space. The results were mixed. On one hand, as with any experimental movement, some silly things happened; when, for example, Roger Zelazny's "For a Breath I Tarry" appeared in seriously garbled form, nobody but the author noticed. On the other hand, writers such as Norman Spinrad, Thomas M. Disch, and Brian Aldiss produced powerful stories that never could have been published in more timid magazines. *New Worlds* itself sputtered out into a series of paperback anthologies.

13-10.   Planet Stories. 1939–1955.

Discussed briefly above, *Planet* was the home of "space opera," the type of adventure that pushed past plausibility to the verge of the absurd, but counted on readers being swept along by emotion and vivid details. At its best, as in the unplanned and unlikely collaboration of Leigh Brackett and Ray Bradbury on "Lorelei of the Red Mist" (Summer 1946), it actually achieved some of opera's larger-than-life power.

13-11.   Science Fiction/The Original Science Fiction Stories. 1939–1941, 1943, 1953–1958.

The publishing history of this title is almost impossible to summarize; see Tymn and Ashley for details. It is typical, however, of the SF editorial production of Robert [A.] W. Lowndes: underfinanced but very intelligent. Lowndes's other magazines include *Future Fiction* and *Science Fiction Quarterly*. They all contain readable fiction and above-average nonfiction, especially Lowndes's editorials.

13-12.   Startling Stories. 1939–1955.

For most of its run, a companion to *Thrilling Wonder Stories* but with the distinguishing feature of running a "complete novel" (45,000–60,000 words) each issue. Most are still readable action adventures, and several were reprinted by Donald A. Wollheim (with magazine source concealed) as halves of Ace Double Novels. Like its companion, *Startling* became a solid, mature magazine in the late 1940s and early 1950s, as shown by its being daring enough to print Farmer's "The Lovers" (August 1952).

13-13.   **Wonder Stories/Thrilling Wonder Stories**. 1929–1955.

Discussed briefly above. Actually begun as *Science Wonder Stories*, the magazine was first edited by Hugo Gernsback (1929–1936), a continuation of his pioneering efforts. Renamed after Gernsback's departure from SF, *TWS* concentrated on juvenile readers; beginning in 1945, however, editors Samuel Merwin, Jr. (1945–1951) and Samuel Mines (1951–1954) raised the level of the contents considerably.

Current Magazines About SF

13-14.   **Extrapolation**. 1959. Quarterly. Donald M. Hassler, Exec. Ed.; Javier A. Martinez, Ed. The University of Texas at Brownsville and Texas Southmost College, Department of English, 80 Fort Brown, Brownsville, TX 78520, Attn.: Javier A. Martinez. fp.dl.kent.edu/extrap.

Oldest of the academic SF journals (founded by Professor Thomas Clareson). Usually an assortment of mid-length critical essays, emphasizing SF but giving some attention to fantasy. Some reviews of scholarly books.

13-15.   **Foundation**. 1972. Three times a year. Farah Mendlesohn, Ed. Dr. Andrew M. Butler, Department of Media and Arts, Canterbury Christ Church University College, Canterbury CT1 1QU, England. www.sf-foundation.org.

Britain's major SF journal, usually lively and sometimes downright bloody-minded. Critical essays of varied lengths, many in-depth book reviews, and letters.

13-16.   **Journal of the Fantastic in the Arts**. 1990. Quarterly. W. A. Senior, Ed. Thomas L. Martin, Managing Ed. JFA. English Department, Florida Atlantic University, Boca Raton, FL 33431-0991. www.artsandletters.fau.edu/jfa.

This journal of the International Association for the Fantastic in the Arts was something of an afterthought, just as the association itself was a byproduct of a successful conference. However, it benefits from being able to draw on an eclectic assortment of conference papers (more than 300 usually attend and participate). See annotations of conference proceedings at the end of Chapter 9.

13-17.   **Locus: The Newspaper of the Science Fiction and Fantasy Field**. 1968. Monthly. Charles N. Brown, Editor-in-Chief, Locus Publications, 34 Ridgewood Lane, Oakland, CA 94611. www.Locusmag.com.

Lives up to its subtitle, having dominated the Hugo category for best semi-professional magazine (26 wins in its 37 years of publication). Covers fantastic literature generally, including the most current and comprehensive reviews of general books and magazine fiction, interview-based profiles of SF pros, and lists of published and forthcoming U.S. and British books. Frequently includes essays on foreign-language SF activities. Its invaluable online companion is www.locusmag.com (see Chapter 8). A lesser rival, *Chronicle* (formerly *Science Fiction Chronicle*) [1979. John Douglas, Ed. DNA Publications, P.O. Box 2988,

Radford VA 24143-2988], does provide coverage of one area *Locus* disdains: movie, TV, and video SF.

13-18.   The New York Review of Science Fiction. 1988. Monthly. David G. Hartwell, Ed. Dragon Press, P.O. Box 78, Pleasantville, NY 10570. www.nyrsf@ attglobal.net.

In-depth reviews rather than an attempt to cover all new books, usually mixed with feature essays. Contributors include active writers and academic critics.

13-19.   SFRA Review. 1970. Quarterly. Christine Mains, Ed. Subscriptions come with membership in the Association; see www.sfra.org.

Since editorship frequently is passed from hand to hand among Science Fiction Research Association members, quality (and frequency) varies wildly. Valuable, however, for lists of scholarly books and some reviews.

13-20.   Science Fiction Studies. 1973. Three times a year. Arthur B. Evans, Istvan Csicsery-Ronay, Jr., Joan Gordon, Veronica Hollinger, Rob Latham, and Carol McGuirk, Eds. Arthur B. Evans, *Science Fiction Studies*, EC L-06, DePauw Univ., Greencastle, IN 46135. www.depauw.edu/sfs.

Originally the most "academic" (theoretical, exhaustively documented, densely written) of the academic journals, though it has enlivened considerably in recent years without losing its solid content. Essays, review-essays, and reviews of scholarly works.

13-21.   Utopian Studies. 1988. Semi-annual. Lyman Tower Sargent, Ed. Utopian Studies, Dept. of Political Science, University of Missouri–St. Louis, 8001 Natural Bridge Road, St. Louis, MO 63121-4499. www.utoronto.ca/ utopia/journal/.

Critical essays and reviews on utopian (and dystopian) themes and fiction, frequently overlapping SF.

13-22.   Vector. 1958. Bimonthly. Tony Cullen, Ed. Estelle Roberts, BSFA Membership Secretary, 97 Sharp St., Newland Ave., Hull HU5 2AE, England. www.bsfa.co.uk.

The British SF Association's critical magazine, featuring interviews, essays, and reviews.

Books about SF Magazines

13-23.   Ashley, Mike. The Time Machines: The Story of the Science Fiction Magazines from the Beginning to 1950. Liverpool Univ. Press, 2000.

First of a three-volume revision of Ashley's *The History of the Science Fiction Magazines* (4 vols., 1974–1978), which was both a history and an anthology of representative stories. The revision is only a history, much more detailed than the earlier work. Volume 2, *Transformations*, scheduled for publication in spring 2005, covers the next two decades. Volume 3, *Gateways to Forever*, remains in the planning stage. Also annotated as [9-10].

13-24. Berger, Albert I. **The Magic That Works: John W. Campbell and the American Response to Technology**. Borgo, 1993.
Careful study of what Campbell did and the context in which he worked. Extremely valuable.

13-25. Bleiler, Everett F. **Science-Fiction, The Early Years**. Kent State Univ., 1991.
Detailed summary and commentary, careful but sometimes harshly critical, on each piece of SF prose published outside the genre magazines from the beginning up to 1930. Also annotated as [7-2] and [9-31].

13-26. Bleiler, Everett F., and Richard J. Bleiler. **Science-Fiction: The Gernsback Years**. Kent State Univ., 1998.
Covers the genre magazines, with even more acerbic tone. Also annotated as [7-3] and [9-32].

13-27. Carter, Paul A. **The Creation of Tomorrow: Fifty Years of Magazine Science Fiction**. Columbia Univ. Press, 1977.
Information about the magazines themselves only in passing, but a thoughtful tracing of themes and motifs in magazine SF stories. Also annotated as [9-46].

13-28. Greenland, Colin. **The Entropy Exhibition: Michael Moorcock and the British New Wave in Science Fiction**. Routledge, 1983.
What *New Worlds* attempted (SF as exploration of inner space, giving up reliance on "hardware," etc.), what it accomplished, why it was resisted, and whether it "failed." Also annotated as [9-85].

13-29. Miller, Stephen T., and William G. Contento. **Science Fiction, Fantasy and Weird Magazine Index: 1890–2002**. Locus Press, 2002.
Annually updated on CD-ROM, a valuable supplement to the Tymn–Ashley handbook (following). Annotated as [7-7].

13-30. Tymn, Marshall B., and Mike Ashley. **Science Fiction, Fantasy, and Weird Fiction Magazines**. Greenwood, 1985.
The basic reference tool for all genre magazines up to 1984. Critical/historical essays on each magazine, including details of publication history, derivative anthologies, etc. Also includes a chapter on academic and major amateur magazines and one on non–English-language magazines.

Books about SF Fandom

13-31. Knight, Damon F. **The Futurians: The Story of the Science Fiction "Family" of the 30s that Produced Today's Top SF Writers and Editors**. John Day, 1977.

Interesting (though not always reliable), informal account of the New York Futurian fan group, which included Asimov, Blish, Virginia Kidd, Knight, C. M. Kornbluth, David Kyle, Robert A. W. Lowndes, Judith Merril, Frederik Pohl, Larry Shaw, Richard Wilson, Donald A. Wollheim, and others. Also annotated as [10-171].

13-32. Lupoff, Pat, and Richard A. Lupoff, eds. **The Best of Xero**. San Francisco: Tachyon, 2004.

Selection of essays, memoirs, and epistolary debates from the Hugo-winning fanzine of 1963. A look at what fans can produce when they rally around one central zine, especially interesting for showing the range of fannish interests.

13-33. Moskowitz, Sam. **The Immortal Storm: A History of Science Fiction Fandom**. ASFO Press, 1955.

A very detailed history of fandom, especially during the 1930s when Moskowitz was a leading fan and took part in many disputes and feuds. The fervor sometimes disguises the fact that only a few dozen people were involved. Also annotated as [9-131].

13-34. Sanders, Joe, ed. **Science Fiction Fandom**. Greenwood, 1994.

A collection of essays *by* fans but written for non-fans; the only book to attempt such connection/explanation/communication. Covers the history of fandom (in America and other countries), and many different manifestations of fan activity. Includes an extensive bibliography. Also annotated as [9-168].

13-35. Warner, Harry, Jr. **All Our Yesterdays: An Informal History of Science Fiction Fandom in the Forties**. Advent, 1969.

Comprehensive, knowledgeable, and good-natured. Also annotated as [9-195]. An enlarged edition (NESFA Press, 2004), edited by Joe Siclari and Deb Geisler, adds photos and an expanded index.

13-36. Warner, Harry, Jr. **A Wealth of Fable: An Informal History of Science Fiction Fandom in the Fifties**. Fanhistorica, 1976.

Continues the above though somewhat more sketchily, reflecting the fragmentation of fandom. Also annotated as [9-195].

CHAPTER 14

Teaching Science Fiction

Dennis M. Kratz

Written primarily for teachers who are currently offering, plan to offer, or hope to offer a course in science fiction, this chapter presents arguments for the value of science fiction in the curriculum, conceptual frames and strategies for designing courses, practical exercises to reach specific educational goals, and a guide to resources that can help instructors reach their goals. It responds to the three questions that I have heard posed most often by teachers and administrators: Why should we teach SF? How can I design an effective course? How can I engage students and help them become more knowledgeable, critical, and appreciative readers? The question I have heard most often from students is more direct. When is the next SF course?

Reasons for Teaching SF

I want to begin by placing science fiction in a broader cultural and educational context. Does science fiction belong in the school and university? The arguments in favor of science fiction are many, varied, and convincing. Science fiction is a major form of literary expression. It is also a vibrant and important form of popular narrative entertainment that reflects American culture in powerful ways. It provides unique opportunities to study the translation of scientific ideas into popular thought. It is a valuable mirror for observing our culture, our selves, and our response to the New and Different. It can help teach about the processes of scientific discovery. It can help develop the imaginative powers of students. It can excite them about science. It is a powerful force in our culture that we are stupid to ignore. This list is far from exhaustive and every one of these arguments implies slightly different approaches and courses.

A more profound and general reason exists that we should declare forcefully and often: the study of science fiction can help, in powerful and particularly appropriate ways, to fulfill the essential goals of a humanistic education for the 21st century. We are preparing our students for a future that will surely be characterized by rapid, disconcerting, unrelenting change in every aspect of their lives—but especially in those areas affected by science and technology. The current digital revolution will continue to transform communication, saturating the environment with multimedia messages in ever-changing formats that will require new types of literacy. These technological advances will inevitably increase the cultural diversity encountered by every student, both personally and through the media.

They will encounter a wider range of attitudes, beliefs, moral standards, social practices, and frames through which to interpret experience than previous generations could have imagined. Finally, the economic environment for which are we preparing our students demands attention. It has been suggested that the United States has recently entered a new economic era—of a "creative economy" characterized by competition in new ideas, new processes, new technology, and new ways of doing business. This economy values entrepreneurship, invention, and the application of disciplined imagination to unforeseen opportunity. Put succinctly, "access to talented and creative people is to modern business what access to coal and iron ore was to steel making."[1]

Properly taught, science fiction addresses all these conditions. It concerns change wrought by scientific discovery and technological innovation. It spans the existing media, from book to film to video game, and even imagines new ones such as the holodeck. Its long fascination with the subject of the alien places issues of cross-cultural understanding in a more embracing context impossible for traditional realistic narrative. Finally, science fiction courses are well suited to approaches that encourage not only critical but also creative thinking.

Approaches to Teaching SF

Having taught science fiction for more than 30 years at the university level, I have reached the conclusion that the most effective approaches have one or more of the following characteristics. First, they embrace science fiction's contradictory nature as both popular entertainment and serious literary genre; moreover, they pay attention to the diverse media in which it appears. Second, they take advantage of its expansive nature that defies clear definition or generic limits. As Jack Williamson has said, "Science fiction has grown and diversified far beyond the reach of any valid general statement about it, including this one."[2] Third, they explore comparatively the treatment, over time and (if possible) across cultures, of specific questions or issues. Fourth, they ignore conventional boundaries separating "creative writing" from other academic courses. Students should not leave a science fiction course without having written a story, drafted a screenplay, designed a game, or participated in exercises that nurture creativity.

Who are these students? Courses at the university level tend to attract a provocatively diverse population. My experience seems typical. My courses fill with students from every major. Usually there is a combination of science students with minimal training in critical interpretation and humanities students with a minimal background in science. Biology and computer science majors (for many of whom this is the one "lit" course they will take as an elective) mingle with students majoring in literature and the humanities. Some students have read a great deal of SF, although often within relatively strict limits. Others have been attracted by the popularity of SF on television and in popular films. Most know little of the history of SF other than through acquaintance with such authors as Asimov, Heinlein, and Dick (generally a result of having seen a movie adaptation of one of their novels). Some arrive ignorant or even suspicious of the genre. They have come out of curiosity, at someone's urging, or because the time of the class fits their schedule.

The situation can be educationally exciting. After all, one of the common aspects of SF is engagement with new ideas and situations. Since the students will be reading about and watching characters encountering strange circumstances that challenge their basic assumptions about themselves and the universe, it seems only fair to place the students in analogous situations within the protected realm of the classroom. Make their discomfort a positive part of the learning environment. I find it useful, for example, to form discussion groups, both in class and electronically, that mix majors and levels of SF knowledge. I try as well to place them in game or play situations where they must imagine their responses to encounters with aliens, time travel, or a radical scientific breakthrough.

Most science fiction courses are designed to address three intertwined topics. Almost all look at the history of SF and engage students in thinking about what might reasonably be called "SF appreciation" or the "aesthetics" of SF. Third, courses devote part or even the majority of time to exploring SF as a means of social commentary or exploring the implications of scientific discoveries and technological developments.

Here is an imagined syllabus from a composite course that touches on all these issues:

Science Fiction

I. The Nature of SF

    A. Defining SF

    B. Some Stories and Ways to Read Them

II. The History of SF

    A. From *Frankenstein* to *Amazing Stories*

For additional information and models, I recommend the more than 400 course descriptions gathered in *Science-Fiction Studies* 23:3 (November 1996). Where to focus depends on the preference of the instructor, the nature of the students, and the place of the course in the overall curriculum.

Every instructor teaching SF is going to face the question of definition. On the one hand, students will ask for a definition. Count on it. On the other hand, as Williamson's statement indicates, SF is too expansive and vital to fit into any restrictive definition. Since the issue of "defining" SF is inevitable, I prefer to start with it. I link discussions to specific stories, using critical discussions as a supplement rather than a focus. We read stories (and see films), then try to extrapolate the qualities that make them SF rather than fantasy or realism. I think it important to set the context by emphasizing that all works exist in multiple genres, just as all individuals can be placed in a wide range of groups.

For example, in what courses could one legitimately read Shakespeare's *Hamlet?* I have received to this question answers that inevitably begin with the obvious: courses on tragedy, Elizabethan drama, English Literature, Shakespeare. With some discussion, the answers broaden to include ghost stories (and therefore fantasy), revenge narrative, and Insanity in Literature, to name but a few. The same exercise can be used to good advantage with the narratives with which I tend to begin courses: modern stories such as Octavia Butler's "Bloodchild," Philip Dick's "We Can Remember It for You Wholesale," or H. G. Wells's novel *The Island of Dr. Moreau.* John Varley's story "The Barbie Murders" served for years as a particularly clear and instructive example of a "double genred" (SF and mystery) tale. Films and episodes from television series (e.g., *Star Trek: Next Generation*) are equally effective. Works such as these can be considered in connection with works of pure fantasy and/or mimetic fiction, depending on the kinds of distinctions the instructor wants to emphasize.

The resulting discussion can lead the students to see what elements all forms of fiction have in common and what elements tend to differentiate SF from other genres. Students can then be guided to theoretical discussions of SF as a genre, as well as attempts to define its essential nature. If it suits your goals, include critical essays by scholar/critics such as James Gunn, Gary Wolfe, and Darko Suvin. Otherwise, use a series of dueling definitions. I have gathered from various sources definitions of SF from the seriously academic to the whim-

sical ("SF is what I choose to publish as SF"). The section on definitions in the
Encyclopedia of Science Fiction [7-21] is extremely useful, as is the entry "Science
Fiction" in *Critical Terms for Science Fiction and Fantasy* by Gary Wolfe [7-29].

My first personal contribution to this ongoing discussion, one that I have
used to good advantage for years, is a proposed definition of SF as "fantasy
made plausible through the rhetoric of science." Granted, the term "rhetoric"
requires some explanation; for I mean by this the use of sufficient references to
science to ease the leap of imagination required of the reader. How valid the
science proves to be is less important, in this view, than how *convincing* it is. Having come to definition from narratives, we then return to the narratives from
the perspective of definition and criticism, assessing both from the rhetorical
view that emphasizes value more than correctness.

This said, I confess that I have always been uncomfortable with any approach
that seeks to establish clear definitions, especially in a genre as fluid and vibrant
as SF. This discomfort has led me, in courses focusing on subjects as diverse as
classical epic and medieval romance to SF, to set up a series of continua and ask
students to place works on each continuum and to explain the reasons for that
placement. One version of a useful spectrum places "mimetic" and "fantastic" at
the poles, with SF in the middle:

Mimetic————————Science Fiction—————————Fantastic

Another places (hard) SF and fantasy at opposite poles, with "science fantasy"
in the middle. The goal of this exercise is to show students that such placement
is to some degree always arbitrary, depending on the perspective of the definer.
The role and nature of the "rhetoric of science" employed by the authors can be
one of the criteria that students are required to consider. Another could be the
conscious allusion to other works clearly identified as SF. The students keep personal journals of their reading during the semester, recording their placements
on an electronic bulletin board. By collating their comparative placements, I
can initiate throughout the semester valuable discussion both about specific
works and about the students' developing notions of what SF is and can be.

However we define SF, I cannot stress enough the importance of recognizing
that the term embraces a spectrum of work ranging from formulaic entertainment to serious literature. It includes film and television. It forms the basis,
along with more purely fantastic themes and is a central element of video
games. By all means transcend the limits of written literature. Take your examples from literature, film, television, graphic novels, and (if possible) games.
Better yet, identify a theme and ask the students to find works from multiple
media dealing with it. As I mentioned earlier, your class will almost certainly
include a mixture of long-time readers and newcomers. The experienced readers will be more than happy to share their knowledge. The challenge is often to
channel their enthusiasm without muting it or allowing them to dominate. If
possible, announce this project early in the semester and set teams the assignment of collecting versions (mingle levels of familiarity with SF if you can).

Again, journals can be effective in promoting both individuals' learning and group discussion.

The very diversity of SF—from space opera to philosophic fable—can play to the instructor's advantage. Consider grouping various treatments of the same theme (e.g., alien encounter, artificial life, an experiment gone wrong), placing intellectually powerful explorations next to second-rate exploitations. In this exercise, as in the consideration of defining SF, placing works along a continuum—in this case with "exploit" on one extreme and "explore" on the other—can prove educationally valuable. What constitutes exploiting a theme? Exploring it? If your syllabus deals with works available in two or more media, does the place on the continuum move as the medium changes? Does this happen regularly?

This brings us to the more general issue of promoting effective interpretive skills. I retain my long-lasting enthusiasm for an approach to interpretation based on the practice of literary translation. Put in simplest terms, this approach asks students to look at a work as if they were going to translate it into another language. The theme of communication across barriers of language and culture (and, of course, species) has made numerous appearances in science fiction. Its treatment ranges from the whimsical humor of the "babel fish" in Douglas Adams's *Hitchhiker's Guide to the Galaxy* to the serious exploration of communication in novels including James Gunn's *The Listeners*, *Solaris* by Stanislaw Lem, and *Timescape* by Gregory Benford. I have used the beginning of Roger Zelazny's classic story "A Rose for Ecclesiastes" ("I was busy translating a copy of my *Madrigals Macabre* into Martian on the day I was found acceptable") to introduce issues of communication across "human" differences and to discuss what a translation tries to accomplish.

Since translation involves the reconstruction of the artistic process that created the original, this charge can lead students to a more complex appreciation of the work. It also provides a practical means of demonstrating that "reading" any narrative (whatever its medium) requires a mixture of imagination and intellect. To demonstrate what I mean, I assign Edgar Allan Poe's story "The Purloined Letter," in which the brilliant Inspector Dupin offers the sensible advice that to catch a thief one must learn to think like a thief. Ender Wiggin, hero of Orson Scott Card's eminently teachable novel *Ender's Game*, expresses a similar view while discussing the reasons for his ability to emerge victorious in the simulated war games of his military training: "Every time, I've won because I could understand the way my enemy thought. From what they *did* I could tell what they thought I was doing, how they wanted the battle to take shape. And I played off to that. I'm very good at that. Understanding how other people think."[3]

I certainly do not intend to campaign for the metaphor of education as a battle, although the metaphor of education as a game has enormous value. Our goal is to evoke contemplation, understanding, and appreciation. Indeed, Ender goes on to argue that understanding nurtures affection: "And it came down to this. In the moment when I truly understand my enemy, understand him well enough to defeat him, then in that very moment I also love him. I think it's impossible to really understand somebody, what they want, what they believe, and not love them the way they love themselves."[4] Reading from a translator's perspective, with the goal of re-creating the vision of the original author rather than (say) writing a paper to prove a point, can lead students to a greater understanding of what constitutes artistic creation, understanding, and the limits of understanding. *Ender's Game*, after all, is about misunderstanding of the Other more than about understanding them.

It follows from this perspective that to appreciate science fiction (or any form of creative expression), we must think to some degree like an artist. To respond with intelligent appreciation to a science fiction narrative, we must learn to think science-fictionally. What characterizes this mode of thought? And how can we as instructors nurture it in our students?

The most obvious source for information about the way that science fiction writers think is the writer of science fiction. Many writers are willing to speak to classes. Consider setting up a funded series of speakers or find a way to include SF authors in an existing one. Recent graduates of writing workshops can provide insights into the ways stories are imagined and brought to completion. Try to become such a recent graduate yourself! To find potential speakers, use the resources of the Internet, your institution, publishers, and the public library. Other resources are listed later in this chapter.

For many instructors (including this one), attempts to write science fiction play an integral role. For this reason, I have annotated several writing guides. I cannot urge strongly enough the value of creative writing exercises. I have expressed my view that development of the imagination should play a more important role in education. Since we claim that SF can develop the imagination of our students, we have an obligation to design our course to increase the possibility of such inspiration.

To evoke the fusion of imagination and logical extrapolation that characterizes science fiction thinking, many instructors devise specific exercises. From published sources, material sent by other instructors, and my own experiences, here is a sampling of possible exercises:

1. Write the future technological history of something that we use now.

2. Write the future history of communication, travel, play, or education.

3. Write a political history of the future. In fact, write two: one optimistically and the other pessimistically.

4. Compose an "alternate" history based on a radically different outcome of a historical event now regarded as significant: e.g., the American Revolution, World War II, the rise of Christianity.

5. Imagine yourself a visitor from another planet: describe your reaction to a specific part of American culture.

6. You have the opportunity to travel in time. Do you travel to the past or the future? If to the past, when and why? If to the future, what do you most fervently hope and fear to discover?

If you decide to employ fiction writing, consider assigning every student to write a story on the same theme. Form writing combines and assign each a different perspective from which to design its story. Ask students to rewrite an assigned story from the perspective of a different character (for example, to offer a sympathetic view of the aliens in a space opera). Or take advantage of the continuing popularity of the franchise novel (also known as "shared world" fiction). Such fiction has proved remarkably valuable in a classroom setting. The instructor, in conjunction with a group of students (or multiple groups involving the entire class), can establish the outlines of a world. Another planet, a future Earth, or an "alternate history" present all can serve this purpose. Students can establish the history, customs, ecology, and other conditions of the world then imagine problems or write a series of connected stories that situate issues discussed in class in the context of that specific world.

In the years since I suggested in the previous edition the use of a mutually developed world, the popularity of the interactive video games known as "sims," where the players build and maintain communities, has exploded. Most students in general and certainly those interested in SF have played such games. SF instruction should lead the way in adapting interactive games for educational use. The power of "sims" to spark imaginative understanding is obvious: "through the creation of new and different worlds and characters, [sims] video games can challenge players' taken-for-granted views about the world."[5] I second Gee's view that we have barely begun to tap the potential of playing (and designing!) interactive games in education.[6] So consider involving interactive games in your course. They are a natural and ubiquitous part of the world for this "screenager" generation. What do the current crop of games based on SF themes tell us about popular culture? What future can we imagine for them? Extrapolating future games, imagining the games of alien cultures, and initiating the design of games based on specific works can all invigorate the learning environment.

Consider also using the theme of "games" and "play" as a subsection of your course. Written in 1985, the novel *Ender's Game* both reflected the then-current use of interactive games by the military and explored its implications for education. Terry Pratchett's 1992 young adult novel, *Only You Can Save Mankind*, provides another example of blurring the line between the world of the game and the real world. Stories like this can be compared with the profusion of computer games based on science fiction works or ideas. "Arena" by Fredric Brown presents another kind of game imposed on "lesser" beings by aliens. The character Q in *Star Trek: Next Generation* represents play of still another kind.

Since science fiction at its best fuses science with fiction, try to incorporate sections on scientific thinking. Invite members of the science faculty into the class. Establish a discussion on the nature of scientific knowledge and on their response to rhetoric of science in a story dealing with their area of expertise. Better yet, emphasize the creative, visionary, even playful aspects of science that attract so many budding scientists to the genre. The biologist Lewis Thomas has identified the common quality of art and science as the ability to make connections among events that seem unrelated. Build on this insight to excite your students about the adventurous leaps made as part of scientific discovery. I recommend most strongly *Sparks of Genius: The Thirteen Thinking Tools of the World's Most Creative People,* by Robert and Michele Root-Bernstein (Houghton Mifflin, 1999), which provides remarkable insights into the processes of creative thinking and how education can nurture them.

This discussion leads us to the nature of SF as an idea-based fiction that can be used to stimulate philosophic inquiry. First and most obviously, it can evoke thought about the implications of science and technology for human culture. The value of specific works for this enterprise can be connected to the exploit–explore continuum that I proposed earlier. *Timescape* retains its power as an intertwined exploration of the process of scientific discovery, academic politics, and the ecological implications of technological innovation. Any discussion of humanness will be enriched by consideration of Isaac Asimov's story "Bicentennial Man" and its subsequent movie adaptation. Issues relating to medical ethics, from genetic manipulation to organ transplants, abound in works of authors from Greg Bear and Octavia Butler to John Varley and Roger Zelazny. I particularly recommend the book *Fantastic Voyages: Learning Science Through Science Fiction Films* [14-5] by Leroy Dubeck and others, as well as Thomas Easton's *Gedanken Fictions* [14-22], for instructors interested in using SF to explore processes and ideas related to science.

In *Cultivating Humanity,* her thoughtful book defending liberal education, Martha Nussbaum adopts the classical notion of education as preparation to become a "citizen of the world."[7] She sees two elements as essential to gaining this more inclusive vision of one's self. First is the development of "capacity for sympathetic imagination that will enable us to comprehend the motives and choices of people different from ourselves";[8] later she suggests that literature can and should "foster an informed and compassionate vision of the different."[9] Second, she argues that to come to an understanding of our own culture we must develop the capacity to become "exiles from our own ways of life, seeing them from the vantage point of the outside."[10]

Science fiction can help educators who agree with these goals to reach them. Encounters with aliens and alien cultures permeate the history of SF. The encounter with the alien can serve as a powerful metaphor for our engagement with differing cultures. Is the Other primarily a threat to "our way of life" to be conquered, or a positive challenge to our myopic assumptions? Some aliens appear in exploitive horror stories in which they play the role of the dangerous outsider who must be destroyed. The careful study of the monster—from King Kong (central figure of assuredly one of the most important movies ever made about race relations in America) to the invading Body Snatchers to the chest-popping creature of the *Alien* series—can tell the students much about what American culture has feared and therefore valued. More sympathetic aliens allow a more positive entrance into examination of the qualities that define humanness. Ursula Le Guin's *Left Hand of Darkness,* which deals specifically with the impact of both gender and environment on thinking, has reached the status of a classic. More recently, Greg Bear's *Darwin's Radio* provides rich food for thought about evolution and the future of "human" values.

It is in this realm of human values that SF can make its most important but far from only contribution to education. It can help create citizens of the world—and universe—whose engagement with Alien Others can make human others less strange. It can help nurture intellectual agility and comfort with change relating to technology and science. That welcoming attitude toward change should characterize teachers as well. The very technology that SF makes one of its most important subjects is transforming education as I write this chapter. Those of us involved with SF and the literature of the future should be in the forefront of developing new approaches to teaching and exploring the potential of new forms of communication and learning, particularly the interactive media associated with digital technology and the new "immersive" environments. Most of these innovations had already appeared in works of science fiction. Now we should take the lead in adapting them for use in science fiction courses.

Resources for Teaching SF

The best resources are books, electronic sources, courses, and people. Fortunately, the electronic media make knowledgeable people more accessible than ever.

Books

I refer the reader to the list of annotated books for valuable sources concerning teaching science fiction (including textbooks and anthologies) and teaching creative writing. Even for books, this is an unstable era. Textbooks and anthologies go out of print. The best broad-based, historically ordered textbook currently in print is *The Prentice Hall Anthology of Science Fiction and Fantasy* [14-25]. It offers a wide range of stories spanning a considerable period of time. Its dual focus on SF and fantasy allows fruitful comparisons of the two genres. Among its most useful features is a listing of film or television adaptations of the stories that are included. Although it is tempting to stick to such historical anthologies, I recommend using the newest literature as well. A current "best of the year" anthology can spark discussion concerning what the professionals (Nebula Awards) or fans (Hugo Awards) prefer at the moment. Most historical or "best" anthologies build in the expectation that the contents have special worth. Since one goal is to hone students' ability to evaluate SF, I repeat the strong recommendation made in *Anatomy of Wonder 4* that instructors assign a current issue of one of the major SF magazines. SF is a literature that celebrates the encounter with the New. Let the "new" include new stories that the students must judge.

Films

Most films or television programs that have any merit or historical importance are readily available in videotape, CD, and/or DVD format. Your library should build a collection. If you are unable to obtain a film at your institution or through one of the major rental chains, I recommend using the resources of the Internet to locate it. Among the Web-based sources for films are www.reel. com and the major Web outlets such as Amazon or Barnes and Noble.

Electronic Sources

By this time, it is reasonable to assume that anyone engaged in teaching science fiction will have at least some familiarity with the Internet and its various search engines. Find a guide to using the Internet. Ironically, the best place to find such a guide is the Internet itself. Go to one of the major search engines (Yahoo, Lycos, Google) and key in "Internet guides." A very useful guide, for example, can be found once you access the Web site of the library at the University of California at Berkeley: www.lib.berkeley.edu/Teachinglib/Guides/Internet.

The Web is so full of evanescent elements that I hesitate to list too many specific sites. The best current site, without question, is that sponsored by the Center for the Study of Science Fiction at the University of Kansas: www.ku.edu/~sfcenter [8-1]. It contains a treasure of information and links to other resources. It is the one place to start for anyone seeking information about teaching science fiction.

The Web site of *Science Fiction Studies* also contains much valuable information about all aspects of science fiction. Click on www.depauw.edu/sfs [8-5]. Particularly useful is the "Wormholes" section, which lists useful sites for scholarly journals, scholarly organizations, library collections, and other resources.

Also useful is the Linkoping Science Fiction Archive: www.lysator.liu.se/sf_archive, which in turn will link you to the Science Fiction Resource Guide at www.sflovers.org/SFRG. An excellent site for those interested in alternate history is www.uchronia.net (Chapter 8). The Science Fiction Writers of America (www.sfwa.org) and the Science Fiction Research Association (www.sfra.org) also have useful sites (Chapter 16).

The University of Kansas continues its role as the leader in science fiction education. I can do no greater service to teachers than to repeat the advice that I gave in *Anatomy of Wonder 4*: you should attend one of the Intensive English Institutes of the Teaching of Science Fiction offered at the University of Kansas each summer.

While professors at many universities offer courses in science fiction and/or fantasy, as accurately as I can ascertain, no American university currently offers a degree specifically in Science Fiction. Three British universities do offer degrees in Science Fiction:

University of Glamorgan: BSc (Hons) in Science and Science Fiction

University of Liverpool: M.A. in Science Fiction Studies

University of Reading: M.A. in Science Fiction

People

The rise of electronic mail potentially puts everyone involved in or interested in teaching science fiction in touch with one another. Attend conferences both locally and nationally. Attend the University of Kansas Institute. Seek out other workshops devoted to teaching SF. If you cannot meet them in person or contact them, you can hear the insights of some of the finest teachers via videotape, CD, and DVD. The Idea Channel (www.ideachannel.com), for example, has video conversations of Jack Williamson and others discussing how to teach science fiction.

Notes

1. Richard Florida, *The Rise of the Creative Class* (Basic Books, 2002), p. 6.
2. Jack Williamson, Foreword to *The Prentice Hall Anthology of Science Fiction and Fantasy*, ed. Garyn G. Roberts (Prentice Hall, 2001), p. xiii.
3. Orson Scott Card, *Ender's Game* [II–217], pp. 260–61.
4. Ibid., p. 261.
5. James Paul Gee, *What Video Games Have to Teach Us About Learning and Literacy* [14-6], p. 140.
6. Ibid., p. 205.
7. Martha Nussbaum, *Cultivating Humanity* (Harvard Univ. Press, 1997), pp. 50–84.
7. Ibid., p. 85.
9. Ibid., p. 89.
10. Ibid., p. 58.

Bibliography

Instructional Guides

14-1.   Allen, L. David. **The Ballantine Teachers' Guide to Science Fiction**. Ballantine, 1975.

High school teachers may still find this volume useful for its analyses, from a teacher's perspective, of selected novels that have become a part of the overall curriculum, especially *Childhood's End* and *Fahrenheit 451*. The rest of the discussions are disappointing, as are the teaching exercises.

14-2.   Behrendt, Stephen C. **Approaches to Teaching Shelley's Frankenstein**. Modern Language Association, 1990.

Highly recommended both as a guide to *Frankenstein* itself and as a stimulus for college instructors to develop similar collections for other SF novels. The essays examine *Frankenstein* from a wide range of perspectives, the majority with insight and intelligence, but some inevitably suffer from too much academic language (i.e., jargon). Reading this collection will not only enhance the reader's understanding of the novel but also provide valuable topics for class discussion. Compare [14-11].

14-3. Carratello, John, and Patty Carratello. **Literature and Critical Thinking: Fantasy and Science Fiction**. Teacher Created Materials, 1990.

Designed for grades 4–6, this book offers teaching units for six excellent novels for the younger reader, of which two (*The Martian Chronicles* and Pamela Service's *Stinker From Space*, 1988) are science fiction. The classroom activities are imaginative and enticing, aimed at improving both students' ability to read and their enjoyment of reading.

14-4. Carratello, John, and Patty Carratello. **A Wrinkle in Time: Literature Unit**. Teacher Created Materials, 1991.

This book is a treasure trove of instructional ideas. It contains pre-reading activities, a plot summary, lesson plans, and suggested projects. It has the same virtues as the Carratellos' curriculum guide annotated above. This is a fine teaching guide for a great novel. See also the 64-page guide by Manuela Soares, *Scholastic Bookfiles: A Reading Guide to A Wrinkle in Time by Madeleine L'Engle* (Scholastic, 2004), which includes an interview and a list of related readings.

14-5. Dubeck, Leroy W., Suzanne E. Moshier, and Judith E. Boss. **Fantastic Voyages: Learning Science Through Science Fiction Films**. Springer, 2003.

An updated version of the authors' 1988 book *Science in Cinema: Teaching Science Fact Through Science Fiction Films,* this version exhibits the same values and limitations of its predecessor. The focus is on using science fiction films and television series (*Star Trek: Next Generation*) for the purpose of building interest in "real" science. Used in this context, it has real value. This limited perspective, however, which can lead to unsympathetic and distorted interpretations of fiction, diminishes its value for SF courses. The approach reminds this reviewer of someone reading a literary translation looking for "mistakes" rather than the process of reconstructing meaning. Nonetheless, *Fantastic Voyages* can be a valuable resource for the SF teacher if used in connection with discussions of science as "rhetoric" in science fiction and occasionally to discuss how certain perspectives can reduce enjoyment.

14-6. Gee, James. **What Video Games Have to Teach Us About Learning and Literacy**. Palgrave, 2003.

Interactive games are already altering the nature of learning in and out of academic institutions. The flow of fine books about this impact has barely begun. Gee's study is among the first and most important because it emphasizes the ways such games are designed to employ basic principles of effective learning. Such principles can be adapted to a wide range of instructional environments. Acquaintance with this and other books on the use of games and interactive digital technology in education is strongly recommended.

*14-7.   Gunn, James E. **Inside Science Fiction: Essays on Fantastic Literature**. Borgo, 1992.

This admirable collection of essays, all originally published elsewhere, is essential reading for every SF teacher. Gunn has made major contributions as a writer, critic, and teacher of SF. Four of the 18 essays are clustered in the category "SF and the Teacher." Although the essays contain much practical advice, they offer something more valuable to the novice and experienced teacher alike: an insight into the overall philosophy that has guided Gunn's teaching over the years. Think of this book as a conversation with a Master Teacher. Also annotated as [9-87].

14-8.   **Other Worlds: Fantasy and Science Fiction**. *English Journal* (March 1990): 25–46.

This admirable collection of four essays gives practical advice on topics that include the importance of "creative writing" assignments, ways to use SF to stimulate discussion of philosophic questions, and tips on using SF to teach feminist issues. Recommended for all teachers.

14-9.   Parrinder, Patrick. **Science Fiction: Its Criticism and Teaching**. Methuen, 1980.

Despite the title, Parrinder devotes only one brief chapter specifically to teaching SF. The remarks on "canons and canon-formation" are old-fashioned but interesting and could prove useful in discussing how SF works become "worthy" of inclusion in academic curricula. More valuable are the implications of his chapter on "Imitation and Novelty: An Approach Through SF Language." Also annotated as [9-147].

*14-10.   **Science Fiction Studies**. No. 19, Vol. 6, Part 3 (1979).

*Science Fiction Studies. No. 70, Vol. 23, Part 3 (1996).

These two special issues of the preeminent academic journal devoted to SF in the classroom will repay careful reading. The earlier issue contains a section on "Science Fiction and Teaching" and an essay by Andrzej Zgorzelski on the relation of SF to fantasy. The section in the latter issue is a treasure house of information and opinion. See especially the essays by Jack Williamson, James Gunn, and Brian Attebury. The issue also contains two excellent resource lists: one of SF and fantasy courses taught in North American colleges and one of the books, authors, and films most widely assigned in SF courses. See also Stephen Potts's "conversation" with Octavia Butler, a writer gaining increasing attention in SF courses. The 1996 issue, in particular, is most highly recommended.

14-11.   Smith, Johanna M., ed. **Frankenstein: Case Studies in Contemporary Criticism**. St. Martin's, 1980.

An excellent companion to Behrend's *Approaches to Teaching Frankenstein* [14-2], this book provides both a clear history of *Frankenstein* criticism and five essays representing different critical approaches: reader-response, psychoanalytic, feminist, Marxist, and cultural. Teachers will be able to use the complementary and occasionally conflicting assessments to good advantage. A glossary of terms is included.

14-12. Spann, Sylvia, and Mary Beth Culp, eds. **Thematic Units in Teaching English and the Humanities**. NCTE, 1980.

Although outdated in many respects, this is still an extremely valuable source for the high school teacher. See particularly the suggested discussion questions for seven SF novels that have reached "classic" status and are often taught: *I, Robot*; *Childhood's End*; *The Gods Themselves*; *2001: A Space Odyssey*; *Planet of the Apes*; *Brave New World*; and *The Martian Chronicles*.

*14-13. Tymn, Marshall, ed. **Science Fiction: A Teacher's Guide and Resource Book**. Starmont, 1988.

Practical and thoughtful, this is a valuable work, especially for the beginning teacher. Tymn's brief introduction gives clear answers to some basic concerns of the teacher designing a course on SF. The book is divided into three sections. The first focuses on the history and culture of SF. The second (now very outdated) discusses important reference texts. The third chapter offers general advice on structuring a course and connecting SF themes to current events.

*14-14. Williamson, Jack, ed. **Teaching Science Fiction: Education for Tomorrow**. Owlswick, 1980.

Essential reading for every SF teacher at every level. The major section of the book consists of 14 practical examples of teaching SF. Robert Myers shows how to integrate philosophy and SF. Martin Greenberg and Joseph Olander deal with political themes in SF. In addition, seven introductory essays discuss the origins of SF in the overall context of American culture. The value of this book resides in part in the breadth of its contributors' experience. Chapters by writers, scholars, teachers, an artist, and a publisher are included. Although originally published in 1980, it remains fresh and informative. Highly recommended.

Writing Guides

*14-15. Card, Orson Scott. **How to Write Science Fiction and Fantasy**. Writer's Digest, 1990.

Card, a widely respected author, provides a clear explanation of how to construct an SF story. He begins by situating both SF and fantasy in the larger context of speculative fiction (that is, all stories that occur in a setting contrary to known reality). He then takes the reader through the steps of creating a world, constructing a story, writing well, and even selling one's fiction. His concept of the MICE quotient (milieu, idea, character, event) is especially useful for discussing published stories as well as for constructing one's own. This is one of several texts that could profitably be used as a supplement in courses that include creative writing exercises or as the main text in an SF writing course.

14-16. Dozois, Gardner, Tina Lee, and Stanley Schmidt, eds. **Writing Science Fiction and Fantasy: Twenty Dynamic Essays by Today's Top Professionals**. St. Martin's, 1991.

Although published more than a decade ago, this is still a valuable guide to writing and selling SF. Contributors include writers and editors. The advice is divided into three areas: storytelling, ideas and foundations, and the business of writing. Especially recommended are the essays by Connie Willis on writing comic narrative and Stanley Schmidt's "Seeing Your Way to Better Stories." If used, supplement with a more recent guide.

14-17. Gillett, Stephen L., and Ben Bova, eds. **World-Building**. F&W Publications, 1996.

Gillett, a geologist, emphasizes the importance of designing scientifically plausible "worlds" (from planets to entire star systems). Most useful for novice writers with the ambition of creating environments based on actual science, Gillett's book would also serve well in a course on using SF to teach science. The tables and diagrams included are among the book's best features.

*14-18. Gunn, James E. **The Science of Science Fiction Writing**. Rowman and Littlefield, 2000.

The best introduction in print not only to writing but also to reading science fiction, Gunn's book could have been listed also in the section on instructional guides. The advice on writing is clear, concise, and to be heeded. Note especially the discussions of the protocols of SF and of "author strategy." Perhaps the most useful section for the novice writer is the appendix, which provides thorough notes and a detailed syllabus (with readings and assignments)—a vicarious experience of attending a Gunn-led writer's workshop. All SF teachers, indeed any teacher of literature, will benefit from the chapters devoted to the reasons people read fiction, the anatomy of the short story, and the creation of believable characters. Gunn blends his expertise as both teacher and writer to fashion a work of value to any teacher or reader of science fiction.

14-19. Schmidt, Stanley. **Aliens and Alien Societies: A Writer's Guide to Creating Extraterrestrial Life Forms**. F&W Publications, 1996.

As the title indicates, Schmidt's focus is on the depiction of convincing aliens and alien societies. His view that writers must pay attention to the potential impacts of biology and the environment on the forms of life and the structure of societies is presented forcefully. Recommended for novice writers as a superior guide to plausible aliens and to the teacher for Schmidt's analyses of aliens in a wide range of SF works.

Themes: Aliens

14-20. Scott, Melissa. **Conceiving the Heavens: Creating the Science Fiction Novel**. Heinemann, 1997.

The title reflects Scott's emphasis on the importance of the generative conception behind good science fiction. The book is structured like a workshop, leading the reader from concept to character and plot development to publication. She also provides a valuable introduction to the various forms of SF along the continuum from "hard" SF to science fantasy. Particularly useful are the exercises Scott offers as ways to resolve a number of typical problems faced by new writers. Scott also offers online writing classes.

14-21.   Stableford, Brian. **Writing Fantasy and Science Fiction: And Getting Published**. NTC Publishing, 1998.

Stableford's book contains both general discussions on the philosophy of writing fiction and practical advice about what will and will not "work" in writing publishable stories. The chapter on marketing SF and fantasy fiction is especially valuable. Part of a "teach yourself" series and aimed at beginning writers needing basic information, it is best when showing how to avoid pitfalls such as excessively conventional themes. Stableford's book will appeal to readers who want discussion of abstract issues involved in the creation of fiction as well as practical advice.

Textbooks and Anthologies

14-22.   Easton, Thomas, ed. **Gedanken Fictions: Stories on Themes in Science, Technology, and Society**. Wildside, 2000.

This is a wonderful collection of stories that dramatize fictional explorations of scientific ideas or technological developments. The title refers to the "thought experiments" that scientists employ when laboratory experiments are either impractical or inappropriate. Particularly useful for classroom discussion are Tom Godwin's classic "The Cold Equations," Bob Shaw's "Light of Other Days," and Charles Sheffield's "Out of Copyright." Highly recommended for courses on "SF and science" or as a supplement to a more comprehensive anthology.

*14-23.   Gunn, James E., ed. **The Road to Science Fiction**. Vols. 1–3 (Scarecrow, 2002), vol. 4 (Scarecrow, 2003), vols. 5 and 6 (White Wolf, 1998).

The best series, historically arranged, of SF anthologies ever assembled, the first four volumes revised from their original appearance as Mentor paperbacks (1977, 1979, 1982). All six volumes belong in the library of every university, school, and teacher and reader of science fiction. Gunn has gathered stories of importance to the development of SF and stories that represent the best writing in the genre. Many of the stories represent both. The question concerning this series is not whether to use it but rather how many volumes to select. A listing of the complete contents of each volume is at www.locusmag.com/index, as are the contents of these other anthologies. Volume 1 is also annotated among the anthologies in this book's Part II.

14-24.   Le Guin, Ursula K., and Brian W. Attebery, eds. **The Norton Book of Science Fiction**. Norton, 1993.

This comprehensive, ambitious, but idiosyncratic anthology includes 67 stories. Teachers should be cautioned about two aspects of the collection. First, since all were published after 1960, it has diminished value for courses that pay serious attention to the historical development of the genre. The emphasis is on "literary" SF. Secondly, as several reviews noted when the anthology first appeared, the choice of stories has an observably ideological focus. (But it must be admitted that every anthology has biases that guide its choices.) On a positive note, women writers are far more widely represented than is usual; on the other hand, the anthology presents "lesser" stories, rather than those for which they are best known, of several important male authors (William Gibson, for example). This having been said, the *Norton Anthology* is a collection filled with riches. Le Guin's thoughtful, often brilliant introduction is reason enough to purchase it. Also annotated in this book's Part II.

*14-25.   Roberts, Garyn G., ed. **The Prentice Hall Anthology of Science Fiction and Fantasy**. Prentice Hall, 2001.

This book fills an important void for teachers. It is comprehensive enough to form the main text in a course. The stories range historically from the early 19th century (e.g., Poe, Shelley, Hawthorne) through 1998. The presence of numerous stories from the pulp tradition is especially welcome. The inclusion of both fantasy and SF offers opportunities to compare the similarities and differences between the two genres; moreover, authors are generally represented by one of their best or at least most representative stories. Several appendixes (e.g., a list of SF/fantasy themes) will be useful to instructors. Highly recommended but with one caution: the book is very expensive.

14-26.   Silverberg, Robert, ed. **The Science Fiction Hall of Fame**, Vol. 1. Doubleday, 1971.

This collection of stories from the 1940s and 1950s is a great anthology, worthy of its title. Arguably the definitive collection of SF short fiction from what I call the Golden Age, it belongs in every teacher's personal library, although it may prove too difficult to find enough copies for use in most courses. Also annotated in Part II's anthologies.

*14-27.   Warrick, Patricia S., Charles G. Waugh, and Martin H. Greenberg, eds. **Science Fiction: The Science Fiction Research Association Anthology**. Harper and Row, 1988.

When in print, this was an ideal anthology for use in SF classes. The stories are arranged chronologically from Nathaniel Hawthorne's "Birthmark" to Octavia Butler's "Bloodchild." Although it contains no teaching apparatus or suggestions, the alternate grouping of stories by theme (biological, technological, environmental, and psychosocial) is useful. It has an attractive mixture of stories from the 19th century (including Wells's "The Star" and Forster's "The Machine Stops"), the Golden Age (with stories such as "Who Goes There?" and "A Martian Odyssey"), and the second half of the 20th century (including some of the most important stories by and about women). A revised, updated version would be most welcome.

CHAPTER 15

Research Library Collections of Science Fiction

Hal W. Hall

Since the first edition of *Anatomy of Wonder* in 1976, the number of large science fiction collections has grown, and the general holdings of many libraries have improved with the popularity of science fiction and fantasy in all venues. Locating required books and magazines has been significantly advanced by access to online public catalogs of virtually all academic and large public libraries. Lib-Web is a gateway to academic and public libraries, and is a useful resource for the researcher (http://sunsite.berkeley.edu/Libweb/). Researchers should consult with their local library and request access to OCLC (Online Computer Library Center) and RLIN (Research Libraries Information Network). These two collaborative resources provide extensive bibliographic access to both printed works and collections of manuscripts and papers. As a general rule, interlibrary loans are not available from special collections in libraries, and photocopying is limited to items that will not be damaged by the process. Old and fragile material is rarely copied. Nonetheless, interlibrary loan continues to be a key tool for the scholar seeking specific texts or editions. Contact individual libraries for special services.

The Eaton Collection at the University of California, Riverside, is the premier collection in the United States, followed by a number of collections in the United States and Canada. Based on monographic (book) holdings, notable

U.S. collections include Texas A&M University, Bowling Green State University, Temple University, Brigham Young University, and the Dallas Public Library. In Canada, the Merril Collection at the Toronto Public Library has long been the premier collection, and is joined by the University of New Brunswick and the newly announced collection at the University of Calgary. Internationally, the great research collections are the University of Sydney; the Science Fiction Foundation collection at the University of Liverpool; the Maison d'Ailleurs in Switzerland, with manuscripts of every French-speaking science fiction author; and the Phantastische Bibliothek Wetzlar, which claims 85,000 items. These collections, separately or together, provide the source material for all manner of scholarship.

Table 15-1.　Statistical Summary of the 26 Largest
SF and Fantasy Library Collections

Library Name	Total Pieces	Mono Titles	Mag Titles	Mag Issues	Manuscripts (Linear Feet)	A/V (Titles)
Univ. of California, Riverside	295,000	85,000	175	—	100	200
Phantastische Bibliothek Wetzlar	130,000	—	—	—	—	—
Univ. of Louisville	100,000	—	—	10,000	—	—
Univ. of Sydney	90,000	50,000	170	41,000	10	—
Toronto Public Library	58,000	30,000	—	23,700	—	710
Texas A&M Univ.	45,000	24,900	200	—	60	—
Univ. of Calgary	40,000	—	—	—	—	—
Maison d'Ailleurs	35,000	—	—	—	—	—
Univ. of Maryland	30,600	10,600	100	20,000	ca. 100	90
Univ. of New Brunswick	27,000	16,000	—	11,000	—	—
Univ. of Liverpool	27,000	—	—	—	—	—
Bowling Green State Univ.	26,000	15,000	500	5,200	60	—
Eastern New Mexico Univ.	23,000	12,800	900	11,695	100	—
Temple Univ.	22,000	15,000	—	7,000	130	—
Univ. of California, Los Angeles	20,000	10,000	100	5,000	5	—
Northwestern	20,000	—	—	—	—	—
Michigan State Univ.	19,500	10,000	—	2,000	—	—
Univ. of Arizona, Tucson	18,000	—	—	—	—	—
Univ. of Kansas	18,000	10,000	128	—	140	500
Dallas Public Library	16,275	16,000	275	—	—	—
Univ. of California, Fullerton	14,000	4,500	221	—	1,241	—
Univ. of Texas, Austin	13,000	8,000	—	250	—	—
San Francisco Public Library	12,000	—	—	—	—	—
Brigham Young Univ.	12,000	12,000	—	—	40	—
Louisiana State Univ.	10,000	—	—	—	—	—
Syracuse Univ.	10,000	4,100	—	5,800	310	—

Data are as reported by the libraries in 2003. Mono = monographs (individual books); mag = magazines.

Not one of the very fine collections just mentioned exists in a national library, largely because such libraries were established long before the study and collection of SF became common. This does not mean to imply that the Library of Congress [15-7], the British Library, the Bibliothèque Nationale, and the National Library of Australia and all the other national libraries do not serve the scholar. Virtually all the national bibliographies are now online, and provide invaluable bibliographic information on the literature of each country. The GABRIEL Gateway (http://portico.bl.uk/gabriel/) provides the researcher a useful pathway to most European national bibliographies. For questions about translations, UNESCO provides the *Index Translationum* online at http://portal.unesco.org/culture/en/ev.php@URL_ID=7810&URL_DO= DO_TOPIC&URL_SECTION=201.html. While not complete, it is the best source for such information.

Three collections offer specialized material of value to researchers. They are private collections serving members, but they offer access to researchers by appointment. Staffing is typically by volunteers, so early advance contact and scheduling is essential.

The American Private Press Association (107 E. Burnett, Stayton, OR 97383. Martin Horvat. 503-769-6088, acquisitions@appalibrary.org) is a collection of 250,000 fanzines published 1965–1980 and 3,000 letters by fans. There is also a very large collection of non-SF amateur (fan) journalism. Photocopies available. Researchers interested in fans and fanzines should consider this collection.

The Los Angeles Science Fantasy Society Library (11513 Burbank Blvd., North Hollywood, CA 91601. 818-760-9234) is a club collection primarily for members' use, with 12,000 volumes and more than 120 magazine runs.

The MIT Science Fiction Society Library (W20-473 MIT Student Center, 84 Massachusetts Ave., Cambridge, MA 02139-4307. 617-258-5126, www.mit. edu/~mitsfs/) is a club collection with a long history and reputation as one of the most complete SF magazine collections in North America. The MITSF catalog (www.mit.edu/pinkdex) indicates good coverage of non–English language periodicals. Around 35,000 total items. The "Pinkdex" to the catalog can be searched online by author and title. The hours are irregular, mostly evenings. Some material circulates to members; room use only for the public.

The collections chosen for inclusion in this edition are of value to research, in their inclusiveness, or by virtue of specialized materials held. All collection descriptions were updated as necessary. Two new collections were added, those at the University of Calgary and the very large Tolkien archive at Wisconsin's Marquette University. A number of smaller collections were dropped from this main listing; see the condensed list that concludes this chapter. Phone numbers and Web addresses are provided for most collections. Advance contact is always advised.

Library personnel will go out of the way to be helpful in discussing your research or reading needs, and will provide photocopies of materials if they are not fragile. Legal restrictions may limit access, either because of copyright law or because writers or their families have requested that a collection be closed for a specified time period. Some collections require individual approval from the collection donor for use. Libraries' needs for public service, adherence to gift agreements, and protection of rare and fragile material require patience and flexibility on the part of both the institution and the scholar. The arrangement here is alphabetical by state for the United States, followed by other countries in alphabetical order.

Library Collections

Arizona

15-1.   University of Arizona Library. Special Collections, P.O. Box 210055, Tucson, AZ, 85721-0055. 520-621-6423. Web address: www.library.arizona.edu/branches/spc/homepage/index.html.

A science fiction collection of 18,000 volumes, with current acquisitions restricted to science fiction as opposed to fantasy and horror. The collection is based on the individual collections of Margaret Brown, Archibald Hanna, and Anthony Boucher. Holdings include complete runs of most American science fiction magazines and strong representation of early pulps. This is a non-circulating collection, and it is 90 percent cataloged. No interlibrary loan.

California

15-2.   California State University. Fullerton-Pollak Library, University Archives and Special Collections, Box 4150, Fullerton, CA 92834. 714-278-3444. Web address: http://library.fullerton.edu/special.htm.

The University Archives and Special Collections Unit holds a science fiction collection of 174 linear feet of hardbacks, paperbacks, and periodicals. A larger circulating collection is distributed throughout the library. The science fiction manuscript collection is contained in 378 boxes (63 linear feet) . The collection holds 146 film or TV scripts and a handful of recordings and pieces of art. The collection has particular strength in the manuscripts and papers of Avram Davidson, Philip K. Dick, Harry Harrison, Frank Herbert, and Robert Moore Williams. Finding guides are available for the manuscripts and papers. The Philip Dick holdings are described in "Philip K. Dick Manuscripts and Books: The Manuscripts and Papers at Fullerton," *Science-Fiction Studies* 2, No. 1 (March 1975), pp. 4–5. The collection was described in McNelly, Willis E., "The Science Fiction Collection," pp. 17–26 of *Very Special Collections: Essays on Library Holdings at California State University, Fullerton,* ed. by Albert R. Vogeler and Arthur A.

Hansen, The Patrons of the Library, 1992. Partially cataloged. Photocopies are available.

15-3. Huntington Library. 1151 Oxford Rd., San Marino, CA 91108. 626-405-2100. Web address: www.huntington.org/.

The Huntington Library is noteworthy for the collections of correspondence held, including: Brian Aldiss, 107 letters to his publishers, 1965–1973; Poul Anderson, 79 letters to his publishers, 1960–1977; Philip K. Dick, 61 pieces, including letters, outlines, and photographs; Frederik Pohl, 91 letters, 1959–1975; Robert Silverberg, 1,700 pieces, 1953–1992, including notes, drafts of short stories, and letters; and Clifford D. Simak, 20 letters, 1961–1974. The manuscript holdings are described in *Guide to Literary Manuscripts in the Huntington Library* (San Marino: The Library, 1979). The Huntington's material is non-circulating, but available to qualified scholars. Photocopying of some of the manuscripts is restricted.

15-4. San Francisco Public Library. McComas Collection of Fantasy and Science Fiction, Civic Center, San Francisco, CA 94102. 415-557-4545. Web address: http://sfpl.lib.ca.us/.

The McComas Collection holds 3,000 volumes of science fiction, plus a strong collection of 92 periodical titles. Portions of the collection were destroyed in 1989, mostly pulp titles at the beginning of the alphabet. The collection is non-circulating and reported as fully cataloged. It is growing by about 30 volumes a year, plus several magazine subscriptions. Photocopying is available but not interlibrary loan.

15-5. University of California, Los Angeles. Special Collections, University Library, Box 951575, Los Angeles, CA 90095. 310-825-4988. Web address: www.library.ucla.edu/libraries/special/scweb/colindex.htm.

The Nitka Collection of Science Fiction and Fantasy has more than 10,000 monograph volumes, including over 400 early editions of H. Rider Haggard. A magazine collection of more than 5,000 issues of 100 titles supplements the monograph collection. Holdings include Ray Bradbury manuscripts (1.5 linear feet), Jean Aroeste (*Star Trek* scripts), George Pal, Gene Roddenberry, Betty Rosenberg, Rod Serling, and other scattered manuscripts. Finding guides to many of the collections are available online. The collection is cataloged.

15-6. University of California at Riverside. Eaton Collection, Department of Special Collections, Tomas Rivera Library, University of California, Riverside, CA 92517-5900. 909-787-3233. Web address: http://library.ucr.edu/?view=collections/spcol/index.html.

The Eaton Collection holds approximately 85,000 volumes of science fiction, plus 100 shelf-feet of manuscripts, more than 200,000 issues of fanzines, more than 200 sound and video recordings, extensive periodical holdings of more than 175 science fiction or fantasy titles, 5,000 comic books, and shooting scripts of more than 500 SF motion pictures. The collection includes the largest holdings of 17th- to 19th-century utopian/dystopian fiction in North America, with a rare copy of Thomas More's *Utopia* as the centerpiece. The collection holds almost 90 percent of all 20th-century American and British science fiction, fantasy, and horror, the largest collection of French science fiction in North America, and representative collections of Japanese, Spanish, Russian, and German science fiction. The collection offers 10,000 reference, bibliographic, biographic, and index volumes pertaining to science fiction, and 75 pieces of science fiction art, including some original artwork. The library contains some 200,000 issues of "fanzines," including the Bruce Pelz and Terry Carr collections, making this the premier location for studies of SF fandom. The manuscript holdings include partial or full manuscript collections of Gregory Benford, David Brin, Michael Cassutt, Philip K. Dick, G. C. Edmonson, Sheila Finch, Robert L. Forward, Diana G. Gallagher, Arthur Loy Holcomb, Gary Kern, Annette Y. Mallett, Daryl F. Mallett, Anne McCaffrey, George E. Slusser, Gary Westfahl, James White, Colin Wilson, and more. The collection catalog was published as *Dictionary Catalog of the J. Lloyd Eaton Collection of Science Fiction and Fantasy Literature* (Boston: G. K. Hall, 1982), 3 vols. The collection is cataloged, except for the manuscripts. It is non-circulating, and is growing by more than 4,000 items a year. It is a Science Fiction Writers of America (SFWA) depository library. Photocopies are selectively available.

District of Columbia

15-7.   Library of Congress. Rare Book and Special Collections Division, 101 Independence Ave. S.E., Washington, DC 20540-4740. 202-707-3448. E-mail: rbref@loc.gov. Web address: www.loc.gov/rr/rarebook/.

The Library of Congress has no discrete science fiction collection, but the sheer scale of the library makes it a resource no researcher should overlook. The library's general collections of books and bound serials are home to the single greatest number of genre-related items. As the general collections number more than 10 million items (there are more than 25 million bound volumes), it is almost impossible to estimate exactly how many of these would be considered works of science fiction, including a number of foreign science fiction titles, which are acquired through exchange. Some 70 percent of the collection is cataloged. The magazine collection contains more than 60,000 titles and 10 million issues. A Jules Verne Collection contains rare Verne volumes donated by Willis E. Hurd (1875–1958). The Rare Book and Special Collections Division holds the only extant copies of the earliest American appearances of one of Verne's earliest novels, *From the Earth to the Moon* (1865), in both a serial (*New York Weekly Magazine of Popular Literature*, 1867) and a book edition (American News Company, 1869). This collection is the largest of Verne material outside France.

   The Pulp Fiction collection consists of issues received on copyright deposit at the time of their publication. It is described in Annette Melville's "Special Collections in the Library of Congress: A Selective Guide" (Washington, DC:

Library of Congress, 1980). A great majority of the issues were held by the Serial and Government Publications Division, although three extremely rare and valuable titles were transferred to the Rare Book and Special Collections Division: *Amazing Stories, Black Mask,* and *Weird Tales.* The collection has now been microfilmed and is available in the Microform Reading Room. The collection contains more than 380 titles, with 10,000 issues. A list of titles can be viewed at www.loc.gov/rr/news/pulp.html.

The Dell Paperback Collection includes a virtually complete set of Dell paperbacks from 1943 to the present. In forming this archival collection, Western Publishing Company tried to document major changes in cover design resulting from marketing strategy, the release of a movie adaptation, fluctuations in price, and in many cases successive reissues of a single publication. The four copies of Kurt Vonnegut's *Slaughterhouse-Five* issued under number 8029, for example, exhibit three markedly different covers. Though approximately 90 percent of the books are reprints of titles previously issued in hard cover, the collection includes the Dell First Edition series, which was begun in 1953. The 6,501 paperback volumes are grouped by series and arranged in serial order. They are described in an author and title file prepared by Western Publishing Company. In 1976, the library instituted a Paperback Copyright Collection, now numbering more than 75,000 items, to provide a unique documentary record of American popular publishing and reading trends. Material related to science fiction and fantasy may be found in the Dime Novel Collection (40,000 titles), the Juvenile Collection (20,000 items), and the Big Little Book Collection (534 items). The Library of Congress holdings were described by Judith Mistichelli, in "Science Fiction at the Library of Congress," *Science Fiction Collections,* ed. by H. W. Hall (Haworth Press, 1983), pp. 9–24.

Georgia

15-8.   University of Georgia Libraries. Humanities Department, Athens, GA 30602. 706-542-7123. Web address: www.libs.uga.edu/.

The general library maintains a circulating collection of 6,041 volumes of science fiction, including reference materials and 50 videotapes. Special Collections holds manuscript collections of Michael Bishop (21.5 linear feet; author permission required), Brad Strickland (2 linear feet), Sharon Webb (9 linear feet) and Tom Dietz (5 linear feet). A representative collection of SF magazines from the 1930s through the 1950s is held in Special Collections. The collection is cataloged. Interlibrary loan and photocopying are available.

Illinois

15-9.   University of Illinois at Urbana–Champaign. Library Rare Book Room, 1408 West Gregory Dr., Urbana, IL 61801. 217-333-3777. Web address: http://door.library.uiuc.edu/rbx/speccoll.htm.

The H. G. Wells Collection includes an extensive book collection from Wells's personal library, with his inscribed and corrected first editions, and files of extensive correspondence both to and from Wells. The Wells manuscripts are in 145 boxes, of which 24 boxes are SF-related (81.5 cubic feet). The collection includes more than 70,000 pieces of correspondence about business and legal affair; diaries, journals, drawings, publication records, manuscripts, and proofs of published works; speeches; unpublished material; and photographs. An online database of the correspondence collection aids access. A grant project supports the cataloging of all of Wells's works on OCLC and microfilming of the collection. Another collection, the Jaffee Collection, specializes in first edition science fiction in dust jacket. The Jaffee Collection is actively growing, and includes more than 500 volumes. Photocopies are available.

15-10. Wheaton College. Special Collections, Buswell Memorial Library, 501 College Ave., Wheaton, IL 60187-5593. 630-752-5705. Web address: www. wheaton.edu/learnres/ARCSC/1/INDEX.HTM.

The library holds more than 200 linear feet of Madeleine L'Engle's papers and writings, supplemented by about 160 of her published works and a selection of media materials. The Madeleine L'Engle Collection is added to regularly through purchases and gifts and is accessible by written permission only. A container list online gives good access to collection contents. The World Science Fiction Conference (Chicon) Collection contains the files (more than 3 linear feet) of Chicon IV, held in Chicago in 1982. The Coleman Luck Collection contains scripts and other materials relating to the *Otherworld* television series, which aired on CBS in the late 1980s.

Indiana

15-11. Indiana University. Lilly Library, Bloomington, IN 47405. 812-337-2452. Web address: www.indiana.edu/~liblilly/.

The Lilly Library has no separate SF/fantasy collections, but has extensive holdings in these areas. Authors' papers in the library include those of Anthony Boucher, Fritz Leiber, August Derleth, Robert Bloch, James Blish, Ray Bradbury, Kurt Vonnegut, Orson Welles, and others. Correspondence from many SF/fantasy writers is scattered throughout the collections, especially in publishers' files such as those of Bobbs-Merrill and Capra Press. First edition collections of many authors are held, including Wells, Verne, Haggard, Chesterton, Derleth, and Lovecraft. A separate catalog of the collection is available. The collection is partially cataloged.

Kansas

15-12. University of Kansas. Kenneth Spencer Research Library, Department of Special Collections, 1450 Poplar Ln., Lawrence, KS 66045-7615. 785-864-4334. Web address: http://spencer.lib.ku.edu/sc/index.htm.

The Spencer Library was established in 1969, and now holds more than 10,000 volumes of science fiction and more than 80 reference or critical volumes. A total 128 magazine titles are held, as well as a large collection of fanzines. The collection holds at least 500 recordings, both audio and visual, miscellaneous pieces of convention literature, buttons, posters, prospectuses, and so forth, and one Hugo award statuette. Over 200 linear feet of manuscripts and papers include the following: Brian Aldiss (13 feet), Lloyd Biggle (17), Algis Budrys (1), Thomas Easton (2), James Gunn (72), Hunter Holly (4), Lee Killough (12), P. Schuyler Miller (18), T. L. Sherred (4), Cordwainer Smith (3), A. E. van Vogt (1), Robert Mills Agency/Richard Curtis Agency (29), and Science Fiction Research Association (7) . The collection is the official repository for the archives of the Science Fiction Research Association and the Science Fiction Oral History Association (audiotapes only received so far). It includes SFWA (Science Fiction Writers of America) official papers from the presidencies of Gunn, Williamson, and Pohl. The collection is the North American Repository for World SF, which deposits non–English-language books and has participated in the SFWA depository scheme since 1970. The collection is described in "The Library of the Future: Science Fiction and the Department of Special Collections," by Ann Hyde, *Books and Libraries at the University of Kansas* 13, No. 3 (Spring 1976), pp. 1–5, and "Records of the Time Patrol: SF at KU," by Ann Hyde, *Books and Libraries at the University of Kansas* 20 (Spring 1988), pp. 1–8.

The collection is active, adding 400 items annually by gift. The collection is non-circulating, and partially cataloged. Materials on-site are accessible by donor lists and shelf arrangement. Photocopies are available.

Kentucky

15-13. University of Louisville Library. Nell Dismukes McWhorter Memorial Collection of Edgar Rice Burroughs, Rare Books and Special Collections, Louisville, KY 40292. 502-852-6752. Web address: http://special.library.louisville.edu/.

The Edgar Rice Burroughs collection of more than 100,000 items is the largest of its kind in any institutional library and includes first editions, personal memorabilia, scrapbooks, Burroughs's school textbooks, comics, posters, photos, manuscripts, fanzines, toys, movies, and related material about Burroughs. The collection includes original art by J. Allen St. John, Burne Hogarth, and others; Burroughs family letters and papers; photographs and notes; and the files of Burroughs biographer Irwin Porges. The Burroughs Collection is supplemented by collections of Ambrose Bierce, L. Frank Baum, August Derleth, Ursula K. Le Guin, and a pulp magazine collection of more than 10,000 issues. The library publishes a journal (*Burroughs Bulletin*) and a monthly newsletter, *The Gridley Wave.* Collecting is active, with regular additions through purchase and gift. Materials are for room use only. Photocopies, but no interlibrary loan. The collection is described in George T. McWhorter, *Edgar Rice Burroughs Memorial Collection: A Catalog,* ltd. first ed. (House of Greystoke, 1991), and George T. McWhorter, "Edgar Rice Burroughs," *Library Review* 30 (May 1980).

Louisiana

15-14.   Tulane University. Howard-Tilton Memorial Library, Special Collections, New Orleans, LA 70118-5682. 504-865-5685. Web address: http://special collections.tulane.edu/.

This is an active special collection of 4,600 books, plus 2,500 magazine issues, and 400 fanzine issues. Specialties include the works of Rosel George Brown, who began the collection, and Robert Heinlein first editions. The archives and papers of the Cheap Street Press were acquired in 2002. The collection is growing at a rate of about 200 volumes a year. The materials are all non-circulating, with some interlibrary loan and photocopying available. Partially cataloged.

Maryland

15-15.   University of Maryland. Baltimore County, Albin O. Kuhn Library and Gallery, 1000 Hilltop Circle, Baltimore, MD 21250. 410-455-6290. Web address: http://aok.lib.umbc.edu/SpecColl/popcul.php3.

The Azriel Rosenfeld Science Fiction Research Collection includes 10,000 volumes of science fiction and 600 volumes of reference and critical work. More than 100 magazine titles are held, along with 20,000 fanzine issues, 790 manuscripts, 4,000 letters, 42 sound recordings, 17 visual recordings, 31 film scripts, and 100 pieces of SF art. The Sapienza collection was acquired in 2003, containing books, magazines, and fanzines. Currently being processed, it will add significantly to the science fiction and fantasy holdings. A collection of more than 6,500 comic books includes some SF and fantasy titles. The collection is particularly strong for authors Roger Zelazny, Thomas F. Monteleone, and David Bischoff. The Bischoff collection of manuscripts, correspondence, personal papers, books, and journals was acquired recently. Individual manuscripts by Roger Zelazny, Thomas F. Monteleone, Charles L. Harness, Brian M. Stableford, E. C. Tubb, and 18 other authors are held. The Walter Coslet fanzine collection is a major strength, mostly dating from before 1960 and including many from the 1930–1950 period. A catalog of the fanzine collection is available online. The collection is active, adding 400 items annually. Cataloging of the books is 75 percent complete, and is searchable online. Photocopies are available, but no interlibrary loan.

Massachusetts

15-16.   Boston University. Mugar Memorial Library, Department of Special Collections, 771 Commonwealth Ave., Boston, MA 02215. 617-353-3696. Web address: www.bu.edu/speccol/.

The Boston University science fiction collection is notable for holdings of manuscripts and papers, but also has 1,800 volumes and two magazine titles. Manuscript holdings include: Isaac Asimov (220 linear feet), Marion Zimmer Bradley (50 linear feet), Arthur C. Clarke (2 linear feet), L. Sprague de Camp (22 linear feet), Samuel R. Delany (60 linear feet), Alan Nourse (60 linear feet), Edgar

Pangborn (18 linear feet), Curt Siodmak (10 linear feet), and Jack Vance (10 linear feet). The collection is active, adding about 100 books annually. The collection is partially cataloged in-house. Photocopies are available.

Michigan

15-17.   Michigan State University Libraries. Special Collections Division, East Lansing, MI 48824-1048. 517-355-3770. Web address: www.lib.msu.edu/coll/main/spec_col/.

Part of the Russell B. Nye Popular Culture Collection is a 12,000-volume science fiction collection that is mostly monographs, but includes samples of most science fiction magazines and some 2,000 fanzine issues. All manuscripts of the Clarion Workshop from 1969 to the present are held. The Clarion manuscripts are arranged by year and by author. A comic book collection of more than 75,000 items includes at least 1,000 science fiction comics, depending on definition. The Vincent Voice Library is a regional depository for the Science Fiction Oral History Association collection, which numbers more than 350 tapes. In 1977, a collection of James Tiptree, Jr. award winners and short-list titles was started. The books, pulps, magazines, comics, and sound recordings are cataloged on OCLC. Cataloging has been enhanced to include publishers' series designations and names of illustrators and cover and jacket artists whenever possible. The collection grows by gifts at a rate of about 300 items a year, and has been an SFWA depository since 1972. The materials are non-circulating. Some photocopies are available, but no interlibrary loan.

15-18.   University of Michigan. Harlan Hatcher Graduate Library, Special Collections Library, Ann Arbor, MI 48109-1205. 734-764-9377. Web address: www.lib.umich.edu/spec-coll/.

The Hubbard Collection of Imaginary Voyages consists of 3,000 volumes of fiction and 130 volumes of reference and critical material, largely of various editions, translations, adaptations, abridgments, and imitations of *Robinson Crusoe* and *Gulliver's Travels*. A few books by such authors as Verne, Bellamy, and Cyrano de Bergerac are included, almost entirely limited to imaginary voyages on Earth with few interplanetary trips. The collection holds a few items by James Branch Cabell, papers of Marge Piercy (14 linear feet), and the Cabell Society archives (2,319 items). The collection is active, adding three to five items annually. It is non-circulating and fully cataloged, and photocopies are available.

Minnesota

15-19.   University of Minnesota Libraries. Manuscripts Division, 222 21st Ave. S., Minneapolis, MN 55455. 612-625-3550. Web address: http://special.lib.umn.edu/manuscripts/literary.html.

The Manuscripts Division holds a *Star Trek* collection of about 9 linear feet of scripts and related materials, including 50 published volumes of *Star Trek* fiction, 100 reference and critical volumes, and 9 sound recordings. The scripts are a pilot script and complete set of shooting scripts for the original television series, and shooting scripts for the first two movies. The Children's Literature Research Collections (Kerlan Collection and Hess Collection) contain many books of interest to students of young adult and children's science fiction and fantasy. Manuscripts and papers maintained include Gordon R. Dickson (60 boxes), Clifford D. Simak (17 boxes), Carl Jacobi (5 boxes), E. Hoffman Price (1 box), and H. P. Lovecraft (17 items). The focus of the collection is authors with Minnesota connections. An attempt is being made to collect material from the old pulp writers, such as Price and Jacobi, but the pulp magazines themselves are not retained in the division. The collections contain notes, correspondence, manuscript drafts, and some galley proofs. The collection is actively maintained and cataloged for use within the Division. Acquisitions are by gift only.

New Mexico

15-20.   Eastern New Mexico University. Golden Library, Special Collections, ENMU Station 32, Portales, NM 88130. 505-562-2636. Web address: www.enmu. edu/academics/library/collections/williamson.shtml.

The Williamson Science Fiction Library originated with gifts from Jack Williamson and now consists of more than 23,000 items. Fully cataloged and circulating are 12,800 volumes of fiction. The magazine collection (including fanzines) includes 11,695 issues of 900 titles. The manuscript collection includes material from Jack Williamson (47 linear feet), Leigh Brackett (8 linear feet), Edmond Hamilton (4 linear feet), Forrest J. Ackerman (13.5 linear feet), Piers Anthony (1 linear foot), *Analog* files 1954–1975 (various authors) (21 linear feet), James Blish, SFWA Presidential (1 linear foot), Marcia Howl (1 linear foot), and Woody Wolfe (1 linear foot). The Williamson collection is a regional depository for the Science Fiction Oral History Association, and 44 sound recordings from the SFOHA are held. The collection is active, adding at least 400 titles a year, and has been an SFWA depository since 1969. The books are cataloged on OCLC, and internal lists and indexes are used to keep track of the rest of the material. Circulating materials will be lent on interlibrary loan, and photocopies are available.

15-21.   University of New Mexico. Center for Southwest Research, Zimmerman Library, Albuquerque, NM 87131. 505-277-6451. Web address: www.unm. edu/~cswrref/enghome.html.

The Donald Day Science Fiction Collection consists of a virtually complete collection of 52 American and three British magazines published between 1926 and 1950. The magazines are those indexed in Donald B. Day's *Index to the Science Fiction Magazines, 1926–1950*. The collection includes Day's original card index. The collection is non-circulating, inactive, and not cataloged in the library sense, although the index serves the purpose. An inventory is available from the center. Photocopying is not available.

New York

15-22. New York Public Library. General Research Division, 5th Ave. and 42nd St., New York, NY 10018. 212-930-0801. Web address: www.nypl.org/research/chss/spe/rbk/mss.html.

The General Research Division has more than 7,000 volumes of science fiction in closed stacks. Current science fiction paperbacks are filmed routinely in the Microforms Division and more than 2,000 are on film. The Microforms Division (separate from the General Research Division but at the same address) holds most commercial science fiction microforms available (pulps and magazines) and 212 sample fanzine titles filmed in-house. The collection is growing by 500 volumes a year. The collection can be searched through OCLC and RLIN. Photocopies and interlibrary loan are available.

15-23. Syracuse University Library. Special Collections Department, Room 600, Bird Library, Syracuse, NY 13244-2010. 315-443-2697. Web address: http://libwww.syr.edu/information/spcollections/rarebooks.htm.

A non-circulating collection of 4,100 monograph volumes of science fiction, 5,800 magazine issues, 25 manuscript collections, and 50 fanzine titles. The manuscripts (in linear feet) include Ace Books (24.5), Forrest J. Ackerman (79), Piers Anthony (10), Hal Clement (2.5), Galaxy Publishing Corporation (33), Hugo Gernsback (50), Gnome Press (0.5), Harvey Jacobs (3), William F. Jenkins (35), David Keller (5), Damon Knight (10), David A. Kyle (0.5), Keith Laumer (12), Anne McCaffrey (4), Mercury Press (1956–1967) (20), Andre Norton (16.25), Frederik Pohl (8), Robert Silverberg (24), Street and Smith (407), Universal Publishing Corporation (0.8), Kate Wilhelm (6), Richard Wilson (20), Donald A. Wollheim (0.5), and Roger Zelazny (5.5). The Mercury Press collection consists of undated responses to questionnaires to determine what kind of people read science fiction, divided by age groups; manuscripts; and a subject file. A description of the collection, "Syracuse University," by Fred Lerner, appears in H. W. Hall, ed., *Science Fiction Collections: Fantasy, Supernatural and Weird Tales* (Haworth Press, 1983). The book collection is partially cataloged on OCLC, and the manuscripts are on RLIN. The catalog is online. Acquisitions are occasional. Some photocopying is possible. No interlibrary loan.

North Carolina

15-24. Duke University. Special Collections Library, Durham, NC 27708-0185. 919-660-5822. Web address: http://scriptorium.lib.duke.edu/#search.

The Negley Collection consists of more than 1,600 volumes of utopian fiction. The basic description of the collection is found in Glenn Negley's *Utopian Literature: A Bibliography, With a Supplementary Listing of Works Influential in Utopian Thought* (1978). This major utopian collection is active, adding 15 to 20 items annually. It is cataloged, and searchable online. (Note: The frequently cited Folcroft edition is reprinted from a partial checklist and should be avoided, according to the library.) The library also holds the papers of Kathy Acker (20.5 linear feet). In 2003, the Murray Collection of popular culture was donated, consisting of 55,000 comic books, "thousands" of fanzines, SF and fantasy books, and other material. A donation of extensive runs of SF magazines will be made later. Contact the library for availability of the material in the Murray collection.

Ohio

15-25.   Bowling Green State University. Popular Culture Library, Bowling Green, OH 43403. 419-372-2450. Web address: www.bgsu.edu/colleges/library/pcl/pcl.html.

The science fiction and fantasy holdings of the Popular Culture Library include more than 15,000 volumes of fiction and related reference and critical volumes; 500 magazine titles; 1,000 fanzine issues; 5,200 pulp magazine issues; and many manuscripts. Manuscripts holdings include Daniel Cohen (18 linear feet), Alexi Panshin (19.5 linear feet), Joanna Russ (7.5 linear feet), Carl Jacobi, and Sheldon R. Jaffery (26 boxes). The collection is a good source for American magazines, 1926–1960. Especially notable are the Michael L. Cook Collection of fanzines and the H. James Horvitz Science Fiction Collection of pulp magazines. The Ray Bradbury collection consists of more than 700 books and 15 linear feet of non-book materials. There are rare Bradbury pamphlets, comic book adaptations, original art by Bradbury, sound recordings, maps, broadsides, photographs, galley proofs, scripts, programs, screenplays, diary notes, posters, promotional material, interviews, speeches, and more than 400 periodicals. The centerpiece of the manuscript collection is the heavily revised 221-page typed draft of *Fahrenheit 451*. Also included are 120 manuscripts in 160 drafts of Bradbury short stories and verse. An unusual item is a 135,000-word manuscript transcribed from tapes forming a complete Bradbury autobiography. The Jaffery collection includes nearly complete sets of Arkham House and DAW books. The Marie Wakefield collection of *Star Trek* material was recently added to the collection, including videotapes, books, models, sound recordings, games, posters, figures, costume jewelry, comic books, and even a McDonald's Happy Meal box. Many items are still in their original packaging. The collection is active, adding 200 to 1,000 items annually. The catalog of the library is searchable online. Photocopies are available; no interlibrary loan.

15-26.   Ohio State University. Special Collections, 1858 Neil Ave. Mall, Columbus, OH 43210-1286. 614-292-5938. Web address: www.lib.ohio-state.edu/rarweb/index.html.

Under the designation "The William Charvat Collection of American Fiction," Ohio State has been working for years to assemble a complete American fiction collection up to the year 1926, and since 1986. The Charvat Collection is primarily valuable for the prehistory of science fiction and fantasy, those books that were precursors to the establishment of the genre in the late 1920s. Few libraries collect comprehensively for this period, as Ohio State seeks to do. The Special Collections also include 105 science fiction magazine titles from 1926 to the present, including a nearly complete set of *Weird Tales*. A collection of a number of the original *Star Trek* series scripts is also held. Photocopies are available.

Pennsylvania

15-27.   Temple University Libraries. Special Collections Department, Philadelphia, PA 19122. 215-204-8230. Fax 215-204-2501. Web address: www.library. temple.edu/speccoll/sfc.htm.

The Science Fiction and Fantasy Collection (Paskow/Knuth) numbers some 20,000 books, 5,500 magazine issues, 2,500 fanzines, and 130 feet of manuscripts. Manuscripts include: Ben Bova, Gardner Dozois, Lloyd A. Eshbach/Fantasy Press, Jack Dann, Tom Purdom, Felix Gotschalk, John Varley, Oswald Train/Prime Press, Miriam DeFord, Richard Peck, Stanley Weinbaum, and Camille Bacon-Smith, with notable manuscripts of John W. Campbell, John Taine (Bell), and E. E. Smith. Of particular note are strong collections of the published works of H. P. Lovecraft, Robert Howard, Ben Bova, and Stanley Weinbaum. Subsidiary collections include the CON collection of SF and fantasy conference booklets, programs, and ephemera; the Sue Frank Klingon/*Star Trek* collection of fanzines and organizational newsletters; and the Enterprising Women Fan Fiction Collection (EWFFC) of amateur fiction. Although most of the collection (90 percent) was cataloged by 1984, the influx of gifts has since reduced the portion of cataloged material to about half. The collection is active, currently adding about 250 items a year. About 50 percent of the published material is searchable online, and much of the manuscript material is accessible through RLIN. The initial fanzine list is available on the Web site, but additions and revisions are on in-house lists only. The collection is non-circulating; photocopy requests are honored.

Rhode Island

15-28.   Brown University. John Hay Library, Providence, RI 02912. 401-863-2146. Web address: www.brown.edu/Facilities/University_Library/libs/hay/collections/index.htm.

The definitive H. P. Lovecraft collection, with more than 700 printed and more than 5,000 manuscript items, half by Lovecraft himself and half by Lovecraft correspondents such as August Derleth, Frank Belknap Long, C. L. Moore, E. Hoffmann Price, and Clark Ashton Smith. A separate Clark Ashton Smith collection includes more than 5,000 manuscripts and 5,000 letters. The George Orwell Collection includes a draft copy of *Nineteen Eighty-Four*, noted as the only manuscript of this work. An H. G. Wells collection contains some 500 items. A complete run of *Weird Tales* is held. Publisher collections include the complete works of Arkham House including most ephemera, and complete Donald W. Grant and Necronomicon Press collections. The collection is active, and cataloged.

Texas

15-29. Dallas Public Library. 1515 Young St., Dallas, TX 75201. 214-670-1668. Web address: http://dallaslibrary.org/.

Since 1974, the library has been building a research collection of science fiction that now includes more than 16,000 volumes, and 187 fantasy and science fiction periodical titles. Some 2,350 of the volumes are in the Brian Aldiss Collection, which also includes personal correspondence, photographs, speeches, illustrations, introductions, posters and cover art, book and film reviews, radio plays, and notes and typescripts for short stories, novels, and poetry. The collection is growing at a rate of about 300 volumes a year by gift and purchase. The collection is cataloged, and most of it circulates. Photocopies and interlibrary loan are available.

15-30. Texas A&M University. Cushing Library, TAMU 5000, College Station, TX 77843-5000. 979-845-1951. Web address: http://lib-oldweb.tamu.edu/cushing/collectn/lit/science/sci-fi/index.html.

The Science Fiction Research Collection was begun in 1970 and now exceeds 40,000 items. An important strength of the collection is a pulp magazine collection, containing more than 200 titles of American and British science fiction magazines from 1923 to the present, plus a growing sample of foreign-language titles including substantial runs of *Fiction* (France), *Galactika* (Hungary), and *Robot* (Italy). The monograph collection of 25,000 volumes is strongest from 1950 to the present, but includes much pre-1950 material. The manuscript collection (200 linear feet) includes Michael Moorcock's Life Collection, 1995–, Chad Oliver's manuscripts, papers, and books, and the papers and books of Bill Crider, Joe Lansdale, Elizabeth Moon, Otto O. Binder, Martha Wells, Steve Gould, Laura Mixon, Frederik Pohl, and Avram Davidson. The Sam Moskowitz collection includes his research files, manuscripts, and some correspondence. Other authors are represented with one or two manuscripts each. The George R. R. Martin collection (120 linear feet) includes his papers, books, and correspondence, with additions coming monthly. A William Gibson collection includes books and his correspondence with his agent from 1981 to the late 1990s. A special effort is made to collect all historical, critical, and reference materials in all languages, including master's theses and doctoral dissertations. A particularly valuable segment of the collection is the "Science Fiction: Collected Papers" file, consisting of more than 10,000 pages of articles about science fiction collected by a local professor in his research. A representative collection of fanzine issues is maintained. The Roy Craig Collection contains the field notes and associated material of the Condon Report, *The Scientific Study of Unidentified Flying Objects* (1965). The collection is described in H. W. Hall, *Science/Fiction Collections: Fantasy, Supernatural and Weird Tales* (Haworth Press, 1983). The collection is active, adding 1,000 or more items annually. Monographs and magazines are accessible through the online catalog of the library. Photocopies are available. No interlibrary loan.

15-31. University of Texas at Austin. Harry Ransom Humanities Research Center, Box 7219, Austin, TX 78713. 512-471-8944. Web address: www.hrc. utexas.edu/home.html.

The Harry Ransom Humanities Research Center has nearly 8,000 volumes of fiction and hundreds of magazines, manuscripts, and letters. The core of the collection is the L. W. Currey Science Fiction and Fantasy Collection, which was the basis for his book on science fiction first editions [7-6]. Supplementing the Currey collection is the Selznik Archive, which includes extensive material on *King Kong* and other fantastic films, and a large collection of motion picture promotional material and lobby cards. The center has hundreds of letters to or from science fiction writers throughout its collections, by Ambrose Bierce, Stapledon, Čapek, Lewis, Orwell, and many others. Manuscript collections include L. Sprague de Camp, Arthur Conan Doyle (23 boxes), Lord Dunsany (6 boxes), Arthur Machen (23 boxes), Ernest Bramah Smith (25 boxes), and T. H. White (36 boxes). The collection is developing along the lines of established strength through purchase and regular gifts. Most books are cataloged. Photocopies are available, but not interlibrary loan.

Utah

15-32. Brigham Young University. Harold B. Lee Library, Provo, UT 84602. 801-422-3514. Web address: http://sc.lib.byu.edu/.

A collection of more than 12,000 volumes of science fiction, of which all but 1,000 volumes are circulating. This is the official Orson Scott Card depository and includes more than 40 linear feet of his manuscripts and papers, and books. Special interests include Arkham House publications, Edgar Rice Burroughs and Orson Scott Card first editions, and Science Fiction Book Club editions. The collection is an SFWA (Science Fiction Writers of America) depository, and is growing by purchase as well, adding more than 600 items annually. The collection is searchable online. Interlibrary loan and photocopies are available.

Wisconsin

15-33. State Historical Society of Wisconsin. Archives Division, 816 State St., Madison, WI 53706. 608-264-6460. Web address: www.wisconsinhistory.org/ archives/geninfo.html.

The August Derleth collection is composed of fantasy and science fiction pulp magazines, together with many detective and genre pulps to which Derleth contributed. The collection also includes some Arkham House books and the bulk of Derleth's manuscripts and personal papers, plus some papers of Arkham House. The collection can be examined in the Archives Reading Room. No appointment is necessary, but it is recommended that researchers call ahead or write.

15-34.   J. R. R. Tolkien Collection, Marquette University Library. Special Collections, Raynor Memorial Libraries, 1355 W. Wisconsin Ave., P.O. Box 3141, Milwaukee, WI 53201-3141. 414-288-7256. Web address: www.marquette.edu/ library/collections/archives/tolkien.html.

The J. R. R. Tolkien Collection is the definitive collection on Tolkien's Lord of the Rings trilogy, and on *The Hobbit.* The collection includes holograph renderings (manuscripts in the hand of the author), various sets of typescripts with corrections by Tolkien, and page proofs or galley sheets, also with corrections in the hand of the author. The manuscripts, 1938–1955, consist of 7,125 leaves (9,250 pages). Included are an advance proof copy of *The Return of the King,* printed maps of Middle-Earth, dust jackets from the original Houghton Mifflin edition, several drafts of a rejected "Epilogue," and manuscript fragments from *The Silmarillion* (1977). Drawings and sketches, often in preliminary form in the margin of the text, can be found throughout the handwritten manuscripts. Linguistic and philological notes relating to Tolkien's invented languages also appear in the manuscripts, often on the verso of the main text. The documents reflect an extraordinary creative process; as many as 18 drafts exist for a single chapter. *The Hobbit* manuscripts, 1930–1937, which consist of 1,048 leaves (1,586 pages), include a holograph version, corrected typescripts, three sets of page proofs with the author's corrections, a watercolor rendering by Tolkien of the dust jacket used by Allen and Unwin, printed maps with corrections, a watercolor of trolls and Gollum by German artist Horus Engels, and the original copy of "Thror's Map." Most of the early holograph is a continuous text with no chapter divisions. The manuscripts for *Farmer Giles of Ham,* ca. 1930–1938, 1948–1949, comprising 173 leaves (201 pages). *Mr. Bliss,* ca. 1928–1932, includes 39 leaves (61 pages). The collection includes a significant collection of Tolkien's published works and associated critical works. Books and periodicals in the collection are described in the library online catalog. Associated collections add significant research value to the Tolkien collection. Taum J. R. Santoski (1958–1991) donated 200 books, dozens of periodicals, copies of Tolkien's academic publications, and notes on the manuscripts, particularly linguistic texts in *The Lord of the Rings.* S. Gary Hunnewell is building an inclusive collection of all periodicals produced by Tolkien enthusiasts. It contains many early U.S. and foreign titles, including obscure publications from Eastern Europe, as well as selected issues of general fantasy and science fiction "fanzines" relating to Tolkien. The collection is being loaned to Marquette with detailed bibliographic descriptions and indexing for microfilming on a continuing basis. Dr. Richard E. Blackwelder (1909–2001) donated a collection of Tolkieniana. Remarkably comprehensive in scope, the Blackwelder Collection is believed to be the largest single body of secondary sources on Tolkien ever to be developed. The value of the collection is greatly enhanced by a well-defined scheme of arrangement and description. Detailed bibliographic information is provided for each item that has been acquired or identified, in conjunction with extensive indexing. The bequest contains many editions and printings of Tolkien's books, including nearly all printings of the Ballantine paperbacks.

Wyoming

15-35. University of Wyoming. American Heritage Center, 2111 Willett Dr., Laramie, WY 82071. 307-766-2070. Web address: http://ahc.uwyo.edu/.

Primarily a collection of science fiction and fantasy manuscripts, about 300 linear feet in extent. Author manuscripts collected, with number of boxes each, are: Robert Bloch (234+), Sam Peeples (50), Forrest J. Ackerman (140+), Martin Caidin (54+), Fritz Lang (30), H. L. Prosser (19), Donald A. Wollheim (14), Michael Kurland (8), Hugo Gernsback (25), Philip José Farmer (8), A. E. van Vogt (3), William Dozier (22), Mort Weisinger (38), George Pal (9), J. Vernon Shea (9), and Jerry Sohl (11). The collections contain books, correspondence, magazines, and fan material collected by Wollheim, Bloch, Shea, and Ackerman. Of particular note in the Wollheim material are many items about early fandom in the United States. Voluminous correspondence relating to Wollheim's editorial experience is extremely valuable in the study of the development of the anthology. His correspondence also reflects important aspects of the market conditions for science fiction over a long period. Much correspondence with well-known writers is included. Some material is restricted. The collection is active, growing through gifts. Catalogs and finding aids are available on site. The collection may be used in-house only, and interlibrary loan is not offered. Photocopying is available.

International Resources

Australia

15-36. Murdoch University Library. P.O. Box 1014, Canning Vale, WA 6155. Web address: wwwlib.murdoch.edu.au/services/research/speccoll.html.

The Alternative and Contemporary Documents collection holds about 5,000 volumes of science fiction, and good periodical runs since 1950. The Leigh Edmonds collection contains more than 300 titles of Australian fanzines. The collection is currently inactive. Photocopies and interlibrary loan are available.

15-37. University of Queensland Library. Special Collections, St. Lucia, Queensland 4072. Web address: www.library.uq.edu.au/fryer/index.html.

This library holds the Donald Tuck collection of science fiction and fantasy, used to compile his *Encyclopedia of Science Fiction and Fantasy Through 1968* [7-9]. The collection includes both monographs and serials as listed in Tuck's work. It is growing through purchase of materials, and is fully cataloged. Hardcover books circulate and are available for interlibrary loan. Photocopies are available.

15-38. University of Sydney Library. Rare Books and Special Collections, Sydney, NSW 2006. 02-692-2992. Web address: www.library.usyd.edu.au/libraries/rare/.

The Science Fiction and Fantasy Collection was established in 1974 as a research collection for scholars, and now holds more than 50,000 volumes:

hardcover 18,000; paperback 28,000; and 1,000 reference and critical volumes. The magazine collection contains 170 English-language titles, and 40 in foreign languages, with a total of more than 19,000 issues. Magazine holdings are virtually complete up to 1978. There are 2,000 fanzine titles, particularly early U.S. fanzines and Australian fanzines. A comic book collection of more than 1,426 titles, with 20,000-plus issues, supplements the science fiction collection. Some audiovisual material. Artwork, film posters, movie stills, and memorabilia supplement the print collections. The library holds manuscripts and typescripts of Aldiss, Brunner, Chandler, Coney, Cowper, Ellison, Irvine, Lovecraft, Leiber, Priest, Tubb, Wilhelm, Wollheim, and others. Original illustrations by Virgil Finlay (6), Kelly Freas, Jack Gaughan, Rick Sternbach, and Donald Wollheim are in the collection. In 1979, holdings were greatly increased with the bequest of the Ron Graham SF Collection, and in 2003 the collection of Colin Steele, comprising a further 5,000-plus volumes was added. The collection is active, adding 150 to 200 items annually. The library has been a Science Fiction Writers of America Depository since 1981. Partial access is provided through local catalogs and through the online library catalog, including the Special Collections Database. The Graham collection has a title card catalog listing all editions, devised by Graham, and a finding list exists for the comics collection. No lending, but photocopies can often be provided.

Canada

15-39.   Toronto Public Library. The Merril Collection of Science Fiction, Speculation, and Fantasy, 239 College St., 3rd Floor, Toronto, Ontario M5T 1R5. 416-393-7741. Web address: www.tpl.toronto.on.ca/merril/home.htm.

The Merril Collection of Science Fiction, Speculation, and Fantasy holds more than 58,000 items, including 30,000 volumes of fiction, 5,000-plus volumes of reference and critical material, and 23,700 issues of English-language magazines (including 1,200 fanzines). The collection includes graphic novels, audio recordings, videocassettes, fantasy role-playing games, fantasy art, and original manuscripts by Phyllis Gotlieb, Guy Gavriel Kay, Cory Doctorow, Karl Schroeder, and S. M. Stirling. Established in 1970 with the donation of Judith Merril's 5,000-item collection as the "Spaced Out Library," it was renamed the Merril Collection on Jan. 1, 1991. Exhibitions in the reading room are changed quarterly. Fanzines and periodicals that are not professionally indexed are indexed in-house. All anthologies are indexed by author and title of each individual short story. The collection is described in *The Encyclopedia of Science Fiction* (Clute and Nichols), and in H. W. Hall, ed., *Science Fiction Collections: Fantasy/Supernatural and Weird Tales* (Haworth Press, 1983). Collecting adds approximately 1,000 books and 1,000 periodical issues annually. A small circulating paperback collection is kept (7,000 volumes). Photocopies are available, depending on the fragility of the item. The fiction collection is being entered into the database of the Toronto Public Library and will be completely searchable in 2005. The Friends of the Merril Collection is online at http://friendsof merril.org.

15-40.   University of Calgary. McKammie Library, Special Collections, 2500 University Dr., NW, Calgary, Alberta T2N 1N4. 403-220-5953. Web address: www.fp.ucalgary.ca/unicomm/news/gibson/.

The University of Calgary received the collection of William Robert (Bob) Gibson in 2002, estimated at 30,000 to 40,000 pieces. The collection contains books and magazines from the 1920s through the 1990s, and is currently being processed.

15-41.   University of New Brunswick. Ward Chipman Library, Box 5050, Saint John, NB E2L 4L5. 506-648-5700. Web address: www.unbsj.ca/library/geninfo1.htm.

The Science Fiction and Fantasy Collection includes more than 16,000 books, with substantial reference and critical materials, and 11,000 issues of periodicals, including microfilm serial holdings, with some audiovisuals and other related material, including science fiction comic books. Manuscripts include three short stories by John Wyndham and *Rite of Passage* by Alexei Panshin. The collection began in 1966 and has been growing actively since, through gifts and purchases. It is an SFWA depository, fully cataloged with an index to its vertical files (pamphlet collections). Items that are not rare circulate locally and through interlibrary loan. Photocopies are available.

United Kingdom
15-42.   Oxford University. Bodleian Library, Department of Western Manuscripts, Oxford OX1 3BG. Web address: www.bodley.ox.ac.uk/dept/scwmss/.

The Department of Western Manuscripts holds papers and books of James Blish, Michael Moorcock, and Brian Aldiss, plus a large general collection of printed science fiction received through copyright deposit.

15-43.   University of Liverpool. Librarian/Administrator, Science Fiction Foundation Collection, Sydney Jones Library, Special Collections, Box 123, Liverpool L69 3DA. Web address: www.liv.ac.uk/~asawyer/sffchome.html.

The Science Fiction Foundation collection of more than 30,000 pieces is housed in the University of Liverpool Library. The collection includes 25,000-plus novels, collections, and anthologies; 1,600 critical works and bibliographies; more than 130 science fiction and fantasy magazine titles in paper and microfilm; some 80 critical magazine titles; and a selection of fanzines. The Myers Collection of Russian SF is an important resource for Russian texts. The library collects heavily in non-English material, with special strength in Eastern European titles. The SFFC and University of Liverpool library hold manuscripts and papers for a number of well-known science fiction writers, including Stephen Baxter, Ramsey Campbell, Eric Frank Russell, John Wyndham, Ian Watson, Christopher Priest, Brian Stableford, Arthur Sellings, Barrington J. Bayley, and the associated Olaf Stapledon Archive. Publication of the journal *Foundation* [13-15] continues. The library offers photocopies, but no interlibrary loan.

Germany

15-44.   Phantastische Bibliothek Wetzlar. Friedrich-Ebert-Platz 3, D-35578 Wetzlar. +49-6441-99792, fax +49-6441-99794, phbiblwz@wetzlar.de.

The Phantastische Bibliothek Wetzlar holds more than 130,000 books, paperbacks, booklets, and magazines of all fantastic genres (science fiction, fantasy, weird, fairy tales, utopias) of the 19th and 20th centuries in the German language. Manuscripts, nonfiction, catalogs, dictionaries, and fanzines are included. A complete set of German-language pulps and magazines is a valuable resource. All German fantastic authors are collected in depth. The materials are non-circulating, but the collection is open to the public and for research. The collection is actively growing, adding more than 5,000 items a year.

Switzerland

15-45.   Maison d'Ailleurs. Case postale 3181, CH-1401 Yverdon-les-Bains. Web address: www.ailleurs.ch/.

The Maison d'Ailleurs holds more than 40,000 volumes of science fiction in 34 languages, of which about one fifth make up a lending library. The magazine collection is substantial, with more than 150 titles in English as well as more than 50 in other languages. Fanzines (more than 300 titles), audiovisual items (more than 1,700), and manuscripts of nearly every French author and some English are held. More properly a museum than a library, the Maison d'Ailleurs contains more than 60,000 items. The remainder includes posters, paintings, music, postage stamps, toys, games, comics, art, autographs, calendars, photographs, and much more, all relating to science fiction. The collection was amassed by Pierre Versins and Martine Thome, and is the essential collection for the study of French or European science fiction. The collection is described in Roger Gaillard's "The Maison d'Ailleurs, a Museum for Science-Fiction," in *Foundation* 53 (1991), pp. 7–23, and more recently in *Locus* (January 1994), p. 40. The collection is active, growing at a rate of about 1,000 items per year. Photocopies are available, but not interlibrary loan.

Addendum

The 23 following collections were judged too marginal or specialized for detailed discussion but are described very briefly as a service to researchers. They are described in more detail in the fouth edition of *Anatomy of Wonder*, and the Web sites provide still more detail.

Alabama

15-46.   University of Alabama in Huntsville Library. Special Collections, Box 2600, Huntsville, AL 35899. 256-824-6523. Web address: www.uah.edu/library/archives/index.html.

Ley collection; inquire about Robert Forward collection received in 2003.

California

15-47. California State University Library. Special Collections and Archives, 1250 Bellflower Blvd., Long Beach, California 90840-1901. 562-985-4087. Web address: www.csulb.edu/library/guide/serv/special.html.

The Masback Science Fiction Collection contains more than 3,000 paperback copies of science fiction, fantasy, and horror novels and short story collections. All volumes are fully cataloged and are available for loan. The David N. Samuelson Science Fiction and Fantasy Magazine Collection contains lengthy, often complete runs of 54 science fiction and fantasy magazines from the 1940s through 1995.

15-48. San Diego State University Library. Special Collections and University Archives, San Diego, CA 92182. 619-594-6791. Web address: http://infodome. sdsu.edu./about/depts/spcollections/.

A 4,000-volume collection of science fiction, 34 magazine titles, and a few dozen manuscripts, letters, recordings, and artwork.

15-49. University of California, Berkeley. The Bancroft Library, Berkeley, CA 94720-6000. 510-642-6481. Web address: http://bancroft.berkeley.edu/info/.

The Bancroft Library holds two manuscript collections of interest. The R. H. Barlow collection contains a selection of Robert E. Howard poetry, correspondence, and related material (ca. 1 linear foot). Described in *The Dark Man: The Journal of Robert E. Howard Studies,* 7 (2003), pp. 15–29. The Ambrose Bierce Collection contains correspondence to and from Bierce, business records, manuscripts, and related material (ca. 3 linear feet).

Colorado

15-50. Colorado State University Libraries. Imaginary Wars Collection, Fort Collins, CO 80523. 970-491-1838. Web address: http://lib.colostate.edu/ archives/.

Some 1,800 volumes, including novels, short stories, and other fictional treatments of future wars.

Delaware

15-51. University of Delaware Library. Special Collections, Newark, DE 19717-5267. 302-831-2229. Web address: www.lib.udel.edu/ud/spec/.

900 volumes emphasizing works of Bradbury, Burroughs, and Heinlein.

Florida

15-52. Rollins College. Olin Library, 1000 Holt Ave., Campus Box 2744, Winter Park, FL 32789. 407-646-2421. Web address: www.rollins.edu/olin/ archives/archives_frm.htm.

M. P. Shiel collection of 450 volumes.

Illinois

15-53.   Northern Illinois University Libraries. Special Collections, DeKalb, IL 60115. 815-753-9838. Web address: www.niulib.niu.edu/rbsc/.

Some 1,000 volumes of science fiction, 105 magazine runs, and a few Lovecraft letters.

15-54.   Northwestern University Library. Special Collections Department, 1937 Sheridan Rd., Evanston, IL 60208-2300. 708-491-3635. Web address: www. library.northwestern.edu/spec/index.html. E-mail: r-maylone@northwestern. edu. R. Russell Maylone, Curator.

Static collection of 6,000 SF paperbacks, some 1930s magazines, and 14,500 comic books.

Iowa

15-55.   Iowa State University Library, Parks Library. Department of Special Collections, Ames, IA 50010-2140. 515-294-6672. Web address: www.lib.iastate. edu/spcl/index.html.

A 479-volume gift collection.

Kansas

15-56.   Pittsburg State University. Leonard H. Axe Library, Pittsburg, KS 66762. 316-235-4883. Web address: http://library.pittstate.edu/spcoll/ndxertman. html.

The Ertman Collection is a non-circulating, fully cataloged special collection of 1,850 science fiction paperbacks, with about 300 added yearly.

Kentucky

15-57.   University of Kentucky Library. Special Collections, Lexington, KY 40506. 606-257-8611. Web address: www.uky.edu/Libraries/Special/.

About 5,550 volumes, with broken runs of 54 English-language magazines, minimally cataloged.

Louisiana

15-58.   Louisiana State University. Middleton Library, Clarence J. Laughlin Library of the Arts, Baton Rouge, LA 70803. 504-388-6572. Web address: www. lib.lsu.edu/special/.

The Laughlin Library is an extensive collection, but only some SF.

New York

15-59. State University of New York. University Libraries, Department of Special Collections and Archives, 1400 Washington Ave., Albany, NY 12222. 518-442-3544. Web address: http://library.albany.edu/speccoll/.

A total 3,266 volumes of science fiction, some critical works.

Ohio

15-60. Kent State University Library. Special Collections and Archives, Kent, OH 44242. 216-672-2270. Web address: http://speccoll.library.kent.edu/.

Paperbacks, 1950–1980, and a large Stephen R. Donaldson collection.

15-61. University of Dayton. Archives and Special Collections, Roesch Library, Room 317, Dayton, OH 45469-1360. 513-229-4267. Web address: http://library. udayton.edu/basics/rarebooks/.

Some 1,500 SFWA depository books, added to regularly.

Oklahoma

15-62. University of Tulsa. McFarlin Library, Special Collections Department, 2933 East 6th St., Tulsa, OK 74104-3123. 918-631-2882. Web address: www.lib.utulsa.edu/speccoll/.

Large collection of R. A. Lafferty manuscripts.

Pennsylvania

15-63. Pennsylvania State University. Pattee Library, Special Collections, 104 Paterno Library, University Park, PA 16802. 814-865-1931. Web address: www. libraries.psu.edu/speccolls/rbm/.

A 3,000-issue magazine collection, which includes many complete runs, Arkham House books, utopian collections; about half cataloged.

15-64. University of Pittsburgh. Special Collections, 363 Hillman Library, Pittsburgh, PA 15260. 412-642-8191. Web address: www.library.pitt.edu/ libraries/special/special.html.

The Archive of Popular Culture includes 2,200 paperbacks, plus fanzines, and comics.

Virginia

15-65. Virginia Commonwealth University. James Branch Cabell Library, 901 Parke Ave., Box 2033, Richmond, VA 23284-2033. 804-828-1110. Web address: www.library.vcu.edu/jbc/speccoll/exhibit/cabell/jbclife.html.

About 1,750 volumes, occasional additions.

West Virginia

15-66.   West Virginia University Libraries. P.O. Box 6069, West Virginia University, Morgantown, WV 26506-6069. 304-293-3536. Web address: www.libraries. wvu.edu/exhibits/asimov/.

Isaac Asimov collection of more than 600 books, games, recordings, videos, and wall charts relating to Asimov.

Wisconsin

15-67.   University of Wisconsin, La Crosse. Murphy Library, La Crosse, WI 54601. 608-785-8511. Web address: www.uwlax.edu/murphylibrary/Departments/archome.html#collections.

The Paul W. Skeeters Collection of fantastic literature, especially 1900–1926 imprints.

15-68.   University of Wisconsin, Milwaukee. Golda Meir Library, Special Collections, Box 604, Milwaukee, WI 53201. 414-229-4345. Web address: www. uwlax.edu/murphylibrary/departments/archome.html#collections.

A total 11 magazine runs, 1926–present.

Canada

15-69.   University of Winnipeg Library. 515 Portage Ave., Winnipeg, Manitoba, R3B 2E9. 204-786-9808. Web address: http://cybrary.uwinnipeg.ca/.

About 3,000 volumes, not all SF, with some children's SF.

15-70.   University of British Columbia Library. Special Collections, 1956 Main Mall, Vancouver, BC V6T 1ZI. 604-822-2521. Web address: www.library. ubc.ca/spcoll/.

A total 30 magazines, mostly from the 1940s to the 1950s.

CHAPTER 16

Listings

Neil Barron

Best Books

Chapter 6 suggests that more than 40,000 works of science fiction have been published since 1700, using a very inclusive definition of SF. Part II annotates about 3 percent of this number, with a higher percentage for the past half century. The approximately 700 works of related nonfiction discussed in Part III include the key earlier works still of value, plus hundreds of more recent studies that reveal SF's growing complexity and variety.

From this highly selective 3 percent sample, contributors asterisked the books they judged best. These asterisks precede the titles in Part II and the authors in this listing. For books in series, contributors most commonly chose only the first book in the series as "best," but in some instances judged the entire series best, designated by the phrase "and sequels." Additional judgments were provided by the four outside readers who were briefly profiled at the end of the list of contributors. If they concurred with the contributors' judgments, their initials follow the title. If they did not, their choices are listed without an asterisk, followed by their initials and, in a few cases, by the year of publication if the book was not annotated. These outside readers selected fiction and some selectively chose nonfiction from those chapters they felt most qualified to judge, as follows:

John Clute (JC) (Chapter 7)
Don D'Ammassa (DD) (Chapters 7, 9)
James Gunn (JG) (Chapters 7, 9, 11, 12)
David Hartwell (DH) (Chapters 7, 9)

To provide additional guidance as well as to illustrate the variety of judgments by knowledgeable SF readers, two additional sources were examined and their collective choices added to the best fiction section:

David Pringle. *Science Fiction: The 100 Best Novels; an English-Language Selection, 1949–1984* [9-154]

T. A. Shippey and A. J. Sobczak, eds. *Magill's Guide to Science Fiction and Fantasy Literature* [7-27]

These are designated Pringle and Magill. Unannotated books from these two sources have the year of publication following the title. SF buffs may also wish to examine the chronological listing, which includes short fiction as well as novels, published 1895–1993, in Edward James, *Science Fiction in the Twentieth Century* [9-99].

Books are listed in the same sequence as annotated, with only the first author/editor shown. See the annotations for more details. See also Table 11-1 for best films.

Part II: Annotated Fiction Bibliography

[Novels and collections are listed first, by author, with anthologies following, listed by title. Young adult (YA) books are flagged]

*Abbott, Edwin A. *Flatland* (JG, DH)
Abe, Kobe. *Inter Ice Age 4* (1959) (Magill)
Adams, Douglas. *The Hitchhiker's Guide to the Galaxy* (Magill) (JC, DD)
*Aldiss, Brian W. *Best SF Stories of Brian Aldiss* (JC, DD, DH)
———. *Barefoot in the Head* (Magill) (DD)
*———. *Greybeard* (Pringle, Magill) (JC, DD)
*———. *Helliconia Spring* and sequels (Magill) (JC, DD, JG, DH)
———. *Hothouse* (Pringle, Magill) (DD, JG, DH)
———. *Non-Stop* (Pringle, Magill) (JC, DD)
Amis, Kingsley. *The Alteration* (Pringle, Magill) (JC, DD)
*Anderson, M. T. *Feed* (YA) (JC)
*Anderson, Poul. *The Enemy Stars* (JC, DD)
———. *Brain Wave* (Magill) (DD, JC, JG, DH)
*———. *Tau Zero* (Pringle, Magill) (DD, JG, JC, DH)
———. *War of the Wing-Men* (Magill) (DD)
Anthony, Piers. *Macroscope* (Magill) (JC)

*Asimov, Isaac. *The Caves of Steel* (JC, DD, JG, DH)
*———. *The Complete Stories* (JC, DD, DH)
———. *The End of Eternity* (1955) (Pringle) (JC, JG)
*———. *The Gods Themselves* (JC, JG)
*———. The Foundation Trilogy (JC, DD, JG, DH)
*———. *I, Robot* (DD, JG, DH)
*Atwood, Margaret. *The Handmaid's Tale*
———. *Oryx and Crate* (2003) (JG)
Auel, Jean M. *Clan of the Cave Bear* and 4 sequels (Magill) (JC)
*Ballard, J. G. *The Complete Short Stories* (Magill) (DD, DH)
———. *Crash* (Pringle, Magill) (JC)
*———. *The Crystal World* (Pringle) (JC, DD)
*———. *The Drought* (JC, DH)
———. *The Drowned World* (Pringle, Magill) (JC, DD)
———. *High-Rise* (Pringle, Magill)
Balmer, Edwin. *When Worlds Collide* (Magill) (JC [and sequel], DD, DH)
*Banks, Iain. *Consider Phlebas* (JC)
*———. *Feersum Endjinn* (Magill) (JC, DD)
*———. *Excession* (Magill)
*———. *Look to Windward*
———. *Use of Weapons* (1990) (JC, DH)
Bass, T. J. *Half Past Human* and *The Godwhale* (1971/1974) (Magill) (JC, DH)
Batchelor, John Calvin. *The Birth of the People's Republic of Antarctica* (Pringle)
  (JC)
Baxter, Stephen. *Anti-Ice* (1993) (JC)
———. *Raft* (JC)
*———. *The Time Ships* (JC, JG)
*Bear, Greg. *Blood Music* (Magill) (JC, JG, DH)
*———. *The Collected Stories of Greg Bear* (DH)
*———. *Darwin's Radio* and sequel (JC, JG)
———. *Eon* (Magill) (DD)
———. *The Forge of God* (Magill) (JC, JG)
*———. *Moving Mars* (Magill) (DD, JG)
*———. *Queen of Angels* (JC, JG)
*Bellamy, Edward. *Looking Backward, 2000–1887* (Magill) (JC, JG, DH)
Benford, Gregory. *Against Infinity* (Magill) (JG, DH)
**Great Sky River* (Magill) (JC, JG)
———. *In the Ocean of Night* (Magill)
*———. *Timescape* (Pringle, Magill) (JC, DD, JG, DH)
*Beresford, J. D. *The Hampdenshire Wonder* (Magill) (JC, DH)
*Bester, Alfred. *The Demolished Man* (Pringle, Magill) (JC, DD, JG, DH)
*———. *The Great Short Fiction of Alfred Bester* (JC, DD, JG, DH)
———. *The Stars My Destination* (Pringle, Magill) (JC, DD, JG, DH))
*Bishop, Michael. *No Enemy But Time* (Pringle, Magill) (JC, DD, JG, DH)
Blaylock, James. *Homunculus* (Magill) (JC)

Blish, James. *The Best Science Fiction Stories of James Blish* (DH)

*———. *A Case of Conscience* (Pringle, Magill) (JC, DD, JG, DH)

*———. *Cities in Flight* (Magill) (JC, DD, JG, DH)

———. *The Seedling Stars* (Magill) (JC, JG, DH)

Boulle, Pierre. *Planet of the Apes* (Magill) (JC)

Boyd, John. *Last Starship from Earth* (Magill) (JC)

*Brackett, Leigh. *The Long Tomorrow* (Pringle, Magill) (JC, DD, DH)

Bradbury, Ray. *Fahrenheit 451* (Pringle) (JC, DH)

*———. *The Martian Chronicles* (Pringle, Magill) (JC, DD, JG, DH)

*———. *The Stories of Ray Bradbury* (JC, DH)

Bradley, Marion Zimmer. *Darkover Landfall* (Magill)

*Brin, David. *Earth* (JC, JG)

———. *Glory Season* (Magill)

———. *The Postman* (Magill) (JC, JG)

*———. *Startide Rising* (JC, DD)

*———. *The Uplift War* (Magill) (JC, JG, DH)

Broderick, Damien. *The Dreaming Dragons* (Pringle) (JC, JG, DH)

Brown, Fredric. *From These Ashes* (DH)

———. *The Lights in the Skies Are Stars* (1953) (Magill) (JC)

———. *What Mad Universe* (JG)

Brunner, John. *The Crucible of Time* (1983) (JG)

———. *The Jagged Orbit* (1969) (Magill) (JC, DD, JG)

*———. *The Sheep Look Up* (JC, JG)

———. *The Shockwave Rider* (Magill) (JC, DD, JG, DH)

*———. *Stand on Zanzibar* (Pringle, Magill) (JC, DD, JG, DH)

Budrys, Algis. *Michaelmas* (Pringle) (JC)

*———. *Rogue Moon* (Pringle, Magill) (JC, JG)

———. *Who?* (Magill) (JC)

*Bujold, Lois McMaster. *Barrayar* (JC, JG)

*———. *Falling Free* (Magill) (JC, DD, JG)

*———. *The Vor Game* (Magill) (DD, JG)

*Bulgakov, Mikhail. "The Fatal Eggs" (JC)

———. *Heart of a Dog* (1968) (Magill) (JC)

Bull, Emma. *Bone Dance* (Magill) (JC)

Bunch, David. *Moderan* (Magill) (JC, DD)

Burgess, Anthony. *A Clockwork Orange* (Pringle, Magill) (JC, DD, DH)

Burroughs, Edgar Rice. *At the Earth's Core* (JG)

———. *The Land That Time Forgot* (Magill) (JC, DD)

*———. *The Princess of Mars* (YA) (Magill) (JC, JG, DH)

Burroughs, William. *Nova Express* (Pringle, Magill) (JC)

*Butler, Octavia. *Dawn* and sequels (Magill)

*———. *Parable of the Sower* and sequel (JC, DH)

———. *Wild Seed* (Pringle, Magill) (JC, DD)

*Cadigan, Pat. *Patterns* (Magill) (JC, JG)

———. *Synners* (Magill) (JC, JG)

Campbell, John W., Jr. *The Mightiest Machine* (Magill)

————. *The Moon Is Hell* (1951) (Magill) (JC, DD)

*————. *The New Dawn: The Don A. Stuart Stories* (JC, JG, DH)

Čapek, Karel. *The Absolute at Large* (Magill) (JC, JG)

————. *Krakatit* (JC)

*————. *R.U.R.* (Magill) (JG)

*————. *War with the Newts* (Magill) (JC, DD, DH)

*Card, Orson Scott. *Ender's Game* (Magill) and *Speaker for the Dead* (JC, JG, DH)

*————. *Maps in a Mirror: The Short Fiction of Orson Scott Card* (JC, DH)

Carter, Angela. *Heroes and Villains* (Pringle) (JC)

*————. *The Infernal Desire Machines of Doctor Hoffman* (Magill) (JC)

————. *The Passion of New Eve* (Magill) (JC)

*Charnas, Suzy McKee. *Walk to the End of the World* (Pringle, Magill) (JC, DH)

*Cherryh, C. J. *Cyteen* (Magill) (DH)

*————. *Downbelow Station* (Magill) (JC, DD, JG, DH)

*————. *Foreigner*

Christopher, John. *The Death of Grass* (Pringle, Magill) (JC, DD, JG, DH)

*————. *The Guardians* (YA) (JC)

*————. *The White Mountains* (YA) (JC)

*Clarke, Arthur C. *Against the Fall of Night* (JC, DD, JG, DH)

*————. *Childhood's End* (Pringle, Magill) (JC, DD, JG, DH)

————. *The City and the Stars* (1956) (Pringle, Magill) (JC, DH)

*————. *The Collected Stories* (JC, JG, DH)

*————. *The Fountains of Paradise* (Magill) (JC)

————. *Imperial Earth* (1975) (Magill)

*————. *Rendezvous with Rama* (Magill) (JC, DD, JG, DH)

*————. *2001: A Space Odyssey* (Magill) (JC, JG)

*Clement, Hal. *Mission of Gravity* (Pringle, Magill) (JC, DD, JG, DH)

————. *Music of Many Spheres* (2000) (DH)

————. *Needle* (1950) (JG)

————. *The Nitrogen Fix* (1980) (Magill)

Clifton, Mark. *They'd Rather Be Right* (Magill) (JC)

*Compton, D. G. *The Continuous Katherine Mortenhoe* (JC, DD, JG, DH)

*Constantine, Murray. *Swastika Night* (JC)

Crichton, Michael. *The Andromeda Strain* (Magill) (DD)

————. *Jurassic Park* (Magill) (DD)

*Cross, John Kier. *The Angry Planet* (YA) (JC)

Crowley, John. *Engine Summer* (Pringle, Magill) (JC, DD, DH)

*Cyrano de Bergerac, Savinien. *Voyages to the Moon and Sun* (Magill) (JC)

de Camp, L. Sprague. *The Continent Makers . . .* (Magill) (JC)

*————. *Lest Darkness Fall* (Magill) (JC, DD, JG, DH)

————. *Rogue Queen* (1951) (JG)

*del Rey, Lester. *Early del Rey* (JC, DH)

————. *Nerves* (Magill) (JC, DD, DH)

*Delany, Samuel R. *Aye, and Gomorrah* (JC, DD, DH)

*———. *Babel-17* (Magill) (JC, DD, DH)

*———. *Dhalgren* (Magill) (JC, DH)

*———. *The Einstein Intersection* (Magill) (JC, DD, DH)

*———. *Nova* (Pringle, Magill) (JC, DD, DH)

———. *Stars in My Pocket Like Grains of Sand* (Magill) (JC, DH)

———. *Triton* (Magill) (JC)

*Dick, Philip K. *The Collected Stories . . .

*———. *Do Androids Dream of Electric Sheep* (Pringle, Magill) (JC, DD, JG, DH)

———. *Doctor Bloodmoney* (Pringle, Magill) (JC, DH)

———. *Eye in the Sky* (Magill) (JC, DD)

———. *Flow My Tears the Policeman Said* (Magill) (JC, DH)

*———. *The Man in the High Castle* (Pringle, Magill) (JC, DD, JG, DH)

*———. *Martian Time-Slip* (Pringle, Magill) (JC, DD, DH)

———. *A Maze of Death* (1970) (JC)

———. *The Three Stigmata of Palmer Eldritch* (Pringle, Magill) (JG)

———. *Time Out of Joint* (1959) (Pringle) (JC, DH)

———. *The Transmigration of Timothy Archer* (1982) (Magill) (DH)

*———. *Ubik* (Magill) (JC, DD, JG, DH)

*Dickinson, Peter. *Eva* (YA) (JC)

Dickson, Gordon. *Dorsai* (DD)

*Disch, Thomas M. *Camp Concentration* (Pringle, Magill) (JC, DD, DH)

———. *The Man Who Had No Idea* (JC, DH)

———. *On Wings of Song* (Pringle, Magill) (JC, DD, JG)

*———. *334* (Pringle, Magill) (JC, DD)

*Doyle, Arthur Conan. *The Lost World* (Magill) (JC, DD, JG, DH)

*du Bois, William Pène. *The Twenty-One Balloons* (YA)

*Effinger, George Alec. *When Gravity Fails* (Magill) (JC [and sequels], DD, JG, DH)

*Egan, Greg. *Diaspora* (JC)

*———. *Permutation City* (Magill) (JC, JG)

*Ellison, Harlan. *Deathbird Stories* (JC, DD, JG)

———. *I Have No Mouth and I Must Scream* (1967) (Magill) (JC, DD)

*———. *The Essential Ellison* (JC, JG, DH)

*Engdahl, Sylvia Louise. *Enchantress from the Stars* (YA) (JC)

Farmer, Nancy. *The Ear, the Eye, and the Arm* (JC)

*———. *The House of the Scorpion* (YA) (JC)

*Farmer, Philip José. *The Green Odyssey* (JC)

*———. *The Lovers* (Magill) (DD, JG)

———. *Night of Light* (1966) (DH)

———. *Strange Relations* (Magill) (JC, DD)

———. *To Your Scattered Bodies Go* (Magill) (JC, DD, JG, DH)

———. *The Unreasoning Mask* (Pringle) (JC, DH)

———. World of Tiers series (1965–1977) (Magill) (DD, JC)

*Fast, Howard. *The Edge of Tomorrow* (JC)

*Fawcett, Edgar. *The Ghost of Guy Thyrle*

Finney, Jack. *The Body Snatchers* (JC)

*———. *The Third Level* (JC, DD, DH)

———. *Time and Again* (Magill) (JC)

*Flammarion, Camile. *Lumen* (Magill) (JC)

———. *Omega* (Magill) (JC)

*Forster, E. M. "The Machine Stops" (JC, DH)

*Fowler, Karen Joy. *Artificial Things* (JC)

*———. *Sarah Canary* (JC)

*France, Anatole. *The White Stone*

Frank, Pat. *Alas, Babylon* (Pringle, Magill) (JC, DD)

Galouye, Daniel. *Counterfeit World* (1964) (Magill) (JC)

*———. *Dark Universe* (Magill) (JC, DD, JG, DH)

Garis, Howard. Tom Swift series (Magill) (JC)

Gernsback, Hugo. *Ralph 124C41+* (Magill) (JC)

Gerrold, David. *The Man Who Folded Himself* (Magill) (JC, DD)

———. *When HARLIE Was One* (Magill) (JC, DD)

*Gibson, William. *Burning Chrome* (Magill) (JC, DH)

*———. *Neuromancer* (Pringle, Magill) (JC [and sequels], DD, JG)

*———. *Pattern Recognition* (JC)

———. *Virtual Light* (Magill) (JC)

*Gloag, John. *To-morrow's Yesterday* (JC)

*———. *Winter's Youth* (JC)

Glut, Donald F. Star Wars Trilogy (1976–1983) (Magill) (JC)

Golding, William. *The Inheritors* (1955) (Pringle, Magill) (DD)

———. *Lord of the Flies* (1954) (DH)

*Gray, Alasdair. *Lanark* (Magill) (JC)

———. *Poor Things* (JC)

*Greenland, Colin. *Take Back Plenty* (Magill) (JC, DD, DH)

*Griffith, George. *The Angel of the Revolution* (JC)

Gunn, James E. *The Immortals* (1962) (Magill) (JC)

———. *The Listeners* (Magill) (JC, DH)

*Haldeman, Joe. *Forever Peace* (JC, JG, DH)

*———. *The Forever War* (Magill) (JC, DD, JG)

———. *Worlds* (Magill) (JC, DH)

*Hamilton, Virginia. *Justice and Her Brothers* (YA) (JC, DH)

Harness, Charles. *The Paradox Men* aka *Flight into Yesterday* (1953) (Pringle,
   Magill) (JC, DD, JG, DH)

———. *The Rose* (1966) (Magill) (JC, DD)

Harper, Vincent. *The Mortgage on the Brain* (Magill) (JC)

Harrison, Harry. *Bill, the Galactic Hero* (1965) (Magill) (JC)

———. *Deathworld* (Magill) (JC, DD, JG, DH)

———. *Make Room! Make Room!* (Pringle, Magill) (JC, DD)

———. Stainless Steel Rat series (1961–1987) (Magill) (JC, DD)

———. *West of Eden* (Magill) (DD, JG, DH)

Harrison, M. John. *The Centauri Device* (1974) (Pringle) (JC)

———. *Towing Jehovah* (1984) and sequels (JC)
———. *The Wine of Violence* (1981) (Magill) (JC, JG)
*Moszkowski, Aleksandr. *The Isles of Wisdom* (JC)
Newman, Kim. *The Night Mayor* (Magill) (JC)
Niven, Larry. *A Gift from Earth* (1968) (Magill) (JC)
———. *Neutron Star* (Magill) (JC, DD, DH)
———. *The Mote in God's Eye* (Magill) (JC, DD, JG, DH)
———. *Oath of Fealty* (1981) (Pringle, Magill) (DH)
*———. *Ringworld* (Magill) (JC [and sequels], DD, JG, DH)
Nolan, William F. *Logan's Run* (Magill) (JC, DD)
*Noon, Jeff. *Vurt* (JC)
*Norton, Andre. *Operation Time Search* (YA) (JC)
*———. *Star Man's Son: 2250 A.D.* (YA) (Magill) (JC, DD, JG, DH)
*Nourse, Alan. *Star Surgeon* (YA) (JC, DD)
*O'Brien, Robert C. *Mrs. Frisby and the Rats of NIMH* (YA) (JC)
*Odle, E.V. *The Clockwork Man* (Magill) (JC)
*Oliver, Chad. *Shadows in the Sun* (Magill) (JG)
———. *A Star Above It/Far from This Earth* (both 2003) (JC, DH)
*Orwell, George. *Nineteen Eighty-Four* (Pringle, Magill) (JC, DD, DH)
*Pangborn, Edgar. *Davy* (Magill) (JC, DD)
*———. *A Mirror for Observers* (Pringle, Magill) (JC, DD, JG, DH)
———. *West of the Sun* (1953) (JC)
Panshin, Alexei. *Rite of Passage* (DD
*Piercy, Marge. *Woman on the Edge of Time* (Pringle, Magill) (JC)
Piper, H. Beam. *Little Fuzzy* (1962) (DD)
Poe, Edgar Allan. *The Science Fiction of Edgar Allan Poe* ed. by Harold Beaver
    (1976) (DH)
*———. *The Works of the Late Edgar Allan Poe*
*Pohl, Frederik. *The Best of Frederik Pohl* (JC, JG, DH)
*———. *Gateway* (Magill) (JC, JG, DH)
———. *Gladiator-at-Law* (1955) (Magill) (JC, DD, JG, DH)
*———. *Man Plus* (Pringle, Magill) (JC, JG, DH)
———. *Midas World* (1983) (Magill) (DD)
———. *The Space Merchants* (Pringle, Magill) (JC, DD, JG, DH)
———. *Wolfbane* (Magill) (JC)
———. *The Years of the City* (Magill) (JC, DD, JG, DH)
*Powers, Tim. *The Anubis Gates* (Magill) (JC)
———. *Dinner at Deviant's Palace* (Magill) (DD)
———. *The Dream Archipelago* (1999) (JC)
Priest, Christopher. *Inverted World* (Pringle, Magill) (JC)
*———. *The Prestige* (JC, DD)
*———. *The Separation* (JC, DD)
Pynchon, Thomas. *Gravity's Rainbow* (Magill) (DD, JG, DH)
*Resnick, Mike. *Kirinyaga* (DD)
Roberts, Keith. *The Lordly Ones* (JC)

*———. *Pavane* (Pringle, Magill) (JC, DD, DH)

*Robinson, Kim Stanley. *Red Mars* and sequels (Magill) (JC, DD, DH)

*———. *The Years of Rice and Salt* (JC)

*———. *The Wild Shore* (Magill) (JC, DH)

Roshwald, Mordecai. *Level 7* (1959) (Magill) (JC)

*Rosny aîné, J. H. *The Xipehuz and the Death of the Earth* (JC)

*Rubinstein, Gillian. *Beyond the Labyrinth* (YA) (JC)

Rucker, Rudy. *Software* (Magill) (JC)

*Russ, Joanna. *The Female Man* (Pringle) (DD)

———. *The Two of Them* (1977) (JC, DH)

———. *The Zanzibar Cat* (1963) (JC)

*Russell, Mary Doria. *The Sparrow* (JC)

*Ryman, Geoff. *Air (or Have Not Have)* (JC)

*———. *The Child Garden* (Magill) (JC, DD, DH)

———. *The Unconquered Country* (1986) (JC)

Saberhagen, Fred. *Berserker* (Magill) (JC, DD)

*St. Clair, Margaret. *Change the Sky, and Other Stories*

———. *Sign of the Labrys* (1963) (JC)

*Sarban. *The Sound of His Horn* (Magill) (JC, DD)

Sargent, Pamela. *Cloned Lives* (Magill) (JC, DD, JG)

———. *Earthseed* (Magill) (JG)

———. *Venus of Dreams* (JG)

Sawyer, Robert J. *Calculating God* (DH)

*———. *Hominids* (DH) (JC [and sequels])

*———. *The Terminal Experiment* (JC, DD, JG)

*Schlee, Ann. *The Vandal* (YA) (JC)

Schmitz, James. *The Witches of Karres* (1966) (Magill) (JC, DD, JG, DH)

Scott, Melissa. *The Roads of Heaven* (1988) (Magill) (JC)

*———. *Trouble and Her Friends* (Magill) (JC, DD, DH)

*Shanks, Edward. *The People of the Ruins* (JC)

Shaw, Bob. *Orbitsville* (Pringle, Magill) (JC, DD, JG)

———. *Other Days, Other Eyes* (Magill) (JC, DD, JG, DH)

———. *The Palace of Eternity* (Pringle) (JC)

———. *The Ragged Astronauts* and sequels (JC)

Sheckley, Robert. *The Collected Short Stories* (1991) (DH)

———. *Dimensions of Miracles* (Magill) (JC, JG, DH)

———. *Journey Beyond Tomorrow* (1963) (Pringle) (JC)

———. *Mindswap* (1966) (Magill) (JC)

*———. *Untouched by Human Hands* (JC, DD, JG, DH)

Sheffield, Charles. *Brother to Dragons* (Magill) (JG)

———. Heritage Universe series *(Summertide,* 1990, *Divergence.* 1991, *Transcendence,* 1992) (Magill) (JC)

———. *Sight of Proteus* (Magill) (JC)

*Shelley, Mary. *Frankenstein* (Magill) (JC, DD, JG, DH)

———. *The Last Man* (JC, JG)

Shepard, Lucius. *Green Eyes* (Magill) (JC, DD, DH)

*———. *The Jaguar Hunter* (Magill) (JC, DD)

*———. *Life During Wartime* (JC, DD)

*Shiel, M. P. *The Purple Cloud* (Magill) (JC, DD, JG, DH)

*———. *The Young Men Are Coming* (JC)

Shiner, Lewis. *Frontera* (Magill) (JC, DD)

Shiras, Wilmar H. *Children of the Atom* (Magill) (JC, DD, JG)

Shute, Nevil. *On the Beach* (Magill) (JC, DD, DH)

*Silverberg, Robert. *The Collected Stories . . .* (JC, JG, DH)

*———. *Downward to the Earth* (Pringle, Magill) (JC, DD, JG, DH)

*———. *Dying Inside* (Magill) (JC, DD, JG, DH)

———. *Nightwings* (Magill) (JC, DD, JG)

———. *A Time of Changes* (Magill) (JC, DD)

———. *Tower of Glass* (1970) (Magill) (JC, JG)

*———. *The World Inside* (JC)

*Simak, Clifford D. *City* (Magill) (JC, DD, JG, DH)

———. *Ring Around the Sun* (1953) (Pringle, Magill) (DD)

———. *Skirmish: The Great Short Fiction* (1977) (JC)

———. *Time and Again* (1951) (JG)

*———. *Way Station* (Pringle, Magill) (JC, DD, JG, DH)

*Simmons, Dan. *Hyperion* (Magill) (JC [and sequels], DD, DH)

———. *Ilium* and sequel (JC)

Siodmak, Curt. *Donovan's Brain* (1943) (Magill) (JC, DD)

Sladek, John. *Keep the Giraffe Burning* (1978) (JC)

———. *The Müller-Fokker Effect* (JC)

———. *The Reproductive System* (JC)

———. *The Steam-Driven Boy* (JC)

———. *Tik-Tok* (1983) (JC)

———. *Roderick* and *Roderick at Random* (Pringle, Magill) (JC, DD, DH)

*Sleator, William. *House of Stairs* (YA) (JC)

*Slonczewski, Joan. *A Door into Ocean* (Magill) (JC, JG, DH)

*———. *The Wall Around Eden* (JC)

*Smith, Cordwainer. *Norstrilia* (1975) (Pringle, Magill) (JC, DD, JG, DH)

*———. *The Rediscovery of Man* (Magill) (JC, DD, JG, DH)

Smith, E. E. Lensman series (Magill) (JC, DD, JG)

———. Skylark series (JC, JG)

*Snyder, Zilpha Keatley. *Below the Root* (YA) (JC)

*Spinrad, Norman. *Bug Jack Barron* (Pringle, Magill) (JC, DD)

*———. *The Void Captain's Tale* (JC, DH)

Stableford, Brian. *The Empire of Fear* (Magill) (DD)

———. *The Fountains of Youth* (2000) (DH)

———. *The Omega Expedition* (2002) (DH)

———. *The Walking Shadow* (Pringle)

*Stapledon, Olaf. *Last and First Men* (Magill) (JC, DD, JG, DH)

———. *Odd John* (Magill) (JC, DD, JG, DH)

———. *Sirius* (Magill) (JC, JG)

*———. *Star Maker* (Magill) (JC, JG, DH)

Steele, Allen. *Clarke County, Space* (1990) (Magill) (JC, DD, DH)

———. *Orbital Decay* (Magill) (JC)

*Stephenson, Neal. *Cryptonomicon* (JC, DD, JG)

*———. *The Diamond Age* (JC, DD, JG, DH)

*———. *Snow Crash* (Magill) (JC, DD, JG, DH)

Sterling, Bruce. *The Artificial Kid* (1980) (Magill) (JC, DD)

*———. *Crystal Express* (Magill) (JC, DH)

*———. *Distraction* (JC, DH)

*———. *Islands in the Net* (Magill) (JC, JG, DH)

*———. *Schismatrix* (Magill) (JC, DD, DH)

Stewart, George R. *Earth Abides* (Pringle, Magill) (JC, DD, JG, DH)

Strugatsky, Arkady. *Hard to Be a God* (1964) (Magill) (JC, DD, DH)

*———. *Roadside Picnic and The Tale of the Troika* (JC, JG, DH)

———. *Snail on the Slope* (1966–1968) (Magill) (JC, DD)

Sturgeon, Theodore. *The Complete Short Stories* (1994–2005) (DH)

———. *The Dreaming Jewels* (Magill) (JC, DH)

*———. *E Pluribus Unicorn* (Magill) (JC, JG)

*———. *More than Human* (Pringle, Magill) (JC, DD, JG, DH)

*———. *Sturgeon Is Alive and Well . . .* (JG)

———. *A Touch of Sturgeon* (1987) (Magill) (JC, DD)

———. *Venus Plus X* (1960) (Pringle, Magill) (JC, DD, DH)

*———. *Without Sorcery* (JC, JG)

*Suddaby, Donald. *Village Fanfare* (YA) (JC)

*Swanwick, Michael. *Gravity's Angels* (JC, DH)

———. *The Iron Dragon's Daughter* (1993) (JG)

*———. *Stations of the Tide* (Magill) (JC, JG, DH)

———. *Vacuum Flowers* (Magill) (JC, DD, DH)

*Sweven, Godfrey. *Rialla*

*Swindells, Robert. *Brother in the Land* (YA) (JC)

*Swift, Jonathan. *Gulliver's Travels* (JC, JG, DH)

*Taine, John. *The Time Stream*

Tenn, William. *Complete Science Fiction of William Tenn* (DH)

*———. *Of All Possible Worlds* (DD)

———. *Of Men and Monsters* (1968) (Magill) (JC, DD, JG)

*Tepper, Sheri S. *The Gate to Women's Country* (Magill) (JC)

*———. *Grass* (JC, JG)

Tiptree, James, Jr. *Brightness Falls from the Air* (DH)

———. *Crown of Stars* (1988) (Magill) (JC, JG)

*———. *Her Smoke Rose Up Forever . . .* (Magill) (JC, DD, DH)

Tucker, Wilson. *The Long Loud Silence* (1952) (Magill) (JC, DD, JG, DH)

*———. *The Year of the Quiet Sun* (Pringle, Magill) (JC, DD)

Turner, George. *Genetic Soldier* (1994) (DH)

*———. *The Sea and the Summer*

Turtledove, Harry. *A Different Flesh* (1988) (Magill)
*———. *The Guns of the South* (JC)
*———. *How Few Remain* (JC)
*Twain, Mark. *A Connecticut Yankee in King Arthur's Court* (Magill) (JC, DD, JG, DH)
———. *The Science Fiction of Mark Twain* (1984) (Magill) (JC, DH)
*Ure, Jean. *Plague* (YA) (JC)
van Vogt, A. E. *Slan* (Magill) (JC, DD, JG, DH)
———. *The Voyage of the Space Beagle* (Magill) (JC, JG, DH)
*———. *The World of Null-A* (Magill) (JC [and sequels], DD, JG, DH)
———. Weapon Shop series (JC, JG)
Vance, Jack. *Big Planet/Showboat World* (1957, 1975) (Magill) (JC, DD, DH)
———. Demon Princes series (Magill) (JC, DD)
———. *The Dragon Masters* (Magill) (JC, DD, JG, DH)
———. *The Dying Earth* (Magill) (JC, DD, JG, DH)
———. *Planet of Adventure* (tetralogy, 1968–1970) (Magill) (JC, DH)
*———. *To Live Forever* (JC, DD, DH)
*Varley, John. *Millennium* (Magill) (JC)
———. *The Ophiuchi Hotline* (Pringle, Magill) (JC, DD, JG)
*———. *The Persistence of Vision* (JC, DD. DH)
———. *Steel Beach* (Magill) (JC, DD)
Vercors. *You Shall Know Them* (Magill) (JC, DD)
*Verne, Jules. *From the Earth to the Moon* (Magill) (JC, DD, JG, DH)
*———. *A Journey to the Centre of the Earth* (YA) (Magill) (JC, DD, JG, DH)
———. *Robur the Conqueror* (1886) and sequel (JC)
*———. *Twenty Thousand Leagues Under the Sea* (YA) (Magill) (JC [and sequel], DD, JG, DH)
*Vinge, Joan. *The Snow Queen* (Magill) (JC, DD, JG, DH)
*Vinge, Vernor. *A Deepness in the Sky* (JC, DD, JG, DH)
*———. *A Fire upon the Deep* (Magill) (JC DD, JG, DH)
———. *True Names* (JC)
*Voltaire. *Micromegas* (JC, JG)
von Harbou, Thea. *Metropolis* (Magill) (JC)
Vonnegut, Kurt. *Cat's Cradle* (Pringle, Magill) (JC, DD, JG, DH)
———. *Player Piano* (Magill) (JC, DH)
———. *The Sirens of Titan* (Pringle, Magill) (JC, DD, JG, DH)
*———. *Slaughterhouse-Five . . .* (Magill) (JC, DD, DH)
Waldrop, Howard. *Howard Who?* (1986) (JC)
*———. *Night of the Cooters . . .* (JC)
*Watson, Ian. *The Embedding* (Pringle, Magill) (JC, DD, JG, DH)
*———. *The Gardens of Delight* (JC, DH)
———. *Miracle Visitors* (Pringle) (JC, DD)
*Weinbaum, Stanley G. *A Martian Odyssey* (JC, DD, JG, DH)
Weldon, Fay. *The Cloning of Joanna May* (1989) (Magill) (JC)
*Wells, H. G. *The First Men in the Moon* (Magill) (JC, JG, DH)

———. *The Invisible Man* (Magill) (JC, DD, JG, DH)

*———. *The Island of Doctor Moreau* (Magill) (JC, JG, DH)

*———. *The Complete Short Stories of H. G. Wells* (JC, DD, JG, DH)

*———. *The Time Machine* (Magill) (JC, DD, JG, DH)

*———. *The War of the Worlds* (Magill) (JC, DD, JG, DH)

———. *When the Sleeper Wakes* (Magill) (JC, DH)

*Westall, Robert. *Futuretrack 5* (YA) (JC)

*Wilhelm, Kate. *The Clewiston Test* (JC)

*———. *The Infinity Box* (JC)

———. *Juniper Time* (Pringle) (JG)

*———. *Where Late the Sweet Birds Sang* (Magill) (JC, DD, JG, DH)

Williams, Walter Jon. *Hardwired* (Magill) (JC)

Williamson, Jack. *Darker than You Think* (Magill) (JC, JG)

*———. *The Humanoids* (JC, DD, JG, DH)

———. *The Legion of Space* (Magill) (JC, JG)

*Willis, Connie. *Doomsday Book* (Magill) (JC, DD, JG)

———. *Lincoln's Dreams* (1987) (Magill) (JC, DD, JG)

*———. *Passage* (JC)

———. *To Say Nothing of the Dog* (DH)

———. *Uncharted Territory* (Magill) (JC, DH)

Wilson, Colin. *The Mind Parasites* (1967) (Magill) (JC, DD)

*Wolfe, Bernard. *Limbo* (Pringle, Magill) (JC, DD, JG, DH)

Wolfe, Gene. *Endangered Species* (1989) (DH)

*———. *The Fifth Head of Cerberus* (Pringle, Magill) (JC, DD, DH)

———. *Gene Wolfe's Book of Days* (1981) (Magill) (JC)

———. *The Island of Doctor Death and Other Stories and Other Stories* (Magill) (JC, DD, JG, DH)

*———. *The Shadow of the Torturer* and sequels (Pringle, Magill) (JC, DD, JG, DH)

*Womack, Jack. *Random Acts of Senseless Violence* (JC, DH)

———. *Terraplane* (1988) (DH)

Wright, S. Fowler. *Dream* (Magill) (JC)

*———*The New Gods Lead* (JC)

*———. *The World Below* (JC, DH)

Wylie, Philip. *The Disappearance* (Magill) (JC, DD, DH)

———. *Gladiator* (JC)

Wyndham, John. *Rebirth* (Magill) (JC, DD, DH)

———. *The Day of the Triffids* (Pringle, Magill) (JC, DD, JG, DH)

———. *The Midwich Cuckoos* (1957) (Pringle, Magill) (JC, DD, DH)

*Yep, Laurence. *Sweetwater* (YA) (JC)

*Zamyatin, Yegevny. *We* (Magill) (JC, DD, DH)

Zebrowski, George. *Brute Orbits* (JG)

———. *Macrolife* (Magill) (JG)

*Zelazny, Roger. *The Doors of His Face . . .* (JC, DD, JG)

*———. *The Dream Master* (Pringle, Magill) (JC, DD, DH)
*———. *Lord of Light* (Magill) (JC, DD, JG)
*———. *This Immortal* (Magill) (JC, DD, DH)

Anthologies

**Adventures in Time and Space* (Healy) (JC, DD, JG)
**The Ascent of Wonder* (Hartwell) (JC, JG)
The Best of Science Fiction (1946) (Conklin) (DH)
**The Best Science Fiction of the Year* (Carr) (JC, DD)
The Best Science-Fiction Stories (Bleiler and Dikty) (1949–1958) DH
**Beyond Time and Space* (Derleth) (JC, JG)
The Big Book of Science Fiction (Conklin) (1950) (DH)
**Conjunctions: 39* (Straub) (JC)
**Dangerous Visions* (Ellison) (JC, DD, JG, DH)
**Full Spectrum* (Aronica) (JC)
**Future Perfect* (Franklin) (JC, JG, DH)
**The Hard Science Fiction Renaissance* (Hartwell) (JC, DD, JG)
**The Hugo Winners* (Asimov) (JC, DD, JG)
**Isaac Asimov Presents the Great Science Fiction Stories* (Asimov) (JC)
**Mirrorshades: The Cyberpunk Anthology* (Sterling) (JC, JG, DH)
**Nebula Awards Showcase* (Kress) (JC, DD, DH)
**The New Hugo Winners* (Asimov) (JC, DD, JG)
**The Norton Book of Science Fiction* (Le Guin) (JC)
**Orbit* (Knight) (JC, DD, DH)
**Pre-Revolutionary Russian Science Fiction* (Fetzer) (JC)
**Science Fiction by the Rivals of H. G. Wells* (Russell) (JC, DD)
**The Science Fiction Century* (Hartwell) (JC, JG)
**Science Fiction Hall of Fame* (Silverberg) (JC, DD, JG)
SF: The Year's Greatest (Merril) (1956–1968) DH
**Starlight I* (Hayden) (JC)
**The Tale of the Next Great War, 1871–1914* (Clarke) (JC)
**A Treasury of Science Fiction* (Conklin) (JC, DD, JG)
**Universe* (Carr) (JC, DD)
**Women of Wonder* (Sargent) (JC, DD, JG)
**The World Treasury of Science Fiction* (Hartwell) (JC, JG)
**The Year After Tomorrow* (del Rey) (YA) (JC)
**The Year's Best Science Fiction* (Dozois) (JC, DD)
The Year's Best SF (Hartwell) (DH)

Part III: Nonfiction

7: General Reference Works

*Bleiler, Everett F. *Science-Fiction: The Early Years* (JC, JG)
*Bleiler, Everett F. *Science-Fiction: The Gernsback Years* (JC, JG)
*Clute, John. *The Encyclopedia of Science Fiction* (JC, DD, JG)

Gunn, James. *The New Encyclopedia of Science Fiction* (DH)
*Hall, H. W. *Science Fiction and Fantasy Research Database* (JC, JG)
*Reginald, R(obert). *Science Fiction and Fantasy Literature* (JC, DD)
*Wolfe, Gary K. *Critical Terms for Science Fiction and Fantasy* (JC, JG)

8: Online Resources

Because of the rapid obsolescence of and changes to online resources, "best" Web sites are not identified.

9: History and Criticism

*Aldiss, Brian W. *Trillion Year Spree* (DD, JG)
*Alkon, Paul K. *Origins of Futuristic Fiction*
Amis, Kingsley. *New Maps of Hell* (DH)
*Ashley, Mike. *The Time Machines*
*Atheling, William, Jr. *The Issue at Hand* (DD, JG)
*Attebery, Brian W. *Decoding Gender in Science Fiction*
*Barr, Marleen S. *Feminist Fabulation* (JG)
*Bleiler, Everett F. *Science-Fiction: The Early Years* (JG)
*Bleiler, Everett F. *Science-Fiction: The Gernsback Years* (JG)
*Brians, Paul. *Nuclear Holocaust: Atomic War in Fiction, 1895–1984*
*Broderick, Damien. *Reading by Starlight* (JG)
*Clareson, Thomas D. *Some Kind of Paradise*
*Clarke, I. F. *Voices Prophesying War: Future Wars, 1763–3749* (DD)
Cogswell, Theodore. *PITFCS* (DH)
*Delany, Samuel R. *The Jewel-Hinged Jaw* (JG)
———. *Starboard Wine* (DH)
*Freedman, Carl. *Critical Theory and Science Fiction*
*Greenland, Colin. *The Entropy Exhibition*
Hartwell, David. *Age of Wonders* (DH)
*Hayles, N. Katherine. *How We Became Posthuman*
*Huntington, John. *Rationalizing Genius*
*James, Edward. *Science Fiction in the Twentieth Century* (JG)
*James, Edward. *The Cambridge Companion to Science Fiction* (JG)
*Jones, Gwyneth. *Deconstructing the Starships*
*Knight, Damon. *In Search of Wonder* (DD, JG)
*Larbalestier, Justine. *The Battle of the Sexes in Science Fiction*
*Lefanu, Sarah. *In the Chinks of the World Machine*
*Malmgren, Carl. *Worlds Apart*
*Moylan, Tom. *Scraps of the Untainted Sky*
*Rose, Mark. *Alien Encounters*
*Ruddick, Nicholas. *Ultimate Island*
*Russ, Joanna. *To Write like a Woman* (DD)
*Stableford, Brian M. *Scientific Romance in Britain 1890–1950* (JG)
*Suvin, Darko. *Metamorphoses of Science Fiction* (JG)

*Wagar, W. Warren. *Terminal Visions*
*Wolfe, Gary K. *The Known and the Unknown* (JG)

10: Author Studies
*Bleiler, Richard. *Science Fiction Writers*
*Aldiss, Brian W. *The Twinkling of An Eye, Or, My Life as an Englishman*
*Asimov, Isaac. *I, Asimov: A Memoir*
*Gunn, James E. *Isaac Asimov: The Foundations of Science Fiction*. Rev. ed.
*Ketterer, David. *Imprisoned in a Tesseract: The Life and Work of James Blish*
*Berger, Albert I. *The Magic That Works: John W. Campbell and the American Response to Technology*
*Barbour, Douglas. *Worlds Out of Words: The SF Novels of Samuel R. Delany*
*Delany, Samuel R. *1984*
*Mullen, R. D., Istvan Csicerny-Ronay, Jr., and Arthur B. Evans. *On Philip K. Dick: 40 Articles from Science-Fiction Studies*
*Palmer, Christopher. *Philip K. Dick: Exhilaration and Terror of the Postmodern*
*Sutin, Lawrence. *Divine Invasions: A Life of Philip K. Dick*
*Weil, Ellen, and Gary K. Wolfe. *Harlan Ellison: The Edge of Forever*
*Gifford, James. *Robert A. Heinlein: A Reader's Companion*
*Keyes, Daniel. *Algernon, Charlie and I: A Writer's Journey*
*Cummins, Elizabeth. *Understanding Ursula K. Le Guin*. Rev. (paperback) ed.
*White, Donna R. *Dancing with Dragons: Ursula K. Le Guin and the Critics*
*Byfield, Bruce. *Witches of the Mind: A Critical Study of Fritz Leiber*
*Dowling, David C. *Planets in Peril: A Critical Study of C. S. Lewis' Ransom Trilogy*
*Merril, Judith, and Emily Pohl-Weary. *Better to Have Loved: The Life of Judith Merril*
*Reilly, Patrick. *Nineteen Eighty-Four: Past, Present, and Future*
*Sheldon, Michael. *Orwell: The Authorized Biography*
*Cortiel, Jeanne. *Demand My Writing: Joanna Russ/Feminism/Science Fiction*
*Esther, Schor, ed. *The Cambridge Companion to Mary Shelley*
*Mellor, Ann K. *Mary Shelley: Her Life, Her Fiction, Her Monsters*
*Sunstein, Emily W. *Mary Shelley: Romance and Reality*
*Tropp, Martin. *Mary Shelley's Monster: The Story of Frankenstein*
*McCarthy, Patrick A. *Olaf Stapledon*
*Cunningham, A. E., ed. *Jack Vance: Critical Appreciations and a Bibliography*
*Butcher, William. *Verne's Journey to the Centre of the Self: Space and Time in the Voyages Extraordinaires*
*Evans, Arthur B. *Jules Verne Rediscovered: Didacticism and the Scientific Novel*
*Martin, Andrew. *The Mask of the Prophet: The Extraordinary Fictions of Jules Verne*
*Smyth, Edmund J., ed. *Jules Verne: Narratives of Modernity*
*Boon, Kevin A., ed. *At Millennium's End: New Essays on the Work of Kurt Vonnegut*
*Klinkowitz, Jerome. *The Vonnegut Effect*
*Huntington, John. *Logic of Fantasy: H. G. Wells and Science Fiction*
*Parrinder, Patrick. *Shadows of the Future: H. G. Wells, SF and Prophecy*

*Smith, David. *H. G. Wells: Desperately Mortal*
*Williamson, Jack. *Wonder's Child: My Life in Science Fiction*
*Wright, Peter. *Attending Daedalus: Gene Wolfe, Artifice and the Reader*

COLLECTIVE BIOGRAPHY
*Aldiss, Brian W. and Harrison, Harry. *Hell's Cartographers: Some Personal Histories of Science Fiction Writers*
*Jakubowski, Maxim, and Edward James, eds. *The Profession of Science Fiction: SF Writers on their Craft and Ideas*

INTERVIEWS
*McCaffrey. Larry. *Across the Wounded Galaxies: Interviews with Contemporary American Science Fiction Writers*
*Platt, Charles. *Dream Makers: Science Fiction and Fantasy Writers at Work*

11: Science Fiction in Film, Television, and Radio
*Hardy, Phil. *The Overlook Film Encyclopedia: Science Fiction*
*Brosnan, John. *The Primal Screen* (JG)
————. *Science Fiction in the Cinema* (1970) (JG)
*Nicholls, Peter. *The World of Fantastic Films*
*Sobchack, Vivian. *Screening Space* (JG)
*Bizony, Piers. *2001: Filming the Future*
*Bukatman, Scott. *Blade Runner*
*Sammon, Paul M. *Future Noir: The Making of Blade Runner*
*Elsaesser, Thomas. *Metropolis*
*Minden, Michael. *Fritz Lang's Metropolis*
*Greene, Eric. *Planet of the Apes as American Myth*
*La Valley, Al. *Invasion of the Body Snatchers*
*Slusser, George E. *Shadows of the Magic Lamp*
*Telotte, J. P. *A Distant Technology: Science Fiction and the Machine Age*
*Telotte, J. P. *Replications: A Robotic History of the Science Fiction Film*
*Warren, Bill. *Keep Watching the Skies!*
*Erdmann, Terry J. *Star Trek: Deep Space Nine Companion*
CFQ (periodical)

12: Science Fiction Illustration
GENERAL AND MULTI-ARTIST STUDIES
*Di Fate, Vincent. *Infinite Worlds* (JG)
*Fenner, Cathy. *Spectrum*
*Frank, Jane. *The Frank Collection*
*Grant, John. *The Chesley Awards for Science Fiction and Fantasy*
*Hardy, David A. *Visions of Space*
*Hartmann, William K. *In the Stream of Stars*
*Lesser, Robert. *Pulp Art*
*Lupoff, Richard. *The Great American Paperback*
*Ordway, Frederick I. *Visions of Spaceflight*

*Powers, Alan. *Front Cover*
*Robinson, Frank. *Pulp Culture*
*Weinberg, Robert. *A Biographical Dictionary of Science Fiction and Fantasy Artists*

INDIVIDUAL ARTISTS
*Artzybasheff, Boris. *As I See*
*Gunnison, John. *Belarski*
*Frank, Jane. *The Art of John Berkey*
*Miller, Ron. *The Art of Chesley Bonestell*
*Cartier, Edd. *Edd Cartier*
*Di Fate, Vincent. *The Science Fiction Art of Vincent Di Fate* (JG)
*Finlay, Virgil. *Virgil Finlay's Strange Science*
*Fenner, Cathy. *Testament: The Life and Art of Frank Frazetta*
*Freas, Frank Kelly. *As He Sees It*
*McCall, Robert. *The Art of Robert McCall*
*Maitz, Don. *First Maitz*
*Frank, Jane. *The Art of Richard Powers*
*Robida, Albert. *The Twentieth Century*
*Richardson, Darrell C. *J. Allen St. John*
*Walotsky, Ron. *Inner Visions*
*Whelan, Michael. *Michael Whelan's Works of Wonder*

13: Science Fiction Magazines and Fandom
CURRENT SF MAGAZINES
Asimov's Science Fiction
The Magazine of Fantasy and Science Fiction

CURRENT MAGAZINES ABOUT SF
Extrapolation
Foundation
Locus
The New York Review of Science Fiction
Science Fiction Studies

BOOKS ABOUT SF MAGAZINES
*Ashley, Mike. *The Time Machines*
*Berger, Albert I. *The Magic that Works*
*Bleiler, Everett F. *Science-Fiction, The Early Years*
*Bleiler, Everett F. *Science-Fiction: The Gernsback Years*
*Carter, Paul. *The Creation of Tomorrow*
*Tymn, Marshall B. *Science Fiction, Fantasy, and Weird Fiction Magazines*

BOOKS ABOUT SF FANDOM
*Sanders, Joe, ed. *Science Fiction Fandom*

14: Teaching Science Fiction
*Gunn, James. *Inside Science Fiction*

Science Fiction Studies, issues 19 and 70
*Tymn, Marshall. *Science Fiction: A Teacher's Guide and Resource Book*
*Williamson, Jack. *Teaching Science Fiction*
*Card, Orson Scott. *How to Write Science Fiction and Fantasy*
*Gunn, James. *The Science of Science Fiction Writing*
*Gunn, James. *The Road to Science Fiction*
*Roberts, Garyn G. *The Prentice Hall Anthology of Science Fiction and Fantasy*
*Warrick, Patricia. *Science Fiction: The Science Fiction Research Association Anthology*

Awards

Most of the awards described below are likely to be unknown to the general reader. They were created to recognize distinguished work in science fiction because the more prestigious literary awards usually ignore popular fiction to concentrate on what is believed to be "serious" work. Those voting for these awards range from a committee to a few hundred readers, sometimes members of the organizations discussed later. Only a handful of the better known or more "significant" awards are discussed below. Annotated adult fiction in Part II shows only winners of the following seven awards. Annotations of some young adult books note additional specifically YA awards, such as the Newbery.

John W. Campbell, Jr. Memorial Award. Given in memory of the long-time editor of *Astounding*, now *Analog*, it is presented each year at the University of Kansas for the best SF novel. This award is distinct from the John W. Campbell Award for the best new author. www.ku.edu/~sfcenter/campbell.htm

Arthur C. Clarke Award. A panel of judges selects the best SF novel published in the United Kingdom, and the writer receives a £1,000 cash prize. www.clarkeaward.com

Philip K. Dick Memorial Award. Created soon after Dick's death in 1982, selected by a five-person jury, sponsored by the Philadelphia SF Society, first and second winners receive $1,000 and $500 respectively for the best original American paperback. www.philipkdickaward.org

Hugo Award. Named after Hugo Gernsback, founding editor of *Amazing Stories*, this is the best-known SF award. It was officially called the Science Fiction Achievement Award until its name was formally changed at the 1992 world SF convention. Attending and supporting members of the convention vote by mail. www.wsfs.org/hugos.html

Locus Award. Voted since 1971 by readers of *Locus* [13-17], these awards generate more votes than any other single award. www.locusmag.com/sfawards/db/locus.html

Nebula Award. About a fourth of the active membership of the Science-Fiction and Fantasy Writers of America, Inc. vote this award in several categories, including several for shorter fiction. The awards are announced a few months before the Hugos and may have some influence on them. www.sfwa.org/awards/

James W. Tiptree Award. Given since 1992 for "science fiction or fantasy that explores and expands the roles of women and men for work by both women and men." Novels and short fiction are eligible. A five-judge council selects the winner and awards a $1,000 prize. See *Flying Cups and Saucers* in Part II's anthologies for a selection of Tiptree-nominated stories. www.tiptree.org/

Just as academics founded organizations devoted to the study of SF, so they began to bestow awards for scholarly distinction. The SF Research Association was the first to offer such awards, beginning in 1970 with the Pilgrim Award for sustained contribution to the study of SF and continuing more recently with the Pioneer Award for best article. *Pilgrims and Pioneers: The History and Speeches of the Science Fiction Research Association Award Winners* (SFRA Press/Jacob's Ladder Press, 2000), ed. by Hal W. Hall and Darrell F. Mallett, collects the presentation and acceptance speeches through 1999.

The J. Lloyd Eaton Memorial Award was given to the best scholarly book about SF published two years previously but is no longer given. The International Association for the Fantastic in the Arts Distinguished Scholarship Award is given to an individual by judges appointed by the IAFA.

Winners and runners-up, which often differ by only a few votes, for three major awards are listed in *The Hugo, Nebula and World Fantasy Awards* by Howard DeVore (Advent, 1998). Arrangement is chronological, all categories are shown, and there is a detailed index by author, book or story title, and other access points. The most comprehensive listing of award winners (only) is *Reginald's Science Fiction and Fantasy Awards: A Comprehensive Guide to the Awards and Their Winners* (Borgo, 3rd ed., 1993) ed. by Darrell F. Mallett and Robert Reginald. Genre awards total 126, non-genre 89. Indexes to award names, to winners, plus appendixes listing SFRA and SFWA officers and locations and dates of World Fantasy and Hugo conventions, plus some statistical tabulations. Most of these awards are obscure beyond belief and were usually short-lived.

Award-winning shorter fiction has been collected not only in author collections but in anthologies, especially best-of-the-year anthologies (see Part II). For award-winning films and TV programs, see Table 11-1. For artist/illustrator winners and nominees, see Table 12-1.

Because a multitude of awards are given every year, every printed source quickly becomes dated. For this reason, the long list of awards in earlier editions of this guide has been omitted in favor of the regularly updated and comprehensive listing at www.locusmag.com/sfawards/index.html. This listing is far more current and flexible than any printed list and permits rapid search by award, individual, category, year, etc. If you use Google, go to the home page, and click successively on more/directory/arts/literature/science fiction. In July 2004, the last category had 22 sub-categories, one of them awards, links to 24 sites, excluding, alas, the *Locus* site. Beginning in 1992, the Golden Duck awards for excellence in children's SF were awarded (see www.goldenduck.org). A committee including librarians, teachers, and "fannish" parents selects a list of five to six titles in each of three categories: picture book (the award is given to the illustrator), Eleanor Cameron award for middle grades (2nd–6th) and the Hal Clement award for young adults (6th–12th). Members of a larger jury vote by Australian ballot, similar to the Hugo voting. Details from info@goldenduck.org. The *Locus* awards listings don't include (yet) the Golden Duck awards.

Series

Listed here are series of three or more books, at least one of which is annotated in this guide. (A single sequel is described in the annotation but isn't listed here.) Some books require or at least benefit from a reader's knowledge of earlier books in the series. Books are therefore listed in their internal reading sequence or by year of publication if the sequence is unimportant. Included here are prequels, works describing earlier events involving characters or settings from a previous work. Series have become increasingly complex, with other writers continuing series, or writing books set in a series universe but formally not part of the series. Such books are listed under the original author's name (see Asimov's Foundation series for example). And see annotations for more details. Reginald's bibliography [7-8] provides fuller details through 1991, including listings of omnibus volumes and books with variant titles not listed here. Following the series listing is an index by keywords in the series titles, cross-referenced to the author. I used the "standard" series title, if any, or followed the series listing in Reginald. Libraries usually disdain series, often for sound reasons, and few make attempts to acquire or retain all books in series. The *Locus* Index, www.locusmag.com/index, contains information on the thousands of SF/fantasy/horror books and stories published 1984 or later and will list the latest books in any continuing series listed here. Series are clearly identified and indexed, with full bibliographic information. While information for individual books is limited to author, title and year, a seemingly comprehensive online series index is www.scifan.com/series/, which claims to list 5,239 series (SF, fantasy and horror) as of July 2004. Searches can be by author or series title; or clicking on a letter brings up parallel columns of authors and series titles beginning with that letter. The general site www.scifan.com/ provides additional book information not restricted to series.

Adams, Douglas. Hitch Hiker
 The Hitch Hiker's Guide to the Galaxy, 1979
 The Restaurant at the End of the Universe, 1980
 Life, the Universe and Everything, 1982
 So Long, and Thanks for All the Fish, 1984

 Mostly Harmless, 1992
 The Salmon of Doubt, 2002

Aldiss, Brian W. Helliconia
 Helliconia Spring, 1982
 Helliconia Summer, 1983
 Helliconia Winter, 1985

Anderson, Chester. Greenwich Village
 The Butterfly Kid, 1967

The Final Encyclopedia, 1984
The Chantry Guild, 1988
Other, 1994

Dowling, Terry. Rynosseros
Rynosseros, 1990
Blue Tyson, 1992
Twilight Beach, 1993

Doyle, Arthur Conan. Professor
Challenger
The Lost World, 1912
The Poison Belt, 1913
The Land of Mist, 1926

Effinger, George Alec. Marid Audran
When Gravity Fails, 1987
A Fire in the Sun, 1989
The Exile Kiss, 1991

Elgin, Suzette Haden. Communipath
The Communipath, 1970
Furthest, 1971
At the Seventh Level, 1972
Star Anchored, Star Angered, 1979
Yonder Comes the Other End of Time,
1986

Elgin, Suzette Haden. Native Tongue
Native Tongue, 1984
The Judas Rose, 1987
Earthsong, 1994

Farley, Ralph Milne. Radio Man
The Radio Man, 1948
The Radio Beasts, 1964
The Radio Planet, 1964
The Radio Menace, 1930

Farmer, Philip José. Riverworld
To Your Scattered Bodies Go, 1971
The Fabulous Riverboat, 1971
The Dark Design, 1977
The Magic Labyrinth, 1980
Gods of Riverworld, 1983
River of Eternity, 1983

Flynn, Michael F. Firestar
Firestar, 1996
Rogue Star, 1009
Lodestar, 2000
Falling Star, 2001
Wreck of the River of Stars, 2003

Foster, Alan Dean. Flinx
The Tar-Aiym Krang, 1972
Bloodhype, 1973
Orphan Star, 1977
The End of the Matter, 1977
Nor Crystal Tears, 1982
For Love of Mother Not, 1983
Flinx in Flux, 1988
Mid-Flinx, 1995
Flinx's Folly, 2003

Foster, M. A. Morphodite
The Morphodite, 1981
Transformer, 1983
Preserver, 1985

Garis, Howard. Great Marvel
Through the Air to the North Pole,
1906
Under the Ocean to the South Pole,
1907
Five Thousand Miles Underground,
1908
Through Space to Mars, 1910
Lost on the Moon, 1911
On a Turn-Away World, 1913
The City Beyond the Clouds, 1925
By Air Express to Venus, 1929
By Space Ship to Saturn, 1935

Geston, Mark S. Starship
Lords of the Starship, 1967
Out of the Mouth of the Dragon,
1969
The Day Star, 1972
The Siege of Wonder, 1976

Gibson, William. Neuromancer
Neuromancer, 1984

Hill, Douglas. Galactic Warlord
Galactic Warlord, 1979
Day of the Starwind, 1980
Deathwing over Veynaa, 1980
Planet of the Warlord, 1981
Young Legionary, 1982

Hogan, James. Minervan Experiment
Inherit the Stars, 1977
The Gentle Giants of Ganymede,
1978
Giants' Star, 1981

Horowitz, Anthony. Alex Rider
Stormbreaker, 2000
Point Blank, 2001
Skeleton Key, 2002
Eagle Strike, 2003
Scorpia, 2004

Hughes, Monica. Isis
The Keeper of the Isis Light, 1980
The Guardian of Isis, 1981
The Isis Pedlar, 1982

Jeter, K. W. Dr. Adder
Dr. Adder, 1984
The Glass Hammer, 1985
Death Arms, 1987

Jones, Gwyneth. Aleutian Trilogy
White Queen, 1991
North Wind, 1994
Phoenix Café, 1998

Jones, Neil R. Professor Jameson
The Planet of the Double Sun, 1967
Space War, 1967
The Sunless World, 1967
Twin Worlds, 1967
Doomsday on Ajiat, 1968

Knight, Damon F. C.V.
CV, 1985
The Observers, 1988
A Reasonable World, 1991

Kress, Nancy. Beggars
Beggars in Spain, 1993
Beggars and Choosers, 1994
Beggars Ride, 1996

Kress, Nancy. Probability
Probability Moon, 2000
Probability Sun, 2001
Probability Space, 2002

Laumer, Keith. R. Retief
Envoy to New Worlds, 1963
Galactic Diplomat, 1965
Retief's War, 1966
Retief and the Warlords, 1968
Retief: Ambassador to Space, 1969
Retief's Ransom, 1971
Retief of the CDT, 1971
Retief: Emissary to the Stars, 1975
Retief: Diplomat at Arms, 1982
Retief to the Rescue, 1983
The Return of Retief, 1984
Retief in the Ruins, 1986
Reward for Retief, 1989
Retief and the Rascals, 1993

L'Engle, Madeleine. Time
A Wrinkle in Time, 1962
A Wind in the Door, 1973
A Swiftly Tilting Planet, 1978
Many Waters, 1986
An Acceptable Time, 1969

Lessing, Doris. Canopus in Argos
Re: Colonized Planet 5, Shikasta,
1979
*The Marriages Between Zones Three,
Four, and Five*, 1980
The Sirian Experiments, 1981
*The Making of the Representative for
Planet 8*, 1982
*Documents Relating to the
Sentimental Agents in the Voylen
Empire*, 1983

Lewis, C. S. Space Trilogy
Out of the Silent Planet, 1938

Perelandra, 1943
That Hideous Strength, 1945

Lowry, Lois. The Giver
The Giver, 1993
Gathering Blue, 2000
The Messenger, 2004

MacLeod, Ken. Engines of Light
Cosmonaut Keep, 2000
Dark Light, 2001
Engine City, 2002

MacLeod, Ken. Fall Revolution
The Star Fraction, 1995
The Stone Canal, 1997
The Cassini Division, 1998
The Sky Road, 1999

Matthews, Susan. Andrej Koscuisko
An Exchange of Hostages, 1997
Prisoner of Conscience, 1998
Hour of Judgment, 1999
Angel of Destruction, 2001
The Devil and Deep Space, 2002

May, Julian. Saga of the Pliocene Exile
The Many-Colored Land, 1981
The Golden Torc, 1982
The Nonborn King, 1983
The Adversary, 1984

McAuley, Paul J. Confluence
Child of the River, 1997
Ancients of Days, 1998
Shrine of Stars, 1999

McAuley, Paul J. Four Hundred
Billion Stars
Four Hundred Billion Stars, 1988
Eternal Light, 1991
Of the Fall, 1989

McCaffrey, Anne. Harper Hall
Dragonsong, 1976
Dragonsinger, 1977
Dragondrums, 1979

McCaffrey, Anne. Pern
Dragonflight, 1968
Dragonquest, 1968
The White Dragon, 1978
(Harper Hall trilogy, above)
Moreta, Dragonlady of Pern, 1983
Nerilka's Story, 1986
Dragonsdawn, 1988
The Renegades of Pern, 1989
All the Weyrs of Pern, 1991
The Dragonriders of Pern, 1978
The Chronicles of Pern: First Fall,
1993
The Dolphin's Bell, 1993
The Girl Who Heard Dragons, 1994
Dragon's Kin, 2003

McCaffrey, Anne. Ship Who Sang
The Ship Who Sang, 1969
PartnerShip, 1992
The Ship Who Searched, 1992
The Ship Who Fought, 1993
The Ship Who Won, 1994
The Ship Errant, 1996
The Ship Avenged, 1997
The Ship Who Saved the World, 2003

McDevitt, Jack. Priscilla Hutchins
The Engines of God, 1994
Deepsix, 2001
Chindi, 2002
Omega, 2003

McMullen, Sean. Greatwinter
Souls in the Great Machine, 1999
The Miocene Arrow, 2000
Eyes of the Calculor, 2001

Miéville, China. New Corobuzon
Perdido Street Station, 2000
The Scar, 2002
The Iron Council, 2004

Moorcock, Michael. Dancers at the
End of Time
An Alien Heat, 1972
The Hollow Lands, 1974

Pournelle, Jerry. The Jupiter Novels
  Higher Education, 1996
  The Billion Dollar Boy (Sheffield), 1997
  Putting Up Roots (Sheffield), 1997
  The Cyborg from Earth (Sheffield), 1998
  Starswarm, 1998

Pratchett, Terry. Johnny Maxwell
  Only You Can Save Mankind, 1992
  Johnny and the Dead, 1993
  Johnny and the Bomb, 1996

Rankin, Robert. Armageddon
  Armageddon: The Musical, 1990
  They Came and Ate Us . . ., 1991
  The Suburban Book of the Dead . . ., 1992

Reynolds, Alastair. Revelation Space
  Revelation Space, 2000
  Chasm City, 2001
  Redemption Ark, 2002
  Absolution Gap, 2003

Reynolds, Mack. Lagrange
  Lagrange Five, 1979
  The Lagrangists, 1983
  Chaos in Lagrangia, 1984
  Trojan Orbit, 1985

Robinson, Kim Stanley. Mars
  Red Mars, 1992
  Green Mars, 1994
  Blue Mars, 1996

Robinson, Kim Stanley. Orange County
  The Wild Shore, 1984
  The Gold Coast, 1988
  Pacific Edge, 1990

Robinson, Spider. Callahan
  Callahan's Crosstime Saloon, 1977
  Callahan's Secret, 1986
  Callahan and Company, 1988
  Callahan's Lady, 1989

  Lady Slings the Booze, 1992
  The Callahan Touch, 1993
  Off the Wall at Callahan's, 1994
  Callahan's Legacy, 1996
  Callahan's Key, 2000
  Time Travelers Strictly Cash, 1981, 2001
  Callahan's Con, 2003

Robinson, Spider. Stardance
  Stardance, 1979
  Starseed, 1991
  Starmind, 1995

Rockwood, Roy *see* Garis

Rubinstein, Gillian. Space Demons
  Space Demons, 1986
  Skyway, 1989
  Shinkei, 1997

Rucker, Rudy. Software
  Software, 1982
  Wetware, 1988
  Freeware, 1997
  Realware, 2000

Saberhagen, Fred. Berserker
  Berserker, 1967
  Brother Assassin, 1969
  Berserker's Planet, 1975
  Berserker Man, 1979
  The Ultimate Enemy, 1979
  Berserker Wars, 1981
  Berserker Base, 1985
  The Berserker Throne, 1985
  Berserker: Blue Death, 1985
  The Berserker Attack, 1987
  Berserker Lies, 1991
  Berserker Kill, 1993
  Berserker Wars, 1994
  Berserker Fury, 1997
  Berserkers: The Beginning, 1998
  Shiva in Steel, 1998
  Berserker's Star, 2003
  Berserker Prime, 2004
  Rogue Berserker, 2005

Utopia Hunters, 1984
The Darkling Wind, 1985

Turner, George. Ethical Culture
Beloved Sun, 1978
Vaneglory, 1981
Yesterday's Men, 1983

Turtledove, Harry. The Great War
American Front, 1998
Walk in Hell, 1999
Breakthroughs, 2000

Turtledove, Harry. American Empire
Blood and Iron, 2001
The Center Cannot Hold, 2002
The Victorious Opposition, 2003

Turtledove, Harry. Colonization
Colonization: Second Contact, 1999
Colonization: Down to Earth, 2000
Colonization: Aftershocks, 2001
Colonization: Homeward Bound,
2005?

Turtledove, Harry. World War
World War: In the Balance, 1994
World War: Tilting the Balance,
1995
World War: Upsetting the Balance,
1996
World War: Striking the Balance,
1996

van Vogt, A. E. Null-A
The World of Null-A, 1948
The Pawns of Null-A, 1956
Null-A Three, 1985

Vance, Jack. Cadwall Chronicles
Araminta Station, 1987
Ecce and Old Earth, 1991
Throy, 1992

Vance, Jack. Demon Princes
The Star King, 1964
The Killing Machine, 1964
The Palace of Love, 1967

The Face, 1979
The Book of Dreams, 1981

Vance, Jack. Dying Earth
The Dying Earth, 1950
The Eyes of the Overworld, 1966
Cugel's Saga, 1983
(plus several short fictions)

Varley, John. Gaea
Titan, 1979
Wizard, 1981
Demon, 1984

Vinge, Joan. Psion
Psion, 1982
Catspaw, 1988
Dreamfall, 1996

Vinge, Joan. Snow Queen
The Snow Queen, 1980
World's End, 1984
The Summer Queen, 1991

Wallace, Ian. Croyd
Croyd, 1967
Dr. Orpheus, 1968
Deathstar Voyage, 1969
A Voyage to Dari, 1974
Z-Sting, 1978
Heller's Leap, 1979
The Lucifer Comet, 1980
Megalomania, 1989

Watson, Ian. Black Current
The Book of the River, 1984
The Book of the Stars, 1984
The Book of Being, 1985

Watts, Peter. Starfish
Starfish, 1999
Maelstrom, 2001
βehemoth, 2004 (in two volumes)

Webb, Sharon. Earthchild
Earthchild, 1982
Earth Song, 1983
Ram Song, 1984

Yolen, Jane. Pit Dragon Trilogy
  Dragon's Blood, 1982
  Heart's Blood, 1984
  A Sending of Dragons, 1987

Zebrowski, George. Sunspacer
  Sunspacer, 1984
  The Stars Will Speak, 1985
  Behind the Stars, 1996

Series Index

Series named after a person are listed by the first name of the person.

Adventure in the Unknown (Claudy)
Aleution Trilogy (Jones)
Alex Rider (Horowitz)
Alliance-Union (Cherryh)
Arabesk (Grimwood)
Arcot, Wade and Morley (Campbell)
Armageddon (Rankin)
Baroque Cycle (Stephenson)
Barsoom (Burroughs)
Beggars (Kress)
Berserker (Saberhagen)
Bird of Kinship (Cowper)
Black Current (Watson)
Book of the Long Sun (Wolfe)
Book of the New Sun (Wolfe)
Book of the Short Sun (Wolfe)
Cadwell Chronicles (Vance)
Callahan (Robinson)
Canopus in Archives (Lessing)
Changes (Dickinson)
Chanur (Cherryh)
Child Cycle (Dickson)
Chronicles of the High Inquest
   (Sucharitkul)
Chung Kuo (Wingrove)
Cities in Flight (Blish)
Colonization (Turtledove)
The Company (Baker)
Confederation (Hamilton)
Confluence (McAuley)
Coyote Jones (Elgin)
Croyd (Watson)
The Culture (Banks)
CV (Knight)
Dancers at the Edge of Time
   (Moorcock)

Darkover (Bradley)
Davy (Pangborn)
Dead Girls (Calder)
Demon Princes (Vance)
Dr. Adder (Jeter)
Dream (Wright)
Dune (Herbert)
Dustland (Hamilton)
Dying Earth (Vance)
Earthchild (Webb)
Earth's Children (Auel)
Eden (Harrison)
Emmortality (Stableford)
Ender Wiggins (Card)
Engines of Light (MacLeod)
Eon (Bear)
Ethical Culture (Turner)
Exiles (Bova)
Falkenberg's Legion (Pournelle)
Fall Revolution (MacLeod)
Faustus Hexagram (Broderick)
Fireball (Christopher)
Fire-us (Armstrong)
Flinx (Foster)
Foreigner (Cherryh)
Foundation (Asimov)
Four Hundred Billion Stars
   (McAuley)
Future History (Heinlein)
Gaea (Varley)
Galactic Center (Benfore)
Galactic Warlord (Hill)
Gate (Corlett)
The Giver (Lowry)
The Golden Transcendance (Wright)
Great Marvel (Garis)

Great War and American Empire
(Turtledove)
Green Sky (Snyder)
Greenwich Village (Anderson)
Hardwired (Williams)
Harper Hall (McCaffrey)
Heechee (Pohl)
Helliconia (Aldiss)
High Inquest, Chronicles of
(Sucharitkul)
Hitchhiker (Adams)
Holdfast (Charnas)
Honor Harrington (Weber)
The Hydronauts (Biemiller)
Hyperion (Simmons)
Isis (Hughes)
Islandia (Wright)
Janus (Norton)
Jerry Cornelius (Moorcock)
Johnny Maxwell (Pratchett)
Jupiter novels (Pournelle)
Known Space (Niven)
Lagrange (Reynolds)
Land and Overland (Shaw)
Legends of Dune (Herbert)
Legion of Space (Williamson)
Lensman (Smith)
Logan (Nolan)
Long Sun, Book of the (Wolfe)
Lucky Starr (Asimov)
Luke (Christopher)
Majipoor (Silverberg)
Manchester Novels (Noon)
Manifold (Baxter)
Marid Audran (Effinger)
Mars (Robinson)
Minervan Experiment (Hogan)
Morphodite (Foster)
Nanotech Quartet (Goonan)
Native Tongue (Elgin)
Neanderthal Parallax (Sawyer)
Neuromancer (Gibson)
New Corobuzon (Miéville)
New Son, Book of the (Wolfe)

Null-A (van Vogt)
Obernewtyn (Carmody)
Orange County (Robinson)
Orbitsville (Shaw)
Otherlands (Williams)
Pandora (Herbert)
Patternist (Butler)
Pellucidar (Burroughs)
Pern (McCaffrey)
Pit Dragon Trilogy (Yolen)
Planetary Tour (Bova)
Plenty (Greenland)
Pliocene Exiles, Saga of (May)
Prelude to Dune (Herbert)
Probability (Kress)
Professor Challenger (Doyle)
Professor Jameson (Jones)
Proteus (Sheffield)
Psion (Vinge)
Radio Man (Farley)
Radix (Attanasio)
Rama (Clarke)
Ratha (Bell)
Retief (Laumer)
Revelation Space (Reynolds)
Riverworld (Farmer)
Robot (Asimov)
Rynosseros (Dowling)
Saga of Pliocene Exile (May)
Schrödinger's Cat (Wilson)
Shadow Children (Haddix)
Ship Who Sang (McCaffrey)
Shora (Slonczewski)
Short Sun, Book of the (Wolfe)
Skolian Empire (Asaro)
Skylark (Smith)
Snow Queen (Vinge)
Software (Rucker)
Song Called Youth (Shirley)
Space Demons (Rubinstein)
Space Trilogy (Lewis)
Star Shards (Shusterman)
Starbridge Chronicles (Park)
Starship (Geston)

Stardance (Robinson)
Starfish (Watts)
Sunspacer (Zebrowski)
Tarot (Anthony)
Technic Civilization (Anderson)
Terraplane (Womack)
The Thousand Cultures (Barnes)
Time (L'Engle)
Tom "Red Clay" (Ore)
Torin (Brin)
Tripod (Christopher)
2001 (Clarke)
Undersea Trilogy (Williamson)

Uplift (Brin)
Venus (Sargent)
Virex (Brown)
Viriconium (Harrison)
Virtual Light (Gibson)
Vorkosigan (Bujold)
War of the Memes (Barnes)
Winterlong (Hand)
Worlds (Haldeman)
Worldwar (Turtledove)
Wraeththu (Constantine)
Xeelee (Baxter)
Xenogenesis (Butler)

Young Adult Books

Because young adult (YA) books are integrated with the adult books in Part II, each clearly flagged, they are listed here for any user wishing to see the range of such books or whether a specific book was annotated. The phrase came into use beginning roughly in 1950 to designate books written for and marketed to teenage readers as distinct from younger children. Books in this listing published earlier than 1950 were chosen by the contributors as likely to appeal to YAs. For series, only the first novel is listed, and for the few multiply authored books, only the first author is shown.

Ames, Mildred. *Anna to the Infinite Power*
Anderson, M. T. *Feed*
Anderson, Poul. *Vault of the Ages*
Anthony, Piers. *Race Against Time*
Armstrong, Jennifer. *The Kindling*
Ash, Fenton. *A Trip to Mars*
Asimov, Isaac. *David Starr: Space Ranger*
Baird, Thomas. *Smart Rats*
Beliaev, Aleksandr. *The Amphibian*
———. *Professor Dowell's Head*
Bell, Clare. *Ratha's Creature*
Benford, Gregory. *Jupiter Project*
Bethancourt, T. E. *The Mortal Instruments*
Biemiller, Carl I. *The Hydronauts*
Bond, Nancy. *The Voyage Begun*
Bova, Benjamin. *Exiled from Earth*

Burroughs, Edgar Rice. *At the Earth's Core*
———. *The Land that Time Forgot*
———. *The Moon Maid*
———. *A Princess of Mars*
Capon, Paul. *Flight of Time*
Carmody, Isobelle. *Obernewtyn*
Christopher, John. *Fireball*
———. *The Guardians*
———. *The Prince in Waiting*
———. *The White Mountains*
Clarke, Arthur C. *Dolphin Island*
———. *Islands in the Sky*
Clarke, Joan B. *The Happy Planet*
Claudy, Carl H. *The Mystery Men of Mars*
Corlett, William. *Return to the Gate*
Cross, John Kier. *The Angry Planet*
Dickinson, Peter. *Eva*

Philbrick, Roderick. *The Last Book in the Universe*

Pinkwater, Daniel. *Five Novels*

Pournelle, Jerry. *Starswarm*

Pratchett, Terry. *Only You Can Save Mankind*

Randall, Florence E. *The Watcher in the Woods*

Reeve, Philip. *Mortal Engines*

Rubinstein, Gillian. *Beyond the Labyrinth*

———. *Galax-Arena*

———. *Space Demons*

Sargent, Pamela. *Alien Child*

———. *Earthseed*

Schlee, Ann. *The Vandal*

Serviss, Garrett P. *A Columbus of Space*

Severn, David. *The Future Took Us*

Sheffield, Charles. *Higher Education*

Shusterman, Neal. *Scorpion Shards*

Silverberg, Robert. *Time of the Great Freeze*

Sleator, William. *The Boy Who Reversed Himself*

———. *The Duplicate*

———. *House of Stairs*

———. *Interstellar Pig*

———. *Strange Attractors*

Snyder, Zilpha K. *Below the Root*

Stone, Josephine R. *The Mudhead*

Stoutenburg, Adrien. *Out There*

Strete, Craig. *The Bleeding Man*

Suddaby, Donald. *Village Fanfare*

Sutton, Jeff. *Beyond Apollo*

Swindells, Robert. *Brother in the Land*

Townsend, John Rowe. *Noah's Castle*

———. *The Visitors*

Tsiolkovsky, Konstantin. *Outside the Earth*

Ure, Jean. *Plague*

Verne, Jules. *A Journey to the Centre of the Earth*

———. *Twenty Thousand Leagues Under the Sea*

Vinge, Joan D. *Psion*

Walton, Bryce. *Sons of the Ocean Deep*

Watson, Simon. *No Man's Land*

Webb, Sharon. *Earthchild*

Westall, Robert. *Futuretrack 5*

———. *Urn Burial*

Wilder, Cherry. *The Luck of Brin's Five*

Williams, Jay. *The People of the Ax*

Williamson, Jack. *Trapped in Space*

———. *Undersea Trilogy*

Winter, Laurel. *Growing Wings*

Wollheim, Donald A. *The Secret of Saturn's Rings*

Wyndham, John. *Planet Plane*

Yep, Laurence. *Sweetwater*

Yolen, Jane. *Armaggedon Summer*

———. *Dragon's Blood.*

Zebrowski, George. *Sunspacer*

The Year After Tomorrow. Ed. by Lester del Rey (anthology)

Translations

English-language science fiction has often been translated into other languages and has frequently served as a model for writers in other languages. The reverse has rarely occurred, and few non-English-language SF writers are well known in North America or Britain. Verne and Lem are the principal exceptions. Readers wishing to read SF in other languages should consult the third edition (1987) of *Anatomy of Wonder* for the sections discussing SF in 13 languages; the *Encyclopedia of Science Fiction* [7-21] for its entries on more than 300 authors and national literatures; the *Survey of Science Fiction Literature* [7-26] for essays on novels and short fiction of 93 authors; and the surveys that appear several times yearly in *Locus* [13-17].

To give some sense, however inadequate, of the range of foreign-language SF, translations of annotated fiction are listed below, preceded by a note by Dennis Kratz, author of Chapter 14, who not only teaches fantastic literature but is actively involved in the American Literary Translators Association. William Weaver won the National Book Award for his translation of Calvino's Cosmicomics. Several of the annotated anthologies include translated SF, notably those edited by Aldiss and Lundwall, Hartwell and Grant, Merril and Nolane. Anthologies with translations from three or more languages are listed at the end of this list under Multiple Languages (anthologies are sequenced by title in Part II, following the novels and collections).

A Note on Translation by Dennis Kratz

Literary translation, always a complex and problematic endeavor, presents additional challenges when the literature involved is science fiction. Stated most simply and ambitiously, the goal of translation is to re-create in a new language the totality of what was expressed in the original language. Where the original is dull, the translation should be dull; where the original crackles with intellectual and esthetic power, so should the translation.

Translation deals, then, not with words themselves but with the artistic vision the words were meant to express and the esthetic response the words were intended to evoke. A translation re-creates not what is "there" but what the translator interprets as being there.

The translator, in other words, is attempting the impossible: to create an equivalent text. Ideally this equivalence will manifest itself both in the new text and in the response of the readers. What characterizes the "equivalent" nature of a translation? A comparison of the two texts will reveal that the translator has found a way to re-create the mode of thinking as well as the use of language found in the original.

For the translator, the text is a complex system of dynamically interconnected parts. Meaning cannot be separated from presentation. Most discussions of translation, interestingly enough, use metaphors of friendship and marriage. We speak of the translator's "fidelity" to the text. But translation also leads to a recognition that this fidelity will be at best partial; for the work of fiction is a complex system that is not only telling a story but also (in all likelihood) impressing the reader with the author's virtuosity. This complexity of the text combined with the differences separating any two languages precludes the ideal goal of total fidelity. Every translator, as a result, is faced with this constant choice: to what part of the text should the translation be faithful? Faithful in what ways?

The issue of fidelity leads to the second goal of the translator: creating a work of art that evokes an equivalent level and quality of response from its new readers. Imagine the challenge of translating a joke from one language to another. Can we really claim to have translated a statement that evokes laughter in one language if it does not also cause laughter in the new version? Consider the choices to which this goal leads the translator, especially if fidelity to the literal meaning of the words would destroy the humor.

The translator of science fiction faces a challenge analogous to that posed by comedy. The best science fiction evokes a sense of wonder that emerges from the author's attempt to describe a setting contrary to known reality in language clear enough to make this new reality plausible and appealing enough to lure the reader into re-envisioning what was in the author's mind. A successful translation would re-create, however imperfectly, both these aspects of the work.

Translation is essential to the growth of SF as an international literature. It makes English-language SF available throughout the world and brings to the American reader works that might expand the possibilities of the genre. Writers such as Stanislaw Lem, the Strugatsky brothers, and Jules Verne are known to most American readers only in translation. Most science fiction in other languages remains unavailable in English. It would be a great service to SF, American literature and the reading public for substantially more to appear.

Czech

Čapek, Karel. *Krakatit*
———. *The Makropoulos Secret*
———. *R.U.R.*
———. *War with the Newts*
Nesvadba, Josef. *The Lost Face*

Dutch

Bilderdijk, Willem. *A Short Account of a Remarkable Aerial Voyage* . . .

French

About, Edmond. *The Man with the Broken Ear*
Boulle, Pierre. *Planet of the Apes*
Cousin de Grainville, J.-B. *The Last Man*
Cyrano de Bergerac. *Voyages to the Moon and Sun*
Defontenay, Camille. *Star*
Farrère, Claude. *Useless Hands*
Flammarion, Camile. *Lumen*
———. *Omega*
———. *Urania*
France, Anatole. *The White Stone*
Hartwell, David, ed. *Northern Stars* (some stories originally in French)
Jarry, Alfred. *The Supermale*
Klein, Gérard. *The Day Before Tomorrow*
Knight, Damon, ed. *Thirteen French Science Fiction Stories*
Maurois, André. *The Thought-Reading Machine*
———. *The Weigher of Souls*

Mercier, Louis Sebastian. *Memoirs of the Year Two Thousand Five Hundred*
Merril, Judith, ed. *Tesseracts* (some stories originally in French)
Merle, Robert. *Malevil*
Renard, Maurice. *Blind Circle*
———. *The Flight of the Aerofix*
Rosny aîné, J. H. *The Xipehuz and the Death of the Earth*
Sand, George. *Journey Within the Crystal*
Tarde, Gabriel. *Underground Man*
Verne, Jules. *The Begum's Fortune*
———. *Clipper of the Clouds*
———. *Dr Ox and Other Stories*
———. *"The Eternal Adam"*
———. *Floating Island*
———. *From the Earth to the Moon*
———. *Hector Servadac*
———. *A Journey to the Centre of the Earth*
———. *Twenty Thousand Leagues Under the Sea*
Villiers de l'Isle, Adam. *Tomorrow's Eve*
Voltaire. *Micromegas*
Vonarburg, Élisabeth. *Reluctant Voyagers*
———. *The Silent City*

German

Gail, Otto Willi. *The Shot into Infinity*
Jeschke, Wolfgang. *The Last Day of Creation*
Kaul, Fedor. *Contagion to the World*
Lang, Hermann. *The Air Battle*
Lasswitz, Kurd. *Two Planets*
Moszkowski, Alexandr. *The Isles of Wisdom*
Pešek, Luděk *The Earth Is Near*
von Hanstein, Otfrid. *Electropolis*
von Harbou, Thea. *Metropolis*
Winterfeld, Henry. *Star Girl*

Hungarian

Karinthy, Frigyes. *Voyage to Faremido and Capillaria*

Italian

Calvino, Italo. *Cosmicomics*
———. *Invisible Cities*
———. *t zero*
Casanova, Giovanni. *Icosameron*

Japanese

Murakami, Harumi. *Hard-Boiled Wonderland and the End of the World*

Latin

Campanella, Tommasso (Italy). *The City of the Sun*
Holberg, Ludwig (Denmark). *A Journey to the World Under-Ground*
Kepler, Johannes (Germany). *Somnium*

Polish

Lem, Stanislaw. *The Cyberiad*
———. *The Futurological Congress*
———. *His Master's Voice*
———. *The Investigation*
———. *Mortal Engines*
———. *Solaris*
———. *The Star Diaries*

Russian

Beliaev, Aleksandr. *The Amphibians*
Brussof, Valery. *The Republic of the Southern Cross*
Bulgakov, Mikhail. "The Fatal Eggs"
———. *Professor Dowell's Head*
Fetzer, Leland, ed. *Pre-Revolutionary Russian Science Fiction*
Magidoff, Robert, ed. *Russian Science Fiction*
Strugatsky, Arkady and Boris. *Definitely Maybe*
———. *Roadside Picnic and Tale of the Troika*
———. *The Snail on the Slope*
———. *The Ugly Swans*
Sturgeon, Theodore, ed. *New Soviet Science Fiction* (anthology)
Tolstoi, Aleksei. *Aelita*
Tsiolkovsky, Konstantin. *Beyond the Planet Earth*
Zamiatin, Evgenii. *We*

Serbian

Zivković, Zoran. *The Fourth Circle*

Spanish

Bell, Andrea A., ed. *Cosmos Latinos* (includes some Portuguese)

Multiple Languages (all are anthologies)

The Penguin World Omnibus of Science Fiction. Ed. by Brian W. Aldiss

The Road to Science Fiction, Vol. 6. Ed. by James Gunn
The Science Fiction Century. Ed. by David G. Hartwell
Terra SF. Ed. by Richard D. Nolane
The World Treasury of Science Fiction. Ed. by David G. Hartwell

Organizations

All hobbies and areas of specialized interest generate organizations of like-minded individuals. Perhaps the earliest such group in SF was the Science Fiction League, founded by Hugo Gernsback to enlarge the subscriber base for *Amazing Stories* in the 1920s. With this magazine, fans had a focus for their interest and used the letters to correspond with one another, later to found amateur magazines (fanzines) in which appeared some of the work of writers who later became well-known. Such organizations often give awards and hold conventions. Described below are some of the principal organizations having SF as a core interest or one of several major interests. Year of founding follows name. More information is available from the Web site.

Association of Science Fiction and Fantasy Artists. 1976. www.asfa-art.org/
An organization of about 500 members, over half of whom are professional artists or illustrators. The rest are a combination of fan (amateur) artists, gallery owners, collectors, convention art show personnel, and art directors. The *ASFA Quarterly* emphasizes convention and gallery art show reports, interviews, and market news, with at least one illustrated interview and art-related article in each issue. Other publications include *ASFA Art Show Guidelines*, the electronic *ASFA Occasionally On Line Update*, and an annual directory, which also lists industry art directors and agent contact information. Awards called Chesleys (after Chesley Bonestell, 1888–1986) are given each year in 12 categories at the annual world SF conventions (see Table 12-1).

British Science Fiction Association. 1958. www.bsfa.co.uk/
An outgrowth of several shorter-lived organizations dating back to the 1930s, the BSFA had about 600 members in 2003. Among its several publications are the critical journal, *Vector; Matrix*, a newsletter; and *Focus*, a magazine for writers. The BSFA presents several awards at the annual National Science Fiction Convention, informally known as the Eastercon.

First Fandom. 1959. www.firstfandom.org
As noted above, organizations celebrating SF were founded in the 1920s. Individuals active in the field by July 1939 ("dinosaurs") are eligible to be full members of one of the first fan organizations, which currently has approximately 200 full members. Associate members qualify with at least 30 years of activity in SF. A First Fandom Hall of Fame award for lifetime contributions to SF is presented at the annual worldcons (see conventions below), and since 1998 the Sam Moskowitz Archive award for excellence in collecting.

International Association for the Fantastic in the Arts. 1982. www.iafa.org

The IAFA's scope is broader than that of the SFRA (see below), as the name suggests. Most of the 300-plus members are academics. Members receive the *IAFA Newsletter*, the *Journal of the Fantastic in the Arts* [13-16], and an annual member directory. An annual conference is held each winter in Florida at which more than 200 papers, panels, and discussions are presented, along with the IAFA Distinguished Scholarship award. Many of the papers have been published in volumes by Greenwood Press (see Chapter 9).

Popular Culture Association. 1970. www.h-net.msu.edu/~pcaaca/

The systematic study of popular culture has attracted a wide variety of specialists from many fields, reflected in the diverse membership of the PCA, which currently numbers about 3,000. The annual conferences held each spring typically attract 2,000 registrants, at which many hundreds of papers, panels, and discussions are presented. Awards are given for the outstanding published article and for work for the PCA. Although no proceedings volumes result, the association is closely linked to the *Journal of Popular Culture* and *Journal of American Culture*, both published at Bowling Green State University, and to the American Culture Association (ACA).

Science-Fiction and Fantasy Writers of America, Inc. 1965. www.sfwa.org

Although many of the approximately 1,500 members write only SF, many also write fantasy, a fact recognized by a change to the current name in 1991. Affiliate, active, and associate memberships are available. Members receive the quarterly *SFWA Bulletin* (market reports, how-to articles, and so on), the bimonthly *SFWA Forum* (for associate and active members only), and an annual directory that lists the agents of the authors. Among the most important awards, the Nebulas, are presented at the annual spring conventions, usually held on either the East or West Coast.

SF Canada. 1989. www.sfcanada.ca

The Canadian counterpart of the SFWA, with which it shares some members. The Web site listed the 118 members in early 2004, most with e-mail addresses and many Web URLs. A handful of members are artists, academics such as Douglas Barbour, or librarians. Members include French Canadian writers, and an official bilingual newsletter, *Communique*, is published two or three times yearly (the Web site is, however, entirely in English). The Webmaster is Ed Willett, ewillett@sasktel.net.

Science Fiction Foundation. 1971. www.sf-foundation.org/

Originally founded to support teaching and research at the University of East London, this semi-autonomous body publishes the journal *Foundation* [13-15] and assembled the largest publicly accessible library of SF in the U.K. [15-43]. The SFF moved from London to Liverpool University in 1993, and the library was integrated with the University of Liverpool library system. The SFF is now a charitable trust that supports the library, produces the journal, and is active in promoting SF through conferences and other means.

Science Fiction Museum and Hall of Fame. www.sfhomeworld.org info@sfhomeworld.org, toll free 1-877-367-5483

This new museum opened in June 2004. It is physically located at 325 5th Ave. N., Seattle, WA 98109, mail to 2901 Third Ave., #400, Seattle, WA 98121. Many changing exhibits, outreach education programs, all described on the colorful Web site.

Science Fiction Oral History Association. www.sfoha.org

Dedicated to preserving the spoken word of the SF community, including authors, artists, and fans. The SFOHA archive contains 2,000 hours of recordings by volunteers maintained at five U.S. libraries: Michigan State, Library of Congress, University of Kansas, Eastern New Mexico University, and the SFOHA archive in Ann Arbor, MI. Most recordings are audiocassettes, but some are reel-to-reel and a few sound-only videos. Users must visit one of these sites, but future plans are to permit copying or lending.

Science Fiction Poetry Association. 1978. www.sfpoetry.com

The SFPA embraces SF, fantasy, horror and "speculative" poetry and gives the Rhysling awards for the best short and long poem. (Rhysling was a blind singer/engineer in Heinlein's "The Green Hills of Earth," 1947.) The award winners are reprinted in the SFWA's annual Nebula anthologies, and winners and nominees in the SFPA's Rhysling anthologies. The 182 members of the SFPA receive *Star*line* (bimonthly), *The Rhysling Anthology* (annual), and occasional special publications.

Science Fiction Research Association. 1970. www.sfra.org/

Founded in 1970 by Thomas Clareson and other academics, this is the oldest organization devoted to the study and teaching of SF. Scholarship is recognized by the annual Pilgrim and Pioneer awards, presented at the SFRA's June conferences. The 275 members, mostly academics (academic affiliation isn't a member requirement), receive the *SFRA Review, Extrapolation, Science Fiction Studies* (see Chapter 13), and an annual membership directory.

Society of Utopian Studies. 1975. www.utoronto.ca/utopia/

An international interdisciplinary group of approximately 350 members devoted to the study of literary and experimental utopias. Papers are presented at the annual fall meetings. Awards include the Arthur O. Lewis award for the best paper presented by a junior scholar at the meeting, the Eugenio Battista award for the best article in each volume of *Utopian Studies,* and the Distinguished Scholar award for lifetime scholarly achievement, among others. Members receive *Utopus Discovered,* a newsletter, and the quarterly *Utopian Studies* (which is also available to non-members).

H. G. Wells Society. 1960 www.hgwellsusa.50megs.com/UK/index.html

Founded to promote appreciation of the life and works of H. G. Wells. The 300 members receive a semiannual newsletter, an annual scholarly journal, *The Wellsian*, and meet regularly, with an annual conference held in London, site of the H. G. Wells Centre at the Kentish Town precinct of the Polytechnic of North London, where the society maintains a large collection of books and other materials by and about Wells. The URL for the American chapter of the society is www.hgwellsusa.50megs.com. It was founded in 2001, publishes an annual, *The Undying Fire*, a semiannual newsletter, and holds regional meetings.

World SF. 1976. www.fantascienza.it/worldsf/

Organized at the first World SF writer's conference in Dublin, this organization's goal is to promote communications among SF writers and editors worldwide. Awards presented at the earlier conferences included the Karel award (after Karel Čapek) for translation, the President's Award for independence of thought in SF, and the Harry Harrison award for individuals who have most improved the international image of SF. As of 2004, the organization appears to be moribund.

Author Index

This index provides access by author/editor to books and other materials that are annotated or substantively mentioned—having at least some critical or descriptive information—in this guide. Simple mentions, such as in compare/contrast statements, are not indexed.

Authors are arranged alphabetically by last name followed by book titles, also arranged alphabetically, and by the entry number. Entry numbers with the Roman numeral prefix II are found in Part II, Primary Literature. Entry numbers starting 6– to15– can be found in Part III, Secondary Literature. References to authors as subjects include simple page numbers from Part I and entry numbers from other chapters, such as Chapter 10's author studies.

All titles by a given author are listed under a single name; cross-references are provided from pseudonyms to real names, or vice versa, as necessary.

Certain items were omitted from this index: variant titles; stories in collections or anthologies (see [7-4] for an extremely comprehensive index); translators; Webmasters; and editors of authored books (as distinct from edited books such as anthologies). Books discussed within annotations, most commonly sequels, are indexed only in the title index.

Alphabetization is word by word, e.g., van Vogt before Vance, Di Filippo before Dick. Mackey comes before McCarthy (i.e., Mac and Mc are not interfiled).

Title Index

Titles of novels and collections and nonfiction are listed alphabetically, followed by the entry number. Entry numbers with the Roman numeral prefix II can be found in Part II, Primary Literature. Entries starting 6– to 14– are found in the relevant chapters in Part III, Secondary Literature.

Subtitles are included only when it is necessary to distinguish between works having the same title. Books with the same title are followed by the author names.

Titles of anthologies are followed by (anth.). All Internet Web sites mentioned anywhere in the guide are listed alphabetically by name followed by (Web site).

Certain items were omitted from this index: stories in collections or anthologies (see [7-4] for an extremely comprehensive index); variant titles; film and TV titles. Translated titles are indexed only under the English title. SF is alphabetized as if spelled out. Titles beginning with numerals are filed as if the number was spelled out, e.g., *2001* is alphabetized as two thousand one.

An index of series titles can be found in Chapter 16.

Theme Index

This index lists recurrent themes in novels, a few collections, and themed anthologies, all in Part II, plus some nonfiction in Part III. The index supplements the "compare" and "contrast" suggestions in individual annotations that refer the reader to other books with similar themes, structures, narrative devices, and so forth. Notes under each heading describe the meaning of the theme and provide cross-references to related themes.

Numbers directly following the theme heading refer to page references in chapters 1 to 5 and 6 to 14. Titles of novels and anthologies are listed alphabetically under each theme, followed by the entry number. Entry numbers with the Roman numeral prefix II are found in Part II, Primary Literature. Entry numbers starting 6– to 14– can be found in the relevant chapters in Part III, Secondary Literature.

ALTERNATE WORLDS, 77

Properly, alternative worlds, but the usage is fixed. Might-have-been worlds or history. *See also* HISTORY IN SF, PARALLEL WORLDS

COMING OF AGE

Most common in young adult novels,
in which a youth is tested and matures.

CYBERPUNK, 73, 74

The "cyber" presumably comes from cybernetics, the study of control and communication in machines (including the "cyberspace" linking computers), and is combined with a downbeat, punk sensibility derived from an outlaw street culture. *See also* STEAMPUNK, HARD SF

CYBORGS

Man-machine hybrids (from cybernetic organism). The machine may be a prosthetic limb or something more elaborate. *See also* ANDROIDS, GENETIC ENGINEERING, ROBOTS

Detective stories. *See* CRIME AND PUNISHMENT

Devolution. *See* EVOLUTION

DISASTER

An event seriously disrupting the social fabric. *See also* END OF THE WORLD, HOLOCAUST AND AFTER

Lucifer's Hammer, II-810
The Machine Stops, II-1055
A Mask for the General, II-452
The Memoirs of a Survivor, II-663
Misplaced Persons, II-494
Nerves, II-308
Noah's Castle, II-1138
Paradise and Iron, II-157
Plague, II-1153
The Prince in Waiting, II-243
Prisoner of Psi, II-572
Radix, II-55
"The Republic of the Southern
    Cross" ("Respublika yuzhnavo
    kresta"), II-177
The Ruins of Earth, II-1386
The Second Deluge, II-979
Sever the Earth, II-1065
Starship and Haiku, II-1104
Stations of the Tide, II-1111
Synners, II-204
Terraforming Earth, II-1262
Time of the Great Freeze, II-1024
The Vandal, II-971
The Wanderer, II-654
The Weathermonger, II-339
When Worlds Collide, II-70
Where Late the Sweet Birds Sang,
    II-1248
The White Plague, II-526
The Year When Stardust Fell, II-579

**DISCOVERIES AND INVENTIONS,
13, 34**
Especially common in earlier SF. *See
also* MACHINES
    Blind Circle, II-897
    Blind Lake, II-1270
    The Clipper of the Clouds, II-1176
    The Doings of Raffles Haw, II-353
    The Flight of the Aerofix, II-898
    The Food of the Gods and How It
        Came to Earth, II-1226
    Frankenstein; or, The Modern
        Prometheus, II-997
    The Invisible Man, II-1227
    Krakatit, II-212
    The Man Who Stole the Earth,
        II-539
    Master of His Fate, II-268
    Mr Hawkins' Humorous Inventions,
        II-422
    Ralph 124C41+, II-431
    Star Dust, II-1194

The Steam Man of the Prairies,
    II-371
They'd Rather Be Right, II-262
The Thought-Reading Machine,
    II-724
Undersea Quest, II-1264
The Weigher of Souls, II-725

DYSTOPIAS
Sometimes called anti-utopias,
depicting societies in which social
pathologies (dictatorships, crime,
environmental pollution) are
prominent. *See also* POLITICS,
UTOPIAS
    The Adventure of Wyndham Smith,
        II-1288
    Ambient, II-1284
    Among the Hidden, II-475
    Anthem, II-886
    Ape and Essence, II-557
    Armed Camps, II-891
    Arslan, II-381
    Brother to Dragons, II-994
    Brute Orbits, II-1304
    Caesar's Column, II-348
    The City of Endless Night, II-504
    A Clockwork Orange, II-190
    Count Zero, II-437
    Dark Horizons, 9-136
    Dark Universe, II-425
    Destiny Times Three, II-651
    Doomsday Morning, II-783
    Fahrenheit 451, II-153
    Feed, II-19
    From Utopia to Nightmare, 9-194
    The Future as Nightmare, 9-95
    The Future Took Us, II-980
    Futuretrack 5, II-1237
    Gathering Blue, II-683
    The Giver, II-684
    The Handmaid's Tale, II-57
    Hell's Pavement, II-608
    House of Stairs, II-1043
    The House of the Scorpion, II-388
    The Humanoids, II-1257
    Invitation to the Game, II-552
    The Iron Heel, II-675
    The Jagged Orbit, II-171
    The Last Book in the Universe,
        II-849
    Limbo, II-1279
    Little Heroes, II-1061
    A Mask for the General, II-452

FEMINIST SF, 65, 82

Usually stories in which female roles
are atypical and/or women are
dominant and/or men are viewed with
suspicion or are absent. *See also*
WOMEN IN SF

HOLOCAUST AND AFTER
More serious than DISASTER, less
serious than END OF THE WORLD.

HUMOROUS SF

LINGUISTICS
Including communication with extraterrestrials, language.

LOST RACES/WORLDS
Common in earlier SF. Includes Atlantis.

MACHINES
See also COMPUTERS, DISCOVERIES AND INVENTIONS, NANOTECH-NOLOGY. *Contrast* PASTORAL

NANOTECHNOLOGY, 75

A future technology emphasizing "machines" that are molecular or atomic in size, a concept that entered SF in the late 1980s. *See also* MACHINES, DISCOVERIES AND INVENTIONS

NEW WAVE, 62, 63

Label applied to work of a number of writers, especially British, whose work in the early 1960s was somewhat experimental and generally rejected the optimistic tone of much earlier SF. *See also* ABSURDIST SF

OVERPOPULATION

See also POLLUTION

PARALLEL WORLDS

Usually situated in an "other" dimension. *See also* ALTERNATE WORLDS

PARANORMAL POWERS

Including telepathy, psychokinesis (ability to influence objects at a distance), precognition (ability to foresee the future) and other "psi" phenomena.

Parapsychological powers. *See*
  PARANORMAL POWERS

Parody. *See* HUMOR IN SF

PASTORAL

Stories depicting a simple, natural way
of life in contrast to a complex, anxiety-
ridden, technology-based one. *See also*
CYBERPUNK, MACHINES, UTOPIAS

Philosophy. *See* RELIGION

THE PLANETS, 76

Of our solar system. *See also* GALATIC
EMPIRES, LIFE ON OTHER WORLDS

RELIGION

Including philosophy, metaphysics. *See also* IMMORTALITY

ROBOTS

Traditionally mechanical or electromechanical in nature. *See also* ANDROIDS, CYBORGS

SATIRICAL SF

See also HUMOROUS SF

SCIENCE FANTASY
Stories combining "rational" elements from SF and magical or fanciful elements from fantasy. Excludes heroic fantasy and sword and sorcery, which generally fall outside SF.

SCIENTISTS AND ENGINEERS, 50
In which the character of a scientist/engineer is a key element. Includes "mad" scientists.

SEX IN SF
Including gender, sexual stereotypes and roles. *See also* FEMINIST SF, WOMEN IN SF

SOCIOLOGY

The study of social relationships on Earth or elsewhere. *See also* ANTHROPOLOGY, POLITICS, UTOPIAS

SPACE FLIGHT

Includes generation starships. *See also* SPACE OPERA, FANTASTIC VOYAGES

SPACE OPERA, 78

Radio dramas sponsored by soap companies came to be called soap operas, and westerns were called horse operas. Adventures in space thus came to be known as space operas. *See also* LIFE ON OTHER WORLDS

STEAMPUNK

In which SF events usually take place in an alternative 19th century. *See also* CYBERPUNK.

SUPERMEN/WOMEN

The superiority may be mental or physical or both, and the gifts may be used for good or ill. *See also* GENETIC ENGINEERING, MONSTERS, MUTANTS

About the Author

NEIL BARRON, editor of previous editions of this popular and critically-acclaimed work, has written extensively in the field of speculative fiction. In 1982 he received the Pilgrim Award for his overall contributions to science fiction and fantasy scholarship.